TO PAUL SHOREY

NON ITA CERTANDI CUPIDUS QUAM PROPTER AMOREM

Preface

The defense of the quiet dead is surely no phantom strife.
For the dead in question are always very much alive, spiritu-
ally active as teachers of the living, and the animus inspiring
the attack is patently some contemporary corruption or abuse for which those
of an earlier time are being held responsible: either (so it is charged) they
were its ancestral advocates or, at the least, they unwittingly provided it with
dynamic symbols, still operative for ill. Thus it is that Plato has been made a
participant in the current conflict of ideals.

The book that lies open before you is, as its title proclaims, a reply to some
of Plato's extremer critics of recent years. It is not intentionally a counterattack; indeed the writer is prepared to make common cause in some respects
with Plato's detractors, sharing the ideals of their allegiance and the avowed
objects of their indignation. Readers of the final chapter will observe my
wholehearted agreement with them when they protest against Plato's dangerously regulative proposals for ordering the good community.

My chief complaints against these critics are that they have not made the
necessary corrections in passing to and fro between the ancient world and our
modern social space-time, and that they have, as a rule, displayed more zeal to
uncover faults than to recognize merit. In consequence, they present a seriously distorted image of Plato both as man and as thinker. The man Plato is
found to possess certain traits of character and of personality, and these discoveries, even when true, are promptly falsified by being set in the frame of
our contemporary culture or in that of an Athens so modified as to be all but
indistinguishable from it. Similarly, his political doctrines are treated as if
they were being proposed in the twentieth century, their acceptable elements
ignored or equivocated away, their affinities with harmful modern ideologies
increased by factitious imputations, with the result that the "great Idealist"
has been denatured into a ruthless advocate of dictatorship and the father of
totalitarianism. Thus the system of Plato's thought is made to revolve around
the axis of its least worth. By parity of treatment every great historic figure
could be robbed of dignity, and we should be taught to distrust and turn away
from most of the spiritual and intellectual benefactors of mankind. The central
aim of this book is to correct these errors of perspective and of fact and, while
stopping short of unqualified acceptance of all that Plato was or taught, to

restore him to a position of repute and potential influence answering to his actual merit. I have written in the conviction that the ancient tree of Platonic philosophy has still deep rootage in our western culture, and that its topmost branches catch the light of a universal sun.

Apology is due the reader for the painful length to which the book has run. The number and magnitude of the questions raised by Plato's opponents has imposed upon his defender the long labor of responsible exposition and detailed reply. To accuse and to raise suspicions are notoriously quicker than to establish innocence; one day in court may suffice for the plausible statement of a set of charges which it will take weeks to sift and evaluate, if a balanced verdict is to be reached. Accordingly it is hoped that the somewhat less than omnivorous reader will employ the table of contents as a guide to the topics of his special choice. Though the book constitutes one continuous and articulated whole, the concluding chapter on Plato's supposed totalitarianism has been so designed that it can be read apart by those to whom Plato's relevance to contemporary issues is of all but exclusive concern.

My main obligations are two, and though disparate, of equal weight. To my revered teacher, the late Paul Shorey, I owe whatever I possess of critical ability to handle Platonic texts, and though I reserve the right to err, and would, for example, treat more seriously than he was wont to do the Platonic metaphysic, it is from him that I have derived my essential vision of Plato. My regarded wife has worked with me as a junior partner during the entire period of composition, and though the responsibility remains mine, has entered constructively into the shaping of many of my central decisions. To her logical sense and special competence in certain areas, particularly psychology, this book stands in unmeasured debt.

It remains to thank a number of persons and institutions for favors and courtesies: the Mahlon Powell Foundation of Indiana University, by whose kind invitation I delivered the core of the present volume in four lectures during the autumn of 1951; the University of Maine for the granting of a sabbatical semester; Mr. Louis T. Ibbotson and the other members of the library staff of the University of Maine for assistance in securing out of the way publications and microfilm; my colleague Dr. Robert K. Sherk for helpful advice on certain points of Athenian history. I must acknowledge also the courtesy of several persons who have supplied bibliographical aid, notably Professors Harold Cherniss, G. C. Field, Walter Solmitz and Theodore C. Weiler; and finally I am indebted to the staff of the Harvard University Press, in particular to Mrs. C. H. Whitman, whose lessons in literary manners prompted me to remove certain polemical asperities which might have grieved the judicious. All the persons mentioned I exonerate from guilt by association with any of my views which may offend.

The following publishers have kindly granted permission to quote from their publications, as specified: Princeton University Press, *The Open Society*

and Its Enemies, by K. R. Popper; Oxford University Press, *Plato Today*, by
R. H. S. Crossman; Charles Scribner's Sons, *The Platonic Legend*, by Warner
Fite; Random House, translations of Thucydides' *History* and of Plutarch's
Lives. The *American Imago* and the *American Journal of Psychiatry* have also
been good enough to permit quotation from articles published in their pages.

RONALD B. LEVINSON

University of Maine

CORRIGENDA

Page 591, col. 2, line 31: For   intention of supplying this very lack in con-

                              Read duty on the Law-wardens of his city to con-

Page 609, col. 2, line 19: For   *Republic*, the gold of the guardian class is

                              Read *Republic*, which is describable, with certain

CONTENTS

IN DEFENSE OF PLATO

1

The Attack on Plato

It would be difficult to specify any major constituent in the vast complex of our cultural tradition that has not, within recent years, been described as standing "at the crossroads," having arrived at the "hour of decision," or confronting its "crisis." Christianity, education, capitalism, individualism, democracy — such is notoriously true of them all, and the list could easily be extended. In such circumstances, it would, indeed, have been strange had Plato escaped challenge; it could only have signified that he had lost all interest to the modern world.

The most casual survey of recent popular and semipopular Platonic literature makes it clear that he has not escaped. The sun of Plato's unquestioned supremacy, as the sublime moralist, the god among philosophers, the son of Apollo, if not set, is at the moment thickly overclouded; Cicero's famous preference for being wrong with Plato, as against being right in any other company, is, to say the least, not the majority view. Plato, in these latter days, has been violently assailed by many sturdy liberals for his hostility to progressive and democratic ideals. Worse, he has been acclaimed and appropriated by some friends of totalitarianism, as the philosophical father of dictatorship. And over and above these political defamations, his claims to affinity with the higher spiritual ideals of our culture have been repudiated.

If such detractions do not, on first hearing, cause a certain shock, the reason may be partly because the artillery of our thunderous times has put our more sensitive reaction mechanisms out of order. The more substantial reason, however, may be that most of us have rather forgotten how highly Plato had been enthroned between the cherubim of Western culture. There have, naturally, been occasional voices raised in dissent. In ancient times, there were the cynic snarls of Diogenes, and the gibes of Lucian, and the malevolent gossip of Athenaeus.[1] Among the moderns, Bacon disparaged what he understood as Plato's high-flying way of speculation; Voltaire ridiculed the Greek philosopher "who invented Christianity without knowing it"; Landor has an imaginary

---

[1] Anti-Platonism in antiquity is further commented on in n. 30, p. 407.

conversation in which Plato is bitterly assailed through the mouth of his ancient detractor Diogenes and charged with almost all the crimes which later critics were to list on the anti-Platonic calendar; Macaulay, in his essay on Bacon, pulls down the placards of Platonic "Truth," "Beauty," and "Good," and replaces them by bright Baconian banners inscribed with the watchwords of scientific progress and the curing of all human ills. And here may be added the more moderate dissents of some accredited scholars of the middle and later nineteenth century, such as Grote and Zeller, who deplored the authoritarian element in Plato's thought, or regarded his political philosophy as distorted at certain points by the prejudices of its author's social station.

But this derogation did not constitute a serious threat to Plato's good name. For such critics as Landor and Macaulay, though intending annihilation, spoke without authority; while those who, like Grote and Zeller, possessed sufficient prestige, were desirous only of setting right certain errors, falling within a general framework of philosophic argument for which, as a whole, they professed a profound respect.

Against these scattered critics was the collective voice of generations, reënforced by the most distinguished among contemporary specialists in each generation. In England, for example, the universities of Oxford and Cambridge forgot their historic differences in their agreement on this point. There were Cambridge Platonists, such as Henry More and the formidable Ralph Cudworth, who fused Platonism and Christian ethics as a potent instrument to destroy the groveling materialism and brutish egoism which they saw focused in the philosophy of Thomas Hobbes. The Cambridge Platonists were supplied with abundant precedents in the Christian Platonists of ancient Alexandria, in Saint Augustine, and in the Florentines of Renaissance times.

At Oxford — to go no further back than the mid-nineteenth century — Benjamin Jowett was inspiring a whole generation of gifted pupils with enthusiasm for Plato, whom he conceived as "the father of Idealism," whose truth, though it "may not be our truth . . . nevertheless may have an extraordinary value and interest for us." In the essays prepended to his translations of the dialogues, and in the graceful and often impressive rhythms of the translations themselves, the thought of Jowett's "poet of ideas" was broadcast throughout the English-speaking world. For the first time the English reader could feel that Plato was an open book, invitingly, even inspiringly, readable, and sympathetic with the deeper moral aspirations of Christendom.

Meanwhile within the same university, but inhabiting a very different universe, Walter Pater was presenting to a small number of the elect his more secular though hardly less imposing version of Plato, published in the cadenced periods of *Plato and Platonism* in 1884. Here Plato appears essentially as the great seer of beauty, the true founder of that cult of harmonious living of which Pater himself was at once practitioner and priest. Much that the earlier poets, from Spenser to Shelley, had suggested of the aesthetic glamor of Plato's philosophy of Love and Beauty, together with what such social reformers as Ruskin and William Morris had just been saying about the high importance for the perfection of the human soul of the shapes and colors that surround it, all this was brought together in Pater's book and through the congenial quality of his style was made effective to all who found Pater's aesthetic sublimations an attractive alternative to the traditional religion.

On our side of the Atlantic, too, Platonism did not lack its altars. Its central temple, it need scarcely be said, was at Concord; Emerson was its most inspired, if not at all times orthodox high priest. Reading his Plato first, perforce, for the most part in the inaccurate and neo-Platonized demi-English translations of Thomas Taylor, the Platonist, he inevitably received Plato's thought distorted at certain points. The wonder rather is, as the reader of the earlier essay on Plato in *Representative Men* may well feel, how Emerson could have found so much inspiration in the Platonic light that struggled through these obscuring clouds.[2]

What Emerson thought he saw in Plato was, in his own words, nothing less than philosophy itself: "Plato is philosophy, and philosophy, Plato." "Out of Plato," he tells us, "come all things that are still written and debated among men of thought." "Great havoc makes he among our originalities."[3] These imposing generalities Emerson was not the man to document in detail, but he will consent to tell us some, at least, of the grounds of Plato's greatness.

To begin with, there was Plato's moral grandeur. Emerson discovered in him "a certain earnestness, which mounts, in the *Republic* and in the *Phaedo*, to piety"; "he has a probity, a native reverence for justice and honor, and a humanity."[4] Plato imparts to his account of moral excellence a geometric quality of precision and definition, becoming thus "the Euclid of holiness."[5] Emerson, like Pater, though to him it is less central, finds in Plato a music of ideas: "His writings have . . . the sempiternal youth of poetry"; and Emerson goes so far as to declare that "poetry has never soared higher than in the *Timaeus* and the *Phaedrus*."[6]

But the crown of Plato's excellence as philosopher, and Emerson's chief reason for putting him among the representative men as the thinker *par excellence*, was his power of combining in the integrity of his metaphysical vision the two opposite poles of Reality: the one and the many, or, as Emerson picturesquely called them, Asia, the principle of unlimited and undifferentiated Being, and Europe, the principle of diversity, of bounded difference. "The won-

---

[2] Thomas Taylor (1758–1835), as the only complete English translator of Plato before the Bohn Library, influenced many other philosophical men of letters, including Coleridge and Shelley, by his accent on the mystical element in Plato, and by his conviction, insisted upon in his extensive commentaries, that the dialogues should be given the arcane theosophical interpretation imposed upon them by the later generations of neo-Platonists.

[3] *Representative Men*, 1876, pp. 39–40.

[4] *Ibid.*, 57–58.

[5] *Ibid.*, p. 87.

[6] *Ibid.*, 88–89.

derful synthesis so familiar in nature . . . the union of impossibilities, which reappears in every object . . . was now also transferred entire to the consciousness of a man. The balanced soul came." [7]

The full measure of Emerson's appraisal of Plato's greatness is set forth with truly devout emotion in the concluding paragraphs of the essay:

Let us not seem to treat with flippancy his venerable name. Men, in proportion to their intellect, have admitted his transcendent claims. . . . How many ages have gone by and he remains unapproached! A chief structure of human wit, like Karnac, or the mediaeval cathedrals, . . . it requires all the breadth of human faculty to know it. I think it is trueliest seen, when seen with the most respect. . . . The great-eyed Plato proportioned the lights and shades after the genius of our life. [8]

This slight sketch could, given sufficient time and knowledge, be amplified into a five-foot shelf. But from that part of the story that has here been told, it is evident that in dealing with Plato, one has to do with a thinker whose ideas have penetrated to the very core of our culture and have since the Renaissance at least become integral parts of our literary and philosophic tradition.

Whoever will grant what has just been said, and to whom it appears credible that even a tithe of the veneration lavished upon Plato has been well bestowed, can hardly fail to feel some degree of concern over the present crisis in Platonism. To do so, the friend of Plato need have no wish to see him defended against the whole spirit of modern philosophy, still less rehabilitated into the standard of philosophical orthodoxy for all time. It is enough to believe that his writings may still be looked to as an unexhausted source of exciting intellectual experience from which genuine insights may still be gained, and to deprecate the arrival of a generation who will regard Plato with hostility and contempt, and hence will misread him or leave him unread.

But has this fixed star in the firmament of history in fact fallen? That is the basic question set for us by the present temper of the world as reflected in the recent literature about Plato. The question is large, indeed formidable, and at this stage of our discussion, unanswerable, unless we are to delude ourselves with opposing dogmatisms. Our first business must be to give a full and impartial hearing to the case against Plato, as it has been urged in its greatest strength by his latter-day enemies in the English-speaking world. We cannot, of course, bring into our court all those who have witnessed against Plato in the recent literature; we shall, however, seek to omit no important charge. Our formal discussion will be chiefly concerned with four writers who have given extended expression to their views, but we shall occasionally turn aside to meet the criticisms of others, wherever their importance requires it.

In the early thirties of our century, there fluttered down upon the heads of Plato's admirers a slender and apparently innocuous volume by that witty and versatile if eccentric man of letters, the late John Jay Chapman, a book with

---

[7] *Ibid.*, 54–55.   [8] *Ibid.*, 78–79.

a title rather bigger than itself: *Lucian, Plato and Greek Morals.*[9] This all but unnoticed attack upon the Platonic stronghold will serve as well as any other as a not wholly arbitrary starting point for our history and appraisal of recent anti-Platonism. Since Macaulay's trenchant critique of Plato in his essay on Bacon, it would be difficult to find anything in English or American literature to compare with the deadliness of Mr. Chapman's intent to destroy Plato as a philosopher. Coming as it did just prior to a whole sequence of blasts and counterblasts, it may not unreasonably be considered as a sort of unconscious declaration of what has threatened to become almost a world war over the Platonic philosophy.

Chapman sustains with grace and verve the paradoxical thesis that the roles assigned by philosophical tradition to Plato and to Lucian, respectively, should be reversed. It is Plato, not Lucian, who must henceforth be regarded as the essentially playful, ironic, morally and logically unscrupulous entertainer; it is Lucian and not Plato whom we are to honor as the pure and ardent moralist-reformer whose brilliant intellect and prophetic insights require us to accord him "a high place among the thinkers of modern Europe."

This spirited if, one might suggest, somewhat hyperbolical estimate of "the Voltaire of antiquity" is the milder half of Chapman's paradox; it could have startled none but the uninformed. Few of Chapman's readers, however, could have been prepared to receive without shock the bland demotion of Plato from the rank of philosophic thinker to that of literary artist, deviser of "drawing-room diversions," and "prince of conjurors." And they might well have asked whether Chapman really meant what he said when, in speaking of the praise of love in Plato's *Symposium*, he branded it "the most effective plea for evil that one can point to or recall."

The plain answer is that Chapman meant what he said, every word of it, in spite of some playful talk in his introduction, wherein the author, in ironical self-depreciation, compares himself to a child scratching his nurse, and presently exhorts himself and his readers to be "ignorant, nimble, and enthusiastic." He is announcing with all the force at his disposal that Plato, the King of Thought, is dead, and completing the formula by adding a *viva* for Plato the Prince of Conjurors.

Thus far we have merely stated the rather strange conclusions that Chapman has reached concerning Plato. It remains, in fairness, to show briefly the sort of evidence that he has adduced in their support. The "formula" of the preceding paragraph suggests the two captions under which the material may conveniently be disposed. We consider first the refutation of Plato the great philosopher.

There has been, Chapman charges, a species of conspiracy among the

---

[9] *Lucian, Plato and Greek Morals*, 1931. Page references to passages quoted from the detractors will not be given in this chapter, but will be supplied in our later discussion of specific criticisms.

learned and devout (from whose ranks have arisen the British and American editors and commentators upon Plato) to "regard Plato as an authority on Divine Truth," and with the aid of Christian theology and mysticism to read into him a "hieratic interpretation" presumed to reveal a "sacred depth" of meaning. This attitude inhibits the attempt to consider first, as in the light of the historical background one ought, "the obvious meanings" of such a document as the *Symposium*. Pursuit of this neglected method has persuaded Chapman of the absurdity of those idealizing interpreters who imagine they have discovered in Plato a foreshadowing of the great mysteries of Christian love, the *fruitio Dei*, and Dante's transfigured passion for the heavenly Beatrice.

We must pause here to acknowledge the satiric skill with which our anti-Platonist has pictured (or caricatured) the incongruous results of these efforts to hold Plato within the boundaries of Christian doctrine. He has asked us to contemplate the truly ludicrous image of "Mr. Jowett, of Oxford," who, confronted by Plato's intractably pagan doctrine of love, "seizes the bull by the tail and is dragged round and round the field by him, sometimes catching at a post of Christian doctrine as it flashes by, sometimes trying to steer the bull by a gallant stubbing of his own toes against a yielding mound of middle class humbug."

The efforts of these well-meaning toreadors are vain, Chapman concludes. The truth is that the *Symposium* cannot be construed into the sublime, devoted as it is to an exploitation of pederasty "as a source of harmless jollification." Its purpose is not to "adumbrate a philosophy" but to praise "a particular practice. . . . The final palinode of Agathon in honor of 'love' is a call not to thought but to action." The claim of the *Symposium* upon our serious, philosophical attention thus disposed of, Chapman gives vent to his distaste for what he feels to be the "strangely heavy" atmosphere in which the dialogue is wrapped, and the repugnance aroused in him by the speech of Diotima, who wears the "thin disguise of Plato himself," and the other "odious characters," all, like "the room itself" stinking "of the poppy."

Confirmation of Plato's lack of moral seriousness Chapman finds in Plato's total inability to grasp the import of that great and grave moralist, whom nevertheless he loved and admired, Socrates. Relying on Xenophon's *Memorabilia* as an honest soldierly account of the historical Socrates, Chapman finds in most of the Platonic dialogues only a phantom, lacking the solid dimensions and the iron will of his original. When face to face with a serious moral question, Socrates advanced on instinct to the attack; Plato sidestepped and covered his incompetence with brilliant but irrelevant brocades.

We are given also a spirited attack upon Plato, the reputed master of logical method. Plato's celebrated dialectic turns out, under the Chapman touchstone, to be merely a species of equivocation, a pretty and ingenious game of verbal shift and quibble, the object of which was, again, entertainment. Plato is thus assimilated and reduced to the lowest class of fourth-century sophist, the eristics, whose antics (though Mr. Chapman does not tell us this) Plato has himself satirically depicted in his dialogue the *Euthydemus*. We are asked to remember the joy that the Greeks, from Homeric times onward, took in subtlety and cunning of every kind, that they were the original inventors of "mock trials, imaginary orations, sophistries, paradoxes," *et id genus omne*, "each of which ended with a laugh and a quiet walk in the public garden." Some crucial passages from several of the dialogues, the *Gorgias, Phaedo*, and *Crito*, are submitted to brief analysis, with special emphasis on their pretense of demonstration, their internal inconsistency, and their contradictions one with another. Truth, we are to conclude, is not the object of a Platonic dialogue, but merely one of its ingredients, to be sparingly employed lest too liberal an application should upset the delicate equilibrium of light and shade.

It is creditable to Chapman's impartiality as a critic that his virulent condemnation of the *Symposium* and his denial of Plato's very existence as a philosopher have not proved fatal to his appreciation of Plato the literary artist. He can even pay tribute to the conclusion of the *Symposium*, "one of the supreme finales in all literature," and characterize the prison scenes in the *Crito* and *Phaedo* as "charming essays, well-imagined and beautiful." In the *Phaedo*, too, he recognizes "a picture by a great artist, wherein everything is falsified, and yet, as in a picture, everything is true." Observe that even amidst these civilities, Chapman will not permit the reader to forget that Plato's literary achievement was at the price of his philosophy.

Nor will he let Plato's purely literary defects go unnoticed. He attacks him at one capital point, claiming that his mastery of the dialogue form is radically defective, sinking, for lack of a character internal to the dialogue and representing the author's point of view, into something below the level of the dramatic, "a *journal intime* of scholarly rumination." Thus, in spite of his concessions, Chapman, in his estimate of Plato's literary art, as in his judgment of Plato as thinker, stands, on balance, as the detractor and the anti-Platonist.

Three years after Chapman's book, appeared *The Platonic Legend* by the veteran moralist and professor of philosophy at Princeton, Warner Fite.[10] This book reports and attempts to document a "discovery": after years of reading Plato in the light of the "idealistic tradition," he happened one day to question his impression that the scheme of education provided by Plato in the *Republic* excluded the ordinary citizens. Pursuing this hint, and relying on the results of his own inquiries, he found his impression confirmed. More, as he continued his investigation, weighing off his own reading of Plato's text against the significance attributed to it by Plato's recent admirers, among them Dean Inge, A. E. Taylor, and Paul Shorey — the "disciples," as Fite delights to call them — he discovered grounds for general "doubt and suspicion

---

[10] *The Platonic Legend*, 1934.

with regard to orthodox interpretation." For now quite another Plato stood before his eyes, a Plato shorn of the inspiration, the infallibility, the divine perfections with which the "disciples" had endowed him, a figure of human proportions, shaped and limited by the historical forces of his day, whose thought was not only bounded by inevitable human limitations, but distorted by partisan prejudice and the small passions of personal embitterment. The objective of the book before us is, then, to "dismiss the idea of a divine revelation, and to treat the words of Plato, if possible, as we should treat the words of any other writer," to destroy "the legend of Plato . . . the consummate artist, . . . the shrewd interpreter of human nature, the stern and lofty moralist, and even of Plato the good Christian." He will touch Plato's metaphysics as lightly as possible, though they are inevitably involved in the general debacle; what is left of them, in Fite's opinion, is chiefly a "landmark," valuable for purposes of orientation to travelers in the realm of philosophic thought. It is Plato's social and ethical doctrine that the book seeks directly to demolish, and along with this, all claims in behalf of Plato's superlative greatness in any department of life or thought.

In presenting Fite's views on these topics, we may seem to imply that all he has said is scheduled for later refutation. On the contrary, it must be emphasized that we shall see reason in our sequel to accept many of his specific criticisms and objections, though this will not entail assent to his more extravagant interpretations. Our summary must also inevitably be defective in failing adequately to convey the atmosphere of cynical disparagement in which his whole discussion moves. Fite has a pretty but mordant wit and a ruthless facility in the caricaturist's art of seizing upon an unlovely feature and making it the center of the physiognomy portrayed, neither of which we can hope properly to reproduce.

For the reader's convenience, we shall tabulate Fite's principal conclusions, and in view of their negative relation to the claims of Plato's "disciples," claims which Fite everywhere sardonically exhibits as the first step in his intended demolition of the master, we shall cast them in the form of denials, as follows:

1. It is denied that Plato's *Republic* contemplates the ideal of maximal happiness and self-development for all the citizens. The community does not offer, save for negligible exceptions, a "career open to talents." It is run in the interests of a small privileged leisure class, say, 10 per cent of the population, guided by the arrogant and esoteric wisdom of a still smaller minority within this, 1 per cent, at the cost of the exertion and sacrifice of the despised and cynically befooled 90 per cent of the citizens. The goal of all this striving is not the humane fullness of a richly cultural existence, which his native Athens could have taught him to love; it is the largely Spartan ideal of a closely regimented state, a stratified caste society, its members carefully bred to type, their quality ruthlessly maintained by infanticide; it is organized largely for the practice of the military virtues, if not for conquest.

2. It is denied that either in the *Republic* or elsewhere in the dialogues does Plato show any anticipation of the Christian, Kantian, democratic sense of the value and dignity of the individual. He fails to discern the very nature of personality, as we conceive it, and the conditions for the development of genuine moral freedom. Even his philosopher kings

THE ATTACK ON PLATO

are impersonal beings; the mass of the citizens are creatures guided only by habit and fear of consequences. "Plato's . . . ideal of a society . . . is then a city of children," in which the small number of "enlightened philosophers" are "the only persons . . . who enjoy an adult status." Plato's suggestion in the *Gorgias* that it is better to suffer than to do injustice, is only superficially in accord with the Christian ideal, resting in reality on prudential considerations of what is materially advantageous in the long run.

3. Plato is far from having anticipated modern sentiment in the relation between the sexes: his conception of marriage is vitiated by the impersonality of the stock-breeder; he had no notion of marriage as a partnership of mutual respect. In this he fell below the standard of his own time and clime.

4. Fite repeats and amplifies Chapman's denial that the Platonic philosophy of "Eros," as expounded in the *Symposium* and *Phaedrus*, admits of the soaring mystical interpretation that Plato's admirers have traditionally imposed upon it. On the contrary, Plato is accepting and glorifying a refined form of sexual perversion, an institution disapproved by the majority of his own contemporaries, and on occasion is condoning and waxing facetious over even its grosser forms.

5. It is denied that Plato had depth of insight into values. Plato labored under the great illusion that it is possible to apply to the moral life a standard of metrical precision which would replace the insights of experience. In so far as such measurement is successful, it reduces moral choice to a species of mathematical calculation. But the method is inapplicable, and Plato's attempt to give it logical and metaphysical support through the never clearly defined procedure known as "dialectic," terminates in mystical obscurity. Plato's conception of social good is so coldly scientific, so intimately dependent on minutely regulated, centrally directed order, that despite differences, it approaches most nearly the iron-clad system of Soviet Russia. The same standpoint applied to aesthetic values results in the reduction of beauty to the single impoverished type of abstract mathematical form.

6. It is denied that Plato is a sovereign master of the logic of argument. He is constantly guilty of fallacies, which the disciples explain as "playful" and deliberate. But this sort of playfulness is often a dishonest debater's trick. And even when he is most serious, as in the *Republic* passage about the divided line, we find him falling into elementary errors of reasoning. The conclusion must be that his power and integrity as reasoner have been grossly overrated.

7. It is denied that Plato possessed a high degree of economic and political wisdom. His scorn of industry and of trade is visible throughout the *Republic*; his plan of the ideal state is not to be contaminated with even the theoretical consideration of such things. The city of the *Laws* is to be planted far enough from the sea to discourage trade, his understanding of which "does not . . . extend beyond the first chapter." As to international politics, Plato, with his backward gaze fixed upon the doomed sovereign city state, was unable to see that the crying need of his times was for federation. In fine, "Plato's political ideals, in the *Republic* or in the *Laws*, are resolutely and bluntly parochial. . . . It would be strange in any case if Plato had anything to tell the modern world about statesmanship."

8. It is denied that Plato has any place among the great masters in the world of art. He would not have been comfortable in such a seat among those for whom he habitually expresses his lively contempt and whom he rates, if the poets be taken as representative, as lowest in the hierarchy of reincarnated souls save for manual workers, sophists, and tyrants. Some artistic achievements stand to Plato's credit, a number of scenes and metaphors; but these are episodic. He has nothing to put beside *Hamlet* and *Don Quixote*. Many of the dialogues, including the *Republic*, far from being finished masterpieces, bear the marks of hasty and careless assembling. Plato is further guilty of shocking incongruities that mar his best effects; witness the anticlimax of the discussion of rhetorical types that follows the myth of the charioteer in the *Phaedrus*; witness also the radical incongruity of introducing the simple austere Socrates into the artificial scenery of Athenian high life in the *Symposium* and making him confide his most intimate thoughts to a group of perfumed dandies. The truth is (here Fite stands with Chapman) that his art is too often a thing of mere artifice and decoration, or a method of ironical evasion of issues. It may be remarked in passing that Fite is of two minds regarding the historical Socrates, sometimes suggesting that he was a great liberal and experimental intelligence whom the

illiberal Plato was incapable of representing fairly, and again presenting Socrates as implicated, along with his disciple, in sophistical dishonesty and posturing mock humility, behind which a colossal arrogance is only half concealed.

9. And finally, Fite denies that Plato was significant either as a man or as a practical moralist. He was "not quite a man . . . his point of view and his attitude towards life were very largely what would today be called adolescent, not to say childish, and what has traditionally been called 'feminine.'" Plato was "a defeated aristocrat" who put "class and party first"; when his claim to personal leadership was rejected, he reacted by injured indignation. These traits are brought into high relief by his impractical and undignified Sicilian adventures in the education of the young tyrant Dionysius, upon whom he inflicted lessons in geometry as a foundation for his wise exercise of royal power, and at whose pretensions to philosophic wisdom, after he had rejected Plato's tutelage, the great philosopher permitted himself to display irritation and jealousy. Believing that of all possible conceptions of the human good only one can be right, Plato is intolerant of any insight but his own. His pessimism and distrust of his fellow men reveals his superficial conception of human motivation. "His one idea of morality is self-restraint; for his imagination is haunted by scenes of debauchery, illustrated unwittingly, and only faintly, by his own *Symposium.*" His total inability to appreciate the aspirations of common men, the humble significance of the intimacies of their daily lives, his exclusively intellectual conception of a spiritual life "to be carried on in terms of logic and mathematics on behalf of impersonally 'great' ends," all this prompts the conclusion that "of all the writers of antiquity he is," so far from being Christian, "the most characteristically and explicitly 'pagan'."

Thus far our report may seem to have spoken as if Platonism and anti-Platonism were matters exclusively determined by the disinterested decisions of individual scholars, due allowance being made for their personal predilections and temperaments. But without commitment to a thoroughgoing deterministic theory of intellectual history, we must remind ourselves of the unblinkable fact that by no miracle of immunity has Platonic scholarship remained untouched by the deeper currents of historical change. Recent anti-Platonism is an outstanding case in point. One might say, without serious exaggeration, that during the decade of the thirties, the interpretation of Plato became a branch of economic and political, not to say, even, of military history. During these years when Fascism was hurling its imposing challenge to the democracies, it was inevitable that the coming war should cast its ideological shadow upon the interpretation of Plato, and that an international *Streit um Platon* should result, by comparison with which the issues raised by Fite were reduced to the proportions of a tempest in an academic inkpot.

It was now suddenly realized, no longer by a minority but by all thoughtful readers, and with a new sense of its full implications, that Plato in the *Republic* had raised in its most radical form the problem of leadership, and as it seemed to many, had advocated as a governmental ideal a pattern of political organization and social control that stood much nearer to dictatorship than to the Lockean program of government by consent of the governed. Fascist propagandists and their counterparts in Soviet Russia were quick to perceive the value to their respective causes implicit in the august name of

Plato.[11] As a consequence, the defenders of democracy presently began to dissociate themselves from so dubious an ally; in such a storm it seemed a dictate of elementary prudence to lighten their vessel by casting overboard this ill-omened prophet whom in an evil hour, mistaking him for one of themselves, they had let come aboard.

Out of the controversy emerged, among others,[12] a book in which the political philosophy of Plato was closely inspected to disclose its bearing on the then current conflict of political ideals. This is *Plato Today*, by R. H. S. Crossman, a one time Oxford Fellow who already, at the date of publication in 1939, was an active member of the British Labour Party, of whose social philosophy he became one of the leading defenders. With his University background and the foreground of his political experience, Mr. Crossman brings to the study of Plato a rare and, one might say, truly Platonic set of qualifications, which have set their mark upon the book. Crossman's major interest, as Reinhold Niebuhr remarks in the foreword, is "in relating Platonic political insights to political issues." And Niebuhr adds his conviction that the book is "a valuable contribution to contemporary political thought as well as to an understanding of Plato's Athens."

How, then, does Crossman stand in relation to our central interest? He has been listed here in a sequence of Plato's all but unqualified opponents. Does the gravamen of his book confirm the complaints of Chapman and Fite? Does it array him with the defenders of democracy against a supposedly fascistic Plato? The answer must be "yes," with some important reservations.

Crossman holds that Plato was wrong, both for his times and for ours, at several major points in his political program, and that the modern world would be dangerously wrong in following the direction he sees indicated in the *Republic*, away from free popular government and toward the thoroughgoing regimentation of society by benevolent aristocrats possessed of supposedly final wisdom. Had Crossman halted his critique at this point, it would be doubtful wisdom to classify him as an anti-Platonist. Few indeed, even among Plato's most ardent admirers, would regard the *Republic*, thus literally taken, as a model for contemporary use. Crossman, however, steps across the line. His anti-Platonism is rendered almost inevitable by his initial assumption that in the political organization of Plato's ideal city we find the sum and substance of its author's recommendations for the Greek world of his day. Crossman's further condemnation of Plato (and by corollary of contemporary efforts to draw instruction from the *Republic*) is expressible in the following theses, maintained explicitly or by clear implication in his book: (1) that the institu-

---

[11] A consideration of the voluminous literature lies beyond the boundaries of our discussion. Further mention of it is made on p. 441 below.

[12] See Appendix I, p. 583 ff., which discusses the work of another Platonic detractor, A. D. Winspear, author of *The Genesis of Plato's Thought*, 1940, and the criticism of Plato contained in Toynbee's *Study of History*, 1934–1939.

tional structure of the ideal city, without basic changes and far-reaching adaptations, was intended by Plato for immediate imposition upon actual communities of ordinary mortals; (2) that in reorganizing these communities, assigning to some of their inhabitants hereditary power, to others permanent subordination, Plato would have followed no higher principle than that of aristocratic class prejudice; and (3) that Plato would have sanctioned the employment, wherever expedient, of the most repellent weapons in the arsenal of political power.

On the other hand, as we shall see, Crossman regards Plato with a very considerable respect, both as writer and as thinker, construing him as a man of great ability and uncommonly good will, sincerely devoted to furthering the general happiness. There is also a sense in which, for all his criticisms, Crossman is himself a Platonist *malgré lui*. We find him sharing Plato's conviction that in the human soul, awaiting only discovery and consistent development, there is implanted a type and standard of justice in accordance with which the life of individuals and community should find their guidance and their rule. True that for Plato those human souls which are capable of awakening of their own initiative, and of holding fast the vision, are the few gifted natures, while Crossman cherishes the Christian faith that all men are potential possessors of this spiritual energy. Both men are committed to the sovereignty of reason in human affairs, as against the prescriptions of custom or the claims of superior power, Crossman, indeed, going so far as to urge upon a democrat the necessity of abandoning such a fundamental article of faith as belief in representative government, if reason and experience condemn its actual value in terms of its contribution to human good. And finally, from their separate standpoints, both men clearly see the extent to which economic and other social institutions underlie and condition the operation of human society and draw the identical conclusion that all such institutions must be subordinated to the authority of a moral ideal.

Throughout his book Crossman preserves to a remarkable degree his judicial poise, and though he has decided views of his own regarding the points at issue, he is misled only on rare occasions into special pleading and the use of an envenomed vocabulary.

Crossman prepares his reader for the understanding of Plato's thought by sketching in the background of several centuries of Greek economic and political change. The life of Plato was cast in a period when the city state had fallen into corruption, and politics had degenerated into ugly strife between equally unprincipled rival factions, while the whole Greek world was threatened from without by the rising empires of Carthage, and subsequently of Macedon. In Athens, Socrates, by questioning and discrediting the beliefs of his fellow citizens in the interests of an as yet undefined higher morality, had still further undermined social stability. Plato, seeing the moral corruption about him, undertook as his life's mission the discovery of this new higher morality, to which Socrates had but pointed, and the development of its consequences for politics, along lines which he wrongly believed Socrates would have approved.

Crossman now addresses himself to describing the tragically mistaken direction in which Plato turned. Being an aristocrat, and scorning the mean employments and pettinesses of the common man, Plato could not hope for a regeneration of the state through a moral awakening of the mass of the citizens. Instead, he dreamed of the restoration of the feudal organization of society, under the absolute control of the existing aristocracy, when once this had been morally reëducated, intellectually enlightened, and imbued with a spirit of dedication to the happiness of all the citizens. The Spartan constitution, with modifications designed to make it an instrument for the general good, would furnish the ground plan for the model state. Plato's own part would be the founding of a university, the Academy, to disseminate this political ideal, and to serve as the training ground for the new governing elite which should provide philosophic rulers for the Greek world. Crossman thus depicts Plato as a practical reformer, convinced of his own rightness and steeled to adopt any measures necessary to bring to his fellow Greeks the benefit of his wisdom; the *Republic*, a book admirably frank and fair in dealing with the reader, is his program of action.

Crossman next imagines the author of the *Republic* as visiting Great Britain, the United States, Russia, and Germany, in 1939. In each country, Plato is represented as examining the national life to determine its ends and values, and as disapproving materialism or barbarism, wherever, as in America, Russia, or Germany, either of these appears to displace the philosophic aim, the virtue and consequent true happiness of the people. But Crossman also depicts Plato as in each country approving, or recommending for immediate introduction, the existence of a small governing class specially trained for political responsibility, and the continued or newly instituted total exclusion of the ordinary citizen from all participation or interest in government. Plato is made to admire the various "noble lies" (Crossman's Plato constantly uses the phrase) by which the common people are deluded into believing what those who wield the actual power wish them to believe: namely, in America and Great Britain, and even in Russia, that the common people themselves have a voice in the government; in Germany, that all ideas and actions which its rulers reprobate are sinister Jewish machinations. Crossman's Plato does demand that the universities where the ruling class is trained must be left untrammeled in their pursuit of the truth, not turned into propaganda mills for inculcating the blind and brutish beliefs of those who now wield power; yet he would also wholly approve the use of violence and murder, as in Germany and Russia, provided only these were employed for nobler ends. In a chapter on modern marriage, Crossman shows Plato setting a correct value on sex as an element in truly personal love between kindred spirits, and credits him with having perceived rightly the necessity of a new type of marriage and sex morality for any social group in which women are to be the equals of men. Of these elements, then, as Crossman conceives it, is composed Plato's message for our time.

Returning to antiquity, Crossman describes Plato's failure to benefit in any way the Greek world of his time, and then analyzes this failure and the uselessness of Plato's message in general, as due to three cardinal errors: Plato's premature despair of the potentialities of the common man; his mistaken belief that a just government can be established by revolution; and his conviction that the final truth can be discovered, and that freedom of thought ought thereafter to be suppressed. Crossman's own faith is in the power of reason and the infinite possibility of self-development of every man; and on the strength of this he would have us alter any governmental form and break down every orthodoxy; in the world today, "it is Socrates, not Plato, whom we need."

This, then, is Crossman's final condemnation of a Plato to whose merits he has nevertheless so honorably borne witness. Though Crossman would no doubt deprecate the sentiment, it is difficult to suppress a word of regret that so enlightened and appreciative a student of Plato should have taken an official position on the opposition benches.

By far the most systematic, detailed attack upon Plato's metaphysical, moral, and political thought is that of K. R. Popper, comprising the first part of his extensive work, *The Open Society and Its Enemies*, which first appeared in 1945.[13] Professor Popper is second to none in his determined opposition to what he regards as the essential Plato; he announces his general agreement with Crossman's strictures, departing from him only in order to go further in the same direction. It is Popper's claim to have revealed, more clearly than any previous writer, the uncompromisingly totalitarian character of Plato's thought.

The plan of our book will not permit a continuous exposition and examination, point by point, of Popper's arguments; we shall consider them separately, under distinct captions, in conjunction with the arguments of the other critics. This, unless we exercise special care, may be unjust to the author of a volume so notable for its systematic character. We shall accordingly attempt in the following outline of his argument to balance this disadvantage by special attention to its logical connectedness.

It may be well to begin with a brief statement of the conclusions reached: Plato was seeking a way to escape from the dangerous instability and moral

---

[13] A second and revised edition, Princeton, 1950, has appeared during the process of preparation of this book, and to this all references will be made. Care has also been directed to bringing all quotations and comments into line with Popper's new version. The changes he has introduced into the new edition will be discussed in n. 17, p. 21 below.

uncertainties of the society in which he lived, an escape into the security of a tribalistic "closed society," in which stability is at a maximum, the interest of the group as a whole becomes the absolute criterion of value, and the life of the individual is rigidly subordinated at all points to tribal prescriptions and taboos. Plato's motivation was psychological: resentment of change, class prejudice, scornful distrust of the common man's capacity for self-direction, and — inconsistently — the desire to benefit the common man by relieving him of strain; the reasons he adduced in support were metaphysical and involved the subordination of moral choice and political action to the supposed laws of historical decay. Plato believed that there had actually existed an aboriginal political state of all but Utopian perfection, to which it was yet possible by a bold reimposition of autocratic rule to effect a return. His *Republic* is to be read not as innovating speculation concerning untried future idealities, but as his serious attempt to reconstruct, as literally as possible, a state which had, he believed, actually existed in the bright morning of the primal day.

Popper's attack upon Plato is the negative aspect of his own positive conviction, which motivates his entire book, that the greatest of all revolutions is the transition from the "closed society" to the "open society," an association of free individuals, respecting each other's rights within the framework of mutual protection supplied by the state, and achieving, through the making of responsible, rational decisions, a growing measure of humane and enlightened life.

Popper sees in the Athenian democracy of the latter part of the fifth century a society that was for the first time in history emerging into relative "openness." The Periclean ideal, as expounded in the famous Funeral Oration, constituted its charter, which was supplemented by the thought of a brilliant group of champions of equalitarian individualism and humanitarianism, including Herodotus, Protagoras, and other outstanding sophists, and Socrates, "perhaps the greatest individualist of all times." These men were breaking down the old barriers, intellectual and moral, and pointing the way forward.

Opponents of the new order, however, remained, the political party of the oligarchs, the privileged or formerly privileged classes of Athens, desirous of regaining the power they had enjoyed before the establishment of the democratic constitution. It was not the excesses of the democracy, inflamed by the reckless rhetoric of the demagogues, Popper would have us believe, but the oligarchic Spartophiles, who by their disloyalty, sabotage, and on occasion outright treason, encompassed the ruin of their native city, the defeat of Athens by Sparta in 404 B.C., which only a revived democracy was able partially to make good.

How, then, did Plato stand in relation to this struggle between reaction and the progressive movement of his time? Popper leaves us in no doubt, if we are to trust his reading of the record: Plato stood, however unwillingly, on the side of reaction. Scion of an aristocratic family with strong oligarchic affiliations, he was early indoctrinated with the love of Sparta, the worst features of which, un-Athenian infanticide and harshness to slaves and under- lings, awakened in him no repugnance. The noble achievements of his native Athens he mocked and denied. Though brought for a time by the powerful moral magnetism of Socrates under the sway of humanitarian, individualist sentiments, he was unable to keep the faith. Frustrated by the turn of political affairs, he found no outlet in the world of action for those consuming ambi- tions which remained with him to the end. The dark struggle in Plato's soul between the Socratic faith and his growing treason to its principles accounts for the "spell of Plato," lending a hitherto unexplained fascination to his writings. For the record of Plato's thought, as Popper reads it, is a story of continuous degradation, in which the noble Socratic gospel, as Plato has sympathetically reported it in the *Apology*, the *Crito*, and others of the earlier dialogues, is gradually and treasonably perverted, against the inner protest of Plato's better self, into the poisonous crypto-totalitarianism of the *Republic*, with its scorn for all that the real Socrates had held dear and its dishonest attribution to him of a dogmatic authoritarianism which blasphemed the memory of the modest and cautious doubter; finally it is transformed into the "theory of inquisition" elaborated in the *Laws*, a polity in which Socrates would, with Plato's full approval, have met the death penalty for presuming to exercise the freedom of rational inquiry.

Popper insists that he does not see in Plato the merely dishonest propa- gandist for the reactionary cause; Plato, he tells us, was dishonest, but he was so in the interests of a cause in which he honestly believed. His hatred of democracy, even his very misanthropy, Popper believes, are not inconsistent with a strangely twisted and abstract love of his fellow Greeks and a zealous wish to procure for them the greatest happiness of which he believed them capable. The grounds upon which this interpretation proceeds will appear from the following exposition of Popper's analysis of Plato's positive beliefs.

At the very base of Plato's social philosophy Popper thinks he has dis- covered a species of fatalism, to which he gives the generic name of "his- toricism." Historicists are all those who believe that the final determiner of the conditions of human existence and the principles of value is a certain nonhuman, self-moving, and (with varying degrees of qualification) inevitable law of historical change. In the modern world Hegel and Marx in their re- spective fashions are examples of what Popper's term denotes. But these men thought of history as a process of forward motion, a vehicle of continuous advance. Plato, on the contrary, is an evolutionist in reverse; from the really perfect eternal Form (the Platonic idea, conceived as a dynamic "primo- genitor"), was born the first and natural, and all but perfect state. This state, Popper asserts, was for Plato no mere ideal, but an actual historical com- munity, from which, through successive stages of increasing badness, the villainous political systems of Plato's own day had been derived. Thus, in Popper's view, Plato imagined himself to be in possession not only of a true conception of how the historical process operates, but more importantly, he thought he had in hand a method of reading off, without further labor of thought or anxiety of conscience, the true scale of values relevant to appraising a human community.

But this knowledge left him still in the domain of bare theory; the facts needed for its practical application were still to seek. Where could the social archaeologist discover concrete examples to help him reconstruct and then preserve the ideal state of the past? Popper credits Plato with bringing great sociological insight and historical imagination to bear upon the solution of this problem. First, Plato arrived by analysis of recent Greek history at the conviction that at the beginning of every revolution, and hence at the very heart of social change, will be discovered a division of economic interest within the ruling class. Plato had here a principle of which, as will soon be apparent, he was to make full use. To this a second principle was added. Casting a shrewd eye about him, Plato noted that among contemporary Greek states were some which, like Crete and Sparta, possessed characteristics which stamped them as survivors from an earlier and hence more perfect time. A third principle, biological and eugenic, completed the theoretical frame. This was the fabrication, by Plato himself, of an occult number lore capable of regulating the quality of all human offspring.

The conditions for a solution of Plato's problem were now clear: he must note and combine the vestigial traces in the ancient constitutions of Crete and Sparta into a whole which, with the addition of the one modern element of Plato's number wisdom, in proportion as it achieved unanimity within its ruling class, would acquire the perfection of the primordial perfect state, and, essential ingredient and preserver of perfection, its stability. Plato himself, sole possessor of the eugenical number and descendant of ancient Attic royalty, would be its rightful Philosopher King, guardian of the purity of its "master race."

The result of these inquiries — the picture of a closed society, kept closed by all the totalitarian devices of censorship, propaganda, racism, autarky, and, for the ruling classes, thoroughgoing communism of wives, children, and property — Plato presented to the world in a cunning disguise of consciously falsified Socratic rationalism and pretended love of truth and justice as his *Republic*.

The preceding summary has conveyed an inadequate measure of Popper's wide and detailed acquaintance with many fields of thought, and it has only suggested his unqualified commitment to liberal and democratic ideals, to the defense of which the entire work is dedicated. It is the more unfortunate that the mistaken zeal of the crusader has, paradoxically, denatured his learning and his good will, the learning passing into a technique for perverting Plato's

basic meanings and distorting the whole context of his life and thought; the
good will passing, by uneasy alternations of attitude, now into moral indignation, now into suspicion or distaste, and on occasion, into what one of his
reviewers has called the "rage to blame." [14]

We may see this process at work in Popper's handling of one particular
weapon of debate. In spite of the high rating one must accord his initial intention of fairness, his hatred for the enemies of the "open society," his
zeal to destroy whatever seems to him destructive of the welfare of mankind,
has led him into the extensive use of what may be called terminological counter-
propaganda. Instances abound. Does Plato speak of his guardians, in the
Republic, under the image of shepherds caring for the human flock? Popper,
seeing in this only an analogue to modern propagandist deception, translates
and transforms the human flock into "human cattle," and by dint of many a
repetition of the phrase, fastens upon Plato's guardians an indelible smear.[15]
The duties and responsibilities of the guardians appear uniformly as their

---

[14] Richard Robinson, mingling praise and
blame in his extensive review of *The Open
Society and Its Enemies* ("Dr. Popper's
Defense of Democracy," 1951).

In this connection a brief review of
Popper's reviewers may be in place. The
extreme diversity of the reviews makes generalization difficult, but the following statements are offered as a conscientious first
approximation. The book has been well, in
some quarters even enthusiastically, received. Almost all reviews have spoken of
its extensive and varied learning and its
obvious friendship to the cause of individualistic liberalism. One eminent authority in
the domain of Platonic studies, Lord Lindsay, in 1945 welcomed the book as "exciting" and "illuminating," and expressed the
wish that it might be widely read; the treatment of Plato he regarded as unfair, though
conceding that "there is a good deal in the
indictment" that Plato had proposed a too
strictly regimented society on the Spartan
model. With a few exceptions in Popper's
favor, however, it is noticeable that reviewers possessed of special competence in particular fields — and here Lindsay is again
to be included — have objected to Popper's
conclusions in those very fields. Social scientists and social philosophers have deplored his radical denial of historical causa-
tion, together with his espousal of Hayek's
systematic distrust of larger programs of social reform; historical students of philosophy have protested his violent polemical
handling of Plato, Aristotle, and particu-

larly Hegel; ethicists have found contradictions in the ethical theory ("critical dualism") upon which his polemic is largely
based. It will be noted, then, that Popper's
attack on Plato cannot be said to have convinced the majority of his best qualified
judges. Yet the partial accord his views
have won justifies submitting them to the
more inclusive and detailed consideration
our sequel will supply.

[15] Popper has acknowledged his indebtedness to Toynbee for this conception of
"human cattle" (Popper, *op. cit.*, p. 498).
He has, however, made it fully his own by
intensification and the implication of sinister motives. In Toynbee's hands the phrase
was disparaging, indeed, but as a reader of
Toynbee's parallel discussion of the Ottoman Turks (Toynbee, III, pp. 26–48) will
perceive more figurative, and not intended
to carry the implication, which Popper has
even made explicit, of deliberate exploitation of a despised subject population (Popper, pp. 47–52). Toynbee at most is charging Plato (Toynbee, III, pp. 90–99) with
sponsoring a benevolently intended ant-col-
ony, in which producers and warriors are so
fully identified with their social functions
as to impair their individual human character, and which was destined to gravitate
into an oppressive system in which the governing directors would inevitably become
parasites upon the exploited animals below. — It is true that with his characteristic inconsistency toward Plato, Toynbee on
one occasion, in unconscious anticipation

"prerogatives" or "privileges." Those citizens whom Plato admits to his city as able to serve only by bodily strength, are labeled, in what purports to be a direct quotation from Plato, as "drudges," though Plato used a milder word (*diakonoi*) perhaps best translated as "servitors." [16] Nor is Plato allowed a myth to be told to all the citizens, including the guardians, about their common birth from the soil and their distinctive differences, typified by the different metals mixed into their souls, without Popper's interposing between us and the just appreciation of Plato's parable, out of the Nazi lexicon, the slogan "Blood and Soil." Such language is doubtless sincere, but only with the sincerity of the partisan, and invites the unwary to draw mistaken inferences of the first magnitude.[17]

---

of Popper, goes the whole way, and speaks (Toynbee, I, pp. 247–9) of Plato's 'myth of the metals' as if Plato were a cynical puller of propagandist wires in the interests of racialism; we shall have occasion to deal with this charge of Toynbee's and of Popper's in a later section; see p. 430 below.

[16] So Shorey renders it, *Republic* 371 D, Loeb Library. It can also be translated "agents" (so Lindsay, A.D., Everyman Library edition, p. 50), or by the Latin word *ministri*. Cf. n. 72, p. 168 below.

[17] See n. 266, p. 357, for an instructive example.

Popper's new edition, or rather that portion of it which deals with Plato, embodies numerous changes, most of which raise no new issue, being merely extensions and corroborations of views presented in the first edition. Three new features, however, deserve comment. (a) Popper has included reference (pp. 485–6) to several authors whom he has found to have expressed views similar to his own. These are Bowra, Fite, Winspear, and Kelsen, with whom the present book will have occasion to deal, and B. Farrington; only with the latter does Popper give warning that he substantially disagrees. Popper's implication that his own view tallies closely with those of the other writers named must be taken to indicate, especially in view of the inclusion of Winspear (see our Appendix I, p. 583), that the essential point of agreement is condemnation or unfavorable criticism of Plato; he does not consider it necessary to reject the support of writers who, like Kelsen, Win-

spear, and to some degree Fite, subject Socrates to the same destructive criticism. Yet Popper's whole interpretation of Plato the man, the reactionary betrayer of the faith of the Great Generation, may be said to depend on the contrast which he draws between Socrates and Plato. These authors in this respect support not Popper, but our own position, in that they show Plato's thought as continuous with that of Socrates; though we should combine this belief not with the joint condemnation in all major respects of both, but with an attempt to show that both were admirable men, whose thought can still be drawn upon for enlightenment. (b) Additional arguments (discussed on pp. 462 and 463, below) have been introduced in support of the thesis that Plato was ambition-ridden and secretly lusting for power. Popper has abated none of his conviction that hidden psychic abnormalities are to be detected in Plato, has indeed heightened the supposed contrast between Socratic modesty and Platonic self-exaltation. (c) Corrections have been made, removing erroneous statements of fact which in the first edition served to underprop essential parts of Popper's argument. Three of these errors, of great importance respectively, as we shall show, for Plato's attitude to racialism, state worship, and the idealization of the past, have been removed, without causing Popper in any case to make the necessary modification in his interpretation as a whole. (Cf. n. 45, p. 519 below, for references to document this statement.) Thus the major issues raised by the first edition, stand.

Our summary statement of the detractors' views is now complete, and we shall in due course undertake our detailed reply. But if the hearing is to be fairly conducted, an initial disadvantage to Plato's cause must be noted and offset: We who read, and those who have arraigned Plato as the enemy of the democratic ideal in some or all of its many aspects are, after all, partners in a common faith, standing together on a platform of convictions and aspirations developed through the centuries, that brings us into a closer relation to each other than can without effort be established between ourselves and any thinker of the ancient world. We are told that this ancient philosopher Plato attacked our common faith, and our hostility is on the alert. It is of some value merely to recognize this fact at this point in our discussion. In ensuing chapters we shall make it a principal part of our business to surmount the obstacle of the years and, although we shall not find in Plato a spokesman of all our values, we shall hope in the light of a closer imaginative sympathy with the cultural situation in which his life was cast to reach a more informed and impartial judgment of what he taught, and still can teach.

But were not most readers left a little breathless by the variety and virulence of the accusations? Who would have thought the old man had so much bad blood in him? Defamer of his native Athens, betrayer of his master Socrates, racist, statist, propagandist unabashed, equivocating, man-hating, boy-loving, frustrated aristocratical snob — one was prepared for an imputation that the marble statue had feet of clay; we hear, instead, that it is composed entirely of mud.

The observant reader may well intervene at this point to say that it is unfair to charge all the chargers with imputing to Plato this whole catalogue of crimes, when even Popper has not included them all, and has, moreover, qualified the blackness of his indictment by including a stray ray or two of benevolent intention on Plato's part. The objection is valid in so far as purely logical considerations are concerned, but it does not take account of the subtler danger. Charges have a way of adding themselves up in a susceptible mind, and even mutually inconsistent charges are capable of psychologically reënforcing each other, when once receptivity to the guilt of a defendant has been established.

A closer examination of the four sets of charges will, in point of fact, reveal an ironical parallel to the situation which Fite describes as existing among those "idealistic" interpreters of Plato, the fabricators of the "Platonic legend," a situation which he turns against their credibility as witnesses. He diverts his readers with the comic spectacle of a Dean Inge finding in Plato a spokesman for the "inner light," after the Dean's own Quakerish fashion, and an A. E. Taylor recreating Plato in the highly admired composite image of a medieval mystic and a Hebrew prophet.

Less diverting, perhaps, but logically of at least equal and opposite weight, is the counterpicture that could be painted of the detractors of Plato, among whom this same procedure is visible in reverse. To Fite, whose moral world revolves about the central axis of personality, Plato's primal lack is his failure to value the uniqueness of the individual. And Popper, understandably enough, sees the Nazi terror lurking at every turn in Plato's thought.

Plato's attackers, also, not content with variety, add a note of mutual contradiction. Thus, we hear Fite deploring the perverse and brutish attitude of Plato towards sexual relations, and Crossman extolling Plato's good taste and practical moral wisdom in this realm. Again, while Fite denies that there is any touch of moral idealism to redeem the prudential spirit of calculation in the *Gorgias*, Popper is busy interpreting the same dialogue as evidence that Socrates, and not his betrayer Plato, could come close to the very spirit of the Christian gospels.

We have here a situation not wholly dissimilar to that contemplated in the opening paragraph of Augustus De Morgan's delightful dissection of mathematical fallacies, the *Budget of Paradoxes*. The passage is here reproduced, prefaced by an urgent disavowal of what may appear to be the condescending implications of the analogy:

If I had before me a fly and an elephant, having never seen more than one such magnitude of either kind; and if the fly were to endeavour to persuade me that he was larger than the elephant, I might by possibility be placed in a difficulty. The apparently little creature might use such arguments about the effect of distance, and might appeal to such laws of sight and hearing as I, if unlearned in these things, might be unable wholly to reject. But if there were a thousand such flies, all buzzing, to appearance, about the great creature; and, to a fly, declaring, each one for himself, that he was bigger than the quadruped; and all giving different and frequently contradictory reasons; and each one despising and opposing the reasons of the other — I should feel quite at my ease. I would certainly say, My little friends, the case of each one of you is destroyed by the rest.[18]

The purpose of the just-cited analogy must not be missed. It is, admittedly, a *tu quoque ad hominem*, spoken by one fly to a swarm of others, beseeching the whole species to be content with a less pretentious buzz. For all that the logic of analogy can tell us, several of us flies may be uttering at least some portion of the truth, and it is conceivable that one is the oracle of unqualified verity. The most that can be validly inferred from the differences of opinion among the various critics and admirers of Plato is the logical impossibility that he can be guilty of all the crimes, or possess all the excellences, that have been ascribed to him. In any case, each specific claim has a right to be considered on its merits, unprejudiced by the company it keeps. This justice we shall seek to secure for our opponents.

In giving priority of consideration to the attack upon Plato we may inadvertently have confirmed the general impression that recent Platonic literature is uniformly a literature of dissent. The truth is rather that the dissenters have had a decided advantage in the contest for the public ear. For theirs was

---

[18] Augustus De Morgan, *A Budget of Paradoxes* 1872, (*sub initio*).

the more newsworthy story, of all but yellow journalistic appeal: "Ancient Attic Sage Exposed." This is the contemporary "Platonic legend," and at this writing, bids fair to have established itself firmly in the general mind.[19]

It is therefore easy to forget the quality and extent of the literature that continues vigorously to maintain the questioned thesis of Plato's greatness and relevance to the problems of our times. The name of Werner Jaeger comes first to mind; his *Paideia,* bearing lightly its load of historical and philosophical learning, is easily the outstanding exhibit here. Jaeger's thought, however, from the very nature of his enterprise — the tracing of the development of the Greek ideal of culture in all its aspects — moves largely within the ambit of the ancient world, and seldom descends from its Olympian detachment to discuss the transcultural values of Greek thought.

At the other pole from Jaeger in this respect is John Wild, whose *Plato's*

---

[19] An image of a "contemporized" Plato, viewed as if in a distorting mirror, is presented by Sherwood Anderson in the preface to his play about Socrates, *Barefoot in Athens,* 1951, and was supplied by him also to readers of the *New York Times* for October 28, 1951 ("Notes on Socrates," Drama Section, p. 1), by way of helping his prospective audiences to view the play, then opening on Broadway, in the desired perspective. When a dramatic artist gives his documented reasons justifying his interpretation of history, he has, by that act, forfeited the protection of his dramatic license. It would be impossible to expose the misconceptions to which Anderson stands sponsor, short of summarizing in advance the entire argument of the present volume. Suffice it to say here that the Andersonian version of Plato plainly bespeaks a close and docile reading of Popper, departing from this author in almost nothing but to make more explicit and to translate, one may say, into the vernacular, Popper's most savage imputations. That Anderson's new-found distrust of Plato did not, as he implies (*Barefoot in Athens,* p. vii), arise solely from his own troubled reëxamination of Plato, assisted only by the chronological ordering of the dialogues achieved by Platonic scholars — that Anderson did not, as it might appear, stumble independently on the self-same "obvious" truths which had previously been uncovered by Popper — is shown clearly by the otherwise incredibly close parallel in sentence structure and thought pattern between Anderson's p. ix and Popper's p. 44; Anderson has even gone so far as to set in quotation-marks, as if they were verbatim utterances of Plato, sentences paraphrased direct, with some resulting inaccuracies, from Popper's already slightly distorted quotations from the Platonic text (see, e.g., our n. 228, p. 340). Anderson accordingly presents to the readers of his play a Plato who is the sinister advocate of "a communistic and brutal dictatorship," "maintained . . . by a ruthless use of assassination" (pp. ix, xii), and who dishonestly attributes these ideas to the liberal, intensely democratic and individualist Socrates; this Plato also advocates most of the other evils and commits most of the other faults found in him by Popper. (It is fair to note that Anderson has also added some errors of his own, e.g., his confusion, on p. x, of the institutions of Plato's *Laws* with those of the *Republic,* and his naive citation of a notoriously spurious Xenophontic letter to Xanthippe.) In his *Times* article, Anderson presented a similarly underhanded Plato, a "homosexual" who championed what was, in practical terms, only a "dictatorship of thugs," prepared to employ without scruple "murder and torture." Since Brooks Atkinson, reviewing this play on the corresponding page of the *Times* for November 11, 1951, twice praises it as revealing Anderson's customary careful "scholarship" — an opinion which may impose itself also upon many other readers of Anderson's learned-sounding preface — it is the more important to show the extent to which Anderson has derived from Popper the discolored Plato he presents.

Theory of Man cuts itself boldly free from the historical moorings of Plato's thought, and attempts, with great dialectical agility, to construct out of Plato's scattered insights the basis for a philosophy of culture, valid for every place and time. Thus Wild, in the interests of what he calls "greater philosophical precision," waives all consideration of the "archaic" questions that concern Plato's relation to Greek society of his period, leaving these to the philologists, and brushes aside in one footnote the whole contemporary literature of attack. The result is a book which, though of great interest and value as evidence of the vitality of the Platonic stimulus and its bearing on the cultural problems of our times, has not chosen to concern itself with meeting the precise attack with which the friends of Plato are currently faced.[20]

The two examples chosen from among the living friends of Plato may serve to suggest the justification for the present book. We have no wish to save Plato from the consequences of any fair accusation. But it is our conviction, born perhaps of tradition, but confirmed by long and anxious thought, that the attack upon Plato has passed the bounds of just criticism. In this crisis, the friends of Plato must not be content proudly to ignore the insolence of the attackers; neither can they further Plato's cause merely by erecting brilliant dialectical structures in his name. They must meet the new charges on their own grounds, accept of the indictment what in conscience they must, repel what in honor they can, confident that in such service they are remaining true to the noblest moral insights of their own epoch and at the same time to the spirit of their master. The furtherance of these aims is, then, the proper business of this book.

---

[20] The two mentioned from among Plato's present-day supporters and admirers serve as examples, illustrative of the direct study and evaluation of Plato's thought; no implication is intended that they stand alone. We shall have occasion on later pages to refer to the work of such men as Morrow and Cherniss, who have testified to the good sense and uprightness of the man, and to the philosophical coherence, subtlety, and fertility of his thought; and the list could be vastly extended.

It is also true that defense of Plato, of the sort here intended, has been made, though to our knowledge only on a smaller scale. As examples, we may cite the article, "On Misunderstanding Plato," by Professor G. C. Field, 1944, and chapter X, "Plato Today," in his Home University Library volume, *The Philosophy of Plato*, 1949. Professor Field is protesting, against Crossman, Hogben, and others, the unwisdom and injustice of setting Plato in modern perspective and identifying the resulting distortion with the actual Plato. Unfortunately, we became acquainted with Professor Field's defense of Plato in these two works only after the present book was largely written, but it is none the less pleasant to acknowledge in him an able and distinguished ally.

Other defenders of Plato, at least against Popper's extreme attack, include two philosophers who have figured among his more notable reviewers: Richard Robinson, mentioned on p. 20, who dissociates himself from the authoritarian element in Plato's thought and from Plato's tendency, as he views it, to exalt the state, but protests sharply against Popper's ascription to Plato of malevolence and fraud, racialism and other assorted totalitarian traits; and H. D. Aiken, to whom we shall later refer (p. 475), who has some vigorous and eloquent words to say in defense of "the Socratic Plato, for whom the polar ideals of order *and* freedom, . . . individual conscience *and* public opinion . . . have their inviolable rights."

2

The Literary Artist

Plato has in several places disparaged the importance of
the written word, but the world has not permitted itself to
be thereby discouraged from placing a very high value on
the words that he has himself written. Indeed, through the centuries Plato
has often been read quite as much for his readability as for reasons more
austere, as foretokened, after the fact, by the legend of the swarm of bees
alighting on the infant Plato's lips. In attacking Plato's literary quality, a contemporary critic is therefore attacking not merely Plato, but, one may say, un-
counted generations of appreciative readers whose judgment, collectively at
least, would seem to outweigh his; for this department of literary appraisal
is one in which there is small advantage accruing to the modern judge as such.

It will be remembered from the preceding chapter that Plato's merit as a
writer is not denied *in toto* by any of the detractors. Crossman, indeed, cannot in this respect properly be classified as a detractor. He pays Plato the
handsome tribute of calling him "first and foremost an artist," and refers
to the little poems that have come down under Plato's name as "among the
most exquisite we possess." Crossman's only detraction here is his addition
that Plato, in the interests of philosophy and the regeneration of Greece,
"deliberately allowed the springs of his imagination to dry up," a statement
which, though it possesses a certain measure of truth, requires modification
in view of the imaginative depth and richness of such late dialogues as
Timaeus and *Critias*. When so corrected, it is tantamount to asserting that
Plato refused to allow his literary imagination to override his philosophical
conscience.

Popper, in other departments the most exuberant of all the detractors, has
very little to say under the present head. His one major reproach is inspired
by his suspicion that Plato's greatest flights of eloquence have for their function precisely to hide the weakness of his thought; and similarly that the
occasional digressions and dramatic hesitations with which the quest of Justice
in the *Republic* is embellished have as their motive the distraction of the

reader's attention from the trickery of the argument, while at the same time unconsciously revealing Plato's sense of guilt and fear of forthrightness of statement. Such interpretations plainly fall outside the categories of literary criticism. We can deal with them only from the standpoint of conclusions reached in later chapters. For the rest, Popper's practice is to ignore, on principle, Plato's literary achievement. We are free, then, to limit our consideration to the faults that Chapman and Fite have found in Plato's artistry.

To have brought clearly to view the element of logical play in the Platonic dialogues would have been to render a service to those readers whose introduction to Plato has taught them to expect nothing in his pages but the sober search for truth. This Chapman has done, but with a vengeance, extending the "element" until it has absorbed into itself the whole. With precisely that quality of clever and witty equivocation which he ascribes to Plato, Chapman, with infinite gusto, devotes several amusing pages to the proving of his hyperbolical paradox.[1] We can follow him all the way in his suggestion that the enjoyment of logical play was no innovation of Plato's, but a deeply rooted addiction of the Greek race, an overflow, one might say, of their superabundant intellectual energies, finding expression in a variety of literary forms.[2] And we will agree, again, with the suggestion, which Chapman was not the first to make, that many passages in the Platonic dialogues may be likened to a contest of wits; — Chapman's analogy is with the game and play of chess.[3]

But at this point we must part company with Chapman. We shall have more than one occasion to remark the cavalier fashion in which moral dissenters from Plato are apt to attribute to Socrates all those good qualities which otherwise they would be obliged to concede to Plato. This is one of the standard devices employed for taking down the dignity of Plato to any desired degree, and doubtless with great effect in the eyes of those readers who are willing to accept the given author's solution of the much vexed Socratic problem,[4] and allow him to rest the weight of his argument upon it. Chapman is a case in point. To him Socrates was the great conscience who solved moral problems by the heroism of the instinctive act,[5] while Plato, in his poverty of moral intuition, was baffled by the martyrdom of his master[6] and could only explain it to himself and others by replacing the Socratic instinct by a shimmering set of ingenious rational equivocations,[7] which in reality explained nothing, but served merely as a highly entertaining substitute for the real Socrates. On this assumption, it was plainly impossible for Chapman to

---

[1] Chapman, *op. cit.*, pp. 141–144.
[2] *Ibid.*, p. 139.
[3] *Ibid.*, p. 148.
[4] The present writer's "solution" of the Socratic problem will be found in later passages in this book, especially Appendix XVI, pp. 632 ff.
[5] *Ibid.*, pp. 165–166.
[6] *Ibid.*, p. 166.
[7] *Ibid.*, p. 164.

ascribe to the iron character of Socrates those playful touches of equivocation which are discoverable in the earlier half of Plato's *Apology*.[8] These must be intruded embroideries from Plato's hand; the veritable Socrates is the voice that speaks to us in the deeper and more solemn tones of the latter portion of his plea.[9]

That this procedure is arbitrary and unfair to Plato need scarcely be argued, since no accredited scholar supports the position to which Chapman (partly, it seems fair to say, by inadvertence) has here committed himself: that Socratic irony is un-Socratic. Nor does Chapman himself offer any shred of evidence for his view; he relies wholly on his literary and moral intuition. If this point is borne in mind, we need not accept Chapman's conception of Socrates as the simple, forthright spokesman of the unvarnished moral truth, in contrast to the evasive Plato. Let us see what will be the consequences of this correction to our estimate of Plato as a literary artist.

The immediate result is an enormous enlargement of stature. From the graceful little Hellenistic juggler into whom Chapman has cunningly transformed him, Plato springs back into his true proportions. The playful element, on the other hand, subsides into its proper minor position in the economy of the dialogues as a whole. Its dramatic function is revealed: to invest these ideally reported Socratic conversations with the atmosphere in which their originals occurred, to depict with sufficient realism the subtle shifts and turns in which reason becomes involved when the theme of thought is socialized and adapted to the exigencies of its occasion and to the perspectives of the individual minds involved. To have dramatized the Socratic quest for wisdom of life in all its rich and often puzzling blend of the ironical with the deadly earnest, this was Plato's artistic achievement in these dialogues of his early period (i.e., the period up to the *Republic*). And it is this that Chapman is denying, when he rates these dialogues as parlor entertainment of the first rank.[10] There is a certain irony in the fact that Chapman's most serious threat to Plato's fame as a literary artist is embodied in his praise. It results, not from denying his skill and deftness, but from so insisting upon it as to preclude his depth and dignity as a thinker. Only when his status as a thinker is reëstablished, is it possible to accord him his literary due.

The only rift that Chapman finds, on his own terms, in Plato's literary lute, is in the handling of the dialogue form. To Chapman's ear there is a lack of resonance; the voice is musically low, at times approaching monologue.[11] This Chapman ascribes to Plato's failure to observe that the dialogue, being a branch of the dramatic art, is subject to the dramatic requirement of bringing upon the stage some character who is in reality the "author-dis-

---

[8] *Ibid.*, p. 155.
[9] *Ibid.*, p. 156.
[10] Chapman never speaks of any of the later dialogues; to judge from anything he says, Plato might never have written them.
[11] *Ibid.*, p. 148.

guised-as-a-bystander," [12] and can thus, by his comments, now represent the feelings of the audience, and again offer an interpretation of the action. This necessity, it is charged, Plato failed to observe, with the results indicated. But perceiving, too late, his need for some equivalent, Plato resorted to the expedient of permitting Socrates, at the end of the dialogue, to emerge from the playhouse, and to speak in another character, that of Plato himself; and in so doing, Plato created simply an ambiguous duplication as between the two persons called by the same name.[13]

This is an ingenious thought, and alluringly expressed, but too fragile to withstand examination. First of all, one may doubt the universal necessity of Chapman's principle even in the domain of the theatre, where it is most obviously applicable. Moreover, is it not a questionable procedure to deduce so jauntily, from the analogy between dialogue and drama, that the former must possess any given element requisite to the latter? And finally, we may deny outright that the Platonic dialogues always fail to employ the desiderated device: Simmias and Cebes, in the *Phaedo*, might reasonably be called the reader disguised as participant (Chapman does not distinguish very clearly between "author" and "reader," in prescribing his principle) ; and in the *Republic*, Glaucon and Adeimantus are similarly employed. Yet that the success of a Platonic dialogue is not dependent upon the observance of Chapman's canon is clear from the universally acknowledged effectiveness of the *Protagoras* (for which even Fite confesses admiration), in which the reader is left without representation. One cannot claim entire success in terms of dramatic excellence for more than a certain number of the dialogues; Plato has often, and as Crossman suggests in reference to his poetry, deliberately given priority to logical and philosophical over dramatic values; but the dramatic insufficiency is due in such cases to reasons quite other than those Chapman suggests. As to the charge that Plato has equivocally duplicated Socrates, it is unfortunately so vaguely stated that we are left to speculate upon its application to any given dialogue and hence cannot oppose it by specific arguments. In general, it might be better to say that Plato has not "duplicated," but, in a sense, complicated his portrait of Socrates, by bringing out his various strangely blended traits.

Fite has, in most respects, adhered to Chapman's formal analysis of Plato as a writer, but has assigned different values to the components: for him Plato, for the most part, is very much in earnest as a philosopher and correspondingly less centrally concerned with the refinements of literary art. The note of playfulness, upon which Chapman had laid such stress, Fite duly observes, but he is not amused. Many of these Platonic playfulnesses, he suspects, are fictions of Plato's idealistic admirers, concocted in order to save Plato from the manifest

---

[12] *Ibid.*, pp. 148–150.   [13] *Ibid.*, pp. 149–150.

absurdity of meaning what he says.[14] The genuine examples he takes to be symptoms of Plato's. addiction to artificiality and prettiness,[15] to this extent agreeing with Chapman; or else he construes them, as we have seen Popper was to do, into unscrupulous devices for concealing the fallacies and softening the audacities of the argument [16] or for dodging the responsibility of defending his thought in a rational manner.[17] Fite finds in Plato a frequently careless literary craftsman, who stitches together his materials into imperfectly unified wholes,[18] a writer who mars his best effects by incongruities [19] and anticlimaxes.[20]

The charges of intellectual confusion and logical incompetence will be met in our later discussion of Plato the man; there, too, we can conveniently deal with the imputation of bad faith, along with the promised reply to Popper's similar accusation. But how shall we meet the imputations of artificiality and prettiness, of incongruity and anticlimax?

Perhaps the boldest procedure here will be the best. Since the *Symposium* has figured as the special target of Fite's attack upon Plato's dignity as literary artist, it would be no slight confirmation of our case for Plato if it could be shown that Fite is mistaken in regarding it as one of the outstanding examples "in literature of empty 'art'; of art consciously artificial," [21] and, moreover, marred by the central incongruity of its "Socrates among the swells," [22] and the "plain anti-climax" of the arrival and speech of Alcibiades; [23] and, further, if it could be shown that the traditional view was warranted in finding in the dialogue the evidence of great and eminently serious art. Such a conclusion does not, of course, admit of demonstration; it may, however, be strongly supported.

We must, first of all, dismiss from our minds Fite's misleading implication that the moral atmosphere of the *Symposium* is simply that of an "all-night drinking party," [24] attended by idly rich addicts of the aristocratic Greek vice of *paiderastia*, and that the program of successive speeches in praise of Love is merely a "parlor game." [25] This is a serious confusion of the cultural perspective, which demands that we view Plato's *Symposium* in the context of Greek tradition. The imputation of moral turpitude, involved in the reference to *paiderastia*, will claim special attention in a later chapter. For the rest, as Jaeger has well shown,[26] the symposium had been developed, even before Plato's time, into an institution of cultural importance, bringing wine, music, poetry, and the personal attachments between older and younger men into a convivial association for the expression and reënforcement of the currently

---

[14] Fite, *op. cit.*, pp. 247–248; p. 285.
[15] Fite, p. 288.
[16] Fite, p. 193.
[17] *Ibid.*, p. 288.
[18] *Ibid.*, p. 279.
[19] *Ibid.*, p. 273.
[20] *Ibid.*, p. 275.
[21] *Ibid.*, p. 272.
[22] *Ibid.*, p. 273.
[23] *Ibid.*, p. 275.
[24] *Ibid.*, p. 158.
[25] *Ibid.*, p. 272.
[26] Jaeger, *Paideia*, p. 176.

accepted notions of manly excellence (*aretê*). In Plato's hand, after his founding of the Academy, the institution appears to have been shorn of its surviving crudities and remade into a genial but carefully regulated form of philosophical seminar and training ground in self-control.[27] In his *Symposium*, he may be said to be suggesting this higher use, by his stress upon the moderation of the drinking in the earlier part, and by the introduction of the feature which Fite belittles with his epithet of the "parlor game"; but he is still working, in general, within the framework of the social practice of the dramatic time and place. The *Symposium*, considered as a work of art, must be judged in the first instance by the degree of its success in capturing a dramatic likeness of a session of this kind or, more precisely, of creating the illusion that we are present there. One may or may not admire the idea of such a symposium, but its existence and general character must be accepted as something given.

Few can come away from even the most casual reading of the *Symposium* without a sense of having been treated to an Attic night's entertainment of unforgettable vividness. This much, perhaps, would be admitted in his more charitable moments by Fite himself. The crucial question is: but is this all? For of itself it leaves standing the more serious literary complaints. We have, however, gained two points which will be useful to our later case: we have cleared the air of some "odorous" comparisons, and we have implicitly made an elementary distinction which should be given explicit statement here: — there is an essential difference between the quality of what is depicted and the quality of the depiction. In so far as the scene of the *Symposium* contains elements of artificiality, elegance, or humorous obscenity, it was the aesthetic duty of its depictor to record them. It by no means follows, however, that the final quality of the artistic representation, i.e., the aesthetic essence of the work of art, must be the same. Let us now see whether, and if so, to what extent Plato as artist has preserved "aesthetic distance" between his vision and the material upon which it has been turned.

The shortest way to see that he has done so is to consider the manner in which the various speakers are carefully differentiated from each other, both by the matter and by the manner of their respective encomia on love. Each man is allowed to speak his piece, but, so to say, at his own risk, and, until the speech of Socrates, without any overt indication of the degree of Plato's approval. Examination reveals that we have here no casual sequence of playful sallies, but an ordered set of progressively serious approaches, with an interpolated Aristophanic extravaganza (itself not without concealed depth of meaning), leading up to the apparent climax of Agathon's rhetorical *tour de force*; this is then employed as the point of departure for the genuine climax, in which, from a dialectically established base, the Socrates of the

---

[27] *Ibid.*, p. 177. Cf. also *Laws* 671 C–E.

dialogue delivers a wholly serious and magnificently eloquent speech. Here, speaking in the name of the prophetess Diotima, Socrates transforms Eros into a passion for self-fulfilment through intellectual experience at once aesthetic and moral, culminating in the "marvelous vision" of Beauty absolute.[28]

It is this speech which Fite has called "an inspired philosophical poem"; [29] his high opinion of it has not withheld him, however, from utter condemnation of the dialogue as "empty art."[30] This procedure is recurrent in Fite's and Popper's pleading. A concession, often, as here, generous to Plato's merit in some department, is initially made, but is soon dropped from view and in the final accounting does not appear. Meanwhile, the concession may be used as a standard by which to condemn Plato in some other respect — in this instance, to emphasize the unfitness of the speech for its vicious setting; it strikes a note of fairness and objectivity, thus strengthening the attacker's case; and it is standing by to serve as "fire-escape," in the event of a counterattack by any defender of Plato.

But to return to our dialogue: — The speech of Socrates is, admittedly, the climax; yet without setting up, as Fite seems to wish to do, an arbitrary and mechanical rule, one cannot rebuke Plato for his failure to end his dialogue on this high note — that is, for anticlimax.[31] The episode of the drunken Alcibiades which follows gave Plato an opportunity to descend, to break the tension, to modulate into a different key.[32] But apart from this apparent intent, there was another motive more certainly to be discerned as operative in Plato's mind. He could not be content to leave the ideal of Eros hovering, where the great speech of Diotima-Socrates seemed to have left it, between the stars. It must be brought to earth and exemplified. This is the function of the remaining speech, in praise not of Eros, but of Eros' true practitioner, Socrates. Alcibiades had been among Socrates' outstanding failures; Plato is here showing how even he was forced to acknowledge the absolute moral integrity and inspiring power of the teacher from whom he had only by an act of self-violation cut himself loose. As Jaeger has effectively

---

[28] I owe much of the substance of this discussion, particularly the account of the plan of the dialogue, to two excellent and closely related analyses, by Taylor, A. E., (*Plato, the Man and His Work*, 1929, Chapter IX, p. 209 ff.), and Shorey, Paul, (*What Plato Said*, 1933, p. 189 ff.). — For confirmation of this standpoint, see Julius Stenzel, *Platon der Erzieher*, 1928, Ch. V, esp. pp. 209–10. Stenzel stresses the point that in the first five praises of Eros there are contained, in less developed form and combined with other, less acceptable elements, "motifs" that achieve their "entelechy" only in the discourse of Socrates-Diotima.

[29] Fite, p. 160.

[30] *Ibid.*, p. 272. As against Fite's verdict on the *Symposium* as a whole, both Shorey and Taylor, *loc. cit.*, offer detailed and abundant evidence. That Fite has seen fit to leave the specific evidence unnoticed gives us the logical right to employ it, in spite of his 'blanket' rejection of these two important "idealizing" interpreters of Plato's thought.

[31] Fite, p. 275.

[32] Shorey's phrase, Introduction, p. lxix, Loeb Library translation of the *Republic*, vol. II.

put it: "The Socratic Eros blazed up in his soul for a moment, but it did not kindle into an enduring flame." [33]

In choosing Alcibiades for the role of encomiast of Socrates, Plato was boldly converting an important liability of the master into an asset, while at the same time avoiding the mawkishness and veritable anticlimax that would inevitably have resulted from putting the speech into the mouth of a "prize pupil." Plato could leave it to his reader to supply the picture of those many less spectacular Athenians whom Socrates had influenced more lastingly for good.

If the foregoing be a true account, Fite's charges of artificiality, emptiness, and anticlimax fall to the ground. There remains the complaint of incongruity. Fite believes that the depiction of Socrates throughout the dialogues and particularly in the *Symposium* is an incongruous blur in which the features of the "inspired prophet and mystic" are unintelligibly mingled with those of "a super-sceptical and more than easy-going man of the world." [34]

It would be fatuous to deny that there are traits in the *Symposium* portrait of Socrates that definitely provide an initial shock. But in the region of art, an incongruity may become the material of which higher congruities are made. One thinks of the role of the ugly in the painter's art, of the satyr play that follows the trilogy, of gargoyles on Notre Dame. Is the moral incongruity of Socrates in the *Symposium* a case in point? Can we refute Fite's charge that Plato has painted for us here two simultaneous and incompatible images of Socrates that simply interfere the one with the other?

We have in this clashing of moral qualities the counterpart of the Socratic irony and skepticism to which Fite also objects, and which so disturbed Chapman. That irony is intellectual: it discounts a knowledge known to be there; the irony of the *Symposium*, on the other hand, is a moral equivalent: it is an assumption of vice, or at any rate, of complaisance, in one whom, following Plato, we are asked to conceive as all but supremely good. From the point of view of practice, the two ironies are the same: they are a tactic of establishing rapport with men as they are and dispelling an imputed superiority that might act as a barrier.

If we look steadily at the two images of Socrates, as Fite would have us believe them to be, with a comprehension of what they are designed to represent, they begin to coalesce. Whether this coalescence will complete itself will depend on our visual strength, our capacity to see the picture as Plato painted it, without the distortion that would result from importing into it contemporary mores, to accept it as the image of a man who could hold together in his nature these two opposing poles.

Is not the gap between easy-going conviviality and moral grandeur a practical measure of immensity? And how can it be spanned? By neither the

---

[33] Jaeger, *op. cit.*, II, p. 197.　　　　[34] Fite, *op. cit.*, p. 274.

one nor the other, taken in their pure natures alone, but only by some hybrid nature with at least a touch of the one and an essential component of the other; that is to say, by an incongruous nature. And it did not require the wisdom of the Delphic oracle to pronounce Socrates "the most incongruous" (*atopos*) man in Athens.

Out of incongruity proceeds a great part of the depth and vitality of the *Symposium*. For it is scarcely an exaggeration to say that the whole dialogue is, from one point of view, describable as a huge adventure in incongruity. There is, for example, the incongruity of the gayety of the occasion with the ultimate gravity of the theme, of the comic spirit of Aristophanes with the tender ideal of unfailing affection that his speech unfolds: the incongruity of the arrival of Alcibiades and of his praise of Socrates — these and countless other smaller touches that a closer study of the dialogue would discover, all show what havoc of appraisal is wrought when the superficial opinion of a critic is confused with the depths of Plato's art. Alcibiades has found us our best metaphor for the art of the *Symposium*: the unseemly statue of Silenus, that opens to reveal the golden images of the gods.

Fite, it will be remembered, is also dissatisfied with Plato's degree of literary coherence, and disparages particularly the *Republic*, as a "nakedly disjointed" "accumulation of afterthoughts." [35] Except for a few small inadvertencies, it would be difficult to point to any other philosophical writing of equal length, ancient or modern, that possesses a more clearly marked structure of organization and development. That a critic like Fite should fail to perceive the well-planned coherence of Plato's book must be construed as a compliment by the left hand to the air of naturalness and spontaneity with which the writer has artfully contrived to make his speakers appear to follow the wayward path of unplanned talk.

By dint of fixing attention upon these apparently accidental turns and shifts in the argument, it is possible to lose sight of the larger contours of continuity, as one may lose the sense of the direction of a winding road. But if at the end of his journey through the *Republic*, the reader will turn around and from a height survey the traveled road, his over-all impression will be one of decided unity. The practical proof of this is the ease with which the book submits to being summarized, as witness Cornford and Shorey, among others. In spite of the dozens of topics involved, from poetry to mathematics, none has been introduced before the reader is logically prepared for it. The *Republic* begins on the level of common sense and common opinion, and rises, by platforms successively built, to the consideration of transcendental themes. A striking example of this, from among many, is that adduced by Shorey [36] and also by Jaeger,[37] explaining the apparent violation of structural coherence

---

[35] Fite, *op. cit.*, p. 279.
[36] Shorey's introduction to Vol. II of the Loeb Library *Republic*, pp. lxi–lxii.
[37] Jaeger, *Paideia*, II, pp. 358–362.

and climactic arrangement occasioned by the reintroduction of the criticism of poetry in Book X, after the subject had seemingly been disposed of in Books II and III. The explanation is that this second discussion constitutes a "relieving interval of calm" (Shorey) between the twin climaxes [38] of the work as a whole — the formal conclusion of the inquiry into the true nature of justice, and the depiction of the fate of the soul after death; and that, moreover, the earlier treatment of poetry had been conducted on the plane of common opinion, presupposing nothing more than the elementary psychology and ethics which the preceding argument had adequately supplied; while the second "banishment of the poets" requires for its justification and proper understanding the elaborate psychology of the tripartite soul and the discussion of the nature of knowledge, in Books VI-VII.

Fite's palmary example of the unfinished state in which the supposedly "consummate artist" left his *Republic,* is the myth of Er, with which the tenth and last book concludes. He professes to be unable, after long effort, to find any relevant meaning for this myth, and is forced to the conclusion that it was something that Plato found in his "barrel" and attached to the *Republic* without any particular concern for the nicety of its adjustment.[39]

What occasioned Fite's criticism was his discovery of some elements in the myth which are, it must be freely granted, not wholly in accord with the boundless promises that Socrates gave to his listeners as he began it. We have been told that the righteous will receive a sure reward in the life to come, and it is disconcerting to discover that the sureness is to some degree contingent on the drawing of an earlier or a later number among the lots, on which the choice of the soul's next life depends. It is also inconsistent with a fundamental postulate of the Platonic ethics to represent the quality of a man's moral nature as determined by a choice preceding birth, thus depriving him, if the myth be taken literally at all points, of the exercise of rational freedom during his life on earth.

There is no reason to represent these inconsistencies as esoteric subtleties of Plato's transcendent art. On the other hand, it is myopic criticism to permit them to distort our view of the major purpose of Plato's myth: to assert the solemn importance of the moral choice between good and evil as reaching beyond the region of the mortal life and exercising its influence upon the fortunes of the soul in the awesome adventures that await it after death, which the mind of man can explore only by conjecture.

This purpose the myth has achieved, in spite of the contradictions. Would the myth have been a finer piece of literary art had they been discovered and replaced, in a "revised edition"? From the point of view of the highest art, combining aesthetic and philosophic truth, we must agree that it would. But

---

[38] A similar structure involving twin climaxes has already been observed in the *Symposium* (p. 31 above).

[39] Fite, *op. cit.,* pp. 279-280.

that the major effect of the prize song is in any measurable degree altered by
its "errors" is a conclusion which may be left to be inferred by the Beckmessers
of Platonic criticism.

The myth moves in an atmosphere that will remind a reader of nothing
so much as one of Michael Angelo's frescoes, or, inevitable comparison, of
Dante's infernal and celestial scenes. For we are shown the stable axis of the
world round which revolve the planetary circles, each with its chanting siren,
to compose the music of the spheres; we glimpse the busy Fates and pass under
the shadow of the spindle of Necessity; and as the souls await the making
of their choice, we hear proclaimed the solemn words, "The charge is with
the chooser, chargeless God." It may be that under the spell of this image,
the sight of all the mortal world grew dim for its author, as for us as we
read, and the logical consistency of his argument was, for an eternal moment,
caught up and dissolved in the splendor of the vision.

Fite believes that Plato cannot draw characters to match Hamlet or Don
Quixote,[40] and that, moreover, such character sketches as that of Callicles in
the *Gorgias* are "slight as compared with even the minor characters of George
Eliot or Thackeray." [41] It cannot be denied that Plato's character creations —
reserving Socrates, for the moment — often fall on the hither side of Hamlet
and Don Quixote, a suggestion which praises Plato by the method of "faint
damns." It must further be conceded that Callicles and the rest, while not below the modern creations mentioned, are indications of talent rather than
proofs of genius.

But Socrates is quite another matter. From the gallery of Plato's portraits
Fite proposes to remove the one on which Plato lavished his richest and
most loving art, on the curious grounds that the suggestion of treating Plato's
portrait as an artistic creation "would hardly be welcomed" [42] (i.e., by the
admirers of Plato). This seems to impute to the friends of Plato the view that
Plato, in depicting Socrates, was simply transcribing from fact; was presenting his picture of the master under a solemn obligation to exercise merely the
function of a camera; and would be discredited in the eyes of his friends if
he were shown to have exercised in the process either intelligence or art.
This incredible conception is to be repelled, however much or little of the
historical figure we may care to recognize in the picture. The Socratic dialogues
bear all the marks of careful selection, arrangement, and focusing of the material; they are artistic elaborations of Socratic conversations, many of which
hark back to the period of Plato's boyhood and beyond. Even the accounts of
the great occasions in the life of Socrates, like the trial, could not have been
stenographic recordings, and owe much of their moving quality to their form.

---

[40] Fite, *op. cit.*, p. 271.   [42] Fite, p. 271.
[41] *Ibid.*, p. 281.

It is too easy to forget that, without the genius of Plato's portrayal, the traditional image of Socrates would be that of the uninspired and prosing sage of Xenophon's *Memorabilia*, and the anecdotal miscellanies of Diogenes Laertius. Meanwhile, European literature would have lost one of its most living characters. He whom the centuries have known and revered under the name of Socrates would not exist.

3

Two Sources for Knowledge of Plato the Man

On the world's calendar of great men are inscribed the names of some whose unquestioned right to honorable remembrance is based upon what they achieved as explorers, chemists, or inventors, or created as mathematicians, musicians, or architects, and not at all upon what they were as men. The world can as well continue to enjoy the fruits of their labors, whether their most recent biographers establish their reputation as saints or prove them to have been monsters of iniquity. Of others, in varying degrees, the opposite is true. Their meaning and value for the world is forever at the mercy of their latest and most authoritative interpreter; one breath of well-attested scandal may wither their laurels for indefinite decades.

In this category, obviously, fall all those great men whose activity was primarily concerned with the moral values underlying the life of man. As one must come into a court of equity with clean hands, so the world has ruled that it will not admire the moral thought of those who are not themselves morally admirable. In this judgment the world may or may not have shown perfect justice. What concerns us here is simply the unarguable fact that, if sustained, the current attack upon Plato would bring him, as man and moral being, under such a cloud of suspicion and distaste as to deprive his moral philosophy of the respectful hearing that tradition has held it to deserve.

It must be made clear that in the ensuing discussion we shall not seek to claim for Plato the sum of human excellence. On evidence forthcoming, we hold Plato to have been a man of high integrity and unquestionable moral dignity. Whether he was equipped with a full set of those personal qualities which one would insist upon in choosing a sympathetic counselor or bosom friend is a consideration that need not be raised. It is not necessary to adore Plato in order to open one's mind to the lessons to be learned from him. Nor need one expect to learn all lessons in his school: the Christian virtues of compassion and humility may be better learned elsewhere. The one thing needful is that one should not be brought, in advance, to hate the man Plato, and thus either close the mind to him or read and distort the dialogues into confirmation of unpleasant opinions already formed.

Nor is it possible to sit long at the feet of a master whom one suspects, however faintly, of deficient mentality. As complaints have been entered by Chapman and Fite against Plato's philosophical intelligence, we must — with the touch of humor inseparable from so fantastic an accusation — undertake also this refutation.

We are not intending an independently organized, full-length portrait of Plato from our own brush;[1] enough if by a careful study of the detractors' pictures and their grounds, we can discover information about the man Plato sufficient to serve as a criterion for judging the degree of their infidelity to their original. What faults, then, of mind and character, are fairly chargeable to Plato? Our opponents seem very sure that they know; yet, in the diverse constructions that they put upon his character (as we have seen), lie the materials for a comedy of contradictions, if not of errors, in the manner of the late Italian dramatist Pirandello, exemplifying his formula that each man is "one, no one, and a hundred thousand." In invoking the shade of Pirandello our intention is not to refute in advance all answers to the central question of this chapter. We shall proceed in the conviction that there really existed a unitary, objective, historical Plato to be approached by thought, who, in a sense to be determined, did or did not possess the faults in question; but a difficult psychographical problem lies between us and a fair rendering of judgment.

If our goal of understanding Plato is to be fairly sought, we must carefully avoid introducing into a corner of our initial statement of the problem a tacit little answer, and after a show of elaboration, unfolding it triumphantly as a conclusion reached. Such a possibility besets those to whom Plato, antecedently to all inquiry, is by definition the disinterested philosopher, the essential man of thought; they will dismiss as accidental to the real man the "external" circumstances of his economic status, political associations, and so on, and will look to his works, finding there his concentrated essence in the thought and the aspirations for which he lived. This way of conceiving Plato's relation to the world may lead, at its most extreme, to the image of a celestial visitor, and may be typified by Emerson's transcendental view, as well as by Goethe's prose-poetic appreciation:

Plato stands to the world as a blessed spirit who has chosen to be its passing guest. His purpose is not so much to become acquainted with it — such acquaintance is presup-

---

[1] The slight sketch to be presented in Chapter 8, p. 483 ff., does not contradict the statement in the text. It is offered tentatively and, as it were, experimentally, for the primary purpose of showing that the biographical data do not require the sinister interpretation put upon them by the detractors.

posed — as to impart to it, in friendly fashion, what he brings with him and what it so sorely needs. He penetrates to the depths rather to fill them with his nature than to investigate them. He moves with longing to the heights to partake once more of his origin. All that he expresses stands in relation to the eternal whole of the Good, the True, and the Beautiful, for which he would awaken a longing in every heart.[2]

To a contemporary, this approach seems antiquated and precritical. It would be an act of daring in these latter times, a defiance of the Zeitgeist, to assume that it is possible to deal adequately with any thinker without taking substantial account of the irrational or subconscious (and mainly discreditable) forces that are held to constitute the determining environment of his conscious thought. The mind of the thinker is thus apt to be reduced to a mere network of intricately interwoven relations, each strand of which it becomes the duty of the conscientious investigator to trace to its sociological and economic sources; and little or nothing is left of the thinker himself.

Equally impious would be the ignoring of the biopsychological determiners of thought. Here, we are often told, lie the major sources of the differences between one thinker and another. A case history of Kant, with, perhaps, special reference to the degree of his father's authority, would, on this view, be more revealing for the comprehension of his "categorical imperative" than the most critical perusal of all his predecessors in the realm of moral philosophy.

So it is that those to whom the postulate of Plato the disinterested thinker is thoroughly unwelcome look first to the external facts, and finding in them grounds for suspecting distorting influences and sinister partisan allegiance, will conclude that these and these alone are the source and sufficient refutation of the imposing philosophical structure beneath which they lie concealed.

We must somehow find a way of combining the merits of the two antithetical methods that have been described. It is obvious that each has hold of an indispensable element of truth. In these circumstances we must, in the name of historical integrity, appropriate from both parties indifferently what our purpose requires. From the older standpoint we will take as indispensable the assumption that, in Plato, we are dealing with a thinker who was in some sense autonomous, whose thought it is our duty to consider on its merits, independently of its origin, and in accordance with the best available criteria of objective truth. To balance this emphasis, we must also take from the more recent school the equally valid and enlightening principle that the spirit of Plato can only be fully intelligible to us if we are willing to study its organic relation to the time and place of its embodiment, to the stimulus of the then paramount problems, and to the limitations and prejudices traceable to its particular social loyalties. And, as we advance, we must be careful not to fall into the counterpart of the fallacy of those detractors who treat Plato's ideas either as inevitably determined, or as the spontaneous generations of Plato's

---

[2] Goethe, *Geschichte der Farbenlehre*, Zweite Abteilung, "Ueberliefertes."

free choice, according as one or the other ascription may work his philosophy the greater harm. In this way alone can one hope to distinguish between the real Plato and the projection of partisan enthusiasms or hates.

We shall need, then, in the chapters that follow, to refer constantly both to Plato's writings and to facts about his life and times, and to this end we shall here provide a brief sketch of each, to serve as a frame of reference. Turning first to the life, we find that the well-attested biographical facts are few — most of our information is affected by a very considerable degree of uncertainty — and that, though our historical knowledge of his period is by no means meager, there are some tormenting gaps, crucial to the events of Plato's life. Moreover, there is available, forcing itself upon the attention of Plato's biographers, but without certain credentials, a mass of material in the thirteen *Letters*. Much doubt is laid to rest in the minds of those who accept at least the most substantial of these as from the hand of Plato. Even for those few who remain doubtful of the Platonic authorship, among whom the present writer wishes to count for one, the *Letters* contain much valid historical and biographical material, as shown by their consistency with trustworthy ancient sources. But in dealing with those passages in the *Letters* in which Plato's inner thoughts and feelings and private conversations purport to be revealed, only those for whom Plato is the unquestioned author will presume to employ them as the basis for judging his character. We are here touching a crucial point, for, as we shall see, the most sweeping conclusions as to faults in Plato's character and judgment have been drawn from this source by more than one of the detractors. Accordingly, the sketch of Plato's life which follows depends upon the evidence of the *Letters* only in those connections where reference to them is explicitly made. Our little biography should enable us to show which charges of the detractors are based upon relatively uncontroverted facts of Plato's life, and to distinguish from them those charges which cannot be either substantiated or, on the basis of the life, refuted, since certain evidence is available on neither side.[3]

Plato was born *circa* 429 B.C.,[4] in the early years of the devastating Peloponnesian war. His was one of the oldest and most distinguished of Athenian families, claiming descent on the paternal side from Codrus, legendary last

---

[3] This account of the life will be an adaptation from Shorey (*What Plato Said*, 1933), and will follow him in utilizing the materials of the *Seventh Letter* but without commitment to the now all but universal acceptance of that document as the product of Plato's own hand. For a discussion of this point I refer the reader to p. 369 below. The need of critical caution in these matters is underscored by George Boas in his historical analysis of the sources and development of the ancient biographical tradition, "Fact and Legend in the Biography of Plato," 1948. It is not untypical, for example, that Plato's ancestral affiliation with Codrus is alluded to by no single source earlier than Diogenes Laertius, more than five centuries after Plato's death (*loc. cit.*, p. 440).

[4] Since the date of Plato's birth is not precise, all statements of Plato's age at the time of any given event are of course

king of Athens, and thus, with the help of mythology, from the earth-shaking Poseidon himself. Through Plato's mother there was affiliation, hardly less honorific, with the great Solon; Plato's stepfather, who was also his mother's uncle, had been an associate and supporter of Pericles.

From birth Plato enjoyed the privileges of aristocratic connections, joined to a moderate degree of wealth. He unquestionably received the traditional education in "music and gymnastic," and is said to have distinguished himself both as wrestler and as maker of verse, a prophecy, perhaps, of the balance he was to hold between gymnastic and "music" in his educational program. In the *Republic*, Plato has pictured for us with fraternal affection and pride his two brothers, Glaucon and Adeimantus, whose union of aristocratic courtesy, manly courage, and zest for sport, with a genuine concern over the true nature of human good, may be said to give us our most intimate glimpse into the social climate of Plato's family connection.

The war with Sparta vastly accentuated the internal party strife between the ruling democrats and their politically disconsolate opponents of varying hue, from the moderates to the extreme oligarchic faction. In this tense and often bitter political atmosphere the boy Plato grew to manhood, an atmosphere, indeed, that must have permeated his home, and have produced in him the deepest interest in the political scene. This was doubtless the more intense in view of his stepfather's former connection with Pericles, and of the prominence in oligarchic circles of his mother's cousin Critias and her brother, Charmides. In Plato's twenty-sixth year, after the Athenian capitulation to Sparta, came the shocking experience of the reign of terror inaugurated by the so-called Thirty Tyrants, and among them Critias and Charmides were leading figures. In the reaction which followed, Critias and Charmides both lost their lives, and the oligarchic faction being thoroughly discredited, the democracy held undisputed sway.

Intellectual influences upon Plato's young manhood apparently included study under Cratylus, the Heraclitean philosopher, and, more momentously, the association with Socrates, whose disciple he is reported to have become at about the age of twenty. After some eight years of close association,[5] there followed the master's execution at the hands of the restored democracy, in 399 B.C. The deep grief and shock which Plato felt was to be a decisive influence upon his entire career.

After the death of Socrates, Plato absented himself from Athens, sojourning first with some fellow members of the Socratic circle at nearby Megara, and spending the remainder of a period of some twelve years, with intervals of return to Athens, in travel. Toward the end of his journeyings, he visited

---

subject to this qualification; but we shall not disturb the reader by constant repetition of the *circa*. The year of his death is similarly only approximate.

[5] For a discussion of the degree of this intimacy see Shorey, *op. cit.*, pp. 18–24, and Burnet, *Plato's Phaedo*, 1911, Introduction, pp. xxvi–xxx.

Sicily, and made the fateful acquaintance of the young Dion, brother-in-law of Dionysius I, the tyrant of Syracuse.

Plato now returned to Athens in 387 B.C., and as if to symbolize the finality of a wanderer's return, committed himself to the life of the city by purchasing a house and garden, just outside the Double Gate; and here he opened the progenitor of the European university, the Academy.[6] As his fame grew, the Academy attracted and held, often for many years, some of the ablest minds in the Hellenic world — instance the astronomer-mathematician, Eudoxus, and, above all, Aristotle. Here Plato lectured and wrote for the remainder of his long life, save only for two intervals, to be described below.

Plato's writings may be listed summarily as follows: By the time of his return and settlement in Athens (387 B.C.), it is commonly supposed that the composition of the minor Socratic dialogues lay behind him. To the next twenty years (though opinion here is divided, some scholars favoring an earlier date) belong his *Republic*, and such other major productions of his literary and philosophical maturity as the *Symposium* and the *Phaedrus*. Later than these, but of indeterminate date, came a whole sequence of less dramatic, but technically rich and important dialogues, embracing the *Theaetetus*, and the *Sophist* and *Politicus*, and ending with the *Timaeus*, the *Critias*, and the *Laws*.[7]

Plato's labors at the Academy were interrupted by two all but sensational adventures, recorded in the *Seventh Letter*, upon which this and the following two paragraphs are based, with some supplement from Plutarch's *Life of Dion*. On these two occasions, at the urgent invitation of his Syracusan friend Dion, Plato accepted the challenge of attempting to put some of his political theories into the harness of practical politics.

Dion's call, and Plato's second journey to Syracuse, in 367/6 B.C., followed the accession to the throne of that city of the young Dionysius II, who by his interest in philosophy had awakened in Dion, Plato's enthusiastic disciple, the hope of realizing the Platonic dream of uniting in one person political power and philosophical wisdom. The young monarch was to be brought to such a degree of enlightenment that he would diffuse virtue through the state by force of his own example, while securing the continuance of good rule by binding himself and all others within his realm to the observance of a scientifically planned code of equitable laws. Plato, as the *Seventh Letter*

---

[6] A. E. Taylor, (*Plato, the Man and His Work*, 1929, pp. 5–6) dismisses the rival claims of the school of Isocrates, founded perhaps a year or two earlier, on the ground that it provided only rhetorical preparation for a political career. The degree to which the Academy may properly be regarded as itself a "university" is considered on pp. 367–368 below.

[7] The probable order of the Platonic dialogues as conceived by a number of recent and contemporary Plato scholars, is displayed in tabular form by W.D. Ross, in *Plato's Theory of Ideas*, 1951, p. 2. From this table it will be seen that, in spite of some divergencies, a very considerable measure of agreement has been achieved.

informs us, though with grave misgivings as to the probable outcome, felt bound to make the attempt. But after an initial success — the tyrant was for a time much impressed and desirous of Plato's good opinion — the plan miscarried. Dion was forced by court intrigue to leave Sicily, and Plato secured permission to depart, promising Dionysius, however, that he would return.

On Plato's third and final journey to Syracuse, six years later, undertaken with even more reluctance than the former, he met with broken promises, jealousies, and even polite imprisonment in the palace grounds, and barely escaped with his life. Dion, now in exile for many years, and despairing of achieving by peaceful means his cherished program of political reform, but having failed to persuade Plato to take any further active part in his plans, successfully invaded Sicily with an armed force, which included many of Plato's former pupils; and after a short-lived and tarnished rule, was himself assassinated.

The death of Dion, Plato's valued friend for more than thirty years, and the unhappy and even discreditable circumstances that attended it, must have struck the now aged Plato a heavy blow. But his spirit did not break under its burden. Still convinced of the sovereign importance of reason in the life of man, and the solemn duty devolving upon the philosopher of discovering the conditions requisite to the exercise of its saving power, Plato continued to bind the sheaves of his late autumnal harvest, the *Laws*. Before he could bring this largest of all his labors to its full completion, death came upon him in his eighty-second year.

Leaving the life, with its uncertainties and gaps, we turn to that other source of knowledge regarding the man Plato, his writings; and here it might be supposed we shall have at hand, available for whatever use we may wish to make of them, his express opinions on countless topics and his implicit approvals and distastes; even the turn and ring of his emphatic sentences will betray the nature of the man.

There is an ultimate truth in this suggestion, but alas, only an ultimate truth of no initial help. To reach it we must somehow swim through clinging subtleties and eddying ambiguities that have swallowed many a brave inquirer. The difficulties are mainly these:

Plato chose for his literary medium the dialogue form; the author is thus necessarily excluded from direct appearance upon the scene. Add to this the circumstance that the principal speaker in all the dialogues of the early and middle period (*Lysis, Laches, Charmides, . . . Euthyphro, Crito, Phaedo, . . . Republic, Phaedrus, . . .*) is a character called Socrates, whose moods and opinions are by no means constant. We see him tenderly and seriously inviting the soul of a young man, and yet arriving at no conclusion for the young man's instruction (e.g., *Lysis*); again, slyly deriding the pretensions of a self-styled expert (e.g., *Euthyphro*); urging an austere dissociation of the soul from all entangling alliances with the sense pleasures associated with the material body (*Phaedo*), but, again, forcing on the reluctant Protagoras, represented as the partisan of a conventional morality, a radical hedonism in which the terms good and evil are to be replaced by pleasure and pain (*Protagoras*). This Socrates wears, habitually, a mantle of modesty, even of deep humility (*Apology*), but does not scruple to style himself (*Gorgias*) "among the few, not to say the only true living statesman." He appeals to reason and the simple love of truth, dissociating himself from the word-catching, victory-hunting sophists (*Apology, Protagoras*), but in the next breath he scores a point by the use of some double-jointed fallacy of which any sophist might well have been proud (*Gorgias*). In short, we seem to be in a Platonic playhouse, in which a tragi-comedy entitled "The Intellectual Adventures of Socrates" is played out before our eyes in a sequence of loosely connected scenes in which the title character undergoes the most bewildering transformations from scene to scene.

Moreover, quite aside from the shifting identity of "Socrates," two further problems beset us, extending into Plato's latest period: his free creation of parables and myths, as a vehicle for conveying "probable" truths about matters beyond the reach of demonstration (*Phaedrus, Politicus, Republic*); and, second, as Shorey has so well pointed out,[8] a habit of formulating definitions and suggesting categories for which, apparently, full conviction is claimed, but which, as we discover later, to our dismay, are either never employed in any subsequent dialogue (e.g., the definitions[9] of the cardinal virtues in the *Republic*), or are so altered or combined with others as to prevent us from treating them as fixed constituents in the "system" of Plato's philosophy.

But there are compensating "probabilities" in Plato's writings, and even, if we are careful enough in method and moderate enough in our demands, "certainties." There is unanimity as to the Platonic authorship of all the major dialogues. There are notably few corruptions in the text, and as a consequence, very few crucial passages upon which a genuine difference among interpreters is possible. Thus we are at least assured, to begin with, that we are not forever excluded from reaching a solution of our problem by radical deficiencies in the material with which we are condemned to work.

More substantial is the positive assurance that comes to us when we note, on repeated reading, that beneath the cross-currents of disagreement that ruffle the surface of the Platonic writings, there is a deep tidal movement of thought and feeling that remains largely (indeed, considering the span of years, amazingly) constant, from the period of the Socratic dialogues through to the *Laws*.[10] We must not beg, and cannot here prove, this assertion, which

---

[8] Shorey, *The Unity of Plato's Thought*, 1903, p. 13, *et passim*.

[9] The four virtues themselves reappear not a few times, but the definitions — e.g., that of civic justice as "doing one's own task" as member of the body politic — are altered.

[10] Shorey, Paul, *op. cit., ubique.*

must gain cumulative confirmation from succeeding chapters. But this much can be said, and provisionally confirmed by reference to readily available evidence: (1) there is hardly a work of Plato's in which there is not a central speaker who either elicits a significant denial or achieves an affirmative conclusion to which Plato's assenting approval is clearly accorded; and (2) an unprejudiced comparison of these approvals will yield, even at a first approximation, an impressive measure of compatibility. What remains to be shown is that (after allowance for wide differences of emphasis in the different dialogues, for differences of dramatic situation which often account for the seeming variability of the Platonic Socrates' opinions, and for some real changes of view on Plato's part) there emerges something that, without possessing systematic rigor, may properly be regarded as "the thought of Plato."

The preceding appraisal of the Platonic writings as a source for the knowledge of Plato's mind will serve our present purpose without our adding to it the unmanageable bulk of a resume of the substantial content of the dialogues. Wherever an anti-Platonist has drawn upon some passage in the Platonic writings, we shall follow him to his source, and discuss the issue in the terms in which he has raised it. With this frame of reference, then, for both the outer and the inner man, we shall hope to reach the closest possible approach to an objective judgment upon the validity of the various accusations made against the mind and character of Plato.

In view of the number and diversity of the indictments, the reader may find it a contribution to clarity to have before him a table bringing together for comparison and contrast the four arraignments of Plato the man.

Plato's Defects of Mind and Character

	Chapman	Fite	Crossman	Popper
1.	Morally frivolous, lacking in seriousness, gently cynical	Serious, in the main, pedantic, but given to prosaic "playfulness" as adornment	Serious, conscientious	Serious to the point of fanaticism
2.	Skillful manipulator of playful fallacies, but confused in dealing with moral issues	Logically inept, blundering, absurd, and fallacious	Very able and talented	Extraordinarily clever
3.	Evasive in a lighthearted way (see 1. above)	Sophistic in serious argument out of love of victory	Fair and open with his readers, giving of his best	Consciously and craftily evasive on the most serious issues (but see 18. below)
4.		Morally immature, troubled to control unruly desires		Exhibiting strong symptoms of repression
5.		Morally petty, jealous, vain, and arrogant	Magnanimous	Morally petty, jealous, vain, and arrogant, full of hate and scorn

	Chapman	Fite	Crossman	Popper
6.	Incapable of understanding noble natures, but sophisticated	Ignorant of human nature, without insight into the meaning of personality	Understanding of human nature (but see 15. below)	Cunning and subtle in the understanding of human motivation (see also 10. below)
7.	Advocate of sexual immorality	Advocate of sexual immorality — perhaps himself immoral	Wise and right in matters of sex	Proponent of sexual immorality for reasons of state
8.		Ignorant of the higher meaning of marriage	Extraordinarily enlightened in regard to marriage	Interested only in breeding the master race
9.		Inhumane, advocate of slavery and infanticide	Inhumane, willing to sanction Nazis' methods (but not their ends)	Inhumane, advocate of slavery, infanticide, and brutal violence (but see 18. below)
10.		Would-be exploiter of the common man; cynical deceiver	Benevolent believer that the common people should do the work; deceiver for the people's good	Inhumane would-be exploiter of the common people; cynical deceiver (but see 18. below)
11.				Prejudiced against barbarians, race-proud
12.		Scorner of manual work	Scorner of manual work	Scorner of manual work
13.	Innocent misrepresenter of Socrates (Socrates was a pre-Christian martyr)	Inconsistent in representing Socrates (but Socrates was in general no better than Plato)	Unconscious misrepresenter of Socrates, a great soul	Conscious or semi-conscious betrayer of Socrates, one of the greatest men of all times (but see 18. below)
14.		Disloyal to Athens, lover of Spartan barbarism	Loyal servitor of the interests of Athens, as he saw them	Disloyal to Athens, lover of Spartan barbarism (but see 18. below)
15.		Class-prejudiced, snobbish	(Unconsciously) class-prejudiced; incapable of understanding the common man	Class-prejudiced, ruthless supporter of privilege, racialist (but see 18. below)
16.		Intolerant	Intolerant out of reasoned conscientiousness	Intolerant out of fanaticism (but see 18. below)
17.		Ambitious, seeking personal influence	Reluctantly accepting the duty of the regeneration of Greece	Wildly, immoderately ambitious
18.		Slightly psychopathic — sexual invert, inordinately vain	Sane and moderate	Psychopathic — repressed, megalomaniac, victim of a guilt complex; inconsistently benevolent; self-supposed cosmic savior

In the next few chapters, we shall examine the compatibility of each of the just-presented "Plato's" with the corresponding evidence from the dialogues, or with that complex of qualities which the historical Plato must have possessed in order to live the life which he admittedly did live. The discussion here (as Popper remarks in a similar connection) must begin and end in the region of "opinion," rather than "knowledge"; yet the restriction leaves standing the distinction between opinion responsible to the evidence, and that wilful play of fantasy and temperament, friendly or hostile, which tells us far more about the writer than of the question under review.

Mental and Moral Stature

In the chapter immediately before us we shall be engaged in the solemn farce of meeting a bewildering variety of charges (those covered by items 1. to 6. in our recent table), ranging from Chapman's accusation of frivolity to Popper's imputation of inhuman hate and scorn. In the process we shall hope to make some advance toward our announced goal of restoring the image of a Plato at once more admirable and more unified.

It is plain that Chapman's view of Plato the man [1] is supported by no evidence beyond what has already been shown to be Chapman's radical misconstruction of Plato's writings. To detach from Plato the quality of moral earnestness and name it Socrates, and to detach from Socrates all playfulness and name it Plato is indefensible. It is perhaps most charitable to suppose that Chapman's image of Plato was evoked from a habitual reading of the shorter and more inconclusive of the dialogues, with their apparent mutual contradictions, and from a confusion between the serious dialectical development of a theme, for the exploring of its possible alternative meanings, and the mere logical embroidering of such a theme, for the intellectual entertainment of a reader. The reality of this difference, and its significance for a proper evaluation of Plato, both as man and as thinker, will be driven home when on later pages our discussion brings us into contact with those works of Plato's middle and later period which Chapman has seemingly not honored with close attention.

Chapman's second most serious charge, that Plato was the poet laureate of sexual perversion, cannot be briefly dismissed and will be given extended consideration, along with Fite's similar charge, in another chapter. As we shall see, Plato's approval of homosexual love, in that limited sense in which he did approve it, was compatible with, indeed was actually an instance of his moral seriousness.

---

[1] For Chapman's view of Plato as morally frivolous and evasive, see Chapman, *op. cit.*, pp. 142–144, 166–168; as confused in dealing with serious issues and incapable of understanding Socrates, pp. 161, 166.

For the rest, we need only point out that Chapman's little Plato is scarcely sizable enough to fill the place reserved for him in history. He could not have organized and kept in active being an institution of higher learning such as the Academy: could he even have maintained order in its halls, or still less likely, could he have held the interest and devotion of his abler pupils? The Academy, in contrast to Isocrates' school, subordinated rhetoric to geometry and dialectic. Chapman is unwarrantably reversing their relations, and altering the inscription over the Academy door to read: Let None Enter Here Without Dexterity.

In taking leave for the present of Mr. Chapman (though we are scheduled to meet him once more, as co-plaintiff in Chapter 5), we must record our gratitude to him for having brought to our attention one of the drollest and most rewarding creatures of literary beast lore, the Amphisbaena. Speaking of "the Attic enjoyment of interminable, non-conclusive discussion," Chapman writes,[2]

The Greeks had even a mythical animal that haunted conversation and was called an *Amphisbaena*,[3] a creature with a head at each end and walking in opposite directions. This animal symbolized that cancellation of one idea by the next which gives you the zero-point of argument. The "horns" of the dilemma stood for the same idea. Plato's *Logos*, that jumps away and hides and is chased by the company, gives a glimpse of the same favorite vanishing point. . . . The same delight in irony which led the Athenians to amuse their leisure moments — which were many — with quibbles that showed how easily Reason defeats itself, led them to enjoy problem-plays; [but, says Chapman, since the problems were solved, this pleasure was bound to pall] . . . till at last, in the days of Euripides, they found a playwright whose aim was to leave the problem unsolved. "Hurrah," said the clever part of the Athenian audience, "we have found the Amphisbaena! This is an entertainment for Gods!"

And Chapman goes on to add: "Plato, in his dialogues, makes appeal to that passion for mystification which Euripides shows in his plays."

After reading this brilliant description, one may recognize the Amphisbaena in many and unsuspected places; he runs — in candor, we must admit — through some of Plato's pages, though it was surely Socrates who instructed Plato in the care and feeding of the creature. Chapman is by far our favorite detractor, a charming and witty writer; but we must not allow him, for all that, to charm us into confusing the double-going of the Amphisbaena with the single and forward tread of Plato's logic in the more serious parts of the dialogues.

---

[2] Chapman, pp. 140–142.

[3] There was no such animal in the imagination of the Greeks — only the very different conception of a dangerous double-headed snake, mentioned by Aeschylus and some obscure late authors. Whether Chapman found his version of the creature in some medieval bestiary, or personally metamorphosed the Aeschylean into the "Euripidean" animal, we should be happy to be informed.

Fite's formal objective, the destruction of the "legend" created by the faith of Plato's adulatory disciples, permits him discreetly to avoid a frontal assault upon Plato's intelligence, while, at the same time providing an opportunity for a series of sharp side-attacks. This gives him the double advantage of reenforcing the plausibility of his argument against Taylor, Shorey, et al., by incidental exhibits of the (supposed) stupidity of their highly magnified master; and ultimately of throwing the accumulated burden of reproach upon Plato, whose combination of rhetorical emptiness and logical infirmity, it is implied, was the first cause of the whole congeries of misconceptions. These ostensibly secondary sallies are thus, from our point of view, the main attack, and to them we shall devote our principal attention.

We may point, first, to Fite's attempt to diminish the magnitude of Plato by denying that he possessed anything properly to be classified as "creative genius." Dividing Plato's major achievement into two main branches, "a system of politics, and a system of metaphysics,"[4] he makes short work of both. The political system is no "fresh poetic creation,"[5] as the unsuspecting reader of the *Republic* may suppose, but largely a transcription of the Spartan constitution, and, for the rest, obvious enough, if one's sole interest is in efficiency. In metaphysics, Plato's only distinction was that which fate gave him, of being first to take up a position which, in the nature of things, must have been adopted by someone.[6] Creativeness is thus denied, but is not the case compatible with a creditable amount of intelligence? Fite is willing to admit this much, and more; he is even willing — hypothetically, to be sure, "if Plato is to be regarded as a creative genius" of any sort — to classify him among the "scientific geniuses . . . of the order of Aristotle and Newton and Darwin, . . . rather than an artistic genius."[7] But this qualified praise is premeditated and short-lived. Its motive is to disengage Plato from the company of the great creative masters of art, Shakespeare, Cervantes, Brahms, and the rest.[8] This objective Fite is apparently willing to purchase at a certain cost; a closer inspection of the accounts will show that no real expense is incurred. For, in the first instance, we learn that even the Newtons and the Darwins of this world are of no peculiar and individual importance. Their results, like Plato's in politics and metaphysics, would have been reached by other men, had they never existed, and were achieved by what, we are led by Fite's language to infer, was no more than a species of "prosaic reflection."[9] And secondly, in Plato's case, even the shrunken honor of being, perhaps, a "scientific genius" is annulled by force of those other passages in which Plato has been taxed with such scientific errors and inadequacies that the comparison with Newton becomes unthinkable and ludicrous. Let us examine these.

---

[4] Fite, *op. cit.*, p. 265.
[5] *Ibid.*, p. 266.
[6] *Ibid.*, pp. 267–268.

[7] *Ibid.*, p. 270.
[8] Fite, *op. cit.*, pp. 269–70.
[9] *Ibid.*, pp. 268–9, p. 271.

On an earlier page, Fite has already asked, "How much of a scientist was Plato, and what kind of a scientist?" [10] And he has answered with the same rapidity with which we have just seen him dispose of Plato's political and metaphysical standing. Dividing science into the natural and the social sciences, he first asserts that to the natural sciences Plato has contributed nothing, nor did he wish to do so; to the social sciences he contributed only confusion. The latter branches of knowledge Fite holds in small esteem, even in the modern world, regarding them as incapable of arriving at truths applicable to the concerns of life, as are those of the natural sciences. His complaint against Plato is, therefore, not only that he failed to advance the social sciences, but that he was so simpleminded as to regard his brand of "pseudo-science" [11] as potentially endowed with authority to regulate the life of man.

But, it will be recalled, Fite's Plato possessed, or rather was possessed by, a "mathematical mind," and was obsessed with a passion for applying, in and out of season, the method of mensuration to all things human and divine.[12] This allegation, alarming if true, would seem at least to endow Plato with the qualities of the mathematician's defect. But no such secondary compliment is intended. Fite accredits to Plato some substantial mathematical achievements, but brushes them aside in the next breath as "not important for our purpose"; [13] furthermore Plato is to be shown in the act of making mistakes in elementary mathematics; the pedant is to be exhibited as guilty also of inaccuracy.

The one example of mathematical incompetence which Fite has been able to adduce is drawn from the description of the "divided line" in the *Republic*,[14] a simile designed by Plato as a pedagogical aid to grasping the Platonic hierarchy of types of being and the correlative types of perceiving and knowing. "Socrates" asks us to divide a line, presumably vertical, into two unequal parts, and again, to divide these divisions in the same ratio, giving four line-segments. The two lower segments we are asked to consider as analogous to the visible world, the lowest denoting the shadows and reflections of material objects, the one next above denoting the things themselves. The two upper segments, taken together, are said to be analogous to the world of the eternal forms, the ultimate, objective, and unchanging patterns which the mind apprehends; the lower segment stands for these as the mathematician handles them, at one remove, without ever getting a direct view of them; the upper section represents them as grasped by a direct mental "intuition," the climax of the cognitive enterprise. Here, says Fite, lies Plato's mathematical blunder: he has built into his line two mutually contradictory demands, one explicit, the other implied. Plato has laid down the requirement that the ratio of the two parts into which the line is first cut, be preserved in the

---

[10] *Ibid.*, p. 219.
[11] Fite, p. 226–227.
[12] *Ibid.*, p. 180; pp. 230–231.
[13] *Ibid.*, p. 231.
[14] *Republic* 509 E–513 E.

second cutting, which would mean that the upper part (call it A + B) is to the lower (call it C + D) as A is to B, and as C is to D. But it is at the same time required by implication that $A>B>C>D$, or (if the topmost segment be taken as shortest) that $A<B<C<D$; for we cannot doubt that the ontological dignity of each section of the line (supposed by Fite to be symbolized by greater or lesser length of line segment) is greater than that of the section below. Yet, and here is the rub, it is mathematically impossible, if the divisions are made as directed, to prevent B from being equal to C.[15]

Should we now agree that Fite is warranted in following those critics who have found Plato in error here, we must ask whether we may not regard it, as some distinguished scholars have done, as a "slight but unavoidable defect," [16] and pass on to matters of more consequence. Fite urges that "for Plato's 'intellectual system of the universe' . . . nothing is more important than the scheme of the divided line," [17] and that therefore, "here if anywhere we may expect 'clear ideas'." There is a portentous confusion here between the unimportant size and shape of the particular symbol employed and the undeniable importance of the referent to which it points. It is the latter only of which it is true to say that it is crucial for Plato's system. The "line" is not, in itself, an argument; it is not adduced as such; and, most importantly, no conclusions whatever are drawn from it. It is the contents of the geometrical frame, the discriminated realities within it, not the frame itself, to which Plato is assigning philosophical significance. So far is he from having constructed the line to scale that we are not even told which of its sections is to be longer, which shorter. It is only, as earlier suggested, an expository device, and it is presently replaced by a completely nonmathematical equivalent, the parable of the cave. Fite's trap has sprung; Plato has flown away.

Fite's Plato not only mathematicizes wrongly; he also, as we have said, intrudes his mathematical method into regions where it does not belong. This special form of stupidity Fite finds conspicuously exemplified in the much-discussed "nuptial number," and the analogous "tyrant's number," in the *Republic*. That either is redeemed by the shimmer of fantasy, Fite treats as the last-ditch defense of the disciples in their forlorn attempt to repel an imputation of absurdity.[18]

In the first of these passages,[19] we find that Plato has put into the mouth of the "tragic Muses" a prophecy of the decline of the ideal city, couched in lofty diction complicated, after the opening sentences, by oracular obscurity. For all its ideality, the city "cannot abide throughout all time"; it will be dissolved. We hear of certain periods or cycles of fertility and sterility, "not alone for plants that grow in earth, but for the animals that live upon

---

[15] Fite, *op. cit.*, p. 251.
[16] *Ibid.*, p. 252.
[17] *Ibid.*, p. 252.

[18] Fite, *op. cit.*, pp. 247–50.
[19] *Republic*, 545 D–547 B.

it." Ever-fortunate human begetting the guardians of the perfect city, despite their wisdom, will not by reasoning and observation attain; the day will come when, in ignorance of the number regulative of human birth, they "will beget children in an unseasonable hour." This will be the beginning of the city's slow but inevitable decline. So much of what the Muses tell us is clear enough; not so the description of the "nuptial number" itself. The more than Cimmerian darkness with which Plato has chosen to wrap it round has been the delight and the despair of Platonic scholars throughout the centuries. Not alone the bare identity of the number, but everything about it remains obscure: does it number days, or years? Does it indicate times favorable, or times to be avoided for prosperous matings? Does it represent not times at all, but combinations of genetic traits and environmental influences? The Muses are indeed, as Plato says, "playing with us and teasing us, as though we were children." [20] And yet, in spite of Plato's unequivocal statement, and in spite of the pronounced stylistic features of the speech, Fite treats the whole as though it were essentially serious, sees only "a languid attempt at playfulness," [21] and charges Plato, in the main body of the speech, with having forgotten the Muses.

We must not dispose of the vexed interpretation of this passage by fiat, but we are within our rights in offering a favorable alternative. What the Muses are saying is neither sense — a structure of completely intelligible meanings — nor nonsense — as Fite takes it to be, sheer absurdity proceeding from the mathematically muddled mind of Plato — but something intermediate between the two: the meaningful use of the unintelligible. On this view the serious and intelligible meaning of the passage is that some day, in some way, the merely human wisdom of the guardians will fail, their eugenic program will break down, and deterioration of the ideal city will inevitably follow. This meaning Plato has chosen, for what would seem to be good aesthetic reasons, to deliver under the form of a veiled prophecy, with dramatically appropriate obscurity, and high-flown literary language. Now it would have been possible for Plato to make his prophecy in the prosaic form appropriate

---

[20] Further discussion of the number will be found on p. 450 ff. below.

[21] Fite, p. 248. In admitting that there is any attempt whatever at playfulness, Fite would seem to have given Plato as much as is needed for defense, and also to have contradicted himself. He says: "Both passages are a part of Plato's long and bitter threnody over the degeneracy of the Athens of his day. . . . In no part of the dialogues is the writer less in a mood for humor. Any real mirthfulness — not to speak of the elaborately planned hoax which is the intention of each passage if it is humorous — is as much out of place here as in the midst of The Lord's Prayer. Yet (this is my verdict) there is a languid attempt at 'playfulness' in the first passage." "In the middle of The Lord's Prayer" would not be an appropriate place for *any* playfulness. But that Plato is not, despite his admitted seriousness throughout the *Republic*, in any specially jest-prohibiting mood in this "part of the dialogues," is shown not only by the two passages mentioned, but by other short jests and amusing similes near by (e.g., *Republic* 548 D, 550 D, 563 C).

to a weather forecast; Fite would perhaps have preferred this style; but dare he demand it on pain of "nonsense"? [22]

The other "number" passage [23] can be more briefly dispatched. Here Plato, having to his own satisfaction completed his proof that the just man is happy and the tyrant miserable, has seen fit to add a little mathematical flourish of demonstration, to dance, as it were, a mathematical jig on the tomb of the tyrant's claim to happiness. By applying a geometry of squares and cubes, quite arbitrarily and in such wise as to arouse the mildly amused wonder of the interlocutor Glaucon, who calls the proof "an overwhelming and baffling calculation," [24] Plato proves the tyrant to be precisely 729 times more miserable than the just man! Fite is, naturally, not impressed; that is his natural right, which we have no inclination to challenge. His wrong in this matter lies rather in his assumption that Plato is unrelievedly in earnest, and hence again displaying, in a particularly fatuous way, his mathematical obsession.

Besides being mathematically obsessed to the point of silliness, Fite's Plato is guilty unawares of using fallacy in argument, and this, too, in matters of crucial import. Fite refers especially to the proof, in the *Phaedo*, just before the death of Socrates, that the soul is immortal. Since one of the "disciples" of Plato, in this case Shorey, has asserted that Plato's use of fallacy in this argument was conscious and concealed by "conscious art," Fite needs only [25] to scoff at the idea that such concealment is thinkable: to Fite's mind it would have appeared to Plato most unfitting in a situation of such solemnity. The use of a fallacious argument cannot have been conscious, and the "disciple" has himself admitted that fallacy is used. In what sense the argument is "fallacious," or what motives Plato may have had for representing Socrates as employing an argument not wholly immune to valid criticism, need not concern us here; [26] our point is that Fite has again, at small cost and as a profitable by-product of attacking a "disciple," tagged Plato with the reproachful name of "unintelligent." [27]

From Plato's writings, Fite has, on occasion, turned to examine the biographical record in quest of further examples of Plato's foolishness. And here he has struck gold of sorts, for in the *Letters*, now so widely accepted as genuine revelations of the facts and motives of Plato's Sicilian journeys, he has found material which, with some selective emphasis and judicious omissions, can be made to fit perfectly into his previously constructed mould. The crown

---

[22] Recognition of passages such as these has prompted Grube (*Plato's Thought*, 1935, p. 29), who characterizes the speech of the Muses as mythical, to declare that "though Plato often speaks in jest, he never speaks in vain." I seize this opportunity of commending to the general reader Grube's temperate and lucid study, with which I find myself in repeated and cordial agreement.

[23] *Republic* 587 B–588 A.

[24] Shorey's translation, Loeb Library.

[25] Shorey, *What Plato Said*, p. 180, quoted in Fite, p. 287.

[26] For treatment of this problem, see below, p. 63.

[27] Fite, p. 285ff.

of Plato's mathematical obsession, for Fite, was his "simplemindedness" in thrusting down the throat of the young tyrant Dionysius II, in preparation for the responsibility of his new political office, a course in geometry. Fite's evidence that Plato was guilty of this alleged folly is drawn from the third *Letter*, which, as Fite is aware, is not one of those most frequently accepted as genuine. Accordingly Fite argues as follows: he appeals to the reader of the dialogues to remember the silly mathematicism they everywhere expound; keeping this firmly before his mind, he will easily accept as genuine the particular mathematical silliness that the third *Letter* contains.[28]

Others have seen in Plato's Sicilian adventures, taken as a whole, an intelligent altruism, a generous and open-eyed response to an appeal to aid the cause of constitutional government,[29] and, beyond that, Greek independence against the threat of Carthaginian power.[30] Fite has turned his blind eye to all that, and with his other eye has, so he tells us, seen into the depths of Plato's silly soul: the Sicilian attempt may be lightly dismissed as a "harebrained venture." [31] Fite has simply used his knowledge of the historical event to discredit Plato's whole relation to the enterprise: Plato "bet on the wrong horse," is Fite's comment. True, but no truer than the relevant truism that hindsight is better than foresight. If Fite's principle were put into effect, not only would there be no horse racing, but all great ventures of faith would cease, in favor of the small certainties of worldly prudence. It is a fair guess that if Plato had not gone to Sicily, Fite would have had some remarks to make about craven cautiousness and unwillingness to expose one's theoretic boldness to the possible humiliation of practical failure.[32]

Reviewing the case that Fite has presented against Plato's right to be respected on intellectual grounds, we may observe certain of its pervasive features. The discussion is marked throughout by a specious consistency of the sort which some of the livelier political columnists have made familiar: a point of view is adopted — perhaps for no more weighty reasons than a temperamental preference for the exhilarating hair-pulling of bigwigs, and the unstuffing of shirts — , appropriate facts and fragments of facts are carefully collected, and these and these only are conscientiously fitted together in such wise as to bring about the scheduled discrediting of the victim. This will explain what otherwise appears to be the miraculous coincidence between an inherently implausible hypothesis and a whole array of facts, tumbling over each other in eagerness to fall into line. Restrict the conditions for admission to sainthood, by requiring all candidates to be members of the Catholic church, and the nonexistence of Protestant saints ceases to be a very strong

---

[28] Fite, p. 253.

[29] Glenn Morrow, "Studies in the Platonic Epistles," 1935, pp. 153, 169, and *passim*.

[30] Taylor, *Plato, the Man and his Work*, 1929, p. 7.

[31] Fite, p. 295–6.

[32] See Fite, pp. 292 and 288–289, where these qualities are attributed to Plato rather in contradiction of his supposed unteachable venturesomeness in Sicily.

argument against Martin Luther. To this principle of restriction Fite has remained faithful: no creditable facts — or only a few belittled ones — are admitted; and out of whatever defective or broken bits he could collect or infer, from dialogues and letters, he has consistently constructed the entire fabric of Plato's mind and thought.

A second principle, for which similar precedent among journalists might be claimed, is that of suggesting — sometimes in forthright accusing tones, again by innuendo — that the view which "I the writer" (in this case, Fite) am maintaining, has, by common consent of mankind, the single alternative of idiocy. The dangers of parting philosophical company with Fite are very real: for the stupidity of having written the *Laws*, Plato may not atone even by admitting "dotage," [33] since the *Laws*, Fite insists, is really not more besotted than the *Republic*, which dates from his maturity. No, there is no help for it: if Fite is right, Plato must admit general mental incapacity. Most readers, it is likely, will find this conclusion logically odd, and will be mystified by the disappearance of intermediate possibilities.

In the fifteenth chapter of Voltaire's *Candide*, we are introduced to one Pococurante — "Like-Little," we might translate him — a master of the art of belittlement. "Poco" resides in a magnificent palace, with spacious gardens and picture galleries, his vast library furnished with *editions de luxe* of the great books from Homer to Milton. But to the astonishment of Candide, "Poco" derives from all this no more substantial pleasure than the fastidious pride of refusing to be pleased. "Homer? His continual repetition of battles, one indistinguishable from the other, his gods perpetually busy in bringing nothing to a conclusion! Virgil? I confess the second, fourth, and sixth *Aeneid* are excellent, but as for his pious Aeneas, his faithful Achates . . . his imbecile King Latinus . . . I do not think anything can be more frigid or more disagreeable. . . . Milton is but a barbarian who made a rumbling commentary in ten books on the first chapter of Genesis. . . . He has turned the stomach of all men of taste. . . ." [34] Will the reader recognize here, despite the exaggeration, some essential resemblance to the author of *The Platonic Legend*?

In effecting his transition from the charge of deficient intelligence and incapacity to recognize a fallacy when he saw one to that of having made constant use of deliberate fallacies, Fite may seem to be stultifying the position he has just defended. It would seem that he is telling over again, with the names changed, the old story of the borrowed bucket: in the first place, the fellow didn't return it, and in the second place, he brought it back with a hole in it. But we may assist Fite in reconciling his charges by admitting

---

[33] Fite, p. 293.

[34] This has been substantially reduced from the original.

the possibility that a man might be unintelligent in general and still possess a certain low cunning sufficient for passing off false mental coins as true.

Such fallacious art runs through all the dialogues, as Fite reads them, but it is not clear whether Plato is the sole culprit or whether the historical Socrates is his accomplice. This ambiguity is, however, of small forensic importance in the present connection, since, on Fite's premises, Plato's guilt would be the same in either case: Plato has either independently practiced the dishonest art, in this case also misrepresenting Socrates; or he has been *particeps criminis*, abetting and approving its practice by his master in chicanery. We will agree with Fite's assertion that it was Plato's wish to stand committed to the entire approvability of his own picture of the "true philosopher," Socrates.[35] Was this Socrates guilty of fraud in argument, and if so, what could have prompted Plato to admire him for his crime?

Our opponents may here point to an apparently serious inconsistency, which we, for our part, accept the obligation to explain. It is this: the Platonic Socrates in many passages professes a great respect for the wisdom of others — he himself is only an ignorant and humble inquirer for their great wisdom; he protests a sovereign respect for truth — he will sacrifice all else to attain knowledge of the true ends of human life; in equal measure, he is the merciless foe of all falsity or equivocation in argument, alert to the slightest deviation from the demands of logical consistency. All this is held up by Plato as being in pointed contrast to those pretensions to final knowledge and that subordination of truth and honest logic to victory in argument which are among the baser characteristics charged upon the sophists. But this same Socrates, as we view him in action in the dialogues, in conversation and debate with a Hippias or a Thrasymachus, seems to fall short of this lofty standard: he is far from any real wish to learn any of the many arts of which Hippias is reputed to be master, and, with Hippias and Thrasymachus both, he is seen achieving a victory in argument[36] by "logical" methods which have just that quality of deliberate and deceptive fallaciousness and indifference to the pursuit of truth, for which the word "sophistic" is especially reserved. Taken seriously, this behavior appears as unscrupulous; taken as playing to the gallery, it seems to be clowning, if not in the church itself, at any rate in the church porch.

In view of this behavior, and supported by the authority of Grote, Fite has been so bold as to charge that Socrates is, indeed, "Plato's best illustration of his own idea of a sophist." [37] Fite points particularly to the *Gorgias* as complete justification of this charge, citing the instance of Socrates' play-

---

[35] Fite, p. 102.

[36] Strictly speaking, Socrates does not argue with Hippias; he merely argues from certain assertions drawn from Hip-

pias, to reach contradictory conclusions from which Hippias is helpless to escape.

[37] Fite, p. 193.

ing hob with Gorgias' pupil Polus, arbitrarily declining to answer his questions and substituting abuse for argument. Further confirmation is supplied in the chapter entitled "Socrates the Martyr" (so called from the fact that he is not a martyr), where attention is directed to those logical devices for shifting the issue with which Socrates conducts the early part of his defense before the court. This ingredient in the *Apology* we have already seen disturbing Chapman — he called it "cup-and-ball practice" [38] — because of its moral incongruity. Fite handles the matter differently, since he assumes, for purposes of argument, that the whole *Apology* is Socratic; for him, the presence of sportive elements, particularly of logical fallacies in juxtaposition with moral sublimities, helps to prove that the sublimities cannot really be sublime. The whole affair is the sorry exhibition of a disgruntled and pretentious man, full of unscrupulous devices, who, if he did not get "what he deserved" when condemned to drink the hemlock, at any rate got what he jolly well might have expected.[39]

Turning now to the defense, let us speak first of the dialogues as a whole. The modern reader is very likely to bring to his reading of Plato the expectation, perhaps even the demand, that a given dialogue be classifiable as a serious contribution to philosophic thought, or, if not, that the work before him waive all right to philosophical consideration and submit itself to be read purely for such poetic or satiric merits as it may possess. He will be the more likely to make this demand if he has become acquainted with the principles of classical art, including literature, where he is often told the classical ideal demands undeviating rationality, order, and clear-cut discrimination of the several literary types, "*les genres tranchés*," as they were later called. Such expectations, applied to Plato, are predestined to defeat. No romanticist could of set purpose more completely have violated the classical tradition in this respect. A highly solemn occasion, such as the last hours of Socrates as depicted in the *Phaedo*, did indeed subdue his imagination to a single key. But the overwhelming majority of the Socratic dialogues are not classifiable in terms of "either . . . or."

It seems that when Plato sat down to write a dialogue, he felt himself free to choose between writing comedy or writing logic and philosophy, all at once or in whatever ratio he might prefer. We find no dialogue without at least some serious component, though a large portion of the *Euthydemus* is definitely presented as an exhibit of eristic legerdemain and the logical lesson of the *Hippias Minor* is so unobtrusive as to permit us to classify it almost wholly as comedy. At the other end of the scale is the *Parmenides*, in whose production the comic muse has had no share; occupying an intermediate position are the greater number of the dialogues, including the *Republic* and

---

[38] Chapman, p. 155.   [39] Fite, pp. 109–10.

the *Politicus*, and even the *Timaeus*, in which the author has reserved the right to indulge a playful impulse whenever he sees fit.

But it would be a mistake in emphasis to treat this playfulness as the sole or even the dominant motive underlying Plato's use of fallacies. Let us consider the situation from a broader base. Plato, as a writer of philosophical dialogues, may be said to have had at least three major objectives. He had first of all to meet every writer's problem: to arrest and retain the reader's interest. Second, he wished to awaken the sleeping philosophic Eros in the reader's soul. And third, in increasing measure as his store of wisdom accumulated, he had much of positive instruction to impart. The first of these is the reason for the great variety in the manner of opening the dialogues; it will account for much in them that is of little or no philosophical importance, e.g. the altercation scene, wherein Socrates and Protagoras come very near to a parting of ways (*Protagoras*), though it should be noted that Plato has managed here to add something to our knowledge of the contrast between the respective methods of the two men. And this motive must have been primary to the time and care Plato obviously spent upon the *mise en scène* of certain dialogues, e.g., the walk along the Ilissus under the plane trees in the *Phaedrus*, and the interior of the house of Callias, with the grand promenade of the sophists, in the *Protagoras*.

More attention to these features, greater sympathy with Plato's intentions to supply more than a minimum set of logical meanings in each dialogue, is a prophylactic against such gratuitous misconceptions as Popper falls into when he imputes sinister motives to harmless little turns in Plato's narrative or the dramatic conduct of the argument.[40] And it will supply a motive other than Plato's malice (though somewhat of stern disapproval may enter as a secondary cause) for the frequent depictions of Socrates engaged in unhorsing the pride of a showy sciolist such as Hippias, or rendering absurd the *soi-disant* religious expert Euthyphro. Such exhibitions were highly relished by Milton, who, speaking in general of the Platonic dialogues, declared, "There is scarce one of them, especially wherein some notable Sophister lies sweating and turmoyling under the inevitable and mercilesse dilemmas of Socrates, but that he who reads, were it Saturne himself, would be often rob'd of more than a smile." [41] Now it would be easier for Plato to steal in his fashion from "Saturne" than from Fite; indeed, it must be admitted that modern sensibility is in general less susceptible to the enjoyment of any sort of discomfiture than was the Puritan poet. But let us not be too Saturnine; all but the thoroughgoing "agelasts" of whom Meredith speaks, will register some degree of amusement, not at the distress of the victim, which receives little emphasis, but at the imperturbable agility and virtuosity of this master of verbal fence.

---

[40] See below, p. 406ff.

[41] Milton, *Apology for Smectymnuus, Works*, 1931, vol. III, part I, pp. 293–294.

Such spectacles have another use which falls logically under our second caption. The sight of "notable Sophisters" laid low for want of a little logic might well strike home to many of Plato's readers and arouse in them misgivings as to their own state of logical grace; young Lysis and young Charmides are similarly shown, under more benign treatment, becoming aware of problems whose existence they had hitherto not suspected; such doubts, pursued, might put them or their like among Plato's readers on their way toward philosophic understanding. Indeed, this remains true of the Socratic dialogues to this day; many an educator ranks them high among books with power to invite the mind, partly by irritation, partly by fascination, to ready itself for the rational adventures of philosophy.

Plato's third purpose as a writer, the imparting of substantial knowledge and understanding to satisfy the impulse thus aroused, is too wide a topic for full discussion here; omitting ethics (with one exception, to be discussed below), metaphysics, and the remainder of his ample curriculum, we speak here, by limitation of our present topic, of logical lessons only. The truly serious constituent in Plato's apparently merely light-hearted play with logical forms is all too easily missed. A critical study of the development of Platonic dialectic will reveal how neat a progression can be traced from the exhibition of fallacies exposed by means of the Socratic "elenchus" (scrutiny and refutation) in the early dialogues, through the analysis of the method of hypothesis in the *Phaedo* and *Republic*, up to the subtle and profound attempts to solve epistemological and ontological problems that characterize dialogues like the *Theaetetus* and the *Sophist*. To appreciate this side of Plato's achievement, one must study under other masters than Fite.[42]

Underlying and reënforcing the three motives we have assigned to the author of the dialogues, there was a fourth, that might well claim to be the first: the impulse of the disciple to present a moving and undying image of his departed master. This is so obviously the primary purpose of the *Apology*, the *Crito*, and (with some reservations) the *Phaedo*, as to need no comment. It is a major theme, as our discussion showed, in the *Symposium*, while such pieces as the little *Euthyphro*, the short *Lysis* and *Charmides*, and the more extended *Gorgias*, might fairly be described as attempts to present Socrates

---

[42] Richard Robinson, in *Plato's Earlier Dialectic*, 1941, has illuminatingly traced the growth of Plato's logic from its Socratic beginnings through its middle period, adding some indication of its final phase, for the fuller treatment of which he refers his readers to Julius Stenzel. It is necessary to add that along with a lively respect for Plato's contribution to the advancement of logic, Robinson displays an exceptionally conscientious recognition of Plato's limitations: he acknowledges that Plato could not have seen, even at the peak of his development, what a contemporary logician is capable of discerning, and argues that Plato sometimes failed to make strict application of the logical principles which he supposed himself to be applying. Thus neither Socrates nor Plato appears to Robinson to have been aware of the illegitimacy of the assumptions on which their conclusions sometimes rest.

in action. If there are in these dialogues, as few doubt, additions and extensions of doctrines from Plato's hand, this is no more than a generous weaving of his own fresh laurels into the master's crown. The depth and intensity of Plato's tribute might, as Shorey has suggested,[43] be compared to Dante's resolution to "praise Beatrice as no woman was ever praised before," a comparison the more just if we remember that, as Dante's Beatrice was metamorphosed into the image of Heavenly Wisdom, so Plato's Socrates tended to become Philosophy itself.

But Plato's portrait of Socrates is no allegorical abstraction. It is a "wart and all" picture of an actual man, the homely traits of person, dress, and speech, no less than the heroic strength of mind and will, all raised no doubt to a higher level of significance by Plato's admiring devotion. Prominent among the traits portrayed are some which modern critics are not disposed to view with admiration equal to that which Plato has lavished upon them. We may smile a little (Fite scoffs) at the glorification of the Socratic capacity for consuming huge bumpers of undiluted wine without losing for a moment the sobriety becoming a philosopher. His general complaisance to the vices of his companions may strike us as incongruous with the transcendent purity of his own conduct. He is shown pressing his "humility" to the point of arrogance, and irrepressibly employing his superb logical powers for the tripping-up of anyone unwary enough to answer in good faith his deceptively innocent questions. That the historical Socrates is here in his own hues, with dramatic truth portrayed, we have every right to believe.

This then was the Socrates who had supplied Plato not alone with the subject for an inspired portrait, but with the ground plan of a philosophical career. Plato's basic motives are, point for point — his function as a biographer aside — projections upon the plane of a more consciously developed program of the central concerns and aims of Socrates. Let us briefly consider this correspondence: Plato's aim of arresting and holding the reader had its prototype in the rather more difficult art required of Socrates, that of diverting his fellow Athenians by a show at least as entertaining as the law courts and the public lecturers. Next it was the task of Socrates to rouse doubts and prime the souls of his listeners for the philosophic search. And finally, for all his disclaimers of knowledge, he had positive teaching to deliver, the crowning feature of his "service to the god": he must excite his fellow citizens to a paramount interest in the well-being of their souls, in moral excellence; and since for him clarity of mind was identical with moral goodness, he had lessons in applied logic to impart, sometimes delivered by shining examples of right method (e.g., *Gorgias*, 450 C–451 D, *Euthyphro* 11 E–12 E) ; again, particularly when he is arguing against some self-satisfied virtuoso of the art of speech (e.g., *Hippias Min.* 364 D–369 B, *Protagoras* 332 A–E, *Gorgias*

---

[43] "The Question of the Socratic Element in Plato," 1927, p. 577.

474 C–475 E), by the most egregious and provoking tricks of debate. We see, then, that fallacies were no idle element in the furtherance of Socrates' mission, and that Plato, his dramatic biographer, could not without damage to his objective have struck them from the record. One will note, however, that Plato, in the interest of his pedagogic aim, has frequently posted warnings of "Fallacy!" along the more dangerous curves of the argument.

Our attention is now claimed by that one element in Plato's ethical message to which we earlier referred (and this element, also, in our view, had its antecedent in Socrates), the use of deliberate fallacies in support of morally approved ends. This forms part of a larger topic, Plato's sanctioning, in certain circumstances, of various kinds and degrees of edifying untruth. With it we shall be busily concerned in a later chapter, since it has appeared to some of the detractors as Plato's odious apostasy from the uncompromising Socratic dedication to truth. Our later discussion will present what is perhaps the best background for answering this objection, an exposition of his complex theory of persuasion and belief. Here we must ask, first, that an important distinction be observed between the readers to whom the dialogues are addressed and two classes of persons, partly or wholly imaginary, to whom Plato in some sense directs his deceptions. His readers Plato addresses as his intellectual equals, and treats with no condescending reserve; to them he presents as much of the truth in his possession as the medium of communication will permit [44] and the situation represented in the dialogue will render plausible. For their benefit he supplies, as we have said, dramatic hints and indications, confirmed often by explicit statements in other dialogues, that he is aware of the difficulties and logical shortcomings which sometimes beset his arguments. The interlocutors are somewhat differently handled; the Platonic Socrates often counsels or requires them, if they cannot refute his arguments, to assent to his conclusions. At a third remove from logical rigor are the arguments presumed acceptable to the supposedly less critical minds of the common citizens who are to inhabit his reformed cities of the *Republic*, the *Politicus*, and the *Laws*.

But in spite of all this open-eyed use of inadequate proofs, we must insist that Plato's central commitment is to the truth as he conceived it: we find him everywhere grounding his ethical theory and his political arrangements upon what he regarded as a true conception of an antecedent reality. He is not oblivious, however, of other humbler considerations and feels the need of mediating, on occasion, between the eternal verities and the limitations of human faculty. Plato's "mediations" are still, in almost all cases, attempts to

---

[44] At *Phaedrus* 275 D–276 D Plato contrasts the written word as a mute helpless image, a sterile hothouse plant, with the living word implanted by dialectic in the soul and capable of self-defense and of perpetuating itself from mind to mind. In conclusion (278 B–E) he disparages the twisting and turning and gluing together of phrases as beneath the dignity of a lover of wisdom, whose distinction it is to be able to establish by word of mouth the inferiority of his own writings.

apply as much truth as possible to the interpretation and regulation of human life. His deepest convictions were no doubt confirmed by argument, but we need not believe that they were originally inspired by it; unless our reading of his life is radically mistaken, they were awakened by the living testimonial of a Socrates and strengthened by the arduous lessons of his own experience. The soul is somehow divine, and has an eternal destiny; and the divine order of the universe is somehow good.[45] To the defense and reënforcement of these spiritual divinations, logical proofs are required to contribute as best they can. Reason and faith are thus enlisted in a common cause, and Plato does not always mark their precise mutual frontiers, something of "myth" creeping at times into his "logos," to balance the rational element that pervades so many of his avowed myths.[46] It is thus that we can understand how it was possible for him, in the *Phaedo*, to give us a Socrates who is willing to admit the fallibility of human reason and the consequent fragility of his proposed "proofs" of the soul's immortality, while yet holding with undiminished ardor to his irrepressible assurance that death is not an end.[47] And the authority of the invincibly surmised, ultimate truths of value, as we may call them, over the secondary forms of truth or falsehood, Plato maintained to his latest years: we find him in the *Laws* (662–663) asserting that he himself is as certain that the good life is one with the pleasant as "that Crete is an island," but adding that were this not the case, a lawgiver worth anything at all would nevertheless manage to convince the young citizens of its truth. And before one totally condemns the manipulation of truth that Plato appears here to sponsor, let it be remembered that Plato is proposing a belief which he thinks it desirable for all men to believe for their own interests as well as for the sake of the community. One may even go further, and see in it a paradoxical and therefore emphatic restatement of his faith in a truth which, like Voltaire's "God," is so necessary that, if it "did not exist," it would "require to be invented."

We may illustrate the application of these considerations by turning to

---

[45] Bertrand Russell (*History of Western Philosophy*, 1945, pp. 142–143) considers that Socrates' determination to believe, at the cost of scientific objectivity, that the universe and man are ethically akin, rather diminishes the glory of his courage in the face of death, and is "the worst of philosophic sins"; in atonement, he recommends for Socrates "a long residence in a scientific purgatory." There is, indeed, an obvious courage in standing up with Russell's "free man," undaunted against the gigantic indifference of an alien universe. But is there not a no less manly courage in the untroubled tenacity with which Socrates stood up to declare his faith that no real harm can befall a good man? Russell will not be the slave of power, Socrates will not be the slave of fear; it cuts no moral difference. Nor can it be said that Socrates is brave because he believes in the divine order; it is at least as true to say that he maintains his belief in God because he is brave.

[46] The rationality of the Platonic myths has been admirably displayed by Frutiger, in *Les Mythes de Platon*, 1930; see especially p. 267: "His myths speak to the intelligence almost as much as to the imagination or to sentiment."

[47] The passages in the *Phaedo* here referred to are listed below, p. 433.

that stormcenter of the charge of dishonesty, the *Apology*.[48] Perhaps it is
not possible to arrange even the terms of fair debate between those who are
shocked by Socrates' intrusion of irony and fallacy into his argument before
the court and those who, like Plato himself, admire it as a badge of courage
and irrepressible *esprit*. This represents, perhaps, a clash of temperaments
past rational resolution. But those who are, like Chapman, disturbed by such
dissonance intruding upon the moral music they have hoped to hear may be
reminded that the shock is more their misfortune than Plato's fault. Socrates,
as the record shows, was like that, and Plato loved him for it and presented
him to the world in his true character. There is little to quarrel with on
either side; whoever wishes Socrates had been Jesus may close the *Apology*
and open the New Testament. The fallacies of the earlier *Apology*, then, are
on the part of Socrates, the outcome of the habit of a lifetime gallantly maintained; that they have reached us unaltered we owe to the pious honesty of
a disciple.

At the very end of the *Apology*, in a universally admired passage, we have
an illustration of that other use of fallacy to which we have referred as
ethical. Socrates turns to those among his judges who have voted for his acquittal and confides to them the mood in which he confronts the world to
come. Death, he tells them, is one of two things, both good: either a long and
dreamless sleep or a transportation to a happier region where one will meet
and crossexamine the great dead. Into the full exposition of the magnificent
peroration, with its closing sentence, held by a great critic and authority upon
the rhythmic structure of prose to be the most beautiful sentence in European
literature, we need not go.[49] What concerns us is to note that the structure of
the argument is founded upon the logically indefensible suppression of possible alternatives to the two that Socrates has chosen to discuss. What we are
offered here is, in fact, a perfect example of that use of fallacy which Plato
has sanctioned and justified by the use he has made of it: fallacy consciously
employed to supply the defects of human reason, and to provide, as in a magical
glass, an image of a transcendent realm which the mind of man can profit-
ably contemplate, but never prove.

It may have been noticed by the observant reader that the name of Popper
has been conspicuously absent from our discussion of the charge of intentional fallaciousness. Had we invited him to participate, he would have told
us, in effect, that the other critics have been rather innocent in regarding
Plato's fallacies, at least those in the *Republic*, as the product of mere desire
for victory in argument, or display of vanity. Those fallacies Plato has con-

---

[48] The diversity of view among the detractors may perhaps do our argument a
little service, here as elsewhere: to Popper,
as we shall see, the *Apology* appears as

our clearest picture of an utterly honest
Socrates.
[49] George Saintsbury, *English Prose
Rhythm*, p. 456; *apud* Shorey, *What Plato
Said*, p. 465.

trived to conceal the structure of his thought, those seemingly playful inter-
ludes, those omissions of logical alternatives, are, in reality, frauds within a
fraud, parts of one systematically planned and carefully discharged deception,
that found its motive in a self-deluding megalomania and sought to achieve
nothing less than the strangling of truth and the closing of the door of a
tribal society upon a considerable portion of the Greek race.[50] We shall offer
Popper a full opportunity to state his case in a later chapter, where it can be
accompanied by his other evidence bearing upon the wider question of Plato's
honesty.[51] Here we must content ourselves with pointing out that, though
Plato would indeed be willing to use fallacies for ethical ends, he limits this
use to those few ultimate questions which reason has led up to, but cannot
answer; and that of the "fallacies" in the *Republic*, some of them are not fallacies, but the necessary patterns of thought when it reconstructs concepts to
serve new needs; [52] while the rest are capable of explanation by one or another of the justifications for the use of fallacy, already listed in this section.

We may now briefly indicate, in the light of the foregoing discussion, the
place of fallacies in the economy of the Platonic philosophy taken as a whole.
The cardinal error, illustrated by Fite, is to treat them as so many sins, by
their very nature offenses against reason and truth. The key to understanding
them is to ask, What are they doing there? and, in each given case, What
function does it perform? Our answer is that they are variously employed to
serve a number of useful and beneficent ends: to amuse and entertain, to
rouse and disturb, to display the swarming confusions generated in an untidy
mind, to display the dramatic truth about Socrates, and *in extremis*, to buttress ultimate truths when human weakness can supply no stouter aid.

In the following section we shall consider those complaints against Plato
which regard primarily not his logical power and his use of it, but the soundness and worth of his character.

Many of the most traditionally admired pages in Plato are those in which
he plies the function, not of logician and dialectician, dissecting and reassem-
bling the objects of human understanding, as we have seen him doing in the
discussion just pursued. They are rather those in which he has reported to us,
often in the form of vivid pictorialization, the results of his acute observations and introspections of the life of the soul, her homesick longing, her
doubts and self-divisions, her desperate struggles with her baser components.
This psychological picture gallery has been admired not alone for the skill of
the painter, but preëminently for the depth of understanding that it reveals

[50] Popper, *op. cit.*, e.g. pp. 96–99, 190–
191, 193–194. This charge of conscious deception is the usual form taken by Popper's
attack, though, as we shall see (pp. 75,
397 ff.), he occasionally introduces partial

extenuations of Plato's guilt. No angry critic
can be held to a strict consistency of accusation: *non semper arcum tendit Apollo.*
[51] See pp. 396 ff. below.
[52] See p. 417 below.

of the essential nature of man and the secret ways of the soul. We have now to counter the attempt by the detractors to turn this achievement against Plato, to neglect or deride his observation and his art, and to interpret the content of his pictures as evidence of the painter's failure both to understand the souls of others and to control, in a civilized and mature fashion, his own.

Whether by intent or by a happy chance, Fite has pursued Plato's "character defects" of this type along the three planes of the Platonic tripartite soul, and has accordingly discovered faults *epithymetic* (concupiscent), faults *thymic* (mettlesome), and faults *logistic* (intellectual). On the concupiscent level, Fite finds Plato overly developed; it would seem that he was barely able to restrain his lawless impulses to acquire and to enjoy. It appears that Plato's "one idea of morality is self-restraint . . . ; and in his imagination self-restraint is occupied exclusively with 'certain pleasures and appetites' (*Rep.* 430 E) . . . . Throughout the dialogues it seems that his imagination is haunted by scenes of debauchery, illustrated unwittingly, and only faintly, by his own *Symposium*." [53] "Child-morality," [54] or a "leisure-class" ethic, suitable only for those who have no serious occupations or imagination to supply the lack of them,[55] — these standards measure, on Fite's stick, the highwater mark of Plato's conception, and offer an illuminating commentary on the practical problem by which Plato was confronted in the management of his own life.

An unflattering self-portrait of a fuming, pride-hurt, "leader" with no following — this is what Fite has discovered in that section of the *Gorgias* in which the great Athenian statesmen of the past are blamed for the behavior of their indocile flock, and in which Socrates (on Fite's view the mouthpiece, here, of the Platonic vanity) is heard to proclaim himself as the one true statesman of Athenian history.[56] In such craven fashion, under the cover of a dialogue, does Fite's Plato strike a dishonest blow at that democracy which he was not man enough to attack directly and in his own person.[57] This deranged inflation of Plato's "thymos," that part of the soul which is the seat of courage or cowardice and by which we feel ambition and covet honor (*Rep.* 581 A–B), Fite finds again expressed in the tradition supported by the *Seventh Letter* of Plato's petty jealousy of his pupil Dionysius, who on the strength of the little that he had absorbed of Plato's esoteric wisdom had presumed to rival his master by writing a treatise on the highest metaphysical knowledge.[58] To this same young man, who "was at least twenty-five, it seems, and an absolute monarch," "Plato's attitude . . . was that of a schoolmistress to a child." [59]

The remaining "failures" in Fite's list — the faults "logistic" — imply

---

[53] Fite, *op. cit.*, p. 305.
[54] *Ibid.*, p. 307.
[55] *Ibid.*, p. 306.
[56] Fite, *op. cit.*, p. 191; *Gorgias* 521 D.

[57] *Ibid.*, pp. 288–289, 292.
[58] *Ibid.*, p. 298; *Letter* VII, 341 B f., 344 D ff.
[59] *Ibid.*, p. 297.

an essential deficiency in theoretic understanding; they are, properly speaking, defects in Plato's ethical theory. But as Fite presents them they are seen growing out of the moral inadequacy of Plato the man and as such deserve mention in this place. Plato "knows nothing" of that regard for one's neighbor and imaginative sympathy for his interests which is the basis of civilized abstention from antisocial actions.[60] Again, he "knows nothing" of the stabilizing function of "a serious aim in life," of "serious purpose and personal responsibility" in the presence of which "the control of appetite is largely automatic"; [61] this, in conjunction with Fite's statement that Plato himself had great trouble in controlling his appetites, constitutes a daring charge indeed. Fite adds that Plato's characters (and, it is implied, Plato) appear to have no private aims, no inner being: they seem to have "suffered a curious amputation." [62] And, closely related defect, Plato has failed to grasp anything of the significance of personality, to recognize the existence and value of the precious differences between one man and another: the individual is swallowed in the type of which he is merely a more or less imperfect reproduction.[63] Thus Fite on Plato's character. Are the other detractors of one mind with him here?

It would be questionable procedure to urge the silence of one accuser against the explicit testimony of the others, but Crossman has contributed much more than silence to the issue before us, as well as to the two issues previously discussed. He offers what amounts to downright praise of Plato for his ability, insight, and fairmindedness; and on the present point, though he denies to Plato, "the natural superior," a tolerant understanding of the common, faulty human being,[64] he applauds his sanity, his balance, and his benevolence.[65]

We have called to our aid an unexpected witness in the person of Crossman. A glance at Popper's deposition, in the table, shows that his charge parallels Fite's to a certain point, but with some omissions and contradictions, and some logical refinements of detail.

There is no suggestion, on Popper's part, of any deficiency in the Platonic intelligence. On the contrary, Popper has transformed Emerson's "great-eyed Plato" into the "many-eyed," a gigantic sinister intelligence, endowed with an unerring instinct for the recognition and ensnaring of his enemies, the true defenders of human good itself.[66] Plato's supposed misuse of his great understanding of human motivation will claim our later attention; at the moment

---

[60] *Ibid.*, p. 303.
[61] *Ibid.*, p. 306.
[62] Fite, *op. cit.*, pp. 318–319.
[63] *Ibid.*, pp. 307–309.
[64] Crossman, *Plato Today*, pp. 102, 301; see also p. 268 below, where this charge again enters our discussion.
[65] For Crossman's praise of Plato's ability and insight, see *op. cit.*, pp. 292, 298, and *passim*; for his fairness and openness, see pp. 98, 292; for sanity and balance in matters of sex, p. 198; for general magnanimity, pp. 97–98, 100–103, 274–275, 278–279.
[66] Popper, *op. cit.*, *passim*; e.g., pp. 40, 83–84, 92, 101, 108, 117, 193.

we will merely note the disagreement with Fite's appraisal, and pass to consider Popper's treatment of Plato's personal morality.

Popper has gone even a little further than Fite, and in the same direction, in quest of Plato's faults concupiscent. He says, "The 'division' or 'split' in Plato's soul is one of the most outstanding impressions of the *Republic*. Only a man who had to struggle hard for upholding his self-control or the rule of his reason over his animal instincts, would emphasize this point as much as Plato did."[67] The significance of this "clamouring for unity"[68] is for Popper reënforced by two other "strong symptoms of repression." In a passage often remarked for its anticipation of some of the fundamental notions in the Freudian psychology, Plato has described certain base desires that awake during sleep, when the soul is released from the sense of shame, and are gratified in dreams of all degrees of folly and turpitude.[69] Plato's creation myth in the *Timaeus* is psychoanalyzed as indicating sexual repression on the ground of the generating power there attributed to the Ideas, or Forms, and the passive receptivity of Space, the mother of generation.[70] Now it is, superficially, very remarkable that after having "proved" all this, Popper makes no extended use of it (as Fite would do) to discredit Plato the man and moralist. The answer is that Popper is not centrally concerned with these objects; his great objective is the demolition of Plato the proto-fascist, and the "split" in Plato's soul is useful to Popper only as confirmation of the supposed consciousness of guilt, the "titanic struggle" in the soul of the betrayer of the democratic ideal.[71]

Despite the apparent similarity between Popper's estimate of Plato's faults of "thymos," and that of Fite, Popper has derived his evidence from quite different sources. It is a somewhat ironical circumstance that the very *Gorgias* passage (Socrates' claim to be the only true statesman) which we saw Fite employing as proof that Plato is arrogant and mad for power, is interpreted by Popper in a contrary sense. The sentence now turns out to be an expression by the historical Socrates himself of the intellectual modesty which, knowing only that it does not know, can rightly claim a unique and useful place for its bearer as the one best qualified to rule.[72] A further difference in sources is Fite's dependence upon the *Letters*, which Popper scrupulously avoids, drawing instead largely upon the *Republic* and the *Laws*. By and large, Fite's is the pettier, vainer man, while Popper's Plato is the more odious and sinister. Pride mounting to arrogance,[73] bitter scorn and hate,[74] an imperious demand to be revered,[75] all these are his in full measure. Popper finds him, in his published works, indulging in thinly veiled sneers, in allusion to the physical defects and inferior social status of his more magnanimous rivals

---

[67] Popper, p. 606.
[68] Popper, p. 606.
[69] *Republic* 571 f.
[70] *Timaeus*, 50 C–D; Popper, pp. 606, 479.

[71] *Ibid.*, p. 191. See our pp. 398, 402.
[72] Popper, p. 128.
[73] *Ibid.*, e.g., pp. 48, 130–131, 565.
[74] *Ibid.*, e.g., pp. 43–44, 95.
[75] *Ibid.*, e.g., p. 44.

in philosophy.[76] Plato is accused of poisonous dishonesty, as we have seen; there are even darker hues, a mad ambition trenching on megalomania.[77] But these wilder surmises we have chosen to isolate in a separate ward; [78] the less spectacular disorders we shall deal with in what immediately follows.

The extent of agreement between Popper and Fite as to Plato's faults of character is such as to permit consideration of the two cases in close conjunction. We shall treat first of Plato's faults of "concupiscence." We found both men placing the main accent upon Plato's unconscious confession of moral mutiny within, implied by his repeated protestations of the beauty of an integrated soul. Fite wants no more evidence of this than that of his own common-sense impressions as a reader; Popper, by a subtler turn of argument, has tried to confirm his suspicion by bringing in Plato himself to offer evidence. In the *Symposium*, Plato has "argued that it is a necessary and not a probable inference that he who loves or desires does not possess what he loves or desires." [79] The implication is that Plato, by his passionate craving for the inward peace of harmonized desire, has shown that he cannot himself yet possess this good.

The problem set for us by this way of viewing Plato is not one of flat disproof, but of separating the true elements from the false and of setting them in their just relation to other important truths about our philosopher. By way of preliminary, we may deal with the suspicion aroused in Popper's mind by the passage in the *Timaeus* (50 C–D), wherein the male principle supplied by the Forms is matched by "space," conceived as the passive, recipient "mother of generation." Now it would require no ingenuity to see in this more than a hint of sexual imagery. What Popper has not chosen to take into account is the significant and no less undeniable fact that this sexual element was a standard part of Greek traditional cosmogony, as any reader of Hesiod's *Theogony* well knows, which lay ready to Plato's hand and which he has largely divested of its anthropomorphic sexual character.[80]

What would be said of a man who should argue that Aristotle shows his essential lack of rationality by "clamoring" continually for the establishment of reason as sovereign in human life? And yet this is the very type of Popper's reasoning when he urges that Plato's longing for unity and harmony prove the want of these in his own breast, and calls Plato to testify against himself from

---

[76] *Ibid.*, pp. 149, 561–562. This point we discuss on pp. 204 ff. and in n. 217, p. 336.

[77] *Ibid.*, e.g., pp. 150, 152.

[78] See pp. 449 ff. below.

[79] Popper, p. 606.

[80] Popper, pp. 478–9, describes at length what he takes to be the sources of Plato's reproductive metaphor, listing Hesiod along with Pythagorean, Heraclitean, and Em-

pedoclean theories. He even adds in his second edition recognition of the fact that in the *Timaeus* the forms are not self-acting generative principles, but require to be impressed on space by the Demiurge. Yet despite this holding of all the threads in his hand, he has used his authorities only to add, psychologically, the weight of learning to his error.

the *Symposium* (200 A f.). As to the Platonic text, within the same Stephanus page Popper might have found it stated that one may desire what one already possesses, in the sense of desiring its continuance into future time, and it is shortly thereafter added (204 A–B) that one may desire more of what one already has. Thus Plato has before him a choice of several avenues of escape from the unrelenting diligence of his pursuer.

It is of course possible, and, as we shall suggest below, not unlikely that the earlier course of Plato's emotional life had not always run smooth. But Popper is talking of the *Republic*, and there, we would maintain, in flat contradiction to Popper, Plato provides no evidence of an unsatisfied longing for inner unity. For civic unity, Plato indisputably longs; but as concerns the individual, we must make a distinction. Plato, speaking, to be sure, in the name of Socrates, appears rather as one who has himself attained moral equilibrium, and who is striving to design the institutional framework that will secure this blessing to others.

This same assumption that we may always take Plato's word as cousin to his deed underlies Fite's belief that in the *Symposium* Plato is revealing his preoccupation with "scenes of debauchery." To judge the *Symposium* in this fashion is to hold the playwright guilty of the crimes committed by his characters, tantamount to denying Plato's existence as a dramatist; moreover, it ignores his right to be considered as a moral teacher, advocating nobler alternatives to existing practices.[81]

We approach more substantial business when we are called upon by Popper to explain those passages in the *Republic* (and we may add, in the *Phaedrus*) which paint the violence of inner conflict or use imagery inspired by awareness of such conflict. Popper appears to have assumed that in all these passages Plato's model was exclusively his own turbid and distracted self. Let us grant the high probability that at least some of the internal tension reflected in the passages cited was Plato's own. The extraordinarily vivid depiction of the unruly steed in the *Phaedrus* argues first-hand acquaintance, at some period of Plato's life, with the ardor and agony of sensual desire. The lawless dreams alluded to in the *Republic* (571 B ff.) appear to be, in their specific content, too traditional, and, one might say, too much in the manner of the tragic hero — Oedipus, Thyestes — to have been dipped directly out of the pool of Plato's own dreams; [82] yet we have his express statement that in every one of us there slumbers a brood of inordinate desires which such for-

---

[81] See our pp. 31–32 and 120–121, where this point is discussed at greater length. The view that all reformers are *ipso facto* confessing their need of moral reform requires its advocates, who are themselves reformers, to hold their own bombshell up to the very moment of its explosion, with consequences no less fatal to themselves than to their victims.

[82] For the frequency of incest dreams in ancient literature, see Dodds' note (*The Greeks and the Irrational*, 1951, p. 61), referring, *inter alia*, to Jocasta's words to Oedipus (*O. T.* 981f.) : "For many a man ere now has in his dreams couched with his mother."

bidden dreams reveal, few and weak, it is true, in some chastened natures, but of greater strength in others. The doctrine of the tripartite soul (*Republic* 437 B f., 439 A–441 C), designed as it is to account for the experienced diversity and rivalry among the functional parts constituting psychic life in its totality, must indeed rest in part upon Plato's own adventures in responsible living; the "many-headed beast" within, with its varied heads, some mild and good, some savage and fierce, and the "lion" (588 C–D), may well be derived to some extent from their author's introspection upon his own private moral menagerie. All this would indicate, it is agreed, that Plato was acquainted with some degree of inner conflict; but we have as yet been given no reason save the vividness of the report to believe that the inner strains implied, are, in an invidious sense, more intense than those of any normally active and honest son of Adam. The vividness it would be plausible, in the case of a creative mind like Plato's, to ascribe to lively imagination and literary power.

There stands among the works of Carl Sandburg a *vers libre* poem [83] in which the poet lists the fox, the wolf, and other beasts, caged within his ribs, all of which he proposes to keep, for the good romantic reason that "the wilderness gave them" to him. No one has yet, to my knowledge, charged this upon Sandburg's quality as moral agent; like Plato, he was probably, in the first instance, elaborating something drawn from his own experience, but under the impression that the insight was valid also for all mankind. But, it is possible to inquire, might not both Plato and Sandburg have been deceived in this?

Our first task here is to dispel the notion, apparently entertained by Fite and Popper, that the presence of any degree of conflict is evidence of abnormality. Against this stands, to all appearances, the full weight of contemporary psychological opinion, regardless of school.[84] It is indeed to be expected that in the personality of any member of Western European culture, traces of the repression of the sexual impulse and other related impulses will be found, and will continue to cause strain, detectable in the adult personality; to put essentially the same point more broadly, it is usual for a member of any culture, when undergoing, in his formative years, the molding effect of the cultural norms, to struggle against such molding and to exhibit in maturity some residual imperfections of "fit." We have, therefore, only to consider whether there is reason to believe that these entirely normal disorders reached in Plato's case an abnormal intensity, and if so, to ask what psychologic or social facts lay behind it.

Note first that Plato was no ascetic seeking the total suppression or mor-

---

[83] "Wilderness," in his volume *Cornhuskers*, 1918, pp. 40–41.

[84] The reader may readily check the view expressed here by reference to two widely available works, *Personality*, by Gardner Murphy, 1947, esp. pp. 763–772, 809–816, and 903ff.; and "Dynamic Theory of Personality," by O. H. Mowrer, in *Personality and the Behavior Disorders*, 1944, esp. pp. 120–121.

tification of all sensual desires. It is true that he rates them low in the scale of goods, and requires them, along with the emotions, to conform strictly to reason. But it is not his policy to deal roughly with these subordinates. He goes so far as to formulate a program for the treatment of our inner animals quite surprising in its humaneness and its spirit of coöperative concession. The "man within us" must be given "complete domination over the entire man." But he must use this domination "like a farmer who cherishes and trains the cultivated plants but checks the growth of the wild — and he will make an ally of the lion's nature, and caring for all the beasts alike will first make them friendly to one another and to himself, and so foster their growth." [85] We have here Plato's goal, his picture of his personal and philosophical ideal. And in it appears no distortion, no sadistic satisfaction in self-suppression.

That this Platonic ideal has also its austere face must be admitted, and we shall later suggest, as a not improbable hypothesis, that in his personal application of it, Plato may have touched at some points the dangerous circle of moral perfectionism, with consequences to be entered on both sides of the ledger. Another Socratic, Antisthenes, had shown to what lengths the Socratic ideal of self-command could be brought by a heavy accent upon the rigors of self-imposed austerity. It may be that the same Socratic precedent had worked upon Plato in a comparable, though by no means identical way. With Plato this could have meant the maintenance of a level of self-control so much above the social norm as to isolate him somewhat from others and thus to produce, secondarily, some further degree of psychic strain. [86]

In presenting their evidence of Plato's conflicts, his critics have conveyed the impression that they have dragged out of its hiding place some shameful secret that Plato had sought with his greatest subtlety to conceal. This procedure generates a double error. Not only does it belie Plato's candor — an obvious feature of his whole mode of treating the animal nature of man — it also prejudges the important question relating to the "ownership" of the experiences in question. We have willingly conceded that Plato entered upon his profession of moralist equipped with some knowledge derived from introspection of the indocile constituents of the human soul. But we are in no way willing to allow, what seems a gross improbability, that Plato limited himself to data derived from his own introspection. Everything favors the assumption that in discussing the subtler modes of psychic life he supplemented his own personal experience with a knowledge of life actively collected from all available sources. Remembering this, we can the more easily arouse ourselves from the dogmatic slumber in which Plato appears to us as a species of patient on the daybed of a psychiatrist. Let us remember that Plato too was in his

---

[85] *Republic* 589 B, trans. Shorey, Loeb Library. Cf. also 571 D–E.

[86] For amplification of this point see pp. 123–124.

manner a psychiatrist, one of the first and boldest explorers of the nether mind, and that it was not until recent decades that some of his findings were fully assimilated into psychological science. In the light of these facts, we had best stop treating all that Plato says of conflict as so much evidence indicative of a perhaps seriously disturbed psyche, and restore him his historical dignity and rights as a "healer of souls," or, in modern parlance, as master of mental hygiene and advocate of the integrated personality.

Coming now to Fite's picture of a Plato ridiculous in wounded pride and petty jealousy, we may first remark that in taking the *Gorgias* passage as "Plato speaking," Fite seems not to have observed due caution. Perhaps he failed to reflect that other interpretations of the passage were possible; at any rate, we have already shown the ease with which Popper could reverse its meaning, to bring it into accord with an interpretation precisely opposite, except in the one point of unfavorableness to Plato; and we may be pardoned for remarking in passing that there exist also possible interpretations which do Plato credit.[87] By drawing upon the *Letters*, Fite might hope to prove, at most, that Plato in his high age, and amidst the overthrow of many hopes held dear, did not always maintain the self-suppression and self-command that most readers have regarded as characteristic of the author of the dialogues. What is quite beyond the evidence is Fite's implication that the real Plato is here revealed, that is, the tacit inference that at every period of his career Plato displayed the petulance supposedly shown in one or two incidents of his decline.

It would be a serviceable part of the preparation for the office of State's Attorney to master the tactical procedure by which Popper, in constructing the image of his malign and subtle Plato, has availed himself of every initial advantage of position. In his preface he warns the reader that in the case about to be considered is involved the very survival of our civilization, and that its defense entails attack upon great intellectual leaders of mankind, who for centuries have been exerting undetected their influence against freedom. In his introduction he warns the reader against certain charlatan prophets of human destiny, "historicists," who make propaganda against democracy, and he affirms "the identity of the Platonic theory of justice with the theory and practice of modern totalitarianism." [88] On the first page of part I, which is subtitled "The Spell of Plato," he prints an extended quotation from Plato, so chosen and presented as to make him seem the most repressive of fascists.[89] Plato is next shown in the intellectual company of those other "historicists," Marx and the racialist Gobineau.[90] When Plato as a historical person first appears on Popper's page, it is as an aristocrat,[91] threatened with loss of his

---

[87] See p. 333 below.
[88] Popper, *op. cit.*, p. 7.
[89] *Ibid.*, p. 9. The quotation, from *Laws*

942 A–C, will be discussed below, pp. 531 ff.
[90] *Ibid.*, p. 13.
[91] *Ibid.*, p. 21.

privileged position, and, like Heraclitus before him (whom Popper has painted for us as an intensely hostile and contemptuous opponent of democracy),[92] motivated entirely, in his whole effort as thinker, by this insecurity. His philosophy, no less than his political theory, is but an effort to arrest all social change.[93] After a few pages of relatively temperate but disapproving exposition of Plato's metaphysics, we are told that, though there is much in Plato which Popper admires, "especially those parts which I believe to be Socratic," [94] this is to be left out of account; only his pernicious political thought, his totalitarianism, is to be demonstrated and for the first time fully exposed. At the head of the next page, we are warned that Plato has been for centuries exerting his influence, and that he is extraordinarily ingenious and acute.[95]

If now it is asked what this accumulation of disapprovals of Plato's political thinking has to do with the appraisal of Plato's character, the answer lies at hand. It is impossible to say of any man, in the present state of world opinion, that he is both extraordinarily clever and a totalitarian, without speaking volumes by way of moral defamation. And so the reader feels no shock when, after some few further pages noting the acuteness and originality of Plato's theory of social change, with its anticipation of elements of Marxist doctrine, the topic of Plato's attitude toward "democracy" is reached and the page begins to bristle with such phrases as "intensely hostile and unjust parody of . . . the democratic creed," [96] "poisonous writing," "invective," "flood of rhetorical abuse" [all against democracy], "Master of the Academy . . . sour and despotic" [toward the young], and "inhuman propaganda" [in favor of slavery].[97] Popper meanwhile has supplied Plato's blackness with a foil, in the persons of a great company of enlightened and humane Greeks, including Pericles and the mass of the plain citizens of Athens, the very ones whom Plato vilified, whose magnificent spiritual achievement, we are given to understand, it was Plato's life mission to annul.[98] At this point the staggered reader may resign the poor remnants of his belief that Plato may escape any portion of the charge; no excuse on the grounds of misguided benevolence, no extenuation seems possible.

On a much later page, after successive and mounting accusations of spleen, pride, and unscrupulous hatred, Popper seems to relent, and we are astonished to hear that, after all, Plato was not wholly malevolent.[99] He felt a certain sympathy for all his fellow Greeks: their mental and moral insecurity, the strain resulting from their new-found freedom inspired him with a kind of twisted benevolence, a desire to lock them up again where they would be at

---

[92] *Ibid.*, pp. 15–16.
[93] *Ibid.*, p. 24.
[94] *Ibid.*, p. 36.
[95] *Ibid.*, p. 37.
[96] *Ibid.*, p. 43.

[97] *Ibid.*, p. 44.
[98] *Ibid.*, pp. 43–4.
[99] *Ibid.*, pp. 165–6. There is also a slight advance indication, on p. 108, of the coming partial exoneration.

peace, in the cage of the "closed society." [100] Concession too little and too late! — for at a second look this benevolence turns out to be only that which is now ascribed by Popper to all advocates of totalitarianism; [101] and, in Plato's case, it is shown combined and contaminated with conscious or half-conscious treachery [102] to Socrates, the apostle of human freedom. This new-found "benevolence" cannot erase the reader's memory of the many preceding pages describing Plato's scorn and hatred and his desire to exploit the common people. The guilt is not sensibly diminished, it is only complicated. We are left contemplating the image of an intensely evil man.

Having seen the method by which Popper has produced his effect, let us make an earnest effort to clear away the mists of prejudice and distaste, and examine the specific evidences and inferences upon which Popper's indictment rests. The vanity of the attempt to infect Plato with historicism, to make him the moral equal of the modern totalitarians, and to deduce his social and moral theories from the fears and frustrations of his aristocratic station, must be the theme of later chapters. But protest must be registered here against the violence done to the spirit of the Platonic philosophy by the arbitrary demotion from its crowning position of Plato's ethical and religious thought. This Popper has achieved in two steps: first, he tells us that he must restrict attention to Plato's political thought; as the case proceeds, we hear strictures upon Plato's characteristically totalitarian suppression of ethics and the substitution for it of state policy, and we suddenly become aware that a postulate of the Popper methodology has been miraculously transmuted into a first principle in the Platonic philosophy. When once this error has been corrected, the ascription to Plato of this essential element of latter-day totalitarianism becomes unthinkable.

There remain for evaluation the particular scorns and hates and prides which Popper believes he has uncovered. These are, in sum, Plato's scorn of the common mass of men, of slaves and non-Greeks, and of those thinkers who championed ideas at variance with his own; his pride in his own family connections and his own status (here would be included his demand for deference), and in his intellectual attainments; and his hatred of democracy as exemplified at Athens, and — though this points in a different direction — his hatred of tyranny. We cannot agree that Plato felt these passions, (save, in part, the hatred of tyranny), in the sense and to the degree in which Popper imputes them; all of them, in a degree, and in a sense to which the rest of this book will give clearer meaning, it is true that Plato felt and expressed, along with other hates and scorns which Popper does not mention. But it by no means follows that he is *ipso facto* blameworthy, as Popper would have us believe. Without wishing to prejudice the question of the ultimate beauty of a soul which has risen to a region of such sacred calm that even for the

---

[100] *Ibid.*, p. 167.   [102] *Ibid.*, pp. 191–2.
[101] *Ibid.*, p. 166.

sake of unselfish aims no ugly urgencies are felt, we may hold that genuine nobility is compatible with many a scorn and hate, provided these are subordinate to a central noble aim; and even that noble souls have felt ignoble hates. The fair procedure, if one is to judge a soul by its scorns and disapprovals, is to list all these without discrimination, to add to them all its loves and aspirations, and then to seek the total pattern. This Popper has not begun to do. His refusal to extend consideration beyond Plato's political thought accounts for, while it does not excuse, some of these omissions, but by no means all; for even in the *Republic* there are hatreds of a sort which, had he given them proportionate weight in his report, he would have been forced to praise; and there are also in the *Republic* expressions of Plato's positive enthusiasms which have not been credited to him.

To cite some outstanding examples: Popper has every right and duty to second Plato's scorn of the ethical nihilism of Thrasymachus, with his cynical equation of justice with the advantage of the ruling class,[103] the very political ethic that Popper so cordially hates Plato for (supposedly) espousing.[104] The traffic in "salvation" — the peddling of "indulgences" — which Plato charges against the Orphics [105] would have awakened Popper's deepest indignation, had he found in Plato a sponsor of the despicable practice.[106] So, too, the contempt poured by Plato upon the lawless violence and greed for wealth of those "timocrats," who resemble the Spartans,[107] and of the oligarchs [108] should have drawn more favorable notice from the man who has so severely blamed Plato for his supposed friendliness to Sparta, and to the reactionary oligarchs of Athenian politics.[109] And why has Popper failed to notice the horror which Plato has so vividly expressed for the shedding of the blood of fellow citizens, in his portrait of the tyrant in the making? [110] Why, unless because it is in conflict with Popper's imputation to Plato of willingness to regard as venial the bloody doings of a Critias,[111] or even to contemplate the realization of his own political ends by "brutal violence"? [112]

Nor is Popper justified in withholding outright enthusiasm for much that Plato loved and praised: the placing of women on a footing of substantial parity with men, with its corollary of higher education for women; [113] the

---

[103] *Republic*, 338 C–339 A. — Instead of approving Plato for his rejection of the view expressed by Thrasymachus, Popper has preferred to accuse Plato of the deliberate trick of degrading the noble ethic of "protectionism" by equating it with the base ethical nihilism of Thrasymachus and thus of craftily concealing his own inability to refute it openly. (See our discussion, pp. 418ff.) And, as a touch of unconscious high comedy in making this charge, Popper's tone becomes for a moment that of the regretful friend who is obliged unwillingly to testify: "But I should not be fair if I did not frankly admit that Plato's method appears to me dishonest" (Popper, p. 105).

[104] Popper, *op. cit.*, e.g., pp. 47–48.

[105] *Republic*, 364 B–365 A.

[106] Cf. Popper, pp. 145–146, 153.

[107] *Republic*, 547 B–C, 548 A–B.

[108] *Ibid.*, 551 C–553 A.

[109] Popper, e.g., p. 182.

[110] *Republic*, 565 D–566 A.

[111] Popper, *op. cit.*, e.g., pp. 594, 610.

[112] *Ibid.*, pp. 560, 194.

[113] *Republic* 456 C–D.

exaltation of reason as the guide to life, with its consequence that rational inquiry is to be the ultimate arbiter of truth and its findings the basis of social control; [114] the honor, reaching reverence, accorded to Socrates, as the exemplar of thought well lived, and life well thought. That Popper has withheld his hearty approval of Plato for his celebration of these themes is, however, no accident; it is the logical result of a quite explicit and systematically wrong construction that Popper has imposed upon Plato. The initial error of conceiving him as the father of the totalitarian state has been, for a logician as systematic as Popper, a fatal step, entailing a distortion of Plato's thought at every point. Those admirable emotional attitudes of Plato which are at variance with this central thesis must somehow be accounted for. They may be overlooked completely or minimized (e.g., Plato's hatred of bloodshed, mentioned above, and of oligarchy); they may be misinterpreted as mere consequences of some other discreditable aim or feeling (e.g., Plato's hatred of tyranny); [115] they may be viewed as cynical deception (e.g., the commitment to reason); [116] or they may be used as evidence of pathological division in Plato's soul (e.g., the loyalty to Socrates).[117] No true picture of Plato, either as man or as theorist of the state, can possibly result.

But if we should mingle, in the fashion earlier suggested, Plato's enthusiasms, fairly judged, along with all his hates and scorns, there begins to emerge the portrait, no longer the caricature of a man. We see a man of generous enthusiasm and soaring hopes, setting out to make virtue and knowledge sovereign over the life of man, confronted by difficulties the magnitude of which it has required the perspective of centuries to measure. How could he but denounce and hold up in his writings to public reprobation those men and those ideas which seemed to him the enemies of the good? So far he

---

[114] *Republic* 537 C ff., esp. 540 A–B. Plato of course conceives such inquiry as possible only for the gifted few, a restriction which Popper would reasonably reject.

[115] *Republic* 555 D–569 C. — Popper, on p. 44, does a very characteristic thing. He has just described Plato's disapproving description of democracy, and is about to give his version of Plato's view on tyranny. Plato hates tyranny, which, on Popper's premises, should be creditable. But Popper says, "Of much greater merit, though it too is inspired by hatred, is Plato's description of tyranny." By this simple sentence he again stigmatizes Plato's attitude to democracy, and, by his adversative "though," implies that hatred of tyranny is also discreditable, perhaps because — we can only guess, at this point — hatred is in itself an ugly trait. Again, on pp. 166–167, Popper is stopped in his intent to describe Plato as unredeemedly evil, by this same

hatred of tyranny; this time, he grants Plato's partial benevolence, solely on this ground; but he qualifies his gift by extending the benevolence to totalitarianism in general. Finally, on p. 193, he explains why the hatred of tyrants is really not creditable at all: tyrants "make concessions to the equalitarian cravings of the people," and no totalitarian, therefore can help hating them! Among tyrants, Popper at this place includes the Thirty Tyrants, whom, on other occasions, he taunts Plato with condoning (e.g., pp. 594, 610). Such windings of logic are the nemesis that overtakes the critic who, having on partial evidence prejudged his victim, is obliged to wrest the remainder of the evidence into a semblance of consistency.

[116] Popper, e.g., pp. 132, 145, 552–3; cf. our Appendix XII.

[117] *Ibid.*, pp. 189–192.

"hated" them, but now and again he paused to express his pity for the unjust: he is convinced that the "many" would not be so, could they be given to behold the beauty of Justice and true philosophy.[118] There remained in his soul some baser deposits from the prejudice-laden atmosphere in which he had grown up; but for the rest his "hates" were the weapons of his ideals, indispensable equipment.

For his display of a knowledge of the seamier side of human behavior, Plato is awarded no honorary degree from Fite's school. Not only does it reveal (as we have heard read in evidence) the muddy places of Plato's own soul; it is also a form of ignorance of that which it professes to know. In support of this charge, Fite adduces Plato's use of the parable of the ancestor of Gyges, the shepherd who, finding that he can become invisible by a simple turn of his magic ring, avails himself of his opportunities to gratify his every desire. This shepherd, Fite would have us believe, represented Plato's idea of what you and I and everyone, with the exception of a few divinely inspired natures, would immediately become, if the persons and property of our neighbors were by some miraculous turn to be exposed to the greed and violence of our invisible hand.[119] A reading of Plato's little story in its context will reveal that Plato has here been maligned. The shepherd is not, as Fite would have us think, Plato's type of the natural man. He is rather the non-natural man, the man misled and corrupted by false instructors, who have taught him that the true measure of life's good is not justice, loved for its own sake, but pleasure, honors, and the means of procuring these. If one wishes to hear Plato's actual doctrine touching the natural man and his natural good, let him turn to the text and read the words, referred to in the previous paragraph, that Plato has put into the mouth of Adeimantus,[120] affirming his faith that, given adequate instruction in the true nature of human good, all men would make justice their sovereign end.

When Fite goes on to tax Plato with failure to understand the sobering and moralizing influence of a profession,[121] one wonders why it has not occurred to him that whatever may have been the situations of Plato's characters in the dialogues, Plato himself had not one but two professions, neither of them exactly a sinecure: the conduct of the Academy, with its heavy and various demands upon his time and thought, and authorship of the long row of the Platonic dialogues, which in spite of their appearance of spontaneity, or because of it, assuredly did not write themselves. We may conclude that between these two major commitments, Plato's mind should have contrived somehow to escape the moral perils of unemployment.

Fite's complaint that the *personae* of the dialogues lack "intimate personal

---

[118] *Republic* 366 E–367 A, 499 E–500 B.
[119] Fite, pp. 300–303, *Republic*, 359 D–360 A.
[120] *Republic*, 366 E–367 A.
[121] Fite, *op. cit.*, pp. 306–307.

ties" and "poignant personal experience" [122] is of a piece with the charge that Plato has failed to grasp the meaning of personality itself, "the all-precious uniqueness of each individual person." [123] Fite, indeed, has not charged this to Plato's individual account; he views it as a defect shared by Plato with the Greek race. Here Fite would seem to be, in part, on solid ground. Greek ethics, like Greek art, was dominated by the typical, the universal, rather than the individual and the unique; it knew little of the Christian reverence for the "person" as such, or of that imaginative exaltation of individual uniqueness that the romantic movement seems to have stamped indelibly upon the modern mind. That Fite has somewhat overstated his case, however, can be seen by anyone who has read the final scene in the *Alcestis* of Euripides, in which Admetus refuses to accept custody of the veiled woman (really his Alcestis) because she reminds him so strongly of the loss of his unique and irreplaceable wife. Plato's own personal relations are here in point: his bereavement when "the peculiar difference" of Socrates (and later, of Dion) was "cancelled from the world of sense." Greek literature, too, from Homer to Plato, abounds in characters, who without ceasing to be typical are genuinely individual persons; Achilles is not confusable with Agamemnon, nor either of them with Odysseus. And what would one say of the critical faculties of the man who could not distinguish Plato's Thrasymachus from his Protagoras, to say nothing of that unique figure who has kindly consented to serve as a convenient illustration of so many of our points, Socrates? The care and skill lavished upon the carving of these distinctive *dramatis personae* show that though the individual did not hold much interest for Plato the metaphysician, he occupied a substantial place in the affections of Plato the man.

---

[122] Fite, pp. 318–9.   [123] *Ibid.*, p. 87.

5

Outlook on Sex and Marriage

Platonic Love: the Theoretical Component

In evaluating the charge that Plato advocates or condones homosexual love, we are plunged into the consideration of what may be called "cultural optics" and defined as the art of making projections from one culture to another with the least possible distortion. A rather trivial example will make our meaning clear: a European visitor to the United States would be pardoned for supposing that his traveler's lexicon had misinformed him when in search of an apothecary shop he stepped for the first time across the threshold of a typical big-city drug store. A confusion of this kind could soon be corrected; our visitor would not be long in discovering a department within the store that corresponded to his anticipation, and allowing for minor differences of available material and traditional practice, he would soon be able to compare his own with the American standard of excellence in the preparation of drugs.

In the case before us, the difficulties to be surmounted before we can properly begin to make relative evaluations are far more complex and emotionally charged. But for these very reasons, it is all the more imperative to undertake their careful consideration, and consequently, the less excusable to engage in cross-cultural comparisons without a diligent and conscientious sociological survey. Chapman's impressionistic method of handling the problem moves on quite another plane.[1] That Fite has made some show of satisfying the demand is to his credit; that he has fallen sadly short of what justice to Plato demands, we hope to make clear.

We may first establish a considerable area of common ground between ourselves and Chapman and Fite. We are none of us in favor of reëstablishing paiderastia,[2] of reverting, under Plato's influence or any other, to the sexual

---

[1] For Chapman's impression of the *Symposium*, see *Lucian and Plato*, pp. 121–137. The burden of his argument has been given previously (pp. 7–8). In consideration of the gay shimmer of his witty wings, we shall not attempt to break his butterfly upon our wheel. Fite, I believe, may be fairly employed as Chapman's deputy in this matter.

[2] For convenience, and in order to avoid unnecessary unpleasantness of terminology, we shall employ the word "pai-

standards prevalent in ancient Greece, or of proving that fundamental differences in the patterns of sexual behavior are merely matters of custom, destitute of significance for the progress of the good life. We may, without undue complacency, congratulate ourselves upon genuine progress as we contrast the cultural degradation imposed upon the women of Athens with the greatly enlarged opportunities for moral and intellectual development open to women in modern civilized societies. And we may well feel gratitude that we are so largely free of the awkwardness and constraints, not to speak of the positive moral dangers, which surrounded the relation of friendship between persons of the same sex in so many Greek communities, including the Athens of Plato's time.

We may also grant that Chapman's and Fite's indignation,[3] when they came to treat of Plato's attitude toward homosexual love, was natural enough as the human response to the almost unanimous evasion of the topic by the reigning English and American interpreters of Plato. It may be observed, in extenuation, that this reticence was necessitated by the taste of the period immediately preceding our own and that this taste became, in the minds of Plato's admirers, first a justification for some mild concealments and misrepresentations, and then a loving blindness to the full extent of Plato's divergence from their own feelings. Chapman and Fite were writing, on the other hand, at a time when it had become possible to express openly and in print the same distaste which had silenced and partly blinded the earlier writers, but before the lifting of the ban on open mention of homosexuality had cleared the way to the full understanding of the cultural setting in which Plato wrote. These facts seem to condone in part the excited repugnance of Fite and Chapman, without requiring us to condemn Plato utterly or to join them in ugly distortion and wild exaggeration of his actual teachings.

It was a sound instinct that led Fite to inquire, as he does in connection with Plato's attitude toward marriage, into the history of the status of women in Greek society, from Homer's to Plato's time;[4] though Fite does not give the benefit of this same connection of ideas to his criticism of Plato's view of paiderastia, where it is also most relevant. We need not dispute Fite's conclusion[5] that the inferior position of women in the Athenian society of the fifth

---

derastia" in a sense broader than that it strictly bears. Literally, of course, it means precisely "boy-love," but even Plato employs it in the broader sense of an erotic relationship between an older and a younger man. We shall follow Plato, also, in using the word to cover any species of amoristic attachment between members of the masculine sex, from utterly pure to utterly impure, leaving it to the context to determine the specific nature of the relationship.

[3] For Chapman's and Fite's indignation, see Chapman, *op. cit.*, p. 120, and Fite, *op. cit.*, p. 153ff.

[4] Fite, p. 61ff.

[5] In which he follows Schmidt, Leopold, *Die Ethik der Alten Griechen*, 1882; cited in Fite, p. 61.

and fourth centuries is not properly representative of Hellenic culture as a whole and may be considered a temporary aberration,[6] "due to the nearly Oriental seclusion imposed upon the women of the better classes in Athens," and exacerbated by "the long duration of the Peloponnesian war." But when Fite charges (as if it were a matter of reproach) that "it is Plato who brings this feature of Athenian sentiment clearly to light," and then fails to see in this any extenuation of Plato's attitude toward the Athenian woman,[7] we begin to lose confidence in the good use that he is making of the valuable material that lies in his hands.

The status of the women citizens (this does not include the resident aliens, who, because their children would not be citizens in law, were not legally eligible for marriage with citizens) is so relevant to the theme of our discussion as to deserve some elaboration here.[8] The central point to be noted may be briefly put: the Athenian woman was not, save for rare exceptions, a possible companion and full partner in the quest of the good life for the educated and intellectual Athenian man. The consequences of this fundamental fact must now be explored.

To begin with, no Athenian matron of repute was to be met with in any public place of resort, save on occasion of certain religious festivals in the company of her fellows. An occasional venture to the market under the protection of a trusted slave represented her maximum freedom. At home, she was confined to the women's apartment, where the greatest part of her time was devoted, in the company of slaves, to the administration of the household. She took no part in the reception and entertainment of guests, certainly not in dining out. Only when her husband chose to dine at home and without company did custom permit her to enjoy a place at his table. On such occasions her conversation must have run almost exclusively to chronicling the small events of domestic history. For not only was she isolated from the sources of more important knowledge; she had always been so isolated. Her original education had been of the meagerest. She could boast ordinarily a training in spinning and weaving and suchlike household arts; with music and letters only in the rarest case did she possess more than mere acquaintance. This ignorance was guaranteed by the early age at which her parent or guardian had arranged her marriage, and underlined by the usual age interval between her and her husband. One degree of freedom she did often possess: the right to leave her husband for just cause; but this right was qualified by the necessity of returning to her original sponsors, at whose pleasure she remained subject to marital reassignment.

[6] Fite, p. 64.
[7] Fite, p. 65.
[8] Our account here owes much to Alfred Zimmern, (*The Greek Commonwealth*, 1924, pp. 334–338); to W. A. Becker, (*Charicles*, 1899, pp. 462–498); and something to Grote (*Plato and the Other Companions of Socrates*, 1865, II, pp. 207ff). Cf. also n. 15, pp. 86–87.

The world that unfolded itself to the view of an Athenian male of good standing and ability was essentially an outdoor world, dominated by the masculine activities of war, politics, and the scarcely less ardent pursuit of those pleasures of the mind and eye that reached so high a pitch in the "school of Hellas." [9] From the scene of these activities women were conspicuously absent; only the unmarriageable flute girls and hetaerae embroidered the edges of his existence. His early schooling had grounded him in the appreciation of the older poets and dramatists. The new education of the sophistic period challenged many of the traditional shibboleths, and opened the mind to audacious speculation concerning all things human and divine; at the same time it supplied him with technical training in that art of persuasive speech fundamental to effective participation in the affairs of a democratic state. The gymnasium and the palaestra were the anteroom to war: in a vivid page of his deeply illuminating account of the typical occupations of a young Athenian, Zimmern depicts the comradeship of the campaign as it carried over into the daily lives of the citizen soldiers.[10] The gymnasium and the palaestra were also, in a sense, galleries, in which living statues remarkable for graceful form and flashing strength inspired appreciation and molded aesthetic taste.

The impact of all this upon the emotional and affectional life of the Athenian youth was inescapable. By more than geometrical necessity (to adapt an expression that Plato applies, in the *Republic*, to the intersexual effect of the proposed close association of youths and maidens in gymnastic training) there would at Athens spring up, exclusively between male and male, intimate friendships and close personal associations; and among these there would be some of a passionate intensity that in our modern society would be abnormal. How the Athenians contrived to bring this situation, to some degree, within the beneficent framework of social control, is a topic to which our later discussion will return.

In this connection the unavailability of the opposite sex, apart from the tawdry charms of harlots and the casual and often vulgar loves of the hetaerae, took its full toll. Apart from his own close family connections, it was scarcely possible that a young Charmides or a Lysis should enjoy more than a veiled glimpse of a young woman capable of arousing his amatory interest. By the date of his marriage to some girl, in most cases hitherto unknown, he would have formed intimacies and commitments in which it was impossible for her

---

[9] For corroboration on this point, we may refer also to the comprehensive work of Hans Licht, *Sexual Life in Ancient Greece*, 1932, especially Chapter I, which describes Hellenic culture after Homer and Hesiod as predominantly concerned with fostering the excellence of the male sex, assigning to its married women, as housekeepers and mothers of lawful children, an honored position, but excluding them from intellectual concerns, as being incapable of sharing in "conversation with men, such as highly cultivated Athenians demanded as their daily bread" (pp. 28–38). The point is reënforced also throughout his book; cf. pp. 418–419.

[10] Zimmern, *op. cit.*, pp. 345ff.

to have any part. Only if he had found in his own mother or sisters one of those occasional examples of developed womanhood, could a young Athenian convince himself that the moral qualities of an acceptable mother of his prospective children and the intellectual powers and social charm he had known among his men friends could come together in a single harmonious personality. That nevertheless Athenian marriages were capable of becoming something much more than impersonal arrangements serving merely practical and biological ends is attested by Plato himself, as we shall see. But of high intellectual intimacy between husband and wife the period has little to show.

Pericles and Aspasia serve to illustrate and reënforce the position that we are maintaining, and that in two respects. For Pericles himself, in the Funeral Oration, has given a most illuminating indication of the accepted Athenian view of woman's place in society, with its uncompromising demand for her self-effacement. In his words of consolation addressed to the families of the deceased, he says, "If I must say anything on the subject of female excellence to those of you who will now be in widowhood, it will be all comprised in this brief exhortation. Great will be your glory in not falling short of your natural character; and greatest will be hers who is least talked of among the men whether for good or for bad." [11] On the other hand, the relation of Pericles to Aspasia provides the outstanding exhibit of the values which Athenian marriage was not ordinarily capable of achieving, a spiritual association on a plane of full equality between two highly civilized persons. Pericles had chosen this woman for himself, and had established her in his household after his divorce from his impeccably Athenian wife, in a position which was regarded by Athenian sentiment as highly unusual, even scandalous.

It is true that in intellectual circles there was in the air during this period considerable discussion of the proper status of women, prompted no doubt in great part by the social fact of Aspasia's existence. Echoes of this discussion are audible in Euripides, that admirer of Anaxagoras, the intimate of Pericles. In the Medea of 431 B.C. (lines 230ff.), Euripides arraigns the injustice suffered by the Attic wife who must set a tyrant over herself and learn painfully to please his moods, while he is free to seek other company than hers and she incurs obloquy if she should venture to leave him. Socrates may well have known and conversed with Aspasia; such Socratics as Aeschines of Sphettus went so far as to represent Aspasia as a moral teacher, including among her pupils no less a person than Socrates himself.[12] It is probable enough that the "virtue" or excellence of women had been a theme of discussion in the Socratic circle and that from this source Plato derived his belief that female virtue was essentially the same as that of men, as well as much of the impetus that was to carry him so far in a feminist direction.

In Aristophanes' Ecclesiazusae of 392 B.C., we are shown in broadest foolery

---

[11] Thucydides II, 45; Crawley translation, Modern Library, New York, 1934.

[12] See Pohlenz, Aus Platon's Werdezeit, p. 260.

a feminist "putsch," and the establishment of a thoroughgoing communism of wives and children under female rule. Obviously there is presupposed here, as elsewhere in the plays of this satirical sharpshooter, some contemporary advocate of the notions under attack, perhaps Plato, in a preliminary edition of his *Republic*,[13] perhaps only some unidentifiable predecessor in this general domain. Thus feminism had become a theme for public mirth as well as for serious advocacy among the intellectuals.

But all these airy discussions had not yet reached the ground, or exerted any measurable effect upon the isolation and limitation to which the Athenian woman remained subject. And here we come upon another example of Fite's failure to make proper use of his adequate material. In his chapter on Plato's view of marriage,[14] he points with approval to the idyllic picture that Xenophon has painted of Ischomachus, the Athenian gentleman farmer, briefing his little bride of fifteen in the rights and obligations of her new position as mistress of his household. The husband's protestations of respect and of willingness to submit on terms of parity to mutually binding standards are indeed touching, and, within their limits, quite sincere. They do not, however, prove the fitness of such a little bride to be the intellectual companion of the usual Athenian of taste and education. Present in this relationship are features which would not be typical in an Athenian household in which the husband had intellectual pretensions or predominant political concerns. For — capital point of difference — Ischomachus is an agricultural enthusiast, primarily interested in the management of his estate, and the area within which equality with his wife is proposed is at the intersection of wheat fields and the domestic granary, and not the point at which the Agora abuts upon the Pnyx. In other words, it is only in so far as he restricts the field of his activities to domestic management that Ischomachus is able to invite his wife into equal association with himself. In suggesting, then, that the Ischomachus menage was representative of the relationship that, given human good will, might normally be expected to obtain between an Athenian husband whose dominant interests were not centered in his home and his wife, Fite is equating a part with a whole.[15]

---

[13] There has been an enormous literature of discussion around and about the supposition of an early edition of the *Republic* as the supposed target of the play. See Pohlenz, *op. cit.*, pp. 207ff. I cannot see any difficulty in assuming that Plato or Socrates before him communicated his feminist ideas by word of mouth to the comic poet, a man with whom, as the *Symposium* implies, both were well acquainted; but admittedly there is no empirical evidence to this effect.

[14] Fite, *op. cit.*, p. 65, referring to Xenophon's *Economicus*, vi, 12–x, 13. Here, as often in the *Memorabilia*, Socrates has been considerably assimilated to the ideas and interests of his reporter, and is shown repeating for the edification of a young friend the recommendations of his agricultural acquaintance Ischomachus.

[15] The position taken above is confirmed, though from a different point of view, by F. R. Earp, in his admirable study, *The Greek Way of Life*, 1929, pp. 51–59. Earp is engaged in interpreting sympathetically the Athenians' treatment of their womenfolk, urging that the position of woman, though unsatisfactory, was

Returning to Fite's understanding of the nature of paiderastia and of Plato's relation to it, we find him talking now and again as if Plato had approved paiderastia *simpliciter,* with no attempt to mark off its several kinds.[16] Fite further construes paiderastia, in the Athens of Plato's day, as something confined to a small circle of class-conscious aristocrats, the esoteric vice of a coterie comparable (we are told in terms) to the decadent fraternity of Oscar Wilde or Marcel Proust; [17] the only exception made in Plato's favor is the ambiguous little admission that in the vice as advocated by Plato, there is nothing of that furtive quality, as of a "guilty thing surprised," which is characteristic of its modern form.[18]

Fite could have found the basis for a juster view of the problem in the little book to which he alludes, in which from the depths of his lifelong intimacy with the monuments of ancient culture, John Addington Symonds has discerningly treated this whole "Problem in Greek Ethics," to quote his title.[19] Symonds has undertaken a historical survey of the entire gamut of affectional relationships between man and man, or man and boy, from Homer to the end of classical antiquity. Setting aside, first, the Homeric ideal of heroic friendship — for, as he shows, this relationship in the Homeric poems themselves is untouched by any admixture of passion or sensuality — he carefully distinguishes the attitudes of the Greeks toward each of several varieties of paiderastia. In general, his conclusions are, first, that in Greek society the toleration of homosexuality of any sort was much greater than it could be in the modern world,[20] and secondly, that there existed a form of this relationship, "mixed paiderastia" or "Greek love," compounded, on the one hand, of sensual attraction and passion (but not necessarily including sexual indulgence), and on the other, of devoted personal attachment, which was entirely respectable, even held to be admirable above other forms of sexual attachment, and widespread among Greeks of good repute.[21] Symonds tells us that within the bounds of

---

not very different from that which she holds in many European lands today, and was not in itself a degraded one. He concedes that her marriage was arranged for her and love between the parties was not presupposed; but then, marital love as we know it was not conceived by the Greeks (pp. 51–53). From participation in civic life she was naturally barred; but woman suffrage is a modernism. From the man's second chief educational experience, his training in athletics and his military service, she was barred; but she had household duties in the place of these to give her self-respect and status. From intellectual interests she was excluded; but such interests were not general among men, either (pp. 55–56). Nor should we believe that the average Athenian found his wife dull by comparison with the "callow boy" in whom

he frequently took an erotic interest (pp. 56–57). It is apparent that Earp, in defending the Athenians, has made his case, but without prejudice to our own. It is entirely possible thus to exonerate the Athenians without disproving that Athenian men who had intellectual interests were more apt to be attracted to promising youths who shared their pursuits than would have been likely in a society which did not treat its women as Earp agrees the Athenians did.

[16] Fite, e.g., p. 153.

[17] Fite, p. 177.

[18] *Ibid.,* p. 158.

[19] *A Problem in Greek Ethics*, by John A. Symonds (first published 1883), privately printed, 1901.

[20] Symonds, p. 6.

[21] Symonds, p. 8. Further documentation of this point will be found below, pp.

this recognized and honorable relationship, public opinion at Athens did not inquire into the personal conduct of the lovers, but regarded bodily union, if such occurred, as a matter of secondary importance.[22] This statement, however valid as a sociological generalization, ignores the presence in Athenian society of certain persons, notably Socrates, Xenophon, and Plato, and probably Euripides as well, for whom this distinction (on which we shall lay some stress below) was by no means trivial. Since, however, we are here summarizing Symonds, we shall follow his usage for the present.

Mythological tradition abounded in stories of the affection inspired in the breasts of the immortals for beautiful youths, of whom we recollect Ganymede, Hyacinth, and Hylas.[23] Even the baser forms of the passion, it is shown, were standard topics of conversation and material for comic representation upon the stage.[24] Poets such as Theognis, Ibycus, and Anacreon alluded frankly to its sensual delights, while Pindar celebrated in exalted language the strength and radiance of the youthful victors in the games, charging that those who beheld such beauty unmoved had hearts "forged with cold fire out of adamant." [25] Nor did the tragic dramatists, from the sublime Aeschylus to Euripides the human, scruple to present with sympathetic understanding the passionate affection of male for male, inciting (so it was held) to manly deeds of war and friendship. A fragment is cited from Euripides, in which an idealized love "of the soul" between man and man is contrasted with the lower love of the body.[26] Xenophon, in his *Symposium*, puts into the mouth of one of his characters (who is, nevertheless, a married man) a glowing declaration of his all-absorbing passion for the beautiful youth Cleinias, for whose sake he would brave any danger or hardship.[27] Among the most honored names on the roster of Athenian national heroes were Solon, whose poems included lines celebrating the love of boys,[28] and Harmodius and Aristogeiton, whose passionate attachment, according to the report, had inspired them to slay the tyrant Hipparchus.[29] Thus, on Symonds' showing, "Greek love" was sustained by the high authority of religious myth and literary tradition, was associated with athletic distinction, military prowess, self-sacrifice and self-denial, and the heroic love of liberty.[30] In short, paiderastia of the "mixed" form, refined but still con-

---

107 and 586, ff. Fite believes that acceptance of paiderastia was not characteristic of the average Athenian, whose way of life is known to us only from the vase paintings; yet the vase paintings in fact offer strong testimony to its acceptance. See Kroll, *Freundschaft u. Knabenliebe*, described on our p. 587.

[22] Symonds, p. 45
[23] Symonds, p. 10.
[24] Symonds, p. 29–30.
[25] *Ibid.*, pp. 22–27.
[26] Ibid., pp. 27–29. The fragment is from the *Dictys* and runs as follows (Symonds'

translation): "He was my friend; and never may love lead me to folly, nor to Kupris. There is, in truth, another kind of love — love for the soul, righteous, temperate, and good. Surely men ought to have made this law, that only the temperate and chaste should love, and send Kupris, daughter of Zeus, a-begging."

[27] *Ibid.*, pp. 39–40.
[28] Solon, Fr. 25, *Elegy and Iambus*, ed. J. M. Edmonds, Loeb Library.
[29] *Ibid.*, pp. 12, 24.
[30] *Ibid.*, p. 44.

taining the element of sensuality, or even, it might be, of physical indulgence, had obtained "moralization, and reached the high position of a recognized social function." [31]

It is this "mixed" form at its most permissive of which the speech of Pausanias in Plato's *Symposium* gives us a classic account.[32] Pausanias views the love between males, including its physical expression, as *per se* higher than the love of man for woman and thoroughly approvable, provided only certain conditions are fulfilled. There must be constancy between the lovers, the intention of passing their whole lives together in intimate friendship. The younger party must be sufficiently mature to insure stability and soundness of character. And the relation must aim, not at material advantage on either side, but at progress in human excellence.

We have spoken of other varieties of paiderastia with which the Greeks were acquainted. The Athenians knew of three major forms, past or present. In addition to the "mixed" form in its two varieties, which, as we have said, Symonds believes the average Athenian did not sharply discriminate, there was also at least the bright legend of an ancient, ideal form, reputed to have existed in its purity among the Spartans and Cretans of an earlier day, whereby an older and a younger man entered, by mutual choice, upon a lasting and honorable relationship, essentially educational and moral in aim, and untouched by sensuality.[33] At the opposite end of the scale, as the records all too plainly reveal, there was a profligate form of paiderastia, simple indulgence of impulse without regard to any principle above that of momentary pleasure; and this vice, at Athens, seems strangely enough to have brought little obloquy upon the older man, the lover, though it was held to be harmful and discrediting to the boy and utterly disgraceful to a boy who submitted for the sake of gain.[34]

It was the sensual forms of paiderastia, the profligate and the mixed, that stood as prominent features of the social landscape in the Athens of Plato's

---

[31] *Ibid.*, p. 72. Between this view of Symonds and that of another scholar, Ehrenberg, who has recently examined the question, there are similarities and minor differences, which we have examined below, n. 95, p. 111.

[32] *Symposium* 180 C ff.; Symonds, pp. 31–33.

[33] Symonds, pp. 13–4. Xenophon, who may be suspected of partiality, but who had certainly lived among the Spartans, roundly asserts the moral purity of the Dorian institution, at least as sponsored by the Lycurgan constitution (*Symposium* viii, 35; *Const. Lac.* II, 12–13). Plato's complaint, cited on p. 97 below, that at Sparta and Crete sexual union between males was regarded as entirely proper, may perhaps refer to prevailing public sentiment in those states, in contrast to the prescribed rule, and therefore need not be taken as wholly contradicting Xenophon's testimony, though it appears to do so. Bethe, in a very persuasive essay, "Die Dorische Knabenliebe," 1907, agrees with Xenophon that the ancient arrangement was socially approved and directed to the promotion of manly excellence, but also shows good reason to believe that the relations between the partners in the alliance involved a sexual component. On his view, the idea underlying the relationship was that of sympathetic magic: the prowess of the older man would pass to the younger only by a direct contact and emanation. See Bethe, *op. cit.*, p. 459 ff.

[34] Symonds, p. 44.

youth. The abomination of the one and the dangers and inadequacies of the other set the moral and educational problem with which Socrates [35] and Plato were deeply concerned. The profligate form "needs but to be seen" to be hated, and Fite does not, save by careless implication, charge Plato with defending it. What excites Fite's indignation is that Plato, as Fite rightly contends against Taylor and others, did not put the mixed form in its indulgent variety entirely outside the pale of his condoning approval,[36] as he might well have done had he followed his own ethical premises in this matter, without regard to the social realities of the Athens of his day. Indignation at this concession has prevented Fite from recognizing what was distinctive in Plato's thought, namely the sharp line by which Plato separates, within the mixed paiderastia, the indulgent from the nonindulgent form, and the spiritualization of the latter, amounting to the conception of a fifth and highest form of the institution, for which alone it is permissible to hold Plato responsible. We shall see that he is fully able to bear the responsibility. But first it will be well to call attention to some features in the other forms which have caused confusion in Fite's argument.

There is, as Fite recognizes, much evidence in Greek literature of the care with which fathers protected their young sons from improper advances, providing "paidagogues" to chaperon them to and from school and to insure their safe return from places of exercise. This fact Fite misuses to sustain his thesis that paiderastia in all its forms was anathema to all but a small aristocratic sect.[37] Plainly it proves no more than what scarcely requires proving, that reputable Athenians deplored the deplorable. It tells us nothing about their attitude toward the only forms of paiderastia relevant to the point at issue.

A second confusion of a sort less extreme: as Symonds remarks,[38] there remained an inconsistency in the Athenian attitude toward even the mixed form of paiderastia, in its indulgent aspect. The institution was itself approved, and, as we have shown reason to believe, widespread among citizens of good standing. Nevertheless, it contained one inexpugnable element which few were able wholeheartedly to accept: the necessity that the younger of the two associates should violate his manly dignity by assuming in the relationship a role analogous to that of woman.[39] The existence of this residual repugnance goes a certain part of the way toward justifying Fite's contention that paiderastia in

---

[35] We have omitted from consideration throughout this chapter Fite's calumnious comments on Socrates and on Plato his admiring depicter (Fite, pp. 178–179, 273–276). He sees in Plato's celebration of the wine-proof sobriety of Socrates only an analogue to a high-school boy's admiration for the iron inwards of his pugilistic hero; and he refuses to accept at face value Alcibiades' tribute to the chastity of Socrates, comparing him to a woman who permits "every liberty but the last." The only "liberties"

permitted were those allowable by a father or a brother (*Symposium* 219 C).

[36] Fite, pp. 165–166.

[37] Fite, *op. cit.*, p. 174. Fite's further assertion that Xenophon considers paiderastia disgraceful may be compared with the passage from Xenophon's *Symposium* cited above, Xen. *Symp.* Cap. iv, 10ff.

[38] Symonds, *op. cit.*, p. 47.

[39] We conclude as much from the speech of Aeschines against Timarchus, quoted in Symonds, p. 46, where several remarks con-

background for both portraits is the parable, among Plato's most notable, of the charioteer and the two ill-mated horses, symbolizing the struggle in man's soul between the rational and orderly principle, seeking to maintain its course, and the plunge of restive and indocile passion.[41] In the account of the beginning of close association between the first pair of lovers, we note the emphasis on the physical intensity of the feelings displayed on both sides. Nothing could be further from the anaemic and cerebral affections traditionally denoted by the term "Platonic love." The inevitable comparison within Greek literature, though even it is too mild, is to the trembling and sweating silence of Sappho's lover in the presence of the beloved. Plato's lovers touch and embrace one another, they are pushed to the utmost edge of erotic consummation; the charioteer and the nobler horse, with reverence and right reason, owe their barely won victory to the blood and sweat of earlier victorious conflicts with the unruly horse.

But the rewards of victory are great. "If the better part of the soul prevails, which leads to an ordered way of life and to philosophy, they pass a happy and harmonious life here below . . . after enslaving that portion of themselves whence arises baseness of the soul, and liberating the springs of virtue." At the end of life, these souls are winged and light, ready to resume their places in the celestial realm.

Of the contrasted pair, Plato speaks more briefly. They have made one, albeit a grievous, error; in forsaking the philosophic life, the pursuit of wisdom, in favor of the more vulgar pursuit of honor, they have lost the assurance of a continued life of self-command. The occasion will arise, perhaps under the suasion of drink, when they will be overmastered by the erotic urge, and will succumb; and having once yielded, will repeat the offence, though infrequently, since the act is not supported by the full agreement of their souls. The fate that awaits them is neither the darkness of punishment beneath the earth, nor yet the undiluted blessedness reserved for those who have remained unspotted. They are on their upward way, though life's end finds them with wings still ungrown; in due course they will get their wings, which for their love's sake will be of the same plumage.

The *Phaedrus*, then, leaves us in no doubt as to its author's attitude toward the mixed-indulgent form of paiderastia. Its indulgent component is definitely listed among practices to be deplored, but not visited with wrath and scorn. And this is because, though its unchastity is *pro tanto* bad, its badness he believes compatible with all but the highest forms of human goodness. If one wished a symbol of its relation to the pure form, that of Launcelot to Galahad

---

[41] For a full interpretation of Plato's parable, the reader is referred to J. A. Stewart's admirable translation and commentary in *The Myths of Plato*, 1905, pp. 306ff. The essential meaning of the myth, corrected for modern readers, is eloquently rendered at the beginning of the second book of Robert Bridges' *Testament of Beauty*.

might serve as a first approximation. But those whose love thus stands on lower ground have already abandoned pursuit of the most admirable ends. And though we cannot draw the line here with any certainty, it seems that even the practitioners of the "lesser mysteries" described by Socrates in the *Symposium* must be understood to transcend the mere love of honor, and hence to stand, as Plato conceived them, with Galahad rather than with Launcelot.

But if we ask what a reading of the *Phaedrus* adds in this respect to our comprehension of Plato's outlook upon the philosophical Eros of the "higher mysteries" celebrated in the *Symposium*, the answer is far more certain. If that dialogue itself left us in any doubt as to the absence of an initial "indulgent" phase in this highest form of paiderastia, the evidence of the *Phaedrus* is decisive against it. The phrase "Platonic love" may properly be employed to denote passionate attachment cleared of sexual intent. The *Symposium* and the *Phaedrus*, taken together, represent Plato's attempt to displace the current fleshly school of masculine loves by a relationship not unlike the reputed ancient Dorian ideal of the lover as teacher, the beloved as pupil, in manly virtue, but with a greater emotional intensity and a widening of its martial and civic perspective into the universal horizon of philosophy.

The *Republic* is not one of those dialogues in which paiderastia is treated at length, but Fite has had something disparaging to say about the two passages in which it is mentioned. This provides a welcome opportunity for us to check our conclusions thus far reached in the light of Plato's mature expression of his ideal sociology. In planning the education of the prospective rulers and soldiers of his city, the "guardians," Plato prescribes as essential the ability to recognize the true forms of the virtues (sobriety, courage, liberality, and so on) and the capacity to be moved appropriately by the contemplation of their personal embodiments. The "true musician," as Plato calls him, will be a lover of persons in whom the virtues are harmoniously embodied; he will be enamoured of such persons even when their beauty is marred by some physical defect, provided the beauty of the soul remains untouched. It is further prescribed that "nothing of madness, nothing akin to licence, must be allowed to come nigh the right love," and there is also to be nothing of the piercing pleasure of gratified passion; all is to be sober harmony. To secure the principles agreed upon, a law is formulated in these terms:

That the lover may kiss and pass the time with and touch the beloved as a father would a son, for honorable ends, if he persuade him. But otherwise he must so associate with the objects of his care that there should never be any suspicion of anything further, on penalty of being stigmatized for want of taste and true musical culture.[42]

It is against the background of this law that we must set the second passage referred to, in which, seemingly, Plato has reversed his ruling in favor of the

---

[42] Shorey's translation, Loeb Library, *Republic* 402 D–403 C.

frankest approval of sensual licence. Here Plato is discussing ways and means of promoting the military virtues. A system of rewards and punishments is planned, and after proposing that the hero be crowned with garlands, and given the right hand of greeting, Socrates, says, "But I presume you wouldn't go as far as this?" Glaucon asks, "What?" "That he should kiss and be kissed by everyone?" This light-hearted suggestion is eagerly caught up by Glaucon (himself something of a man of pleasure, as the dialogue has previously made clear), who exclaims, "By all means, and I add to the law the provision that during that campaign none whom he wishes to kiss be allowed to refuse, so that if one is in love with anyone, male or female, he may be the more eager to win the prize." "Excellent," says Socrates.[43]

It is not my intention to suggest that this just quoted remark deserves inclusion in an anthology of "shining passages" in Plato. Some readers will agree with Shorey's evaluation: "deplorable facetiousness . . . almost the only passage in Plato that one would wish to blot." [44] Others may choose to think of the kisses publicly presented to home-coming American soldiers on Fifth Avenue. Having said this much, one is strongly tempted to pass on to matters of more importance; but the misuse of the passage by Plato's detractors obliges us to prescribe an antidote.

Fite has presented first the later, facetious passage,[45] and then has exploited the distaste and suspicion that it is calculated to arouse to persuade his reader that the restraint of the earlier passage was merely a conventional front, concealing the vileness within. In the enforcing of this point, he suggests that Plato's demand, "that there should never be any suspicion," denotes a mere polite concealment, a keeping-up of appearances, and not anything like the avoidance of even the appearance of evil.[46] Such a construction is indeed grammatically possible but, aside from *parti pris* consideration, quite lacking in probability of any kind. To a fair-minded reader who knows anything, moreover, of the extreme sanctity attached by the Greeks and especially by Plato to the filial relation, the restriction to the behavior proper toward a son is suffi-

---

[43] Same, 468 B–C. Popper, who in general is not concerned with Plato's attitude to sex (for exceptions, see our pp. 69–74 and n. 59, p. 98), has not failed to take up the interpretation of the present passage to Plato's discredit, importing overtones of Nazi promiscuities and treating the suggestion of Glaucon as serious public law proposed by Plato. He renders the word here translated "kiss" (*philein*) as "make love to," and interprets it as a transparent euphemism. He then goes on to say that Plato expects the state, in consequence, to obtain an "increased number of children from heroes" (Popper, p. 148). It is true that *philein* may be a euphemism. But in this context, where

the disputed action is represented as being suggested, on a voluntary basis, by "Socrates," this is not at all certain. And Popper is surely wrong in reading into Socrates' next remark the assertion that this "making love" will result in offspring. What Socrates does is to add to the list of rewards that are being planned for the brave man, the earlier-announced promise of more frequent participation in "marriage." It is from such regularly scheduled and sanctioned "marriages" that the hoped-for children are to result.

[44] Shorey, footnote *ad loc.*
[45] Fite, *op. cit.*, p. 167.
[46] *Ibid.*, p. 168.

cient proof of the intent of the law. It should be further noted that the penalty proposed for infraction — the stigmatization as tasteless and unmusical — represents a far stronger deterrent among the guardians of the *Republic* than among other men. In so far as this passage departs from the teachings of the *Phaedrus*, it is in the direction of lessening the emotional intensity of the love permitted; Fite, inconsistently, notes this, but turns his admission into a backward reproach to the *Phaedrus*.[47] The *Republic* passage also rescinds the partial acceptance granted in the *Phaedrus* to the second-best love, the mixed-indulgent paiderastia. In his ideal community Plato can order such matters better than in feverish Athens. It should be noted, too, that whereas the *Symposium* states, and the *Phaedrus* implies, that an initial madness of love aroused by beauty is the only entrance to the philosophic life, the *Republic* makes no such assertion. True that all those educated as Plato would educate his guardians will be lovers of beauty; but in his ideal community, Plato can dispense with the intensity of passion which he perhaps felt to be required, in an ordinary Greek city, to draw young men away from their worldly pursuits into the philosophic life.[48]

The wiser procedure, then, in comparing the two *Republic* passages concerning paiderastia, is to reverse Fite's order, taking them in their original sequence in the book, and to observe that, in the light of Plato's established principles expressed in the earlier passage (and elsewhere throughout the dialogues), the facetious passage can be nothing but a joke, albeit an unpleasant one, forming part of the characterization of Glaucon, and of the depiction of Socrates' attitude toward all these young men whom he wishes to reform and ennoble, but must first charm and hold as listeners.

---

[47] Fite, p. 170.

[48] I find myself in reluctant dissent from the majority view, recently reaffirmed by Hackforth (*Plato's Phaedrus*, 1952, p. 3ff.), which regards that dialogue as a later composition, though only slightly later, than the *Republic*. Although I recognize the substantiality of the arguments upon which Hackforth rests his case, to me they still seem less than conclusive. With Pohlenz, whom Hackforth cites (p. 5), I must reject a theory that requires us to believe that the *Phaedrus* was composed by a man in his later fifties, or, as I should put it, by a man who had already composed the *Republic*, with its serene and tempered ideal of love and beauty, its failure to sanction *mania* even in its noblest form, and its substitution of moral earnestness and love of knowledge, as motives propelling to philosophic understanding, for the winged flights of the *Phaedrus*. The empathy of the depiction in the *Phaedrus* of the "tiefbewegte Brust,"

the lively color and the swing of the prose rhythms in the myth, all bespeak a younger and less tranquil psyche than that which finds expression in the corresponding passages of the *Republic*. We may also note that the *Laws* essentially continues what I take to be the development seen in the *Republic*.

This is an eminently "subjective" opinion, and I shall not urge its adoption by others. To those for whom Hackforth's array of arguments is more convincing, I can concede (as I have suggested in my text above) that the difference in the environments contemplated for the future philosophers and soldiers, on the one hand in the *Phaedrus*, on the other in the two political works, may go a considerable way in accounting for the appearance of change in the doctrine of love. The difference in general tone and literary color, however, will still embarrass those who put the *Phaedrus* after the *Republic*.

Our conclusion that there is no indulgent paiderastia in the city of the *Republic* receives what seems complete confirmation from a comment of Aristotle's,[49] who, despite his distaste for this practice, and for all his ingenuity of objection to Plato's ideal state, can find nothing more damaging to say on this head than that Plato has legislated only against the physical expression of the love between males, and hence, because his abolition of the family has made it impossible for fathers and sons, or brothers, to identify one another, has not precluded the possibility of passionate attachments arising between persons thus closely related.

Coming at last to Plato's *Laws*, Fite would have us believe that the aged author — sin and he having wearied of one another — retired from his profession of apologist for paiderastia and roundly rebuked it as an unnatural vice.[50] He will not charge Plato with having personally practiced the vice; but he sees no reason for believing he had abstained. In any event, Fite thinks, the passion had been for Plato too exclusively based upon a sensuous delight in beauty, the attraction of which had palled.[51] And it is convenient to his case against Plato to make use of Plato, in his later years, as a sort of star witness for the prosecution. Let us search for the proportions of truth and error which are compounded here.

The *Laws* contains two passages devoted to the discussion of the theme of sex regulations. In the first and shorter one,[52] the Athenian Stranger, i.e. Plato, sharply criticizes the institutions of Crete and Sparta for tending to suggest and encourage the practice of union between those of the same sex, which, Plato says in terms, is as unnatural among men as among beasts. This would on its face lend color to Fite's contention. At a second glance, however, one sees the cause of the confusion: Plato is here talking of the gross form, which he has never countenanced, and of the mixed-indulgent form, which he deplored, even in the *Phaedrus*,[53] and has already banished from his *Republic*.

The second passage [54] deserves a full report. In returning to the problem of framing laws for the regulation of sexual relations, Plato expresses grave concern; the leisured conditions of living, the frequent close association of the young members of his community of both sexes set a problem more difficult for the legislator than that encountered in other states. No help is forthcoming from the Spartan and Cretan codes that he has found so helpful in other connections, for these permit sexual intercourse between men and boys. If now, Plato continues, we test the Spartan and Cretan practice by our sovereign criterion, namely, virtue, it is found deficient; no one could maintain that the

---

[49] *Politics* II, 1262, 32ff.
[50] Fite, p. 170.
[51] Fite, p. 171.
[52] *Laws*, 636 A–D.
[53] Even in the *Phaedrus*, Plato had con-

demned sexual union between the lovers as "terrible and unlawful" (254 A) and apparently also (251 A) as "contrary to nature."
[54] *Laws*, 835 B–842 A.

"lover" of this sort is improved in self-control by such physical indulgence, or that the object of such attention becomes the manlier for it.

The situation requires an analysis of the whole genus of those emotional relations between persons, which are called friendship, if mild; love, if intense. A three-fold classification is suggested: (1) The relation subsisting between equals in point of virtue; it is "gentle," in the sense that it contains nothing savage or violent, though it may possess its own sort of intensity; such a lover, who "counts bodily desire as but secondary, and puts longing looks in place of love, with soul lusting really for soul, regards the bodily satisfaction of the body as an outrage, and reverently worshipping temperance, courage, nobility, and wisdom, will desire to live always chastely with the chaste object of his love." [55] (2) The relationship between opposites; it is "terrible and fierce"; such a lover, who "is in love with the body and hungering after its bloom, as it were that of a ripening peach, urges himself on to take his fill of it, paying no respect to the disposition of the beloved." [56] (3) The relationship compounded of (1) and (2), in which it is difficult "to discover what the man affected . . . really desires to obtain" and in which "the man himself is at a loss, being dragged in opposite directions by the two tendencies." [57] Plato would, so far as possible, put (2) and (3) outside the pale, but he desires to preserve in his State the first form, namely: "that kind of love which belongs to virtue and desires the young to be as good as possible." [58]

Plato next points out that the whole problem of regulating the sexual life would be solved if the legislator had behind him, as he has in the prohibition of incest, that unanimity of public opinion which makes all men voluntary servants of the unwritten law. This happy ideal would be the source of countless blessings, could we but attain it, and we must not shrink from the attempt to establish, by every educational means in our power, the universal consecration of "the natural use of reproductive intercourse, — on the one hand, by abstaining from the male, and not slaying of set purpose the human stock, nor sowing seed on rocks and stones where it can never take root and have fruitful increase; and, on the other hand, by abstaining from every female field in which you would not desire the seed to spring up." [59] Failing this, we will fall back upon a "second best" state of public opinion, or universal attitude of disapproval or approval, which will sanction some deviation from strictest chastity, provided it be kept from public knowledge, be infrequent, and remain unhonored. Plato now states his twofold law: In its ideal form, it will forbid all sexual intercourse with males and all extra-marital relationships. In its

---

[55] *Laws*, 837 C, Bury's translation, Loeb Library.

[56] *Laws*, 837 C.

[57] *Laws*, 837 B.

[58] *Laws*, 837 D.

[59] *Laws*, Bury's translation, 838 E–839 A. It is a remarkable fact that Popper, p. 583, in his pursuit of similarities between Sparta and Plato's political thought, has been led to list this very passage, along with *Laws* 740 D–741 A, which is equally innocent, as evidence that Plato "recommended . . . homosexuality" as one of the "means for keeping the population constant."

second-best form, it will still forbid all intercourse with males, but it will not take note of other deviations [60] if these are, as stated earlier, entirely discreet; if, however, the offender is detected, "he shall be disqualified from all civic commendation, as being really an alien." [61] It will be noted that this second-best form of the law fails to correspond to what a reader of the *Phaedrus* would have expected, by rejecting wholly, and no matter how discreet, converse with males.

From the foregoing summary the following points emerge:

(1) Plato in the *Laws* is retaining as a fully approvable institution that relationship of impassioned friendship, utterly devoid of sexual indulgence, between an older and a younger man, to which he had given sanction both in the "erotic" dialogues, and in the *Republic*.

(2) There is in the *Laws* a deprecation of the turbulent and tumultuous quality of the feelings, sanctioned for even the "philosophic" lovers in the *Phaedrus*; though it should be remembered that there Plato was dramatically describing the violence of the initial phase of the relationship, and tells us plainly (*Phaedrus* 256 B), that after the unruly horses are once brought under control, the subsequent journey of the two souls through life is marked by orderliness and self-command. If comparison is made with the serious treatment of the subject in the *Republic*, no contrast with the *Laws*, in this respect, appears.

(3) It is, however, true — and here we are about to find the slight but actual basis on which Fite has built — that in comparison with the *Symposium*, and particularly with the handling of the second pair of lovers in the *Phaedrus*, Plato in the *Laws* is more censorious, certainly less condoning, of the mixed-indulgent form of paiderastia. Whereas the occasionally guilty lovers in the *Phaedrus* are tardily but definitely to be "saved," they would win no such forgiveness in the *Laws*. Even Plato's "second-best" law forbids entirely any sexual indulgence as between males, and the mixed-indulgent form of paiderastia is banished, as in the *Republic*, from the state.

What, then, in retrospect, may we with justice conclude, as to Plato's guilt as an advocate of homosexual love? It remains to collect the answers we have already given in reply to each charge, into a general statement applicable to all.

If our discussion has not been wholly vain, it must have succeeded in one important respect: it must have lifted the question above the plane of personal dislike, provincial indignation, and forensic accusation, and into the region

---

[60] Plato in the preferred form of his law has expressly condemned concubinage, an institution not unknown at Athens; see, e.g., Demosthenes lix, 118, and 122, quoted in our n. 81, p. 106. But the language in which he has expressed his second-best law invites the reader to suppose that on this level he intended to sanction it. This, however, is most improbable, as England in his note *ad loc.* observes. Taylor in his translation has boldly rephrased the passage so as to remove the implication.

[61] *Laws*, 841 E.

of intercultural comparison, historical understanding, and philosophical appraisal. This is not to say "beyond good and evil," or to some Olympian region "*au dessus de la mêlée*," for we have not sought to abolish or obscure genuine differences in moral value wherever we have encountered them.

Our discussion should also have succeeded in counteracting, to some extent, that blindness to distinctions of kind and degree within the field of paiderastia which are occasioned, in great part, by our inveterate association between the notions of "homosexuality" and "pederasty," and of depravity and vice; these are gorgon words, which turn our critical judgment into stone.

We have made plain that Plato wrestled manfully with what he rightly recognized as one of the gravest problems of his day, seeking always to redeem from sensuality the existing practices, and to convert what could be redeemed, or partly redeemed, into an agency of emotional and intellectual training. From first to last we found him sharing the common sentiment of his period and culture, that some, at least, of the more than "friendly warm" attachments between man and youth were permissible, and even precious strands in the fabric of the good society. We saw him as having reached, in the latest period of his thought, his nearest approximation to our own way of thinking in these matters, but still maintaining as a valued institution one highly moralized and carefully delimited form. Reserving our right to reject, for ourselves, even this last deviation from the masculine friendship which we, in our society, accept and honor, we should not therefore scorn and despise the Greek thinker of an earlier day, from whom we can learn, at least, some noble ends toward which "the marriage of true minds" may be directed.

Platonic Love: the Biographical Component

The course of our discussion has brought us to a position from which it is both necessary and convenient to consider a recent monograph on "Platonic Love" [62] by a writer of high distinction in the domain of constitutional law and philosophical jurisprudence, Professor Hans Kelsen. In an earlier study, Kelsen has sought to show the difficulties and limitations in the Platonic ideal of justice.[63] Here, however, he has come to grips with the problem of Plato's personality, conceived as determined by his sexual orientation. Not content to view Plato as a thinker for whom paiderastia, as an existing practice in the life about him, set an educational and moral problem, Kelsen regards the paiderastic impulse as the central personal problem in Plato's life, and as such the hidden root of the whole Platonic philosophy. We shall return to a consideration of the wider problems herein involved in our own attempt to evaluate the reputed abnormalities of Plato's personality, in a later chapter. In the present context our discussion will be limited, so far as the

---

[62] "Platonic Love," 1942, pp. 3–110.   [63] "Platonic Justice," 1937–8, pp. 367–400.

tightly knit structure of Kelsen's argument permits, to what specifically concerns the problem of paiderastia.

Kelsen has drunk deep of the well of latter-day psychoanalytical theory, and accordingly his study breathes a more clinical air than is perhaps customary in philosophical, to say nothing of philological, discussion. He is no intentional detractor, professing as he does a great veneration for Plato, both as man "great in the domain of the spirit" [64] and as poet-thinker.[65] Nevertheless, the extent to which he has attempted to derive the essential values of Plato's philosophy from the desperate and pathological efforts at self-justification of a consciously guilty deviant from the approved sexual mores of Athenian society will appear to many readers to leave little more room for the recognition of genuinely philosophic thinking on the part of a supposed philosopher than would the interpretation, based on class loyalty and economic determinism, of Winspear or of Popper. That in fact Kelsen's position can be interpreted as an indictment of Plato, an accusation against him as psychologically abnormal and mad for autocratic power, is shown by Popper's welcoming of Kelsen as an ally.[66] But let us have a closer look at Kelsen's assumptions and their supporting evidence.

Kelsen opens his argument with a descriptive listing of those traits which he believes to constitute the essential psychic structure of a particular variety of homosexual male who has passed beyond the period of youthfulness at any place and time within the framework of a civilized community which is "still viable," and hence necessarily hostile to homosexuality.[67] The central characteristic of this socially rejected individual is a painful sense of difference and isolation resulting in an ambivalent outlook upon society, alternating between hostile rejection and an attraction towards it as an object to master and to serve. In cases of the type under consideration, "the unconquered incest wish," suppressed but still powerful, produces "indifference, even hostility, to the mother" and a strong tie to the father and brother, while the constant necessity of repression nourishes the "melancholic-depressive component of the character." "A certain infantilism" arising from the feeling of inferiority leads to the conversion of the wish to dominate men into a desire to dominate the less formidable young, and "love of youth and education" remains the lifelong concern of such a man: "he . . . becomes a teacher." Idealizing his own past, when he was innocent and safe, he becomes in politics an archaist and conservative; aware of his own singularity and valuing it, he regards as unjust the dominance of the common mass of mankind and is therefore undemocratic; wishing to overturn the existing dispensation, he preaches that the first shall become last and the last first, and becomes, like Jesus or like Plato, the prophet of a new order.

---

[64] Kelsen, "Platonic Love," p. 6.
[65] *Ibid.*, p. 6, pp. 22–23.
[66] Popper, p. 570.

[67] Kelsen, "Platonic Love" (henceforth cited as "Kelsen"), pp. 7–9, 38–39.

We shall not attempt to evaluate directly the correctness of this supposedly typical case-history,[68] contenting ourselves in the main with questioning its applicability to Plato. As we shall see below, Kelsen himself later importantly qualifies his statement that homosexual attitudes are never countenanced in a viable society, and this precisely in relation to the Athens of Plato's day. Moreover, Kelsen has imputed to his classificatory principles a universality and necessity which should be reserved for use, if at all, in such authenticated disciplines as mathematical physics. Similarly, he has in practice ignored the possibility of "the plurality of causes," implicitly claiming that the characteristics ascribed to homosexuals are producible in no other way.

Kelsen, accordingly, proceeds with the utmost confidence to the fitting of Plato into his framework, establishing what seems to him a complete correspondence. We may list the grounds of Kelsen's argument as chiefly these:

Kelsen finds in the tradition what he appears to regard as evidence that Plato's physique was somewhat effeminate, stressing his delicate features and weak voice, unfitted for oratory. Evidence is produced that he experienced alternations of mood. Kelsen suggests that Plato had so deeply loved his father, who died apparently in Plato's early childhood, that he exalted him in thought to the skies, there to become the invisible Good, "God himself, God Father," of whom Plato conceived himself to be the earthly representative; similar processes, he suggests, were at work in the mind of Jesus. In an enigmatic short paragraph, Kelsen declares that the psychological function of this deification of the father figure is to "set aside" the father, to ensure that "the Hero and Redeemer" shall "have no, or at least no earthly father," and in confirmation of this notion, cites the idea, current in Athens after Plato's death, that the divine philosopher had been the son of Apollo. This manner of interpretation seems able, thus, to employ ideas existing solely (so far as is known) in the minds of other persons for the understanding of the most intimate thought processes of the person under investigation.

The complimentary references in the dialogues to Plato's other male rela-

---

[68] As authorities to be examined in connection with the maternal incest wish, Kelsen cites Otto Rank, *Das Inzestmotiv in Dichtung und Sage*, 1912, and Rolf Lagerborg, *Die platonische Liebe*, 1926. What Kelsen has taken from Rank is apparently only the general theory of ultimately Freudian origin (Rank, pp. 274–275) that homosexuality may arise from a disruption of the delicate balance normally maintained between the rival attractions toward the two parents. If in a male the normal incest wish directed toward the mother becomes a fixation and is repressed under the thrust of social condemnation, then, so runs the theory, a defence-mechanism (*Abwehr*) is found in a rejection of all love of women; and a redirection of the erotic impulse toward the male parent lays the foundation for homosexual love. But at the application of this theory to Plato is at Kelsen's own risk; there is no mention of Plato in Rank's discussion. Lagerborg, who is aware of Rank's theory, specifically rejects its application to Plato, and offers no support for Kelsen's attempt to identify Plato's further personality components with those of a sexual invert such as Kelsen describes. For other major points of variance between Kelsen and Lagerborg, see our note on the latter, p. 124 below.

tives are, as one might expect, duly collected.[69] Kelsen remarks upon the lack of any open reference to Plato's mother; but as his only trace of evidence for the supposed hostility to her, cites as possibly valid Wilamowitz' suggestion that she is portrayed anonymously in the *Republic* (549 C ff.) in the person of the vain and complaining wife of the high-minded and rather aloof man who dwells in an ill-governed city.[70] Finally, the portrait of the tyrant in the *Republic* "may well be Plato's own hated and repressed second self," and Plato's description of the desires set free in dreams, including the incest wish, is, in agreement with Popper, unhesitatingly interpreted as autobiography.[71]

Our answer here must be that what seems to be a consistent and impressive picture of an extreme degree of abnormality in Plato's family relationships is being built up, partly by omission, partly by exaggeration, out of material adequate only to indicate a far lesser degree (probably within the normal range) of a similar orientation toward the male and away from the female members of his family. Kelsen omits mention of Plato's traditional youthful prowess as a wrestler,[72] which surely weighs against his extreme effeminacy in respect to physique. No allowance is made for the inferior and shut-in status of women in Athenian society; in fact Kelsen does not betray any awareness that women were otherwise situated in the Athens of that day than in our own culture, a serious omission indeed; for this cultural inferiority (to psychologize in our turn) may well have induced many boys to identify far more strongly and feel far more sympathy with the more honored and more privileged father, brothers, and uncles than is customary in our mother-centered homes today.[73] Custom may even have provided a socially approved basis for Plato's silence in his works regarding his mother: Pericles, as we have seen, had declared the highest honor was due to that woman who was least talked of among the men, for good or for ill. One may perhaps discount as mere adherence to traditional Greek sentiment those passages in which Plato speaks with filial piety of the reverence and service due to a mother as well as to a father, but this explanation cannot do entire justice to Plato's expression of the honor due to a mother or a nurse as to one who performs "dear and lovable" services (*philon kai agapêton*).[74] Further, it should be regarded as a warning circumstance that it

---

[69] See our listing, pp. 261 f., 267 f.

[70] This passage is discussed in another connection, p. 117 below.

[71] Kelsen, *op. cit.*, pp. 10–14; see pp. 71 ff. and n. 21, p. 403. Kelsen argues that the statement of Socrates-Plato in the *Republic* that he has "dwelt in the same place" with the tyrant, and hence knows his ways, is to be interpreted as Plato's admission that he himself is the tyrant; the force of this is diminished by the known fact that Plato had visited a tyrant, Dionysius I of Syracuse and that he again refers to this experience in the *Laws*, 711 A.

[72] Diogenes Laertius, iii, 4.

[73] That in Plato's Athens greater sympathy was customary between male, than between male and female, members of a family is concluded, chiefly from a study of the orators, by Earp, *The Way of the Greeks*, 1929, p. 51.

[74] *Laws*, 918 E. For the honor due to both parents, see *Laws*, 931 A ff., and for the extreme seriousness of crime against them, *Laws*, 869 A–C. At *Republic*, 470 D, Plato makes appeal to the sanctity of a mother or nurse to enforce the wrong of ravaging the motherland of the Greeks.

was necessary, in order to establish a case, to catch at straws as Kelsen has done: to utilize the possibility that an uncomplimentary depiction of a woman may be that of Plato's mother; and to see as autobiographical and confessional any vivid description of evil promptings of a particular sort, without controlling it by careful consideration of other equally vivid depictions for which no relevant confessional value could reasonably be claimed.[75] When it is further necessary to interpret Plato's psychic state in terms of a later legend of his supposed divine origin, it should become evident that a considerable ingredient of fancy has been needed to eke out the data.

Kelsen next attempts to show that Plato's attitude toward women is incompatible with the supposition of any degree of normal feeling toward them. Since we shall treat Plato's view of women and of marriage at greater length in the next section, we may here proceed in somewhat summary fashion. Briefly, Kelsen shows first, what no one denies, that women are often spoken of by Plato as of lesser human worth and dignity than men, particularly in the myths of the *Symposium* and the *Timaeus*.[76] Second, he takes exception to Plato's treatment of women in the *Republic*, where, Kelsen complains, equality between the sexes is granted only on the basis of "ignoring the woman as such." Here Kelsen expresses his own rather quaintly moralistic distaste for Plato's suggestion when he "seriously proposes" that women be permitted to exercise naked in the palaestra; Kelsen declares further that this indicates "sexual indifference to women." Plato's proposal to abolish for his guardians the monogamous family "must have sprung from no very deep experience of a love relationship to a woman nor of . . . intimate participation in marriage and family life"; the state control of marriage in the *Laws* "would violate every normal feeling." [77] As his crowning example of Plato's lack of comprehension of women, he asserts that Plato has decreed in his ideal state only that no father is to know his own offspring, and has totally ignored the even greater necessity, if his scheme of producing one big, happy family is to succeed, of debarring the

---

[75] For example, the constant deprecation of money-getting (e.g., *Laws*, 831 C ff.), and the scorn and distaste for the merely bodily pleasures in general, when indulged to excess (e.g. *Rep.* 586 A–B). There is also frequent strong condemnation of violence and bloodshed (pp. 226, 344–48). The *Phaedo* provides a condemnation of "misology," or distrust of reason (89 C ff.), which, though gently urged, in keeping with the tone of that dialogue, is also very earnestly expressed.

[76] Several of these passages are quoted below, pp. 127, 130.

[77] Kelsen appears here to have been misled by Warner Fite's misreading of a Platonic passage (see n. 181, p. 131, below). Kelsen acknowledges, in his note, p. 6, his indebtedness to Fite, as "one of the few authors who dare to call things" (i.e., Plato's praise of "pederasty") "by their right name," and in one or two further passages follows Fite's lead, to his own cost. Whether or not the state control of marriage prescribed in the *Laws* violates our own feelings is beside the point; "normal" is here by implication employed to indicate a capacity to accept moral and physical intimacy with a woman. And that acceptance of such supervision of marriage as Plato recommends is not incompatible with this capacity is suggested by the policy of the Catholic Church in regard to the duty of parenthood, and its acceptance by Catholics.

mother also from such knowledge. "The man who is silent about her here shows that nature has denied him all knowledge of motherhood." Kelsen, finally, makes rather a point of the sexual situation presented in Plato's myth in the *Politicus*, where in the Golden Age men are depicted as originating as gray-haired elders from the earth and then as growing progressively younger till they fall as seed into the earth again. Here, Kelsen observes correctly, "sexual propagation is expressly excluded"; but he adds without justification the further suggestion that Plato contemplated the entire absence of women from this paradise: "women were here superfluous." [78]

We shall show below that Plato's view of women is by no means in the main scornful or derogatory. Again we find that Kelsen has been able to make a strong case only by the aid of omission and exaggeration. His failure to take into account the Athenian depreciation of women is here particularly harmful, depriving him as it does of a valid means of measuring Plato's relation to the Attic norm. Further error results from his inadequate weighting of parallels in mythology: we must not forget that the primitive folk imagination in many lands has drawn pictures of the beginning of things which do not set the female on a par with the male principle, or which envisage creation without the aid of any female principle whatever; mythology (particularly in Greece) has represented woman as a later creation than man, and as of lesser worth and importance, and has also pictured a Golden Age without child-bearing. Kelsen's surmise that women were probably omitted from Plato's equivalent of the Garden of Eden is gratuitous. Instead, Plato may fairly be said to have taken their presence for granted; for he makes no provision for their sudden appearance on the scene at the moment (*Politicus* 271 A–B, 274 A) when the Divine Helmsman lets go the tiller and the present era of the world, complete with sexual reproduction, begins its operation.

Plato's program in the *Republic* of permitting women to participate with minimal exceptions in all the activities of the men is undoubtedly out of line with Athenian custom. But it does not prove what Kelsen supposes. Kelsen's belief that Plato's recommendation of naked exercises for women rests on a failure to perceive what this would mean to a normally constituted male is hard to accept in the light of cultural anthropology (many cultures permit their women to go naked); it ignores also Plato's remark (*Republic* 458 D) that this intimate commingling of the sexes will inevitably arouse the desires, and the extended passage in the *Laws* (835 D ff.) in which he foresees that similar arrangements in that city will require the lawgiver to take particular care in establishing safeguarding attitudes and beliefs among his citizens, if promiscuity is not to result. Kelsen's crowning instance, Plato's supposed failure to observe the necessity that the mother, too, shall be kept from knowing which child is her own, is simply an error: three pages later than

---

[78] Kelsen, "Platonic Love," pp. 14–20.

the passage quoted, Plato makes this very provision (*Republic* 460 D). Plato has, in fact, a considerable comprehension of parental tenderness for the small child. He can speak in the *Lysis* (212 E–213 A) of the fact that parents love the baby most before it has begun to love them, and even when perhaps, having been punished by father or mother, it hates them; and in the *Laws* (776 A–B) he paints a pretty picture of the newly married husband taking his wife to their future home, there to make "the nest and home of his chicks." It is true that Plato did not possess a deep and overriding sense of the value of a close and intensely personal marital relation; but as we have seen and shall see below, in a certain sense, neither did the typical Greek of Plato's day.[79]

In short, Kelsen's evidence is sufficient only to support a weakened form of his contention that Plato fails fully to treat woman as man's equal (he was, indeed, far above most of his contemporaries in this respect). It does not prove his insensibility to the meaning of sexual attraction between men and women, or of motherhood. If the evidence shows that Plato fails to measure up to modern feeling in his attitude toward marriage, this, in the absence of intracultural comparison, is valueless. Kelsen fails to prove what his case requires, namely: that Plato's treatment of women in the dialogues proves him lacking in all capacity for normal heterosexual feelings.

Kelsen's next step is to collect from the dialogues many of those passages with which we have already dealt, showing Plato's idealization and celebration of paiderastia as a path to the life of philosophy.[80] Here we may complain of his failure to represent clearly the sharp discrimination which Plato makes in the *Phaedrus* between the philosophic lovers and that less worthy pair who indulge their sexual impulses. And we may express some doubt as to the significance of the fact, to which Kelsen points as if it proved Plato's sexual peculiarity, that it is only to homosexual love that Plato denies all bodily gratification; might not this mean that Plato sympathizes, as we today, rather with the satisfaction of the heterosexual impulse, feels less revulsion from it?[81] But in general, we need not quarrel with Kelsen's main contention in

---

[79] Julius Stenzel, *Platon der Erzieher*, 1928, p. 206, points out that the family, "in the present-day sense of an individual spiritual community of living," did not exist in the Athens of that day.

[80] Kelsen, *op. cit.*, pp. 21–28.

[81] It may be also suggested that Plato and Socrates were not in a position to discountenance the gratification of both heterosexual and homosexual impulses, since they, like other Greeks of their day, considered some bodily satisfaction of the sex urge, as of hunger and thirst, necessary to health, and therefore not to be omitted by the good man, who is obligated to care for his body's

minimum needs. There is no reason to believe that they regarded as virtuous its entire suppression, as did the Christian tradition for many centuries, and as modern society still requires, under special circumstances, e.g., in the case of unmarried women. We can instance the passage in Demosthenes' *Against Neaera*, lix, 122 (or 1386.20): "We have courtesans for our pleasures, concubines for the requirements of the body, and wives for the procreation of lawful issue"; the remark put into the mouth of Antisthenes, that advocate of abstention from all unnecessary pleasures, by Xenophon (*Symp.* iv, 38): "If ever my

this section, which is that paiderastia, untouched by indulgence, is the proper meaning of "Platonic love." We are in agreement, therefore, with Kelsen, thus far, in his belief that Plato presents nonindulgent paiderastia as an ideal exemplar of love of knowledge and as a desirable life pattern, and we may accept enough of his case to assent that it is not unlikely that Plato exhibited to a certain degree a tendency to attachment to the male as contrasted with the female — although probably not beyond the range deemed normal in the Athenian society of his day.

But just here we reach our basic divergence from Kelsen. His argument, be it noted, requires for its success the existence of a strong social pressure against homosexual deviation; for the sense of unworthiness, of isolation and rejection, is the origin of all the peculiarities which are supposed to develop in a personality thus affected. And this strong social disapproval of paiderastia (or "pederasty" or "boy-love," as Kelsen calls it, thereby confounding its various kinds), Kelsen believes himself able to demonstrate as historical fact.[82]

Kelsen, too, has read Symonds, and cites him continually in his footnotes, in apparent confirmation of his own contentions. It is illuminating, therefore, to observe the highly selective use he has made of Symonds.[83] From Kelsen's exposition of the state of affairs at Athens, the reader would indubitably derive the impression that on the whole, and very strongly, paiderastia "was in conflict with the moral and legal views of the Athenian society of his" (Plato's) "time"; "every variety was held to be morally objectionable." [84] Moreover, the reader would naturally suppose that this was the view of the frequently-cited Symonds. Only on careful inspection might he detect, in a footnote, Kelsen's citation of one of Symonds' contrary contentions, namely: that "boy-love [was] . . . a characteristic which distinguished warriors, gymnasts, poets, and philosophers from the common multitude." [85] Nowhere

---

body is in need also of sexual satisfaction, I am . . . well satisfied with whatever woman chances to be at hand . . ."; the reported retort of Diogenes, when reproached for public indecency (Diogenes Laertius, VI, 69) : "I wish it were as easy by rubbing the belly to be rid of hunger"; Plato's provision in the *Laws* (930 C, trans. Bury, Loeb Library) that a widow who has children to care for may be permitted to remain unmarried unless "it be deemed that she is unduly young to be able to live healthfully without a husband"; Plato's frequent remarks about directing and ordering the sex impulse, never, even in the *Phaedo*, denying it all expression (e.g., *Phaedo* 64 D, *Rep.* 458 D-E, *Laws* 784 E, 782 E-783 A). All

these imply clearly that the activity is regarded as necessary, the only question being that of choosing the form it is to take, with regard to the rights of the persons involved and of the community as a whole, and also to the quality of the children that may be engendered.

[82] Kelsen, *op. cit.*, pp. 28–39.

[83] Appendix II, pp. 586ff., examines the other authorities cited by Kelsen and concludes that in the main they, too, fail to support Kelsen's position, and testify instead to the widespread acceptance of decently conducted paiderastia in Plato's Athens.

[84] Kelsen, pp. 28, 36.

[85] Kelsen, p. 37, n.4; Symonds, p. 67.

does Kelsen so much as mention Symonds' central thesis, his belief that there existed a form of paiderastia which had achieved widespread social recognition and approval among Athenians of good standing; though Kelsen does go the length of admitting, in one paragraph of this section, that at Athens, "clearly, there was an opposition of two different opinions" as to the respectability of serious homosexual relationships. In a later section, as we shall see, he will admit much more.

In his survey of the Athenian sentiment, Kelsen spends much space, to no purpose, in depicting the attitudes taken by Athenian law and custom toward sexual outrages against boys, toward the prostitution of the sons of the citizens, and toward what we have called the profligate Eros generally. Here he emphasizes the protection against improper advances which careful parents provided for their young sons. These concerns may be said to be irrelevant to the question before us, just as the protection of young girls in present-day society against rape and seduction are irrelevant as evidence of American hostility to heterosexual love.

Kelsen's brief sketch of the sexual relationships among figures in Greek religion and myth very one-sidedly minimizes or omits mention of the beautiful youths beloved by the gods, and concentrates on figures like Hera, who typify heterosexual love. But this is to ignore the point at issue. No one wishes to maintain that Greek religion was predominantly or solely expressive of love between males; what is claimed is only that divine sanction for this passion could be found in Greek mythology.

Kelsen has denied by implication [86] the existence of passages surviving from a lost play of Aeschylus (cited by Symonds), in which what we have called "mixed-indulgent" paiderastia was presented sympathetically, and has omitted to mention many striking instances cited by Symonds of honored figures in Athenian life of whom paiderastia was believed characteristic. And he too easily credits Antisthenes, one of the followers of Socrates, with opposition to paiderastia,[87] citing the statement of Diogenes Laertius that Antisthenes recommended "the wise man" to "marry in order to have children from union with the handsomest women." Plato could be shown to have said in his *Republic* substantially the same, if Antisthenes' word "handsomest" (*euphuestatais*) be taken to include moral and intellectual as well as merely physical beauty.

But Kelsen's special inadequacy, his failure to distinguish between the kinds of paiderastia, is clearly illustrated by his claiming as a proof of the attitude of right-feeling Athenians, the example of Xenophon, in whom he sees "an unmistakable tendency to decry boy-love and to honor marital sexual

---

[86] Kelsen, p. 31.

[87] *Ibid.*, p. 33. Kelsen also cites, as authorities for his inclusion of Antisthenes, Bruns and Kroll. We have already seen (App. II, pp. 586–587) that Kroll does not document his assertion regarding Antisthenes, whereas Bruns documents it only with a mutilated quotation.

love." [88] Anyone who reads Xenophon will see that whereas, like Plato's Socrates in the *Symposium*, and more strongly than in the *Phaedrus*, Xenophon deplores sexual indulgence as between males, he by no means deplores or fails to honor, even eloquently to preach the ennobling effect of passionate attachment between men and youths, stirred into being and sustained by adoration of the youth's beauty of body as well as soul. The self-confessed passion of Critobulus for the lovely young Cleinias (iv, 10–21), the hush that falls over the entire company in contemplation of the beauty of the boy Autolycus (i, 8–10), express on Xenophon's emotional scale something almost as intense as Plato's own depiction of these feelings in the *Symposium* and *Phaedrus*. It is true that Xenophon permits none of his speakers, as Plato permits several of those who precede his Socrates, to praise the indulgent Eros; Xenophon does not see fit to dramatize the social attitudes against which Socrates, by his own practice and teaching, waged his crusade of spiritualization. And it is true that there is in Xenophon one sentence in which recognition is given to devoted love between man and wife.[89] Moreover, at the end of the piece there is a depiction of the "homeward ho!" of those married men of the company who have been watching an affectionate and amorous (heterosexual) pantomime enacted by a youthful pair of paid entertainers, and have been stirred to emulation — surely a not too lofty conception of the ennobling relationship of marriage.

But the main emphasis of Xenophon's piece is on paiderastia, or passionate attachment between a man and a youth, which is honored by Socrates, who, as in Plato's *Symposium*, is the author's principal mouthpiece. It must not be accompanied by any sexual indulgence — Xenophon is most emphatic on this point. And it must be a love of the soul's excellence rather than the body's; yet here there is more tolerance; for it cannot be regarded as a mere accident that Autolycus, and the other beloved youths who are mentioned, possess in addition to beauty of soul, bodily beauty, on which much emphasis is laid. With these provisos, such love is extolled in the strongest terms, as inspiring and beneficial to both parties in their pursuit of virtue (viii, 6–41). Nor does it even appear to occur to Xenophon that love between the sexes, which he here represents as a matter of mutual affection (*philein*) and enjoyment of the delights of love, could serve, like the love between a man and a youth, to inspire lofty ideals and accomplishments. In short, Xenophon is no opponent, but rather the advocate, of paiderastia, in the only sense in which Plato sanctioned it fully.

Kelsen's other witnesses against the Athenian acceptance of "pederasty" are three: Prodicus, as quoted in Xenophon's *Memorabilia*, Euripides, and

---

[88] *Ibid.*, p. 33.

[89] Xenophon refers (viii, 3) to the love between Niceratus and his wife, of whom the latter, according to Todd, Introduction to his Loeb Library translation, p. 377, "would not survive her husband when he was killed by the Thirty Tyrants."

Aristophanes.[90] And here the confusion between the different varieties of paiderastia is the main strength (or weakness) of Kelsen's position. For the opposition of Prodicus, so far as the brief phrase in which it is embodied permits of definite interpretation, is solely to the profligate form.[91] The Euripidean fragment on which Kelsen bases his demonstration that Euripides "expressly condemns pederasty" is precisely that fragment which Symonds quotes to prove Euripides' acceptance of passionate attachment between males provided that it be kept free of sexual indulgence.[92] Aristophanes, too, fails to provide clear testimony for Kelsen's contention. In him we have to do with a man who behind his comic mask disliked moral irregularities of all kinds, as measured from the standpoint of an older Athens which he believed had been free alike of sophistic teachings, disrespect to elders, religious skepticism, adultery, and profligate associations between older men and boys. But in the plays it is the profligate Eros, like the profligate Aphrodite, that is rejected.[93] Aristophanes' attitude toward passionate attachments decently conducted between a man and a beloved youth, kept clear of indulgence or even "mixed-indulgent," would scarcely be a fertile theme for comedy; the plays will not help us to discover it. But Plato's *Symposium* is here in point. Since it was published either during the lifetime of Aristophanes, or only shortly after his death, in an Athens which knew him well, it seems unlikely that it would ascribe to him opinions diametrically opposed to his real views. And from the speech ascribed to him, one would necessarily classify him as approving paiderastia in its more temperate forms.[94]

---

[90] Kelsen, pp. 32–34.

[91] Xenophon, *Mem.* II, i, 29–31. Prodicus represents Virtue as reproaching Pleasure as follows (Kelsen's trans., p. 33) : "Thou dost not even tarry for the desire of pleasant things, but fillest thyself . . . before thou desirest . . . Thou dost rouse lust by many a trick when there is no need, using men as women."

[92] See our citation of this fragment, p. 88 above. It appears to be too easily interpreted in contrary ways, to possess much weight on either side. Obviously it condemns unchastity and celebrates the love of the virtuous soul, rather than the body; therefore, it may be argued, it speaks of friendship. Obviously, however, it speaks of love which tempts to the abandonment of chastity, love which must guard against being led to "Kupris"; it therefore signifies, so the contrary argument runs, the passionate attachment of paiderastia.

[93] Aristophanes, *Clouds* 973–980, and (perhaps) 1084–1104; and *Birds*, 137–142, 704–707. The *Birds* passages are much less condemnatory of homosexual love than those in the *Clouds*; Pithetaerus, the self-confessed advocate of irresponsible boy-love in the *Birds*, is generally a sympathetic character, and the morals of Birddom are represented as not wholly disapprovable, in contrast to those of the seriously condemned "Unjust Argument" of the *Clouds*. A similar attitude of jesting toleration toward a very earthy form of paiderastia is conveyed at the end of the *Knights* (ll. 1384ff.) in the indecent suggestions made about the slave boy who is there presented to the reformed and rejuvenated Demos. But from all this we can no more infer the personal moral approval of the playwright than we can prove him the unqualified advocate of the various other forms of sensuality his characters so engagingly display.

[94] It will be seen in later sections of this book that remarks ascribed to various persons in Plato's dialogues, e.g., the sophists Hippias and Protagoras, are generally taken by scholars as evidence, with some

We are now in a better position to judge whether, in the Athens of Plato's youth, there existed sufficient social disapprobation of paiderastia to make of Plato a soul "tortured by guilt feeling," as a result of his own recognition within himself of paiderastic impulses. It must be remembered that it is not required, in order that an individual shall feel himself accepted, for all groups in the society in which he lives to sponsor the same values; it is enough if he feels himself in accord with his family and friends, in childhood, and later, with his social group; witness the successful development into self-confident adults of many members of minority groups within our own culture. If, then, as Kelsen has confessed, Plato had available to him in Athens a reputable social group in which paiderastia of a restrained and honorable kind was accepted, he need not have developed any sense of "painful isolation," any more than the usual boy in our culture develops abnormal guilt feelings as a result of discovering his own heterosexual tendencies, which must in their different fashion be subjected to social restraint. It follows that Kelsen's proof, which requires the two supports of demonstrated homosexual tendencies on Plato's part (some degree of which we recognize) and of demonstrated near-universal reprobation of these tendencies, fails conspicuously for lack of its second half.[95]

---

allowance for satirical depreciation or dramatic improvement on Plato's part, of the actual opinions of these persons.

[95] The opinion of a high authority on Athenian social life claims our attention here. Ehrenberg, in *The People of Aristophanes*, 1951, using the plays of Aristophanes as unconscious mirrors of the general Athenian attitude to life, finds in them evidence (pp. 100–102) that "paederasty" was commonly regarded as the outstanding characteristic of the aristocrats. To them it appeared as highly honorable, a part of their inheritance from the great past, closely connected with the whole atmosphere of the palaestra. Ehrenberg recognizes, however, that this ideality of aim was often permitted to lapse into a more realistic and even venal practice; it is in this latter aspect that it is prominently attacked in the comedies. The ordinary citizen, himself no paederast, viewed its wealthy practitioners with scorn. And the middle-class man who had grown rich and had adopted the practice as part of his self-assimilation to the nobility, would be inclined to be ashamed of it. Yet it played a large and significant part in the lives of upper-class Athenians, by whom it was openly pursued. Ehrenberg further states (p. 180) that "no slave is ever mentioned as the object of homosexual love," which remained at Athens "exclusively a relationship with free and noble boys."

With much of this interpretation the present writer is obviously in full accord. It is clear that Ehrenberg's position offers all that is necessary to answer both Kelsen and Fite, depicting as it does a large and influential section of Athenian society as fully approving passionate attachments between men of good standing and boys who were their social equals. We must, however, reject or modify other parts of Ehrenberg's description. The scorn which the ordinary Athenian felt for the wealthy paederasts did not cause him to regard it as unthinkable that a common man like himself should look lecherously upon a boy, whether slave or free, as shown by the passages in the *Birds* and the *Knights*, mentioned in n. 93, p. 110, and in the *Plutus*, ll. 155ff. Ehrenberg's evidence that the bourgeois lover of a boy felt ashamed of his passion is unsatisfactory. It is drawn from Lysias' oration iii, where the boy is shown living as the dependent of his wealthy lover, and in his house; he is not an Athenian of equal standing, and may even have been a slave; so thinks W. R. M.

Two further observations may serve to illuminate our general problem. The first is the possibility that, far from experiencing shame and the necessity of concealing and denying his readiness to feel passionate attachments to males, Plato in his youth may have experienced some social pressure toward the development of such feelings, and may have received approbation and encouragement.[96] The highly honored military and athletic tradition had, as Symonds shows, some tendency in this direction, and the tradition of poetic achievement in Plato's family, combined with the precedent of Solon's sensitivity to male beauty, would have reënforced the effect. Moreover, there was Socrates, who professed to teach the "Science of Love."

Second, there is, we may agree, a serious instability inherent in an erotic passion which, though it may be accepted or even artificially stimulated by social pressure, is not, in the ideal case, destined ever to be given bodily satis-

---

Lamb, the Loeb Library editor, Introduction, pp. 70–71. Such a relationship would not have met with the approval, say, of the speaker Pausanias in Plato's *Symposium* (181ff.) ; this fact sufficiently explains the embarrassment of the older man. As against Ehrenberg's statement that no slave is ever mentioned as the object of homosexual love, if the passage already cited from the *Knights*, ll. 1384ff., is not enough, there is Xenophon's *Symposium*, which is oddly enough cited by Ehrenberg to prove that slave boys could be acrobatic entertainers, but which plainly shows also (iv, 52–4) that the person of such a slave boy required vigilant protection by his owner. Furthermore, there were houses of prostitution inhabited by male slaves, in one of which, so the tradition goes, the Phaedo of Plato's dialogue, captured in war, had once been an inmate. The scorn of wealthy paederasts shown by Aristophanes to have been felt by ordinary Athenians, then, was real, but it was not a revulsion from homosexuality as such. It would be more proper to say that they viewed the romanticizing and exaltation of the relationship with ribald skepticism, and saw in it only a bodily pleasure, somewhat harmful to the development of manly hardihood in the boy, which among the wealthy debauchees of Athens was, like other luxuries, carried to excess.

[96] That males who loved youths were regarded by many intellectual Greeks of Plato's day as more masculine and hence more admirable than males who loved women only, can be rendered probable by the testimony of the Hippocratic school of medical science, if we are permitted to read the myth told in the *Symposium* by Aristophanes in the light of the Hippocratic treatise *On Regimen* I, 28ff., and to extend somewhat the parallel drawn by Bury in his edition of the *Symposium*, pp. xxxi–iii. (I am indebted for this suggestion to R. S. Brumbaugh, "Early Greek Theories of Sex Determination," 1949, pp. 49–50.) For in the Aristophanic myth, the male formed by the division of the original global male creature is a lover of men when a boy, and a lover of youths when a man, and is also represented as the most manly and admirable of human creatures (*Symp.* 191 Eff.). The double male, who most closely corresponds to him in the Hippocratic scheme (though his sexual inclinations are not mentioned) is also the most admirable and manly male. It is true that the Hippocratic scheme includes, in addition to the normal male, an effeminate male who is said to be greatly inferior. And so far as can be seen, this role is not distinguished in Aristophanes' myth from that of the masculine male *par excellence*, except in so far as the age interval justifies and excuses it in the youths of whom he speaks. But the formal parallel between the six sex gradations recognized by the Hippocratic writer and the four sex gradations of the somewhat simplified Aristophanic scheme is in general so close as to have suggested to Bury a relation of parody, and it is therefore not unlikely that in the Hippocratic, as in the Aristophanic scheme, those males who loved other males in masculine fashion were regarded as most masculine and most honorable.

faction. It is as if we preached marriage as the highest form of personal intimacy, while demanding within it, so far as possible, total abstinence from sexual communion. Such a position would inevitably lead to perturbation of spirit, not least in those who successfully fulfilled its difficult conditions. This success, we have no reason to doubt, was attained by Plato himself; and the perturbation expressed in the *Phaedrus* is thus sufficiently explained without the necessity of positing social disapprobation of the homosexual nature of the passion. We may infer on general principles that another and more frequent consequence of attempting to maintain so unstable an equilibrium would be the breakdown of the restraint; and from this would result in time, in the mind of a discerning observer, a questioning of the validity of the original conception and a tendency to frown upon the intensity of passion which so obviously favored sensual excess. Thus without injury to Plato's personal repute, certainly without the imputation, which Kelsen has taken over perhaps from Symonds,[97] that Plato's Eros had simply grown old and deserted him, we can explain Plato's denial in middle and old age that the madness and passion of love, honored in the *Phaedrus*, was in itself a good; and we can understand his withdrawal of all tolerance whatever from the sexual concomitants of paiderastia, as simply the result of his observation of the destructive effects of such tolerance.

Our answer to Kelsen's basic thesis would now be complete, were it not that at this point he has complicated matters by shifting his ground. Not content with classing Plato among the (supposedly despised) Athenians "who were not inaccessible to masculine beauty, like Solon, Aeschylus, Sophocles, . . . Socrates . . . Alcibiades," and the Critobulus of Xenophon's *Symposium* (most of whom Kelsen did not previously list among the "pederasts," in his section describing the Athenian outlook upon this predisposition), Kelsen now declares that Plato obviously exhibited a more extreme degree of homosexuality than any of these. They were able to marry and breed children; they were, therefore, not liable to develop distorted personalities: "such bisexuality . . . would not at all be perceived subjectively as an inferiority."[98] We welcome the admission, thus so unexpectedly and inconsistently made, that the presence of paiderastic tendencies, even when these were publicly known, did not lead to personality difficulties, and look to see how it is possible to maintain that Plato's case was so exceptional. Plato, Kelsen explains, held the political conviction that the good citizen must "serve the fatherland by the establishment of a family and of successors."[99] Yet he "never thought of founding a family"; he must, therefore, have "experienced the tragic destiny

---

[97] Kelsen, p. 39; Symonds, p. 52. But Symonds also recognizes the possibility that observation had revealed to Plato the unworkableness of this "halting place" between license and austerity.

[98] Kelsen, p. 41.

[99] *Ibid.*, p. 39.

of a onesided homosexuality." [100] In a footnote this is then called "a feminine predisposition," and identified with that "disease of effeminacy" which, he says, quoting Symonds as authority, was "described by Herodotus and Hippocrates as something essentially foreign and non-Hellenic." [101] And it was in consequence of this extreme affliction that Plato endured "the torture of a pathologically cursed Eros." This is a truly extraordinary extravagance, as well as a misrepresentation of Symonds. What Symonds is talking about, as he says explicitly, is the psychological phenomenon presented by men who abandon male clothing and the masculine way of life and live openly in all respects as women; as such he interprets the persons described by Herodotus and Hippocrates as occurring among the Scythians.[102] To think of Plato in these terms occurred to none of his contemporaries. Aristotle, who on Kelsen's own showing regarded homosexual indulgence as a distasteful perversity, spoke of Plato as "a man whom it is not right for the evil man even to praise." [103]

Kelsen, however, will attempt to show from the dialogues that Plato thought of himself in these abject terms. The movement of Kelsen's argument may be analyzed as follows: Up to a certain point, we had been following a line of reasoning which was apparently designed to prove that Plato must have suffered inward shame and guilt as a result (a) of his experiencing of paiderastic emotions (clearly exhibited, we agree, in the dialogues), and (b) of the Athenian condemnation of all forms of paiderastia (supposedly demonstrated by Kelsen's survey of the state of affairs at Athens). We are now urged to believe, instead, that Plato must have been effeminate to the point of im-

---

[100] *Ibid.*, p. 41.

[101] Kelsen, p. 41; Symonds, p. 18.

[102] Herodotus I, 105; Hippocrates, *Aër.* xxii. It is possible, however, that no primarily psychological condition was actually involved, and that Symonds has misinterpreted the ancient authors; possibly the Scythians in question were simply the victims of a wasting disease, infectious in nature. Whatever the case, however, there is no relevance to Plato!

[103] Jaeger (*Aristotle*, 1934, pp. 106–110) discusses the applicability of this tribute to Plato and concludes that it is surely his.

At this point some account should be taken of the views expressed by Wilamowitz (*Platon*, 1920) which are so similar to those of Kelsen and yet so importantly different. Although Wilamowitz conveys no hint of effeminacy — indeed he rather stresses Plato's athletic youth — he regards him in his sexual orientation as one whose "life no woman ever entered, not even to disturb" (I, p. 37); "that women remained alien to Plato his whole life long, is everywhere indicated; it is perhaps his

most serious deficiency" (I, p. 49). Wilamowitz concludes this from the dialogues, relying also upon the elegy on Dion traditionally ascribed to Plato, while neglecting the lines addressed to women (Diogenes Laertius, III, 31–32). On the other hand, Wilamowitz is no less certain that Plato grew up in a society in which a compromise had been reached in regard to paiderastia, between Spartan acceptance and Ionian rejection, the "mixed-indulgent" form which Pausanias defends in the *Symposium*. Such an environment could not have imposed upon the young Plato any necessity of developing conscious guilt as a result of paiderastic impulses. But Wilamowitz recognizes also that Plato's outlook was significantly altered by the influence of the Socratic ideal of self-control. So Wilamowitz could explain Plato's attitude in the *Phaedrus* and *Symposium* as that of one looking down, with mild and sympathetic understanding, at mistakes and confusions from which he had been able, at the cost of great effort, to win free.

potence because (a) Athenian opinion did not condemn paiderastic tendencies sufficiently to produce personality-distortion, unless these precluded marriage (a marked change in Kelsen's view), (b) because Plato nevertheless exhibits in the dialogues extreme symptoms of shame and guilt, and (c) because he never married. Helped by Kelsen's own change of view regarding Athenian opinion, we may consider that we have refuted the earlier argument. If now we can show that Kelsen's evidence from the dialogues of Plato's self-condemnation is unconvincing, and that his failure to marry can be otherwise explained, the second argument must also fail.

In order to show Plato's self-condemnation, Kelsen points first to the struggle attending the repression of the urge to sexual union, described in the *Phaedrus*, a perturbation which, as we have already shown, was inherent in the nature of the "mixed-nonindulgent" paiderastia, not distinctive of Plato alone. Kelsen's only other evidence of Plato's inner misery is the portrait of the tyrant in the *Republic*, which he again brings forward as Plato's self-portrait. Plato depicts the Eros of the tyrant as the ruling passion in the soul of a man given over wholly to profligate excesses of lust of every kind, to violence, and to disregard for all prohibitions regarding food (cannibalism is probably implied, in line with the Thyestes legend); [104] the tyrannical man, Plato says, is like a drunken man, or a madman, or one under the dominion of lust (Eros); the Eros in his soul, that tyrant within, has "madness for his body-guard." [105] On Kelsen's interpretation, Plato here "confesses" that the deepest impulses of the tyrant's soul, which is his own, are "just that Eros," and that "madness," which he glorifies in the *Symposium* and the *Phaedrus*.

We must again protest that Plato is not, in all his condemnations of assorted vices, admitting a special personal temptation to commit each one of them. It is explanation enough that he feels within himself a general kinship with humanity, that he knows something of Greek history, actual and legendary, and that he adds thereto the elaborating intelligence of a dramatist, able to fill in a general concept with vivid details. It is to beg the question to assert with Kelsen that in the portrait of the tyrant we have to do with "the same" Eros and the same madness which Plato elsewhere praises. Obviously we do not have here to do with that madness which in the *Phaedrus* is called the "gift of the gods" (244 A), or with that love "sent from heaven for the advantage of lover and beloved alike" (245 B), but with that other sort of each

---

[104] *Republic* 571 D–E, 574 E–575 A. The combination of these various proverbial crimes, suggestive of the themes of Greek legend and of tragedy, rather lessens the probability that in one of them, and one only (that of incest with the mother), Plato is revealing his private preoccupation. Nor can it be said that Plato is innovating on the basis of his own inner experience in

making lustfulness, along with violence, a defining characteristic of the tyrant; this may be seen from Herodotus III, 80, where in the description of the tyrant as such, the habit of "violating women" is set beside that of "executing men without trial."
[105] *Republic* 573 C, 573 A–B (trans. Shorey, Loeb Library).

from which, in each case, and at some length, the Socrates of the dialogue is careful to distinguish them (by implication, at 238 A–E, and again at 265 E ff., esp. 266 A–B). The Eros of the tyrant is self-seeking lust, similar to that mundane and harmful passion described in the earlier part of the *Phaedrus*, or to the "Vulgar" Love condemned both in the *Symposium* (181 A, 185 C, 187 E) and in Xenophon's work of the same name (viii, 9–10). Plato, with the aid of a clear context, can use the word in either sense without confounding the meanings.[106] Kelsen's hypothesis also requires that the tyrant's Eros — if it be Plato's — shall be exclusively, nay effeminately, homosexual; and this is certainly not the case, since courtesans are more than once referred to in association with the tyrant (573 D, 574 B). As Kelsen has himself earlier shown, when Plato depicts disapprovable love, he is most likely to introduce adulterous heterosexual love. In short, Kelsen has not shown, in the tyrant's Eros, that limitation to purely female impulses which he supposes to be the inmost secret of Plato's tortured spirit; thus, on his own hypothesis, he has diminished the probability, already slight, that Plato's abhorrence of the Eros-dominated tyrant constitutes an unconscious self-revelation. The hypothesis of Plato's inner suffering is left, thus far, without support.

But what shall we say of Plato's failure to marry? We must certainly agree that had he been either a guardian in the *Republic*, or a citizen of the proper age in the *Laws*, he would have imposed upon himself the duty, if he were in any way capable of it, of fathering children.[107] But it is not lightly to be assumed that in Athens he must have felt such an obligation, and that therefore his failure to marry proves incapacity. Socrates had married, late in life, and had given sons to the city; by so doing he had proved, he said (*Crito* 52 C), that the laws and customs of the city were acceptable to him. But for Plato

---

[106] We have seen "Kupris," in the fragment of Euripides cited above, p. 88, used as a synonym for illicit sexual union; yet it was simply an epithet of Aphrodite, the "Cyprian" goddess. In Plato, too, it is not infrequent for a word to have two values; he does not, typically, "technicalize" his terms. Thus we shall see below (pp. 174–76) that *douleia*, "slavery," has both a favorable and an unfavorable use in Plato.

[107] It is noteworthy that in neither of his ideal states does he contemplate the possibility that some citizens may be incapable of marriage (with one exception, mentioned below), or may justifiably choose to remain single. In the *Laws*, foreseeing that some may refuse to marry, he condemns such persons to the payment of annual fines, and further to have no honor or regard paid them by any of the younger men, and to possess no authority over them.

This does not sound like Plato's statement of his own just deserts. In the one passage which might initially be interpreted in favor of Kelsen's hypothesis (*Laws* 925 D ff.), Plato is making legal arrangements for the marriages of girls who inherit land allotments (discussed on p. 132 below), requiring them to be married to their next of kin, and pauses to recognize the insuperable obstacles to such unions which may occasionally exist, imperfections of body or mind in either of the proposed partners. This could be taken as Plato's justification of his own case. Yet when he exemplifies the possible defects, he speaks of "madness or some other dire affliction of body or soul, such as makes life intolerable" for the husband or wife (Bury's translation, Loeb Library). It seems utterly improbable that Plato regarded himself as thus afflicted.

the very fact that this city had rejected Socrates made matters different. The depiction in the *Republic* (496 C–D) of the morally enlightened man in a morally unacceptable environment, seeking shelter from the storm in the cover of the wall, reveals clearly enough Plato's sense of estrangement from what he regarded as the corruptions of contemporary Athens. In such a city, even a man most ardently anxious to be of service could not on Plato's view expect to achieve real benefit to himself or to the city, by direct participation in its affairs.

This sense of helplessness to do good would apply with special force to the duty of parenthood. We may recall once more the wife of the high-minded man in the ill-governed city (*Republic* 549 C–E) and the general situation in that family group. If this woman cannot safely be identified as Plato's mother — she is indeed a type — her portrait and the account of her influence upon her son can suggest for this very reason what Plato may have felt likely to happen in the event of his own marriage; for she is depicted simply as one who shared the commonplace values of the city, and who, as such, was necessarily incapable of participating in her husband's more ideal concerns.[108] Even granting, what is not altogether likely, that Plato could by inquiry have discovered among the young daughters of his fellow-citizens a congenial spirit, the capital difficulty would still have remained. In the existing Athens, as Plato saw it, the whole community constituted an agency of miseducation, against whose pervasive influence, unless by divine chance, no parents could hope to rear a virtuous son. Even choice seed, Plato avers, when sown in alien soil, will take on the characteristics of the local variety (*Republic* 492 A, 497 B); and since, we are also told, "*corruptio optimi pessima*" (491 D), should his sons be able, they would be only the more likely to do harm. The educational failures even of Socrates, against the prevailing forces of corruption, could not be overlooked: Critias, Charmides, Alcibiades! There is, therefore, no ground for believing that Plato felt a civic obligation to leave successors; it is far more likely that he felt an obligation to avoid any commitment that would interfere with his propagation of the message which, he thought, might yet save the Greek world; and such being the case, the last

---

[108] Another Platonic passage mentioning disharmony in marriage as seen in the usual Greek city is *Laws* 774 C, where Plato, prohibiting dowries, remarks that this will prevent the haughtiness of a rich wife and the humiliating servitude of her husband. Yet despite these unfavorable comments, Plato did not reject marriage as such, but regarded it as a fortunate state, much to be desired, as is shown in the *Phaedrus*, in that passage in which the Socrates of the dialogue is cataloguing the sins of the selfish and sensual lover (239 E–240 A). Such a lover, wishing to keep his beloved youth dependent on him, will wish to see him bereft of parents and friends, and shorn of any wealth he may possess, and finally, will wish him "to be as long as possible unmarried, childless, and homeless" (trans. Fowler, Loeb Library) — a situation which, it is implied, is not to the youth's true advantage. In the *Laws*, too, there is a passage (776 A–B) to which we have referred above, depicting the newly married young couple in their home, visiting and being visited by their parents, "handing on life, like a torch," in placid piety.

supposed proof of his special degree of homosexuality fails to win credence. We need believe neither that Plato was more effeminate than an Aeschylus or a Socrates, nor that he suffered from a sense of guilt or inferiority as a result of such paiderastic impulses as he did experience.[109]

Denying, thus, Kelsen's basic contention, we shall be in a position to reject, without further ado, many of the consequences which he has elicited. But we shall still find that some of his conclusions remain acceptable on other grounds. We may illustrate this situation by reference to Kelsen's picture of Plato's relation to Socrates. For Kelsen, Plato's devotion was based on his great need for moral support in the "struggle against Eros"; Plato honored in his master specifically the lover of youths who conquered himself, who embodied that "ideal of chastity which he" (Plato) "never fully attained." [110] (Parenthetically, Socrates himself, for Kelsen, was no ideal seeker after disinterested knowledge, but, as we shall see later in another connection, a man ambitious of personal ascendancy over the golden youth of Athens,[111] seeking "justice" only in order to justify his exercise of this ascendancy.) [112] Neither of these two theses, so far as they concern Plato, requires our assent, and the imputation to him of unchastity seems particularly gratuitous, being in the nature of the case unprovable.[113] Yet we may agree with Kelsen's more

---

[109] If something of the spirit of reconstructive romance which we have seen operating in Kelsen and Heinrich Gomperz should now descend upon us, we might here introduce the thesis that Plato entertained until nearly middle life a cherished dream of marriage, which he, like others of the bisexually inclined Athenians, held to be not incompatible with, but rather complementary to the pursuit of intellectual concerns in company with ardently admired male friends; and we might hold that the *Republic* should be read as Plato's final renunciation of this intent. We could point, first, to the *Phaedrus* passage in which he speaks — "longingly," as we should say — of wife, children, and household as among the greatest of human goods, the enjoyment of which should not be too long deferred. In the *Republic*, we could point to the extended metaphor of philosophy as a young maiden to be wooed and wedded, and to the promise of frequent marriage-connections, bestowed as a much-desired privilege upon the best and bravest of the younger guardians. On the other side in the supposed struggle with himself, we could set Plato's gloomy recognition of the attitude which

would be taken toward himself and his projected activities by any probable Athenian wife and her family, and his discouraged view of the educational environment in which his children would necessarily be reared. We could then see, in the passage written in his old age, describing the young married couple in their home, surrounded by their children (*Laws* 776 A–B), Plato's backward look at this golden dream of his younger manhood, which he now vicariously enjoys, pictured as the happy lot of those surrogate sons of his, the well-reared citizens of that safe educational environment, the city of the *Laws*.

[110] Kelsen, p. 44.

[111] Kelsen, p. 78.

[112] Kelsen, pp. 78–80.

[113] It must be granted that Kelsen can here claim the support of Lagerborg, *op. cit.*, pp. 85–87. The latter, however, offers his suggestion as mere probability, supported by Plato's understanding forgiveness of human frailty, and emphatically disclaims the significance of such a hypothetical lapse as against the certain integrity of Plato's spiritual striving. Amid much that is obscure, it remains clear that Kelsen has overdrawn his evidence. Not

generalized formulation of what bound Plato to Socrates, as the latter's tireless "affirmation that the good and the right existed," and his "realization
of virtue, the living justice," in the program of his life.[114] Again, we cannot
accept the assertion that Plato was already alienated from the democratic society of Athens "through his own predisposition" to a socially condemned
homosexuality. Yet we assent to the shattering effect upon Plato of the death
at the hands of this society, of "the only just one" whom he had known.[115]
Using this as premise, we might then reverse the order of arguments, and
after pointing out that a "predisposition" of the sort does not necessarily lead
to an antidemocratic attitude — witness Walt Whitman — we might argue
instead that the criticism of democracy by Socrates, reënforced by the execution of Socrates by that democracy, suffice by themselves to account for this
aspect of Plato's political outlook.

Kelsen's analysis of Plato's supposed struggle for self-justification now
leads him to a long discussion [116] of the deep cleft which after the death of
Socrates (so Kelsen avers) threatened to split the world for Plato into two
irreconcilable halves. He depicts first what he regards as the earlier stage of
Plato's thinking, a deep pessimism, the utter condemnation of the body, of
mortal life, and of society, which he finds in the *Gorgias* and in the *Phaedo*;
he then discovers in the *Lysis*, the *Symposium*, and the *Phaedrus*, Plato's
palinode, the triumphant justification of the body and of the material world
as the preconditions of love, and of love, in turn, as the means to true knowledge and blessedness. Thus the cleft is healed, and Plato is restored from
self-condemnation and the practice of death to the search for social justice
and for power over men.

Kelsen has twisted to his purpose [117] a passing remark made by the Socrates of the *Gorgias* in response to Callicles' assertion that to live without feeling the want of anything — without desires to be constantly satisfied — is
no better than to be a corpse (492 E). Socrates is willing to concede (and it
is this that Kelsen takes as evidence of Plato's despair) that those poets and
sages may be right who have declared that this mortal life is indeed death,
and that death is life; but, he continues, they tell us also that the most miserable souls are those of incontinent persons, the uninitiate, who strive always
with a sieve to fill the leaky jar of desire. To balance this comparison, he
adduces a second: the life which is sober and content with enough wine, honey,
and milk to fill its sound jars is better than the life which must always be pour-
ing more and more of these into its leaky jars (493 Eff.). This is no black

---

wishing to commit the same error in a contrary direction, we can only point out once
more that in the *Phaedrus* (256 A–C)
Plato plainly says that those lovers whose
lives are directed by ambition will fail,
while those who set wisdom as their goal
will be enabled to win self-mastery. And

except upon the assumption of deep-dyed
hypocrisy, we have every reason to assign
Plato to this latter class.

[114] *Ibid.*, p. 45.
[115] *Ibid.*, p. 46.
[116] *Ibid.*, pp. 46–76.
[117] Kelsen, pp. 46–47.

pessimism, but it is merely another expression of the pervasive Socratic-Platonic belief in the possibility of immortality, and another affirmation of the doctrine that the tendance of the body is necessary and good, but that it must not impede or preclude the tendance of the soul.

To be deplored in Kelsen's reading of the *Phaedo* [118] is first of all his failure to note its organic blending of idea, occasion, and manner into a unified poem, certainly the greatest in ancient literature, on the theme of death. The pleasures of the senses, the mundane pursuits of daily existence, even those larger interests of communal life which Plato was never willing long to disregard, all this is subordinated and deliberately pushed out of view to permit our gaze to fall undistracted upon the soul in its awareness of its own divine nature and its happy foreboding of the world to come. The balancing of the resulting deprecation of the values of the earthly existence could not, without aesthetic violence, have been included in the dialogue itself; that Plato did not attempt such a violation, proves not that he had not yet attained the necessary ideas, but that he possessed an aesthetic conscience. And we shall see below that even in the *Phaedo*, rightly read, can be found justification of the body, of the senses, and of mortal life as parts and participators in an ordered universe.

To read the *Symposium* as Plato's search for moral justification of his "peculiar Eros," as "an apologetic pamphlet," [119] has led Kelsen into many a misinterpretation. (Plato, as we have maintained, neither possessed, in his time and place, nor felt that he possessed, a "peculiar Eros"; nor was he "apologetic," either on his own behalf or on Socrates'.) Showing no recollection of his admission that there existed at Athens a group of "bisexually" inclined men, of good social standing, and that there were also those who engaged in "frank advocacy" of paiderastia, he overlooks entirely the possibility that Plato intended a dramatic depiction of various representative Athenian attitudes in regard to paiderastia, at the conclusion of which he would present, through the words of Socrates, and through the device of Alcibiades' encomium, his own teaching; for it need not be forgotten that Plato believed he had a message, developed out of the life and teaching of Socrates, and of this message the doctrine of Eros formed part. Instead, Kelsen simply takes it for granted that in their different fashions all the speakers are put forward by Plato to deliver apologies for his peculiarity; they are simply mouthpieces, and Plato is made fully responsible, both for those motifs in their encomia which he could accept, and for those other elements which in the concluding portions of the dialogue he explicitly rejects. Presumably Kelsen's hypothesis of self-justification requires him to regard the more indulgent views of these other speakers as statements of what Plato wished or needed to have expressed, in view of his own supposed lapses from chastity; [120] but this we

---

[118] *Ibid.*, pp. 47–51.   [120] Kelsen, p. 59.
[119] Kelsen, pp. 55, 68.

have no need to accept. In most of the dialogues, indeed, there are speakers
whose opinions are first set forth, to undergo refutation or correction as the
argument unfolds, and it would be hard believing that all of them have been
put forward to justify Plato's secret sins.

That Kelsen's central preoccupation can produce blindness to the obvious
is shown in his humorless dealing with the speech of Aristophanes. The serio-
comic extravagance of its myth, over which he exclaims in several passages,
seems to him particularly revealing of Plato's hidden motivation. In thus attempting to justify as natural a homosexual passion, by a "more than paradoxical phantasy," [121] Plato indicates his need to cover "the shame arising
in eroticism, the shame . . . of showing oneself, one's innermost being,
naked." [122] That Plato could have wished either to entertain his readers, or
to portray an attitude which Aristophanes would recognize as akin to his real
view, or to perform the *tour de force* of inventing an Aristophanic notion
worthy of the comedian himself — none of these possibilities seems to have
entered Kelsen's mind.

For Kelsen the speech of Socrates, too, is but the justification of "the
Platonic Eros," conceived exclusively as Plato's personal problem; the only
motivation of Plato's doctrine of Eros as "a great *daimon*," himself neither
fair nor foul, but in a mean between these extremes, serving as intermediary
between men and the gods, "transporting human things to the gods and divine
things to men," [123] is but to aid Plato's struggle with his conscience, which
condemned "his Eros" (always "his" alone, for Kelsen) "as sinful and repudiated by society." [124] The doctrine of spiritual creation through love seeks
"to prove nothing else than that the Platonic Eros," more than the love which
generates human descendants, is "a fructifying and productive love." [125] This
is to ignore the dialogue's explicit statement (202 E ff., esp. 206 C) that all
love, not homosexual love alone, is thus intermediary between the human and
the divine, and brings to pass "birth in beauty"; all love is justified, not
merely some special flaw in Plato's nature. In seeing spiritual creativity as
arising only out of love, Plato was undoubtedly overstating his case, and was
destined in other contexts to alter his emphasis. [126] But in believing that only
the love between males in its higher forms could thus inspire its participants,
who shall doubt that in terms of Athenian society he was near the truth? And
as to the greater honor which Plato claims for spiritual paternity as contrasted with the begetting of children, we must admit that he here undervalues
the service of those who keep alive the human race and contribute material
and moral support to successive generations; yet we cannot deny that the

[121] *Ibid.*, p. 61.
[122] *Ibid.*, p. 65.
[123] *Symposium* 202 E, trans. Lamb, Loeb
Library.
[124] Kelsen, pp. 66–67.

[125] *Ibid.*, p. 68.
[126] For Plato's somewhat different attitude in the *Republic* and in the *Laws*, see
pp. 94–96 and p. 98.

intellectual and moral services of great men in general far outweigh their services as parents, and have often been attained only by their renunciation of family responsibilities.

Plato in the latter part of the *Symposium* is writing a plea for the primacy — above the pursuit of pleasure, wealth, and power — of poetic and legislative productivity, and on a still higher plane, of philosophic contemplation, which renounces even the personal warmth of intimate friendship with one beloved person in favor of communion with impersonal beauty and good. Though he has started from the love of the beautiful embodied in one fair youth, he has in the climax demanded that the true lover, he who rightly "practices paiderastia," shall scorn all merely bodily and particular beauty; as in the *Phaedo*, where the body is condemned as the soul prepares itself tranquilly for death, so here visible beauty occupies only the lowest level from which the soul must free itself as it mounts upward. We may wholly agree with Kelsen that the *Symposium* is Plato's binding together of the depth and height of the universe through Eros. But this does not commit us to construe it as merely Plato's surmounting of a peculiar personal shame. Instead, it can be seen as the delineation of a pathway by which confused and ignorant souls can be taught to set in due order the various human goods, and, in the most fortunate cases, to develop insights enabling them finally to attain knowledge of the highest good. As such, it is but one of several such pathways to be found in Plato's works. Another is described in the *Republic*, leading upward first through ordered and virtuous living and later by means of studies of increasing abstractness, through dialectic to the vision of the good. In the *Theaetetus* there is a brief but memorable sketch of the upward path of "becoming like to God" through the pursuit of justice, piety, and wisdom (175 C–177 A). And in the *Phaedo* itself, which Kelsen believes to represent Plato's despair of the body and of the world, what is called "the practice of death" is nevertheless, despite the difference in color and emphasis appropriate to the occasion, entirely comparable to the "right practice of paiderastia" in the *Symposium*. It is a path or ladder for the soul; as its first step (*Phaedo* 74 A– 77 A), the soul must learn to recognize the ideal forms as they exist embodied in the material world; progressively, thereafter, the soul learns to recognize and contemplate them in their purity.[127] In both dialogues the "gradient of value" is clearly marked and very steep. But both alike present the totality of existence as a potential value which Plato emphatically affirms.

We cannot then accept Kelsen's shame-ridden Plato, driven to desperate expedients of finding cosmological excuses for his own socially despised sexual abnormality. Must we then replace the rejected hypothesis by another

---

[127] *Phaedo* 64 C–68 B. The *Phaedo*, being organized as a series of arguments for the immortality of the soul, does not present in order the stages in the soul's progress. They are, however, referred to, as stated in the text.

constructed at our own risk? It would indeed be futile to destroy one dogmatism to the end of substituting another. But it is a fair demand that we should show that there exists at least one alternative to Kelsen's view, compatible with the limited data at our disposal and free of the violence to probability that led us to reject the Kelsen hypothesis.

The crucial point to be explained is plainly the intensity of Plato's high enthusiasm for spiritual perfection, and his repudiation of all violation of measure and self-control, whether in the gratification of appetite or (something Kelsen does not sufficiently stress) in disregard of the rights of others. We have also to account for the inner strength and determination with which he pursued his goal throughout his long and productive life, and for the energy of his resistance to the standards of the contemporary Athenian culture — that gap between himself and the society of which he might have been an acquiescent and comfortably mediocre member. (We shall discuss his eagerness to impart his vision of excellence to others in a later section.)

The trend of psychological opinion in recent years (at least in America) has led consistently in the direction away from the search for exclusively and narrowly sexual causes of individual variations in personality structure. Nor is there need to postulate prior abnormality in the individual in order to explain exceptionally strong inhibitions. It is commonly recognized by latter-day Freudians, as well as by adherents of other schools of thought, that even very exacting standards of behavior, including but by no means limited to sexual prohibitions, which are originally enforced by a parent or other member of the family group, may, if mingled with affection and admiring approval, be gradually so internalized in the child as to become a living part of his "super-ego," or of what Kelsen would call his "social-moralistic consciousness." [128] These standards, if they are by some combination of cir-

---

[128] Kelsen, p. 67. A succinct statement of the nature of this process as it is conceived by many contemporary Freudians to operate in the general case may be quoted from a recent psychiatric writer: "The social control of the child is initially external in the control exercised by the parent. . . . In its negative side this parental control is maintained by actions felt as punishment by the child. If these actions are balanced by sufficient love and emotional security, and the expected pattern is made sufficiently clear, possible, and tolerable to the child, the parentally enforced standards become internalized in what Freud called the superego. This early superego, gradually modified and extended by education, reflection, and usually religious training, becomes the conscience of the adult." — Richard L. Jenkins, "Psy-

chiatry at the Crossroads," 1949. For an account, generally Freudian in its orientation, of the modification of this process in individual cases, see "Personality Patterns in School Children," by R. Nevitt Sanford, 1943.

When in particular persons the just mentioned process of reflection, modification, and extension has been carried so far that the socially imposed standard of conduct has been transformed into an independently adopted ideal, then the resulting "superego" would seem to have much in common with the "humanistic conscience" desiderated by Erich Fromm ("Conscience," in *Moral Principles of Action*, 1952) and the "moral autonomy" of Jean Piaget ("The Child and Moral Realism," *ibid.*). But Fromm apparently has also maintained (e.g., *op. cit.*, p. 176) that any willingness

cumstances set sufficiently high (but not too high), can account for strong repulsions and earnest strivings; if they are accompanied by unusual abilities, they may lay the basis for high achievement; and if, in the child's later experience, they are found to be more strict than those commonly honored in the wider social environment, they may produce, in varying degrees of intensity, the "symptomatology" of conflict, which the older psychologists, inferring a narrowly sexual origin, were, it seems, too often tempted to label as pathological.

In Plato's case, we need assume no further initial pressures than this inner striving after all excellence, as he had been given to conceive it. Beyond the sense of liability to err, which is a usual concomitant of such an ideal, there is no necessity to posit conscious guilt, or an awareness of some special defect or failure. The interactions between his efforts to excel and the recognition or lack of recognition which his successes were given by his social group will have provided outer pressures in plenty. That Socrates in due time supplied Plato with welcome support and with independent testimony to the validity of his self-imposed striving for "virtue," and gave him also the basis for reinterpretation and widening of the meaning of this goal, we need not doubt. Here again, the special sexual explanation of Socrates' attraction for Plato is unnecessary and ultimately false.[129]

---

to sanction coercion applied to the moral judgments of others (examples of which are to be found among Plato's legislative proposals) is itself enough to prove that an "authoritarian conscience" in its extremest form has been at work. That Plato was prepared to carry the principle of rational and benevolent authority to excessive lengths we have conceded (e.g., pp. 547ff. below). On pp. 483-495, however, we have attempted to justify our belief that the "authoritarian personality" in Fromm's sense cannot without important qualifications be made to fit Plato.

[129] Lagerborg (Die platonische Liebe, 1926) and Kelsen share common ground in according an important place in the scheme of Plato's thought to his doctrine of Eros. But apart from their agreement, noted on p. 118 above (for Lagerborg a probability only) that Plato's own loves were not always platonically conducted, they are at variance with each other in their interpretation of Plato's doctrine at almost every essential point. Their central differences will emerge from the following enumeration of theses defended by the Swedish scholar.

(1) Nothing in Plato's practical or theoretical treatment of sexual matters requires for its explanation the assumption that Plato was a born or deep-rooted sexual invert (p. 86).

(2) Plato's rejection of the love of women, his relegation of such love to a position inferior to that of the philosophically interpreted worship of Eros, was a natural result of the cultural position of women in Athenian society. While it is not true that the Athenian woman was so destitute of appeal as to drive the ordinary man into homosexual love (p. 37ff.), she fell short of the possibility of such idealization as would engage the imaginative enthusiasm of a highly intellectual man (pp. 41, 86), and thus was excluded from participation in the "mysteries" of Platonic love.

(3) A certain "gallantry" was the expected thing in the relations between older and younger men, in the polite Athenian society of Plato's day (not a mere clique, but the great number of the educated persons). And although the line between the permitted degrees of freedom and excess was in that day not an easy one to draw, public opinion among the educated accepted without scruple the "respectable"

To conclude: In our dealings with Kelsen, as elsewhere in the course of our investigation, we have found that a thesis novel, striking, and seemingly able to unify a wide range of facts, rests upon a narrow selection of evidence, so chosen as to support an extravagant or even a narrowly doctrinaire theory.

Women and Marriage

The world of the Athenian citizen in the fifth century, the theatre in which, for the most part, the Platonic dialogues are laid, was as we earlier noted pre-

forms of stable amorous friendship, reserving its disapproval for promiscuous or venal forms of sensual indulgence (pp. 44–45).

(4) Plato's praise of paiderastia was not the misuse of reason to throw a color of ideality over a condemned practice of sensual love. It was rather a desperately sincere effort to purify an existing institution (pp. 57–8).

(5) The tensions and strains discernible in Plato's personality are not a consequence of guilt and concealment in the face of social disapproval. They are the price of a moral perfectionism which has carried its denials to a point beyond that which nature is willing to endure (pp. 80, 86).

(6) Following the blameless precedent of Socrates (pp. 57ff.), Plato employed Eros as a pedagogical aid to the young men gathered in his Academy (91ff.). Herein the goal was moral and intellectual sublimation of the amorous impulse in himself and others. (Lagerborg thus views Plato as pursuing a conscious and highly approvable aim, while Kelsen sees him as essentially a shame-ridden puppet at the mercy of his strongest, blindest desire.)

(7) And, finally, Plato's endeavors were crowned with significant achievement (197–198). Whether or not he was able to keep himself at all times unspotted from the world, Plato elaborated a rich and noble philosophy of Eros, culminating in a transcendent ideal which has refreshed and inspired the moral and religious imagination throughout the centuries.

A book very different from Lagerborg's temperate study, but presenting an instructive formal parallel to Kelsen's effort to interpret Plato's whole life and thought as a result of homosexuality, is *Treason Complex*, by René Allendy, English trans., 1949. This book, upholding a similar thesis

in regard to Aristotle, adduces "positive proof" (p. 35) of his abnormality, and depicts his entire life and work as the consequent betrayal, in succession, of every cause and every person to whom he rightly owed allegiance and gratitude, not excluding Plato. Modern psychoanalytic theory has flexibly supplied Allendy, too, with pronouncements regarding the necessary interconnections between love relationships with parents and intellectual and social outlook. Yet along with some similarities to Kelsen's views, we find important differences; thus for Allendy, Plato's supposed incest wish directed toward his mother shows that, despite his surface homosexuality, Plato was "psychologically entirely masculine" (p. 72); in consequence, Allendy is able to depict Plato as possessing the admirable qualities of an essentially undogmatic mind and an outlook, relatively speaking, democratic and equalitarian. Allendy's book progresses from psychoanalytic extravagance to scandalous gossip and suspicions of duplicity; thus, in order to find room in Aristotle's life history for a purely hypothetical secret mission to Persia in the interests of Philip of Macedon, Allendy suggests that this trip took place when Aristotle purported to be living on Lesbos studying biology, and that the many references found in Aristotle's later writings to natural phenomena observed in that region have, in that case, been inserted merely to keep up the original pretense. We need not charge Kelsen with having gone so far in the direction of wild surmise as Allendy. But the two books are based, with similar recklessness, on doctrines regarding homosexuality which are at once too much trusted, even while their reference is limited to contemporary European society, and too far afield when applied in the very different social setting of fifth- and fourth-century Athens.

dominantly a man's world. That this masculine dominance is reflected in the Platonic dramas is not matter for surprise, particularly in view of the all but complete exclusion of women from the practice of philosophy. No woman can really be counted as a character in a Platonic dialogue; Diotima of the *Symposium* is rather an incarnation of the divine wisdom than a woman; while Xanthippe, in the *Phaedo*, is allowed only a single ejaculatory line. But woman as a theme of sociological inquiry, as a project in reform, is another story. How far Plato has done justice to it and to his own repute as a man of good will and moral insight will best appear as the substance of our reply to his critics, who have not left untroubled the topic of Plato's outlook upon woman and marriage.

The chief complainant here is Fite, roused as ever by the claims of a "disciple" (in this instance Shorey) that in his treatment of sexual morality in the *Laws* Plato has expressed "essentially the most scrupulous modern sentiment." One thousand pities that in setting out to correct an excessively friendly extravagance, Fite has succeeded only in losing the friendliness, while increasing the extravagance in the opposite direction. Fite's principal objections are as follows:

(1) Fite denies that Plato had anticipated the modern ideal of love as involving deep personal intimacy, communion of minds, and life-long affectionate fidelity, at least as this applies to marriage. We have seen above that Fite has denied to Plato any appreciation of the preciousness of individual persons; it is now rather curious to find him implying the direct opposite in his statement that Plato "knows full well" the meaning of this highest type of love, but only in the perverted form which runs between man and man.[130]

(2) Sex, Fite says, is for Plato purely an appetite, along with the desire for food and drink, to be held within moderate bounds. Plato's attitude toward sexual union is "the point of view of the stock farm," and his aim in regulating it is solely the breeding, for the public interest, of appropriate numbers of children of the best stock.[131]

(3) Fite scoffs at Plato's proposal, in the *Republic*, to sanctify by appropriate religious ceremonies those temporary unions, for one occasion only, between members of the class of guardians, which are to be arranged by the rulers and called "marriages"; and at Plato's idea that, because no one can identify his own parents or children, all his guardians will feel for one another the appropriate emotions of filial reverence or parental affection.[132]

(4) Fite, having examined, as we have reported above,[133] the contemporary Greek code of marriage, especially as illustrated by Xenophon's Ischomachus and his young wife, contrasts this with the "unconcerned brutality" displayed by the Platonic Socrates toward his wife Xanthippe, in the one Platonic dialogue (the *Phaedo*) in which a wife appears, an incident which shows us, in Fite's view, Plato's ideal of the philosophic attitude toward marriage.[134]

Though Popper does not directly treat the subject of marriage, Fite could find, here and there in Popper, a few passages in his support, chiefly the complaint against Plato's treating the relation of husband and wife as a branch of

---

[130] Fite, *op. cit.*, p. 52; pp. 42–52.

[131] *Ibid.*, pp. 57–59.

[132] *Ibid.*, pp. 54–55.

[133] See pp. 82, 86, above.

[134] Fite, pp. 61–68.

animal husbandry.[135] Of Crossman, who is, in this connection, rather a "disciple" (though a somewhat heretical one) than a detractor, we shall speak below.

Before giving our reply, let us look at the record of what Plato has actually said about women and marriage. The *Phaedo* first claims our interest here because it is, as earlier mentioned, the occasion of that rarest of rare phenomena, a woman on Plato's stage. At the beginning of the reported dialogue, the friends of Socrates, who have come early to the prison on this, the last day of their master's life, find Xanthippe there, seated beside him, holding her infant son. On seeing them, Xanthippe cries aloud, and exclaims, "O Socrates, you will be speaking to your friends for the last time, and they to you!" Her open expression of grief prompts Socrates to arrange that she be escorted home, and she is assisted out, "weeping and beating her breast." [136] We hear no more of her until near the end. Socrates has bathed, in order to spare the women, he explains, the trouble of washing what will presently be his corpse. We are told also that his three sons, including the youngest, are brought to him along with "the women of his household," and that after talking with them, and delivering his final charges, in the presence of Crito, he bids them depart; these things have taken some time.[137] He rejoins his friends, and soon afterward drinks the poison. In all this the modern reader may well feel that the importance of Xanthippe's emotion has been undervalued; but to follow Fite in discovering here only a callous affront to a sorrowing woman in the shadow of bereavement requires, as we shall presently see, the neglect of some important particulars in the Platonic account.

One short but striking sentence in the earlier part of this same dialogue must also be listed here. In it Plato's Socrates reveals his imaginative sympathy for the love that has prompted many a man "to go gladly down to the house of Hades" that he might there see and be with his lost "human darling or wife or son, for whom he longs." [138] It involves no denial of the strength and sincerity of this pathos to note that the context puts these longings on a plane inferior to the love of true wisdom unclogged by the body, for the sake of which the philosopher welcomes death.

In the *Symposium*, some honors, albeit second honors, are accorded to the loves of male and female. Aristophanes' jocoserious fantasy of the cutting in two, by Zeus, of the aboriginal spherical human creatures, explains all love as the mutual longing of the now separate halves to revert to their former condition of undivided union.[139] There is, beneath all the foolery, a note of tenderness in the poignant longing of each severed pair to be once more members, one of another. True that this is shared by all the types of loving pairs

[135] Popper, *op. cit.*, pp. 146–147.

[136] *Phaedo*, 60 A; cf. also 117 D.

[137] *Phaedo*, 116 A–B.

[138] *Phaedo*, 68 A.

[139] *Symposium* 189 D–193 D.

described, male-male, female-female, and male-female; true that the love of male for male is given a far higher status, spiritualized and ennobled above the others; yet the fact remains that this sort of affection between male and female is recognized as above considerations merely practical or pleasurable; and it is said that for the human race, men and women both, true happiness can only result from a restoration of the original unity of the loving pairs, each after its own kind. Later in the *Symposium*, as we have seen, comes the speech of Diotima, in which the love of men for women is said to be the love of those who, desiring to beget children, are pregnant in the body only, as contrasted with the nobler love of those who are pregnant in the soul, and seek out fair youths in company with whom they may beget fair thoughts and deeds.[140] Thus we dare claim no more for the *Symposium* than that in the speech of Aristophanes it reveals its author's capacity to recognize, in at least a secondary degree, the kind of personal attachment to which we in the modern world give the name of love, and to see in it something different in kind from the subhuman biologism of the stock farm.

In the *Republic*, we find a very striking change of scene, and correspondingly, of attitude. In the first place, the love of male for male, as we have seen above, is so altered and restricted as to lose the poignancy and momentousness for the individual of the love celebrated in the *Symposium* (though the devotion to beauty and the shared pursuit of virtue are still presupposed), and the love of men for women, itself almost entirely depersonalized, alone remains. In the second place, Plato has gone all but the whole length of recognizing the equality of the sexes, thus further altering the conditions of marriage. The Socrates of the dialogue maintains the view that woman's natural necessity of childbearing is irrelevant to her fitness for participation in the duties of the state; there is, he believes, no human occupation, including war, from which women are by natural incapacity excluded. Woman is, it is true, the weaker vessel, and in every department of human activity men are the masters. The best women, however, excel the inferior masculine performers.[141] And it is even contemplated, as a proper part of the ideal state, that women are to be found among the very small number of its ablest members, who are to be its rulers, its "philosopher kings." [142] As a consequence the *Republic* provides for the selection and education of women in accordance with the same standards and in preparation for the same functions as those that are prescribed for the male members of the community.[143]

The *Republic* tells us nothing of Plato's ideal of marriage for the bulk of the citizens; we are told only of the institution, applicable to the class of the guardians, of the "sacred marriages," [144] temporary unions, for severely procreative purposes, under the careful direction of those selected members of

---

[140] *Symposium*, 208 E–209 E.
[141] *Republic* 455 B–456 B.
[142] *Ibid.*, 540 C.
[143] *Ibid.*, 456 B–457 B.
[144] *Ibid.*, 459 A.

the guardian class, the rulers, who are themselves beyond the prescribed ages of generation. These unions, the sole form of marriage in which the guardians are permitted to engage, are in the highest degree impersonal; no account is taken of personal preference; all is singlemindedly directed at what is taken to be the public interest.[145] The resulting offspring are to be removed from their mothers at birth; those deemed worthy [146] are brought for rearing to a *crèche*, whither the mothers are required to come to nurse them, but without the satisfaction of knowing which are their very own.[147] As if in anticipation of a charge of irreligion, the Delphic oracle is to be consulted; with its approval, the new institution is to be invested with the sanctions of religion; hymns are to be composed, and we are asked to think of the whole occasion as a religious festival.[148] There is also, as Fite reported, the expectation that as the children grow up they will regard, with the suitable filial piety, all members of the age group to which their unidentified parents belong, as fathers and mothers; on the same principle, they will be abundantly equipped with brothers and sisters and all other relations.[149] But the parents of these children, after they pass the ages ordained for marriage in the interests of the state, may enter freely into such intimate unions with the partners of their choice as they see fit; of such permissive unions the state takes no cognizance, provided only that no children result [150] and that such unions be conducted in a seemly manner.[151]

Now despite these notable departures from the Athenian customs and attitudes, and also from the attitudes depicted in the *Symposium*, Plato occasionally reverts, especially in the matter of regard for woman's abilities and claim to equal treatment, to the level of customary belief. Some of these lapses are hardly more than idioms of the Greek language, as who should say "womanish" as a traditional and thoughtless synonym for "cowardly"; others refer plainly to women as they are in the ordinary Greek society of Plato's day, as contrasted with what they might be under ideal conditions; [152] but occasionally he seems to be speaking on his own responsibility and deliberately, as if for the moment he had forgotten his own more advanced beliefs. What may be an instance of this occurs in the description of the "democratic" state, where among the excesses of disorder inherent in such a constitution he lists "the spirit of freedom and equal rights in the relation of men to women and women to men."[153]

---

[145] *Ibid.*, 459 A–E.
[146] It is not said here what will be done with the infants not judged fit. We know from the *Timaeus* that some will be reared as common citizens; others (those that are defective) will probably be exposed. See pp. 196–97 below for discussion of this question.
[147] *Republic*, 460 B–E.

[148] *Ibid.*, 459 E.
[149] *Ibid.*, 463 C–E.
[150] See below, p. 197, where we discuss Plato's proposed measures for dealing with these matters.
[151] *Republic*, 461 C.
[152] *Republic*, 431 C.
[153] *Ibid.*, 563 B. But this passage may refer particularly to disorderly behavior as

A clearer instance of this unreconciled duality in Plato's judgment upon woman is found in the *Timaeus*. She whom we have seen enthroned among the philosopher kings in the *Republic*, is here half-seriously presented, in a sort of appendix on the creation of "the other animals," as the outcome of the moral deterioration of men who, lapsing into "cowardice and injustice, were suitably reborn as women in the second generation."[154]

In approaching now the *Laws* we should be employing a lawyerly tactic if we confined attention to the specific issues Fite has raised. But there is so much of Plato's accumulated life-lore to be discovered in that labyrinthine treasure house, that we may yield to the temptation to explore its windings at some length, regarding as relevant whatever Plato has to say of woman from infancy to the end of her days.

The view of women taken in the *Laws* has, first of all, much in common with that in the *Republic*, tinged slightly with the pejorative attitude expressed in the *Timaeus*. In an earnest plea for the establishment of common meals for women, as well as for men, which is, on his view, a necessary means of ending the seclusion of women and bringing them out into participation in the common life of the community, Plato reiterates his belief in the lesser excellence of the female members of the human race, stating it, this time, in terms of a tendency to secretiveness and wiliness,[155] and if they are untrained for war, to cowardice.[156] But he believes, also, that they need not be left in this state of unworthiness. Since it is the lawgiver's first and paramount aim to produce the best human beings, women as well as men,[157] and since women are the weaker vessels, it is to neglect more than half his task to fail in bringing them to the highest pitch of excellence which they can attain.[158] To this end the lawgiver must contrive that the women shall share as far as possible in all those activities which, because they seem best fitted to produce human excellence, he has ordained for the men.[159]

The *Laws* as a whole concerns itself much more than the *Republic* with the earliest stages of education; hence we hear much more of how the children, girls as well as boys, will be brought up. Education will be provided by the state, and will be compulsory.[160] At three years begins the daily attendance at the local temple, both boys and girls being brought there by their nurses for play under the supervision of a woman official.[161] From six onward, boys and girls have separate lessons, but study all the same subjects — supervised games,[162] gymnastics,[163] horseback riding,[164] singing and dancing,[165] reading

---

between men and women, as contrasted with ordered and responsible equality such as he approves.

[154] *Timaeus*, 90 E.
[155] *Laws*, 780 B–781 D.
[156] *Ibid.*, 814 B.
[157] *Ibid.*, 770 D–E.
[158] *Ibid.*, 781 B.

[159] *Ibid.*, 805 C.
[160] *Ibid.*, 804 D–805 B.
[161] *Ibid.*, 794 A–B.
[162] *Ibid.*, 795 D, 797 A ff.
[163] *Laws*, 795 E–796 D, 814 D–816 D.
[164] *Ibid.*, 804 E.
[165] *Ibid.*, 795 E–796 D.

and writing,[166] playing the lyre,[167] arithmetic, geometry, and astronomy,[168] — all under the direction of officials, both men and women, who are citizens,[169] but with the aid, also, of paid expert teachers, brought in from outside.[170] At the proper ages, both boys and girls become liable to military service and learn all the arts necessary for war.[171] Both participate, with choral dance and song, in the festivals and ceremonies, take part in the athletic contests,[172] and march in the processions, to which, in the city of the *Laws*, so very large a share of the citizens' lives is devoted.[173]

A girl, when she arrives at the proper age,[174] will be given in marriage by her father or guardian,[175] as we shall see below, and she will be enjoined to bear children;[176] but she will continue to participate in the common meals, taking her daughters with her,[177] as the sons accompany their father; and she will continue her military training, her athletics, and her participation in the choruses and festivals, as before.[178] During the period allotted to the pro-creation of children, both she and her husband are forbidden all extramarital relations under legal penalty, but thereafter the law will take no notice of derelictions, provided these are discreetly conducted.[179] This relaxation of control appears at first sight to reproduce the granting of personal freedom in the Republic to the guardians who have finished their procreative service to society. Yet since we know that in the city of the *Laws* Plato's aim is the public acceptance of an ideal of marital fidelity, we can see in it only two principles: his wish to avoid legal enforcement in areas which he believes best controlled by voluntary conformity (*Laws* 788 A–B, 790 A–B); and his continued recognition of the equality of the sexes — there is to be no "double standard." The woman of the *Laws* is eligible to hold office in the state; there are several types of women officials,[180] among them the teachers already mentioned, and the "marriage supervisors," whose duties include the admonition of young couples who refrain from having children.[181] A woman who is widowed, and has already borne sufficient children, may remain unmarried, and in this case may manage her own affairs, and even sue in court[182] (an

---

[166] *Ibid.*, 810 A–B.
[167] *Ibid.*, 812 D–813 A.
[168] *Ibid.*, 817 E ff.
[169] *Ibid.*, 813 C.
[170] *Ibid.*, 813 E.
[171] *Ibid.*, 805 C–806 C, 814 A.
[172] *Ibid.*, 796 D.
[173] *Ibid.*, 803 E.
[174] Sixteen to twenty years; 785 B.
[175] *Ibid.*, 774 E.
[176] *Ibid.*, 783 D.
[177] *Ibid.*, 780 B, 806 E.
[178] *Ibid.*, 814 C, 803 E.
[179] *Laws*, 784 E–785 A.
[180] *Ibid.*, 759 A–B, 794 A–B, 795 C–D, 813 C.

[181] *Ibid.*, 784 A–C. Fite, p. 48, has mis-read Plato's requirement of daily meetings of this board of officials, and declares that the young couples are to be placed "under the daily supervision" of the commission, adding, "What this means, heaven knows!" The picture evoked, of a regular morning visit of inspection to each household, is sufficient to justify the exclamation point, but is not in Plato, whose supervisors are doubtless intended to rebuke those who wish selfishly to escape or postpone in-definitely the onerous responsibilities of parenthood, while offering advice and as-sistance in cases of involuntary barrenness.
[182] *Ibid.*, 937 A.

unprecedented capacity).[183] At death, those women who have lived lives worthy of honor are eligible, equally with men, for state burial, attended with pomp and circumstance.[184]

In all this, Plato carries forward his ideal of the independent and equal woman of the *Republic*, but the *Laws* has also made many concessions to Greek custom. One of these is private marriage, as we have seen. Still, even when making concessions, Plato has wished to improve the adopted institutions. During the girlhood of our typical woman of the *Laws*, there have been monthly "parties," with "sportive dances" for the boys and girls, attended by all the families in each tribe; these are instituted for the express purpose of allowing the young people to become acquainted.[185] At twenty-five,[186] each young man is enjoined, on pain of fines and loss of civic honor, to choose a bride,[187] in order to raise up children for the state,[188] and for the service of the gods.[189] He is exhorted not to aim at a wealthy alliance, or to choose solely for his own satisfaction, but to select wisely a future mother for his children.[190] There is no talk of allowing the girl to choose, but it is said that her father, in choosing for her, will consider not only the degree of kinship and the keeping of the family land allotment in the family, but also whether the character and conduct of the prospective bridegroom fit him to be a desirable son-in-law and husband for his daughter.[191] Dowries are prohibited.[192] If the girl is an orphan, however, the guardians may be unable to take into consideration, in selecting a husband for her, more than kinship and the inheritance of the land.[193] In cases where such marriages, arranged with a view to settling the inheritance upon the proper heirs, involve unions which are repugnant to either of the parties — and, point of special significance, Plato speaks very strongly of the myriad reasons which might enter into such unwillingness to marry a designated person — those involved may appeal the decision again and again.[194] Plato says nothing of what voice in the selection of a husband may be given an orphan girl who is not an heiress (i.e., not the inheritor of her father's land allotment) ; it may be that he assumes that her wish will be considered; but he does provide, in the case of an heiress who has no available kinsman in the state, that she may choose her own husband,[195] and this, though he might easily have enjoined that the Law-wardens should choose on her behalf some worthy citizen.

Once married, she is, in the usual case, her husband's wife for life; there

---

[183] Becker, *Charicles*, 1899, pp. 463–98 and 236, will give an idea of the extreme divergence of most of these provisions from ordinary Greek practice and feeling.
[184] *Laws*, 802 A.
[185] *Laws*, 771 E.
[186] *Ibid.*, 772 D; but cf. 721 B, where thirty to thirty-five is the age prescribed.
[187] *Laws*, 772 D.
[188] *Ibid.*, 783 D.
[189] *Ibid.*, 773 E.

[190] *Ibid.*, 773 A–E.
[191] *Ibid.*, 771 E, 924 D.
[192] *Ibid.*, 774 C.
[193] *Ibid.*, 924 D–E. The Athenian woman in Plato's day was also often thus regarded by the law as the appanage of the property which she would confer upon her husband.
[194] *Ibid.*, 925 D ff.
[195] *Laws*, 925 B–C.

are here no temporary unions. The young couple are to live alone in their own house.[196] It is the wife's responsibility to set an example to the slave women of her household by early rising and to manage this household well,[197] in addition to performing all her civic duties. She is not mentioned, however, as a voter, or a juryman, nor are most of the state offices within her reach. If what Plato considers the best law for the regulation of sex is adopted, she and her husband will both be obligated permanently to abstain from all other sexual relationships; Plato hopes thus to secure that the married pair will be on the best of terms with one another.[198] If only the second-best law proves feasible, she will at least be spared the injustice of a one-sided restriction.[199] If there arises grave disagreement between them, or if there are no children, divorce is permitted or, in the second case, encouraged. And in the event that there are already sufficient children, remarriage is to be arranged with a view to securing companionship between the husband and wife, and mutual assistance in old age.[200]

We may note, in these provisions, that the usual marriage customs have been altered from motives which are not far to seek. First of all, it was necessary to bring them into accord with a requirement peculiar to the city of the *Laws* — the unbroken inheritance, within each family connection, of its particular land allotment. More importantly, Plato was also motivated by a desire to attain ends which he would have considered good in any state: the development of human beings possessed of the most complete and rounded virtue; the handing on of the "torch of life" to the best possible descendants; and a marriage relationship, which, if it was not a personal devotion and a spiritual communion of minds, was to regard the rights of personal choice so far as this did not conflict with the just-mentioned ends, and was to be in itself a serene and affectionate association for the joint attainment of sacred ends.

And now, with all this exposition behind us, what shall be our reply to Plato's critics? In general terms, this: that they need not so much a refutation — save for some secondary faults of inadvertence — as a correction of perspective; they have looked at Plato through a badly focused lens.

In answer to Fite's first objection, we may agree that, though Plato clearly understood the name and nature of deep, life-long devotion to a beloved person, between self-chosen partners, he never proposed its embodiment in the code of marriage. In framing his marriage legislation, he did not look to those instances of spiritual attachment of which, as we have seen, he was aware; rather, like the makers of Attic law who preceded him, he thought of marriage as an institution arranged by and for the social group, not primarily the individuals concerned. But, as our discussion of paiderastia sought to make evident,

[196] *Ibid.*, 776 A.
[197] *Ibid.*, 808 A–B.
[198] *Ibid.*, 838 E–839 B, 841 D.
[199] *Ibid.*, 841 D–E; 784 E.
[200] *Ibid.*, 784 B, 930 A–B.

this implies no lowering of aim, no degradation of Plato's personal character. It is a cultural phenomenon, reënforced by a temperament and a highly serious moral philosophy.

Fite has asked us to believe that the *Phaedo* is to be read in evidence of the "unconcerned brutality" of the Platonic Socrates, who prior to passing his last day upon earth in philosophical discourse with his companions, curtly disposes of his wife "in four words."[201] Neglect of three elements in Plato's record has brought Fite to this harsh and erroneous conclusion. He has failed to notice that Xanthippe had been given priority over all others in taking leave of Socrates: it is a virtually certain inference that she had passed the entire night in his presence, since the dialogue describes her as already with him at the opening of the prison. Again, Fite has not observed that Xanthippe reappears at the end of the dialogue. True, she is not mentioned by name, but the inference that she is counted among the "women of the household" is strong in itself, and is reënforced, as Burnet also points out,[202] by the inclusion of the child in arms among the three sons. This explodes the noble indignation of Fite's reproach and destroys the pointed contrast which Fite draws between the "brutality" to the wife, and the "fine courtesy shown by Socrates . . . to his jailer and executioner."[203] Surely Fite should have mentioned, for its bearing upon the issue he had raised, what we in our turn may call the "fine courtesy" shown by Socrates to the women of his household, by his thoughtfulness in bathing, to spare them trouble, in his last hour.[204]

The charge of impersonality may be carried to a deeper level than that of failure to conceive the heights of the modern ideal. This Fite has done with special reference to the *Republic*, in accusing Plato of having outraged the basic conditions of personality by the regulated promiscuity of his proposals for the conduct of sexual relations, and also in branding the so-called "sacred marriages" worthy only of the farmyard imagination of the stock breeder. The

---

[201] Fite, *op. cit.*, p. 68.

[202] In his edition of the *Phaedo, ad loc.* (116 B).

[203] Fite, *op. cit.*, p. 67.

[204] It will be noted that Fite's failure to remark the return of Xanthippe strengthened his case against Plato in this instance. Another example of a helpful error is found in the different renderings of the same word, *oikeios* (friendly, familiar, intimate), as this is employed in two passages, one from Plato, the other from Isocrates. Fite thinks Plato devoid of any true appreciation of the marriage relationship, and Isocrates is being pointed to as expressing the more admirable attitude which Fite believes to have been usual in the Athens of Plato's day. Therefore, when Plato, who is advocating marital fidelity, says that it will make men *oikeious kai philous*, "familiar and dear" to their wives, Fite translates this "chummy and friendly" (p. 52), and sees in it the utter absence of any proper feeling; on a later page, quoting Isocrates, Fite has translated a similar expression, concerning marriage, *oikeioterai kai meizous*, which means "more familiar and important," as "more intimate and precious" (p. 62). I think it will be agreed that the result of this change in the rendering of *oikeios* is to put Plato below Isocrates in his appreciation of the deeper levels of human association, and thus to give the latter a considerable undeserved advantage.

Republic being no ordinary city, it will be appropriate to accord it the privilege of consideration apart; in what follows, we shall evaluate Fite's criticisms only in so far as they are directed at the very special conditions postulated for Plato's city of the ideal.

Now, after one has swallowed down his initial distaste for the idea of assignment for marital duty, inherent in even the most carefully solemnized form of the sort of temporary unions that Plato has sponsored, so soon as one's sociological imagination (and conscience) regains its equilibrium and goes back to work, a number of qualifying reflections suggest themselves. It is, first of all, as unfair as it is uncritical, in estimating the moral quality of a "sacred marriage," to forget the base-line of the available alternatives in the Athenian society of Plato's day. We must not permit Mrs. Ischomachus — or rather, her husband, or rather still, her literary creator, Xenophon — to mislead us here. It is easy to forget that what is offered to this girl (for girl she is), is not a free choice of a husband after her own heart. Should Ischomachus one day leave her a widow, she would be returned to the house of her father, pending remarriage to the next Ischomachus of whom her father might approve. A Greek woman would, it is true, be thus given in marriage in the usual case but once in a lifetime, but the arrangement would be none the less mandatory. In every instance, when we look to the basic elements, we see that a girl has under compulsion been assigned to a designated male whose rights include that of propagation — and all this with the full sanction of society, reënforced (it was believed) by cordial approval from on high. Such being the case, the prayers of the bride should have concentrated on the hope that the gods might see fit to increase the virtue of the coming Ischomachus. Plato's provisions, once these facts are recognized, seem rather less harsh.

Fite was in some doubt, in the presence of Plato's attempted sanctification and moralization of his marriage arrangements and projected family relationships, whether to find in them evidence of the arranger's failure to understand the nature of such social institutions as the family, or to view them simply as an example of Plato's cynical humor amusing itself. He skeptically inquires whether Plato can really believe in the practicality of his system of relationships, designed to produce reverence, order, and universal accord; and how could any sensible man suppose that this outlandish system would ever receive consecration?

But this is to overlook a point quite as familiar to the educated Greeks of Plato's day as to the contemporary sociologist. What reader of Herodotus, familiar with his tale of that Oriental people who, as a filial duty and a sacred rite, were accustomed reverently to eat the bodies of their dead fathers, could doubt the practically unbounded capacity of all but a small, highly civilized minority of the human race, to accept as part of the nature of things whatever social arrangements and institutions are presented to it from childhood as sanctioned by immemorial tradition or divine wisdom? [205] Plato's marriage provisions even had direct precedent in the known usages of more primitive non-Hellenic peoples, as is clear from Herodotus' account of the Agathyrsoi, who "make commerce with women communal, to the end that they may be brothers, one to another" — an eminently Platonic motivation! [206] As Grote declared, the sovereign difficulty (which he reasonably enough regards as insurmountable) in the way of realizing the Republic, lies in its very inception, its initial collision with the existing beliefs and practices of mankind, not in its maintenance.[207] Without implying that Plato was contemplating the immediate legislative realization of his ideal state, we must pronounce him even here, in this perhaps most extravagant of its features, to be innocent of talking self-contradiction or mere nonsense.

To chide Plato with cherishing stock-breeders' ideals is strictly parallel to the procedure of those opponents of "Planned Parenthood" who find it in their hearts and minds to brand the whole modern movement of the intentional control of the number and times of birth of one's children by any means other than abstention from sex activity as "organized obscenity." The parallel is rather instructive. Let us assume the standpoint of a man of good will who happens to be, on principle, a thoroughgoing opponent of birth control; he will then stand in the same relation to birth control which our reasonable reader may be assumed to occupy *vis-à-vis* the Platonic scheme for regulating the size and quality of population in his ideal community. Now, by hypothesis, there will be no question of converting the opponent in either case. But to both opponents it would be fair to say: the scheme that you denounce may be wrong, but at the same time, it is responsibly and thoughtfully wrong, wrong in such a way as to inspire the unprejudiced with an admiration for the high end envisaged, and the moral energy employed in its pursuit. The Western world has moved only slowly and with great misgivings toward Plato's principle that the procreation of children is not to be passively regarded either as simply a God-given mystery or as the outcome of a beneficent instinct, but is to be coördinated with responsible thinking, regulated by such norms as population-needs, the individual family situation, and the best possible en-

---

[205] It is to be noted that Plato says the approval of the Delphic oracle will be necessary before his plan can be carried out. Doubtless he believes the god will approve; but he shows himself in this only as the reverent believer in the wisdom and benevolence of the god.

[206] Herodotus IV, 104. What may fairly be challenged in Plato's position is his assumption that the mutual affections engendered by the traditional Greek family could be preserved essentially unaltered in quality in his new social order. Recent psycho-

logical study of the effects of social institutions on personality (for example, *Psychological Frontiers of Society*, by Abram Kardiner and Associates, 1945) suggests that a family organization as unusual as Plato's would produce within it mutual attitudes and feelings differing to an indeterminate degree from the traditional ones, though affection in some form might well survive.

[207] Grote, *Plato and the Other Companions of Socrates*, III, pp. 218-9.

dowment for the children themselves. The standpoint we have just been urging upon the two hypothetical objectors is not without affinities to that of Crossman, who shows great respect for Plato as the ancestor of much modern good sense applied to social problems.[208]

We may also claim for Plato the credit of having given recognition, sharply at variance with the Athenian mores, to the right of personal choice in the matter of a partner in love. If he felt it necessary to forbid such choice in the arrangement of marriages, he at any rate gave it free scope where it seemed possible, in later life, after the period of procreation had ended. This, while it does not satisfy the demand that marriage be made a permanent bond, should commend Plato to anyone who regards love as an intensely personal matter, dependent for its full value on the complete assent of both partners and on mutual congeniality and sympathy.

It remains to evaluate Fite's criticisms as they apply to the marriage regulations of the *Laws*. Our labor is lightened by the removal from the docket of the charges that Plato's aims in this reformed community are merely those of regulating appetite [209] and breeding blooded stock, or that he has failed to consider personality and the rights of individual choice; these we have already sufficiently discounted in our exposition of the treatment of women in the *Laws*. But we must still compare Plato's proposals here for the semipractical reform of the Greek code of marriage, with that same picture of Xenophon's ideal husband and wife to which we have more than once referred; a picture which, though Fite declares it "may be said to represent the Greek tradition," [210] may more fairly be described as Xenophon's own proposal for reform.

Now it is indeed true that Xenophon's Ischomachus and Plato would make a strangely ill-assorted pair. Ischomachus has an unreflecting piety and simple virtue rivaling those of Southey's Father William, the thrifty diligence of a Poor Richard, and a passion for order and comfort in the household worthy of the senior members of the Swiss Family Robinson. He professes in all sincerity, as we have seen, to make his young wife his equal and partner in the management and enjoyment of his estate. There is to be an equality, but

---

[208] Crossman, *op. cit.*, pp. 197ff. Crossman, however, is not in accord with some other views maintained in this chapter, asserting, e.g., that Plato did not condemn the indulgent paiderastia (p. 204) and that he wished to "depersonalize the sexual act," to treat it as "a passing pleasure, like a glass of good wine" (p. 199). Nor can we agree with all that he has to say of social standards valid for the contemporary world.

[209] In referring (*Laws* 782 E–783 A) to the "three dominant desires, hunger, thirst, and sex" as "morbid states (*nosêmata*) which the lawgiver is called upon to con-

trol"—something for which Fite, p. 51, reproaches him—Plato is laying a rational foundation for that modern concept of dynamic psychology, the "drive," an inner force impelling the individual to act in such a way as to achieve a satisfaction. The same conception is expressed at *Rep.* 437 B–C, and 439 C–D. Compare H. A. Murray, *Explorations in Personality*, 1938, p. 54ff., esp. p. 60. Fite adds that Plato wishes these three urges to be mainly suppressed. This is, however, simply not in the Platonic text.

[210] Fite, *op. cit.*, p. 66.

Ischomachus himself will supply and interpret it. We presently hear that hers is to be the indoor part — the gods have so arranged it. What emerges, in spite of the access of enthusiastic good will and the novel program of practical and persuasive instruction by the husband,[211] is really, *au fond*, the conventional picture of the Athenian woman, country style, given in marriage, taken as wife, and restricted — in this case, all but unconscious of her limitation — to a sharply bounded area of traditional duties, within which her "freedom" is only the brighter side of her lifelong obedience to her husband.

Now in comparison with Xenophon's ideal, Plato appears almost as a social revolutionary, the traditionalist elements in him dwindling to vestigial proportions. For Plato has, after all, both in the *Republic* and in the *Laws*, advocated smashing the old frame of feminine seclusion and subordination. In this he is the continuator of the Pythagoreans, who first among the Hellenes accorded women equality of rights, by admitting them to their sodality,[212] and of those discussions of the status of women which, as we have seen, probably occurred in the Socratic circle in Plato's younger days. But Plato pressed on beyond the Pythagoreans, beyond anything that we know of the Socratics, and far beyond the Spartans — so often misleadingly adduced as Plato's complete exemplars in this matter.

Plato favors disengaging woman from the personal and often selfish and degrading authority of one man, and subjecting her to the far more uniform and equable direction of the laws. He wishes to submit her to the civilizing influence of education, up to its topmost reaches, embracing (perhaps to her sorrow) even participation in training for defensive war, and to enlarge her theater of activity to include the holding of public office and the entailed opportunity to win public honors, entitling her to heroic burial. Plato never spoke woman "near so fair" as did Ischomachus — sometimes he forgot himself and abused her a little, in an old-fashioned way. But, in compensation, he was the first great thinker to lend his intelligence and authority to the furtherance of her claims to be recognized as man's all but fully equal partner in every human and rational enterprise.

---

[211] H. D. F. Kitto, in his little book *The Greeks*, 1951, p. 231, supposes that Xenophon (*Economicus* iii, 12–13) has testified to the absence of "arguments" between the ordinary Athenian man and wife, and therefore to the high status of the wife as a partner in the household enterprise. But plainly the Xenophontic Socrates is criticizing the ordinary Athenian husband, in the person of his friend Critobulus, for failure to supply his wife, through frequent "conferences" (not "arguments"), with the education that will fit her to become his partner. It is by way of showing Critobulus and the rest of Athens how Athenian marriages may be most effectively reformed that "Socrates" will presently describe the novel educational methods of the exceptional Ischomachus.

[212] Wilhelm Nestle, *Vom Mythos zum Logos*, 1942, p. 106; citing Iamblichus, *V.P.* 267.

6

Plato and Humanitarianism

The Status of the Slave

A formidable array of charges pressed by Plato's recent critics, Popper in particular, falls under the general heading of inhumanity. These we shall deal with in the present chapter under four subheads, of which the first concerns Plato's guilt in accepting the institution of slavery. The mixture of historical truth and fiction in Popper's indictment will require us to pursue him through a long and tortuous argument. We shall first allow him to state his case as to the prevailing attitude toward slavery in Plato's day, offering our reply forthwith; this done, we shall present the results of our own survey of Athenian sentiment. Using this as our standard, we will next examine Plato's outlook upon the problem, and attempt an evaluation of Plato's view of slavery in its bearing upon the point at issue: Plato's quality as a man.

In developing his discussion of slavery, as in many other connections throughout his book, Popper has employed a most effective device, of which we have already briefly spoken. He has called together a cloud of witnesses from among Plato's contemporaries or near contemporaries at Athens, to whom he has given the name of the "Great Generation." These range from Pericles and Herodotus through most of the leading sophists, Socrates, and Euripides, to Antisthenes, the traditional founder of the Cynic school; together they are exhibited as champions of the great principles of democracy, individualism, equality before the law, and humanitarianism. From among them he summons forth to testify against Plato, at each stage of every argument, those who can most plausibly be presented as having had a better or more forward-looking view than that of Plato. One would not object to this procedure, if it were carefully and critically employed, and if it were balanced by an equally just presentation of Plato's own points of superiority over these others; it would then constitute one possible standard for appraising Plato's achievement as a thinker. In Popper's hands it is far from that; it is not an instrument of measurement, but a weapon of destruction.

And let us pause to remind the reader of the manner in which Popper's regiment of noble thinkers was originally recruited. In calling them a regiment, we are suggesting that they constitute something of a stage army, in virtue of the frequency with which they are made to appear and reappear; but this is far from being the whole account of the matter. We must look behind Popper to the relevant labors of some generations of (largely) German scholars, to whom he seldom alludes,[1] but to whom he would no doubt be the first to admit his profound obligation. To these colossi of research we owe the reconstruction, from fragments and citations preserved in other authors, of many of Plato's neighbors in time, and the extension, by similar methods, of our knowledge of other figures already well represented by surviving works. To this labor of collection, these scholars have added interpretation and conjecture, and have brought before us, as the finished products, outlines of points of view coherent and consistent, and in many cases morally and intellectually admirable; did we not know the methods by which a few fossil bones, so to speak, have in some cases been construed into the likeness of an entire organism, we might often believe ourselves to be reading summaries of extensive literary productions by the men in question.

These labors have been, often enough, labors of loving admiration, in which the deficiencies and inconsistencies of a fragmentary sage have been supplied and corrected by the broader and more enlightened perspective of his learned sponsor. Such generosity of temper[2] has both its values and its limitations, which come home to the interests of our inquiry at one decisive point: the generous tribute paid to one thinker can readily become a grievous depreciation of another, when applied in setting an invidious standard of comparison, that is, when the putative merits of the one are employed to prove the limitations and "betrayals" of another. Peter is thus robbed of justice in order that Paul may be paid honors which he might not — if the full facts were known — deserve. That Popper has done just this should gain confirmation as our tale unfolds.

Among Popper's witnesses will be found some whose fragmentary testimony is not self-contained, but requires completion by a set of conjectural inferences, all favoring the not otherwise established assumption that the objective of the thinker in question was moral truth and the alleviation of the misery of the oppressed. Again, when scholarly interpretations of a given thinker are in conflict, Popper has chosen that alternative which represents the thinker as the advocate of humane principles, thus swelling his ranks by the addition of some whom scholars at least equally well accredited have enlisted in the opposing camp.

---

[1] Popper explains (p. 467) that war conditions prevented access to many authorities whom he would otherwise have consulted. There are occasional references to such German scholars as Duemmler, T. Gomperz, and Nestle, but these are obviously insufficient to measure the full extent of his obligation.

[2] Wilhelm Nestle's scholarship seems to me (as will be illustrated here and there in the sequel) to be open to this reproach.

To each of his witnesses Popper contrives to give a spurious authority on the strength of all the rest: Pericles seems to endorse Antiphon, and Antisthenes to gain strength from Alcidamas. Popper's common practice is to take from each witness the best pieces, so to say, and thus make what seems a concerted movement out of a number of viewpoints which are in some respects mutually incompatible, some of which are in large part conjectural, and others neither liberal nor humane unless given the benefit of every doubt; while Plato, his best passages ignored, any passages susceptible of misinterpretation distorted to his disadvantage, and his least liberal passages advanced to the foremost positions, does unequal battle with the whole regiment.

We would not for a moment seem to depreciate the service to the cause of civilization rendered by even the slightest of those voices. Great ideas, as Whitehead has imaginatively reminded us, seldom make their first appearance in full-blown generality; they gain a foothold in a limited form, adapted to the society within which they are sheltered, and there they await the ripeness of the time of their fulfilling, meanwhile inciting to the perception of the limitations and defects in the existing order to which custom makes men blind. Whitehead's insight will make us more generous in appreciation, more sensitive to distinguish the living seed of an idea from the dead shell of traditional inadequacy within which it comes into the world. But it is much to our purpose to remember that it was of Plato, first of all, that Whitehead was thinking, in that magnificent first chapter of his *Adventures of Ideas*; and, by happy accident, in especial he was thinking of the inner persuasive force of Plato's notion of the rational soul in its historical career as a solvent of the brute material "necessity" of slavery. The "Great Generation" of whom Popper speaks planted many a fertile seed, for which we are still grateful. We must not mistake the seeds for the full-grown plants; nor must we forget our debt to the seminal thought of Plato.

Now Popper would have us believe that there was at Athens, before and during Plato's lifetime, a practical and very nearly successful antislavery movement. Among the many voices raised against the injustice of slavery, calling for its abolition as a violation of nature, he lists several members of his enlightened thinkers of the "Great Generation," and includes in the movement, as well, most of the plain citizens of Athens. That Plato both knew and combated this noble movement, Popper lays as a most grievous charge at Plato's door. We shall take special care in treating Popper's contention in this instance, in an endeavor to show the kind of evidence he has employed and the manner in which it has assisted him to reach erroneous conclusions by successive stages of probable or possible truths.

Popper's chief evidential exhibits for the existence of a strong antislavery movement at Athens may be listed and replied to briefly, as follows:

(1) There is the saying, credited by an ancient commentator on Aristotle's

Rhetoric to the sophist Alcidamas, that "God has made all men free; no man is a slave by nature."[3]

This sentence from Alcidamas is beyond reproach both as to its authenticity and as to the nobility of its sentiment. Its context is lost, yet something is known of the oration in which it occurred. This was an oration, or rather a political pamphlet — for such orations were composed with a view to publication — written in about the year 366 B.C., to recommend that the Spartans, who had been defeated in war by the Thebans, should acquiesce in the liberation of Messene. The territory of this city state, conquered hundreds of years earlier by the Spartans, had ever since formed part of Sparta's lands and was cultivated by serfs who were descendants of the original Messenians. Now Thebes was seeking to weaken Sparta by loss of territory and serfs, and to set up Messene as a fortress to hold Sparta in check. It was this reëstablishment of Messene that Alcidamas was defending.[4] Under these circumstances, it seems extremely unlikely that he would have been led on to make a universal application of his principle to the liberation of all slaves everywhere,[5] or even of any others than the Messenians; to suggest to the Spartans the simultaneous liberation of their remaining serfs, at such a time, would scarcely have been tactful. It seems more probable that he employed a sweeping affirmation, as other orators have done, in support of a limited plea. We may observe that large moral generalizations of this kind are not in themselves fair indications of the actual legal and political system to which the speaker is committed, even when there is strong conviction behind them. Let it be remembered that the proposition "Slavery is contrary to natural law; for by natural law all men were originally born free"[6] was a fundamental premise in that Justinian Code in which the rights of the slave-owner are securely and minutely expounded, and that many American southerners, slave-owners on a large scale, felt no contradiction between their practices and the spirit of the Declaration of Independence.

An effort has been made to interpret Alcidamas' reproach against slavery as the outgrowth of a consistent philosophical position which has been reconstructed with the aid of two further unconnected fragments preserved by Aristotle (who cites them as examples of Alcidamas' literary style, not at all as illustrations of his thought), fragments which consist respectively of the phrases "laws, the kings of cities" and "philosophy, the border-outpost of (or against) law." By combining these two, and by a judicious choice of interpretation of each, it is possible to present Alcidamas as the consistent opponent, in the name of philosophy and of "nature" or "God," of all oppressive and legal institutions, of which slavery is but one.[7] This leaves out of account,

[3] Schol. to Aristotle's *Rhet.* I, 13, 1373 b 18; Popper, p. 70.

[4] R. C. Jebb, *The Attic Orators*, 1893, p. 45; *Cambridge Ancient History*, 1927, vol. VI, pp. 90–97.

[5] So thinks Zeller, *Gr. Ph.*, I, 1007, 2;

quoted in W. L. Newman, *The Politics of Aristotle*, 1887, vol. I, p. 141.

[6] Justinian, *Institutes*, book I, title II.

[7] As does Wilhelm Nestle, *Vom Mythos zum Logos*, Stuttgart, 1942, pp. 344–345. Others regard Fragment 1 as referring not

however, the only other surviving fragment of Alcidamas' political thought, in which he lists among those who are "wise," along with men of such varied claims as Homer and Anaxagoras, the lawgivers Solon and Lycurgus, and the Theban generals Epaminondas and Pelopidas. In short, the evidence does not suffice to determine whether Alcidamas was a consistent thinker at all, much less to define his standpoint with certainty. His declaration against slavery is left standing like a spire without a church below, and must be admired for itself alone. We cannot, on the evidence, affirm that it was animated by more than a limited intent, or, if it was designed for wider application, that it was accompanied by any attempt to think through the consequences for society at large; in short, that it was more than a piety of the theoretical intellect, or even a rhetorical device, adopted for effect in pleading a particular cause. The saying of Alcidamas was indubitably an achievement; it was memorable, and it may have become a seminal thought in other minds, as Jefferson's words were to become and to remain in our own society. But it does not constitute Alcidamas a practical abolitionist in the Athens of his day.

(2) There are the lines from the *Ion* of Euripides: "The name alone brings shame upon the slave, who can be excellent in every way and truly equal to the freeborn man"; and from the *Phoenissae*, "Man's law of nature is equality." [8]

Popper is certainly right in claiming that the deep human sympathies of Euripides were extended to include the slave. But he is as certainly wrong in reading the notion of humanitarianism, or concern for slaves, into the line, "Man's law of nature is equality." This line is taken from the speech of Jocasta, the queen mother, who is attempting to dissuade her son Eteocles from making himself a tyrant by usurping the equal right to the throne of his brother, Polyneices, and forms part of her development of a series of Greek commonplaces, among them the thought that excess of power breeds hostility and violates the cosmic law of measure. The bearing of this idea on Euripides' general political outlook will be discussed later.[9] The quotation beginning, "The name alone brings shame upon the slave," has at least the merit that it concerns slavery; but the lines, put into the mouth of a noble slave, devoted to his mistress' interest, assert only the possibility that a slave may be the equal in virtue of a free man and the unfairness of failing to recognize the virtue of such slaves; there is no protest against the office of the slave, no proposal for

---

to the tyrant law, but to laws as honorable kings, which weakens the view favored by Nestle; others, again, on grounds of Greek usage, would render Fragment 2, "bulwark of the laws," which, if accepted, quite finishes Nestle's case. What all this demonstrates, *me judice*, is that all this cannot be demonstrated.

[8] *Ion* 854ff; *Phoenissae* 538; as translated by Popper, p. 70.

[9] See pp. 280–81. If Euripides' lines have any relevance to contemporary Athenian affairs, they may be taken as his admonition to the oligarchs (the year is 409 B.C.) that usurpation of power is unjust and self-defeating, and to the opposing faction that civic bloodshed is never justified, even when it is perpetrated for the sake of enforcing just claims. But this is highly speculative.

the removal of the institution. Plato himself, as we shall see,[10] comes close to asserting as much about individual slaves, while remaining wholly within the limits of the system. Euripides is here the champion of the right of virtue to be recognized for what it is, wherever it may occur. For the rest, as we shall see below,[11] he is first and foremost the troubled and deeply sympathetic observer of the strange ways of Necessity and the contradictions that beset the mortal state, and he speaks with pathos of the wrongs that pride in its ruthless strength inflict upon the vanquished. Frequently, again, he presents in lively dramatic conflict both opposing aspects — and here the sophistic influence is very evident — of the chief questions alive in the Athenian mind. Yet he never ventures to condemn the contemporary institution of slavery, or even to hint at the emancipation of all existing slaves.

(3) There is the declaration of the sophist Antiphon (we give the passage as translated by Popper): "The nobly born we revere and adore; but not the lowly born. These are barbarous habits. For as to our natural gifts, we are all on the same footing on all points, whether we now happen to be Greeks or Barbarians. . . We all breathe the air through our mouths and nostrils"; [12] and of the sophist Lycophron: "The splendor of noble birth is imaginary, and its prerogatives are based upon a mere word"; [13] and of the sophist Hippias, in Plato's dialogue the *Protagoras*: "Gentlemen, I believe that we are all kinsmen and friends and fellow citizens; if not by conventional law, then by nature. For by nature, likeness is an expression of kinship; but conventional law, the tyrant of mankind, compels us to do much that is against nature." [14]

In invoking Antiphon as an opponent of slavery [15] and upholder of the moral rights of man, Popper has called in a veritable fox to guard the hens. The deftly handled quotation reveals its true nature, reveals "the fox it drags behind," as the Greek saying went, if one reads the rest of the two fragments from the same treatise "On Truth" from which it and Popper's other quotations from Antiphon are taken. For, first, it becomes apparent that it is not natural "gifts" which Antiphon is asserting to be the same for Greeks and for barbarians so much as natural needs or tendencies to seek necessities; this is a small misinterpretation of the passage by Popper, but it obscures the essentially

---

[10] See pp. 178, 180.

[11] See pp. 158ff.

[12] H. Diels, *Die Fragmente der Vorsokratiker*, 1922, vol. II, p. xxxvi; fr. B, col. 2. Quoted by Popper, p. 70.

[13] Aristotle's *Fragm.* 91 (Rose), as translated by Popper, p. 70.

[14] *Protagoras* 337 E, as translated by Popper, p. 70.

[15] Popper, on first introducing Antiphon (p. 70), calls his position only "humanitarian" and "equalitarian," and does not call him in so many words an oppo-

nent of slavery. But in referring his reader back to the page for the "Athenian antislavery movement," he constantly includes him, by implication, in the movement, and does the same for Hippias and Lycophron; and on later pages in the notes, includes these persons explicitly (Lycophron on p. 614; Hippias and Antiphon on p. 563). The "movement" indeed needs them, since of all Popper's witnesses supposedly opposing slavery, only two, Alcidamas and Euripides, actually refer to slaves.

biological nature of the kinship which is asserted by Antiphon.[16] In the other fragment, we find that among the things that are "contrary to nature" (and which therefore, on Popper's assumption, are to be cast into outer darkness, along with the institution of slavery) are the very foundations of civilization, of moral culture in any form. For, we are told, "in hostile opposition to nature" stand "conventional prescriptions to the eyes, what they shall and shall not see, to the ears, what they shall hear . . . tongue . . . hands . . . feet . . ." and finally "to the mind, what it shall and shall not desire." [17] Occurring later in the fragment are the lines, quoted also by Popper in his account of Antiphon's ethical position, "Of the actions here mentioned [i.e., those in accordance with unnecessary human convention], one would find many to be contrary to nature. For they involve more suffering where there should be less, and less pleasure where there could be more, and injury where it is unnecessary." [18]

The true meaning of this is all but hidden from the reader under the high-sounding phrase used by Popper to describe it, "utilitarian ethics." It would be a sheer error to assume that the "suffering" here described is that of others, slaves perhaps, whom we ought to relieve. Its real meaning, since Antiphon is here approving "nature," is that, unless there is a chance of getting caught, no inconvenient restraints are to be laid upon the urgencies of the self-regarding individual, no painful actions performed for the sake of justice or human decency. If this be "utilitarian," in any sense, it must be in that of the greatest good of the greatest rascal.[19]

---

[16] Diels, op. cit., vol. II, pp. xxxvi, frag. B, col. 2. Popper (p. 563) does not agree with Tarn ("Alexander the Great and the Unity of Mankind," 1933) that the passage is biological; but in the absence of any specific mention of a mental or moral trait, the argument in favor of a biological interpretation remains unanswered. In general agreement with the view here adopted may be cited, e.g., Ernest Barker, Greek Political Theory, 1947, p. 69, and Paul Vinogradoff, Historical Jurisprudence, 1922, vol. II, pp. 29–30. Jaeger (Paideia, vol. I, pp. 324–325), despite his inclusion of Antiphon, along with Hippias, among "the first cosmopolitans," in the following volume has a different tale to tell: we now hear (p. 141) that he is to be classed with the Callicles of Plato's Gorgias and the Athenian envoys of the Melian dialogue in Thucydides, as the advocate of self-regarding egoism. The two passages together form a view of Antiphon's position in general agreement with the view here maintained: "cosmopolitanism" founded on the wreck of morality. We welcome also the confirmation provided by Glenn R. Morrow

("Plato and the Law of Nature," 1948, pp. 26–27), to whom Antiphon appears, in the strongest contrast to Plato, as the evangelist of self-regarding expediency.

[17] Diels, op. cit., vol. II, pp. xxxii–xxxiii; translation the writer's own.

[18] Diels, p. xxxiv; translated by Popper, p. 70.

[19] Our discussion has sought to avoid, as far as possible, involvement in the moot question of the relationship between Antiphon the author of the On Truth, and Antiphon the author of the fragments that have survived under the title of On Concord (Peri Homonoias) (Diels, 1922, vol. II, p. 298ff.). The difficulty of assuming a single author appears from the variety, nay incompatibility, of the moral standpoints expressed, which range from the cynicism mentioned above to the idealism of fr. 59, which declares that he who has neither himself desired nor come into contact with evil cannot claim to have won self-mastery. If only one Antiphon be permitted us — I personally feel the need of two — some hypothesis of the rhetorical development of opposing points of view seems indicated.

Returning now to Antiphon's critique of the traditional "barbarous" discrimination of Greeks from barbarians, how great an achievement must we consider it? Remembering the egoism upon which his theory of man is founded, we might without manifest injustice liken the unity upon which he lays stress to that disreputable "touch of nature" (as Shakespeare employed the phrase), which, while it "makes the whole world kin," does not precisely assist the moral progress of the race. But to this it could be replied that Antiphon was not seeking to create or to increase human excellence, but merely to discover the truth about man; and part of that truth, as he construed it, was that the principle of self-interest, conceived as the natural and proper driving force behind all human behavior, cuts across all racial boundaries. Taken on this level, as a tentative contribution to philosophical anthropology, we may well allow his dictum to claim its credit due. Meanwhile, we choose to remember that only by conjecture can Antiphon's breach with tradition on the question of the barbarian be first extended to embrace the slave, and then inflated into a moral condemnation of the practice of slavery.[20] And it is precisely this extension of an extension that must be assumed in order to validate Popper's title to list Antiphon among the champions of human freedom.

Popper's next exhibit, the quotation from Lycophron about the hollowness of nobility of birth, is, like the earlier quotation from Alcidamas, a fragment, a fragment within a fragment, preserved in a citation by a later anthologist from a lost work of Aristotle's *On Nobility of Birth*. Lycophron, indeed, is hardly more than a philological phantom. The fragment is clear enough in itself, being embedded in a context sufficient to leave us in no doubt as to its general meaning. Aristotle is asking whether we are to classify nobility of birth among "things valuable and worthy, or, as Lycophron wrote, an utterly empty thing. For, comparing it closely with other human goods, he [Lycophron] asserts 'unseen is its beauty, in words lie its high claim,' implying that it is preferred in view of its appearance, while in reality there is no difference between those who have noble birth and those who have it not." [21] The same anthologist has preserved for us Aristotle's answer to Lycophron, which introduces the notion that the truly well-born are those who have inherited not

---

In any event, the cynical utterances contained in the fragments of the *On Truth*, and inseparable from the meaning of the very passages which Popper has employed as proof of this Antiphon's noble universalism, remain a sandy foundation for the towering inferences he has built upon them.

[20] The interested reader can pursue Nestle through the details of his argument (*Vom Mythos zum Logos*, pp. 377–378) tending to show that Antiphon was the source of Euripides' attack on nobility of birth and on the obloquy attached to

slavery, in his lost play *Alexander*. Nestle interprets surviving fragments of this play as confirming his conviction that Antiphon had condemned slavery in some further passage, now lost, of the papyrus *ms. On Truth*. On the interpretation of Antiphon which is here followed, Nestle's hypothesis is unthinkable. Euripides could scarcely have been inspired to praise that equality among men of all ranks, which is based on moral worth alone, by the self-regarding "naturism" of an Antiphon.

[21] Aristotle's Fragments, fr. 82 (Rose).

merely "noble traits" but also "the natural capacity to engender many children like themselves." [22]

Taken by itself, Lycophron's truly admirable dictum will not appear revolutionary beyond the measure of Euripides and his very similar denial of the connection between birth and worth, presently to be discussed. It gains dynamism by its imputed relation to the only other relevant idea we are able to associate with his name. This is a version of the social-contract theory of the state, alluded to by Aristotle in the *Politics*, according to which the state is no more than a compact between citizens for guaranteeing mutual justice.[23] The combination of these two ideas — the denial of the claims of birth, and the circumscribed area assigned to the activity of the state — has yielded Popper his idealized image of Lycophron, the proponent of liberty and equality. It is apparently on this ground, plus the supposed influence of the school of Gorgias, with which Lycophron was at one time probably associated, that Popper has justified his inclusion of Lycophron among those "who developed the fundamental tenets of anti-slavery and of anti-nationalism, i.e., the creed of the universal empire of men"[24] and that he has, climactically, and with entire originality, credited Lycophron with announcing the principle that "there should be no slaves at all."[25] Let us pause here to catch breath and to observe that Lycophron, in outlining his "laissez-faire" state, has not surrendered his privilege of appealing to the authority of the state for protection of his property rights over his slaves. In fine, there is no solid reason for supposing that his theory was in any way concerned with the status of the slave.[26]

The speech of the sophist Hippias, quoted by Popper from the *Protagoras* of Plato, will be found to add nothing to the case in hand. Plato has represented Hippias as smoothing out an altercation between Socrates and Protagoras by referring to the likeness, kinship, and fellow-citizenship, by nature, of all the guests present at the house of the wealthy Callias on the occasion of the conversation reported in the dialogue. We must begin by assuming that Plato is here reflecting faithfully a well-known sentiment of Hippias. This done, we find Hippias to be the advocate of "nature," which unites like to like, and the opponent of "law" or "convention," which, in conflict with nature, forcibly imposes upon men its arbitrary commands. The only other indication of Hippias' opinions upon a related theme is Xenophon's report of a conversation between Hippias and Socrates, in which we learn of a further criticism directed by Hippias against law: it is man-made, and marked by such diversity

---

[22] *Ibid.*, fr. 85.

[23] Lycophron will be discussed further in connection with Plato's supposed misrepresentation of his political theory, on pp. 418ff. The passage in Aristotle is *Politics* 1280 b 4.

[24] Popper, p. 180.

[25] Popper, p. 614.

[26] Nestle (*Vom Mythos zum Logos*, pp. 342–344) regards Lycophron as having used the concept of natural right toward the abolition of governmental constraint and traditional class privilege; but he does not suggest that the slavery issue came under his view.

from people to people, and by such inconstancy, that it cannot be taken seriously.[27] Hippias' achievements in mathematics, his encyclopedic educational
program, his rather bizarre doctrine and practice of "self-sufficiency" — all
these are aside from our issue. Our question is: In what sense and to what
degree do Hippias' convictions about nature and convention, so far as these
are reasonably well attested, justify Popper in including him among the opponents of slavery?

It is clear that one might argue, *a priori*, from the major premise, "Social
custom is bad," and the minor premise, "Slavery is a thing of custom," to a
syllogistic conclusion condemning slavery. But it would be equally consistent
with our meager knowledge of Hippias to conjecture that by combining the
major, "Nature indicates as fellow citizens, friends, and kinsmen, only those
who are alike," and the minor, "Phrygian slaves are unlike their masters," he
may have reached the contrary conclusion. In short, we are not in a position
to state how Hippias would have developed his principles, or how he would
have evaluated slavery; there is no evidence that he discussed it at all. *A fortiori*, Popper is beyond warrant in asserting that Hippias was its factual opponent.

(4) In addition to the list of opponents of slavery explicitly claimed as
such, there are some others whom Popper has recruited by dint of repeated
inclusion of their names in loose association with the others and in juxtaposition to the discussion of slaves. Thus the Socrates of Plato's *Meno*, whom
Popper regards as the real, as opposed to the Platonic Socrates, elicits
from a young slave by appropriate questions a proof of the Pythagorean
proposition in geometry; from this Popper deduces that Socrates believed in
the rationality of slaves, making them in this essential respect the equals of

---

[27] Xenophon, *Memorabilia* IV, iv. —
Later in this same conversation the Xenophontic Socrates extracts from (the Xenophontic) Hippias the concession that certain unwritten laws, e.g., "Venerate the
gods," "Honor thy parents," cannot be the
issue of a social contract, but must emanate
from the gods themselves. If Xenophon is
assumed to be reporting faithfully an actual assent by Hippias, and if Hippias'
position as pieced together out of Plato's
and Xenophon's reports is to be made consistent, it may be argued that Hippias
must have classed these "unwritten laws"
along with the prescriptions of that "nature" which he mentions approvingly in
the *Protagoras*; and from this, and from
his rejection of force, that his conception
of "nature" was constructive and promotive
of wide human unity and mutuality; so
Nestle (*Vom Mythos zum Logos*, pp. 367–
370) has argued. But this is to overlook

Xenophon's obvious purpose in reporting
the conversation: he intends to show Socrates as undermining whatever in Hippias'
thought may have appeared dangerous to
conformity to Athenian moral and political
principles, and hence to depict Socrates as
skilfully drawing from Hippias admissions
which could then be used to refute and
convert him. The real Hippias was by no
means guaranteed to make the concessions
Xenophon reports. Nestle, by a chain of
conjecture based principally upon the language used by Hippias in the *Protagoras*
to describe law, is led to conclude, also,
that Hippias was probably one of those
whom Aristotle was later to mention (see
p. 155 and cf. n. 178, p. 209) as opposed to
slavery because it was against nature, and
based on force. It is possible that we are
here in the presence of the "evidence"
upon which Popper has tacitly built.

free men; and thus Socrates' equalitarianism and humanitarianism are demonstrated, in contrast to the narrow racialism of Plato.[28]

That Popper should choose the passage about the slave in the *Meno* as an example of the moral superiority of Socrates to his renegade pupil Plato is a further instance of the device, earlier mentioned, of making the word "Socrates" mean whatever among its possible meanings can be best employed for the discrediting of Plato; since Popper is highly systematic in his method of drawing the line, we shall have to discuss this device as he uses it in several later passages.

In the present instance, even granting that the Socrates who examines the slave is the simon-pure historical Socrates, the only relevant and valid conclusion to be drawn from the examination is that Socrates takes it for granted, in the interests of his argument, that the slave is a *bona fide* member of the human race, and hence endowed with the ability to recollect, under the necessary guidance, the eternal patterns or forms seen by the soul before birth which are the basis of rational knowledge.[29] Nothing more is claimed for him than what Plato elsewhere presupposes as the necessary "condition of (the soul's) passing into human form," [30] the ability to refer particulars to their appropriate universal ideas. Clearly, then, this incident in the *Meno* offers no support for a contrast of Socrates with Plato, to the latter's detriment.

Nor has Popper observed the following awkward consequence entailed by his view. If the *Meno* shows us the veritable Socrates, then the latter must be responsible not alone for the implied doctrine of the rationality of the slave, but also for the manner of treating him, with all its social implications. And that manner conveys no hint of a recognition of the slave as in any social or personal sense the equal of the freemen present. He is called into the dialogue by his master's brief word of command; no explanation is offered him of the purpose he is to serve; he is addressed merely as "boy" (*pai*), remains anonymous throughout, and is finally dropped from the dialogue without thanks or appreciation. In all this there is very little suggestion of the equalitarian.

And if we are to judge the opinions of the man Socrates on the basis of those ascribed to him in the earlier Platonic dialogues, then the Socrates of the *Crito* cannot be omitted. This Socrates solemnly compares his obligation to the laws of Athens with the duty of a son toward his parents, or a slave toward his master; like them, he is bound to endure harsh words or blows without possessing the right to retaliate: he must even submit to death at the laws' command, and "this is just." [31] We would not remotely suggest that Socrates in this passage condones the unjust punishment of slaves; yet what he says

---

[28] Popper, p. 127; *Meno* 82 B.
[29] *Meno* 81 A. The ideas are not here referred to as such, though they are clearly implied.
[30] *Phaedrus* 249 E.
[31] *Crito* 50 E–51 C. At *Crito* 52 C–D

Socrates also voices the usual Greek scorn of "slavish" behavior when he speaks of escaping from prison, contrary to his contractual obligation to the laws of his city, as something only the "meanest slave" would do.

implies an acceptance of the institution of slavery, and an affirmation of the slave's duty to submit. If slavery was condemned at Athens in Socrates' day as against "nature," Socrates has here apparently set himself on the side of obligations imposed by "law" or "convention."

(5) There is the supposed fact that Antisthenes, a former associate of Socrates and a teacher of rhetoric and philosophy at Athens, was a great equalitarian and exponent of the brotherhood of all men; this is often the reason for the addition of his name to the honor roll of such a group as "the great equalitarian movement which . . . did not even shrink from attacking slavery." [32] This implies, though it does not state, that Antisthenes was also an attacker of slavery. In such lists, too, appear sometimes Pericles, Protagoras, and Herodotus, again without assertion, but with implication of antislavery sympathies. [33]

An "argument" of this sort is too nebulous to permit dissection; Popper is really not arguing with his reader, but conditioning his reflexes, so that when presented with the stimulus "Antisthenes," for example, he will automatically think "opponent of slavery." Antisthenes, the "humanitarian philosopher," will claim our attention in a later section of this chapter. As for Pericles and Herodotus, it is safe to say that they would be startled and indignant at the free use Popper has made of their names in this connection.

(6) A further proof that there was a strong antislavery movement at Athens in the late fifth century which brought slavery there to "the verge of dissolution," [34] rests upon evidence supplied by Plato in his *Republic* of the very great indulgence accorded their slaves by the Athenians; on similar testimony from the "Old Oligarch," an anonymous author with strong antidemocratic leanings; and, finally, upon some statements made by Aristotle, bearing upon the disorderly behavior of Athenian slaves. [35] Be it said at once that we are here in agreement with Popper, so far as concerns the relatively humane treatment of slaves at Athens. Nevertheless, from this recognition Popper has drawn consequences from which we shall now show reasons for dissenting.

It is Popper's contention that kindness to slaves at Athens was a conse-

---

[32] Popper, pp. 94–95.
[33] *Ibid.*, pp. 95 and 180.
[34] Popper, note 18 to chapter 10, p. 586.
[35] *Ibid.*, p. 44, and note 18, p. 492. One can only conjecture how Popper would employ, in support of his contention that Athens was humane to slaves, the passage which he here cites from Aristotle's *Constitution of Athens* 59, 5, in which it is said that the "Thesmothetes" hear private suits involving merchandise and mines, or the slander of a free man by a slave. It may be pointed out that a slave was under Athenian law in some respects a piece of

property, like a cow or a dog, and that damage done by him could be assessed against his master; on the other hand, because the slave was valuable, the law protected his master against summary retaliation upon the slave's person. In case Popper is arguing that the very existence of slanderous slaves proves Athenian humanity, we may answer that it is hard to see how a slave could be prevented by any degree of inhumanity from tale-bearing, and that he might even spread slander at his master's bidding.

quence — hence a proof of the existence — of a vigorous antislavery movement there.[36] Zimmern has set the situation in what seems its true light. On his showing — he can find partial confirmation of his view in the cynical tributes of the Old Oligarch to Athenian policy — the treatment of slaves at Athens was largely dictated "by the nature of the work which the slave is called upon to do."[37] With the expansion of industry and commerce during the fifth century, the Athenians needed willing and responsible workers whom they could trust to perform, under a minimum of supervision, tasks that required in many instances intelligence and even spontaneity. Quite obviously one could not whip a slave into the state of mind requisite for decorating a vase. Nor could slaves engaged as their masters' financial agents go without legal protection from physical assault. Slaves employed in the silver mines at Laurium illustrate Zimmern's point from the other end: these unfortunates worked under onerous and unwholesome conditions, rented out in gangs to mining-concessionaires, as Xenophon tells us,[38] at so much per head per day, with the stipulation only that the concessionaires should keep the number of slaves on foot always the same. Surely here was a situation not conducive to kind treatment, and one which any genuinely humanitarian abolition movement would have been quick to exploit.

Though by any modern standards unbelievably harsh and callous to slaves,[39] Athens still offered them far more protection and consideration than other Greek cities, and was proud to have the reputation of so doing;[40] not only did the slave walk about the city in confidence, protected by his master's right to sue on his behalf anyone who injured him; there was also the possibility at Athens that an outrage done to a slave, even by his own master, might be punished, if a free citizen should bring a suit for outrage (graphê hybreôs) in the slave's behalf (a thing no slave could do himself); and by taking sanctuary in a temple, a misused slave could force his owner to sell him to another. Yet there is no indication that either of these privileges was a recent innovation in the late fifth century; one, the protection against outrage, was very old. Unfortunately, moreover, these remedies seem to have been seldom invoked,[41]

---

[36] Popper, op. cit., note 48 to chapter 8, p. 563.

[37] The Greek Commonwealth, 1924, p. 386ff.

[38] Xenophon, Ways and Means iv, 14–16. We have attempted to avoid involvement in the controversy over the degree of unwholesomeness of the mines themselves (see Pauly-Wissowa, art. "Sklaverei" by W. L. Westermann, Supplementband VI, col. 917), basing our case on the slave gang conditions and what would seem to be their inevitable consequences.

[39] Glotz. G., Ancient Greece at Work, 1926, p. 192ff.

[40] Glotz, op. cit., pp. 196–197; Glenn R. Morrow, Plato's Law of Slavery, 1939, pp. 124ff. Zimmern, op. cit., p. 136, speaks of the pride of the Athenians in their reputation for mercy and generosity in general. Cf. also our discussion, p. 164 below.

[41] It is necessary also to observe that the graphê hybreôs was much more limited in its application than a modern reader might suppose. In the first place, severe beatings and general ill-usage of slaves were certainly not considered instances of hybris. A vase painting reproduced in Glotz, Ancient Greece at Work, 1926, p. 205, shows a slave in a Greek pottery-works tied up by arms

and in any case their application was practically limited to city-dwelling slaves. Athens remained a city employing great numbers of slaves, many of them in the inhuman bondage of the mines; along with land and buildings, slaves constituted a recognized medium of investment and a staple means of production; the slave traders waxed rich. And imperial Athens, by selling conquered populations as slaves, contributed substantially to increasing the numbers of these unfortunates.

(7) Popper has so entirely overlooked these facts, and has so convinced himself of the average Athenian's moral disapprobation of slavery, that he has misread a Platonic passage, and then used it to prove again his central mis-

---

and legs to the ceiling to be flogged; at Athens, some such lifting up or "hoisting" was sufficiently customary for Aristophanes to employ the word as a jesting synonym for flogging (see *Knights* 1129 and the notes on this line and on 1362–1363, in the edition of R. A. Neil, 1901).

That *hybris* did not include forcing a slave to accept sexual relations is shown, if proof be needed, by the master's power to send his slave concubine away to a brothel (Antiphon i, 14). Ehrenberg, *The People of Aristophanes*, 1951, pp. 184–190, gives a generally balanced and fair account of the Athenian slave's liability to mistreatment without redress, from which the conclusion plainly emerges that to be accounted *hybris*, mistreatment must have had to be extreme. How, in fact, could we imagine it to be otherwise under a legal system which envisaged the torture of slave witnesses, even in cases where the slave himself was not suspected of any wrong?

In the second place, it is not to be lightly assumed that even killing by violence could necessarily be dealt with by *graphê hybreôs*. A case is reported in one of the Demosthenic orations (xlvii, 70) in which such a crime could not be punished because, as the citizen who wished to prosecute was advised by the official expounders of the law, he was not legally entitled to bring the usual private suit for homicide; Athenian law permitted only a kinsman or, in the case of a slave, a master, to bring such a suit, and this citizen was neither. The expounders of the law do not even mention the *graphê hybreôs* as a possible recourse, nor does the citizen himself refer to it, despite his insistence that he had wished to do all that could legally be done to punish the killers of his old nurse. We cannot

therefore agree with Morrow ("The Murder of Slaves in Attic Law," 1937, p. 218) that the *graphê hybreôs* was certainly applicable here; on the contrary, this case (along with others in which the *graphê hybreôs* is known to have been employed) goes far to suggest that *hybris* was not, as Morrow maintains (*op. cit.*, p. 215), "the legal genus" which included homicide and assault and, beyond this, all insults to the person, but that special aggravating circumstances, in some extended sense religious in nature, had also to be involved.

Further, we must bear in mind the implications of certain Athenian attitudes stressed by Bonner and Smith (*The Administration of Justice from Homer to Aristotle*, 1938), and not denied by Morrow ("Plato's Law of Slavery," 1939, p. 48). To the conscience of the Athenian, homicide remained primarily a matter for the family of the dead man to attend to, and though the law provided also certain indirect means which could be employed for bringing to justice a person who had committed the impiety of killing a member of his own household (cf. n. 26, p. 404), Athenians in general would continue to regard such suits in the main as "none of their business" (Bonner and Smith, *op. cit.*, vol. II, p. 214ff.). Where a slave was the victim, such unconcern would be reënforced by the generally low esteem attached to slaves (cf. *ibid.*, p. 224), and only religious scruples of unusual intensity (or perhaps, as we have said, special circumstances attending the crime) would induce an outsider to intervene.

For further discussion of the protection afforded slaves by Athenian law, see pp. 186ff. and Appendix III, pp. 589ff.

conception. In the *Republic* Plato, expressing his deep disapproval of what he considered the disorder and license of a "democratic" city such as Athens, remarks scornfully on the admiration accorded there to those who flout the elected officials, and on the too great equality with their "betters" permitted to young persons, women, foreigners, and slaves. (Popper is right enough in citing this to prove that Plato dislikes insubordination in slaves, as we shall see below.) But Plato then goes on to sum up all this license in a sentence which Popper translates as follows: [42] "And what is the cumulative effect of all this? That the citizens' hearts become so very tender that they are irritated at the mere sight of slavery and do not suffer anybody to submit to it, not even in its mildest forms." What honest and unsuspicious reader could doubt, after reading this, and assuming it to be correctly translated, that Athens came close to abolishing slavery? [43] Yet it is all a mistake; though Plato uses the word *douleia* (slavery or servitude), it bears only a figurative allusion to slavery in the usual sense. Plato is talking in this sentence about obedience to law, and to propriety in general, as he conceives propriety, not at all about the institution of slavery. What Plato says is: "And do you note that the sum total of all these items when footed up is that they render the souls of the citizens so sensitive that they chafe at the slightest suggestion of servitude and will not endure it: For you are aware that they finally pay no heed even to the laws written or unwritten, so that forsooth they may have no master anywhere over them." [44] It is servitude to law, for themselves, which Plato says the citizens reject.

In the light of the evidence presented in the last several pages, what, then, can fairly be said to remain standing in Popper's case for the existence at Athens in the late fifth century of a strong antislavery movement, all but successful in abolishing slavery there? The simplest answer is "Nothing," if words are taken in anything like their literal sense.

It is our intent to show, before we have done, that this method of treating the evidence at his command is typical of Popper, whose whole apparatus of learning and exhaustive documentation of his case against Plato are misused and vitiated by just such wilful judgment as we have shown here. As a consequence, a book which according to its preface aims "not so much to popularize the questions treated as to solve them," solves nothing, at least so far as Plato is concerned, and can serve but to popularize error, unless it can, by patient and thorough refutation, be shown for what it unhappily is: an intolerant plea for tolerance, and, as regards Plato, a monument of systematic misconception.

---

[42] Popper, p. 44.

[43] This misreading has borne fruit in the preface to Sherwood Anderson's play, *Barefoot in Athens* (cf. our n. 19, p. 24), where the unsuspecting playwright, following Popper, passes on to his own readers in turn the illusion, and declares flatly (Anderson, pp.

ix–x), as on Plato's own authority, that the Athenians — differing in this from the inhumane Plato himself — "advocate[d] the manumission of all slaves."

[44] *Rep.* 563 D–E, Shorey's translation, Loeb Library. Cf. for the same conception, *Laws* 701 B.

But leaving refutation aside, we must now assume the burden of positive assertion, and at the cost of some repetition attempt a general analysis and description of the Athenian attitude toward slavery and the slave, from the beginning of the sophistic movement down to the period of Plato's death.

(1) During the latter half of the fifth century at Athens, that "school of Hellas," a thousand questions concerning man and human society were eagerly asked and answered and asked again. Among the protagonists of this movement were those very sophists to whom we were unable, just above, to accord the kind and degree of honor which Popper has claimed for them as apostles of freedom, but to whom we can conscientiously and cheerfully accord the credit for having applied their speculative and ingenious minds to the raising of many new and fruitful problems.

Controversy has raged, however, over the seriousness of their thought. Some modern scholars[45] have seen in the activity of these men primarily the sort of deft juggling of ideas for rhetorical effect which, we remember, Chapman discovered in the Platonic dialogues. Others[46] have vigorously maintained the essential earnestness of the sophists and the clarity, audacity, and liberalism of their ideas, and have treated their rhetoric as, on the one side, a contribution to artistic tradition, and on the other, an effective accessory to their serious ends. Perhaps no single phrase could strike a fairer balance between these contending points of view than that of an ancient author, Philostratus, who in the introduction to his *Lives of the Sophists* characterized the sophistic of the fifth century as "rhetoric philosophizing." This epigrammatic utterance we take to mean that, by and large, these sophists, as Plato would have us believe in his *Gorgias*, were concerned essentially with the art of persuasion, sometimes in highly decorative forms, in which the art predominated over the substance. Some among them were completely indifferent to public, objective truth, or denied outright its existence or attainability (e.g., Protagoras and Gorgias). This position itself these sophists were obliged to defend by the use of more or less serious philosophical argument (e.g., Gorgias' subtle equivocation in his treatise *On Being*, in which he both proves and disproves the existence of objective reality). Others, again, like Hippias, would seem to have accepted the existence of a verifiable reality (for him, nature and its commands) and to have employed philosophical arguments for its justification at the expense of law and custom, though in which directions he may have carried his crusade on behalf of nature we cannot tell. Meanwhile, an Antiphon, while accepting with Hippias nature as the validating standard, interprets it as a means of justifying, for all men alike, the morally untrammeled satisfaction of individual instinct and the evasion of social obligation.

---

[45] The outstanding modern advocate of this view is Hermann Gomperz, with whom Leon Robin, *La Pensée Grecque*, is in substantial accord.

[46] Grote led the way here, in his *History of Greece*. Among recent champions of the sophists may be counted Dupréel and Nestle.

It appears from this diversity of aim and of conviction between one sophist and another, even within the group of those whom Popper claims as the friends of enlightenment, that we should be very rash in accepting Popper's picture of a unified band of liberal thinkers advancing with singleminded purpose to overwhelm the bastions of social wrong. Instead, there rises the image of the Cadmean warriors, at war with each other quite as much as with the institutions of that society that paid their fees. In the face of these considerations, then, we have need to remember that isolated sophistic utterances may neither be serious proposals, presented in recognition of and willingness to accept responsibility for their consequences, nor form part of a humane or morally acceptable whole. And sweeping conclusions, drawn from fragmentary evidence, will often collapse when it is possible, as in the case of Antiphon, to examine their frame of reference.

Among the most frequent themes of debate among the sophists and their followers, was, as we saw above, and as Popper has greatly stressed, the "nature-law" antithesis, the relation between the whole body of accepted beliefs and customary prescriptions (*nomoi*), obviously the product of human action and preference, and the working of that great independent scheme of things, lying possibly beyond man's knowledge, and certainly beyond his control, on which the name of nature (*physis*) is bestowed. This distinction invited application in many fields — to the origin and nature of language and religion, as well as to government and the whole complex of human relations within the framework of the state.

And here we know that, at some period, the discussion of the institution of slavery took its place among the others; but when this first occurred, or by whom the nature-law distinction was applied to the denunciation of slavery, except for the one definite fact of Alcidamas' declaration in (about) 366 B.C., we have no certainty. What is past doubt here — so far we may agree with Popper — is that before the time when Aristotle sat down to write the third chapter of the first book of his *Politics* (written at some date between the death of Plato in 348 and his own in 322) slavery had been condemned by some persons as morally wrong, on the ground that it was in contravention of nature, merely conventional, and the result of violence; others had raised objections against specific forms of slavery, such as the enslavement of Greeks, or of captives in war. This much Aristotle has himself been generous enough to tell us, but, alas, no more. We are left to speculate as to the identity (except for Alcidamas) of these opponents, and even in his case, we cannot be sure that he intended the application of his principle to go beyond the freeing of some circumscribed group of slaves. The limitation on all discussion of Greek thought concerning the moral status of slavery is underscored by recognition of these facts.

It is, then, uncritical to attribute to definite, named predecessors or contemporaries of Plato ideas which (so far as our evidence goes) may quite as well have belonged to men of a later generation, and which may thus have been formulated too late to have made an effective entry into Plato's mind. If our *caveat* appears austere to the point of pedantry, our defense must be that inherently trivial material, when allowed the status of historical fact, can (and has) become a means of drawing inferences that are far from trivial in their effect.

But by no means should we allow the virtue of precaution to deteriorate into an ungenerous withholding of credit due. Let us offer our tribute to the "Unknown Sophist-Abolitionist," adding our regret that the great words of Alcidamas could find no echo in Plato's thought.

Returning from this mood of mingled envy and admiration, we must next remember that it is one thing to cast out fertile suggestions and to champion splendid principles, and something else to work out a comprehensive plan of reform that takes into account the consequences of drastic changes in the fabric of society. To use a domestic parallel, it is indeed one thing to accept the practical responsibility of running a household, and another to enjoy the privileges of bachelor freedom while suggesting sweeping changes in someone else's *ménage*. We have no right to affirm that anyone among Aristotle's critics of slavery had thought through the consequences of its abolition. We have still less warrant to believe that they set about practical measures looking to its removal.

Another set of possibilities for interpreting Aristotle's report that there did exist some who argued against slavery, has been brought into view by those who have suggested that he was referring to the Cynics,[47] with whose denial of the necessity of an organized community his own beliefs stood in the sharpest contrast. From them we might expect, if from any Greek sect, coincidence of theory with at least personal practice. There is no evidence that the Cynics subjected slavery to any special criticism, beyond distant inference from the spectacular personal asceticism which they practiced, and from the accepted fact that Diogenes called himself a citizen of the world, and refused his allegiance to the traditional mores of any actual state. From his premises there could certainly be drawn (whether he himself drew it or not) a repudiation of slavery,[48] as it appears that the Stoic school, which grew out of the Cynic with some admixture from Plato and Aristotle, actually did, in their doctrine of the ideal brotherhood of man.[49] And if Diogenes himself, like the Stoics,

---

[47] Zeller, e.g., cited by Newman, *The Politics of Aristotle*, 1887, vol. I, p. 140.

[48] Perhaps the best argument that Diogenes opposed slavery, is the statement in Strabo that one Onesicritus, who had been a pupil of Diogenes, later spoke with approval of the absence of slavery among an oriental people (Strabo, 15, p. 710, cited in Newman, *op. cit.*, vol. I, p. 140). This, how- ever, shows at the most, and assuming no other influence upon Onesicritus than that of Diogenes (an unlikely assumption), what might be inferred from Diogenes' position; it does not show that Diogenes himself had inferred it.

[49] Morrow, in his note, p. 131, *Plato's Law of Slavery*, is a little too generous to the Stoic Zeno, when he quotes with ap-

repudiated slavery, it is also possible that he, like many of them, accepted it as an actual existing institution, merely denying it any moral importance. And this would be confirmed if we accept the tradition that Diogenes, in his later years, was himself enslaved: he accepted his position without protest, contenting himself with maintaining that he, as the truly wise man, was the true master: the position of de facto slave or de facto master was irrelevant to the proper business of life, the practice of virtue. The Stoic doctrine of the brotherhood of man was a seminal idea; but in the tub of Diogenes, it had — so far as we have any evidence — hardly begun to sprout.

It is needful also to recollect that the discussion of slavery, whatever its direction, could never in the ancient world have become a practical movement for the freeing of slaves in general. It is easy to imagine the swift silencing of any private person who should have ventured publicly to propose and to set about collecting fellow proponents looking to the actual freeing of all slaves. In a city like Athens, where one out of every three or four persons was a slave, where the adult slaves almost equalled in number the adult citizens,[50] considerations of public order and safety, not to mention the immediate economic self-interest of almost every citizen, would have supplied sufficient reason for putting such an advocate beyond the border.

A further prerequisite to abolition was the clear envisagement of some more just and efficient alternative to slavery, not too painful in its results, and within reach; and here it is illuminating to note that the only positive suggestions for a slaveless society (unless we may include Plato) [51] made by the Greeks near the time of Plato, are those of the Old Comedy playwrights, and, oddly enough, Aristotle. The playwright has imagined a golden age, in which food will cook itself, water for the bath will automatically say "turn off the tap," and the slippers and sponge will come of themselves.[52] The graver imagination of Aristotle limited itself to the assertion that we would not need slaves to do our work if, like the fabulous self-moving statues of Daedalus, and Homer's "tripods of Hephaestus," instruments would come when called, and shuttles were able to throw themselves through the web.[53] The wholly unintended prophecy of this last example will not escape the notice of any modern reader.

---

proval, as evidence of opposition to slavery, Zeno's declaration that "it was as great a crime to strike a slave as to strike a father." As shown by the references given by Morrow (Diogenes Laertius VII, 120; Cicero De Fin., IV, xxvii, 76), Zeno was exemplifying the Stoic paradox that any moral lapse, no matter how small, is as bad as any other, no matter how large. The choice of examples implies how small a lapse it is to strike a slave, how large to strike a father. Another comparison is between the fault of a ship's pilot in losing a cargo of straw, and

in losing a cargo of gold. The Stoic accent fell on the character of the man who struck, not on the injury to the person harmed.
[50] Zimmern, op. cit., pp. 178, 381. Cf. W. L. Westermann, "Athenaeus and the Slaves of Athens," 1940, p. 469.
[51] See pp. 167–171 below.
[52] A. W. Pickard-Cambridge, Select Fragments of the Greek Comic Poets, 1900, pp. 176–177.
[53] Politics A, 4, 125 b 33; and Newman's note, ad. loc.

There could not, indeed, as the British scholar Heitland has argued,[54] have been an abolition movement in Greece, or elsewhere, until these two conditions were satisfied: the existence of a group of persons convinced that slavery was wrong and inefficient, and their possession of some degree of power to bring about the change. On Heitland's showing, the second of these conditions was wholly absent in the ancient world; the first was only partially satisfied by the uneasy stirring of conscience over the abuses of the system, and by a recognition, on the part of a few individuals, that the institution itself was somehow not in accord with nature and the will of God. There was, accordingly, no such thing undertaken by anyone, at any time during Greek or Roman antiquity, as an abolition movement; [55] there is no need to take seriously the conclusion of any argument whose premises assume its existence.

(2) In addition to the sophists, there was, as Popper has said and as we have seen above, Euripides, who spoke with genuine moral sympathy for the undeserved obloquy which slavery entailed, and shows us in many scenes that the fate of those whom war had reduced from freedom to servitude did not leave him undisturbed. As Zimmern has well said,[56] the poet did not let

---

[54] W. E. Heitland, *Agricola*, 1921, pp. 445–448.

[55] The one possible exception to this rule known to us is the short-lived attempt in 133 B.C. of Aristonicus, a claimant to the throne of the last Attalid king of Pergamum, to establish a regime at Leucae in Asia Minor by the aid of dispossessed persons and revolting slaves whom he called "Sun-citizens" (Strabo XIV, i, 38). Tarn, in his article "Alexander the Great and the Unity of Mankind," states his belief that Aristonicus' venture was based upon the "Sun-state," a Utopia devised by a writer called Iambulus at some date after 290 B.C.; in this ideal state each citizen was to perform in turn all social functions, and wives were to be held in common. What success Aristonicus might have had is unknown, since he was promptly crushed by Rome, which claimed the Attalid domains by testamentary right. One other apparent exception reveals itself, on closer view of the evidence, to be unproven. Athenaeus states (VI, 264), on the authority of Timaeus, that the Locrians and the Phocians, in accord with their ancestral customs, had no purchased slaves until the mid-fourth century, but were served in their household affairs by their own young people. Timaeus' whole account of the Locrians, however, is severely condemned by Polybius (XII, 5–

12) as a friendly fiction. Whoever still takes Timaeus' statement as true may claim for the Locrians and Phocians fidelity to an austere ideal of eschewing luxury. But it must be remembered that the absence of purchased slaves leaves open the possibility that, even so, these peoples may have possessed serfs or bondsmen, who would be slaves in the extended sense in which we have been employing the term.

[56] Zimmern, *The Greek Commonwealth*, 1924, p. 388.

Two lines spoken by the chorus in Euripides' *Hecuba* (ll. 332–333) are cited by Edith Hamilton (*The Great Age of Greek Literature*, 1942, p. 161) in support of her view that "to Euripides belongs the glory of being the first to condemn" slavery. The lines are these (quoted as from Murray's translation, though we have been unable to verify this):

That thing of evil, by its nature evil,
Forcing submission from a man to what
No man should yield to.

But a careful reading of what Euripides wrote shows that the English version has greatly modernized the author. In calling slavery by nature an "evil" (*kakon*), Euripides does not say, "How naturally wrong it is to make slaves," but "How wretched in its very nature is the life of a slave." The phrase used in the second line, "what should

his privileged spectators forget that they themselves were not certainly exempt from this ultimate misfortune, should disaster overtake the state. But, Zimmern further reminds us, this is not to say that the dramatic exhibition of a Hecuba or an Andromache enslaved, roused Athenians into a critical and resentful attitude toward the institution of slavery; it touched, rather, the springs of sentiment, prompting the master to a more humane sympathy for the slaves whom the unpredictable reversals of man's lot had made members of his own household.

But Euripides does not limit his appeal to sentiment. He was also the great rationalist, and among the themes of argument of this most argumentative of ancient dramatists was that of the name and nature of the slave: is it just to scorn the slave simply as slave, to impute to him a lack of that human excellence which a free man can possess? In our earlier discussion, we met one Euripidean answer to this question, drawn from the *Ion*. A combing of the other eighteen plays and the hundreds of surviving fragments [57] will strengthen the conviction that in the *Ion* passage Euripides has given once and for all his own personal and deeply felt answer to the question he has raised. It comes down to his conviction that the antithetical terms "freeman" and "slave" cannot be fairly said to correspond to the antithesis "noble" and "base." In the lost *Phrixus* (Fr. 828, Nauck, 1895), we are told that there are even slaves with souls freer than the free. This same lesson clearly emerges from the debate in the arbitration scene in the *Alexander*, a play in which a supposedly common slave is on his merits judged the victor in a contest with the sons of Priam.[58] A fragment from this play (Fr. 53, Nauck, 1895) is interesting for its anticipation of later equalitarianism:

---

not be" (*ha mê chrê*) does indeed express moral disapproval, but what is being disapproved, as the context reveals, is the infliction upon the luckless captive in war of the grossest sort of wrong — in this instance, the slaying of Hecuba's daughter as a sacrificial victim — wrongs that have little or nothing to do with the institution of slavery as such. It is really war and the sufferings of prisoners of war that the poet is condemning here; the status of the slave at Athens is simply not in question.

[57] A convenient gathering of passages, including the fragments, in which Euripides treats of slavery, is A. Douglas Thomson, *Euripides and the Attic Orators*, 1898. The discussion in this section draws also on Paul Decharme, *Euripides and the Spirit of His Dramas*, 1906, and on Wilhelm Nestle, "Untersuchungen über die philosophischen Quellen des Euripides," 1902.

[58] We may note in passing that Nestle (*Vom Mythos zum Logos*, pp. 377–378) re-

gards it as probable that Euripides in this play was building on foundations supplied by Antiphon's supposed rejection of the slave-freeman antithesis, a view which I am for reasons already given (pp. 144–146) unable to accept.

The critical labors of such scholars as Snell ("Euripides Alexandros," 1937) and Scheidweiler ("Zum Alexandros des Euripides," 1948), valuable as they are as contributions toward the integration of the papyrus fragments of the *Alexander*, along with the quotations from the play surviving in later writers, into an ordered and intelligible whole, do not throw any further light upon the special topic of Euripides and slavery. They are, however, of great importance in helping us to see that the theme of the *Alexander*, which runs into that of the entire trilogy, is not primarily the sociological problem of slavery as a just or unjust institution, but rather the frequent tragic disharmony, in this wayward world,

> For when we were in ancient time first born,
> And Mother Earth sent forth her mortal sons,
> One self-same aspect she bestowed on all;
> We've nothing all our own.

in the lines that follow, the main point is driven home:

> Noble and base-born are one progeny.
> Time and convention have accomplished Pride.
> Wisdom *is* noble birth; 'tis God that gives
> A true discernment — it is never wealth.

For Euripides, character and not birth, moral understanding and not wealth, are the realities to which we should look in forming our estimate of human worth, and these, he insists, are sometimes to be found in slaves.

This same Euripides, however, also presents the case against the slave in the *Alexander,* though we may believe with less conviction; and throughout his plays he does not scruple in numerous passages to reveal the shoddier aspect of the slave, to stigmatize his weak and craven spirit (*Ion* 983), and to show the disloyal facility with which he will turn from an old master to that master's murderer (*Electra* 632). He has given us a revealing picture of a Greek freeman's reaction to affront, and incidentally the ordinary Greek outlook upon slaves in the quarrel scene in the *Alcestis* (675–678). Here Pheres, provoked by the unreasonable and insulting words of his son Admetus, blazes at him: "And do you imagine, boy, that you are loading this heap of abuse upon the head of some Lydian or Phrygian purchased slave? Are you not aware that I am a Thessalian, and the son of a Thessalian, a free man, genuinely free?" It would not be difficult to infer from this speech what Euripides regarded as the language in which a free man might be expected, not improperly, to express his mind to an offending slave. More revealing is the fact that the great humanitarian has made comic capital, in one extended scene (*Orestes* 1510–1526), of the dastard and cringing mendacity of the appropriately anonymous Phrygian slave before Orestes, representative of the masterly Greek race.

Thus Euripides reveals what is truly significant to our inquiry, namely: that when the mood of imaginative sympathy is not upon him, he shares with his audience precisely that contempt for the slave nature which we shall presently find Plato expressing when his moral sympathies are not awake, to the scandalized indignation of his modern critics.

(3) In turning from Euripides to the comic playwright, Aristophanes,

---

between merit and rewards, and the bewildering reversal of roles by which a proud, slave-scorning Queen Hecuba passes beneath the spear of the Greek conquerors as herself captive and slave (Snell, *op. cit.,* esp. p. 66 *ad fin.*). The trilogy, presented just after the Athenian capture and depopulation of Melos (cf. p. 320 below), is often viewed as a warning to imperial Athens of the inevitable moral consequences of the abuse of power, and of the instability of that power itself.

we must be on our guard lest we place too naive a reliance upon what may turn out to have been only a piece of Rabelaisian foolery. But with the proper caution, we are at liberty to use to our purpose even the broader scenes of comedy, just as the contemporary student of racial prejudice can employ as data the folklore of "comics" and vaudeville skits. Slaves are not prominent in most of the Aristophanic comedies; when they do claim a greater share of attention, it is only to achieve the bad eminence of obscenity, greed, cowardice, and intrigue. Their humanity is fully recognized, but only at the complete cost, after all allowance for comic license has been made, of their human dignity. They are, in spite of all, invincibly likable in their genial, pot-companionable way; the implication would seem to be that they are so far below the level of potential competitors for equality and social recognition, that everyone, including Aristophanes and their masters, the spectators, can enjoy the fun, with no infringement of their social dignity. They grumble and complain, hunger and thirst right mightily, yield to animal impulse at a moment's notice; their wagging tongues are stopped only by fear of a beating, and then are more interrupted than subdued. Witness the slave Xanthias in the *Frogs*, revealing his comically exaggerated joy in spiting his master, something, he says, that "drives him crazy with joy," and the slave Cario in the *Plutus*, who taunts his old mistress with her fondness for wine.

We may touch lightly here upon the New Comedy of Menander and Philemon. It dates from a generation following the death of Plato, but resumes and amplifies those more serious vindications of the humanity of the slave which we found first expressed by Euripides. Two frequently cited passages of Philemon, whose plays survive only in fragments, declare that no man is born a slave, but chance has enslaved his body; and that a slave is still a man, and human.[59] The plays of Menander, whose literary remains are more abundant, give us something much more substantial with which to work. In these plays there is no longer any portrayal of the heroic age; we are not asked to weep for Hecuba, once queen, now slave; we are rather in the atmosphere of every-day life of Greece in the late fourth and following century, and the slaves in question are all but direct transcriptions from the social milieu, though the plots themselves depend upon improbable coincidences, mistaken identities, and rediscoveries of long-lost, exposed infants. There is recurrent recognition of the slave as a fellow traveler with his free master along the uncertain and unhappy road of human life. We are impressed by the substantial roles Menander has assigned to slaves of both sexes. Thus the flute-girl Habrotonon, in the *Shorn Lady*, inspired by a mixture of genuine benevolence with a wholly defensible self-interest looking to her own freedom, contrives and carries through to a successful issue an

---

[59] Philemon, frags. 95 and 22 in Kock's *Com. Att. Fragm.*

ingenious device for discovering the parents of an exposed infant; in the *Hero* Menander has given us something truly surprising, almost Rousseauistic, the image of a noble slave, Daos, who to shield the reputation of the girl he loves, takes upon himself the responsibility for her misfortune, yet loses his prospective happiness as she marries her violator.

But in the society depicted in Menander's plays the slaves' own Utopia has not yet been reached. We must remember that the quarries are still in operation and that large estates are being worked by slave gangs, whose members are social miles below the slaves whom Menander puts upon the stage. And even these favored few are shown still in fear of irresponsible and unjust corporal punishment; we see also the helpless situation of the female slave in her sexual relations. On the other side, it is notable that slaves almost control their masters' destinies by their involvement in their masters' love-affairs. Indeed, there is little to choose, in education, manners, or ideal of life, between slave and master.[60] The slave has risen substantially above the old level, but his near equality has not been achieved without the downward leveling of the freeman.

(4) Besides those who, like Euripides, felt the pathos of the slave, there were those who raised emphatic voices to protest (as we shall see Plato do) against the enslavement of Greeks by their fellow Greeks. Among these the names of Callicratidas, the Spartan admiral, and of the two Theban generals Pelopidas and Epaminondas, have been preserved,[61] and these men seem also to have gone some little way toward carrying out the prescription.

(5) There were the laws of Athens, giving the slave more protection from abuse than did the laws of other Greek states, laws of which the Athenians were justly proud; [62] there were the working conditions which encouraged humane treatment; there was the recognition, on the part of many masters of slaves, of the advantages of holding out to them the hope of freedom as the reward of loyal service; and there was the growing acceptance into the general body of resident aliens at Athens of those who had been slaves.

(6) In order to measure Plato by what came immediately after his lifetime, as well as before and during it, it may be well to give some account of Plato's most distinguished pupil. Aristotle advanced the hopeful idea that slavery could be limited, at least in a reformed society, to those who were "natural slaves," i.e., those who were incapable of independent rational existence, and hence would be benefited by being in tutelage to a wise master.[63] His double error lay in his supposition that such beings exist in large numbers (but chiefly among the barbarians), and that wise masters, again

---

[60] Gilbert Norwood, *Greek Comedy*, 1931, p. 351n., quoting Wilamowitz.

[61] Cf. W. L. Newman, *The Politics of Aristotle*, vol. I, p. 142.

[62] Cf. Euripides, *Hecuba* 291; and see our discussion of the same subject just above, pp. 151–152.

[63] For an exposition and critique of Aristotle's conception of the "slave by nature," see Newman's *Politics*, I, p. 146ff.

in a well ordered society, would be available. But his defense of slavery, so restricted, as "natural," was based upon these suppositions, not upon failure to recognize the injustice of slavery where slaves were fully rational beings. Aristotle's prescription, if carried out even in rough approximation, would have resulted in an enormous amelioration of the institution. But it remained in the universe of philosophic discourse, except in so far as it was misused by men of later generations, who appealed to the great name of Aristotle in support of their anachronistic views.

(7) On the other side of the ledger, there is evidence that by no means were all Athenians ready to recognize the moral right of slaves to considera- tion on their own account. It can be maintained with probability that, in any age, granted reasonable freedom of expression, an excellent mirror of public opinion at an average level of society is to be found in the speeches of its successful courtroom orators; for here, by the very nature of the case, a deliberate effort is afoot to gain a favorable judgment through appealing to precisely those beliefs and prejudices which the skilled pleader knows to be present in the minds of the majority of his hearers. If, then, we would know how representative Athenian jurymen felt about the rights and the character- istics of slaves, we may find the matter made startlingly clear in the fortunately well-preserved speeches of the Greek orators who span the period that runs (roughly) from the death of Socrates, in 399 B.C., to the years shortly after the death of Plato in 348.

Following the order of time, we begin with Lysias, an especially signifi- cant and credible witness in view of his outspoken championship of the cause of Athenian democracy. Lysias had lost a brother to the greedy violence of the Thirty Tyrants; in his speech written to be delivered [64] against the freed- man Agoratus, their guilty tool, he expresses with vehemence the general hatred of their criminal regime. The crimes of Agoratus have been enumer- ated; the high character and virtue of his victims have been asserted. And now, to drive home his point, the base character of Agoratus must be dis- played. Lysias proceeds to his business in these words: "And who, then, is he? You must know that he is a slave born and bred, so that you may know what manner of man it was that grossly maltreated you." The contemptuous appellation "a slave born and bred" is a phrase of which the orator is here making use for the second time.[65]

As the decades passed, Athenian prejudice against slaves did not subside. Aeschines, whom Demosthenes has immortalized by abusing him, has some- thing much in point to tell us in his *Plea against Timarchus*. The law which permits suit to be brought against those who have outraged the person of either boy or girl, man or woman, whether free or slave (the *graphê hybreôs*),

---

[64] The courtroom speeches of the Attic orators were written to be delivered by the plaintiffs or defendants in person.

[65] Lysias, *Against Agoratus* 64 and 18; translated by Lamb, Loeb Library.

has just been read before the court, and Aeschines thinks it necessary to explain to his fellow Athenian democrats why a sensible lawgiver should have bothered to speak of slaves in this connection. He says:

Perhaps someone might wonder, at first hearing, why this word "slave" is included in the law dealing with outrage. But if you will ponder the matter, men of Athens, you will discover that this is the crowning feature of the law. For the framer of this law was not seriously concerned about the welfare of slaves; it was out of a desire to accustom you to abstain absolutely from the violation of the bodies of free persons that he enacted the provision that not even slaves should be so abused. In short, it was his conviction that in a democratic state whoever commits an outrage upon anyone whatever — such a man is not fit to be a fellow citizen. (*Against Timarchus* 16.)

One need not seek for a clearer reflection of the Athenian denial of the slave's importance as a person than we find in this view which a shrewd analyst of public opinion confidently submitted as acceptable to his representative Athenian listeners.

An interesting passage in Demosthenes appears at first blush to express an attitude identical with that of Aeschines. The *graphê hybreôs*, he urges, is a wise institution, even when pushed to the "extreme limit," i.e., when invoked in behalf of a slave. For "the legislator thought he ought to look not at the rank of the sufferer, but at the nature of the act." [66] This is almost so much pure Aeschines; for the absence of Aeschines' overt scorn of the slave is all but balanced by the implication of the phrase "extreme limit" (*tosautei hyperballei*). But now a surprising thing happens: without transition, Demosthenes turns from callous disregard of the slave's welfare to a bold characterization of this law as unprecedented evidence of admirable humanity to slaves. After calling for a reading of the law, he congratulates the men of Athens upon its humaneness (*philanthrôpia*) and in a swelling passage avers that, were the barbarian nations, the natural enemies of the Hellenes from whom the Hellenes procure their slaves, to hear of a law so merciful, they would invite the Athenians to act as their protectors. How is this shift in attitude to be explained? We must consider what was expectable in a forensic pleader addressing himself both to the vanity and to the prejudices of Athenian jurors. Thus Demosthenes indulged his hearers in a double treat: he exhibited to them the merciful morality of their legal generosity to the slave, and he showed them how the law could be interpreted without any diminution in the immense superiority over the slave which the Athenian free citizen must under all circumstances maintain.

In the passage just considered, the topic of the slave figured only indirectly; it was precipitated, one might say, out of a law in which the slave had been incidentally included. Fortunately, there occur elsewhere in the Demosthenic corpus two speeches which bring the social standing of the slave to the focal point of the discussion. In the one we are shown the scornful

---

[66] Demosthenes XXI, 46.

attitude deemed appropriate to the ordinary "run of the mill" slave, while the other pays a substantial tribute to the merit and respectability of a member of the small class of extraordinary slaves whose abilities and public services had earned them their freedom and even their full citizenship.

Pasio, the outstanding Athenian banker, had risen thus from the status of barbarian slave to that of citizen, and, dying, had chosen Phormio, one of his own freed slaves, a man of extraordinary ability, who had himself attained the citizenship, to be his business successor, appointing him in his will the guardian of his family and estate, and directing, as was customary in such cases, that he marry his widow. A bitter dispute arose over the disposition of the estate, and Pasio's elder son, Apollodorus, brought repeated legal action against Phormio. Demosthenes writes a very effective speech in favor of Phormio, which makes evident the very considerable respect which one who had acquired citizenship and wealth through display of the commercial virtues could command, regardless of his origin. Apollodorus is reminded by the speaker that Pasio, his father, "did not acquire his fortune, any more than did Phormio, by good luck . . . but gave proof to the bankers . . . who were his masters, that he was a good man and an honest, and so won their confidence." [67] Demosthenes goes on to assert that Pasio would have been fortunate if he could have imparted these virtues to his son, Apollodorus.

This plea is countered in a later speech, possibly also from the hand of Demosthenes, in any case delivered by Pasio's son, Apollodorus. A touch of high comedy is provided here by the circumstance that Apollodorus, in his vicious denial of Phormio's right to the social prerogatives of a citizen (he feels it particularly an affront that Phormio has married his mother), is himself in closely similar case, as the son of an ex-slave. For all that, he will not let the jurors forget that Phormio was born a barbarian, and was purchased in the Athenian market. His climactic plea to the men of the jury is this:

I will tell you . . . how I think you will all best come to know the enormity of the wrongs that have been done me. You must each of you consider what slave he left at home, and then imagine that you have suffered from him the same treatment that I have suffered from Phormio. Do not take into consideration that they are severally Syrus or Manes or what not, while this fellow is Phormio. The thing is the same — they are slaves, and he was a slave; you are masters, and I was master. Believe, then, that it is fitting now for me to exact the penalty which each one of you would claim; and . . . punish the man who has robbed me of a verdict.[68]

In conclusion, we may note that there is no real contradiction between the two passages. There is only the difference to be expected between the standing attainable by the rare exception, and an angry and overly emphatic statement of the rule — the scorn which the master had purchased the right to feel for his animated instrument, his slave.

---

[67] Demosthenes *Oration* XXXVI, 43; translation by Murray, Loeb Library.

[68] [Demosthenes] XLV, 86–87, translation Taylor, Loeb Library.

The just concluded review of the Athenian outlook on the slave is designed to serve as an inventory of the helps and hindrances, so far as we can collect them from the records, which met the mind of Plato as his own thinking on this topic matured, and to provide a species of rough base-line against which to measure his achievements and his deficiencies or failures. The Athenian attitude toward slaves at the start of the period in question, covering roughly the century from 450 B.C. to Plato's death, rested basically on three presuppositions. The permanence, necessity, and entire propriety of slavery were taken for granted; the privileges of citizens, jealously guarded even against free foreigners, could not without pious horror be thought of as open to slaves, except in the most extraordinary instances, and even then with grudging reservations; slaves were thought to be — again, except for the exceptions — naturally endowed with cowardice, duplicity, greed, laziness, insolence, and the rest of the catalogue of slavish vices. Affecting the level determined by these attitudes, as the years passed, we find a rise in popular feeling and in the practical treatment of slaves, caused by changing conditions of industry and trade, and reënforced by the suasions of a dramatic poet like Euripides. War conditions no doubt generated, from time to time, a greater solidarity between the citizens and the city-dwelling slaves. There was the eloquent fact that, at the time of Arginusae, slaves had helped to man the ships which won Athens that last victory in the Peloponnesian war, and had helped also in the restoration of the democracy after the tyranny of the Thirty. But making in the opposite direction was the steady downward tug of the increasing preponderance of barbarian slaves, particularly those from despised areas such as Phrygia.

At some time during this period, and extending perhaps beyond its close, occurred those discussions concerning the general justifiability of slavery which we found reported with tormenting anonymity and vagueness as to date in Aristotle's *Politics*; we cannot cite chapter and verse of any specific preachment against slavery as an unjust institution before the definite, if perhaps limited denunciation of Alcidamas, when Plato had already passed his sixtieth year.

The end of the period found the three basic suppositions in the Athenian view of the slave unchallenged by the mass of Athenian citizens. For a very few of the educated, we may believe, acceptance of the institution was qualified by an uneasy doubt as to its rightfulness, while another few believed that a slave, though remaining a slave, was still unimpaired in moral or intellectual stature. A large number of reflective persons were concerned to limit the incidence and mitigate the evils of slavery. But even for these few (provided they were concerned at all for the maintenance of civil society), the conviction remained that in some form slavery was both a necessary and a permanent institution.

Let us now consider the picture of slavery that Plato has himself given, piecing it together from various passages of the dialogues, remembering that our primary purpose is to use his picture of slavery to help us get our picture of him.

We were already making a start toward our goal, when we noted, with regret, a certain lack of humanity in the attitude of the Platonic Socrates toward the slave in the *Meno*. Read in the light of other passages in which Plato discusses the proper treatment of slaves, the *Meno* incident seems to be most reasonably interpreted as a very fair expression of Plato's own attitude: his standing conviction that a slave is not to be harmed, either in word or deed; neither is he to be spoiled by undue familiarity and indulgence. The Socrates of the dialogue is entitled to his remark, after the first round of questioning: "We have not harmed him. . . . We have advanced him on the road to self-knowledge." If the slave had been permitted to speak, one might venture the guess that he would have been willing to forego this advancement in exchange for a little human kindness, or for a joke, perhaps even at his own expense. But that is precisely what Plato would not, on principle, bestow. The word principle, in this connection, is important because, as we shall presently show, we should not do justice to Plato if we presuppose the right to explain his behavior by calling it prejudice. We may feel the important difference between the sort of unintended and incidental benefit conferred on the slave and the active benevolence which would have been displayed had a youthful Charmides or Lysis been playing the same role. For all that, if we remember the base-line of Athenian sentiment, all that we can fairly charge against Plato is that he has failed to rise as high above it as we might have expected from a man of his moral intelligence.

But what of slavery under the ideal auspices of Plato's *Republic?* Here, if anywhere, one might suppose, we shall be able to take Plato's full measure as critic of existing practice and as charter of new ways.

First of all, it is necessary to ask, "Does Plato contemplate slavery in his ideal state?" On its face, it appears strange that we should need to ask this question; but the fact remains that it has been variously answered, and the discussion has apparently not yet reached an end. Thus, in his recent *Plato's Theory of Man*,[69] Wild asserts his belief that there is no slavery in the *Republic*. Plato's ideal state "is a 'classless society' supported not by slaves but by workers possessed of legal rights and protected by governmental authority." The few references to slavery that occur in the course of Plato's discussion, Wild treats as casual, illustrating a point by reference to individuals and situations in an ordinary Greek state.[70] He is arguing against Morrow,[71] a leading authority on Greek slavery and Plato's political thought,

---

[69] John Wild, *Plato's Theory of Man*, 1946, p. 107.
[70] In this respect, I am heartily in agreement with Wild, despite the contrary view expressed in passing by Newman, *The Politics of Aristotle*, vol. I, p. 143.
[71] Glenn Morrow, *Plato's Law of Slavery*, 1939–1940, pp. 130–131.

who speaks for the view which may be fairly called the majority opinion. We need not pretend to offer a definitive decision in this dispute. We may draw some conclusions, however, from the curious and significant fact that such a dispute should be possible. For it would appear, in the circumstances, that credit may accrue to Plato whether he has omitted slavery from his ideal commonwealth, or has not. In the first event, all criticism of Plato, the philosophical slave driver, is obviously absurd; he is instead to be crowned as the great abolitionist. Alternatively, he has so minimized its function, so assimilated the service of the slaves to the common life of mutual service of all the inhabitants of his city, that it requires the microscopic eye of the specialist to determine its very existence. A rapid glance at the relevant parts of the *Republic* will provide the support necessary to sustain this rather bold assertion.

It will be remembered that Plato's ideal state is presented as an end product of an imagined social development. We start from a hypothetical minimal community, thought of as arising out of the insufficiency of the individual to supply his own needs, and consisting of a few workers, each devoting himself solely to the practice of his specialty, such as a farmer, a house builder, and a weaver, exchanging their commodities and services to their mutual advantage. This minimal community is allowed to grow into the unspoiled agricultural stage by the addition of further specialized workers, such as cowherds, some few importers and exporters, shopkeepers, and lastly common laborers, those persons whose lack of mental ability leaves them only their physical strength to contribute to the commonwealth; in exchange for this they are to receive wages and the status of citizens.[72]

From this first unspoiled city develops "the inflamed city," the city with a fever, in which the multiplication of desires brings into being the luxury

---

[72] Popper, p. 48, translates this "nasty remark," as he calls it (*Republic* 371 D–E), "Are there not drudges who possess not a spark of intelligence and are unworthy to be admitted into the community, but who have strong bodies for hard labor?" The word which he here translates as "drudge" is *"diakonos,"* which is revealed by a survey of the word and its cognates as used by Plato to have as its basic meaning service, subordination, and the performance of tasks at another's bidding, as contrasted with activities which are authoritative or independent. Thus Plato contrasts the work of a clerk or administrator with that of a ruler, and of a cook with that of a physician. Often used of slaves, *diakonos* can also be used of merchants, who are thought of as paid agents of their customers, and of children who act as apprentices and helpers of their fathers (*Rep.* 466 E–467 A). It is used on one occasion (*Laws* 782 B) of the hero Triptolemus, who has been the "servant" of men in providing them with the culture of grains. The present passage, then, if translated without rancor, reads as follows: "Are there not other servants or helpers" (or "agents") "who in intelligence are wholly unworthy" (or "not wholly worthy") "of our fellowship, but who . . .?" The reader is asked to note that the faults of Popper's translation, while slight in themselves, are in the direction of putting Plato in a worse light; and that, as is also typical, he attempts to clinch this effect by the description he applies to the passage: "nasty remark."

trades and war as an instrument of acquisition and defense of wealth.[73] In this second city it is apparent that slavery plays a part, though Plato does not speak of slaves as such, and the same word (*diakonos*) which was used for the merchants, shopkeepers, and laborers of the unspoiled city, is again employed to designate the children's nurses and cooks of the luxurious city.

We have thus far had no hint of social reform of any sort, only descriptive analysis, and what might be called "poligenetics." What we are now to see, in the foundation of Plato's ideal state, is an attempt to bring the inflamed city into a condition of health by removing the causes of its disorder, so far as possible, and by establishing that proper mode of functioning which later is to be identified with Justice, the harmonious, healthy interaction of all the constituent parts. Since Plato believes that the key to this cure is the provision of ideal rulers, he will give no more account of the necessary workers, whom we must assume to continue their functions in supplying the basic needs of the whole city. But the case is different with the cooks and serving maids, and the luxury trades generally; these, it is reasonable to believe, will tend to disappear or reach a minimum, with the disappearance of extreme wealth and the growing simplicity of living established and enforced by the rule of the philosopher kings.[74] With the disavowal of an expansionist foreign policy — population is to be deliberately kept small [75] — soldiers will be required for defense only. The work of the city appears to be provided for in terms of the activity of those free citizens, previously mentioned, among whom are included, at the humblest level, the common laborers. Where, then, is slavery, or the need for slavery?

Here the detractor may have ready a reply along several lines. He may urge that the rough and dirty work, presupposed for the full-time operation of Plato's state, is largely carried on behind the scenes by slaves, of whom Plato does not even speak, so much are they taken for granted. And such may be the case, for all that can be demonstrated to the contrary. It gains part of its plausibility from the admitted fact, made evident in our discussion of the *Meno*, that it was not Plato's habit to put slaves very near the center of his picture. There is, secondly, the argument from silence: would not Plato have "hired a herald," if we may employ his own expression in the *Republic*, to announce to mankind the momentous emancipation? We do not wish to undervalue this argument, which appears to possess substantial weight. It is not Plato's way to allow points of importance to pass unmarked.

A third type of argument seeks to show the existence of slavery in the Republic on the ground that slaves are mentioned in several passages in

---

[73] The minimal and the unspoiled cities, *Rep.* 369 B–372 C; the inflamed city, 372 C–374 D.

[74] *Rep.* 399 E, 404 C–405 A. The philoso-

pher kings are, of course, first described only later, in Book VI.

[75] *Rep.* 460 A, and for the ill effects of the growth of population, 373 D.

Plato's book. It seems fair to say that none of these passages possesses full probative force. Those adduced by other commentators prove, on examination, to refer to slavery as a generic Greek institution and make no reference to the specific state of affairs contemplated in the ideal city.[76] There is, it is true, one passage, not mentioned by other commentators to our knowledge, in which slaves are briefly included among the social ingredients of the Platonic city. Plato, praising the principle which he proposes to denominate

---

[76] Morrow (*Plato's Law of Slavery*, 1939, pp. 130, 132), arguing that the presence of slaves is "taken for granted" in the *Republic*, also cites three references to slaves (*Rep.* 495, 563 B, and 549), two of which we shall discuss on pp. 176–177. These show, Morrow feels, such agreement in "tone and temper" with Plato's general attitude towards slavery in the *Laws*, as to exclude any principled opposition to the institution on the part of the author of the *Republic*. The passages themselves seem to us to show only the traces of the common Greek attitude of superiority to slaves, with which, as we have said, as with the similar Athenian superciliousness toward women, Plato was to some extent infected. To Morrow's conclusion, however, that Plato in the *Republic* shows no opposition to slavery as such, we may consent, reserving the right to add the qualification presently to be expressed in the text, that despite his acceptance of slavery as necessary in an ordinary Greek city, concern for the moral welfare and unity of the whole community may have influenced Plato to plan an ideal city in which slavery would sink to insignificance.

Popper, however (pp. 48–49), has rashly employed one of the three passages cited by Morrow (*Rep.* 549) as the basis of what he considers a simple and conclusive proof that there are indeed slaves in the ideal state, as follows: Plato, after describing the "timocratic state," which arises from the deterioration of the ideal state, has occasion to describe also the "timocratic man," the typical leading citizen of such a state, and says of him (I quote Popper's own translation), " 'He will be inclined to treat slaves cruelly, for he does not despise them as much as a well-educated man would.' " Popper comments, "But since only in the best city can education be found which is superior to that of timocracy, we are bound to conclude that there are slaves in Plato's

best city, and that they are not treated with cruelty, but are properly despised. In his righteous contempt for them, Plato does not elaborate the point." Now Popper is misleading here not so much because of translation unfavorable to Plato, though this element is present, to some slight degree, in the word "despise" thus overemphasized by Popper's subsequent remarks. Nor does he mislead principally because of his ungenerous interpretation of Plato's motives, though this is present in high degree. He is wrong here because of neglect of context, and hence of Plato's meaning — another not infrequent cause of Popper's errors. (See his misuse of the passage from Antiphon, mentioned on our p. 144f. his misinterpretation of Socrates' arguments against Callicles, p. 416, and the forced meaning he ascribes to a passage from the *Laws*, p. 624f., as other instances of his neglect of context.) A reading of the entire description of the timocratic man, *Republic* 549 D–550 D (and similarly of the passage concerning the oligarchic man, etc., which follow), will show that Plato, in the passage quoted by Popper, is in process of shifting his frame of reference, and is no longer describing the timocratic man solely as he would arise in the ideal state, at the beginning of its degradation. He is describing him also as he would arise in an ordinary Greek city, "badly governed," as Plato says; he arises in such a state as the son of a noble father who holds aloof from the public life of the city, absorbed in his own mind and keeping himself to his own affairs. It is a man such as this father who "despises" or "thinks down from above" (*kataphronein*) on slaves, and hence is never rough with them, as his son, the timocratic man, is apt to be. Since this father exists in an ordinary Greek state, and is, in Plato's terms, undoubtedly a "well-educated" man, Popper's proof that slaves must exist in the ideal state is invalid.

"justice," asks whether anything can contribute more to the excellence of the city than "the principle embodied in child, woman, slave, free, artisan, ruler and ruled, that each performed his one task as one man" (433 D, trans. Shorey, Loeb Library). What can one make of this? It is possible, that Plato in this passage has for the moment forgotten his reference to the ideal city, as he can be shown to have forgotten on one other occasion in the *Republic*; [77] if this is the case, his list is simply a standard enumeration of all the possible conditions of man, a carry-over from language applicable to any ordinary Greek city. On the other hand, it is possible that Plato has here revealed his presupposition that slaves will have a place, however slight, in his ideal community.

Nevertheless, it remains true that Plato's city, more than most Greek cities of the time, could have been operated without slaves. Zimmern believes that until the time of Athens' commercial expansion, even at Athens the slaves constituted but a small part of the population, and that most of the work was done by the citizens.[78] And the citizens of Plato's state were mostly workers, debarred from participation in government — something to which the Athenian citizens necessarily devoted much time; they were therefore free to devote themselves wholly, as Plato believed right, each man to his own work. Plato makes no mention of slaves, then, because the logic of his scheme has robbed them of meaning and function. Whoever wishes to speak of Plato's Republic as a "slave society" must be prepared to face the paradox that nowhere in its construction is there any need of slaves; they would come dangerously near to being a leisure class! Plato has reserved the work for his citizens, who must be saved from the idleness, profligacy, and flitting about from one occupation to another, which Plato believed he had seen, and had disliked, at Athens.[79] The presence of slaves in any numbers would have endangered his ideal of a simple, hardy, and wholesome community in which each man does his own work. On this understanding, then, and with this limitation, we wish to be included among those who do not believe there are slaves in Plato's Republic.

It may be added, if we may extend our hypothetical reasoning one stage further, that by omitting slavery as a functional part of his ideal state, Plato was not, in our judgment, advocating the immediate abolition of slavery in the world, or in the Greek world. The author of the *Republic* liked to think

---

[77] *Rep.* 425 A; at 460 A, also, Plato forgets that he has restricted himself to laying down regulations affecting the guardians, and speaks as if he were dealing with the whole city.

[78] Zimmern, *op. cit.*, pp. 394–395. In these days also, the public affairs of the city required far less of the citizens' time than later to be the case. To those who believe

that Plato is modelling his city on Sparta it should be said that Sparta apparently was operated without slaves other than Helots; so perhaps was Locris (cf. n. 55, p. 158). In Plato's city the Helots or serfs are replaced by citizens, and no further change is functionally required.

[79] *Republic* 561 C–D.

of his city as possible and offers it by implication as a model which other cities might approach in excellence; but he had no expectation of reforming into ideality the whole Greek world of "inflamed cities." [80] Nor was he, in the analogous case of war, an internationalist, or a crusading Isocratean Panhellenist; [81] his little community, ruled by her philosopher kings, was to carry on the pursuit of virtue behind the wall of an eternal preparedness for defensive war, much as he has pictured for us the virtuous man, living retired from public affairs in an ordinary Greek state of Plato's day. He had some hope that the Greeks, under the influence of their common reverence for the Delphic Apollo, might come to refrain from the worst atrocities toward one another, as we shall see in a moment; but perpetual conflict, or the threat of it, between Greek states, and between Greeks and barbarians, was taken for granted, as was the eternal enslavement or death of barbarian captives and, within the Greek cities themselves, of at least the noncitizen destitute and criminal. To hope for better things would have meant either total impracticality or the conception of vast mechanisms of social machinery which our modern world has, indeed, conceived, but has not yet brought into full operation.

But before leaving the discussion of Plato's attitude, as expressed in the *Republic*, toward the institution of slavery, properly so-called, it will be our congenial task to call attention to an eloquent passage (*Republic* 469 B–471 C) in which Plato expresses his vigorous opposition to the enslavement of Greeks by Greeks; Greek cities, says the Platonic Socrates, bearing in mind the danger of enslavement by the barbarians, should not enslave one another. The citizens of his ideal city will not own Greek slaves, and will urge other Greek cities, also, to refrain. This Glaucon, replying to Socrates' question, approves, adding that it will encourage the Greeks to keep their hands off their fellows, and to make war on the barbarians instead. Socrates, a few sentences later, asserts that any struggle between Greeks is to be regarded as a social sickness, a civil strife between fellow citizens; only against barbarians, the natural enemies of the Greeks, ought we to speak of waging war. The people of our state will be philhellenes, lovers of their own kind. They will not fight with Greeks as if they were enemies, but as men expecting later

---

[80] The author of the seventh Platonic *Letter* (cf. p. 369) speaks with conviction of the light that would spread to all quarters of the world from one state governed in accord with true standards of morality and obedience to law. But Plato did not in general allow himself to hope that more than a small portion of mankind could attain high moral excellence; cf. our discussion of this attitude in both Socrates and Plato, p. 258.

[81] Isocrates (436–338 B.C.), among other not always mutually consistent ideals, cherished the hope of a union of Greece against Persia, under the leadership of some new "Agamemnon," who, after his heroic campaign was completed, was apparently expected conveniently to wither away and permit the little Greek cities to resume their normal way of life. Plato's prescriptions of behavior proper to Hellenes in their relations with their fellow Hellenes in general are discussed on p. 229, and the ideal of a defensive alliance of autonomous Greek cities in Sicily, entertained by the author of the Seventh *Letter*, pp. 384–385 below.

to be reconciled; they will refrain from burning and laying waste.[82] Popper recognizes the existence of this passage, saying, "I agree that Plato in the *Republic* (469 B–C) opposed the enslavement of Greek prisoners of war; but he encouraged that of barbarians by Greeks, and especially by the citizens of his best city." [83] We in turn agree that Plato implies no objection in the actual state of international affairs in his day to the enslavement of barbarian prisoners of war (whether he "encouraged" it is not so certain; Glaucon must not always be taken as Plato's mouthpiece; his own temperament colors more than one of his remarks). But surely Popper, the accuser of Plato as inhumane, ought, in fairness, to have scored one count in Plato's favor here. It is our opinion that Plato is here advocating a reform which might have had some chance of practical effect [84] (which was not, like the discussion of the unnaturalness of slavery, doomed to remain merely theoretical), and for which he deserves, as a man, high credit; we can still wish that Plato had gone further and, admitting that war with the barbarians was inevitable in his day, had at least expressed regret at this unfortunate division in the wider kinship of mankind.

But whether or not there are slaves, in the full literal meaning of that word, in the Republic, there remains another possible line of attack. The detractor, trying to convict Plato of inhumanity, may also, like Popper, and with or without the latter's imputation of violent methods and vicious motivation, charge that Plato has reduced all but the minority of the citizens of his misnamed commonwealth to a virtual state of slavery; [85] for, the argu-

---

[82] Plato is here adding his voice to the plea for Panhellenic unity against the barbarians made by Gorgias, in his Olympic Oration of 408 B.C. (see our mention of this, p. 298 below), and perhaps also to that of Lysias, who championed similar ideas either in 388 or 384 B.C.; Isocrates' manifesto calling for a crusade against Persia was to be given to the world in 380. In expressing his concurrence, however, Plato lays stress on the refusal to enslave Greeks, either as cities or as individuals, rather than on the common enmity to barbarians.

[83] Popper, note 29 to chapter 4, p. 495. On p. 150, also, Popper refers to this same passage, but here he may be said to have distorted it to the point of disguising it completely, alluding to it only as an "attack . . . launched immediately before" the passage he is discussing (*Rep.* 473 C–E), against "the equalitarian creed" of Alcidamas, Lycophron, and Antisthenes, "by correlating the natural inequality of Greeks and Barbarians to that of masters and

slaves." Could anyone have recognized beneath this disguise Plato's plea for mercifulness in warfare with fellow Greeks?

[84] See *Cambridge Ancient History*, vol. VI, p. 443, where reference is made to a law passed in Athens at the instance of a former pupil of Plato forbidding any Athenian "to purchase as a slave any free man taken in war," a law which "may have influenced those cities which in the next century bound themselves not to enslave each other's nationals." This interpretation of Lycurgus' law has, however, been questioned. Some see in it a more limited aim; cf. Westermann, Pauly-Wissowa, col. 927.

[85] Popper, p. 48, has even confused temporarily the sharp distinction which Plato clearly draws between common citizens and slaves (see *Republic* 547 C–D, discussed on pp. 175–176 below). Engaged in discussing whether there are slaves in the Republic, Popper notes Plato's statement (*Rep.* 463 A–B) that the common citizens of the ideal city are not to be *called* "slaves" (Italics

ment runs, he has deprived them of all voice in government, subjecting them to the necessity, backed by a monopoly of the armed power of the state, of obeying absolute rulers.

That, in some sense, this charge is true, Plato himself would admit, nay, has himself asserted. We are all, high and low, ruler and ruled, rightly the slaves of God. The man in whose soul the principle of right reason is naturally too weak to maintain its proper control over the bestial element in his nature, must become for the benefit of all, himself not least, the "slave" of the nobler man, who has within him, as his ruling principle, servitude to the divine order; because it is better that all things should be ruled by divine wisdom so that all in the city shall be as like as is humanly possible, and friends one to another, under the same governing rule (*Republic* 590 C–D). It is, of course, easy to adopt a cynic attitude in the face of this noble protestation and, with Popper and Fite, to see in it only a rationalizing evasion of the issue. But that Plato is not improvising bad theology to cover worse social ethics is confirmed by any comprehensive survey of his thought. Here it will be sufficient to point out that the sincerity of Plato's ideal of "servitude to the divine" (he uses the ordinary Greek word for "slavery," *douleia*) is confirmed most substantially by the weight of Plato's later writings. In the *Timaeus*, as Vlastos [86] has well shown, the whole realm of matter is viewed as so to say the slave of divine intelligence, which finds its very *raison d'être* in accepting the directive persuasion of its master, God; in the *Laws*, as Morrow notes,[87] "Plato is never weary of preaching 'slavery to the laws' . . . as the saving principle of all political order." Earlier, in the *Phaedo*, the Platonic Socrates declares that men are "to be listed among God's chattels," [88] an expression of unqualified subordination, unsurpassed even in the *Laws*.

If Plato is thus willing to describe his citizens as the "slaves" of their rulers, then Popper's charge that Plato has regarded them as the rulers' "human cattle" [89] may not be so damaging as Popper would like us to think it; for this figure of speech, like that of "slaves," can be shown to have two faces: the same referent may be viewed as "cattle" and as "flock." Popper imports

---

Popper's) by the rulers, as is the practice in other Greek cities, but "Supporters" and "Employers." But this, Popper says, is done only for "propagandist reasons." He thus manages to imply that these workers are in fact slaves, deceptively and cynically called by another name. That Popper does not, however, intend to maintain directly that all the common citizens *are* slaves, is shown by the necessity he still feels of demonstrating that slaves exist in the Republic.

[86] Gregory Vlastos, "Slavery in Plato's Thought," *Philosophical Review*, 1941, p. 294ff.

[87] Glenn Morrow, "Plato and Greek Slavery," *Mind*, 1939, p. 188.

[88] *Phaedo* 62 B. The matrix of this mode of thinking is visible as early as the *Apology* 23 B, in the Socratic "service to the God." It is true that the word used, *latreia*, suggests in this context free and voluntary attendance. But even in the *Laws*, citizens are to be "the *willing* slaves" of the laws. Willing slavery to the laws would not be unlike the Socratic *latreia*.

[89] A phrase used to describe the common citizens of the *Republic* by Toynbee, also; see our discussion, p. 20. For Popper's use, see, e.g., pp. 52, 55.

the former term and exploits its implications. But if we change the phrase to "human flock," the sting of the accusation is drawn, and Plato's meaning becomes clear. The object of the good ruler *qua* ruler, as of the shepherd or herdsman, is the good of the ruled; and Plato's rulers, be it remembered, are to have no admixture of private motives and interests beyond the modest provision of their own livelihood; they are to be disinterested and self-controlled to an almost superhuman degree.

Further indications that Plato's ordinary citizens were not to be condemned to a servile condition, in any literal sense of the word, are the following points, upon which Plato has laid stress:

There are to be no idle rich in the Republic, any more than idle poor. Plato in language that anticipates Disraeli's famous "two cities," denounces extremes of wealth and of poverty as bringing idleness and inefficiency and as making of the city not one, but two at least, at enmity with each other, the city of the rich and the city of the poor (422 E). Every man and woman will work and work hard, rulers, soldiers, and all; hence it is irresponsible to suggest, as does Fite, that Plato has provided a country-club existence, with polo ponies thrown in, for his privileged few, idleness purchased at the price of the grinding toil of the many; or to speak always, as Popper does, of the "prerogatives" and "privileges" of the ruling class, never of their obligations.[90] The guardians are to be particularly interdicted from wealth; if there are to be degrees of affluence among the citizen body, it will be some of the citizens of the third, nongoverning class, and not the rulers, who will enjoy the privilege of moderate wealth; for economic power is not to be the determiner of distinction or the measure of blessedness in this commonwealth.

A further bulwark against servility is to be the belief, shared by all the citizens, that they are blood-brothers, though possessed of different talents and destined to different stations; and, to implement this belief, there is to be the practice of rearing, as rulers or as ordinary citizens, all children, regardless of parentage, who are seen to be fit for either station. That this is true to Plato's intention, in any case, we shall hope to establish in later chapters;[91] it is mentioned here, so that the reader may provisionally list it as evidence of Plato's honest intent to benefit the common citizens, as he conceived benefit for them. As a final indication of Plato's benevolent and scrupulous attitude here, we must remind the reader that the first downward step in the deterioration of the perfect state, following immediately upon the corruption in the characters of the rulers, is the reduction of the common citi-

---

[90] Popper, e.g., pp. 50, 73, 90. The way of life assigned to the guardians of the second rank, the soldiers, is seen by Plato in one aspect as an arduous and ennobling form of leisure; in another, it is a set of activities required for maintaining their fitness for their social task, essentially those of a professional army kept continuously in training. Cf. pp. 544 and 546.

[91] See pp. 424ff. and 535ff.

zens from a free estate to slavery.[92] They had been free men, friends of the rulers, whose modest material support they supplied in return for the benefits of government received; they are now sunk to the condition of *perioeci*,[93] and serfs or slaves. Surely Plato could not have told us more plainly that, in his city, no member of the class of the governed was to be exploited or contemned.

We come now to the consideration of those passages in the *Republic* which the detractors will not willingly let die, i.e., those in which Plato speaks slightingly or even with stern contempt of slaves, and thus is held to be chargeable with inhumanity, even quite aside from the imputed odium of having sponsored slavery, open or disguised, in his ideal state. Plato has given a lively picture, alluded to above,[94] of the excessive freedom of the unstable and anarchic denizens of the "democratic" state, in the course of which he writes, "The extreme limit of license, my friend, arises in a state of this kind when purchased slaves, male and female, are no less free than their purchasers." And, as a crowning touch, we are presently told, with playful gusto, that the very horses and asses will jostle you off the street unless you yield the right of way (563 B–563 C). Let us contribute the just-quoted passage to help fill the modest inventory of Plato's social sins. We are to remember that his sin was not the egregious betrayal of an acknowledged ideal, and not the perverse innovation of a moral saboteur. It was in part the deposit in a noble soul of a prevalent miasma of his moral climate, in part the reverse of the medallion of an essentially religious reverence for order and submission to what he, like Socrates before him, genuinely felt as properly constituted authority.

It is rather piquant to discover a close parallel [95] to this Platonic "doulophobia" in, of all writers, Euripides. In an eminently serious speech by Ion, that thoughtful spokesman of the playwright's own opinions, Euripides has stigmatized the Athenian streets and the insolent rabble that swarms them. Ion will not go to Athens; he will stay in the decency and leisure of his quiet small town, where "no base fellow pushes me off the road, a thing insufferable, to yield and make way for one's inferiors" (*Ion* 635–637). The word "slave" does not appear, but population statistics for Athens would indicate that among the jostlers there would be no lack of slaves. We have, then, the warrant of Euripides to prove that Plato's picture of Athenian traffic was not simply the peevish dream of a disconcerted aristocrat.[96]

---

[92] *Rep.* 547 C–D.

[93] This term, as employed at Sparta, designated noncitizen inhabitants, occupying an intermediate position between citizens and Helots. In Crete, however, it was applied to agricultural serfs like the Helots (Aristotle, *Politics* II, ch. X).

[94] See p. 153.

[95] Pointed out in Shorey's note on 563 C.

[96] Glotz (*Ancient Greece at Work*, p. 197) seems to have interpreted Plato here, as Popper does, in the light of the similar but far more testy passage in the work of the Old Oligarch, who regrets that Athenian

Another instance of Platonic *hauteur* in the *Republic* is found in the lively parable of the upstart would-be philosopher who rushes in to fill a place left empty by his betters, who have deserted philosophy for more worldly pursuits. Plato has drawn him in caricature in the likeness of "a little bald-headed tinker who has made money and just been freed from bonds and had a bath and is wearing a new garment and has got himself up like a bridegroom and is about to marry his master's daughter who has fallen into poverty and abandonment"; the children of such a union (i.e., the philosophical ideas of the upstart philosopher), says Plato, will be inevitably "bastard and base." [97] We need not ask who, if, indeed, anyone, is the personal target of Plato's abuse.[98] As Morrow has pointed out, Plato is here incidentally expressing scorn of those overly ambitious slaves who somehow manage to work their way to freedom and then aspire to become the equals of freemen [99] — a feeling which we saw exemplified in the speech of Apollodorus against Phormio.[100] It will be noticed that Plato's attitude is here incidentally revealed. The more convincing evidence, then, of the sincerity of the feeling, says the detractor; to which the friend of Plato may perhaps reply: the more convincing evidence of Plato's moral achievement when, directly confronting the difficult problem of the slave, he rises in some degree above those prejudices which, in Morrow's language, were "deeply rooted in Greek consciousness and in Greek practice." [101]

Turning now from the consideration of slavery in Plato's *Republic*, we must discover what will be his disposition of the problem in the *Laws*, wherein the discussion is confined to what Plato regarded as practically workable within the limits of Greek time and space.

It is not easy to appraise what Plato has to say of slavery in the *Laws* and this for many reasons: Plato is avowedly drafting a "second best state," one that must come to terms with the actualities of his day: internal disharmony and social injustice, external insecurity darkened by the shadow of the sur-

---

slaves may not be struck by free foot-passengers. Glotz is not an admirer of Plato, yet it may be pointed out that he yields no support to Popper's view of the Athenians as active abolitionists; see his pp. 192–219.

[97] *Republic* 495 E–496 A, Shorey's translation, Loeb Library.

[98] Popper, in a passage we shall discuss below (p. 205), disregards the phrase "just . . . freed from bonds," and cannot use this passage to prove Plato's inhuman attitude toward slaves or ex-slaves, because he is using it to prove Plato's equally ignoble hostility to Antisthenes, who was a half-citizen, not an ex-slave. It is Morrow who makes the application to slaves. He, how-

ever, takes the "bald-headed tinker" as of more serious importance for Platonic eugenics, than I am able to do; for the tinker's setting is simply any ordinary Greek city, with citizens not especially selected for eugenic excellence; and the remark about the baseness of his offspring is no more than the utilization of a common prejudice to make a point in disfavor of philosophical views which Plato, believing his own views to be alone true, regarded as unsound.

[99] Morrow, *Plato's Law of Slavery*, pp. 46, 94 and n., 110 and n.

[100] See p. 165.

[101] Morrow, *op. cit.*, p. 110.

rounding barbarian world. His reforms are thus restricted to the limited area of the practicable, and must be judged with this in mind. Further, he has so intimately mingled innovations of his own with traditional Greek legal and social institutions, Attic, Spartan, and other, that to isolate his own contributions, or even to understand the full significance of the proposals made, we must appeal to the specialist in Greek legal history, and even he is frequently embarrassed by an insufficiency of evidence from which to draw more than a conjectural conclusion. And finally, there is the fact that the *Laws* itself alone among Plato's unquestioned works was left in some degree unfinished and contains some ambiguities and omissions which we can well suppose a final redaction would have cleared.

The most extended passage in the *Laws*, or, for that matter, in the whole of Plato, devoted to a continuous discussion of the problem of slavery (*Laws* 776 B–778 A), will serve as the basis of our discussion here; to it we shall attach the substance of the many slighter, often incidental results of his reflection on the matter that are scattered up and down the twelve books of this, the longest of the Platonic dialogues. As always, the Athenian Stranger is to be understood as speaking directly for Plato. What he tells us is this (we paraphrase) :

The slave is a species of possession, altogether the most difficult and problematic thing a man can own. The cause of the difficulty lies in the first instance (we shall later hear of a more basic cause) in the only partial agreement between what is commonly said, i.e., the current beliefs and practices, and our experience with the slave. The controversy over the various forms of serfdom, especially Helotry, which some approve and some condemn, is widespread and bitterly contested throughout Greece. We should all agree that it is necessary to own slaves as docile and as virtuous as possible, but opinion as to their nature and treatment is divided between two schools of thought. Slaves have often proved themselves "superior in every form of virtue" to the brothers and sons of their masters, and have preserved their masters and their masters' whole household; [102] such things are said by those of the first school. (It is stated presently, by implication, that those who say this of slaves repose confidence in them and deal with them mercifully, eschewing the degrading violence of the lash.)

The opposing school of thought utterly mistrusts the soul of a slave, believing that there is no health in him; and appealing to our wisest poet, say that "Zeus takes half of a man's mind away on the day of his enslavement." To them the slave is a wild animal to be controlled with the goad and the

---

[102] It should be a sobering reflection to those who engage in the facile construction of large humanitarian movements from fragments of lost writings, to imagine how loud a chorus of admiration for its "noble humanitarianism" would have resounded in Popper's halls, had this single half-sentence of Plato had the luck to be quoted by a scholiast as from some anonymous thinker of the late fifth century, or deciphered from the charred papyrus fragment of an Antiphon or an Antisthenes.

lash; in consequence, the souls of their slaves become many times over as slavish as before. But those who think otherwise, act in the opposite way.

What, then, are we to do about owning and controlling slaves in our new state? In his reply, the Athenian touches those deeper springs of the difficulty to which reference was just now made. He assumes without argument that slaves there are to be, in accord with the "necessary distinction," as he calls it, "between slave and freeborn master." It is in respect to this distinction that the primal difficulty arises, springing from the nature of man generically, that "intractable creature," and not merely from the nature of that "difficult chattel," the slave.

Leaving the two schools, the Athenian now strikes boldly out for himself. The frequent slave uprisings, as in Spartan-dominated Messenia, and particularly where slaves employ a common language, point up the problem of forestalling revolt. Two remedies suggest themselves: we must see to it that our slaves are of diverse stock, so that diversity of speech will make insurrection less likely; and we must supply them with a just and proper regimen,

and that not only for their sakes, but still more for the sake of ourselves. Proper treatment of servants consists in using no violence towards them [hybris is Plato's word], and in hurting them even less, if possible, than our own equals. For it is his way of dealing with men whom it is easy for him to wrong that shows most clearly whether a man is genuine or hypocritical in his reverence for justice and hatred of injustice. He, therefore, that in dealing with slaves proves himself, in his character and action, undefiled by what is unholy or unjust will best be able to sow a crop of goodness, — and this we may say, and justly say, of every master, or king, and of everyone who possesses any kind of absolute power over a person weaker than himself. We ought to punish slaves justly, and not to make them conceited by merely admonishing them as we would free men. An address to a servant should be mostly a simple command: there should be no jesting with servants, either male or female, for by a course of excessively foolish indulgence in their treatment of their slaves, masters often make life harder both for themselves, as rulers, and for their slaves, as subject to rule.[103]

With the passage now before us, we may proceed to our comments.

We may first ask what was Plato's reason for accepting the dichotomy between "slave" and "freeborn master" as a "necessary distinction"; some explanation seems required of the apparently facile establishment of the city of the Laws upon a basis of slave labor. There is ambiguity here, arising from the precise meaning of Plato's word "necessary." Some, finding in it a hint of the "necessity" that one deplores, would interpret the passage as evidence of Plato's philosophic hostility to slavery. Others find in the word an implicit indication of Plato's wholehearted approval, reasoning that, in calling it "necessary," Plato has incorporated it into his basic political theory. It is possible, however, to maintain a position intermediate between these two views, if we remember that in the entire program of the Laws, Plato is making concessions to the "necessity" of the imperfect sociological background of his citizens (Laws 740 A). They will never consent, he tells us, to hold all

---

[103] 777 D–778 A, trans. Bury, Loeb Library.

possessions in common. Nor will the more prosperous consent to a flat equality in the holding of offices with their economic inferiors (*Laws* 744 B–C). *A fortiori*, then, Plato was barred from rising to heights of ideality from which the distinction between slave and free could have appeared as no longer necessary. Thus on balance, Plato would seem to be the convinced upholder of slavery, but only in consequence of his intention to design for this, his second-best state, a constitution with good hope of realization.

Of particular interest is his criticism of the Spartan practice. This criticism, in view of the presence of the Spartan Megillus (it will be remembered that Megillus, the Athenian Stranger, and the Cretan, Clinias, are the persons of the dialogue), was fated to be politely made; it is so to the point of indirection. But this should not blind us to the importance of the contrast between the Spartan arrangements and those of the new colony. Plato's citizens are to be freed, if Plato's precautions against insurrection are effective, from a continual preoccupation and a brutalizing dread, to which Spartans were so unfortunately bound, and which dominated life in their city. The slaves in turn are to be freed from the corresponding oppression and degradation. This twofold criticism of Sparta illustrates Plato's own dual attitude toward slavery, his moral idealism, on the one side, and, on the other, his hard-headed, rather unsympathetic practicality. Let us consider these in turn.

We may fairly credit to Plato for righteousness three important recognitions, clearly conveyed in the just summarized passage. The first is that the slave, albeit a chattel, is a person capable of moral excellence. The Athenian has all but signed his name to the view of those who believe that many slaves have been conspicuously better "in every form of virtue" than free members of their households. A careful reading of the passage will show the necessity of the qualifying "all but"; for the conclusion of the sentence, carrying the actual assertion, is put in the form of an appeal to the fact that "such things are said" about slaves; yet his emphatic rejection of the school of thought of those who distrust and hence terrorize their slaves implies his far greater sympathy for the favorable view of the slave's potentialities. One might suggest that some unhappy practical considerations intervened between the premise and the far-reaching conclusions that might so easily have been drawn. Yet we have seen the direction in which Plato's moral instinct was pointing him; alas that he was unable to pursue the journey to its end. This incipient recognition is confirmed and amplified by those remaining to be listed.

Plato is to be honored, secondly, for his recognition that the attempt to secure the proper behavior of slaves through sheer physical coercion and animal training, without recognizing the human nature of the slave and the demands of justice, is self-defeating. In deploring violence as a means of "schooling" the slave into a rude animal obedience, Plato has taken a further step (perhaps logically and psychologically prior to his recognition that the slave is capable of virtue) away from the denial of the slave's essential moral oneness with the free. It is especially gratifying that he here recognizes and deplores the paradox inherent in the notion that some men are so very bad that they must be beaten into being very much worse. (In a later passage, *Laws* 793 E, he similarly and in more explicit terms bans the infliction on slaves of punishments that will enrage the recipient.) Not that Plato has disavowed corporal punishment, still less the corporal punishment of slaves; in point of fact, he has taken over from traditional Attic law, and with added emphasis, the principle that the offenses of slaves, in contrast to those of free men, are to be commonly visited upon the slave's body. What we are applauding here is his departure from the Spartan practice of generalized terrorization and of mistreatment divorced from and disproportionate to misdeeds on the slave's part, and above all, Plato's demand for meticulous justice (at least on his own schedule), in the infliction of punishments.

Third, Plato has recognized that a master's relation to his slave, like that of a political superior to those over whom he holds power, entails the obligation to practice the most scrupulous justice; and this not only for the slave's sake, but even more for the sake of his own soul's justice. In this declaration we are offered the most emphatic and deeply felt expression that he has left us of his conscience manifesting its condemnation of the misuse of power, his concern for the victims of social injustice, and his belief in the moral oneness of slave and free.

But though the passage has by no means been overlooked by the friends of Plato, one of the most thoughtful and technically qualified among their number, Professor Morrow, has found what he thinks good reason for equating Plato's position here with the attitude of the orator Aeschines, in the passage we have quoted above.[104] Since Plato's position is morally superior to that of Aeschines, it will be worth our while to examine the passage with particular care.

Morrow calls attention to that part of Plato's statement in which he says that the right treatment of slaves is "not only for the sake of the slaves, but more for our own sakes." From this, and from the inadvertent addition of the words "so much" to his paraphrase of Aeschines' statement that it is not to protect the slaves that the Athenian law was aimed (so that Morrow gives it as "not so much"),[105] Morrow draws his conclusion that the ideas expressed are identical.[106] But to this there are two objections.

The meaning of the Platonic phrase "for our own sakes" is ambiguous at first sight, suggesting an "either-or" relation between "our" interests and those of the slaves. Nothing, however, could be less Platonic. The true good

---

[104] Above, p. 164.
[105] Glenn Morrow, *Plato's Law of Slavery*, 1939–1940, p. 39. In the ensuing discussion, Morrow will be our most valued guide, though we shall not be able to follow him in some particulars, later to be specified.
[106] Same, p. 41.

of the slave, on Platonic principles, is inseparable from that of the master, and both are inseparable from the true good of the community, itself the instrument of the supreme Good, of which God himself is the measure. "Our interests," then, are in becoming better men, not merely in forestalling revolt; as, in the *Gorgias*, the receiving of injustice is a lesser evil than the doing of it to another. A recognition of moral value is not absent from the Aeschines passage; but in the Platonic passage considered, the idea of virtue receives the major stress.

The other reason against Morrow's view is that Aeschines, as we saw, treats the offense against the slave as of no importance in itself; the aim of the law, he says, is solely to prevent the formation in the citizens of evil characters. Plato, on the other hand, is clearly concerned, though to a lesser extent than for the masters' characters, with the effects of just and unjust actions upon the slave, in whose mind the seeds of virtue are to be planted by his master's example; whereas unjust actions, as we learned in a preceding section, degrade the slave, making him many times more slavish. This is again an assertion that slaves are capable of virtue (of some sort, at any rate), and shows plainly that Plato considered the virtue of the slave important in itself.

There remains the unwelcome task of inquiring: How grave are Plato's shortcomings here? Our first complaint is at the harsh consequences which seem implicit in Plato's refusal to permit community of race and language among his slaves. This prohibition suggests to a modern mind the sort of happenings which opponents of slavery in our own country particularly deplored, the disruption of family ties by the forcible separation of the members; for manifestly, the mere continuance in family association for the period of one or two generations, would automatically produce a degree of unity among the slaves in excess of what the Platonic principle would tolerate. Had Plato thought through his principle and foreseen these results? As we shall see in a moment, it is quite plain that he had not, and yet it would be sentimental to suppose that he would have allowed such a consideration to stand between him and the realization of his cherished goal of the good community. After all, Plato's proposal was no innovation; the Athenian slaves of the fourth century were, in fact, mainly barbarians of mixed origin, subject to resale at their masters' convenience; nor was it expected that slaves should enjoy family life, except in rare instances, or rear children. That a good society should so basically disregard the interests of a large part of its population is one of those contradictions which admittedly appear in so many parts of Plato's (or any other) slave-based society. But, as we shall have occasion to repeat, the contradictions emerge, for the most part, from an existing situation which Plato confronted; they were not of his invention.

Plato's provision that slaves be of mixed origin entails, in fact, a basic inconsistency in Plato's treatment of slavery. For, as Morrow has pointed out,[107] if slaves were mere bought outsiders, not bred in the household, and if they were continually shifted from owner to owner, it would seem impossible that there should exist that sense of fellow membership, shared by master and slave alike, in the household and in the religious community, on which Plato is largely depending for the slave's education in virtue, and (as we shall presently argue) for his protection from abuse. Throughout the *Laws*, Plato continually enjoins that the slaves shall share the moral and religious views of the citizens, even to the extent of helping to keep their masters in the path of virtue (e.g., 665 C, 838 D, 808 A). We have here a clear indication of oversight on Plato's part. Whether he would have modified his requirement of diversity of origins and languages for the slaves, had this difficulty been apparent to him, cannot be said; but it appears probable that he would have taken the risk of home-bred slaves, so great is his regard for virtue; yet again, not so much for the sake of the slaves' virtue, as for that of the citizens.

Nor is it pleasant to hear Plato, the grand admonitor of the citizens, disclaiming admonition in favor of punishments and curt imperatives for slaves. True, this disclaimer may reasonably be taken to mean only that the "slave in use," if one may so speak, must be directed and not advised, a meaning which would be compatible with the master's devoting attention at other periods to his moral instruction.[108] But at best this education would not be on a parity with that offered to the citizen himself. Just as the bodies of free men are kept in health by the application of rational rules, prescribed by a physician who has made his patients his genuine partners in research, while the bodies of slaves are cured by a fellow-slave who perfunctorily prescribes the remedies which crude experience recommends, so to free men only are addressed the rational persuasions of the *Laws*, justifying those rules by

---

[107] Morrow, *Plato's Law of Slavery*, p. 129.

[108] Morrow (*Plato's Law of Slavery*, pp. 43–45) has developed the idea that Plato does intend the master to admonish the slave in the sense of giving moral instruction; it is only that admonition is not to be mere rebuke and warning, used in place of punishment. In support of this, Morrow adduces six or seven passages in the *Laws* which he believes document the assertions that the slave child is to be "educated along with free children up to the age of six years at least," that slaves are to take part in the choric festivals, and that they are to be indoctrinated in virtue. — We are able to follow Morrow's guidance here only with reservations. His inclusion of slave children unfortunately seems to rest upon a statement (794 A–B) about the education of "all little children" from three to six, which may mean only free children — it is impossible to be sure —, plus a backward reference, at a later stage of education, to a prior grouping together of slave and free (817 E); but as there intervenes a discussion of the training of both slave and free in choric dances and representations, even this does not prove that slave children were among the three-to-six-year-olds mentioned. The training in choric performances, to be sure, is intended also for slaves; but its value as moral education is much diminished by the fact that for them is reserved the enactment of roles unseemly for citizens. — But we are in full accord with Morrow that some degree of moral instruction imparted to the slave is presupposed in Plato's state, in which the virtue of each is presumed to be in great part a multiple reflection of the moral excellence of all.

which they are to guide their lives. In the matter of law, the slave will, it is true, be somewhat better served than in medicine; for he will have before him the enlightened example of his master's conduct, and probably, as we have seen, his instruction also. But he will not participate in the rationality of his master's commands; he can rise no higher, on Plato's plan, than loyal conformity to a principle stated and understood by someone else.

This implication of the slave's inferiority will recall that figurative passage in the *Republic* in which the rule of the better man over the worse is justified: a man who lacks that higher component of virtue which is of the reason, it is said, should rightly be the "slave" of the man who possesses it.[109] And here in the *Laws* this lack is assumed, without proof, to be characteristic of the actual slaves. The citizens of the *Laws*, to be sure, are with rather more reason presumed to be capable of moral wisdom than either the common citizens of the *Republic* or their own slaves; for they are no ordinary body of Greeks, composed of persons of mixed abilities. They have been carefully selected from among the applicants as being "sound" and "well-bred" and "good," possessing bodies and souls which nature and nurture have combined to make excellent. Except for the members of the Nocturnal Synod, who correspond roughly to the philosopher rulers of the *Republic*, they do not, it is true, rise to philosophy. Yet, as we have just noted, they are not without rational insight. Probably, if we may extend without expectation of exact correspondence the categories of "gold" and "silver" natures of the *Republic*, we should so classify these citizens, while their slaves must correspond to the lower levels of the common citizens in the *Republic*, possibly possessing "iron" natures.

It is unfortunate that Plato, who had, in the *Republic*, shown his awareness that slaves might owe their status to no more rational principle than that of conquest, who, even in this very passage in the *Laws*, has not denied that some slaves are nobler than some freeborn men, should here impoverish his discussion by speaking as if the term "slave" denoted always a class of persons possessing the common characteristics entitling them to be thought of as a natural group, and, further, by ascribing to them as a group the qualities of their least worthy members. The reader of the *Republic* will agree that, even if Plato had recognized here the possibility of the appearance of gifted natures among the slaves, he would have anticipated only their infrequent occurrence; still, we may regret that he left it to Aristotle to draw the distinction, implicit in his own incompletely unified thought, between the "natural slave" and the man who should justly be free. For, in that event, Plato might well have felt an obligation, as he did in the *Republic*, to devise some means of doing justice to such "silver" or "golden" natures.

The modern reader, to whom the mention of the doctrine of the "natural slave" will perhaps recall its use by the American champions of slavery in

---

[109] *Republic* 590 C–D; mentioned above, p. 174.

the old South, is not likely to feel that Plato would have been taking a forward step, had he proclaimed it. And yet a forward step it would have been, as measured by the practice of his time, if he had done so, and had then proceeded to devise means for carrying it into effect; particularly so since Plato was attempting to frame a constitution for a realizable city, not, like his earlier self in the *Republic*, advancing proposals which might be dismissed as merely ideal. We may amuse ourselves by imagining how Plato might have introduced his proposal for the emancipation. The Athenian Stranger is imagined as speaking: "And, Clinias, must we not exert our care here to avoid a great and baleful unholiness?" Clinias: "I do not entirely understand." (He seldom does, and where justice to slaves is concerned, would be more than usually obtuse.) Athenian Stranger: "I am thinking of the impiety of those who subordinate the better to the baser, inverting that right order of things which alone is worthy to be called divine. And that would be the consequence, were we, by careless haste or gross ignorance, to assign to men of our city their natural superiors or their equals, as their slaves." Such an argument, naturally, would have failed to satisfy a radical opponent of slavery, if such there was in Plato's day. The point is that we can be quite sure that it would have satisfied Plato, both intellectually and morally. To be a slave, even to a truly virtuous master, would be in Plato's view, a misfortune, certainly, as compared with the lot of even the meanest citizen in his Republic; but outside of Utopia it would be not without its advantages for one incapable of full self-mastery. And to those who were neither fellow citizens nor kinsmen, no more was felt as due.

Was it, perhaps, because they were to be barbarians, that he did not provide for, because he could not admit its possibility, the emergence of the highest human types? As we shall see later, there is no evidence, except the fact that Aristotle expressed this view, for any opinion on Plato's part, that barbarians as such were incapable of intellectual virtue, and there is much evidence to the contrary, particularly in the *Laws*. There is on the other side, evidence, in the *Republic*, that Plato held the highest moral capability to be extremely rare, among the Greeks; and he based his refusal to approve the enslavement of fellow Greeks not upon their mental and moral capacities, but upon the pieties of kinship. Plato's views upon slavery are not based upon any neat dichotomy of mankind into Greeks and barbarians, but rather upon this notion of kinship, combined with his moral classification of mankind into those capable, in varying degrees, of self-direction in virtue; it is this that we may urge as his excuse, and this that we must regret as inadequate.

Plato's ban on all forms of playfulness in a master's relation to his slaves will strike most genial Americans as among his frostiest blunders. The friendly smile, the little joke, are such familiar lubricants of our social machinery, that it is difficult for us to imagine that the wheels would go round without them. Yet it would never be possible to attach an equalizing smile to a privileged countenance without at least incongruity of effect. It is worth remembering that so thoroughgoing a social realist as George Bernard Shaw [110] would interdict, as futile and mutually embarrassing, all attempts within the framework of our current capitalist society to overcome class barriers by inviting one's cook to sit down at the family dinner table. And though we may well reject the framework of Plato's proposed society, we must not in justice fail to see that there was a considerable realism in his proscription of playing fast and loose with the structure. There is an element of positive practical kindness in the reason offered: such familiarity will make slavery more difficult on both sides. There is involved perhaps the moral repugnance which Plato would feel for the shared impropriety and ribaldry which such jesting could easily invite, regret for the liberties which it would seem to encourage and the resulting punishments, all of which consequences of jesting with slaves the Greek comedies abundantly attest. In the *Frogs* of Aristophanes, the slave Xanthias offers to entertain his master Dionysus by retailing to him the usual jokes at which the spectators in the theater always laugh. But Plato's design required a choice between slaves and their jokes, and chose slaves.

We must consider now the gravest charge against Plato's attitude toward slavery in the *Laws*, supported as it is by Morrow's able and painstaking researches, namely that Plato's actual law of slavery, as distinguished from his merely ethical prescriptions, falls at almost every point where comparison is possible measurably below the level of liberality and humaneness that characterized the contemporary legal code of Athens, and often below some other ancient codes of comparable date and place.[111] The first of Plato's departures from Attic precedent was his common prescription of heavier punishments for slaves; his worst was his proposal that slaves guilty of such offenses as wounding a freeman be punished not in a manner determined by the discretion of a court, but by being delivered to the injured person who might inflict such punishment as he would (879 A). Grimly analogous is the treatment indicated for the slave who has killed his master: he is to be turned over to his master's family to do with as they please, with the sole proviso that he be put to death (868 B). Merciful, in comparison to the provision just described, is the law that children resulting from unions between free and slave shall either rate as slaves, or, with the slave parent, be sent out of the land; and that freedmen whom their ex-master deems remiss in their duties to him may be directly by him reclaimed, precisely like runaway slaves. There is no mention, in Plato's existing text, of those legal actions against persons guilty of outrage to slaves which, as we have seen, were possible at Athens (by means of the *graphê*

---

[110] *Intelligent Woman's Guide to Socialism and Capitalism*, New York, 1928, p. 95.
[111] Morrow has conveniently condensed his monograph, *Plato's Law of Slavery*, in his article, "Plato and Greek Slavery," 1939; the above is taken from pp. 194–198.

hybreôs), or of any right of asylum and sale to another master. And the penalties proposed for the killing of a slave in some cases seem to fall below the Attic standard, and again appear simply to be left unspecified, a silence open to possible disturbing interpretations. When Plato's law does specifically grant the slave greater legal rights than the law of Athens, it is in connection with the slave's right to testify in court and to lay information in criminal cases, rights which are intended to increase his usefulness to the cause of justice, but not (so, at least, Morrow maintains) to enlarge his own privileges or immunities.

Can we, without the acrobatics of special pleading, say anything substantial in extenuation of Plato's reactionary legislation? In no sense do we wish to obstruct critical justice in its proper task of passing sentence upon whatever is reprehensible in Plato's thought. But a distinction cries out to be made between the motive of action and the reprehensible act. This distinction is the more pertinent in view of the central issue before us in the present sequence of chapters, the quality of Plato as man. What we are asking is not whether there is a standpoint from which we can delude ourselves into seeing bad things in a good light. We are asking, rather: From what standpoint, compatible with the degree of moral intelligence claimed for Plato, could he have looked with favor on social arrangements which to us appear as obviously bad? Briefly, then, we shall undertake to show that the shortcomings of Plato the legislator do not shatter our image of Plato the good and intelligent man. The difficulties of our *probandum* will be diminished, moreover, in so far as we are able to show that the difference in liberality between the Attic and the Platonic code was somewhat slighter than Morrow has supposed.

How, then, could Plato have brought himself to leave the punishment of slaves so largely in the hands of private persons, and to visit upon slave offenders so much harsher penalties than did Athenian law? Perhaps it was partly because, in planning the life of an agricultural community, he felt that urban Athenian precedents were unsuitable. His knowledge of the comparative law of the Greek cities, some of them in circumstances similar to those of his intended colony, may have persuaded him of the unworkableness in such a state of some of the Attic provisions, while indicating the necessity of providing more rigorous sanctions for offenses against the persons of freemen, if his citizens were to walk abroad in safety. As we saw, the need of guarding against insurrection and the obligation to deal justly with the slave were his two chief concerns.[112] The course of history has revealed to us what remained, apparently, still hidden from Plato's view, that these two aims are incompatible: no amount of "justice" can offset the ineradicable human impulse to be free, and on the other side, the restrictions necessary to prevent the slaves' uprising cannot be just. But if slavery was to be maintained under

---

[112] See p. 179.

the conditions contemplated by Plato, perhaps his legal solution of the contradiction was foredoomed to fall below the Athenian achievement.

The motives prompting Plato's legislation against the interests of children of parents one of whom is a slave are not far to seek. As a convinced believer that heredity conditions the excellence of human stock, Plato was opposed to adulterating his carefully selected citizen body by admixture with the haphazard heredity of the slaves. True, there was open to him the alternative of bestowing freedom upon such children without the citizenship, the status of resident aliens. But this would have resulted in the creation of a group of non-citizens, closely related to citizens and naturally pressing for admission to the citizenship, the very privilege which Plato could not have allowed them. There is also the possibility that Plato intended to discourage irresponsible propagation by visiting a penalty, though but a mild one, upon its issue, a policy which, while not approvable, has been also that of most modern societies until nearly the present day; and this is made plausible by the stern opposition to such irregularities that marks his whole discussion of the problem of sex in the *Laws*.[113]

Dismissing these practical considerations, we must now examine certain moral and religious principles bearing upon the problem at hand. A most pervasive characteristic of the Platonic legislation, in contrast to the Attic, is unquestionably the great degree of autonomy that Plato accords to his private citizens, as the heads of households and as the agents of public order. In the area of legislation affecting the slave, this means an increase in the independent authority of the master. The extension of the citizen's autonomy supplements the practical necessities of a rural environment in accounting for Plato's earlier mentioned regulations requiring freemen to act as part assessors and agents in the punishment of offending slaves, and explains the power of a master to reclaim directly his delinquent freedman. Morrow has fully recognized the importance of this motive in Plato's slave legislation, and has even employed it to cover some matters which we shall see in a different light. The same principle is discoverable in many of Plato's provisions not directed primarily at the control of slaves. Thus, we find him according to all adult freemen the right and duty of disciplining offending free children and their (slave) "pedagogues," wherever encountered; so, too, we observe the many occasions on which bystanders are enjoined to intervene for the prevention of crimes, by whomsoever attempted. All these laws are, to a considerable degree, inspired by an admiration for an older Athenian polity, a pre-industrial, agricultural Athens, in which the structure of society was largely partriarchal,[114] and for the code of Solon, which also laid upon citizens the obligation of intervening to prevent crime.[115]

---

[113] *Laws*, 835 C–842 A. This topic is discussed also on pp. 98–99.

[114] Morrow, *Plato's Law of Slavery*, pp. 128–129.

[115] *The Administration of Justice from Homer to Aristotle*, Bonner and Smith,

But it is all-important to assign its true weight to a second principle which underlies Plato's legislation. As the corner-stone of all his social and political institutions, Plato is installing a state religion, so conceived as to pervade the whole life of every citizen and to provide the mold within which his life-long education in virtue will be cast. This is largely the traditional Athenian religion, with most of its anthropomorphic and some even of its superstitious and magical components still unrationalized, though it has been purged of its ethical crudities, and provided — so Plato believed — with a firm foundation in a theory of conduct and a natural theology capable of rigorous demonstration. The result which Plato anticipated was nothing less than the creation of a climate of moral and religious opinion which would reproduce, with greater depth and purity, the atmosphere of the earlier Athens at her Marathonian best. Accordingly, we may both agree and disagree with Morrow's conclusions: with him we may recognize that Plato has accorded to the master a very considerable (even dangerous) degree of authority over his slave; our departure from Morrow is measured by our conviction, soon to be defended, that this jurisdiction is not as absolute as he has supposed, and by our insistence that it is not the master as such to whom the power is given, but the master as the embodiment and agent of a solemn code of patriarchal responsibility.[116] We may thoroughly doubt the practicability of Plato's ideal; it is not, on that account, incompatible with the benevolence of its designer.

But how far did Plato wish to extend the master's patriarchal jurisdiction over his slave? We must now confront Morrow's contention that in two vital areas beyond those we have recognized as within the master's competence,

---

1930, I, p. 170. These writers also note (II, pp. 271-3) the surprising extent to which the Athenian legal system continued into the fourth century to rely upon the action of the individual citizen both for the initiation of suits in the public interest and for the carrying out of the decisions of the courts in civil suits for damages. Plato thus had Attic precedent for many features of his code which might otherwise be mistaken for eccentric deviations from juristic good sense: e.g., the permission extended (*Laws* 762 C) to any citizen who pleases to punish with blows persons who have failed to attend the public meals finds its parallel in the Attic provision ([Demosthenes] lix, 86) that the woman who has been taken in adultery, if she dares to attend a public sacrifice, may be visited by whoever pleases with any outrage short of death. We know of no parallel in the Athenian law of slavery to Plato's unlovely provision leaving the execution of a slave convicted of killing a freeman to be carried out by those adversely affected by the deed and "in whatever way they wish," but the same Demosthenic oration (lix, 66, trans. Murray, Loeb Library) cites a law declaring, in the case of a convicted adulterer, that the injured party who has caught him in the act, "in the court-room may inflict upon him . . . whatever treatment he pleases, provided he use no knife," and we can judge from the scholiast on Aristophanes' *Clouds* 1083 that the indignity inflicted might be extreme.

[116] Morrow (p. 129) has noted Plato's wish to reinvigorate the older religious sources of protection for the slave, but without recognizing fully that to Plato at least they may have seemed adequate to insure against injustice the slaves in his community, even though these were to be impermanent and of alien stock.

Plato has deliberately deprived the slave of legal protection, subjecting him to his master who in turn is answerable only to his conscience and his religious scruples. Thus, Morrow strongly inclines to see the operation of this motive in Plato's failure to make specific provisions for suits in behalf of slaves who have suffered outrage (the *graphê hybreôs*) and for the right of asylum.[117] We shall not argue the question of intention respecting the right of asylum, except to point out that Plato may well have assumed it to be included, as a matter of course, among the city's religious usages, and confirmed by the special sanctity which, he warns his citizens, attaches to all promises made to suppliants (*Laws* 730 A). The *graphê hybreôs*, however, is another matter, and we hold the conviction that Plato had no intention whatever of omitting it, or its equivalent, from his code. True that in that part of the *Laws* where he is enacting legal penalties for crime, he fails (885 A) specifically to list offenses against slaves as instances of *hybris*. We find, indeed, no reference in terms to a *graphê hybreôs* in any application whatever. But Plato has provided the most serious penalties against a wide class of actions and sayings, sweepingly defined as the outward signs of disbelief in the existence of the gods and in their watchfulness and unswerving justice, and called indifferently (885 B, 907 D–E) *hybris* (outrage or insolence) or *asebeia* (impiety). Just such conduct we have heard him solemnly denounce, particularly as practiced against slaves.[118] Plainly it will not do to say that the slave's protection is left wholly to the master's conscience, since that master's conscience is itself the concern of the law; not for nothing is the religion of the *Laws* a state religion. It is hardly conceivable, therefore, that Plato can have lagged behind the Attic code in determination to condemn insolence or outrage against whomsoever committed, or that he can have intended to set acts of this nature against slaves beyond the reach of law.[119]

We wish to call special attention in this connection to one further highly

[117] Morrow, *Plato's Law of Slavery*, pp. 55–56, 126–127.

[118] See p. 179. According to the interpretation here adopted, the essence of *hybris* in Platonic law consists not in injury to the dignity or rights of the person harmed, but in defiance of the divine law, which not only sanctifies certain relationships within the *polis* but also "holds a hand uplifted" over the helpless, so that wanton violence against a slave is felt as directed against the gods; so, too, with "Strangers" (foreigners) (*Laws* 729 E–730 A).

[119] That at Athens all too many offenses against slaves were probably not within the ambit of the *graphê hybreôs* has been argued in n. 41, pp. 151–152, and we must admit that in Plato's state the concept of

hybris or *asebeia* would probably not have embraced a much wider variety of such offenses; though we may surmise that in view of Plato's great concern for the avoidance of "unholiness" of every sort, and his determination to regulate in detail the behavior of his citizens, more protection would have been afforded. But whereas at Athens, even when the law was applicable, it must often have happened — so our authorities agree — that no citizen came forward to bring suit, Plato, by requiring the magistrates on pain of prosecution to bring suit against all perpetrators of impious and insolent acts, and by omitting the penalty which at Athens was assessed against the complainant who failed to secure a fifth of the judges' votes, has done what he could to make his law a live letter.

interesting Platonic omission, that of the torture applied to slave witnesses. This unlovely and unintelligent practice, to which Attic law permitted frequent recourse, is not mentioned in the *Laws*, and in one province, that of homicide trials, it is clearly ruled out by conflicting provisions.[120] Morrow holds the view that in other types of cases Plato is tacitly accepting the Athenian rule of admitting slave testimony only when it has been given under torture.[121] But it is difficult to see why anyone who regards as significant Plato's omission of the *graphê hybreôs* and the right of asylum should deny him the benefit of the same inference here. The disuse of torture would be in accord not only with the greater legal capacity of the slave in Plato's city, but also with another principle that runs through the *Laws*, namely: that no avoidable suffering shall be brought upon an innocent person in consequence of another's guilt.[122]

The relative inadequacy of Plato's legal sanctions against the killing of slaves, which for Morrow is a distinctive feature of the *Laws*, is a matter of grave potential importance; that Plato's provisions are not as inadequate as Morrow has pronounced them is a conclusion to which we have been brought by considerations set forth in our note.[123] The main point is this: certain apparent gaps in Plato's homicide legislation raise the question of how best they may conjecturally be filled. Morrow has appealed exclusively to the two principles which he thinks paramount in Plato's law of slavery, the paternalistic autonomy of the master and the social utility of the slave as a potential public informant. As a consequence, he asks us to believe that the lives of slaves other than potential informants would be left by Plato almost wholly destitute of legal protection. But that Plato did not intend to leave the slave to this degree unprotected is evident from that other Platonic principle to which we have already more than once appealed, a principle far more deeply grounded in Plato's legislation than either of the other two: the city of the *Laws* is to be a community of righteous men. Accordingly, to take but a minor example, we find Plato expressing dismay at the thought of perjurers attending public gatherings; to avert this evil in his city, he will abolish the oath for litigants (*Laws* 948 D–E). *A fortiori*, it cannot be seriously supposed that Plato would have tolerated, as members of his community, men who had deliberately and from base motives taken the life of a slave. Again we must recall that, on Plato's view, injustice to a slave was also moral injury to the agent of the injustice. That Plato designed the legal code of his second-best of all cities to remain benignly neutral in the face of such fundamental violations of moral integrity, itself the very *raison d'être* of the Platonic

---

[120] Morrow, *Plato's Law of Slavery*, p. 77ff.; *Laws* 937 A–B.

[121] Morrow, *op. cit.*, pp. 80–81; and "Plato and Greek Slavery," p. 192.

[122] See our n. 124, p. 192.

[123] Morrow's comparison of Platonic and Athenian legislation bearing upon the killing of slaves is examined in our Appendix III, pp. 589ff.

community (*Laws* 770 C–D), is the surprising and unwelcome consequence of Morrow's view.

Evidence that ethical considerations, and not partisan sociological principles alone, have guided Plato in his legislation is found in the punishments he imposes upon those guilty of temple-robbing. This is a very grave offense in Plato's eyes, as at Athens, and ranking it beside the worst crimes against parents and the mother-city, he proceeds (*Laws* 854 D f.) to lay down correspondingly severe penalties. The striking point in what follows is the differential treatment of slaves and citizens. It is the guilty citizens who, in view of the life-long education that has been lavished upon them, must now accept the consequence. They are adjudged incurable; after their proper execution, they are to be ingloriously buried beyond the frontiers of their native city, and their names buried with them in oblivion. But for slaves guilty of the same offense, there is still hope; they, too, are to be cast out of the city, with the brand of their deed upon them, but alive, in the belief that their punishment may have "sobered them into better men." [124]

---

[124] Since our topic in this chapter has been slavery, we have been debarred from direct consideration of the general spirit of Plato's penal legislation, yet a few points in regard to this deserve mention. That Plato's law of slavery is harsher than the Athenian we have seen; that this is true also of his treatment of offenses within the family has perhaps not been sufficiently stressed, either by Morrow in his account of Plato's slave-legislation or by our defense. The parallel may be documented by reference to the monograph of A. H. Chase, "The Influence of Athenian Institutions upon the *Laws* of Plato"; see his pp. 172–180, 191. As an example we may cite Plato's refusal to condone violence against a parent even in self-defense; here we are reminded of Socrates' insistence in the *Crito*, 50 E–51 C, that a son has no such right against his parents, a slave against his master, or a citizen against his city. Plato is also more severe regarding offenses against elders, who are to be regarded by each younger person as if they were his own parents, and he is more scrupulous in forbidding mistreatment of Strangers; cf. Chase, p. 180, *Laws* 879 B–880 D, 872 A–B. We would suggest that, though the penalties laid on slaves seem marked by a special deterrent intention, the principle uniting these diverse instances is a kind of piety, the sense of a particularly solemn obligation interdicting violence against superiors in

the patriarchal household, or against those especially protected by the gods (Plato's legislation shows special tenderness for the interests of other classes of the helpless also; cf. n. 130, pp. 295–296).

Plato's excessive severity to those who violate the obligations of piety is balanced by another principle, namely: his particular care to avoid the penalizing of the innocent. Even in respect to slaves, who are denied equal justice so far as this denotes equal penalties for equal offenses, justice is to be done, as we have seen, in the sense that no punishment is to be inflicted on a slave who has done no wrong. And in respect to the innocent children of criminals, Plato has extended his care for justice beyond the achievement of Athenian law, not employing confiscation of goods as a penalty, where Attic law would have done so, and taking care in all cases to specify that no blame shall attach to the children, even when their fathers have been condemned for the most serious offenses; see Chase, pp. 151, 166, and *Laws* 855 A, 856 C–D, 877 C, 909 C–D. That this scrupulousness is not derived from Plato's wish to preserve undiminished the 5040 citizen households is shown by his method of dealing (*Laws* 856 C–E) with the extreme case of children whose forefathers and fathers for three generations have been executed by the state. They are to be sent back to the land of their ancestors, with all their property except the value of the land-

In Plato's treatment of slavery in the *Laws*, we have found him earnestly and conscientiously pondering the insoluble problem of fitting the institution into the framework of a just state. He had arrived at a solution adequate, in his own terms, to abolish, on the theoretical level, the invidious distinction between slave and free, by the theological expedient of conceiving all men as alike slaves of the divine will. But from this principle he was able to build no satisfactory bridge into the sociological domain; he ended where he began, by failing to observe that there exists no justification for slavery which does not violate his basic principle of social order that, under God, authority must be proportional to moral intelligence. It is not perhaps surprising that the *Laws* provides no machinery — a thing unprecedented in the Greek world — for permitting gifted slaves to follow justice in interchanging positions with

allotment, and a son of one of the other citizens shall hold the lot in their place. This method of restoring the proper number of households could have been more widely employed, had Plato been less observant of justice to individuals. The one exception to this rule of not punishing the innocent is the sending into exile of the illegitimate child of parentage half-slave, half-free, mentioned on p. 186 above; this penalty, however, is not severe.

We see the same concern for justice in Plato's provision that whoever, from the motives we have discussed on p. 590, kills a slave "when he is guilty of no wrong," shall be condemned just as if he had killed a citizen. The same spirit appears in Plato's law that a man shall be held guiltless for slaying another in order to defend against attack his own father, provided only that the father "is committing no unrighteous act" (*Laws* 874 C). Plato's apparent omission of the torture of slave witnesses may well constitute a further case in point. In these and similar features of his legislation the purifying influence of Plato's life-long concern for justice, with its ethical and religious reenforcement, makes itself felt.

Other creditable features of Plato's legislation include his humane theory of punishment. This, as he sees it, is intended not as retribution but as beneficial to the criminal, serving in mild cases to improve him morally, while even for the incurably unjust man it is better that he should live no longer; in addition, punishment deters others and, when the punishment is capital, relieves the state of the presence of the malefactor (*Laws* 862 D–863 A, 934 A–C).

Plato somewhat inconsistently regards death as a penalty likely to have a strong deterrent effect on observers, despite his own declaration that it is the "least of evils" (*Laws* 854 E), and despite his intention as lawgiver to teach the citizens this same belief. This attitude may serve to mitigate his treatment of the just atheist, who belongs to the class of offenders whom he has committed himself (863 C–D) to treat with the greatest leniency. — We find also no explicit mention in Plato's *Laws* of cruel punishments such as *apotympanismus*, which were legally inflicted at Athens; with the possible exception of those indeterminate penalties exacted of offending slaves, to which we have alluded, his most severe sanctions, imposed respectively upon those guilty of violence against parents and upon deceitful atheists, are not death, but the status of outcast, or life imprisonment in an isolated prison. Plato is careful to avoid the use of oaths in situations which invite to perjury; apparently he would make little use of the favorite Athenian penalty of disfranchisement (cf. Chase, pp. 156, 164, 180, and *Laws* 855 C), not wishing, as we know from the disapproval expressed in the *Republic* (555 D), to have men in the city but not of it. He makes an advance over Athenian law in his infliction of lighter penalties, in ordinary cases, upon those who are brought by passion to commit crimes of violence. In short, Plato's failings in the matter of slavery are very considerably offset by his achievement, in other areas of his legislation — and even in two areas affecting slaves — of greater wisdom and justice than even Athens displayed.

less gifted masters; but we could wish that Plato had expressed regret that this juster way was not practicable. We may further regret that his fear of insurrection and his confidence that his colonists were to be men of irreproachable virtue should have led him to deprive their slaves of that fuller measure of public protection under law which Athens accorded to her slave population.

In these respects Plato's great intelligence and moral insight failed him; not, however, for lack of honest if misguided consideration of the slave's welfare. The taproot of his failure was his inability to think of the interests of the slave, or those of the metic, as on a parity with those of the citizen. He was a man of his time in thus weighing the welfare of the different groups on unequal scales, an unequal valuation which, though it was expressed in concretely different forms, underlay the social structure at Athens as well.

It is interesting to observe, also, that the extensive dependence upon slave labor which characterizes the city of the *Laws* — it is indeed, as Popper has said, a slave state — results from a basic similarity between its constitution and that of Athens, taken in conjunction with two important differences. The historian Freeman has pointed out that ancient democracy, though far kinder to slaves than ancient aristocracy, apparently required them, as aristocracy did not, for its very existence: "It is hard to conceive that a large body of men, like the qualified citizens of Athens, can ever give so large a portion of their time as the Athenians did to the business of ruling and judging . . . without the existence of an inferior class to relieve them from at least the lowest and most menial duties of their several callings." [120] Pending the invention of modern representative government and devices for making the small jury an instrument of justice, democratic societies had no other recourse. Thus by moving in the direction of democratic government in the *Laws*, Plato was for this very reason moving away, *pari passu*, from the (at least relatively) slaveless economy of the *Republic*: in the absence of the philosopher kings and their specialized military assistants, every citizen must become both a soldier and a responsible participant in government. And to the degree that his citizens were to be better prepared for these responsibilities, as Plato understood such matters, by a life-long and time-consuming education not required of Athenian citizens, slavery was in his community so much the more necessary. Since, moreover, the city of the *Laws* was to be no recipient of imperial tribute, as Athens had been at her flowering-time, its material support required what its free citizens were too preoccupied to supply, a body of men prepared to toil, and these could, in the circumstances, be nothing else than metics and slaves.

In taking leave of the topic of slavery, we may express the hope that we have not sought to justify any of the unjustifiable features of Plato's far from satisfactory legislation. Enough if we have shown some grounds that will help

---

[120] E. A. Freeman, *History of Federal Government in Greece and Italy*, p. 30.

the modern reader to make sense of what otherwise would be the painful and unintelligible paradox of Plato in the role of immoralist.

Preservation of Life and Relief of Suffering

Further grounds for asserting Plato's radical inhumanity have been found in his apparent lack of reverence for the sanctity of the individual life, and his indifference to suffering. Both offenses are sustained by evidence drawn principally from the *Republic*, with incidental support from other dialogues; they may be dealt with the more conveniently in this place in view of their affinity with the theme of the preceding discussion.

Popper has an initial advantage in being able to make his first objection to Plato here turn upon Plato's commitment to an institution peculiarly repugnant to the modern Christian world: to put Plato in the position of advocate of infanticide, is almost to have won his case as tried in any modern court. Nor will Popper allow that Plato may have been upheld in this matter by the Athenian conscience of his own day. That Plato should have sponsored the exposure of unsanctioned or substandard infants in his ideal state, Popper declares a horrendous lapse from the merciful practice of Plato's contemporary Athenians; "Infanticide was not an Athenian institution"; [121] here again, it is supposed, Plato has been misled by his tendency to imitate the worst features of the Spartan state. Popper finds it an instance, too, of Plato's crude animal-breeder's degradation of the dignity of human life. On both these points, he is in full accord with Warner Fite.[122]

In thus stating flatly that Athens did not practice infanticide, Popper is declaring his adherence to a view which, with distinct limitations, has indeed been upheld by certain recent authorities. But he has failed to indicate the disputed nature of the opinion, and to delimit sharply the circumstances under which infanticide was either countenanced by Plato or alleged to be practiced by the Athenians.

It is, first, not disputed that Athens, unlike Sparta, did not delegate to public authority the right to decide which infants should be reared and which should not. But the question of the extent to which exposure was practiced by private individuals at Athens in the fifth and fourth centuries is more difficult of decision. Evidence exists which has been held by some scholars to indicate more frequent resort to the practice in Athens at that particular time than anywhere else in Greece, by others to prove at least its very frequent occurrence; the same evidence has recently been scornfully rejected by still other scholars as untrustworthy; and the dispute seems unlikely to be resolved in the near future.[123] But it is interesting to note that despite the

---

[121] Popper, p. 52.

[122] Fite, p. 56.

[123] For the view, generally accepted until recent decades, that the Athenians of Plato's day freely practiced infanticide both for eugenic and for personal economic reasons,

wide differences of opinion, there seems to be no doubt entertained by anyone
that exposure under certain circumstances was generally practiced and accepted by the Greek world in earlier centuries; there is what appears to be clear
testimony, also, to the prevalence at Athens in the early years of the third century of the exposure of girl babies,[124] and soon after, evidence in plenty of the
widespread destruction of infant life throughout the Greek world in general.
For the particular centuries and place in which we are interested, it is generally agreed that no law prohibited infanticide, and even those scholars who
are most contemptuous of the supposition that Athenians made constant use
of the practice, admit that deformed children or weaklings were probably exposed without public obloquy and that the head of a family might reject a
child whom he did not acknowledge as legitimate; nor were there foundling
hospitals or any certainty of rescue for such exposed infants.

In the light of these generally admitted Athenian attitudes and practices,
it may be well to see what Plato actually recommended. Describing the "sacred marriages" in the *Republic*, and the disposition to be made of the babies
that are born of them by the public authorities, who are to arrange matters
so that the parents will not know which of the children growing up are their
own, he proposes that the officials shall distinguish among the parents the bet-

---

see Zimmern, *The Greek Commonwealth*,
1924, pp. 330–331, and note, Glotz, *Ancient
Greece at Work*, 1926, p. 193, and Hum-
bert, article "Expositio," in Daremberg-
Saglio; a similar position is taken by
Busolt-Swoboda. The protest against this
reigning opinion was urged by H. Bolkestein, in "The Exposure of Children at
Athens and the *Engchytristriai*," 1922;
Bolkestein appears to be the most extreme
in his repudiation of the ascription of such
actions to the Athenians of the fifth and
fourth centuries, admitting hardly more
than that fathers of families may have been
legally empowered to refuse to rear illegitimate children (p. 237). A less wholesale
rejection of the earlier view is found in the
article by La Rue Van Hook, "The Exposure of Infants at Athens," 1920, where
Van Hook, energetically denying the frequency of the practice at Athens, nevertheless acknowledges that "in recommending
exposure in extreme cases" Plato and Aristotle "were not running counter to general
Greek feeling and to occasional contemporary practice" (p. 143). In opposition,
again, to these two writers, A. Cameron,
in "The Exposure of Children and Greek
Ethics," 1932, has maintained, p. 107, that
exposure was undoubtedly "familiar in the
Athens of the classical period," existing

continuously from early centuries to later
ones, though perhaps rendered by prosperity less common at that time than at others;
Cameron has also supposed Plato to be
commending exposure in the *Laws* (cf. our
n. 126, p. 198). The question has since been
reviewed by A. W. Gomme (*The Population
of Athens in the Fifth and Fourth Centuries
B.C.*, 1933, p. 75 ff.) ; Gomme is mainly concerned to show that exposure was not sufficiently frequent to affect Athenian popula-
tion-figures; he does not doubt that weaklings and defectives were exposed at Athens,
accepting for this the evidence of the passages in Plato's *Theaetetus* (160 E; for the
metaphor, cf. 151 C and 210 C), which
clearly reflect the possibility that at Athens
a young mother might be refused the right
to keep and rear a child judged by the midwife or her husband to be unfit. Finally, we
may mention Bonner and Smith, *The Administration of Justice from Homer to Aristotle*, 1930. These writers, having reviewed
the literature listed above, except apparently Cameron's article, appear to be in general
accord with Van Hook; see their pp. 80
and 201.

[124] The fragment of the comic poet Po-
sidippus, *apud* Van Hook, *op. cit.*, p. 238:
"Even a poor man rears a son, even a rich
man exposes a daughter."

ter from the worse, and rear the offspring of the former, but those of the latter they shall not rear: "The offspring of the inferior, and any of those of the other sort who are born defective, they will properly dispose of in secret, so that no one will know what has become of them." [125] In the *Timaeus*, where Plato is recapitulating briefly the laws of the *Republic*, he writes, "we said that the offspring of the good were to be reared, but those of the bad were to be sent privily to various other parts of the state" (19 A, trans. Bury, Loeb Library), and goes on to describe how this assignment, like the decision to rear as guardians "the offspring of the good," is merely tentative, and will be reversed if the children as they grow up prove themselves fit for other stations.

These passages show, first, that secret disposition of the rejected babies born of the "sacred marriages" was probably in most cases to mean no more than placement among the common citizens; the supposition that in the case of the defective babies it means exposure is based wholly upon the supposition that no Greek would rear such an infant. It should be emphasized, therefore, that Plato's reputation stands and falls *pari passu* with our judgment of his contemporaries, and that only those who believe infanticide in such circumstances to have been acceptable to the Athenians of Plato's day have reason to charge Plato with having accepted it.

But the *Republic* envisages still another class of infants for whom, or so it appears, exposure is contemplated. After enacting that "marriages" shall not be permitted between persons above certain age limits, he provides that if conception results from unauthorized unions, abortion shall be procured if possible; if a child is nevertheless born, the parents shall "dispose of it on the understanding that we cannot rear such an offspring" (461 C). These children correspond to illegitimate children in an ordinary Greek state, and as in the former case, only in so far as we presume that such babies were probably exposed by Plato's respectable fellow-citizens need we assume that this is his meaning; we have seen that when he speaks of "not rearing" babies, he may mean only that they are not to be reared as guardians, but are to be offered for adoption by common citizens.

We have seen, thus, that either we need not believe that Plato advocated exposure, or we may believe, as does the present writer, at least in the case of the defective children, that he did, and that so also did the Athenians of his day. But it is important to note also that the circumstances justifying the practice in Plato's eyes, if any did, are those which probably justified it in Athens also. For limitation of population, Plato recommends only (*Republic* 460 A and, by implication, 372 C–D) that excessive children shall not be begotten.

In the *Laws* the situation is somewhat different in that there is to be no

---

[125] *Republic* 459 C–D and 460 C, trans. Shorey, Loeb Library.

thoroughgoing state control of marriage or of child-rearing, and therefore no occasion for such regulations as those of the *Republic*. But even so, Plato could easily have adopted the Spartan law that the state should decide the fitness of infants for rearing, and he makes no mention of such a law. Believing, as in the *Republic*, that the state must neither increase nor decrease in size, he points out that there are many "devices" or "measures" for controlling the number of births, and recommends "holding back reproduction" (literally, *epischeseis geneseôs*), or encouragement of reproduction, by means of honors conferred or withheld, or admonitions from older to younger citizens; in case there are, even so, due to the mutual affection of husbands and wives, too many citizens, colonization may have to be employed (*Laws* 740 D–E).[126] There is certainly here no explicit reference to infanticide, nor does the context naturally suggest it. Only as we judge the practice to have been almost universally taken for granted as a means of population-limitation need we read into Plato's words such a meaning, and to the present writer it seems that the passage as a whole, with its suggestions that colonization may have to be resorted to, strongly implies the contrary.[127] The *Laws*, therefore,

---

[126] Without claiming special competence to weigh most of the evidence for or against the practice of exposure by the Athenians, we feel it none the less necessary to take issue with Cameron (*op. cit.*, pp. 106, 108) on his use of Plato's remarks in the *Laws* as evidence that Plato approved the practice. The "devices" to restrict or encourage the growth of population to which Plato has reference are simply those which he himself immediately mentions, namely: honors and admonitions; to use this nonexplicit reference as Cameron does, is circular: he assumes as a principle of interpretation what he believes the passage proves. Objection must also be made to his statement (p. 108) that Plato at *Laws* 930 C "proposed to limit the family to two." In this passage Plato, discussing divorced persons and widows and widowers, is naming the "bare sufficiency of children" (so Bury in my judgment correctly translates the phrase) which is to make it unnecessary that remarriage shall be arranged with a view to further childbearing. Elsewhere he plainly shows, e.g., at *Laws* 740 B ff., and 923 C ff., that he expects families to vary in size, some containing more than two children, and that he expects also to allow for mortality from war and disease, both of which expectations are indeed necessary if a constant population is to be maintained.

[127] The *Laws* also contains several other references (e.g., 923 D, 925 B) to colonies sent out by the city, and even a mention (929 C–D) of the officials whose duty it is to have charge of younger citizens destined for such colonies.

We may protest in this connection Popper's distant conjecture (p. 521) that Plato may have believed population increase "equivalent to a decrease in quality" of the people themselves, caused, in fact, by nothing else than "racial degeneration"; this assumption is designed to support Popper's belief, criticized also on pp. 424ff. and pp. 535ff. below, that Plato regarded the maintenance of racial purity as the key to all political stability. Such an ascription of racialistic motivation is especially gratuitous in view of the following considerations: (1) Plato in the *Laws* explicitly suggests, as we have seen just above, that overpopulation originates in connubial affection, a thing which in itself he heartily approves (*Laws* 839 A–B); and in the *Republic* (458 D–460 B), he implies by his restrictions on the matings which are to be permitted, that excess numbers would arise if the normal sexual impulse were simply to operate unchecked. (2) Plato had nonracialist reasons in plenty for disliking what he considered overpopulation in his ideal cities, e.g., his dear ideal of civic unity (*Rep.* 422 E–423 C); his determination to abolish poverty (*Rep.* 421 D–422 A, *Laws*,

would seem in no way to incriminate Plato as an advocate of infanticide; if there is any change from the *Republic*, it is in the direction away from the practice.[128]

The charge of indifference to suffering finds its evidence in Plato's denial, in the *Republic*, of the right of chronic invalids to the time and care of the sons of Aesculapius (*Republic* 405 A–408 B). On Popper's reading,[129] Plato is here expressing the totalitarian doctrine of the supremacy of the state over the lives of its individual members, combined with the merely stolid indifference of a selfish man in good health to the physical ailments of those less fortunate than himself; Popper adds the uncharitable suggestion that Plato lived to reverse his judgment on this point (*Laws* 720 C), when, in his high age, he himself became the sufferer.

But this is a substantial perversion of what Plato has said in both works. In the *Republic*, Plato was asserting his belief that life receives its value from the active use to which it is put, health being prized not primarily for its sensuous delights, but because it is the necessary condition of a useful life. Plato is entirely in earnest in denying that it is right for the rich man to employ his wealth for hiring medical aid in neutralizing the noxious results of sensual indulgence. He is no less earnest in his denial of anyone's right thus to protract a life which is no more than an extended illness. In all this there is, indeed, a quality which today would be popularly called "Spartan." But it is not Spartan in any literal sense; it is simply a rather austere application of a fundamental principle in Platonic ethics: the superiority of the soul and its interests — virtue, the good life — to the body and its craving for mere physical existence. All this is so far from being denied by Plato in the *Laws*, that it is simple truth to say that Plato has there reasserted it with, if anything, added emphasis (*Laws* 726 D–728 D, especially 727 D). There is neither more nor less support of the rights of the incurably sick to be kept alive, and the reader will search the pages of the *Laws* in vain (it is certainly absent from the passages cited by Popper) [130] for any confirmation of

---

e.g., 744 D, 936 B–C), and his belief that men devoid of any property were a harmful element in the state (*Rep.* 555 D–E, 562 B–D); his provision in the *Laws* that land shall be the sole means of the citizens' support (741 E, 919 D) and that each shall possess a plot adequate for the purpose (737 D, 855 A–B), regulations sufficient in themselves to necessitate either the cessation of increase, or a constant policy of colonization; and, again in the *Laws*, the whole machinery of elective government, which, in the absence of the modern device of representation, presupposes mutual familiarity among all the members of the citizen body (*Laws* 753–768, and for the need of familiarity, 751 D).

[128] It is to be noted also that Plato does not propose, in the *Laws*, the destruction of illegitimate children, the offspring of forbidden unions between citizens and slaves. His disposition of such infants, though it does not commend itself to us on other grounds (cf. p. 186), is not that of a callous destroyer of infant life.

[129] Popper, pp. 136–137, and note 5 to chapter 8, p. 552.

[130] *Laws* 720 C, 857 C–D, cited by Popper, note 5 to chapter 8, p. 552. In interpreting 857 C–D as Plato's complaint against

Popper's suggestion that an ailing Plato was demanding for himself any more right to medical consideration than he would have accorded to the citizens of his Republic.

We may conclude that, though Plato's heart is far from vibrating in unison with the tender string of Christian humanitarianism, neither was it the receptacle of cold indifference to the well-being of others, joined with self-indulgence, as Popper charges. The simple truth is that moral excellence, which a man might possess while undergoing the torment of the rack (*Republic* 361 E), was to Plato a far more central concern than were his health and bodily comfort. But he is not willing to see a good man suffer, and states his conviction (*Laws* 936 B) that even in a moderately well ordered city, no man, slave or free, who possesses any share of virtue, can be permitted to suffer the pains of destitution.

In concluding this section it is our rather unwelcome duty to deal with what might best be described as a temporary lapse into irresponsible journalism, on the part of the author of an otherwise generally thoughtful and temperate book. Crossman, in conducting his "Plato" (supposedly the Plato of the *Republic*) on an imaginary tour of the modern world, stops him off in Nazi Germany and again in Soviet Russia, to show his appraisals of these two contemporary versions of the authoritarian state. After listening to Goebbels denouncing the Jews and Jewish reason as the enemies of Aryan virtue and the chief dangers to German world domination, and urging all good Germans to "have your revolvers ready," Crossman's Plato expresses himself as "well pleased" with this obvious piece of rhetorical mythology, recognizing in this Nazi propaganda the precise counterpart of the (ig) "noble lie" in his own *Republic*, and adding, with complete cynicism, the further compliment that in it the speaker had "displayed an irony worthy of Socrates himself." [131] This depth of self-betrayal "Plato" is made to equal, if not to excel, in the compliment he pays to Stalin, who has employed the " 'noble lie' of democracy and proletarian freedom," which, having served its purpose, he has now suppressed, and has "quietly put away" "those innocents who mistook myth for reality." [132] These two passages substantially contradict Crossman's own ascription to Plato, in many passages,[133] of humaneness, hatred of oppression, by whomever practiced, and a longing for a social order which would bring to each man his just dues. They amount to Crossman's assertion, without proof, that Plato, in the *Republic*, would have been willing to utilize numerous members of the citizen body as mere propaganda fodder to be brutally sacrificed without regard to justice; they imply, secondly, that Plato would

---

an actual physician who talked "too much philosophy" to him (Plato) "when he fell ill while writing the *Laws*," Popper is wrong beyond his usual custom. For he supposes Plato himself to be making the complaint which, in fact, Plato ascribes to an ignorant empiric doctor.

[131] Crossman, *op. cit.*, pp. 246–248.

[132] *Ibid.*, p. 231.

[133] *Ibid.*, e.g., pp. 257, 235, 287.

have put quietly to death those citizens who were simple enough to have persisted in believing his myth of the metals, and who inconveniently pressed the rulers for the carrying out of its provisions with regard to the "golden" offspring of the common citizens.

Such formal repudiation as Crossman's own "noble lie" deserves, it will receive in our Chapter 8. A lively imagination and the puckish impulse to "streamline" the ambassador from antiquity seem to have overwhelmed, for the moment, the good sense and the good will of the writer, and moved him to give his readers a sadly jazzed version of a classic. But whether consciously or not, he has by imputing such ideas to Plato most unfairly branded him with a degree of inhumanity that should be reserved for use upon the brows of international gangsters.

Greeks and Barbarians

It has been maintained that no man can be properly humane without a proper notion of humanity,[134] i.e., without the concept of the unity of mankind as a principle transcending ethnic and cultural boundaries, suffused with reverence, and confessing moral obligation. Such a thesis might lead one to ask whether this concept was familiar to the thoughtful Greeks of Plato's time, or was, perhaps, a later notion, first developed by the Stoics, and given a deeper and more practical meaning by confluence with Christianity.

A British scholar, Tarn, has entered the (to most persons) unexpected name of Alexander the Great, as deserving of the high honor of priority in this field.[135] To many persons, to whom the name of Alexander recalls the violence of conquest and a private life brimming with passional excesses of anger and of love, this will seem as surprising as if they were to be told that Nero, and not St. Paul, has a right to the title of "Apostle to the Gentiles." The heart of Tarn's contention is that in Alexander we meet, for the first time in Greek history, a man who was pledged, both in theory and in practice, to abolish the old dichotomy that had so long divided the Aegean peoples, into Hellenes, racial and cultural superiors, and all others, huddled indiscriminately together under the blanket of the unflattering name "barbarians," and pledged also to develop a mutual "harmony of hearts" throughout the known world.

Tarn has not arrived at his conclusion without making what he considers a careful examination of the claims of all previous candidates for the honor, in the course of which he dismisses in turn, as having made only negligible contributions, all the sophists and teachers, predecessors and contemporaries of Plato; Plato himself and Aristotle, taken together, are charged with negative influence: any early gropings after a conception of human unity were

---

[134] See our discussion, p. 231, and Appendix VII, pp. 601ff.

[135] Tarn, W. W., "Alexander the Great and the Unity of Mankind," 1933; and "Alexander, Cynics, and Stoics," 1939.

"strangled by the idealist philosophies"; [136] and Alexander is left to develop the conception almost unaided.

But Popper will not allow Alexander priority of conquest here, though he expresses great admiration for Tarn, approving especially his condemnation of Plato and Aristotle; he has other claimants to promote, who, if successful, will naturally bring profit to their sponsor by furthering, in turn, his charges against Plato. As, in the context of slavery, we found Popper conjuring up spirits of light, champions of human freedom, to set off Plato's black-hearted defense of slavery, so here, he would find it highly serviceable to his case, could he reassemble from its surviving fragments, a noble soul, contemporary with Plato, who had discerned and made manifest what the partisan Plato could not and would not see: the great truth of human brotherhood, the unity of all mankind. Fortune smiled, and put in Popper's way the very man to fill the office, Antisthenes, whom certain boldly speculative scholars had already contrived, in spite of what has appeared to other scholars to be the lack of reliable evidence on many essential points, to equip with a full complement of significant doctrines.[137] Popper, unhesitatingly taking sides in the controversy, has accordingly adopted this greatly enlarged and improved Antisthenes, and has attempted, principally in three long footnotes,[138] to adduce his reasons for his faith.

For Popper, we must note, the idea of the "unity of mankind" means primarily the recognition of a basic similarity in worth and dignity among men, as is shown by his use of the invidious distinction between Greeks and barbarians as a touchstone for detecting opponents of "unity"; but when he employs interchangeably with it, the phrase "brotherhood of all men," he adds to the idea of similarity an element of mutual obligation and helpfulness akin to Tarn's idea of "the harmony of hearts," but conveying also, as no attentive reader of Popper's book can fail to note, a suggestion of Christian love. It is the advocacy of human unity in this fuller sense of brotherhood, that Popper has attributed to Antisthenes.

The complex pattern of Popper's argument, with its warp of fact, and its woof of fantasy, and sometimes outright fallacy, is dissected in our Appendix IV.[139] What deserves place in our text is a brief word of warning to who-

---

[136] We are unable to credit Tarn with any careful regard for the rights of the case as it concerns Plato, to whom in his discussion he is notably unjust (see our note, p. 243 below). For this reason we shall not be able to appeal to Tarn's authority in support of our qualified disbelief in the supposed priorities of other pre-Alexandrian thinkers; we shall be indebted to him, however, for evidence and reasons which seem to us cogent in themselves.

[137] The scholarly enlargement of Antis-

thenes which forms the background of Popper's view is discussed in our note, p. 209 below. See also the mention of the controversy, with references, in Tarn's "Alexander, Cynics, and Stoics," 1939, p. 42.

[138] Popper, op. cit., notes 37, 47, and 48 to Chapter 8, pp. 560, 561–564.

[139] This Appendix, which examines in detail Popper's arguments for regarding Antisthenes as an equalitarian, a humanitarian, etc., may be found on pp. 592ff.

ever would avoid being caught in Popper's web. Let the reader notice especially two logically questionable procedures, upon whose use much of the apparent strength of Popper's case depends.

There is, first, the implicit assumption that we may accredit to a given thinker, without specific evidence, adherence to any one of the doctrines identified with a teacher or school of thought with which the thinker in question is known to have been in any way associated. This would be comparable to attributing to Plato a belief in the Pythagorean ban on bean-eating, on the strength of Plato's known association with the Pythagorean Archytas; or, as Popper would certainly not wish to do, attributing to Plato all the noble ideas which Popper believes were truly Socratic. Popper employs the assumption mentioned, both forward and backward in time. First it serves him to prove that Antisthenes must have shared the (supposed) equalitarianism of Alcidamas and Lycophron, because he can be shown to have had contact with the school of Gorgias, by whom they can be shown to have been influenced in some (not specifically relevant) respects. This same assumption lends a specious color, also, to Popper's suggestion that the humane element in Roman Stoicism is indirectly owing to Antisthenes. The pedigree can indeed be traced from Socrates through Antisthenes and the Cynics, and down to the Roman Stoics. But to infer that such continuity of descent proves the special humaneness of Antisthenes is to violate our knowledge of the natural history of ideas, to neglect their Protean character: the kaleidoscope of history sometimes requires but the addition of a few more beads, and one or two unexpected shakes, to reveal patterns never yet seen by the eye of man.

A second practice employed concomitantly with the one just described to establish the equalitarianism of Antisthenes, is the misuse of modalities, that is, the tacit abandonment of originally admitted qualifications to the truth of crucial assertions.[140] To some degree, we are all inevitably guilty of this prac-

---

[140] Popper has at his disposal another means of escaping servitude to historical authority and caution. In the domain of ethics (as we shall see below, p. 475) he denies the existence of any "facts" to which moral judgments must conform, and feels free, within certain wide and ill-determined limits, to make "decisions" beyond the reach of refutation. In somewhat parallel fashion, he denies (reasonably enough) that history is a "science" — since it can neither experimentally verify its conclusions nor predict the future — and hence feels himself free to present under the immunity of a "point of view" or "interpretation" (Popper, pp. 167, 586) his own conclusions, affirming himself "fully" to "believe" that which he nevertheless does not "dogmatically" assert. He tells us further (p. 450)

that though historical "points of view" may differ in the number of "accepted records" or "facts" which they successfully unify, and in the number of auxiliary hypotheses which they require for their support, no historian can offer anything essentially different. But in his application of this theory he has revealed an important weakness. For he seems to have been so preoccupied in destroying the imposing structure of scientific history that he has failed to notice a humble edifice, housing that lesser but still necessary "science" of history which is pledged to the achievement of maximum historical objectivity through the conscientious application of critical methods of handling data and evaluating rival probabilities. In ignoring this discipline, the investigator may find himself unifying under his "point

tice, since it is manifestly impossible to repeat on each occasion all the previously admitted qualifications of the statement made. But in Popper this mild necessary fault has been pushed to its extreme. Thus, in adducing his evidence regarding Antisthenes, as he does principally in his footnotes, Popper may state frankly its "highly speculative" nature, and in drawing out what he supposes to be consequences, often uses phrases like "it seems to me extremely likely" or "if so, then the case must have been thus." Yet in other notes, and particularly in his text, he repeatedly makes the unqualified statement, even the emphatic statement, that Antisthenes was an equalitarian and an exponent of the brotherhood of man; [141] and in his final chapter, with no new glint of evidence, and having established, to his own satisfaction, and on similarly tenuous grounds, the conscious or semiconscious guilt of Plato as betrayer of Socrates, he roundly delares that "Socrates had only *one* worthy successor, his old friend Antisthenes" (Italics his).[142]

By applying such methods, then, and on the avowed basis of only that evidence which we have examined in our footnote, Popper believes himself to have established the right to assert, in sum, that there was at Athens in Plato's time a man, Antisthenes, who, inspired by Socrates, enlightened by the school of Gorgias, and made wise by his own half-barbarian birth, saw the unreality of the prevalent distinction between Greeks and barbarians, and, believing that there was but one God, believed and taught also that under this God, all men are brothers. And this man Plato knew, and scorned, and shamefully misrepresented and vilified in his writings.

And here, parenthetically, we will consider the likelihood and the textual grounds of Popper's conviction that Plato has indulged in bitter and unworthy personal abuse of Antisthenes in the *Republic*.[143] In the first passage adduced,[144] Plato is considering a favorite theme, the personal qualities necessary to students of philosophy; in this case, the students in question are those who are to be trained as rulers of the ideal state. The discussion is perfectly general and even tranquil; but presently there is a little dramatic thunderstorm of indignation, carefully controlled, against unfit aspirants to philosophy in the ordinary Greek state, who bring public disesteem upon this noble pursuit. Socrates begs to be excused for his vehemence: the sight of philosophy reviled made him forget his intended gentleness to those who are at

---

of view" not "facts" but conjectures, and accounting by his "interpretation" for the "accepted records" only by the aid of unobserved auxiliary hypotheses of the most dubious kind. It is thus that we find Popper unifying his interpretation of Plato by such extravagances as his magnification of Antisthenes and the Athenian opposition to slavery, and his fantastic inflation of Plato's single reference to King Codrus (discussed on pp. 462f. below) into Plato's

claim to kingly power in Athens; in this fashion the *ignis fatuus* of an enthusiastic amateur is presented as on a parity with the carefully focussed light of even the most judicial historian.

[141] Popper, *op. cit.*, pp. 180, 561.

[142] *Ibid.*, p. 189.

[143] See our Appendix IV, (b), p. 592, for Popper's assertions.

[144] *Republic* 535 A–536 C.

fault.[145] (The standard of propriety here observed is nearer to that of an ecclesiastical tea party than to the dog fight — "an attack of extreme violence" [146] — that Popper is implying.) Socrates has declared that the proper "aspirant to philosophy must not limp in his industry, in the one half of him loving, in the other shunning, toil. This happens when anyone is a lover of gymnastics and hunting and all the labors of the body, yet is not fond of learning. . . . And he too is lame whose industry is one-sided in the reverse way." [147] Likewise maimed in respect of truth are those who hate the voluntary lie, but do not shun the involuntary lie of ignorance and mistaken knowledge; nor are those fit who lack the virtues of courage, sobriety, and the rest; but only those are to be chosen, either as friends or as rulers in a state, who, possessing all the necessary excellences, are true-born, not, like the unworthy, "crippled and bastard" (chôlois te kai nothois).

Catching at some points of correspondence between Plato's language and the characteristics of Antisthenes,[148] for example, the word nothos (bastard, or person-not-of-citizen-birth-on-both-sides, such as Antisthenes), Popper finds here an "undoubtedly personal attack." [149] Meanwhile he leaves unnoticed the several points at which what is said is patently inapplicable to Popper's own conception of Antisthenes, the plain man and the anti-aristocrat, for example, the reference to a fondness for hunting, which, as Popper has noted on another occasion,[150] was typically rather an upper-crust pursuit.

We have discussed elsewhere the second passage in which Popper supposes Antisthenes to be the object of attack.[151] This depicts the bald-headed tinker who marries his former master's daughter. By a similar forcing of conjecture, Popper has been able, here again, to discover the well-concealed features, despite the rather incongruous fact that our tinker has just been released from bonds. Again Plato's real subject is the general class of those who unworthily aspire to philosophy; but again Plato uses the word nothos, along with phaulos (trifling, of small account, base), this time employed to describe the imaginary children of the tinker, and his bride Philosophy, who represent in the parable the philosophical beliefs of such a would-be philosopher.

---

[145] Cf. Rep. 539 A, where this leniency is again expressed.

[146] Popper, op. cit., p. 562.

[147] Shorey's translation, Loeb Library.

[148] Popper, p. 562, seems to argue that the adjective "crippled," also, was intended by Plato to point to Antisthenes; at any rate, he cites several Platonic passages which refer to persons with crippled or limping souls, or souls and bodies, as if the use of this metaphor proved an intent to "attack" Antisthenes. It is well to note that Plato employs similar metaphors wherein

spiritual faults and failings are figuratively represented by bodily defects, in other passages where no possible reference to Antisthenes exists; e.g., in the Gorgias myth (523 C–525 A), where the souls of the wicked are said to be maimed and deformed by their evil deeds, though their material bodies may be fair, and their birth noble.

[149] Popper, p. 562.

[150] Ibid., e.g., pp. 504, 616.

[151] Republic, 495 C–496 A; see also our p. 177 and p. 239.

Much of the force of Popper's implication is lost if it be remembered that the word *nothos*, though it was also employed as a generalized expression of reproach, as in the first passage cited above, signified for Plato something much more remote from the vocabulary of vituperation than our word "bastard," as currently employed. In Plato's second context, just cited, it went, along with *phaulos*, to describe the plebeian and noncitizen status of the children, and also, by a neat pun, to denote the false and illegitimate character of philosophical ideas, a use which may be supported by the application of the same word to what the *Timaeus* calls the "bastard concept" of space,[152] meaning simply that properly speaking, in the true, legitimate sense of the word, we have no "concept" of space, but only a false and spurious notion.

What survives as probable truth in Popper's imputation, then, comes down to this: that Plato indulges in some spirited satire upon a miscellaneous class of unfit aspirants to philosophy, so described as to make the inclusion of Antisthenes in one of its subclasses (that of those excessively devoted to the toils of the body) a not impossible conjecture. Of gibes at racial impurity or civil disabilities there are none. If we look beyond the *Republic* to other dialogues, we find a similar situation: there undoubtedly exist passages seriously undertaking to refute, or even on occasion satirizing, views that may well include those of Antisthenes.[153]

We return now to consider the status in Plato's Athens of the idea of the unity of mankind, and Antisthenes as its supposed advocate. The difficulty of dealing with Popper's argument consists briefly in this: he has chosen, in

---

[152] *Timaeus* 52 B. Cf. *Apology* 27 D, where "daemons" or spirits are said to be perhaps the "bastard," i.e., semidivine, children of gods.

[153] It is a generally accepted opinion among scholars that Antisthenes was among those in Plato's eye when he speaks (*Sophist* 251 B–C, 259 D) of the numerous callow youths and "late-learning" old men who, through poverty of intellectual possessions, rejoice in the magnificent wisdom of asserting that only propositions of identity are possible, a doctrine which we know from Aristotle that Antisthenes actually held. Suppose it so, but notice that in spite of a tinge of ironical derision, Plato names no names, and uses a plural form; he is still moving on the plane of philosophical argument — he gives reasons for what he ridicules; and in his mention of poverty of wisdom, he has done all he could to prevent an ingenious reader from supposing that the material poverty of Antisthenes or of anyone else is here in view. In further extenuation, one may urge that it was in any case a serious conviction of Plato's that

the study of philosophy should be begun after adolescence and before maturity, and should presuppose the study of mathematics.

After all this talk of possible "attacks" by Plato upon Antisthenes, it may be permissible to mention that there were ancient reports of the converse relation: Diogenes Laertius reports that Antisthenes directed against Plato a controversial dialogue, *Sathon* (Diogenes L., vi, 16, and iii, 35). Another late compiler, Athenaeus, has even insisted (220 E and 507 A) that the title *Sathon* is an indecent pun (see Liddell and Scott, *s.v.*) on Plato's name. We speak of the caution to be employed in using Diogenes, n. 155 below, and Athenaeus, n. 30, p. 407. Since in particular "Sathon" was apparently also a man's name in common use (cf. Licht, Hans, *Sexual Life in Ancient Greece*, 1932, p. 416), this scandalous intention need not be regarded as proved against Antisthenes. The situation, however, underscores the dangers besetting those who, like Popper, have leaned heavily on the more sensational passages in these two ancient sources.

Antisthenes, a man whose thought is no longer available to us in the requisite detail, but who maintained some views that are consistent with his having been, in some sense, a proponent of the "unity of mankind." By further interpretation and baseless amplification, he has constituted Antisthenes a moral saint and an inspired advocate of human brotherhood. Next, having discovered a point or two of contrast between this man and Plato, he has constructed a full-fledged antithesis, as between virtue and vice. And he has then said to his opponents, in effect: prove that I am wrong, or else accept in silence the damning consequences to Plato's cause. Now we must freely admit that Plato's preëminence as moralist among the Hellenes would be diminished, though by no means as much as Popper suggests, could it really be shown that Antisthenes was the zealous, beneficent champion of the ideal of human brotherhood, with its recognition of rights and duties, the great equalitarian-humanitarian of Popper's dream. Nevertheless, we shall not need to accept Popper's proposed alternatives. It is no part of our necessity to prove that an insufficiently grounded assertion must be false. It is sufficient answer to Popper to have shown, as we have done in our footnote,[154] that he himself has failed to make his case.

But not to rest satisfied with a debater's victory, let us make the best of the scanty and often precarious evidence which is available to bring into view a more credible Antisthenes.[155] We need not, for the sake of doing justice to Plato, be led into being unfair to Antisthenes. He was, unquestionably, a man of merit, a *vir Socraticus* of whom Socrates need not have been ashamed. With his logical and epistemological theories we are not here concerned, though they have won him common, if limited, recognition from the historians of thought.[156] He was a successful teacher of rhetoric and an accomplished writer, exhibiting here the fruits of that early training in the school of Gorgias which Popper, by strained inference, regards as having encouraged his supposed "equalitarianism." [157] Apart from a certain virulence, sometimes running through the gross into the obscene, we may admire his pungent wit and his playful instructive humor.[158] Certain of his fragments show that he

---

[154] Appendix IV, pp. 592ff.

[155] The principal source here is Diogenes Laertius, whose *Lives of Eminent Philosophers*, third century A.D., is a compilation of compilations, containing along with much true gold an indeterminate amount of apocryphal alloy, especially in its "anecdotal" sections. As the standard accounts of Antisthenes depend very largely upon this book — without it, indeed, he would scarcely be a recognizable man — we are methodologically within our rights in drawing from it material required for correcting the

distorted and magnified image that results from its partial and partisan use.

[156] For a brief discussion of the extent and validity of Antisthenes' achievements in this field, see Appendix V, pp. 595f.

[157] Popper, note 48 to Chapter 8, p. 562.

[158] Two anecdotes will illustrate the type of saying which is ascribed to him, with what veracity we cannot tell: someone having said, "The war will destroy the poor," his Shavian comment was, "On the contrary, it will produce them in droves"; of an Orphic priest expatiating on the glorious

could use language with great facility and imaginative force, as when he wrote, "Insight is the mightiest of forts; it can never fall, never be betrayed. Its walls must be built of our impregnable conclusions." [159]

As a moralist, he commands respect by his single-minded devotion to his ideal of a self-sufficient morality, which he called "Socratic strength," [160] achieved through insight, and through strenuous austerity and exertion (*ponos*).[161] As hindrances to attaining the goal stand the traditional popular views of how life should be lived and what makes life satisfactory, for example, pleasures of sense, which must therefore be "shot dead" in the person of Aphrodite; [162] the encumbering appurtenances of civilization — clothing and houses, beyond the bare necessities — are to be eschewed.[163] The goal of life is freedom from illusion.[164] If in pursuit of this ideal one is slandered by men of ill will, well and good; it is a kingly thing to do good and be reviled.[165]

It is to such doctrines as these, and their partial embodiment in Antisthenes' life, that Diogenes the Cynic acknowledged his debt, when he said of Antisthenes, "Since he freed me, I have not been a slave . . . He taught me what things are mine and what are not"; [166] and again, in jocoserious complaining compliment, "He clad me in rags, and made me turn beggar, a man without house or home." [167]

Antisthenes dismisses with a quip his own semibarbarian birth; [168] the Athenians' pride in their "authochthony" seems to him to set them on a parity with grasshoppers and snails.[169] The politics of the wise man are in accord not with the existing laws but with the law of virtue; [170] the virtue of a man is the same as that of a woman; [171] the truly well-born are the virtuous; [172] the just man should be valued above a kinsman; [173] the good man deserves to be loved.[174] He who has once acquired virtue can never lose it, for his virtue is a weapon that cannot be wrested from his hand; [175] he is entirely self-sufficient, since all that others have belongs to him.[176] Such a man we may find prefigured in Heracles among the Greeks, and Cyrus the Elder among the barbarians.[177]

---

after-life in store for initiates, he inquired, "In that case, why don't you go and die?" (Stobaeus 50, 11; Diogenes Laertius, vi, 4).

[159] Diogenes Laertius, vi, 13.
[160] *Ibid.*, vi, 11.
[161] *Ibid.*, vi, 2; vi, 11.
[162] Clem. Alex. *Stromata*, II, 175. The complete fragment is as follows: "Antisthenes . . . says, 'I would shoot Aphrodite dead, if I could get within range of her; for she has corrupted many of our very best women.' And he says that Eros is a corruption of nature, and the wretches who succumb to it call the disease a god."
[163] Xenophon *Symposium* I, 4.

[164] Clem. Alex. *Stromata* 179.
[165] Diogenes Laertius, vi, 7, and vi, 4.
[166] Epictetus, *Diss.* III, xxiv.
[167] Plutarch, *Quaes. Conviv.* II, i, 7.
[168] Diogenes Laertius, vi, 4.
[169] *Ibid.*, vi, 1.
[170] *Ibid.*, vi, 11.
[171] *Ibid.*, vi, 12.
[172] *Ibid.*, vi, 11.
[173] *Ibid.*, vi, 11.
[174] *Ibid.*, vi, 12.
[175] *Ibid.*, vi, 12, and 105.
[176] *Ibid.*, vi, 11.
[177] Antisthenes' writings included works dealing with each of these "wise men."

It is from this area of the thought of Antisthenes, apparently, that the Antisthenes of Popper and of various German scholars on whom he may have drawn, takes his origin.[178] The just-mentioned praise of Heracles has been interpreted by some scholars as evidence that Antisthenes was an advocate of "*philanthrôpia*," that trait which is often closely connected with the cult of the hero who is said to have performed his famous twelve labors in the service of mankind. Of course, it is possible that the philanthropic motif (in the same sense of the relief of suffering and the saving of lives) was involved. But nothing that Antisthenes is known to have said suggests this interpretation. The center of Antisthenes' ethical theory lies in the individual's pursuit of his own goal of self-sufficiency, and the good of others (apart from

---

[178] As partial explanation and perhaps extenuation of what otherwise might appear as Popper's spontaneously generated Antisthenes, we may point to certain premonitory extravagances in the earlier German literature. Wilhelm Nestle, in his *Sokratiker*, 1923, pp. 9–17, provides several good examples of the art of improving an ancient philosopher by introducing his isolated opinions into a wider frame of reference and then, by extrapolation, reading off favorable results. Thus, finding in Antisthenes various condemnations of traditional prejudices about birth and rank, he sets this in the frame of a universalistic altruism and concludes that Antisthenes advocated the principle of philanthropy, rejected slavery, and was the opponent of war. All these positions, as we have seen, are consistent with some of Antisthenes' utterances; none of them is actually found in any existing fragment. Charity is not a cardinal virtue in historical writing, but if it must be indulged, let it not be at the expense of authors who do not enjoy the privileges and immunities of those who survive only in fragmentary form.

Perhaps we should add here, in further extenuation of Popper, that his earlier-noted implied inclusion of Antisthenes among those who opposed slavery (see p. 150 above) may have sprung originally from the unsupported ascription to Antisthenes of this very opposition, by one of Nestle's confrères or by Nestle himself. Nestle offers a particularly glaring example of his own generosity to Antisthenes by stating, first (*Sokratiker*, p. 15), that Antisthenes "must have" denied the validity of slavery, and then by putting in parentheses after this assertion the bare citation "Arist. *Pol.* I,

2, 3." The Aristotelian passage cited makes no reference to Antisthenes; it is merely the statement which we have discussed at length, pp. 155f. above, that "some persons" had opposed slavery. Thus Nestle had seemed to claim the support of Aristotle for his own baseless conjecture.

But Nestle was neither the first nor the worst romancer in this field. To Duemmler, it seems, goes the honor of priority, in his *Antisthenica*, 1882; while for Joël it remained to achieve a speculative altitude that has moved Praechter (Ueberweg-Praechter, *Philosophie des Altertums*, 1926, p. 135) to say of Joël's account of Antisthenes: "By far the greater part rests upon a high and swaying structure of hypotheses which collapses before the smallest breeze of criticism. Under Joël's hand Antisthenes grows into a mighty giant whose significance and influence become enormous: 'Antisthenes rises before us as the first preacher on Greek soil, as the first pure moralist, and the first philosopher of the will, as the spiritual bridge between Hellas and the Orient, and as the prophetic precursor of the most important movements in life and thought of the post-ancient, nay, of the modern world.'" Wilamowitz (*Platon*, 1920, I, p. 263) warns against manufacturing philosophical doctrines out of such individual catchwords as those reported from Antisthenes. Elsewhere (*Die Griechische u. Lateinische Literatur* u.s.w., 1912, p. 131) he has expressed his conviction that the attempt to build up Antisthenes "out of pure blue air" into a thinker and writer of special significance, was one of the "windiest illusions" of nineteenth-century philology.

their progress toward a like self-sufficiency) can scarcely have occupied more than a subordinate place in his scheme. In any case, it is doubly arbitrary to impute an idea which Antisthenes is not known to have held, and then to reorganize what is known of his ethical system in order to make room for it.

Similarly, his exaltation of the claim of virtue above those other customary claims of birth and of civic and family obligation which we have listed above, has moved these same sympathetic interpreters, despite the lack of any further evidence, to credit him with denunciation of all restrictive discrimination between classes and races, and between slave and free,[179] and with the cherishing of a vision of mankind as one community of mutual service and good will. It would be false to deny that Antisthenes had gone some steps along this noble path, and ungenerous to refuse him credit for having helped to inspire others — certain later Cynics and the Stoics of later date — to travel further along it. But once again, it is only by a generosity that has crossed over into extravagance that one can transform his isolated insights into a universal bill of human rights.

Furthermore, even a measured admiration for the insights and achievements of Antisthenes must not distract our attention from certain other equally well-attested features in his physiognomy, sharply at variance with the estimate of him that Popper has made. As mentioned above, Antisthenes composed a treatise (now lost) in which he is supposed to have presented the *beau ideal* of human excellence in the person of an idealized King Cyrus the Elder, who founded and administered his empire through the exercise of insight and moral strenuousness. From the fragments that remain it is beyond even German ingenuity to reconstruct the details; what is sufficient to our purpose is embodied in the mere fact (if it is a fact) that the man whom Popper construes into a great libertarian and democrat should have chosen to connect politics and morals through an application of the principle of leadership. Consistent with this positive approval of the rightful rule of the morally most intelligent individual was Antisthenes' negative attitude toward the Athenian democracy. This appears in humoristic form in his suggestion that the Athenians should elect asses to be horses, since they are able by show of hands to convert nongenerals into generals,[180] and is more soberly stated in the complaint that it is strange business to clear wheat of weeds and reject the unfit for military service, but not to exclude evil men from public life.[181] To the same effect he declared, "If a state is not able to separate its virtuous citizens from the less virtuous, it is in a bad way." [182] Cited also among the fragments is a curious bit of evidence that Antisthenes' disapproval of Athenian practices found its positive counterpart in an admiration of Sparta; having traveled from Athens to Sparta, he said, "I have gone from

---

[179] This attribution has been noted in the preceding note.

[180] Diogenes Laertius, vi, 8.

[181] *Ibid.*, vi, 6.

[182] *Ibid.*, vi, 5.

the women's apartment to the men's hall."[183] Our argument here does not depend on the assumption that the just-quoted dicta are indisputably authentic utterances of Antisthenes, though as regards democracy, they are among the best attested. The point is that they go on all fours with the rest of what has come down to us in his name, so far as this involves morals and politics, and that they make evident the arbitrary principle upon which Popper has proceeded in choosing the materials for his portrait of Antisthenes.[184]

If among the best attested opinions of Antisthenes stands the declaration, warranted by Cicero, and made central by Popper, that there is one God by nature, though there are many by convention,[185] we must be careful not to be lightly overawed by what, beneath the paint of its expression in terms of the nature-convention antithesis, had not been news to any educated Greek since the sixth century.[186] Moreover, Antisthenes has unfortunately told us singularly little about his god. He is one, in some unspecified sense; and on the negative side, he is not like anyone, not to be seen with eyes, and not capable of being depicted.[187] In speaking of Antisthenes as a monotheist, we are, therefore, in great danger of saying more than we have a right to mean. And this is precisely what Popper has done. For him, there appear to be two, and two only, forms of monotheism, one good, one bad, one narrow and tribalistic, and one universalistic, with the brotherhood of man as its natural complement. Since Popper, adducing Antisthenes' supposed denunciation of racial prejudice, views Antisthenes as eminently untribalistic, there seems to be no halting of the inevitable conclusion.[188] The radical defect of Popper's argument is, as we have indicated, its failure to take into account the *tertium quod datur*, the possibility that the broad monotheism of Antisthenes might, quite consistently with his known materialistic leanings,[189] have been a form of partial or thoroughgoing pantheism, equating God with the sum total of

---

[183] Theon, *Progymnasmata* 5, 45.

[184] One other possible element in Antisthenes' message, neither more nor less probable than several of those which Popper has adopted, he has done well to leave unmentioned. Gomperz and Nestle both have emphasized those ideas of Antisthenes that, by a breach with the customary institutions of civilized society, suggest a "return to nature," to the simple conditions of animal existence typified perhaps by the life of the herd or of the hive. Something of this sort was definitely advocated by later Cynics who looked back to Antisthenes as their exemplar. And thus, reasoning on Popper's usual pattern, we should find exemplified with a vengeance that social ideal so abhorrent to Popper (and to Toynbee), a "return to the beasts," but with Plato replaced by Antisthenes as its dangerous advocate.

[185] Cicero, *De Natura Deorum* I, 13, 32.

[186] See Jaeger, *Theology of the Early Greek Philosophers*, 1947, esp. p. 31.

[187] Cited by Nestle from Theodoret. Graec. aff. cur. I, p. 713.

[188] The actual course of Popper's argument is complicated by a greater number of steps, and by appearing, not in one passage in his book, but scattered through footnotes (note 37 to chapter 8, p. 560, and note 48, pp. 562–564). It will be apparent, I think, that the reasoning is logically equivalent to that indicated in our text. Popper seems also to believe (p. 360) that the mention of a "great soul" whose "home is the whole world" (which he quotes from Democritus) is an essentially monotheistic expression.

[189] Asserted by Ueberweg-Praechter, *op. cit.*, p. 162, with the support of Fragment 33, Mullach.

materials and energies of the universe, and thus incapable (without the addition of further principles) of supporting the brotherhood of men, because it has emptied the fatherhood of God of any intelligible meaning. Again we disclaim certainty; we claim only immunity from the unwarranted certainties of others.[190]

Let us now, in the role of interested but impartial observers, fix our attention upon the progress of this strenuous Socratic, with the aim of noting how far at the farthest he may with reasonable probability have traveled toward a conception of human brotherhood; and let us then judge what would be the consequence to Plato's good name, of granting the existence of such a man.

We may assume, to begin with, that Antisthenes really wore the clothes, literal and moral, in which his biographer Diogenes Laertius has arrayed him: that is to say, that he really said most of the penetrating things and believed most of the creditable doctrines as reported; that these were not mistakenly referred back to him from among the dicta and the insights of later thinkers. Along with this, we may assume that, while not engaged in logical and rhetorical refinements, he spent much of his great energy in exemplifying in practice and in putting others on the way toward his accepted ideal of self-sufficiency and insight. In all this we have found him conceiving of human excellence in terms applicable in principle to all conditions of men, with the sole proviso that they possessed sufficient strength of understanding and rigor of will to follow along his arduous path. In so far as he devoted himself to preaching and teaching this ideal (we are neglecting here his activity as teacher of rhetoric), he made practical acknowledgement of the claims of others to share the benefits of his insights.

The initial handicap under which Antisthenes labored — his exclusion from full participation in the life of his native Athens — must have worked to his ultimate advantage as a moralist, in making him poignantly aware, in his own person, of the artificial nature of discrimination based upon the accident of birth — though at a price; for it should not be forgotten that belonging to a closeknit human group confers its own moral benefits, promoting sympathy and social concern. That Antisthenes extended the scope of equality to include barbarians, that is, complete non-Greeks, would in the circumstances have been a short step that he may well have taken. Save for the silence of the record as concerns slaves, we may then regard it as likely that his thought chimed with humanitarianism or equalitarianism to the extent that his conception of human worth took no account of status or of birth.

---

[190] Popper's claim that he is certain of nothing, though he believes firmly in his "point of view," is discussed on p. 203.

But no final appraisal of Antisthenes is possible without reference to the standpoint of the man whose influence on his career was paramount, Socrates. For in his admiration of Socrates, Antisthenes had been admiring a man whose life-long interest lay in awakening the intellectual consciences of all who came within his reach, a preacher whose gospel was a moral reason, in essence perfectly neutral as regards class or race.[191] Socrates, it is true, in carrying out his mission did acknowledge one special obligation and, apparently, omit one application. Speaking to his judges of his determination to continue plying his function as cross-examiner of souls, he had said, "This I shall do to whomever I meet, young and old, foreigner and citizen, but most to the citizens, inasmuch as you are more nearly related to me." [192] Young and old, foreigner and citizen, but be it observed, no mention here or elsewhere in the Socratic biography [193] of a ministry to slaves. Now we should be very ill-advised to make capital of this omission in a depreciation of Socrates as a moralist — it will be much wiser to regard it as an inadvertence due to custom, the unleisured condition of a slave's life, or the like. By parity of reasoning, we need not violate probability by the arbitrary assumption that from among the various convictions of Socrates, Antisthenes must have selected only those that favored humanitarianism and then have drawn from them all of the consequences required to complete the full-blown modern conception. The fact of Socrates' omission of slaves warns us that logical consequences are not always drawn, or full consistency in practice always attained; and what a Socrates could fail to do, his pupil without fatal consequences can dispense with. Both Socrates, and, in his more limited and secular way, Antisthenes, survive scrutiny as advocates of an ethic fundamentally universal, and aimed without intended discrimination at mankind in general.

Here, then, we have reached a conception to which the phrase "unity of mankind" in a limited sense — we shall call it "moral unity" — may properly be applied: the recognition of a common pattern of human excellence in terms of which alone the true worth of any man is to be judged; and the corollary acceptance of an obligation to impart a knowledge of this pattern to at least those members of humankind, without distinction of race or class or sex, with whom one may be associated. The substance of this conception we have found in Socrates, and, we may grant, in his pupil Antisthenes too.

And if Antisthenes believed thus in the moral unity of mankind, in a unitary pattern of the good life which it was his zealous intent to impart to others, what was, for him this pattern? The exaggerated individualism which he taught would find its logical expression in the self-production of a tiny

---

[191] See our note on *Meno* 73, p. 217 below.

[192] *Apology* 30 A, trans. Fowler, Loeb Library.

[193] The trivial reënforcing exception to this rule, also found in the *Meno*, is noticed on p. 148 above.

minority of the self-sufficient "wise," practicing hardihood and rejoicing in
social ostracism, respecting and admiring one another, contemning and holding themselves aloof from the majority of mankind. His *Cyrus* may well have
contained an account of the manner in which the welfare of the masses was
secured by the all-sufficient wisdom of their king, but of this we have no
knowledge. There is no trace of his having striven, in the circumstances of
actual Greek society, to advance the cause of coöperation, or to promote mutual helpfulness and loving-kindness among men in general, such as is implied
in the word "brotherhood." The friendly critic is obliged to pass lightly over
the indications of vulgarity and intolerant rudeness which are reported. Earnestness, moral rigor, and the zeal of the disciple and the teacher, yes; a universal ethical ideal, within the limits of its meaning, yes again; humanitarianism, brotherhood, or any other splendor of self-transcending altruism — unproven, even unadumbrated.

If now we were to set Plato beside this not impossible image of his one-
time rival, to whom we have given the benefit of every reasonable doubt, does
he lose all moral luster by contrast? By no means; for over against every excellence with which Antisthenes has been endowed — except for his entirely
conjectural explicit disavowal of the traditional Greek contempt for barbarians — one may point to a corresponding achievement of insight by Plato,
established by abundant textual confirmation. The proof of this will presently
concern us at some length, and the importance of Plato's influence as the dis-
seminator and persuasive advocate of the moral unity of man, and as a vital
contributor to the growth of the later ideal of humanitarianism, will there
be indicated. From the conclusions there to be reached, we may borrow the
assertion that Plato cherished an abiding belief in the moral unity of mankind; that in spite of a realistic recognition of the hostility subsisting between
Greeks and barbarians in international affairs, he made no invidious distinction between them in personal dignity and worth; and finally, that Plato believed in the oneness of God, as the one paradigm of goodness to whom all
men must become like. Plato's ideal of the good life, which lent content to his
belief in moral unity, like that of Antisthenes, was lacking in Christian tenderness, but it did not lack depth and high aspiration; and in the same measure
in which Plato's ideal of the good life was more balanced and inclusive than
that of Antisthenes, his conception of the moral unity of mankind was richer,
wiser, and more fruitful in the centuries to come. To those for whom the
vastly greater richness and complexity of Plato's philosophy of man do not
overshadow the merits imputed to the champion of a strenuous and single-
minded virtue — those for whom the final choice remaining to be made lies
between two thinkers whose merits, in the case before us, appear to be roughly
equal, or even weighted in Antisthenes' favor, we would offer this practical
counsel: remember that of the two thinkers, one is a documented reality; the
other remains, in most relevant respects, the meager outline of an ethical

position, and the scanty record of a life, amplified to an indeterminate degree by the combined efforts of his ancient and modern partisans.[194]

But were there, perhaps, others at Athens in Plato's day, from whom he could and should have learned a more active and benign conception of human unity and concord than that which he possessed? Several other candidates have been proposed, by Popper and others, for this honor, though on similarly meager grounds.[195] In particular, Diogenes the Cynic, a younger contemporary of Plato, whose reverence for Antisthenes we have noticed, has been frequently hailed as a full-blown cosmopolitan; and rejected; and hotly defended, and attacked.[196] Without entering at length into this second unfinished controversy, we think it fair to say that Plato's repute as a man of good will has little to fear from any reasonable estimate of Diogenes' claims. Suppose, first, that Diogenes was actually a contemporary of Plato at Athens — a point on which there has been considerable doubt; let us allow him to have championed the idea of the moral unity of mankind, as we have defined it, and further to have deprecated political allegiances as introducing artificial divisions among mankind. What follows? That Plato might have encountered a pithy aphorism flouting the claims of any community short of the Cosmos, to be the proper abode of the wise man. Seeking to find, in the way of life and in other utterances of the witty sage, a more precise interpretation of this dictum, Plato would have discovered that it implied a duty of imitating the animals in the public conduct of private business, of disowning the artificial prejudices which forbid cannibalism, incest, and temple-robbing, and of deprecating, as matters of indifference, all arts and sciences, human and divine, save the practical art of satisfying, with a maximum of independence, the minimum of self-regarding desires. A moral unity of mankind (or of the "wise" part of it) on such terms could hardly have had claims on the attention of a man busy with the planning of a city in which human life should flourish in its most comely and enlightened form.

For all the hue and cry, the only outright denier of the naturalness of the Greek-barbarian antithesis yet produced from the period was Antiphon, a man whose own particular way of using the antithesis of nature versus convention reveals him as what we would be likely to call an immoralist or nihilist;[197] a social analyst, perhaps; a "social reformer,"[198] never.

---

[194] The logical and epistemological achievements which Popper claims for Antisthenes and the relation which he implies exists between "methodological essentialism" and intolerance, are treated in Appendix V, pp. 595f.

[195] Appendix VI, pp. 597ff., discusses others who, it has been claimed, championed cosmopolitan views in Plato's Athens.

[196] See Tarn's article, "Alexander, Cynics, and Stoics," 1939. For further discussion of the status of Diogenes see *A History of Cynicism*, by D. R. Dudley, 1937.

[197] See pp. 144ff. above.

[198] So Popper, note 48 to Chapter 8, p. 563, has called him. Reference is here made to the Antiphon of the papyrus fragments; cf. n. 19, p. 145.

It is now time to redeem our pledge and to display the elements in Plato's thought which justify the rather far-reaching claims made in his behalf as a proponent of the moral unity of man and as a philosophically important source of the later full-blown idea of human unity. Since Popper has employed the distinction between Greeks and barbarians as a touchstone for distinguishing the friends from the foes of human unity, we shall focus attention on the significance for Plato of this distinction. But here it simply will not do to limit ourselves to the half a handful of passages in Plato's works in which the problem of Greeks versus barbarians (which, for convenience, we shall hereinafter refer to as the "barbarian problem") is specifically discussed.

A thinker of Plato's range, complexity, and philosophical coherence can confidently be expected to cast much sidelight on any one of his topics by his treatment of other superficially unrelated themes. This will be particularly the case in the instance before us because the topic is so extraordinarily rich in ethical and metaphysical implications. One could wish that there had come down to us under Plato's name a dialogue called the "Anacharsis, or the Barbarian," in which the problem of the moral unity of mankind was directly broached. But in its absence, we need not complain; no ancient thinker before the Stoics has rivaled his contribution towards the treatment of the theme.

That Plato's theory of man was grounded in an implicit conviction of human moral unity is the conclusion to which we hope the openminded reader will be brought. The important inequalities which Plato recognizes are those which exist within any group between individual men, or between groups of persons reared under different educational influences; but the differences exist without destroying the unity of that larger group to which all men belong.[199]

Attention may first be called to the strongly "unitarian" implications of all that Plato tells us in the great myths about the creation of the human soul and the beginnings of its terrestrial career. When, in the *Timaeus*,[200] the high God (the Demiurge) delegates to the junior gods the task of framing the mortal soul, it is noticeable that there is no suggestion of any second-rate prescription for souls of low degree. All mortal souls are from one and the same formula; their mutual differences are subsequent deteriorations not contemplated in the plan of their creation; and from these deteriorations result, not barbarians, but, we are whimsically told, women and the animals. We observe the same absence of any distinction in the *Phaedrus*, and again, in the *Protagoras*. In the former,[201] we hear of certain souls following with difficulty the procession of the immortals, and enjoying, in various imperfect degrees, the vision of the eternal forms. These are the souls which, falling and acquiring a material vehicle, are to populate our world as men; those souls

---

[199] The inconsistent position of slavery in this scheme is discussed in n. 226, p. 223.

[200] *Timaeus*, 69 C–D.
[201] *Phaedrus*, 247 B ff.

which have not seen the forms at all are incapable of human incarnation.[202] The souls which have shared the vision are, it is true, distinguished into nine groups, according to their capacity for clear, steady seeing of the forms (that is, on the basis of their innate intelligence and ability to control the unruly steed of passion). What this might mean for an eager champion of racial inferiority is obvious, but of that there is no hint; what it means for Plato is suggested by his statement that those of the first rank will become "seekers after wisdom" or followers of the Muses, those of the second, virtuous kings or commanders in war, and so on, a hierarchical division quite as possible for a barbarian society as for a Greek. So, in the *Protagoras*,[203] when recently created man has been equipped with the arts that will secure his sustenance and his defense against the elements (and it is of man generically that Plato speaks),[204] as if to make the accent on a unitary conception of human nature the more unmistakable, Plato tells us that Zeus in pity, desiring to prevent the extinction of the human race — threatened by inability to cooperate against the animals, and by mutual strife and injustice —, bestowed upon all men indifferently the great gifts of Justice and Reverence. True that, as we presently learn, in the exposition following the myth, this gift is not developed in all individual men in equal degree. But no radical and insurmountable differences between one variety of the human race and another, are contemplated.

If we look at Plato's mythical account of the far end of human life and the rewards and punishments awaiting individual souls, again we find no

---

[202] Cf. p. 149 above. The slave in the *Meno* would be more centrally introduced into our discussion here, had not Popper contended that he is the exclusive property of the historical Socrates, and hence, on Popper's view, a reflection not of Plato's thought, but of the Socratic humanitarianism that Plato treasonably abandoned. On my own view, there is nothing to prevent taking the striking implications of human unity throughout the *Meno* as genuinely Platonic. The "virtue" of which the dialogue is in search is required to be equally applicable to man and woman (73 A), young and old (73 B), bond and free (73 D) — in fact, to "all human creatures" (73 C). This is entirely consistent with the more elaborate analysis found in the *Republic*, where Plato, while retaining the conception of the unity of virtue, takes account also of what he believes to be important differences in human capacities; in his ideal state, he expects to secure a harmony of virtue in all his citizens by the development in the souls of the less gifted of right opinion and good

habits, replacing the autonomous wisdom of the most highly endowed men and women as the governing principle of the soul; every individual will thus possess a well-ordered and rightly ruled internal polity.

[203] *Protagoras*, 320 C–323 A.

[204] I follow Shorey (*What Plato Said*, pp. 124–125) in regarding this myth as Plato's composition, and agree with his further statement that "this does not mean that Plato may not have taken suggestions from Protagoras' treatise 'On the State of Things at the Beginning.'" In view of the extraordinary correspondence (noted, again, by Shorey) between the major ideas of the speech of Protagoras and the themes of Plato's *Republic* and *Laws* (cf. p. 294 below), I think it justifiable to present the myth as evidence, confirmed by the parallels presently to be adduced, of Plato's own convictions. The absence of satire and the exaltation of the style are further indications of Plato's agreement with the essential standpoint of the myth; and this would hold, even were one to regard Protagoras as the "onlie begetter" of the ideas expressed.

hint of racial differentiation. In the *Gorgias* myth (523 E ff.) we are told that Zeus appointed three of his sons to act as judges in the nether world, one to judge the souls that come from Asia, another to judge those from Europe, while the third, Minos, adjusts all cases in which the other two have found any point of doubt; after the judgment has been rendered, all the souls take their appointed ways alike, according to their deserts. There is no suggestion of special accommodations for any racial superiors or inferiors. Nor in any other of Plato's eschatological myths — *Phaedo, Republic* — though the *dramatis personae* are exclusively drawn from Greek mythology, as could hardly have been otherwise, is there anything to which the ardent opponent of discrimination could take exception.

Before considering Plato's account of the beginnings of history and the cultural achievements of the race, we may pause to gather a bit of evidence from a dialogue now first to enter our discussion, the *Cratylus*, in which the rival claims of "nature" and "convention" are examined in relation to the parts they have respectively played in the development of language. For all its play with the fancies of extravagant etymology, the *Cratylus* is no irresponsible farce. We can readily distinguish in it the philosophy from the fun. In one of the more obviously serious divisions of the argument, we find Socrates paying the "barbarians" an indirect but sincere and substantial compliment.[205] He is arguing in favor of the notion that there is a standard according to which the correctness of a name must be measured. Now if a man knows and understands the essential form or nature of a shuttle, he may choose to make a shuttle out of any one of various materials, according to his special purpose, and each will be truly and correctly a shuttle, embodying the same form in different materials; just so, the giver of names, the so-called "lawgiver," must first have understood the form and then have embodied it, whether in Greek or in a barbarian language. Putting the issue in more nearly contemporary terms, this is to ask whether the same "concept" can be equally well expressed in two different linguistic media, which is equivalent to asking whether a non-Greek (barbarian) language can be intellectually as respectable, as logically adequate, as Greek. The Socrates of the dialogue maintains the affirmative. Neither in this nor in any other part of the dialogue are the "barbarians" treated with cultural condescension. Their languages, as the measure of their insights, are regarded, in all the respects that are considered, as going on all fours with Greek. In view of Plato's sovereign regard for the values of rational discourse, this is no slight concession made to those whose unintelligible "ba-ba's" had inspired the contempt of the haughty and provincial Greeks who originally bestowed upon them the unflattering onomatopoetic soubriquet of "barbarians."

In the *Politicus*, on his way to the logical discovery of the ideal statesman

---

[205] *Cratylus* 390 A.

by the method of successive divisions, Plato has introduced an arresting passage, in which the traditional division of man into barbarians and Greeks is rejected as logically inadequate on the ground that "barbarian" is a mere congeries of classes bound together by no common natural tie; the distinction is satirically compared to a division of the animal kingdom which might be suggested by that intelligent bird, the crane, intent upon self-aggrandisement, into cranes and other living creatures.[206] Now, as Shorey has contended,[207] Plato is here essentially interested in the logic of definition; he is not advocating dropping the expression "barbarian" from the vocabulary of everyday life. But it is still true that in objecting to jumbling together under a common appellation "all the other races, which are countless in number and have no relation in blood or language to one another," Plato was measuring the distance between himself and the dogmatic racialist, whose distinguishing trait it is to cut off discussion and to substitute easy labels, like "barbarian," for the nicer discrimination that can be had only at the cost of honest inquiry and patient thought. The passage also provides us with a second indication that Plato would have been incapable of asserting the superiority of the Hellenes over all other races. It would, of course, have been possible for him to have surveyed with care the cultural achievements of all the peoples of whom he knew enough to form a judgment, and he might then have emerged with the conclusion that first honors belonged to the Hellenes of his day. Something of the sort, on a modest scale, he does indeed attempt; and even this does not imply racial bias.[208] But we must not suppose Plato guilty of the provinciality of believing such local and temporal preëminence to be absolute, in the face of this passage in the *Politicus*, which expresses his cosmopolitan awareness — Plato, be it remembered, was a traveled man — that there were vast numbers of peoples in lands beyond his knowledge. As we shall presently show, by the aid of other passages,[209] he contemplated the possibility that in these wide reaches human communities and individuals of the highest types might well exist.

Plato has, then, equipped barbarians with souls and languages equal in dignity to the Greeks', and has rejected as provincial the proposal to classify them all together as lacking the merit of being Greek. If now he still cherishes any deep conviction about an unbridgeable cultural gap, one would expect it to emerge in his discussion of the origin of handicraft and the practical arts, and the historical differentiation of the various forms of social or political organization which fell within his view. But the record, though otherwise abundant, shows no such difference. The picture, in the *Politicus*,[210] of the undifferentiated "human flock," under the immediate direction of one com-

---

[206] *Politicus*, 262 A–263 D, trans. Lamb, Loeb Library.

[207] Paul Shorey, *What Plato Said*, p. 600.

[208] See pp. 221 and 603 below.

[209] See pp. 230–231 below.

[210] *Politicus* 268 D–274 E.

mon "Divine Herdsman," belongs rather to the mythical background of human history than to history itself. We need say of it only that it adds one
more instance of Plato's philosophic neutrality as between Greeks and other
races.

To the student of history and, in particular, to the philosopher of history,
the third book of the *Laws* is certainly the most interesting section in all Plato.
Were we more fully at leisure, there would follow here a comparison of its
basic categories with those of Arnold Toynbee; the three-fold pattern of the
influences exerted by the environment, the play of moral forces, and the hovering presence of God in the background, is not unlike in the two men. What
directly concerns us here, in Plato's historical account, is the remarkable
breadth of vision, the display of the "modern" historiographical virtue of
universal perspective. Who speaks, a barbarian or a Greek, in the whole first
part of the discussion,[211] no one could tell by the criterion of internal evidence, save perhaps by such indications as the illustrative use of a quotation
from the *Odyssey*: there is no claim to special favor of the gods or to peculiar
moral or intellectual distinction entered on behalf of the Greeks. The forces
recognized as regulative of history are, with the exception of one pious reference to Providence (working in behalf of the human race at large), natural
forces, such as floods and pestilence, the availability of the materials requisite
for the development of a technology, the bulk and distribution of population,
and the like. We are given a remarkably shrewd speculative reconstruction
of the recurrent rhythm in the development of governments, from the primitive
patriarchy, typified by Homer's Cyclopes, who "deliver judgment, each one
over his own wife and children, and heed not one another," through the stage
of the combination of clans and the building of the city by the sea, typified
by Troy, up to the formation of *ententes* among strong monarchical states.
And now moral forces are added in the covering generalization that the dis-
solutions of states are universally traceable to moral failure on the part of the
rulers.[212] Sparta, Messene, and Argos have been founded, and have arranged
a multilateral pact, the security of which is endangered by the just-mentioned
moral failure on the part of the rulers of Argos and Messene. We are told [213]
that this pact had been intended as a protection for all Hellas in the event of
an invasion by the "barbarians." It is the first appearance of the word, and
it comes almost as a shock to the reader; on a second look, we see that the
expression refers to the Trojans, about whom we have long been hearing,
together with those who, Plato says, were their allies, the Assyrians, fore-
runners of his contemporary Persians. And in thus setting in the frame of
history the enmity between Greece and the Persians, showing the contemporary conflict as but the modern descendant of the war with Troy, Plato

---

[211] *Laws*, Book III to 685 C.   [213] *Ibid.* 685 B.
[212] *Laws* 683 E.

makes no implication of cultural or ideological differences. Troy, itself a barbarian city, has been used as a type of all early cities beside the sea.

In view of this impartial attitude toward the barbarians of prehistory, it will not be surprising to find Plato speaking on equal terms, and in some respects with admiration, of the historical deeds and contemporary practice of men of other nations than his own; Persia and Egypt are the chief examples.

Persia, in spite of the fear it still inspired, and its many faults, of which Plato was well aware,[214] is drawn upon as a source of moral and political instruction and inspiration. Cyrus the Great is praised as having tempered absolute power with popular freedom; he considered the interests of his own people, and listened to their advice, with the consequence that the Persians became united and powerful.[215] The subsequent decline Plato attributes to the corruption of Cyrus's son and successor by early flattery and indulgence. The power of the Persians, he tells us, was later restored by the commoner Darius and his six companions, who divided the rule of the kingdom amongst them. In his wisdom, Darius introduced once more a measure of "shared equality," and won the loyal devotion of all classes, including the common people. But after him, the corruption of his son, in turn, was the cause of a second inevitable decadence: the unity and loyalty of the state is destroyed by excessive despotism, the deprivation of the commoners' rights and disregard of their interests. Here, as in Argos and Messene, we are being shown the operation of the principle that moral failure in the ruler is the ruin of a state. The point for us to observe here is that the political experience of the Persian people is being treated, with no looking down the Hellenic nose, as typically human, its lessons valid for all mankind.

Mention of Egypt occurs in connection with three topics in the *Laws*. "There are evils in Egypt," Plato tells us; [216] what he considered to be one of these, we know: the love of gain is said in the *Republic* [217] and again here in the *Laws* [218] to be especially developed among the Egyptians and the Phoenicians. Plato, reflecting gravely upon the possible cause of this unfortunate tendency, makes no slightest suggestion that bad racial inheritance may be to blame. Instead, he weighs and rejects the possibility that it is an evil necessarily attendant upon the study of arithmetical calculation, something which he has been commending for the citizens of the *Laws*. And he concludes that the observed illiberality is probably "due to their having had a bad lawgiver, or to some adverse circumstance that befell them, or else, possibly, to some nat-

---

[214] *Ibid.* 697 D.

[215] Plato disturbs the modern reader by seeming to regard the victories of the Persians over other peoples solely from the point of view of the advantage to the Persians themselves. It must be remembered that he was engaged in a discussion aimed at illustrating a particular point. That he did not in general approve the building of great empires by conquest will be seen below, pp. 229 and 567ff.

[216] *Laws* 657 A.

[217] *Republic* 436 A.

[218] *Laws* 747 C–D, trans. Bury, Loeb Library.

ural disadvantage" in their situation, that is, to the superiority of some dis-
tricts over others "for the breeding of men of a good or bad type" — a doctrine associated with the Hippocratic school.[219] This, he thinks, is a matter
which must be looked to by any lawgiver who wishes to offset the possible
unfortunate effects of some particular region. But despite his reservations
regarding the Egyptians in some respects, Plato admires their achievement
in preserving art forms by sanctification, so that they show no change in ten
thousand years.[220] The teaching of arithmetic by means of games to "countless crowds" of little Egyptian children is another device which he approves
and wishes to adopt into the system of his model colony.[221] It is worth noting,
before leaving the *Laws*, that Carthage, that other barbarian power which,
like Persia, so threatened the Greeks of Plato's day, had also, on Plato's view,
something still to teach: the strict regulation of drinking practices, in which
the Carthaginians excel even the Spartans.[222]

In the *Timaeus*, we have, as testimonial of Plato's respect for the Egyptians, the famous and colorful passage [223] at the beginning of which is reported the just rebuke, administered to the unripe wisdom of Plato's ancestor
Solon, by the Egyptian priest: "O Solon, Solon, you Greeks are children ever,
neither is any man among you grown hoary with age." Solon has revealed
his typically Greek ignorance of the order of magnitude represented by the
millennia of past history, and his ignorance of that history itself. The priest
goes on to inform Solon that nine thousand years ago, before the most recent
deluge in Greece, the Athenians themselves were a most notable people, possessing institutions of great excellence; these, it appears from what is told of
them, strikingly resembled the scheme of the Platonic *Republic*. In confirmation of his words, the Egyptian priest bids Solon note that many existing
Egyptian laws and institutions are closely parallel to those asserted to have
been in use in antediluvian Athens. Thus in Egypt Solon may observe that
there is strict separation of priests, warriors, and craftsmen, and no man may
meddle with another's calling; and the laws encourage the pursuit of wisdom
and all science to the utmost. This is a more honorable distinction than Plato
grants the Egyptians when, in the *Republic* and again in the *Laws*, he accuses
them of putting first the love of property. It may serve to warn us of the free
use Plato may choose to make of his supposed historical facts when he composes utopian romances; since he wishes here, for fairy-tale purposes, to
strengthen to the utmost the parallel between Egyptian institutions and those
of the *Republic*, he prefers to neglect essential discrepancies, both between
methods of insuring specialization of occupations, and between kinds of wis-
dow and science. But in any case, there is no separatist scorn of Egyptians as

---

[219] Cf. the Hippocratic treatise, *On Airs,
Waters, and Places*. The same connection
between human types and climate is asserted at *Timaeus* 24 C–D.

[220] *Laws* 656 D–657 B.
[221] *Ibid.* 819 A–D.
[222] *Ibid.* 674 A.
[223] *Timaeus* 22–25.

men. It is institutions, and perhaps also climates, which make the important differences.

Plato's idea of the international relations to be contemplated between Greeks and barbarians has incurred much censure. In a passage in the *Republic* to which we have already referred,[224] Plato declares that Greek cities should not reduce other Greek cities to slavery, but should remember the common danger of enslavement by the barbarians. The word "enslavement" or "slavery," here denotes not the selling into slavery of the individual citizens, though the one was often a concomitant, in some degree, of the other, but the loss of independence by the city as a whole; to Plato it was so much the same idea that he refers to both kinds of "slavery" in one breath, and goes on in the next sentence to preach that Greeks should not possess individual Greek slaves. Plato asserts that the Greek peoples are by nature friendly to one another and alike and akin: the barbarians, on the other hand, are unlike and not akin to the Greeks, and the two are enemies by nature. The Greeks ought to regard all Hellas as their own, their motherland and nurse, and to remember the holy places which they have in common; it should be held an accursed thing for Greeks to devastate and burn one another's lands and dwellings, or to enslave their fellow Greeks. Yet against the barbarians, it is implied, these will be among the usual methods of waging war; and Glaucon, at least, expresses the hope that the abandonment of the practice of enslaving their fellows will encourage the Greeks to fight against the barbarians instead. Thus war with the barbarians is thought of as inevitable, and perhaps, even, if Glaucon speaks here at all for Plato, as meritorious in the circumstances.

It is said that Plato is here inhumane; in asserting that Greeks should not enslave Greeks, but only barbarians, he has "correlated the natural inequality of Greeks and barbarians to that of masters and slaves";[225] he thus shows his logical agreement with Aristotle's doctrine of the "natural slave," and reveals his own anti-equalitarianism and disbelief in the ethical concept of the oneness of man.[226]

---

[224] *Republic* 469 B–471 D; see also pp. 172–173 above.

[225] Popper, p. 150.

[226] For Popper's discussion of this Platonic passage, *Republic* 469 B–471 D, and for the unwarranted conclusions cited in our text which he derives from it, see Popper, pp. 71, 150; and notes 13 to chapter 5, pp. 510–511, and 48 to chapter 8, pp. 562–564. The matter will require our careful attention here.

Popper is confounding a recognition of the enmity and threat of aggression between Greeks and barbarians with an assertion of moral inequality or a doctrine of racial superiority. He seems to have a feeling that barbarians in Plato are, as it were, poor immigrants, whom Plato regards with scorn and prejudice, or, like unhappy neighboring peoples of a Nazi state, looked upon as having no rights that can be weighed against the interest of the master race. This would be to import into Plato ideas that are not there. That barbarians, taken as groups — e.g., the Persians — might justifiably be regarded as extremely dangerous and hostile

to the Greeks, Popper seems to have overlooked entirely.

It is also overlooked that in speaking of
enmity between barbarian peoples and
Greeks as "natural," Plato was not alone.
Thus Demosthenes, in the speech from
which we have quoted above, p. 164, praises
the Athenian regard for the rights of their
slaves (who were almost entirely barbarians), as something quite contrary to what
would be expected by the barbarian peoples
themselves, between whom and the Athenians there exists a "natural enmity" (Demosthenes XXI, 46).

In asserting that Plato, like Aristotle,
believed that Greeks are natural masters,
while barbarians are natural slaves, Popper
is, as often, attributing to Plato what is
undoubtedly to be found in Aristotle,
though even Aristotle admits exceptions to
his rule. To this practice of attributing,
backward or forward in time, the doctrines
of one thinker to another with whom the
one was associated, we have already had
occasion to advert; in Popper's hands it is
employed always to discredit Plato, never to
exonerate or to credit, so that Plato is not
exonerated on grounds of having perhaps
learned from Socrates this or that Platonic
belief of which Popper disapproves, but is
confidently assumed to be the source of any
disreputable belief expressed by Aristotle.

In all Plato there is no assertion that
barbarians are by nature slaves. In the particular passage in the *Republic* which we
are discussing (*Republic* 496 B–471 D), he
has said that, as barbarians are "naturally
enemies," it is proper to enslave them when
captured in war. Slavery was the almost
universal fate of such captives (when they
were not summarily executed or, if wealthy,
reserved for ransom) in all the ancient
world, and the Greeks did not contemplate
a world in which there would be no slaves.
It may be regrettable that Plato did not
recommend enslaving nobody at all, but to
assert that barbarians might be enslaved, if
captured, is not to assert that they are naturally slaves.

Plato possessed, if he did not, indeed,
invent, the concept of the tripartite soul,
and in terms of his own modification of this
concept, Aristotle defined the natural slave.
Plato also believed, as we have seen in our
discussion of the common citizens in the
Republic, p. 174 above, that some men are
naturally so weak in the moral and intel-

lectual power of self-control that they require for their own good to be directed by
others. Yet he does not equate these weaker
men with slaves, but in fact states that in
the ideal city they will be free. In the
Politicus 309 A, he says that the wise statesman will enslave those who are wallowing
in all ignorance and baseness; this may
refer to demotion into a class of slaves, such
as Plato was to include in his second-best
state, depicted in the *Laws*. But it does not
equate barbarians with slaves.

In the *Laws*, as we have seen, Plato
bases the economy of his state largely upon
slave labor, and strongly suggests that the
slaves are all to be of non-Hellenic origin
by proposing that, for the prudential purpose of forestalling revolt, they shall be required to be of diverse stock and to speak
different languages. We thus find nothing
here at variance with his pious belief, stated
in the *Republic* passage we are considering,
that Greeks should not capture and enslave
Greeks in war. Plato's employment of barbarian slaves in the *Laws* implies no conviction that barbarians are by nature slaves.
Plato had a great regard for the sanctities
of kinship, and might easily have recommended to the Egyptians, had he been in a
position to speak to them of such matters,
that they should not enslave fellow Egyptians, and that they should follow the same
rule regarding diversity of origins, merely
reversing the position of Egyptians and
Greeks.

It may be added here that to take the
step taken by Aristotle, and to declare the
existence of natural slaves and their virtual
identity with certain readily available types
of barbarians, would have been logically
most convenient in dealing with the particular question of slavery, though it would
have introduced (did introduce, in Aristotle's case) into other parts of the philosophical system numerous and insuperable
difficulties of another sort, which Plato
avoided. Nevertheless, Plato's thinking, because he had no such doctrine, was rendered inconsistent when, as in the *Laws*, he
contemplated the existence of a class of
slaves, and made no provision for elevating
gifted members of the class to freedom and,
beyond this, to citizenship and to office in
the state (see p. 184 above). But Plato
never, so far as our evidence goes, took the
step taken by Aristotle.

It may be repeated here from our pre-

It is also said, by another critic,[227] that Plato is parochial in his outlook upon international affairs, since he has failed to advocate an actual federation of the Greek states, which alone could have saved Greece from that conquest from without to which, weakened by internal discord, it was so soon to succumb.

Still another observer [228] holds that Plato was insufficiently aware of the barbarian menace, not recognizing that only a military dictatorship could save desperately endangered Greece from Macedon in the north and Carthage in the west; that the city states, jealous of their independence and hostile to one another, could not coöperate; and that Plato's proposals for an independent and reformed city state, founded on impartial justice, showed his utter blindness to the imperative need of military discipline and the value of powerful and ruthless city governments, like that of Dionysius I, tyrant of Syracuse, which would be able to compel the coöperation of large groups of Greek communities against the common foe.

Plato is also visited with implied disapproval, from a third quarter,[229] because he had no conception of a world state, ruled by a benevolent emperor, whose business it would be to promote concord and community of feeling amongst all his multifarious subjects. By some, also, he would have been more honored, could he have envisaged (as Diogenes is supposed to have done) the disappearance of the city state, and the substitution for it of a world state, not apparently ruled at all, without any laws or government or civic obligations, consisting merely in the universal pursuit by each man of his own self-discipline in "virtue."

Doubtless Plato did not build up a federation of Greek states, or look to a dictatorship or an empire as the salvation of Greece, or wish to dispense with civil government. Perhaps if the reach of his imagination had been extended further into the future, he could, at least, have spoken with regret of the impossibility of urging the immediate mitigation of the brutalities of warfare against barbarians, proclaiming as the grounds of such a policy that barbarians, too, are alike and akin and by nature friendly to Greeks; and we may wish that he had done so. But the reasons why he did not so urge it, for immediate adoption,[230] seem perfectly obvious. When Plato is attacked si-

---

vious discussion, pp. 193–94 above, that slavery cannot be rationally justified, and that it introduces unavoidable inconsistencies into the thought of anyone who makes the attempt. The failure of ancient thinkers to suggest a realistic escape from the difficulty was perhaps due to the fact that, with few if any exceptions (cf. n. 55, p. 158), no actual ancient society rejected slaves.

[227] Fite, p. 294. Popper, also, as we shall see, pp. 309ff., 320, has chided Plato for not appreciating realistically the possibilities of

the Athenian empire, as a means of forcibly unifying the Greek cities.

[228] Crossman, p. 278.

[229] Tarn, op. cit., passim.

[230] The passage in the *Republic* (469 B ff.) of which we are speaking, is concerned with a proposal for immediate action and marshals its arguments consistently from this point of view; for this reason Plato cannot properly be held blameworthy for failing to state in this connection his views concerning warfare, or the grounds for de-

multaneously, for not having done or advocated so many contradictory things
— in this particular, for not having recognized the extreme peril from the
barbarians in which the Greeks stood, and, on the contrary, for not attempting, by unilateral restraint, to abolish the customs of devastation, burning,
and enslaving, as used in war against barbarian enemies, and certainly as employed by barbarians against Greeks — we may be tempted to step aside and
allow the attackers to strike at one another.

But a more constructive procedure is required. We may here assert (on
evidence to be adduced in our later discussion of political theory) that Plato
was never an advocate of imperialism or aggressive war of any sort.[231] He
cherished the life of peace, the *"irenic"* life, as among the rewards of that
complete virtue which alone could make it possible.[232] To conceive of Plato
as the advocate *simpliciter* of war against the barbarians, or of war at all, has
no foundation in any Platonic text. Furthermore, Plato has not left us without clear indications of his reasons for using the phrase "natural enemies"
in speaking of the barbarians. In a passage in the *Laws*,[233] speaking of what
would have happened to the Greeks if the Persian invasion in the days of
Marathon had been successful, he envisages a veritable loss of national identity: all the Greek races would have been mingled and confused, and the
Greeks confused and confounded with the barbarian peoples; he speaks of
the scattering and transplanting of races and peoples which had been practiced by eastern conquerors as a device to secure pacification; perhaps, too,
the selling abroad into slavery of captured populations was in his eye. If this
result was to have been expected in the past, it was no less a threat should
Greece now or in the future be overrun. Even in Plato's mature years, the
Greek cities of Ionia had been reduced from independence to a deeply humiliating subjection to Persia. To urge the obvious: one need not be a haughty

---

siring peace in general. That he did not
elsewhere in his works explicitly advocate
more humane relations among various
peoples and states is another matter; in a
way, perhaps he did. His picture in the
Timaeus of the ideal Athens of the days before the flood, mentioned below (see p.
229), shows a Mediterranean *pax Athe-
niensis* enforced by Athenian arms, but — in
contrast with the *pax Romana* — leaving
each state or nation unenslaved and independent. In the *Laws* (645 B) he speaks of
a moral law governing the intercourse between states, as well as their internal ordering (cf. p. 520 below). Here is no un-
derwriting of the rule of force in international affairs.
[231] On pp. 510 and 515ff., we shall distinguish Plato's aims from those of Spar-

tan militarism and, on pp. 567ff., show the
error of conceiving Plato's Republic as an
aggressive menace to neighbor states.
[232] *Laws* 628 C, "The highest good, however, is neither war nor civil strife — which
things we should pray to be saved from —
but peace one with another and friendly
feeling"; *ibid.* 803 D, "It is the life of peace
that everyone should live as much and as
well as he can" (trans. Bury, Loeb Library).
At *Laws* 742 D ff. Plato lists as the popularly accepted measures of a state's well-being
wealth, imperial power, virtue, and happiness, accepting the last two as inseparable
expressions of his own ideal, but unhesitatingly rejecting extreme wealth and, by
implication, empire, as incompatible with
these sovereign goals.
[233] *Laws* 692 E–693 A.

racialist to dread enslavement, loss of national identity, or even mere conquest by a foreign power.

There is also in the *Laws* that passage, already quoted,[234] in which Plato speaks of the war between the Trojans and the Greeks of that earlier day, as strictly parallel to the enmity in his own day between Persians and Greeks: after the Trojan war the Greeks feared that they might be attacked, in reprisal, by the Trojans and their allies, the Assyrians, "as we today fear the Great King." The barbarians, especially those to the east, were the immemorial enemies of the eastern and mainland Greeks, as the Carthaginians were of the western Greeks. In all this, the struggle between Greeks and barbarians, at least since the days of Troy, is thought of as defensive on the side of the Greeks, or at the most, as preventive attack. It is true that the Greeks had enslaved barbarians, or at least had made raids against them; but the Greece of the city states was not a conquering nation, and Plato, in particular, never wished her to be, as we shall see below.

Much material bearing on the barbarian question presents itself in the *Menexenus*.[235] But one must use what is there said with great care and at one's own risk; for in it Plato has mixed the moods of earnest and of ironic jest. We find him extravagantly praising the Athenians for having pursued, in their historical relations with other Greeks, precisely that policy of moderation in war, and that racial piety, which, in the *Republic*, he was to hold up as a Panhellenic ideal, and by the same token, castigating the other Greeks for their willingness to call in the barbarians (i.e., the Persians) as allies in their wars against fellow Greeks, and for their readiness to enslave one another. Plato swellingly declares that the unfailing benevolence of the Athenians, their desire to help all who stood in danger of enslavement, had prompted them to save the great King himself, although the reverence for their ancestors who fell at Marathon, Salamis, and Plataea, had restricted them to permitting Athenian volunteers and exiles to aid him. Later, the Athenians, alone of all the Greeks, refused to surrender to the Persian King, for money, their fellow Greeks of the Ionian cities; this they could not do because, Plato is swept into saying, they are pure-blooded Greeks beyond the common run of Greeks, and therefore have no divided loyalties, but feel for the barbarians pure and wholehearted hatred. Under the impulse of the spirit of hyperbole implicit in the oration, Plato has managed here to praise Athens, almost in a breath, both for her noble generosity to barbarians, and for her pure hatred toward them, based on her purity of race.[236] What seriously un-

---

[234] *Laws* 685 C–E.

[235] *Menexenus* 242–245. For further comment on the *Menexenus* and an indication of the writer's interpretation of what Plato meant it to convey, see pp. 335ff. below.

[236] Similar praise of the Athenians for their (supposed) almost extravagant gener-osity toward barbarians, we have seen expressed by Demosthenes (see p. 164 above); and in his oration in favor of Phormio, Demosthenes compliments the Athenians of the jury upon their nobility of birth, their proper pride in their pure Athenian family lines. (Dem. XXXVI, 30).

derlies these rhetorical commonplaces of patriotic pride is the sense that the
barbarians, whether attacking independently as in the past, or called in by
factions among the Greeks themselves, were a constant source of danger to
the Greek world.

In view of all this, it is pressing a word to see in the phrase "natural
enemies," used by Plato of the barbarians, anything more than a recognition
of the actual situation in Plato's day. The enmity between Greeks and barbarians was immemorial and ever-present. It had brought death upon the ancestors of the Greeks and had enslaved their contemporaries. And every Greek
was born and lived his life in danger of conquest by the barbarians, as likewise these barbarians were "born" knowing that they might be led against the
Greeks. The phrase itself can be no warrant for any far-reaching conclusions
as to Plato's thought about mankind.

Also relevant to international affairs is a disputed sentence in the *Republic*
which concerns a young Greek of splendid natural abilities, usually identified
with Alcibiades, who, it is said, might have become a worthy philosopher;
but spoiled by flattery, he believes himself, instead, fitted for ruling over
"both Greeks and barbarians." [237] Plato's satirical use of this proverbial-
sounding phrase, expressive of unbounded ambition, has been interpreted,
like the *Menexenus* passage above, as an "attack upon cosmopolitan or similar tendencies," [238] as if Plato were here obstructing the kind of benevolent
desire to unify East and West which Tarn sees and admires in Alexander. Yet
Plato's expression can certainly contribute nothing to any charge that he
scorned barbarians. It is quite true that Plato had no wish that Greeks and
barbarians should be cosmopolitically united under the universal sway of
any man, be he an Alcibiades or an Alexander, nor was Plato in general am-

---

These were compliments which the Athenians expected from their orators. So too
Lysias, in his Funeral Oration, which in
many of its themes closely resembles the
Menexenus oration (cf. p. 337), derives the
excellence of the Athenians from their
origin, *not* by descent from a miscellany of
peoples "gathered from all quarters," but
by autochthonous birth from Attic soil
(Lysias ii, 17). What Plato has said of the
racial purity of the Athenians is thus patently no upwelling of his own inveterate
prejudice. Plato's awareness of the actual,
mixed origin of himself and his fellow citizens is revealed in the *Theaetetus* (cf. p.
263), where everyone is declared to be
descended from partly barbarian ancestry.
But autochthony, though recognized as false
in fact, was for Plato an acceptable mythological vehicle of the true ideal, supplying
a regulative injunction to all members of

the *polis* to extend brotherly consideration
to one another — the very lesson enforced
in the *Republic*'s "myth of the metals" (cf.
pp. 424ff. below).

[237] *Republic* 494 C–D.

[238] Popper, note 48 to chapter 8, p. 563;
see also note 50, (5), p. 566. Since the only
result recorded in the *Menexenus* of the
"pure hatred" there said to be felt by the
Athenians for the barbarians, was their
refusal to take money for abandoning to
them the Greeks of Asia Minor, such "pure
hatred" might seem to be less an anticos-
mopolitan tendency than Popper implies.
But in any case one should not forget that
the meaning of Plato's phrase is severely
limited by the context in which Plato has
employed it. "The barbarians" here are
simply the Persians, in their hostile and
despotic aspect.

bitious for the Greeks, even the best of them, to become conquerors and rulers over barbarians. His own picture of the ideal behavior of a Greek state in international affairs is very similar to the behavior of the idealized Athens described in the *Menexenus*, namely: that of a universal liberator of the oppressed, with a special piety for fellow Greeks; he has described it for us in the *Timaeus*, where another idealized Athens, this time in the far distant past, is said to have driven back the barbarians of Atlantis (who had sought to conquer both the Greeks and the barbarians of the Mediterranean basin, among them the Egyptians) and then to have set everybody "free." [239] Similarly in the *Laws* (737 D) Plato remarks in passing that the citizens of his state must be able not only to defend themselves, but to offer aid to neighboring states, if these are unjustly attacked. This seems at least as reputable an international ideal from an ethical point of view, as that of an Alexander, striving, after conquering various peoples, to give them some sense of kinship and unity under his own self-appointed rule.

In the *Republic*, in the midst of that same satirical description of the unbridled license characteristic of a lawless democracy to which we have had to refer in connection with women, slaves, and the impertinence of the young, there occurs also a sentence which has been pointed to as antihumanitarian: [240] the complaint that in such a city, the resident alien and the foreigner are considered and consider themselves the equals of citizens.[241] It is true that Plato considers such "equality" as improper; we may understand him to believe that outsiders should not exert influence in the affairs of a city like Athens, or be given rights equal to those of the citizens, who have admitted these others on no such understanding, and on whom rests, or should rest, the responsibility for governing the city rightly, according to the laws.

We can better understand this feeling if we imagine an America inhabited by citizens and unnaturalized aliens in proportions comparable to those obtaining at Athens. If Athens had been for centuries in the habit of regularly and continuously, year by year, admitting to citizen status her resident aliens (a thing which she had on one occasion done, on a large scale, in the years long before Plato's day, and which we may wish she had done more extensively), the situation might have invited more tolerance on Plato's part. It might have been more like that in America today, where most of us who are citizens are the descendants of yesterday's or day-before-yesterday's aliens, and are confident, therefore, that aliens can be assimilated. Even America, however, would hardly have cared to open wide the doors to all immigrants from every land, and at the same time to obliterate, or even to blur, the distinction between citizens and noncitizens. Athens did freely admit strangers

---

[239] *Timaeus* 24 E–25 D.   [241] *Republic* 563 B.
[240] Popper, note 48 to chapter 8, p. 563.

from any land; and to feel that they should not be the equals in influence of citizens in a democratically governed state, may not have been so hidebound as it sounds. No national culture or ideal of life could long exist, subject to such dilution.[242]

That Plato believed such noncitizens should be protected from all injustice is attested by a passage in the *Laws*,[243] in which, again invoking that special moral sanctity which, as we have seen, he felt attaching to all those who are unable to defend themselves, he speaks in the strongest terms of the special retribution which a just God will visit on anyone who wrongs a foreigner.

We come now to two passages in the *Republic* which, since they seem patently to express in high degree a recognition of the oneness of mankind, require to be explained away by those who, like Popper, are unwilling to "idealize Plato" by finding in him "anything but hostility toward the humanitarian ideas of a unity of mankind which transcends race and class." [244] In one of these passages Plato states his belief that unless philosophers become kings, or kings philosophers, "there can be no halting of evils, either for the cities or, I think, for the human race" (*tôi anthrôpinôi genei*) ;[245] in the second passage, he says of his ideal city, that wherever or whenever philosophic natures are the rulers, the city may have had actual existence or be about to have it, in infinite time past or in the future; or perhaps it may exist even now, in some far off, unknown barbaric region.[246]

The first of these Popper has attempted to discount by claiming that in this famous sentence, introducing the central idea of the *Republic*, long prepared for and acclaimed by Glaucon as the most revolutionary possible pronouncement, Plato means nothing of importance by speaking of the benefits

---

[242] Here we really have Popper's poor immigrant, being denied privileges held to be open, properly, only to citizens. We may wish that Plato had envisaged naturalization processes for admitting aliens to citizenship. Perhaps, in an ordinary Greek city, he did; there is in this passage no proof that he disapproved the Athenian policy of admitting, to various degrees of civic rights, resident foreigners who had done signal service to the city. He would still wish such rights to be restricted to those who had been granted them. It is at least as probable that Plato here has in mind that undue influence in politics which seems to have been exerted by certain wealthy resident foreigners or metics, e.g., the enormously powerful merchants and bankers, as that he is speaking of poverty-stricken freedmen. (See G. Glotz, *Ancient Greece at Work*, 1926, pp. 313–315, 184–

186.) It may be added that the Athenian policy of welcoming foreigners, and the Athenian policy (taken over by Plato in the *Laws*) of considering any freed slave as simply a resident foreigner, would hardly have been possible if such resident foreigners had been thought of as persons entitled, after a few years' delay, to claim citizenship. It is probably true that never in the world's history has any nation, except, perhaps, for a few years in an empty, unsettled land, admitted all comers, and also extended to all of them citizenship. Some degree of exclusion, either from entrance in the first place, or from citizenship-rights, is universal.

[243] *Laws* 729 E–730 A.

[244] Popper, note 50 to Chapter 8, p. 566.

[245] *Republic* 473 D.

[246] *Republic* 499 C.

which philosophic rule will confer on the "race of man," — that this is, in fact, "an afterthought." [247] In the first place, Popper asserts, Plato had not the ethical conception of "humanity"; he was (as we have already quoted) the unsparing opponent of the equalitarian Antisthenes; in the second place, Popper adds, Plato, as a racialist, was alluding merely to his belief in the importance of avoiding racial degeneration in the ruling class, which was, after all, to be the chief task of the philosopher kings.[248] The second passage, concerning the possible occurrence among the barbarians of philosophic natures, Popper can only discount as Plato's expression of extreme unlikelihood: if even among the barbarians philosophic rulers should arise, such a remote contingency would still serve to give actual existence to the ideal city.[249] Popper's arguments will be discussed in detail in our note,[250] and, so far as they concern "racialism," in later chapters.[251] These discussions, taken in conjunction with our exposition in this section of Plato's whole attitude toward the barbarians, and his conception of man, will, we believe, sufficiently exhibit Popper's distortions and belittlements of Plato's meaning. Here we need only say that when, in his *Republic*, Plato asserts the possibility that among the barbarians there may exist men of the highest type which he can conceive, and when he also speaks of the benefit which such men, acting as rulers, may confer upon the "race of men," there is no doubt that the "race of men" includes all men everywhere, and that for all of them Plato holds at least a wistful hope that good may come.

One further passage concerning Plato's attitude toward barbarians will complete our list. In the *Phaedo*, on the last day of Socrates' life, he and his friends are speaking of immortality, in which Socrates believes and would have them believe. Cebes has been saying that there is in each one of us a child who fears that at death his soul will be blown away into nothingness, and Socrates replies that they must sing spells to the child each day until the fears are charmed away. Cebes asks where, when Socrates is gone, they will find someone to charm the child within into security. Socrates answers, "Wide is Hellas, Cebes, and in it there is many a good man; and many are the races of the barbarians. And all of them you must examine closely, searching for a singer of such incantations, not sparing your money or your toil." [252] Plato did not believe all individual men to be equal; — to find one to take the place of Socrates would not be easy. But such a man must be sought also among the barbarians.

---

[247] Popper, p. 149.

[248] Popper, pp. 149–150.

[249] Popper, note 50 to chapter 8, pp. 564–566.

[250] Popper's arguments intended to show

Plato's lack of the conception of "humanity" are met in Appendix VII, pp. 601ff.

[251] Chapter 8, pp. 424ff.; 9, pp. 535ff.

[252] *Phaedo* 78 A.

We are brought, then, to certain conclusions, contrary to much that has been written about Plato, both by friend and foe, which we may state in summary fashion here. We have seen that Plato did not entertain the notion that the whole wide world should or could be organized into a single community; neither did he express the ideal of fostering, in the actual world of his day, that concord and union of hearts among all men which should make war impossible; nor did any other Greek of his day of whom we have record. So far Tarn is right. It is none the less false to cite Plato, on the evidence of his recognition of the hostility between Greeks and barbarians, as having "strangled" any gropings toward an ideal of human concord.

As against Popper, for whom a belief in "human unity" is not so much an ideal of concord among men, as of equality in rights and in worth, we have shown that Plato was no believer in eternal cleavages in spiritual equality and worth between divisions of mankind; Plato does not represent the barbarians as the natural inferiors of the Greeks.

For Plato, the human soul, that "divine plant" of the *Timaeus*, has its habitation in every human frame, despite differences in intelligence and in moral direction; each soul has its momentous choice to make, to which God is not indifferent; the music of the spheres orchestrates its destiny, and the stage of its action is the circuit of the heavens. In the furtherance of the moral life Plato felt himself under the most solemn imperative, an obligation extending as far as his voice could reach; and this obligation, laid upon each private citizen, requires him to consider the effect of his acts upon even his humblest slave, and on the stranger within the city gates. Throughout the dialogues, happiness is represented as the goal of all men; virtue, defined in rational and hence universal terms, is the means thereto; and the universe is one in its nature, and unified to the last detail by the concern of divine providence. To demand, in the face of all this, that Plato should have brought to full maturity the ideal of human unity, shows little either of gratitude for his enormous service rendered, or of understanding of the process by which the world has slowly accumulated its moral treasures.

The Manual Worker

It will be remembered that "scorner of honest toil" was one of the charges made against Plato. The specific complaints listed are, in this instance, so similar that we may present them collectively, noting only the degrees of vehemence or moderation that reflect temperamental differences among the plaintiffs.

As aristocrat and man of property, Plato was incapable of grasping the real meaning and dignity of labor — so runs the unanimous arraignment. This was a constitutional incapacity, thinks Crossman,[253] due to the sheltered

---

[253] Crossman, *op. cit.*, pp. 95–96, 100–102.

isolation of Plato's existence, and entirely compatible with benevolence for the common man, whose interests, as he saw them, moved Plato to genuine concern.[254] On the contrary, urge Fite and Popper, Plato knew very well what he was about; prejudice makes men blind, but not so blind that they cannot see their own material advantage. There is even an element of cynical amusement on Plato's part, thinks Fite, at the cleverness with which the real state of affairs has been concealed from the workers in his *Republic*: they are dupes and drudges, undertaking all the mean and onerous labor from which the do-little guardians have exempted themselves on the pretext of other and more important avocations.[255] And with Fite's cynicism Popper stands agreed; he differs only by representing Plato as more bitterly in earnest in organizing his technique of fraud and oppression, and by according him a strangely inconsistent sort of pity for his victims.[256] But of this we must treat at large in other chapters. All are agreed on the scornful condescension with which Plato regards the worker and those degraded and degrading mechanic arts which Plato will not let his guardians touch.

Popper, again, as with slavery and the unity of mankind, would darken Plato's guilt by contrast; two men, Socrates and Antisthenes, he tells us, did all that was humanly possible to show Plato the error of his ways, by preaching a gospel of work. "While Plato . . . insisted that manual work is degrading, Socrates seems to have adopted a very different attitude. (Cp. Xenophon, *Memorabilia* II, 7; 7–10; Xenophon's story is, to some extent, corroborated by Antisthenes' and Diogenes' attitude toward manual work.)" [257] Popper reiterates these statements, together with the Xenophon reference, in several further footnotes,[258] but without documentation of the claim that Antisthenes and Diogenes approved of work.

Let us deal first with the second count. Was Plato playing renegade to a noble gospel, preached to his deaf ears by men of his own day? The question involves us once again in the thorny problem of the historical Socrates, as well as in the doubts and difficulties surrounding Antisthenes. What we shall seek to show here is only how far Popper's partisan imagination has outrun the evidence.

We have earlier mentioned [259] the ill repute of Xenophon as a reliable reporter of Socratic opinions, uncontaminated with his own, a contamination particularly pronounced when practical matters near to his heart are in question. In supporting his suggestion that Socrates was the advocate of work, by

---

[254] The topic of Plato's attitude toward the common man, in so far as it is separable from his attitude to the laborer, will be discussed later; see pp. 253ff.

[255] Fite, *op. cit.*, pp. 26, 93, 136–138.

[256] Popper, *op. cit.*, pp. 48, 52, 76, 166–167, 193–194, etc.

[257] Popper, note 26 to chapter 5, p. 516.

[258] *Ibid.*, note 47 to chapter 8, p. 562; note 4 to chapter 11, p. 615.

[259] See n. 14, p. 86.

the testimony of Xenophon, Popper has leaned on a witness whose strength he has himself recognized as insufficient to bear much weight [260] and has also found in Xenophon's report substantially more than Xenophon intended to put there. Among Xenophon's many pictures of Socrates as the practical and down-to-earth adviser of all who listened to his counsel, we find one in which "Socrates" advises that a household of impoverished gentlewomen be not ashamed to earn their bread by spinning and weaving for the market, an activity useful in itself and honorable for women; it is this anecdote to which Popper refers. In the following chapter Socrates similarly advises that an old soldier swallow his pride and hire himself out to do what he considers the slave's work of acting as farm supervisor to some estate owner. To neither occupation does Socrates consider the term "slavish" applicable. In the *Economicus*, a still more transparently Xenophontic Socrates shows where he would draw the line dividing the liberal occupations from the illiberal. The wives and daughters of citizens (we are told with approval) are all taught to spin and weave, and indoor tasks are divinely ordained for women; [261] but for men, only outdoor tasks are proper, and of these only such as keep the body fit, prepare a man to serve his country in war, and leave him leisure for the affairs of friends and city; all others are "banausic," sordid and base. Elsewhere, Xenophon's Socrates brands the tanner's trade "fit for slaves." [262] Nor did he recommend that the male relative of the poor gentlewomen assist them in weaving; enough that he, their "watchdog," supply them with protection. We see, then, that the Xenophontic Socrates approves work, but only under strict limitations. The neat correspondence between these limitations and the pattern of Xenophon's own career should not escape notice.

Nor need we be surprised to discover that Xenophon's Socrates is shown (*Memorabilia* III, 10–11) conversing with the practitioners of unpretentious arts, with an armorer and even with a courtesan. His concern is always with the principles underlying these arts; he is no nearer practicing or encouraging his followers to practice them than was Plato, as we shall see below. And he does not scruple to refer (*ibid.* III, 7) to the smiths, carpenters, and farmers of Athens, gathered in the Assembly, as so many "dunces" in civic affairs.

Besides Xenophon, no one among the contemporary and near-contemporary "Socratographers" whose writings have survived, has anything to say about a Socratic belief in the moral excellence of work. The comic poets, including especially Aristophanes, had apparently never heard of so novel a

---

[260] Popper, note 53 to chapter 10, p. 596; note 56 to chapter 19, p. 598–599.

[261] Xenophon, *Economicus* vii, 6, and 18–22.

[262] *Ibid.* iv, 2–5; Xenophon, *Apology* 30. One might also refer to *Mem.* I, ii, 56–57, where Xenophon ascribes to Socrates praise of "working" (*ergazesthai*) and the "work-

man" (*ergatês*). The latter word might seem to imply physical toil like that of a farmer, but in Xenophon can be used of a soldier or even a general. We have here only Xenophon's insistence that Socrates approved beneficial activity, as opposed to laziness or such useless activities as gambling.

doctrine, else in all likelihood they would have made capital of it in their caricatures. They had heard of bare feet, pallor, and grime, but these were symbols of austerity and asceticism rather than badges of toil. The "work" which Aristophanes ascribes to Socrates is done not with hands and back, but with tongue and brain; it is a "reflectory," not a factory, of which the Socrates of the *Clouds* is manager. Nor is there evidence of any practical intent to be extracted from the tradition that another contemporary, Simon the Cobbler, wrote dialogues — the so-called *Leather Talks* — in which Socrates was shown conversing in his shop, but to what purpose and with what result we are left to surmise; if, indeed, Simon himself is not wholly fictitious.

Plato's evidence on this point can be used only with caution, on pain of begging the question at issue, since Popper has charged him with complete and wilful misrepresentation. But there is no bar to mentioning that in the *Apology*, which even Popper regards as genuinely Socratic, when Socrates recounts the principal motives of his life, we hear nothing of work in the service of mankind, or of any mission to exalt the workman as such. When he does speak of the craftsmen, it is with no sense of special approval of their way of life, still less does he claim membership in their class; he accredits them with knowledge, excellent in itself, of their own crafts, but taxes them, as Plato would have done, with the grievous error of imagining, because of the knowledge which they do possess, that they know also many more important things of which, in fact, they are ignorant.[263]

One characteristic of Socrates, as both Plato and Xenophon portray him (we touched upon this just now, in mentioning the comic poets), is his capacity to bear up under deprivation of food and rest, or extremes of heat and cold.[264] It is necessary to lay stress upon this point here, in spite of its great familiarity, because it seems to have been the principal source of one major confusion on Popper's part. When Popper tells us that Antisthenes praised manual labor, "and practiced what he taught," [265] and adds Diogenes as well, he supplies us with no supporting evidence. We are obliged to go where Popper himself doubtless went, to those late compilations of quotations and uncertain anecdotes upon which we have previously drawn.[266] And here we find the probable source of the error. For in these pages, it will be remembered, Antisthenes appears as rejoicing in a kind of exaggerated Socratic rigor and austerity; toil or labor (*ponos*) was his watchword, and Heracles of the twelve labors, his patron hero. Antisthenes wore but one single garment, a folded mantle, was much given to the toil of wrestling, and threatened to shoot Aphrodite. Traditionally, "the indifference of Diogenes, the continence of Crates, and the hardihood of Zeno," [267] were inspired by him. He was outdone by the spectacular austerities of his reputed pupil Diogenes, who is said

[263] *Apology* 22 C.
[264] Xenophon, *Memorabilia* I, v and vi; Plato, *Symposium* 220 B.
[265] Popper, note 47 to chapter 8, p. 562.
[266] See n. 155, p. 207.
[267] Diogenes Laertius, vi, 15.

to have sallied forth from his famous "tub" (more properly burial jar) and on hot days to have rolled vigorously in the burning sand; in the cold season he would clasp marble columns to his bare chest.[268]

In all this, need we insist, there was much toil but no work, no glorification of that manual labor for pay which — so far as the evidence goes — both men were Greek enough to despise. Let it be remembered, for its later bearing on Popper's argument,[269] that Antisthenes and Diogenes were both reputed to cherish, for this reason if for no other, a marked admiration for Sparta; [270] nor must it be forgotten that Plato had also admired the austerity which was characteristic both of Socrates and of Sparta, and though he never encouraged its wilder exaggerations, in his *Republic* prescribed the "toil" of gymnastic for all his guardians, including the future rulers, who must love *ponos* both bodily and mental; in higher degree, it served as model for the hatless and shoeless campaigners of his city of the *Laws*.[271] For himself, he seems to have practiced at least one Socratic austerity (and perhaps others, for we have scant knowledge of his personal life), that of rigorously reducing the hours spent in sleep, rousing himself from his superfluous slumbers by an alarm clock which he had made for himself and which was found among his effects at his death.[272] We see, then, that there is no basis for the notion that either Socrates or Antisthenes admired or practiced workaday work of the sort required for the success of Popper's argument.[273]

Turning now to evaluate Plato's own attitude, we begin by assuming, charitably, perhaps, that no one of the accusers is blaming Plato for not having become at least a part-time cobbler or manufacturer of alarm clocks. They are blaming him for defective and prejudiced thinking, accusing him of having lapsed from the plane of critical, philosophical thought, into that of an aristocratic "common sense" that settles questions of value by appealing uncritically to the instinctive preferences and claims to privilege sanctioned by the genteel tradition. Clarity of thought requires that we distinguish two senses in which such a charge might be made: (1) that Plato never arrived at the degree of philosophical maturity required for making the distinction

---

[268] D. R. Dudley, in his *History of Cynicism*, 1937, warns against undue reliance upon the Diogenes saga, particularly the anecdotal material contained in our prime source, the *Life* by Diogenes Laertius, material which Dudley characterizes (p. 29) as belonging "rather to an anthology of Greek humour than a discussion of philosophy."

[269] See pp. 304, 638–639.

[270] For Diogenes' praise of Sparta, see Diogenes Laertius, vi, 27; for Antisthenes' admiration, see pp. 210–211 above.

[271] *Rep.* 410 B, 535 B–D; *Laws* 792 D.

[272] Wilamowitz, *Platon*, 1922, I, p. 715, quoting Athenaeus, 174 C. Cf. also *Laws* 807 E ff.

[273] Ironical in this connection is the fact that in the old aristocratic educational program, of which Pindar was the poet laureate, "*ponos*" was accorded an important place. See Eduard Schwartz, *Ethik der Griechen*, 1951, pp. 50–51. As an appropriate translation for "*ponos*," in this context, Schwartz suggests "training," and adds the notion of "hard discipline." Even more directly to our purpose is his discovery of this same meaning in the word as used by Antisthenes himself (pp. 120 and 141).

between objective value, and the values of aristocratic common sense; or (2) that having reached the distinction, he permitted his better reason to be overcome, either chronically, or on occasion, by the rhetoric of his baser self. The answer to these charges will emerge from the discussion which follows.

Plato's most emphatic recognition of the confusion of thought that results from allowing our "instinctive" repugnance to certain sorts of experienced objects to guide our metaphysical thought about them, occurs in the *Parmenides*. In this dialogue, Socrates, still a very young man, is encouraged and courteously reproved by the aging master of dialectic, — encouraged for the vigor of his philosophic "drive," and rebuked for his error of allowing popular prejudice to misshape his thought. Socrates, it appears, has scrupled to admit into the honorable society of the eternally subsisting Forms such disreputable members as "hair, mud, and filth." This regard for the "opinions of men," Parmenides avers, is due to his youth; "philosophy has not yet laid hold of you, as one day, in my opinion, it will; then you will dishonour none of these." [274]

These words are, indeed, put into the mouth of Parmenides; they possess an obvious propriety to the thought of the man who defied common sense, branding it in his poem as "the false way of opinion," in favor of an audacious theory of the unqualified One. Nevertheless, that Plato is fully endorsing the view here expressed is clear, from the fact that, as we shall presently see, its substance is reasserted elsewhere in the Platonic writings.

In another of the dialogues of Plato's later period, when philosophy had had time enough to lay tightly hold of Plato, at any rate,[275] we find him engaged in a logical analysis which preserves the most perfect neutrality of outlook in the face of a subject matter ranging from the general's art of capturing men to the very humble little art of destroying lice.[276] The *Sophist* might almost be taken as an extended footnote by Plato on the meaning of Parmenides' advice to the young Socrates: thought has a job to do, important and difficult enough in itself; trust it, and do not hamper its operation and pervert its result by intruding extraneous difficulties in its path. On occasion, that is, thought must think of lice, on occasion of the divine providence; thought alone can determine the propriety of each; to pure reason all things are pure.[277] We may find Plato further applying the same rule when, in the

---

[274] *Parmenides* 130 E.

[275] To my reading, the opinions of the Socrates of the *Parmenides* are simply some of the doubts and surmises of Plato about his own theory of ideas. So Ross, D., *Plato's Theory of Ideas*, pp. 84–85.

[276] *Sophist* 227 B. The art of weaving is illustratively employed in a similar fashion in the *Politicus* 279 B ff.

[277] That the theme of the arts, high and low, their structural relation to each other and to the pattern of human life, occupies

no small place in Plato's thought, is a thesis vigorously maintained and subtly argued by Professor Wild (John Wild, *Plato's Theory of Man*, 1946), who has gathered from a comprehensive survey of the dialogues a truly astonishing number of passages to support his conviction that Plato as philosopher of culture has much to say still pertinent to the modern world. Professor Wild has had the daring — and I would add, the philosophical insight — to seek the heart and spirit of Plato's social philosophy

Laws, he gives his mind indifferently to the high theme of natural theology, in Book X, and to minute prescriptions for the regulation of orchards, market practices, and hot water for temple baths. Our conclusion must be that Plato had by no means failed to make the distinction between "common sense" and critical objectivity, in dealing as a theorist with value situations, and that he has heeded the warning of Parmenides in an honest endeavor to preserve his thought from the perverting influence of human prejudice.

But, it will be objected, thinking about the art of louse-catching and the application of the art to the catching of real lice, by Plato himself, or, vicariously, through his guardians in the *Republic*, are quite different matters. Could Plato have envisioned himself, or one of his social equals, in the role of louse-catcher, and does he show scorn and contempt for those upon whom such tasks do devolve? The answer to these questions cannot be entrusted to a simple "yes" or "no." We shall be the better able to answer after the few preliminary explanations that follow.

Plato in every line of his *Republic* makes clear the first and all-important distinction that concerns us here between those privileges or prerogatives that one may be born to — hereditary wealth or power, without account of merit or social utility — and that stewardship or position of public responsibility that one is born for, in the sense of being endowed by nature with capacities which, when sufficiently developed by appropriate and, if one is to become a Platonic guardian, rigorous education, qualify their possessor to serve the common interest with maximal effect. Privilege is banished as firmly as are the irresponsible imitative poets from Plato's state; responsibility is its rock and foundation. It follows that all reference to the special "prerogatives" and "privileges" of Plato's rulers, without reference to their obligations, to say nothing of their outright deprivations, is indefensible.[278] "Men of good will" have a right to differ within the confines of decency over where to draw the line of demarcation that, in practice, is difficult to draw, between obligation and privilege.

That Plato did, in fact, regard the activity of his rulers as an obligation, and an onerous one, he tells us plainly in a passage (quoted by Popper in disparagement of Plato as anti-individualist, but not in this connection) which declares that not for their own special happiness is any class reared in his state, but in order that they may serve the common interest; and prescribes that to this end the guardians, when fully trained, must forego their uninterrupted absorption in intellectual delights and repay with dedicated service

---

behind the letter of his sociological law; and though he has sometimes gone a little further in this direction than appears compatible with a full respect for historicity, he has set what I cannot but regard as a noble example of how to go about saving the living thought of a great thinker from premature burial at the hands of those interpreters who confuse the small defects of time and place with the lack of philosophic vision.

[278] Popper, pp. 50, 73, 90.

the expense of their nurture and education. With the extraordinary assumption that Plato is here speaking with tongue in cynic cheek,[279] we shall later deal. In concluding this section of the argument, we ask the reader to note that nothing that has been said in Plato's defense requires assent to the truth of his conviction that acceptable government can be contemplated in the absence of participation on the part of the majority of its mature citizens.

But if Plato did not claim privileges in his ideal state for his "aristocrats," did he, nevertheless, scorn the workers and the work? Since, as in a suit for libel, so here, in this closely parallel charge, so much depends not alone on what was said, but upon the manner of the saying, it will serve the cause of justice to put before the reader a concrete exhibit or two of Plato's *ipsissima verba*. Perhaps the fairest procedure will be to cull from Plato's miscellaneous utterances those representing his least favorable appraisals, employing the least flattering epithet at the disposal of the Greek language (we have already found Xenophon using it) for describing the life of toil: "banausic," that is, sordid, base, illiberal.[280] There are three such places in the *Republic*, two of which will be recognized as near neighbors of passages dealt with in our discussion of slavery.[281] The first of these immediately precedes the simile of the bald-headed tinker: we read of certain "miniature men," the most skilled in their little arts, who, attracted by the dignity and splendor that Philosophy, even in her present forlorn condition, yet retains, leave the prison house of toil and skip away to woo the fair orphan maiden to be their bride; "this is what these many unfit natures are aiming at, men whose souls are bent and maimed by their sordid and illiberal (banausic) arts, even as their bodies are disfigured by their trades and crafts." [282] — In the succeeding book Plato is speaking of the higher education of his guardians, to follow upon their gym-

---

[279] See Popper's warning, p. 52, that we must "keep in mind" Plato's real meaning when we read his description of the guardians as "shepherds of men."

[280] The word *"banausos"* carried with it from its origin (the root is generally considered to be *"baunos,"* furnace, plus *"auô,"* blow) displeasing suggestions of soot and sweat. The notion of physical deformity was also associated, as one may perhaps infer from the lameness of the Homeric Hephaestus. Following a familiar semantic path, the term was extended to denote all the illiberal "base mechanic arts," deemed unworthy of the freeman.

[281] See pp. 174, 177.

[282] *Republic* 495 D. In qualified agreement with Adam's note *ad loc.* we suggest that the persons symbolized by the tinker are the whole class of sophist-rhetoricians of Plato's day and those whom they had trained. The bent and maimed souls of the many unfit claimants to philosophy resemble the stunted and warped souls of the courtroom pleaders of *Theaetetus* 173; similarly the illiberal arts in which they have been engaged suggest the kind of rhetoric, uninformed by inquiry into "the nature of the whole," which at *Phaedrus* 270 A is called "mere routine." The physical disfigurement is harder to account for, but Plato may mean no more than the absence of that physical vigor and hardihood which the unathletic training and pursuits of a rhetor or speech writer could not produce and which to him were prerequisites of the highest philosophical achievement.

nastic and "musical" training. What must come next in the curriculum? Surely not the arts and crafts (*technai*), "for all these, we held, are sordid and illiberal." [283] The third passage brings Plato's conception of the banausic into clear relation with his ethical theory, correlated with the dominance of the least worthy constituent of the soul. The Platonic Socrates asks, "Why, do you suppose, do the terms 'banausic' and 'manual art' carry a reproach? Is it not solely when a man is naturally so weak in his noblest part that he is not able to discipline the turbulent beasts within him, and is able only to learn the art of flattering them?" And Socrates-Plato goes on to tell us that such a man requires, for his own welfare, to be the "slave" of another, in whose soul the godlike principle of reason holds sway; thus both are brought into a friendly likeness, since both are under the same just rule.[284]

On a very different philosophical level, but employing the same key word, are two passages, in the *Symposium* and *Theaetetus*, whose close agreement in form and content will be apparent in the quotations that follow. In the *Symposium*, Diotima has been speaking of the intermediate nature of Eros, a mighty Daemon through whom is the whole converse of the gods with men. "He who is wise in such matters is a man inspired, but he who is wise with any other wisdom, whether in the arts or in the handicrafts, is base and sordid" (banausic).[285] In the *Theaetetus*, the Platonic Socrates declares the absolute justice of God; "becoming like to God," assimilating oneself as far as possible to this perfect justice — that is the supreme knowledge and the highest virtue: "in contrast to this, the semblant clevernesses and wisdoms, when they appear in governments, are vulgar, when in the arts and crafts, sordid and illiberal" (banausic).[286]

We must turn now to our task of appraising Plato's attitude. As with slavery, so with this closely related question of manual labor, we cannot judge with fairness and understanding save as we view it in the context of the society within which Plato lived. We must ask what was the status commonly accorded to the manual laborer in the period in question. Putting this inquiry to two of the highest recent authorities, we receive a clear and consistent answer: "Honest labour as such, commanded no respect. How could it?" [287] This contempt is largely due to the corroding influence of slave labor, "the gangrene of which spreads to the whole of society. The sight of the slaves at their drudgery modified ideas about work in a deplorable way. Already the aristocracy of the wealthy had only disdain for the craftsman and the agricultural labourer. All free men now felt contempt for slaves' tasks. To pass your days as a workman, to resign yourself to the trade of a *banausos*!" [288] If a free citizen did undertake to earn a livelihood as a manual worker, the dead

---

[283] *Ibid.* 522 B. A similar sentiment is implied, though without the use of the word "banausic," at *Republic* 396 A, D.

[284] *Republic* 590 C–E.

[285] *Symposium* 203 A.

[286] *Theaetetus* 176 C.

[287] Heitland, *Agricola*, p. 452.

[288] Glotz, *Ancient Greece at Work*, p. 86.

weight of slave labor was there to drag him down to the bare level of sub-sistence. In these circumstances, small wonder that many sought escape down the avenue of adventure provided by the career of mercenary soldier, an occupation regarded as honorable by contrast with what was felt as servitude. Such was the starting point of Plato's thought about the laborer, and the word banausic, like the word slavish, carried with it and tended continually to reinforce a prejudice from which it was all but impossible to escape.

This initial disparagement of labor and the laborer, found throughout Greek society, had presently to come to terms, in Plato's mind, with other principles derived from other sources. Among these was the contrast — for Plato, even the antithesis — between activities beginning and ending in material wants and their satisfaction, and those higher wants, as he had heard Socrates term them, of the soul and its need of tendance. We shall find him overcoming this dualism, in some degree, as for that matter, Socrates too, in his fashion, had contrived to do; and yet the contrast reappeared, at all stages of his thinking, as a necessary distinction between the higher ruling principle, the rational and the divine, and that which, at best, is the agent or slave of the divine. Sometimes the two appeared to him to be divided by an unpassable gap. Thus we saw how, in the *Symposium*, the divine wisdom which Eros purveys has as its only alternative a wisdom which is, in reality, only a sordid craft, an antithesis reaffirmed with undiminished audacity in the *Theaetetus*. From this altitude of observation, it is implied, all those distinctions that bulk so large in the human perspective of ordinary existence disappear: there is no longer a distinction between the king's art and the toiler's; all mortal pretenses are rebuked with one common opprobrium; all occupations are banausic, save only the contemplation of the divine. The startling extremity of this position Plato seldom chose to maintain; indeed, it would hardly have been compatible with his vocation as philosopher of human culture. Yet it is no piece of empty rhetoric. It is an upwelling from the depths of Plato's religious consciousness, a hymning of the life lived by men blessed by the gods. Its relation to his more secular conception of social organization is a problem to which we shall presently return.

Plato believed, further, that individual men have different innate capacities for intellectual and moral development, different moral-mental I.Q.'s, so to speak; and he believed that men of the highest capacity are correspondingly rare. From this and the former principle, he could not but draw the consequence, decisive for the schedule of human relations established in the *Republic*, that those "golden" and "silver" natures, upon whom, as special organs for securing the realization of the higher values, devolved the proper ordering of the commonwealth, were themselves of the highest value; he could not permit them to be impaired by what he believed to be soul-deforming tasks. By contrast, the merits of the less gifted, the average members of society, received from Plato less than their due honor. Since manual labor had, in any case, to be performed, he was willing to tolerate for the common citizens, who were not, in any case, to be soldiers, its bad physical effects; its spiritual harmfulness he hoped to neutralize by proper guidance.

The laborer was further diminished in esteem by a third principle, basic to the scheme of the *Republic*, that of the specialization of social functions. Developed from the Socratic quest for the true expert in government and the other arts of life, this principle was not in itself a mere uncriticized prejudice; yet it cannot but seem to us to be pushed here beyond its proper bounds. From it Plato derived the necessary limitation of the cobbler to his last, and the life-long restriction of his guardians, also, to their proper tasks. Thought was their special function, to think, if need be, about the weaving art or the art of catching lice, but not for the sake either of practicing these arts or even of understanding them for their own sakes. It is to be done only in the service of developing the method and power of dealing with the "greatest and noblest" objects, that is, the bodiless realities and their relations, of which no sensuous image can be formed.[289] The principle of specialization appeared to justify again the uncrossable social chasm which prohibited to the guardians any participation in manual labor, made an ex-tinker unthinkable as a philosopher, and rendered it impossible for Plato to picture himself as a weaver. *Les extrêmes se touchent*, the high principles of a disinterested philosopher are in such cases brought into momentary identity with the prejudices of the Athenian leisure class, and the baser voice of his place-time speaks through Plato's lips. The detractors are, *pro tanto*, right.

It is now time to cry out "nevertheless," for in spite of the concessions made, there is much in the record highly creditable to Plato, evidence once more of the integrity of his thought, maintained against heavy odds in the face of the limitations and prejudices of his class and time.

One may point, first, to his stated ideal of the relations that are to obtain between the guardians and the workers in the *Republic*. In an earlier connection we pointed out the concern for the workers' welfare and dignity as citizens which Plato regarded as one of the distinguishing features of the best state. It is a little ironical to discover that Heitland, who compares the condition of the workers in the *Republic* to that of serfs, because they have no voice in the government, balances this by likening the status of the guardians themselves to that of slaves, in that they receive for their labor only the usual pay of slaves, namely: their subsistence and nothing more.[290] The truth is that neither group of Plato's citizens is enslaved to the other, on Plato's view, or,

---

[289] *Politicus* 285 D–286 A, *Sophist* 227 A–B; similarly *Laws* 769 B, in regard to the art of painting. It is a noble contradiction in Plato's conception of his philosopher-kings that they are also required to make practical application of the theoretic insights thus attained; cf. p. 545.

[290] Heitland, *Agricola*, p. 75. For the board-wages of the guardians, see *Republic* 420 A. The slaves referred to would be the public slaves, temple custodians and the like.

if one prefers the expression which we have seen was Plato's preference, both are "enslaved" to right rule.[291] Plato, who presumably knew at least how he wished matters to be arranged, prescribes that the common citizens shall speak of their rulers as "Saviors and Helpers," while the rulers are to address the citizens as "Wage-givers and Nurturers."

That these are intended to be no mere courteous formalities hiding the relation between exploiters and exploited will be evident to any open-minded reader of the *Republic*. For to what end the lifelong arduous devotion of the little band of guardians, and the perpetual readiness for literal self-sacrifice of their military auxiliaries, if not the achievement of the best life Plato thought achievable for the total community, of which the principal beneficiaries in point of number, if not, as might well be argued, in point of need, are certainly the workers? They are conceived as secure and happily busy in the performance of their tasks, not without a sense of their own dignity and importance as the brothers, as well as paymasters, of those whose duty it is to lead and to defend. This is not democracy, but neither is it cynocracy — nor yet Sparta. It is, rather, a genuinely benevolent paternalism, with an abundance of gratitude and mutual good will.[292]

In concluding this section we may draw upon the two earlier quoted sentences from the *Symposium* and the *Theaetetus*, for further evidence that in

---

[291] Popper would say, to the almighty state. We shall meet this objection later, pp. 518ff.

[292] Tarn, in his article "Alexander the Great and the Unity of Mankind," 1933, seeking for any conception of human unity before Alexander, has declared himself unable to detect more than a negative conception of civic harmony or "homonoia," consisting only in the absence of faction (*stasis*). This ideal, he declares, still merely negative, was then extended, first by Gorgias, then by Isocrates, to the Greek world, in an attempt to end the mutual strife of the Greek cities. But of any conception of a positive "homonoia," either within a city or in the wider world, of that "mental attitude which should make . . . faction impossible because the parties were at one," he has been able to find "hardly a trace" (p. 125).

Tarn is here unfair in failing to credit Plato's appeal to the Greek cities to mitigate their mutual struggles by recognition of their basic oneness, which he compares to that of the citizens of a single city; like such citizens, they must recollect that they are not to be enemies forever, but are destined some day to be reconciled, and they must fight only in such a way that reconciliation shall be made easy. We have summarized this passage in more detail, on pp. 172 and 223 above. Surely this is the equivalent of the achievement credited by Tarn to Isocrates.

Worse, Tarn entirely neglects the dominating ideal both of the *Republic* and the *Laws*, the designing of a city which shall be "one" and "friendly to itself." We noticed above, p. 174, how highly Plato valued harmonious relations between the members of his *Republic*. His discussion of the virtue of Temperance (*Republic* 431 B–432 B) is an impressive expression of the same ideal in the musical metaphor of *harmonia*: each citizen is attuned, both inwardly in his own soul, and in the harmony of his relations to the social order. Mutual amity to the highest degree possible is of the essence of Plato's ideal in the *Laws* (e.g., 743 E). Both works thus proclaim that positive ideal of civic harmony sought in vain by Tarn. Nor was it necessary for Tarn to go as far down the centuries as the date of Iambulus, to discover an ideal commonwealth in which civic harmony was fostered by kings; Plato's *Republic* lies at hand.

his appraisal of human arts and activities Plato was measuring "high" and
"low" in terms of *bona fide* moral and metaphysical values, as best he could
conceive them, and not employing a double standard in favor of his own
social class. Freely interpreted, we may find in the two passages an arresting
suggestion for the overcoming of the banausic. For in both passages it is implied that all arts, including the high arts of the practicing statesman and of
the educator, are base and sordid, when contrasted with the philosopher's
solitary contemplation of the divine; and yet, in the *Republic* (and elsewhere
in Plato), these arts, when illuminated by that very insight into the divine
which the two passages are exalting, are ranked as chief among the saving
forces in human life. Thus, it would appear, the recognition of the divine is
the supreme solvent of all that is base and unworthy in life and art. One
might well wish that Plato had further explored and applied the fine implications of this suggestion, which he has done no more than to adumbrate.[293]
If we draw out those implications for him, what we find Plato saying in effect is this: the only true meaning of banausic, on any philosophic standard
of value, is that element in human life which ignores or defies the gracious
and just nature of the divine, and which, accordingly, loses its likeness to
God. Let us, then, build "Callipolis" upon foundations both beautiful and
just, a city in which every work that requires to be done is well and rightly
done; in such a city, and there alone, the banausic will be looked for and
not found.

---

[293] Cf. also his remark in the *Laws*,
quoted on p. 260 below, regarding the services rendered by the craftsman and the
soldier.

7

Plato and the Ethico-Political Issues of His Time

The Aristocratic Starting-Point

"Defeated . . . irreconcilable aristocrat," advocate of expensive special privilege,[1] regarding the masses as "not worth talking about," [2] believer in government reserved for gentlemen "to whom the pretensions of the demos are a vulgar intrusion"; one to whom the murderous Critias and Charmides appeared worthy of exoneration because, after all, "they were gentlemen"; one who hoped, perhaps, that if his own political program of enlightened aristocracy were adopted by the Athenians, it would "only reinstate and justify" the old ruling class, himself and his friends; [3] treasonably pro-Spartan, admirer of Spartan narrowness and scorn of lesser breeds, despiser of the "unexampled liberality and enlightenment" of "the 'age of Pericles'" and "all of its works." [4]

The voice, as the reader will recognize, is that of Fite, presenting in part his recurrent assertion that Plato's whole political outlook was determined by partisan prejudice. With one important exception, presently to be considered, this is the gist of the charges against Plato which it will be the task of the present chapter to appraise. We have allowed Fite to sound the keynote, and we shall return to discuss his argument, but we must first allow the other detractors to reënforce his case, by the special way in which each one has used and misused the evidence in support of the common charge.[5]

After our hearing of Fite, the bland and moderate tones of Crossman

---

[1] Fite, pp. 135–136.

[2] *Ibid.*, p. 26.

[3] *Ibid.*, pp. 291, 132–135.

[4] *Ibid.*, pp. 142–152.

[5] In view of his eminence as philosophic thinker in his own right, mention may be here made of the comments of Bertrand Russell, in his *History of Western Philosophy*, on Plato's supposed aristocratic prejudice. For an exposure of the errors into

which, for all its incidental wit and wisdom, this unhistorical history is pleased to fall, I must refer the reader to Professor Boas' able review (*Journal of the History of Ideas*, VIII, 1947). Since there appears to be nothing of more than stylistic significance, relevant to the issue before us, to differentiate Russell's disparagements from, say, those of Warner Fite, we shall not attempt any separate answer to Russell.

strike the ear as a wholly friendly voice. There is, indeed, as earlier noted, much approval and even admiration in Crossman for Plato's political motives and aim. This does not, however, prevent him from stressing the part played in the shaping of Plato's political mind by "the atmosphere of counterrevolution" in which he grew up,[6] and from interpreting as a natural and inevitable consequence of his aristocratic origin, Plato's alleged conviction that "government was the perquisite of the gentry," and that "the peasant, the craftsman, and the shopkeeper were incapable of political responsibility"; [7] and from asserting that, in practice, for all his struggles to introduce reforms, Plato's final prescription for the ills of the Greek world was simply that "the best of the existing aristocracy should become dictators." [8]

The suggestion latent in Crossman, and to some degree, in Fite, that political opinions are the fated consequences or functions of the individual's social class, and are thus not genuinely free options determinable by reason and thought, is explicit and central in the view of Plato expounded by Winspear, a detractor whom we have recommended as collateral reading.[9] For him, indeed, this derivation is not confined to the area of political theory; it is invoked to explain Plato's whole philosophy. Winspear's readers have been well prepared for this sort of ideo-analysis by the manner in which he has handled Plato's philosophical predecessors, the Ionians, penetrating to the supposed heart of their doctrines by an ingenious decipherment of the cryptic symbolism with which it is overlaid.[10] It is instructive to observe the divergent results that may be reached by applying this method to Heraclitus. This pre-Socratic thinker, the philosopher of the universal flux, we shall see Popper treating as a reactionary, embittered aristocrat, whose "historicist" theoretical position is but an embodied protest against the lost stability of tribal status; [11] Winspear discovers in his thought the climactic expression of that progressive mercantile development which both he and Popper so warmly approve; to Winspear, Heraclitus was indeed the opponent of the lower classes, but in the interest of the class of wealthy merchants, whose problem is that of "trade expansion, with its philosophical counterpart — motion." [12]

Winspear, like all the others, has underscored the fact of Plato's family commitments to the oligarchic interest. But certain further exhibits are of his

---

[6] Crossman, p. 92.

[7] *Ibid.*, pp. 92–95.

[8] *Ibid.*, pp. 280–281.

[9] See our account of Winspear's book, *The Genesis of Plato's Thought*, p. 583 below. It should be remembered that while Winspear acknowledges other influences on Plato, e.g., psychology and family relationships, as needed for the "proper evaluation of a thinker" (Winspear, p. 162), these are plainly "dispensable"; for Winspear contrives to reach dogmatically untroubled conclusions without their aid.

[10] Anaximander's cosmology is, in this way, revealed as a sort of economic allegory in which "sea and land are put forward as the central realities, notions conforming with . . . the great rise in productive capacity and markets," while "the earth, which we may conjecture, corresponds to Ionian mercantile enterprise, is 'in the middle' and in equilibrium" (Winspear, *op. cit.*, p. 120).

[11] Popper, pp. 15–16, p. 22.

[12] Winspear, *op. cit.*, p. 127.

own arranging: Plato found in Pythagoreanism, with its diaphanously disguised espousal of the interests of the landed aristocracy, an impressive rationalization for his own antidemocratic prejudice. So confident is Winspear of the strength of this affiliation, that he regards the political oppressions accredited to the brotherhood in the sixth century during their dominance in Magna Graecia as all but certain evidence of what Plato would have done, had his fair city descended from heaven into social fact.[13] Winspear stands alone (though Fite, one suspects from occasional innuendoes, could be induced to repeat the words of the accusation after him [14]) in naming as traitor to his class and as senior partner in Plato's aristocratic prejudice, none other than that Socrates whom Crossman and Popper have claimed as the great libertarian.[15] And in natural association with his corrupt and corrupting love of Socrates, Winspear, following Fite's precedent, sets Plato's slightly qualified approval of Critias.[16]

A scrutiny of the arguments offered by Popper as proof of Plato's aristocratic bias will show that his charges, while wider than those of any other single critic, do not extend beyond their collective range. But it has still been possible for him to develop his case in his own unmistakable way. Two traits are pronounced. There is, first, the technique of exposition, by which repetition, undertone, overtone, and contrasts of light and shade achieve a heightening of effect, with a corresponding lowering of Plato's reputation. Second, there is the uncompromising effort to integrate the evidence of aristocratic prejudice into a larger, all-inclusive picture of Plato's moral and intellectual distortions. Popper, as will be remembered from our earlier synopsis,[17] is engaged in an attempt to show that Plato's whole vision of the world was dominated and determined, like that of Heraclitus, by a peculiar "inverted" form of "historicism," which, again, was inspired by a self-interested hostility [18] to that process of social change which had already destroyed most of the privileges of aristocracy, and which, Plato believed, must at all cost be prevented from completing its ravaging work. Thus the goal of Plato's political program was that of "arresting change" in the interests of the privileged few, with a secondary form of psychological security incidentally included for the benefit of the exploited many. The other elements in Popper's case are dealt with in other chapters; meanwhile it is important to notice how much the initial plausibility of Popper's imputation to Plato of class prejudice owes to the interrelation of the various distorted components of his total picture.

The following samples will illustrate the tenor of Popper's view. Plato "suffered desperately under the political instability and insecurity" of Athenian political life; all his family antecedents were aristocratic, running back

---

[13] Winspear, pp. 228–229; also pp. 248, 85, 79.

[14] Fite, p. 101; 169, 173, 273–274.

[15] Winspear, p. 107; also pp. 106, 166–167.

[16] Winspear, p. 168, 188–189.

[17] See pp. 18–19.   [18] Popper, p. 84.

to the lawgiver Solon and to Codrus, a legendary Attic king; his connections included "Critias and Charmides, the leading men of the Thirty Tyrants." Disappointed in his expectation of entering politics, Plato experienced "the feeling that society, and indeed 'everything', was in flux," a feeling from which arose "the fundamental impulse of his philosophy as well as of the philosophy of Heraclitus." This flux, with its downward trend, was condemned by "the aristocrat Plato," who described that degenerate form of political (dis)organization, democracy, in "an intensely hostile and unjust parody." [19]

In his program of political reform, Plato proposes a "master class" which requires training in "the specialized art of keeping down its human sheep or human cattle" whom it is to "shear"; these working-class citizens are to find happiness in "slaving" and to do the "dirty work" for those superior natures, the rulers.[20]

In harmony with this denunciation of his native city is Plato's "general tendency to prefer Spartan customs to Athenian ones," a tendency shared with the "subversive and pro-Spartan oligarchic party," composed of "the privileged, or of the formerly privileged, classes of Athens." Plato allied himself with this party, which hated "the trade of Athens, its monetary commercialism, its naval policy, and its democratic tendencies," and opposed its imperialism; this imperialism Popper regards on the whole (and despite the partisan misrepresentation by which Thucydides has blackened its memory), as moderate in its demands, beneficent, and likely to have developed "into a universal empire of man." Plato remained at bottom, and despite all, loyal (Popper drives this home by his repeated use, in every possible connection, of the phrase "Plato's uncle Critias," "Plato's beloved uncle Critias") to the most "ruthless," "morally rotten," "hypocritical" "example of . . . nihilism" of them all, Critias.[21]

For these reactionary tendencies Popper will hold Plato responsible; for in his day there had already been announced to the world "the new faith . . . in man, in equalitarian justice, and in human reason," the faith of the "Great Generation," Pericles, Herodotus, Protagoras, Democritus, Alcidamas, Lycophron, and Antisthenes, including "perhaps the greatest of all, Socrates." All these Plato brought himself to oppose, and in so doing "was led along a path on which he compromised his integrity with every step he took . . . to the same point to which once the Thirty had been led" — "the return to the beasts." [22]

In replying to all this the great point is to maintain perspective, to keep one's critical temper. On hearing Plato called a "bad" man, one must not be

---

[19] The quotations in this paragraph are assembled from Popper, pp. 21, 22, 85, 42, and 43.

[20] References for this paragraph: Popper, pp. 52, 48, 165, 76.

[21] Popper, pp. 54, 174, 173, 192, 173, 175–178; on Critias, pp. 140, 179, 186, 189, 538, 594, and by implication, 182, 187, and 610; and p. 179.

[22] Popper, pp. 183, 184, 499; pp. 184, 180, 189, 194, 195.

irritated into denying that he was a man at all. Yes, Plato was born, and well-born, into an old Athenian family that had, if you please, a King Codrus at one end of it, and a Critias (and a Plato) at the other. Plato, like most of the makers of Greek literature and thought, enjoyed a privileged social position, which served him both for good — in his absorption of all its benefits of education and stimulating social experience — and for ill, in his initial absorption of limitations and prejudices. He belonged, indeed, by birth and association, to that very social and economic grouping from which the leaders of the counterrevolutionary party were also drawn. Doubtless the "admitted folly of democracy" [23] (at least in its post-Periclean form) was a frequently heard catch-word among the associates of the young Plato; only his own growing experience and the course of political history enabled him, with painful effort, partly to sift and separate its mixture of truth and falsity.[24] Family loyalty and sentiment may well have guided the hand that drew the engaging retrospective portrait of the young and still blameless Charmides, in the company of his cultivated older kinsman Critias, in the dialogue that bears his name, and added the encomium upon their family, in whose distinction, till then unsullied, Plato himself could share.

With Plato's critics one must agree that affiliation with the party of privilege left its mark on his political outlook in the form of limitations and prejudices. But we shall hope to show that as his life ran on and his wisdom increased, this element in his thought, never central, dwindled in importance, and though it was not destined to be quite overcome, was pushed into a steadily more marginal position by the weightier principles of his thought. That Plato if put in power would have followed, as the detractors have averred, the unhappy precedents of the early Pythagoreans (Winspear) or of the Thirty Tyrants (Popper), is a sheer assumption. In the immediate sequel, then, the non-partisan reader will not permit our agreement with an important premise of Plato's enemies to pass for assent to the extravagant conclusions at which they have arrived.

After this interval of partial concession, we wish to resume the argument by entering a protest against a widespread assumption, held by many who are properly counted among the friends of Plato — the assumption that practical politics, the achievement of a definite program of political action, was the overwhelmingly primary and absorbing aim of Plato's life and thought.[25] This alluring and perilous half-truth can be and has been employed to the in-

---

[23] A phrase employed by Alcibiades, according to Thucydides.

[24] For Plato's later and limited expressions of appreciation for democracy, in the *Politicus* and especially in the *Laws*, see our pp. 330–331, 513, 514–517. That Plato, in his earlier period as well, shared with the best advocates of democracy an active concern for the welfare and happiness of the ordinary citizen, we have argued on pp. 173ff, and pp. 242–243.

[25] The way may be prepared for this assumption by using the seventh Platonic *Letter* (as do von Fritz and Kapp, in their *Aristotle's Constitution of Athens*, 1950) to show that up to his fortieth year, Plato's

jury of all just and positive appreciation of Plato, and is so fundamental to the whole issue of the present book that its refutation is, in a sense, our major theme.

Plato, in the view here adopted, should be listed among the topmost members of that small number of philosophers in the western world to whom the *unum necessarium* was the winning of an adequate metaphysical and religious standpoint capable of serving as the basis for the theory and practice of the moral life, an objective rendered doubly urgent, on the one side, by the inadequacy and decay of the traditional Greek morality during the late fifth century, and secondly (contributory to the just-mentioned decay) by the danger to all morality, as he conceived it, of the compound of skepticism, relativism, and naturalistic nihilism, which he saw as the meaning of the sophistic movement. The single bulwark standing against this menacing tide appeared to him in the person of Socrates, whose unfinished business of establishing human life upon a rational and righteous foundation it would be the business of his life to bring to consummation.[26]

It is at this point and in this context that "politics," in the only sense in which the term is applicable to Plato, entered his system of ideas. The form and content of the *Republic* are the best illustration here. Setting out as a Socratic search for the definition of a virtue, it develops into a Platonic de-

---

thought was dominated by the problem of practical politics, to a degree radically "inconsistent with that picture of the 'born philosopher' and his attitude toward life which is familiar to us from the best known of Plato's works" (p. 218). These critics then require us to read the *Apology, Crito,* and *Gorgias* as works that "concentrate upon Socrates' conflict with the Athenian democracy" and "do not presuppose the philosophical contents of any other Platonic work" (p. 219). From this position it is but a step (not taken by these writers, but, as we shall see, taken by several of the detractors) to assert that what is central and alone expressive of the author's intention in the *Republic,* is the securing of practical political ends; whatever elements in the work are found in contradiction with this interpretation, must then be disposed of as either psychologically instrumental to the grand aim, or conscious or unconscious misrepresentation.

In my judgment there is no need to be led, by acceptance of the seventh *Letter,* to such a conclusion for the reason that the harsh contrast between "practical" politics and philosophical theory did not constitute a significant alternative in Plato's thought.

There is, as we shall show at some length (pp. 333–34, 644), a genuine continuity between the "Socratic" self-scrutiny and pursuit of individual virtue, and the Platonic vision of the perfect state. Both are in one sense practical and in another, not. Furthermore, to hold with von Fritz and Kapp that the *Apology, Crito,* and *Gorgias* are dominated by the Socratic conflict with the democracy is to lose sight of the virtual identity between their ethical doctrines and constantly recurring constituents of Plato's thought. Indeed, the *Gorgias,* with its use of the language of the theory of Ideas (497 E, 503 E–504 D, 560 C), and the conception of the soul and its ordering in conformity to the orderliness of the cosmos (507 E–508 A), seems to destroy the sharp contrast between the purely political and the philosophic dialogues required by those who deny that a philosophical motive was at work during Plato's earlier period.

[26] This view is in substantial agreement with that of Crossman (pp. 97, 100), dissenting, however, from the excessive accent, running through Crossman's book taken as a whole, on the practical, political aspect of Plato's aims.

piction of an ideal social order. This order is designed to fulfil all the Socratic demands for righteousness and rationality; in becoming "political," it has by no means abandoned the ethical end. Indeed, it is Plato's endeavor, by setting the Form of the Good in the crowning position, to bind ethics and politics together in an indissoluble metaphysical knot, in the service of the rational and moral order in the universe. Thus the *Republic*, as it were, recapitulates the phylogeny of Plato's thought. The step beyond Socrates can be seen as constituting, for Plato, a moral obligation, owing to his master, to himself, and as he seems to have felt, to mankind at large. Taken in this perspective, it can be seen that such aristocratic prejudice as remained in Plato's outlook could not have usurped the importance it would have possessed, had the problem that Plato set himself been merely or primarily political.

The detractors with whom we have to deal have apparently made this very assumption; and this fact will now help us to explain their unanimous assertion that in Plato's birth and class affiliations they have found the sovereign key to understanding his motivation as a man and to interpreting his thought, so far as this is political; and some (Popper and Winspear) have even claimed thus to explain the direction and goal of his entire philosophy. In consequence, they have, as it were, reckoned the mere facts of his origin and background as items on their list of charges; by adding that he has shown pride in his relationship to Solon, and has praised members of his family, like Glaucon in the *Republic* (we postpone for the time, discussion of the case of Critias), they have made the implication of *hauteur* more damaging, and have heightened the probability that the modern reader will share their own readiness to expect the worst in the way of prejudice on Plato's part and will be predisposed to see, with them, this prejudice as determinative of his thought.

The genetic approach to the criticism of philosophical arguments, as is well known, is beset by special dangers. But, as is clear from the continued and fruitful use of this method by biographers and historians of every sort, the method itself is not to be condemned. The question, as ever, comes back to the concrete use made of it on each occasion. We have already noted the paradoxical, not to say contradictory, results reached by Winspear and Popper, respectively, in their genetic derivation of the Heraclitean philosophy. We must now consider how it is that this method has apparently been found so useful by the detractors as applied to Plato.

We do not believe any of the detractors — even including Winspear, whose reliance upon the possibility of deducing philosophic ideas from socio-economic origins is maximal — has gone so far as to rest his charge that Plato's thought was basically motivated by class interest, upon pure *a priori* genetic principles. They have used the hypothesis as a logical springboard or signpost, have pursued its consequences out into the text of Plato and back home to the hypothesis, in the usual way in which scientific hypotheses are employed; with all this one finds no fault. And out there, in Plato's text, they have indeed discovered confirmatory instances of prejudice. But here, to our reading, they have gone astray. We must assume, in order to explain the end results, that some preconception of their own has led them to construe these discovered traces as indicating the existence of a far larger mass of prejudice, and also of class interest, lying concealed (we speak primarily of Fite and Popper, of Crossman to a far lesser degree). Perhaps unconsciously they have forgotten the lapse of centuries, and have thought of Plato as a modern like ourselves, one who, supposing that he felt such emotions as prejudice against the commonalty or pride of birth, would not, except by occasional inadvertence, reveal the feeling; perhaps a given critic has even begun his study of Plato as a search for the unwholesome origins of modern dictatorship. We know, at any rate, that the detractors have felt justified in ascribing to Plato prejudice and selfish scorn of great intensity. This supposed prejudice, applied as an explanatory principle to the text and to the events of Plato's life, has led in turn to the discounting or outright misconstruction of data pointing in the opposite direction; assisted by the assumption, mentioned above, that political action was a primary concern to Plato, and by some subsidiary hypotheses, such as the imputation of deceptive tactics, it has provided a consistent formula for forcing Plato's political message to fit the required pattern. This distortion, helped on by the neglect of those elements of Plato's thinking which are nonassimilable to the design, can then give apparent grounds for presenting the original hypothesis as validated, or even (in Popper's case) as congruent to the total area of Plato's thought.

Out of the matrix of this method emerge a number of plausible and internally consistent, if somewhat curtailed and remodeled Platos: a rather nice Plato, despite his old-fashioned assumption of belonging to the best people, whom you would like to have tea with in an Oxford college room (Crossman's) ; [27] a narrow-minded, self-satisfied, intolerant, and tiresome Plato (Fite's) ; and one to whose propaganda devices in the interests of privilege and oppression you would be wise not to expose yourself, without Popper's prior warning to distrust him. This last Plato is, paradoxically, at once incredible and overwhelmingly convincing, an extraordinarily unified and coherently interrelated pattern of prejudice and counterrevolutionary strategies; such is the cogency with which this malignant system is composed, that one feels that here he has, at last, found the logically consistent Plato. And so he has, with a vengeance, far more logically consistent than any other, for it is Popper, the consummate artist in logical articulation, who has caused us here, as Bacon might say, to mistake a stage play or show of art for a work of nature.

This counter-charge against the detractors, of prejudiced ascription of prejudice, cannot in this place be adequately sustained: it must gather evi-

---

[27] Crossman's Plato is, however, marred, both in consistency and charm by the atrocity of approving, hypothetically, the modern brutalities of a Hitler and a Stalin and the supposed cynicism of a British class of "titled wealth"; see p. 15 above.

dence cumulatively as in successive chapters (some of them already behind us) we come to closer grips with the actual "rulings" of Plato's thought on matters where aristocratic prejudice is presumed to have determined his decisions. In this way we shall hope, first, to introduce inconsistencies into these too-consistent Platos, and then to validate another, more approvable, though still humanly limited man.

It may be helpful, before further advance, to review briefly the course of the discussion in the present chapter. In general reply to the charge of aristocratic prejudice and political reaction, we were able, first, to reduce the area of the dispute by admitting the partial truth of the detractors' case. We then showed reason for believing that the detractors had overvalued the genuine data at their disposal by (1) the assumption that Plato was dominated by a practical political aim, and (2) (closely associated with this error) the misuse of the genetic method. There remains the task of determining how much of Plato's reputation for openmindedness will remain, after due and proper weight is given to all the available evidence. We shall divide the discussion under three heads, Plato and the common man, Plato and the Athenian political scene, and, finally, Plato at the tyrant's court.

Plato and the Common Man

That Plato was innocent of the graver inhumanities against the common man in the *Republic*, we have a right to claim on the grounds of our previous discussions. We have shown, for example, that he accorded the status of citizen, with full civil rights, within the limits of the contemplated "constitution," to even those least gifted persons whose sole claim to association lay in their bodily strength and capacity for arduous toil, and that the whole body of workers were to be treated with respect and benevolence. That such humbler members of the community did not occupy the center of his discussion, and that their needs have not been adequately provided for, have also, however, been made matter for reproach, and this charge we must now patiently refute.

Friendly interpreters of Plato have often argued that his cardinal principle of "each to his proper task" requires as a condition of its fulfilment a basic education common to all citizens; to include the children of workers in the program of liberal education planned for the guardians was, therefore, part of Plato's intention. This Fite has denied as part of his severe arraignment of the social justice of Plato's city, and he has offered supporting arguments of considerable weight. Because of the uncertainties here, we think it wiser and fairer to grant Fite this much of his case, that Plato probably did not envisage the inclusion of the workers. But to attribute this, with Fite, to the promptings of an envious spirit, grudging, in the interests of its own differential advantage, a minimum standard of educational decency to those from whose toil the fruits of leisure are derived — this is a cruel distortion, which a little comparative sociology will be sufficient to set right.

We shall maintain, then, that what the *Republic* sponsors is an education adapted to the anticipated needs and presumed capacities of the functional divisions of the community: a visual-manual training for those who will be called upon to make shoes or pots or statues, and a musico-gymnastic education for those who will be called upon to make war and civic peace, with a higher conceptual level of training for those who will be called upon to make decisions and formulate policies. We may suggest that many a contemporary progressive educator would be charmed to provide for his young learners-by-doing a semester or two of association with those "sons of potters" whom Plato mentions as learning their father's art by observation and tentative experiment. Such an educator might also envy the assurance Plato has given (*Republic* 423 D) that each individual worker will be conscientiously assigned to the trade or craft for which his native aptitudes have shown him fit.

It may further be asked whether our own American educational scheme, for all its genuine pursuit of the ideal of equality, is not to a considerable degree, above the level of the elementary school, still fairly describable as limited in its practical aims, and certainly in its achievements, to a radically differential schedule: trade-schools for the "many," and college and graduate schools for the privileged few. We do not wish to equate the two unequals, but we believe it is not only a sobering exercise in actuality to view our own practice in the perspective of antiquity; it is also more likely that we shall do justice to the ancient world, if we can discover beneath the mask of its radical differences some of the features so familiar to us in our own.

We may venture a further suggestion as having, at least, an initial probability: modern technology has so completely destroyed the sort of handicraft industry to which the apprentice system was the natural concomitant, that those early years of life, which otherwise might have been largely allocated of necessity to the learning of a trade or craft, are now largely free for the broader program of the elementary school. Had this same condition confronted Plato, who dares to say that he might not have availed himself of it as an opportunity for "planting a crop of virtue" (to adapt a phrase from the *Laws*) in otherwise idle and unplanted minds? On the supposition here envisaged, then, Plato's failure to provide an education like that assigned to the guardians may be ascribed less to aristocratic prejudice than to the unavoidably cramping limitations of ancient craftsmanship. If the detractor feels that since it would not have been possible for Plato to give to each of his citizens the benefit of a broad and humane education up to the limit of his powers, nobody should have got one, it can be argued that Plato did what he believed best for the others, by providing them with enlightened public servants.

But how if, by a mingling of aristocratic scorn and neglect, Plato has explicitly deprived the many, not of education alone, but of such protection of their basic human rights as would accrue to them under the rule of law? It is Popper's belief that Plato has done just this, forbidding "his rulers to leg-

islate for them and their petty problems." [28] The evidence for this statement
apparently consists in a misreading of a *Republic* passage (roughly from 425
C to 427 A), in which Plato is merely relieving his rulers (and himself and
his readers) of the advance provision of burdensome detailed legislation about
harbor dues and actions for slander and the like, while explicitly assigning to
his enlightened rulers the framing of such enactments as may be needed (*Republic* 425 D–E); adding that these will be few and simple, since, in a well
governed city, many regulations designed to prevent fraud will be superfluous
(*Republic* 427 A).

There is left the "argument from silence," employed by both Popper and
Fite, the assertion that Plato's lordly scorn of the workers is audible in the
extended treatment that he does not give them. "The workers . . . do not
interest him at all, they are only human cattle whose sole function is to provide for the material needs of the ruling class . . . This is why our information about the lower classes is so scanty." [29] Similarly, Fite, who has pictorialized his notion of Plato's scornful neglect of the masses by likening their
position in the panorama of the *Republic* to that of the common soldiers in
Velasquez' picture, "The Surrender at Breda": they are merely there by way
of a foil to the central figures on whom the painter has lavished his art, lay
figures perfunctorily sketched and shading out into an obscure fringe of pack
animals, outsiders, and slaves.[30]

That Plato has devoted less space to discussion of the working class than
Fite and Popper, counting pages in the interests of social justice, consider
appropriate, is not necessarily to be explained in terms of aristocratic prejudice. Another reason which might occur to a nonpartisan reader is simply that
Plato had something else in mind to say, a something which until recently,
few qualified critics have regarded as either unimportant or unjustifiable.
That "something" was a compound of ethics, educational theory, metaphysics,
with other ingredients too numerous to enumerate here, and to the saying of it
an extended account of the occupations and the training of the workers in
his state was not, in Plato's view, indispensable. We may remind the reader
of a fact mentioned in our discussion of Plato's attitude to the "banausic," [31]
namely: that some time after the composition of the *Republic*, as evidenced
particularly in the *Sophist* and *Politicus*,[32] Plato had descended from the
higher spheres of speculation and had immersed himself sufficiently in the
study of the mechanic arts to be able to discourse, in a surprisingly well-
informed manner,[33] of the technical process employed, for example, in the
wool-worker's and the angler's occupations. He would, therefore, presumably

---

[28] Popper, p. 48.

[29] Popper, p. 48. For our discussion of
the damaging implications of exploitation
and scorn of the workers, see pp. 173ff.

[30] Fite, pp. 90–94.

[31] See p. 237.

[32] *Politicus* 279 C ff.; *Sophist* 220 B f.

[33] Commented on admiringly by Wilamowitz, *Platon*, 1922, I, pp. 576–577; 1948, p.
455.

not have drawn back in disdain from discussion of the crafts and professions, needed in his city, had the design of his book required it. If it still seems inexcusable to the critic of Plato that he should have been mainly concerned with a type and level of education and of theoretic pursuits open and applicable only to the leisured and intellectual few, we are again driven to take shelter in the obvious: we will leave it to a jury of contemporary "common men" to decide whether the present writing and the writings that provoked it are not all, by the same measure, guilty of the same offense. Such benefits as may accrue to the ordinary citizen from our discussion will be indirect; they will reach him, if at all, after a long interval during which the social percolator has had time to do its job.

We may now for awhile shake free from the company and atmosphere of the detractors and turn to a project of our own, gathering for inspection in the hope of setting the whole matter of Plato's aristocratic prejudices in a fairer light a reasonable number of passages in which such prejudice is involved, either as exemplified or as opposed. The material can be arranged under three heads, of which the first is scorn of the "many" or of the "multitude."

There is scarcely a Platonic writing, from the *Apology* to the *Laws*, in which one could not find, verbally or conceptually, the contrast between "knowledge or true opinion" and "the beliefs of the many." The recurrence of this antithesis should not, however, be permitted to conceal from view a certain diversity in the connotation of its second member; in the instances to be adduced we shall ask the reader to note this variety.

In the *Apology*, reporting his search for a man wiser than himself, Socrates comes at last to question the artisans. He finds them wiser, indeed, than those more highly esteemed, in that they are wise in their own crafts; yet in their mistaken supposition that their wisdom extends to other "matters of highest import," they too fall into ignorance, and their claim to wisdom fails (22 D–E). Later, in justifying his abstention from political life, he asserts that no just man, struggling against the many unjust and lawless acts that are done in cities "by you [Athenians] or any other multitude" could long survive (31 E–32 A).

Crito, in the dialogue of that name, protests Socrates' refusal to break prison, urging, as a secondary reason, that "many people" will suspect him, Crito, of having withheld the necessary bribes, out of avarice or fear. "The many," he avers, "will not believe that you were unwilling to escape" (44 C). Socrates, replying, contrasts the many with the most reasonable or best, and by a brief induction (47 A f.) proves that it is only the expert and never the many whose praise or blame are to be taken seriously. True, the many have the power to take our lives, but this, in comparison with our justice, which they cannot take, is a trivial matter (48 A–B). Further, the many imagine that for an injured man to return an injury is just, a belief which, Socrates declares, all but a few will always continue to hold, but to which he and Crito will never assent (49 D–E).

In the *Gorgias*, Socrates, maintaining against Polus the unhappiness of the unjust tyrant, agrees with him that this is not the view of "the Athenians and the Strangers" (that is, of the whole of Athens), and that they and all of their political leaders with them will testify in favor of Polus' view; but questions of philosophy, of ultimate right and wrong, are not to be solved by these forensic methods (472 A–B). On the same principle, a little later, Socrates again refuses to accept the verdict of numbers: he is "not a politician," he says; he does not take the vote of the many as to the truth of his words. Instead, he offers to submit his case to the judgment of one respondent, Polus, whom he will crossexamine; "for I think that both you and the rest of mankind really believe that it is worse to do wrong than to suffer it" (473 E–474 B). In a later section of the dialogue, Socrates makes use of "the many" in order to lead the immoralist Callicles, believer in the natural right of the stronger, into a contradiction: The many, collectively taken, it has been admitted, are by nature stronger than the few; the many also hold that "justice is equality and that doing injustice is more disgraceful than to suffer it"; it follows that the truth of these two propositions can claim the sanction of nature, and not of convention only (488 E–499 A).[34]

"The many" appear in the *Republic* in a great variety of roles. "The many" mistakenly suppose that individual sophists, as educators of the young, are capable of doing any damage worth speaking of, compared to the "great sophist" — who is indeed himself "the many" gathered in assemblies and courtrooms, whose approvals and dissents, cheers and boos, impose their erroneous standards upon the impressionable youth. "The many" may indeed be likened to a "great beast," whose moods and appetites it is the mistaken business of the individual sophists to make into the subject matter of their instruction (492 A–493 E). With less of picturesqueness but with greater sympathy, we are told, however, that though forever incapable of philosophy (493 E–494 A), the multitude will be capable of admiring and loving philosophers, when once these are no longer degenerate pretenders but veritable sons of light (499 E–500 A). The many, in their pursuit of sensual pleasures, appear in a later book, in wanton aspect: "without experience of wisdom and virtue . . . bent over their tables they feed like cattle, . . . for very greed kicking and butting each other with iron horns and hooves" (586 A–B).

Some concluding examples may be drawn from the *Laws*. The many suppose that the aim of music is simply to give pleasure to any man, be he bad or good (655 C–D, 658 E, 700 E); when they were no longer strictly controlled, at Athens the many set themselves up as judges in the theatre, and

---

[34] The relation of this conclusion to Plato's own serious ethical and political theory will claim our attention on later pages, 416 and 422–423.

thus engendered a corruption in taste, which in turn sapped the foundations of the state, and introduced a lawless democracy (700–701). The many have no conception of the natural order of human goods (661 A, 742 E); they hold mistaken opinions about the virtues (662–63). They believe that there are occasions when the adulteration of commodities is a justifiable practice (916 E), and entertain the perverse notion that the study of astronomy is the road to atheism (967 A). Yet Plato will still insist that no man does wrong willingly (860 D–E); and he tells us again, as in the *Republic*, that though themselves not virtuous, nay even sometimes when they are quite evil men, the many can yet distinguish the virtuous man from the wicked (950 B–C).

In sum, we see that occasionally "the many" are simply most-people-within-a-certain-limited-group; in the first passage cited from the *Crito*, they are simply most of those whose good opinion Crito desires to retain. Another frequent use is the one in which we are particularly interested in this chapter: the common people, as distinct from the well-to-do or the educated — more specifically, the *dêmos* of Athens, gathered in its assemblies and courts. "The many" in this sense are spoken of as dangerous and lawless, and as believers in the advantages of power (in the *Gorgias* passage) and in false values generally, from the first dialogue to the last. But this "prejudiced" or "political" meaning blends insensibly into a third use, which we may call the "philosophical": "the many" as the antithesis of "the few who know" or even of "the one who knows." In this sense, also, the concept spans the entire series of the dialogues; with the exception of the few wise, it includes all of mankind, rich and poor, noble and commoner alike. And here we find both Socrates [35] and Plato displaying a strange union of intolerance and sympathy. "The many" will always be mistaken about the true good (*Crito*). Yet "no man does wrong willingly"; in every man, rightly questioned, will be found true wisdom; and "the many" can and will judge rightly of virtuous men, if virtuous men are shown them. To save "the many" from their folly becomes at once the end despaired of by both Socrates and Plato, and the chief end of their lives, to which their own achievement of justice would also contribute. It would be most uncritical to pass over unnoticed Plato's animus against the political party of "the many," Athenian democracy. But it is more uncritical, and unfair as well, to ascribe to this motive all Plato's condemnation of human error and wickedness, and to see in his desire to help the common man only a desire to put him securely in his despised and exploited place in the social frame.

We must now spread our inductive net a second time, for the catching of Plato's utterances expressing his scorn or appreciation of craftsmen or wage workers; and here, to do justice to Greek usage, we must note that the term

---

[35] We here assume the preponderantly Socratic character of the *Apology* and *Crito*; cf. p. 632. For the "philosophical many," see also n. 228, pp. 340–341.

"craftsman" is employed in a sense much wider than we in the modern world would give it: a sophist, for example, falls within its ambit. Our labor here will be much lightened by the results reached in our examination of Plato's attitude toward the "banausic." But for the greater security of building on a wider base, we wish to add a few supplementary examples.

A blush rises to the cheek of the aristocratic young Hippocrates in Plato's *Protagoras* (312 A) when he is asked by Socrates whether it is in his mind to become a professional sophist. In the *Republic* (434 A–B), we are not surprised to hear that cobblers may interchange crafts and tools with carpenters with less injury to the state than would result from the intrusion of an artisan-by-nature upon the office of a soldier, or of the latter upon the function of supreme guardian.

There is a passage in the *Theaetetus* (175 B–176 A) with which we shall presently be concerned again, in which Socrates employs some relevant metaphors: the petty skill of the courtroom lawyer is a mere trick of "rolling up a pack," "sweetening a sauce or a fawning speech": lacking the ability of the true philosopher to discourse about the chief ends of life in the interests of truth alone, he cannot "drape his cloak" like a freeman, or hymn aright the life of men loved by gods. There is an unmistakable touch of social haughtiness in all this; perhaps, as often happens in imaginative writing, the figure has claimed more attention than its due. In any case the central meaning of the passage concerns a distinction between two types of mentality which, it is arguable, are only accidentally relevant to the social distinctions here employed for their vivid dramatic depiction.

The *Laws*, as ever, will provide a court of highest instance on Plato's balanced conclusions on the proper attitude to craftsmen. Prejudice we still find; pilots, captains, and rowers, are, as in the *Republic*, a motley crowd, "not wholly respectable" (707 B); even the painter's art is one which a man will be just as well off for never having seriously considered (769 B). Citizens are completely banned from engaging in any technical craft (846 D, 919 D–E), from any manufacturing, mercantile, or other profit-making enterprises, except farming, and here only vicariously — the actual work is to be done by other hands; and the citizens' wealth is not to exceed a certain measure (745 A).[36] There is, however, a curious passage (919 B ff.), in which, with entire

---

[36] There is another source of corruption from which Plato is happy to think his citizens of the *Laws*, unlike those of Athens, will escape (*Laws* 705 D ff.). The inland situation of the colony will preserve them from the deleterious effect of naval warfare, with its invitation to cowardice, offered by the ships standing ready to provide escape. Plato further rejoices (707 A–B) that, not being compelled to owe their safety in war to persons like pilots and oarsmen, they will not suffer that perversion of values that results whenever greater honors are accorded to the less deserving. Plato is manifestly not here appearing at his liberal best. Yet he is hewing valiantly to the line of a genuinely noble if misplaced ideal. He is here, as in the *Gorgias* (511 C ff.) declaring that the most honorable of human arts is still virtue and not that of securing safety.

seriousness, Plato speaks with warm and sympathetic approval of retail trade as naturally good; along with the services of the laborer and the innkeeper, it comes into being to supply the satisfaction of human needs. He adds a daring suggestion, appropriately guarded: "if the best men should be compelled for a season to keep inns or peddle or follow any such trade," which "Heaven forbid!" — then we should see these callings "enjoying the honors that we give to mothers and to nurses." But Plato recalls regretfully his old conviction: it is the weakness of all but a few select natures to be unable to withstand the clamorous voice of gain. The citizens of the model city (who are to be responsible for its government) must not be subjected to such moral risk. No citizen, on pain of being judged to be "sullying his paternal hearth" [37] shall engage in trade. These tasks, since they are necessary, must be carried on, but to the least extent possible, and by those (the resident aliens) who would least damage the state were they to become corrupt, and finally, under careful supervision. And Plato adds to his legislation a price-fixing law designed to guarantee a fair profit to the traders, for the express purpose of guarding their moral safety; for "the Law-wardens must bear in mind that they are guardians not only of those who, being well-trained both by birth and nurture, are easy to guard from lawless and evil ways, but also of those who are otherwise, and who follow pursuits which greatly tend to urge them on the road to vice; and these they must guard the more." [38] Immediately after this, Plato pays equal honor to the artisans, coupling them with soldiers: "Sacred to Hephaestus and Athena is the class of the craftsmen who have furnished our life with the arts, and to Ares and Athena belong those who safeguard the products of these craftsmen by other defensive arts"; by their callings, "these all continually serve both the country and the people." Plato enacts that each shall be justly rewarded by the citizens of his state, the artisan with fair payment for his work, the soldier with "those honors which are the soldier's wages." [39] Remembering the high status of the soldier in the *Republic* (and that in the *Laws*, too, the soldier's task is held fit for the citizens themselves), we can recognize the high respect for the artisan which this combined treatment implies.

In fine, Plato's attitude to the craftsman exemplifies again that tempering of prejudice with principle of which we have spoken; and even in the realm of principle, it cannot easily be brought to a brief formulation, involving as it does so much of his whole theory of man and of the good society. To the end of his days, particularly in his *obiter dicta* and in his metaphorical passages, Plato drops into the scorn-laden language so prevalent among all privileged classes of his day, as we have seen him do, also, in relation to slaves and women; this is an indication of prejudice, aristocratic prejudice, if the de-

[37] *Laws* 919 E, trans. Bury, Loeb Library.
[38] *Laws* 920 A–C, trans. Bury, Loeb Library.
[39] *Laws* 920 D–922 A, trans. Bury, Loeb Library.

tractor likes; but, as we have seen, it was neither Plato's personal invention, nor merely a tradition in the Plato family.

On the other hand, from early till late, this same man showed himself aware of the value and dignity of the crafts: in the *Apology*, he reports the belief of Socrates that workmen, as workmen (but not as supposing themselves to know of higher matters) are to be honored; [40] in the *Republic*, they are to be the friends and the only less talented brothers of the guardians; [41] in the *Laws*, the arts are sacred and the trades are naturally good; the artisans serve the country in their way as truly as do the soldiers. Yet a wide range of principles prevent Plato from admitting the worker to full participation in the highest human excellence. These include the beliefs, earlier mentioned, that soul and its attendance are of higher worth than body, that men capable of complete virtue are rare, and that competence in any art requires specialization; added to these is the belief in the specific damage and danger to body and soul brought by the crafts themselves on those who practice them. Plato pities and wishes to protect those who must be exposed to these ill effects. He does not, when he looks the problem full in the face, scorn the worker or the work. But when it is proposed that working men shall participate in government — to him the crucial and the crowning art, to which all others are subservient — then the workman merges with the *dêmos*, the many in the political sense; and not from prejudice, but from principle, Plato will resolutely bar his entry.

Let us turn the pages of the dialogues once again, this time looking for reflections of Plato's feelings about noble birth and the prestige accruing to a man through membership in a distinguished family; here, too, we shall include ancestral wealth. Perhaps it will be simplest to set out passages under the captions of approval or disapproval, reserving, as before, questions of interpretation to a final paragraph of appraisal.

The Platonic Socrates knows how to pay little compliments to the young men with whom he talks, as he does to Lysis and Menexenus (*Lysis* 207 B–C), to whom he delicately imputes beauty and noble birth by eliciting from them the admission that it is a matter of dispute between them which of them possesses these qualities to the higher degree. Similarly, by way of illustrating the importance of determining the essential nature of a thing before disputing about its qualities, he playfully tells Meno that it is impossible for one who is utterly ignorant of who Meno is, to know whether Meno is handsome, wealthy, and well-born, or, he mischievously adds, knowing the young man's vanity, the reverse of these (*Meno* 71 B).

Broader praise, with no admixture of irony, is bestowed upon the family to which Charmides and Critias (and, as we remember, Plato himself) be-

---

[40] See p. 235 above.   [41] See pp. 175, 242–243 above.

longed. The young Charmides, in the dialogue so named, is pointed out to Socrates by Critias, and Socrates, having exclaimed over his beauty, asks whether he is also noble in soul, adding, " 'I should think, Critias, he ought to be, since he is of your house.' " Critias vouches for this, and adds that Charmides is also a poet; " 'That, my dear Critias,' Socrates replies, 'is a gift which your family has had a long while back through your kinship with Solon.' " A little further on, Critias praises Charmides as preëminent in all respects, but principally in temperance, and Socrates says to Charmides that this was only to be expected; " 'for I do not suppose there is any one else here who could readily point to a case of any two Athenian houses uniting together which would be likely to produce handsomer or nobler offspring than those from which you are sprung.' " And Socrates goes on to mention the fame for beauty and virtue and all else that is called fortunate, on both sides of the family, concluding with praises of Charmides' own beauty, and the exclamation, " 'But if your nature is really rich in temperance and those other things, as our friend here says, blessed is the son, dear Charmides, that your mother has borne in you!' " [42] Beside this we may put the sincere compliment paid by Socrates in the *Republic* to Plato's brothers, Glaucon and Adeimantus, who, having just concluded their restatement of Thrasymachus' case in praise of injustice, now urge Socrates to refute their arguments: "It was excellently spoken of you, . . . in the beginning of the elegy which the admirer of Glaucon wrote when you distinguished yourselves in the battle of Megara — 'Sons of Ariston, whose race from a glorious sire is godlike.' This, my friends, I think, was well said. For there must indeed be a touch of the godlike in your disposition if you are not convinced that injustice is preferable to justice though you can plead its case in such a fashion." [43]

In a later dialogue (*Timaeus* 20 A), the philosopher Timaeus is commended as one well fitted to discourse of statecraft and the noble conduct of war, possessing as he does wealth and birth, as well as political experience and philosophic training. Combined with the compliment, we have perhaps in this passage Plato's recognition of the favorable differential entailed by exposure to those influences for moral and intellectual development which in Plato's society, as still to a large degree in our own, accrued to those who possessed wealth, and to those whom the Greeks called "well-born." There was thus what we may call an incidental relation between birth and wealth and educational and cultural advantges, which commended the former.

As to wealth, if we may neglect for the moment its frequent concomitant, birth, Plato makes no objection to it as such; his excoriations are reserved for it in process of being unscrupulously acquired or intemperately consumed. He includes it in his "table of goods," as we shall presently see, but at the

---

[42] *Charmides* 154 D–155 A, 157 D–158 B, trans. Lamb, Loeb Library.

[43] *Republic* 368 A, trans. Shorey, Loeb Library.

bottom of the list, and as strictly subordinate to moral control. In the *Phaedrus* (279 C), he reports or invents a little prayer in which Socrates prays that he may think wisdom true wealth, and that he may possess "as much gold as only the temperate man can support and manage." As has been well remarked, "Socrates neither prays for wealth with the worldling, nor deprecates it with the Cynic," [44] but values it in its place. Marxists will scoff and socialists will imagine a vain thing; nevertheless there is, we submit, something more than snobbism residing in Plato's principle.

Being "well-born" has thus far appeared as simple matter for congratulation, but *audi alteram partem*. The *Gorgias* is strewn with passages breathing contempt for wealth, power, and the distinction conferred by even the highest political offices in the Athenian state. Until near the end, there has been no explicit depreciation of the claims of noble birth, but in the myth with which the dialogue closes, all the just-mentioned vaunted measures of value, together with that of birth, are combined and collectively condemned in ringing terms. In older times, as Socrates has heard and takes for true, it was the custom of the gods to assign men to their future punishments or rewards after a trial held on earth, on the last day of a man's life. Frequent miscarriages of justice occurred, and complaint was referred to Zeus, who said: " 'The cases are now indeed judged ill; and it is because they who are on trial are tried in their clothing, for they are tried alive. Now many . . . who have wicked souls are clad in fair bodies and ancestry and wealth, and at their judgement appear many witnesses to testify that their lives have been just.' " Zeus prescribes that henceforth they must be " 'stripped bare of all these things before they are tried; for they must stand their trial dead . . . bereft of kin and having left behind on earth all that fine array, to the end that the judgement may be just.' " [45]

We come again to the passage in the *Theaetetus* from which we drew the pair of contrasting pictures of the lawyer and the philosopher just above. The philosopher, after furnishing matter for amusement to the hard-headed realists, *habitués* of the courts, by his general ineptitude in such affairs, has his turn to be amused when he listens to the empty speeches and boasting of the others.

When he hears a panegyric of a despot or a king he fancies he is listening to the praises of some herdsman — a swineherd, a shepherd, or a neatherd, for instance — who gets much milk from his beasts; but he thinks that the ruler tends and milks a more perverse and treacherous creature than the herdsmen, and that he must grow coarse and uncivilized, no less than they, for he has no leisure and lives surrounded by a wall, as the herdsmen live in their mountain pens. And when he hears that someone is amazingly rich, because he owns ten thousand acres of land or more, to him, accustomed as he is to think of the whole earth, this seems very little. And when people sing the praises of lineage and say someone is of noble birth, because he can show seven wealthy ancestors, he thinks

---

[44] W. H. Thompson, in his note *ad loc.*, to his edition of the *Phaedrus*, 1868.

[45] *Gorgias* 523 C–E, trans. Lamb, Loeb Library.

that such praises betray an altogether dull and narrow vision on the part of those who utter them; because of lack of education they cannot keep their eyes fixed upon the whole and are unable to calculate that every man has had countless thousands of ancestors and progenitors, among whom have been in any instance rich and poor, kings and slaves, barbarians and Greeks. And when people pride themselves on a list of twenty-five ancestors and trace their pedigree back to Heracles, the son of Amphitryon, the pettiness of their ideas seems absurd to him; he laughs at them because they cannot free their silly minds of vanity by calculating that Amphitryon's twenty-fifth ancestor was such as fortune happened to make him, and the fiftieth for that matter. In all these cases the philosopher is derided by the common herd, partly because he seems to be contemptuous, partly because he is ignorant of common things and is always in perplexity." [46]

The same issues recur, involved in the problem of constructing the best practicable city of the *Laws*. No reader of that book can well have forgotten its repeated insistence on the primacy of moral intelligence as the unique prerequisite to honor in that austere state. Government will be entrusted, and the name of "wise" be given, not to those of agile intellect, "trained in all accomplishments," who, however, lack the love of "what they perceive to be noble and good"; but rather to "those whose mental condition is the reverse of this . . . even if — as the saying goes — 'they spell not neither do they swim.' " [47] There is a small shock of surprise awaiting us, in what seems a manifest contradiction, on the following page: the tabulation therein offered (690 A) of the various "claims to rule" includes that of the "well-born," which, by the manner of its presentation, seems to be accorded the warrant of a just claim. But we soon observe that also included is the claim of the stronger, a claim that Plato proceeds at once to treat with ironic ridicule, and to contrast, in its supposed naturalness, with the veritable naturalness of the rule of law, without force, over willing subjects, which is here equated to the rule of the wise over the ignorant. When, in the following book, Plato returns to the tabulation of the "claims," it is to call attention to the relation of logical conflict between them, and above all to declare with unequivocal clarity that, in his state, "we shall assign office to a man not because he is wealthy, nor because he possesses any other quality of the kind — such as strength or size or birth; but . . . to that man who is most obedient to the laws." [48]

If now we find Plato in fact according some differential advantages in political representation to his wealthier citizens,[49] it must be remarked that these

---

[46] *Theaetetus* 174 D–175 B, trans. Fowler, Loeb Library. Popper in his revised edition, p. 566, takes note for the first time of this passage, acknowledging that it stands "in flagrant contrast" to his own account of Plato's attitude, which nevertheless he does not retract. See our Appendix VII, p. 603.

A pithy sentence reënforcing Plato's point is at *Theaetetus* 173 D: "As to who in the city is well born or ill born, . . . he [the true philosopher] knows even less of that than he does of the proverbial

pitcher-fulls that make up the sea."

[47] *Laws* 689 B–D, trans. Bury, Loeb Library.

[48] *Laws* 715 B–C, trans. Bury.

[49] *Laws* 744 B–C, 757 A–E. — Careful reading of 757 will show Plato at pains to distinguish three modes of distributing offices, the inequality based on wealth, the simple arithmetical equality of the lot, and the proportionate equality of the "judgment of Zeus," based on virtue and cultivation (*paideia*). The third is his aim, but

are reluctant concessions to human imperfection, justified only on practical, prudential grounds. Plato's own preference is for a thoroughgoing equality of possessions (744 B–C). His rating of wealth in the hierarchy of human goods is stated in several places in the *Laws*,[50] but with especial neatness as follows: "It shall be laid down that the goods of the soul are highest in honour and come first, provided that the soul possesses temperance; second come the good and fair things of the body; and third the so-called goods of substance and property." [51]

But our books are not yet balanced. There are three more entries, all approvals of good "birth," though as we shall see with referents importantly different from that which the *Theaetetus* has condemned. There is, to begin with, a sense in which it is true to say that Plato places a very high value upon birth, using it as a directive principle for organizing, preserving, and even improving, his reformed communities of the *Republic* and the *Laws*. This is birth in the biological, or, better, the eugenical meaning of the word. How far Plato had gone toward an organized theory of human genetics is a topic reserved for later pages.[52] In the present context we need only note that Plato clearly distinguished between heredity and "noble birth."

A second ground upon which Plato can be shown to have approved "good birth," this time in the sense of good family environment, is the advantage it provides of growing up in a household where approvable ideals are honored as they were exemplified in the ancestors, put into practice by the living adult members, and inculcated in the young. Such a family, if it had also enjoyed public recognition, could both confer the name of "well-born" in the popular sense, and constitute the matrix for favorable moral development. We cannot offer complete documentation in the form of a passage specifically asserting the principle, but we may point to Plato's shrewd eye for the importance of the *êthos* of a family (though to his mind its influence was rarely strong enough to withstand the pressure of false ideals in the community) on the developing characters of its scions, shown in the passage in the *Republic*, where the misguided youth who is to become the "timocratic" man, is described as responding still to the restraining influence of his virtuous and philosophic

---

even so good a thing must be employed in moderation, if discord is to be avoided. Thus it must be tempered with the other two. Popper's statements (pp. 534–535, 548–549) that Plato "much preferred" plutocracy, and that he "demands" that political office shall depend in part on wealth, birth, height, and comeliness, are most unjust. "Concedes partially and reluctantly" would be the proper expression. As to Popper's further remarks anent Plato's "conquering war horde" morality, shown in his believing, as Popper implies he does, that bodily

strength entitles a man to greater influence — this is first to overlook the obvious advantages of family connections, size, and good looks when it comes to success in an election in any age, and the particular sensitivity of the Greeks in general to bodily beauty; it is also to ascribe to Plato approval of what he merely recognizes regretfully (cf. 690 B, cited just above) as influential.

[50] E.g., 631 B–D, 831 C–D, 727 E–728 A.
[51] *Laws* 697 B, trans. Bury, Loeb Library.
[52] See below, pp. 537ff.

father, who is "watering and fostering the growth of the rational principle in his soul"; [53] this influence, however, is unable wholly to protect the son from the false values of his vain mother and the house slaves, and of the citizens of the ill-governed city which is their home (550 A–B). A few pages later we hear of the similar situation of the young son of the "oligarchic" man, who, tempted by base companions, is admonished by his father and his other kinsmen; sometimes such a youth is thus reformed and restored to the (relative) virtue in which he was reared (560 A). From these and other passages in which Plato recognizes the all-importance for growth in virtue, of the values which are held up to the young by those with whom they are associated, it seems a fair corollary to assert that Plato valued the sort of moral and cultural environment in the home, under which a Theaetetus, a Polemarchus, or he himself had grown up, as more frequently promotive of the good life of virtue and reason, than any other this side of Utopia.

A third sense in which Plato valued high birth is closely related both to Plato's piety for those of kindred blood, and to his admiration for the virtuous life, two interests never far from the center of Plato's affections. In the most serious portion of the often satirical and deliberately rhetorical *Menexenus*, the notion of pride of ancestry confronts us in a different form. It is now the heritage of honor which it is the duty of a descendant to preserve, to enhance, and to pass on. Plato imagines the dead whose obsequies he celebrates as addressing their descendants, bidding them strive to outdo their fathers in virtue. You will win this victory over us, they say, "if ye are careful . . . not to trade upon the glory of your ancestors nor yet to squander it, believing that for a man who holds himself of some account there is nothing more shameful than to find himself held in honor not for his own sake but because of the glory of his ancestors. In the honors which belong to their parents, the children truly possess a noble and splendid treasure; but to use up one's treasure, whether of wealth or of honour, and bequeath none to one's children, is the base and unmanly act of one who lacks all wealth and distinctions of his own." [54]

Now it would be little short of an affront to a reader's intelligence to spell out for his benefit the significance, for an estimate of Plato as a man, of what he himself has so clearly and magnificently said of aristocratic birth. We have noted the small contradictions, but for the rest we may let Plato's own explanations stand. That they are sufficient to justify the rewriting of some passages in Fite's and Popper's books should be clear. In the case of the "many" and of the workman, Plato was held back from admitting them to full excellence by principles which, while we can respect the integrity of their application, we cannot accept; in the case of nobility of birth, however,

---

[53] *Republic* 550 A, trans. Shorey, Loeb Library.

[54] *Menexenus* 274 A–B, trans. Bury, Loeb Library.

Plato achieved full emancipation, and his declaration of contempt for its pretensions, but for the fact that it is longer and more explicit than that of Lycophron, and therefore less neatly quotable, could be inscribed equally well on the banner of any equalitarian movement.

But one subtopic deserves a word to itself: how shall we interpret the apparently rather special honors that Plato has incidentally but effectively heaped on his own head by the praise of his own family? (We shall reserve for later discussion [55] Popper's remarkable suggestion that Plato was celebrating the fountain of his own royal blood, when, in the *Symposium*, he makes passing reference to King Codrus, though Plato does not mention the supposed connection between his father's family and this legendary hero.) The most obvious interpretation of the praise bestowed would seem to be that the principle suggested in the *Menexenus* is here in point: Plato accepted from his ancestors the "treasure" of an honorable name, valued it accordingly, and sought by the achievement of his own life to add to its luster. This suggestion, while in substance true, is open to one serious objection: why, then, did he evoke the tarnished images of Critias and Charmides, and perform his rites of piety in their blood-stained presence? To this we may in turn reply that he has appealed back beyond their later shameful time to the halcyon days when Critias was a brilliant and cultivated if somewhat overconfident and contentious intellectual, and Charmides his statuesque and exemplary young *protégé*. If now it still be asked why Plato has brought them before us at any stage, and on any page of his writings, when he was free to choose the characters who should appear upon his literary scene, we are limited to conjecture, for in such matters no possibility of demonstration exists. But a possible answer is simply that Plato was, behind his proudly impersonal mask and beneath his well-draped mantle, a man, also, and one who, if he has not made us the confidants of his humiliations and griefs, has not thereby cut himself off from the fellowship of human sympathy. And Plato must have suffered deeply from the discrediting, through the violence charged upon his kinsmen, of his family name. He was not, in consequence, led into any criminal complaisance with the offenders, or lame apologetics in their behalf.[56] What he has done, in his own vindication and in that of his surviving family, is to have presented for us in all their erstwhile comeliness, these "boughs that might have grown full straight," had they but continued in the old path, established for them by their proud Solonian tradition and pointed out for them with unmistakable clarity by Socrates.[57] Read in this

[55] Popper, p. 475. See our discussion, pp. 462–463 below.

[56] An apparent exception to this statement, *Menexenus* 243 E–244 B, will be discussed on p. 346 below; we shall also again discuss Plato's relation to Critias, pp. 358ff.

[57] Plato was within his rights also, in representing Socrates as having associated on terms of friendship with these kinsmen of his, in their earlier times. Xenophon, too,

light — and we are not without title so to read them — the allusions to the
splendor of the family past no longer appear as instances of Plato's vainglory.
They become, as it were, scenes in a tragedy of understatement, in which the
pity of the latter end is reënforced by contrast with the bright promise of
Act One. Herein Plato was no more honoring the dishonorable deeds of Critias
and Charmides, than he was in the *Symposium* congratulating Alcibiades
upon his subsequent iniquities. In both cases, he was showing Socrates as
achieving what was humanly possible, in the circumstances, toward preventing
the disaster that engulfed all three blindlings in the later years.

A word will serve to acknowledge the essential truth of Crossman's assertion that Plato was by association and by temperament debarred from understanding the common man, whom Crossman equates roughly with the working classes of Plato's *Republic*. Crossman does not censure Plato for observing
the degradation and ignorance of the common man — Crossman feels himself
constrained to acknowledge that, through the conditions of an unequal society,
the common man even in the modern world has often been plunged into
such degradation. He blames him, rather, for failing to understand the potential goodness and intelligence lurking in the mind and heart of the ordinary
citizen, and entitling him, despite all appearances, to be given, in continually
growing measure, full and equal rights of participation in the management of
the human enterprise. It cannot be denied that Crossman's charge is deserved,
— that, for Plato, the ordinary run of men in an ordinary community are
what is left of human nature when the light of philosophy has been removed,
or rather when this light is darkened by ignorance within. The unhappy consequences for his social theory of this defective insight we must consider in
due course. One may ascribe it, in part, to the social conditions and political
crises of his time, and in part, with Crossman, to a certain aesthetically and
intellectually grounded aloofness of Plato's personality. One may even, in dia-
metrical denial of Crossman and Popper alike, mention among the contributing causes one Socrates: for had not Socrates turned him from the unexamined opinions of the "many" to the search for the one expert, the one who
knows? And for the acquiring of this knowledge, a lifetime was not too long.
The intellectual few alone could companion Plato in his search, and from
their association Plato could not come to know the worth and potentialities
of the actual common man. In consequence of this ignorance, the principles
which we have described as standing between Plato and the extension of political rights to workmen, went uncorrected by counter-principles which, equally
Platonic, might have served to alter much that we find unacceptable in his

testifies in his *Symposium* to the fact of
this relationship as it concerned Charmides,
who is there depicted as an agreeable and
unassuming companion, accepted by Socrates on equal terms of intimacy with Antisthenes. (It is to be remembered that Popper makes much of the closeness of the
friendship between Socrates and Antisthenes.) Similarly in the *Memorabilia* Socrates likes and approves of Charmides.

social arrangements, particularly those of the *Republic*. For Plato has given us also the principle that participation in the formation of policies must be proportional to moral understanding. Whoever, then, could have shown Plato that he was materially mistaken in having imposed too low a ceiling on the intellectual and moral potential of the common man, would have had Platonic consent and gratitude for altering Plato's conclusions in this matter.

Plato and Athens

No responsible attempt to measure the integrity of Plato's criticism of contemporary Athenian democracy and his relation to the political movements of his day is possible without reference to the logically prior standard of an "objective" estimate of the political and cultural pattern of the Athens in which he lived. All the detractors, recognizing this, have, each in his own characteristic way, given clear indications of the standard employed.

For Fite the Athenian culture of the fifth century was a brilliant achievement, particularly as the expression of intellectual enlightenment, of which Plato himself is cited as an example. But Athenian glory was marred by certain moral deficiencies.[58] The Athenian bid for supremacy had converted the cities of the erstwhile league into subjects of an empire. The value of Athenian democracy was limited by the restrictions upon admission to citizenship and the jealous guarding of rights and privileges which gave it something of the character of "a gentleman's club" [59] and produced "a leisure class of gentlemen-rulers, supported by the dole." [60] The clash of "democratic" and "oligarchic" party interest which constituted Athenian politics was a dangerous and often utterly unscrupulous game, played out with a calculating self-interest on both sides. The advantage of the oligarchic party, which lay in immunity from the heavy burden of taxation and from that destruction of agriculture which war and imperial adventure imposed primarily upon them, was pursued by ruthless violence and even, we may suspect, by treachery; the advantage of the politically-conscious, city-dwelling *dêmos* lay in war and the profits of empire, upon which their pay depended. But rising above the battle, and measuring the spirit of Greek democracy at its greatest height, stands the Funeral Oration of Pericles,[61] "a noble picture . . . of an enlightened civilization, and one of the finest of all time." [62] This picture Fite asks us to consider in significant juxtaposition, or opposition, to the narrow oppressions of Plato's *Republic*.

Crossman's Athens is recognizably the same city that Fite describes,[63] but more incurably torn by internal strife, and not so much enlightened as

---

[58] Fite, Chapter VI, pp. 113–127.
[59] *Ibid.*, p. 122.
[60] *Ibid.*, p. 127.
[61] *Ibid.*, pp. 148–152.
[62] Fite, p. 150.
[63] Crossman: for the Athenian empire,
pp. 29–31; for the policy of imperial expansion, pp. 32–34; for the excesses of the democrats, p. 33; for the ruthless class-war, pp. 34–35; for the defects inherent in Periclean democracy, pp. 35–46.

morally confused and bewildered by the rapid succession of dissolving life views which had replaced the older morality of custom. The new rationalism had brought skepticism in its train, leading to a cynical nihilism and ruthless power politics against which the Socratic appeal to Reason and the authority of virtue were unable to prevail.[64] Indeed, Crossman is prepared to believe that for all his nobility of aim, Socrates had on balance simply amplified the confusion, and his "effects on Athenian life had" — in the light of their political consequences — "been disastrous." [65] To carry forward the unfinished business of his dead master, first applying the Socratic dialectic to the positive definition of the virtues, and then founding upon them the just political order which Socrates had demanded, was the self-imposed task of Plato.[66]

From this report on Plato's Athens as viewed by our two critics, one gathers that it would have been very possible for a citizen of good sense and good will to have urged fundamental changes in its constitution looking to the removal of the serious evils and dangers with which it was beset, in short, to have maintained a position comparable in its general features to that which Plato was led to maintain. To this extent, then, we have been treated to a partial justification of Plato. But for this indulgence the third critic, Popper, has made full compensation. So thoroughgoing is the contrast that Popper has set up between the spell of Plato and the spirit of democratic Athens, that it includes, along with its own abundance, whatever of reproach, direct or implied, was conveyed in Fite's account. In consequence, we may omit the task of answering Fite (Crossman hardly needs an answer) and proceed direct to our consideration of Popper.

It will be necessary now for us to follow Popper's lead in traversing a considerable stretch of Athenian history and political cabal, with special reference to the relations of democratic and oligarchical programs and action. A brief foreword will prevent a possible misunderstanding. We shall be entering an area of discussion the greater segment of which is common ground. To much of what Popper will be heard to say in approval of Athenian democracy and in condemnation of its oligarchical enemies, our text offers its unqualified agreement. But we must beg to be excused from agreement with a certain number of what we hope to show are mistakes in matters of fact, together with some important omissions; we must reject the oversimplification of the issues, the attribution of motives, and the exaggeration, favorable and unfavorable, which heighten the effect of contrast between opposing political factions. Our main protest must be directed against the manner in which every oligarchic sin has been laid at Plato's door, while every item of Plato's political or ethical creed has been made to appear as his denial of a

---

[64] *Ibid.*: for the prevailing confusion and immoralism, pp. 65–76, esp. pp. 73–74.

[65] *Ibid.*, p. 77.
[66] *Ibid.*, pp. 97–98.

splendid spiritual achievement of democracy. In the light of Popper's explicit disclaimer of the wish to treat Plato as an historical villain (he quotes Shaw's preface to *Saint Joan* as his precedent), it is the more surprising and the more important to note that the moving cause of this whole historical section in Popper's book is precisely to establish Plato's inexcusable, or almost inexcusable guilt.[67]

It will help us to keep our eyes on the main issue amidst the clutter of historical detail, to present here a brief schedule of Popper's chief objectives in his historical section, in the order in which we shall deal with them, as follows:

(1) The representation of the opponents of the democracy at Athens, the so-called oligarchs, as the would-be preservers of the "closed society" against the new spiritual forces of "openness"; and an enumeration of what Popper considers their defining characteristics.

(2) The undermining, as an oligarchical partisan, of the historian Thucydides, the chief source of the prevailing view that Athenian democracy displayed weaknesses responsible for its defeat at the hands of Sparta in the Peloponnesian war.

(3) The discovery in the teachings of the "Great Generation" at Athens of the "new faith . . . of the open society"; and the defense of the Athenian democracy, from Pericles to the period of Plato's maturity, as the bearer of this faith.

(4) The proof that Plato was in all essentials a typical oligarch; the discovery in his political philosophy of all the oligarchical stigmata listed in (1) above, made blacker by treachery to the teachings of the Great Generation.

As will be remembered from our *résumé* of Popper's book in our opening chapter, he describes as the primordial form of social organization the "closed society," which provides its members with a sense of security, based upon predetermined personal status for everyone and readymade answers to all moral problems through customary taboos and prescriptions. The "open society" takes its beginnings from contact with other societies of differing mores, which leads to questioning of taboos; within the society, commerce supplies the chief leverage, widening the area of contact with the outside world, enabling individuals to compete, and by changing their relative status abolishing the old hereditary division into privileged and unprivileged persons. There results a sense of insecurity, but along with it there is born moral responsibility, which is the basis of progress toward humanitarianism, individ-

---

[67] Popper, in his earlier edition, p. 165, spoke gravely of "the way in which we may blame" those who, like Plato, still opposed Athenian democracy after its implications had been fully developed by Socrates and its other champions. In his second edition, p. 184, he has added the words "to some extent" to his condemnation, but without altering his ultimate assessment of Plato as blameworthy in high degree (pp. 191, 194).

ualism, and the remaining virtues of a free society. This change was being accomplished, for the first time in history, in fifth-century Athens, brought about by the friends of democracy, against the diehard opposition of the party of the privileged, the so-called oligarchs.[68]

Accordingly, the first and most significant characteristic of Popper's oligarchs (defined as "the privileged, or formerly privileged" classes of Athens) is self-interested opposition to social change, their second, opposition to the liberalizing forces of trade and commerce, particularly seaborne commerce. For these reasons they were the special foes of the progressive policy of Pericles, that unified and coherent program of an Athens democratically governed, made safe from landward attack by her Long Walls, and occupied with trade, the operation of a great navy, and the administration of a maritime empire.[69]

It should be noted that Popper recognizes the existence of a group of moderate oligarchs, among whom the historian Thucydides is included as a "representative leader," who displayed to the full the above-listed hostilities, but who were, withal, "upright men," the defenders of the "old virtues, and the old religion." The watchword to which they rallied was "Back to the old paternal state"; to these men, who were unwitting tools, "used for their own ends" by the Spartans and the extreme oligarchs, and whose fortune it was to live when "the new faith of the open society . . . was not yet [fully] formulated," Popper extends his forgiveness.[70] He holds them not guilty of the remaining faults of the oligarchs *par excellence*, to which we now return.

Characteristic of these extreme antidemocrats, from first to last, in Popper's eyes, was treacherous pro-Spartan sympathy. They championed the "arrested oligarchic tribalism of Sparta" against Athenian democracy, and were prepared to betray the vital interests of Athens, even in wartime, in return for Spartan help against their democratic fellow citizens. And in due time, Popper tells us, they succeeded: "the main responsibility for the lost war rests with the treacherous oligarchs who continuously conspired with Sparta." [71]

Irreligion and nihilism were associated characteristics; despite his admission that many adherents of the movement were religious conservatives, Popper insists in the same breath that the movement "was itself morally rotten." He ascribes views similar to the ones held by Plato's Callicles and Thrasymachus to those young aristocrats, who, he implies, were the actual oligarchic leaders, though they professed to be democrats; and he cites as climactic proof the case of Critias, who (as Popper has told us in a previous chapter) "was the first to glorify propaganda lies" by celebrating "in cynical

---

[68] References for this paragraph are Popper, pp. 167–173, and 179.

[69] *Ibid.*, pp. 173–174. The Long Walls

connected the city of Athens proper to her seaports.

[70] Popper, pp. 178–179.

[71] *Ibid.*, pp. 173–175, 179, 187.

verses" the invention of religion, as the fabrication of a "wise and cunning man" who wished thereby to keep mankind within the boundaries of "law and order." [72]

Finally, Popper shows us the extreme oligarchs as brutal and ruthless. The repressive and murderous behavior of the Thirty Tyrants, whose "leaders" were Critias and Charmides, is presented as no more than the logical outcome of the program of the movement from beginning to end — that movement, which, he tells us, Plato came at last to join and to abet.[73]

As an illuminating example of the species oligarch, Popper calls our attention to that pamphlet formerly attributed to Xenophon, the work of the unknown "Pseudo-Xenophon" or the "Old Oligarch," as Zimmern has taught us to call him, whose views on the improper management of slaves at Athens will be remembered from a preceding chapter. Popper tells us that the "central idea" of this writer, which was also "an article of faith with Thucydides and Plato," is the indissoluble connection between the hated Athenian democracy and naval imperialism; the writer also tries to show, according to Popper, that there can be "no compromise" between the two worlds of oligarchy and democracy, and that "only the use of ruthless violence, of total measures, including the acquisition of allies from outside (the Spartans)" can put an end to the democratic system — a program which, Popper implies, the Old Oligarch is in favor of immediately putting in practice. We are asked to regard him as only the first of the "intellectual leaders of the revolt against freedom," who included, of course and particularly, Plato.[74]

Have the oligarchs of Athens been rightly described and delimited in Popper's pages? Before answering this question, we may pause for a moment to discuss the meaning of the terms "oligarch" and "oligarchy." Etymologically, of course, "oligarchy" means simply the "rule of the few." In Plato's day it was possible to employ the word in a generalized sense, covering the predominance in the state of any minority or limited group of citizens. This gives the word a fairly simple meaning, although even here there might be dispute as to whether the term could properly be applied to a government in which the limited group of participants exceeded half of the citizen body. But beyond this point, all simplicity is lost, for a bewildering variety of so-called "oligarchies," actual or merely advocated or described, meets our gaze, differing in the persons or groups to whom predominant power is assigned, in the

---

[72] *Ibid.*, p. 179 and p. 140. As with others of whom he disapproves, so here with Critias, Popper has further blackened his character by exaggeration. For the verses cited represent religion, though a fabrication, as being aimed at the general good of society, not at the selfish benefit of the cunning fabricator himself. They are not by any means, in themselves, cynical, nor is religion thus conceived properly to be described simply as a "propaganda lie." Also to be borne in mind is the possibility that the verses, surviving from Critias' play the *Sisyphus*, express the opinion of a *dramatis persona* rather than of the dramatist.

[73] Popper, pp. 192–194.

[74] *Ibid.*, pp. 182–183.

degree and distribution of the powers, and in the interests, economic and other, which these arrangements were in each case designed to serve.[75] In these circumstances, a given user of the word "oligarchy" may, as he prefers, employ it in the broad sense, or he may specify the particular variety to which, in his pages, the word is to be understood to refer, and then detail the particular interests which, according to his analysis, this variety subserves. But having made the latter choice, he must beware of extending his application of the word to governmental forms which may be "oligarchic" only in some other sense.

Popper has permitted himself to transgress this rule in more than one way. On an earlier page, engaged in sketching in the background of Plato's life, he has defined the form of oligarchy which Athenian dissidents were constantly endeavoring to restore as "a rule of the leading aristocratic families." [76] Given this definition of "oligarchy," the term "oligarch" will denote, we may suppose, a person who favors the rule of such families, either in a particular case (his own) or in general; and this is what Popper intended it to mean at that point in his argument, since it is part of his intent to prove that Plato claimed such a prerogative.[77] But the word "oligarch," thus narrowed, would by no means cover all who were during Plato's lifetime included among the opponents of the Athenian democratic form of government. Popper, accordingly, though he does not withdraw his earlier definition, makes no mention of it in his discussion of the Athenian political scene. His intention here is to identify Plato with the actual proponents of oligarchy at Athens (who were by no means all advocates of the supremacy of aristocratic families), particularly with the more extreme of these; he now introduces, as we have seen, other and more inclusive specifications. It is these new criteria which we have now to examine, and in which we shall find further reason for dissatisfaction.

We note first that Popper's classification of Athenians is strikingly and suspiciously simple. He has divided Athenian society into two camps, and only two; for though he recognizes two subspecies of oligarch, he attaches small moral importance to the distinction, and he mentions no other significant

---

[75] Whoever supposes that any single specifiable "few" or kind of "rule" will determine all Greek forms of oligarchy is advised to consult the introduction to Newman's monumental edition of Aristotle's *Politics*, where (vol. IV, pp. xxiff.) the learned diligence of the editor has added to the four varieties formally recognized by Aristotle eleven others that figure incidentally in various parts of the *Politics*. Plato himself in two different dialogues applies the term to two differently specified forms, and actual proposals made by Athenian op-

ponents of the democracy varied widely. Of one such constitution, classed by Popper unhesitatingly as "oligarchy," in which all governmental functions were to be performed by a chosen body of five thousand citizens, the democratically sympathetic historian Grote says that it was rightly regarded as "tantamount to a democracy" (*History of Greece* (condensed), 1907, pp. 707–708).

[76] Popper, p. 21.

[77] For our discussion of this charge, see pp. 459ff.

groups. On the one side are the oligarchs, all of them privileged or formerly privileged, antidemocratic, foes of the open society, and of its causes and accompaniments, progressive change, commerce, naval enterprise, and empire; on the other are their opposites in all these respects, the friends of openness, the democrats. By this division he has implicitly alleged that the basic characteristics named as a set of related traits may be found conjoined in all, or almost all (we will not require exactitude) of the large number of Athenians, over a long span of years, who opposed the democracy or favored serious changes in the Athenian form of government. And he has further implied that these traits were not significantly characteristic of the democratic interest itself.

This excessive simplicity finds expression in the second feature of Popper's picture of oligarchy, the attribution of uniformly bad motivation to all who thus opposed democracy at Athens. For it will be observed that the criterion of privilege is prominently displayed, and imparts to the oligarchic position the color of self-interest, while the democrats are tacitly relieved of any charge of seeking more than justice: they are but the foes of special favors for any group. And whereas the democrats, by implication, favor commerce and empire for entirely justifiable, even for admirable reasons, the oligarchs appear as motivated in their opposition to all these civilizing activities solely by a clutch after their own vanishing privileges.

The third feature of oligarchy as Popper depicts it is the intensity of wickedness which, by selective emphasis on the activities of its least admirable members, is made to pervade the whole movement. For though Popper has specifically exempted some of its adherents in the earlier years from personal participation in the sins of its extremer members, as we have seen, he has nevertheless said in effect: there is no middle ground. Those who opposed democracy as it was exemplified at Athens lent themselves to the purposes of its most unscrupulous enemies, and if blindness cannot be urged in their favor, they must be equally condemned. Thus oligarchs without distinction are constantly called "treacherous," are said to be, as a whole, "morally rotten," and are typified repeatedly by Critias and the Old Oligarch.

In short, this entire classification, with its simplicity, its damaging ascription of motives, and its intensification, is fitted to serve less as an instrument of understanding than as a basis for condemnation. It is an adaptation to the Athenian political scene of a pattern of inquiry that has become all too familiar in recent decades: the political witch hunt. This consists in designating by a common label a group of persons to whom as a whole are ascribed the combined disapprovable tenets of its severally most extreme members, and then in classifying as an adherent of the group any intended victim whose opinions can be shown to be in any degree similar to these. Such a method, while admirably adapted to secure neatness and clarity of compartmental thinking, is unfitted to take account of the uniqueness of almost any individual, and preëminently so in the case of a man like Plato, who by originality and independence of thinking defies simplicity of description and rises above party allegiance.

Now there will be no argument as to the existence at Athens of oligarchs favoring the rule of the few; nor will it be doubted that among these were some who took active, practical steps to secure a change in the constitution, and to establish in power themselves and their friends. Twice during the period discussed, these men inaugurated by revolutionary means their own versions of oligarchy. There were, as Popper has said, clubs to which men of oligarchical sympathies belonged, and on both occasions the clubs formed the nuclei of the sedition.[78] We shall agree that these actual oligarchs included many who displayed one or more of Popper's set of traits — many who were privileged, many who opposed change or commerce or empire, many even who were in addition pro-Spartan, unscrupulous, or violent.

But we shall submit that in simplifying and schematizing, as he has done, the political situation at Athens, Popper has exceeded the margin of error to which the framer of historical generalizations is entitled. We shall ask the reader to note, first that opposition to democracy might be theoretical, not active or applied to the Athenian scene, and especially that it might not envisage as desirable the installation as rulers of oneself and one's friends, or any existing Athenian "few." Something like this we shall in the end establish as true of Plato. Secondly, turning to consider the practical advocates of a change in the Athenian constitution, we shall show that there were many ways in which a man could display or fail to display any of Popper's listed oligarchic traits, and that these traits and their opposites are not to be found only on that side of the line to which Popper has assigned them. There were, in fact, many intermediate positions and combinations of interests and ideals, held by actual Athenians of the period in question, and there occurred

---

[78] A detailed study of these clubs is *Athenian Clubs in Politics and Litigation*, by G. M. Calhoun, 1931. The picture given is of organizations which served several purposes in Athenian life, combining social activities with mutual assistance in seeking political office and in handling legal affairs. The primary purpose varied from club to club, and might change as the members' interests changed. Citizens of all walks of life and of all political colors belonged to them. Pericles belonged to a club, and so did many quiet citizens of moderate views. But greater notoriety attached to those clubs to which dissolute young men like Alcibiades belonged, or to that club of wealthy oligarchic sympathizers to which, it was believed, the crime of mutilating the square stone images of Hermes was traced in 415 B.C. Some of them were actively engaged in revolutionary activities preceding the oligarchic revolutions of 412 and 404, the clubs to which men of oligarchic sympathies belonged forming convenient closed circles for the confidential interchange of treasonable views before the *coup* was openly avowed. Because of this, clubs as such were after these events thought of by some as likely to be antidemocratic. And it was recognized that they could enable their members to pervert the ends of justice in the courts. But that they did not cease to be common features of Athenian life we know from Socrates' reference in the *Apology*, 36 B, where he lists them among the usual preoccupations of politically active Athenians.

marked shifts in the composition and alignment of political groups, as the years passed. And although we shall not be able to take the reader through a review of the many decades of Athenian history which would have to be traversed if we were to document this case in detail, we propose to present sufficient evidence in connection with each of Popper's criteria to show their inadequacy and unfairness in the use to which he has put them. Let us begin with that trait which, on Popper's scheme, since for him opposition to the birth of the "open society" is the worst crime against humanity, is the most basic oligarchic characteristic — opposition to social change.

It is of course true that in so far as democracy itself was relatively a new thing, all those who opposed democracy, as such, were the opponents of social change; and in so far as Athenian democracy seems to us good, and in the direction of openness, they were the opponents of progress. Democracy, however, as Popper is also aware, does not appear except in conjunction with other social changes, and it is in respect to these that differences of attitude are to be examined. Is it true that all antidemocrats are opposed to all these concomitant changes, democrats to none? And is it morally indefensible to oppose, for any reason or to any extent, any of them?

To restate with some modification Popper's exposition, we can indeed observe in Athenian development an example of that close companionship between the growth of trade and the coming about of those conditions of urban social organization out of which alone "high cultures" of the type accredited in the Western world have taken their rise. And, as always, the achievement of this progress was at a cost, indeed at a double cost: the destruction of some of the old values and the generation of some new evils. The older values, as Popper has acknowledged, were not without their honest and disinterested defenders. But we must also recognize, what Popper denies, that it was still possible to wish to conserve the older values even after the new values had become established. It was possible to believe that some of the old might be retained along with the best of the new; it was even possible, for those who saw the new accompanied by and vitiated by what appeared to be inherent evils, to idealize the old, and to wish in some degree to reverse the change — all without vicious intent or selfishness. A conservative Athenian of Plato's day, even in Plato's latest years, could thus desire to restore not alone the security of that older society, but also what he believed to be its hardihood, its courage, its regard for the sanctities of oaths and the ties of common citizenship or blood, its rural simplicity, and its purity of religious faith — any or all of these. He could reject the competitive struggle for gain, the fickle and irresponsible conduct of public affairs under the leadership of demagogues, the vindictiveness and violence of political conflict, the prejudiced administration of justice, and the grasping after imperial power which appeared at times to be inseparable from the new order.

And if the antidemocrats could thus oppose change for what seemed to them virtuous reasons, so, too, could the Athenian democracy itself. Popper makes no mention in this connection of the existence of a democratic desire to arrest change or to oppose progress, with especial reference to the "openness" of Athenian society, yet such there was — the bigoted suppression, even the putting to death of religious innovators and supposed blasphemers, and the pride of pure Athenian blood, the jealous refusal to extend the rights of citizenship, which characterized the Athenian *dêmos*.[79] We see thus that the desire to arrest change, and in particular to arrest change in the direction of greater tolerance and universalism, will not serve as a simple criterion by which to divide Athenians into oligarchs and democrats.

But what of hatred of Athenian commerce and empire, the desire to return to the stable agrarian society, which is also set forth as an illiberal oligarchic aim? We concede that some degree of this feeling was frequent among oligarchs. But here, too, we shall meet complications, tendencies, and interests which cut across the simple line of cleavage. Popper has presented to us the Old Oligarch as the type of the extreme antidemocrat, ready to let loose, it is implied, the dogs of civil war and foreign intervention, in essence the upholder of what was later to be Plato's position, and sharing with both Plato and Thucydides the heart of his doctrine, the condemnation of naval imperialism as inseparable from democracy. Let us, with no intention of giving this unlovely and unsympathetic ancient writer a clean bill of health, look a little more closely at what he has said.

One can take no exception to the accuracy of Popper's report of the Old Oligarch's dislike of the common man and the political power and advantage perforce accorded him in the democratic scheme of things at Athens. The commoners uniformly appear in stark opposition to the "noble" and the "good," as the "bad" or the "worthless." The fundamental fault in the Athenian constitution is the perfectly necessary (for otherwise the navy could not operate effectively) but otherwise entirely objectionable granting of freedom and power to the commoners; and if a proper constitution were desired, it would be necessary to entrust the framing of new laws to wise men, who would at once demote these creatures to the position of slaves.[80]

But as one reads on, his attention is attracted by some features which Popper's review had not taught him to expect. He is scheduled for a surprise in chapter II, where he will learn of the advantages (as Pericles also describes them, in his Funeral Oration, reported by Thucydides) to be derived from life in Athens; of its wealth, its enjoyment of imported luxuries, made possible by control of the sea. There may indeed be irony in the assertion that the Athenians have a diet, a costume, and a language enriched by contributions from both the Greek and the barbarian nations.[81] But there is straightforward congratulation in the mention of Athens' security from the effects of crop fail-

---

[79] See pp. 316, 322, and n. 236, p. 227.   [80] Pseudo-Xen., *Constitution of Athens* I, 8.   [81] *Ibid.* II, 7.

ures, and there is pride and admiration in the depiction of Athens' immense power as mistress of the sea to dictate to other nations and to ravage their territories at will.[82] True, it is admitted, Athens has one weakness, in that Attica is not an island: though the *dêmos* is secure within the Long Walls, the farmers and the aristocrats suffer when Attica is invaded, and there is also danger that, if internal sedition should arise, a foreign army could be introduced by land; but the Athenians consider these disadvantages unimportant in comparison with the very great advantages of naval power.[83] From Popper's account, we should hardly have expected the endorsement, implied in the celebration of Athenian wealth and power, of the Long Walls, the harbor, and the fleet — in short, the praise of (democratic) empire.[84]

We have seen here the apparently opposing views that may be brought together in the mind of a single man who, so far at least as his sympathies are concerned, is an undoubtedly genuine example of the oligarchic tribe. But what of Popper's suggestion of this same man's treasonable intent to call in the Spartans to overthrow the democracy? We have seen that the Old Oligarch recognizes the possibility that some dissidents might wish to summon foreigners to their aid. And in a later chapter, he says also that the Athenian *dêmos* have learned from their unsuccessful experience the unwisdom of trying to coöperate with states, like Sparta, whose constitutions differ radically from their own.[85] But he does not advocate the opening of the city gates to the enemy, nor does he propose to improve relations with Sparta by appropriate changes in the Athenian constitution. Instead, the conclusion of the whole little work is a passage denying that within the Athenian state there exists any appreciable number of malcontents, deprived unjustly of their political rights, with whose aid it would be possible to overthrow the state.[86] Surely this assertion of the impregnability of Athens would form a strange conclusion to a pamphlet aiming at inciting her enemies to an attack. No, the message of the Old Oligarch is not a call to arms; quite the reverse, it is, in its strange and caustic way, a "peace pamphlet," warning those who live under an opposite rule that though they may congratulate themselves upon the excellence of their constitution in point of true virtue, nevertheless the Athenian way, in spite of its one great flaw, has many merits, and above all, strength.

The foregoing discussion of the Old Oligarch shows, first, that Popper's list of oligarchic traits constitutes an oversimplification so extreme that it cannot even be used to describe his type case; second, that Popper has here, as in other connections, mixed with a considerable quantity of learning a small but active principle of arbitrariness sufficient to infect the whole; and

---

[82] *Ibid.* II, 6, and 11–13.
[83] *Ibid.* II, 14–16.
[84] A. W. Gomme, "The Old Oligarch," *Athenian Studies*, 1940, p. 231, agrees that the Old Oligarch "is not, like Plato, averse

to the material advantages of Athens' unique position."
[85] Pseudo-Xen. III, 10–11.
[86] *Ibid.* III, 12–13.

thirdly, that by this distortion he has created an impression full of malign implications for the character of Plato, as well as of Thucydides. For though Plato, and in some sense Thucydides also, were opposed to democracy as it was exemplified at Athens in the years of the Peloponnesian war, we have already displayed enough of Plato's views to show that his opposition to democracy was not of the same sort as that of the Old Oligarch; we shall show the same for Thucydides below. And though the Old Oligarch was undoubtedly in sympathy with oligarchy, he was not averse, as Plato was, to the profit and power of commerce and empire.

Another instance of the realistic love of empire and naval power among the extreme Athenian oligarchs, meets us in Thucydides' account (VIII, 91) of the oligarchic conspirators of 411 B.C., the so-called "Four Hundred." These men had seized power in Athens, but had failed to win over the Athenians of the fleet, which at that time was based on Samos. Seeing that they were liable to be attacked at any moment by their own fellow citizens of the fleet, they were making desperate efforts to negotiate a peace with Sparta on the most favorable terms to themselves: "For their first wish was to continue as oligarchs and hold sway over their allies; failing that, to be independent and in possession of the ships and the walls; but should this too be cut off, then at any rate to avoid being the first victims of the restored democracy, by calling in the enemy and making shift without walls and ships, let the city's affairs go as they would, so long as their own persons were secure." We have here a clear demonstration that the oligarchic heart could vibrate to the iron (and golden) string of empire.

Once we have shaken off the illusion that the line of cleavage drawn by Popper will enable us to place every man Jack of the Athenians on his proper side in the struggle, the sooner we shall be able to see that even though a given man (Plato, for instance) displayed in some sense every one of the traits which Popper lists as essentially oligarchic, he was not necessarily at all like Popper's typical oligarch.

It will also become apparent that among those who may be roughly described as conservatives — men who wished to preserve the values of the older social order, and who must therefore in Popper's terms, be classified as oligarchs — there may be found earnest champions of some of the more enlightened values of the new order. On a later page, Popper has admitted to membership in the Great Generation two "great conservatives," Sophocles and Thucydides — both oligarchs; and he has recognized in Thucydides some traces of humanitarianism. Nor is he blind to the existence in the "period of transition," as he calls it, of the "wavering" Euripides, and the "skeptical" Aristophanes.[87] Our quarrel with Popper here is mainly that he has not taken account of them in drawing his picture of oligarchy, has not modified its

[87] Popper, p. 180.

blackness by the addition of their splendor, and in consequence has failed to do as justice would require, namely: to agree that "oligarchs," even as he defines them, were often men of insight and human worth, and that Plato was one of these. That he has not done so he justifies by his special principle of limitation, according to which those oligarchs are to be forgiven, and only those, who lived before that rather vague date after which the message of the open society was fully formulated — a proviso which, as we have said above, and as we shall show further good reason to believe below, need not be accepted.

We may with full justice ask the reader to recollect the attitude of Euripides toward the possibility of human excellence in the slave or in the lowly-born, and to observe simultaneously that Euripides, as is well-attested,[88] was an opponent of the extreme democracy, the advocate of a moderate oligarchy, somewhat on the lines of Thucydides. As another example of the very common tendency among able and good Athenians to combine the traits which Popper sees as distinctively oligarchic with others which he reserves for the democracy, we may also claim Aristophanes, who could nurse the sweet dream of restoring the old agricultural economy, with its associated virtues of temperance and piety, and deplore the dangers that he thought inseparable from the new education, and yet in the midst of his jesting could espouse, as simple common sense, such liberal and humane measures as the granting of citizenship rights to resident aliens and allies, and the raising of the allied cities from the status of subjects to a position of parity.[89] Having observed these men, we may be able to understand the attitude of Plato, who felt that democracy as it was exemplified at Athens must be rejected almost *in toto*, yet could nevertheless accept no form of government in its place which did not preserve one of the prime benefits of that democracy, the security from injustice, the welfare and dignity of the common man, in striking contrast to the Old Oligarch's bitter conviction that a rightly ordered state would see him every inch a slave.

Our discussion thus far will have fulfilled its intention if it has shown that there were antidemocrats who were not at the same time opponents, as the case might be, of empire, or of commerce, or of the welfare of the common man; that there were antidemocrats, as well as democrats, with whose enthusiasm for unbounded power and wealth Plato could no more have sympathized than with a Callicles or an Archelaus; and that there was more than one spirit in which a man could oppose democracy, or change, or commerce

---

[88] *Supp.* 238ff., *Orestes* 917ff., *Electra* 380ff.

[89] This is the interpretation put upon *Lysistrata* 574–586 by W. S. Ferguson, *Cambridge Ancient History*, V, p. 325. In another passage also cited by Ferguson (p. 360), *Frogs* 686–737, Aristophanes, in the midst of a rather race-proud plea to the Athenians to forgive the citizens who had participated in the oligarchic revolution of 412–411, incidentally approves such measures as the granting of citizenship to the slaves and aliens who had manned the ships at Arginusae.

and empire, without being the enemy of all that was good in the life of contemporary Athens.

To Popper's succeeding ascriptions to the extremer oligarchs of being
treasonably pro-Spartan, morally ruthless, and cynically irreligious, the pattern of the preceding discussion is also applicable. In each case the neglect of
significant diversities among those who are held to exemplify the given characteristic has produced not portrait but caricature. There were "pro-Spar-
tans" at Athens, as we learn from Plato's *Protagoras*, whose cachet of Spartan superiority was a military mantle and a cauliflower ear; [90] there were
others, like Socrates [91] and perhaps Antisthenes,[92] who saw other and deeper
values in the Spartan way of life. There was the historian Herodotus, who
could accord Sparta admiration second only to his approval of Athens, and
dream of a united Greece under the leadership of both.[93] There were also men
like Thucydides, who in their banishment could visit Sparta and study im-
partially her point of view, weighing her outmoded strengths against the new
but precarious strength of Athens,[94] and men like Xenophon, who could serve
Sparta's interests even in war, without losing, in some sense, their attachment
to Athens, and (in Xenophon's case) his loyalty to Socrates and hatred of
the Thirty Tyrants.[95] There were also the betrayers of Athens to Sparta to
save their own skins, like Alcibiades, who served, as he said, that city which
gave him security, but would doubtless have preferred that the city should be
Athens.

As to moral rottenness, the only monopoly that the evidence warrants us
in imputing is that which sociology would lead us to expect: while poverty
and the need to make a livelihood in a hard world sometimes produces its
own sort of moral blight, the rarer "fleurs du mal" of elegant skepticism and
self-indulgence would seem to have been cultivated at Athens, as elsewhere,
in the "Adonis gardens" of the leisured few. In Xenophon's account of Critias,[96] there is evidence of a sensuality that exceeded the bounds of what
Athens was prepared to accept; and in the mocking of the Mysteries and the
mutilation of the images of Hermes, we have record of what may fairly be
called profligate irreligion. But again, these are isolated examples which we
cannot permit Popper to identify as attributes of the "movement itself." Repression and the readiness to resort to murder and violence are indeed proved
against the Thirty Tyrants, but before we extend this trait to all adherents
even of the extremer oligarchic position, three things should be taken into
account: that revolutions are apt to throw up into positions of leadership the
more resolute and fanatical adherents of the victorious party, and further to
corrupt these men by the unwonted exercise of absolute power; that at Athens,

[90] *Protagoras* 342 B–C.
[91] See p. 304.
[92] See pp. 210–211.
[93] See p. 290.
[94] See pp. 606–608.
[95] Xenophon, *Hellenica* II, 3–4.
[96] Xenophon, *Memorabilia* I, 2, 29–30.

successive alternations of democrat and oligarch had produced increased vindictiveness on the part of the victors; and that, as Thucydides has told us, in the Greek world of that date, political murder and the wholesale putting to death of defeated factions in civil strife had become the order of the day, and was no monopoly of oligarchs.

We have thus shown that Popper's picture of the oligarchic interest has been so far oversimplified as to be seriously inaccurate, and that it has been overintensified in its disapprovable aspects in such a way as to do injustice to almost any individual who should subsequently be described as an adherent of the oligarchic movement. We must now deal, as promised, with Popper's account of Thucydides as a historian, since he is a principal source of our knowledge of the period. In three words, Popper's thesis is that Thucydides is himself an oligarch, showing the traits Popper has assigned to oligarchs in general; and that Thucydides' *History* is a party book, and its strictures upon the Athenian democracy not worth our credence. We shall herewith offer a summary reply, relegating to our note [97] the task of a point-for-point examination of Popper's argument.

Thucydides has chosen a method of writing history which reduces to a minimum his own explicit comments upon the action. He seldom stops to cheer the players, or to speak sternly to those guilty of a breach of rules. For the most part his judgments are, so to say, embodied in the events he has chosen to report, in their bearing upon the course and consequences of the great struggle, the Peloponnesian war, which is his subject. He concedes much to the operation of impersonal forces which in his belief man cannot abolish, though it is often possible, given the necessary knowledge and decisiveness of action, to channel them in a direction of advantage. Many of his finest effects are achieved dramatically through directly reported speeches of the political and military leaders on both sides, speeches which he has told us are not always precise reports, but rather reconstructions of what was or might most illuminatingly have been said in the circumstances. Again he will employ a sort of dramatic irony, as when he juxtaposes the episode of the Athenian attack upon Melos — extreme example of selfish imperialism, naked and unashamed — with the solemnity and high hopefulness of the sailing forth of the Athenian expedition to Sicily — the tragic rushing upon inevitable doom. Throughout, the historian has been at obvious and self-declared pains to collect and to verify his raw materials, the outward facts, the wheres, whens, and by whoms. But — point crucial to our interest — has the historian remained a historian on the level of his serious judgments of the causal interconnections of events, or is Popper justified?

---

[97] Our attempt to answer Popper's arguments against the trustworthiness of Thucydides as witness to the faults of the Athenian democratic government, appears as Appendix VIII, pp. 604ff.

It would, of course, be worse than idle to deny that Thucydides is through-out his work maintaining a point of view. He was far from indifferent to the shattering events in progress around him. He can even be shown to have yielded in one instance (VIII, 73) to the human frailty of gratuitously gibing at a demagogue who was, to him, particularly offensive, thereby violating his own rule of omitting from the record everything that was not organically re-lated to his theme. But aside from such rare departures, his maintenance of a point of view is far from proving what Popper's case demands. For it is not possible without begging the question to assume that the point of view in question was substituted for a set of unequivocal and contrary facts which any honest observer with half an eye could not have failed to see. How if the facts were substantially as Thucydides has interpreted them? Should Thu-cydides' final judgment, which issued in what may be called "oligarchical sympathies," have been suppressed? And who is in a position to go behind Thucydides to offer an objective criterion by which to measure the essential fairness of his mind? Again, we remind our reader that we are not engaged in arguing, on the authority of Thucydides or any other, that Athenian democ-racy ought never to have seen the light. Our more modest intention is to show that serious criticism of it, even the rejection of many of its essential features, does not prove moral turpitude, or a mind blinded by prejudice and self-interest.

We must not be led beyond the limits of the quite limited degree of cer-tainty here available. But unless one is willing to ignore the all but unanimous ruling of ancient and modern readers, it is surely a violation of historical probability to throw out of court a document so rich in evidence as Thu-cydides' *History*, without the authority of any other more reliable witness, and merely on the grounds of what appear to be highly precarious subjective suspicions.

The truth is that every one of Popper's assertions touching the quick of the issue — his picture of Thucydides the oligarch, filled, as such, with the partisan desire to arrest change, and to fight the empire and commerce, is substantially at odds with the conclusions reached by those qualified special-ists whose arguments we have been able to examine. Bury viewed Thucydides as a species of ancient Machiavelli, for whom power and pragmatic efficiency formed the standard of approvable statecraft. Finley and Gomme, in impres-sive mutual agreement, have stressed his appreciation of the Periclean regime, with its prerequisite of power, especially naval power, as constituting an ad-vance over the old static agricultural economy still represented by backward Sparta, and have found in him the regretful spectator and analyst of the de-terioration of Athenian national life in consequence of its corruption at the hands of the less enlightened and selfishly disunited party leaders who as-sumed control after the death of the great statesman. More recently, Grene has asked us to view Thucydides as the cold, proud, aspiring achiever of an "everlasting possession" in his own flawless history, a counterpart to the memorable, almost inhuman grandeur of the Athenian empire under Pericles.

And so Popper is left alone in undisputed possession of a Thucydides largely of his own contriving (at least, he has given us no indication of any supporting authorities), a Thucydides tailored in strict conformity to the fashion that Popper has decreed an oligarch of his subvariety must wear. The imperfections that may be found in the historian prove little more than his human imperfection; they do nothing to impair his essential reliability as historian of his own time, in experience, ability, and devotion to his task, second to none.

We have seen how, in the treatment of the oligarchical interest at Athens, the rough edges of political history have been smoothed over under Popper's hand into conformity with a simpler and more logical scheme. We must now expect the same sort of recrystallization of intellectual history around the axis of his preference, in his account of that group of outstanding men whom he has called the "Great Generation," and of the Athenian *dêmos* during the corresponding period.

In our examination of this subject we shall ourselves be cast in a rather unseemly role. We shall have to appear as diminishers of the glory of some really glorious names; in these circumstances we may be permitted to say a word of deprecation. In what follows, we shall strive to pluck no stars from the crowns of the great ones in question save those that adulation has unwarrantably put there, and which serve by contrast to darken Plato, but it will also be incumbent upon us to take the initiative in pointing out some limitations upon the greatness of the Great Generation, for the similar reason that injury is done to Plato if he is measured by a standard set higher than the true level of his time.

We must begin by calling attention to what is doubtless an inadvertence, though it functions as a fallacy: an illegitimate concentration in the lighting which serves to enhance the brilliance of effect. For what Popper has called a generation actually spans a tract of time more nearly equal to a century. By including Protagoras and Pericles as well as Antisthenes and Alcidamas, he has been able to bring on the stage, as if contemporaries, men who were born some half a century before Plato, along with men whose activity reaches into the latest period of Plato's life. By this extension of his range, Popper is able to extend correspondingly the number and luminosity of Plato's rivals and reputed superiors. We shall review these persons briefly, one by one.

Pericles worked steadily and, few would question, effectively, in behalf of the rights and interests, as he saw them, of the citizens of Athens. For many years he led them with supreme authority without overriding them, remaining at all times subject to the electorate. We recognize in him (but let us not forget his obligation to the genius of the historian Thucydides, who has so persuasively reported him) a great voice lifted in behalf of the splendid cultural ideal which his own practice furthered: an Athens beautiful and free, in which citizens, each according to his capacity, could share the direction of their common concerns in mutual toleration, holding up to the whole of Greece a model of what human life could be at its most intelligent and gracious best. This in all conscience is a sufficient basis upon which a monument to Pericles the democratic statesman has been firmly reared. But it is insufficient to support the claim that Popper has entered in his behalf,[98] that he championed a universalistic democracy. When, in 451–450 B.C., Pericles secured the passage of a law restricting the Athenian citizenship to those descended from citizen parents on both sides, he was acting as clearly within the ambit of democracy in the ancient sense as he was violating the spirit of what the term signifies in the modern world. To deprive some five thousand persons of their citizenship for no other offense that this seems to us essentially undemocratic. But if, with Pericles and his contemporaries, we mean by democracy the special interest of all members of a closed society of citizens, then plainly this diminution of the number of "shareholders" was a democratic measure, since it raised the quotient of advantage left when the number of citizens is divided into the quantity of available privilege; but it was not democracy in the universalistic sense. Popper has indeed anticipated this criticism, but he has not neutralized it by his entirely undocumented reference to Pericles' having toward the end of his life "revised his attitude toward these matters, probably under the influence of such men as Protagoras." [99]

Just here we may notice in passing an ambiguous quotation which tends to extend beyond defensible limits the "openness" of Pericles' ideal Athens. Quoting from the Funeral Oration sentences which do honor to its author both in his eyes and in ours, Popper includes among them the proud boast: "Our city is thrown open to the world; we never expel a foreigner . . ." [100] The harm here is done by the three dots. One might well suppose from Popper's avowed purpose in introducing the quotations, that is, to exemplify the "humanitarian and universalistic" spirit of the Oration, that Pericles is here heard announcing a policy of universal admission of foreigners to the privileges of citizenship, or at least magnanimously extolling the Athenian policy of admitting them freely to residence. What the three dots have obscured from view is that Pericles is not here talking within the context of citizenship or permanent residence. He is speaking of military policy; the omitted sequel is his boast that Athens is not afraid of what foreign spies may learn from observation on the ground, of her state of military readiness.

Basic constituent in the intellectual program of Popper's Great Generation, as we saw at length in an earlier chapter, was an antislavery plank, or at

[98] Popper, p. 181.　　　　　　　　　　　　　　[100] *Ibid.*, p. 181.
[99] *Ibid.*, p. 533, note 16 to chapter 6.

the least a theoretical denial of the basis of a natural distinction between slave and free. But one searches the record in vain for the slightest indication of Periclean opposition to this institution, without which his whole political system, as actually organized, could scarcely have functioned. Nor does Popper report the discovery of any such evidence. And the same may be said of another supposed tenet of the Great Generation, namely, the cosmopolitan denial of the "natural" difference between Greeks and barbarians. But by a series of overlapping pronouncements Popper has so associated the name of Pericles with democracy, and democracy with freedom, and freedom with antislavery and antinationalism,[101] that no reader could be expected to refrain from drawing from the sorites the unwarranted conclusion that Pericles was to some degree, at least, an abolitionist and, toward the end of his life, a believer in racial equality.

Nor is there any indication that Pericles had any plan for the emancipation of that other oppressed group, Athenian women. This is perhaps surprising in view of his own practical preachment, by his relation to Aspasia, of the liberal ideal. But what is arresting almost to the point of dramatic irony, is that passage in the Funeral Oration upon which we earlier commented, in which he pronounces most worthy of honor that Athenian matron who is least talked about among the men. One can but wonder whether the implications of this for the most talked about (and against) woman in Athens, had crossed the great statesman's mind.

Since, as we have already heard, and are scheduled to hear at greater length, one of Plato's major offenses was that he cherished an "organic" theory of the state, in contrast to the free individualism of the Periclean ideal, it is a matter of some importance to inquire whether it is true that, as Popper supposes, this ideal was one of undiluted individualism, or was perhaps itself "infected," to some degree, with organicism. In considering the Funeral Oration with this question in mind, one must, of course, make due allowance for the nature of the occasion, an honoring of the city's dead, and for the underlying motivation of a speech in war time, delivered by the war leader himself. Both considerations would prompt us to expect accent on the enduring life of the fatherland, for which it is sweet to die. But the thought of the statesman-orator is not content to rest at this point. He appeals to his auditors to contemplate an Athens that transcends all other goods, all other affections: "You must yourselves realize the power of Athens and feed your eyes upon her from day to day, till love of her fills your hearts; and then when all her greatness shall break upon you . . ."[102] Is it too much to say that this Athens, under the glowing imagination and devotion of her great custodian, has become something, may we say, metaphysically more than the sum of its human parts, past and present, that it has been reified and deified into an end-in-itself, and, as it

---

[101] Popper, p. 180–181.

[102] Thucydides II, 43, translated by Craw-   ley, Modern Library, New York, 1943, p. 107.

were, is conceived not as the claimant and recipient but as the source of values? This impression is strengthened when, just before the close, he offers to those bereaved parents who are still of an age to have children the (to him) consoling hope that further offspring will not only help them to forget those whom they have lost, but "will be to the state at once a reënforcement and a security." [103] We would not press the point beyond a certain minimum, but this suggestion of state worship, untempered even by subordination to any higher law, may help us to reach a juster estimate of Plato's lesser commitment when on occasion he speaks of the common interest over against the individual, in a manner that Popper has sharply rebuked. We shall then do well to remember that it is not within reason to expect any Greek, whether Plato or Pericles, to have reached that deeper appreciation of the individual person which the Christian centuries have so slowly and so painfully achieved.

The speech of Pericles contains a suggestion of another attitude deeply condemned by Popper, the concept of the state — one's own state — as standing above the moral law and measurable only by its power. There is a sentence in which Pericles celebrates the invincible power of Athens and of her citizens, declaring: "We have forced every sea and land to be the highway of our daring, and everywhere, whether for evil or for good, have left imperishable monuments behind us." [104] The Athens for which Athenians are invited to die is not, then, simply the moral ideal embodied in the justice and liberty accorded its citizens. In its external aspect, it is frankly an amoral glory.

Nowhere, perhaps, do we find Pericles falling more clearly short of the exaggerated moral heights on which his admirer has fondly conceived him to stand, than in his relation to the development of the Athenian empire. We are not suggesting that on the standards applied to other empire-builders, Pericles' policy was particularly reprehensible. Neither was it beyond reproach on contemporary Greek standards, and *a fortiori*, it was far below the level suggested by such words as "universalistic" and "humanitarian."

Popper has asked us to think of the revenues flowing into the Athenian treasury not as tribute, but as a sort of moderate tax paid out for services received.[105] Herein, if Plutarch is to be believed, Popper has the support of no less a man than Pericles himself, who is said to have reassured the Athenians that they were "in no way obliged to give any account of these moneys to their allies, so long as they maintained their defense," adding that "they should convert the overplus . . . to such undertakings" (temples and other public works) "as would hereafter . . . give them eternal honour, and for the present . . . freely supply all the inhabitants" (of Athens) "with plenty." [106]

---

[103] Thucydides II, 44, translated by Crawley, Modern Library, New York, 1943, p. 108.

[104] *Ibid.*, II, 41. In Pericles' later oration,

Thucydides II, 64, a similar attitude is taken.   [105] Popper, p. 177.

[106] Plutarch, *Life of Pericles*, ch. XII; translated by Dryden, Modern Library, New York, 1932, pp. 191–192. Plutarch, however,

In Plutarch's report, Pericles is represented as speaking as of right; in Thucydides, in an oration delivered in the second year of the war, he is shown speaking with less righteousness and more realism. Warning the Athenians that they must, whether they will or no, fight to retain their empire, he says, "For what you hold is, to speak somewhat plainly, a tyranny; to take it perhaps was wrong, but to let it go is unsafe." [107] That Thucydides has on the whole not misrepresented the convictions of Pericles here is, we believe, past doubt, particularly for those who with Popper are convinced that the Funeral Oration is in all essentials pure Pericles; it is indeed unthinkable that Thucydides could, even had he the motive so to do, have imputed to so thoroughly well known a leader views obviously other than his own.

Pericles is also, like Winston Churchill, quite willing to remind his fellow citizens that material values tremble in the balance when empire is at stake.[108] In the Funeral Oration itself, one notes the reference to the fruits of empire and trade, which Athenians, so to speak, could have for breakfast.[109] The city upon which he asks his hearers to turn their eyes is not merely an imponderable ideal; it is the "megalopolis," also, that his mind dwells upon, a city great in material size and wealth; [110] and he even speaks with satisfaction of what we may call the "stately homes of Athens." [111] We need not presume to "cast sour looks" upon the worldly standards herein implied, and from our heights expect the Athenians to have borne the burdens of empire out of sheer ethical obligation. It is merely that we are here presented with one more obvious aspect of Periclean "democracy" which neither Plato nor conscientious democrats today are under any moral necessity to applaud.

Following the precedent set by Popper, we can very briefly deal with Herodotus, who enters the scene merely as one who was "welcomed and hailed in Pericles' city as the author of a work that glorified" the Periclean principles of "equality before the law, and of political individualism." [112] That Herodotus celebrated Athens, and was welcomed there, is not in dispute; what I shall show cause to deny is that the qualities celebrated were in any real sense identical with those that Popper has defined as the faith of the Great Generation.

The *Histories* of Herodotus are, in general, more profitable to enjoy than to dissect: the mingling of irrepressible curiosity, narrative skill, broad sympathies which did not exclude barbarian peoples,[113] genuine and generous

---

is not nearly so dependable a source as Thucydides, cited below; cf. Gomme, *A Historical Commentary on Thucydides*, 1945, p. 65 ff., esp. p. 66.

[107] Thucydides II, 64, translated by Crawley, Modern Library, New York, 1934, p. 118. That Pericles' attitude toward the allied cities was that of "master" rather than "friend" is also the conclusion of Merritt, Wade-Gery, and McGregor, *The Athenian Tribute Lists*, III, 1950, pp. 278–281.

[108] Thucydides II, 62.
[109] *Ibid.* II, 38.
[110] *Ibid.* II, 38, 43, 64.
[111] *Ibid.* II, 38.
[112] Popper, p. 180.
[113] This is not to say that Herodotus was without a lively sense of certain capital points of Hellenic cultural superiority. He regards barbarians as typically prone to violations of human decency in the treatment of the dead (IX, 78), and to a "silly

hatred of tyranny — in the presence of these qualities, criticism dissolves into appreciation. But for the sake of just perspective, we must observe that though fully contemporary with Pericles, his mind and imagination belonged to an earlier day. Upon the surface of his book there float expressions of the "enlightenment," borrowed, perhaps, from Protagoras, whom he probably knew; [114] but at a deeper level he remained faithful to the standards political, moral, and religious that the "men of Marathon" had proclaimed. The liberty of which he speaks is freedom from tyranny and from foreign rule, his praise of "*isagoria*" — equal freedom of speech, or, generalized, equality —, though applied to Athenians, contains nothing distinctive of the "new democracy," [115] and might, indeed, have been pronounced, with slight verbal alterations, in an encomium upon Sparta. The war that he is prepared to fight is not the war between Athens and Sparta on whose brink he stood — he witnessed the first few years. His war is still that of the free Greeks under the leadership of Athens and Sparta against the barbarians, the Persians, who do not know true freedom; a war, we may notice, whose principle was to be approved by the author of the *Menexenus* and of the *Republic*, and an Athens which was to be a source of inspiration to the author of the *Laws*, without in the least commending him to Popper's favor.

A frequent and distinguished visitor in Periclean Athens was the sophist Protagoras, who was honored by Pericles in a dual capacity, by appointment to an important legislative commission and by being given the task of furthering the education of his two sons.[116] That Protagoras was among the most gifted of the sophists, that his educational program, designed to impart the skills required both for private life and for participation in public affairs, deserves honorable mention in any history of education, and that he cast out, by way of underpropping his practical platform, some stimulating if undeveloped ideas bearing on the nature and origin of knowledge and of culture, is the almost unanimous verdict of modern scholarship,[117] in which probably Plato himself (with important reservations) would concur. To Protagoras' credit, also, is the candor with which he declared his inability to judge whether or not gods exist or what their form might be, a declaration for which, as

---

superstitiousness" which the "clever Greeks" have outgrown (I, 60, 3). And the abhorrence of despotism is, he thinks, a distinctively Hellenic achievement (VII, 102). In all this, Herodotus reflects what Shorey has called "normal Greek feeling" (*What Plato Said*, 1933, p. 600).

[114] W. Nestle, *Vom Mythos zum Logos*, p. 509.

[115] I owe this admirable observation to How and Wells, *A Commentary on Herodotus*, 1936, vol. I, p. 7. See Herodotus, V, 78, and the praise of Spartan *isokratia*, V, 92;

also VII, 101ff.

[116] These are probable inferences from Diogenes Laertius, ix, 50, where it is said, following Heraclides, that he "gave laws to Thurii," an Athenian colony founded in 443 B.C.; and from Plato, *Protagoras* 314–315, where the sons of Pericles appear among his pupils.

[117] Jaeger, *Paideia*, I, bk. 2, ch. 3, contains a fine appreciation of Protagoras, which however is not blind to the limitations of Protagorean humanism; see especially pp. 298–299.

tradition has it, he was prosecuted and found guilty under the same Athenian law that later was invoked against Socrates.[118]

The world at large remembers him best for his relativism, with its famous watchword, "Man is the measure of all things." What precisely Protagoras meant by this radical-sounding formula has been subject to much dispute. At its maximum, it would leave each individual the infallible determiner ("measure") of his own "truth"; at its minimum, it involved the repudiation of a discoverable objective truth valid for all mankind. Our most responsible account of the Protagorean relativity, particularly as applied to ethical problems, is contained in certain sections of Plato's *Theaetetus*. From what is there said, and also from a related passage in the *Cratylus*, it is clear that in strict theory Protagoras had committed himself to according equal truth to the opinions of all individuals: "What seems true to each man really is true for him." [119] It is equally clear, however, that the disruptive social implications of this theory were hedged about by Protagoras himself, at the cost of consistency, with a conservative identification of justice and holiness, for any given community, with what "seems" just and holy to that community, that is, with its laws and customs. His first task as educator, therefore, was to make his pupils "better" in terms of the accepted norms of their own states.[120] When, as fully educated participants in political life, his pupils should advocate modifications in the existing laws, then, on Protagoras' assumptions, no question of just or unjust need (or, strictly, could) arise to trouble them. The proponent of such a change must urge his case on grounds of "advantage" to the state; if adopted, the new law will both seem and be just.[121] Thus Protagoras could avoid collision with

---

[118] Fr. 4, Diels, *Vors.*, 1922. For the charge of atheism, see Nestle, *Vom Mythos zum Logos*, p. 278, and esp. pp. 480–481. The chief ancient source is Diog. L., ix, 54, 55, 51.

[119] *Theaetetus* 170 A; *Cratylus* 386 A.

[120] *Theaet.* 167 A–D; cf. also *Protagoras* 318 E–319 A, taken in conjunction with 326 C–D and 328 B. It should be noted that this view would make the state — any state — the custodian of its citizens' consciences, a conception which, when he thinks he has discovered it in Plato, stirs Popper's deepest indignation.

[121] *Theaet.* 167 C, 172 A. The allusion at 172 B to those persons who "are willing to affirm that none of these things [i.e., just and unjust, holy and unholy] exists by nature or has an essence of its own," Cornford interprets as referring not to Protagoras and his followers, but only to those thinkers mentioned immediately afterward, "who do not argue altogether as Protagoras does" (Cornford, Plato's *Theory of Knowledge*,

1935, pp. 81–83). But two considerations make substantially against this view: (1) at 172 A, in a passage admitted by Cornford (p. 89) as "genuinely Protagorean," justice and all other moral and religious values are equated with whatever any state may choose to decree, a position in substantial accord with the opinion of those who deny that justice has a nature and an essence of its own; and (2) a passage in the *Cratylus*, 386 A–E, in language closely resembling that of our disputed sentence, presents the Protagorean position as involving the denial that things such as virtue and vice have a fixed essence according to which they naturally come to be. To my mind the least difficult assumption is that Plato intended to put Protagoras in a group whose common property was the denial of a "natural" justice, or objective standard of moral validity by which laws could be evaluated. The members of this group, however, were marked by specific differences, some of them, like Protagoras, following tradition

traditional opinion within any community he honored with his presence, and
without recognizing the existence of any absolute moral norms, could practice
his profession of improving his pupils and their several cities by offering instruction in how to manage effectively both private and public affairs, and to
speak persuasively on either side of any question.[122]

But in the thought of Protagoras, as we know it, a more basic inconsistency
remains. Not only does Plato attest and offer objections against his relativism;
he also attributes to him certain doctrines impossible to bring into accord with
the basic tenet of moral relativism, and far more acceptable in consequence to
a thinker like Plato, who maintained the objective reality of a universal standard of human good. Even in the *Theaetetus* there is perhaps some hint of this,
when Protagoras is shown describing those advantagous new laws which a
wise public speaker will cause to be enacted as instruments for inducing his
city to hold more truly "wholesome" opinions concerning what is just, and is
heard comparing the activity of such a speaker to that of the physician, who
really knows how to produce better health, and therefore more healthful per-
ceptions, on the part of his patient.[123] We cannot tell whether or in what
direction Protagoras thought fit to develop this analogy. Clearly there is nothing in the analogy itself to prevent the identification of political health with
such nonmoral goods as prosperity and power. But that it may carry suggestions of a wider and more spiritual significance, implying the existence of a
standard of moral value, is shown by the ethical use to which Plato himself
puts it in the *Gorgias* and the *Republic*. It is in Plato's dialogue the *Protagoras*,
however, that we find positive indications that Protagoras did sometimes appeal, by implication, to objective moral standards. True, the dialogue contains
important elements avowedly relativistic; there is the little speech in which the
sophist seeks to escape from the logical clutch of Socrates through the side-
door of the merely relative truth of all applications of the word "good" (334 A–
C), and, prior to that, there is the approving description of the typical civilized
community indoctrinating its young citizens in its own mores and in its traditional laws, "invented by good lawgivers of old" (325 C–326 E). It is observable, however, that even in this latter passage there is a strong implication of
an underlying quality common to all communities, though present in unequal
degrees, and serving as a criterion by which they may be distinguished and

---

in regarding the institutions of the state as
genuinely binding upon its citizens, while
others, like Thrasymachus, regarded moral
prescriptions as mere devices whereby the
ruling class enhanced its power. In effect,
then, Plato is saying: Protagorean relativity leads logically into radical immoralism.
Protagoras stopped short of the abyss; others have plunged into it.

[122] It seems to me highly probable that

Protagoras, in announcing his relativism,
was not interested in developing its epistemological consequences, but that, like
Gorgias (see p. 154), he philosophized in
the interests of his rhetoric, employing
philosophical arguments in refutation of
the rival claims of philosophy, to clear the
ground for the practice of his essentially
nonphilosophical art.

[123] *Theaet.* 167 B–C.

preferred to the condition of the wild men of Attic comedy (327 D). Most striking of all is the evidence of the myth which Plato ascribes to Protagoras; here we are told that in primeval time, Zeus bestowed upon all men individually some share in the basic social virtues of *dikê* and *aidôs*, justice and reverence (322 C–D). There are thus provided in the generic nature of man (as we have seen in an earlier chapter) theoretic grounds for the discovery of a moral code binding upon all men, independent of the "seemings" and diversities which characterize the experience of particular communities and their individual members. The consequences of this element of his thought, had Protagoras followed them home, would have made of him in many respects a Platonist before Plato, and would have forced him to abandon his relativism and his comfortable impartiality as between all opinions about right and wrong. It is perhaps this unresolved conflict among his views, as they have come down to us, that has tempted several modern interpreters to construe him into consistency by assimilating him to their own philosophical outlook.[124]

Popper appears to be a case in point. Out of the fifth-century Protagoras whom we have just portrayed, he has constructed a much improved modern thinker under the same name. In absolute antithesis to a backward-looking Plato, hidebound in rigid adherence to tradition, this neo-Protagoras is presented as the forward-looking sponsor of a high ethic, "critical dualism," according to which "man the moral being" superimposes "norms . . . upon the original or natural state of affairs," and creates institutions "not natural but conventional," institutions for which "we are responsible," and which therefore, we may change. Popper further credits Protagorean theory, in thus justifying changes in social practices, with the intention to "improve things," which in Popper's terms implies the aim of developing societies progressively more democratic, more individualist, and more humane. The same implication attaches to the title Popper confers on the sophist: "theorist of the open society." This admirable Protagoras is the forerunner and spiritual kinsman of that other and still greater "critical dualist," Popper's Socrates. And more than this, Popper assures us on several occasions that Protagoras' ethical position was founded on a sincere religious belief. From the myth we have just mentioned, with its machinery of gods and demigods, Popper concludes that the self-announced agnostic Protagoras believed "God to work through man," and that "the laws, which are our making, are made with the help of divine inspiration."[125]

---

[124] For example, F. C. S. Schiller, the Oxford humanist, hailed him (chapter II of his *Studies in Humanism*, 1912) as the daring founder of the pragmatic method, itself capable of yielding objective truth measured in terms of publicly shared values; and Paul Elmer More saw him (*Hellenistic Philosophies*, 1923, pp. 325–327) as the antithesis of what he, More, approved and made of him the major prophet of a radical moral skepticism.

[125] The quotations in this paragraph are assembled from Popper's discussions of Protagoras on pp. 61, 65, 67, 132, 180, 184, and 509.

There is a certain element of humor in this situation, arising not simply from the extravagance of the claims, but rather from the curious circumstance that what is intended as a furious attack on Plato displays itself, when the necessary corrections are made, as a profound compliment to him. For the Protagoras whom Popper bids us admire owes most of his authentic substance to that aspect of Protagorean doctrine which Plato presents sympathetically, as we have seen, in the early part of his dialogue *Protagoras*; and to put the matter shortly, it is not possible to separate the Protagoras of this particular section of the dialogue from Plato sufficiently to permit of glorifying the one without according simultaneous and substantial honor to the other. Whoever will study the views there expressed in comparison with Plato's thought in many of the other dialogues, up to and including the *Laws*, will find a truly surprising measure of agreement.[126] We recommend to our reader the rereading of our earlier presented brief summary of the myth from Protagoras' speech by way of illustration of this point.[127] The basic ideas that without the virtues of justice and reverence no community, however technically competent and abounding in warlike strength, can long endure, and that albeit in unequal degree, all men must participate in them and live lives guided by their fundamental rule — these ideas no reader of Plato can fail to recognize as inseparable components of his thought. The mythical description of the two virtues as the gift of Zeus is matched by Plato's genuine conviction that the human soul has a divine element, and that laws, though of man's making, are rightly made only in conformity to a divine paradigm. Platonic, too, is the notion of the entire community as educator; though Plato would regard the value of the education as dependent upon the quality of the moral standards to which it conformed. Plato, and Socrates as well — witness the *Crito* — would concur in regarding the laws of the Greek cities as the primary vehicles of moral instruction for their citizens, and as expressions, in the main, of traditional wisdom. And in considering this parallelism, one will do well to remember, in justice to Plato, what Shorey has so well said: that there is no reason to attribute to anyone other than Plato himself, "the wealth, the refinement, the concatenation of the ideas and the systematic composition of the whole." Popper shows some marginal awareness of the similarity between the views he ascribes to the two men,[128] but has all but totally obscured it in his zeal to convert Plato into the contrary of that which he approves.

Between the historical Protagoras and Plato there remain, indeed, vital points of contrast, rooted in the Protagorean denial of objective truth. But Popper has brought us no nearer understanding either man. It is surely unhistorical to see in Protagoras a pioneer in the advocacy of responsible improvements in the legislative structure of a state, when, since at least Solon's

---

[126] See Paul Shorey, *What Plato Said*, p. 124.

[127] See p. 217 above.

[128] Popper, n. 27 to ch. 5, p. 516.

time, such activities had been a conspicuous feature of the Athenian political landscape. Conceiving Protagoras as a forward-looking progressivist, Popper has failed to note the sophist's appeal to ancient and traditional wisdom, and his consistent failure to espouse any program of social values as *per se* more worthy of furtherance than any other; to this extent Popper is endorsing a thinker committed to a strict moral neutrality between communities of such opposing characters as, say, an "open" Athens and a "closed" Sparta. In his assimilation of Socrates to Protagoras, Popper has expunged from the record the notorious opposition between the Socratic quest for valid and universal knowledge of the moral good, and the Protagorean assumption that no such knowledge is possible. By ignoring Protagoras' explicit agnosticism, Popper has been enabled to equip an eminently secular relativist with a spurious halo of sanctity. Not only has he lavished upon his favorite merits supposititious and, in the ancient world, as yet unborn. He has also glorified Protagoras at Plato's double cost, bestowing upon him much that has every right to be thought Plato's own, and according to Plato only the usual misunderstanding and abuse. Protagoras may have his laurels; but they need not be filched for him from another's crown.

Morally equivalent to the putting of leading questions to a witness is the practice of making an author say what you want him to say by selectively emphasized quotations. This is what our adversary has done for the sake of raising the illusion of an extreme modernity in the ethical outlook of Democritus, that near contemporary of Socrates, whose fame as advocate of the atomic theory, and builder of a materialistic world scheme in which causal determination holds universal sway, has for most readers obscured his importance as among the first of the great philosophers to address himself to ethical problems. Out of the mass of fragments which unhappily is all that remains of the vast output of this extraordinarily prolific man, Popper has assembled a little sermon [129] on the text of humanitarian universalism, in which the several separate constituents, aptly combined, and enhanced by occasional modernisms in the translation, produce an apparently overwhelming effect. A few examples of this method are in order.

When one reads, "Virtue is based, most of all, upon respecting *the other man*" (italics ours), it is difficult not to feel that we are listening to one of our contemporaries. But when one examines the original, he sees only the statement that "Reverence (*aidôs*) is that which chiefly comprises virtue," a sentiment noble enough in itself, but scarcely a novelty in Greek thought.[130] And now,

---

[129] Popper, pp. 180–181.

[130] Fr. 179 (Diels). The appeal to *aidôs* occurs frequently in Homer (e.g., *Il.* XIII, 95), and in a deeper moral sense in Hesiod (*Erg.* 192, 324, 200), not to mention other uses of the term in Theognis and the tragedians. A valuable discussion of *aidôs* in Greek thought generally, as the shame or ruth man feels at the thought of dishonoring himself by a base deed, or by wrong done to those who are helpless (suppliants, strangers, the aged, orphans), will be found

by the sheer juxtaposition of another fragment, with a quite different context, inaccurately rendered [131] as "Every man is a little world of his own," a spurious ethical enhancement is induced. For here the reader is brought to thoughts bordering on a sermon by John Donne, and a piece of cosmological anthropology merges into a mystical Christian awareness of the sanctity of Everyman. Of most of the other ethical dicta that are quoted, we may simply say that so far are they from reading "as if directed against Plato," [132] that their spirit and almost their very letter can easily be found in many a Platonic dialogue.[133]

One citation, indeed, remains, which Plato could not have said without qualification: "Better poverty in a democracy than high good fortune, so-called, under an autocracy, by just so much as freedom is better than slav-

---

in Gilbert Murray's *Rise of the Greek Epic*, 1911, pp. 103–112. Here, however, some slight injustice is done to Plato: Murray explains that the more intellectual and authoritarian Plato not unnaturally made less appeal to the emotional virtue *aidôs*, turning rather to virtues based upon principle and insight, and to civic control of conduct. While there is truth in this contention, there is also implied oversight of the many passages in Plato, particularly in the *Laws*, where the same feeling is expressed, sometimes in the very word *aidós*, sometimes by means of such near equivalents as *aischynesthai*, or *sebesthai* (e.g., 729 B–C). Plato speaks of "reverencing justice" in one's dealing with the helpless, especially slaves (777 D). See also 729 E and the references given in note 133 just below, for examples of Plato's attempt to protect the helpless in the city of the *Laws* with the aid of reverence and pity, reënforced by religious sanctions, law, and social pressure.

[131] Fr. 34. The fragment says". . . in man who is a little world (microcosm)," meaning that there is an analogy between the structure of man and that of the macrocosm, and conveying no reference to ethical relations obtaining between one man and another.

[132] Popper, p. 181.

[133] Fragments 41, 62, and 55, "To refrain from wrongdoing, not through fear but from a conviction that one ought to refrain," "Good is not merely not doing wrong, but not even wanting to do wrong," and "Works and deeds of virtue, not virtuous words, should be our concern," are collectively reaffirmed in the whole purport and substance of the *Republic*, but particularly in Book II.

Socrates is there asked to refute precisely the standpoint that Democritus rejects, the supposition that fear of consequences is the sole consideration inducing man to virtue; he is asked to prove that being just is not merely a prudential alternative that men reluctantly accept only because what they really want (i.e., violation of the persons and property of others), is not consistent with their own security. The superiority, over the mere "word," of the good "deed" and the virtuous intention (Aeschylus' "being rather than seeming good," *Rep.* 361 B) is tacitly asserted in every line.

With fragment 261, "One should to the best of his ability redress the wrongs of those who have suffered injustice, and not permit it to happen" (or "to pass unpunished"), there are numerous parallels throughout the *Laws*, where willingness to intervene in behalf of the victims of injustice is enjoined upon all citizens, and even upon slaves, with particular solemnity in the case of orphans or the helpless aged; see *Laws* 730 D, 880–882, 926 D–928 D, 932 C–D.

To Democritus' injunction (not mentioned by Popper, but well worth our admiration), "Learn to feel far greater shame (*aidós*) before thyself than before others" (fragment 244), there is, to my knowledge, nothing quite equivalent in Plato, though it is consistent with his many expressions of the idea that one ought to honor reason and self-consistency more than public opinion (*Crito* 46 B, 49 D), and with the doctrine expressed in the *Phaedo*, 83 A, that the soul should honor her own conviction and intuition of value.

ery."[134] Yet if "democracy" be qualified as constitutional and law-abiding, Plato could have given his full assent; in any case he matches Democritus in scorn of worldly fortune bought by subservience to a despot, and when choosing among states existing in his day, ranked democracy of any kind above a government without law, whether exercised by one man or by "the few." But in drawing upon the surviving political fragments attributed to Democritus, Popper is on dangerous ground; the impossibility of reconciling their diversity of standpoint, some of them being sharply antidemocratic,[135] has led to doubt as to their Democritean authorship.[136] It is special pleading to flourish the democratically inspired fragment while leaving unmentioned the existence of fragment 267, that asserts, "Rule belongs by nature to the superior man." Nor should fragment 252 remain unmarked, in which Democritus declares in the strongest terms the preëminence of "the interest of the city over all else," a mode of expression which, when found in Plato, is deemed totalitarian, but which, fairly viewed, may be only an emphatic rejection of selfish interests threatening the common weal.

From this discussion we hope no reader will emerge with the impression that he has been reading an attack upon Democritus; the present writer yields to none in admiration for the profundity and versatility of his thought and (subject to the indicated uncertainties) his liberality and humanity of outlook. What has been attacked is, as so often, not the ancient philosopher but the modern critic who has made use of him to improper ends. We know him as the proponent of an ethical ideal in which a certain "tranquillity" (*euthymie*) is identified as the good for man, an ideal which was to be adopted by Epicurus for the chastening of the hedonism of Aristippus, and by him transmitted to its most persuasive advocate, the poet Lucretius, himself a staunch admirer of Democritus. Popper has not made use of what seems to me perhaps the finest evidence of his ethical insight, his impressive admonition, previously cited, "Learn to feel far greater shame before thyself than before others" (fragment 244). This appeal to the sacred self-respect of the individual offered a standard and a support to those for whom the sanctions of the human community and of the gods no longer were available.

We approach the end of the roll call of the Great Generation: now, if ever,

---

[134] Fragment 251. Popper translates (p. 180), "The poverty of a democracy is better than the prosperity which allegedly goes with aristocracy or monarchy . . ." The word translated "aristocracy or monarchy," and which we render "autocracy," is "*dynastai*," a word which sometimes means simply "rulers," but can also mean "ruling oligarchs" who possess hereditary and unrestricted power; in Democritus' sentence it plainly has more than a tinge of despotism. (We shall discuss Popper's

reasons for his special translation of this word on p. 461 below.) Plato was far from admiring such forms of government, except in the one respect of furnishing a remote possibility of the establishment of the ideal state, by the fortunate conversion of one such ruler to true philosophy (*Republic* 473 D).

[135] Fragments 49, 75, 254.

[136] Nestle, *Vom Mythos zum Logos*, p. 203.

Popper must produce the definitive formulators of the "new faith," whose activity marks the dividing line between the forgivable oligarchs and the unforgivable. Next on the list appear "the school of Gorgias — Alcidamas, Lycophron, and Antisthenes," originators of "the creed of the universal empire of men." [137] Perhaps we should interpose here the comment that the frequent approving references to Gorgias himself, and to the school [138] might excusably lead the reader to suppose that the latter was the place to which Athenian citizens betook themselves to receive instruction in universalistic humanitarian ethics. A correction is in order.

Gorgias was, first and foremost, a master of discourse, a teacher of the art of persuasion through the medium of artistic prose.[139] But he left his pupils free to choose their own application of this skill. This will explain what would otherwise be the anomaly that among his "followers" are found men moving in opposite directions. There are, as Popper keeps reminding us, some who seem to have been on the right side of certain great issues of their day, but there is also a Thrasymachus, and perhaps a Critias and a Callicles, who in spite of their profession of contrary principles, have equal right to be classified as belonging to Gorgias' school. The only well-attested positive deliverance of Gorgias himself on a question of political import, was his speech at Olympia, in which, as a Panhellenist, in glaring contradiction to the ideal of universalism as Popper conceives it, he sought "to turn the Greeks against the barbarians . . . advising them to take for the prizes of their arms not each others' cities but the land of the barbarians." [140]

Of Alcidamas we have already spoken.[141] Except for his classic sentence against slavery, nothing significant remains. Lycophron denied the claims of birth (as did Plato), and spoke importantly, as Aristotle indicates, of the state as guarantor of mutual justice, although incapable of supplying moral education to its citizens.[142] But what further elements, if any, were included in his theory, cannot be reliably determined. We do not know whether either man was in Athens during the greater part of the period in question, nor whether ethics and politics were among their central interests. With Antisthenes we have previously dealt at length.[143] It will be remembered that we found in him, as in Socrates and in Plato, an ethic applicable in principle to any man, but along with the outline of this ethic, the fragments attest an equally cordial repudiation of democracy, not acknowledged by Popper, and show no championship of that broadly conceived "brotherhood of man," which Popper has ascribed to him. Leaving out of our present concern his nominalistic materialism, we should be hard put to discover any originality of doctrine. One might

---

[137] Popper, p. 180.
[138] *Ibid.*, pp. 112, 149, 560, 562.
[139] See p. 154; cf. also p. 337.
[140] Quoted from Philostratus, *Vit. Soph-*

ist. I, 11, by Jebb, *Attic Orators*, 1893, vol. I, p. 198.   [141] See pp. 141–143, 155.
[142] See pp. 146–167, 418–424.
[143] See pp. 202–215.

say he rendered a service to his master, of a sort different from that rendered by Plato, by his dramatic imitation and exaggeration of the ascetic and strenuous element in the Socratic manifold. But this achievement was at the price of a rejection of civic and religious pieties to which Socrates had assigned a central place.

"The greatest contribution to this faith was to be made by Socrates, who died for it." With these words Popper reveals the paramount importance, for his conception of the faith of the Great Generation, of the man whom he believes Plato was destined to betray. Now, as with Democritus, so here the present writer refuses to be outdone by Popper in the measure of his admiration, as our discussion of Socrates in Appendix XVI will make evident. Few would dissent [144] from the judgment that in Socrates human reason found one of its noblest and most fruitful embodiments. And yet such a blanket agreement may conceal important differences in emphasis; and the same differences will be found reasserting themselves at other points in the Socratic message, with important consequences for the interpretation of the whole. Let us detail here the picture of Socrates which Popper has drawn.

The man whom Popper is admiring is first of all a believer in "human reason as a universal medium of communication," a practitioner of "intellectual honesty and self-criticism." [145] He is the modest agnostic, whose wisdom "was simply the realization: how little do I know!" therein displaying "the true scientific spirit." [146] Moreover, "this Socratic intellectualism is decidedly equalitarian. . . . Everyone can be taught. . . . Any uneducated slave has the capacity to grasp even abstract matters." "And his intellectualism is also anti-authoritarian. . . . Real knowledge, wisdom, and also virtue, can be taught only by a method . . . of midwifery." [147] In sharpest contrast to Plato, who demanded that the wise should rule, Socrates, disbelieving in "all professional learnedness" [148] prescribed only that "statesmen should be . . . conscious of their limitations." [149] Socrates held that "there is nothing more important in our life than other individual men"; we are to cherish a "belief in the human individual as an end in himself"; [150] from Socrates' "doctrine that it is better to be a victim of injustice than to inflict it upon others," we can perhaps "best understand the core of his teaching, his creed of individualism." [151] "He was . . . a critic of Athens and of her democratic institutions," but his criticism "was a democratic one"; [152] "in fact, he had tried to give it" (democracy) "the faith it needed. This had been the work of his life." [153]

Though Socrates talked much of the "soul," Popper argues, he thereby

---

[144] Certain of Plato's detractors, however, rightly perceiving the organic relation between the thought of Plato and Socrates, have tarred both men with the same stick. See, e.g., n. 17, p. 21, and pp. 446, 466ff.

[145] Popper, p. 184.

[146] *Ibid.*, p. 127.

[147] *Ibid.*, p. 127.

[148] *Ibid.*, p. 127.

[149] *Ibid.*, p. 130.

[150] Popper, p. 185.

[151] *Ibid.*, pp. 184–185.

[152] *Ibid.*, p. 184.

[153] *Ibid.*, p. 188.

committed himself to no metaphysics: his "theory of individuality (or of the 'soul,' if the word is preferred) is . . . a moral and not a metaphysical doctrine." By it, he is reminding us that "there is . . . in man a divine spark, reason; and a love of truth, of kindness, humaneness, a love of beauty and of goodness." [154] In view of all this we may speak of "Socrates' advocacy of the autonomy of ethics . . . expressed especially in his doctrine of the self-sufficiency or autarky of the 'virtuous' individual"; [155] we may call him a "critical dualist," "who felt compelled by his conscience as well as by his religious beliefs, to question all authority, and who searched for the norms in whose justice he could trust," or in a more familiar vocabulary, "perhaps the greatest apostle of individualistic ethics of all time." [156]

To the truthfulness of some traits in this depiction, to the humanity and sincerity of the entire man, one can take no exception. There is even a sense in which one might agree with every single part of the whole. But, on the other hand, it is also fair to say that there is a sense in which the whole thing is wrong, wrong as our author (*me judice*) so often is, in an eminently coherent and systematic way. To illustrate: we agreed with Popper when he listed among the attested characteristics of the historical Socrates his habitual admission of ignorance, with its twofold implication of intellectual honesty and critical caution. But it was without our knowledge and consent that this undeniably Socratic trait should be supposed to have entailed for Socrates what it has come to imply to the modern mind, the recognition of the equal validity of other points of view. By joining this "ignorance" to the practice of spiritual midwifery, as applied by Socrates to all comers, including a slave, Popper thinks he has gone far toward establishing his view of a nonauthoritarian, equalitarian Socrates, inspired with a democratic regard for the opinions of all others, and a willingness to treat their opinions as naturally the "equals" of his own. Need it be said that no text is available to document this preview of nineteenth-century ethics? The Socrates preference for suffering rather than dispensing injustice has been subjected to a similar transmutation: for Popper this is the supreme exhibit of Socratic individualism, that a man should so love and value the interests of others that he would prefer to suffer at their hands rather than to infringe the sanctity of their individual rights. This Socrates, so modest intellectually, so morally determined, has now been made fully ready for the act of dying "for the freedom of critical thought" and for "free speech" itself, "for the right to talk freely to the young," or in order to attest his "loyalty to the state, as well as to democracy," as Popper has arranged for him to do, on later pages.[157] It is a wind blowing from the same quarter that has inspired what we heard Popper say about Socrates and "souls." No good "critical dualist" should have a soul. But if, by any chance, a critical

---

[154] *Ibid.*, p. 185.
[155] *Ibid.*, p. 509.

[156] *Ibid.*, p. 67, p. 127.
[157] Popper, pp. 188–189, 601.

dualist, otherwise in good standing, is overheard talking about a soul, well, fortunately there are devices for explaining that away.

In fine, Popper's Socrates has been washed in the waters of modern liberalism until every odor of his historical Greek origin has been removed. He has been put into modern dress, and would now be mistaken, at a distance, for the author of "A Free Man's Worship" or even for Jean Paul Sartre; or, most plausibly of all, for Popper's ideal self. But how such a projection could find something solid to identify itself with in the original Socrates, we have now to explain.

As a first approximation, we may say that what permits Popper or anyone else to make so fair an initial show of evidence supporting his case is just that duality or polarity in the personality and thought of Socrates which figured in our earlier discussion under the name of "incongruity." [158] The perennial charm and the perennial problem of Socrates lies, I believe, just here, in his most distinctive and baffling gift of seemingly breaching logic by attaching to himself what, when listed separately, appear as contradictory predicates. Is he a lonely spirit, given to mystical abstraction? Yes, and also the most eminently social of human animals. A great commoner? Yes, and an aristocrat of the intellect. The satirist of the popular religion, and its most pious practitioner; modest in his claims to know, but believing himself to possess the only key to true and universally valid knowledge; anarchist, putting his devotion to his "mission" above the command of the laws, and yet believer in the divine right of the personified Laws of his native city to his unqualified obedience, even unto death; — and the list of apparent contradictions could be further extended.

We can join Popper in finding in the *Apology* [159] and in various of Plato's "Socratic" dialogues, clear and ample evidence of the intellectual modesty of Socrates, his dissociation of himself from those self-styled experts whose conceit of knowledge had never subjected itself to critical inspection. We confirm, also, his attribution to Socrates of a genuine interest in promoting enlightenment, awakening the moral consciences of all who came in his way, citizen and foreigner. In such "sidewalk talks" and in his interviews with the artisans (*Apology* 22 C–E), there is a certain flavor, at least, of what Popper has called "equalitarian," a suggestion of the common touch. Nor can we doubt that the man who chose the alternative of suffering injustice to that of inflicting it on others, was expressing a humane ideal, consistent with the highest ethical conscience of the race. And finally, we will cordially agree that in refusing to

---

[158] See pp. 33–34 above.

[159] An arresting interpretation of the *Apology*, according to which Socrates made no actual speech, and the great speech we possess is from first to last a product of Plato's dramatic imagination working upon his memories of his conversations with his departed master, is considered on p. 632 below, together with a brief statement of our reasons for not dealing at length with this challenging hypothesis.

abandon his calling as teacher and public conscience at Athens, or, when condemned, to avail himself of the proffered opportunity to escape, he sealed his career in the true blood of martyrdom.

But as our indication of the Socratic polarity has taught us to expect, we can find other things as well. We can find in the *Apology*, along with the disclaimer, a more fundamental claim to know. The skepticism of Socrates reveals its granite foundation in an unshakable, a dogmatic conviction that there is a divine law or standard set for human reason to discover, and that by taking earnest and careful thought man is not merely employing a "medium of communication," as Popper would have it, but is pursuing an appointed way leading by successive steps nearer to knowledge of the true end which all men seek. We find no hint that this divinely sanctioned good is for Socrates identified with human action and its free principles of choice, as on Popper's interpretation it should be. On the contrary, it is an objective referent, and though Socrates is willing to suggest that it may be very close to human consciousness, revealing itself in dreams and oracles and, for him personally, in the inhibiting admonition of a "divine sign," it is certainly not conceived as either the creation of human aspiration or as deriving its authority from a mandate issued by the rational will of man. It speaks, and we listen, though, Socrates would insist, we must be actively intelligent listeners.

The *Apology* shows us, accordingly, a Socrates who, despite his asserted ignorance, claims to possess already the ground plan of the most important knowledge. He knows and proclaims the universally valid schedule of values which sets soul highest and body and wealth below (29 E ff.) ; he has no hesitation in asserting the dependence of the soul's well-being upon its achievement of moral good (29 B–E) ; he is convinced of the justice and benevolence that run providentially through the universe (41 D), in happy accord with the moral interests of man. He is confident that those who are able to confer moral benefit upon the young are not the many, but the few experts, perhaps even the one expert (25 B–C). And through his whole defense he shows no scruple in presenting himself as the uniquely competent, the perhaps irreplaceable man (28 E f., 29 D ff., 31 A–B), whom the god has selected for the improvement of the city.

If we turn to the *Crito*, we find again not the message, "Each man of us, whoever he may be, must make his own decision," but rather the appeal to the moral expert, and the implication that the expert will be recognized by his consistent enunciation of the same doctrine (46 B). Again the call for the one who knows is hedged with the proviso, if there is such a man (47 D), and again the proviso is then quietly dropped, and Socrates proceeds, as if he had himself, through reason, access to truth (48 A), affirming, as in the *Apology*, the primacy of moral goods and the certainty of their cosmic validation.

The *Gorgias* repeats with more assurance the self-same teaching. As in the *Apology* we had a Socrates determined to benefit the citizens whether they would or no, so here we have a Socrates who conceives of statecraft as the moral betterment of citizens by the expert, the trained and experienced physician of souls, a task to be undertaken only by one who has had long practice in the private pursuit of the art (513 E–515 C), and who has arrived at self-consistency (482 A–C, 527 D–E) upon all matters of moral importance. When the Socrates of the *Gorgias* claims to be "the only statesman" whom Athens has produced, it is to neglect the entire context to construe this, with Popper, as meaning that the true statesman is, first and foremost, the man who "knows his own limitations." Every line of the dialogue breaths the moral certainty with which Socrates adheres to his convictions, in the face of what he sees as the radically false opinions of almost all his fellow citizens. The constant comparison of the true political leader with the physician, trainer, and builder, imply the existence of just such objectively valid moral knowledge as the Socrates of the *Apology* proclaims himself almost uniquely to possess. The dialogue is an impassioned call for the placing of none but those who possess this knowledge, and are able to impart its benefits, at the helm of the state.

When Popper interprets Socrates' preference for suffering rather than dispensing injustice as evidence of altruistic individualism, he is neglecting the actual Socratic argument, and has drawn his conclusion from the mere psychological implications of the *probandum*. For Socrates conducts his proof entirely from the side of the interest of the given individual in preserving the health and order of his own soul from the corruptive action of injustice. He is speaking from a standpoint that abstracts from the equal rights and interests of "others," and concerns itself with the "self-regarding" question: Will you, or I, or any man, be ultimately better off for having a corrupted soul? Having answered with an emphatic "no," he can then turn to persuading others to pursue, in the same fashion, each man his own best interest.

If in the preceding, we have protested Popper's discovery of altruistic individualism in the Socratic preference for suffering over doing injustice, this is not because of any wish to deny that Socrates was everywhere displaying a genuinely altruistic interest in his fellow men as individuals. The Socratic attempt to help each man to discover through self-scrutiny a standard of value common to all is very different from what Popper supposes to be his encouragement to each man, in the absence of any such objective universal standard, to make decisions for which he is individually responsible. The discrimination of these two standpoints is of great importance from every point of view, and basic to a right reading of Plato's relation to Socrates; in this connection it will reënter our discussion at a later point.

One further correction should perhaps be made in Popper's interpretation of the Socratic paradox concerning injustice. Popper speaks of Socrates' refusal to "inflict" injustice upon others, and shortly after, presents him as including among the highest human virtues, "humaneness" and "kindness." If there is in these phrases the suggestion that Socrates enjoined pity for those who suffer pain, correction is in order: there is no text for such an attribution. To punish wrongdoers appears to the Socrates of the *Gorgias* (469 B) as "unenviable," but the elimination of suffering is not indicated as any part of the urgency that inspired him; the evils of the soul — ignorance, injustice — were what he sought to cure.

New wine is again poured into old bottles when the motivation of the Socratic marytrdom is found in the furtherance of free thought and free speech. True that Socrates in the *Apology* is demanding what we may call his freedom to follow the dictates of his conscience against the authority vested in his judges; but it is very important to notice that Socrates does not think of it as a freedom at all. For him it is only a necessary disregard of a human authority, entailed by obedience to a divine command. The suggestion that he is here demanding freedom not merely as a personal right but as a general human right is even less tenable. Is it thinkable that a man should die for the sake of a principle that he neglects to mention? Would he not have said that it was not he alone whose rights were in question, that his protest was rather against the larger unwisdom and injustice of silencing anyone at all, however different from himself, who might arise among the Athenians to teach new doctrines or to speak out in favor of unpopular causes? Clearly, neither his own "freedom" nor that of others is here in question.

Nor can we follow Popper in his reading of the *Crito*, which he interprets as Socrates' attestation of his unbounded loyalty to democracy. Here the contestants are, one may say, an innocent individual, tempted to protect his own material interests at the cost of an illegal act, and the ideal city of Athens, represented by its personified Laws, claiming unqualified obedience from those whom she has bred and reared, and who have accepted her protection. And, as all the world knows, Socrates in his decision subordinated the individual to the social order. He finds the highest good of the individual in justice, which demands of the citizen (where obedience to God does not conflict) his reverent cherishing above life itself of the orderly institutions of his own city (*Crito* 50 A–53 C). There is no suggestion that Socrates regards the laws of Athens as more binding upon an Athenian than are the laws of other states, even "oligarchic" ones, upon those have been born and have chosen to remain their citizens; there is even commendation of Crete and Sparta, of Thebes and Megara, as well-governed (*Crito* 52 E, 53 B). Neither in the *Apology* nor in the *Crito* is there any praise of the democratic form of government. In both dialogues there is expressed reprobation of the lawlessness, irresponsibility, and false values, of "multitudes," in assemblies or in courts of justice (*Apology* 31 E–32 A, *Crito* 44 D, 47 E–48 C). Furthermore, there is an outright inconsistency between the depreciation of wealth and material interests, voiced by Socrates in the *Apology* (29 E) and attested by all our other knowledge of his life and teachings, and the conception of Socrates as the banner-bearer of an Athenian democracy which, as Popper insists, included among its essential

traits commitment to the twin ideals of commercial enterprise and naval imperialism. And thus we are brought to the conclusion that we can accept
neither a Socrates-Voltaire who would die in preservation of any man's right
to disagree with him, nor a Socrates dying because of a particular esteem for
Athenian democracy as such.[160]

There is a further consideration making against Popper's Socrates, as the
man who lived and died the humble advocate of equal rights for the opinions
of all, who in any other than an ironical sense believed himself ignorant of all
ultimate moral and religious truth, and who was therefore the thoroughgoing
individualist and democrat. This is the singular circumstance that these traits
appear not to have been reproduced or taken into account by any of his
disciples. Among the fragments of Antisthenes there are preserved no echoes
of such beliefs; Popper himself makes no claims to have found here the needed
confirmation. The same could be shown to be true of Aristippus. And it is
therefore possible that Plato's "treachery" was not to the historical Socrates,
but to the modernized version only.

But even though Popper's Socrates were ten times more historical than he
is, we still cannot allow him to be used as a measure of the level of toleration
which Plato should have attained. For Popper's Socrates has been derived almost entirely from Plato's depiction of him in the *Apology* and *Crito*, whereas
Popper's Plato is primarily the architect of the Republic and the city of the
Laws. And in contrasting the libertarian Socrates with the authoritarian Plato,
Popper has not allowed for this fact; in neglecting the very different conditions
under which they are being observed, he is violating a basic canon of scientific
method. We will, of course, agree that it is not possible, as Popper has clearly
seen, to use the Socrates of the *Republic* as a reliable informant as to the views
of the historical man, since we have no means of purging him of his Platonic
increments. But it is none the less indefensible to neglect the fact that we see
the unadulterated Socrates (if we see him anywhere) only as he stood accused
and in opposition to the existing state of affairs, as a private citizen in the
actual city of Athens; and it is unsound to infer, from what he then said, what
he would have prescribed had he faced the problem of drafting an ideal polity.[161] We may be sure that in it he would have preserved the freedom of anyone who in all earnestness desired to obey the Delphic god. But even here,
there was room for different interpretations of the god's meaning, and are we
to be certain that Socrates would have allowed any unspecified citizen freedom
to interpret an oracle as he saw fit, and thereby perhaps to endanger the

---

[160] For our replies to Popper's arguments
concerning particular passages in the *Apology* and *Crito*, we refer the reader to Appendix XVI. For the relation between the
Socratic schedule of values and Plato's allegedly oligarchic hostility to commerce,
see n. 215, p. 334.

[161] That it would in Popper's view have
been possible for a libertarian to describe
an ideal polity (largely in negative terms,
it is true) is shown from Popper's belief
that Lycophron did so, at least in germ;
Popper, pp. 540–541.

stability of the common life? It is pleasant to imagine the difficulty such a citizen would have encountered in achieving this freedom, had it been made conditional on his ability to defend his opinion against a scrutiny as exacting as any Platonic censorship, namely the Socratic *elenchus*, from whose bourne few travelers ever returned. What would have been the Socratic edict upon atheists, or anarchists, or moral nihilists, must be matter of conjecture only. In a community in which moral belief was, to his way of thinking, sound, in which the common citizens unanimously taught the young to value justice above all else, and taught them, too, that God would watch over them, alive or dead, we cannot know that Socrates would have desired to see the young perplexed by questioning, or would have admitted the teachers of new doctrines. Whether he would even have used untruths for the good of his citizens is uncertain; there is a passage in Xenophon, paralleling Plato's well-known statements in the *Republic*,[162] in which Socrates justifies the medicinal use of lies in behalf of the sick or the insane, and Socrates, as we have seen, took toward his fellow Athenians somewhat the attitude of a physician. In sum, it outruns the available evidence to assert that in his legislation, he would have avoided all Plato's errors.

We should like to close our discussion of Socrates by filling in what seem to us two important omissions in Popper's sketch. There is, to begin with, his blindness to a trait which is very evident in almost all of the Platonic dialogues, and not absent even where one might least have expected it, amid the solemnity of the *Apology* and the *Phaedo*. We refer to that artful mode of self-deprecation to which the name of irony was given by his contemporaries, his constant assertion of his own ignorance as contrasted with the supposed great wisdom of others. For Socratic irony was not simply a source of harmless fun; it was an instrument that he employed in his logical business, a device which he found useful in enticing his dialectical victims. It is absolutely necessary to recognize this for any proper awareness of what is actually taking place beneath the innocently smooth surface of the advancing dialogue, as Popper naturally is, in general, aware. But what is of equal importance — and Popper has given his readers not the slightest hint of it — is this: that irony and Socratic modesty cannot be kept apart, and that, if one may put it so, the irony of the situation is that, though perhaps the irony itself is a little modest, there is no doubt that the modesty is very considerably ironical. Popper's failure to observe this fact may indicate that the irony of Socrates is still in effective operation, and that the latest victim of its deceptive power is Popper.

The second neglected facet of Socrates may be indifferently referred to logic or to ethics; for it is their meeting place. In an earlier chapter of his book, Popper made reference to the Socratic quest for universal definitions of

---

[162] Xenophon, *Memorabilia* IV, ii, 17; *Republic*, e.g., 331 C–D, 382 D, 389 B.   Xenophon, of course, is not necessarily an independent witness.

the virtues, but on the later pages in which he gives his account of the Socratic message as part of the "new faith," this indispensable ingredient has been dispensed with. The result of this omission is unfortunate in more than one respect. By leaving out of view the process of inquiry, with its interest in the pursuit of moral knowledge not yet attained, we may slip easily into the error of supposing that Socrates had a completed message which it was the duty of a faithful disciple simply to preserve. Socrates had, it is true, convictions; but these he did not habitually hail as conclusions. Seeing, then, that in the teaching of Socrates the search for knowledge is usually declared to have been fruitless, and combining this observation with the mistaken interpretation of the Socratic irony as simply modesty, it is possible to infer that the suspension of judgment is what Socrates meant us to recognize as the full maturity of his wisdom, and to proclaim in the name of Socrates a law forbidding any conclusion, claiming to be valid beyond the limits of the individual conscience, ever to be reached. This is to dismiss entirely what a Plato might judge to be the positive core of the Socratic doctrine: the demand that life be rationally examined with a view to discovering objective truth, and that the resulting conclusions be accepted as the bases of belief and act, even as the bases for planning the good community. That Plato honored this demand in his treatment of his master's teaching, according to his full lights and best conscience, is at the least a defensible interpretation.[163]

We have come to the end of the list of the "Great Generation," and we must

---

[163] Bowra (*Ancient Greek Literature*, 1933) has this to say (p. 169) of Plato's relation to Socrates: "Plato's view may be partial, but he cannot be suspected of distorting the truth." And he adds, "For Plato, Socrates represented all that mattered in life, and to this ideal philosopher he pinned his faith, pursuing his course with consistency from youth to advanced old age." This passage, interestingly enough, is taken from a book which Popper has included as first in a group of authors who, as he says, have expressed "similar views of Plato" with his own. It is entirely true that Bowra's appraisal of Plato is not without some sharp disparagements which resemble Popper's; e.g., he deplores (p. 187) the rigorous punishments and inquisitorial discipline advocated in the *Laws* (we have sought to meet this criticism, pp. 351f., 355ff.), and finds himself tempted at times to regard Plato's transcendentalism as "a lifeless mirage" and his arguments as "based ultimately . . . on fear" (p. 189). It is these judgments to which Popper has exclusively appealed. But when we read Bowra's account as it should be read in its organic entirety, Popper's omissions become as intelligible as they are indefensible. The truth is that the great part of the exposition is devoted to celebrating Plato's intellectual and moral virtues in glowing terms. Thus we are shown Plato adopting his life's mission: "He must follow his master and try to make men better." "Plato purified and sublimated the simple faith of his master and identified the end of the good man's life with the attainment of absolute truth" (p. 178) ; the great myths "convey a picture of man's place as a moral being in the scheme of things." In the *Republic*, "the ethical doctrines of Socrates are taken to their logical conclusion" (p. 181) ; Plato, "starting from the conviction that power must be combined with justice," depicts an "ideal ruler . . . perfectly given to the service of the state"; "in his anxiety to be perfectly fair," he sets out an uncompromising ideal, "no matter how impracticable it may seem" (p. 182). In such utterances Bowra would seem to have quite disqualified himself as Popper's ally.

now summarize the results of our inspection. We have thus far been required to concern ourselves so closely with discounting exaggerated claims that our recognitions of positive contributions may have lacked an emphasis which we propose now, in summarizing, to supply. What, then, were the modes of thought and feeling, truly valuable in whole or in part, which Popper has claimed for the thinkers on his list, but which Plato was not able to accept, or to which he accorded, for whatever reasons, something less than their due?

Taking our start with Pericles, we can but regret that so many of the fine aspirations of the Funeral Oration were so little possible of admission into the circle of Plato's beliefs. To us, the Periclean definition of Athenian democracy, with its confident assertion that all citizens are capable of sharing the task of rational decision, and able, by virtue of their "happy versatility," to turn readily from immersion in their private lives to undertake the public business of politics and war, appears as a sort of prophetic vision of our own political faith. We too are committed to the temper of "live and let live," that forbids "sour looks" cast at our neighbor when he deviates slightly from the beaten path. And we are perhaps even a little too prone to share the Periclean enthusiasm for the splendor of wealth and power, and to agree with his tacit presupposition that civilization and material prosperity are related to each other in no merely accidental way. In short, it would not be possible to formulate the essential assumptions underlying the somewhat differently organized institutions of our own culture without an implied approval of much of the contents of this classic speech.

So much Popper can justly claim, and by so much Plato must be diminished. But from this point on we have found little substance in Popper's report. For the truth is that only the Periclean ideal among Popper's whole list of new and shining ethical insights comes through the ordeal of critical inspection substantially uninjured. Herodotus, as we saw, adds nothing to the purpose. Protagoras has suffered what is in Popper's terms the humiliating experience of having been found in agreement at some important points with the "historicist" Plato; where he differed, it was not to propose progressive norms of conduct, but to accept those which he found in use, as proper for the community which imposed them, except where considerations of utility might justify a change. His priority as a "critical dualist" has been lost with the disclosure that the term itself is a misnomer when applied to a traditionalist such as he. The most fertile theme in his thought, his epistemological relativity, escaped neither Plato's appreciation nor his censure; but it was not in itself an ethical message; and in so far as it was not part of the ethical teaching of the period, it is not here in question. Democritus, again, was set over against Plato exclusively in the character of moralist, in an antithesis which our argument was able to convert in large part into a harmony, citing parallels from Plato's text to show how far, despite his materialistic metaphysics and his ethic which dispensed with divine sanctions, he has gone toward agreeing in morals with the great idealist Plato. Of the others we need hardly speak, or of the oft-repeated tale which, under examination, turned out to be almost a ghost story: Alcidamas, the man of one noble fragment, Lycophron, surviving only in agreement with Plato's scorn of noble birth, and as the recorded announcer of so brief a form of the contract theory of the state that it offers almost no restrictions on the freedom of conjecture as to what he "must" have meant. Antisthenes adds nothing reasonably well attested which goes beyond that part of the teaching of Socrates which he adopted, except what we may admire in his increased emphasis upon bodily exertion and moral force. As to Socrates himself, Plato is best understood as the passionate advocate of all that he conceived his revered teacher to have believed. In so saying, we are not, of course, denying that Plato reserved the right to grow. But even growth, for him, lay in the direction in which he believed Socrates would have gone. Popper's "new faith," after Pericles, has turned out to consist in part of a few scattered insights which Plato did not share, plus a far larger number which Plato fully honored, refined, and sent forward upon their way.

Another fact has also become apparent from our discussion. The thinkers whom Popper has chosen to honor are either men whose opinions are in large part unknown, or men who can be shown to have entertained, side by side with their approved beliefs, others which, if they had been mentioned by Popper, he would have had to count as illiberal or even oligarchic. Like Plato, these men are not made up according to the strict recipe of democrat or oligarch, but display in their thought elements which we are unable fully to accept, along with those for which we honor them. On any reasonable basis of choice, Plato deserves a high place among the great men whom Athens produced in her time of intellectual greatness, and himself contributed and championed many of its most admirable ideas.

We turn from talk of individuals to the use of larger terms — the Athenian democracy, and the empire. But at bottom the issue is the same: our opponent will be selling democracy dear and buying Plato cheap, as part of a single operation. Let us, as our habit is, hear first his argument. The grounds on which it chiefly rests will be familiar to us from the earlier discussion of the oligarchs and of Thucydides.

The democracy is first of all, as we know, the protagonist of the open society, the very opposite of the reactionary oligarchs: it is inevitably, therefore, the party of trade, the navy, and the empire.[164] That it is also, for Popper, the very heart and glowing center of the essential Athens, we may learn from the fact that on a single page Popper employs interchangeably the expressions "Athenian democracy," "Athens," and "the Athenian people, the demos." These terms are thus endowed by their employer with an almost mystical ca-

[164] Popper, p. 173.

pacity to contract or expand, not without serving the practical purpose of excluding from consideration the interests and excellences of the nondemocrats. This denial of the minority rights of the Athenian "oligarchs" becomes on occasion the denial of their very existence as Athenians. The demos is Athens, and one who like Thucydides is said to be (as we have seen above) "a friend neither of the . . . demos . . . nor of its imperialist policy," is *ipso facto* declared disloyal: "his heart was not with Athens, his native city." [165]

Athens, Popper complains, has been represented by the historians, under the influence of the partisan Thucydides, as "a ruthless democracy, a place ruled by the uneducated, who simply hated and suppressed the educated, and were hated by them in turn. But this view . . . makes nonsense of the known facts, and above all of the astonishing spiritual productivity of Athens in this particular period." [166] The period is the first decade of the war with Sparta, a period which did show a great flowering of Athenian genius, some of the flowers being left over from the Periclean age, others springing up for the first time, like Thucydides and Aristophanes. Popper does not call to his reader's attention any other decade, or the suppressions or persecutions which occurred in this very decade, but leaves his comment to stand as a characterization of the state of affairs which obtained at Athens throughout the time in which the democracy ruled. The democracy is thus credited with having provided the necessary conditions for the free flowering of the Athenian culture in the fifth century, and with having maintained relations of mutual cordiality and respect with the Athenian "educated."

There follows a defense of the Athenian empire, chiefly on the ground that "it is necessary . . . to see that tribalist exclusiveness . . . could be superseded only by some form of imperialism"; [167] the Athenian empire, therefore, we conclude, is to be regarded as a historical necessity and a force making for an even wider "open society"; it is to be judged solely in terms of its degree of enlightenment compared with other empires, particularly that of Rome, and in the light of what it "might have" developed into. As examples of enlightenment he cites Athens' abstention from seizing the "cultural possessions" of her subjects, and her offer of equal citizenship to the people of Samos in 405 B.C. He celebrates also the novel imposition, in the year 413, of a 5 per cent duty on all the seaborne exports and imports of the cities of the empire instead of the former tribute. As a result, Popper declares, "the Athenians became interested in the development of allied trade, and in the initiative and independence" of the allied cities. (Since he cites no evidence of this interest, we may suppose that he is reasoning in terms of the expectable long-term results of such a policy, rather than reporting an actuality; yet he uses the indicative mode.) [168] On such grounds, he refers to the dominance of Athens as

[165] Popper, p. 173.
[166] *Ibid.*, p. 176.
[167] Popper, p. 176.

[168] Bury, *History of Greece*, 1931, p. 486, is apparently Popper's source for this praise of the change in Athenian financial meth-

merely "temporary," and hails the empire, "with its possibility of developing into a universal empire of man." [169]

In diametric opposition to this empire, he sets Sparta, whose methods in foreign affairs are characterized under six headings as (1) "tribalism and arrestment," (2) the banning of humanitarian ideologies, (3) "autarky" or independence of trade, (4) "particularism" or refusal to "mix with inferiors," (5) "mastery" or domination over neighboring states, and (6) restriction on the size of the city itself.[170]

And now by a truly spectacular example of that complete mastery over the meaning of the word "democracy" of which we have earlier spoken, Popper apparently reconciles two contradictory propositions in the assertion that, far from having lost the Peloponnesian war as a result of its own dangerous weaknesses, the democracy (a) was deprived of victory only by the treachery of its oligarchs, and (b) won the victory. This last he supports by the fact that democracy was reëstablished by the peace which followed the reign of the Thirty Tyrants, as the Athenian form of government. "It had proved its superior strength. . . . Nine years later . . . the Athenians could reërect their walls. The defeat of democracy had turned into victory." [171]

Finally, in his account of the condemnation of Socrates, Popper condones the prosecutors on the double ground that they intended only "to prevent him from continuing his teaching," not to put him to death; and secondly, because, though "they well knew" he had not intended what his oligarchic pupils had done, "they could hardly regard" his teaching as "otherwise than as dangerous to the state." [172]

Fortunately, the case for Plato does not depend upon a blacking out of the glory that was Greece and the brightness that was Athens. It depends rather upon the ability of his apologist to show that there was a point of view that could be taken by a man of intelligence and good will, from which the splendor of Athenian democracy appeared heavily overcast, and that Plato shared that point of view. To establish this contention it is neither necessary nor desirable to appeal to the so-called verdict of history. In what follows we are preparing to remain within the historical space-time in which Plato lived and to answer

---

ods, but Bury says of it, with proper historical caution, that it "might" tend toward the conversion of the empire into a more mutually advantageous institution. For the early abandonment of this much-heralded fiscal change, see p. 321 below.

[169] Popper, pp. 177–178.

[170] Ibid., same pp. In attributing this last trait to Sparta, Popper makes illegitimate use of a sentence quoted from Plato's Republic, in which Plato prescribes this limitation of size for his ideal city; Popper's

use of this sentence implies that it may be taken simply as Plato's description of a Spartan policy. This is an example of that circular method by which Popper, having shown to his own satisfaction that Plato's ideal city is essentially similar to Sparta, then draws upon either one to supply unattested characteristics of the other. Cf. our n. 59, p. 98; n. 23, p. 510; n. 104, p. 541; pp. 564, 567–568.

[171] Popper, p. 187.

[172] Ibid., p. 188.

Popper's criticism in the light of the events and circumstances of Plato's own experience.

In our earlier discussion we saw how Popper has admired and praised the Athenian commerce-navy combination as the leaven which cracked the cake of custom and made possible the "open society"; and we argued that this may well be true, and yet that a man might value the old pieties and the old hardihood, and dislike what seemed to him the new scramble for gain and the new oppression, without forfeiting his claims to moral decency. We wish now to leave the immediate plane of ethics and explore this same situation from the point of view of the economic interests which created conflicting groupings among the Athenian citizenry, in addition to those two, trade-hating oligarchs and trade-favoring democrats, of which we have heard so much.

Commercialism as the joint cause and consequence of the Athenian empire must indeed have seemed to many an Athenian statesman or voting citizen an excellent good thing. We remember how Pericles had implied his cordial approval, and how even the dour visage of the Old Oligarch had relaxed into a smile at the thought of the material advantages that ensue. The hum and stir of shipyard and factory made a brave music in the ears of the city-dwelling Athenians and their near neighbors, the men of the Piraeus.

But there was another class of citizens, by no means negligible in numbers, though in general they lacked political cohesion and influence as a group, to whom the new prosperity was a mixed blessing, destined to become a misfortune. These were the landowners of Attica, a far more numerous class than from Popper's account it would be possible to guess, and by no means principally composed of wealthy aristocrats, masters of large estates. Attica was, more than most Greek states, a country of small farmers,[172] of the sort so vividly typified for us, with comic exaggeration, by their spokesman of genius, Aristophanes, in the person of the genial grumbler, the long-suffering, hearty, down-to-earth, indomitable Dicaeopolis. Aristophanes shows him to us as he was in the first years of the war, cooped within the walls of wartime Athens and longing for the war to end that he might resume the joys of rural life. Perhaps the interests of a Dicaeopolis and of his fellow farmers large and small might have been compatible with the mercantilism of the new age, but only in so far as that mercantilism was itself consistent with a public policy which permitted long periods of peace, or at any rate provided protection from widespread and continuous devastation of the rural areas. But under the policy announced by Pericles for the conduct of the Peloponnesian war, it was prescribed that the whole outlying population of Attica should retire within the safety of the walls, leaving the enemy free to carry out, unopposed and year

---

[172] The following account of the rural element in the Athenian state is based in the main on insights derived from Thucydides, esp. II, 14–16; from Glotz, 1926, especially pp. 245–262; from Heitland, 1921, especially pp. 41–53, 48–50; from Aristophanes, especially the *Acharnians*; from Gomme, 1945, p. 9.

after year, his ravages of the countryside.[173] The devastation thus wrought —
the burning of homes and other buildings, the cutting down of orchard and
vineyard (grimly attested in the passionless record of Thucydides) [174] — we
can visualize with the aid of news-reel pictures of Korean refugees. The consequences to a small farmer with no other source of livelihood and with no accumulated capital, can readily be imagined, especially when the high ancient
interest rates on loans are taken into account; it would often mean the loss of
his farm; and this would be particularly the case with those specialized grow-
ers of wine and olives, numerous in Attica, who could not, like farmers of grain,
go some way toward repairing their losses at the next season's planting. That
Plato was aware of the plight of sufferers such as these, is a not distant inference from the *Republic* passage, earlier examined, in which he pleaded for the
mutual observance among all Greeks of a code of civilized warfare, under which
such predations would be outlawed.

The number of Athenians whose interests were herein involved comes home
to us when we are told by a modern authority that "the great majority of
Athenian citizens lived on or from their land." [175] It is the group of small
farmers which, as Plato also says (*Republic* 565 A) constituted the most numerous group of citizens; though, Plato adds, they lose the power which this
might give them because they will not often come out in force for the assemblies. Whether or not the disregard of the legitimate interests of these men
which was involved in the Periclean plan for victory was a necessary tactic, it
was bound to impress many Athenians, with or without vital personal stakes in
the issue, as a partisan decision, based, despite high-sounding justifications, on
a one-sided conception of the national welfare. As the war dragged on, the impact of this policy on the Athenian body politic was in more than one respect
unfortunate. The dissatisfaction of the agricultural part of the population was
a principal support of the movement to alter the constitution which won temporary success in the two oligarchic revolutions. Further, as the dispossessed
farmers lost their hopes of return to the soil, they ceased to exert a sobering
influence upon public affairs, and joined the urban poor who had always favored the more adventurous state policy, thus strengthening the hand of those
demagogues whose inflammatory recklessness and narrow partisanship invited
the empire in the direction of the *débâcle* of 404 B.C. The stage was being set
for the "do-little" Athens of the fourth century, in which the mercenary soldier and sailor were required to exercise those functions which civic devotion
had grown too feeble to perform, and the impoverished assemblyman of necessity voted himself doles, while trade stagnated and Attica became increasingly
a land of large estates worked by slave labor.

---

[173] Thucydides I, 143; II, 21–22.

[174] *Ibid.*, in the case of Athens II, 21–22;
of Plataea, II, 75.

[175] Glotz, *Ancient Greece at Work*, 1926,
pp. 250–251.

We are, in short, suggesting that it is undemocratic to talk of "Athenian democracy" and its interests while excluding from consideration the economic welfare of some one thousand large landowners and some twenty-two thousand small farmers, the greater number of whom were unable, in the circumstances, to continue making their living from the soil. Popper has been showing us the ancient analogue of the New Yorker's map of the United States, with its exaggerated seaboard and its conspicuously absent prairie states. When we restore proportion to the picture we can begin to feel a sympathy extending beyond the sphere of trade and naval enterprise, and to recognize as legitimate parts of the social landscape the blank places on Popper's map. We may even come to view as falling on the hither side of treason the objections felt by the wealthier citizens, whether landowners or merchants, to being crushed under the ever-mounting burden of war expense, just as, at the other end of the economic ladder, we gain a more realistic grasp, and see the natural necessity, of the motives that guided the poorer citizens to vote themselves maximum advantages at the assembly. We are brought, then, to understand that it is a gross simplification to explain the disruption of Athenian civil unity as due exclusively to the malign influence of a few "old devil" oligarchic landowners, diehard supporters of ancient privilege, who constituted the collective snake in an otherwise paradisiacal, commercial-naval, wholly public-spirited, democratic Athens. Surely if one is searching for explanation, he will be more likely to stumble upon something to his purpose in the tug and pull of vital interests, affecting large numbers of citizens, than in the "demonology" that Popper has introduced.

We have just seen that it is doubtful practice to identify the Athenian democracy with the commercial and naval policy, unless one specifies exactly what one is including within the term democracy. Similarly, it is partly a terminological problem to determine how far one may validly go in calling the great flowering of Athens in the several decades following the mid-century, the product of Athenian democracy. If we are using "democracy" in the narrower political sense to denote the advocacy of government by what was, in effect, the city-dwelling demos, such a statement is more than questionable. It would be a difficult assignment to establish a correlation between devotion to this political ideal, and degree of cultural productivity. We are forced, then, to speak in broader terms. And when we do so speak, we are obliged to put high on the list of the cultural immortals the names of the "conservative" Sophocles, the "waverer" Euripides, the "skeptical" Aristophanes, and the "oligarch" Thucydides. It is a fair penalty exacted from those who, like Popper, have drawn narrow party lines, to discover to their chagrin that they have seriously impoverished their party and enriched the opposition.

If it be objected in reply that it was in any case Athenian political democracy which made possible all this free cultural expression, including what was reactionary within it, we must protest that this is to mistake the part for the

whole. We must not forget that government by the Athenian demos was not
interchangeable with that far wider and richer thing, the living body of Athenian beliefs, traditions, and institutional practices, which trace the clear line of
descent at least as far back as Solon. The literature, the moral ideals, the plastic
imagination that astonish the student of the Athenian fifth century, are the
results, under democratic auspices, of that larger complex. We may go further
and assert that the demos itself, in what concerns cultural life, is also its living
product, schooled in political understanding by its elder statesmen, the aristocratic proponents of democracy, in the meaning of art and drama by the
cumulative effects of decades of exposure to the creative products of a great
tradition. But when Plato formed his earliest impressions of Athens, the tremendous urge of the Athenian upswing was slackening; he could well have felt
that its energy had been inherited from that earlier epoch, and that evils which
had been latent in the system from the beginning had now come to full development. Plato reached manhood in a time when the evidences of Athens' decline
were inescapable. Her very existence she owed to Spartan forbearance; the
rebuilding of her walls she owed to Persian gold and the calculating Persian
desire to keep Greeks in check by means of other Greeks.[176] Plato even witnessed, in 389, the repetition on a small scale of the shortsighted mistreatment
of Athenian allies in a revived Athenian league of cities, by Thrasybulus, the
hero of the restored democracy.[177] True, Athens was still the "school of
Greece," but in a much slighter, more academic sense than Pericles had intended. To Popper, from the vantage-ground of the twentieth century, it is clear
that the principle of democracy was destined to renew and vastly to extend its
triumphs in the modern world. To an observer standing where Plato stood, and
knowing democracy in the form it then displayed, it might well have appeared
that, on the contrary, democracy was only the unchecked rule of the least competent, and that what needed preservation was rather the way of life of that
older Athens, with its traditional virtues deepened and extended and clarified
in the light of the philosophic insights of the great age, insights which, for him,
had been made possible by Socrates.

　And what of the record of the Athenian people for supporting and tolerat-
ing the great men of the great age, or freely permitting the dissemination of
new ideas? It is certainly true that Athens gave scope and appreciative reward
to artists and thinkers, statesmen and generals. The Parthenon was built, the
plays were performed and applauded, the sophists were attracted from the far
corners of the Greek world. Pericles was kept in office for many years. But this
sunlit picture, in the interests of fidelity to its original, requires some shadows.
There were also dangers to which intelligence and a disposition to liberal
thought *ex facto* exposed their possessors, dangers threatening also all persons

---

[176] *Cambridge Ancient History*, V, p.　　[177] *Ibid.*, VI, p. 52–53.
364; VI, p. 49.

conspicuous in the public eye whose policies or acts might chance to incur the disfavor of the public will.

When in the Funeral Oration Pericles uttered those famous words in praise of Athenian toleration for citizens who wished to go their own way, he had not yet himself experienced to the full Athenian capacity for violating that great principle. His political enemies apparently were those chiefly responsible for the legal harassing of his friend, the sculptor Phidias. The legal persecution of his venerated teacher in philosophy and intimate friend, Anaxagoras, however, was actively assisted by the religious intolerance of the ordinary Athenian, shocked at the impiety of the godless thinker who in looking up at the sun and moon beheld stone and earth where piety saw gods. Pericles had also to endure much malicious slander directed at his domestic life and relations with the noncitizen woman Aspasia, whom, as a result of his own law, he could not marry; he might almost have been describing such slander when he spoke of "sour looks, which though they do not injure, are yet unpleasant." Real harm was threatened in the capital suit for impiety brought against Aspasia, whom he was able to save only at the cost of a personal appeal before the court. And to crown all, he suffered in his latest year at the hands of that demos whose political freedom he had done so much to advance, the humiliation of a demotion (later reversed) from his position of command, and the indignity of a trial on a charge of embezzlement, with the imposition of a heavy fine.[178]

We see in all this — and other comparable cases are written into the record [179] — how dangerous it is to treat the demos and free-thinking democracy as synonymous terms. To cast doubt upon the existence of the city's gods or to neglect their worship was ground both for public suspicion and for legal prosecution. That the bringers of such suits mingled political motives with religious sentiment shows only that the latter was strong enough to be serviceable to the purposes of those who exploited it, at the same time revealing the close relation the ordinary Athenian conceived to obtain between his city and its traditional gods — between enmity to the one, and denial or disrespect of the others.

For an outstanding example of the intensity and virulence that could result from a full working partnership between political suspicion and religious animosity, we must consider the mysterious case of the mutilated Herms, which still awaits its definitive solution. Whether it was but a midnight frolic of young blades "swoln with insolence and wine," or in some oblique and obscure way

---

[178] Plutarch, *Pericles* 35.

[179] Diagoras the atheist was convicted of verbal impiety and condemned to death *in absentia*, a price being set on his head, in about the year 415; Protagoras, according to a widely accepted tradition, which, however, Burnet questions (John Burnet, *Greek Philosophy*, I, p. 117), was prosecuted for expressing doubts whether the gods existed or not, and copies of his book burned by the public executioner in the market place. There existed a law forbidding atheism or the teaching of astronomy, on which these prosecutions were grounded. See Nestle, *Vom Mythos zum Logos*, 1942, p. 479.

a symbolic act perpetrated by oligarchic enemies of the democracy, or the outcome of some yet more hidden motive, we shall perhaps never know. What we do know is that the responsibility for the desecration was laid at the doors of those to whom irreligion could plausibly be imputed, to the well-to-do, the social group to whom association with the sophists had attached in many minds the suspicion of godlessness. Information was unearthed against a club of men suspected of oligarchic leanings, and a plot to overthrow the democracy was inferred therefrom.[180] The incident grew to serious proportions, with consequences that reverberated for years in the political mind of Athens. And in the process it made very clear the sinister element in the exacerbated democracy. For men were put to death on the flimsiest of evidence, and a military expedition of the first magnitude was deprived, when actually in operation, of its ablest leader, whom the same demos had appointed. In the lurid light of such ways of conducting public business, the democracy did not show to its best and soberest advantage; and citizens of means were warned of the danger in which they stood, should any occasion for suspicion arise against them.

We see, then, that the demos did, in a way, hate and distrust the "educated" sufficiently to make insecure the very lives of prominent Athenians who might attract their suspicion or displeasure. Numerous instances could be displayed in which lesser public displeasure resulted in banishment or fining of generals or ambassadors who failed to achieve the successes expected of them.[181] It is clear that the picture of an Athens where the "educated" were hated and suppressed, though not true *simpliciter*, is not "nonsense." It was, in fact, sufficiently true to affect seriously the sense of mutuality in Athenian political life. After 411 B.C., when the revolution of the Four Hundred had given the democratic sympathizers in their turn reason to fear for their lives, the natural reaction expressed itself in the so-called "democratic terror," and no one who reviews the record of confiscations and banishments arising, often enough, from mere or even merely alleged association with the antidemocratic regime, will be moved to style that appellation a complete misnomer. These abuses, it is true, were greatly exceeded by those of the second oligarchic revolution yet to come, for which in their turn they had sowed the seed, and in consequence the general reader of Greek history is apt to be almost unaware of their occurrence, and thus tends to fall the more easily into an uncritical idealization of the democracy. The situation had become one in which there was little trust or sense of civic unity to be found anywhere. It is not without significance in this connection that Euripides, whose sympathies after about 421 B.C. had become alienated from the trend of Athenian democracy, accepted the invitation of the Macedonian tyrant Archelaus, and removed himself permanently from the Athenian scene.

---

[180] *C.A.H.*, V, p. 324.

[181] *C.A.H.*, V, p. 245, Thucydides; p. 351, Anytus (who, however, escaped by bribery); VI, p. 51, Andocides.

The fate of the generals after Arginusae is a grim reminder of this loss of civic unity. A really substantial naval victory had been won. The generals in charge had dispatched two officers to rescue those Athenians still alive aboard the disabled vessels and to gather up the bodies of the dead, when a sudden storm (so it was maintained) rendered their mission impracticable. We need not repeat in detail the whole of the distressing tale. What needs to be stated here can be briefly told: six generals, men of high standing and credence, against whom no substantial case had been made out, were deprived of their constitutional right of separate trials, and, after a certain Socrates the philosopher, who chanced to be the presiding officer on that day, had refused to put the illegal question to the vote, were nevertheless collectively condemned to death by his majesty the people of Athens. One of the condemned was the son of Pericles; two others were men whose services to the cause of democracy, both Athenian democracy and Samian, had been outstanding. It was the possession of power such as this and the disposition to use it, when crossed in its purposes and under the sway of passion, as a lethal weapon against those who had fallen from its grace, that justified many thoughtful men in likening the demos in action to his reputed opposite, the tyrant in power.

Here we may briefly raise a question not directly confronted by Popper,[182] but compellingly germane to the interest of any thoughtful friend of free and democratic government. We have just seen that the Athenian law sought, unsuccessfully in the case of the Arginusae generals, to interpose some safeguards between the demos and the individual who had excited public indignation. But it is equally important to ask whether this same law provided any protection for individuals or groups who were dissatisfied with the existing institutions and wished to introduce changes looking to some further limitation on the direct power of the demos. What, if any, opportunity existed for even the most moderate opposition party to urge by orderly legal methods a change in the constitution?

After the revolution of 411, with the introduction of a compulsory oath taken by all citizens to support the existing democracy, and in view of the prevailing suspicion and hostility against all oligarchs or near oligarchs, such a possibility plainly did not exist.[183] But even apart from this, dating probably from the time when the court of the Areopagus was shorn of its powers as guardian of the constitution, there was included among the basic laws of Athens the "graphê paranomôn," whereby whoever introduced a measure believed to be contrary to existing law was open to indictment, and in sufficiently serious cases, liable to the death penalty. This provision, which served many a harmless and useful purpose,[184] had in it also the potentiality of dis-

---

[182] Popper assumes at one point in his argument that Athenian law was freely open to revision; see our p. 640 below.

[183] *Cambridge Ancient History*, V, p. 349.
[184] See Grote, *History of Greece* (condensed), 1907, pp. 323–324.

couraging effectively the introduction of measures of reform. Concrete evidence of the operation of this principle as a defense against constitutional change is largely lacking, but it is arguable that its general effect must have been in the direction of driving into the conspiratorial underground all serious advocates of substantial change.[185] There is thus reason to believe that Athenian democracy would have been saved some of its excesses and would have gained in inner security and concord, could it have found some alternative way of safeguarding the legal foundations of its power.

In introducing his defense of the Athenian empire, Popper has disclaimed any intention to justify the evils or brutalities incidental to its beneficent activity, mentioning certain "wanton attacks" of which it has been held guilty, but rendering the phrase innocuous by the instant qualification, "if such have occurred." We wish to tear away this hypothetical screenwork and take a glance at the methods of compulsion employed, not wantonly but from calculation, in the maintenance and extension of Athenian imperial power, methods the harshness of which was of course intensified by the chronic state of war. Two examples will suffice. In the fourth year of the struggle with Sparta, Mitylene, one of the supposedly free allies, as distinct from subject cities of the Athenian empire, attempted with the promise of Spartan aid to break away, and was finally induced to surrender after a siege which had been exceedingly costly to the Athenians in pride as well as in pocket. At the assembly held to determine the fate of the captured city it was voted, on Cleon's motion, in order to dissuade other cities from revolting, to put to death all men of military age, and sell into slavery the noncombatants. On the following day the matter was reconsidered at a second meeting of the assembly and by a very narrow margin the vote was rescinded. The ship bearing the revocation of the original vote arrived at Mitylene barely in time to stay the execution.[186] The Athenians thus, by good luck and on second thought, were able to withdraw their condemnation of these many thousands of persons. But the narrow margin by which the more merciful proposal was carried shows that even on the second day a number amounting probably to several thousand Athenian citizens were still willing to follow Cleon's cold-blooded policy. This incident displays also

---

[185] Instances of the application of this law in the fifth century apparently are few, being limited to its use, or attempted use, on behalf of persons threatened with illegal prosecution, or against a measure introduced in the assembly without due formality. See Bonner and Smith, *The Administration of Justice from Homer to Aristotle*, I, pp. 225, 265–266, 267. But in 411 B.C. it was felt necessary formally to suspend it before the measures constituting the new oligarchic government were openly proposed; obviously, therefore, it was regarded as a formidable barrier to constitutional change (*Cambridge Ancient History*, V, p. 328). In the fourth century, it degenerated into a source of nuisance suits brought against prominent politicians. But the fear of being suspected as an "oligarch," if one should propose such a measure as the restoration of the Areopagus, was still alive in the fourth century, as is evident in the cautious tones of Isocrates, *Areop.* 58ff.

[186] *Cambridge Ancient History*, V, 213–218.

one of the unfortunate features of the Athenian democratic system, which put such decisions in the power of a large popular assembly liable to be swayed by the tempestuous eloquence of a Cleon.

But the outstanding example of the self-regarding coercion underlying Athenian imperialism is undoubtedly the notorious Melian incident, the Lidice, one might say, of the Peloponnesian war. In its simplest terms, here was an application of the imperialist principle in its most ruthless form, "*Obedite aut obite*"; and the latter alternative, having been chosen, was remorselessly enforced: the male population executed, the women and children sold as slaves.[187] "The Athenians" were "on the whole the most humane people in Greece," as Grote has truly said; but, Grote also acknowledges, "humanity, according to our ideas, cannot be predicated of any Greeks."[188] Against the background of these two episodes, one may marvel at Popper's ability to believe that the ordinary Athenians were so "tenderhearted" that they were "on the verge" of abolishing slavery.[189] In both cases we see the subordination of any regard for mutuality of interests within the empire, or for human rights, to the absolute ends of Athenian prestige and power.

But quite apart from evaluation of the specific evils of his favorite imperialism, Popper has quietly provided a principle designed to atone for them in advance. It is assumed, of course, that the overcoming of tribalism is an eminently justifiable end; imperialism, it is asserted, was the "only" means thereto; it is now the servant of that end, and as such endowed with full moral authority. It has become a necessary organ of historical advance. Now, this is an extraordinary doctrine to emanate from the man who has shown no mercy to the historian Meyer for adopting a form of this very principle. Meyer, it appears, had expressed his scorn for the "flat and moralizing evaluation" of those who judge "great political undertakings with the yardstick of civil morality." This Popper declares to be an obvious piece of Hegelianism, a form of historicism, and as such condemned by the whole gravamen of his book.[190] By what warrant, then, can Popper justify his own practice when he gives a right of eminent domain to Athenian imperialism to pursue its way untroubled by the yardstick of the moral standards with which Plato had measured it and found it wanting? One may ask how Popper would judge the case of some contemporary political "democracy," with perhaps a creditable colonial record behind it, which should today declare its aim of forcibly uniting the nations of the world into one community under its benevolent hegemony. Could he consistently refuse allegiance to this forward-looking program, pre-

---

[187] *Cambridge Ancient History*, V, p. 281.

[188] *History of Greece*, 1907, p. 436.

[189] Popper, in making his modest list of admitted defects in Athenian imperialism (p. 176), includes recognition of the existence of slavery at Athens, but apparently overlooking the Athenian practice of selling into slavery conquered populations, hastily reminds us again in a footnote (p. 586) of his unshaken faith in a popularly-supported Athenian abolition movement.

[190] Popper, p. 586.

senting itself as the "only" way of superseding "nationalist exclusiveness"? And were he to yield to the understandable, even creditable, impulse of rejecting this crocodile claim to historical necessity, would he not be owing something of an apology to Plato?

Enough has perhaps been said already of Popper's defense of the empire on the ground of the supposititious interest taken by the Athenians in the "initiative and independence" of the allied cities, as a consequence of the duty imposed upon goods transported by sea by these cities. In the face of the centralized control by the Athenian assembly and law courts of the conditions under which the affairs of the empire should be carried on, this reference to "independence" is in any case a curious way of expressing the idea of the Athenians' assumed active concern for increasing the volume of allied trade. What Popper has contrived to convey to his reader is the image of the Athenian empire in the likeness of a mutual benefit society, holding out to its free members security and numerous other attractive features in return for a modest contribution. It is almost superfluous to remark that an invitation to join was quite as mandatory as the payment of the duty. And it is significant that only some four years after the duty was imposed, it was under fully democratic auspices withdrawn, and the tribute reinstated.[191]

Popper's further defense of the empire is conducted largely in terms of two comparisons, the first with Rome, the second with Sparta. He objects against the historians of antiquity in general, especially his disliked Meyer, that they have failed to observe the superiority of Athenian imperialism to that of Rome. Now it is hard to imagine that Popper is really asking us to blame Plato for the lack of clairvoyance. But the fact remains that the discussion manages to imply that it was blameworthy for a contemporary to have failed to observe the liberal quality of Athenian imperialism which he, Popper, has demonstrated by means of a comparison with Rome.

Nor is the contrast as clearly indicative of Athenian liberalism as we are asked to believe. To suggest that it was highly creditable to the Athenians to abstain from the later Roman practice of shipping home the "cultural possessions" of conquered cities, is to forget that Athens was already well supplied with that species of owl. As to the offer of citizenship to the people of Samos, it may well have been a "very interesting instance" of a political invention; [192]

---

[191] See Merritt, Wade-Gery, and McGregor, *The Athenian Tribute Lists*, II, 1949, p. 45, and III, 1950, p. 363. These same scholars also offer evidence (pp. 364–365) to show that the Athenians continued, into the latest days of their empire, to regard themselves as the sovereign determiners — and chief beneficiaries — of the uses to which the imperial revenues should be put.

[192] Popper, p. 586, complains of the in-justice of Meyer's failure to "credit . . . the Athenians with a constitutional invention of the first order," and of his giving the credit to Rome for a less liberal form of it. But that is to shift the issue from the question of political history and action to one of political theory. No one doubts the primacy of the Greeks, particularly Athenian Greeks, in this latter domain. We were, however, asking quite a different question.

but it will not greatly help the Athenian democracy to a reputation for true, practicing liberalism. It should, first, be remembered that a very special intimacy obtained between the Athenian democracy and the citizens of Samos, dating from the time of the oligarchic revolution of 412–411, at which time the Athenian fleet, headquartered at Samos, had sponsored an overthrow of the Samian oligarchs, and having established the rule of the native democrats, had entered with them into a solemn compact of mutual support. And the desperate eleventh-hour gesture of offering them the citizenship was heavy with tragic irony. This bid for the continued favor of her last ally against Sparta, on the eve of her collapse, was the beginning of a policy which, undertaken in time, might have forestalled the disasters that now brought it to this futile birth. For universalism in the area of citizenship was precisely what the Athenian demos in its prosperous times had been most determined not to permit. We have seen that Pericles himself had supplied the narrow exclusiveness of the Athenian citizenship with a legal base. From that time on, the hard and fast line was drawn between those of pure Athenian blood, the superiors and hereditary rulers, and those who were disqualified by even a trace of the impure blood of any other origin. And this line the Athenians had with difficulty been able to bring themselves to breach even in isolated instances when disaster overtook them. If we are in search of seasonable advocates of equal rights for citizens of the allied states of the empire, we shall have to turn to the chronic satirist of the new democracy, Aristophanes, whose Lysistrata's advice we have already heard. A comparison between the Athenian demos and this mouthpiece of conservatism would disclose the advantage in liberalism to be on the unexpected side.

Bearing more immediately on Plato's political opinions is Popper's second comparison, that between Athenian imperialism and Spartan "methods in foreign affairs." As will be seen by a glance at the earlier given tabulation,[193] the first two, together with the last, of his six methods, are not primarily matters of foreign policy; number (3), independence of trade, while it may be so in some respects, was, in the case of Sparta, aimed more at securing simplicity of living than at influencing the affairs of other states, and hence was, by intent, domestic, like the first two. Taken together, these four add up simply to Popper's unfavorable description of the Lycurgean constitution of Sparta. They are not properly a description of her foreign policy. Numbers (4) and (5), refusal to mix with inferiors and domination of neighbor states, respectively, are not points of contrast between Athens and Sparta. They are actually common features. Our text has already had occasion to underline Athenian pride in racial purity and refusal to grant parity of citizenship to those not born to it. This and Athenian domination over neighboring states were basic rules in the book of the Athenian empire. The completeness with which they were enforced

---

[193] See p. 311 above.

left little to be desired, as the names of Antisthenes and of Melos (strange pair) will serve to remind us. Sparta's actual foreign policy, if Popper had chosen to describe it, was not endearing — witness the imposition of close oligarchies of Spartan choosing on cities of the former Athenian empire, after the Spartan victory in 405 B.C.[194] Plato would be open to criticism had he approved such methods, but he did not; which is perhaps why, in describing Sparta, Popper chose instead to point to Lycurgean provisions which he believes he has established as being favored by Plato.

At first glance it is not easy to make sense of Popper's assertion that Athenian democracy won the Peloponnesian war: that to represent this war as ending in 404, when Athens capitulated, is in fact a "distortion," "for the democrats fought on"; and that in the end, as we have reported above, they turned "defeat . . . into victory." One gasps at this deft juggle that seems to twist history to its purpose. But on second thought, what has happened becomes quite clear. Popper has fused the war of Athens against Sparta with the struggle between the Athenian democratic party and the Athenian oligarchs. He views them both essentially as efforts of the democratic way of life against the advocates of the closed society. And he judges the success of both by their outcome, the date of this outcome to be chosen arbitrarily by himself, and the influence of coöperating causes of the success to be neglected.

Now, we can admire, with Popper, the heroism and devotion to the cause of popular government displayed by the Athenian democrats under Thrasybulus, who ended the oligarchic rule of terror. We can share Popper's deep disapproval of the Thirty and their bloody and short-sighted regime. We can rejoice with him that the democratic form of rule was reëstablished and proved itself, on the whole, so moderate in its conduct. And we can accept his judgment that within Athens itself the moral victory rested with the upholders of popular government. But we need not join him in his blindness to the defects and therefore also to the failures of Athenian democracy. We can look steadily at the fact that the war with Sparta was lost: that the purposes for which Athens entered the war were not achieved, and that after the loss of her empire and the expenditure of much blood and treasure, she found herself blockaded by land and sea, starving, and at the absolute mercy of whatever terms her conquerors should impose. And when these conquerors, after the defeat of the Thirty, for their own purposes permitted the democracy to resume functioning, and when, a little later, the Persians, again for their own purposes, made possible the rebuilding of the walls, we cannot permit this restoration to be called the victory of democracy. Our own confidence in the democratic principle does not require to be bolstered by the mistaken proof that in the fifth and fourth centuries B.C., in the form in which it was then embodied at Athens, it enabled its supporters to win wars. Unless we recognize that the Athenians of this

---

[194] *C.A.H.*, VI, pp. 27–28, 44.

period were conscious of having suffered a major defeat, of having lost not only empire but their earlier pride in their national strength and confidence in their national security, we can not understand why Plato and others among his contemporaries could have supposed that democracy, like the unrestricted oligarchy of 404, had been discredited.

There remains one sizeable stain upon the Athenian democratic scutcheon, which Popper has done his desperate best to remove, the judicial murder of Socrates; his condemnation, while it was by no means the unanimous verdict of the court, still serves to remind us of the less liberal component within the democracy. This cleansing is not merely a difficult operation; it is an embarrassment. It requires a tacit retraction of some previously made claims; for manifestly, if Socrates and the Athenian demos that condemned him were both as advertised, animated by the liberal democratic spirit, why, then palpably the trial could never have resulted as it did. And so Popper, in order to resolve the dilemma, has chosen to blame the teaching of Socrates himself, representing his accusers as mild and moderate men, who desired only to exile this teacher of doctrines which they could hardly regard as other than dangerous to democracy itself. Popper's assertion that death was not the penalty sought by the accusers, though he is not alone in the opinion, is rather in the nature of a compliment to their reputation; at any rate, they proposed the death penalty, and no accusers could do more.[195] We need not regard their intended moderation as proved. But for Popper to imply that Socratic teaching could reasonably be regarded as dangerous to democracy is matter for astonishment. The reader may recall the declared judgment of Crossman, earlier quoted, that the mission of Socrates had in fact undermined

---

[195] Burnet argues in his note on *Apology* 35 e 1–38 b 9 (*Plato's Euthyphro, Apology of Socrates, and Crito*, 1924), and we do not doubt his contention, that accusers who intended only exile were well advised to propose death as a penalty, since in that case the convicted defendant, wishing at all events to save his life, was fairly certain to offer to go into exile as the alternative. But accusers who intended in all earnestness to encompass the death of the defendant had also to propose death. There seems, indeed, no possibility of knowing Anytus' or Meletus' intent. It could be maintained with more reason that the judges of Socrates would have accepted his banishment, had he proposed it (see *Crito* 52 B–C). But three-fifths of these judges obviously preferred to condemn him to death, rather than to permit him freedom to teach; if Diogenes Laertius is to be trusted, 300 of 501 so voted. The remaining two-fifths, however, have genuine claim to our respect, and to the exoneration which Burnet and, following him, Popper, have sought to extend to the court as a whole and to the accusers.

It appears certain that the condemnation of Socrates, like the earlier attacks upon Anaxagoras and Aspasia, was grounded upon both political and religious motives, the relative strength of which can scarcely be precisely measured. Burnet has insisted upon the essentially political motivation of Socrates' accusers, and it is therefore the more interesting to find him recognizing that the success of their attack was dependent upon the existence among the common citizens of hostility to disturbers of the popular religion. Thus he speaks, in his edition of the *Euthyphro*, note on 2 a 1, of the "accusers of Socrates and the religious prejudices to which they appealed."

democracy, and that his death, however regrettable, was "justified"; no society could be expected to tolerate such exaltation of the search for truth
above the necessity of social stability. Now Crossman, one must observe, is
true to his own assumptions in so regarding Socrates. On his view, each society lives by institutions which embody and preserve its values; within it
there arise individuals with vision to discern values yet unrealized; the tragic
choice perennially confronting mankind lies between preserving the old, and
permitting the destructive criticism which dissolves the old in order to make
place for the new. But Popper has no right to such an argument. To him,
freedom of thought and of expression is of the essence of the new, the open
society, which once for all provides the institutional framework within which
alone humanity can rightly live. To tamper with this basic requirement is, in
his own vocabulary, to turn back, and back inevitably "the whole way," "to
the beasts" — repression by "brutal violence." By accepting the principle of
the death penalty for heretical opinion, the restored Athenian democracy is
thus condemned by Popper's own ruling. He has merely withheld the admission from his reader.

We may add that Popper's democracy is not helped by the "proof" that he
has offered, that Socrates was himself its stanchest advocate. There is essential incredibility in the combined picture of this Socrates, a devoted democrat,
explaining his lifelong devotion with crystal clarity across the centuries to
Popper, but failing to communicate it to his democratic listeners; and of
these listeners, who, as reasonable men, could hardly fail to see the danger
to their humanitarian individualist ideals, which arose from this man's championship of these same ideals.

Let us rejoice in our new freedom from the tormenting complexity of these
converging errors, and ask our usual and basic question: how could Plato
reasonably have regarded the trial and condemnation of Socrates? To Plato's
eyes it must have appeared a subversion of all values. We have seen that
Socrates had not figured in Plato's eyes as the advocate of democracy, but
rather as its critic. Plato had interpreted his teaching as pointing in the direction of a quite different political ideal. But to Plato, Socrates was none the
less the loyal son of Athens, who had made it his life's work to teach humane
and universal wisdom to his kinsmen the Athenians and to all others who
could receive it. Whether or not a death sentence had been originally intended, the fact remained that in the end agents of the Athenian democracy
had invoked and executed the final penalty upon "the best and wisest of the
men of that time." By this action they seemed to Plato to have convicted
themselves of that veritable ignorance which is wickedness. If he could not
accept the oligarchs, whose representatives, the Thirty, had stained their
hands with the blood of so many innocent fellow citizens, neither could he
accept these "many" who had put to death Socrates. Popper may be able to
condone the democratic prosecutors, against his principles, by putting him-

self in their places and thus seeing how Socrates must have looked to them. We must do as much for Plato, if we are to understand how this catastrophic event must have affected his judgment of popular government.

Standing now at the end of our review of Popper's defense of the Athenian democracy, we may conclude with a generalization. Underlying Popper's whole argument is the conviction that opinion has been led by partisan misrepresentation into a systematic error in its appraisal of the Athenian achievement: the world had read "gray" where the true reading was, humanly speaking, "white." We are urged to make this one simple change; then History will be herself again, and all may yet be well. But, as our argument has sought to establish, this reversal will not do. If put to a forced option between the two, we would do better to rest in the conviction that something more solid than "a tendentious distortion" underprops the accepted view that real weaknesses, moral and practical, were inherent in the Athenian version of democracy, and contributed substantially to its overthrow.

All that Popper has told us of the aims and beliefs of the oligarchic party at Athens is presumably designed as a help in understanding the political loyalties to which Plato was predestined by family and class ties, and the dark significance of the party allegiance to which, Popper believes, he had, before he wrote the *Republic*, committed himself. And now he describes for us a Plato who, resolved upon the necessity of overthrowing the Athenian democracy, approves in all essentials the program of the Old Oligarch (as Popper has interpreted it) and of Critias, who had only attempted to carry it into effect.[196] By this one assertion, Popper has identified Plato with the most extreme class of oligarchs, and has attributed to him, one should note, their qualities of treacherous willingness to call in the Spartans and to murder citizens by the hundreds. This Plato, unappalled by "the most ruthless use of violence," asks only the question why Critias failed.[197]

The answer that Popper imagines Plato as giving is that Critias had ignored the strength of sentiments, the necessity of wedding people to their chains. Plato saw that this could not be attained by defying the love of justice; on the contrary, "men must be taught that justice is inequality, and that the tribe . . . stands higher than the individual." [198] Thus did Plato anticipate, "perhaps unconsciously, the great secret of the revolt against freedom," the principle of Pareto, which is to present oneself as the champion of all those noble sentiments which one is seeking to destroy; and this aim Plato set himself with marvelous skill to effectuate. Beyond the addition of this new prin-

---

[196] Popper, p. 190. This is a necessary inference from what Popper represents as the train of thought followed by Plato in contemplating the failure of Critias. We have not wished to burden the reader with the lengthy quotations of Popper that would be required were we to employ his precise words.

[197] Popper, p. 190.

[198] *Ibid.*, p. 190.

ciple, Popper finds nothing of consequence to distinguish Plato from his predecessors in the ugly confraternity of oligarchs.[199] This Plato it would be a misnomer or a euphemism to call a philosopher; he is rather a practical crypto-counter-revolutionist, who directed the energies of a lifetime to framing propaganda, disguised as dialogues, for a new Athenian oligarchic revolution which should succeed where Critias had failed.

But where, we may ask, is Popper's proof that Plato did so ally himself with the Athenian forces of reaction? Where is Plato's proposal for the reform of Athens, the new oligarchic constitution which Plato hoped to see put into effect, the program which "in the political field," as Popper has told us, "added but little to the old oligarchic program"? [200] And here we come upon a discovery which is at first sight inherently incredible; yet there is no escaping a conclusion which, for whatever reasons, Popper has not seen fit explicitly to state in this connection: Popper is implying that the *Republic* itself, interpreted as Plato's major expression of the oligarchic faith, was a species of blueprint of the oligarchic political order that Plato hoped that he, himself, might be able to establish in the place of the democracy, at his native Athens. It is not only propaganda, it is itself the program. And Popper is also implying (since, it must be recollected, we have no other sources for such knowledge), that indications exist, in the *Republic* and in Plato's other dialogues, sufficient to prove that Plato would have approved its installation, if necessary, by violent means.

What we have been asked to see is, one might say, an optical impossibility save to an eye in frenzy rolling: to bring together in one view the streets and market places of the real Athens, and the "airy burgomasters," as Milton called them, of Plato's political and philosophic dream. The truth is that we have been finding it more and more difficult to see what Popper has successively asked us to see, as he has developed his panorama of Plato's Athens. It will be remembered how progressively different from our own was Popper's vision of the oligarchs, of the Great Generation and the Athenian demos, and finally of Socrates; and now in the conjunction of Platonopolis and the actual Athens, and of Plato and the Thirty Tyrants, made only more cynically sophisticated, the ultimate disparity is reached.

Popper has not recalled to us explicitly, here in his discussion of the po-

---

[199] *Ibid.*, pp. 190, 193–194.

[200] Not content with ascribing to Plato the items in the oligarchic creed, Popper has also (note 64 to chapter 10, p. 609) committed himself to the view that "most of Plato's political proposals, including the . . . communism of women and children, were 'in the air' in the Periclean period" and (Popper, p. 193) were those very proposals "against which Pericles had once argued." We are told (cf. Popper, p. 182)

that it is in the Thucydidean Funeral Oration that this argumentation was carried on: "Pericles' speech is . . . a defense . . . perhaps even an attack . . . directed [in part] . . . against the totalitarian ring" at Athens. This conception of the Periclean Funeral Oration as directed against utopian ideal constitutions, complete with communism of women and children, is an airy construction for which no solid foundation is supplied.

litical scene, what he has told us in his earlier chapters about Plato's *Republic*. Undoubtedly, however, he is expecting us to recall the elements upon which he laid such stress in his analysis of the ideal city. If, then, we think back to those earlier chapters, we shall see that these elements, in their out-of-focus fashion, correspond to the items on the creed he has ascribed to the oligarchs of Athens, almost every item having its quasi-equivalent; the one important exception is that in Plato's state alone is found that insistence upon aristocratic birth, as prerequisite to privilege, which, as we have seen, Popper could not consistently ascribe to the Athenian oligarchs in general. It is in view of this formal correspondence, achieved by selective emphasis and distortion, that he has been able to bring his "witch hunt" to its predetermined close, and to identify Plato's "program" with that of the most extreme oligarchs. He has construed the *Republic* as an archaic, an arrested state, the very antithesis of an open society, the bulk of its population degraded into "human cattle," drudging doers of the "dirty work," held to their tasks by a combination of deceptive propaganda and the actual armed might of the race-proud and racially distinct master class; a city aping Sparta and rejecting Athens, self-sufficient, without trade or other liberalizing contact with the outside world, cemented into collectivist unity by the mere contrivance of a state religion.[201] To clear the way, "clean the canvas," for this new construction, Plato was prepared to "purify, purge, expel, deport and kill. ("Liquidation" is the terrible modern term for it.)"[202] And at its head stood a medicine man in the mask of a philosopher, Plato himself, scion of ancient royalty, exclusive master of the abracadabracal nuptial number, by means of which he intended magically to control the destinies of all the inhabitants.[203]

Another truly remarkable consequence arises from Popper's assertion that, except for the Pareto addition, Plato's political program contains almost nothing beyond "the old oligarchic program" which he has also described as "the theory . . . of the Old Oligarch and the Thirty." Turning the statement around, we see that the Old Oligarch and the Thirty have been credited with nothing less than the creation in all essentials, of Plato's *Republic*. For however much Popper is prepared to trim away from this work of theoretical construction and analysis, in order to arrive at what he regards as its essential message, he is still leaving it much substance; witness his long description of its provisions, in many a chapter. And now this substance is said to have been contained in the "program" of the Old Oligarch (who, as we have seen, made no constructive recommendations and did not even advocate any action),

---

[201] As examples of passages in which Popper makes these assertions, we may here mention for the opposition to change, p. 39; the caste state and "human cattle," p. 52; hatred of the virtues of the open society, p. 117; hatred of trade, p. 87; opposition to naval imperialism and democracy, p. 182; love of Sparta, p. 47; religious opportunism, p. 140; use of force, note 44 to chapter 8, p. 560.

[202] Popper, p. 163.

[203] *Ibid.*, p. 150–152. We discuss this notion of Plato's royal descent on pp. 462–463 and the "number" on pp. 450ff.

and in that of the Thirty — presumably their intentions regarding the constitution to be set up after they should have pacified the city. In so doing, he has outrun any documentation which he has made available.[204]

This picture of a conspiratorial Plato, hardly distinguishable from a Critias, hoping to be summoned at any moment to direct the forcible restoration of his fellow Athenians to the tribal cage, presents us with a perhaps insoluble problem in refutation, except in so far as our entire enterprise achieves a solution. From the nature of the case Plato never had an opportunity explicitly to disclaim it. The best one can do is to bring it out of the midnight atmosphere in which it was generated and expose it to the action of the charities and serenities of Plato's available self-expressions in his writings, from which gradually a different and quite incompatible portrait will emerge. We shall now examine some of the more important passages in the dialogues bearing on the Athenian political scene as Plato knew it from report or at first hand, from Solon up to the time of his own maturity. It will be convenient to arrange his opinions according to subject matter, under the following heads: (1) the assembly, the popular courts, and election to office, (2) the statesmen of Athens and the working of the Athenian constitution, (3) reform of the Athenian constitution, (4) revolutionary violence, and (5) the career of Critias.

(1) The assembly, the popular courts, and election to office. We have earlier referred to Plato's disparagement of the collective behavior of Athenians in their democratic assemblies and courts. His chronic complaint, and the *Apology* and the *Crito* are evidence that Socrates had here set him the precedent, was that these bodies were guilty of fickle and irresponsible reversals of opinion, suggestibility to nonrational appeal, and even of lawless behavior, to the danger of the just man who had chanced to incur their displeasure; and this he might bring upon himself, perhaps, as Plato averred in the case of his master, by his very justice itself. Over the material man and the breath in his nostrils their control was absolute, but they were powerless to affect the true good of a man, which has its inaccessible locus in the human soul.[205]

---

[204] The Thirty included Theramenes and Critias, along with others about whom far less is known; of most of them only the names survive. Theramenes is associated with the constitution of the Five Thousand, which, as we have suggested, pp. 343–344, was certainly not that of the *Republic*. Of the constructive political views of Critias nothing survives. He apparently intended to suppress the teaching of the art of discussion (Xenophon, *Memorabilia*, I, 2, 31). Ferdinand Dümmler, in *Hermes*, 1892, p. 260ff., has sought to show that Critias, in his lost *Constitution of the Athenians*, had calumniated Solon and the group from whom some of his (Critias') political opponents were descended, but for all his speculative skill and boldness contents himself with a report of Critias' antidemocratic activities and does not venture into a reconstruction of his positive program.

[205] Especially *Apology* 31 E, 34 C ff., and 41 C–D, and *Crito* 44D, 47E–48 C.

In the *Gorgias* the rhetoric commonly employed in the courts for the attainment of the speaker's ends, regardless of truth and in defiance of moral values, is branded a pseudo-art, the deceptive shadow of the true art of justice (463–465). Ignorance is ironically charged upon the Athenian assembly in the *Protagoras* (319 B–D), when Socrates drily infers that this august body must believe that virtue, in the sense of enlightened public policy, can not be taught, from the fact that although only the expert is allowed to speak to issues involving professional knowledge, all sorts and conditions of men are allowed to hold forth upon the larger questions of state. We recall in this connection an earlier adduced passage from the *Republic* (492 B–C), in which the power of the assembly, or other large functional grouping of the demos, to pervert the attitudes and value judgments of the young men is likened to that of a great sophist. What the *Gorgias* told us of the defeating of justice in courts and assembly by the counterfeit presentments of rhetoric, the *Republic* reaffirms; we hear also of the sinister machinations of the political clubs, whereby a man can escape conviction for his crimes. The same criticism of the courts is evidenced in the sharp Hogarthian picture of the shrewdly ready pleader in the *Theaetetus* (172 E), his soul made slavish and stunted by the pressures of the harsh environment to which it has been subjected, practicing his crooked little art of ingratiation (it is hinted that bribes have been given and received) in competition with a "fellow slave," before their common master (the judges) who stands over both "holding some case or other in his hands." It might seem the final proof of Plato's hostility to courts and assemblies that in the ideal Republic, there is no actual or conceivable provision for an assembly, and we can infer from 433 E that he is replacing the Athenian dicastic system with tribunals conducted by the guardians themselves.

We see in Plato's criticism of these inseparable elements of Athenian political life a vindication of that "apolity," abstention from active political participation, which he shared with and perhaps originally derived from Socrates, an abstention in principle from the inequities and unmeaning dangers of the political arena. The attitude finds its most striking expression in the famous simile of the man "waiting out the storm in the shelter of a wall," in *Republic* 496 C–D. It is therefore by no means surprising that in his plan for an ideal polity he should have removed precisely these features which were associated in his mind with the most serious dangers. But from all this unsparing criticism it would be as easy as it would be erroneous to conclude that Plato would have recommended the abolition in the city of Athens or in any other city where ideal rulers were not at hand of popular assemblies and courts. The *Laws* shows us that Plato looked to reformed versions of both these institutions as two main pillars of his reformed state (764 A, 768 A–C, 956 B–958 A). To rid them of their faults, he relied upon the raising of the educational level of all of the citizens,[206] the outlawry of morally irresponsible rhetoric (937 D–938 C), and, in relation to the courts, the enjoining upon the presiding officer of a special duty to restrain those very abuses noted in the *Apology* as frequent in the Athenian courts (949 B). There was, it is true, to be change in the method of selecting the Council which, as at Athens, supplied guidance to the Assembly, and above the popular courts a higher court of appeal was to be added. But with these alterations, Plato was prepared to believe that the popular assembly of all the citizens, and the popular courts, had still substantial contributions to make to the improvement of the life of Greece.

Of some importance is Plato's attitude toward another feature of the Athenian political system, the choice of officials by election. Plato does not regard this practice as typically democratic, in this respect differing markedly from ourselves; to him and to his fellow Greeks it was the lot which characterized democracy. Nor does Plato express disapproval of election, even in the *Republic*. Certainly he does not leave room for it in his ideal city; the guardians are a self-perpetuating body, like many a professional group in our own day. But in any other city, as with the popular assembly and courts, so in the case of election, Plato is its convinced advocate, and believes that ideally all citizens should be eligible to every office, and that all who have not shirked their duty of military service should possess the vote. In the *Laws* he yields to practicality, as he conceives it, by setting up property qualifications for some of the Councilmen and for those competent estate-managers in the service of the city, the City-stewards and the Market-stewards; yet it is on completely open elections that he rests his hope of securing the best men for the highest offices in the state.[207]

(2) The statesmen of Athens and the working of the Athenian constitution. Here first a word is in order about a man, Solon, who by virtue of his essentially moral approach to the political problem, and his strenuous endeavor to rise above partisan commitments, set Plato a great and, as we shall see, immensely influential precedent.

> Holding my shield between, I would not let
> This side or that unjust advantage get —

so Solon had, not unfairly, described his own efforts to reëstablish Athens on a foundation of social justice.[208] There is, in this context, significance in Plato's proper pride in tracing his family relationship with Solon,[209] and in

---

[206] The elaborate provisions for public education are laid down principally in Book VII. The laws themselves, however, with their persuasive prefaces, and the festivals, are also to have educational effect.

[207] These regulations are discussed again,

pp. 344 and 514–515.

[208] There is a finely illuminating account of Solon's contribution to the ethics and religion of the city state, in Jaeger, *Paideia*, I, chapter VIII.

[209] See pp. 261–262 above.

the many passages in the dialogues in which Solon's distinction as the Athenian legislator *par excellence* is gratefully acknowledged, or his achievement in poetry celebrated by citation or general allusion.[210] It is interesting, and perhaps an indication of the consecrated status accorded him, that Plato nowhere in his writings debates the wisdom of any particular piece of Solonian legislation, and this is the more significant because, as we shall see, he has actually drawn much from Solon's precedent in framing the *Laws*.[211]

If now it be asked how Solon appeared in the perspective of the Athenian of the late fifth century, no simple answer is forthcoming. The extreme oligarchs, it appears, would have none of him, even spending their energies, when occasion offered, in darkening his memory by inventing tales of his sharp practices. By the full-time democrats Solon was honored as one of the founders of the democracy, but only as one who had sowed the seeds but had by no means brought to maturity their cherished freedoms. This left room in the middle for a group of moderates of either persuasion, as evidenced by the appeal to the name of Solon made in the early stages of both the oligarchic revolutions, by those among the leaders who were seeking the support of citizens of moderate views. The name Solon connoted, as part of its public meaning, the conviction that the state could be stably founded upon nothing else than conformity to the eternal laws of the moral order. There was also connoted, on the practical plane, the advocacy of firm and impartial constitutional government, with a property qualification for office, but with important powers, exercised through the assembly and the courts, at the disposal of all citizens. These powers were, in fact, so extensive that they have been held by most students to amount to effective sovereignty of the state.[212] The Solonian constitution was entirely incompatible with the unchecked rule either of the wealthy or of the well-born. For this reason, Plato's informed admiration for Solon should go far to show that he was never an extreme oligarch,[213] and that except in such a case as the ideal Republic, where ideal rulers were to be provided, Plato was always in favor of some degree of popular control.

The *Gorgias* stands as Plato's major indictment of the statesmen whose

---

[210] E.g., *Laches* 188 B, *Republic* 599 E, *Laws* 858 E, *Symposium* 209 D, *Timaeus* 20 E.

[211] See n. 30, p. 514 below.

[212] Cf. *Solon the Athenian*, by I. M. Linforth, 1919, pp. 85–6. If it can truthfully be said that Plato deprived the common citizens in the *Laws* of some powers which Solon had given them, it is also true that Plato has compensated for this by greater liberality, e.g., in leaving open the highest offices in the state to citizens possessing only the minimum property qualification.

[213] For a most favorable judgment upon Solon as man and political thinker, the reader may see the chapter devoted to him in C. M. Bowra, *Early Greek Elegists*, 1938, pp. 73–104. Bowra concludes, "Solon . . . combined . . . a strong belief in individuality with a belief no less strong in duty to the community . . . It is no mere fancy to discern his influence in . . . Aeschylus . . . Sophocles . . . Pericles . . . Among the many good fortunes of Athens not the least was that . . . it produced a man so honest, so fair, so scrupulous, so public-minded as Solon."

acts and thought had laid the foundations of the Athenian empire. It will be recalled from our earlier discussion that the "Socrates" of this dialogue — to the indignation of Warner Fite, who suspects Platonic megalomania, and the admiration of Popper, who sees only the declaration of the true Socrates that none but the man who knows his own ignorance can safely rule — voices his claim to be the only proper statesman that Athens has produced. Though we do not accept Popper's interpretation of Socrates' meaning we need not deny that Socrates himself may well have expressed, in his own less vehement way, ideas which Plato has here elaborated, in condemnation of the materialism and moral indifference of the political leaders in question. But from the form and content of what is said we can hardly resist the inference that the criticism has been made Plato's very own. What the Platonic Socrates is demanding is the recognition of the priority, one might well say the absolute sovereignty, of moral goodness in all the arts, including especially politics and its pendent art of rhetoric. The only rhetorician or statesman that Socrates will accept is he who sets as his aim the moral betterment of the citizens. Callicles, answering Socrates, is prepared to admit that "our contemporary" politicians (the dramatic date of the dialogue is 405) fail to pass this test, but puts forward as satisfying the Socratic demand four of the greatest names in the Athenian record: Themistocles, Miltiades, Cimon, and Pericles. To no purpose! — for Socrates, like Satan the accuser in the book of Job, is hard to convince of human merit. Beginning with Pericles, with whom he is particularly severe, he charges them all with failing in the one and only duty of which we have spoken (515 C–517 C). Wars they may have won, harbors and docks they may have built. But to the virtue of the Athenians they made no positive — nay, even a negative — contribution; this is shown by the acts of the Athenians, who in the end, like the cattle of an unskilful herdsman, turned on them and threatened them with destruction.[214] They have aimed only to procure for the city the satisfaction of material wants, where true statesmen would have struggled to inculcate virtue, and like mere cooks and vintners have overfed the citizens as if they were so many children, on the sweetmeats of indulgence; the citizens, their digestion now seriously upset, in their simplicity do not know whom to blame (519 A), and will condemn Socrates, who has attempted to serve as their true statesman, like children condemning a doctor on a charge brought by a pastry cook (521 D–E).

Beneath the exaggeration and satire of this, runs the current of a des-

---

[214] It is interesting to find in the *Meno*, supposed to have been written not much later than the *Gorgias*, a similar criticism of the great Athenian statesmen as having been unable to transmit their virtues, this time to their own sons. In this slighter dialogue, the almost prophetic intensity of the *Gorgias* is not to be found, and there is even the suggestion that the substantial achievements of the statesmen in question are given recognition. But the tone is lightly ironic, and the whole discussion is conducted in terms of what Socrates thinks Anytus, whom he has drawn into replying to his questions, is likely to accept as true; we therefore have no reason to believe that the favorable judgments expressed are those of Socrates or Plato.

perately earnest Socratic morality, convinced that virtue is effective knowledge of the art of ordered life, and that without virtue, politics is poltroonery. The heart of this critique of the democratic system of government, as it is expressed in the *Gorgias*, is that it fails to make knowledge of this sort its guide, and that, in consequence, it runs off in quest of false values.[215] One remedy for the evil (the remedy which Plato first proposed) is formulated in the *Republic*, whose lords of right rule, the guardians, are nothing if not moralists in action.

But Plato, it seems, was not willing to end the *Gorgias* without finding some statesman of an earlier time upon whom he could with a clear conscience bestow a word of genuine praise, and his choice of a recipient is not without significance. In the concluding myth, describing the sanctions in the next world of conduct good and bad, Socrates remarks upon the small number of good men whose goodness survives the corrupting influence of power. Among these few he points out, as an outstanding example "among us and in the eyes of all Greece, Aristides the son of Lysimachus." This praise of a political figure who had certainly the reputation of a loyal servant of the Athenian democratic constitution [216] points to the conclusion that Plato inside the field of Athenian politics did not distribute praise and blame in accord with the degree of a man's willingness to bring in Spartan aid to overthrow the democracy, or, like the Old Oligarch, look with haughty scorn (tempered with admiration of wealth and power) upon the whole picture of an Athens under popular rule.

In refusing his approval to the elder statesmen of Athens and their followers, the Socrates of the *Gorgias* made at least a clear statement of his

---

[215] In this connection we may directly confront Popper's recurrent charge that the many restrictions laid on the commercial activities of citizens in both of Plato's ideal states are evidence of his kinship with the oligarchic enemies of Periclean commerce and empire, the docks, the Long Walls, and the ships. Since Popper sees this commercial expansion as enabling gifted individuals to move from class to class, and as freeing men's minds from blind tradition, he will allow Plato no other reason for his restrictions than opposition to these good things. Inconsistently, however, he has allowed Socrates to deprecate Athenian concern with commerce, excusing his denunciation (p. 593) as arising from "his anxiety to stress the things which, in his opinion, mattered most." Apparently Popper is willing to accept the same excuse for the exaggeration of Socrates' austere attitude as seen in Antisthenes. There appears

to us no reason to doubt that precisely similar reasons moved Plato to embody in his ideal constitutions the Socratic recommendation that, so far as practicable, men should turn aside from seductive material concerns to seek spiritual improvement.

[216] A recent authority on Greek political history, upon whom we have earlier drawn (Gomme, *A Historical Commentary on Thucydides*, 1945, vol. I, p. 47), has said something to our purpose here: in the fourth century, the moderate democrat praised Clisthenes and Aristides, without approval of the leaders of the subsequent development; the moderate oligarch repudiated Clisthenes but accepted Solon; and Solon himself was discountenanced by the extreme oligarchs. If we are to follow Gomme's classification, Plato apparently would be placed among the "moderate democrats"; which is not far from where, in the *Laws*, we find him.

reasons. In the *Menexenus*, the case is more difficult. Along with other aims, Plato has set himself to criticize the Athenian form of government and its chosen leaders, particularly Pericles. But here we are obliged before making any use of the dialogue, to dissociate the two elements of irreverent irony and earnest idealism of which it is subtly compounded, a task which, were we limited to the *Menexenus* itself, would be insoluble. In our search for Plato's serious meaning, we must look beyond the work itself, chiefly to other Platonic writings where, in contexts untouched by irony, comparable ideas are expressed. Patiently pursued, this method will yield a little new-found gold. But in the main we must be content if it permits us to show that, granted our interpretation of Plato's serious works, the *Menexenus* can be read in accord with it, a demonstration the more necessary because Popper, reading the *Menexenus* in the light of his own pejorative interpretation of Plato's serious works, has employed it to Plato's hurt.

Be it said at once that the *Menexenus* is not among the happiest achievements of Plato's genius. We have earlier claimed substantial value for its concluding section, the message of the ancestors to their descendants, and it is not without other eloquent passages, though they will not figure in our discussion. But modern taste does not easily tolerate such extreme interpenetration as we have here of jest and earnestness. For us there is possible only a one-way passage from the serious into the frolic, or the reverse. At any rate, let us say that only a transcendent comic genius (Aristophanes, for instance) can for us successfully turn the trick of repeated comings and goings between the two poles. And so as we read our *Menexenus* we find the experience, to say the least, a trifle disconcerting.

More serious in its implications is the second hindrance to our appreciation. Our moral taste is offended in beholding what appears to be a rather frivolous satirical belittlement of a very great man, Pericles, who is associated in our minds with most of what is of highest value and, one might say, sanctity, in Greek tradition. We see in Pericles, if not a Greek saint, like Socrates, at least a dedicated statesman, and the added fact that his dedication so importantly corresponds to our own, through the shared ideal of democracy, heightens our revulsion to ironical merrymaking at his expense. That the imagined occasion of Plato's parody, like that of the historical speech of Pericles to which the parody is presumed to be attached, was an honoring of the war dead, is a consideration that carries our feeling further in the same direction. What can be said in mitigation of this apparently grave offense?

Unfortunately there has been much dispute over the motives that impelled Plato to compose and publish this controversial book. Wilamowitz, for example, believed that in it Plato was making a bid for his new school by a demonstration that he could, so to say, outsmart the sophists at their own rhetorical game. It has also been suggested that possibly it had no more serious purpose than the amusement of its author in proving to himself his own literary ingenuity in subding his imagination to the requirements of this special literary form. Popper seems very sure that it was composed with no other end in view than to discredit Pericles, democracy, and enlightenment in general.[217] In the midst of the obscurity which has caused this diversity of interpretation, there are, nevertheless, some clear areas. There is at the very least light enough to permit us to see, as in what follows, the inadequacy of Popper's view. Further, we shall maintain without denying the possibility of some of the other proposed interpretations, that at least one clear and creditable motive can be shown to be involved.

To begin with, it is perfectly clear that Pericles is not the single object of Plato's satirical attack. The greater portion of the speech in the *Menexenus* is a deliberately garbled version of Athenian history, in which the valiant deeds of the Athenian ancestors of the war dead, their singleminded devotion to the general good of Greece, their glorious victories over all who opposed them, are celebrated, and their defeats and failures glossed over and reduced almost to the vanishing point, in sublime disregard of historical perspective. Now all this bad history has little or nothing to do with Pericles, no point of attachment to his speech, in which only a brief general mention of the ancestors was given a place. Even in Plato's encomium upon the Athenian constitution, some of the points made have no direct relevance to the Periclean speech.[218] The target of the oration is rather the whole class of those patriot-orators, of whom Pericles is one, whose indifference to truth and blindness to

---

[217] Popper has called the *Menexenus* "that sneering reply to Pericles' funeral oration" (p. 192) and has in several other passages in text and notes made play with this unproved assumption that Pericles is Plato's sole target in the dialogue. Popper's whole discussion is discolored by such expressions as "Plato gives himself away," "maliciously" (p. 192), "hatred," "open scorn," "ridicule" (all of admirable things) (p. 534). The charge is made that Plato's praise in the *Menexenus* of the "pure hatred" of the Athenians for the barbarians (245 D) is ridicule "by a pro-Spartan partisan" of the "liberality of Athens" to foreigners (p. 534), which Popper has chosen to present as a particularly Periclean trait (cf. our p. 286). Plato is talking of the Athenians' refusal to ally themselves with the Persians in war against other Greek states, and is perhaps ironically exaggerating a commonplace of the usual patriotic address (see our discussion of the expected topics of praise for Athenians in the orators, n. 236, p. 227). On p. 95 Popper explains the reference in the *Menexenus* to

the traditional origin of the Athenians from the soil of Attica as due to Plato's desire "to impute the naturalistic argument" unjustifiably to Pericles. The climax of this sort of vilification of Plato is reached in Popper's statement that not improbably Plato's reference to the "equal birth" of all Athenians "is meant as a scornful allusion to the 'low' birth of Pericles' and Aspasia's sons" (p. 533). In the light of the similar talk of the equal birth of Athenians from their soil, found in Lysias' funeral oration (see our discussion, pp. 337, 345), this suggestion is revealed to be as baseless as it is mean. For the record, it may be well to note here the erroneousness of Popper's reiterated assertion (pp. 534, 585) that in the *Menexenus*, 236 A, Plato represents Socrates as the pupil of Antiphon the Rhamnusian, which is based simply upon a misreading of the text, and also the error of his statement (p. 534) that this Antiphon was not an Athenian: Rhamnus is the name of an Attic deme.

[218] These are the points we discuss in n. 217 above, and Appendix IX, p. 609.

the true good of their country as Plato conceived it revealed itself in their dangerous idealization of the actual and imperfect Athens. Such orations were staple productions of the period; time has spared us only one other example,[219] a speech with some uncertainty assigned to Lysias, wherein the kind of encomiastic hyperbole in describing Athenian history and institutions against which Plato is protesting is admirably illustrated.

To point out the falsity and unwholesomeness of these rhetorical constructions is the clear purpose behind the irony in that passage of the introduction to the dialogue (235 A–C) in which Socrates expresses his admiration of their authors, whose carefully prepared encomia, compounded of the true and the false, and most beautifully tricked out in words and phrases, practice sorcery upon our souls; and as we listen, especially when those who are not Athenian citizens are by our side, we ourselves and our city grow more splendid and majestic in our eyes, and we imagine ourselves dwelling in the Islands of the Blessed, rather than in the actual Athens. Plato thus serves notice upon his reader that one major purpose in the speech to come will be to provide an exaggerated example of rhetorical deceits of this kind.

Detailed examination of the oration in the *Menexenus* will disclose in addition many passages, especially near the beginning of the speech, but here and there throughout, in which the standard tricks of rhetorical embellishment, artificial antithesis, alliteration, and assonance,[220] have been obviously overdone for satirical effect. These shots are fired not primarily at Pericles; for his speech, as Plato read it in Thucydides, was only a moderate example of the decorated style. They come much more closely home to the style of Gorgias and his school, in which such exuberance reached full flood.

What touches Pericles most nearly is, first, the (to our taste) rather displeasing horseplay of the introductory passage (235 E–236 C) in which Socrates gives us the farcical picture of a Pericles whose speeches were written for him by his schoolmistress in the art of rhetoric, Aspasia. We are not amused, but neither need we draw too solemn a face about it if we remember that Pericles in the earlier fourth century, while certainly looked back to as among the greater greats, had not yet been put upon a pinnacle as he has been in the modern world (we shall presently see that Plato was willing to recognize his greatness as an abstract intelligence, apart from the question of his political program), and, secondly, that Plato would hardly have supposed that anyone would be taken in by his facetious words. At the end of the dialogue (249 D–E) he makes it sufficiently plain that Aspasia is not the author of the *Menexenus* oration, nor probably of any other speech. In other words, we do not here have to do with serious, malicious gossip.

---

[219] The Funeral Oration in the Demosthenic corpus ([Demosthenes] lx) is generally assigned to a later period. The oration of [Lysias] referred to is Oration ii.

[220] F. Blass, *Die Attische Beredsamkeit*, 1892, vol. II, p. 470ff., discusses these rhetorical features in detail.

The second main reference to Pericles in the *Menexenus*, and at the same time to the Athenian constitution, is the short and breathtaking passage (238 B–239 A) in which we seem to have a sort of exaggerated paraphrase of the central political message of the Periclean Funeral Oration.[221] A first reading of this passage leaves one with the impression that Plato is offering us an unqualified satire upon democracy and all its works. For the orator seems to have pilfered fineries from many a political wardrobe, including monarchy, democracy, and aristocracy, for the adornment of an Athens never seen on land or sea. We hear of the unexampled excellence of her citizens, and of the corresponding excellence of her government; of the unbroken continuity of her constitution, from the time of the earliest kings; and of the willingness with which the "many," holders of power, accord office and influence only to those whose merits, unhampered by considerations of wealth and birth, qualify them to contribute to the common good. At the root of this admirable harmony lies the common origin of all Athenians from the womb of their mother Attica, and their consequent equality: as brothers, they will not endure that any one division of the population be enslaved to any other. Taken in its literal application to the Athens of Plato's experience and appraisal, this is obviously a fancy picture; mingled with the exaggeration of Athenian excellence there is, clearly, a note of irony. The problem set for us, then, is to discover the nature and scope of this irony, and to determine the justice of Popper's conviction that Plato is herein holding up to cynical derision the noblest of Athenian ideals.

If, now, we call to mind what we know from Plato's other writings to have comprised his political ideals, and set them in point-for-point correlation, as we have done in our footnote, with the topics developed by "Socrates-as-orator" in the *Menexenus*,[222] the main object of Plato's irony comes plainly into view. One trait of the Athenian polity he could not accept as ideal, or even, without substantial qualification, as the best practicable arrangement: the vesting of direct and final power in the mass of the people. But with this exception, what one reads in this part of the *Menexenus* is a kind of Athenian "Republic," a serious congratulation of the Athenians, on the part of a fellow believer, upon the nobility of the ideals to which they stood committed, together with an ironical declaration that those ideals were, forsooth, perfectly embodied in the actual Athens. In effect, Plato is saying: "The glories for which our Fourth-of-July orators are in the habit of praising Athens are indeed for the most part glorious; but alas! today they have largely ceased to be." The passage constitutes one further expression of Plato's feeling that Periclean democracy had failed, and that particularly as contrasted with its more splendid aims, taken over, as Plato believed, from an earlier and more admirable

---

[221] Thucydides II, 37.
[222] An analysis in detail of the political   section of the *Menexenus* may be found in Appendix IX, pp. 609ff.

Athens, it was a sad disappointment and a mockery. It shows us, too, that in his eyes little good was accomplished by the periodic restatement of these ideals, in the guise of actualities, with added extravagance and embroideries of diction, before an Athenian audience, but that this practice stood in the way of a serious attempt to improve matters.[223] In so far as the remembered figure of Pericles stood before the world as the chief spokesman for the claim that the developed Athenian democracy was the best possible, indeed the only answer to the political problem, it was Plato's wish to discredit him. But our understanding of Plato's purpose is only impeded by the atmosphere of "scornful allusion" and "hatred" that Popper has evoked.[224] Plato's indictment is quite a different thing from the malicious, "sneering reply" into which Popper has construed it. Indeed, it is continuous and in large part identical with that Socratic criticism of the leaders of the democracy "for their lack of [true, moral] wisdom," of which Popper has so strongly approved.[225]

The glorification of the Athenian polity standing complete, the historical section of the oration now begins. And here we should make it plain that in spite of the sometimes fantastic romancing of Athenian history, there are portions of the record in which, Athenian glory being actually attested and requiring no imaginary coloration to improve it, Plato can and does express with enthusiasm and persuasive power some of his own cherished appreciations of the true greatness of his native city. Such, notably, is the long account of the courage and nobility that Athens displayed in the Persian wars.

Toward the end of the *Menexenus* oration (246 D ff.), there occurs the earlier mentioned speech of the ancestors. This speech borrows nothing from any of the ironical sections that have gone before, contains no hint of irony, and could be sustained by a formidable array of parallel passages from other dialogues; it is therefore to be regarded with confidence as carrying a straightforwardly Platonic message. And this message offers a key to the positive value of the dialogue. For Plato is in effect telling the living through the voice of their ancestors speaking from the tomb, how a city may escape the perils which flattery and self-complacency are setting in its path. Glory, we hear, in language that almost reminds us of Faust,[226] is not a treasure that can be simply given by one generation to the next. It is a thing that must constantly be renewed and rewon, if it is not to turn into its contrary, and become a reproach. And glory is the fruit of virtue and of this alone. Without virtue, those reputed goods, knowledge, riches, and all the rest, are nothing worth.

Leaving the *Menexenus* behind us, we turn briefly to the *Phaedrus* for a passage, unnoticed by Popper, in which Plato has given a final proof that his

---

[223] Crossman (p. 300) has warned us, in our own day, against this same folly of equating our "millennial vision" of what our democracy aims to be with the far less ideal realities of contemporary politics.

[224] See n. 217, p. 336 above, for references.

[225] Popper, pp. 194, 188, 190.

[226] *Faust*, part II, ll. 11575–11576.

criticism of Pericles was an affair of principle unclouded by the prejudice and malice of the mere partisan. Here the Platonic Socrates, with all earnestness and with judicial calm, bestows upon Pericles the fine compliment of styling him "the most perfect orator of the day," finding in him the product of high native intelligence ripened by philosophic training into "lofty-mindedness, in every way effective of its ends" (269 E–270 A). It is only by adding the implied reservation that for all his gifts and training, Pericles had not employed his rhetoric to the highest end — the purpose of pleasing the divine rather than of "speaking and acting before men" [227] — that Plato sets in the perspective of his thought as a whole praise which otherwise would have been near to adulation.

We need carry no further in this place our exposition of Plato's attitude toward the Athenian constitution. We may sum up our findings in the section just ended, in the statement that Plato's criticism of democracy, reported immediately above, and also those other criticisms of democracy which have been so much stressed by Popper,[228] should not lead to the conclusion that

---

[227] *Phaedrus* 273 E, 274 A, trans. Fowler, Loeb Library.

[228] We may protest in this place against Popper's report (p. 44) of what Plato says in the *Republic* about democracy. Plato, we are told, identifies "freedom with lawlessness, equality before the law with disorder." So Popper represents Plato's complaint that what is called by the honorable name of freedom, in a democracy such as the Athens he knew, too often means disregard of law and decorum, and his objection on principle to such "equality" as the choice of public officials by means of the lot. Plato does not prove himself by these objections, even if we judge them excessive, to be an opponent *simpliciter* of freedom, or of all that is usually meant by equality before the law. Popper continues: "Democrats are described as profligate and niggardly, as insolent, lawless and shameless, as fierce and terrible beasts of prey, as gratifying every whim . . ." Anyone who will examine the relevant passages will see that these qualities have been chosen by Popper in part from Plato's description (559 D ff.) of the youthful excesses of the "democratic man," his wild-oats period, so to speak, from which he later recovers, to a considerable extent, in the normal case (561 B); the "insolent" and "lawless" persons mentioned (560 E) are personifications of the young man's profligate habits and opinions; the "beasts of prey" (559 D) are his evil companions; in so far as they rep-

resent also elements in a democratic state, they are the "drones," the ruined and reckless men who, Plato says, are bred in oligarchies (555 D f.) but become powerful only in a democracy, through the failure of the mass of the citizens to pay sufficient heed to public affairs (564 B ff.). They are not Plato's typical "democratic man," nor do they constitute the largest element among the people; to represent these, Plato has given us elsewhere the simile of the worthy old skipper, bewildered and befooled by the ignorant self-styled navigators (*Republic* 488 A ff.). In the passage which Popper purports to be summarizing, only the indiscriminate gratification of whims is truly charged by Plato against the democratic man. Popper then declares that Plato depicts the democrats "as living solely for pleasure, and for unnecessary and unclean desires," and adds: "('They fill their bellies like the beasts,' was Heraclitus' way of putting it.)" This is, first, an error, since Plato's democratic man is expressly said to alternate between indulging his various appetites and impulses, and exercising virtuous restraint. (The "democratic man," it should be noted, is himself largely a metaphorical being, his fickleness in maturity symbolizing the democratic custom of allotting office now to a worthy, now to an unworthy citizen, as his early excesses symbolize the civic disorders attendant upon a revolution from oligarchy to democracy.) Popper's charge is, secondly, an injustice, since no matter what Hera-

"democracy," in the sense of popular exercise of specified political powers, was a political expedient for which he had no use. How much he was willing to concede to its claims will again concern us in our later examination of the parallels between his *Laws* and the institutions of Sparta, and his evaluations of democracy in both *Politicus* and *Laws*.[229] Doubtless these later dialogues register some actual change in Plato's political theory, but if due account be taken of the differences in the degree of freedom to mold the environment to his will, which the earlier and the later dialogues respectively contemplate, the change in evaluation is all but lost in a change in perspective. Except when he was contemplating the ideal conditions of the Republic, Plato never failed to grant some degree of approval to democracy, and as we have seen, introduced many of its characteristic features, shorn of what he regarded as abuses, into the city of the *Laws*.

(3) Reform of the Athenian Constitution. Within the Athenian polity, as we have seen, Plato believed major alterations to be in order — so the dialogues were one after another informing the Greek world. Was he then in favor of abandoning the democracy at Athens for some form of rule by the few?

Of Popper's belief that Plato intended in his own person to install the *Republic* at Athens, we may remark that he leaves the steps by which Plato supposedly expected to reach dictatorship completely vague. Plato does say in the *Laws* (710 E) that if an ideal state is to arise, the easiest and quickest method would be to convert a tyrant, the next a king, and the third, the popular leaders in "some form of democracy"; and by this he means, as he explains, a form of democracy in which such leaders are few in number and possess great power (and, therefore, presumably, could induce their people to accept the required surrender of sovereignty). But at Athens, where the people were most jealous of their power, it would have been necessary to convert large sections of the demos itself; and this, Plato is implying, is impossible (*Laws* 712 A).

But if, as Popper's case requires, Plato designed the dialogues as Pareto-propaganda for inducing the rank and file of democratic Athens to accept the political miracles he was promising to perform, they are singularly ill adapted to this end. They are no sugared popularizations, but everywhere presuppose a willingness and a capacity to follow an argument to any level of logical abstraction. And were the common citizens expected to pursue the windings

---

clitus may have said of the many or the "mob," Plato does not thus condemn the "democrats." The true parallel with Heraclitus' saying in Plato's thought is Plato's condemnation (e.g., at *Republic* 586 A f.) of the "philosophical many," of whom we have spoken on p. 258. These unenlightened souls, however, need by no means always be "democrats"; they would include tyrants and most oligarchs, not to mention many a "timocrat" (cf. *Rep.* 548 A f., cited on our p. 511). Plato does not approve Athenian democracy, but his picture of its faults is not Popper's.

[229] See pp. 513 and 514–517 below.

of Plato's logic in order to learn in the end that "the many are incapable of philosophy" (*Republic* 494 A)? Or was Plato perhaps aiming at the popular leaders of his own day, whom he constantly represents as led and determined in their policies and judgments by the "great beast," to whose moods and appetites they are the indulgent servitors? Ought not Plato, on the Pareto principle, to have effected a politic concealment of these opinions in order to win over democrats to his unrighteous cause? Popper does not stay for an answer to these difficulties. Instead, he vaguely indicates as those whom Plato aimed to deceive, "all intellectuals" and "all righteous men" and all who cherished the "freedom of thought for which Socrates had died." [230] The class of Athenian contemporaries of Plato who could satisfy all these conditions must have been small. But at this point Popper seems to have forgotten Plato's supposed Athenian conspiracy, and speaks as if Plato had been casting spells consciously intended to bind generations of readers yet unborn.[231]

But one can spare himself the pains of such distortion by reverting to the simpler view that we have been all this while maintaining: Plato's basic aim was no conspiratorial perversion of truth. He was honestly endeavoring to carry forward the Socratic quest and to set forth the pattern of a political order in conformity with the highest demands of morality. The dialogues are "propaganda," but only in the sense that they constitute an attempt to spread a knowledge of this rational faith. The *Republic* is literally addressed as advice and guidance to two young men, Glaucon and Adeimantus, touching their choice of principles for the management of their lives. Behind and beyond them Plato was addressing not the body of Athenian citizens, rich or poor, but the intellectual few, whom he hoped to convert from nihilistic doubts or selfish ambition to a preference for the upright life, at any sacrifice. Within Athens this might mean the giving up of all hope of political influence and the acceptance of obscurity and probable poverty. Somewhere in the Greek world, however, the message might reach the ears of persons who had power to establish better laws. And from the spectacle of their success, a light might shine capable of illuminating even the ignorant many. That such a program was impractical cannot be denied; yet it was not beyond the horizon of Plato's hope.

If Plato did not, then, expect to see the embodiment at Athens of the Republic, would he have favored the installation there of an oligarchy of a frequent Greek type, a government controlled wholly by the wealthy few? What Plato thought of such constitutions, "in which the rich govern and the poor

---

[230] Popper, p. 193. In speaking of "all righteous men" Popper might of course claim to be including the nonintellectual righteous. But the dialogues, being, as they are, intellectually demanding, would seem unfitted to lead astray these persons.

[231] Popper has apparently converted his own belief (discussed on pp. 447–449) that Plato has in fact poisoned innumberable generous minds down to our own day, into Plato's foreknowledge of the countless thousands who would read his works, and his deliberate intention to befool them all.

man does not share in the government" [232] (*Republic* 550 C–D), is plainly and indignantly told in the eighth book of the *Republic*. This type of government, according to Plato's announced classification, is one degree less evil than democracy. But it is interesting to note that it actually receives at his hands a more bitter castigation.[233] Wealth and virtue, we hear, lie in opposing pans of the balance. Wealth is no more a valid criterion in the selection of those who are to hold political power than in the choice of a ship's pilot. Inseparable from oligarchic rule is the division of the city into two bitterly hostile cities, "dwelling together and always plotting against one another." The greed of the wealthy leads to the existence of a class of men who are in the city but in no sense of it, complete destitutes or paupers, from whose ranks are drawn the professional criminals in which such states abound. These are the evils, Plato says, "or perhaps even more than these," [234] that afflict the oligarchic state. Was Plato, in this sense, an oligarch?

Slightly more worth the asking is what would have been Plato's response to an invitation to join a movement seeking by nonviolent, constitutional measures (assuming that such proposals would have been tolerated by the democracy) to restore Athens to a regime comparable in essentials to that of the Solonian time. His "apolity" would have stood in the way of active political participation. Would he then have approved it in theory? It could be argued that such a goal would have appeared too meager to the author of the *Republic*; even the less hopeful author of the *Politicus* and the *Laws* believed that new levels of insight into the problems of government should make possible advances over those older political forms.[235] Or it could be argued that he would doubtless have welcomed the removal of the evils that he saw flowing from the uncontrolled democracy, and the restoration of such an Athens as had conquered at Marathon.[236]

Would he, like Thucydides, have approved the constitution of the Five

---

[232] The word here translated "government" is *archê*. This form of constitution would be distinguished from the Solonian type by the exclusion of the poorer citizens from all, or almost all, rights of participation, among which are included the exercise of voting rights and a seat in the Assembly or in the law courts. Plato in the *Laws* 767 A, 768 C) regards the prerogative of sitting as a juror as not technically an "office" (*archê*), yet still in a sense an "office" of real importance. He makes it a basic prerequisite to the citizen's feeling of membership in his city; cf. p. 525 below.

[233] In a later dialogue than the *Republic*, what Plato calls "oligarchy," defined in that place as the "rule of the few without law," is in fact set lower in the scale of value than democracy (*Politicus* 303 A–B).

[234] Shorey's translation, Loeb Library.

[235] In the *Politicus* (299 B–E) he speaks of the necessity of constant investigation of the problems of all arts, particularly that of government, if civilization is not to stagnate. The whole enterprise of the *Laws* (*pace* Popper) is an adventure along new paths of practical legislation. See the discussion of Plato's *Laws* in A. E. Taylor's *Plato, the Man and His Work*, 1929, p. 464. Taylor has also provided in the introduction to his translation of the *Laws* a tabulation of Plato's legislative originalities.

[236] At *Laws* 698 A, Plato begins his account of the excellence of the Athenian constitution at the beginning of the fifth century, which he refers to as a moderate form of government under elected rulers, or (701 E) a moderate degree of freedom.

Thousand, established at Athens in 411 B.C., following the failure of the more extreme rule of the Four Hundred? It was doubtless Thucydides' approval of this government which caused Popper to classify him as an oligarch; Thucydides says of it (VIII, 98) that it combined wisely the interests of the few and the many. Plato, we can be fairly certain, would not willingly have accepted it. If it had been provided with a well-devised set of mutually adjusted laws, and had been administered with due respect for these laws, he would in so far have approved it (*Politicus* 300 B ff.). And he might have approved, in part, its assignment of power to those able to serve the state as cavalry or heavy-armed soldiers; in the *Laws* (753 B) he assigns the right to elect Law-wardens to persons similarly qualified.[237] But also in the *Laws*, he countenances no limitation of the right to participate in government to a minority of the citizens, constituting not more than a quarter of the whole,[238] but instead gives every citizen active rights; nor had Solon made any comparable restriction. In this respect, therefore, the constitution of the Five Thousand would have resembled the "oligarchy" which Plato so firmly rejects in the *Republic*, as breeding "two cities" within the city, and would not have met his mind.

Such speculations are not very nourishing, and do not end very far from their starting points. They probably go as far as the facts will take us toward revealing Plato's outlook upon peaceful reform of the Athenian government.

(4) Revolutionary violence. But Popper has added a second, highly damaging charge in his assertion that Plato felt no revulsion against the violence that had accompanied the two oligarchic revolutions of 411 and 404, and would have approved an equally violent third. Can we find in Plato's writings passages that will tell us what he thought of these events?

There comes immediately to mind the strong condemnation of oligarchic violation of law expressed by the Socrates of the *Apology* (32 C–D). Popper, of course, will not allow this Socrates to be our Plato. And yet, as we have earlier argued, he is beyond his rights in so refusing. Plato's implied approval of this part of the speech is inextricable from his implied approval of the entire speech. We may repose our confidence in it as genuinely expressive of Plato's own personal conviction.

There is another passage in which Plato specifically refers to this same oligarchic revolution of 404, in which Critias was involved. But as ill-luck

---

[237] These foot- and horse-soldiers in the city of the *Laws* will, however, include all citizens except criminals, cowards, etc., since here there will be no sailors, and no impoverished citizens unable to provide themselves with arms.

[238] Though called the Five Thousand, the governing class, defined by the qualifications set up, appears to have been larger;

see Lysias xx, 13. We do not wish to blink the fact that in the *Laws* (737 C–E) Plato sets tentatively at approximately five thousand the number of adult male citizens. He will keep the citizen body within the chosen limits not by disfranchisement, however, but by a continuous policy of population restriction and colonization. Cf. our p. 198 and n. 257, p. 353.

will have it, it is in the *Menexenus*, and we are warned, therefore, that it will have to be employed with caution, and in subordination to more positive indications drawn from other sources. Nevertheless, when thus read, this part of the *Menexenus*, like those passages which we have already examined, admits readily of an interpretation in perfect accord with the general trend of our evidence. To establish this result we shall make use of a triangular comparison between what is said in part of the historical section in the *Menexenus*, what Plato has elsewhere committed himself to, and what Lysias,[239] in the corresponding section of his funeral oration, has said on the same topics.

Lysias, recounting the glories of Athenian history, skips lightly down the decades, celebrating at length Marathon and Salamis as victories over the barbarians, and then expatiating upon the beneficence of the Athenian empire. No mention has been made of the very existence of the Peloponnesian war, when suddenly we hear that at Aegospotami, either through the "badness of the commander or through the will of the gods," the Athenian power was destroyed, and the other Greek cities, their protector being laid low, now found themselves enslaved by the Spartans. Lysias next praises the "men of the Piraeus," the embattled Athenian democrats, for their refusal to accept this enslavement, for their compelling their fellow citizens to share with them their restored freedom, and for their magnanimity in pursuing, not vengeance, but a policy of reconciliation in the interests of civic concord. It will be evident from this partial *résumé* that the funeral orator chose his own historical proportions, and could omit or dilate at will, so long as he took care to evoke in his listeners only welcome memories. We shall be able, therefore, to take Plato's selective emphasis in his speech in the *Menexenus* as a partial index of the speaker's own views.

Covering the same period as Lysias,[240] Plato praises Athenian achievements at Marathon, Salamis, Plataea, and Eurymedon, all of them being interpreted as the saving of the whole of Greece from the barbarians; only at Plataea, he remarks, did the Spartans lend aid. He then speaks in an injured tone of the envy felt by the other Greeks for the Athenians, and of the latter's services in defending Hellenes against enslavement by fellow Hellenes (the Thebans, aided by the Spartans). He proceeds to praise the generosity of the Athenians in making peace with the Spartans (the peace of Nicias, which ended the first half of the Peloponnesian war) without seeking utterly to destroy them, and praises also the triumphal valor of the Athenians, who thus conquered those same Spartans with whose aid they had formerly beaten off the barbarians. Of the Sicilian expedition he says only that having gone too far afield in this altruistic enterprise, the Athenians abandoned it, meeting with "ill fortune," but bringing honor upon those who conquered them. He com-

---

[239] The use of the name Lysias in this passage is a practice adopted for brevity, and is not meant to imply a judgment that the oration is genuine. The sections summarized are 20–66.

[240] *Menexenus* 239 D–244 B.

ments bitterly upon the ingratitude of the Spartans, toward the end of the Peloponnesian war, in bringing in the Persian king as their ally against Athens. He celebrates the victory of Arginusae as proof of Athens' true invincibility; Athens was, in fact, he says, laid low only by her own internal dissensions.

Plato has now brought us to the fateful year 404; we look eagerly to see what he will reveal of his attitude toward the oligarchic revolution. But like Lysias, he leaves it for all practical purposes unmentioned. The listener could never guess that terrible slaughter had taken place. Quite unlike Lysias, however, he makes no reference to the heroic action of the men of the Piraeus. In hushed tones, he speaks at some length of the reconciliation, founded, he says, on the sense of kinship among the Athenians, who are of one blood. The struggle between the two parties, he says, was caused not by "wickedness or hatred" on either side, but only by "misfortune." We, the living, are witnesses of the forgiveness that has reunited us.

There were several points during this recital at which our attention had reason to be alerted. Was it not interesting to note how the speaker not only omits every faintest reference to the activities of the Thirty, but makes the exaggerated statement that no blame attached to either side in the civil war? Lysias, in spite of the inhibition imposed by the spirit of the occasion, could plainly hint of his hatred of the tyranny. No doubt Plato might, consistently with his own principles, have found a missile or two to fling at the Thirty Tyrants; so much the *Apology* makes clear. But he could scarcely, as the same *Apology* makes equally evident, have joined Lysias in praising without serious reservations the democratic system supported by the opponents of the Thirty.[241] We may believe that he wished seriously to condone neither side in the struggle, yet he could not turn his swelling Funeral Oration into a sour distribution of blame. For this reason he may well have chosen to pass over the unpleasantness with a pious phrase — not incompatible with his own principle that no man does wrong willingly — and to direct attention solely to the admirable, following the same pattern of patriotic extravagance seen in his unrecognizable picture of the Sicilian expedition.

Examining the praise bestowed upon Athenian achievements, we observe the stamp of sincerity and of Plato's personal evaluation upon the praise of Greek loyalty to Greek against the barbarian, and of Athens' moderation in concluding peace with Sparta. Plato's irony, it seems, in this passage has limited itself wholly to whitewashing national faults and failures, exaggerating national virtues, and amplifying to mythical proportions the kinship bonds between the Athenians themselves and the Hellenes generally; the ideals he upholds are expressed in hyperbole, but remain his own. In the celebration

---

[241] At *Apology* 32 A–C is mentioned the condemnation, contrary to law, of the Argi- nusae generals; cf. our p. 318. See also our pp. 304, 638–639.

of the amnesty after the defeat of the Thirty, with its mutual forgiveness by those who are of one blood, we surely hear the veritable voice of Plato, uplifted in a species of thankful prayer for that "harmony of hearts" which, as we know, was to be the theme song of his *Republic*. And to this we may point in evidence that he could never have given assent to the violent misrule of the Thirty, and that the renewal of civil war and internecine bloodshed had no place in his hopes and plans for the future of his native city.

We shall not dismiss this passage of the *Menexenus* without noting the several slaps and rebukes administered to the Spartans, and to the pride expressed in the Athenian victory of Arginusae. We shall ask that these be remembered, as we shall find use for them at a later point in the argument.

Plato's abhorrence of civil violence may also be inferred from the well-known autobiographical passage in the most reliable of the Platonic letters (VII, 324 E ff.), in which "Plato" revives, after the passing of many years, the repulsion and shock that he experienced as a young man when what seemed the fair promise of the party to which Critias had joined himself degenerated into a brutal violence that made the democratic administration that preceded it shine with the brightness of the age of gold. The letter records also the attempt of the Thirty to implicate his friend Socrates *nolens volens* in their crime. "But he refused, and ran every risk rather than become a partner in their unholy deeds." And the writer of the letter adds a generous appreciation of the moderation and restraint of the restored democracy. Now if the author of this letter has been speaking — as many believe — with the authority of Plato,[242] we have in these citations a valuable *a fortiori* confirmation of our right to believe that the deprecation of civic discord and appreciation of the restored democracy, expressed in the *Menexenus*, were sincere.

A few pages later in this letter we come upon something which reads almost like a direct answer to the question we have raised. It is as if someone had put to Plato the direct question, "What would you do, Plato, if you thought that the political institutions at Athens were out of order and that you had the knowledge requisite to set them right?" "Plato's" answer is one which he thinks befits "a man of sense": "If his native city seems to him badly governed, he will offer his counsel, provided his advice has any chance of being heard and he will not be put to death for his pains. But he must not attempt to force a change of government upon his mother city. If it is not possible for the best constitution to arise without the exile and slaughter of citizens, he should hold his peace and pray that heaven's blessing will be upon him and his city" (VII, 331 D).

We have now exhausted our knowledge of Platonic, or reputedly Platonic, passages from which anything explicit can be learned touching Plato's judg-

---

[242] The attitude taken in this book toward the Platonic *Letters* is discussed in our note 287, on page 369 below.

ment upon oligarchic violence inside Athens. If we wish to discover anything further under this head, we are, like Popper, reduced to inference and interpretation. We are forced to search Plato's works for remarks that may apply to Athens past and present, even though such remarks may be without specific reference to Athenian history.

Among the first fruits of such a search and pointing in the same direction as the passages above, is Plato's strong deprecation of shedding the kindred blood of fellow citizens, in the *Republic* (565 D). There we hear of the "protector of the people," who on his way to becoming the tyrant, "does not withhold his hand" from this crime, or from proposing the redistribution of lands and the abolition of debts. He is likened to the worshipper at the shrine of Lycaean Zeus in Arcadia, in the terrifying legend, who having tasted "of the one bit of human entrails minced up with those of other victims, is inevitably transformed into a wolf." If this passage stood alone as the vehicle of Plato's moralizing reflections on the use of violence for the attainment of political ends, further discussion of the topic would be superfluous.

But what are we to make of the several passages to which Popper has pointed an accusing finger, in which Plato apparently accords to the wise statesman a hand free to "banish and to kill" whom he thinks fit?

We must here make objection to Popper's including in this category [243] the procedure suggested in the *Republic* (540 E–541 A) for accomplishing, in the first instance and with the greatest speed, what has been admitted as the near impossibility of launching the ideal city. This is the "sending out into the country" of all the inhabitants of the chosen city above ten years old, and the educating of the children, thus "removed from the influence of their parents' temper and habits," in the laws and customs of the new polity. The purpose in view, that of effecting a fresh start, unencumbered by the traditional mores, is one that Plato seriously regarded as important. But the highly fanciful tactic proposed should not be treated too solemnly. The suggested picture of a handful of philosophers left alone with a city-full of young children, like Boswell's Dr. Johnson locked up with a baby in a tower, shows us that Plato cannot have carried his thinking beyond the first stage of tentative suggestion, keeping his attention fixed wholly upon the end proposed, without due reflection upon the means. This being the case, it would be absurd to suppose that he had seriously determined upon the ruthless use of violence, and we should be wrong to hear the knock upon the door, the heavy boot upon the threshold, which Popper's words "deport" and "expel" evoke. The word Plato used can equally well be employed (*Symposium* 179 E) for "sending away" to the Islands of the Blessed, and the "country" into which the parents

---

[243] Popper, p. 162. Popper reënforces his interpretation of the Platonic passage by slight inaccuracies in the translation, tending to give the impression of greater scorn or violence in Plato's attitude. Thus he translates "send away" (*apopempô*) as "expel and deport," and makes Plato refer to the "mean" character of the children's parents, where no corresponding word exists in the Greek text.

are to be sent may be their own farms or country estates, outside the city proper.

The second passage to which Popper has directed attention is not so easily disposed of, and indeed contains implications of an attitude which, though it is not the partisan ruthlessness of an oligarch, nor the special ruthlessness of a heartless aesthete, as Popper suggests, still does not, for several reasons, commend itself to our acceptance. Let us first see what this attitude actually is, and then set it in relation to the temper of the times in which Plato lived. As Popper has correctly reported,[244] Plato in the *Politicus*, speaking of those rare and almost hypothetical beings, the true statesmen, who rule in accord with the art or science of statesmanship, asserts (293 D–E), "Whether they purge the state for its good by killing or banishing some of the citizens, or make it smaller by sending out colonies somewhere, as bees swarm from the hive, or bring in citizens from elsewhere to make it larger, so long as they act in accordance with science and justice and preserve and benefit it by making it better than it was, that must at that time and by such characteristics be declared to be the only right form of government." [245]

Fair interpretation of this stated principle requires at least a brief indication of the general pattern of the dialogue. The *Politicus* has set out, in true Socratic fashion, to define the statesman, but employing an elaborate logical method (*diairesis*) of Plato's own invention. Exercise in the use of this method, Plato tells us (286 D–E), is the primary purpose of the entire discussion. The atmosphere in which the dialogue moves is one of disinterested, theoretical, in short, "scientific" inquiry, focussed on a topic of broad human concern which is nothing less than what we should call the theory or science of government. For we need not be misled by Plato's use of the apparently personal term "statesman." The "man" here is really no man; he is only the postulated possessor of knowledge of a specified sort, a kind of useful fiction, like a frictionless surface or a perfectly straight edge, supplying a hypothetical standard from which measurements can be made. After several attempts to define the statesman have been exposed as inadequate, Plato has reached the point at which he is attempting to show that only the possession of knowledge of the truly good for man and the community, can serve as the defining mark (*horos*) of the true statesman. Other traditional and currently accepted criteria, such as whether rule be exercised by few or by many, over willing or unwilling subjects, or in accord or not in accord with law, are rejected as irrelevant or nonessential.[246] In the passage just quoted, Plato is carrying to its logical extreme the test of knowledge alone. Plato does believe, as we

---

[244] Popper, p. 162. Popper, however, as before, employs the unfavorable word "deport" in his translation, in place of "send out."

[245] *Politicus*, trans. Fowler, Loeb Library.

[246] Grote (*Plato and the Other Compan-*

ions of Socrates, 1865, vol. II, p. 478) has well observed the close parallel of this definition of the true statesman with that given by the Xenophontic Socrates, *Mem.* III, 9, 10.

know from other passages, that the actual lawgiver will be justified at times in exercising the functions of banishing or condemning citizens, but it is only with the proviso that the best available knowledge is actually his, and that he stands to profit nothing by the result of his decisions.

In seeking a just understanding of Plato's handling of this problem of political coercion, we must first introduce a distinction, and then point to a widespread characteristic of the Greek world of that time. Plato has used language which runs together two matters that we in the modern world are in the habit of keeping distinct, namely: criminal jurisprudence and political reform. In the *Politicus* passage, the sending out of colonies or the calling in of new citizens belongs obviously in the second field. Pericles, we know, made frequent use of the device of emigration, which was subsidized by the city; Popper's word "deport" again introduces sinister associations, where favorable overtones would be in order.

The "killing" and "banishing" we can not so immediately place. Popper assumes without question that it, too, belongs in the realm of political measures, signifying the removal of political dissidents; but it could equally well have no reference to such persons. Plato, as usual when he is considering the inauguration of good government, appears throughout the dialogue to be proceeding upon the assumption that the statesman is not required to struggle for his power. He is thought of as appointed for the purpose of effecting needed reforms in some existing city — like the board of commissioners mentioned at *Politicus* 300 B — or, perhaps, as was Plato himself,[247] called upon as a recognized expert in law, to assist in the creation of a new city. Plato's language is wide enough to include among those who are to be killed and banished, what we should think of as gangsters and racketeers, the criminal population in general, particularly that part of it whose activities had not been checked by the existing imperfect laws. In reading Popper, one is never reminded of the presence in Greek society of this class of persons, of whom the orators have so much to tell.[248] No more political motive need be seen in Plato's recommendation here than would be reasonable to find in the action of a new mayor of one of our great cities who might inaugurate his administration by urging his prosecuting attorney to redouble efforts against the vice rings.

The inclusive character of Greek law, which embraced so much moral and religious prescription, and, in dealing with a particular defendant, did not hesitate to take into account his general moral character, even his military service record, rather than to hew to the line of the particular charge, would

---

[247] See Taylor, *Plato*, p. 464, where this tradition is reported. The tale records, however, that Plato refused.

[248] See e.g., Bonner and Smith, vol. II, the chapter on sycophants *passim*, esp. p. 47. Calhoun, in his discussion of Athenian

clubs (*op. cit.*), includes a revealing section on the clubs in litigation, and describes (pp. 95–96) groups of persons whose sole business was sycophancy and venal pettifoggery.

make the task of Plato's statesman easier than is that of the modern prosecutor, who may be reduced to seeking the conviction of a notorious gangster for evading the income tax. That Plato's thinking is pervaded by this amalgamation of law and morals is illustrated by what is later said (*Politicus* 308 E–309 A) of the duty of the statesman to arrange that only such persons as are capable of achieving moral goodness shall be educated to full citizenship in the new state, the morally vicious to be banished or put to death or deprived of their chief civic rights,[249] the morally incompetent to be reduced to the status of slaves.[250]

These are bold prescriptions, indeed, and unless applied with the greatest care likely to defeat their own high ends. We shall have occasion later to evaluate and to express our reservations regarding this kind of paternalism. But though Plato conceived the authority and the principles directing the weeding out of unfit citizens as being handed down from above, whereas we conceive them as arising from the community acting through its elected officials, we should not fail to note that the process itself is carried on in every society by its courts and the admission boards of its institutions; it is a continuous process, a necessary part of government. In the case imagined by Plato, the numbers to be rejected as future citizens need not be greater than the number usually disqualified in some fashion in any state. And Plato's statesman, like that modern sovereign the people, was to entrust to others possessing the requisite special skills the application of his principles to the concrete case (*Politicus* 305 B–C, 308 D–E).

But the contemporary conscience is likely to be troubled also by the severity of the penalties and the apparent readiness to resort to final sanctions. Our judgment of Plato in this matter must in fairness take into consideration the standards and practice of Plato's contemporaries. We are apt to think of the Athenians much as they were pleased to consider themselves, as conspicuous in their day for their humanity and kindliness; and in spite of an element of exaggeration,[251] there is no reason to question its over-all correctness. But on closer view we see the necessity of recognizing some considerable exceptions. There were still survivals of the ancestral cruelties, such things as the torture of slave witnesses and, in some cases, of free men who were simply not of "pure Athenian" descent, and there was the abomination of the method of execution known as *apotympanismos*.[252] The great number and unimpor-

---

[249] A similar view regarding the divinely-sanctioned necessity of putting to death those men who are incapable of acquiring "justice and reverence" is expressed by the Protagoras of Plato's dialogue of that name, 322 D.

[250] See our remark on this passage, p. 224 above.

[251] See our pp. 151, 164.

[252] The torture of slaves is frequently referred to; e.g., Lysias VII, 34–38. The torture of free non-Athenians is referred to in Lysias XIII, 25–27, 59. *Apotympanismus* is mentioned as being inflicted after the restoration of the democracy in 403, in Lysias XIII, 56, 65. Cf. Bonner and Smith, *The Administration of Justice from Homer to Aristotle*, 1928, vol. II, pp. 126 ff. and 279 ff.

tance of offenses for which the death sentence was invoked is disconcerting to the modern temper. The rigors of Leviticus are rivalled in such provisions of Attic law as death to the wretch who has laid a suppliant's branch on the altar at Eleusis during the seasons of the Mysteries,[253] banishment and confiscation to him who rooted out the stump of a sacred olive tree (Lysias, Oration VII), and, to leave the zone of religious offenses, death as one of the penalties applicable to the Athenian citizen who sat as juryman while still owing money to the city.[254] Enslavement might legally be visited by an irate father, even at Athens, upon an unchaste daughter, and slavery was also the penalty awaiting the non-Athenian found living as husband or wife to an Athenian citizen.[255] Looked at in this context, Plato's statesman, with his apparent readiness to kill, banish, and enslave, where we should prescribe either the penitentiary, at one end, or psychiatric social service, at the other, loses much of his sanguinary coloration.

But what if among those who are to be killed and banished are included political opponents, as such, of the program of the "true statesman"? Plato's language does not exclude this possibility. We have already remarked upon the freedom with which leaders of the political opposition were regarded by the victorious party in the Greek cities as outright enemies, to be treated accordingly. But as we have also shown, there is good reason to believe that Plato was not infected with this cultural brutality. And in the *Politicus*, the statesman is regarded as a mediator, perhaps an outsider, without personal stake in the outcome and not involved in the enmities and bitterness of the parties. If he banishes or puts to death those whose continued presence will endanger the success of the new constitution, he is exercising a function which neither we, nor in other passages, Plato,[256] would entrust to any individual, but he is at least acting on disinterested principle. And in granting to his ideal statesman this power, if he does so grant it, Plato is not approving its exercise against fellow citizens by the all too human Athenians whom circumstance might have endowed with arbitrary mastery.

But must we with Popper believe that the highly magnified statesman is none other than Plato himself? We shall return in a later chapter to the ques-

---

[253] See Moses Hadas, *History of Greek Literature*, 1950, p. 163.

[254] Cited in Paul Vinogradoff, *Outlines of Historical Jurisprudence*, 1922, vol. II, p. 188; from Dem. xxi, 182. Vinogradoff also cites several fragments from Democritus (Diels, Frs. 257–260) in which it is interesting to find that thinker using the analogy of destroying noxious beasts and reptiles to justify the killing of criminals and other enemies of the community.

[255] On the sale of a daughter, Glotz, p. 193; on the fate of the pretended Athenian spouse, [Dem.] lix, 16–17. Aristotle's *Constitution of Athens*, ch. 42, has been commonly understood to declare that any eighteen year old claimant to citizenship disqualified by the official examiners as of partly non-Athenian origin was also enslaved. Gomme, however, has sought ("Two Problems in Athenian Citizenship Law," 1934) to interpret Aristotle as testifying only that Athens thus sold into slavery youths shown to be of partly servile birth.

[256] E.g., *Laws* 875 A–D.

tion of how far and in what sense Plato considered himself to be possessed of the philosophic wisdom whose saving power for the Greek world he so often celebrated. In this place, we can only say that there is no evidence to indicate that Plato, confronted with an actual occasion in which philosophic rule appeared attainable only at the cost of violence, would have accorded himself the right to intervene — particularly if such violence would have been directed against his fellow citizens. Nowhere in his writings, even in the most remote region of supposition, does he contemplate such action. On the evidence, we must suppose that he would have awaited that more propitious hour which haunted his imagination, when some person or small group of persons, already in possession of recognized and stable power, should extend him an opportunity to offer his disinterested counsel. And if to these considerations we add what light the letters throw upon him in his hour of decision during the Sicilian adventures, we may conclude, with as much certainty as the nature of the case admits, that throughout his life Plato adhered consistently to his high principle of restraint.

In the *Laws* occurs a discussion, parallel to the passages in the *Politicus* which we have been discussing, but with some interesting differences of aim and emphasis. Here (*Laws* 735 A–737 B) there is no question of defining the lawgiver and finding his ideal nature; the legislator (or legislative commissioner) is conceived as neither necessarily all-wise nor all-powerful; he is, one may say, whatever responsible person possessing knowledge of statecraft he may happen to be, and Plato is simply describing one of the functions which he must perform to the extent of his power. We hear again of the necessity of culling out from the human flock the undesirables, before proceeding with the founding of a new city or the reform of an existing one. This a tyrant-legislator may do in an already established community, by the drastic methods of death and banishment of the incurably bad, useful methods not available to others. (It is worth noting that Plato, relying, perhaps, upon his reader's familiarity with his earlier expositions, does not pause here to make the all-important distinction between the tyrant as such, the very nadir of morality, and the gifted and uncorrupted young tyrant, of whom he hoped so much.) Weeding out by colonization is proposed: the dangerously disaffected poor, on the brink of revolutionary violence, may be encouraged to leave town in this fashion.[257] As to the more deserving poor, landless and crushed by a burden of debt to the great landowners, the legislative reformer must offer them aid. Outright confiscation or cancellation of debts is disallowed; the method recommended, a practice apparently falling somewhat on the hither

---

[257] At *Laws* 740 E, Plato again refers to the possibility that colonists may have to be sent out, this time after the establishment of the city, in the event that the citizens become too numerous for the available land allotments. Again he speaks of the process, not at all as a deportation, but as "the sending forth, in friendly wise from a friendly nation" (trans. Bury, Loeb Library) of suitable persons.

side of social realism, but one which had been exemplified in the Greek world, is piecemeal voluntary resigning, by the rich, of their excess of land and credit in favor of the dispossessed.[258] In this passage, as in the *Politicus*, the central topic of discussion is not the elimination of political enemies; the standard of "good citizen" is severely moral, or perhaps, we should say, penological. Where political reform is in view, as in the case of the revolutionary or landless poor, the measures advocated are not violent, and are directed to secure, in some degree, the interest of these persons themselves, as well as the good of the state as a whole. In both passages, there is evidence of Plato's participation in the general Greek attitude of severity toward the criminal, and of Plato's own scientific-authoritarian viewpoint in government. In neither is there indication of Plato's approval of revolutionary violence directed to the imposition by force of any sort of ideal state.

One of Popper's most extravagant assertions is that Plato had viewed as a "favorable circumstance" the presence in Athens of Spartan troops, summoned to assist the Thirty in maintaining themselves and their iniquitous regime [259] and had felt no other emotion than approval at the thought of Athens beneath the Spartan yoke; he would have been prepared, we are led

---

[258] This same end is to be made effective in the new city of the *Laws* by legislation preventing any citizen from selling his land, and setting a ceiling on individual wealth. All these measures, whether practical or not, show Plato's unwillingness to accept the *de facto* enslavement of any class of citizens to another class — something which Popper by his identification of Plato with the Old Oligarch most flagrantly ignores.

For an instance of the voluntary resignation of property rights in favor of the poor, see Aristotle's *Politics*, VI, 1320 b 9 ff., where it is reported of the Tarentines that "they gain the good will of the populace by sharing the use of their property with the poor." I am indebted for this citation to Minar, *Early Pythagorean Politics*, 1942, p. 90. It may be added here that Minar is at one with Winspear (cf. App. I, p. 583; p. 247) in interpreting the Pythagoreans as by no means essentially religious or philosophical-minded, but as a sort of international conspiracy of political conservatism dedicated to upholding, in the name of religion, the ideal of government by landed aristocrats; he agrees with Winspear also in seeing Plato's political thought as anticipated at most essential points by the Pythagoreans. The first of these theses, which rests largely on a tendency to inter-

pret ideologies as determined directly by class interest, plus the contention that the most influential Pythagoreans were aristocrats, is at variance with the view of the school generally taken by scholars in the field; see the reviews of Minar's study, *Am. Hist. Review*, XLIX, 1943, p. 870 f., by W. A. Oldfather, and *Pol. Sci. Q.*, LVIII, 1943, p. 304, by Kurt von Fritz. The second thesis presupposes the authenticity of late and probably spurious Pythagorean treatises which contain Platonic and Aristotelian ideas. One must also object to such a passage as that on pp. 103–104, where Plato's provisions in the *Laws* that private citizens shall act as public prosecutors are depicted solely as parallels to the cynically interpreted Pythagorean justification of enmity to lawbreakers, and to the Spartan system of spying on the Helots. The real parallel is clearly with the Athenian public suit, brought by an interested citizen (cf. the *graphê hybreôs*, mentioned on p. 151 above). Minar's theory of economic determinism, combined with his reasonable dislike of government by a cynically self-interested aristocracy of birth and wealth, seems thus to have led him to join Winspear in misplaced suspicions of Plato's political ideals.

[259] Popper, p. 190.

to suppose, to summon them again, if their presence could aid him in achieving his neo-oligarchical revolution. There is no text which Popper can cite
in support of such a charge; it arises solely from his picture of Plato as a
third head upon the double-headed monster whom he has created, called "the
Old Oligarch and Critias"; it is guilt by association, the very ultimate example of the witch-hunt technique. Plato's pride as an Athenian,[260] and his
obvious friendly contempt for the ordinary Spartan illiterate,[261] joined with
his serious philosophic conviction that the Spartan training aimed only at a
part of virtue and failed to inculcate self-command in the face of temptation
to license and brutality,[262] would have made him bridle at the very notion
of subordinating Athenian institutions to Spartan control. And once more,
such an act would have contravened that refusal to employ armed might to
the attainment of desired ends, against which he had so definitely set his face.

And here, with apparent inappropriateness, we must consider the treatment
proposed for atheists in the tenth book of the *Laws*. Before considering the
extent of Plato's guilt in this matter, we wish to enter a strong protest against
what we feel to be Popper's unfair tactic of introducing this topic in the degrading context of "brutal violence" and in the shadow of implied oligarchic
leanings.[263] One is tempted to remind Popper, at this point, that the death
penalty for atheism was no innovation of revolutionary oligarchs, and that
with slight verbal exaggeration one might more properly style it a "good old
Athenian democratic custom" to which Plato reverted in his old age. And as
to the suggestion that it is comparable to the arbitrary and illegal executions
for convenience and profit committed by the Thirty, be it remembered that
Plato has not proposed that summary violence be applied to the disbeliever.
On the contrary, the laws dealing with religious offenses of this class are made
part of the fundamental legislation of the city. There is, first of all, the "prelude" to the law itself, by far the most elaborately thought out of all these
persuasive introductions by which Plato hopes to establish a spirit of friendly

---

[260] In the *Laws*, Plato praises the older
Athens, as we have seen, and indicates his
belief that good Athenians are very good
(698 B ff., 642 C). In the *Menexenus*, we have
parallel praise of the Athens of Marathon,
and also much patriotic celebration of
Athenian prowess and service in the cause
of Greek freedom, down to and including
the peace of Antalcidas. In the *Menexenus*
(244 C–D), also, there is evidence of a feeling of bitterness against Sparta, who has
not only failed to match the magnanimity
of Athens, but has meanly deprived Athens
of her walls and fleet, in 404 B.C. These expressions of patriotic feeling are in the
Menexenus and therefore not necessarily
dependable at face value; they are con-

sistent and continuous, however, with the
attitude toward the events at the time of
Marathon, which we know from the *Laws*
to be Plato's own. In the *Timaeus* (24 C–
D) Plato makes the Egyptian priest declare
the climate of Attica best fitted to produce
men of supreme wisdom, who should also
be good warriors.

[261] The Spartan lack of cultivation is
made matter for jest at *Protagoras* 342 A ff.

[262] At *Laws* 633 D begins a long discussion tending to show the deficiencies of the
Cretan and Spartan laws in these respects.
Similar views are expressed in *Republic*
548 E–549 B. See pp. 510f. below.

[263] Popper, pp. 189, 194–195.

understanding between the citizen and the laws under which he is to live. In the present case, the prelude amounts to a substantial essay in natural theology, seeking to prove the existence of the gods, their inflexible justice never to be swayed by sacrifice or prayers, and their providential control of the universe, extending to the last detail. This preamble, which its author evidently regarded as constituting a clear and irrefragable demonstration, is the rational basis upon which the legislator proceeds.[264] We are not here concerned with details, but the following points require note: Plato provides for those accused of impiety public trials of three days' length before the city's highest court, corresponding roughly to the Athenian Areopagus. The law recognizes the occurrence of virtuous and candid atheists, as well as those who are hypocritical and vicious. The latter are confined, upon conviction, to lifelong isolated imprisonment in the penitentiary — to Plato's mind, the harshest of penalties. The good atheists are more considerately dealt with. For five years or more, they are reprieved, and during this time are confined to the reformatory, and there visited by the enlightened members of the Night Council, which is so named from the time (before sunrise) prescribed for its meetings, and is no secret, black, and irresponsible conclave, but is composed, in effect, of the teachers and students of jurisprudence and philosophy in the state (*Laws* 951 D ff., 961 A ff.). The councilors endeavor by all rational means to turn disbelievers from the path of error. If these suasions are successful, the reformed atheists are restored to their normal membership in the community; if not, they are put to death.[265] And here we

---

[264] *Laws* 907 D ff.; and for the court, 855 C ff., 767 C–E.

[265] It is interesting to notice the similarities and differences between Plato and a thinker who stood much under his influence, Rousseau. In the *Social Contract*, Rousseau also would condemn atheists, sharing Plato's conviction that God and the immortality of the soul are realities beyond dispute, and belief in them the necessary foundation of the moral life and of the community. The great difference is that Rousseau would give admitted atheists the right to go into voluntary exile, reserving death for those who conceal their disbelief. That Plato did not make the same provision is regrettable, but is explicable enough in view of the fact that the penal legislation of the *Laws*, unlike that of Athens, apparently contemplates the exile of citizens only in cases of homicide (the comedian of 935 E–936 A may be thought of, like the tragedian of 817 A f., as a noncitizen). Presumably, however, those who were accused of atheism could, like those accused of murder, choose to escape abroad rather than to stand trial.

A further comparison between Plato, Athens, and the Inquisition of Christian centuries will help to dispel the unjustified notion that Plato is to be considered the originator of persecutions for heresy, in a sense entirely distinct from Athenian precedent and basically identical with the methods and aims of the Inquisition. We start from the uncontested fact that both Plato and Athens in some sense countenanced religious persecution. Our further comparison of these two may be disposed under four chief headings, as follows:

(1) Plato, as elsewhere in his legislation and with even greater intensity in this general area (cf. p. 190, above), wishes to ensure that his laws shall be fully enforced, and intends, we may assume, to penalize even the private and inconspicuous expression of disbelief or disrespect; Athens, with secular unconcern, in general took no note of privately expressed disbelief,

must not allow our imaginations to be excited by Popper's word "inquisition," and especially by his ambiguous use of the phrase "the 'treatment,' " referring to the discussions and admonitions employed by the councilors. There is nothing in Plato's text to suggest cruelty, no hint of thumbscrews and the rack, nor of the more modern techniques of forced confession.[266] Plato's

---

though demanding public conformity and on occasion actively persecuting the open dissemination of irreligion or of doctrines thought conducive thereto (cf. p. 315 and n. 195, p. 324).

(2) Plato and Athens are alike in employing no harsh methods to elicit confession, inflicting no cruel punishments on those condemned.

(3) Both Plato and Athens provided public trials in the regular courts, with no special disabilities imposed on the accused.

(4) Plato in the method he prescribes for selecting the judges and in the procedure laid down for the conduct of the trials has sought to supply fuller protection than Athens afforded against hasty and unjust condemnation for all persons accused of capital crimes, including impiety.

It must also be noted that the minimum religious creed which Plato prescribes under penalty is a form of theism immeasurably more rational and ethical than the crude polytheistic cult to which Athens required conformity.

The relation between Plato, Athens, and the Inquisition may now be summarily stated, under the same numbered headings.

(1) On this point Plato will be found closer to the Inquisition than to Athens, since he will penalize inconspicuous impiety and privately expressed disbelief; yet he constructs no such machinery as was available to the Inquisition for invading the privacy of every man's conscience and ferreting out secret heresies.

(2) and (3) On both these points, Plato's kinship is with Athens, his distance from the Inquisition immense.

(4) Here Plato has attempted to do better than Athens; the Inquisition with its closed hearings and the all but unbounded discretion it assigned to the Inquisitors fell vastly below Plato's juridical level.

A further gap between Plato and the Inquisition is found in Plato's principled refusal to impose confiscation of property,

with its entailed injustice to the families of persons condemned, as a penalty for any serious crime, and his care explicitly to exempt the children of condemned atheists from suffering any disability; the Inquisition, as is notorious, made great use of confiscation.

References in the *Laws* for these statements include those given in the preceding note, and for the scrupulousness toward descendants, 909 C–D, 856 C–D.

On balance, then, Athens, Plato, and the Inquisition all persecute religious dissenters and nonconformists, but differ in the degree and manner of this persecution. In (1) above, we find Plato less liberal than Athens and closer to the Inquisition; he falls below Athens, also, in not allowing such milder penalties as exile. In (2) and (3) he resembles Athens. In (4) he rises or attempts to rise above both. In the quality of the creed he imposes and in his care to exempt the innocent, he outstrips now one, now the other. If Plato is to be called the father of the Inquisition, he is also both for good and for evil the son of Athens.

[266] The implications of Popper's invective terms, here as in other cases (e.g., "liquidation" and "brutal violence") have not failed of being caught by such a reader as Sherwood Anderson, who, demonstrably under Popper's spell, accuses Plato of proposing to employ "assassination" and "torture"; cf. our n. 19, p. 24. Nor should we permit modern sentiment to obscure the fact that Plato himself regarded the proposed death penalty as mild: he consistently teaches that death is the "least of evils," and in the case of the incurable offender, beneficial even to the man himself (*Laws* 862 E). For Plato, the honest disbeliever is "just" in terms of his own belief in what is best (for the inconsistency in Plato's thought on this point, see pp. 526–27); but being mistaken, "ignorant," on matters of the highest importance, he is none the less a wrong-doer, and harmful to himself and others.

inclusion of honest atheists among those worthy of the death sentence remains, even when presented in its fairest light, a matter not for lame justification by his adulating admirers, but for sincere regret. But without retracting anything of our dissent, we think that our survey of the facts of the case reveals that the law of death to atheists is neither a repudiation of the enlightened practice of Athenian democracy, nor an endorsement of oligarchic violence, nor a barbarous anticipation of medieval cruelty. Nor is it, as Popper has elsewhere implied, an expression of doubtful sincerity, by one who perhaps was himself a greater atheist, of a wish to restrain "other (lesser) atheists" in the interests of the master class.[267] It is, instead, the consequence of an excessive strength of conviction on Plato's part, and an excessive trust in the persuasive power of patient philosophic argument to turn honest but misguided souls about toward the light.

(5) Critias. In Plato's favorable allusions to his uncle Critias, both Fite [268] and Popper [269] have found sinister confirmation of Plato's sympathy with oligarchic violence. Accordingly, we must devote more attention to the charge of Plato's unreserved admiration for Critias than its inherent incredibility warrants, particularly because there are not wanting circumstances which, when regarded with a jaundiced eye, have some real chance of doing serious injury to Plato's reputation.

We may pass lightly over those nonpolitical evidences of Plato's friendly judgment of Critias as a younger man, which we noticed in the course of our earlier discussion of Plato's family pride. It would be merely arbitrary to insist that Plato should have gone out of his way by introducing condemnation in advance, any more than in the case of Alcibiades, of the wrongs that Critias and Charmides were scheduled later to commit. But the situation is different with a passage in a much later dialogue, the *Timaeus*, the political implications of which are unmistakable.

We have there (19 C–20 B) to do with a very substantial compliment paid by the Socrates of the dialogue to a character named Critias, who is said to be "no layman in these matters," that is, war, diplomatics, and philosophy, with an implied inclusion of the gifts of poetry and eloquence. Plainly, he is a distinguished gentleman, for whom Socrates-Plato cherishes a high regard. How great is this regard we can infer from the importance of the task assigned him: he is to be permitted to satisfy the wish of Socrates to have the citizens of the ideal Republic brought to life and action, in a narrative description of

---

[267] Popper, pp. 140–141. It is, as often, difficult to cite fairly what Popper has said, since he has so intricately compounded straightforward accusation with a show of generosity which, in turn, leads into further accusation. If anyone will read carefully the paragraphs at the foot of p. 140 and the two at the top of p. 141, he will see that the admission that there "may" be some genuine religious feeling in Plato, is promptly neutralized by the assertion that it is in all cases subordinated to "political opportunism" and to strengthening "the rule of the master class."

[268] Fite, p. 132.

[269] See p. 248 above.

that city engaged in a war worthy of her, and of "achievements . . . answerable to her education and training both in deeds of war and in diplomatic intercourse with various cities." [270] One may well feel that Plato could never have entrusted such a commission to anyone but one with whose standpoint and values he felt himself in cordial sympathy. Were these conditions satisfied by Critias? And if so, what becomes of the sincerity of Plato's idealistic program, with its radical condemnation of oligarchic violence? There are two ways of escape from this dilemma.

We may, with Burnet and Taylor,[271] return to a closer scrutiny of the opening pages of the *Timaeus* and find reason to doubt that the Critias there presented is one and the same with the tyrant Critias who was Plato's uncle, and cause for identifying him instead with that Critias' grandfather, an otherwise all but unknown older contemporary of Socrates who might have fought at Marathon. A major argument supporting this view is based on a substantial error in the chronology of Plato's family tree inseparable from the assumption that the Critias here introduced is indeed the tyrant. At *Timaeus* 21 B, "Critias"

---

[270] Quoted from Taylor's translation, *Plato: Timaeus and Critias*, 1929, 19 C.

[271] The identification of the Critias of the *Timaeus* as the grandfather of Critias the tyrant, apparently first made by Burnet (*Greek Philosophy from Thales to Plato*, 1914), is discussed in some detail by A. E. Taylor, in his *Commentary on Plato's Timaeus*, 1928, pp. 23–25. In the dialogue, "Critias" says that when he was ten years old, a time at which the poems of Solon were "new," he recited from these poems in the presence of his grandfather Critias, who was then close on ninety, whereupon this grandfather told him a tale which he had himself heard as a child from Solon, his father's friend and kinsman. If we take the customary view, and regard the Critias of the dialogue as the tyrant, of course the references made by Socrates to his literary gifts are appropriate enough. But this Critias was born somewhere near 450 B.C. (he was about the same age as Alcibiades), and would therefore have been ten years old in 440, hardly a time when Solon's poems were new. The grandfather would then have been born in 530, whereas Solon died ca. 558 B.C. On the other hypothesis, the Critias of the dialogue is himself about ninety. He was ten, therefore, in about 500, at which time the Peisistratid tyranny had been recently expelled, and the poems of Solon, presumably not current during the tyranny, would have been but newly revived. This supposition, therefore, saves the

chronology. A second strong argument derives from the distinct impression of venerable age which is conveyed by the Critias of the dialogue; his stress on the clarity with which he remembers the events of his long-ago childhood is important here. As justification for the praise bestowed by Socrates upon the Critias of the dialogue, Taylor and Burnet assign to the elder Critias authorship of some of the literary fragments which have come down under the name of Critias, and interpret as referring to the older man two comments on "Critias" in Aristotle. These arguments lend some support to the main contention, but in themselves are of slight importance. In short, it appears that the Taylor supposition receives its substantial support from the error demonstrably present in Plato's genealogy, if the Critias be taken as the tyrant, and from the dramatic depiction of the Critias of the dialogue as advanced in age; and it suffers from the substantial disadvantage that the elder Critias, though we know in either case that he existed, is otherwise unknown to have achieved personal distinction.

Dorothy Stephans in her doctoral dissertation, *Critias, Life and Literary Remains*, 1939, pp. 4–5, after careful consideration of the evidence, reaches the conclusion that the Burnet-Taylor view is "unquestionably" correct. It would be premature, however, to regard the point as definitely settled.

is made to say that his grandfather had learned from Solon, who in turn had heard from the Egyptian priests, a tale of ancient Athens, as she had been before a great flood which had destroyed the civilization of those days in Greece. A little arithmetic applied to this situation reveals that the grandfather of Critias the tyrant, at the time of Solon's death, was and would for some 25–30 more years remain unborn. Could Plato have made so gross an error in recounting an incident in the history of his own family, that family of which he was (we saw) rather pathetically proud? The anomaly is removed by the simple assumption, supported by further considerations of internal evidence, that we have here a case of mistaken identity, and that the Critias of the *Timaeus* is, appropriately enough, a very old man, linking his hearers in imagination to a very remote period verging on the legendary past. And so Plato has drawn him for us, depicting a man of dignity, who moreover lays stress on the very long time that has passed since he heard the tale, which he recollects with the clarity characteristic of the bright impressions of childhood (*Timaeus* 26 A–C). If Taylor and Burnet be judged to have made their case, the detractors have, *pro tanto*, lost theirs. But we dare not build upon this conclusion, favorable as it is to our interest, while reasonable doubt of its validity remains.

We must, therefore, consider the alternative possibility that "Critias" was Critias Tyrannus. Our knowledge of this man's political misdeeds derives principally from Xenophon's *Hellenica* and *Memorabilia*, reënforced by the orations of Lysias.[272] From these sources, enough evidence is available against Critias to procure his hanging in effigy before the most merciful court of historians. Once a popular leader and supporter of Alcibiades, his criminal career dates from his return from exile in Thessaly, along with his fellow oligarchs of the extreme persuasion, after the fall of Athens in 404, his heart burning with the hate of the accursed demos that had exiled him. Chosen one of the Thirty, who were originally a provisional government appointed with Spartan approval to draft a reformed constitution for Athens, the so-called "constitution of our fathers," he forced his way to the head of those least willing to employ constitutional methods. We hear of the summoning of a Spartan garrison, under whose protection he and his fellow extremists carried out a reckless program of confiscation and killing, including the murder of advocates of moderation within their own party (e.g., Theramenes), the execution of wealthy metics on false charges for their money, and the mass murder of the citizens at Eleusis. He met his end, after five months of misrule, fighting against the democratic forces led by Thrasybulus. This, then, is the man, and this his policy, that we are asked to put morally equal to the author of the *Republic*. This is the final underlining of our riddle: how could Plato, subsequent to the

---

[272] *Hellenica* II, iii, 11–56; iv, 1–19.   *Memorabilia* I, ii, 12–39; Lysias, XII, 43–45, 55; XIII, 59.

end of such a career, have put Critias in the honored seat of an elder statesman — the same Plato, moreover, who had written the condemnation contained
in the *Apology* of the deeds of the Thirty? One or other of two possible answers must, we think, be adopted.

It is possible that in the *Timaeus*, as in the *Charmides*, Plato was asking his
readers to think historically or dramatically, in terms of the implied date of
the conversation reported, and thus to think of a Critias yet unembittered by
exile and uncorrupted by power, in short, the Critias that he himself no doubt
remembered from the now far off and happy Socratic season of his youth. The
Timaeus, we saw, unless we make the assumption that it presents the older
Critias, is extremely careless of chronology, and even if we assume a relatively
early dramatic date, the younger Critias might be supposed to have had a
sufficent military and political record, combined with his substantial achievements in letters, to justify, with some exaggeration, the commendation of his
claims in these respects. In those times Critias had been the gifted and apparently high-principled man whom Socrates had honored with his friendship.[273] Plato must, then, have believed that in the interval Critias had been
radically corrupted, perhaps as a result of that process vividly described in
the *Republic* (565 B–C), whereby those who were at first not plotting against
the democratic constitution are converted, by the constant accusation that they
are oligarchs, into oligarchs in very truth, or in consequence of the exiled years
in that lawless Thessaly of which Socrates had spoken so disparagingly in the
Crito (53 D). Looking backward, Plato might well have discovered the seeds
of this corruption even before the exile, in Critias' period of service as popular
leader, an activity which, as we know from the *Gorgias* (512 E–513 B) and
from the *Republic* (492 B–D, 493 D), Plato regarded as morally perilous in
high degree. To this we may add the conviction we have earlier cited from the
Laws (875 A–D) and which may also be quoted from the *Gorgias* (526 A):
"A difficult thing it is, Callicles, and worthy of all praise, to reach a position
of great power to do wrong, and to live one's life through in justice, and few
indeed achieve this."

---

[273] An unprejudiced reading of the surviving fragments of Critias (Diels, 1922,
vol. II, p. 308ff.), after exposure to Popper's
comments upon them, should awaken surprise and suspicion of Popper's judgments.
The twin charges of "treacherous pro-
Spartan leanings as well as . . . oligarchic
outlook" (p. 594) are discovered to rest, so
far as Popper cites his evidence, solely upon
Critias' indictment (Diels, Fr. 45) of Athenian democratic leaders, e.g., Themistocles
and Cleon, for self-enrichment during office,
a charge which in itself may be partisan and
unjust but which has nothing to do with
treachery or Sparta; the "ambition" rests

upon the verses (Diels, fr. 15) in which,
like Horace in the first of his Odes, the poet
briefly describes the many several ideals of
human felicity, noble birth, wealth, etc.,
and concludes with a declaration of his own
preference for "the credit of fair fame";
the "blunt nihilism" is grounded on the
supposititious cynicism of the verses concerning the origin of religion, of which we
earlier (n. 72, p. 273) disposed. We do
know from Critias' later history that he was
infected with most of these faults, but it is
not the case that they are to be discovered,
as Popper has said, in his "extant writings."

We have still to consider the second possibility: Plato may not have believed that Critias ever really became the monster of iniquity that Xenophon and Lysias have painted. To employ a little freedom of psychological interpretation, we may point out that a too loyal admirer of one charged with grave wrongdoing is confronted with a choice between bringing himself to accept wrong as right — this would be Popper's supposition — and believing that somehow the admired person was not guilty of the wrong. One way in which Plato could have accomplished this latter feat is suggested by a passage in the *Politics* (1305 b 26) in which Aristotle asserts that Charicles, another of the Thirty whom both Xenophon and Lysias link with Critias as particularly influential, made himself the predominant member of the group by exercising a species of demagogic skill upon them. This statement of Aristotle contains no specification of date and makes no mention of Critias (indeed, Aristotle makes no mention whatever of Critias' activities as one of the Thirty); we have, therefore, little to guide us to a conclusion here; and unless Xenophon is wholly wrong, Critias cannot be substantially cleared. Nevertheless, it is possible that Plato may have persuaded himself that Critias was acting under the compulsive direction of Charicles, and was thus led into deeds contrary to his own will. One should note that both of these alternatives are in accord with the evidence of the Seventh *Letter*, and of the *Apology*, which condemn unequivocally the actions of the Thirty, but without specification of persons.

Our conclusion then would be: Plato in the *Timaeus* is either praising the tyrant's grandfather, or else commending a Critias either not yet, or (to Plato's fond belief) never destined of his own will to become a tyrant. To which we may add that one decisive fact is clear beyond contest: whoever the Critias of the *Timaeus* was or became, Plato does not make him an occasion for commending or justifying tyrannic rule.

There remains unexplored in our treatment of Plato's relation to the Athenian political scene and that of Greek politics generally, an area of his activity to which political significance may have attached, his direction of his famous Academy. The detractors have unhesitatingly ascribed to it this meaning. Crossman regards the Academy as "an 'open conspiracy' to clean up Greek politics," Plato's instrument for converting young aristocrats "into statesmen who voluntarily submitted to the law of reason" and who were then, so Plato hoped, to be "vested with absolute power in the cities of Greece." [274] Popper holds essentially the same view, but with more bitterness and less concession to the rationality of Plato's aims, remarking that not a few of Plato's chosen candidates for absolute power later became tyrants.[275] Neither critic offers any documentation of this view of the Academy, which they derive apparently from

---

[274] Crossman, pp. 116, 125–126.   [275] Popper, pp. 134–135. Cf. our note 291, p. 370 below.

the *Republic* by adding together the higher education of the Guardians and Plato's statement that even a single philosophic inheritor of absolute power would suffice to realize the ideal city.

In the discussion to follow, we shall hope to present evidence sufficient to disprove these particular charges; it will also become apparent in the process that the founding of the Academy was not, as Popper conceives it, a crime against the freedom of the human mind,[276] but a memorable step in the progress of higher education and a credit to the intelligence and conscience of its founder. Materials for reconstructing a full, circumstantial account of life at the Academy are not available. But inferences sufficient for our more modest purpose may be drawn not alone from the Platonic writings but also from references in fourth-century literature, eked out by cautious use of traditions surviving in later writers.

Whoever might wish to prove that the founding of the Academy was inspired by a desire to engage in oligarchic conspiracies, or to impose philosophic rule upon Athens or Greece at large, might appeal to the passage in the Seventh Letter (325 D–326 B) where Plato (if it is he) declares that in the lack of "friends and trusty associates" he was forced to abandon his earlier hope of active participation in politics and of improvement in the Athenian government, and that he came finally to declare the impossibility of governmental reform in general until philosophic wisdom should be united with political power. This statement appears to leave open the question of revolutionary intent. The question, however, is decisively closed later in the same letter (331 C–D) by the declaration, previously mentioned, that a man should stand ready to advise but must never offer violence to his native city. If, then, we are to use this letter as a key to Plato's purpose, we shall be within our rights in arguing that the Academy was not intended to serve as a headquarters for revolution,

---

[276] *Ibid.*, pp. 133–134. An instructive instance of Popper's temperamental readiness to condemn *in toto* whatever is in his eyes infected with any degree of fault, is provided by his rather extraordinary feat of crediting Plato with the invention of "both our secondary schools and our universities," only in order to discredit both him and them. "This devastating system of education," he declares, offers the best proof of basic human decency in the bare fact that it "has not utterly ruined" all its victims. Plato, he asks us to note, proposed to select the "best" from among the students in his ideal city to serve as rulers, and, Popper implies, designed and operated the Academy along similar lines. By so doing, he has vitiated all subsequent institutions of learning, substituting crude "personal ambition" as the student's motive in studying, for "a real love . . . of inquiry," and stifling originality by causing students to be judged in terms of conformity to the opinions of those in authority. We are in accord with Popper's view that universities should not select rulers; universities today, it is also agreed, have not solved the problem of separating their accrediting function from their function in teaching and stimulating. But these objections do not appear to justify the wholesale condemnation either of the existing institutions or of the act of their originator in summoning them into existence. Nor is it proved that Plato's educational principles led in his own practice to the ill consequences which Popper believes their inevitable outcome; see App. XII, p. 619, where reference is made to Cherniss' proof of Plato's wide tolerance of dissent among the members of his Academy.

either at Athens or elsewhere, but as a little colony of peaceful men, fitted to offer sound advice on political affairs, or to support the responsibility of public office, by reason of their possession of true philosophy.

The dialogues are, of course, our best means of discovering what, for Plato, was the promise of that philosophy which the Academy was designed to propagate. The *Phaedrus* describes the finished dialectician and master of rightly directed speech, who can both distinguish and combine, teach and persuade, and who "has knowledge of the just and the good and the beautiful." [277] Such a man, Plato declares in a passage of great depth of conviction (276 E–277 A) "employs the dialectic method and . . . sows in a fitting soul intelligent words . . . which are not fruitless but yield seed from which there spring up in other minds other words capable of continuing the process forever, and which make their possessor happy, to the farthest possible limit of human happiness." [278] This citation expresses *in nuce*, as we shall hold, Plato's aim in establishing and maintaining his school throughout the years. Such teaching found its initial application to the private individual, who, if endowment and effort sufficed, was to be brought simultaneously to become good and to know the good (for Plato never admitted that the two, in the highest sense of each, could be kept apart). Again in the *Republic* we encounter the just man and private citizen of an ordinary Greek state, who (591 C ff.) will establish first and guard as his chief treasure the order in his soul, and will participate in the politics of his unregenerate home city only by some providential chance; such a man (496 E), we have already heard, "will take his departure with fair hope, serene and well content when the end comes," though he may have been compelled to spend his whole life in retirement. Education for such a life the Academy would certainly supply.

And concurrently, by the self-same training, the Academy aimed also to fit its pupils for political life, since, on Plato's view, the just man in private life was also the man best fitted to direct affairs of state. The master of true rhetoric, in the *Phaedrus*, we cannot doubt is such a man. The whole *Republic* may be said to assert that the just man, the philosopher, if conditions permit, will serve best both his own and his country's highest interest by taking public office. And the same identity of qualification is asserted, as we shall see, throughout the dialogues. We may then truly call the Academy from its very beginning a school of politics, but only in this highly Platonic sense.

We have also the testimony of one of Plato's contemporaries, Isocrates, who has reported to us from his own known standpoint how the Platonic Academy appeared to him in its bearing upon political life. As head of a competing school, he may be trusted to have been well acquainted with the general character of the educational program of his distinguished rival. It is, therefore,

---

[277] *Phaedrus*, 266 D–E, 271 D–272 B, 276 C.

[278] *Ibid.*, 276 E–277 A, trans. Fowler, Loeb Library.

of considerable interest to find that his most serious objection to that program was precisely its impractical and unpolitical character, its insistence upon argumentation and mathematics, which, if long pursued, Isocrates believes, must "ossify" the mind, and its neglect of those realities of daily living and the contemporary political scene which, he does not hesitate to let us know, are best learned in his own school.[279]

Searching for more concrete indications of the conduct of Plato's school, its methods and subject matter, we find that for the earlier years of the Academy our sources are disappointing. It has been suggested that Plato turned to educational purposes in his Academy a regulated conviviality, less exuberant, we may suppose, than that depicted in his *Symposium*, and resembling more closely the sedate spirit underlying the prescriptions for the use of wine in the *Laws*.[280] Few would dispute the probability that the curriculum proposed for the higher education of the Guardians in the *Republic* is an idealized reflection of that followed in the Academy, with adaptations dictated by the difference between the actual and the ideal environments; in the Academy, for example, there could have been no possibility of delaying till the age of thirty the pupils' first encounter with criticisms of law and accepted moral beliefs, or of providing fifteen years' experience after the age of thirty-five in war and public administration.

We are on ampler but by no means always undisputed ground in approaching the Academy as it was during the last twenty years of Plato's life. A contemporary comic poet has poked fun at the pedantic methods of definition and division employed by the youthful pupils of Plato, who are shown dividing and classifying the world of plants and animals (with logical, not with biological intent), with a refinement that reaches its comic climax in determining the genus of a pumpkin. A rude interruption is ignored, and Plato, unperturbed, mildly bids the youths go forward with the task.[281] When we examine the dialogues of Plato's later period, we make no doubt of what is being scoffed at here. It is the identical method that we saw exemplified in the *Sophist* and again in the *Politicus*.[282] The comedian confirms the inference from these dialogues that Plato was faithfully applying to his students the high standard of rigorous intellectual training without which he believed no one could attain mastery either of private virtue or of the true art of politics.[283] The conformity which is indicated to exist at this one point between Academic practice and the contents of the later dialogues encourages us to go further in the same direction, and to hold that the later dialogues, though there is no reason to believe

[279] *Antidosis* 258–268, *Panath.* 26–28.
[280] See pp. 30–31 above.
[281] Epicrates, Fr. 11 (Kock), Athenaeus ii, 59 C.
[282] Cf. p. 349.
[283] Harold Cherniss, in his Sather Lectures, *The Riddle of the Early Academy*, 1945, is occupied in disallowing the claims of those who assume that Aristotle, or anyone else, has given adequate evidence of the existence of any other "philosophy of Plato" than that contained in the dialogues. He accepts none of the *Letters* as genuine and repels all suggestions of an oral tradition

they give a rounded picture of Academic teaching, can yet be drawn upon substantially for a knowledge of its spirit and subject matter. On the basis of this probability, let us see what relevant conclusions may fairly be drawn.

Our attention is engaged first by the training the young respondents in several of the later dialogues are shown receiving at the hands of the older man who, in each case, is guiding the discussion. They are being relieved of false preconceptions, and introduced, by example, to the turns and technical refinements of dialectic; [284] they are warned of moral dangers and edified by being made parties to demonstrations of noble truth. These young men are depicted as eager and docile learners, a little too close to the educator's dream. But their appreciativeness is fully matched by the engaging courtesy and affectionate consideration with which they are treated by their preceptors, reminding us of the attitude of Socrates in the *Lysis* and *Charmides*, though

---

supplementing the dialogues. On his way to establish this position, he has touched several points of concern to our present discussion. For Cherniss (pp. 62–63), the evidence of the comic playwright regarding activities of the Academy is negligible: its substance could have been drawn directly from Plato's published works, its form and satiric point are borrowed from his older brother-comedian's *Clouds*, ll. 191 ff. The great weight of Cherniss' authority might dismay us here were it not that this point is peripheral to his argument. If I were to risk debate, I should stress the following points: (1) Two other names are linked with that of Plato; the poet undertakes to tell what Plato and Speusippus and Menedemus are doing. This looks in the direction of the Academy, and could not have been derived from the dialogues. (2) The borrowing from Aristophanes is limited to the surface and does not deprive the satiric picture of a distinctive realism of its own. (3) First- or second-hand observation, enlivened by the talk of the town, seems on general principles a more likely basis for a popularly acceptable comedy than such abstruse and widely unknown documents as the later Platonic writings.

[284] Again, and this time on a major issue, we have taken a position in apparent opposition to that of Cherniss. I say apparent, for it is my belief that most if not all of the contradiction can be removed by careful attention to terminology. Cherniss, *op. cit.*, basing his argument upon the educational provisions of the *Republic* which

forbid dialectic to those below the age of thirty, has denied that Plato would have been more permissive to his younger students in the Academy. Premature requests for explanations of metaphysical points would have been met with recommendation of more time devoted to "abstract thinking and debate," and with the answer, "first, more of the preliminary studies, the exercise of the mind and the cultivation of the character; metaphysics is for the mature!" We may inquire in this connection whether it is necessary to assume quite so precise a transplantation to the environment of actual Athens of the schedule designed for the citizens of the ideal city; we have pointed out above (p. 365) two discrepancies which might have rendered some modification necessary and desirable. Cherniss proceeds to draw the conclusion relevant to his particular interest, namely: that on his premises, it is unthinkable that Plato "came before pupils under thirty years of age . . . and glibly lectured to them on the doctrine of ideas; in fact, . . . [it seems] highly improbable that he lectured on the doctrine or tried to *teach* it at all" (pp. 69–70). And with this I fully agree. What is required for the security of our position is simply that the ban on "dialectic" which Cherniss supposes to have been operative in the Academy shall not be construed to have excluded young men from engaging, under responsible direction, in dialectical and metaphysical discussions comparable to those exemplified in the *Theaetetus*, the *Sophist*, and the rest.

now containing no hint of gallantry.[285] All this on our premises may be seen as an expression of the paternal interest taken by the master of the Academy in the progress of his young wards.

We have mentioned the curriculum of the *Republic* as a most probable indication of the course of studies in the earlier Academy. We find plentiful evidence in the later dialogues of Plato's unflagging interest in the mathematical sciences which figured so prominently in the list. In the *Laws* Plato insists that every citizen must learn enough of geometry to grasp the incommensurability of certain magnitudes, and of astronomy to recognize the periodical regularities of the heavenly bodies, thus to avoid "swinish" ignorance and blasphemy (819 D ff.), while the Law-wardens and their younger associates must pursue a course of study (965 A ff.) substantially at one with that prescribed for the guardians in the Republic. Since it cannot be supposed that Plato would be content with any less knowledge for those under his charge, we are required to think that mathematics in all its branches retained to the end the importance Plato had accorded it in the earlier days of the Academy. The *Laws* also confirms what the other late dialogues tell us of the continued importance of dialectic and of its application to the structure of the good for man; we are also reminded of Plato's overweening certainty that dialectics thus applied would infallibly demonstrate the priority of souls and the divine ordering of the universe.

While the younger members of the Academy pursued these basic studies as far as their capacities and their leisure allowed, the maturer men conducted more advanced inquiries of their own. For we must not forget that the Academy contained notables other than Plato, among them that versatile genius Eudoxus, whose contribution to the theory of planetary motion was one of the major achievements of ancient science, not to speak of the young Aristotle, whose researches seem to have been in progress in the last years of Plato's life. That Plato himself engaged in extensive researches, whether alone or in company with others, is made evident by the acquaintance with scientific speculation in many branches of physical and biological science shown in the *Timaeus*, and by the extensive knowledge of history, sociology, and comparative law embodied in the *Laws*. If we are not justified in calling the institution that sheltered and guided these manifold activities by the name of "university" in the full encyclopedic sense of that word, it was, nevertheless, the *alma mater* of all subsequent *alma maters*, and if the descendants have evolved be-

---

[285] See *e.g.*, *Sophist* 234 C–E, 266 D–E, *Politicus* 268 D–E, *Parmenides* 130 A–B. This attitude in the later dialogues is close cousin to that shown in the *Theaetetus*, and also in the *Phaedo*, where as Popper, p. 492, n. 17, has commented, Socrates' manner to the young men is "pleasant, kind, and respectful." We cannot, however, permit Popper to claim the credit solely for Socrates. What Socrates is shown to do and say in the *Phaedo* has Plato's earnest concurrence.

yond the ancestral form, the Academy loses thereby nothing of its native luster.[286]

We have here, then, the picture of a community of scholars and scientists engaged in lifelong study, among whom came and went an indeterminate number of younger men, differing in ability, remaining for varying lengths of time, and progressing in their mathematical and dialectical studies to correspondingly different levels of attainment. That Plato intended all of these to acquire absolute power and rule alone, without law, as do the philosopher kings of the *Republic*, only a rash man would maintain. More credible is the supposition that Plato hoped his alumni would emerge enamored of intellectual insight and moral truth, and less inclined to confuse the holding of power with the possession of the good. That he expected the best of them to become capable at last of the disinterested exercise of power one must also believe. In the exceptional case, this might mean personal sovereignty, employed to impose just and constitutional rule; in the millennial instance, even the founding of a city akin to the ideal. More expectably, it would take the form of service in the capacity of legislative expert for new colonies or for the reform of existing constitutions.

In sum, our review of the evidence has, we hope, made clear the robbery

---

[286] Ernst Howald (*Die platonische Akademie und die moderne Universitas Litterarum*, Zurich, 1921) sharply attacked the then prevalent picture of Plato's school as something very like a modern Institute for Advanced Study, where specialists in the various fields of inquiry carried on research under the direction of a Plato before whose "royal superiority of intelligence the greatest mathematicians bowed" (Usener, *apud* Howald, *op. cit.*, p. 4). Howald did good service in removing the exaggeration that pious Platonists had interposed between us and the reality, but he also laid heavy hands upon the reality itself. For Howald, Plato is the eternal type of the unscientific transcendentalist, for whom the "facts" held neither interest nor authority; and he sees the Academy as a religious association of like-minded mystics on the Pythagorean model.

In my judgment, Jaeger (*Aristotle*, 1934, pp. 13–23) has retained what is valid in Howald's overcorrection. Jaeger leaves standing a considerable part of the Academy's scientific reputation, e.g., its contributions to the progress of mathematics and astronomy, and without adulating Plato's supposed scientific genius or leaving out of sight his basically ethical aim, recognizes the extent to which Plato in the later period of his life turned in the direction of more empirical and scientific inquiry, creating in the Academy an atmosphere in which Aristotle's empiricism was made possible. There is also in Jaeger confirmation of the point of view developed in our text, as suggested by his statement that the later dialogues present a picture of the work of the Academy "that lacks no essential feature" (p. 15). But Jaeger goes further than I should wish to follow him in speaking of the Academy as "a communion of the elect" (p. 23), a phrase which seems to me unfortunate in implying an extreme exclusiveness which nothing in the record supports. Jaeger is quoting from the Seventh Letter a passage which has no necessary application to the Academy (341 C–E). No doubt Plato exercised a considerable discretion in his "admission policy," but the question who were the elect could only have been solved, we must suppose, subsequent to admission. Even in the *Republic*, Plato did not imagine it possible to determine the future guardians without recourse to a series of rigorous tests spread over a period of many years.

by omission committed by those who endow the Academy with a purely political intention, to the neglect of the richness of its aim. And not less clearly we have sought to show the calumny of those who have discovered in it nothing more than a hissing nest of fledgling tyrants.

The Sicilian Venture

Our knowledge of Plato's political experience and activity is fortunately not restricted to his almost wholly passive and theoretical relation to the Athenian scene. We are able to follow him onto the wider and more exciting stage of his Sicilian journeys, where he became in the fullest sense a participant, almost a protagonist. Our sources here are troubled with uncertainty; we must rely, for all practical purposes, exclusively upon those among the collection of thirteen letters traditionally ascribed to Plato which contemporary scholarship generally regards as genuine, or at the very least as composed at an early enough date and by a sufficiently well-informed person to possess historical authority. In the opinion of almost all scholars, these conditions are satisfied by Letters VII and VIII, by all odds the most substantially informative among the collection. Several other letters have won a considerable degree of acceptance.[287] But we shall draw only upon the two mentioned, with two exceptions, to be explicitly noted.

---

[287] See R. S. Bluck, *Plato's Life and Thought*, Routledge and Kegan Paul, London, 1949, p. 189, for a summary of the opinions of authorities upon the authenticity of the letters taken individually, upon which the assertion in the text is based.

Because of my somewhat anomalous relation to the problems of interpretation rising out of the Platonic *Letters*, documents with which willy-nilly any writer about Plato the man must deal, I offer here a short explanation of my standpoint and the reasons (and causes, so far as I am aware of them) underlying it. As a pupil of the late Dr. Paul Shorey, I came under the influence of a master of Plato's language and thought whose attitude toward the *Letters* was one of uncompromising, but, I believe, discerning objection. As Shorey has made the grounds of his disbelief publicly available (see *What Plato Said*, 1933, p. 40 ff.) I need deal with them but briefly. For Shorey all the letters save the Seventh and Eighth are obviously vitiated by such un-Platonic traits as gross superstition, affectation of a secret, incommunicable doctrine, and sophistical triviality. Letters VII and VIII he could not accept in view of what

seemed to him lesser faults; even these two, however, and *a fortiori* all the rest, seemed to him "incompatible with what we can infer from Plato's undisputed writing was probably his own moral character, and certainly his moral tact" (p. 41). But though unable to believe that these two best letters were from Plato's own hand, Shorey agrees that if not Plato's, they "must have been composed not later than a generation or two after his death by some Platonist who must have had access to the facts and who was himself so steeped in Plato's later writings that he could plausibly imitate their style."

Accepting Shorey's general position, then, I have treated the major letters, i.e., VII and VIII, as probably reliable sources of knowledge in respect to all external facts and plans and intentions which must have been known to Plato's associates in the Academy; I have also indicated the conditional nature of my argument whenever it is based upon the *Letters*. But in deference to the collective wisdom and authority of the majority of latter-day interpreters, who, like Field, Bluck, and Morrow, would accept as genuine the greater number of the Letters, and who regard VII and VIII as unques-

We are now about to submit these letters to a brief inspection, in order to extract from them what they are able to tell us of Plato's attempt at a practical application of his political ideals. We are the more obligated to this fuller scrutiny in view of our having drawn from the Seventh Letter in confirmation of Plato's moral disapproval of the Thirty. Impartiality of method demands that we include whatever else creditable or discreditable the record may contain.

The bare facts of Plato's three Sicilian journeys have been incorporated, with a minimum of interpretation, in the *Vita* of Chapter 3,[288] and need not be repeated here. But we must give some account of how these facts have appeared to the detractors. Fite, as we have seen,[289] treats the whole story as a record of Plato's pedantic ineptitude and childish vanity. He pays no heed to the specific political intentions or results. Popper has abstained from any substantive concern with the letters, having made a compact with himself to rest no part of his argument upon writings not assuredly genuine,[290] and having, moreover, preferred to interpret Plato as preoccupied with conspiring to establish himself as the philosopher king of Athens. Nevertheless, he has found in Plato's relations to Sicilian affairs, especially through the participation of his pupils from the Academy in Dion's armed overthrow of the tyranny at Syracuse, what he thinks good reasons for reasserting Plato's advocacy of an indefensible use of power.[291]

Crossman, regarding letters VII and VIII, at least, as unquestionably

---

tionably Plato's own, I have given more space to arguments based upon the personal and subjective details of Letters VII and VIII than my private conviction would warrant.

[288] See pp. 42–44 above.

[289] See pp. 55–56, and 67 above.

[290] Popper, p. 475, note 5 to chapter 3. Popper does on one occasion utilize the letters (p. 606, note 57 to chapter 10) in conditional corroboration of his own theory that Plato in the dialogues consciously misrepresents the views of Socrates.

[291] Popper, pp. 134, 550, and 610. Popper, following Athenaeus (XI, 508), lists with relish several members or supposed members of the Academy who were subsequently involved in usurpations or assassinations. Athenaeus, to whom Zeller (*Plato and the Earlier Academy*, 1888, p. 30, n.) refers as an "adversary" of Plato, is a biassed and almost irresponsible source where Plato is concerned, directing against him an often grossly inaccurate and scurrilous diatribe (XI, 504 C–509 E), of which the passage in question forms part. We need not doubt that

some of Plato's pupils turned out to be unprincipled men. But we may still object that Popper has given undue weight to these unhappy instances by his failure to list also the pupils or associates who are said to have had honorable success as legislative experts (Plutarch, *Adv. Colotem.* 1126 C, apud Taylor, *Plato*, 1929, p. 464). Further, Popper has not observed that in the Greek world of that day, many a young man of wealth and influence became an unprincipled and ambitious seeker after power, without benefit of any philosophic teaching; it was this general breakdown of the old social bonds and moral influences that set for both Socrates and Plato the problem of finding new grounds for the threatened values. Popper has urged in defense of Socrates, the teacher of Critias and Alcibiades, a plea which we may borrow for use in Plato's behalf: "He went out of his way to attract young men and to gain influence over them, especially when he . . . thought that some day they might possibly hold offices of responsibility" (Popper, p. 186).

genuine, has treated Plato's Sicilian experiences with seriousness and respect, but finds in them grounds for the gravest indictment of Plato's political philosophy as impracticable, and destined to achieve only illiberal results. Crossman's Plato, on setting out for Syracuse at Dion's and Dionysius' invitation in 367 B.C., carried in his satchel the *Republic*, which was his political program, "composed with the possibility of an invitation from Syracuse constantly in view.[292] Plato did not, however, anticipate its immediate realization in Syracuse. The steps which were to precede and to condition the embodiment of the ideal state were three: (1) the education of Dionysius as a philosopher was to be begun; (2) the governing clique at the Syracusan court were to be morally reformed and induced to abnegate their wealth; (3) the Greek cities of Sicily were to be restored,[293] supplied with aristocratic constitutions, and set under the young king's rule. Once Dionysius should be successfully educated into a philosopher, Plato believed, "everything else would follow of its own accord," that is, the *Republic* would become a political fact.[294]

Crossman reports without malice the collapse of these hopes, representing Plato's motives as honorable and his plans, while doomed to failure, as not absurdly visionary. But after the unsuccessful third trip, in 361 B.C., Crossman believes, Plato's faith in the program of the *Republic* "collapsed like a house of cards." Despairing of the possibility of ideal rulers, he turned to the planning of constitutional governments in which "the freedom and liberty of the subject" are preserved, as giving "at least some protection against tyranny." [295]

We are now told of Dion's attempt, after his successful *coup d'état* and expulsion of Dionysius from Syracuse, to introduce there "a modern system of cabinet responsibility to a popular assembly," [296] and of the failure of this type of constitutional government to win the support of any of the major pressure groups in Syracusan politics. The resulting bloodshed and civil turmoil marks, for Crossman, "the end of the attempt to put Plato's philosophy into practice." [297] Dion met death at the hand of an assassin. To Plato was left only guilt, frustration, a turn to pacifism, and death.

Crossman presently gives us in retrospect what he regards as the three major assumptions underlying the *Republic* as a political program: (1) the ordinary man is incapable of self-government; (2) there do exist individuals capable of absolute rule; (3) these individuals will most often be found in the ranks of the gentry. From these three taken together, Crossman believes, Plato drew a conclusion which "transforms the *Republic* . . . to an aristoc-

---

[292] Crossman, p. 107.
[293] The Greek population of these cities had been compulsorily removed to Syracuse by Dionysius I, in pursuance of his policy of centralization.

[294] Crossman, pp. 267–268.
[295] Crossman, p. 272.
[296] *Ibid.*, p. 274.
[297] *Ibid.*, p. 275.

racy of *birth*" in which the claims of the abler members of the inferior class are quietly dropped from view. In consequence, Plato's message, despite its author's intentions,[298] becomes simply "the practical proposition, 'the best of the existing aristocracy should become dictators.' " [299]

Having heard Crossman's view, we may now proceed to our own interpretation, to be followed by a final balancing of accounts. We must first ask what meaning is to be attached to the mere fact that Plato permitted himself to participate as he did in the political affairs of Syracuse. Apart from the particular policies that he attempted to carry out, what significance is there in the type of association which Plato consented to enter with the two Dionysii, and with Dion? Even before he first visited Syracuse, in 389–388 B.C., as a man of about 40, he must have known by report how affairs were managed under the ruthless Dionysius I, and the Seventh Letter (326 B–D) records his first strongly unfavorable impressions of life at the Syracusan court. The blistering word picture of the tyrant in the *Republic* (565 C ff.), however much or little it may have borrowed from the physiognomy of the man whom Plato met,[300] would in any case make it difficult to understand how its painter could enter into a lifelong idealistic friendship with a man, Dion, who was doubly related by marriage to the despot, and was later to serve him for many years as his admiral and trusted minister. We must explain, too, how Plato could consent to involve himself, at Dion's instance, in the affairs of that tyrant's son, Dionysius II.

As to Dion, he must have seemed, when Plato came to know him on his first voyage to Sicily, to have been a soul well worth the saving, young, able, passionately responsive to the philosophic stimulus that Plato gave [301] — in short, a sort of stabler Alcibiades with a conscience. But what shall we make of the ensuing friendship running through the years, between Plato the tyrannophobe and Dion, the servant of a tyrant's will? There is, obviously, something here to be explained. But without doing violence to any of the attested facts, Plato's defender can urge the following: the evidence shows only that Dion continued to perform the duties that devolved upon him as an officer of the existing government, which Plato had taught him to disapprove. In the making of this government, perhaps the most powerful in the world of that

---

[298] For Crossman's testimony to Plato's good intentions, see his p. 284.

[299] Crossman, p. 281. Crossman's belief that Plato's actual plan in Syracuse was simply to moralize the existing upper classes and confirm their tenure of power, has apparently influenced his interpretation of the *Republic* so far as to cause him to discount Plato's plain statement in the *Republic* that in the ideal state the most highly endowed children of whatever social origin are to be educated as guardians. It is our conviction, defended on p. 540, that Plato meant precisely what he said.

[300] Some elements in the portrait of the tyrant in the *Republic* are closely paralleled by characteristics of Dionysius I; others, notably sensual indulgence, do not seem to have been drawn from this source. Cf. Wilamowitz, 1948, pp. 343–344.

[301] *Letter* VII, 327 A–B.

day, Dion had had no hand; it was fully established by the time Dion reached maturity, and had incidentally been honorably recognized by a decree of the Athenians in 394–393, during Dion's boyhood.[302] If we may believe Plutarch's moralizing tale, Dion was also the only person at the court with the hardihood of speaking out his disapproval in the face of the tyrant himself.[303] Chief point of all, as soon as the realities admitted of taking definite action, upon the death of Dionysius I, he unhesitatingly moved in the direction of his political ideals and sent for the admired Plato to help him train Dionysius II for the role of constitutional monarch and pattern of all human excellence (we shall justify our assertion here on a later page). It would seem unreasonable to ask more than this from Dion, unless one takes the view that in the interests of pure Platonic ideality, he should have abandoned all hope of contributing to future reform and have gone forth, an impoverished exile, to accept perhaps board and room at the Academy, or more realistically, to find precarious employment as a soldier of fortune.[304]

But if Plato's friendship with Dion has thus seemed to require explanation, Plato's own intervention in Syracuse needs no defense. It was consistent with all that was best in Plato that he should have been prepared to face the realities of power in the hope of turning it in a beneficent direction. And in coming to the court of Dionysius II in 367 and again in 361 B.C., Plato was propelled, as the letters show us, by highly creditable motives. He was responding to the call of Dion, to whom as friend he felt an obligation. Even more compelling was his basic commitment to the principles of his philosophic creed, which obligated him to help in the peaceful and persuasive creation, wherever possible, of communities enjoying a happiness based upon virtue.[305] These principles he had proclaimed, and where they bade he would

---

[302] *C. A. H.*, VI, 132–133.

[303] Plutarch, *Life of Dion*, v, 4–5.

[304] The particular criticism of Plato which this paragraph has attempted to answer is found in a recent semifictional "double biography," *Plato and Dionysius*, by Ludwig Marcuse, 1947. The little book is rather more inclusive than its title suggests, covering the relations, as its author sees them, between Athens, Socrates, Plato, the two Dionysii, and Dion, with an epilogue on Plato's message for the world today. It is a witty and readable performance in spite of what to my taste is its unfortunate attempt to tell a solemn tale with journalistic flippancy. Mr. Marcuse has made free use of his apparently extensive learning; one did not expect and does not get documentation for his sometimes breathtaking interpretations, for example his notion that the *Republic* is a love letter addressed to Dio-

nysius I, wooing him to become the perfect ruler. Though on occasion Marcuse figures as a Platonic detractor, and throughout exempts none of the persons dealt with from his condescending ridicule, on balance the book is a substantial approval of Plato as a man who set the example of refusal to accept tamely the unacceptable *status quo*, and instead championed the Deed, even the dangerous and perhaps mistaken Deed, which, Marcuse affirms, is the only hope even today of escaping intolerable evils.

[305] Here we may recall Toynbee's rebuke (vol. VI, pp. 255–259) to Plato for thinking he could remain a philosopher with a sword concealed in his mantle. I do not think Toynbee's criticism is separable from his fundamental tenet that the Lord has supplied the only fit guide for humanity in the person of a Christ crucified; in rejecting Plato as savior, Toynbee has done him the

follow, despite the uncertainties of the enterprise (VII, 328 B–C, 329 B) and even the very real risk which was involved: it should not be forgotten that those who incurred a tyrant's displeasure might count themselves fortunate to escape with their lives (VII, 350 C). Plato felt, for all these reasons, that his self-respect was deeply involved. Some have seen in the last-mentioned motives no more than the vanity of a self-regarding wish to show the world that he was no obscure schoolmaster "whispering in a corner to three or four striplings" (*Gorgias* 485 D), but a professional counselor of kings. To say this is to confuse self-respect with self-regard, and to ignore the nature of the self in question.

We approach now consideration of the actual program that Plato and Dion attempted to set up in place of the existing tyranny. And here we confront our basic disagreement with Crossman. We cannot follow him in his belief that it was Plato's hope and expectation, after a period of preparation lasting perhaps (Crossman does not specify) no more than a decade or so, to see rising from the reform of the tyranny the whole shining fabric of the Republic,[306] complete with the communism of the ruling class and the dictatorship of a philosopher in the person of the converted Dionysius II.

We cannot accept the notion that the *Republic* bears clear traces of having been written with any such application in view. Syracuse, like Athens, and in even higher degree, was extremely ill-fitted for conversion into the compact, ordered, and austere city of the *Republic*. And as to Dionysius II, nothing in the record could have suggested to Plato that he possessed that extraordinary endowment of intellect and moral genius by which the philosopher kings had been defined, and on the basis of which they were to have been selected from among the most promising members of their generation. It must be remembered, too, that those exalted beings were to have been trained and protected from all untoward influences from earliest childhood; the environment of the court had supplied Dionysius, who was already some thirty years old at his accession, with an education opposed to this at all points. Judging from the *Republic* alone, then, it appears probable that Plato's initial program for Syracuse, so far as he permitted himself to have one in advance, would have

---

honor of placing him in a position immediately below that accorded to the Savior of mankind. The older Plato believed strongly in Providence, but not to the exclusion of the use of swords for the maintenance of order against enemies without and within. Plato's standpoint is nearer to that of Pascal (*Pensées*, Première Partie, Art. IX): "La justice sans la force est impuissante: la puissance sans la justice est tyrannique . . . Il faut donc mettre ensemble la justice et la force; et pour cela faire que ce qui est juste soit fort, et que ce qui est fort soit juste."

[306] Our view here agrees with that of R. S. Bluck, the most recent English editor of *Plato's Seventh and Eighth Letters*, Cambridge, 1947, p. 6. Bluck, in turn agrees with G. R. Morrow, *Studies in the Platonic Epistles*, 1935, p. 160 ff. To Morrow's lucid and otherwise admirable inquiry our whole discussion of Plato's Sicilian journeys owes a substantial debt.

been far less ambitious than the creation of the ideal city, with Dionysius as philosopher king.

An inspection of the letters themselves will reveal, however, the difficulty of arriving at certainty regarding Plato's political objectives in Syracuse, and will show how it is possible for highly responsible observers to reach opposing interpretations; how Crossman can hold his view, while Morrow can argue forcefully that the aim was never other than the establishment of a constitutional monarchy.[307] We shall seek to marshall first the reasons for this latter view, as derived from the Seventh Letter.

Letter VII is an open letter, or pamphlet, purporting to be written by Plato, shortly after the death of Dion, to Dion's friends and supporters in Syracuse, in response to their request for advice concerning the settlement of Sicilian political affairs. It combines a few paragraphs of this advice with a brief account of the development of Plato's own political principles, leading into a more detailed record of his entire relationship to Sicily, particularly to Dionysius II and to Dion.

As to the making of Dionysius into a fit person to serve as enlightened ruler of Sicily, the letter contains no evidence that Plato had been led to expect in Dionysius any very unusual gifts of mind or spirit; [308] none had been asserted of him by Dion in his initial appeal to Plato (327 E–328 A). The young tyrant had come to feel, Dion had reported, a longing for philosophy and education; and Dion had thought it possible that he might become sufficiently inspired with a desire for the virtuous life, to coöperate in establishing good government, in accord with Plato's political principles, in Syracuse. Thus the tyranny would be abolished "without massacres and murders" and the other evils of civil strife (327 D). Accordingly, we are not surprised to hear of Plato's and Dion's efforts, undertaken on Plato's arrival, to convert Dionysius from his dissolute way of life, employing every resource of the teacher and moralist and holding out to him an alluring picture of the fruits of reform: troops of friends upon whom he could depend as loyal supporters of his rule, and by whose aid he could hope to extend his power against the Carthaginians (331 E). The attempted conversion failed; but Plato expresses his conviction that if it had succeeded, or if Dion's later attempt himself to establish a government of laws in Syracuse had been successful, the highest interests of philosophy and of mankind throughout the world would have been served;

for if . . . philosophy and power had really been united in the same person, the radiance thereof would have shone through the whole world of Greeks and barbarians, and fully imbued them with the true conviction that no state or any individual man can ever become happy unless he passes his life in subjection to justice combined with wisdom, whether it

---

[307] Morrow, *op. cit.*, p. 150 ff.

[308] This is not meant to imply that Plato, at least after personal contact with Dio-

nysius, thought him stupid; at 338 D he calls him "naturally well-endowed for learning."

be that he possesses these virtues within himself or as the result of being reared and trained righteously under god-fearing rulers in their ways (335 D).[309]

Noticeable in all this is that though the ruler is to possess philosophy, the primary stress is laid upon moral goodness and the transforming effect of the sovereign's virtue (and of the good laws, which, as we are told in the case of Dion, he would have established) upon public morals, with the resulting benefit to all.

In mentioning law as a feature of the Syracusan government-to-be, we have touched upon a recurring theme in the Seventh Letter. On the opening page we read the declaration that Dion's opinion from the very first (and Plato's own, for he had derived it from Plato) had been that "the Syracusans ought to be free and dwell under the best laws" (324 B). Again in his advice to the friends of Dion, Plato announces as his third repetition of the doctrine, the advice he had urged first upon Dion and then upon Dionysius: "Neither Sicily, nor yet any other State . . . should be enslaved to human despots but rather to laws" (334 C). Dion, who had accepted this teaching, would have brought "freedom" to Syracuse, and would then have endeavored "to set the citizens in order by suitable laws of the best kind" (336 A). Dion, we hear again near the end of the letter, aimed only to establish "a moderate government" (*politeia*) "and the . . . justest and best of laws" (351 C). To be noted in passing is the vehement rejection of any intention to redistribute property, either by violent seizure or by popular decree (351 B).

This repeated assertion of the primacy of law, coupled with the idea of an exemplary ruler,[310] implies, it would seem, the establishment of what we should call constitutional monarchy. We shall see, when we come to examine the Eighth Letter, that Plato approved highly the voluntary relinquishment by a king of a large part of his power for the good of the state. And we need not doubt that Plato had originally expected to superintend this relinquishment and relying on his own experience and insight as moral and educational expert,[311] with the help of Dion as the expert in Sicilian affairs, himself to take the major part in the drawing up of the new constitution. In the light of these considerations, it is not unlikely that Plato intended the function of the ruler, once he had employed his power to instate the government of laws, to be chiefly that of setting the moral tone and standard of the state, and ex-

---

[309] We have followed Morrow in rendering *hosios* "god-fearing" where Bury renders it "holy"; otherwise the translation is Bury's, Loeb Library.

[310] In the *Politicus*, 302 B–E, Plato was to express the opinion that in the absence of the ideal statesman, the least imperfect form of rule is that of one man under the restraint of a written code of law. Since

the dissolute young monarch could not, as we have argued, have been readily mistaken by Plato for a potential instance of the ideal ruler, the *Politicus* adds confirmation to the view defended in our text.

[311] For the moral and educational functions of the lawgiver, cf. *Politicus* 309 D, and *Laws* (e.g.) 770 B–771 A, 688 A–B, 743 C–744 A, 718 C ff.

pected him to relegate the actual conduct of affairs, with certain specified exceptions, to the magistrates, himself remaining thenceforth, like all others in the realm, subject to the laws.

The resettling of the Sicilian cities is viewed from the standpoint of Plato's usual concern for the preservation of the values of Hellenic culture against barbarian encroachment (336 A). These cities were to be resettled, equipped with codes of "equal laws" (*isonomia*) (336 D), and linked to one another and Syracuse in bonds of friendship by "laws and constitutions" (332 E).

From the Third Letter, if we may trust it, we hear (316 A) that Plato labored, during the early months of his first stay at the court of Dionysius II, in constructing "preludes" to laws, those moralizing and persuasive little prefaces which were Plato's own invention and of which we hear so much in the *Laws*. This occupation, if shared with Dionysius, or if the preludes were presented to him for examination and approval as they were composed, would seem to have been well suited to the elementary instruction of the royal pupil in the principles of morals and legislation, and implies that the promulgation of laws was at the heart of Plato's plan for Syracuse from the beginning.

We have assembled from the Seventh Letter the principal evidence which suggests that Plato's original plan for the reform of Syracuse was the more moderate one of constitutional monarchy. But we are not at liberty to brush aside Crossman's assumption to the contrary, which must be allowed to possess a considerable initial plausibility.[312]

(1) In support of the view that the ideal Republic was to be attempted, the Seventh Letter provides, as its second repeated theme, the coupling of the notions of philosophy and political power. We have already quoted one such passage. There is also the impressive reassertion, included in Plato's brief account of his own intellectual history, of the familiar central sentence of the *Republic* stating the necessity that philosophers shall become rulers, and conversely (326 A–B). Dion, too, in urging Plato in the first instance to come to Syracuse and attempt to win over Dionysius II, had argued that this was the long-awaited opportunity to combine in the same persons philosophy and the rule over great cities (328 A). These expressions undoubtedly suggest, at first blush, that the realization of the ideal city was definitely intended. Dion's prediction of the unbounded happiness throughout Sicily (327 C, D), which was to result from the new philosophical regime, points in the same

---

[312] This appears to have been a prevalent view and well worth refuting when A. E. Taylor wrote (*Plato*, 1929, p. 7). Post (*Thirteen Epistles of Plato*, 1925), while leaving the question of Plato's precise expectation in going to Syracuse undetermined in his introduction, encourages Crossman's view by speaking (p. 68) of Plato's "attempt to convert Dionysius and so to set up the ideal commonwealth." The Loeb Library translator of the *Letters*, R. G. Bury, also appears to lend countenance to this view, in speaking (p. 470) of Plato's hope of "realizing the philosopher's dream of the Ideal State."

direction, and recalls that "cessation of evils" promised on the same terms in the *Republic*.

(2) At a later point in the letter, Plato has occasion to disparage attempts to expound in writing ultimate metaphysical principles, as Dionysius has purported to do, in a book which he has published; and in this connection Plato mentions the prerequisites to grasping these principles: love of wisdom, disposition to sober living, long application in association with a master, or, later on, independently (340 C–D).[313] Presently Plato adds the all-essential precondition to any degree of success in the enterprise: the candidate must have natural goodness of soul, kinship to the objective goodness of which he is in search, as well as the necessary intellectual powers; without these, "Lynceus himself could not make him see" (344 A). It would be open to Crossman to argue that the educative ideals here under discussion are essentially those of the ideal rulers of the *Republic*, and that Plato's association of them with his own attempts to promote the education of Dionysius proves that Plato had all along, up to the moment of ultimate failure, been grooming Dionysius for the office of philosopher king in the full sense. Also lending support to this view is the passage in the third letter (319 C) which records that Plato had prescribed for Dionysius the study of geometry as a preliminary to the carrying out of legal reforms.

(3) One other sentence in the letter lends support to Crossman's view. Plato, it will be remembered, is offering advice to the friends of Dion as to the settlement of Sicilian affairs, now that Dion has passed from the scene. He has recommended the summoning of a legislative commission to draw up laws for Syracuse and the lesser cities of the island. But in the sentence in question (337 D) he declares that such an arrangement is only the "second" best, in contrast to what he had hoped to accomplish in association with Dionysius, the "first" or truly best plan, "good things common to all."[314] This

---

[313] Something should here be said of the so-called "tyrant's test," which, on the evidence of the Seventh Letter (340 B–341 A), Plato administered to Dionysius II on his second arrival at the monarch's court. Reports had reached Plato in Athens that during his absence Dionysius had been seized with a renewed passion for philosophy and had been making great progress in his studies. Plato, wishing to verify these rumors, thought fit to apply the test in question, a species of combined aptitude and interest test, designed to reveal whether or not the candidate's reported interest in philosophy was more than a superficial vanity. It consisted in part in "pointing out what the subject" (i.e., philosophy) "is as a whole, and what its character, and how

many preliminary subjects it entails and how much labor" (Bury's trans., Loeb Library). One might argue that the delay in administering this test until the second visit shows that a thorough-going grounding of Dionysius in philosophical disciplines had been no part of Plato's original project. There is, I think, weight in this argument, but, on the other side, it is conceivable that pedagogical caution inspired the delay. We shall therefore not build any part of our case upon this argument.

[314] Plato's word *agatha*, which we have translated as "good things," is a broadly inclusive term capable of embracing all genuine values, whether moral or material; so we find him employing it at *Laws* 697 B. — This intricately ambiguous sentence,

latter phrase, standing in loose connection with the rest of the sentence, is commonly interpreted as a brief description or identification of the first plan. The sentence, then, can be understood to mean that the "first," or truly best, is identical with the basic pattern of the *Republic*, and can be read as Plato's explicit statement that his original intent at Syracuse was the establishment of the ideal city. The chief support of this interpretation is found in the *Laws* (739 A–E), where, referring to the constitution of the *Republic*, or to one that differs from it only by going further in the same direction of communism, Plato puts it "first," in contrast to the type of city aimed at in the *Laws*, which is "second in point of excellence."

We must now weigh one against the other the two interpretations of Plato's plan for Syracuse, beginning with the part assigned to Dionysius. In the face of the evidence, it cannot be denied that Plato originally hoped, on the strength of Dion's recommendation, to turn Dionysius into a philosopher or lover of wisdom, in some sense of that adjustable word. Absolute power, or so Plato believed,[315] lay already in his hand; and thus he would fulfill the requirement of the combination of power with philosophy. But here we must not be led into accepting a choice between the rival errors of "all" or "none," with no permission to accept a modest intermediate "some," in respect to the degree of philosophic wisdom required. It is no doubt true that Plato would have been delighted to carry Dionysius as "high as metaphysic wit could fly," had that young man exhibited the requisite strength of wing; later on, on his second visit to the young monarch, Plato did make trial of his fitness for the higher flights, and found him wanting. No doubt, also, Plato was well aware of the long and arduous discipline the candidate would have to endure in order, first, to overcome his moral miseducation, and then to acquire the minimum intellectual grounding for exemplary virtue, and for this purpose he may well have considered geometry a useful study. Yet it is very unlikely that Plato felt it a necessary condition for the substantial success of his venture that Dionysius should complete a program of studies in all branches of mathematics and in dialectics, culminating in the immediate vision of the Good, such as that sketched in the *Republic* for the higher education of the guardians.

Our contention may be enforced by reference to the case of Dion. Plato's confidence in him was apparently unlimited, and his death, Plato pronounces in the Seventh Letter, was as great a blow to the cause of philosophic rule as the refusal of Dionysius II to enter upon the life of philosophy. Dion, though

---

mentioning three apparently distinct alternative plans for Syracuse, which, however, are classified under only two degrees of excellence, is discussed by Morrow, p. 150ff., with much clarity; it is his interpretation which we essentially follow.

[315] Crossman (p. 285) has pointed out that even a tyrant has power only in so far as his rule serves the interests and receives the support of important groups within the state, and that probably the carrying out of such reforms as Plato contemplated was beyond the power of any tyrant.

not himself in the strategic position of ruler, had been able to spread the right appraisal of values among some of the young men of the Syracusan court, with Plato's full approval (327 B–D) ; we even hear of his having imparted some knowledge of philosophical doctrines (338 D). Yet Dion, to all appearances, had enjoyed only a very limited opportunity to pursue philosophy into its more advanced and technical reaches. True, there is every reason to suppose that he had eagerly read and pondered Plato's dialogues as they successively appeared, and had in the process developed fuller insight into the principles of the Platonic philosophy. But his claims to be a "philosopher" appear to have reposed for Plato, who so styles him (336 B) in the Seventh Letter, primarily upon his noble enthusiasm for virtue and his steadfast subordination of all opposing claims to those of justice. No more than this, possibly less, is what Plato would have felt it necessary to achieve in the education of Dionysius. And this would be much; for should this be realized, then Plato could hope that power joined to the wisdom of virtue, accompanied by the promulgation of good laws, and resulting in the morality and happiness of a nation, would stand as a beacon for the illumination of "the whole world of Greeks and barbarians" (VII, 335 D, 336 B). (Herein is contained explicit indication of awareness and concern on Plato's part, if the Seventh Letter is genuine, for that wider community of mankind for which, we remember, Popper was unable to detect in him anything but hostility.

We have not yet met the argument derived from the parallelism between the prerequisites to philosophical insight as described in Letter VII and that combination of qualities and pursuits exacted of the candidates for the highest office in the *Republic*. What in my view goes far to turn the force of this argument is the context of the passage in the letter, which is nonpolitical. Plato is talking epistemology and metaphysics. The question is how a knowledge of first principles can be reached, such as would be requisite for describing them in a treatise like that which Dionysius was reported to have written (an attempt that Plato deprecates in any case). Plato is describing something far above that minimum "love of wisdom" which he would have felt necessary for any sort of philosophic ruler, even assuming him to be assisted by skilled and philosophically trained advisers, as Dionysius would have been by Dion and Plato. Nor is he describing the basic level of conceptual competence which the beginning study of geometry was intended to promote — if the third letter and Plutarch are correct in reporting that this formed part of Plato's curriculum for Dionysius.

What we are here arguing, in short, is the perhaps somewhat uncustomary view that Plato, in speaking of his great hope that a true love of philosophy should arise among the mighty, was willing if necessary to accept in such exalted persons an equipment less than maximum, if only the king in question was amenable to instruction and was, himself, virtuous, and to adjust, accordingly, the type of political organization which should be adopted. A sort of symbiosis of the ruler and his philosophic advisers was tacitly assumed, for at least the period during which the new constitution was being shaped and imposed; and the future course of affairs was left vague, possibly on the assumption that the ruler, having submitted himself to the laws, would withdraw so far as his duties permitted into those more delightful occupations of the spirit of which in the *Republic* Plato speaks with such conviction, thus coming in time, perhaps, to possess in his own right philosophic insight. Plato has not confided to us his plans or expectations in this respect. But he may consistently with his principles have believed that such a king would by his blameless and disinterested conduct so win the esteem of the citizens that, as occasion arose, he would be consulted in national crises, and so would continue to exert a beneficent influence despite his abandonment of absolute power.

There remains in support of the view that we are maintaining what is, I think, our least disputable piece of evidence. We are offered in the *Laws* (711 E ff.) a brief sketch of the coöperative relationship between a young tyrant, who is "temperate, quick at learning, with a good memory, brave, and of a noble manner," who is also "fortunate . . . only in this, that in his time there should arise a praiseworthy lawgiver, and that, by a piece of good fortune, the two of them should meet"; from such a conjunction there arises, more quickly and easily than in any other way, the best state. And this is effected primarily by the example and influence of the monarch, who distributes honor and dishonor, reward and degradation, in accord with the true and valid standards of "reason's dictates, called by the name of 'law' " (713 E). It is possible to see in this Plato's retrospective comment on his Sicilian experience, his reassertion that what he had hoped to accomplish was still highly desirable and, in a favorable case, possible. We are also, on this assumption, given a clue to exactly what it was which to Plato's mind was responsible for the failure with Dionysius: the tyrant must possess temperance, not of the philosophic kind which is identical with wisdom, but that "ordinary kind . . . which by natural instinct springs up at birth in children and animals, so that some are . . . continent, in respect to pleasures" (710 A). It seems to be plain from this passage that Plato did not expect the young tyrant to supply from within himself the necessary wisdom, at least in the early stages; though it is provokingly obvious, also, that Plato does not draw so precise a line as could be wished between the respective functions of the partners in the association.

But if Dionysius was expected to acquire only a limited philosophical insight, there is no longer any reason to suppose that Plato would have sanctioned a code of laws which left such a ruler in possession of absolute power. That is to say, once the supposition is abandoned that Dionysius was to become in his own person the completely trained lawgiver, we may revert to our earlier stated view, and take in its obvious sense Plato's statement that

Syracuse must be enslaved not to men but to laws. The aim of Plato was to abolish the tyranny as such, and from his repeated coupling of the contemplated government that was to replace it with the "rule of law," we feel justified in rejecting any identification of Plato's plan for Syracuse with a program in which law was overshadowed by the benevolent omniscience of its idealized rulers, and in concluding, as we have said above, that constitutional monarchy, with the right of hereditary succession, was the intended form of rule.

This view is reënforced by a consideration which Crossman has not confronted: if the *Republic* was to have been realized at Syracuse, an absolute prerequisite would have been the voluntary renunciation by Dionysius of all right to transmit his power to his descendants, and the handing over of authority to choose future rulers of Syracuse to a self-perpetuating group of philosopher-guardians, which, if we follow Crossman, would have been set up under Plato's direction by selection of candidates from among the sons of the nobility or members of the court circle of Syracuse. The abdication of Dionysius himself would also have been entailed, had the scheme been carried out consistently, as soon as among the crop of new philosophers one or more should be found who were his superiors. To have proposed to a reigning tyrant any such idea would certainly have been wildly unrealistic; and there is, in fact, no hint that either Dion or Plato ever included it in his most distant plans.

If, then, we assert that Dionysius was not expected to become, in the full sense, a philosopher king, and that the new government of Syracuse was to be a constitutional, hereditary monarchy, it may be felt that we have still not sufficiently accounted for Plato's and Dion's predictions of "unbounded felicity" for Sicily; it may be argued that the author of the *Republic* could have anticipated so happy a result only if the reformed government of Syracuse were to correspond closely with the particular institutional arrangements of his ideal state. Crossman, as we have seen, relying apparently on the sentence in Letter VII describing Plato's original plan as "first" in excellence, and particularly on the phrase "good things common to all," takes it for granted that Plato expected this pattern to be established in some detail, and that at no distant date. Yet this supposition is not as solidly grounded as at first appears. The phrase "good things common to all" has been plausibly rejected by Morrow as an intrusion into Plato's text of a marginal gloss by some early commentator.[316] If this view be accepted, we are no longer re-

---

[316] We are again in close agreement with Morrow (pp. 151–152). His rejection of the phrase "good things common to all" is based not alone upon the difficulties of material interpretation which it entails, but also upon its highly anomalous grammatical status in the sentence. On Morrow's view the ancient commentator was adducing (wrongly) the very parallel by means of which a modern interpreter may seek to justify the presence in the text of the disputed phrase, and was suggesting that this

quired to believe that the "first" or best plan included the distinctive social institutions of the *Republic*. Had it done so, surely we might have looked for extensive indications, both earlier and later in the Sicilian letters, that Plato intended making so remarkable an alteration in the social landscape; but apart from the disputed sentence, they maintain an unbroken silence.

The notion that Plato's reforming imagination was inseparably attached to the particularities of the *Republic* is further weakened by a second consideration. The concluding section of the *Politicus,* a dialogue written some time after Plato's first visit to Dionysius II, sketches institutions markedly divergent from the scheme of the *Republic*. The account is short and by no means explicit, but it is clear that there is no separation of the citizens into three classes, nor is there any mention of communism of property or of wives. And yet, as truly as we so term the Republic, it is an ideal state, designed and supervised by the Statesman in person. Again, how very different are the institutions of the *Laws*, a state to Plato's mind only once removed from ideality. The conclusion of the matter would seem to be that Plato reserved the right to employ in his political planning as much or as little of the pattern of the *Republic* as the fitness of the occasion might suggest, keeping always to the principle that the laws and institutions of a state, in proportion to its excellence, must be so devised as to place power at the service of wisdom, embodied either in ideal rulers or in good laws, and to issue in the maximum attainment by its citizens of the whole of virtue, and of the highest degree of mutuality and harmony.[317] The constitution of Syracuse might therefore, under its Platonic reformation, approximate the pattern of any state which should embody this principle. And in anticipating such a consummation, Plato and Dion might well have felt cause for rejoicing.

Great inequality of wealth between citizens — witness the *Republic* and the *Laws* — Plato always regarded as a major source of disunion, and this he would certainly have wished to eliminate, but he would not necessarily have approached the goal in the manner that Crossman supposes, by demanding the abnegation of wealth by the Syracusan court, preparatory to converting them into a communistic sodality of civil servants. Plato might more probably have expected to work toward the reduction of economic inequality first by vigorous efforts to lower the place of wealth in the general esteem by the example of an austere king, and by the educational effect of the re-

---

sentence be understood in the light of *Laws* 739 A–E, where, as we have seen, community of wives and property is treated as belonging to the essential nature of the best state. Morrow takes no note of an alternative way of rendering innocuous the offending phrase, followed by Howald, Bury, and Post. This is to interpret the three Greek words as conveying the notion of "blessings" or "benefits enjoyed by all," an interpretation that does no violence to the Greek and removes the strong implication that Platonic communism is intended.

[317] This principle, which we find pervading the argument of the *Republic*, may be found stated in the *Laws*, e.g., at 630 E, 688 A–B, 770 D and 739 C–E.

vised laws and their persuasive preambles. At this point it might have appeared to him possible to apply the sort of legislative restrictions on wealth and poverty that we find him building into the constitution of the *Laws*, and to encourage that voluntary surrender of surplus wealth to which we earlier referred.[318]

Reverting now to the sentence containing the enigmatic reference to "first" and "second best" plans, we have seen that there is no certainty that these terms are used in the full sense they bear in Plato's theoretic writings. The alternative reading of the riddle, confirmed by the whole tenor of the letter, is that by "first" Plato meant "first under the circumstances," and that the term embraces, over and above the excellences common to all the plans, the unique advantages of the original hope, chief among which had been a code of expertly designed laws, the undisturbed continuance of civic peace, and the wholesome influence upon the Hellenic and barbarian world of the spectacle of so momentous a revolution achieved by persuasion, not by force. These high aims Plato could not have thought beneath the dignity of a true philosopher; he would not have scrupled to call them "first" in excellence among plans possible of accomplishment.

What has just been said contains an implied answer to Crossman's suggestion that Plato hoped to reorganize the Greek cities of Sicily into a brood of ideal states under the headship of Dionysius the philosopher king. If, as we have sought to show, Plato did not think it possible to attempt an undiminished ideal state at Syracuse, he would surely not have ventured upon the wholesale manufacture of Republics throughout Sicily. We may conceive these cities rather as so many constitutional monarchies, or perhaps, Solonian aristocracies. And it is also improbable that Plato would have wished to keep them under Dionysius' rule. In the Seventh Letter Plato pictures his ideal of the rebuilt cities as bound together in friendship, by "laws and constitutions" and by loyalty to the reformed Dionysius, into an alliance against the threatening barbarians.[319] If we are permitted here to read in evidence

---

[318] See pp. 353–354. There is no direct depreciation of wealth in Letter VII, though Plato's disapprobation of luxury and the unbounded pursuit of pleasure is emphasized. In the Eighth Letter (355 A–C), the pursuit of wealth in preference to the goods of the soul and of the body is strongly denounced and it is recommended that the principle of the subordination of wealth be made the basis of the legal system.

[319] VII, 331 D–332 E. It is true that both the Persian empire under Darius and the Athenian empire are mentioned as proofs of the advantages to a ruler of having loyal friends who help him maintain his power

(332 A–C); but there is also strong disapproval of the practice of exacting tribute from subject states for the benefit of the sovereign city (351 B). It is probable, therefore, that the element of loyalty was being singled out, in the case of the two empires, for its edifying effect on the mind of Dionysius, and that the power in question was to be not imperial power, but the power of defeating the barbarians by means of the loyal coöperation of the reëstablished and emancipated Sicilian cities. In the *Laws* (684 A–B) we have Plato's picture of a league between Argos, Messene, and Sparta, of a type which he strongly approved, in

from the *Timaeus* and the *Laws*, we can write him down as a champion of autonomy among Greek states, and of leagues for mutual coöperation, as against hegemony of one powerful state over smaller neighbors.[320]

We have thus presented, principally on the basis of the Seventh Letter, what appears sufficient evidence to dispel the notion that Plato's project in Sicily constituted a "hare-brained venture," as Fite would have it, into the naive blue, or, to speak with Crossman, a plan for establishing a dictatorship of "the best of the existing aristocracy." Further confirmation of this result awaits us in a source of which as yet we have made little use, the important Eighth Letter, which in the process of describing Plato's later political proposals for Syracuse, will cast a backward light upon his original hopes and intentions. But before passing to the consideration of these later plans, we must stop to consider a matter of the greatest concern to the defender of Plato's character, the question of his responsibility for Dion's *coup d'état*, and the tragedy of Dion's subsequent career.

Is it justifiable, with Crossman, to speak of Plato's guilt in sending Dion to his death, and the direful international effect of his policy in weakening the protective power of the Syracusan empire and thus preparing the downfall of Sicilian Greece before the Carthaginians? And what of Popper's accusation that in the concluding chapter of Dion's life is written a final indictment of Plato and his whole Academy, as, respectively, the sponsor and the training-ground for tyrants preparing the most ruthless use of power?

The Seventh Letter tells of the meeting between Plato, freshly returned from Syracuse, and the exiled Dion, deprived of family and fortune, at the Olympic festival in 360 B.C. On hearing of Dionysius' continued refusal to restore his rights, Dion resolved upon a punitive expedition against the tyrant, and invoked the aid of Plato and his friends. Personal participation Plato declined, urging his age and his reluctance to involve himself in violent action against a man whose hospitality he had received, and with whom he would prefer to help Dion to a reconciliation; but he made no attempt to prevent Dion from appealing to their mutual friends for assistance in his enterprise.

We may pass rapidly over the events immediately following this interview: Dion's gathering of a heroically small band of friends and mercenaries, their entry into Syracuse almost unopposed, and the subsequent naval and military engagements leading to Dion's complete victory. But we must look more closely at the events that now ensued. Dion's position, though externally supreme, was insecure at the foundation. He was separated by temperament and by principle from the Syracusan populace, who were clamoring for a restora-

---

which each state was bound to assist the others against any internal threat to their constitutions, while together they were to stand opposed to the Persian danger. Mor- row has suggested (pp. 144–145) that Plato may have had in mind such an arrangement in Sicily.

[320] See also p. 229 above.

tion of democracy and a redistribution of land; he lacked the support of the wealthy, who had little sympathy with his soaring principles and still less with the heavy taxation which he was forced to impose upon them in order to pay the mercenary troops in his employ. And worse, his authority was increasingly threatened by the maneuvers and intrigues of his associate Heraclides. Repeatedly this man's endeavors to displace Dion in popular esteem (as, for example, by proposing the redistribution of land, and by spreading personal calumnies), and even his communication with the enemy, were magnanimously forgiven by the principled moralist Dion, until at last, forced to an issue, Dion connived at his rival's assassination. From this time on, he appeared to the public mind hardly distinguishable from the usual tyrant.

But Dion had not abandoned his intention of setting the city under the reign of law, an ideal to which, as we have seen, Plato had converted him at the very outset. He had, in fact, already sent to Corinth for a deputation to assist him in his work of legislation when he was struck down by a group of conspirators headed by his unfaithful friend Callippus, who then usurped his rule. Callippus (so it is reported) had been associated with the Academy, though but distantly; and the whole incident could be interpreted to Plato's hurt, and to the discrediting of his political ideals.[321]

These, then, are the hard facts of the case, as nearly as they can be gathered from the record. The rest is a problem in casuistry, a balancing of rights and wrongs one against another. As to Plato's responsibility for Dion's attempt to overthrow the rule of Dionysius, it is to be remembered that Dion was no ingenuous youth to whom Plato stood in *loco parentis*. He was a free moral agent, a man in middle life with a long experience of the world behind him. His previous behavior to Dionysius would seem to have been exemplary. We have seen the benevolent program he had hoped to realize for Sicily under the rule of a philosophically reformed Dionysius II; there was in this no attempt to secure the power, as he might well have done, for himself or for his nearer kinsmen. And now, it would seem, he had every provocation and justification, both personal and in the interests, as he saw them, of the people of Syracuse, for wishing to end the existing regime, which was, after all — let us not forget — a tyranny. If Plato, as we have seen, refrained from prejudg-

---

[321] Plato's enemies in antiquity did not fail to exploit the supposed connection to infer an inner bond between tyrannic violence and Platonic philosophy. Wilamowitz, *Platon*, Berlin 1948, p. 432, while accepting the tradition that Callippus was associated with the Academy (based on Athenaeus XI, 508, and Diog. Laertius, iii, 46), argues that his immersion during the same period in military, political, and legal activities precluded any real participation in the life of the school. Taylor (*Plato*, p. 8) is inclined to question the tradition, arguing that it conflicts with the statement in the Seventh Letter (333 D–E) that Dion's acquaintance with Callippus was not grounded in the common pursuit of philosophy but upon comembership in a club and shared religious rites. It does appear unlikely that the author of the letter would have laid himself open to a charge of insincerity by glossing over a public fact of this nature, if it was a fact.

ing what Dion or his own friends ought to do, this was perhaps because on both sides of the question he could see approvable motives as possible determinants of action.

But what of Dion's later acts, which despite their apparent violence and injustice, did not shake Plato's approval of their author? Our interest in all this lies not so much in the presumed degree of Dion's guilt as in Plato's estimate thereof; we are concerned with the judging of Plato's judgment of Dion, as we were earlier concerned with his judgment of Critias, for the light it throws upon his moral standpoint. And we possess in this case of Dion one distinct contribution to clarity which was lacking to us in the case of Critias: we have under Plato's name (and from his hand, if the letters are indeed Plato's) an evaluation of the man in question, clearly related to Plato's view of those very acts and policies upon which others have grounded their attack.

Is it conceivable that Plato approved what Dion did to the full extent of justifying the assassination of Heraclides as a necessity to right rule? This man stood between Dion and his goal; he had shown himself "incurable" by his incapacity to respond to Dion's example of enlightened forbearance; he had proved himself to be one of those impurities that a good legislator must purge away for the sake of the public health. These are plausible considerations, and with some adjustment we may accord them our assent. Plato has given us a clue in the Seventh Letter (351 D–E), in his statement that Dion's fall was not caused by his failure to recognize the iniquity of the men he had to deal with, but by his failure to judge the extreme degree of their iniquity. This might be interpreted to imply not only that had Dion possessed this discernment, he would have guarded himself against his assassins, but also that he would (and should) have dealt more firmly with Heraclides in the first instance, and would not then have been forced into a position which only tyrannical acts could maintain. In short, it is probable that Plato would have endorsed the execution of Heraclides after an open inquiry and establishment of his guilt. If Plato is to be indicted for this judgment, it must be on the premises of a thoroughgoing opponent of capital punishment or of violent revolution. *Inter arma silent leges* is a principle of obvious application to the state of things in the midst of a revolution, when, in the overthrow of accustomed authority, courts martial alone can sit.

In addition to the assassination of Heraclides, other offenses have been laid at Dion's door. But these charges are not very well evidenced. Dion, it appears, had a "bad press" in the persons of contemporary observers and recorders whose hostile accounts found their way into the works of later historians.[322] In these circumstances, it is entirely possible that the picture of

---

[322] See Morrow, *op. cit.*, pp. 167, 28. We have, however, been unable to find in the chapters of Nepos (*Dion*, 6, 7) cited by Morrow any reference to Dion's use of his mercenary troops against the citizens, which Morrow found there, and which Bluck (*Plato's Seventh and Eighth Letters*, p. 17, n. 4) also reports.

Dion which we possess shows features that Plato had no need to condone, for the sufficient reason that they were absent from the original. Dion may have done nothing more tyrannical than to impose heavy assessments upon the wealthier citizens, necessary for the support of his soldiers. The employment of such mercenaries was in itself no badge of tyranny; in the fourth century it was the established practice, followed at Athens as well as elsewhere, and always they had to be paid. If Plato knew of these reports of Dion's high-handed actions, as he did know that Dion had been accused at Syracuse of intending to make himself tyrant, we cannot doubt that he interpreted them in the light of what he believed to be his own knowledge of Dion's character, as calumnies.[323] They thus become matter of indifference to us in our investigation of Plato's standards of the morally approvable.

But after all possible discounts of hostile exaggeration, there remained in the record of Dion's revolution the stubborn fact that by his overthrow of Dionysius he had touched off a train of events that kept Sicily embroiled in civil turmoil for many a year. When Plato composed his defense of Dion, included in the Seventh and Eighth letters, this disorder was in full career. We must ask: did Plato regard it with complacency, as perhaps a negligible price to pay for the noble risk of attempting the venture of philosophic government? No attentive reader of the letters can carry away the impression that Plato had urged Dion to the enterprise. At Olympia he had still spoken of a reconciliation. His account of Dion's aims repeats with emphasis his conviction that Dion had sought to achieve his purposes without causing the death of a single citizen.[324] If Plato was willing to condone some mistakes of Dion, even some injustices, this forgiveness is founded upon his confidence not alone in the unselfish excellence of Dion's aims, but also in the scrupulousness of his choice of means.

It will be recalled that Crossman has held Plato accountable for the subsequent collapse of the Sicilian empire and the later victory of the barbarians. This is what seems an unmerited compliment to the stability of the Sicilian tyranny in the ineffective hands of Dionysius II or his hypothetical successors. Quite possibly one might have found, in the fourth century, more reliable

---

[323] In Letter VII, 351 A–C, Plato seems to be defending Dion against calumnies by repudiating the notion that Dion could have been guilty of such actions as confiscating the wealth of the few to distribute it to the many, proscribing wealthy citizens in order to enrich his friends, or collecting tribute from subject cities for the benefit of the capital city. We know from Plutarch (*Dion*, xxxvii, 3) that Heraclides had in fact proposed the redistribution of wealth, and it is therefore possible that some other person or persons involved in the Syracusan disorders had committed the other acts which Plato disapproves; but there is more reason to believe that Plato is here making counter-accusations against the fellow partisans of the critics of Dion than that he is defending Dion against charges of having been guilty of the injustices mentioned.

[324] VII, 351 C. The Loeb Library translator, Bury, by an emendation apparently supported by no *ms.*, reads *ho ti* for *ou ti*, and accordingly translates, "by means of the fewest possible exiles and executions."

forecasters of coming events, better guides to prudential political policy, than was Plato; the court of history has ruled that he was in error in pinning his faith on the viability of the independent city state under the pressure of the coming conquerors. But our concern is not with Plato as historical prophet or far-seeing practical statesman, perceptive beyond the level of the well-informed and sensible man of his day. His attainments in these respects do not affect our purpose of showing him clear of the imputations of frenzied ambition, criminal complaisance, and general bad faith, which threaten to hide from us the actual integrity of his political commitments.

We may treat more briefly the record contained in Letter VII, and also in Letter VIII, of Plato's later plans for the ordering of Syracusan institutions, called forth by the failure to convert Dionysius and by the death of Dion. We are told (VII, 337 D; VIII, 357 A) that these plans were, in essence, the same which Dion while he lived had hoped to accomplish for Syracuse, but they clearly contain some adaptations to later circumstances. The situation obviously required still further abatement from Plato's maximum demands. Accordingly we shall be able to see what things he was prepared to sacrifice and what things he felt indispensable to a decent arrangement of political affairs. We shall find that he believed it necessary and possible even now to attempt the realization of a considerable part of the basic requirements laid down in the *Laws* for a "second best" state.

In the Seventh Letter Plato, seeking to heal the breach between the relatives and friends of Dion, to whom the letter is immediately addressed, and their opponents in Syracuse, recommends the calling in of a legislative commission,[325] chosen from the whole of Greece, not excluding Athens, "for there too there are those who surpass all men in virtue" (336 D). These commissioners are to be

men who are in the first place, old, and who have wives and children at home, and forefathers as numerous and good and famous as possible, and who are all in possession of ample property . . . These men they should fetch from their homes by means of entreaties and the greatest possible honors; and when they have fetched them they should entreat and enjoin them to frame laws, under oath that they will give no advantage either to conquerors or conquered, but equal rights in common to the whole city. And when the laws have been laid down, then everything depends upon the following condition: . . . if the victors prove themselves subservient to the laws more than the vanquished, then all things will abound in safety and happiness (337 B–D).[326]

It is interesting to note that Plato has, by his choice of prerequisites for membership in the commission, both excluded himself and all but the senior members of his Academy, and as a loyal Athenian included some of his fellow citizens. Plato's patriotism is also attested in a passage of Letter VII, 334 B,

---

[325] Or perhaps one commission for Syracuse, and one for each of the other cities to be reëstablished in Sicily.

[326] Trans. Bury, Loeb Library.

where Plato, concerned lest the depravity of Dion's Athenian assassins work injury to the good repute of his native city, with pardonable pride adduces himself and his freedom from corruption as a contrary instance of Athenian good faith.

The Eighth Letter purports to have been written some months later, when the conflict had become a three-cornered civil war between the party of Dion and that of the exiled Dionysius, with the advocates of a restored democracy taking the field against both. The recommendation of a legislative commission is again made, this time with the addition of a constitution briefly outlined (356 C–357 A). There are to be three kings, the respective heads of the three factions, but their powers are more symbolic than substantial; they are denied the right to exile, banish, or put to death citizens. For the rest, what we are told of the constitution strikingly resembles that of the *Laws*, upon which Plato was supposedly working at the time. This is the system to which Crossman refers as that of "cabinet responsibility to a popular assembly." It is to be a mixed or balanced government, with power divided between a board of Law-wardens, a council, and an assembly of the citizens.[327] There are to be popular courts, but all capital cases are to be decided by a higher court composed of Law-wardens and exmagistrates.[328] And this constitution is averred (357 A) to be that which Dion, after his capture of power, had intended to institute.

Plato retains his interest in the resettlement of the Greek cities of Sicily; his philhellenism is still in full flood (357 A–B). Meanwhile he urges immediate cessation of internecine conflict and a policy of conciliation (352 E ff.). There is much talking down of the importance of wealth (355 A–C), again in conformity with many passages in the *Laws*. And throughout, the utmost importance is attached to the rule of law, which is to exercise "despotic sway over the kings themselves as well as the rest of the citizens" (355 E).[329] Of great interest to us for the backward light it throws upon Plato's and Dion's original plan for Sicilian reform is the declaration that Plato's present advice is the same as "the counsel I gave of old. And now also my word of advice to every despot would be that he should shun the despot's title and his task, and change his despotism for kingship" (354 A).[330]

By the aid of these statements regarding Plato's and Dion's earlier intentions we are enabled, by stages, to infer our way back to the general nature of the original plan. The finally proposed constitution is declared to be the same, with minor exceptions, as the program that Dion would have carried out after the expulsion of Dionysius; in the Seventh Letter, as we have reported, Plato had declared that what Dion would have accomplished under

---

[327] The assembly is apparently open to all citizens, without property qualification. This is rendered probable by the consideration that property restriction would have made the "compromise" (VIII, 355 C–E) unacceptable to the democratic faction at Syracuse, and by analogy with the *Laws*.

[328] The similar arrangements in the *Laws* are described at *Laws* 752 D ff., 756 B f., 764 A, 766 D, 767 C, 855 C f.

[329] Trans. Bury, Loeb Library.

[330] Trans. Bury, Loeb Library.

these same circumstances would have contributed as much to the cause of philosophy and to the benefit of mankind as could have been achieved had Dionysius proved capable of all that Plato hoped. We must, of course, not mistake these substantial similarities for outright identities. The final plan was, admittedly, a dilution of a second plan (the one in which Dion was central), which was itself an unwelcome alternative to the original, which revolved about Dionysius. But enough remained to determine an important measure of agreement. There was, in any case, to be a constitution, which would impose substantial limitations upon the power of the king. The powers thus lost would necessarily have been transferred to certain other legally established authorities. The Seventh Letter did not tell us how these other authorities were to be constituted, but from the assertions of the Eighth Letter, quoted above, it is a reasonable inference that the framework of kings, Lawwardens, council, popular assembly, and courts of appeal was part of the original scheme, with the single structural difference that, in the first and second versions, there would have been but one king. If these inferences are sound, the conclusion that no attempt to reproduce the Republic was ever under view, needs no further proof, and it is clearly the framework of the city of the *Laws*, with the addition of a philosophically virtuous monarch, which Plato's original plan for Syracuse had more closely resembled. And now, from this he had been obliged to accept a reduction and again a further reduction.

It is plain to see how the two "second-best" plans for Sicily represent an abatement from Plato's ideal of the practicable best. In the first place, while Plato was by no means willing, as Crossman has said he was, that "the best of the existing aristocracy should become dictators," it appears that he was willing to concede, as a practical expedient and part of the "second-best" plan, that they should serve as legislative commissioners. As we have seen, Plato believed, not without some justification in the actual social conditions of his day, that effective intelligence was more likely to be found among the wealthy, who could afford the luxury of leisure and education, and believed also, apparently, that a distinguished family was a fairly reliable index of human quality as judged at a distance. Presumably he also thought that wealth would render the commissioners proof against the influence of bribes, and that their lineage would lend prestige to the results of their labors. We can regret that Plato failed to see, as we so clearly discern, that fifty men of property, chosen neither as social philosophers nor as philanthropic saints, however disinterested they might be in relation to persons and to local issues, would be very likely to legislate in favor of their own economic class. As at least a partial offset to this tendency, however, we may remember that the Eighth Letter (and perhaps the Seventh Letter intended to do the same) [331]

---

[331] At VIII, 356 C, just before proposing the calling of the commission and outlining the constitution, Plato says that this settlement of affairs "has been described to you before," and at 357 A, says that this had been Dion's plan while he lived.

makes it a basic requirement that in the framing of the constitution the interests of the democratic principle shall be conserved. And he plainly saw the interval between these laymen and the intellectually trained and practically experienced legislator, with eyes fixed on the harmony and virtue of the whole state, whose place he and Dion might have supplied. His second point of concession was the substitution for the originally intended, highly moralized monarch, of the three kings, one of them in the tarnished person of the philosopher *manqué*, the no longer young Dionysius II. And of course, it was necessary for Plato to forego all mention of those educational, sociological, and economic innovations characteristic of the theoretic city of the *Laws*, which it would have been pedantically unrealistic to introduce into such a context.

On the opposite side of the ledger, Plato was able to declare his faith in the following principles: (1) The necessity of tempering aristocratic rule by a moderate recognition of the democratic principle, or conversely. This idea, to which we find Plato giving full and emphatic expression in the *Laws*, was none the less sincere despite the fortunate circumstance that in the context of the Sicilian situation he was able to advocate the offering of it as a concession to the partisans of democracy. On occasion, a philosopher also can be a diplomat. (2) The prime necessity of putting an end to civic division and turmoil, and the constitutional safeguarding of all citizens against summary violence and oppression. (3) The subordination of the concern for wealth to higher values. (4) And, finally, the principle upon which we have found him constantly laying the greatest stress, subservience, equally binding on all classes and factions in the state, to the rule of law.

The application of these four principles in the imperfect form alone possible in the face of the factional division that had developed, could not have seemed to Plato the full equivalent of what he and Dion had originally hoped to procure for the Sicilian realm, or even of what Dion alone might have accomplished; yet the resulting polity would have been in its degree acceptable and consonant with his ideals. Syracuse, so strikingly like Athens as to have prompted Thucydides to compare the two in mentality and outlook — a great maritime, commercial city, and thus liable, as was Athens on Plato's view, to all the resulting moral infections — and, moreover, a city undoubtedly actual, not theoretically existing only — was thus to be provided with a constitution resembling in general outline that of Solon.[332] It seems probable, therefore,

---

[332] The chief difference (aside from the institution of the three kings, irrelevant to Athens) would seem to be Plato's provision that citizens should be tried for all offenses involving serious penalties before a court composed of magistrates and ex-magistrates, and thus resembling somewhat the Areopagus. Plato, having seen Socrates put to death by a popular court, regarded this provision as a safeguard against unjust condemnation. A convinced democrat might, of course, have ascribed this advantage rather to the popular courts.

that this would also have been his minimum plan for the reformation of Athens, with the solemn proviso that it must be achievable without bloodshed.

We have now to summarize what we have learned from our Sicilian journey, of Plato's political ideals in relation to the practical issues of his day. We may do this on two successive assumptions, beginning with the assumption that the letters (i.e., VII and VIII, upon which we are essentially relying) are Plato's own. In this case, we shall be compelled to admit that in laying down the requirements for membership in his proposed legislative commissions, he yielded more to the claims of birth and wealth than we could have wished or should have expected from his pronouncements elsewhere. This we are able to explain only as a concession to what he considered the practicalities of the existing social order.

For the rest, Plato's reputation in the relevant respects has emerged not only uninjured but positively improved. He showed himself immune to the luxury and the opportunity for enrichment that the Syracusan court supplied, remaining faithful to his Socratic schedule of values, which he continued both to practice and to preach. We saw him expressing concern for the spread of true beliefs throughout the whole of humanity, attempting to further the causes of Hellenic unity and the preservation of Hellenic culture, and, to the refutation of his enemies contemporary and to come, speaking a clear and proud word in defense of his native Athens. He has been heard insisting upon the importance of just and equal laws, to which rulers and ruled alike are to be subject. We have seen him prepared to temper his ideal demands to meet the exigencies of an actual situation, while at the same time maintaining his determination to benefit equally all classes in the state, and as a means to this end, his faith in the mixed or balanced constitution. And we have shown that at no time was he the advocate of achieving high ends by violent means.

On the assumption that the letters are not genuine, they may still be shown to yield a harvest of honor for Plato's name. We may no longer claim any of the more intimate self-revelations and evaluations. But we are still warranted in saying that if he went to Syracuse with the intention of converting a tyrant to the love of wisdom, and if the other events of which the letters tell are in general accord with fact, then we have testimony to his active willingness to serve what he regarded as the highest interests of the Greek world of his time. And, furthermore, we have solemn attestation to the candor of Plato's commitment, so often expressed in the dialogues, to the principle of persuasion as the only approvable path to governmental reform and the only one which he himself was prepared to follow. For all Popper's suspicion of Plato's secret approval of oligarchic terror at Athens, no evidence can be found to show that Plato ever took the first tentative step in the direction of revolution in his native city. On the other hand, the letters show that he journeyed twice to Sicily in the hope of carrying out just what his writings had led their readers to expect he would attempt, namely: the conversion of one person in authority, or at most of a few such persons, to sympathy with his aims, in the expectation that their already existing power would then suffice to achieve reform. As practical policy, this may not have been wise. But as the honest and energetic effort of a man who, having abandoned hope of finding support among the common people, and having also renounced violence, had left himself no other avenue toward his cherished goals, it commands respect and puts beyond question his sincerity.

In the chapter just behind us we have defended Plato as man and political philosopher against the charge that Plato the aristocrat had corrupted both. We have agreed with all the detractors and with all the world beside, that Plato was born and died an aristocrat. Our thesis has been that in the interval between these two events something of importance happened, namely, a life devoted in great part to an honest, able, and fruitful effort to develop a system of universally applicable political principles embodying the Socratic demand that moral wisdom should be sovereign over appetite, passion, and power, principles possible for adoption, in whole or in part, by his sadly distracted or blindly self-complacent fellow countrymen. We have expressed our regret that his understanding of the common man and of the moral values of democracy fell short of the general level of his thought; but his deficient trust in the common man did not imply a lack of concern for him and the protection of his interests. The principles he sought were not for the particular benefit of any group, but were designed to serve the interests of all classes of the community. In his pursuit of these aims, his thought more and more divested itself of prejudice, and though to the end of his life one can find him guilty of lapses into the old familiar mode, his conscious thought had so far transcended aristocratic bias that, with some concessions to social inertia, he could treat as hollow all claims to special prerogatives based on wealth or birth, and could regard as worthy of respect, though in some cases likely to be morally harmful, any socially useful task.

As an Athenian among Athenians, he cast off all party allegiance, scorning the selfishness and venality and repudiating the violence of the oligarchs, no less than he deplored the inconstancy and blind passion of the democrats. It is, we saw, an illusion to suppose that the right course had been clearly and unequivocally charted for him by a unanimous band of *illuminati* whose wisdom he rejected and betrayed. Instead, he was confronted with a welter of conflicting claims and creeds unable to stand up against the merciless scrutiny of the one man, Socrates, who seemed to Plato to have founded the method and indicated the goal which alone could lead out of the intolerable confusions and miseries visible to him on every hand, miseries inseparable, he believed, from all existing polities. What Plato hoped, then, was not a rejuvenation of the Old Oligarch or a restaging, with improved scenery, and with himself as protagonist, of the crimes of Critias. He disavowed the way of violence and continued by all legitimate roads open to a philosopher to promote, by his writing and his influence upon his pupils, his cherished dream of civic mutuality and virtue founded upon wisdom. His first meeting with Dion had given him, however, a point of attachment to the world of political reality, and when the call to action came, clear of all commitment to revolutionary violence, he responded, sacrificing personal convenience and incurring mortal risk to vindicate the cause he held most vital to the welfare of mankind.

It was our pleasure to observe the development of his political thinking as it moved toward fuller recognition of the value of the once slighted democratic principle. He had, indeed, never seriously held that a community this side of political paradise could endure without a substantial degree of popular control. But in the *Laws*, the ripest fruit of his thought, we find him explicitly advocating, for the government of his semi-ideal city, the "well-tempered" constitution, in which all citizens possess not merely civil but also active political rights. We may say of him that his opposition to democracy was for subjectively right reasons, that he did not consciously turn his back on any clearly envisaged human good, and that through it all, he was pursuing ends which, though we today seek them through the medium of democracy, we must still pursue.

8

Was Plato an Abnormal Personality ?

The Charge of Duplicity and Inner Division

In this final chapter on Plato the man we must answer on his behalf the last and most extreme of the accusations preferred against him. These charges have almost all been foreshadowed in our earlier discussion. Some further extensions and intensifications of Plato's supposed guilt will be examined, but the important novelty will consist in a more detailed reporting of the evidence adduced, and in our point-for-point reply. We shall be dealing principally with Popper, reënforced at some points by Plato's other critics; and it is our intention to allow the very intensity and extravagance of the accusations to play a major part in the drama of their own refutation.

It will be remembered from previous citations that the Plato who has excited Popper's moral indignation is no ordinary villain in simple and single-minded pursuit of wicked ends. What Popper sees in the soul of Plato is a conjunction, an interaction of impulses and ideals, some tinctured with nobility, others (and these by far the more numerous) frankly despicable. The principal basis of this conception of Platonic duality is not far to seek.

Popper has discovered in the *Republic* a Platonic Socrates who expresses "righteous contempt" for slaves, scorn of "the human cattle whose sole function is to provide for the material needs of the ruling class," "oligarchic inclinations," and all the other iniquities which we have reviewed in previous chapters. These same views Popper finds reappearing in Plato's later dialogues, expressed sometimes by other speakers. Even in some passages of the *Gorgias*, an earlier dialogue, Plato presents us with a Socrates whose utterances constitute "treacherous oligarchic propaganda against the open society, and especially against its representative, Athens." [1]

On the other hand, we have seen how, for Popper, Socrates was in his

---
[1] Popper, p. 593.

proper person the very incarnation of the values of "openness," the foremost champion of humanitarianism and the democratic cause which was sponsored by the Great Generation and supported by the mass of the Athenian citizenry. And for his knowledge of this great man, Popper relies chiefly upon certain of the earlier Platonic dialogues, hailing as Socrates' veritable "last will" and testament the *Apology* and *Crito*, in which (though Popper does not stress the point) this same Plato displays his full and reverent acceptance of the Socratic message. Nor could Popper, indeed, dispense with Plato as witness for this individualist, this libertarian, this admirably undogmatic Socrates; for were Popper required to extract the essential Socrates from Xenophon and Aristophanes, he would find it difficult to canonize him as the saint of critical dualism.

From the dilemma posed by this antinomy between opposing Platonic pictures of Socrates, neither term of which he was prepared to deny or modify, Popper has found it possible to escape by the construction of a hypothesis: Plato genuinely, under the inspiration of the Socratic teaching, abandoned for a time his oligarchic predisposition, and during this blessed interval had been able truly to depict his admirably democratic master. But he soon reverted to his sympathy for the program of the Old Oligarch and Critias, and began a progressive misrepresentation of Socrates resulting in the transformation which we find fully achieved in the *Republic*.

Even in the *Crito* there may be, Popper feels, one or two traces of Plato's deceiving subtlety; in the *Meno*, he detects surviving traces of Socratic humanitarianism.[2] Though the *Gorgias* is still largely Socratic, it contains also, as we have heard, an admixture of Platonic illiberalism which Socrates himself, had he lived to know of it, "would . . . have loathed." Plato, in short, the "least faithful" disciple, has "betrayed Socrates," has "tried to implicate" him in his own oligarchic endeavors, has wrongfully made into the semblance of an ally an opponent, helpless because he was dead, "whose overwhelming strength he would never have dared to attack directly."[3]

Popper had now to decide whether this misrepresentation was intentional-vicious or unconscious-forgivable, and chose both. In the space of three or four pages, he tells us in uneasy alternation, that Plato "retained Socrates as his main speaker even after he had departed so widely from his teaching that he could no longer deceive himself about this deviation"; that Plato "discovered, perhaps unconsciously," the Pareto device of cynical propaganda; and that Plato "succeeded in persuading himself" of the beauty and justice of his antihumanitarian aims. By virtue of one term of this unresolved contradiction, Popper must be supposed to justify the bitter indignation which, as we have seen, he so frequently expresses against Plato's "treachery," "dishon-

---

[2] See pp. 148–149 above.
[3] Other references for this paragraph are

to be found in Popper, pp. 593, 596; 189–191.

esty," and "libeling" of his master. He reads the *Republic* and other dialogues of Plato's later periods with a suspicious eye, and discovers evidences of despicable chicanery, calculated to deceive a guileless reader,[4] on many a page.

On the other hand, the possibility of unconscious, almost unwilling desertion of the Socratic teaching gives rise to the conception of a "titanic struggle in Plato's mind,"[5] a soul "disunited and inharmonious,"[6] deep suffering, and a conflict which "touches our feelings" also, and enables us, though we cannot approve, to sympathize and forgive. This second explanation of Plato's duplicity permits Popper to appear in the role of tolerant spectator of human frailty, while accounting also for the presence of those unspecified traces of genuine humanitarian zeal which Popper professes to detect in the whole tendency of Plato's political message.[7]

We touch here upon what is certainly one of the strangest features of Popper's whole book, the fact that after all the pages in which are described Plato's inhumanity, scorn, and callous disregard of the interests of the common people, his claim to aristocratic privilege for himself and for his "master class," Popper in his final chapter looks back over his demonstration that Plato wished to establish a regime in Athens indistinguishable from the most ruthless totalitarianism, and comments that he feels this view to be "defective," since it fails to account for "Plato's sincere belief in his mission as healer of the sick social body." We have not been properly prepared for his declaration, "I . . . grant his fundamental benevolence," nor for the sudden disclosure that Plato's strongest motive was the desire to help the people, who, "frightened by the breakdown of their 'natural' world," suffered and were unhappy.[8] This generosity on Popper's part is somewhat tempered in its effect by his further statement that the example of Plato has taught him to see in a new light totalitarianism in general: it has made him aware that totalitarianism attempts to answer, though in a mistaken way, "a very real need," and hence is to be viewed with a large tolerance. This forgiveness he extends in equal degrees, apparently, to both the Platonic and the modern forms.[9]

Popper's demotion of Plato's benevolence to the level of a Hitler's or a Stalin's cannot be welcome to Plato's friends. And it is rendered still less acceptable by the notable fact that Popper, in thus altering his general characterization of Plato's political thought, has cited no Platonic passage in which he is willing to recognize evidence of Plato's good will. We think back over some of the passages we ourselves have cited — the myth of the metals,

---

[4] *Ibid.*, pp. 191–194; e.g., pp. 148 and 103.
[5] Popper, p. 191.
[6] *Ibid.*, p. 606.
[7] Ibid., pp. 108–109. Popper here says that his "personal impression" favors the hypothesis of inner struggle in Plato; yet he leaves unaltered the numerous expressions throughout the book which testify to his predominant assumption that Plato is cynically deceptive; and such, despite his intermittent assertions of his contrary "impression," is the effect of his exposition as a whole.
[8] Popper, pp. 166, 172, 192.
[9] Popper, p. 166.

in which the citizens of the ideal state are enjoined to regard one another as brothers; the provision that the rulers shall receive no more than a modest maintenance from the common citizens, in return for devoted service; the prescription that the rulers are to regard their humbler fellow citizens as "Nurturers," while these are to think of them as "Helpers." On which of these passages (if he has mentioned them at all) has Popper not cast implications of cynical pretense, calling them "propaganda" or worse? [10]

We seem forced to the conclusion that Popper did not begin with a recognition of Plato's benevolence, but that his new insight has arisen out of his acquaintance with the recently developed concept of the strain of decision entailed by freedom, and the corresponding release offered by sheltering authority. Having first seen in this concept an explanation of the willingness of many millions of our contemporaries to submit themselves to totalitarian direction,[11] he has next miraculously inferred from the need of the submissive many for shelter, a benevolent aim on the part of those who offer them this baneful protection; and he has then admitted Plato to the same exoneration. In any case, we cannot accept his amazing offer on Plato's behalf. Plato is indeed in need of some forgiveness for his advocacy of paternalistic government. But his benevolence is not that which Popper accredits to totalitarianism, nor is there any slightest evidence that the concept of the "escape from freedom" ever entered his consciousness.

We are thus brought to see that Popper's hypothesis of Plato's duplicity in presenting the thought of Socrates, his entire conception of Plato as either dishonest or self-deceived, or, perhaps, as deeply self-divided, rests primarily on the following foundations: on the one hand, upon the ascription of black totalitarianism to the later Plato; on the other, upon the shining picture of Socrates as chief embodiment of the faith of the Great Generation and of democratic Athens, and upon the just-described airily insubstantial attribution to the later Plato of that supposed remnant of Socratic humanitarianism, his desire to relieve the common people of the strain of decision. Only if these three premises are granted, is there any ground for Popper's conclusion.[12] In

---

[10] *Ibid.*, e.g., pp. 48, 552.

[11] This concept has been employed for explaining the psychological appeal of fascism in our day (but without imputing "benevolence" to the dictators themselves), by Erich Fromm in his *Escape from Freedom*, discussed in our text, pp. 483f., 493f.

[12] In order to render his hypothesis of Plato's betrayal of Socrates less "fantastic" than "it may appear to Platonists," Popper has also adduced (pp. 653-654) what he deems Fichte's perfidious perversion of the thought of his "master," Kant. Yet this supposed parallel may lend probability rather

to a quite different hypothesis, namely, Popper's transfer of the pattern of betrayal from the one case to the other. There can be observed in Warner Fite a readiness to discover the littleness of a great man, be he Plato or be he the founder of Christianity; see his deflationary *Jesus the Man*, 1946, *passim*. Popper has a readiness, apparently, to see a great man's thought wrongfully misrepresented by those who come after and pose as his admirers. The extent to which this tendency can carry him is measured by his ability to believe that Burnet and Taylor, Platonists that they are, have

so far, then, as we have succeeded and shall succeed in destroying the picture of the blackly totalitarian Plato and in tempering with factual reservations that of Socrates and his contemporaries, we shall have accomplished, in major part, our refutation of Popper's hypothesis: there is simply no need of it. The great betrayal of Socrates turns out to have been, rather, a heroic effort on the part of a loyal disciple to carry to its fulfilment the change in outlook upon human concerns, individual and social, which Socrates had inaugurated, and Plato's effort to do so is shown to have been motivated, not by some special totalitarian benevolence, but by that same desire to share with others the happiness of a virtuous life which had led Socrates himself to question and instruct his fellow citizens.

But Popper has brought into the field subsidiary arguments in support of his hypothesis of betrayal, chief among which is a thesis which, though it is open, as we shall hope to show, to severe objection, possesses sufficient truth to be worthy of our close attention. Popper holds that it is possible to arrange the Platonic dialogues in a rough sequence on the basis of their progressive departure from an original Socratic base, established in the *Apology* and *Crito*, in the direction of an essential Platonism, observable in pure form in the *Laws*. (Readers of Jaeger's *Aristotle* will recall that scholar's brilliant if sometimes precarious reconstruction of the stages of Aristotle's gradual retreat from Plato and establishment of his own characteristic philosophy.) It is further claimed that these departures are systematic, displaying their influence in many crucial departments of Plato's thought, nine of which Popper specifies.[13] Now in so far as these touch matters of moral and political import, our earlier discussion of the thought of Socrates has shown reason to deny the very existence of any such essential alteration;[14] Popper's belief is indeed made possible largely by his blindness to any evidence of tendencies which he himself disapproves in the Socrates of the early dialogues, and by his corresponding and converse refusal to understand the later Platonic writings. In Appendix XVI, we have argued that differences between Plato and

---

been guilty of misrepresenting Socrates, charging him by implication with lying in his own defense upon the witness stand (p. 600). All this tempts one to say that Popper's use of the analogy of Fichte's betrayal of Kant — whatever may be the facts of the case — suggests precisely that "fantastic" quality of Popper's argumentative mind which it is adduced on purpose to deny.

[13] Popper, pp. 599–603. The first three criteria of change listed by Popper are not said, like the remaining six, to make possible the systematic ordering of the important dialogues as Plato's age advances, but

merely to differentiate decisively between the *Apology* and later dialogues. The list is as follows: (1) absence of interest and knowledge, *vs.* presence of both, concerning natural philosophy. (2) uncertainty *vs.* certainty regarding survival after death. (3) belief that the tolerant *vs.* the wise, should rule. (4) tolerance and trust *vs.* distrust, toward men, especially young men. (5) belief *vs.* disbelief in truth, free speech, and free thought. (6) intellectual modesty *vs.* dogmatism. (7) individualism *vs.* collectivism. (8) equalitarianism *vs.* belief in social status. (9) belief *vs.* disbelief in democracy.

[14] See pp. 299–307; cf. also App. XVI.

Socrates in respect to Popper's two remaining indices of change [15] are non-existent or irrelevant to the question of misrepresentation or "betrayal." But we would not wish to be understood as sponsors of the contrary error, blankly denying all differences between two closely related men who were nevertheless two men. We agree that the Platonic dialogues reveal evidence of progressive change. The compatibility of this agreement with the denial of the essential truth of Popper's thesis we must explain.

That a philosophic mind of the first magnitude such as Plato's should have spent its energies in the mere loyal reassertion of Socratic truths, is in itself incredible. Departures of some kind were inevitable. First and most natural of these would be the attempt to carry forward the results reached by the master, by the further application of his methods of inquiry to problems and situations to which Socrates had addressed himself only partially, or not at all. For example, there is no certainty that Socrates had ever attempted to delineate that type of social community which would arise, were his criticisms of the existing Athens to be written into one single, coherent constitution which would make possible the recommended improvement in the moral standards of all its citizens. In making that attempt, Plato produced his *Republic*, for Popper a betrayal of Socratic modesty and skepticism, for us a royal instance of a pupil's creative piety.

But it would be unfair to Plato as a creative thinker to represent his thought as merely the extension of that of Socrates. The dialogues constitute abundant evidence of insights extending into fields into which, to our best historical knowledge, Socrates had never stepped. Fertile elaboration of Pythagorean speculations about nature, such as the *Timaeus* provides, advanced mathematical knowledge, displayed even in the *Republic*, the metaphysical and epistemological refinements suggested in the *Sophist* and in the *Theaetetus*, move in a world far from that of Socrates. As this change progressed, it would become for Plato a matter of taste and judgment to decide, in connection with any given topic, whether new material should be put into the mouth of Socrates, or quoted by him as told him by another, or expressed by some other central speaker. And we may conjecture that whereas some extensions of Socratic ideas appeared to Plato so clearly in line with Socratic thought as to make their attribution to him not only fitting but due, others permitted only that Socrates should appear as interested listener, while still others required either a dramatic setting inappropriate to Socrates, or a method of treatment foreign to the Socratic ethos.[16]

---

[15] See pp. 634 and 634–635 below.

[16] Stenzel believed himself to have traced the course of Plato's philosophical development from his Socratic period to the period of the *Parmenides*, *Sophist*, and *Politicus*, dialogues which "show a fundamental change in Plato's doctrine" (*Plato's Meth-* *od of Dialectic*, English translation, 1940, p. 16). In the light of his theory, he has suggested reasons for the changing role assigned to "Socrates" in the various dialogues. His case, though presented with great subtlety and skill, is unacceptable to me for reasons of which two may be men-

Yet in all Plato's growth and accumulation of trans-Socratic wisdom, the thought of his old master did not ever really lose its key position, was never shorn of its proper honor. It is in fact more surprising to observe the continued centrality and emphasis given to ideas already present in the earliest dialogues than to note the changes; [17] and even in the work of Plato's latest years, were one to remove from it all that may fairly be called the Socratic base, it is no exaggeration to say that the entire structure would collapse.

For the reasons offered, then, we may reject Popper's thesis in the sense in which he has asserted it, while remaining free to agree that a process of orderly change can be traced from the *Apology* up to the *Laws*. Plato was no changeless Platonic idea; his "morning state" was not identical with that of his eventide. New interests emerged, his confidence rose and fell, he was, in short, subject to all the conditions of humanity. But from first to last, unswerving fidelity to the Socratic ideal of moral knowledge as the means to human happiness and as the key to the ordering of the universe was the unifying motive of his long and fruitful life.

As earlier mentioned, Popper now and again treats Plato as the divided soul in tragic conflict with its baser component; the alleged conflict itself is then employed as confirmation of Popper's thesis of betrayal. Popper feels this struggle by sheer intuition, with overtones of Faust, divining the existence of "two worlds" within the single soul of Plato. By a second intuition, he divines that generations of readers have shared his identical perception, that in fact this conflict is "the main secret of Plato's fascination," and an explanation of his great influence. Thus Popper's hypothesis of Plato's losing struggle with his inhumane impulses is given, or so it seems, collective confirmation.[18] And to this Popper adds that the depth of Plato's suffering, his self-division and inner disharmony, are revealed by his conception of the human soul in the image of "a class-divided society." [19]

To all this one is tempted to make the briefest of all logical replies, *non sequitur*. One can grant, in some sense, all the premises, not the conclusion.

---

tioned here: (1) He has assumed too great a discontinuity between Plato's earlier and later thought. (2) His position requires him to put the *Phaedrus* among the late dialogues. As I have elsewhere explained (p. 96), I find it difficult to believe that the tumultuous Eros of the *Phaedrus* is the work of a man who had already depicted, in the *Republic*, the tranquil Eros with folded wings, or that the literary quality of the *Phaedrus* is compatible with a late date. The advanced position assigned to the dialogue by Stenzel to my mind accentuates these difficulties.

[17] The reader is invited to compare the ideas we have pointed out in the *Apology* and *Crito* (pp. 302–304 above) with those affirmations in the *Republic* and *Laws* described, e.g., on pp. 519–521, and with the pervasive elements in his thought summarized on pp. 232 and 250–251.

[18] Popper, p. 191, appears also to be implying that Plato's fascination for his readers arises from their own unconquered love of power and impulse to oppress others. See our discussion of this charge against Platonists, pp. 447ff. below.

[19] Popper, pp. 108, 191, 606.

Plato had tensions in his soul; "two worlds" (properly interpreted) are in strife for its possession; Plato has been fascinating to many readers. We have elsewhere discussed some of the tensions and their significance, and again in the next section of this chapter we shall return to them.[20] No doubt the fascination of Plato is in part due to the urgency and force of his beliefs, the intensity of his emotional life, and the conflict within him between allegiance to ideal values and acceptance of actuality. Plato does indeed conceive the human soul, when unjust, as a "class-divided society"; by the same token, he conceives the soul of the temperate and just man as a society united to the uttermost by good will and mutual piety; and this unity, we agree with Popper, Plato struggled to attain. Between the full possession and the utter lack of what is good, we have heard Plato tell us, in the *Symposium* (204 A–B), is that intermediate state, proper to philosophers, the state of striving toward the good. It is extravagance to describe Plato's pursuit of inner harmony as a "division" or "split" in his soul, as it is a sheer assumption to diagnose it, with Popper, as the agonized conflict between oligarchic inclinations and the humanitarian faith.[21] Plato's betrayal of Socrates receives no confirmation from any of these arguments.

But Popper has collected also certain specimens which we must not neglect to examine: there are Platonic works in which traces of the internal struggle itself, he believes, can be detected. The earliest of these traces Popper discovers in the *Euthyphro*, assumed by Popper, as his interpretation requires, to have been written after the *Apology* and *Crito*. This is a little dialogue wherein Socrates and Euthyphro, a professional diviner, discuss the nature of true piety or holiness, starting from a case of conscience complex enough in its legal and moral bearings to perplex a Hellenic Solomon: a blood-guilty laborer, or serf, of Euthyphro's, has been left fettered in a ditch by Euthyphro's father while a messenger was sent to Athens to determine what shall be done with him, and has died of the neglect; Euthyphro, fearing the ceremonial pollution which will come upon him from association with his father, is prosecuting him for homicide (4 A–E, 9 A–B). Socrates implies his doubt as to the propriety of this action by his ironical admiration for the exact knowledge of true piety which alone could embolden Euthyphro to such an act. What Popper conveys to his reader is the idea that the major purpose of Plato in writing this dialogue was to claim the authority of Socrates in support of his own antihumanitarian political program; for is not Socrates shown as arguing symbolically in favor of the oppressive ancestral social order by questioning the righteousness of extending protection to a

---

[20] See pp. 122–124 above, pp. 483–498, especially p. 492, below.

[21] As we said above, p. 69, Popper in his note, p. 606, describes Plato's psychic state as a difficulty in controlling "animal instincts," and by his comparison with Freudian doctrines implies that these are libidinous; yet in his text (p. 191) he cites the same evidence as proof of the struggle against oligarchic impulses.

mere serf as against the sacredness of a father who had murdered him? [22]

We must first pay tribute to the extreme logical neatness of this way of reading the dialogue, and then protest that Popper has achieved this neatness by imposing his own conception of the central aim of the dialogue, instead of permitting Plato to determine that center for him. That Plato should intend presenting a dramatic picture of the Socratic method applied to the examination and clarification of conflicts in traditional notions of piety — this accepted view of the purport and scope of the dialogue Popper brushes aside as the usual misinterpretation. At the focal point he places the social status of the victim, which we shall agree does possess a real if peripheral importance, but which Popper implies was the sole reason why Euthyphro's action was questioned by Plato. The fact that the man left to die had himself in a drunken rage killed Euthyphro's father's slave, and the further fact that the death was due to neglect and not to intention, Popper has not seen fit even to mention, with the result that Euthyphro's father is made to appear as a simple murderer, and in consequence Plato appears as one in whose eyes the murderer of a humble citizen is quite blameless in comparison with the impious prosecutor of a father.[23] No allowance is made for the possibility that the dialogue has reference to an actual occurrence, or that Socrates had in fact made it the occasion of such an inquiry as is here reported. Popper follows Grote in asserting that "every citizen was bound by Attic law to prosecute in such cases." [24] This, however, is open to serious doubt; Euthyphro perhaps had not even the right to bring suit for homicide, though he believed he did.[25] And in any case, it gives a false picture both of Euthyphro's motive, which was ceremonial-religious, and of Athenian actuality. The general moral sentiment did not enjoin the suing of a kinsman and would apparently have required Euthyphro to be silent and to run the risk of himself being sued for "sacrilege" (*asebeia*) rather than to bring suit against a father.[26] Popper's

---

[22] Popper, pp. 191–192, 608.

[23] To most readers the disturbing feature of Plato's account will probably be the apparent insensibility of his Socrates to the suffering of the man in the ditch. We can see this in perspective only by remembering the rather widespread indifference to suffering among the Athenians of Plato's day, especially when the sufferer could be viewed as criminal. See our discussion of this, pp. 351f. above. The victim's status as common laborer does in our judgment increase for Plato the extravagance of Euthyphro's action, and this reflects Plato's (and also the general Athenian) estimate of the relative importance of persons; the tension is enhanced also by the high age of Euthyphro's father (4 A). But neither is given

equal weight with the violation of filial duty, the guilt of the laborer himself, and the nearly involuntary character of the father's crime.

[24] Popper, p. 608.

[25] Cf. Burnet, notes on *Euthyphro* 4 c 3, 5 e 3.

[26] For a discussion of similar cases, see Bonner and Smith, *The Administration of Justice from Homer to Aristotle*, 1938, pp. 216–217, where, following Glotz, it is declared that there is no record of the suing of a kinsman. It was necessary in such cases for a third party to bring a suit against some member of the homicide's family, in the settling of which the guilt of the supposed homicide was determined.

interpretation of the *Euthyphro* need not, in view of all these facts, be seriously regarded, and the curious set of circumstances involving Euthyphro and his father may once more be reasonably viewed as but an appropriately selected starting-point for a dialogue intended to clarify notions of piety.

A second and outstanding exhibit of sedition in Plato's soul Popper finds in the *Menexenus*, a dialogue which, as we have seen, he interprets as Plato's scurrilous attempt to pour ridicule upon Pericles and all that his name connoted of the high principles of Athenian democracy. What we must note here is Popper's assertion that Plato has revealed his own inner struggle, has "given himself away," in the declaration, put into the mouth of the Socrates of the dialogue, that after listening to such a patriotic speech, he hardly realizes where he is for several days, so great is the exaltation produced. Plato, we are to understand, thus pays an involuntary tribute to the influence that the Periclean ideals still wield over his reluctant soul, and reveals that he is not yet so bad as he is destined to be, and that he still retains some vestigial traces of the old Socratic holiness. How much less expensive and more valuable would be the obvious alternative, that Socrates is here deriding that false elevation of spirit, so readily awakened in the midst of great public gatherings on solemn occasions, when the orator pours forth his wine of flattering words! The trance thus induced is for Plato one of the unwholesome products of that rhetoric described in the *Gorgias* (464 D) as a subdivision of the art of flattery, which "dangles what is most pleasant for the moment as a bait for folly," and distracts the citizens from the pursuit of civic good. It is not without interest to compare to this ironical handling of the oratorical trance the quite serious words of Alcibiades in the *Symposium* (215 B ff.), confessing the far more powerful effect of listening to the piping of the Marsyas whose name was Socrates. The *Menexenus* as a whole may be read, despite its somewhat scattered manifold of motives, as a contribution to the study of the uses of rhetoric, good and bad, a theme frequent in the dialogues from first to last. Again Popper's attempt "to read between the lines" (which he says is "not at all difficult") evidence of Plato's inner conflict, has only prevented him from seeing clearly the meaning of the lines themselves.

But Popper has still other proofs of Plato's internal struggle, which can "be found in nearly every place where he turns against humanitarian ideas, especially in the *Republic*." These are, in brief, "his evasiveness and his resort to scorn in combating the equalitarian theory of justice, his hesitant preface to his defence of lying, to his introduction of racialism, and to his definition of justice," [27] to each of which Popper has devoted a detailed discussion through which we must follow him.

Before doing so, we must post a warning against an unannounced incon-

---

[27] Popper, p. 192.

sistency in Popper's standpoint. He lists these "evasivenesses" and the rest as traces of the conflict in Plato's soul between the still surviving "better self" and the "Old Oligarch" within him. But when we examine Popper's presentations of the alleged hesitations, we hear only of planned delays, dishonest silences, adroit calculations on the part of one who is concerned only with how best to distract and hoodwink his reader, and it is plain that the struggle, in its original internal sense, is assumed to be wholly at an end. What remains is a very different thing, a struggle against liberal opinions supposedly existing in the souls of others, a battle of propaganda. And as such Popper, without the requisite explanations and qualifications, presents it. Herein is illustrated what we earlier described as Popper's choice of both alternatives to the question of whether he should present Plato as tragically self-deceived or as the cynical and crafty deceiver of others, against whom, to use a Platonic phrase, it is right "to give free course to wrath." As a consequence, we shall be forced into a joint discussion of the two disparate things which Popper has inextricably intertwined.

It will be convenient to examine first the dissection which Popper makes of Plato's manner of introducing his definition of justice, in the fourth book of the *Republic*; for nearly all the supposed earmarks of fraud and equivocation are there detected. The search for justice, toward which this entire section of the *Republic* is directed, is nearing its close; the ideal state has been sketched and outfitted in the process with the basic institutions required for its material and spiritual well-being; two of the four virtues upon which its excellence is presumed to rest have been sufficiently accounted for, i.e., wisdom and courage; temperance and justice remain undefined. And now (430 D) begins what Popper calls the "lengthy preface," which he describes as "an ingenious attempt to prepare the reader for the 'discovery of justice' by making him believe that there is an argument going on when in reality he is only faced with a display of dramatic devices, designed to soothe his critical faculties." The two pages that follow in Popper's text make clear the *modus operandi* of these devices, imputing to Plato a shrewdness and dishonesty worthy of the wily Ulysses. Glaucon, it appears, is Plato's stooge, his function that of going through the motions of keeping careful watch over the "intellectual honesty" with which Socrates conducts the argument, so that "the reader himself, need not . . . watch at all." [28] It is he who (on Popper's construction, presently to be denied) prevents Socrates from indulging his avowedly "dishonest" impulse to skip over the definition of temperance. Following a sneerful little paragraph on the definition of temperance, — a definition in which Popper has apparently not been able to find evidence of fraud, but only of Plato's scorn and contempt for the common man, who is to be taught to know his place — we reach the exposé of the major hoax.

---

[28] Popper, p. 98.

In figurative language borrowed from the vocabulary of the chase, Socrates exhorts Glaucon to keep a close watch, for the quarry (that is, justice) is lurking in the covert close by. The lively imagery that follows, — Socrates entering the dark thicket, followed by the helpless Glaucon whom he continues to encourage, the "halloa" of discovery, leading after a teasing final delay, to Socrates' proposal that justice be defined as "to do what is one's own," "to perform one's proper actions," — all this, Popper insists, is merely a distraction, a diversion of "attention from the intellectual poverty of this masterly piece of dialogue." [29] In fine, Popper is suggesting that it was the naive reader and not justice that Plato caught.

The cracked stone at the base of Popper's argument is unquestionably the incredible degree of roguery that it imputes to a man whose fundamental honesty was never questioned in his own day by those who, like Aristotle, knew him well. Or are we to suppose that they, too, were members of the conspiracy, and that to a man they kept the secret of Plato's skilful chicanery? [30] But

---

[29] Popper, p. 99.

[30] That Plato was not, among his contemporaries or immediate successors, suspected of duplicity is clearly shown in a study of the personal criticisms directed against him in antiquity, "Hostility to Plato in Antiquity" (typewritten, unpublished doctoral thesis, University of Chicago, 1916) by Edwin L. Theiss. Tracing to their probable sources the various gibes and slanders found especially in Athenaeus, and also in Diogenes Laertius, Theiss finds little or no indication of unworthy personal animosity between Plato and such men as Antisthenes, Eudoxus, Aristotle, Xenophon, and Isocrates. Their genuine divergencies in belief, however, involved them in active controversy and competition, and their pupils and successors, members of rival schools, developed these relatively impersonal and decent disagreements into outright calumny and attack. They searched the dialogues in no spirit of equity for passages to be employed against Plato and emerged in triumph with such gems as the charge that Plato slanders Socrates by representing him in the *Symposium* as enamored of Alcibiades, and that in the *Republic* he banishes Homer out of jealousy of his greater literary merit. Theiss groups the personal attacks on Plato as directed against (1) Plato's character (sexual license, involving both youths and a mistress, love of pleasure, love of praise, unworthy pupils), (2) harsh disposition toward contemporaries, including Socrates, fellow Socratics, and some of his own pupils, (3) Sicilian journeys (luxury, lack of tact, flattery, ambition, venality), (4) plagiarism, (5) political inactivity at Athens and impracticality. It is noteworthy that there is here no confirmation of Popper's charges of deceitful propaganda or of conspiratorial relations to Athenian oligarchy. On two points only does Popper appear to have the support of any of the ancients. There is a sentence in *Rhetoric* II, 23, 1398 b, in which Aristotle, illustrating the rhetorical use of an appeal to a recognized authority in support of an argument, reports an appeal made to the authority of Socrates after the latter's death. Plato, as it seemed to Aristippus, had spoken somewhat magisterially, and Aristippus said, "Our friend, at least, would not have said such a thing." This remark may be interpreted in confirmation of Popper's contrast between the modesty of Socrates and the dogmatism of Plato, but since it was spoken by Aristippus, who differed markedly with Plato as to the meaning of Socrates' teaching, and who was known for his cosmopolitan grace and adaptability rather than for zeal and passion, the rebuke must be discounted to an indeterminate degree. The other point of agreement between Popper's case and that of the ancient critics is the animosity reported to have existed between Plato and Antisthenes; Antisthenes directed diatribes against Plato, and Plato, so it is said, showed to Antisthenes, as to other Socratics, arrogance and injustice. Theiss is unwilling to believe Plato guilty, except in so far as

we need not appeal to such general considerations, to the neglect of the specific evidence that lies at hand.

Why, one may ask, has Popper not considered the many places in Plato's writings in which a stretch of argumentation is followed by a passage whose obvious function it is to refresh and to relieve the strain of prolonged attention? Platonic dialogues were not, even for Plato's later period, Aristotelian treatises, still less the prototype of Euclid's *Elements*. One would surely make sad work of their interpretation were he to proceed on the principle that a departure from the strict track of logical continuity is to be regarded as a danger signal that their author is about to perpetrate, either uneasily or with cynical cunning, some deviltry.

Popper's account of the manner in which Socrates leads the reader, in the person of the poor bewildered and impatient Glaucon, about in the wood of his mystification is not without a certain sardonic humor of its own. One would not complain of that, save that it serves as a device (not necessarily conscious) for screening from the reader another form and instance of humor, of whose existence Popper seems not to be aware, namely, Plato's own humor in writing the same passage. One does not need a diagram to see the ludicrous position of Glaucon, stumbling after Socrates in the dark, in helpless dependence upon his ironical guide who insists on treating him as his hunting companion on terms of parity with his knowing self. What Plato has, in fact, created here is not in any serious sense the illusion of an argument, but the reality of a comedy which comes to an appropriately whimsical close with the absurd discovery that the object of their desperate quest all the while lay quietly within their grasp.

In suggesting that Plato has made use of the character of Glaucon in his unscrupulous conspiracy against the intelligence of the reader, Popper has given us a wry version of what is perhaps one element in the truth. It is quite true that Glaucon in several ways helps Plato to carry his reader along with him. But there is nothing sinister or conspiratorial in this. It is, of course, as Chapman long ago reminded us,[31] one of the most harmless and necessary

---

he may have been outspoken both orally and in the dialogues in his opposition to Antisthenes' philosophical tenets, and he believes the evidence similarly insufficient to prove unworthy abuse of Plato by Antisthenes; again, the rivalry of the schools, he thinks, provides sufficient explanation. The untrustworthiness of such sources as Diogenes Laertius and Athenaeus is underlined by Theiss' research, which serves to remind us of the many centuries that lie between these writers and the period of Plato's and Antisthenes' lives, and provides abundant evidence of the animosities and irresponsible attitude to facts which had

already corrupted their sources. It should be noted that Theiss has limited his inquiry to the literature of Platonic detraction and has excluded from his report the counter-exaggerations of the adulators who devised the apocryphal tales of swans and of bees that prophetically announced Plato's glory to the world. Had it not been for the accident that Athenaeus has been preserved, while writings correspondingly biased in Plato's favor have been lost, we might know more than we do of the facts and fancies favorable to Plato.

[31] See pp. 28–29.

tricks of the dramatist's trade to bring some character upon the stage whose outlook and interests coincide with those of the auditor or reader sufficiently to permit imaginative identification. But when Popper himself points out this very principle in relation to Glaucon, he gives it a gratuitous and malicious turn and thereby misses what seems the entire point: Glaucon is "worth his keep" to Plato by his infectious display of eager interest in the course of the dialogue, which sets a good example to the reader. Simultaneously, he serves as a species of scapegoat, taking upon himself the responsibility for what might seem the pedantry of Socrates in protracting the discussion into the most meticulous detail. Glaucon is, in fact, exercising just this function when he dissents from Socrates' suggestion that they omit discussion of temperance: "Oh, no, let us have the whole story!" But Popper, mistaking a Greek idiom and ignoring the context,[32] permits himself to talk of Glaucon as keeping watch over the "intellectual honesty" of Socrates, whereas Glaucon is watching, instead, to be sure of losing no part of the promised investigation. This whole question of "honesty" has no foundation here in Plato's text; it is a projection, not to say a "plant," for which Popper alone must be held responsible.

Glaucon is again enacting the enthusiastic and impatient reader-disguised-as-a-listener when he complains (Rep. 432 E) of the delay in reaching the description of justice: "That is a lengthy preface for one who is eager to hear." Note that this complaint refers, not, as Popper supposes, to the entire passage beginning with the protest against omitting discussion of temperance, and including the adventures in the underbrush, but only to the teasing delay that Socrates inflicts upon him, following the "halloa" of discovery, in continuing to ring changes upon the confession "How stupid we have been, we knew it all along," while refusing to communicate to his tormented listener the identity of the "it." Only by ignoring this natural and obvious motivation, is Popper able to discover in Glaucon's little reproach an indication that Plato has for the past several pages been playing a deliberate trick.

And, finally, Popper has neglected to mention one quite literally climactic point. The definition of justice was, by the very nature of the case, destined to be the climax of this entire section of the Republic. It could not be allowed to pass unsolemnized: somehow bells had to be rung and salvos fired. Parallels to this method of emphasis abound elsewhere in Plato. One of the most striking occurs later in this same dialogue: approaching the introduction of three features of his ideal state whose importance he wishes to underscore,

---

[32] What Popper renders, "It would be dishonest were I to refuse," is the phrase *ei mê adikô,* which (see Shorey's note to *Rep.* 430 E) means, "It would be wrong of me to refuse"; this, in the light of Glaucon's attitude of eager interest throughout the dialogue, and in particular, of Glaucon's previous reminder to Socrates (427 E) of his initial promise to lead them in the search for justice, sufficiently indicates the correct interpretation.

he has availed himself of the vivid and sustained metaphor of the three waves of objection and ridicule with which, he anticipates, his proposals will be met. And it is interesting to note that this metaphor permits him to throw the greatest emphasis upon that one of the three whose significance he regarded as paramount, namely, the rule of the philosopher kings, since the "third wave" was, in Greek popular belief, the greatest. Again, in Book IX, to mark the formal completion of the proof that justice is *per se* the highly preferable alternative to injustice — the *probandum* of the entire *Republic* — he makes the fanciful suggestion (which Grote, construing it with undue literalness, rebukes as immodest on Plato's part) that "we hire a herald," or let Socrates "proclaim that the son of Ariston has adjudged that man the happiest who is most just" (*Republic* 580 B). Such ceremonies take time, time enough to account for what Popper calls a "lengthy preface." But there is nothing dark and devious about them which elaborate hypotheses are required to explain.

Closely tied to the attack upon Plato's diversion of attention is the critique of the three arguments on which the Platonic theory of justice is made, at this point in the dialogue, to rest. Two of the three are conceived by Popper as part and parcel of the attempt to distract, the hems and haws and "look yonders" of a man furtively awaiting the safe moment for introducing, at last, a "straightforward and consistent" plea for the "collective clockwork" of totalitarian justice, "in all its barrenness." [33] Popper expresses his (ironical) reluctance to consider the first of these an argument at all, and in this expression, apart from its intention, we can find something substantial with which to agree. The so-called "argument" is the statement (*Republic* 427 E, 433 C) that if three of the supposed four virtues, wisdom, courage, temperance, and justice, have been accounted for, and justice has not yet been found, then whatever virtue is further discovered must be justice itself. (As we shall presently see, there is here present the tacit assumption that each of the four virtues must be a basic and vital condition to the excellence of the city.)

Now clearly there is present in this form of inquiry something of definite logical interest, the germ, at least, of what Mill formulated as the method of Residues. [34] But quite as clearly, Plato is not leaning any substantial weight upon it as a validation of his result, is not, in short, using it as an argument in the full sense. It is employed rather as an expository device to indicate the path that the mind of Socrates may be supposed to follow in bringing him to a "conclusion," which conclusion is, however, not regarded as demonstrated but rather as brought clearly into view, as recommended, for that closer inspection which it presently receives. Plato makes it clear (433 C–E) that to be judged acceptable as the missing member of his tetradic scheme,

[33] Popper, p. 107.

[34] In so saying I may still, with Shorey (note on *Republic* 427 E, Loeb Library) deplore as "pedantry" the attempt to discover in Plato Mill's celebrated canon. Plato is not trying to analyze the methods of induction, but merely to direct and to expound a particular train of thought.

the proposed virtue must show itself of equal if not superior importance to the three virtues already identified; there is implied also the requirement that it must characterize the city as a whole and every group of its inhabitants.[35] It is next subjected to the test of the two succeeding arguments listed in Popper's complaint. We are then told (434 D ff.) that this proffered conception of justice, if it is at last to be approved, must show its adequacy to describe the corresponding excellence of the individual. And before the final acceptance is pronounced, it has been shown (442 E ff.) clearly to exclude the ordinary civil crimes and iniquities of theft, adultery, and bad faith. It thus appears that the seemingly odd but actually not uncommon mixture of psychology and logic, of heuristic and proof by which Plato has arrived at what may be called a likely hypothesis — for as such his proposed definition truly functions — justifies some hesitation over the classifications of the form of reasoning involved. But it is only the imputation of bad faith to Plato's procedure that has permitted Popper to treat it with cynical contempt.

Plato's second argument receives even rougher handling; Plato is detected in the attempt to derive his "antiequalitarianism" from the "equalitarian . . . view that justice is impartiality"; his argument "is nothing but a crude juggle," whose "sole purpose" is the illegitimate attempt to show "that justice, in the ordinary sense of the word, requires us to keep our own station," i.e., " 'our own' class," forever. "This is how the greatest philosopher of all times tries to convince us that he has discovered the true nature of justice." [36]

What Plato has actually done is to point out that it is possible to confirm his suggested definition of justice by observing that judges in the courts of his city will seek in giving judgment to render to each his own, "both the having and the doing of what is properly his" (Republic 433 E) ; that is, we may interpret, to restore the balance that has been disturbed by crime, by assigning repayments or penalties, or by restoring status to those unjustly accused. Plato is showing that the suggested formula can be extended to include the justice of the courts, something that a definition of justice would naturally be expected to do. We are reminded of the meaning of justice which is employed in the Gorgias (464 B, 478 A–D), where justice (dikê and dikaiosynê, interchangeably) is made the correlative of medicine, as legislation is that of the trainer's art; and as the trainer and the legislator minister to healthy souls and bodies respectively, the physician and the judge minister to and assign the remedies to those that are sick or in need of healing punishment. To call the judgments given by the just judge, the assignment to each of "having and doing his own," is fully in accord with this point of view, and Plato's second proof is seen as not without weight, in terms of his thought

---

[35] We recollect from the Protagoras (322 D–323 C) that reverence and justice, aidôs and dikê, are required of all members of any human community, and are not, like flute playing, excellences to be dispensed with by any man.

[36] Popper, pp. 96–97.

as a whole. We shall agree with Popper that its intention here in the *Republic* is to lend strength to the suggested formula for justice. But since we shall not agree that this formula amounts to the assertion that in the actual world, as distinct from the ideal city, everyone must keep forever his "own station," we deny the truth of Popper's further remarks concerning the "sole purpose" of this argument.

Plato's third argument is the assertion that it would be harmful in the highest degree to the ideal city, and therefore correspondingly unjust, for a member of one of the three functional classes to intrude into a class whose duties his natural capacities do not qualify him to perform; that it is just, therefore, for him to do his proper task; and that thus again the formula for justice is sustained. It is in this third argument, Popper believes, that Plato, putting off all disguises, confronts us with a serious appeal to the principle of collectivism, and to its discrediting Popper accordingly devotes much space. The issues raised reach the very center of Plato's moral and political thought, the theme of our discussion in a later chapter. But a few comments are indispensable in the present context.

For the success of Popper's interpretation of what Plato has been concealing and revealing in this fourth book of the *Republic*, it is, of course, essential that the revelation, when it comes, shall possess the proportions of a mountain, not a mouse. To secure this result, Popper has done all that was humanly possible to enlarge and underline what is unacceptable in the concept of Platonic justice. To this end, he has done two things that must not be allowed to pass unchallenged.

Popper asserts that in this argument, "Plato recognizes only one ultimate standard, the interest of the state." In thus unwarrantably narrowing Platonic justice, restricting it to the service of the state's interest, Popper has given a specious color to his declaration of the "barrenness" of the concept. But this is, as Berkeley puts it, "to raise a dust and complain we cannot see." The advocate of any form of civil organization whatever, not totalitarians alone, must regard it as part of injustice to undermine the stability of his approved form, part of justice (and an important part) to maintain it. And Plato, as we have seen, extends his concept of justice to include legal justice, and is on his way to test his definition against the demands of the psychology and ethics and social behavior of the individual, both within and without the ideal state. Plato, in calling it "just" to do what serves the interest of the city, is stating no more than that this is part of justice; and Popper has no warrant for treating Plato's statement as a definition of the whole.[37] To put this in another

---

[37] To be listed as part of this same error is Popper's further statement (p. 104) that in Plato's city "it is simply nonsense" to say "that it is better to suffer than to commit injustice," because injustice is an act against the state and nothing more, and therefore an individual cannot "suffer" an injustice. A man can be injured or cheated in Plato's state, just as he could be put to death in the Athens described in the *Gor-*

way, Popper has no right to interpret Plato's statement as the assertion that the interest of the state is by nature, essence, and definition equal to Platonic justice. To do so is to avenge Thrasymachus upon Plato, by re-erecting his overthrown thesis, "justice is the advantage of the stronger," and making it serve as the corner stone of Plato's temple.[38] The reasoning which has engendered this conclusion involves an arbitrary identification of "property" and "essence," in which, despite his efforts to avoid it, Popper has involved himself throughout his discussion of Plato's political thinking.[39] This is particularly easy to do because for Plato "advantage" (e.g., happiness, beauty, stability) in the normal case attends upon moral excellence. But this is not to say that moral excellence is only for these reasons to be sought. That so gifted a logician as Popper should be chargeable with neglecting so gross a distinction is a commentary upon the dyslogistic power of partisanship. It is not true, as Popper supposes, that the eye of hate sees clearest.[40]

Secondly, we cannot allow Popper to distract his readers into transferring to the justice which Plato has proposed the indignation naturally aroused by applying the Platonic formula, in its political aspect, to an unreformed city, such as Athens or Megara, with the result of freezing in perpetuity all existing inequalities of ownership and status. Plato's political justice, of course, has its only proper home and application in a city shaped and molded initially by conformity to its canon, namely, the principle that each should really be where he belongs, in view of his capacity, and have what he requires, in view of his needs and contribution to the common life. It was in fact largely for

---

gias, and he will in either case "suffer injustice," but only in the terms of Socrates' paradox; since his soul is unimpaired, he will suffer no real injury. Alternatively, in the *Republic*, the man who commits injustice harms both the state and his own soul by disturbing their respective internal orders, and is truly worse off than he to whom injustice has been done (*Rep.* 366–7).

[38] Oddly enough, Woodbridge maintained (*The Son of Apollo*, 1929, pp. 90–91) in a whimsical sense, that Plato has actually done this very thing — though with no disposition to abolish the distinction between might and right.

[39] Elsewhere in his book (e.g., pp. 72–73), Popper has shown himself well aware that Plato's ethics are rooted not in political but in metaphysical soil, or, in other words, that Plato is what Popper calls a "spiritual naturalist," whose ethics rests upon a normative theory of man. True that Popper has, in a sense, anticipated this objection, and argued (pp. 76–81) that though Plato appeals to the norm of human

nature, that norm was itself political in view of the insufficiency of the individual man. This has merely shifted the incidence of the fallacy; for it by no means follows that the economic and political organization of individuals into a state has displaced moral control, has set up its own peculiar norm free from moral responsibility. On the contrary, as the account of the education of the philosophic rulers in *Republic* Book VII shows at length, and as Plato states succinctly at *Laws* 645 B, quoted on p. 520 below, the state must hunt and find a moral principle for its guidance, namely, justice, which cannot be defined in less than cosmic terms.

[40] "Plato hated tyranny. Only hatred can see as sharply as he did in his famous description of the tyrant" (Popper, p. 193). In an earlier passage, it is true, Popper had implied (see n. 115, p. 78 above) that hatred even of tyranny is somehow discreditable. But he himself professes "frank hostility" (p. 36) to "historicism," and therefore to Plato's political thought.

the sake of formulating this ideal and drawing out its full implication for
the life of man that Plato wrote the *Republic*. Plato's sense of the organic relation between his definition and its contemplated sphere of application is
shown by his practice in subsequent dialogues, e.g., in the *Laws*, where without altering anything in his fundamental value scheme, Plato assigns to justice a meaning better fitted to take account of changed relations of the citizens to each other and to the common weal.[41]

Plato has also, in clearing the way for his totalitarian scheme, been guilty
in Popper's eyes of another crime, that of ignoring what he could not hope
successfully to combat. Thus, in the *Republic*, while appearing to omit from
consideration "none of the more important theories" of justice "known to
him," he fails even to mention the view "that justice is equality before the
law" (*isonomia*). That this omission is tactical and no mere consequence of
ignorance, Popper infers with certainty from allusions to the theory in the
Gorgias, where, he asserts, Socrates defends it, and also from the "few sneers
and pin-pricks" it receives in a part of the *Republic* "where justice is not the
topic of the discussion." This "almost unbroken silence" is a part of Plato's
attack, conducted "not squarely and openly," against his "arch-enemy,"
equalitarianism.[42]

In all this we think it fair to say there is no single element which supports
the conclusion in favor of which it is adduced; it is more nearly true that
the destined conclusion has forced the selection and interpretation of the
"facts." Let us then see whether what Plato has done in the *Republic* can be
more easily explained without the violence of assuming Plato's bad faith.
The *Republic* begins and ends with a concern for the individual soul, and in
the conviction that its present and future well-being depend upon its "justice,"
i.e., its righteousness during its mortal career. The aged Cephalus introduces
this theme at the beginning of Book I (330 D ff.) and expounds it in the
language of traditional Greek religion; Socrates reaffirms it at the end of the
final book: "If we are guided by me . . . we shall pursue justice with wisdom
always and ever, that we may be dear to ourselves and to the gods . . . and
thus . . . we shall fare well." [43] In the interval, it is true to say Plato has
evaluated every important theory of justice known to him, including the current "equalitarianism" associated with Periclean and post-Periclean democ-

---

[41] In the *Laws* the ideal of political
justice is not indeed essentially different
from political justice in the *Republic* (or
for that matter, in the *Gorgias*): it is defined (757 C) as the principle of assigning
political offices and honors in proportion
to a man's moral and intellectual worth.
But Plato reluctantly tempers this ideal in
practice, to meet the circumstances imposed by a "second-best" state, with the
result that the measure of civic worth becomes the spirit of obedience to the existing laws, and the incitement of others to
a like attitude (715 B–D, 730 D).

[42] Popper, pp. 92–96; p. 116.

[43] Trans. Shorey (slightly altered), Loeb
Library.

racy, but he does so in an order chosen by himself. In Book I, he passes rapidly over the inadequacies of various traditional notions of what right conduct is — paying one's debts, benefiting friends and injuring enemies, etc. (331 C ff.). The standpoint here is still that of the individual man. With Thrasymachus' definition (338 C), we enter upon considerations involving political as distinct from moral questions, but, as is indicated by the manner in which the proffered definition is handled, the basic question (e.g., 343 C ff., 348 B ff.) remains the same: what does it profit a man to possess this quality rather than its contrary? This becomes especially clear in Book II, after Thrasymachus has been overthrown, when Glaucon and Adeimantus restate his case with supplementary reënforcement, for Socrates to refute in its fullest possible strength. What is called for, therefore, at this point of the argument, is just what Plato has provided: the most persuasive of current arguments known to him, purporting to show that a man is a victim of his own naiveté if he permits his interest to be interfered with by moral and religious principles.

It is thus true that Plato has not put into the earlier part of his *Republic* what Popper supposes he was under obligation to put there, the discussion of the organizing principles of various forms of political constitutions, e.g., democracy, with its principle of "equality before the law." Why Plato should have followed Popper's order in the construction of his book one fails to see. What is clear, however, is that in Book VIII, after the lineaments of his ideal state have been clearly drawn, Plato does offer a discussion of the types of government and an appraisal of the degree of human excellence and social fairness attainable in each. Certainly he makes clear his judgment that the contemporary democracy, despite its advocacy of equality, was very unequal and unfair in its actual distribution of rights and benefits. Popper has belittled Plato's treatment of democracy here [44] in view of the satiric tone that pervades it. But for reasons we have earlier expounded, Plato was not in a position to sing the praises of democracy. The only relevant question concerns not appreciation but honesty, and though one may well doubt that Plato's satire does full justice to the case for Athenian democracy, it is certainly an honest and unabashed attack, from a clearly indicated base, upon the principle of equality regarded as the essence of political justice.

The construction of the ideal state begun in Book II is undertaken by Socrates as a means of clarifying the nature and function of justice. Doubtless this shows that Plato was interested not merely in the moral problem as it confronts the individual, but in the political question as well; it is no

---

[44] Popper in another passage, pp. 43–44, does not belittle but emphasizes and exaggerates (as we have seen, n. 228, p. 340) Plato's scornful description of democracy, calling it "a flood of rhetorical abuse" "identifying liberty with licence, . . . and equality before the law with disorder." In charging "almost unbroken silence" on this topic, therefore, Popper seems to have overlooked his own earlier assertions.

mere afterthought. Doubtless, also, the moral and the political aspects of the ideal state are, for Plato, not to be torn apart. Within their indissoluble unity, however, this much of duality may be discerned: the political institutions are for the sake of the moral life of the citizens, and not — Popper's capital error — conversely. And since it is recognized that this moral striving can be carried on, at least by gifted individuals, without the support of a well-ordered state, political justice, for Plato, cannot absorb without remainder the totality of justice. We may remind ourselves again of the just man in the evil state, who stands aside from political affairs, like one who takes shelter behind a wall in a storm.[45] It is scarcely necessary to insist that the *sine qua non* of the existence of this man is the separability of ethics and politics, and that unless there is a meaning of justice stateable independently, he could not be described as just. In view of this requirement, it would not have been possible for Plato to pursue his search for a comprehensive definition of justice among definitions of political or juridical justice, such as *isonomia*. His failure formally to consider its claims needs, therefore, no further explanation.

The sole remaining support of Popper's belief that Plato dishonestly refrains in the *Republic* from giving due consideration to equality as justice, is his reputed discovery (other critics are said to have "overlooked" the fact) that in the *Gorgias* Plato had shown Socrates defending this very theory, for which, in the later parts of the *Republic*, he is made to express his scorn. On quieter inspection, this will be seen to involve a misreading of a passage (*Gorgias* 488 B ff., esp. 488 E–489 A) in which Socrates makes a purely dialectical use, against Callicles, of the notions that equality is just, and that injustice is shameful, as opinions admittedly approved by the many. Socrates does not here state to what degree he himself is in accord with them; he merely proves that since the many are collectively the stronger, these opinions will, on Callicles' own premises, constitute natural justice. When, later in the *Gorgias*, Socrates comes to grips with his theme, his standpoint is in no respect at variance with that of the *Republic* or later dialogues: the equality that he defends is proportional or "geometrical," not of the simple "arithmetical" variety, beloved of Athenian democrats.[46]

We have also to consider the weight of another of Popper's imputations

---

[45] More extreme instances of this lack of dependence between individual moral attainment and the interest of the state are mentioned by Plato in the passage from the *Laws* (770 C–D) quoted on pp. 520–521. On p. 643 we discuss also Plato's conception of the relation between individual moral attainment and the state as a moral and educational influence.

[46] The real basis of our statement here is not the passing mention of "geometrical equality" (508 A), for all the importance

which Plato assigns to it elsewhere (e.g., *Rep.* 558 C, *Laws* 757 A–D). That basis is, rather, to be assembled from the dialogue as a whole, particularly those passages in which Socrates compares the statesman's art to that of the public trainer or physician of souls (e.g., 513 E–515 A, 502 E–505 B), combined with the further conception of the physician as the man who knows how to apportion to each his appropriate kind and amount of nourishment or medicine (e.g., 490 B–C, 464 B–C).

of underhanded practices, this time the important charge that Plato had no right, and knew he had none, to apply the term "justice" to his theory of the proper principle of social organization and its application to the individual. To Popper this is no mere question of verbal propriety. Plato was, it is granted, sincere in his opposition to humanitarian forces; but he is declared unscrupulous in his choice of means. Not daring "to face the enemy openly," he sought to capture the strong and admirable existing sentiment in behalf of the good thing which was equalitarian justice, and enlist it in behalf of "totalitarian class rule," by a dishonest verbal trick, in short, by a use of the Pareto principle.[47]

Nothing could be more plausible than this suggestion, with the one proviso that Plato may be antecedently defined as "a reptile capable of discourse." For why should Plato be denied the right to apply to the outcome of his efforts to clarify and purify what was to him the most approvable plan and purpose of human life, individual and social, the name of justice? Nor is this simply a matter of sentimental right. There is a principle of logical and general philosophical importance at stake, easily to be illustrated at every stage of the growth of human enquiry. We may call it by the somewhat high-sounding name of "the right of conceptual reëssentialization," and illustrate its use by pointing to the semantics of such words in the scientific vocabulary as "sugar" and "angle," in which the attainment of new heights of generalization has involved doing a radical violence to their traditional, commonsense meanings, denying that sugar is sweet, and speaking of angles greater than 360°. We may even claim the founder of Christianity as a practitioner of this art: witness his "reëssentialization" of such terms as "my neighbor"; while in contemporary political discussion, "world citizenship" is an instance of the same process in mid-career.

Returning to Plato, in the light of what has just been said we can read a reply to Popper: by including in his wider formula for justice the traditional juristic meaning of the concept, Plato was not making an insidious attempt to capture popular affection. In just the same way, as we have shown, he has included other popular acceptations of the term which Popper has not noticed (*Republic* 442 f.), e.g., the observing of oaths, abstention from thefts and betrayals, respect for parents. He has provided for the inclusion of the solitary conscientious objector, and for the description of the state as a whole, both in its internal ordering and in its international conduct; he has accounted, with some modification, for the justice of the common citizens in his ideal state, as well as for that of the rulers. In all these ways Plato is "reëssentializing"; he is effecting junctures between new and old that enrich both terms of the relation. The conventional ideal is deepened and extended by being caught up into a wider pattern of systematic totality; at the same time the

---

[47] Popper, p. 92.

philosophical ideal gains in solidity of relevant content. There has been no juggle, no wrenching of context, only the sort of clarified enlargement of significance that always results when philosophy discovers a more comprehensive category for the coherent ordering of the miscellanies of human experience. Whether Plato's ideal is in all its applications acceptable to the modern reader is another question; but there can be no doubt that the effort to construct it constitutes a legitimate and even noble attempt, in line with a progressive method of inquiry.

We have witnessed the insufficiency and failure of Popper's suspicions of bad faith in Plato's way of introducing and defining justice in the *Republic* and have traced them to their respective foundations in Popper's deliberate blindness to literary considerations, his neglect of the logical distinction between definition and description, his misreading of a Platonic passage in the *Gorgias*, and above all, his inflexible and unimaginative requirement that Plato shall arrange his topics, employ his terms, and conduct his discussion along lines predetermined for him by Popper. In so doing we have illustrated the general arbitrariness and the busy inventiveness of Popper's method, and we have thus, it is hoped, established the probability that Popper's other imputations of guile to Plato could be shown to be similarly baseless, were it possible to examine them all in equal detail. This we do not intend to do; yet there are still some of these which merit attention.

Popper maintains that Plato has knowingly misrepresented and has thus caused to be misunderstood and undervalued a noble theory of the proper function of government, conceived by Plato's near-contemporary, the sophist Lycophron, whom we recall as an admired member of Popper's Great Generation and a supposed but unverified opponent of slavery; we have also seen [48] that he was in fact the author of a denunciation, preserved by Aristotle, of the claims of noble birth, and of one other relevant fragment dealing with the proper end or aim of the state and embedded in Aristotle's discussion of this topic. It is this latter with which we are here centrally concerned. Aristotle is occupied at this point in his *Politics* [49] in rejecting the view that a state can be constituted by an association of individuals or households bound together only by agreements, like trade treaties and nonaggression pacts between states, which regulate the exchange of goods and prohibit mutual aggression. To him it appears that the only association worthy the name of state is one which includes among its aims the promotion of virtue in its citizens. In the midst of his argument, he quotes, in order to deny it his approval, the saying of "the sophist Lycophron," that "law is the guarantor of just mutual dealing, but is unable to make the citizens good and just."

---

[48] See pp. 146–147 above.   [49] *Politics* III, ix, 6 ff.

It is well to remember that these two fragments and their Aristotelian contexts constitute our entire basis for judging Lycophron's political thought. Popper himself has declared, "Any opinion of Lycophron must be highly speculative, owing to the scanty information we have"; [50] yet he has not hesitated to speculate boldly upon the two fragments, and on Lycophron's behalf has announced the claim that he was the first proponent of "the protectionist theory of the state." [51]

This theory, which Popper regards as even today the only valid justification of government, does not attempt, we are told, to answer the question, "How did the state originate?" — a question which Popper regards as fatally "historicist" — or the "essentialist" question, "What is the state?" but only, "What do we demand from a state?" It appears to assume the existence of a group of persons who regard themselves as associated upon equal terms for the purpose of attaining rational ends. Each of its members, in so far as he is a "humanitarian," is conceived as saying, "What I demand from the state is protection; not only for myself, but for others too. I demand protection for my own freedom and for other people's . . . against aggression from other men . . . I know that some limitations of my freedom are necessary. . . But I demand . . . protection of that freedom which does not harm other citizens." [52] It is a further essential part of Popper's conception of the protectionist state that it shall not concern itself with, or attempt to control the morality of its members; such an attempt on his view would necessarily "destroy morality," and replace it with "the totalitarian irresponsibility of the individual." [53] It is this protectionist view of the state, equalitarian, individualist, and altruistic, which Popper finds to have been Lycophron's great discovery, and of which "we have been robbed" by Plato's dishonest misrepresentation.[54]

That Plato knew the theory well, Popper concludes from a passage in the *Gorgias* (483 B ff.), in which Callicles, who believes that natural justice is "that the strong should rule and have more," is made to speak scornfully of the usual laws and customs which decree that no man shall get the better of his neighbor and that it is unjust and disgraceful to attempt it; for, Callicles declares, the weak men, who are in the majority, make these laws in their own interest in order to deter the strong, and "are well content to see themselves on an equality, when they are so inferior." [55] Popper supposes (a) that Callicles is here opposing (without naming) Lycophron, quoting and criticizing his equalitarian doctrine of protectionism; (b) that the Socrates of the dialogue, merely by opposing Callicles, by implication "comes to the rescue of

---

[50] Popper, p. 541.
[51] *Ibid.*, p. 112.
[52] Popper, pp. 108–109.
[53] *Ibid.*, pp. 111–112.
[54] *Ibid.*, pp. 112–113.
[55] *Gorgias* 483 C, trans. Lamb, Loeb Library.

protectionism"; and (c) that Socrates' subsequent use of Callicles' own premises to disprove Callicles' doctrine of natural justice,[56] constitutes the explicit defense, by Socrates himself, of several elements in protectionism. Thus Popper believes he has presented proof at once of the nobility of the true Socrates as contrasted with the counterfeit "Socrates" of the *Republic*, and of Plato's knowledge of Lycophron's protectionist doctrine in its equalitarian and unselfish form.[57]

Turning now to the *Republic*, in the speech of Glaucon (358 E ff.) Popper finds a second but seriously altered sketch of protectionism. Here Glaucon is maintaining, for the sake of the argument, the thesis that injustice is advantageous to its possessor, and in presenting his case he is made to expound the views of some persons who say that justice itself is of no lofty origin or nature. Best of all things, they say, is the doing of injustice to others with impunity; and this in the beginning all men sought to obtain. But the majority, being weak, had no success, and in consequence banded together to relinquish by a social compact the most desirable thing in order to secure for themselves the second-best thing, which is immunity from being wronged at the cost of doing no wrong; and this they call justice. In Popper's opinion, Plato has here, as also in the *Gorgias*, given the theory of protectionism a "fatal historicist presentation." But in another respect, his treatment of it in the *Republic* reveals "a tremendous difference," for whereas in the *Gorgias* Socrates defends protectionism, in this later dialogue he has dishonestly, but with "astonishing success" and cleverness, made it to appear identical with cynical nihilism, to the disadvantage of Lycophron's fair fame and to the lasting hurt of the humanitarian cause in general.[58]

We are now ready to appraise the degree of credence which Popper's argument deserves; and a second look discloses that it rests principally upon one base, that is, the altruism and other ethical excellences which, Popper assumes, originally were inherent in Lycophron's doctrine, distinguishing it from the ignoble form presented by Glaucon in the *Republic*. And Popper has further assumed that in its original form there was no talk of origins, nor any suggestion of a historical social compact. Without these assumptions it would be impossible to prove anything to Plato's discredit in this whole matter; for then the difference between the *Gorgias* and the *Republic* (if such there be) loses all significance. Since this is so, we must examine closely the evidence on which Popper's high claim is based.

We are thrown back upon that passage from Aristotle's *Politics* in which the sentence from Lycophron occurs. As has been said, the general theme is the separation of the state, properly so-called, from other associations with which it may be confused, among them limited associations resembling

---

[56] We have discussed this argument above, p. 416.

[57] Popper, pp. 114–116.
[58] Popper, pp. 116–117.

treaties between nations. Aristotle is not discussing the motivation of the nations which enter into such treaties, or of the persons who may be imagined to do the same. He implies nothing, either favorable or unfavorable, concerning the reasons for which Lycophron's "guarantor of just mutual dealings" exists. It is perfectly compatible with Aristotle's presentation to believe that Lycophron, in describing his social compact, had taught that it was maintained by its members not out of a desire to protect others, but out of the purely prudential desire of each man to secure his own personal safety and profit. Nor does Aristotle go into sufficient detail to enable us to see the reason why Lycophron denied the state's fitness "to make the citizens good and just." To speculate upon this is not very profitable, but we may at least observe that there is no foundation in Aristotle's text for Popper's implication that Lycophron must have denied on principle the propriety of the state's intrusion into the domain of individual responsibility.[59] And once this supposition is eliminated, Popper's claim that Lycophron's theory was "individualist" loses all foundation. Whether Lycophron depicted the social compact as a historical event is similarly undiscoverable. Aristotle, it is true, presents it as part of his own discussion of the aim or purpose of the state, without reference to origins. But he would be perfectly within his rights in referring to a doctrine which had spoken of the purpose for which law was originally established, as a doctrine regarding the purpose or nature of law.[60] Nor can it be assumed that Lycophron's law guaranteed equality among the citizens. There is certainly no mention of equality, nor any implication of it in Aristotle's context: treaties between nations are by no means always concluded on an equal basis. And depending on what is regarded as "just," a social compact could pledge its members to maintain inviolate any inequalities of status, rights, or possessions. True that Lycophron is on record as having denied the claims of noble birth, but we do not know his attitude toward other inequalities, e.g., the claims of wealth. The characteristics for which Popper so highly honors Lycophron are thus not attested by Aristotle.

---

[59] Other possible reasons for denying the state's fitness to produce virtue in the citizens lie near at hand. Lycophron may have maintained what was almost a postulate of the sophist's trade, that training by a qualified sophist was requisite. He may have believed that it would be highly desirable for the state to inculcate virtue, but that it was unfortunately impossible, since, as Antiphon observed in a passage adjoining the one quoted on our p. 145 above (Diels, II, pp. xxxiv–xxxv, fr. A, col. 6), legal penalties for crime come late and are uncertain; as Diodotus (Thucydides III, 45) had also observed, threats of punishment for crime have never constituted effective deterrents. He may have agreed with the sentiment expressed in the play of Critias (who had also, apparently, been a pupil of Gorgias) that religious sanctions were indispensable (see pp. 272–273 above).

[60] If Lycophron had said, "The state originated when men established law as the guarantor of just mutual dealings," Aristotle could still have quoted him as he does. Popper, p. 111, says that conventionalists, wishing to describe the state in terms of a demand, often clumsily speak of its origin or its essence. It could be concluded from this that unless there is particular reason for precision, a given expositor may employ these concepts interchangeably.

Nor can the *Gorgias* be pressed into service to establish the original excellence of Lycophron's theory. Callicles' version of the social contract theory is indeed very different from what Aristotle tells us of Lycophron's. There seems in fact to be no similarity except that both involve a compact. In Callicle's version there is no mention of the state's unfitness to produce virtue, and thus at a blow half of what was known of Lycophron's is eliminated. In Lycophron's version, so far as can be judged, all citizens unite to establish law; in Callicles', it is the weak alone who do so, in opposition to the strong. In Lycophron's version, equality is left unmentioned; in Callicles', it is prominent, though cynically regarded as the self-interest of the weak. The *Gorgias* contains further important additions. There is the supposition throughout that all men aim simply at power and wealth, and there is the cynical identification of conventional justice with the selfish interest and the moralistic pretense of the weaker men. The theory has been altered and has grown so much that it cannot properly be called the same; it is either Callicles' own (if he is a real person), or that of some other man; Antiphon the sophist has been suggested as a likely candidate.[61] It has indeed become ethically equivalent to that presented in the *Republic*.

Popper, brushing aside all these new and cynical elements as simply Callicles' misrepresentation of a noble theory, still sees at its core what he imagines to be the altruistic, equalitarian doctrine of Lycophron. He assumes that in so far as Callicles speaks of law as a compact between the many weak men who ordain that equality is just and brand injustice as foul and disgraceful, he is simply restating Lycophron's view; yet there is no evidence, as we have seen, that Lycophron ever thought in these terms. Popper then adds, as before, the assumption that Lycophron had imputed generous motives and individualist scruples to those who establish law, and behold! "protectionism" is before us. Yet there is not in the *Gorgias*, any more than in Aristotle, any indication that Lycophron, or indeed anyone in Plato's Athens, had ever ascribed such other-regarding motives to the participants in a social compact.[62] Callicles does not say of the weaker men, even in scornful derision, that they refuse to intrude on the field of private morality, or that they desire justice, each man for his neighbor as well as for himself, because they do not wish anyone at all to suffer wrong.

Nor does the Socrates of the dialogue, simply by the fact that he opposes Callicles, imply the existence of a noble compact theory which he defends.[63]

---

[61] See our discussion of Antiphon, p. 144f.

[62] Plato's own version of the social compact (*Rep.* 369 B ff.), while it rests upon the assumed self-interest of the participants, is at least free from any suggestion of a desire to overreach, and is as amicable a theory as any that has come down to us from that period.

[63] Popper's thesis that there is "a tremendous difference," hitherto overlooked by the commentators, between the *Gorgias* and the *Republic* in the attitude adopted toward the "protectionist theory," is difficult either to state clearly or to refute because of the complications resulting from the quotation, by one speaker, of another's be-

Popper, as we have seen throughout our acquaintance with him, too easily assumes that there are only two positions possible, and that a man who denies one must support the other; he overlooks the existence of positions which combine elements of both, or contain elements foreign to either. Socrates, as we have seen, does later in the *Gorgias* take a stand which differs both from the equalitarian theory of the state and from Callicles' doctrine of self-interest. As to Popper's demonstration that Socrates "upholds . . . several features" of the compact theory which Callicles unfairly misrepresents, we may say first that Socrates-Plato, in every dialogue in which the question is directly raised, believes that to do injustice is fouler than to suffer it,[64] which is one of the features referred to; and for the rest, it is simply not true that Socrates upholds what Callicles denies: we have shown that Popper's proof of this rests upon his failure to observe the dialectical nature of Socrates' initial refutation of Callicles.[65]

The form of the compact theory of justice which appears in the *Republic* is, as we have said, closely akin to that in the *Gorgias*, and is presented by Plato as thoroughly unacceptable, its affiliation with the doctrine that self-interest is the only determiner of human action brought strongly to the fore. We remember that for Popper this fact is the damning proof that Plato has dishonestly misrepresented Lycophron. But where is Lycophron's altruistic theory presented to our view? We have sought for it in vain in Aristotle; it has not been found in the *Gorgias*. There is simply nothing for Plato to have misrepresented. Instead, there is every likelihood that Plato was only too well acquainted with the existence in Athens of a nihilistic version of the compact theory, developed by some person or persons whose names he refrains on principle from recording. Plato has chosen in his *Republic* to present this dangerous doctrine, which could be used to convince young men like Glaucon

---

lief; nevertheless, that it rests on a confusion can be shown, if sufficient patience is exerted. Popper says, in brief (p. 115), that in the *Gorgias*, Lycophron's theory is presented by Callicles as one which he opposes; Socrates opposes Callicles and thus *ipso facto* supports Lycophron. Popper next states that in the *Republic* Lycophron's theory is presented by Glaucon as an elaboration of Thrasymachus' nihilism; Socrates opposes this Thrasymachean nihilism, and thus opposes Lycophron's theory. The confusion here apparently arises from the word "presents." In the *Gorgias*, Callicles does not *present* Lycophron's theory, even if we accept Popper's belief that Lycophron had enunciated a noble compact theory which Callicles is opposing. Let us assume, with Popper, that Lycophron did so announce it,

and let us then attempt to restate what Callicles, and Glaucon, do with Lycophron's noble theory. Callicles announces as his own an immoralist theory of the social compact in which Popper sees embedded elements of Lycophron's theory. Glaucon too sets forth a nihilistic theory of the social compact in which Popper sees embedded elements of Lycophron's theory. Thus in both dialogues, Lycophron's theory appears only in combination with immoralist or nihilist elements. In both dialogues, it is thus identically related to Socrates, in that he refutes the nihilistic doctrine with which it is combined.

[64] Cf. our pp. 412–413 and notes, and for a corollary principle, p. 439.

[65] See p. 416 above.

that to be unjust with impunity was the "smart" thing to do, as a prelude to his attempt to set forth a more persuasive ideal of self-realization combined with altruistic concern for social well-being. That he had every right to do so, without being accused of misrepresenting or intending to deceive anyone, seems obvious.

We see, then, that with Lycophron, as with Antisthenes and Socrates, Popper has built up an ancient thinker by the simple process of making all modern and creditable additions to his doctrines which do not conflict with his recorded sayings, or which can be added, as he has done for Socrates and Antisthenes, by ignoring some of these. Having built up this thinker with the utmost generosity, he then not only contrasts Plato with him, to Plato's disadvantage, but also ascribes to Plato misrepresentation or vilification of his noble opponent. The charge that in dealing with Lycophron Plato has robbed us of a valuable ethical insight is seen to be particularly baseless, since there remains of Lycophron only enough to establish him as the proponent of some form of the compact theory of the state, whether altruistic, or in all respects equalitarian, or individualist, or nonhistorical, we cannot say. This being the case, Plato's reputation for honesty can suffer no harm.

The "myth of the metals" in the fourth book of the *Republic*, which Popper calls a "propaganda lie," and to which he has affixed the name of the "Myth of Blood and Soil," has provided another opportunity to press the charges of duplicity and guilty hesitation. Again Plato is seen trembling before the anticipated indignation of his libertarian Athenian reader and, in the hope of deluding him, practicing sleights and turns of rhetoric. Yet Popper in his exuberance of accusation has permitted himself to charge Plato simultaneously with making the "blunt admission" to this same reader of his intention to hoodwink not only the common citizens of the ideal state, but *"the rulers themselves"* (italics his). Popper divides the myth itself into an uneasy "lengthy preface," and the exposition of two false notions which are to be imposed upon the citizens. The first of these notions is the relatively innocent idea that the "warriors" are born of the earth of their country, and therefore bound in duty to defend it; the second is the guilty racialistic tenet that the citizens possess differing innate capacities — "metals" infused in their souls — which fit them to hold differing stations in the community. Since Plato's "lengthy preface" and expression of uneasiness in introducing the myth appear to have reference only to the first of these ideas, Popper adds the subsidiary hypothesis that Plato has intentionally arranged it thus, in order to distract attention from the really unacceptable second idea. And although Plato, in describing the differing innate capacities of the citizens, explicitly states that these capacities alone, in whatever class in the state they may arise, are to determine social functions, Popper hastens to assert that "this concession is rescinded in later passages in the *Republic* (and also

in the *Laws*)." [66] Elsewhere Popper comments on Plato's supposed behavior
in thus speaking "as though a rise from the lower classes . . . were permissible," and then withdrawing the permission, as further evidence of Plato's
guilty hesitation in introducing his "racialism." [67]

We should by this time be able to recognize the distinguishing marks of
Popper's approach. There is, first, his tendency to employ a partisan vocabulary: "blunt admission" for "frank statement" that a myth is to be told;
"propaganda lie," used as if it were a synonym for "myth," without regard
for the fact that a myth may be intended to symbolize a truth; and "Blood
and Soil," with its Nazi overtones. We should expect his readiness to scent
deception, and observe without surprise his prompt improvisation of a further hypothesis to account for a weakness in his argument; even the fact that
this hypothesis involves further discredit to Plato was expectable. We should
be forewarned against his assertion that Plato withdraws his stated intention
to transfer citizens from station to station as befits their capabilities. "This
may be true," should be the vigilant reader's initial reaction, "but I had best
not accept it on the strength of so partisan a plea."

We must first consider what, if any, signs of guilt are discernible in
Plato's introduction of the myth (*Republic* 414 B ff.). Socrates has proposed
that a medicinal lie be told to the citizens. Asked by Glaucon to name it,
he goes on to say at some length that it is but a "Phoenician tale" such as
is told by the poets, of what befell in olden times,[68] a thing not easily credible
today. Glaucon, thus kept waiting, says that Socrates seems to shrink from
telling, and Socrates replies in mock fear, "You will think that I have right
good reason for shrinking when I have told." Glaucon humorously bids him
be brave, and Socrates explains that when the first group of guardians shall
have been made fully ready to guide and guard the city, all the citizens are
to be told — in what bold and persuasive words he hardly knows — that they
have dreamed their whole prior lives up to this moment, and that they have in
reality been fostered within the earth, where also their arms and all their
possessions have been fashioned; and now they have been brought forth as
sons to their native soil and brothers to one another, owing protection and
piety to both. Glaucon remarks, "It is not for nothing that you were so

---

[66] Popper, pp. 137–139.

[67] *Ibid.*, pp. 50, 496, 192.

[68] This follows Shorey's and Cornford's
rendering, which implies that the miraculous origin of men from the soil, as the poets
say, occurred in the early days. It could be
rendered to imply that it was the telling of
such tales and the successful persuasion of
men into believing them, which happened
in early times. The Greek can be read in
either way. The meaning of the epithet
"Phoenician" seems to be adequately ex-

plained by the Phoenician origin of Cad-
mus, with whom is associated the tale (mentioned again, *Laws* 663 E) of the sowing of
the dragon's teeth and the earthborn warriors that sprang from them. Popper's suggestion (p. 555) that Plato refers to a division of mankind into four races, "utilized
in Egypt for purposes of political propaganda" and imported into Greece by the
Phoenicians, seems overingenious, and dispensable by anyone not bent on finding
reasons to discredit Plato.

bashful about coming out with your lie." Socrates, replying, "It was quite natural that I should be, but all the same hear the rest of the story," goes on to aver that though they are brothers — so the citizens are to be told — yet infused in their souls are different metals, gold, silver, bronze, or iron, as the case may be, destining them to different tasks. In general their children will inherit their parent's natures, but since the citizens are all akin, exceptions may occur; and these the guardians must diligently transfer to their rightful stations, raising or lowering them as required; "for there is an oracle," the tale must add, "that the state shall then be overthrown when the man of iron or brass is its guardian." [69] When Socrates again expresses his doubt that the citizens can in any way be induced to believe the story, Glaucon agrees, but suggests that their descendants may come to accept it. And Socrates concludes by saying that any success will be helpful in increasing the citizens' loyalty to the state and to one another.

With Plato's myth now in outline before us, we can perceive another unjustifiable procedure that has served to lend support to Popper's argument. Twice in this passage Popper has been guilty of a "criminal negligence" which, until it is observed, works great injury to Plato. He has passed over in silence the fact that Plato asks his citizens to think of each other, all classes alike, as brothers! When Popper analyzed the myth and found in it two ideas, he should have found three; for the citizens' obligation to one another is made equal in importance to their duty to their common land. But Popper, maintaining that Plato wishes above all to keep wide the cleft between the "master caste" and the "human cattle," and even that he secretly regards the rulers as a "conquering war horde" who have subjugated the mass of the citizens,[70]

---

[69] Trans. Shorey, Loeb Library.

[70] Here is involved another of Popper's complicated imputations of guile which is perhaps deserving of discussion, though we cannot cut off individually every head of this hydra. Plato, after describing the training of the first group of guardians and the myth of their origin from the soil, which is to be told to all the citizens, guardians and commoners alike, employs the little dramatic device of imagining their first entry, armed and under the command of their leaders, into the city, which may be conceived as already in full existence, or may be thought of — Plato does not say — simply as a designated site for the settlement, as yet unoccupied. Within it, the guardians must select the place of their encampment, which is to be the spot best suited to enable them, literally, "to hold in check those within, if anyone should be unwilling to obey the laws," and to ward off enemies from without (415 E). Popper, filled with his conception of the ideal city as a near replica of ancient Sparta, which originated by "forceful subjugation," as Plato well knows, though he wishes to conceal these facts, calls this passage "a description of the triumphant invasion of a warrior class of somewhat mysterious origin — the 'earthborn.'" Popper next examines that part of the Laws in which Plato describes the origin of human communities out of the scattered survivors of a great flood, discovering there reference to "war bands" where Plato describes only peaceful communities; and as Plato approaches the time when Sparta is to be founded, and describes the social turmoil which uprooted the Dorians and sent them forth, this time as real war bands, to seek new homes, Popper detects that "Plato becomes evasive": Plato does not state plainly that these Dorians conquered the Peloponnese, but continually

would not wish to see the myth of the metals as the myth of brotherhood. He has, in fact, made it appear that only the "warriors" are to be told that they are autochthonous, and has thus made the myth serve to divide the very citizens whom it is intended to unite.

---

digresses to talk of other matters, as, says Popper, Plato himself admits, speaking of the "roundabout track of the argument." At last, however, "we get a hint that the Dorian 'settlement' . . . was in fact a violent subjugation." Popper adds that Plato "preferred for obvious reasons to veil in mystery" this discreditable fact (Popper, pp. 51–52, 497–498).

One of the remarkable things about all this is the idea that Plato hesitates to admit that Sparta originated by conquest. Plato, it is true, does not emphasize the historically obvious, but he makes it perfectly plain in the passages which Popper cites (*Laws* 682–683), that this was the case. It would certainly have been an inanity for Plato to attempt to conceal from the Greeks of his age the facts of former invasions of Greece by their ancestors. The "roundabout" course of Plato's argument in the early books of the *Laws*, of which Plato himself speaks, does not require explanation in terms of "evasiveness." He has in his eye that involved structure of the conversation, seemingly artless and natural, like the rambling talk of old men, which nevertheless describes several times a circle and comes back to the same point, namely, the supreme importance for the success of any state that its laws shall aim not at courage alone and success in war, but at the whole of virtue (cf. *Laws* 688 B); Plato has skilfully contrived to reach this conclusion by following more than one line of reasoning.

Nor does Plato, in fact, appear to regard the Dorian conquest as in any way discreditable. Similarly, the conquests of the Persian Cyrus appear to awaken in Plato no commiseration for the conquered populations (694 A–E), but only admiration for the institutions of the Persians which made possible their success. This attitude does not commend him to the modern reader, and in order to absolve him we are forced to remind ourselves that his ideal cities do not engage in conquest, and that in discussing the origins of Sparta and the Persian empire, he is talking history, not urging contemporary policy. But Popper, we must remember, believes that Plato's *Republic* is a proposal to recreate at Athens a proto-Sparta, and that (though Plato does not intend his fellow Athenians to notice this) its common citizens are to be made correlative with Helots; he therefore thinks that in admitting even by a "hint" that Sparta originated by conquest, Plato has made a slip, and that in allowing "a short but triumphant tale of the subjugation of a settled population" to appear in his *Republic*, Plato has given himself away to the discerning eye.

But there are other and, I think, more plausible ways of explaining this greatly exaggerated march of the "earthborn." In the first place, the title "earthborn" applies to them no more than to the common people, since all the citizens alike are to be told that they are born of their soil; nor is their origin more "mysterious" than that of the rest of the inhabitants. Plato has not told us the origin of any of his citizens. The march into the city may, as we have said, be no more than the arrival at the designated site of a new settlement. Or, if the city is conceived as already existing, the picture in Plato's mind may be derived from the ceremonies attending the conclusion of the first year of military training of the Athenian *Ephebi*; Aristotle describes the custom in his day of their appearing at the festival on that occasion, and giving an exhibition of their military evolutions (*Const. Ath.* 42). Or Plato may have imagined a city which had, a few years earlier, determined to adopt the ideal constitution and had then authorized the selection of some of its youth for training as guardians. And now the day has arrived when the training is completed and the new constitution is to be inaugurated. This is an innocent alternative of at least equal weight to Popper's fantasy of guilt and deception.

The mention of the guardians' task of guarding the city from external enemies and from internal disobedience to law, which Popper calls the "decisive" passage proving conquest and oppression, is not different from a minimum description of the

No less damaging and no less unfair is the omission of another feature of Plato's myth, namely, that it is thought of as being boldly told to living persons about themselves, in defiance of their own immediate memories of their previous lives. From Popper's presentation, it would be quite possible to suppose that the tale told to the citizens concerned the distant past, describing perhaps the origin from the soil of their earliest progenitors. Popper's omission tempers the myth's audacity and thus strengthens his own hypothesis of Plato's guilty hesitancy at introducing his racialism by weakening a dangerous competitor — the possibility that Socrates' hesitation and humorous expressions of dismay have nothing to do with ethical considerations, but are grounded on the very obvious incredibility of the tale itself.

Our suggestion that the hesitation of "Socrates" reflects Plato's concern for the credibility of his tale may be strengthened by consideration of his practice elsewhere. No author of a dramatic dialogue can afford to lose the credence of his audience in the dramatic probability of what he is presenting; the theorist, also, if he is to carry conviction, must not seem unaware of the degree of likelihood of his explanations or recommendations. That Plato gave careful attention to both these points, the evidence of the dialogues as a whole abundantly prove. A dramatic device from a later book of the *Republic*, to which we have already pointed as an instance of Plato's careful preparation of his climactic effects, will serve also to illustrate our present point, his discounting in advance of the reader's doubt as to the practicality of a proposal, or the naturalness of the interlocutor's reaction. This is the extended introduction in Book V (450 A–D, 457 B–D) to Plato's three most controversial proposals, the equality of woman, the marriage and property regulations, and the philosopher kings. Here Socrates hesitates again and again, and requires reassurance from all the company; and here again Glaucon helps Plato, by his ready expressions of surprise, to dramatize the reader's sense of the improbability that such measures could ever be carried into effect. In these three instances Glaucon is helpful also in converting the reader eventually to a belief in their plausibility, by his later acceptance of them as advisable and right.

To revert to the tale of the citizens' birth from the soil: Plato does not require Glaucon to agree, when he has heard Socrates' tale, that the idea of

---

task of any modern government: to defend the nation, uphold the constitution, and keep down crime. The brief phrase here must be read in the light of other passages which describe the responsible and benevolent relations of the guardians to the bulk of the citizens; it must not, as Popper would have it, be first arbitrarily interpreted, and then employed as evidence of the falsity of good intentions expressed elsewhere. Pop-

per has, in fact, created almost wholly out of his own preconceptions this picture of a triumphant subjugation, has given the term "earthborn" a mysterious signification where only a plain reference to the myth of the metals is involved, and has attributed evasiveness to Plato, regarding both the origins of Sparta and the functions of his guardians, where only frankness exists.

convincing the first group of citizens is practicable, but only that in later generations the myth may be believed; [71] and this marks Plato' own doubt on the point. There is no need to assume any other than these daylight and aboveboard causes of Plato's "hesitation." [72] And we may claim every right

---

[71] That such a myth related of distant ancestors might be believed by the common people, at least, Plato had full proof in the tradition of the Athenians' own origin from the soil of Attica (mentioned, e.g., in Aesch., *Eumen.* 13; Eurip., *Ion* 589; Aristoph., *Wasps* 1076; Isocrates, *Panegyr.* 24, *Panath.* 124; Lysias ii, 17–19; Plato, *Menexenus* 239 B). But it is quite certain that by Plato's day and for some time before, largely as the result of Ionian science and the sophistic influence, the educated Athenian had come to doubt as a matter of course the literal truth of all mythological tales. Some could be successfully allegorized, like the tale of Boreas carrying off a nymph in the *Phaedrus*; some could be otherwise rationalized into credibility, as we apparently see Thucydides doing with this very tale of the Athenians' autochthony (I, 2, 5); still others were simply disbelieved. And in the *Gorgias*, when Socrates is about to tell his myth of judgment in the afterworld, he is made to say to Callicles (523 A, trans. Lamb, Loeb Library, slightly altered), "You will regard this as a fable, I fancy, but I as an actual account." In a similar fashion, Glaucon could well be expected to doubt whether it was reasonable to imagine that even after lapse of time, the rulers of the city would believe the myth of their origin from the soil.

But Plato, and Socrates, it seems, were in a somewhat different position from that of the average skeptical Athenian of good education. Plato's attitude is well summarized by Shorey (*Republic*, Loeb Library, vol. II, pp. lxiv–vii). Plato was able to disbelieve the particularities of myths, while believing in the basic validity of truths which they contained. In consequence of this attitude, it is not always possible to say with confidence whether a particular element in a Platonic myth belongs to the symbolic dress or to the underlying truth; to put this in another way, a reader unacquainted with the whole range of Plato's thought cannot easily gauge the degree of credence Plato asks for his myth as a whole. Popper has been misled by this Platonic

ambiguity more than once, particularly in relation to the myth in the *Politicus* (see our pp. 463–464, 612, 623–624). On p. 555, he asserts that Plato proffers the idea of men born from the earth, contained in that myth, "as a true story." As against this, Plato has warned his observant reader (*Politicus* 268 D) that his myth is an instructive and entertaining tale for boys; cf. also *Laws* 713. But the best proof that Plato does not literally believe his own myths lies in the varying symbolism employed in different myths which express the same basic truths (e.g., in *Phaedo* and *Republic*).

Popper has gone astray also in another respect systematically connected with his misinterpretation of Plato's *Republic*. It is an essential part of his case to prove that Plato's guardians are a "master caste," racially distinct, and superior to the other citizens. Hence, just as Popper speaks throughout of the "earthborn" as including the "warriors" only, misleadingly ignoring Plato's inclusion of all the citizens, so also, by way of corroboration, he asserts (p. 555) that "the Athenian *nobility*" (italics ours) claimed to be earthborn, "as Plato says in the *Symposium*, 191 B." This is a simple misstatement of fact, combined with a most misemployed citation. Athenian citizens were supposed to be autochthonous regardless of whether they were noble or not. And in the *Symposium*, the reference leads only to Aristophanes' humorous myth, where he tells of the early days when men were globeshaped creatures with four arms and legs, and when all alike originated from earth. There is no statement anywhere that the Athenian "nobility" claimed to be autochthonous.

[72] Now that we have shown that Plato displays no moral shame on proposing his lie, we may revert to the "idealization" of which Popper complains in Cornford's note *ad loc.*, and express our agreement with Cornford's description of the myth as a "harmless allegory." For Plato's *gennaion pseudos*, we should favor the translation "lie" (or "falsehood") "of generous propor-

to point out that Socrates' delay and "bashfulness" are definitely related by Plato to the idea of the citizens' birth from the soil, and are not in evidence when Socrates tells the part of the myth that concerns the different metals. For this latter idea, which parallels the division of mankind described in the *Phaedrus* on the basis of their differing degrees of moral insight, Plato shows no shame, either here or elsewhere.[73]

The rest of Popper's argument regarding the myth of the metals can be briefly answered. In the first place, since Plato does not, as we shall show, withdraw his intention to elevate "golden" and "silver" children into the guardian class, his supposed hesitation in so doing cannot exist. The added assertion that he withdraws it "also in the *Laws*" is a false parallel. In that state, there are no classes of guardians and of citizen-workers; there are

---

tions." In this we neither demand the translation "noble lie," nor accept Crossman's ironical use of this same phrase as the equivalent of "ignoble lie" (meaning a propaganda fiction of any degree of falsity which a ruler may find useful), nor approve the implications of pride and oppression which attach to Popper's "lordly lie."

In this connection it is appropriate to mention a curious semi-parallel between Popper's treatment of the myth of the metals and Toynbee's. Popper (p. 498) acknowledges, despite fundamental divergencies, some indebtedness to Toynbee, and it is probable therefore that the two interpretations are not entirely independent. Toynbee has been engaged, to use his own phrase, in "drawing the covert" of race, to see whether racial differences can account for the wide range of human cultural achievement, and he is about to announce that they cannot. It is his belief that other thinkers before him have been aware of the emptiness of racial claims, and in this connection brings in Plato's myth of the metals (I, pp. 247–249) — wrongly, we think, since Plato is not at all discussing the ethnographic divisions of the human race, e.g., "Alpine," "Nordic," or "Mediterranean," with which Toynbee has been dealing. He regards Plato as "half-humorous, half-cynical" in propounding his myth, which is put forward frankly as a fraud designed to reconcile the common citizens to their necessary lot, by "mendaciously" ascribing to innate differences the effects of divergent upbringing and education. To Toynbee it is apparently inconceivable that Plato believed in the reality of innate differences sufficiently great to justify autocratic gov-

ernment; as he sees it, Plato makes quite plain to his reader his knowledge that such differences cannot exist, and thus gives "the fallacy of Race . . . its final exposure." Toynbee and Popper agree, therefore, in seeing in this passage cynicism, and in talking of "race"; they are alike also in overlooking the reason which lies closest to hand for Socrates' hesitation, namely, his doubt that contemporary adults can reasonably be expected to swallow a fairy-tale with themselves as central characters. Against both Toynbee and Popper, we submit that there is here no question of race, but only of differences in endowment conceived as occurring within a racially homogeneous population, much as variations in I.Q. were believed until recently in America to be almost entirely hereditary (cf. p. 241 and p. 537). And there is no cynicism, only the (to us) unacceptable notion of telling the citizens an edifying falsehood which embodies what Plato believes to be an ethical truth (their mutual obligation) and a fact of nature (human variability in endowment). To the extent that Toynbee and Popper agree, therefore, we can answer both with confidence. On the other hand, Toynbee is clearly at odds with Popper as to Plato's message to his reader: Popper sees him attempting to dupe the reader into accepting as true the existence of "racial" differences, while, for Toynbee, Plato scoffs visibly at the very idea. This contradiction may help us to show that neither interpretation is necessary, but that Plato honestly shares with his reader his intent to tell his citizens, in symbolic fashion, what he believes to be two basic truths.

[73] See pp. 216–217 above.

only citizens, metics, and slaves. The fact that Plato does not provide in the *Laws* for freeing and elevating into the citizen class able and virtuous slaves is regrettable, but it proves nothing about the different situation in the *Republic*.[74] The horrendous charge, put into italics, that Plato intends to deceive by his myth even the rulers, can be regarded calmly by one who recollects that for Plato the tale embodies, along with its literal falsity, important truths, and that it symbolizes the ideal not only of willing workers, but also of rulers looking with fraternal concern to the well-being of their lesser brothers. It is eloquent proof of the value that he imputes to loyal devotion to the common good, that Plato should propose, albeit in a passing and half-serious way, to dilute by mythological admixture the philosophic omniscience of his philosopher kings.

One of Plato's highest honors in the modern world has been the reverence shown him as the foremost champion, against brute force, of the humane power of persuasion, which Whitehead has taken as the measure of man's moral progress through the centuries. But Popper would rob him of this credit also. In introducing his myth of the metals, Plato speaks of the possibility of "persuading" by this lie of generous proportions, the people of the ideal city. And Popper has taken the occasion to warn us against being ourselves "persuaded" by Plato's use of this fair-sounding word, in many other passages in which it occurs. We are to recollect that in political contexts, and particularly "where he advocates that the statesman should rule 'by means of both persuasion and force,'" "by 'persuasion' of the masses, Plato means largely lying propaganda," and probably has in mind his customary conception of "the doctor-politician administering lies." [75] Against this implication that Plato has again been caught covering over and concealing from his reader his true and disreputable meaning, we shall contend, on the contrary, that he has nothing to conceal, that by "persuasion of the masses" he does not mean lying in more than an infinitesimal number of cases, and that even here he has been perfectly open with his reader. Without attempting a complete listing of the numerous distinguishable senses of the versatile word *peithein*, to persuade, and its derivatives and cognates, we shall offer instances sufficient to show what damage Popper has done to a fair statement of the case in representing Plato's use as preponderantly suggestive of deceit. In

---

[74] Popper believes (p. 497) that Plato intends to judge "goldenness," etc., in the *Republic*, from the mere fact of a child's parents' status (his arguments to this effect will be discussed on pp. 535ff.), and consequently believes that the slave status assigned in the *Laws* to the child of parents one of whom is a slave, the other free, proves that Plato, in the *Republic*, would have assigned worker-status to the child of parents, one of whom was a worker, the other a guardian, or, *a fortiori*, to any child born of worker parents on both sides. Since Popper's major premise is here completely unfounded, his conclusion may be reasonably dismissed.

[75] Popper, pp. 138, 552, note 5, and 553–554.

the process of refuting the errors of his critic, we welcome the opportunity of revealing some of those Platonic uses of persuasion which prompted Whitehead to present Plato as its patron saint.

Plato is naturally at liberty to employ the Greek word in any of its recognized Greek uses; and it is not his doing that, like many other words, it has shades of meaning ranging from the most unsavory to the fully honorable. We shall agree with Popper in finding near the bottom of the scale, as the word is employed by Plato, the meaning illustrated in *Republic* 364 C, where it is said that soothsayers promise to secure indulgence for the crimes of their patrons by "persuading" the gods with spells and incantations. But the case is less simple when Popper implies that hardly higher in the scale is that meaning which he has so much stressed in his criticism of the myth of the metals, to "persuade" someone to believe an untruth. The use of the concept in this passage is so bound up with the whole question of the function of myth and of rhetoric in Plato's thinking, that we shall best approach it in the light of a wider discussion.

Plato has made it very clear in the *Gorgias* that he can use the word in varying senses in close proximity to one another. "Persuasion" first appears (453 A–D) as the function of all arts which produce conviction in the minds of hearers, including on the one hand true teaching, as of mathematics, and on the other, rhetoric, as the sophist Gorgias conceives it. This rhetoric, which must convince large numbers of persons in a short time, imparts opinion only, and is shown by "Socrates" to be an art of "persuasion for belief" (453 E–455 A), exercised upon the ignorant by the ignorant and the unprincipled (455 E–460 D), for the sake of private interest (452 E, 456 C–457 C). Here, then, we have seen Plato employ "persuade" both in the broad sense, which includes an honorable use of persuasion for imparting knowledge, and also in a degraded sense, to describe an ignorant, irresponsible, and self-interested rhetoric of which Plato fully disapproves. In this latter sense we meet it often in the dialogues. But we have not yet done with Plato's use of the word "persuade" in connection with rhetoric. For further meanings we may turn to the *Phaedrus*.

Here Plato is discussing and illustrating what he calls, literally, "the soul-leading art of words," rhetoric, conceived broadly as the whole art of winning consent or convincing by means of speech. There is no limitation as to topic, or intent, or number of hearers; both written and spoken kinds are included. And here again forms of the word "persuade" are employed more than once to describe the whole art (e.g., 271 D). Plato, however, divides rhetoric into true and false: the false rhetoric of the sophists and orators is again identified with the art of persuading, without knowledge, those who are equally ignorant, and again it is implied that its purpose is selfish and irresponsible (260 A–261 E). The true art, on the other hand, must be based upon knowledge; its practitioner "must know the truth," and must be able to divide things into classes and to comprehend particulars under a general idea (273 D–E, 277 B–C); he must adapt his speech, if he is to win assent, to the kinds of souls addressed, and offer to the complex soul discourses complex and harmonious, but "simple talks to the simple soul" (271 D, 277 C). Such knowledge, once acquired, is best employed in the pleasing of "our divine masters"; but it must be acquired even by those who are to attain the baser aim of pleasing men (273 E–274 A).[76] Of those employing fully-developed and perfected rhetoric for this latter purpose, the dialogue seems to imply, Pericles is the outstanding example.[77]

Up to this point in the *Phaedrus*, Plato has spoken of the whole art of speech as that of persuasion; but now as in the *Gorgias* he employs the word in a narrower sense. We find him speaking of the finished artist in words as one who will be able by means of his art to teach — and this is its noblest use, to which it is put by true philosophers, imparting sound and fruitful knowledge to receptive souls; or it may be used, alternatively, to "persuade" (277 C). Here again we have "persuasion" contrasted with "teaching"; yet — and this is what we wish to emphasize — here it is not persuasion of an ig-noble sort. It is a method of producing belief which may be rightly employed by the true artist in words, in cases which do not admit of prolonged and personal instruction; and, when the souls to be persuaded are simple, it is itself simple. But it has no selfish aims, and it seeks to inculcate what is pleasing to God.

Another use of persuasion with which Plato is in sympathy is found in the *Apology*, where Socrates, describing the heart of his mission (30 A), says that he goes about doing nothing but "persuading" old and young among the Athenians to care for their souls, above all else. Again in the *Phaedo*, "persuasion" is honored. The talk is of death and of the immortality of the soul, and Socrates, though confident and serene, is not by any means dogmatically certain of the truth of his belief, nor does he seek to demonstrate it to his friends. Simmias at one point, expressing the general view, says that if truth and certainty are not to be had, the brave man must take "whatever human doctrine is best and hardest to disprove," and sail through life upon it as on a raft (85 D). And throughout the *Phaedo*, there are many passages in which Socrates and his friends speak of being "persuaded" or of "persuading" themselves that the soul indeed survives (e.g., 91 B, 92 D, 108 C–E). Near the end Socrates offers to tell a myth whose truth he says he would not be able to prove, yet he is "persuaded" that it is true. When he has finished, he says again that though the myth cannot be taken literally, yet "that this, or something like it is true," a man "may properly and worthily venture to

---

[76] Quotations are from the translation by Lamb, Loeb Library.

[77] Another example of a finished orator cited by Plato is "*Adrastus*," a legendary figure who may represent the orator Anti-phon.

believe" (114 D).[78] Where Socrates can thus "persuade" himself and his closest friends and employ thereto a myth, there can be no suggestion that persuasion and the use of myths constitute the administration of lies.

In the *Timaeus*, we find two striking instances of "persuasion." One occurs in the account of the origin of the Cosmos (48 A). Here Reason is said to control Necessity — conceived as the mindless and purposeless ground of the universe — to the end of making created things as good as possible, by "intelligent persuasion." A little later (51 E) the existence of the eternal changeless forms, in addition to material objects, is rendered probable by the parallel distinction between reason, which is firm and unalterable, and partaken of by the gods and by very few men, and true opinion, which is alterable, shared by all men, and derived from "persuasion." Here the province of "persuasion" lies in the relation between intelligence and the irrational, or the imperfectly rational. Yet it is the means to good and to truth.

Summing up, then, the uses to which we have seen Plato put the concept of persuasion, we find that these may be roughly classified thus: (1) the function of speech which wins assent, in all its kinds; (2) the unworthy persuasion of the ignorant by those who are themselves ignorant and self-interested; (3) persuasion by those who know, but who put their complete knowledge of the art to uses pleasing not to god, but to men; (4) the approvable use of speech to win consent, by those who know and whose motives are irreproachable, but (a) under conditions which preclude teaching, or (b) upon topics which make proof impossible, or (c) when those who are to be persuaded are not fully rational. If we examine those occurrences of the word which Popper cites to prove that, in Plato's pages, "persuasion" is linked with deception, we find that many of them refer to class (2), and express only Plato's disapproval of the sophist's use of persuasion, not his own intent to employ it similarly; others belong to class (4) and do not involve any intention to deceive, but merely the impossibility under the circumstances (so Plato believed) of imparting fully rational knowledge.

We have now to investigate how Plato's use of the concept of persuasion is related to the lying propaganda which Popper sees in it. First of all, we must agree that the use of lies in certain circumstances is advocated in the *Republic* for purposes of government and that though the word "persuade" is not used in connection with them, there can be no doubt that some use of the persuasive art of speech would be required to make the auxiliaries "blame chance and not the rulers" when they are told that the fall of the lot has determined their marriages, whereas really these are engineered by the rulers for eugenic reasons. In this instance we have the only sanctioning

---

[78] Quotations are from the translation by Fowler, Loeb Library. The citations in the text include some passages in which the idea of persuasion is conveyed without the use of the Greek word *peithein* or its cognates.

by Plato of an outright practical lie, to be told, to be sure, for benevolent reasons (and only for such purposes does Plato sanction the telling), but a lie and nothing more. We, like Popper, find this policy distasteful. This lie, then, and any others like it which Plato's rather general permission might justify, constitute such basis as exists for Popper's charge that Plato proposes to use "lying propaganda" in his city. But they do not justify the charge that it is "largely" lying propaganda which Plato means by "persuasion of the masses," as can be well illustrated by the myth of the metals itself.

In another part of the *Republic*, speaking of the education of young children, Plato proposes to use at the earliest ages, "lies" (or "falsehoods"), by which he means, he explains, the fable or myth, "which is, taken as whole, false, but there is truth in it also" (377 A). In these tales, however, there must be no misrepresentation of the gods, for "the young are not able to distinguish what is from what is not "allegory" (378 D).[79] Plato thus does not intend his myths to embody essential falsehood. Nor, in the *Phaedo*, was Socrates' myth of the afterworld intended to deceive. In the same way, the myth of the metals is a fable to be believed by adults, and the "persuasion" of the citizens to accept it is Plato's way of teaching truth. We may dislike its attitude of intellectual superiority, but it is not properly described as "lying propaganda."

Similarly, though in differing degrees, Plato intends both his Statesman and his Statesman's assistant, the rhetorician, in the city of the *Politicus*, to inculcate not lies, but truths, the one by his laws, the other by his "mythology" (309 C–D, 304 C). If politic lies for the good of the citizens are also to be dispensed by the rhetorician at the Statesman's behest, they are not mentioned; in any case, there is no reason for supposing that they would be employed more than very occasionally, just as there is seldom need for the strong drugs to which in the *Republic* Plato compares them.

In the *Laws*, we hear of no medicinal lies, as distinct from myths, to be administered to the self-governing citizens. There is only the one passage already mentioned, in which Plato says that even if the virtuous way of life were not also the happy one, any lawgiver of the slightest worth would teach this to the citizens; but that since, fortunately, it is true, such teaching will be no deception.[80] Plato adds here, too, that myths — again he refers to the myth of origin from the soil — may perhaps be devised, such as will bring the greatest good to the city by inducing the citizens to the willing practices of virtue, if they are persuaded to believe them (663 C–664 A); and the citizens must "charm themselves" unceasingly (we are reminded of the same word, used in the *Phaedo*, 77 E, of the belief in immortality) to think that goodness and happiness are one (665 C). Popper has seen sinister "persuasion" embodied in the "preludes," those short homilies which, taken along

---

[79] Trans. Shorey, Loeb Library.   [80] See p. 64 above.

with the actual laws, constitute one important instance of the combination of "persuasion and force" to which Popper has referred. But the preludes are emphatically not the utterances of the "doctor-politician administering lies"; whoever doubts this is advised to read one or more of them (e.g. 721 B–D, 773, 854 B–C). They are examples of the art of the true rhetorician as Plato conceives him in the *Phaedrus*, fitting simple discourses to simple souls, persuading them not to false but to true belief.[81]

As one reviews the course of the just-completed argument, two points should emerge with special prominence. (1) The lying use of persuasion is to be slight in extent, and is to be rigorously restricted to the most responsible and disinterested persons. One may doubt the possibility of drawing a *cordon sanitaire* around the serpent of deception and preventing it from spreading its infection into other areas, corrupting the rulers and spreading distrust among

---

[81] Popper inserts a long footnote (pp. 553–554) dealing with persuasion in Plato, and intended to show that Plato, in advocating its use, is advocating lying propaganda; the note, however, shows only the dangers of general statements about Platonic usage, not founded upon a thorough and nonpartisan use of lexicography. Popper sets up two uses of the word, (a) the influencing of opinion by fair means, and (b) "taking [*sic*] over by foul means." He then seems to say (p. 554, top) that it is occasionally correct to take "persuasion" in Plato in sense (a), but unaccountably gives as his only example of such an honest use a passage (*Republic* 365 D) in which, as he himself says a few lines below, an apt paraphrase of the meaning would be "cheating." To cite no other favorable uses of the word in Plato is, in effect, not just. In political contexts, however, Popper says, Plato employs the word in sense (b), and in illustration of this use, cites many passages, in all of which, he declares, "the 'art of persuasion' as opposed to the 'art of imparting true knowledge' . . . is associated with rhetoric, make-believe, or propaganda." This, while literally true, is most misleading. For, as we have shown, none of these three is for Plato necessarily false; even "make-believe," as in myths, can be basically true. On investigation about half of Popper's list of passages (*Gorgias* 454 B–455 A, *Phaedrus* 260 B, *Sophist* 222 C, perhaps *Philebus* 58 A) are found to involve reference to the "persuasion" of the sophists, a thing which Plato would have scorned to advocate or imitate. Others (*Theaetetus* 201 A, *States-*

man 296 B ff., 304 C–D, *Timaeus* 51 E, *Rep.* 511 D, 533 E) involve persuasion employed *faute de mieux*, in situations which, in Plato's opinion, preclude true teaching, and do not portend deception. But perhaps the most glaring example of Popper's failure to deal fairly with his reader in this connection is his citation of *Gorgias* 454 B–455 A, a passage which prominently employs the word "persuasion" in the broad and neutral sense in which it covers all speech which wins assent, specifically including what Popper calls "the art of imparting true knowledge." To have cited this passage only as illustrating Plato's use of "persuasion" in the "foul" sense (it does illustrate this use as well) is special pleading.

On p. 610, Popper suggests (note 69) that Plato, in recommending the use of "persuasion and force," is merely proposing to add consciously deceptive propaganda ("this would indicate that Plato was well aware of Pareto's recipe") to the violence of the Thirty Tyrants, and with this one addition, to accept their record of ruthless coercion as a model of proper political action. This allegation, so far as it concerns persuasion, rests on no further evidence than the passages discussed above, and so far as it concerns the Thirty Tyrants, rests on the identification of Plato's views with those of the extreme Athenian oligarchs, an identification which we have shown to be at fault on pp. 326ff. Altogether it constitutes an excellent instance of the way in which unsound conclusions may be pyramided into sheer illusion.

the ruled; one may not deny Plato's intention to do so. And one may argue that had good reason been presented to him for anticipating so self-contradictory a result, he would have cast deceit utterly out of his ideal kingdom. (2) One is impressed with the orderly diversity and richness of the concept of "persuasion," and its fruitful use in Plato's hands. From cosmology to politics, from mathematics to immortality — only a master of a dialectic at once flexible and firm enough to retain its structural identity from dialogue to dialogue, could have spanned so wide a gap. It is evident, therefore, that Popper's fusion of Plato's carefully discriminated types of persuasion into one amorphous whole is an extreme oversimplification.

But we have yet to adduce what Whitehead seems to have regarded as Plato's chief credential as advocate of the honorable practice of persuasion.[82] This is the method and character of the Platonic dialogues themselves, which in the main exemplify the use of persuasion in its most rational form. The right of objection, of counterproposal, is everywhere recognized. No one is bludgeoned or threatened into the acceptance of a point of view. So far as such a thing is possible on paper, Plato has sought to put his interlocutor on a parity with his Socratic self, and to leave the issue to the arbitrament of that personified "argument" whose aim and outcome no man is empowered to coerce.[83]

The method of the dialogues appears as the closest possible literary approximation of the method of philosophical instruction which Plato recommends for those whom alone he regarded as truly educable in the higher reaches of philosophical instruction, and which in all likelihood he applied to the students at his Academy. It would have place within the city of the *Republic*, it is true, only as employed in the higher education of the guardians; here again we confront that honest but unfortunate belief of Plato that most men are natively incapable of being brought to the full exercise of reason; but for them he hoped to obtain the benefit of conclusions rationally reached, so presented as to win their unconstrained consent. In either case, what Plato champions is an ideal of persuasion, responsibly employed for

---

[82] *Adventures of Ideas*, e.g., pp. 64–65, 105–109.

[83] Popper, p. 413, acknowledges the "reasonable spirit" in which arguments are conducted in Plato's writings, but limits his concession to the Plato of the earlier dialogues and does not abate his contention that, even so, Plato intended to prevent the free use of reason by the philosopher kings of the Republic. We shall again confront Popper's opinion on this point, pp. 618f. below. Here we may point out that the spirit of reasonableness in argument is clearly in evidence in the *Republic*, as attested by

Crossman (cf. our p. 493) and in the *Phaedo*, as attested by Popper (cf. our p. 367, n. 285); yet these are dialogues in which Popper has maintained that the undogmatic and modest attitude of Socrates toward others' opinions has given place to Platonic authoritarianism and dogmatic certainty. Popper's position thus entails an obvious inconsistency which can, however, be easily avoided by assuming with the present writer that a commitment to accept the verdict of reason was always a fundamental principle of Plato's thought.

the sake of the highest attainable good, and rejecting so far as may be the blind compulsions of force and fear.

We have seen how Popper would reduce Platonic justice to the moral nullity of a fraudulent device for luring unwary lovers of democratic equality to the acceptance of a program founded on the radical denial of equalitarian principles. In attempting this transvaluation, Plato, as Popper views him, was practicing upon his readers, ancient and modern, that same dishonest art of persuasion which he cynically admitted his intention of employing for gulling the citizens of his perfect state.

Popper has also not failed to point out the contrast between the permission Plato accords his rulers to tell medicinal lies to the citizens, and the stern prohibition of the citizens themselves from meddling with untruth. Plato's religion, too, is seen to be little more than a political fraud.[84] Popper's conclusion, thus, is that for Plato all truth is "subordinated to the more fundamental principle that the rule of the master class must be strengthened." Though Plato may mean by truth what is commonly denoted by the concept, his love of truth, that primal virtue in a philosopher, so nearly synonymous with philosophy itself, can be seen for what it is, a shameful pretense.[85]

Having destroyed to his own satisfaction two of Plato's historic strongholds, justice and truth, Popper pauses to consider what remains. Still standing, he notes, are a number of "ideas, such as Goodness, Beauty, and Happiness," to which presently "Wisdom" is added. Popper has assigned himself the task of reducing these supposed Platonic splendors to sordid actuality by showing how in each case this Athenian Pareto has, with varying degrees of conscious or unconscious deceitfulness, exploited moral sentiments to cover totalitarian actualities. Goodness, thus, is found to be hardly more than a synonym for the stability of the arrested state. Happiness for the privileged master race is equated with their position of authority, for all others, with the impoverished security of accepting and liking the servile position assigned to them by the rulers. The wisdom, too, with which Plato endows his misnamed philosophers, is a most dubious quality, exhausted in the discharge of three questionable functions: to cling with dogmatic tenacity to sterile and abstract truths, to separate themselves prestigiously from all ordinary citizens by their aura of esoteric knowledge, and to preserve, by the use of a mysterious pseudo-genetics invented by Plato for the purpose, the purity of the master race, thus triply reënforcing the permanence of the arrested totalitarian state. Finally, beauty is an ideal even more vicious in its effects. It has led Plato to conceive the politician as one who "composes cities for beauty's sake," who in his ruthless search for personal aesthetic satisfaction

---

[84] See n. 267, p. 358, and n. 50, pp. 521f.   [85] Popper, pp. 136–141.

is willing to use as his medium other men's lives, and to "liquidate" those who object to forming part of the composition.[86]

Plato, an aesthete who has sacrificed the highest interests of morality to make an aesthetic holiday! There is a colossal irony in this when we remember how this same Plato has been brought to book by the same complainant for having sacrificed in the interests of Spartan austerity the aesthetic richness of poetry and the other arts. Surely this is more than a paradox.

At the root of the confusion are two supplementary errors. First, there is the failure to see that beauty for Plato is not something externally related to moral values. On the contrary, the virtues, for Plato, cannot adequately be described in abstraction from their aesthetic qualities. We have seen how basic to Platonic "temperance" is the essentially aesthetic notion of "harmony" or "consonance," [87] how for the Socrates of the *Gorgias* it is both better and "fairer" — "more beautiful" — to suffer than to commit injustice. A striking example is supplied by the description in the *Phaedrus* (247 C–D, 250 B–C, trans. Fowler, Loeb Library), of those divine principles of justice, wisdom, temperance, and beauty perceived with piercing joy by the soul before birth, "shining in brightness," "perfect and simple and calm and happy apparitions," "visible only to mind, the pilot of the soul," and ever after longed for and sought in their earthly embodiments by men below. In the Platonic universe it has been providentially arranged that among these ideals themselves there is no conflict: in achieving virtue, man attains at once happiness and moral beauty.[88] It is to tear asunder these inseparables to demand that Plato should not feel aesthetic satisfaction in the contemplation of the city or the man who in his terms embodies all excellence and enjoys the highest happiness.

What, then, has prompted Popper to suppose that Plato was sacrificing the interests of others in his search for beauty? The answer seems to be a perverse literal-mindedness in construing Platonic metaphors. Plato speaks in the *Republic* (500 C ff.) of the philosopher as a sort of artist who molds himself, and others also, if reluctantly he comes to power, "stamping on the plastic matter of human nature" the images of sobriety, justice, and the other forms of moral good, including beauty of soul. Such an artist, Plato tells us, must be permitted a clean tablet upon which to paint the ideal constitution and the corresponding individual character. Now in this Plato is clearly employing aesthetic categories, but quite as clearly he is subordinating them

---

[86] References for this paragraph are to be found in Popper, pp. 132, 142, 143, 144, 145, 148–150, 161–163, 165, 193–194, 558–559.

[87] See p. 243, and note.

[88] Further passages in the *Republic* expressing the unity of beauty and virtue are 484 C–D, 588 A; in the *Laws*, e.g., 705 E– 706 A, 859 D–E. That these two concepts were linked by the Greeks generally is attested by R. W. Livingstone, *Portrait of Socrates*, 1938, p. liii, and is again asserted, with a wholesome warning against confusing Greek feeling with modern aestheticism, by Kitto, *The Greeks*, p. 170.

to the moral qualities which form their ground. The beauty which emerges from the painting is not created to please the painter; it is merely the structure of moral goodness shining by its own light.

But Popper has built also upon another part of the metaphor. By laying undue stress upon the single element of "canvas cleaning," by bringing in from other Platonic contexts and misinterpreting Plato's remarks on the methods of selecting suitable candidates for membership in an ideal or reformed state,[89] and by adding his own belief that it was at Athens that the "Republic" was to be immediately installed,[90] Popper has embued Plato's demand for a clean tablet with a gratuitously sinister quality. It is to be recalled once more that the *Republic* is a sketch of a fully ideal community, the limiting case, as it were; to say that such a community would have to be without commitments to previously existing, imperfect institutions and mores is hardly more than a tautology. If we look to the city of the *Laws*, the founding of a new colony with carefully selected citizens involves no selfish aesthetic ruthlessness. Even the reform of an existing community beginning with the removal or execution of criminal elements is not necessarily brutal, unless all Greek penology is so.

It is, therefore, worse than idle to talk of Plato's indulging his aesthetic predilections at the cost of morals. We may criticize justly his ideal of moral goodness for the common citizen and regret the absence from the painter's image of elements of political activity and self-direction which to us form part of that ideal picture. But for Plato, these elements did not admit of embodiment, were without the region of possibility. For him the ideal city shone with a beauty inherent and proper to its own perfected nature, the "beauty of laws and institutions," indistinguishable from the good.

In behalf of three of Plato's specified ideals — justice, truth, and beauty — we have now offered the major part of our defense against Popper's suspicions that they are deceitful glass gems. To perform in this place a like service for Platonic goodness, happiness, and wisdom, would involve an unwarranted duplication of our own earlier and later discussion of these themes. But we may at least set ourselves on record as having said that nothing in Plato's text obliges any reader, however, vigilant, to accept Popper's exposé of the actualities behind the Platonic façade, or to believe in the Machiavellian motivation that Popper has suspected. It is only on the supposition that he has already established the foulness of Plato's actual aims that Popper can demand the right of construing the fair names attached into a corresponding dishonesty and can then present the difficulty of penetrating these disguises as a proof of the diabolical cunning, mingled with self-deception, of the mind which so successfully concealed its evil nature from the eyes of centuries of deluded readers.

---

[89] See pp. 348–354.

[90] See pp. 327–329.

But, we must ask, what is the predisposing cause that leads Popper chronically to indulge these sinister imaginings? We may be helped toward answering this question by examining the comparable discoveries of an older compatriot of Popper's, the late versatile Austrian philosopher and sociologist, Otto Neurath. Neurath had occasion to consider the difficult problem, following the second World War, of controlling the textbooks suitable for use in the German schools, and in this connection he published in collaboration with J. A. Lauwerys his appraisal of the political tendencies of the *Republic*.[91] It would indeed be presumptuous to doubt these writers' first objection to the book, namely: the dangerous use which, he foresaw, Nazi-minded educators might be expected to make of it. Such a prophecy had, as he acknowledges, the great security of experience behind it; for, as is well known, during the period that witnessed the rise of National Socialism, the *Republic* was more than once subjected to a "Nazified" interpretation.[92] What concerns us more nearly is the agreement with Popper, on the part of Neurath and Lauwerys (henceforth for brevity referred to as Neurath), that the Nazi view is correct, that any fair reading of the *Republic* will reveal essentially an etherealized philosophical anticipation of the major abhorrent tenets in the Nazi creed.

To Neurath, Plato is "after all, a totalitarian reformer," callous to individualist values, to whom "the main purpose of the state is to preserve the purity of the race and to organize the people for war against foreign barbarians, who are to be looked upon as natural enemies."[93] This statement he documents very much as Popper has done in favor of his somewhat different thesis, by a gathering together of the scarce passages in which Plato takes account, without enthusiasm, of the necessity of war; by pointing to the existence of a specialized and highly trained class of warriors, which he does not fail to call a "caste"; and by dwelling on the importance which Plato attaches to the guardians' breeding, which for him, as for Popper, is a matter of "race." Having set forth Plato's "specific political plans" in this fashion, Neurath de-

---

[91] The two articles referred to, by Otto Neurath and J. A. Lauwerys, are as follows: "Nazi Textbooks and the Future, II," *Journal of Education* (British), 1944; and "Plato's *Republic* and German Education," *Ibid.*, 1945. The appearance of these articles was followed by a lively controversy in the pages of this same journal, April–August, 1945, which came to my attention only when the present section of the book stood complete. Neurath and Lauwerys were answered first by G. C. Field, in a soberly persuasive article which closely parallels the point of view which we have maintained, and far less happily, in my opinion, by C. E. M. Joad. Among other defenders of Plato, John

Pilley of Wellesley College, U.S.A., subjected the positivistic assumptions underlying Neurath's and Lauwerys' attack to a penetrating critique. The two anti-Platonists, however, remained, on their own statement, "unrepentant and unabashed," and ended with the recommendation that at least Plato should not be set before young students on a pedestal.

[92] Of this literature I am acquainted only with Joachim Bannes, *Platon, die Philosophie des Heroischen Vorbildes*, Berlin, 1935. Glenn Morrow, *Philosophical Review*, L, March 1941, p. 105, lists other works of this type.

[93] Neurath, 1944, p. 575.

clares, like Popper, that we must utterly distrust Plato's "lofty declarations." He doubts "whether Hitler would reject Plato's ideals," and urges us to observe the "many fine statements on the common good" in the official program of the Nazi party. He warns us to be on our guard against a writer whose work is full of "brutal, coarse, and undemocratic statements," who is, however, too often presented to us in fair disguise by persons in our midst who are attracted to him by their own private ambitions and subconscious longings; and we must take care lest, "more than we realize today," our youth be corrupted through Plato's pages.[94]

We have thus in Neurath and in Popper two Austrian liberal thinkers, both of whom not only see in Plato a totalitarian reformer whose program is at one with National Socialism, but discover in him also an indirection and a speciousness which turns his idealism into a cynical pretense. To take these two complementary misconceptions in order, the identification with Hitlerism can be adequately explained if we observe the presence in the situation of three mutually reënforcing factors. There is, to begin with, the historical circumstance that both Neurath and Popper saw and suffered, under Hitler's temporary triumph, the shames and wrongs of a regime for whose principles the authority of Plato had been claimed. One may well ask whether it was

---

[94] Neurath, 1945, pp. 57–58. In order to show the conquering aim of the ideal state, Neurath cites the passage in which Plato is describing the "fevered city," from which the discussion of the ideal state takes off; this luxurious city, Plato says, will be compelled by its expanding wants to "cut off a parcel of its neighbors' land." In thus charging Plato's city with crimes committed before it was born, Neurath joins the company of Fite, who fell earlier into the same pitfall. We shall discuss the general question of the "militarism" of the Republic, pp. 566ff.

Neurath makes a point of Plato's recommendation that children who are to be warriors are to be taken out with the army to within sight of actual battles (466 E–467 E), and uses the metaphor of young hounds who are given a "taste of blood" to train them as hunters (537 A); this Neurath intensifies by making the children "very young" (Plato says "when they are sturdy") and by saying that Plato intends them to "develop a proper blood-lust," whereas there is no reason to suppose that more is intended than the necessary readiness to fight and to face danger. In Plato's deprecation of war against fellow Greeks and his calling of barbarians, by contrast, "natural enemies" of the Greeks, against whom it is

proper to wage war and to practice enslavement (469 B–471 C), Neurath, like Tarn and Popper, has seen only the reference to barbarians, and has interpreted this contingent and comparative approval of war against them by vast exaggeration as Plato's statement of one of the two chief aims of his state. Neurath also, like Toynbee and Popper, sees racialism in Plato's belief that, within a race, mental as well as bodily characteristics vary enormously and are inherited. An error less far-reaching but equally conditioned by preconceptions is Neurath's misreading of a Platonic passage (410 A), approving of capital punishment of "incurable" criminals (an idea frequently expressed elsewhere in Plato, e.g., Laws 862 E); in this Neurath, for understandable reasons, but with no foundation in the text, sees the sanctioning of killing mental defectives. With much greater accuracy Neurath points to the politic deception of the citizens regarding the marriage lots, and comments unfavorably on the censorship and generalized control from above of the citizens' lives. But where so much disproportion, distortion, and even downright error has gone into the making of a description, despite the presence of some truthful elements, we can deny truthfulness to the resulting whole.

possible to retain balanced judgment of the Platonic philosophy during those years when a subtly Hitlerized version of the *Republic* was actually functioning as a part of the symbolical machinery of Nazi rule.

Secondly, quite apart from the Nazi misinterpretation, there are actually parallels, despite the all-important differences, between the officially formulated aims of the Nazi party and the political ideals of the *Republic*. That such should be the case need excite no surprise if one refuses to allow the sensational nature of the issue to inspire partisan emotion; for it is notorious in politics no less than in chemistry that slight changes in ingredients and in the internal relations of the parts can produce sensationally different results. The nature and significance of the similarities and differences between Platonism and Nazism it will be our concern to treat at some length in our final chapter. Hypothecating upon the results of that discussion, we may here affirm, by way of example, that militarism and racialism, those baleful portents in the murky sky of Hitlerism, are simply not visible from the latitude of Plato's ideal city. But Popper and Neurath, in their concentration upon likenesses which are actually present, have not observed the differences, or have even distorted them into further similarities; and Neurath has carried the process so far that he has seen the closest kinship between Plato and the Nazi state as residing in the two qualities mentioned, which, on our view, are not present in Plato. To explain how this could happen, we may point by analogy to the psychological principles of "set" in perception, and of "closure," according to which an expected whole can be mentally constructed out of a minority of its known elements and perceived as if present in its entirety. Where all prior expectation and many details suggest the identity of Plato's picture with Hitler's, the interpreter may "hallucinate" what is needed to complete the outline; and this is apparently what Neurath and, in his slightly different way, Popper, have done.

But the supposition of Plato's duplicity remains to be explained. And here Plato's own declaration of his honorable, even his impracticably idealistic aims, combined with the historical situation, offer ample cause. Since Plato's detailed proposals have already been identified with those of Hitler, what can be more obvious than that his fair outward appearance is deceptive? And reënforcing the surmise thus aroused there was, in the historical situation, a prepared attitude of mind which confirmed it and added apparent probability to its unlikeliest development. The suspicion of hypocrisy, conscious or unconscious, in the political field, of sordid realities masquerading behind "lofty declarations," and more than this, the conception of a systematically planned program of deception, in the light of which both critics see Plato — this attitude, in its intensity and its accompanying sense of danger to our whole society, has been contributed to the study of Plato by the atmosphere of central Europe in the early decades of our century and by the events which followed Hitler's rise to power.

The existence of a widespread and contagious attitude of suspicion in the Vienna of those days can be shown by an example drawn from an unexpected quarter. It is really astonishing, after immersion in Popper's book, to reopen *Mein Kampf*, and to note the similarity in this particular respect between Hitler and his fellow countrymen, Neurath and Popper. Not far from the beginning of the book, Hitler records his discovery of the chicanery that underlay the "glittering phrases about freedom, beauty, and dignity" of the literature addressed by the Marxist-inspired Social Democratic party of Vienna to the "simpletons of the middle class," and the "lies and slanders" of the "brutal daily press," aimed by this same party to entrap the masses.[95] A few more pages, and Hitler has detected the sinister racial origins of Marxism itself, has uncovered the aim of the Jews to dominate the world — the Jews, those enemies of mankind who write or speak "in order to conceal or at least to veil their thoughts; their real aim is not therefore to be found in the lines themselves, but slumbers well concealed between them." [96] These suspicions were not of Hitler's invention, but were seething about him in the atmosphere of Viennese politics.

And even behind Hitler, with his distrust of Marxists and Jews, rises a third rank of adepts in the detection of political treachery. The Marxist Social Democrats themselves, objects of Hitler's suspicions, were at one with Hitler and Popper and Neurath in their disbelief in the good faith of their opponents. As Hitler has reported, the Marxist spokesmen in the Vienna of his young manhood depicted "the nation as an invention of the 'capitalistic' . . . classes . . . the authority of law as a means for oppressing the proletariat; the school as an institution for breeding slaves and slaveholders" [97] — and the indictment was, he tells us, extended to include the entire sum of capitalistic institutions and ideals.

As the Marxism of the street-corner was thus everyman's teacher of suspicion, so, for the educated, the subtler and more intellectual Marxist conception of ideologies, arising out of and supporting systems of economic organization, cast doubt upon the disinterestedness of moral and political principles. Whoever still preserved the innocence of his understanding had also to confront the sociological relativism of Pareto, according to which ethical principles are mere "derivatives," that is, rationalizations of existing sentiments. More importantly, there was the new Freudian analysis which seemed to reveal moral systems as mechanisms of escaping into illusion from the menace of unconscious desires. And dating from the nineteen-twenties, there was a minority movement of which Neurath was a member and to which Popper owes a substantial debt, "logical positivism," which promoted the view that ethical propositions, being "noncognitive" and purely emotive, are neither

---

[95] *Mein Kampf*, translated by R. Manheim, 1943, pp. 41–43.

[96] *Ibid.*, p. 64.

[97] *Ibid.*, p. 40.

true nor false; from this position, it is easy to show how grossly deluded have been all the great moralists. In the midst of such plots and counterplots, it would not be difficult to develop an illusory X-ray vision into the deceitful or self-deceiving soul of any political and ethical thinker, such as Plato, particularly after it had been accepted as proved that his proposals resembled Hitler's official program.

And as if this were not enough to damn Plato as a hypocrite, another shocking historical influence was added as a consequence of Hitler's accession to power and the unfolding of his career. Plato's principles having been equated with the theory of Nazism, his hypothetical practice, that is, what these principles would have come to had they been acted upon, could readily be identified with Hitlerism in action, as Neurath and Popper appear to have done. This interpretation is given color by its superficial resemblance to the method of "operationalism," which some logical positivists regard as the true criterion of meaning.[98] And as, admittedly, nothing in the original program of the NSDAP or even in the most frankly confessional passage of *Mein Kampf* gave adequate warning of Nazism's later demoniacal repudiation of the basic assumptions of common humanity, this has thrown the most evil implications back upon Plato. Suspicion has been confirmed, the validity of extending the merest hints of oppressive intentions into full-fledged inquisition has been proved; in the full energy of alarm and outraged humanitarian sympathy, "closure" is attained, and Plato is seen as Hitler in ancient dress.

In thus seeing in Plato's pages the outline of Hitlerism, Neurath and Popper are not alone. The same invitations to suspect, the same historical object lessons have been shared by us all, though not experienced with such intensity. Neurath and Popper are merely among the extreme examples of a reading public whose membership threatens to include virtually the entire class of libral-democratic readers, as once, at the end of the eighteenth century, the Terror of the French revolution threatened to make anti-Republicanism coextensive with humanitarian scruples and belief in legal justice and decency. Today friendship for Plato is to be found chiefly among those scholars (and their friends and disciples) whose vision of him antedated the rise of Nazism, and thus remained clear of the psychic impurities and "conditioning" that we just now described. The reading of Plato has become a difficult art, requiring critical restraint and firm resistance to the lure of easy analogies and deadly historical parallels. But the difficulty is substantially reduced by the mere recognition of its existence. The real danger here is that of being taken unawares by an irrational suspicion of whose operation we are only dimly conscious.

---

[98] Popper's departures from the tenets of logical positivism, as established by leading members of the school, are not crucial to the present discussion, but may be found *passim* in his notes to Part II of the *Open Society*, esp. p. 632 ff.

An egregious instance of the extravagance into which a suspicious approach to Plato can lead is found in the attempt to interpret him by means of Marxist principles made by Winspear and Silverberg. In *Who Was Socrates?*,[99] these writers have developed the hypothesis of the economic determination (and deterioration) of the thought of Socrates, who on this view was led, through the corrosive influence of his friendship with representatives of the propertied class at Athens, to renounce in their favor the fine democratic-mercantile sympathies of his earlier time. Accordingly, when the betrayed democracy had executed him, Plato invented, in his *Apology*, the speech that Socrates should have made (Winspear and Silverberg believe that Socrates actually made no speech at all), and in it Plato shows himself master of the hypocritic art: attention is skillfully directed away from the real charges, the suspicion of "being the head of an antidemocratic conspiratorial club" and of introducing the "militant" Pythagorean deities of "international conservatism." Socrates is made to appear to posterity, instead, as the victim of prejudice directed against him because of his being mistaken for a "democratic" sophist and materialist (our authors think Thrasymachus and Anaxagoras great exponents of the "democratic" viewpoint). Plato's aim is "subtle"; he "deliberately confounds two quite separate things"; "he has done this with such success that . . . all the labors of scholarship have not served to extricate them" [100] — until, fortunately, Winspear and Silverberg achieved it; we remember that in Popper's book it was Popper who was required to uncover Plato's quite different villainy!

Thus Winspear and Silverberg supply another, perhaps the crowning example, of the wild work that can be made of Platonic interpretation, if one consents to follow the whispers of suspicion. Hypotheses are soon built, and, with the help of other often unnoticeably small *ad hoc* assumptions, easily "verified," rendered, as these authors say of their own interpretation, "necessary." But Nemesis awaits them in the persons of other no less malignly disposed interpreters whose suspicions happen to run in opposing directions. And so we may once more leave these Cadmean warriors to their fate of blind destruction at one another's hands, reflecting that suspicions which can thus project themselves adaptably upon the object are more the misfortunes of their possessors than valid indicators of actuality.

---

[99] A. Winspear and T. Silverberg, 1939.
[100] *Ibid.*, pp. 76–78. In holding that the *Apology* is a Platonic invention, our authors are building upon the thesis propounded by H. Gomperz and defended by Oldfather, discussed below on p. 632. Be it observed, however, that neither of these scholars has lent the sanction of his name to the notion that the author of the *Apology* was making dishonest propaganda, or in any sense distorting the fundamental issues involved.

Another example of modern sleuthing which supposes itself to have uncovered ancient deceptions and betrayals of noble causes — this time committed by Aristotle — is the book by Allendy described on p. 125, n.

But there remain still other persons against whom it is not impossible that suspicion may be aroused, chief among whom are (1) the friends and admirers of Plato, including our blessed selves, and (2) the suspicious detractors. As to (1), (2), in the persons of Popper and Neurath, have warned their readers to suspect all those who, like the present writer, essentially approve the philosophy of Plato. As Popper sees us, either we are the well-intentioned dupes of Plato, unconscious but dangerous carriers of the poison which Plato has slid into our souls (under this caption Popper apparently includes most modern commentators),[101] or we are in some sense Plato's partners in crime, his fellow conspirators against liberal and equalitarian ideals, whom Plato has paid off in the small coin of flattery or won by his appeal to our baser motives. Popper is here thinking on the one hand of teachers, philosophers, and musicians, whose professional pride Plato has gratified by magnifying their functions,[102] and on the other hand of the snobs and would-be beneficiaries of an unequal society whose claims Plato has so soothingly justified.[103] Among these, Popper and Neurath, too, have asked their readers to believe, are not a few in whose hearts Plato has awakened "secret dreams" of personal power and mastery over others.[104]

The injustice of this wholesale calumny must not pass unchallenged. On its face, such a claim is largely unverifiable. Of the two lonely examples cited in proof of personal ambition, let Popper retain possession of his one showpiece, Nietzsche, whom reading of Plato undoubtedly reënforced in his dream of power. We may merely note that, as a matter of fact, it was Callicles, champion of nonmoral power, whom Plato rejects, and not Socrates, whom Plato loved, to whom Nietzsche's sympathies were attracted.

Popper is much more unhappy in his other instance. Some imp of the perverse inspired him to select from among Plato's admirers the late scholar and moralist A. E. Taylor, and to fasten upon him the fantastic charge of "hinting" (Popper sees "hints" easily in Plato, too, we recollect) that in England, in the year 1939, a true Platonist like himself, if given the opportunity, would have done what he could to install the Platonic Republic in place of the existing government. Evidence for this slur upon Taylor's motivation does not, properly, exist. On examination of the passage cited by Popper from Taylor's article, we find that Popper has simply transferred to Taylor a notion of Plato's that Taylor was expounding, as if Taylor had himself asserted it, with reference to Britain, in the year 1939! Taylor, remaining wholly within the context of the ancient Greek world, was recounting *Plato's* belief that men born into an "oligarchy" or a "democracy," but cherishing an ideal such as Plato's own, would, if good fortune gave them

---

[101] Popper, pp. 43–44, 87–88, 103, 510.
[102] *Ibid.*, p. 500, n. 39.
[103] *Ibid.*, pp. 95, 191.

[104] *Ibid.*, pp. 152, 570; Neurath, 1945, p. 57.

power, seek to actualize at least in part the philosophic commonwealth.[105] Seldom, in our experience, has so microscopic a base of evidence been assigned the function of supporting so huge a superstructure of assertion. Taylor's remark dealt with a different topic, was applied to another age, was quoted as the opinion of another man. There is no proof of Popper's charge against Taylor, no proof of his ascription of dreams of power to Platonists in general.

Moreover, even had Taylor been in some way revealing an intention of his own, it is only on the principles of a rabid anti-Platonism that such an intention partakes of guilt. It is no crime to wish, or to be willing, to put what political idealism one cherishes at the service of one's country. Had Popper contented himself with the suggestion that so ardent a Platonist as Taylor, if returned to Parliament, would have sought to apply Platonic principles for the benefit of the British people, as Masaryk did for Czechoslovakia,[106] we should have accepted the suggestion and applauded the contemplated act. One could readily imagine Taylor urging educational equalization or introducing a bill for subsidizing political research, and quoting appropriate passages from the *Republic* by way of precedent. But such moderation is not at Popper's command. He is inviting his reader to think of Taylor as seeking to put into practice the complete program of the *Republic*, interpreted, moreover, as he, Popper, sees it — and that, we know, is a different matter indeed. The bare fact is that Popper is not here advancing an argument. He is merely spinning his vicious circle of suspicion, to Plato's hurt.

To discount the testimony of all friends and admirers of Plato, as Popper and Neurath have done, attributing it to their credulity or without evidence blackening their characters with charges of secret pettiness or ugly ambition, has the advantage of seeming to dispose of the otherwise embarrassing fact that many able men of undoubted allegiance to liberal principles have greatly admired Plato, an admiration which has been shared even by some of those who, like Crossman, have been compelled to dissent from Plato's authoritarianism and distrust of the common man. Write it down as another advantage of this tactic that it discredits in advance the efforts of all who may seek to answer. For who of us is prepared to present himself as the unerring embodiment of pure and disinterested Reason? The present writer does not claim more than an honest effort to see clearly and to present his evidence without suppression or distortion. By way of answer to Popper's implicit charge of secret pride or ambition, we shall appeal to a principle of civilized communication. Without for one moment seriously questioning Popper's and Neurath's right to present themselves as disinterested friends of liberal de-

---

[105] "The Decline and Fall of the State in *Republic*, VIII," *Mind*, 1939, p. 31.
[106] *Masaryk on Thought and Life*, Conversations with Karel Capek, 1938, pp. 72, 162.

mocracy, we will point out that they enjoy this status as a presupposition which they are under obligation to extend to their opponents who have entered a like claim. We may see in their pages or in the setting of their lives presumptive evidence that they have succumbed to the influence of a pervasive atmosphere of suspicion, or have been led to weigh evidence wrongly, by excruciating experience. We may even judge them totally incapable of serving as reliable guides to the interpretation of Plato, and may cite evidence and marshal arguments to prove it. But we must not without specific grounds accuse them of discreditable motives which are secret, and hence by definition unverifiable.

To return to Plato, our final statement must be that he has emerged from his ordeal unstained. We have with meticulous care examined typical cases of all Popper's charges, weighed his evidence, and tested his arguments. The imputations of conscious and unconscious guilt and struggle reveal themselves as no more than projections; the depiction of the imaginative symbols of Plato's deeply cherished beliefs as cynical propaganda has shown itself to be based on omission and distortion of evidence, and on preconceptions derived from false historical parallels. Of Plato's deceitfulness nothing remains but an honest proposal to make a limited use of deception for the higher communal ends. In view of this, the least that can be asked for him from his responsible contemporary readers is that they accord him the moral respect and supposition of good faith with which alone it is possible to read, justly and with good hope of essential understanding, a great, if sometimes, from our modern standpoint, greatly mistaken mind.

The Charge of Self-Aggrandizement and Lust for Power

To complete their "pathographic" analysis of Plato's soul, our analysts, Popper, and another who is now to reappear in our pages, Kelsen, have much to say of his feverish ambition and the fanatical certitude of conviction that supported it, traits so clearly incompatible with his reputation for judicial calm and philosophical indifference to common esteem, as to require a radical revision of the traditional view. The two unfavorable interpretations, though in broad agreement, are sufficiently different in detail to warrant separate treatment. We will give our first hearing to Popper.

Heretofore, in the interests of exposition, we have dealt separately so far as possible with the individual traits into which Popper has analyzed Plato. But if one is to receive the full import and impact of his analysis, one must combine these *disjecta membra* into the image of a single whole. Thus the tortured guilt and the cold-blooded guile, the impulse to exploit and at the same time, in some sense, to benefit the common man, must somehow be brought together by the reader within the framework of one personality, if the impression conveyed by Popper's book is to be adequately reproduced.

And into the same complex whole must somehow be worked a further trait or group of traits of a dark, discolored hue, which will justify us in applying to its functional totality the predicate pathological, if not outright insane. This element in Plato's makeup is, in its most generic aspect, exaggerated self-assertion, which expresses itself in a "lust for power," issues in extreme dogmatic certainty, and justifies itself by an all but megalomaniacal "claim to rule."

Of Popper's arguments supporting this charge, we shall deal first with his new and quite unsatisfactory interpretation of the "nuptial number" in the *Republic*. It will be remembered from our earlier discussion [107] that Plato makes the Muses, "jesting with us and teasing us as if we were children," describe this number in complicated and obscure mathematical language, and foretell that failure to know and to employ it in regulating marriages will one day pervert the eugenic practice of the guardians, with consequences fatal to the continued existence of the ideal state. We have indicated in the same place our general attitude to the vexed problem of the number; here we have no intention of clearing away the darkness that still surrounds the impregnable citadel of its (presumed) serious significance. What is contemplated is the much less pretentious task of expounding and evaluating Popper's reading of its meaning as evidence for Plato's desperate and either unscrupulous or, if sincere, deluded claim to power. We must follow the path of Popper's argument, which will lead us steadily downward from his initial rejection of the "idealized" conception of Plato, as the sober proponent of moral reform implemented by rulers possessed of philosophic vision, via the degradation of the rulers into medicine men and sham eugenic experts, to arrive finally at the identification of Plato himself with these rulers at their worst.

Popper tells us that the modest Socratic conception of the philosopher was radically corrupted by Plato, who ascribed to his philosophers definitive insight, and literally "supernatural" knowledge. The philosopher king is "not like other men." He is in the first place set apart from the common herd and confirmed in power by esoteric pseudo-wisdom. But he possesses also a practical political function, upon which depends the whole hope of permanent happiness, the recovery, never again to be lost, of the paradisiacal happiness enjoyed at the dawn of time, by the inhabitants of the first and best city, before the "Fall of Man"; this function is to keep pure the guardians' aristocratic blood, and to breed from among their descendants a race of supermen, forever guaranteed against degeneration. Under the administration of such breeder kings, Athens is to be reconstituted a replica of the primeval ideal city, imagined as the actual ancestor of the Spartan state, with the single but all-important addition of immunity to decay. The nuptial number, unknown before the "Fall," will be acquired by these new guardians as part of their

---

[107] See pp. 53–54 above. The passage is *Rep.* 545 D ff.

mathematical and dialectical training, and will enable them to fix the new city into permanence.[108]

The number is, Popper believes, a determinate figure, known to Plato, though he may not have chosen to reveal it completely in his published page.[109] It is Plato's own invention, computed by the aid of the newer mathematical knowledge of solid geometry and harmonics, upon the basis of certain primitive Pythagorean superstitions concerning the numerical nature of reality and human happiness.[110] It is designed to secure the permanence of that racial excellence which is shown by anticipatory references in important passages of the *Republic* to be regarded as a matter of desperate importance, worthy to constitute the central concern of the city's rulers.[111] And Plato, by his description of it and by his insistence that if it is unknown, the city cannot endure,[112] is obscurely recommending himself to his fellow Athenians as the only possessor of this practical key to ideal guardianship, which is to be theirs on condition that they shall summon him to be their ruler. Thus did Plato, as Popper holds him up to our derision, attempt to ply "the sorry trade of every shaman, the selling . . . of breeding taboos . . . for power over his fellow men." [113]

In an effort to break the spell of this coherent and even somewhat fascinating illusion, let us first attempt to conceive the state of mind of a man who, residing in the outskirts of Athens, seriously believed himself capable, at any moment, of beginning the swift and inevitably successful conversion of his native city into an eternal paradise. Could a man whose head contained so explosive a notion have kept quietly on the track of an academic and philosophic life, without confiding the results of his "research magnificent" to those who might be in a position to aid in its realization? Could he have refrained from forming a little committee of enthusiastic promoters? Is it conceivable that when the invitation to Sicily arrived he would not have given the idea a conspicuous place in his earliest proposals for reform, a fact which (even if the letters are not genuine) could hardly have escaped the attention of contemporary observers? Can one believe that throughout the length and breadth of his writings not a word of this unparalleled discovery can be found, save this one short passage in the *Republic*? In this passage, too, the number is by no means presented as an enticement, held out to prospective buyers with loud and confident insistence. Instead, it is introduced by the sportive and teasing Muses, as a means of explaining, by its absence, the fated dissolution of a city which has nowhere been plainly and unequivocally identified as a city of long ago; indeed, the very existence of this supposed proto-city has been so well concealed that its dissolution has

---

108 Popper, pp. 81–83, 145–150.
109 *Ibid.*, pp. 82, 518.
110 *Ibid.*, pp. 145, 150.

111 *Ibid.*, pp. 148–150, 566–567.
112 *Ibid.*, pp. 148, 520.
113 *Ibid.*, pp. 150, 152–153.

for millennia been taken by Plato's readers to be the fated decline of a dream city of the future. Even the dissolution itself is spoken of exclusively in the future tense: "the rulers will not attain fortunate births"; "the children will not be well-born." Such tactics suggest an advertisement written in invisible ink, and would constitute extraordinary and self-defeating reticence in any shaman. Popper's hypothesis is thus seen to be initially unlikely in the extreme, opposed to all psychological probability and historical evidence, and unsupported by anything that Plato, in his other writings, proposes or describes as the functions of government, or the methods of eugenics.

If we now examine the grounds Popper has offered for his crucial contention that Plato believed himself possessed of such a number, we see that it rests first upon a series of inadmissible contentions basic to Popper's whole case. First of these is his conception of Plato's as dishonest, a conception which permits the ascription to Plato of almost any unproven beliefs and intentions; on this principle, it is always possible to reject what Plato says, and to search for "hints" and enigmatic revelations. It gives Popper, in effect, a fourth dimension into which he can escape when the time comes to produce evidence. It permits him in dealing with the number to brush aside Plato's explanation of the essential purpose of the guardians' higher education, to substitute his own discreditable analysis of their functions, and to add elements of which Plato never speaks; it also enables him to explain, as intentional concealment, the obscurity with which Plato describes the computation of the number itself. Colored and supported by the concept of dishonesty are further general theses: the notion of the aboriginal, proto-Spartan, ideal city which Plato, without openly admitting it, is describing throughout most of the *Republic*, and the belief that Plato secretly intended the immediate realization of the reconstituted city at Athens, with the existing Athenian oligarchs and *demos* frozen into inviolable castes. We have already dealt with these general misconceptions, except that of the primeval city, the disproof of which, since it turns upon the consideration of vermiculate details, may, in spite of its importance to Popper's case, be relegated to an Appendix.[114]

But before leaving this topic we must not fail to walk once around the monument that Popper has erected here to Plato's naïveté. For Plato is represented as believing that the first city, in the full sense of the word, which ever existed upon this earth, was a civic structure elaborately complete with its three ordered classes of rulers, warriors, and workers, equipped with an educational system comprising the two branches of music and gymnastic, nourished upon a highly edifying mythology and literature which ascribed no evil to gods or to good men, permitting to its guardian group no property and no emolument beyond subsistence, and displaying in approximate form

---

[114] See Appendix X, which argues in disproof of Plato's supposed conception of a   primeval "best state," pp. 612ff.

all the other features of Plato's city of the *Republic*, as described in Books III and IV. Besides the manifest absurdity of this elaborate primitivism, we may mention a logical difficulty. Popper has told us that "Plato had a fairly clear idea" that the first and best city had originated when the Dorian "war horde" marched triumphantly into a "city, previously founded by the tradesmen and workers," and imposed themselves as masters upon a "settled population." [115] The city which resulted — the perfect city — is for Plato, so Popper believes, the earliest embodiment of the Idea of the City.[116] Of what lineage, then, was the city or the settlement which was thus overwhelmed?

But the main absurdity entailed by Popper's supposition is the truncated time schedule on which it assumes that Plato's parochial mind was operating. For if at the time he wrote the *Republic*, Plato regarded his aboriginal perfect city as the immediate progenitor of the Spartan and Cretan forms of government, this would set an interval of not more than a few thousand years (probably much less) between it and Plato's own day. No longer ago than this, then, Plato must have believed, there had existed upon this earth an almost unblemished perfection, embodied in the primal city. Assume it to have endured unchanged for other millennia preceding its decay, still, since it is the "first" city, it must reach back to the time of man's first organized association in cities.

Plato, then, for Popper, believed all past time numbered by a handful of millennia. We invite Popper's attention to Plato's statement in the *Theaetetus* (175 A), a dialogue he has himself suggested may antedate the *Republic*, that, as the philosopher well knows, every man now living is descended from "unnumbered thousands" of forefathers, among them rich and poor, kings and slaves, Greeks and barbarians.[117] We cannot agree that there is reason for assuming the *Theaetetus* earlier than the *Republic*, yet neither can we believe that Plato, when he wrote the *Republic*, should be suspected of believing the origin of time distant by but a few scores of millennia. There is no reason to suppose that between the *Republic* and the *Theaetetus* Plato first discovered time's immensity. Was not the philosopher of the *Republic*, too, the "spectator of all time and all existence" (486 A), a phrase sufficiently vast in its implications? If Popper has recourse to his suggestion of a serious Platonic belief in epochs,[118] and would argue that it is the beginning of the present epoch which Plato believed thus recent, he will be involved in other difficulties. For he has argued that Plato's best city is the first embodiment in time of its Idea, one of the products of that contact of the Ideas with time at time's start, and of their paternal operation to produce as their first-

---

[115] Popper, pp. 498, 51, 55.

[116] *Ibid.*, pp. 28, 30, 41.

[117] That Plato means thousands in direct line (father, grandfather, great-grandfather, etc.), not the thousands quickly achieved by the spreading increase of the powers of two, is clear from his reference to a twenty-fifth and a fiftieth ancestor.

[118] Popper, pp. 22–23, 475–476.

born offspring nearly perfect material copies, which forms part of his interpretation of the Platonic metaphysics and the very basis of his belief that
Plato's perfect city is also Plato's notion of the earliest city.[119] The moral
of this fable would seem to be a *caveat* against underestimating the intelligence
of your adversary, especially if your adversary happens to be Plato.

There remain, however, Popper's arguments dealing more immediately
with the number. It is, Popper argues in sum, vital to the breeding program,
which is in turn vital to the welfare of the city; it is based upon the very
mathematical knowledge with which Plato proposes to equip his guardians;
Plato plainly implies that it could, if known, be employed to obviate the city's
decline; and Plato himself, though obscurely, announces its formula. Surely,
he would have made it the cornerstone of his new edifice!

This chain of reasoned error could be cut at many of its links, but we
may begin with pointing out its major weakness: It neglects, or rather denies,
a fundamental tenet of the Platonic philosophy, the necessary corruptibility
of all things that share in generation. Popper is aware of Plato's adherence
to this belief, even of Plato's reassertion of it as affecting the ideal city in
the very passage concerning the number; [120] yet, in some fashion not made
clear to the reader, he has convinced himself that Plato did not mean the
corruptibility to apply to the perfect state, and that with the one addition of
a scientific breeding program, this state will, if reconstituted, escape decay —
apparently in perpetuity.[121] This fundamental violation of Platonic first prin-

---

[119] We shall discuss Popper's analysis of
the Platonic theory of the Ideas on pp. 627ff.

[120] *Timaeus* 52 A provides another statement.

[121] Popper, pp. 81–82. Popper's belief
that for Plato "the perfect, the 'natural'
state" can have no necessity of dissolution,
his insistence (p. 520) that Plato could not
conceivably have spoken of it as "a thing
of human generation," appears to be closely
connected with some of his other misconceptions of the Platonic philosophy. Thus it
is probably no accident that Popper also
thinks of Plato as a political "holist," who
attributes no independent value to the individual human being, and locates all value
in the state; it is in consonance with this
that Popper supposes Plato to have set the
state above and apart from all other mundane beings and structures. On an earlier
page (p. 38), engaged in expounding the
Platonic theory of ideas, with its teaching
that all material copies of the ideas partake
of mutability, he has gone so far as to add
the words "except perhaps the most excellent ones," thus providing without textual

justification a little niche for the perfect
state as he conceives Plato to regard it.
Popper has failed to take account of the fact
that it is the human soul alone which Plato
has thus set beside the World-All and the
gods, as a creation, indeed, and not, like the
eternal forms, in essence incorruptible, but
as having been created by the Demiurge
himself, deathless and everlasting (*Timaeus*
41–42, 69 C). The state, it is true, is not in
the *Timaeus* mentioned along with the mortal and corruptible beings created by the
junior gods. But the absence of any specific
exception in its favor is notable. This being
the case, its status, sufficiently indicated
even in the *Republic*, as a mere earthly copy
of its form or idea, suffices to classify it
among the things generated and subject to
corruption, even if the Muses did not specifically declare it thus corruptible. Plato's
hope and desire of stabilizing and preserving to the utmost whatever is excellent in
the world of flux have led him in the *Laws*
(960 B–E), under the audacious figure of
irreversible Fate, to speak as if his well-
founded state were destined to endure. In

ciples is but another consequence of that initial neglect of the Platonic philosophy as distinct from political theory which has made possible so many of Popper's misinterpretations of this political theory itself.

If signs of life remain in Popper's serpentine argument, after this fatal objection has taken effect, we are willing to destroy *seriatim* or render harmless its surviving segments. First of all, we may agree that the eugenic function of the guardians, though quite different from Popper's conception of it, is to Plato of the greatest importance, and that he deems it vital to the continued existence of the ideal city.[122] But this alone does not prove that there is

---

the *Republic* (424 A), he even looks forward, once the city is established, to a continuous cycle of improvement, an upward development in human and institutional excellence; in the *Laws* (769–770, 951–952, 962), he is hopeful of including among the city's institutions one which will provide for cautious future improvements, even perhaps for radical transformation closer to the ideal.

But we must remember Plato's lively awareness of the uncertain element in human history, the recurrent fires and floods and pestilences which have so often in times past hurled man backward into barbarism (*Timaeus* 22 C, *Laws* 677 A), not to mention those lesser vicissitudes which are of commoner occurrence (*Laws* 740 E–741 A). It would seem, therefore, that when Plato allows himself to speak in terms of an apparently unbounded "historical" future, one must assume that he has appended the tacit proviso, "barring contingencies." Popper's exemption in Plato's name of the ideal state from corruptibility is related intimately also to his treatment of Plato as a "historicist," a mistaken view treated obliquely in our App. X, pp. 612ff., and confronted directly in App. XIV, pp. 622ff.

[122] In his endeavor to show the great significance of the number passage and to strengthen his thesis that in it Plato reveals his own claim to serve as philosopher king, Popper has asked us to see it as the culminating member of a series of passages in the *Republic* which voice Plato's great concern with "race" in the special sense of racial exclusiveness, and reveal Plato's belief that good breeding consists entirely in keeping certain noble racial strains uncontaminated with base infusions of lower-class or degenerate blood (Popper, e.g., pp. 81–82). On pp. 149–150 and 566–567, Pop-

per lists these passages, claiming as racialistic the plea (*Republic* 470 ff.) that Hellenes shall not war on or enslave one another, but only barbarians, and seeing the same racialism in the great sentence (473 C–E) which declares that until kings become philosophers there shall be no cessation of evils for the "human race"; a "bridge" is discovered in the passage (536 A–B) which prescribes that fit aspirants to philosophy must be "true-born," not "cripples" or "bastards"; all these "foreshadow" the number, which is to prevent the entry of racial imperfection into the guardian class. We have already removed most of these passages from Popper's racialistic series by arguments presented on earlier pages. That the philosopher-king sentence speaks universally of the human race has been argued on pp. 230f.; we have presented on pp. 172f. reason for believing that, in the passage on war and enslavement, the note to which Plato's sympathy is attuned, and on which the emphasis is placed, is the recommendation of mercifulness toward Hellenes, while the sanctioning of harshness toward barbarians is only incidental, representing an uncorrected survival from the widespread Greek attitude toward enemies of either sort. On pp. 204ff. we have already commented upon the passage concerning "cripples" and "bastards," in the course of discussing Antisthenes, who was at that point in Popper's argument supposed to be the personal target of Plato's remarks; it was then shown that these apparent terms of prejudice or abuse are used in a purely figurative sense, to describe persons unevenly balanced, "loving toil," as Plato puts it, with either body or soul, but not with both. The passage has no reference to any particular person, nor has it racialist bearings: though Plato undoubtedly would consider the qualities of

any reference to the breeding program in those passages elsewhere in the *Republic* in which Popper has detected it, or that Plato believed himself possessed of a magically efficacious nuptial number. Next, the fact that the guardians are to have mathematical knowledge of the sort involved in Plato's description of the number does not prove that they will also possess the number. It is well to observe that in Plato's text, no one is credited with knowing it except the Muses. "The rulers whom you have educated," the Muses say, "will not for all their wisdom hit upon fortunate begetting and barrenness for your race"; their powers of "reasoning combined with sense-perception" will not forever avail, but "in ignorance" they will permit the begetting of unworthy and unfortunate children. Even if we assume for the moment that "the rulers whom you have educated" are, in fact, Popper's imaginary Ur-guardians, Plato has said at the most that they did not possess the number; he has not asserted the contrary of the mathematically educated guardians of Popper's supposed second city. If we believe, on the other hand, that Plato describes but one ideal city, and that the guardians referred to are the fully-trained philosopher kings, we have the simple assertion that even they will not attain it.[123]

---

body and mind to which he refers to be largely hereditary, this does not mean that he is thinking of them for the moment as hereditary, or that he ascribes their presence to "purity" of blood, as we shall argue on pp. 535ff. As regards the number passage itself, we shall show similarly that the racial excellence which Plato says will fail and by its absence bring about the downfall of the city, is not "racialism" in Popper's sense of the word. In short, of Popper's series three passages are not, properly speaking, "racial" at all; the fourth proves genuine racial interest, but of a different kind.

[123] Throughout this discussion I am maintaining the view that it is the *number* of which the guardians are to remain ignorant. The Greek seems to imply this (546 C–D), reading "the number . . . is master over . . . better and worse births, and when, in ignorance of these, the guardians unite brides and bridegrooms inopportunely," etc. Nevertheless, I am prepared to grant the possibility, though it seems to me scarcely probable, that it is not the number which will be lacking: that the guardians' *logismos*, reasoning or calculation, will be adequate, and will on this supposition include knowledge of the number, whatever it may represent; the error will arise from false observation of particulars, from *aisthêsis*, a

faculty which in the Platonic theory of knowledge is radically liable to error. Whichever alternative one adopts, the consequences are the same: the guardians will commit the inevitable mistake, the snake will find its way into the garden.

Popper advances the argument, set forth on his pp. 81–83 and 518–520, that guardians equipped with the modernized higher education which Plato is planning to provide will not be liable to the error of which the Muses speak, since they will not be limited to the faulty "empirical method" which for Popper is conveyed by the phrase "calculation (or reasoning) combined with observation" (*logismos met' aisthêseôs*), and will not be compelled to "hit, *accidentally*" (Popper's italicized translation of *teuxontai*) upon the method of getting good offspring, but will have at their disposal a "purely rational method" (Popper, p. 82). We may point out first that Popper's emphatic phrase, "hit, accidentally," is not a necessary interpretation of the Greek, which could equally well mean "hit, by aiming at" or simply "obtain." Even more surprising is the notion that mathematically trained guardians could be conceived by Plato to dispense, in their supervision of marriages, with *aisthêsis* or observation. For all activity relating to the material world, "particulars" are indispensable, and "particulars" are derivable

Deserving of more serious consideration is Popper's next argument. The Muses assert that since the guardians are ignorant of the number, the city must inevitably be destroyed, and in so saying seem to imply that knowledge of it would suffice to avert this catastrophe; the city's destruction is not, therefore (or so it appears) unconditionally determined. But consider: the Muses have already told us that since the city is of the class of things which are generated, it must inevitably pass away. We are not at liberty to construe the statement about knowledge or ignorance of the number in such a way as to contradict this categorical assertion. And precisely as in the first case it is not implied that the city might somehow cease to be a thing of generation, so in the second there is no implication, and indeed no logical possibility, that the number, if it is indeed capable of averting destruction, might pass into the class of the known.[124]

---

from the universals which alone reason can supply, no more for Plato than for modern logic.

It is true, as Popper has been at pains to point out, that Plato in prescribing the higher education of the philosophic ruler (*Rep.* 523 ff.) bids him leave behind the region of sense perception and mount to lay hold on essences alone, thus to become a "true reckoner." This is the upward pathway from the cave of Plato's metaphor. But there is the downward pathway also, by which the guardians are compelled to return from the heights of reflective reason and confront the actual world, that they may accustom themselves once more "to observe the shadowy things" of sense (520 C), and "may not fall short in experience" (539 E). In another metaphor, the "painter" of the ideal city or character looks off to the heavenly model, but must again direct his eyes upon his work (501 B).

That Plato did not suppose that observation, *aisthêsis*, despite its limitations, was dispensable, appears again in the *Phaedrus* (271 D–272 A), where discussing the conditions under which the knowledge of rhetoric may become effective, he affirms that after the types of discourse applicable to different men and occasions have been learned, the student must also be able to recognize these persons and occasions by observation (*aisthêsis*). Again, near the end of the *Laws* (960 E ff.), engaged in justifying the institution of the Night Council which is to serve as the "savior of the laws," he ascribes the preservation of every living being to its "mind and senses" or "reason and observa-

tion" (*nous met' aisthêseôs*) (961 D), and explains that the elder and younger members of his Council are to exercise respectively these two functions on behalf of the state (964 E–965 A).

In short, in the passage about the number it is proper to read the Muses' phrase *logismos met' aisthêseôs* as Plato's expression for rational scientific method (in the modern sense of "scientific"), the best available combination of human faculties for dealing with the world of experience and material fact. It is this which the Muses say will not suffice to save the guardians from eventual error.

[124] Cf. our note 123, p. 456 above. If the number is known to the guardians, and if, therefore, their blunder is occasioned by ignorance of another sort, we are required merely to believe this other ignorance equally inevitable.

But Plato's reference to the guardians' ignorance may be explained in yet another way. If one supposes that neither knowledge of the number nor any other human skill or accuracy can avail to save the city, and that decline will inexorably begin when the cycle or period of fertility and barrenness for human creatures, of which the Muses speak (cf. p. 53), shall have turned through its appointed orbit — on this supposition, the ignorance of the guardians is brought in simply as a piece of dramatic irony: all unaware of the futility which attends their efforts, on that unhappy day they will continue to do their conscientious best, alas! without effect.

The final argument from the fact that Plato himself is obviously able to state the formula of the number, and therefore must himself possess the knowledge, though to be sure he ascribes it only to the Muses, is an instance of the loss of aesthetic distance which deceives the spectators in the theatre into believing the scene literally, not dramatically, real. If a character upon the stage declares aloud what he asserts no one except himself will ever know, does the existence of the author and the spectators belie him? Whether or not Plato has given directions capable of yielding a definite number,[125] — if knowledge of the number would avert decay, does he not make the Muses declare it will remain unkown?

But it is time to make an end of refutation and to combine our previous scattered suggestions into a summary statement of an alternative interpretation clear of the difficulties under which Popper's hypothesis labors. Whatever the actual number in itself may or may not be, it is functioning in this passage essentially — we would say exclusively — as a dramatic device. It symbolizes those inevitable and uncontrollable forces or powers beyond human wit or wisdom, operating on a periodic principle worthy of what was to Plato this mysterious but mathematically ordered universe, which are scheduled in the end to overthrow the mightiest and fairest structures of human contrivance. As we read the passage, nothing of significance for our purpose hangs on the identity of the number, or upon what units of time or of genetic com-

---

[125] The chronic disagreement among scholars as to the identity of the number persists, despite A. E. Taylor's hopeful prediction ("The Decline and Fall of the State in *Republic*, VIII," 1939) that it would be brought to an end by the solution of Diès (*Le Nombre de Platon*, Paris, 1936, cited by Taylor). Still in the field, though somewhat damaged by adverse criticism, is the double interpretation which Adam has given (in his notes and Appendix on *Republic* 545 C), discovering first an embryological number, 216, and second a cosmological number, 60^4, or 12,960,000, which is taken to indicate days, and, assuming Plato to have counted 360 days to the year, is read as 36,000 years; this in turn is interpreted in the light of the *Politicus* myth, as the supposed duration of the world's half-cycle, as it moves from better to worse and conversely. Diès has argued in favor of a single number, identical with Adam's second number, or 60^4, and this is taken by Taylor, *op. cit.*, to represent the number of years, 36,000, in which would be accomplished the entire declension of the perfect state into tyranny. Then there is Brumbaugh's assignment of genetic significance to the mathematical expression or diagram — hardly a number in the usual sense — which he detects in the passage (see Appendix XI below, pp. 616f.). That Plato should have had some determinate number in mind as he wrote the speech of the Muses seems to me likely on any conceivable hypothesis. Even a "painted dagger" must share with its more substantial prototype certain particular qualities of size and contour, if it is to perform the illusory function devolving upon it. One can imagine Plato starting with a number chosen partly, like the number 5040 in the *Laws*, for its facile factorability, and partly for its astronomical or other cosmical associations, and proceeding to involve it in the pomp and obscurity required by the character of the speakers (the Muses) and the nature of the occasion (a prophecy of doom). That Diès' inquiry (and Adam's in part) should lead to the number 60^4 makes possible what is to my mind a happy compromise between the "occult significance" and the "merely literary" schools of interpretation. See our suggestion of the number's "meaning," in our text, immediately below.

binations it enumerates. It may even be, one may say, no more than a package so artfully and significantly wrapped that we are content, and Plato's purpose is served, even though it should turn out that nothing whatever remains after the last wrapping has been removed. All that is necessary is that the transience of the ideal state should be oracularly announced,[126] and that its corruption should be traced to the loss in native perfection of its rulers.[127]

We are not required, therefore, to believe that Plato conceived himself possessed of esoteric number wisdom and that he thus announces himself as the indispensable man, the uniquely qualified philosopher shaman. From our portrait of Plato we may happily delete one more disfiguring trait.

If Plato did not try to purchase a position of power with the counterfeit coin of a breeding taboo, had he no other grounds on which to rest his claim? Popper believes that he had, and that a Lyncean reading of the dialogues will leave readers in no doubt as to their nature: Plato was obsessed by the conviction that by virtue of his descent from the Athenian aristocracy, he possessed the right to rule. The evidence for this, Popper has ferreted out from the dialogues, pointing first to Plato's celebration of his maternal lineage, in the *Charmides* (and again in the *Critias*), as a disclosure of his pride of race.[128] The same trail leads on into the *Republic*, where Popper notes as significant the assignment of the exclusive right to rule to the master caste, the

---

[126] Plato's manner of introducing his myth of the number, which we are asked to imagine as being told to us by the "Muses," "playing with us . . . as if we were children" and speaking "in lofty, mock-serious, tragic style" (trans. Shorey, Loeb Library), finds a striking parallel in the *Sophist*, 242 C–E, where various pre-Socratic theories of being are about to be passed in review. Of the authors of these theories, who have spoken in fanciful metaphors and have not troubled to make their meaning clear, Plato says, "Every one of them seems to me to tell us a story as if we were children," and he presently refers to two of the rival sects, the Heraclitean and Empedoclean, as "some Ionian and Sicilian Muses." What may we validly infer from this close similarity? Perhaps two consequences emerge: (1) In speaking of "Muses" in the number passage, Plato has in mind a conflation of earlier thinkers, blending together for his purposes their cosmological speculations and mathematical lore; Empedocles and Pythagoras suggest themselves. (2) From the parallel passage in the *Sophist*, and from *Theaetetus* 180 E, we know that Plato deprecated oracular obscurity in seriously-intend-

ed metaphysical doctrines, since it produces confusion in the minds of listeners, whether or not it indicates a similar lack of clarity in the mind of the thinker himself. Plato's own use of high-flown and obscure language in the number passage, therefore, implies that his intention is not wholly serious, and that his reference to those earlier thinkers is somewhat ironical: when impressive obscurity is what is wanted, they are the ones to call upon! And on topics which are beyond human wit — when myth alone can aid us — such impressiveness is all that can be asked. So, at least, I would interpret this parallel.

And finally, it is interesting to note that Plato's use of the Muses as symbolic agents of possible deceit can be traced back as far as Hesiod's *Theogony* (ll. 27–28), where the Muses are made to say: "We know how to speak many a falsehood like unto truth and, when we so wish, to tell the tale of truth."

[127] Another recent interpretation of the Platonic number, by R. S. Brumbaugh, is discussed in our Appendix XI, pp. 616f.

[128] Popper, pp. 22, 475.

guardians, and the corollary concern for keeping pure the blood of the guardians, which for Popper is almost the central motif of the *Republic*, the end and aim of the secret racialism which Plato was so "hesitant" in bringing forward, and for the sake of which alone so-called "philosophers," as distinct from soldier-administrators, were required as kings. Expressive of the same spirit of exclusiveness, Popper finds, are those passages in the *Republic* where "bastards" and "bald-headed tinkers" are scornfully rejected in favor of the "true-born" aspirants to philosophy.[129] When the Socrates of the dialogue explains how a small number of elect souls have been preserved from the prevalent corruption, Popper's ear discerns a more personal note, indeed a reference to Plato himself, in the mention of a "certain nobly-born and well-bred character who was saved by flight" (or "by exile")[130] from involvement in the politics of his native state. When Plato presently urges the possibility that his ideal state may be realized in at least one instance, if a single descendant of kings or "aristocrats" (Popper thus renders *dynastai*), having been born with a philosophic nature, should escape corruption, Popper again detects a personal reference, since Plato's family, on Popper's special interpretation, are describable as "*dynastai*." From this it is but a step to his climactic discovery in the *Republic*, that the famous sentence concerning the philosopher kings is, again, Plato celebrating Plato. For when this sentence declares that philosophers must become kings, or failing this, that "those who are now called kings or rulers" (*dynastai*) must genuinely and sufficiently become philosophers — here too, in the word *dynastai*, Plato reveals that he is thinking of just such members of aristocratic families as himself.

How shall we separate and distinguish the elements of undoubted truth in the just-stated theory from the fabric of error in which they are interwoven? We may first refer the reader to our earlier discussion of the *Charmides* and the mingling there displayed of family pride with something that we may almost call apology. It is not denied that Plato would have liked to take satisfaction in the high standing of his family, as he doubtless had done in his boyhood, and that after its disgrace in the time of the Thirty, he liked to hark back, in his dialogues, to the days when it still stood high in public esteem, to stress its connection with Solon and its other honorable distinctions, and to show that his subsequently disgraced kinsmen had once enjoyed the friendship of Socrates. This degree of family pride does not prove a haughty racial exclusiveness. In the *Republic*, we shall categorically deny that there is any intent to distribute power on the basis of descent, or, in the usual acceptance of the term, to keep "pure" the guardian breed.

The passage referring to the "nobly-born and well-bred character" saved by flight or exile (496 B) comprises a listing of the several influences that

---

[129] *Ibid.*, pp. 149, 561–562.

[130] *Ibid.*, p. 568. The reference is to *Rep.* 496 B; the translation given is Popper's.

might preserve a man for philosophy. It enumerates the "divine sign" of Socrates and the ill-health of Theages, and in addition mentions three typical situations which would be similarly effective. If Plato has here provided one category in which he himself could properly be included, that would not be matter of surprise, still less of scandal. He may, however, have thought of himself as belonging to that small group who, as he says, "by natural affinity" are drawn to philosophy "from other arts which they justly disdain"; accordingly, there is no certainty that he has referred to himself as "well-born." That he did not think "good birth" in the usual sense prerequisite to inclusion among the small remnant of the saved is plainly shown by the identity of its chief member, Socrates.

One of Popper's most gratuitous conjectures is the discovery of reference to Plato himself [131] in the philosopher-kings sentence, which we herewith reproduce for convenience of reference:

Unless . . . either philosophers become kings in our states or those whom we now call our kings and rulers (*dynastai*) take to the pursuit of philosophy seriously and adequately, and there is a conjunction of these two things, political power and philosophic intelligence, while the motley horde of the natures who at present pursue either apart from the other are compulsorily excluded, there can be no cessation of troubles, dear Glaucon, for our states, nor, I fancy, for the human race either. [132]

To begin with, Plato is already sufficiently included in the first clause, among philosophers; there is no need, in order to prove him a claimant to kingly power, ingeniously to insert him into the alternative clause which follows. Secondly, we must point out with emphasis that Popper's interpretation breaks down the symmetry and even the sense of Plato's sentence. The two specified conditions for the realization of the ideal state must be in equilibrium: "until philosophers become kings" (i.e., actual rulers) must be balanced by a clause meaning "until actual rulers become philosophers." And to interpret *dynastai* in the second clause, as referring to hereditary aristocrats who, like Plato's family, were among the politically unemployed, is literally to strike the bottom out of Plato's meaning. Examination of the later passages reaffirming the central meaning of our sentence, two of which Popper cites as again employing the words *dynastai* or *dynasteia*, will show that if Plato's meaning is not to be violated, these words must in these contexts signify rulers actually entrenched in power. [133]

---

[131] Popper, p. 568.
[132] *Rep.* 473 D, trans. Shorey, Loeb Library.
[133] The passages in question are *Republic* 487 E, *498 E, *499 B, 500 E, *501 E–502 A, 536 A–B, *540 D–E, those marked with an asterisk being the ones in which the words *dynastai, dynasteia,* or *dynasteuô,* occur. It is not denied that the words *dynastai* and *dynasteia* can bear the meaning that Popper assigns them (p. 568), viz., "hereditary oligarchic families" or "aristocratic families"; to Popper's list of passages we may add Lysias II, 18, an excellent example of this use. But in Plato the word occurs with the greatest frequency in its more closely etymological meaning of "the (politically) powerful"; see especially *Gorgias* 526 B;

But Popper has still further surprises in store for us; wilder things are yet to come. We have heard much of Plato's claim to power, both as author of the indispensable breeding number and as member of the hereditary ruling class. Now Popper offers us an additional claim, wholly unprecedented in the literature of Platonic scholarship and reading for all the world like an excerpt from the case history of a megalomaniac: Plato was reaching for "the power which he thought his due," as "descendant and legitimate heir of Codrus the martyr, the last of Athens' kings who, according to Plato, had sacrificed himself 'in order to preserve the kingdom for his children.' "

What possible foundation in Plato's text supports this dizzily baroque fabric of interpretation? In that portion of the *Symposium* in which Socrates is reporting the wisdom of Diotima, there is reference to the desire of noble fame as the motive prompting those who went to their deaths for others' sakes, as Alcestis did for Admetus, Achilles for Patroclus, and Codrus to

---

and also *Laws* 711 D, where the substance of the philosopher-kings sentence is restated.

We may answer here two more footnotes in which Popper (p. 569) further supports his charge that Plato in the *Republic* reveals his personal ambition to become king of Athens. In the *Politicus* he detects "a revealing self-reference" in the statement (292 E–293 A) that the sole criterion of true statesmanship is possession of the appropriate knowledge: "the man who possesses the kingly science, whether he rules or not, must be called kingly, as our previous argument showed" (trans. Lamb, Loeb Library).

We shall discuss on pp. 496–498 the general question of Plato's conception of himself in relation to political knowledge. This particular passage, however, so far as it is supposed to constitute a special personal revelation, can be more easily disposed of. Much evidence converges on the probability that the historical Socrates and his associates pursued definitions and drew distinctions between real and apparent law, power, justice, and the like (cf. *Gorgias* 469 C ff., real power; *Apology* 40 A, the true judge; *Republic* Book I, 341 C ff., the true ruler). And Xenophon reports, not incredibly, that Socrates had made the very distinction found in the *Politicus* (*Mem.* III, ix, 10): "He affirmed that kings and rulers were not those who held scepters, nor those who were elected by any chance persons,

nor those who obtained power by lot or violence or deceit, but those who possessed the science of ruling." This type of reasoning was indeed implicit in the Socratic search for the man who knows, the expert. It is not Plato's invention, and cannot be employed to "illuminate" Plato's psychic state.

Popper's next discovery is Plato's statement in *Laws*, 704 D–E, that only "a mighty savior and divine lawgivers" (trans. Bury, Loeb Library) could preserve from luxury and depravity a city situated on fine harbors on the seacoast — as Athens was in fact situated. Popper begins by translating tendentiously, converting the "divine lawgivers" into *one* "superhuman legislator," and then reads the passage as "an indication that Plato had once dreamt of becoming the philosopher king and savior of Athens," and is now explaining away "his failure." Such a search for hidden motives prompting Plato's remark is superfluous; plain reasons lie at hand. Plato tells us in this very passage, and confirms it elsewhere, that in his opinion commerce above a certain necessary minimum is promotive of greed and luxury, and sea battles destructive of manly courage and discipline. If anyone's "failure" is being explained away, it would be more plausible to suggest that of Solon and the other framers of the earlier Athenian institutions, whose laws, good though they were, had not been able to preserve Athens against such odds.

preserve the kingdom for his sons.[134] The choice of persons cited was plainly determined by one single consideration: their value as classic instances of self-sacrifice. To see in the introduction of Codrus into this context the personal motive of reminding Plato's Athenian readers of his kingly prerogatives is to offer violence to a passage whose moral and spiritual atmosphere transcends the personal and the mundane, and, *a fortiori*, the calculations of political effect. And if it be suggested that the allusion to Codrus is not a deliberate but a subconscious revelation of Plato's fanatic dream of power, our answer must take the form of a warning to the critics against the irresponsible use of so dangerously two-edged a weapon, which is likely to cut more deeply into the hand of him who "taketh it up" than into the body of the intended victim. Plato's many hundreds of pages contain hundreds of names, from Cronos to the younger Socrates; among them the name of Codrus occurs but once, and in a context where it is objectively relevant. If one must apply the methods of psychoanalysis to the understanding of Plato's dreams, one should observe its prescription of drawing no conclusions not supported by frequently recurrent themes.

We approach now the veritable climax, in which the last full measure of Popper's devotion to his fanatical effort to prove Plato a fanatic is made manifest. Popper has abstained from a full-length and direct statement of the charge, which, indeed, is so shyly and obliquely put as to remind a reader of Popper's own description of a guilty Platonic hesitation. And yet there is no possible doubt of the meaning intended: Plato believed himself to be potentially the very hinge on which the portals of History would swing open to admit the millennium; he conceived himself as the destined lawgiver whose moral insight and mystic knowledge of the "number" would literally bring to a close the hemicycle of the world's downward motion and inaugurate a

---

[134] Popper's interpretation demands that the sons for whom Codrus died should be construed as including the entire line of his descendants, running down the centuries to Plato and his collaterals. This receives no support from the legend, as supplied by the scholiast *ad loc.*, according to whom Codrus had two sons, Medon and Neleus, the former of whom actually inherited his father's rule, while the younger became the founder of "twelve-citied Ionia" (and, we may add, was traditionally the ancestor of the Codrids in Ionia, mentioned in Bury, *History of Greece*, 1931, pp. 81–82, 168–169). The context, indeed requires that Codrus' act of sacrifice, like that of Alcestis, should have an immediate relationship to some person or persons in whose behalf it was tradition-

ally supposed to have been performed. There is a small anomaly, tangential to our issue, in the inclusion of Achilles, since it is hardly true to say that Achilles died for the sake of Patroclus: at most one could say that loyalty to Patroclus prompted him to return to that war in which he ultimately met his death; but the specific personal relationship is undoubtedly present in Achilles' case. Codrus' act, furthermore, was no private tradition hardly known outside of Plato's immediate family. It was generally accepted and acclaimed in Athens, as shown by the reference to it in Lycurgus, *Against Leocrates*, 84–87, and might have occurred naturally to anyone engaged in listing famous instances of self-sacrifice.

return of the golden age, in which change would be abolished and the primal perfection would be itself again.[135]

It will be sufficient refutation of Popper's view to show that in all three of the major political dialogues, Plato makes clear his belief that throughout the foreseeable future, change will remain a permanent element in human affairs. Thus in the *Republic* (424 A) he ventures the prediction that the establishment of the ideal community could become the starting point of a cycle of favorable changes, better nurture and education producing men who, in turn, are able to produce offspring better than themselves. The city must also at long last decay. In the *Politicus* (294 B), it is denied that even the best conceivable code of laws could forever retain their fitness to their sphere of application; "for the dissimilarities both of men and actions, and what may be termed the absolute unrest of human things, suffer no art whatever to lay down in any matter any simple rule which shall be applicable to all cases for all time." [136] And in a notable passage in the *Laws* (951 B) Plato has, as it were, refuted in advance all suggestions that he regarded himself as the one and only indispensable legislator, whose enactments must stand unaltered to all time. The well-ordered state, we are told, must not

---

[135] This charge, like the idea that Plato considered his descent from Codrus a valid claim to rule as king of Athens, appears for the first time in the revised edition of Popper's book; Popper's belief in Plato's sanity has diminished in the intervening years.

It is possible that Popper has wished to answer critics of his argument that Plato maintained the necessary superiority of all that is past, and with this in mind has sought by his additional hypothesis to reconcile Plato's supposed belief in the steady decay of all excellence in the present epoch, with the obvious fact of his effort to establish reformed states or even his hope of an ideal city, in the future. This hypothesis is developed by stages, of which the first consists in giving serious weight to Plato's mythical picture in the *Politicus* of alternating ages of decay and ages of gold, and supposing further that Plato believed the period of his own lifetime sufficiently depraved to make it ripe for the cosmic reversal (Popper, pp. 22–23). The next step is to assert, "Plato may well have believed that . . . the advent of the cosmic turning point would manifest itself in the coming of a great lawgiver whose powers of reasoning and whose moral will are capable of bringing this period of political decay to a close"; "it is likely" that Plato's belief in

this function of the lawgiver in restoring the age of gold, which could know no change, is expressed in the *Politicus* myth (pp. 23–24). Then, on a later page (p. 38), discussing Plato's supposed belief that in the current epoch increasing corruption infects all human souls with almost no exception, Popper adds, "Plato mentions the possibility that 'a soul gifted with an exceptionally large share of virtue can . . . become supremely virtuous and move to an exalted region.' The problem of the exceptional soul which can save itself — and perhaps others — from the general law of destiny, will be discussed in chapter 8." Now Popper's chapter 8 is entitled "The Philosopher King," and contains his revelation that Plato is himself this exalted being, and that he claims by knowledge of the mysterious number to have the power of counteracting the general law of destiny; this Popper asserts, it will be remembered, without reservation. The two premises now unite, and we see that Popper is asserting without any attached "perhaps" that Plato believed himself to be the destined man for whom the world was waiting.

[136] Campbell's translation, *ad loc.* This recognition of the necessity of revising legislation does not stand alone; cf. *Laws* 769 D–E, cited on our p. 507.

remain in ignorance of "the doings of the outside world." It needs such knowledge, not only as an example of avoidance and for confirming the sound elements in its own legislation, but in order "to amend any that are deficient." For "amongst the mass of men there always exist — albeit in small numbers — men that are divinely inspired; intercourse with such men is of the greatest value, and they spring up in badly-governed states just as much as in those that are well-governed." As Socrates in the *Phaedo* had denied his own irreplaceable uniqueness,[137] so here, whether or not Plato would in some sense include himself in the small number of the divinely inspired, he is so far from identifying himself with the embodiment of unalterable wisdom that he is willing to subject his own political constructions for ultimate confirmation and improvement to the insights of these gifted men. Such an expectation is in complete contradiction to the fantasy of a cosmic lawgiver under whose magical hand the world will be transformed into the perfection of immutability.

But it is time for us to leave this wonderland of impossible surmise and return to the realm of historical probability. Plato did, beyond question, regard himself as able to speak with authority on the great questions of moral and political reform. He may, for an occasional moment of exaltation, have trespassed briefly upon divine assurance, but he habitually pauses to confess that both he and those for whose benefit he is speaking fall short of the divine perfection. Thus in the *Laws* (853 C), contrasting himself and his fellow lawgivers, and their prospective citizens, with the "sons of gods" of the golden age, he says, "We are but men, legislating for the seed of men," and again, as the immediate prelude to his cosmological flight in the *Timaeus* (29 D): "I who speak and you who will judge my words are but of mortal nature."

The critics of Plato have not contented themselves, however, with discovering in his works specific justifications of his right to rule; these are seen as part and parcel of a general demand for recognition and authority, expressive of the deepest nature of the man. Behind and lending urgency to the claim based on the nuptial number and upon royal descent, Popper discerns a personal ambition, a sour, despotic authoritarianism.[138] It is presumed as underlying Plato's oligarchic inclinations, and as making use of that "fundamental benevolence" whose sincerity, in some sense, we have seen that Popper is willing to grant, as further ground for his right to impose his will. His dishonesty and self-divided deceitfulness were in the interests of this same ambition.

Popper invites us also to remember the kindly genial way that Socrates had with the young men who followed him, and his constant endeavor to lead

---

[137] *Phaedo* 78 A, quoted on p. 231 above.   [138] Popper, pp. 150–153 and notes.

them through unrestricted discussion of basic ethical concepts along the open
path of individual development; in contrast he underscores Plato's haughty
disdain, the sour distrust displayed in both the *Republic* and the *Laws*, by the
ban upon free discussion of philosophical topics with the young.[139] Tending
in the same direction are Plato's restrictions upon the freedom of artistic
expression in which Popper finds him guilty of legally imposing his own likes
and dislikes upon the community at large.[140] He is shown as denying what
Protagoras and Socrates (it is said) so clearly saw, that questions involving
moral values are not matters of absolute knowledge, but depend upon the
free exercise of personal decision; in consequence, Plato retained possession
of a dogmatism which served as a certificate for inflicting his own will upon
others.[141] And for general psychological underpropping of his charge that
Plato's soul panted after power, Popper has appealed to Kelsen's earlier-
mentioned monograph, "Platonic Love." [142]

We have already in another connection considered this psychoanalytic
study of Plato, the homosexual, whose attitude toward society was basically
determined by an ambivalence arising from his inner sense of guilt, a retreat
and rejection balanced by a desire to dominate and to serve. This conflict,
as Kelsen sees it, found its ultimate sublimation in Plato's pedagogic program
with its theoretic extension into government. The central relevance here for
the understanding of Plato's personality is the accent on domination. The
theory purports to explain, almost without residue, the reputedly objective,
theoretical, disinterested philosophy of Plato, in terms of an abnormal
psychic condition, one of whose major manifestations is the quest for personal power. In the process of illustrating and defending his theory, Kelsen
has made a number of acute observations mingled, as we shall hope to show,
with much cavalier imputation, a procedure that sets a difficult problem for
one who wishes to do simultaneous justice to him and to Plato. The chief
points in his analysis are these:

Plato's dominativeness, though springing from its own root in the deep
soil of Plato's being, was directed and mightily strengthened by an outside
force. It may come as something of a shock for a reader of Popper to learn
that this force was named Socrates, that modest and self-effacing inquirer,
pledged to the defense of the intellectual freedom of others. What Kelsen sees
in the bearer of this name is a man whose ruling passion was "the urge to
dominate," a "bourgeois" who had forced his way by sheer strength of will
and intellect into the highest stratum of Athenian society, where he spent

---

[139] *Ibid.*, pp. 44, 132, and notes.

[140] Popper, p. 54 and notes, esp. p. 502.

[141] Popper's thesis that a belief in the
objectivity of moral truth leads to intolerance is conveyed chiefly by his extravagant
praise of Socrates, who supposedly (see our
p. 300) had announced "critical dualism"

as his personal creed and had derived from
it his all-embracing tolerance of the views
of others. See, e.g., Popper, pp. 128–131,
62–67, and, for Plato's use of his dogmatic
"spiritual naturalism," p. 78.

[142] *Ibid.*, p. 570; for our previous discussion, see pp. 100ff. above.

much of his tireless energy in the mere process of humbling and lowering the aristocratic youth and those who were his competitors for their admiration, the sophists. This does not preclude a heroic element in his thought, the conviction that an absolute norm of justice exists, though beyond his power to demonstrate.[143]

At this point the task of summarizing Kelsen's rapid and elliptical argument becomes a serious responsibility. But what Kelsen seems to be saying is that in the very act of thus affirming the existence of an absolute standard of justice Socrates exhibits the urge to dominate. Particularly in the doctrine that "virtue is knowledge" both Socrates and, at least, the younger Plato display an altogether exceptional will to power. For no intelligent person could have believed, against all experience, that knowledge alone can determine action, that is, that knowledge possesses coercive power over the will of its possessor. What the formula expresses is the assumption that there is no knowledge worth the name save that which is serviceable to the end antecedently determined by the will. This will to virtue, then, tacitly replacing the intellectually unknowable absolute norm, claims as of right the conditions of its own fulfilment, inflicting upon others, under the name of "knowledge," whatever opinion is required to validate its own ungrounded claim to authority. In reality, Kelsen asserts, "a pure and true knowledge" cannot serve as "the basis for virtue. The will as will to power, however, needs a legitimatization, and finds it in the idea that to master men means the same as to better them, to change them from evil to good. . . . In consequence virtue must be transferable from master to mastered . . . must be knowledge, must be teachable." And so the Socratic right to teach is justified.[144]

This Socratic identification of virtue and knowledge was taken over by Plato, but not, Kelsen tells us, without significant modification and enlargement. Plato had emerged from the struggle with his own sense of unworthiness by the process, recorded in the *Symposium*, of learning to accept both himself and the actual world as a mixture of good and evil capable of movement toward the ideal. Thus set free and strengthened, he rose to the full measure of his capacities, vastly exceeding, in emotional energy and in will to power, the "stunted" Socrates, who remained "stuck in pedagogy." Plato, aspiring to the government of men, and unwilling to accept the positive law of the state as the ultimate political justice, adapted the Socratic formula "virtue is knowledge" to the purposes of a "preacher of justice," and a "prophet of the ideal state."

Some points in the argument thus far presented require our immediate attention. What must one say of Kelsen's assertion that the Socratic formula "virtue is knowledge" is conceivably nothing more than an attempt to lay

---

[143] Kelsen, pp. 77–80.   [144] Kelsen, pp. 81–83.

the foundations of a dictatorship over the beliefs and actions of others? It would seem that Kelsen is so deeply entrenched in what may be called his positivistic voluntarism, his belief (if we understand him correctly) that virtue can be based only upon private acts of will, that he is simply incapable of imagining how an intelligent ancient could have believed knowledge alone capable of determining the will, unless because his desire to dominate misled him.

This plainly passes by the commonsense possibility that Socrates, at the beginning of his career, should have felt a genuine need of finding an external rational ground for the guidance of his own conduct. In the historical circumstances this was precisely what was expectable of so intelligent a man. The sophists, by their claim to teach "virtue," had already implied that virtue is a kind of knowledge. What could be more natural than the determination to find another kind of knowledge capable of validating "virtue" in the deepest and highest sense, i.e., the improvement and perfection of the soul, which for Socrates was the highest good for man (*Apology* 29 D–E)? And the knowledge under pursuit, as the ally and servitor of the soul's interest, could be counted upon to move a will already committed to that sovereign good. Whether the hoped-for results of this quest should be put to any use beyond self-direction was an issue undetermined by anything in the quest itself and thus falls outside the import of the Socratic equation of virtue and knowledge. Even the teachability of the knowledge sought, assuming its discovery, had not been left for Socrates to assert. Our conclusion then must be that the Socratic search for a teachable knowledge which could underprop virtue, and the Platonic claim to have found it, arose as responses to the challenge of the intellectual environment, and were in their origin not dictated by the distinctive psychic structure of either man; the identification of knowledge and virtue thus loses all value for the very purpose for which Kelsen has invoked it.

If, as seems to be the case, Kelsen is also maintaining that anyone who believes in the existence of objectively knowable moral truth has revealed the authoritarian structure of his soul, then one may say that Kelsen has the evidence of the greater part of history against him. Certainly this is true of Greek ethics, with its notoriously teleological character. Let us note two conspicuous examples: Popper's much-magnified individualist Antisthenes could on this theory be proved an authoritarian; and a like fate would overtake even the gentlest association of Epicurean friends, who, reclining on the tender grass, are fondly imagining that they have learned from the master of the Garden the knowledge of nature and of man in the light of which they pursue the true virtue of tranquillity.

After expressing this major disagreement with Kelsen, we may begin to list our qualified agreements. That Socrates was no mere dutiful incarnation of the voice of God, but was sustained in the exercise of his extraordinary energy and ability by a lively enjoyment, is confirmed by all the evidence. Doubtless, too, he welcomed the tribute of admiration, especially from the golden youth of whom Kelsen speaks, and valued the warmth and jollity of an occasional symposium. For Plato one could tabulate a suitably adjusted schedule of greater and lesser satisfactions which combined with the hope of furthering his more ideal aims to motivate the activities of his life. But these concessions do not require us to join Kelsen in finding Socrates' primary motivation in the pursuit of victory over other persons, or Plato's in a fantasy of political power. Kelsen has in no way justified his selection of these as their respective dominant motives. If Kelsen's choice is based upon the inadequacy of his psychological principles to supply a basis for the understanding of personality other than self-interest or the operation of purely self-centered urges, we shall suggest at least a possible alternative below.

On one important point we can emphatically assent to Kelsen's view. This is his awareness that if Plato is to be convicted of dogmatically asserting the absolute validity of moral principles on the basis of which he was prepared to undertake the direction of other men's lives, guiding them educationally or governing them, then Socrates must share to some extent in the condemnation. For Kelsen has correctly seen that the thought of the one was but a development and extension of the other's. And the skepticism of Socrates, his refusal to admit that he possessed knowledge, must not be permitted to obscure either his constant presupposition that such knowledge can and must be found, or his fundamental affirmation of principles already known to him, which he believed central to the conduct of life, both for himself and for other men, could they but be persuaded to adopt them.

As corollary to this agreement with Kelsen, we may consent also to attribute to both Socrates and Plato the desire for dominance over men. But we must stipulate a use of the term "dominance" which Kelsen does not centrally intend, though on occasion his use approaches it. "To influence others helpfully and from a position of superior insight" is an approximation to what is meant. Any one who considers himself able to help others, possessed of a point of view which it would benefit them to adopt, claims at least a limited superiority; to make the effort to win them to its adoption is then to attempt domination. In this sense, Kelsen and Popper, despite their denial of objective validity to the moral values which they uphold, join with Socrates and Plato and the myriad other champions of significant human causes in a common motivation which we may hail as admirable while we deny that it is peculiar or abnormal. Plato, it is true, was willing at least in theory to go further, and to assume responsibility for planning a community which should exemplify the values which he honored. The degree of blame attaching to this willingness we shall later attempt to assess.

But to complete our report of Kelsen's argument: In further confirmation of his thesis that Plato was dominated by the desire for power, Kelsen draws for us the picture of Plato as a would-be tyrant, on the deepest level of his personality fearing his own ruthless impulses should he attain power: the Callicles of the *Gorgias* is Plato's symbol at once for Critias, whom he feared to become, and for his rejected inner self. Plato therefore in the *Gorgias* renounced politics and chose philosophy.[145] But in the *Republic*, conditionally reversing his choice, he made passionate appeal to his native Athens to let him serve her as her ruler. And here he reveals naively his utter certainty of his own rightness, presupposing as self-evident his philosophy as the foundation of the state, and imagining himself as the only possible ruler, from above, over even the philosopher kings themselves. He shows no awareness of the difficulties in the way of the realization of the ideal state, for is not the uniquely qualified man at hand? Nor, once established, will it go to ruin, for he obscurely reveals his knowledge of the nuptial number. He even divulges to his intended protégés his proposal to lie to them for their own good and thereby unconsciously renders his own project unworkable.[146]

In the *Politicus* and the *Laws*, Kelsen discovers, if anything, clearer and more emphatic evidence of Plato's hypertrophied will, declaring that Plato shows no recognition of the value for all men of freedom of personality, as such.[147] And finally, the Syracusan experience is displayed as Plato's vicarious adventure in political power, with Dion simultaneously in the characters of his *inamorato* and his other self. Thus we are shown, through Dion's deterioration from philosophic ruler to red-handed tyrant, the calamities that must befall when the fantasies of Platonic philosophy become vested with actual political power.[148]

We are now ready to consider Kelsen's evaluation of Plato's will to power as distinct from that of Socrates. We may be excused from further comment upon Kelsen's presentation of the *Symposium* as marking a crisis and a turning-point in the fever-chart of Plato's self-condemnation, since we have already given our reasons for doubting the correctness of Kelsen's diagnosis of extreme homosexuality.[149] But in any case it remains to determine how far Kelsen can be followed in his conviction that Plato's subsequent life and thought were basically directed by his "will to power."[150]

---

[145] Kelsen, pp. 89–94.

[146] Kelsen, pp. 94–103.

[147] *Ibid.*, pp. 103–105.

[148] *Ibid.*, pp. 105–110.

[149] See pp. 113ff. above.

[150] One point in Kelsen's interpretation of the *Symposium* bears directly on Plato's supposed love of power, and may be mentioned here. Kelsen maintains (pp. 76–77) that even in this dialogue, Plato makes "intensely personal avowal" of his passion for dominance by declaring, through the mouth of Socrates, that the noblest offspring of the spiritual Eros are the proper ordering of states and households, and such achievements as the laws of Solon and Lycurgus. Now, as the reader will see by reference to the dialogue (209) or to our p. 91 above, these spiritual products are said by Socrates to be attainable by souls which rise only to the level of the "lesser mysteries." Above them (210–212 A) Plato sets the ascent to the vision of ideal Beauty and the true virtue and bliss which are the offspring engendered thereby in the soul of the beholder. In the *Symposium*, therefore, Plato exalts philosophy above power even such as Solon's. By his failure to make this clear in

It is not wholly irrelevant to note a certain ambiguity — one might say 'ambivalence" — in Kelsen's evaluation of Plato's supposed love of power. On the one hand there are indications of approval; it is the ground, as we have seen, of a contrast, to Plato's advantage, between "the narrow confines of Paideia," to which Socrates was restricted by his personal deficiencies, and "the wider realms of Politeia" in which alone Plato, whose "dimensions were greater in every respect," could "gain his satisfaction." [151] Yet Kelsen also presents it as a distortion of personality resulting from a psychic malady, scarcely a trait worthy of commendation either in a philosopher or in a man. Combining these two views, we reach an apparent contradiction. Knowing Plato's defect, should not Kelsen in all reason have deplored any attempt on his part to pass from Paideia to Politeia? To escape contradiction, there is, as we see it, only one answer that Kelsen can give. He can say to Plato: "I approve only your aspiration to govern men; I deplore the assumption upon which you approach power, namely, that it is possible to know the good and to impart it from master to subject. Go ahead and rule, only don't attempt to justify it in terms of ultimate human good."

To this we may reply on Plato's behalf that to Plato a mandate to govern without commitment to a schedule of values would have appeared the equivalent of tyranny or unprincipled demagogy, and that he could only have regarded Kelsen's suggestion with pious horror. There is tragic irony in this situation, with its implication of radical disparity between two outlooks upon the responsibilities of power. We cannot attempt anything like an adequate account of the difficult problems to which it gives rise, though a little later we shall have something to say on the subject. But this collision of convictions makes clear how little justice one does to a political attitude like Plato's, with its deepest roots in an ethical and metaphysical theory, when one attempts to measure it by a standard such as Kelsen's, which is unable to do anything with Plato's first principles save to reduce them to symptoms of a psychic malady.

No one need dispute Kelsen's right to revive, with modern psychological improvements, the old idea that the character of Callicles in the *Gorgias* is in reality a portrait of Plato's one-time paradigm, his uncle Critias, and hence (herein lies Kelsen's innovation) a portrait of Plato's rejected self. Such intuitions, though from the nature of the case indemonstrable, are enlivening and may be said to possess at least a species of analogical truth. The danger is that the vividness of the analogy may so captivate the imagination as to efface the memory that the "self" in question was fought against and rejected, leaving only the impression that an intimate relation, perhaps even an identity, has been established between the real Plato and his supposed antithe-

___

his discussion of Plato's yearning for power, Kelsen has represented as highest in Plato's regard that which Plato, on the contrary, has expressly relegated to a lower plane of value.

[151] Kelsen, pp. 83–86.

sis. This is what we found Kelsen doing with the picture of the tyrant in *Republic* IX, and most of what we wrote in that context is applicable here. It is not sound to identify Plato with those of his characters whom he abhors, while neglecting his affinity for those, like the "apolitical" Socrates and the philosopher kings who unwillingly descend, whom he approves.

The postulate that the real meaning of a psychologically emphatic rejection is simply the rejector's own basic attraction to the thing he denounces, leads to a choice of evils. For if it proves that all generous opposition, as, for example, to Hitler in our own day, rises out of an inner tendency to emulate a Hitler, still it does not help us to understand why, in a given person, this inner tendency is rejected and transformed into a force for good. Or if, by interpreting all a man's strenuous rejections of evil into evidence of his kinship for this evil, it turns into hypocrisy or self-deception all his corresponding enthusiasms for good, it leaves us no excellence to be admired in any ardent soul and condemns us either to cynicism or to the admiration only of indifference and stolidity. It appears wiser to rise from these underground chambers and to argue that Plato in the *Gorgias* has shown not his suppressed longing for power, but his rejection of power misused, and that in the *Republic* he has accepted not power, but power employed for approvable ends. Again, as in the case of Eros, Kelsen has failed to observe that Plato has demonstrated two species where Kelsen has seen only an ambivalence.

That a man of Kelsen's acknowledged acumen should have failed to respect the principle of perspective in literary art, may seem surprising, yet in his reading of the *Republic* he has been led — apparently by his zeal to penetrate Plato's hidden meaning — into just such an error, in more than one respect. In an obvious sense, Plato is of course present on his own stage, sharing his every belief with the Socrates who is his mouthpiece. Granted too, that Plato has endowed his philosopher kings with all the wisdom he himself possesses; granted even that in some sense they are, as Kelsen insists, a collective portrait of the artist (and we must add, of Socrates as Plato conceived him). Even so, Plato must not be conceived as one or more of the characters in his own play, knowing and doing all that he ascribes to them. Just as we have seen Popper assume that the Muses, when they describe the nuptial number, reveal Plato's own knowledge of its identity and use, so Kelsen makes the same unnecessary assumption that Plato is himself the Muses. Kelsen goes on to imagine that Plato has put himself on the examining board of those who select the future rulers and on the committee for controlling marriages; Plato has given himself, too, the task of telling the assembled citizens the myth of the metals. Is it so difficult to see that if the *Republic* was to be written at all (and Plato was not the first to compose such a work,[152] he would have to describe the institutions of the ideal state? And

---

[152] Hippodamas and Phaleas, Plato's predecessors in describing ideal constitutions, are discussed by Aristotle, *Politics* II 7, 1266 ff.

if it was to be vivid and delightful reading, the choice of an imaginary founding of the city "in words," by Socrates and his young companions, was a
happy device, in line, moreover, with the common Greek practice in the establishment of a colony.

Given this approach, the fact that the city was to be absolutely ruled does
not in the least affect the degree of authority assumed to be possessed by
the framer of its constitution; for if Plato had set out to found a democracy,
complete with a bill of rights, he could equally well in his book have imagined
Socrates figuring as lawgiver, and could through him have enacted that its
constitution should be held inviolate, particularly in this matter of civil liberties, thus arrogating to himself — or so it could be said — supreme authority over the otherwise all-powerful citizens; and in describing the conduct
of this democratic government, Plato could be charged with imagining himself
electing officials, handing down judgments, and making administrative decisions. By placing the government of his imaginary city in the hands of a
small self-perpetuating minority, Plato does show his belief that such power
would be beneficial, and to this extent proves himself able to sympathize with
and to identify himself with absolute rulers. But why must we disregard, or
with Popper, treat with scornful irony, his assertion that they will rule reluctantly, in order to escape the evils of being ill-governed and because of
the obligation imposed upon them by their rearing? For it is mere cynicism
to deny that this is an integral part of the role with which Plato sympathizes.
It is true, as Kelsen says, that Plato believed an ideal state could be established only upon the assumptions basic to his own philosophy, and this we
shall discuss below. But here we must ask the reader to note one further
blindness in Kelsen's interpretation. If Plato's failure to provide any realistic
means of transition from actuality to his ideal state can be construed as his
simple offer of himself to be its architect, and if, moreover, his open avowal
of his proposal to use deceit for the good of its citizens can be interpreted
as his naive and self-frustrating revelation of his dream of power, both can
also be read as indications that Kelsen is mistaken in believing that Plato
had any expectation of installing the Republic at Athens, with himself as its
deceitful ruler.

Kelsen's strictures upon Plato's political thinking and doing after the
period of the *Republic* need little comment here. Of Plato's relation to Dion
we have had our say; how far the *Politicus* and *Laws* justify Kelsen's talk of
"will-less puppets" pulled about by a "godlike philosopher" is considered elsewhere in this book with reference to the method and aim of these two works
and, in the case of the *Laws*, to the social arrangements proposed; [153] to the

---

[153] In introducing the *Politicus* as expressing Plato's reluctance to restrict "the
truly wise, royal sovereign . . . by any kind
of constitutional laws" (Kelsen, pp. 103–
104), Kelsen has combined accuracy with
misdirection. For while it is perfectly true

imputed motivation we shall shortly devote further attention. We may remark again that the semblance of will-lessness is imparted to the citizens described in these two dialogues largely by the exigencies of their literary birth; as we observed in the case of the *Republic*, since Plato is writing a description of an ideal community in its cultural entirety, his general procedure must be to represent its members as abstract vehicles of his cultural ideal. He does, significantly, explicitly recognize in the *Laws* (746 A) that no concrete persons could become such "citizens of wax" as he describes. We may enter one further objection: that Plato's oppressiveness was "unexampled," either in the cruelty of the prescribed penalties for crime or, with reservations, in his religious enactments, may be doubted in the light of our discussion, on earlier pages, of Athenian practices,[154] to which Kelsen seems to pay too little heed.

In the course of the preceding discussion we touched now and again upon the edges of certain large assumptions that were serving our critics, apparently, as general grounds upon which their specific criticisms reposed. Let us deal more centrally with these, as perhaps the best immediate preface to our reading of Plato's personality relevant to his claim to authority. The first

that Plato urges such immunity for his ideal Statesman, it will be remembered from our discussion, p. 349, that this Statesman is rather a norm than a man, and that in his absence reliance must be placed upon the "second-best," which we found Plato so earnestly recommending to the Sicilians, government according to law. In other words, so far from constituting an endorsement of rule by the "free judgment" of an individual ruler, the *Politicus* is preponderantly a plea for a "government not of men but of laws," a government into which Plato would recommend the introduction of as much genuine knowledge of political relations as the community is able to procure. Kelsen, p. 103, has also fallen into the error which we have pointed out and attempted to set right in Popper's case, in n. 133, page 462 above: when Plato declares the possessors of the science of kingship, and them alone, to be true kings, whether they rule or no, Kelsen supposes that Plato is simply asserting his own claim to rule, despite his unfortunate lack of present power. A conception arising out of another man's thought (that of Socrates), inspired, moreover, by the highly impersonal ideal of framing logically adequate definitions, can hardly be simplified into a mere expression of inner urges.

In earlier discussions of the *Laws* (pp. 353, 464–465) we noted that the legislative expert of that work, the Athenian Stranger, with whom Plato clearly wishes to be identified, is not presented as omniscient or all powerful. We have acknowledged our dissatisfaction in the face of the overly regulative constitution he proposes (see also below, pp. 549f.). But we must also in fairness call attention to the provisions Plato has made for securing to his citizens personal participation in the community and individual rights, mentioned elsewhere in this book, as follows: to vote and hold office (pp. 330–331, 514–515); to sit as judge (p. 525); to appeal unwelcome decisions (e.g., p. 534); to have the rationale of the basic laws clearly and publicly explained (pp. 525–526); to hale offending officials into court (p. 561).

[154] See pp. 351f., 355f. The stringent criticisms directed by Bowra (see our note, p. 307 above) against the "ruthless punishment" and general repressiveness found in the *Laws* are in partial accord with Kelsen. We ask the reader to consider the rights and wrongs of Bowra's case, also, in the light of these same pages in our text, and of pp. 550f. and 560f. below.

of these assumptions figured in the discussion of Plato's conception of virtue and knowledge. It is the repudiation as logically untenable and even pernicious of what we shall call for convenience, "moral dogmatism," or the belief that moral truth can be and has been in all essentials discovered, and that it is actually known to the person who proclaims it, for instance, to Plato. Must we assent to this condemnation? [155]

For my part this is one of those questions best dealt with by contemplating the results that would necessarily follow from assuming an affirmative answer. If moral dogmatism has always been the pernicious thing that our critics seem to see in it, which of the great ethical and religious systems would escape whipping? The skeptics, relativists, and nihilists, and in addition the critical dualists of our own times, would alone remain as approvable movers of human history, against the dead weight and outright opposition of the proponents of other modes of thought. But this is to forget that man has struggled up the long trail of his cultural development almost always with

---

[155] Popper's own position of "critical dualism," or the "dualism of facts and decisions," described on his pp. 60–67, has already been mentioned, pp. 293 and 300. It involves the assertion that the moral life must rest upon free decisions, based upon a knowledge of facts but not derivable from them. Moral standards are creations imposed upon nature, not derived from supposed facts such as "man's spiritual nature" or the "will of God." At the same time, Popper feels himself entitled to insist that the substance of these decisions is by no means arbitrary; they are highly important choices, for the proper making of which "we are responsible"; further, they may be made with the aid of "faith," and "because of your conviction that it is the right decision for you to take" (p. 66). Since he has, thus, a foot in either camp, Popper has the not inconsiderable advantage of denouncing as a "spiritual naturalist" any particular disapproved thinker who believes it possible to know that certain ethical decisions are, or are not, in accord with man's spiritual nature, while himself claiming at will the support of any religious believer who can be interpreted as grounding his firm belief upon an act of choice.

But this tactical advantage is won at a cost; critical dualism, consistently maintained, must abandon any claim to apply to basic moral decisions such predicates as "right" and "wrong," and can attach no ethical meaning to talk of our "responsibility." It reveals itself as impotent to condemn the momentous "decisions" embodied in the collective actions of any group, e.g., the Germans under Hitler, except by appeal to other "decisions" for which no greater objective validity can consistently be claimed. In spite of Popper's dissociation of himself from the positivist position, it appears that an essential kinship remains. (For a recent instance of the positivist inability to condemn Hitlerism on grounds other than those of expediency, see Richard von Mises' *Positivism*, 1951, pp. 338–339 and 365–366.) The critical dualist asks us to abandon moral dogmatism in favor of a standpoint which, in spite of his good intentions, lends itself with equal facility to a high ethic of universal humanity, or to moral nihilism — if one so decides! Meanwhile, an intermediate position (that to which the present writer adheres) can easily drop from sight, a view well expressed and defended by Morris Cohen (*Reason and Nature*, 1931, pp. 446–449), according to which we may assume an absolute norm and engage in active quest of it, while nevertheless entering no dogmatic claim that at any stage of the inquiry we are in complete and final possession of it.

Whoever wishes further exhibition of the contradictions latent in Popper's ethical program should read pp. 469–471 in H. D. Aiken's admirable review of the *Open Society and Its Enemies*, 1947, to which our discussion would have been substantially indebted had it come earlier to our notice.

the assistance of guides for whom the goal toward which they pointed was good beyond the reach of doubt. As we have seen above, moral dogmatism was the anchor of the gentle but unyielding faith of Epicurus, in this respect at one with his Stoic rivals. In neither case can any evils be shown to have resulted from the certitude, apart from blindness to the excellences of other views, and in both cases it supplied a serviceable energy of conviction. If it is true that moral dogmatists lighted the fires of the Inquisition and sought to glorify God by repressing man in Calvin's Geneva, it is no less true that moral dogmatists, some centuries later, were among the prime movers of the abolition of slavery. It is even true, despite the paradox, that the establishment of religious freedom itself was attained largely through the confident assertion that it was God's will to be worshipped without constraint. And though one may deplore the errors, one must not ignore the immense contribution to the life of the spirit that has entered history through this often tragic door. What history might conceivably have been without intense convictions about ultimate right and wrong is matter of conjecture, but these have been too deeply involved in the spiritual achievement of the race to justify any member of our species in treating them as aberrations which we might have dispensed with altogether, to our profit.

Let us not lightly pass over the impoverishment to our heritage that a ban on moral dogmatism would entail. Consider the historic function of those preachers whose moral eloquence and sublimity have won for them the name of Prophet in the most exalted sense. They speak out of a burning conviction, for which dogmatism is almost too light a name, that through the channel of their being an absolute truth has been dispatched to mankind. Their message we tend today to translate out of a literal language that speaks of a just and merciful Jehovah into the more sophisticated language of projected moral ideals of justice and mercy, and in these terms even a convinced atheist can continue to honor them. But this is true only with a qualification which, we suggest, has equal relevance to Plato. We must assume that their dogmatic conviction was a measure of the energy of their devotion to an ideal truth, and not, primarily, an assertion of "how right I am." They must be understood (to paraphrase an admirable dictum) as wishing to be on God's side rather than merely claiming to have God on theirs. And to this end we see them flinging their whole heart and soul and mind into the momentous struggle. Just so, if in a less tempestuous and more philosophic key, and hence with more tolerance for opinions other than his own, did Plato testify to his faith in the spiritual ideal.[156]

---

[156] A fair measure of Plato's way of dealing with doctrines which are in basic conflict with his own is discoverable in his treatment of the sophists. We have earlier commented upon his outlook upon some of the best-known bearers of this name, e.g. Protagoras, pp. 291–295, Hippias, pp. 58 and 60, Gorgias, p. 432. Here we wish to make as clear as the still controversial character of the question will allow how far

Unwilling to condone Plato's claim to know, Popper has yet arranged a means of saving from the ranks of dogmatists and enlisting under his own banner two of the greatest moral teachers in the persons of Jesus and Socrates. But this cannot be justified. Socrates, as we have seen, was not a "critical dualist"; [157] he did not declare that no faith can claim universal validity, but rather testified that the universal human values into which he had insight and for which he stood must take precedence over the values to which the Athenians had enacted that he should bow. His confession that he was unable to frame definitions of the virtues and specify their mutual relations must

---

what we have been terming Plato's moral dogmatism permitted him to estimate at its true worth their contribution to the life of Greece.

Since Grote's famous vindication of the sophists from the exaggerated collective condemnation of them that had so long remained the orthodox view, and for which Plato's depiction of them was taken to constitute sufficient evidence, the sophists have had an almost uniformly "good press." Their kinship at so many points to the interests and sympathies, and even prejudices, of nineteenth- and twentieth-century liberals, has won them many able and enthusiastic vindicators, and out of an abundant literature has come genuine proof of their intelligence, their good will, and their fertile *aperçus* and discoveries in many fields from grammar to sociology. But in consequence of this revision there has been a tendency to "white out" some of the blacker spots that really belong in the historical picture, with the further result of seemingly throwing out of focus the view taken of them by some of their less appreciative contemporaries. It is thus that it has become difficult again, and for the opposite reason, to understand in its true light what now appears as Plato's perverse failure to assign them a higher rating.

What then can be fairly said of Plato's justice in this matter? It cannot be denied that he has given them less than their due in some respects. Take Hippias: From the two dialogues that bear his name, one carries away the impression — which may, indeed, have had some basis in the character of the man — of a pretentious pedant, boasting of his universal proficiency in every art, craft, and science. But who would suspect that this man, as the most authoritative contemporary opinion now holds (cf. Burnet, *Greek Philosophy*, I, p. 118), was also

a genuinely creative mathematician? It would be difficult, too, from the formal analysis of the dialogue called the *Sophist*, to infer that any honest and intelligent thinker could be discovered in the group.

On the other hand, this same Plato, we remember (cf. pp. 217, 294), has credited to Protagoras in the dialogue of that name a myth of exquisite literary art, loaded with ideas many of which are impossible to discriminate from those that he has elsewhere advanced in all earnestness under his own name. And in the *Theaetetus* 152 ff., esp. 166 ff., we have seen him generously offering of his subtlest epistemological insights for the elaboration and defense against banal objections of the Protagorean relativity, as a prerequisite to its fair evaluation. Notice, also, that Plato can show a respectful courtesy to Gorgias, in the dialogue of that name, 448–460, and recognize the honorable intention behind ideas and practices to which he himself is thoroughly opposed, postponing their refutation until their consequences are presented patently and blatantly by a disciple, Polus, for whom Plato holds no restraining respect.

Furthermore, if we remind ourselves of some of the actually nihilistic doctrines proclaimed by an Antiphon, or by a Polus and a Thrasymachus, we should have no difficulty in seeing how, to an ethical idealist such as Plato, it must have appeared mandatory to "crush the infamy" of "sophistry." It becomes at least fully understandable also why Plato, who had inherited from Socrates the task of vindicating objective truth and goodness against subjective relativism and cynical nihilism, should, in the heat of conflict, have been deficient in his appreciation of the genuine merits of those whom he regarded collectively as the enemy.

[157] See pp. 302–304 above, 635–637 below.

not obscure the certainty with which he affirmed his knowledge of the basic values and goals of human life.

That the founder of Christianity could be made to appear as a forerunner of "critical dualism," one might have thought impossible, but Popper has given the impossibility a brief semblance of actuality by the apt choice of a quotation. He cites the familiar contrast between "Ye have heard that it was said by them of old time . . ." and "But I say unto you . . .," as indicative of the essential contrast between "mere formal obedience" and "the voice of conscience." That this contrast has a central place in the religious ethic of Jesus we take to be common ground to all interpreters. What is unwarranted, however, is the implication that in thus denying the authority of tradition, Jesus was disavowing a knowledge of the ground of human good in the will and law of God. There was, for Jesus, no suggestion of a dualism between "fact" and "norm" or "decision." Nor is there any basis for the supposition that he regarded moral norms as in any sense created by human conscience. There is for him one Father whose will should be done on earth as it is in Heaven. And conscience, if we may employ a term absent from his vocabulary, was the opening of the inward eye to the seeing of God's truth. If the sentiment quoted by Popper establishes the compatibility of the fundamental position of critical dualism with Christianity, then it will do the same for Plato, who himself denounced the traditionally received beliefs on many a vital question and sought to win his hearers' honest assent to his own newer insights. But these two equal errors will not correct each other. They merely prevent us from seeing what is basic, namely, that these two men were, each in his own way, affirming a prophetic message that fused value and truth.

Speaking thus in behalf of those who have claimed a universal knowledge of good and evil, we do not mean to legislate for all future ages, or even to deny that certain enlightened thinkers of our time have shown that for themselves, at least, and possibly for a certain number of our contemporaries, no loss in moral earnestness is entailed by their announced abandonment of all "belief" or "knowledge"; though it is the opinion of the present writer that so long as they continue, like Popper, to champion as right certain "decisions" and to denounce others with equal ardor, they have in effect changed rather the verbal form than the substance of certainty, and are equally involved with the dogmatists in passing judgment upon the acts and opinions of others. Such persons are surely within their rights, and are even, one may believe, performing a service by thus attempting to find a philosophic base for proclaiming new charters of freedom for mankind. But they are serving no good end by writing their program into history and asking us to condemn all our other spiritual guides for the fault of claiming knowledge.

But it is quite possible that Popper and Kelsen will object that they have not condemned all certainty in all ages, and will assent to the proposition that some forms of moral dogmatism have, in times comfortably remote, made contribution to human progress. They would, however, one is very sure, stoutly deny that in any age a moral dogmatism can retain anything of human worth when combined, as they see Plato combining it, with the attempt to "compel them to come in." And in this denial they would as certainly be sustained by the convictions of a large part of the liberal world. Must we then agree that Plato shall suffer condemnation as the enemy of freedom of conscience? Yes, with a large proviso. Plato was wrong, and has exemplified here that intolerance of which we spoke above, which Whitehead has called "the besetting sin of moral fervour." [157] In extenuation, it can be said that Plato had not lived through the centuries intervening between him and ourselves, and was insufficiently aware of the futility of attempts to enforce opinion and of the horrors to which they lead; that he required under penalty of the law the acceptance of only a minimum religious creed, hardly more than that expected by John Locke in his establishment of the minimum limitations upon religious toleration; [158] that he was indeed too hopeful of the powers of example, precept, and rational argument, but that he envisaged no use of cruelties, such as were used against heretics in mediaeval times. As we have earlier argued, nothing in his Socratic heritage had put his feet firmly on the road leading to a tolerance permissive of all beliefs. And finally, in rejecting the usual Athenian inattention [159] to what a man believed, so long as his actions conformed to the civic requirements, Plato may well have felt that he was correcting a blindness in the Athenian outlook which had failed to observe with sufficient clarity that acts arise from beliefs and that good citizenship cannot be manufactured out of nihilism and indifference, nor mutual loyalty out of creeds which lead to radically different ideals of conduct. This problem shifts its locus, but in our day as in Plato's finds no simple solution; witness Popper's own sanctioning (and ours) of the use of force against active advocates of the totalitarian overthrow of freedom. We can and should see Plato's error, therefore, and condemn his proposal, but we need not see it as evidence of depravity or special tyrannousness, or because of it fail to see the moral fervor from which it grew.

A third position open to Plato's attackers is that taken by Kelsen, namely: that the particular form of moral dogmatism which affirms the immediate identity of knowledge and virtue is inevitably more oppressive than those forms which admit the interposition of the will between belief and act, since

---

[157] *Adventures of Ideas*, p. 63.

[158] This statement is not designed to obscure the overwhelmingly liberal character of Locke's ideal of religious toleration, the freedom he would grant (and Plato would not) to the various modes of worship, and his deprecation of ecclesiastical sanctions beyond the gentle exercise of excommunication. Yet he states in terms that atheists are "not at all to be tolerated," averring that "the taking away of God, though but even in thought, dissolves all" (*A Letter concerning Toleration* (1689), Oxford, 1946, p. 156).

[159] It will be remembered that we have discussed the Athenian attitude toward religious dissenters on pp. 316f. and 355–358.

especially if it is made the foundation of government, it must attempt to control men's minds. This contention is not merely a challenge to Socrates and Plato; it is equivalent to the assertion that no member of the Socratic family could have supplied an adequate basis for a constitution for the reason that the entire line of ethicists, Antisthenes and Aristippus, no less than Zeno and Epicurus, busied themselves with ingenious transformations of the equation "V–K." Nor is it true that governments based on other ethical theories would be automatically precluded from inquiry into the inner recesses of men's minds; for the identification of virtue with faith or right opinion, or with the good will, could equally well appear to justify an attempt to control the source of action rather than merely to regulate action itself. No, the sources of Plato's error must be sought elsewhere, as we have suggested above. And before leaving this topic, we may call attention to the tolerant and universalistic implications which underlie this definition of virtue in terms of knowledge, springing as it does from the Socratic faith in the native affinity of men to reason and the good. Such virtue is not dependent on the privilege of birth or special divine favor, owes no allegiance to unexamined custom, and is communicable from man to man by the gentle suasions of discourse. If any moral dogmatism is to supply a basis for government, this would appear to be among the best.

And finally, there is the position which Popper has implicitly taken, in which the moral dogmatism of an ancient thinker, though *per se* undesirable, is regarded as venial or damnable, according to the company it keeps. Thus Popper could justify his acceptance of the moral dogmatism of Antisthenes or Alcidamas, while rejecting Plato's, which he sees as a defense of totalitarian oppression. To this we must reply: it is granted that moral dogmatism multiplies by its own intensity the evils in any evil program to which it is applied. But unless all our doctrine is vain, the Platonic program as a whole can scarcely be so described. When Plato is being most dogmatic, he is commonly declaring a rational faith which makes human excellence independent of race or time or social class, which sets the same divine law over all mankind and seeks only to discover that good end which the universe subserves and man can join in serving. If Plato also taught some doctrines we cannot accept, shall his moral certainty still be utterly condemned?

One other large and dubious assumption seems to underlie the criticism offered by Kelsen and Popper of Plato's claim to authoritative knowledge, namely: the tacit postulate that one is entitled to pass directly from the detection of abnormalities and distortions in the personality of a thinker to the condemnation of his thought.[158] In its most general form this raises the truly

---

[158] Kelsen has put on record (p. 6) his repudiation of this procedure, which, however, he ignores in his own subsequent argument, as we have noted in his deflation of the Socratic-Platonic equation of virtue and knowledge into a mere "pretext" (page

abysmal question of the value relation between the psychic structure of a philosopher and the quality of his ideas and beliefs. Are the two things independent of each other in such fashion as to permit the coexistence in a given thinker of "bad," that is, abnormal or pathological motivation, and "good," that is, philosophically valuable doctrines? Or, excluding as obviously untenable both this and its extreme opposite, must we hold that some degree of distortion of a man's personality will appear inevitably as an equivalent disfigurement in the substance of the thought?

The situation recalls our mention at the beginning of our discussion in Chapter 4 of Plato's alleged defects of mind and character, of the world's demand that moral teachers shall themselves be morally admirable. We are now encountering a far more extreme demand laid upon the philosopher, who is expected to be a veritable Caesar's wife, above not only "crime" but "suspicion." An instructive parallel may be found in the various attempts to interpret the Christian gospel as the product of a disordered — hysterical — perhaps homosexual — what-you-will mentality, attempts to which one of the Platonic detractors has lent some support.[159] These researches have uniformly failed to cast doubt upon the value of the Christian message, and the chief cause of the failure is applicable, in essence, if less flamboyantly, to Plato: It is very difficult to believe that a distorted personality is capable of preaching a Sermon on the Mount or composing the ten books of the *Republic*, if these are rightly interpreted; and if by any chance one has finally succeeded in believing this, he confronts the new and equal difficulty of believing that what has achieved so remarkable a result is rightly to be classified as a disordered personality, or must accept the paradox that disordered personalities are among the highest human goods. Thus, whether or not Plato had delusions of personal grandeur, or suffered from a pathological desire to dominate, his message must be construed in the terms in which he has himself stated it: we must hold him responsible for those and only those ideas to which he stood philosophically committed. In so far as this message is then found to be promotive or destructive of what we believe to be humanly or divinely good, we may say that the personality which sustained it and made it possible was to this degree and for these purposes good or bad. Whoever refuses to accord primacy to the doctrines as against the personality of a given thinker may find himself in the embarrassing situation of the critics in *Fanny's First Play*, unable to pass judgment on the quality of the piece until they know who has written it.

But we cannot leave this complex relationship between mental peculiarities and philosophical achievement without some indication of their positive

---

85) for that excessive urge to dominate which he sees arising out of the peculiarities of each man's Eros.

[159] Kelsen, as we have remarked on p. 102 above, appears to see in Jesus psychic abnormalities similar to those which he detects in Plato.

correlation. In spite of our denial of any simple relationship between the most distorted, even the "sick" personality, and the value of ideas, we would not deny that the thinker's personality is one factor in determining the content of his thought, and that distortion in the one will tend to introduce alterations in the other. This influence, however, will inevitably be intricately combined with the familiar effects of cultural environment, historical events within his experience, all the accidents of his biography, and the juncture in the history of thought at which he reaches reflective maturity. Various personality traits may hinder or further the logical working out of his premises, as we have seen in Plato's case, for example, in the barrier posed by his intellectuality and personal aloofness to his understanding of the common man, and on the other hand, in the urgency of his desire to bring the full benefit of Socratic insight to the service of his fellows.

Some help toward measuring Plato by an appropriate psychological standard may be found in Herzberg's thoughtful study,[160] in which the psychic structures of thirty "kings of philosophic thought" throughout the centuries were investigated and compared, to the end of determining what mental characteristics form the common basic equipment for major contributors to the history of thought. One need not accept the radical "psychologism" of this author, according to whom the approvable function of philosophy is its contribution to mental health, providing, as it does, an outlet for inhibited impulses, an escape from "harsh and intractable reality" into a "painless" and "satisfying world," and a creative satisfaction in achieving and expressing so imposing a system of ideas. Nor need we accept entire his treatment of Plato, whom he sees as a homosexual and depicts in the light of the exceedingly doubtful Second Letter, which he believes to be genuine, as a highly inhibited, even an absurdly timid person; [161] fortunately, for most of the others among his philosophers, more dependable data were available. Herzberg's general conclusions, grounded upon the broad base of a dispassionate survey, remind us powerfully of the fact that within our Western culture, at least, the most fruitful philosophic results more often than not appear as the outcome of tormented mental processes. In most of these philosophers Herzberg believes it possible to demonstrate the presence of powerful impulses held in check by equally powerful inhibitions which, by the mechanism of "sublimation," he supposes to have supplied the indispensable energy; and in all cases, he believes, some degree of rebellion against authority, as embodied in traditional belief, has driven its possessors to enunciate their novel doctrines. Through it all, he has directed our attention to the intricate transmutation of initially "bad" into terminally good qualities. On this view, then,

---

[160] *The Psychology of Philosophers*, by Alexander Herzberg, 1929.

[161] *Ibid.*, pp. 68, 140. Herzberg would seem to have reached his view of Plato as a homosexual by interpreting in this sense the findings of Wilamowitz; cf. our n. 103, p. 114.

if we find in Plato something other than the serenity of the phantom hero of a textbook on mental hygiene, we need not be shocked into wild surmises as to his hidden and unwholesome purposes. We are left, if we so desire and if sufficient data can be had, to search a little more deeply into the sources of his tensions, and to remember that the great thinker is commonly one who has paid a great price for the message which he holds out to us. These considerations may then keep us from doing Plato perhaps the greatest injury that can be offered any thinker: to ignore what he has sought to say to us, in our zeal to prove that its meaning must be sought on the level not of validity but of pathology.

In an early chapter we offered a brief *vita Platonis* restricted to the external facts of his career. We need now to supplement that account by describing a conceivable structure of personality traits and purposes underlying his attitude to power and authoritative knowledge, using as a criterion in selecting our material our best notion of what a contemporary psychologist of personality would wish to know and would be willing to credit. In view of our rebukes to the detractors for their audacity in drawing maximal conclusions from minimal data, be it hereby known that no apodictic certainty for any of the conclusions reached in the following section is claimed, and that the purpose of this section is to show that the hypotheses of the detractors are by no means the only construction that can be put upon the "facts of the case." In other words, the implicit challenge to accept these damaging interpretations or provide a better is hereinafter accepted. And since the challenge cannot be met without attempting to construe the meager facts concerning Plato's life into a rounded conception of his personality, we are constrained to enter upon that dark and slippery ground. We shall be as economical as possible in drawing support from conjecture, but we shall not hesitate in the circumstances to make use of probabilities, properly labeled.

But before beginning our psychograph, we must pause to describe a certain complex of character traits to which under the title of the "authoritarian personality" the *Zeitgeist* of our era has devoted anxious attention. The relevance of this semiclinical personality pattern to the understanding of Plato is a problem upon which our psychological portrait may hope to shed a little light. That Plato exemplifies this pattern none of our detractors has formally charged, but both Kelsen and Popper have employed concepts trenching closely upon it, and it is quite possible that at this very moment some indignant person is composing an article on authoritarianism in which Plato is shown as its original avatar. We wish, therefore, to include this complaint against Plato, entered collectively in the name of the twentieth century, and herewith submit two descriptions of the "disease," abbreviated from the contemporary literature.

Fromm has described the "authoritarian," or what he more horrendously calls the "sado-masochistic" personality, as characterized by the desire to dominate others so completely as to deprive them of all independence and simultaneously to submit to a power overwhelmingly stronger than oneself.[162] He implies that in those individuals who emerge as leaders, and who display this disposition in its extremer forms, it arises typically from suppressed resentment and fear of a too strict and threatening parent or parent-substitute.[163] The authoritarian believes that man's destiny is determined by inexorable forces beyond his control; it is even said that all worship of any power outside the individual self is akin to authoritarianism, though worship of a forgiving God and belief in man's fundamental goodness and freedom of will mitigate this type of submission.[164] The authoritarian hates the powerless, whom he desires to attack; he rationalizes his hatred by declaring them to be basically inferior and by imagining them as humiliated. He also hates himself, particularly his own appetites, and can therefore not love others.[165] His nature is made clearer by contrast with the truly free, confident, and spontaneous individual, who, as Fromm paints him, can be known by his faith that man can direct his own fate, by his self-activity in work, and by his love and sense of duty toward others, whom he regards as his equals and whose independence he wishes to preserve. He may still wish to guide others, but only as a teacher, whose aim it is to benefit them and to help them become, like himself, independent beings.[166]

In a short discussion of the same theme, Murphy [167] lists the processes whereby he conceives the authoritarian personality to be produced; he notes (1) an overdependence, carried into adulthood, upon parental attitudes regarding right and wrong; (2) an identifying attachment to the parent "anchored" primarily upon his aspect as lawgiver, at the cost of his affectionate and comradely aspects; (3) compensation for some initial damage to the self-esteem by a perpetual attempt to see oneself as admirable, resulting in excessive attachment to socially approved norms; (4) and (5), the development of a persistent adoring attitude towards rules as ends in themselves, and a naive moral realism, in accord with which "rightness" and "wrongness" are attached simply to definite actions, these two traits serving as means of achieving and justifying "petty and major despotisms" over others.

In contrast to these two pictures of unwholesome domination, we may quote briefly from the psychiatrist Schilder, who is describing the psychological essence of the parental impulse itself. He sees the emotional basis of parenthood as having been acquired by each successive generation through identification with the attitudes of its own parents, and as essentially the wish

---

[162] Fromm, Erich, *Escape from Freedom*, 1941, pp. 141–142, 162–163.

[163] *Ibid.*, pp. 65–66.

[164] *Ibid.*, pp. 69, 73, 170–172, 174, 265–267.

[165] *Ibid.*, pp. 89, 96, 115–117, 168.

[166] Fromm, *Ibid.*, pp. 97, 157, 164–166, 261–263.

[167] Gardner Murphy, *Personality*, 1947, pp. 857–865.

"to experience not only love but also power" over another person. "The wish to have a child" is in both men and women, "the wish to create something going out from themselves, something which has a life of its own yet remains a part of the parent. We need an outer world, we want to have power over this outer world, we want to recreate this world into its true self, but this projected self should be better adjusted to reality than we ourselves are." [168] This benevolent and necessary "authoritarianism" is another attitude which we shall find reason to recognize as akin to Plato's own.

As an initial contribution to the determination of Plato's personality, we may say very confidently, the dicebox of heredity had seen to it that from the start the boy Plato should be isolated somewhat from his playfellows, set apart as an exceptional individual both in his own awareness and in theirs by his possession of an enormously able mind. Furthermore, two traits in the personality of the mature Plato are so insistently visible in the dialogues as to drive us to the conclusion that they rest upon a psychic structure established in his early age. These are an uncompromising demand upon himself and others, for the realization of a high, even rigorous, standard of moral excellence, and tempering the austerity of this ideal, a deep concern, no whit diminished by the infrequency of its sentimental expression, a truly paternal impulse, to champion against injustice, and to enlighten and direct to their real good and well-being all members of the human family within reach of his voice. These qualities may well have originated from the idealized image of his father, whom he early lost, or of some other authoritative and protective male member of his primary group, to whom he was attached in bonds of affectionate and quasi-filial intimacy, and who set for him that exacting standard of achievement which he presently made his own.

It has sometimes been suggested that a close affinity exists between Plato's "father image" and his conception of the divine; Kelsen, for example, has spoken of Plato's idea of the Good in the *Republic* as an exalted symbol for the dead Ariston.[169] In so far as this connection is accepted, it can be made to yield an interesting reflection from the celestial back to the terrestrial parent. For in the *Timaeus*, as we have seen, Plato speaks of a "Maker and Father of this Universe" who "was good . . . and . . . desired that all should be, so far as possible, like unto himself" (28 B, 29 E), and who by "intelligent persuasion" induced blind Necessity to bring "to the best end the most part of the things coming into being" (48 A).[170] Nor does the Platonic Form of the Good operate despotically, but rather by force of its own splendor and loveliness it compels the love of the beholder (*Republic* 517 B–C, 508 E–509 A, *Phaedrus* 250 D). Surely, if anything of the suggested connotation

[168] Paul Schilder, *Goals and Desires of Man*, 1942, pp. 176–178.

[169] Cf. p. 102 above.
[170] Trans. Bury, Loeb Library.

is valid, we have here evidence that the father-figure whom Plato revered was no such stern task-master as the father-figure of the supposedly typical authoritarian has the logical duty to be.

These assumptions would throw light upon a much disputed region of Plato's personality. The high standard he had set for himself, reënforcing the isolating tendency of his exceptional intelligence, would be sufficient to account for that mixture of a clear consciousness of his own superiority with doubt of his acceptance by others, that ambivalent attitude toward social approval, and that sense of tension and struggle in the control of his passions, to explain which Kelsen has superfluously invoked his hypothesis of Plato's extreme homosexuality.[171] On the positive side, the supporting relationship with his father or father-substitute, and the protective affection and approbation that he probably enjoyed in addition from mother and nurse, brothers and cousins, supplied him with the key to understanding the value of intimate human relationships, while providing him with a firm basis of inner self-confidence. Not improbably, his membership in a close-knit wider kinship group, with which he gladly identified himself, taught him to feel the worth of solidarity. His self-confidence would be further enhanced by his good physique, and, as his awareness grew, by the pleasant discovery of his family's prestige and of the honors and advantages conferred by full Athenian citizenship.

With our hypothetical psychologist closely in view, we may now change our tactics, and carry forward our attempt to account for major strands in Plato's adult personality by distinguishing the several "identifications" with other persons or with social "roles" which he seems to have made during his formative years, and which were not sloughed off almost without trace (like the schoolboy role, for example) as the years passed. The first of these, the identification with the father, or protective and authoritative older relative, we have already discussed, but we shall return to it because of its paramountcy: on our assumption, it was permanent, and it stood in close, supporting relationship to major elements of his personality which were later to be added.

Three other identifications will claim our attention, of which the first was Plato's self-assimilation not so much to a particular person as to a composite which we may call the "Euphues" role. In spite of its misleading association with the Elizabethan master of "conceits," I venture to employ this name not only because Plato had a special fondness for it, but because he applies it in the *Republic* to those young men whose joint excellence of mind and body set them apart as uniquely qualified to undertake, after rigorous training, the

---

[171] It is not doubted that Plato experienced homosexual emotion. But it will be remembered that Kelsen saw in him a degree of homosexuality far in excess of that which was accepted among Athenians of Plato's social group, and this we have shown to be unproved.

high function of intellectual and moral direction in the ideal state, or to take an important part in the affairs of any properly conducted city. Alcibiades is all but named (*Republic* 494 B) as a *manqué* instance of a Euphues, a born philosopher, distinguished by "quickness in learning, memory, courage and magnificence." Such a one, "even as a boy . . . will take the lead in all things, especially if the nature of his body matches the soul." We may note, from its similarity to what was later to be Plato's own case, the fact that "his kinsmen and fellow citizens . . . will desire . . . to make use of him when he is older for their own affairs." It is from among the small number of such natures as these (495 B) that "those spring who do the greatest harm to communities and individuals, and the greatest good when the stream chances to be turned in that direction." [172]

As it stands, this description is an indispensable part of the structure of the *Republic*; has it corresponding significance as a reflection of a stage in the development of its author's personality? In order to elicit meaning of this sort from the Alcibiades passage, we must remember first that Alcibiades for Plato was no abstract example introduced into a formal exposition of the qualities expectable in a potential philosopher. He was rather a memory of one whom at an impressionable age Plato had doubtless seen in the flesh, and with whom he may also have conversed. Apart from the bond of social class, he was related to Plato as an older one-time pupil of his admired teacher Socrates and as a fellow pupil, friend, and associate of Plato's uncle, Critias. We remember how vividly Plato in the *Symposium* has depicted Alcibiades as still a wavering follower, "faithful in his fashion" to the Socratic ideal. The intensity of the later report argues that the rise and fall of this brilliant but ultimately lost leader had deeply moved the young Plato. Had it also held up before him in his earlier years a role which, with certain alterations and improvements in the acting, he felt himself qualified to play? It is not possible to answer this question with a categorical "yes," but I think this is one of the points at which a limited display of audacity is in order. If ever a gifted and imaginative boy had set before him materials for his heroic and tragic imagination to elaborate into an example of conjoint imitation and warning, the conditions were here fulfilled, and the common relation to Socrates would have facilitated identification. It is at least a colorful hypothesis that the example of Alcibiades had inspired Plato with the short-lived hope of succeeding where Alcibiades had failed as the follower of Socrates in politics, the statesman who should reëstablish the ancient dignity of Athens on a new and unshakable base of philosophic knowledge, and should set before the world the example of her virtuous greatness.

But Alcibiades, if the "shiningest," was not the only embodiment of this role. There was also that other tragic failure, the much disputed, two-valued

---

[172] Shorey's translation, Loeb Library.

near relation, also a Socratic in his earlier time, Critias. How much of a Euphues was he, and could he also have served Plato as model for any identifi-
able part of his personality? From what was said in an earlier discussion, it
will be remembered that at least until after the period of his life represented
in the *Charmides* and in the *Protagoras*, Critias possessed an unblemished,
even enviable record as man of intellect and artistic talent, combined with
social facility and political promise. In the former character he might well
have dazzled his young nephew by the profusion of his gifts: poet, playwright, even philosopher, with a theory of time and of knowledge and an
interest in the comparative anatomy of constitutions. And that this man was,
during the years in question, the pupil and familiar of the revered Socrates,
must have appeared to his youthful admirer the final seal of moral validation.
Ardent, energetic, unquestionably intelligent, supposedly high-principled, and
no doubt of handsome presence, Critias, it thus appears, would have merited
a high rating on the Platonic scale as a Euphues.

We must now turn over the medallion to consider its tarnished side, which
is fully as revealing to the student of Plato's personality as the obverse. For
if in the Critias we have considered thus far, Plato found reënforcing allure-
ment toward the role and goal of man of thought, of letters, of high principle,
and of action, it was quite as clearly the Critias of 404 who gave Plato, at
the very threshold of his political career, his best reasons for not entering
upon it. A man of Plato's moral commitments could find no compromise
with the regime of the Thirty, or with any of its surviving supporters; nor
could he, with his principled opposition to democracy as it existed at Athens
and his known family affiliations, have been either a willing or a welcome
addition to the ranks of the restored democrats.

A third and most momentous identification had, even before the debacle
of the Thirty, achieved lodgment in the personality of a Plato then approaching his twenty-fifth year. It would not be difficult to argue (as Kelsen has
also done) [173] that the first psychic gift of Socrates to his young pupil was
that of a second "father image," extending its warmth and protection to him,
and beyond him to the elastic circle of all who chose to submit themselves
to its benevolent sway, and that along with this, he offered Plato an anchorage
for his belief in the possibility and supreme importance of moral excellence.
Here, too, was a man — the Socratic dialogues, written long after, vibrate
with the astonished conviction — in whom reason was quietly at work in
seeking to impress its image upon all human activities and passions. This was
a role which the deepest impulses in Plato's soul desired to play, for the sake
of which he would renounce or modify all conflicting aims, a renunciation
well expressed in the traditional story of his burning of his tragedies after
meeting Socrates. Legend might also have reported further symbolical burn-

---

[173] Kelsen, p. 46.

ings; for if he was to make himself fully one with this admired teacher, he must disavow the elements of self-claim so conspicuously contained in the Euphues role as enacted by Alcibiades and Critias: he could never share their elegant skepticism, or emulate such self-indulgence as was inseparable from their way of life. Furthermore, Socrates, in striking contrast to these young aristocrats and to Plato's father as well, was a commoner. To this fact Plato may well owe much of his success in purging his human ideal of irrelevant pomp and circumstance and in reaching the Euphues conception as we see it in the *Republic*, that of a man well-endowed, not well supplied with noble or wealthy ancestors.

The death of Socrates was the decisive event which at once widened to a chasm the gap between Plato and the Athenian democracy, and thrust upon him the duty of preserving and strengthening the memory, of spreading and confirming the doctrine of this "justest man of his time." This is the birth of that double star which Emerson thought it beyond the power of the critical telescope to separate, the combined role of Plato-Socrates, which consolidated all the elements in his previous experience not in conflict with the new aim, and provided full scope for all his rich endowment.

We have spoken in an earlier chapter of one other life-long object of Plato's imitative regard, his revered ancestor Solon. As Plato's life advanced, it is fair to say that he came more and more closely under the Solonian influence. For in his two most monumental works, and we may add, for good measure, the *Politicus*, Plato was enacting, ideally, the role of legislator, and for the reasons earlier given,[174] it can be stated that in large part the great prototype that inspired him was that of the Athenian lawgiver and poet who sought justice and civic harmony before all else, and expresssed this quest in memorable and persuasive literary form.

While it is not contended that the complete Plato can be conjured out of the psychic constituents thus far suggested, we do submit with some little confidence that our hypothetical construction comports well with the great problems with which he chose to concern himself and the solutions with which he stood content. But if our fundamental contention is right, Plato's personality, no matter how completely we might be able to delineate it, cannot be looked to as the exhaustive source of the Platonic message, which contains elements derived from many objective sources; and to these we now turn.

We must first remind ourselves of those features of the Athenian environment that left their mark upon Plato's mind, setting problems and establishing the orbit within which his ethical and political thought was to move. After every allowance has been made for Athens' great cultural and political achievements, there were grave defects objectively present in Athenian society. During his most plastic years, from boyhood to early maturity, Plato had seen

---

[174] See pp. 262 and 331–332.

little else than war and civic convulsions, bitter fruit that might well have appeared to him to reveal unsoundness at the heart of the tree — the Periclean and post-Periclean democracy — upon which they had grown.[175] Nor did the fourth century, as it advanced, confute this opinion. The restored democracy, it is true, for a time followed more cautious and enlightened international policies, but the passion for imperial domination was destined to show itself again when opportunity offered. The utter discrediting of the extreme oligarchic faction had produced a general agreement to let the constitution stand, in the main, unaltered, as the sole alternative to civic chaos; but again, so great was the jealousy of the demos to preserve its every prerogative, that even moderate reforms could not be proposed without extreme danger to the proponent. The irresponsible power of the orators at the Assembly and in the courts remained at least as great as it had been at the time of Cleon, and was often exercised to seek the banishment or death of political opponents, however meritorious their record of service to the state, or was employed simply for purposes of extortion. Small wonder that cynical antimoralism still had its advocates and practitioners, and that a prudent regard for personal safety and survival remained necessary equipment for any man in public life, to the detriment of civic harmony and devotion to the common good. And the unity of the Hellenic world, in defiance of the sacred bond of kinship and shared cultural and religious tradition, continued to be sundered by recurrent and unrestricted wars.[176]

To one who, like Plato, saw in all this the evidence of perverted values and the repudiation of mutual obligations, the situation called for radical reform, reform which must be grounded in the moral truths he had accepted from Socrates, and must also be implemented wherever possible by decisive changes in the social order. Political action, in the circumstances, was for Plato impossible; not so the continued attempt to strengthen and extend the theoretical basis of ethics, and to develop norms by which, at some more propitious time which providence might one day supply, a genuinely moral commonwealth might be set up.

But the course of Plato's development cannot be simplified into the history of a temperament reacting to the Athenian scene; a second set of objective influences demands recognition. He was born into a culture in which ideas were pursued and actively manipulated by individual thinkers versed in the technique of critical and speculative inquiry. Around the young Plato swarmed a medley of philosophical and scientific views and systems, the

---

[175] This statement has received full documentation in Chapter 7, especially pp. 331–326.

[176] This account of the situation in the fourth century owes much to Field, *Plato and His Contemporaries*, 1930, ch. VIII, and is confirmed by the rather scattered report on Athenian affairs of the period, given in the *Cambridge Ancient History*, VI, principally on pp. 25–26, 34–35, 55–57, 70–75, and 103–107.

achievement of the nearly two centuries since Thales. Plato, throwing himself eagerly into the congenial task, selected, assimilated, and reshaped those elements of this medley which he deemed valid into a vision of what was, for him, compelling truth.

From the Parmenidean principle of unshakable Being, from the Heraclitean flux, from the Pythagorean worship of number and measure and the Orphic-Pythagorean dualism of soul and body, Plato drew the materials for building his ordered universe, wherein the reluctance of matter is brought by the divine persuasion to partake of the excellence and order of the eternal forms. The Socratic belief in the primacy of the soul and in knowledge as the way to virtue, and his practical postulate that all souls are in some degree capable of such knowledge, provide the channel through which the ideal values pass into human life, while the diverse capacities of individuals, in their particular embodiments, make it necessary and right that in the political realm some shall exercise guidance over others, always inviting and in individual cases, if necessary, compelling them toward justice. The city-state as the pattern of organization and the distinction between citizen and metic and slave, are taken over from existing practice, and along with them are carried into the social system such dross as the tolerance in certain circumstances of infanticide and of harshness to criminals, and the acceptance as inevitable of perpetual warfare, if not among Greeks, at least between Greeks and barbarians. The Platonic social structure is a hierarchy, running from top to bottom. But even the lowest member has an interest which the highest is bound to regard, and in his eternal destiny shares equally the hope of rising to the full height of the ideal. In sum, Plato had carried through to the best of his ability the colossal task (never, indeed, brought to systematic completion) of framing a synoptic theory of Being and of Value, in terms of which to fulfill the Socratic demand for knowledge of the virtues and their interrelationship, and, moreover, had shown the possibility of designing on the basis of this knowledge forms of political organization capable of maintaining, along with the spiritual welfare, the safety and material interests of all their members.

A philosophical moralist may rightly be held strictly accountable for those principles with which he begins and which he must be assumed to have seen clearly and to have chosen for their own dear sakes, but he is less to be condemned, though still accountable, for what that beginning may appear later to entail, especially if the bright initial "truths" have dazzled him a little by their luminosity. Plato did not begin with the aim of banishing Homer, condemning atheists, or refusing to permit the young to hear objections to their city's laws or morals, but when these procedures appeared as the necessary costs of overwhelming benefits, they took on, for him, the moral quality of the ends they served. If this is the logic underlying the rejected doctrine, "*Finis medium justificat*," it is also, we may add, the logic justifying such "necessities" as the execution of criminals, an end for which no society exists. Plato unfortunately had no access to those principles, moral and prudential, which today forbid us to accept those of his proposals which we judge illiberal. Whether Plato would have actually carried out all his own unhappy recommendations may be doubted; it is too easily forgotten that Plato did not rule the Republic, or put into effect the regulations of his *Laws*. But what is certain, and of importance for our judgment of his character, is that these flaws in Plato's scheme tell us only what he did not, unfortunately, reject on instinct; they support no inference as to his instinctive purposes and positive aims.

Plato's deep and passionate conviction that there was an ethico-political problem to be solved, urgent, all-important, for which his Socratic insights had adequately prepared him to offer solutions, was met by the counterthrust of an antipathetic, even hostile environment. Could not this war of mighty opposites have generated a tension in his soul sufficient to account for all the inner struggle that Popper has entered under the gratuitous caption of guilt, and has proposed as explanation of Plato's otherwise inexplicable fascination? If more than this is needed, we may appeal also to the tension between the ideal of personal conduct, set, as we have seen, so high in Plato's case, and man's passional and appetitive nature, to which Plato, though wishing to satisfy its legitimate claims, was determined not to yield control.

If Plato grew to his full maturity under stresses and strains such as we have surmised, it is then not at all remarkable that a close eye should detect some deviations from the norm of the complacent bourgeois. What is more worthy of comment is the over-all sanity of the man. We are once more reminded of Emerson's oracular dictum: "the balanced soul came." Plato's response to the challenge of his environment would seem to have been all that a professor of mental hygiene could have prescribed: he adjusted his goal to the possibilities of achievement, which in his circumstances meant renunciation, or at least indefinite postponement, of public action, and the devising for himself of a way of life which would permit him a working expression, in a narrower sphere, of his basic purposes. We are not surprised, then, to find him adapting to his own use in the Academy the Socratic technique of education through the living word, the illuminating interplay of mind with mind, directed to the Socratic end of bettering the soul; similarly we find him carrying forward that interest in the technique of clear and precise thinking whereby Socrates had sought to pass through knowledge to virtue. When the Sicilian summons came, Plato set forth, so to say, in the character of a Solon-Socrates, whose legislative program was designed to realize the values of both men.

Part of his energy throughout the years went into his literary creations, which, beginning apparently as a monument to Socrates, served also to acquaint the Greek world with the growing body of his thought, and, in the following decades, with the spirit of his Academy. He has referred to the dialogues (*Phaedrus* 274 B ff.) as of secondary importance, a judgment with which most of us find it difficult literally to agree, but one that does credit to its author's modesty, and underlines the seriousness of his purpose, which refused to honor the semblance of mind equally with the living reality. Roughly speaking, we may characterize the dialogues as essentially Socratic conversations, increasingly elaborate; in their social content, they are also importantly guided by a Solonian aim, and, taken as a whole, they fulfil their author's picture of himself as a man of letters, which may have been initially inspired by Critias and, more remotely, by Solon. In spite of occasional thunderbolts of moral indignation and prophetic denunciation of the "Lord's enemies," there runs through all the dialogues a recognition of the limitations upon human knowledge, an urbane note of intellectual openness to suggestion, which Whitehead has contrasted, to Plato's advantage, with the unrelenting dogmatism of an Augustine controverting a Pelagius.[177] This quality has won from Crossman, despite his "hatred" of Plato's political teaching, the fine praise — he is speaking of the *Republic* — that Plato has supplied "a pattern of . . . disinterested research" which "never bullies or deceives its reader or beguiles him with appeals to sentiment, but treats him as a fellow philosopher for whom only the truth is worth having." [178] These admirable qualities have their expression in the *Republic* and in equal measure in the continuing stream of Plato's productions. Their permanent home, since we cannot regard them as transient dramatic fictions, was the mind and personality of Plato. There is every likelihood that they found further expression in Plato's manner of treating his maturer associates in the Academy. As to his conduct toward the younger minds under his direction, we may remind ourselves of what we earlier said, and note again the kindly consideration and encouragement that the young men seen, for example, in the *Sophist* and *Politicus*, receive at Plato's hand. Nor is it amiss to add that in dealing with those who are his fellows in age but not in capacity, as is the case in the *Laws*, he observed a fine courtesy in tempering the wind of his doctrine to the shorn and lamb-like capacities of Clinias and Megillus. In short, there emerges in contradiction to Popper's dyspeptic construction of the sour and despotic Master of the Academy,[179] the likeness of a man who may well have commanded not only the admiration and respect but also the affection of those willing and able to learn geometry and enter the high fellowship of the Academy.

If now we venture to apply Fromm's criteria of authoritarianism to our version of Plato's personality, we should be obliged to note as significant Plato's submission to the Divine, and, on the human level, to Socrates; but

---

[177] Whitehead, *Adventures of Ideas*, pp. 134–135.
[178] Crossman, pp. 292.
[179] Popper, p. 44.

no less significant is the fact that it is not power as such to which Plato submits, but persuasive Reason and justice, and that neither his God nor, *a fortiori*, his martyred master, had coercive power over Necessity. It might be noted, also, that Plato wishes to dominate others, that he regards the mass of men as natively inferior beings who are, ideally, to be regulated in action and in thought, and that he himself lays down the aims which even the rulers are to regard. But here we should remember, from our earlier discussion, that Plato's handling of his guardians is in literary perspective; we could show, as we shall see below, that in fact he invests them with an ideal wisdom far beyond his own; even his wish to dominate the mass of men is mitigated by the desire to protect them from their own incapacity, and by his belief that they too, *sub specie aeternitatis*, are his equals. As for Plato's subjection of his own emotions and appetites to a rigid control suggestive of self-hate, plain to be seen is the qualifying fact that he condemns *per se* no impulse or appetite, but only its antisocial or excessive indulgence, and that he seeks rather to harmonize than to extirpate them.

Murphy's account of the processes by which authoritarians may be produced, unlike Fromm's list of criteria, is presented for use only in societies like our own, and Murphy should, therefore, not be held accountable for discrepancies resulting from an attempted transfer to the ancient world. Since, however, such transfers are all too likely to be made, we shall try to neutralize their injury to Plato. For if it should be argued that Plato carried with him throughout life beliefs and standards acquired in his youth, from Socrates, Solon, and perhaps from his father, it may be answered that these beliefs were certainly subjected to active criticism and interpretation, and that quite apart from their origin they have a right to be considered on their merits. If his picture of himself as "lawgiver" is held to indicate undesirable "anchorage" on the lawgiving aspect of the parent, and a love of rules for their own sakes, we may point to the fact that in the Greek world such a picture of oneself could arise in another way, from self-identification with the ancient, honorable and still surviving social role of lawgiver, and that this role perforce entailed the proposing of rules. To the suggestion that Plato's sense of isolation, through injury to his self-esteem, may have turned him toward moral perfectionism, we answer that conversely, Plato's persistent adherence to a moral ideal was itself promotive of isolation, a major cost borne by the moral reformer in any age. And if Plato's assertion of absolute standards of right and wrong is taken as equivalent to a naive realism, the most casual reading of the dialogues will show how far Plato was from a naive acceptance of traditional morality.

We see then that the strait-jacket of the "authoritarian personality" in its technical or semitechnical sense, cannot be made to fit Plato without very considerable alterations. He stands in fact far closer to the legitimate teacher recognized by Fromm. While for the common people it cannot be held that

Plato hoped to do more than benefit them from above, as head of his Academy and as the imagined educator of philosopher-rulers in the *Republic*, he was claiming an interim authority, which is legitimately exercised, as Fromm agrees, by any teacher who strives to assist his pupils to become rational independent beings and his own full equals. True, Plato shows a marked conservatism by extending the years of intellectual nonage well beyond the arrival of adulthood, but this fact need not blind us, as it has blinded Popper, to the goal he held in view.[180]

Closely bordering upon this will to teach is that paternal impulse which Plato, in the absence of children of his own, seems to have extended to the people of his imaginary cities. We speak only of one aspect of Plato's feeling, for he stands to the citizens in many other relations; he is, after all, planning political communities complete with all the powers of enforcement. But something of the fatherly attitude was among his proudest contributions to civic law.[181] Again with only modest hopes for his less gifted sons, he cherished a paternal dream that his more fortunately endowed offspring, both male and female, would rise to levels of excellence beyond his own. And in the prevision of such a family, working out, in harmonious and amicable interaction, the fulness of their respective powers, Plato must have felt some vicarious fulfilment of that impulse to create what is at once one's own and endowed with its own independent life, which Schilder finds at the heart of parenthood.

Our just completed construction of Plato's personality was inspired and dominated by the wish to show that one need not for lack of better accept Kelsen's and Popper's reading of Plato as a soul hungering and lusting after illicit power. One important piece of unfinished business remains. Can we, on our assumptions, account for those indications in Plato of undue certainty, intolerance of alternative views, and claim to expert knowledge of right rule, which fit with such facility into the Kelsen-Popper scheme?

We have already laid the broad foundations of our answer to this question in what was said of the relation of Plato to Socrates. From this standpoint

---

[180] For a discussion of Popper's charge that Plato wished to deprive even his philosopher kings of the freedom of critical thought, see Appendix XII, pp. 618ff.

[181] The incompleteness of the parallel is further evidenced for those who accept the *Seventh Letter* as Plato's own by what is there said (331 B) of the writer's unwillingness to employ anything more than good counsel for the direction of a misguided son. Yet that Plato in his role as lawgiver conceived himself to be emulating also the good teacher and the good parent is shown with

particular clarity at *Laws* 857 E ff., esp. 859 A, where he recommends that laws shall attempt to give wise counsel to the citizens about "what is noble, good, and just," and shall "resemble persons moved by love and wisdom, such as a father or mother," rather than to "order and threaten, like some tyrant or despot" (trans. Bury, Loeb Library). In this the Plato of the *Laws* is employing a metaphor and extending a principle approved by the Socrates of the *Crito*, 51 B, E (cf. p. 643 below) and of the *Apology*, 41 E (cf. p. 637).

two of the three qualities in question — certainty and intolerance — take on a somewhat different look: certainty becomes in great part the rapturous assent of a disciple to the authority of his master's vision, intolerance his effort to defend the cherished doctrine against all hostile comers. In putting the matter in this way, we are no doubt exaggerating; Plato was certainly not merely a disciple. But we suggest that if we have our eyes open to the increment of certainty and intolerance generated in this way, we will see a Plato importantly different from the man whom Kelsen and Popper have depicted.

Every moralist and every prophet, in proportion to the depth and intensity of his insight, in a manner becomes the "thing he contemplates," ever more closely identifying himself with the nature of the power in whose name he speaks. At its maximum, as in the Hebrew Prophets, the prophetic utterance is equated with the voice of God, the prophet saving his religious humility by assuming the role of the recipient and reporter of the divine word. Something of this sort, though more modest in its manner of expression, we have seen Socrates claim, when in the *Apology* he speaks of the command laid upon him by the god. Plato, as we read him, was a prophet of this same Delphic revelation, at one remove, his conviction confirmed by the testimony of a great life heroically ended. There is humility as well as generosity in the temper of a man who for many years attributes to another his own best and most deeply felt insights and ventures his most confident assertions only in this other's name.

We have postponed consideration until now of the third quality on the list of Plato's seeming vanities, the claim to expertness in government and legislation, because it differs somewhat from the other two. We have maintained that Socrates had, implicitly, presented himself as one with expert knowledge of the soul and its true interests, and in the *Crito*, as one qualified to speak of justice with authority, a claim which Plato with added emphasis repeated on his behalf. But he did not, so far as is known, develop an ideal constitution, nor devote particular attention to the study of laws. In the *Gorgias*, Socrates (if our view be accepted, it is Socrates speaking here) is shown demanding that moral knowledge shall be made the basis of the communal life, that statesmanship shall be directed not by the aim of giving the public what it wants but by some art or science of the health of the soul, devoted like medicine to securing the true good of those it serves.[182] This demand, implying as it does the possibility of attainment, formed the point of departure for that development and systematization of the thought of Socrates which Plato felt it his duty to supply. In the *Republic* we see the Socratic premises, supplemented by Platonic insights, organized into an imposing structure and "rounded with the dream" of a complete and certain knowledge possessed by

---

[182] In the *Euthydemus*, 290 B–292 E, a   similar description of the "kingly art" is implied.

the ideal guardians. It is here that suspicion has arisen, reënforced by the appearance in the *Politicus* of an ideal Statesman; and the question is raised, to which we earlier promised to suggest an answer: was Plato, in describing these patterns of excellence and incarnations of eternal truth, who are fit to rule without check or trammel, tacitly defining himself?

We may answer without hesitation: "yes," in so far as by "himself" is meant Plato's ideal, the standard of excellence and aspiration to which he stood committed and which remained the ultimate goal of his pursuit. We may say "no," if reference is made to the actual Plato, as he stood at any period of his long life. We of course agree that in the *Laws*, behind the transparent mask of the Athenian Stranger, Plato presents himself as fitted to legislate for a new colony; for such a more limited enterprise, he felt himself in knowledge of actual laws at least equal, and in wisdom, by virtue of his Socratic moral principles, far superior, to any contemporary of his likely to be called upon for such services.

But with the rulers in the other two dialogues the case is different. The guardians in the *Republic* are set in a frame of ideality; in addition to their moral wisdom, they are provided with superlative skills, such as the ability to discern in the young child, even perhaps in the infant, the future dispositions and abilities of the adult, and the knowledge of the best genetic combinations; being by definition perfect rulers, why should they not possess all possible knowledge? In the *Politicus*, the situation is similar. No "divine shepherd" is available for the tending of the human flock. Nevertheless, an ideal standard of moral excellence exists, and the "Statesman" is the name given, *ex hypothesi*, to whoever — individual or small group — possesses the knowledge which can bring men in cities closer to this ideal standard (296 E–297 B, 300 D–E). Such knowledge must be continuously pursued, and as it is progressively discovered, must be permitted without let or hindrance to exercise authority over human life. Under existing circumstances, this knowledge is best applied to the framing or revising of legal constitutions, since men do not believe that there exists such a being as the true Statesman who could be trusted to rule without law (301 D–E). That Plato is thinking primarily of Socrates as the possessor of political knowledge is shown by the unquestioned reference to him (299 B–C); that Plato considered Socrates the "true politician" we know also from the *Gorgias*. Plato is claiming himself to be the "Statesman" only as the living representative of the Socratic knowledge of man's true good, and as the diligent student of the institutional means to its maximal attainment.

In neither dialogue is Plato the hero of his own tale. He is in a position like that of a physician (he himself would approve this analogy) who should write a pamphlet on "Medicine and Human Welfare," claiming that medical science possesses a beneficent knowledge in no way dependent for its validity upon the action of statesmen and parliaments, but able, potentially, to eliminate contagious disease, reduce maternal and infant death rates almost to the vanishing point, and give every child an adequate diet, whether or no the governments of the world can be brought to contribute to it the necessary funds and authorization. Such a writer might believe that he himself, or another like him, approximated the human vehicle of "Medicine," without revealing a lust for personal power, or believing himself the Medicine Man in person.[183]

And yet, in candor, we must make a small concession at this point to Plato's critics. The mind of Plato was a platform of dispute on which his hopes and aspirations, enkindled by the Socratic vision of the good life for man, declared with confidence, "The city of perfection must and can exist, and this is the plan of its building," while from the opposite quarter, his knowledge of life and of mortal frailty asserted with no less energy, "Such a blessed community, save under the rarest of favoring conditions, is not accessible to man — its pattern is laid up in heaven." It is not possible to deny that Plato in his dialogues on occasion permits himself to speak as if the external circumstances alone — perhaps a simple invitation to himself from a docile tyrant — were wanting for the immediate realization upon earth of the perfect community, in which a philosophic master of the "royal art" would be given an unhindered hand.[184] To avoid the error of taking this for his true meaning, it is necessary to bear in mind his own pronouncements in other more sober passages, and to strike the balance.

We reach the end of our consideration of Plato the man and personality. We may perhaps express the modest hope that during this long period of association, our acquaintance with Plato has progressed into something like an intimacy, bringing with it a greater appreciation of the very much in Plato that is highly admirable and a compensating understanding and forgiveness of what is not.

---

[183] We are here interested in Plato's ideas as expressions and revelations of his personality, and accordingly will forego any discussion of the validity of the ideas themselves. Please note also that in drawing our analogy between medicine and Plato's conception of the science of statesmanship, we should not be understood as maintaining that medical values necessarily take precedence over all competing cultural interests.

[184] We have discussed a misunderstanding of this nature in connection with Plato's intentions in Sicily, pp. 374ff. above.

9

Was Plato a Totalitarian?

The Meaning of the Term

Unless we have been grossly misled, the theme of the chapter before us broaches what for most readers is quintessential to all contemporary discussion of Plato's thought. It is not, as the reader well knows, here first introduced; it has been the leitmotif running in and out of our whole argument. The question whether Plato was a totalitarian — whether his political ideal was substantially identical with whatever is held to be the common and distinctive basis of Fascism, Nazism, and Russian Communism — this question is, I think, certainly the hinge upon which turns the fate of Plato as a possible companion for the liberal intelligence of our time. An unqualified affirmative answer would deal him a staggering blow; as, *per contra*, a fair disclaimer on his behalf would go further perhaps than anything else, to restore a confidence which repeated accusations have gone far to destroy.

But first a word of apology, addressed jointly to Plato and to the reader. In the preceding chapters the order and substance of our argument was largely determined, as must always be true for the defender, by the tactics of the attackers. In consequence, our major task was the vindication of Plato the man, our minor concern was with Plato the thinker. The inherent injustice in this way of dealing with a professional thinker needs no further comment, but cries out for what, alas, is beyond our reach in the present book — full treatment of the various areas of Plato's thought from ethics to metaphysics. Such an undertaking seemed demanded by the depreciatory comments upon his philosophical achievements, and on several occasions we have given at least an implicit answer, or have suggested the line that could be followed in a full reply. But in the main we have left the performance of this service to other and more technically competent hands, and shall limit ourselves to meeting the spearhead of the present attack.[1]

In discussing Plato's relation to totalitarianism we are, be it noted, no

---

[1] An evaluation of Fite's criticism of Platonic ethical theory appears as Appendix XIII, pp. 620f.

longer replying only to Crossman's severe but scrupulous condemnation or to Fite's ironical deflations and sprightly innuendoes; we no longer enjoy the luxury of answering charges which are the private imaginings of an extravagant accuser such as Popper. Although these specific attackers will not be forgotten and Popper's voice will continue to be heard rising above the rest, we shall not be content to have answered them alone. It is, in fact, not only the enemies of Plato who must be met on this issue, but on occasion also some among those who would count themselves in principle his friends. We shall assume, therefore, that our reader is already numbered among these friends, or that we have in large part made our case with him against the detractors, in favor of Plato the man. The issue is sharply focussed: was Plato, however honest, and however single-mindedly devoted to his aims, nevertheless an instance of the noxious breed of totalitarians?

Our first business is with this particular word, and our first concern must be to avoid falling into one or another of the several "word-traps" that lie directly along our way. There is spread temptingly before us the possibility of accepting complacently the public meaning of our term as specified in the latest edition of the most authoritative dictionary. The 1951 edition of Webster's International offers the following definition of "totalitarian": "Of or pertaining to a highly centralized government under the control of a political group which allows no recognition of or representation to other political parties, as in Fascist Italy or in Germany under the Nazi regime." [2] Now that is certainly an admirable formulation or fixation of current usage, clear, self-consistent, and as far as it goes, unobjectionable. But even so, we may not appeal to it as our platinum bar of measurement. It remains on a level of such particularity as to be applicable only to the contemporary political scene. And if we should attempt to remedy this defect by remodeling Webster's definition into some such form as "of or pertaining to government by a small, rigorously limited governing group which allows no voice in the determination of policy to any other group within the state," we should then have a definition of our term undeniably applicable to Plato but now so ample in its generality as to embrace indifferently all forms of narrowly-based authoritarian government known to man.

One other definition deserves mention here, seldom employed in its strict purity in popular or even in technical discussion, but undoubtedly valid and important and, in addition, admirably suited to the making of what is from our standpoint a distinction of sovereign importance. A clearcut instance of this use is provided by a recent authoritative writer on political theory who describes Russian Communism and Fascism alike as "totalitarian in the sense that they obliterated the distinction between areas of private judgment and of

---

[2] By permission. From *Webster's New International Dictionary*, Second Edition, copyright, 1934, 1939, 1945, 1950, by G. & C. Merriam Co.

public control." [3] And just here we wish to assert, as conspicuously as can be managed, that if anyone is willing to employ the term "totalitarian" deliberately and scrupulously within the area of meaning thus defined, reserving all questions concerning the nature and purpose of the state which is to exercise such comprehensive regulation over the citizen, then it is permissible and indeed necessary to call Plato by this most dangerous of names. To the defense and illustration of this "agreement" between ourselves and Plato's critics, we shall later return. Here we remark, however, that in this sense, as in that we just now adapted from Webster, the term is applicable to a very wide range indeed of political systems.

What most of us have in mind, however, when the word is pronounced, may be illustrated from those formulations of the meaning of totalitarianism that took their origin in the warfare of ideas waged for more than two decades by the leaders of democratic thought against their ideological and military enemies in Italy and Germany and, with an armistice of mutual alliance, against Russian Communism. Vigorous efforts were made to discover a complex of essential characteristics capable of serving as a common denominator for the first two, or for all three of these political systems, and able also to differentiate them from other autocracies on the one hand and from what is held to be the essence of democracy or of liberalism, on the other. In examining any collection of such descriptions, one notes a considerable community, qualified by a wide difference in emphasis — they are not all built around the same center — and by variation in the traits chosen for mention. This unity in diversity may be illustrated by several such descriptions, drawn from the writings of men who are unquestionably qualified representatives of the liberal and democratic faith, and who are, moreover, not centrally involved in the current conflict over Plato.[4] These we have abbreviated with care to prevent distortion and present here as sample formulations by responsible observers of the central meaning of the term today.

Totalitarianism has been described, with special reference to Nazism and Fascism, as a fabric of three strands: (1) nationalism, (2) the doctrine of the racial superiority of the people in question, and (3) emphasis upon a ruler, conceived as the embodiment of power, and a small group of elite surrounding him and combining with him to enforce a strict discipline upon the masses; when Communism alone is considered, the first two traits are omitted.[5] Another writer holds totalitarianism to be the combination of two primary elements: (1) authoritarianism, or a strong forceful government, centered in a single person or in a minority group, either for the sake of pragmatic efficiency or on the ground that the state should be governed by

---

[3] George H. Sabine, *A History of Political Theory*, 1950, p. 905.

[4] At the risk of seeming arbitrary in our choice of authorities, we may gain something in objectivity by choosing almost at random from the available list.

[5] Adapted from *Ideas and Men*, by Crane Brinton, 1940, pp. 471–472, p. 489.

the wise few; (2) "etatism," or the doctrine that the state is an end in itself to which individual interests must be subordinated or sacrificed, and in the interests of which all individual liberties must be abolished.[6]

A professional philosopher and veteran interpreter and defender of democracy presents an interesting four-fold definition of this "catch-word," whose meaning, he tells us, is largely "emotive": (1) uniformitarianism, the enforcement by the state of an all-pervasive creed which supplies the sovereign aim, whether this be the service of God, national aggrandisement, or some international cause; (2) anti-intellectualism, the dethronement of reason in favor of the belief that will and emotion give validity to thought; (3) tribalism, or the determination of all values by the collective: truth and other norms are regarded as intracultural or intranational and the state becomes the supreme moral end; (4) technologism, or the worship as an end in itself of whatever "works" or is efficient.[7]

As previously remarked, these definitions or descriptions have much in common, though they are differently centered and not in full agreement as to which traits must necessarily be included. But all alike, since they attempt to get at the irreducible minimum, fail to express the cloud of connotations which for most users surround the word, and contribute largely to its emotional aura. Concentration camps, sudden disappearances of persons not known to have committed any crime, "purges" even of those in high authority, death by starvation and cold, by poison gas and firing squad; great mass meetings and the emotional elevation of the leader and the cause, and as the counterparts of these, hostility to supposed enemies, the glorification of war or of permanent revolution — all these are psychologically inseparable from our concept of totalitarianism, as the reader will probably agree. And in addition there is a group of traits, no longer central but well remembered as having formed part of the program of one or more of the totalitarian regimes, such as the encouragement of illicit sex relations for the purpose of breeding "heroes," or the attempt to alienate children from their parents for purposes of indoctrination. Some shadows of these survive in the word as we use it and help to identify and to blacken its meaning.

Meanwhile we must not lose sight of what our familiar detractors have told us of their various conceptions of totalitarianism. All of them, to the degree of their interest in political matters, are of course affronted by totalitarianism. But they differ from such advocates of the liberal faith as the authorities previously listed in that their conceptions of totalitarianism are in each case centered in some group of traits which they believe central also to Plato's political thought. Crossman presents an anomaly in that he has not accused Plato of being on all fours with the totalitarians, being careful always

---

[6] Similarly adapted from *From Luther to Hitler*, by W. M. McGovern, 1941, pp. 14–17.

[7] From "The Philosophical Roots of Totalitarianism," by R. B. Perry, in *The Roots of Totalitarianism*, by MacIver, Bonn, and Perry, 1940, pp. 20–31.

to distinguish Plato's aim of virtue and happiness for all from the crass or brutal aims of the modern dictators, and even from the unjust and mistaken purposes of the ruling classes of the so-called "democracies." Yet he regards as basic both to Plato and to communism and fascism the belief that the common man cannot be trusted to participate in self-direction, and must therefore be subtly controlled by propaganda; as further common traits, he points to Plato's recommendation that an elite shall be selected and trained to do the necessary directing, and he detects in Plato a willingness to employ propaganda devices and government policies of any degree of falsity, injustice, and cruelty. Crossman also believes, though he does not make this part of Plato's kinship with totalitarianism, that Plato was guilty of racialism of a sort in proposing that membership in the governing class be made the hereditary monopoly of chosen persons of birth and wealth.[8]

To Fite the basis of Russian Communism is the worship of organizational efficiency for the sake of economic success, just as other hierarchical systems, like the Roman Empire, an army, or an American business corporation are organized with a view solely to efficiency in the pursuit of their respective aims. Plato's aim, so Fite declares, is "distinction in war, if not . . . conquest," and his design for the ideal city is merely the expression of "technological efficiency" in its pursuit. On another page, Fite identifies as "true Platonism" the Russian Communist belief that the correct opinion on all subjects should be determined by those in authority and publicly proclaimed for docile acceptance by all; in this connection we recall also Fite's contentions that the "freedom" of Plato's citizens is no more than a "habitual respect for authority," and that the Republic is, except for the handful of rulers, a city of "greedy children," kept in order solely by external restraints. Fite draws no further parallels between Plato and any totalitarian regime; he does, however, believe he has found in Plato's state various traits, such as the just-mentioned militarism, admiration for Sparta, and the cynical deception and exploitation of the common people, which those who see Plato as the proto-Nazi have charged against him.[9]

We may recall also the identification of Plato as a "totalitarian reformer" by Neurath and Lauwerys. They have succinctly declared that for Plato, as for Hitler, "the main purpose of the state is to preserve the purity of the race and to organize the people for war." [10]

Popper has directed far more detailed attention to the problem and brought against Plato a correspondingly more systematically articulated charge. In Popper's value system, the making by individuals of free moral choices is of paramount importance, and correlative with this is the requirement that these choices shall be humanitarian, looking to the achievement of freedom and to the abolition of pain, so far as possible, for all men every-

---

[8] Crossman, e.g., pp. 172–179, esp. p. 179; 232, 247–249; 281.
[9] Fite, pp. 216–219; 244, 80–81, 304; 147–148, 29–30, 137–138.
[10] For the reference to Neurath and Lauwerys, see n. 91, p. 441.

where.[11] The chief obstacle to the realization of these values he has found in advocacy of the "closed society." This advocacy, combined with certain other doctrines, he would apparently call "totalitarianism"; yet to this word, frequent throughout his book, he nowhere assigns a definition. We are compelled, therefore, to gather together the various separate qualities which he has assigned to it, to make up a ten-fold description, as follows: (1) "historicism," or the doctrine that historical events are determined by inexorable laws; (2) Spartanism, the exaltation and imitation of Spartan institutions and ideals; (3) "holism," or the belief that the interest of the group or the collective is the criterion of morality, and that it entirely supersedes the welfare of the individual; (4) the doctrine of racial superiority; (5) advocacy of the direction of the state by a specially trained and disciplined ruling class; (6) the "closing" of the society, or the attempt to stabilize the state and to give security and peace to its members by predetermining all their choices and beliefs; (7) readiness to employ violence for achieving radical reforms; (8) inhumanity; (9) the recommendation of "autarky," to keep out the liberalizing effect of trade; and (10) militarism, exercised against neighboring states, employed to unify the people and to prevent the entry of liberal beliefs from outside sources. All these traits, or modifications of them, Popper believes to be actively present in Plato's political thought.[12] There follows as a necessary consequence the obligation of denouncing Plato as a totalitarian and as the fountainhead of political evil, likely unless checked to continue spreading his dangerous infection in the modern world.[13]

Ten Proposed Measures of Plato's Guilt

We have before us, now, all the materials necessary for the hearing that it is our intention to conduct. We shall deal first with the descriptions of totalitarianism which we have assembled from the detractors, analyzing these into their separate components and weighing Plato's "guilt" under each, then measuring the degree of his conformity to each of the descriptions in question taken as a whole. It will then be a matter of no great difficulty to show in similar fashion his relation to totalitarianism as formulated by our nonpartisans. What should emerge from all this, we trust, will be a reasonably

---

[11] Popper, pp. 65–66, 508–509.

[12] For Popper's description of these elements of totalitarianism and his attribution of them to Plato see, e.g., on historicism, pp. 5–8, 11–13, 25–27, 37–40, 486–488; on Spartanism, pp. 42, 47–55; on holism or "tribalism," pp. 12, 97–105, 468, 537; on racialism, pp. 50–52, 81–83; on the ruling class or "caste," pp. 47–55, 86–87; on the "closing" and the benevolent reasons for it, pp. 86–87, 132–133, 166–167; on radicalism and violence, pp. 161–163, 194; on inhumanity, pp. 48–49, 52, 564–567; on Plato's recommendation of autarky, and on the reasons for autarky and conquest by totalitarian states today, pp. 86–87, 177–178. On p. 36 he declares roundly, "It is the totalitarian tendency of Plato's political philosophy which I shall try to analyze, and to criticize."

[13] Ibid., pp. v, vii, 7, 36–37.

objective judgment upon the question whether the term "totalitarianism" as employed by responsible observers, and Plato as interpreted with correspond- ing care, can be conjoined without a contradiction.

What the reader of the section that follows may expect is neither simple denial nor confession on Plato's behalf. Our earlier expressions of indigna- tion at what we felt, and still feel, to be the perverse exaggeration of the de- tractors must not cause the reader to expect that we are undertaking a total refutation of their claims. In point of fact, our findings with regard to the separate components of Plato's alleged totalitarianism will show the widest possible range of result, from total contradiction of individual items to al- most complete agreement, through an important middle range in which like- ness and difference are in virtual equilibrium. It may be that our result will please neither friend nor foe, but we must resolutely attempt to set partisan considerations to one side and, adapting the Platonic precept, follow the argu- ment wherever it may lead.

"Historicism." — The first of the proposed criteria which we shall con- sider is "historicism," a charge of Popper's devising which he stands alone in urging. For this reason and because its consideration will require pro- longed attention to detail, we shall pass rather rapidly over it in our text, referring the interested reader to Appendix XIV.[14] To claim prophetic knowl- edge of the course of history, derived from a knowledge of the "laws" which govern its movement, is to be what Popper calls a "historicist." The moral harm entailed is twofold: the historicist will allow the supposed "laws" to determine his ends, and, further, will be in danger of excusing himself from strenuous attempts to remove evils; for he will be tempted to believe such efforts either superfluous, if in accord with destiny, or, if they invite to action contrary to destiny, futile.

That Popper has not adhered to the rules of judicial logic and equity in his manner of affixing the guilt of historicism upon Plato will be seen from a simple analysis of the structure of his argument. He has made his defini- tion and claimed Plato as coming under it by virtue of his belief (ascribed to him by Popper) that "all social change is . . . degeneration." Popper has thus by implication fastened upon Plato the guilt of resigning his rights and duties in the choice of ends, and shuffling off responsibility for action upon the law of destiny. But presently we find him charging Plato with whole- sale "social engineering" in an effort to "arrest change." But, but, one must exclaim, this second charge annuls at least one half of the first! For it shows Plato manfully shouldering the moral responsibility of a great decision, made to counteract the entropy of historical decay,[15] and should wring from Popper

---

[14] Appendix XIV, p. 622ff., deals with Popper's charge against Plato of histori- cism.

[15] Popper's new charge, added in his second edition, that Plato believed himself the predestined turner-about of the world's moral weather (discussed on our pp. 463– 465 above) will not solve the difficulties of

iron praise such as should be paid to a Henleian "Invictus" or a Russellian "Free Man," "building his temple on the unyielding foundation of despair." In the face of Plato's marked deviation from the type of the historicist as described by Popper himself, Popper's perseverance in affixing this label may be fairly called an egregious example of another wrong he has charged upon Plato. Popper has turned, for the moment, into a "methodological essentialist," treating "historicism" as a kind of Platonic Idea, which retains its essential identity and essential harmfulness under all its varying phenomenal disguises.

What, now, of the other half of obloquy, that which is incurred by permitting ends to be determined by the sheer givenness of the march of historical events? We cannot see how this fault can remain in one who has, by Popper's own supposition, taken it upon himself to call the reversal of history a good, and to adopt it as the supreme goal of endeavor. And again assuming that Plato ever made the supposed adoption, how could anyone know that it was Plato's adoption of this goal that dictated his values, and not his antecedent conception of the good that prompted him to accept it as a worthy goal? But we ourselves, relying upon conclusions reached at an earlier stage of our argument, have no need of speculatively inferring Plato's concept of "good" from what he might have thought about history, since we can see it so unambiguously emerging out of the interaction of his moral consciousness with the ethical ideals of Socrates.[16]

Now, as we have shown at some length in our Appendix, the various Platonic texts that genuinely encourage the idea that Plato regarded the earlier as *eo ipso* the better, are disputable in point of doctrinal seriousness, while other passages are made to support the thesis only by forced interpretation and neglect of context. It is also true, unfortunately for the strength of Popper's case, that we never find that Plato thought of applying a historical measuring-stick to events and personalities of the known past or of the living present. His ethical teaching is indeed permeated by the belief in the possibility of attaining in the present, by strenuous effort, justice and philosophical insight. These views are out of line, both positively and negatively, with what Plato should believe, if for him, as Popper's theory requires, the historical principle were the great and overarching law of human destiny.

We can go further. The *argumentum ex silentio* is crowned by a number

---

his position. It of course implies that Plato conceived his own Utopian engineering as predestined by historical necessity, and to this extent, if true, adds to the consistency of Plato's presumed historicism. But it still leaves Popper under the necessity of showing that Plato believed all past change to have been preponderantly degenerative; moreover, since Popper teaches that, for Plato, the world's new age was to be static, it still requires him to demonstrate that, in Plato's ideal cities, there would be no change. Neither of these propositions can be supported, as our next few pages will show.

[16] Cf. pp. 400–402, with cross-references, and Appendix XVI, pp. 632ff.

of clear positive examples. At the beginning of the third book of the *Laws*, Plato has, so to say, opened the door of his study at the Academy to permit us to see some of the results of his historical and archaeological research. He is proposing to throw light upon the origins of governments by a long-time survey of the ways in which cities change for better or for worse. Plato is operating with a theory of "cultural catastrophism": through the vast, perhaps infinite reaches of time past, civilized communities have arisen by slow steps from rude beginnings to various degrees of cultural maturity (he formulates no periodic law requiring perfection at any point), and then, through the agency of catastrophic floods, plagues, and the like, have been thrown back to their primitive conditions. Applying this theory to his own epoch, he imagines that after "the great flood" our species was represented only by certain "scanty embers of the human race," consisting for the most part of "herdsmen of the hills," men of simple virtue, but destitute of almost all knowledge of the mechanical and social arts. The account reaches its peak of interest from our point of view at 678 B, where we read: "Do we imagine, my good Sir, that the men of that age, who were unversed in the ways of city life — many of them noble, many ignoble, — were perfect either in virtue or in vice?" That this was impossible the interlocutor heartily agrees. And Plato continues, "As time went on and our race multiplied, all things advanced — did they not? — to the condition which now exists . . . not all at once, but by small degrees, during an immense space of time." This, need one say, is a picture of cultural ascent, a process which entails much evil, but is necessary to the achievement of the highest human excellence. The idea of the increasing possibility of humanly directed progress is carried out in the whole plan of the *Laws*, which seeks, finds, and then attempts to implement in legislation designed for an actual city, the basic principles of good government, and, as England has called it, "the secret of political vitality." And Plato adds to his projected legislation the expression of his hope (*Laws* 769 D–E) that later lawgivers may amend his work, "in order that the constitution . . . he has organized may always grow better, and never in any way worse." [17]

To take what constitutes perhaps the clearest and most overwhelming example, we can quote once again the progressive optimism of *Republic* 424 A, which contemplates, on the basis of a proper social order once set in operation, progress from generation to generation of better and better men in a better and better city. To Plato's standpoint as herein expressed, the last word to suggest itself as applicable would be Popper's word "historicism."

"Backward, my brave Spartiates! One collective leap backward and the frozen future will be ours!" These are Plato's marching orders to his regi-

---

[17] The several quotations in this paragraph are from Bury's translation of the *Laws* in the Loeb Classical Library.

ment of political reactionaries, stated at great length in the *Republic*, and repeated with no essential change in his other political writings — so they are interpreted for us with varying emphasis by most of Plato's recent critics. Our earlier exposition of their views will permit us here to rival the brevity of the slogan-maker. Popper sees Plato's goal as paradise regained, with slight pseudosophical improvements, by means of the construction on the model of Sparta and Crete of a still more immobile society whose leading principle is "arrest all change." [18] Toynbee, to whose analysis Popper has expressed some indebtedness, speaks of the *Republic* as a desperate attempt to "peg" a disintegrating city-state at the level of an "arrested society" such as Sparta, "worked out to logical extremes" and directed by a "sovereign intellectual caste" of philosophers.[19] Crossman and Fite, while they do not employ the concept of social arrest, are not far behind the others in their emphasis on Plato's dependence upon the Spartan model.[20]

If our discussion appears to have strayed from its official track of totalitarianism, a word of explanation: among our detractors, Popper has brought Spartanism and "arrestment" into intimate relations with the totalitarian state through the concept of the "closed society," which for him is a description applicable alike to Sparta, Plato, and the dictatorships of our time. (The other elements of this conception of the closed society will be separately discussed below.) And to Popper we must add Toynbee, who starting from the resemblance between Plato's state and the "arrested" societies of Sparta and the 'Osmanli Turks, was brought, *via* a consideration of the function of censorship in assuring stability, to compare the *Republic* with Nazism and the U.S.S.R.

Of the two elements comprising this charge we may dispose at once of the suspicion that Plato was an archaist, aiming primarily to reproduce the pattern of the past. In Popper's scheme "archaist" is "historicist," and we have given our reasons for regarding this latter term as inapplicable to Plato. Toynbee, though he has not here applied the word "archaist" to Plato, has undoubtedly applied the meaning. Classifying Plato's cities of the *Republic* and the *Laws* among the literary Utopias, he lays it down that in common with others of their class they express only the felt need to arrest the downward movement of the society within which they were produced; their authors can aim no higher than "holding the ground which has been won for them by their fathers." [21] As evidence, Toynbee points to the passage in the

[18] Popper, pp. 42, 46–55, and *passim*.

[19] Toynbee's views have been described on our pp. 583–585. The relevant passage for our purpose here is vol. III, pp. 90–99.

[20] Crossman, pp. 114–117; Fite, pp. 142–148, 266.

[21] Toynbee, III, p. 89. One Utopia, that of More, Toynbee exempts from this stigma, expressing his astonishment (p. 90 n.) that in an age when the admiration of Greek models stood so high, More was able to resist the restrictive prejudices of Plato and Aristotle to so great a degree, and to espouse "the opposite ideal of elasticity and growth."

Laws in praise of the Athens of Marathon, and says that Plato in both the *Republic* and the *Laws* shows himself the docile pupil of the Spartan statesmen of two centuries before.

Now, we have great admiration for Toynbee's sweep of historical vision; his feat of combining in one *coup d'oeil* nomads, Esquimaux, and Plato, is spectacular and charming. Even his theory of Utopias displays the fertility of its author. But what he has fitted into his scheme is not quite Plato. Toynbee's category of "arrestment" is central to his interest in this section of his inquiry; it can be made central to Plato's political thinking only by displacement of Plato's own center. Indeed, as Toynbee has himself implied, Plato was innovating when he superimposed upon the rank-and-file guardians of the *Republic*, who are the analogues of the nomad's "watch-dogs," the detached philosophers, self-denying servants of the community, whom in other sections of his book Toynbee duly appreciates and acknowledges. Surely this novelty alone (and there are others) provides more than sufficient warrant for classifying Plato in respect of past and future as an eclectic, blending elements of the past with the utterly unprecedented.[22] Who then shall say, save for convenience of classification, that so radical an innovator was content merely to "hold the ground" won for him by his ancestors?

In bringing against Plato the charge that his *Republic* is fundamentally a "Laconizing pamphlet," reaffirmed in all essentials by his *Laws*, the detractors are illustrating the type of charge which eludes classification under the simple headings of "true" and "false," and requires a careful balancing of considerations; since it reproduces *in parvo* the pattern of the larger indictment with which this whole chapter is concerned, identifying Plato substantially with what he undoubtedly in part resembles, it requires a similarly

---

Granted that More's social and economic outlook on some important questions, e.g., slavery, is (as the lapse of eighteen centuries might lead one to anticipate) substantially nearer than Plato's to the accepted standards of the modern world; Toynbee has, none the less, greatly amplified the antithesis, by a simultaneous and opposite misreading of both authors, in more than one respect. Thus, against Toynbee's implication that More favored a growing population may be cited More's regulation requiring limitation of the size of families, and his intention of keeping constant the number of the inhabitants of the state itself (More, *Utopia*, ch. v). And precisely at the two points stressed by Toynbee as evidence of More's superiority, the contrast fails, at least as regards Plato's city of the *Laws*; the marriage ages for Utopian men and women, twenty-two and eighteen re-

spectively, and the control of excess population by the sending out of colonies (More, chs. viii and v), are not, as Toynbee would have us believe, opposed to all Platonic precedent, but could in fact have been copied with minor alterations from the *Laws*; see our pp. 131 and 132, and n. 127, p. 198.

[22] Cassirer (*The Myth of the State*, by Ernst Cassirer, Yale University Press, New Haven, 1946) has supplied a fine appreciation of the fertile novelty of Plato's political philosophy in his chapter VI, esp. pp. 68 ff. He shows Plato's refusal to ground the state either upon sheer tradition or upon sheer power, and accredits to him the creation of the "Legal State," whose foundations are laid in rational theory. "To break the power of the 'eternal yesterday' became one of the first and principal tasks of Plato's political theory" (p. 73).

discriminating reply. If sustained, the charge would find Plato guilty of taking over bodily from Sparta the basic institutions of his ideal city,[23] in so doing choosing the baser part of Spartan boorishness, brutality, and authoritarian narrowness in preference to Athenian humanity and liberality, and by his example and prestige launching on its long career the myth of Sparta, which, it is affirmed, "had a great part in framing the doctrines of . . . national Socialism" and other similar systems of false values.[24]

Fortunately we are not left to infer Plato's outlook upon Sparta from his discussion of other themes. There are many texts, but none more illuminating than the account in *Republic*, Book VIII (547 B ff.) of the deterioration of the ideal state into the species of state called "timocracy," of which Sparta has been named as an example, and the description of this state and its typical citizen. To my reading, the most interesting thing about this passage is the ambivalence of its attitude toward the Spartan way of life. We note the high formal honor implied by its immediate derivation from the perfect state,

---

[23] Crossman and Fite have been somewhat less unfair than this implies, acknowledging to some degree Plato's divergencies from Sparta. — Popper, p. 42, asserts, what would be difficult to document, that "most of Plato's excellent description of their institutions" (i.e., the Spartans' and Cretans') "is given in certain parts of his description of the best state, to which timocracy is so similar." (Timocracy is the name Plato has assigned to the type of state to which Sparta belonged.) Purporting to be summarizing Plato's description of the sequence of states which originate successively from the ideal city, Popper then omits Plato's actual description of timocracy completely, except for mention of its ambition and its instability, and goes on to describe the transition to oligarchy, into which it degenerates. In this way he avoids the necessity of apprising the reader that Plato, in further vital respects, condemns and reprobates the Spartan form of government, an omission which, in the circumstances, amounts to suppression of evidence.

[24] The quotation is from Bertrand Russell, *A History of Western Philosophy*, Simon and Schuster, New York, 1945; Popper has said much the same, p. 42. Few if any contemporary critics have equaled Bertrand Russell in the strength of his conviction, expressed in the book named, that the *Republic* is of Spartan inspiration. The curious feature of Russell's presentation of his case is this: after two preliminary chapters on "The Influence of Sparta" and "The Sources

of Plato's Opinions," in which he declares in the roundest terms that the *Republic* is of purest Spartan pedigree (pp. 94, 104–105), and highly "illiberal," we come to a chapter on "Plato's Utopia" in which Sparta receives but one mention. Russell makes the assertion — not extravagant in itself, though open to reasonable doubt — that Plato's city "will almost certainly produce no art or science, because of its rigidity"; he then adds, "in this respect, *as in others*, it will be like Sparta" (p. 115, italics ours). What these other points of identity may be, we are left to conjecture. From Russell's general comments on Plato's ethical standpoint, pp. 115–118, we should conclude that Russell condemns Plato chiefly as believing in an objective standard of goodness, the knowledge of which is attainable by some few wise persons, not by all, which is to be employed as the basis of social organization in preference to the consensus of opinion or the arbitrament of force; and to this again we need not object. But Russell's scornful and indignant depiction of an inhumane, militaristic, and benighted Sparta, and of a Plato aping and admiring it without reservation, has added to the indictment many counts which, being left unsupported by specific argument or evidence, are unfairly set beyond the reach of reasoned rebuttal by Plato's defender. We shall be forced, therefore, to meet these shadowy arguments indirectly, by exhibiting their conclusions as incompatible with what we hope to establish as true.

which ranks it two degrees above democracy. And that the honor is not wholly formal appears from Plato's specific approval of certain of its characteristic features, such as the respect for rulers, the exclusion of the warriors from all gainful pursuits, and the institution of the common meals for men. Though not enamoured of the philosophic Muse, they have a certain love of music. But, as the most casual reading of the record shows, this is by no means the whole account. The defects of timocracy are many, and, as our general knowledge of Plato's standards allows us to say, severe. Timocracy is born of what Plato everywhere deplores, the love of gain, which overmasters some of the rulers of the ideal state; the resulting struggle terminates in the betrayal of the interests of those "of whose freedom they had been the guardians" (547 B–C). As Plato elsewhere in the *Republic* tells us (416 A–417 B), from now on they will be the "enemies and masters" of their former fellow citizens, "hating and being hated, plotting and being plotted against . . . fearing far more and rather the townsmen within than the foemen without," and, as if to mark their utter contrast to Plato's philosopher kings, transformed from trusty shepherd dogs to "wolves." They become preëminently contentious, ambitious, and preoccupied with war, in which they spend the greater part of their time (548 A, 549 A). These timocrats have further vices of which Plato has shown his detestation and scorn: clandestine violation of law (548 B), "fierce secret lust for gold and silver" finding gratification in "private nests in which they can lavish their wealth" upon their favorites (548 A–B). He marks their harsh treatment of slaves and subservience to superiors, and the absence from their souls of "that best guardian, . . . reason blended with culture." [25] These, manifestly, are not the sentiments of an undiluted Spartophile.

Not only does the *Republic* comment directly upon timocracy. There are also implicit criticisms, favorable and unfavorable, embodied in the institutions of the ideal city. As the detractors have noted, there are similarities to be observed: the unquestioned, willing acceptance of the order of ruling and being ruled, in Plato's city, corresponding to the outward Spartan respect for rulers and for law; the division of the population into the two distinct groups of guardians and workers, corresponding, formally, to the Spartan division into Spartiates and their classes of servile helpers; the prohibition of gold and silver (albeit somewhat differently managed in the two cases); the communal life of the guardians, which can be regarded as an extension of the Spartan messes; the "sacred marriages," remotely resembling the Spartan sanctioning of occasional extramarital relations for eugenic purposes, and the delegation to the state of the power of deciding which infants are to be reared, a decision at Athens apparently exercised by the father.[26] The public educa-

---

[25] 549 A–B. The translations in this paragraph are from Shorey, Loeb Library, slightly altered.

[26] Some of Plato's critics, e.g., Popper, would add the "Glauconic Edict" of *Republic* 468 C. We have given our reasons for

tion of both sexes can be viewed as an extension and development of the
Spartan precedent; the inuring of the young to the spectacle of war is much
in the spirit of Spartan training; and the list could be enlarged by many minor
particulars.

But we cannot fairly weigh the significance of these common traits until
we have observed the alterations Plato has introduced into almost every item.
Whereas at Sparta the land, the houses, the very persons of the lowest class
of the population belonged to the Spartiates and were administered and exploited for their exclusive benefit, Plato's guardians own nothing individually
and as a group receive board-wages only. Their social function is to serve the
common welfare (*Republic* 416 C ff., 420 B ff.); their living together in
common is an expression of this purpose and a guarantee of its scrupulous
fulfillment. Plato's education includes women, up to its topmost reaches;
it lays far more stress upon music, and subordinates gymnastic to the building of character; it is to be conducted by persuasion and play (536 E) and
not by the harsh, resentment-provoking methods of the Spartan disciplinar-
ians (548 B–C). Music is to be strictly censored, but it is noteworthy that
Plato retains as the two permitted modes of music not only the mode suited
to the brave man, steadfast in toils and dangers, but also that suited to that
same man living the life of peace, persuading or teaching, or listening with
open mind to the persuasions of another, "not bearing himself arrogantly,
but in all this acting modestly and moderately and acquiescing in the outcome." [27] Though Plato's guardians are to be tested in endurance of toils
and pains (413 D), he lays no Spartan stress on suffering, and his citizens,
unlike Spartans, are to be exposed also to the suasions of pleasure and to
be tested for their ability to resist its charms (413 E). The very censorship
is different in spirit, aiming at building an ordered soul (411 E–412 A)
rather than at courage alone and conformity. And above all, there is the
higher program of studies with which Plato crowns the education of his
guardians, both men and women, a thing as far beyond even the highest
level of Spartan culture as metaphysical speculation transcends the narrow
boundaries of traditional common sense. The vision of the good thus reached
is the ultimate sovereign authority in Plato's state, as against the blind tyranny of unalterable law. Despite the similarities, and despite the admiration
which Plato, like Socrates before him, feels for the Spartans' virtues, the ad-

---

regarding Glaucon's legislative proposal as
a *jeu d'esprit*, pp. 95–96. — The question of
the exposure of infants at Athens has been
discussed on pp. 195ff.

[27] *Republic* 399 A–B, Shorey's trans.,
Loeb Library. The existence of this second
mode in Plato's state would never be
guessed by any reader who should rely on
Popper for a picture of Plato's proposed

use of music. On p. 54 and again on p. 501
he denies the existence in Plato's scheme
of any modes except such as are designed
to "make the young . . . braver, i.e. fierc-
er," and then speaks of Plato's views as
"almost incredible in their superstitious
intolerance." Our comment must be that
Plato's rather wrong prescriptions have
been wrongly represented.

miration is matched by condemnation, and the similarities are offset by enormous differences in structure, spirit, and aim.

We have still to comment upon the severe censure of the Athenian democracy which Plato implies by placing the Spartan state, with all its recognized flaws, so high above it in his scheme of cities. Undoubtedly he does mean to express his decided preference over democracy for timocracy, abstractly defined as the pursuit of honor rather than of indiscriminate desire. But when the two forms are corrupted into lawless perversions of themselves, the case is altered. In the *Politicus* (302 E f.) the assertion occurs that democracy or the rule of the many, when accompanied with law, falls below the level of the rule of the few with law, and is the least approvable of lawful forms of government; but Plato adds that among the lawless forms, lawless democracy is best, as capable of working the least harm. If we may read the *Republic* in the light of this principle that degree of obedience to law is an essential measure of constitutional excellence, we can explain why, in spite of its official position in the *Republic* so far below timocracy, it does not receive a correspondingly severe arraignment. If we compare the detailed descriptions of the several states, we see plainly that while the democratic man has stirred Plato's ironic contempt, the oligarch and the timocrat have moved his deep moral indignation. If our parallel with the *Politicus* be accepted, this would be because, inconsistently with his avowed intention of exhibiting each one of them at first in its uncorrupted form, Plato has allowed himself to train the batteries of his criticism upon their lawless (and familiar) manifestations.

The impression of Plato's estimate of Sparta which is left by the *Republic* is confirmed and its detailed evidential foundation greatly extended by a reading of the *Laws*.[28] Having doffed the mask of "Socrates" and donned that of the "Athenian," Plato is again alternately, almost simultaneously, praising and blaming the Spartan state and, it should be observed, subjecting Athens to a like treatment. We find in the *Laws* an intricate compound of Spartan institutions and those of the Athenian, particularly the older Athenian constitution, rectified by some political inventions of his own, the whole being informed and directed by Socratic-Platonic moral values.

Although the *Laws* distinguishes no more sharply than did the *Republic* between the "Lycurgan" constitution conceived as operating in its pristine perfection and the realities of fourth-century Spartan life, it is quite clear

---

[28] As we have said, Plato does not tell us in the *Politicus* where he would classify Sparta, which apparently would hover uneasily between the types, both as to the number of rulers and as to lawfulness or lawlessness. Other Platonic dialogues need not detain us long. *Crito* 52 E is an indication of Socrates' appreciation of Spartan obedience to law, and also of Spartan law itself, though in what respects we are not told. *Protagoras* 342 A ff. satirizes the superficiality of Athenian Spartophiles who ape the outside of Spartanism by wearing short cloaks and displaying cauliflower ears. The ascription, in the same passage, of a profound but riddling wisdom to the Spartans, is of course a pleasantry.

that Plato's approvals pertain to the earlier time. He approved the structural complexity or balance of the Spartan constitution, seeing in it an instance of that "mixed" state, tempering "monarchy" with "democracy," which he so highly valued, and which he had found exemplified also in the older Athens and in Persia under Cyrus the Great. He praised it also as aiming at the virtue of its citizens, though, to be sure, only at the fourth and least important part of complete virtue. Among his imitative adoptions, in each case with some modification, these may be listed: (1) the equality and inalienability of the land-lots, a further democratization of the structural basis of the Lycurgan system; (2) the common meals, extended by Plato to women also; (3) prohibition to the citizens of participation in trade and commerce, of travel or communication with foreigners except under severe restrictions, and of the use of a common coinage; (4) censorship of all art and literature; and (5) the encouragement of marriage (of the usual sort) and of the production of children in proper numbers and of good endowment: (6) and (7) universal public education and military training, adopted from Sparta with drastic changes immediately to be noted.[29]

Turning to the departures from Spartan precedent, some of which will be seen to be identical with those observed in the *Republic*, we may list the following:

(1) The classes of inhabitants. — The citizens proper are equal, as at Athens, except for a property qualification for certain offices, similar to a provision of Solon's.[30] The highest office in the state, however, that of Law-

---

[29] References in the *Laws* for these similarities with Sparta are as follows: (1) 745 D, 740, 741 B; (2) 780 A–781 D; (3) 919 D, 953 A–C, 950 D, 942 A; (4) 801, 817, 829; (5) 721 B–C, 783 D–E; (6) Book VII, 804 C–D; (7) 942–943.

The restrictions which Plato imposes upon the admission of strangers to the city of the *Laws* and upon foreign travel by its citizens are certainly un-Athenian and illiberal, but it is perhaps worth noting that they are in large part un-Spartan also; here as elsewhere Plato has consciously refused to adopt unaltered the Spartan way. He will, it is true, keep visitors to the city under supervision, yet they are to be admitted and made welcome (952 D ff.). Delegations as "numerous, honorable and good as possible" are to be sent to the various Hellenic games and congresses of peace (950 E). And approved citizens above the age of fifty are to be allowed to travel abroad at will (951 B ff.), though when they return they are to make no unfavorable comparisons of their own city's laws with those

they have seen elsewhere, except in their confidential reports to the Night Council (cf. our p. 517). Plato believes that thus his city will avoid both stagnation and blind adherence to tradition (951 B–C), and will escape the bad reputation of the Spartans among the rest of mankind as "boorish and harsh" (950 B).

[30] The detailed provisions relating to voting, eligibility to vote and to stand for election, the use of the lot, and the like, regarding each particular office, are too complex for exposition here. The reader is referred to the valuable monograph by A. H. Chase, "The Influence of Athenian Institutions upon the *Laws* of Plato," 1933, pp. 131–192. The author characterizes, in advance, his conclusion, in the telling sentence, ". . . if it be true that the *Laws* savor of earth, the earth is chiefly that of Plato's native Athens" (p. 131), and offers at the close an inclusive list (pp. 189–190) of some sixty parallels between the legal and political features of the two cities. Our earlier promise, p. 332, to show that Plato's legislation

warden, is open to all male citizens, and voters for this purpose likewise include all.[31] It is curious to note that election, thus employed, was regarded by the Athenians as undemocratic, and must be counted among the "oligarchic" features of Plato's state.

(2) *Helotry.* — As we have shown,[32] Plato is well aware of the dangers and injustice of the Spartan institution. He hopes to establish in his Magnesian colony a system free of its evils, in which, though he gives the slave less legal protection than did Athenian democracy, Plato hopes to bring it about by the strong pressure of moral unanimity that he shall be treated with scrupulous justice by a master who feels that his power has not lessened but increased his responsibility for his slave's welfare.[33]

(3) *Militarism.* — We have discussed Plato's "irenic" ideal,[34] and have mentioned the passage (628 D–E) in which, tactfully, in the presence of the Spartan, he rebukes the Spartan tradition for its preoccupation with war: no man will ever make "a finished lawgiver unless he designs his war legislation for peace rather than his peace legislation for war." The aim of his state, as he tells us (962 E–963 A), is not victory over other states, or any of

---

in the *Laws* is heavily indebted to the Solonian code may be vicariously paid by a reference to pp. 190–191 of Chase's monograph, where ten specific parallels are listed. At one point we may dissent from Chase's interpretation, namely, the assertion, p. 134, that Plato has made the amount of a man's landed property the basis of the property classification of citizens. In view of the equal number of citizens and of land allotments, and the inalienability of the allotments, it would be impossible for any citizen to acquire more land than any other, within the state, nor is there any evidence of expected encroachment on neighboring states — rather the reverse (*Laws* 737 D). On the other hand, it is plain (744 B–C) that Plato expected wide variation among the citizens in amount of movable property. That it is this variation which is to be the basis of the property classification thus appears clear from the *Laws* itself, and is confirmed by Aristotle's testimony (for what it is worth), *Politics* II, vi, 1265 b 15.

[31] Plato says (*Laws* 753 B) the voters shall be all men who serve or who have served according to their ability as horse-soldiers or as foot-soldiers, which would seem to include all except cowards or criminals. This fact makes clear the injustice of Popper's sneer (p. 489) that the Law-wardens are to be elected only by the "military class" in Plato's state, though Popper charges Plato elsewhere (p. 538) with making the illiberal requirement that all citizens shall receive military training. In point of fact the election of Law-wardens comes as near as anything in Athenian political practice to satisfying modern standards of democratic government, its only departure from the Athenian democratic ideal being its failure to employ the lot. (It is to be noted that we here refer to the election of Law-wardens as provided for at 753 B–D, not to the arrangement described at 966 C–D and 968 D; this later arrangement we take to be a step toward that possible transformation of the city of the *Laws* into the ideal Republic which Plato permits himself to contemplate at the end of the final book; cf. n. 38, p. 517, below.) Similarly unjust is Popper's charge against Plato of militarism, based on the fact that both of his approved states are to be ruled by "wise ex-soldiers." This is as true for Athens as for Plato's city of the *Laws*.

There exists also in Plato's city the post of Examiner, which, though its duties are restricted, consisting only in ensuring that no official shall transgress the bounds of his office, might be held by virtue of this fact to outrank all other offices. This position also is open to all citizens, and all citizens participate in the election (*Laws* 945 E f.).

[32] See pp. 178–181.

[33] See pp. 179, 181, 182.

[34] See p. 226, and n. 232.

the other commonly pursued aims, but simply "virtue," or, as he elsewhere (701 D) formulates it, independence, internal harmony, and indwelling wisdom. Now it is true that Plato is about to frame a city whose citizens will seemingly devote the greater part of their time to arduous gymnastics and military training. Does this deprive him of his right to criticize Sparta from above? From our modern standpoint, it might appear that it does, so doubtful have most of us grown of the compatibility of continuous active "preparedness" and a genuinely pacific national temper. But not so, if we do Plato the courtesy of distinguishing the probable and contradictory outcome of his intention from the intention itself.

Plato's plan for reconciling military preparedness with a way of life that owed its central allegiance to the ideal of peace might, with some extravagance, be called a prophetic anticipation, with a huge extension in the sphere of application, of Boy-Scoutism. As the Boy Scout, ideally, not only perfectly enjoys what he is about, but is receiving a most admirable moral education and at the same time is strengthening his body and acquiring the various skills that will prepare him to become, on demand, a highly efficient soldier in defense, so Plato conceived that his citizens, with their gymnastic contests and war games, their riding and hunting, and their participation in the athletic but equally aesthetic and morally improving festival dances and choral performances, would be simultaneously preparing for any war that need ever be, achieving their maximum happiness, and fulfilling the divine purpose for man.[35] One might search the literature of antiquity all a long summer's day without discovering a statement of a more pacific ideal.

(4) Education. — The range and depth of purpose marking Plato's plan of education in the *Laws* (described in our text above) [36] is by its very nature an implicit condemnation of the Spartan scheme. True that Plato has not freed himself from all its unfortunate features, deeming them necessary for his communal purposes — for example, censorship — but wherever he has departed, as he so often has, from the Spartan model, he has moved in a direction approvable on modern principles. He could not copy Athens, which had no public system of childhood education.

Other features of the city of the *Laws* which are not Spartan in inspiration include the basically Athenian framework of government, comprising the following set of institutions: its popular Assembly; its Council, adapted, with the addition of the modified property-qualification above mentioned, from the Athenian Council; its elected military officials and its city- and market-stewards; and its council of Law-wardens, corresponding roughly to one

---

[35] For a full exposition of these interpenetrating purposes of Plato's prescriptions regarding athletics, military training, virtue, religion, and happiness, see R. C. Lodge, *Plato's Theory of Education*, 1947, chapter IV, "Education for Citizenship," and for Plato's central thought developed in our paragraph, *Laws* 803 C–E.

[36] See pp. 130–131, 367.

aspect of the court of the Areopagus in its day of power.[37] Add to these the carefully articulated legal system based on the Athenian dicasteries, whose defects did not blind Plato to their many merits. Finally, there is the unique institution of the Nocturnal Council, composed of the ten eldest Law-wardens, the Examiners (all these being popularly elected officials), a few others who have served the state well, and an equal number of their chosen younger companions. This body, despite its alarming name — it should, indeed, have been called the Dawn Council — and its unhappy association in our minds with the death of atheists, is designed by its creator to serve a variety of benign and important purposes. It will be a species of philosophical institute, a practical adaptation of the Platonic Academy, its members presumed to possess philosophic insight and a degree of educated understanding scarcely inferior to that of the philosopher kings. It will be an agency of stabilization and social control, but it will serve also, within carefully restricted limits, as an organ of reform; for it will sit as a perpetual committee on the revision and improvement of the laws, and will supervise the official journeys to foreign parts to bring home news of discoveries which may be of use for the perfecting of the life of the community.[38]

In the light of what we have shown to be Plato's joint incorporation of so much Athenian excellence and his rejection, partial but, as we have seen,

---

[37] No implication is intended that each of these institutions, taken separately, is specifically Athenian; thus the Spartans too possessed an Assembly. It would also have been possible to include in the list the "land-stewards," or "watch-captains" and the system of military training (760 B–763 C) which they conduct, an institution bearing roughly equal resemblance to the Spartan "secret service" and to the training of the Athenian Ephebi. Cf. Chase (op. cit., n. 30, p. 514 above), pp. 151–154. The institutions and offices mentioned are described, in the order given, at Laws 764 A f.; 756 B f.; 755 B f., 759 A f.; 753 B f. The popular courts are described at Laws 767–768.

[38] The references documenting these statements on the Night Council are 769 A ff., esp. 769 D; 951 C–952 C; 960 B–968 B. A word is here in order regarding the change in the status and function of this institution, introduced at the end of the Laws, 969 B ff., and engendering in the entire fabric of Plato's second-best city a contradiction which no quantity of explanation can entirely remove. The sovereign power to form and reform the state in the light of its definitive wisdom which is conferred, thus late in the day, upon this organ

of government, would render idle the whole complex structure of legal and political institutions that Plato has been at such pains to build and for which he had planned so extensive a future. Perhaps the least unsatisfactory disposition of the difficulty is psychological: Plato has never at any time really abandoned his ideal of the philosophic state; he has merely postponed its realization sine die. Coming, at long last, to the concluding section of his extended description of the second-best, with the end of his own mortal career not far from view, he saw and took the opportunity for one last profession of his faith in the attainability of the true human goal. And what better device could the imagination of the ageing dramatist conceive than this most characteristic curtain to his last act of his final play? Our assumption, therefore, is that prior to this final rebirth as a committee for the realization of the Republic, the Night Council was designed to be an important but not omnipotent part of the city, and our remarks in the text refer exclusively to the Council as engaged in activities which leave undisturbed the basic structure of the state.

far-reaching, of so much that is most repellent in the Spartan scheme, the charge of Spartanism reveals itself in the full mendacity of its "half-truth-fulness." It was Xenophon, with the fairy-tale coloration of his *Constitution of the Lacedaemonians,* and bless his innocence, Plutarch with his moralizing *Life of Lycurgus,* and not Plato, who gave the myth of Sparta its pair of wings.

"Holism" and collectivism. — In an earlier chapter we touched upon some aspects of a theme which we must now submit to a more extended analysis: Popper's critique of Plato's so-called "holism," [39] a term which Popper has applied in at least three distinguishable aspects of meaning, whose range and mutual consistency it will be our first task to explore. We shall consider first that part of Popper's interpretation which seeks to bring Plato into complete agreement with a central tenet of totalitarianism as conceived not only by Popper but by all three of our nonpartisan authorities.[40] This is Popper's imputation to Plato of the doctrine that "it is the end of the individual to maintain the stability of the state" [41] and its counterpart, "the criterion of morality is the interest of the state. . . . 'Good is what is in the interest of my group; or my tribe; or my state.'" And from this Platonic-totalitarian theory of morality, we are told, "it is easy to see" that there follows the consequence, destined to be explicitly drawn by Hegel in later centuries, "that the state can never be wrong in any of its actions, as long as it is strong." [42]

To Plato's "holism" thus conceived, Popper has added the advocacy of the famous "organic" theory of the state, as a "permanent collective," a "'natural' unit of a higher order," "within which the different individuals and groups . . . , with their natural inequalities, must render their specific and very unequal services." Combining, now, this doctrine of functional variety among citizens with the exaltation of the state's interest immeasurably above the individual's, Popper ascribes to Plato the belief that "the individual is nothing but a cog," his virtue wholly comprised in his fitness for his social task.[43]

Thus far "holism" has had reference to the whole which is the "tribe" or "state." But Popper has found in Plato another and a wider application that enables him to describe Plato's holism as his "demand that the individual

---

[39] In Popper's lexicon, the term "holism" is graced with no suggestion of emergent novelty and creative advance, ideas which its use in the cosmological system of the late General Smuts has taught many readers to associate inseparably with the term. Nor does Smuts' holism in any sense exemplify what for Popper is the essential viciousness of holism as he employs the term, that is, the brutal indifference of the "whole" to

the rights and values of its parts, its tyrannical disposition to exploit.

[40] Brinton, as will be recollected, included among the characteristics of totalitarianism "nationalism," of a brand which "exalted one national group into masters, all others into slaves" (*op. cit.,* p. 420). Perry lists "tribalism," and McGovern, "etatism."

[41] Popper, p. 97.

[42] Popper, p. 106.

[43] *Ibid.,* pp. 80, 107.

should subserve the interest of the whole, whether this be the *universe"* (italics ours), "the city, . . . or any other collective body." [44] With disapproval he quotes, as "a truly classical formulation of moral holism," a sentence from Plato's sermon addressed in the *Laws* (903 C) to the young disbeliever who is unaware of the moral unity of the World-All: "all partial generation is for the sake of the Whole, . . . it not being generated for thy sake, but thou for its sake." [45]

In the inconsistency of the meaning which Popper has thus assigned to Plato's "holism" lies the first and most fatal weakness of Popper's position. For how can a "moral holist," whose "whole" is the universe, be simultaneously a political holist, for whom "the criterion of morality is the interest of the state"? The contradiction is palpable, but from it there is one escape open to whoever is willing to commit the supreme anachronism of endowing Plato with modern, quasi-Hegelian categories. On this audacious assumption it could be argued that the universe is so controlled by the High God, whose delight is continual contradiction, that each state as a political "whole" is rightly the master of its own "parts," and at the same time is rightly the opponent of all other "wholes," the moral oneness of the universe manifesting itself in God's unfailing approval of each successively victorious whole. This is a path few would venture upon; nevertheless some such attribution to Plato of ideas of which he was, so to say, systematically unaware, alone can provide escape from contradiction for anyone who, with Popper, would press upon Plato the charge of holism both political and cosmic.

It is our privilege, therefore, by an odd turn of the argument, to accept (with the reservation presently to be noticed) [46] Popper's charge that Plato

---

[44] *Ibid.,* p. 99.

[45] *Ibid.,* p. 80. We give the *Laws* passage as translated by Bury, Loeb Library. Certain alterations that Popper has introduced into his second edition constitute recognition of an earlier error in fact, but substitute for this error the inconsistency noted in the text above, between Plato's alleged doctrine that state-interest is the criterion of right, and the "moral holism" now added to the charge. In the first edition, p. 69, Popper cited as "a truly classical formulation of political holism" the admonition to the young atheist; in the second edition, p. 80, the word "moral" has replaced "political." Similarly, on p. 87, where originally the only wholes mentioned as those to which the "holist" will sacrifice the individual, are city, tribe, and race, there has now, on p. 99, been added the universe as well. In a rewritten footnote, p. 517, while acknowledging the cosmic reference of the admoni-

tion to the atheist, he has contented himself with reiterating his conviction that, even so, the "underlying tendency" of Plato's holism is political. (Ast's lexicon and I have been quite unable to verify Popper's assertion, made in this connection, that "Plato often uses 'holon' (esp. the plural of it) to mean 'state' as well as 'world.' ") By thus recognizing the absence of a principal prop on which his argument had been sustained without making the entailed adjustment in his interpretation of Plato's thought (except for the attempt noted to broaden the charge), Popper exemplifies a tendency shown also in other changes made in the second edition (see pp. 603 and 629, and cf. n. 17, p. 21, and n. 121, p. 454) to correct factual errors without abandoning or altering in Plato's favor the conclusions to which they had originally served as premises.

[46] See pp. 528–529 below.

is a moral holist, and to employ this as a premise in demonstrating that Plato did not sponsor the theory that the state's interest is the ultimate criterion of right. Such a theory is clearly a form of ethical particularism, to be classified under the general heading of moral relativism. Can it be shown that Plato's ethical doctrine is rooted in a universalistic absolutism radically opposed to relativism in all its forms? We have earlier maintained precisely this position,[47] and the very passage that Popper has cited from the *Laws* as proof of Plato's moral holism will serve well to remind us of the cosmic universalism of Plato's ethics. For Plato, there was no world but one, the "only-begotten" of the *Timaeus* (31 B), and no set of moral principles but those everlastingly implicit in the nature of that world; and the young disbeliever is admonished, in language that mingles popular religious imagery and Plato's own theological doctrine, that one cosmic law determines the fate of every soul for good or ill, in accordance with its own free moral choices. Divine providence is at work (903 B–C) looking to "the preservation and excellence of the whole," and every soul "tends therefore always in its striving toward the All." That the life of man is bound to the divine order is specifically asserted again (*Laws* 645 A), in the striking image of the "golden cord" of reason or *logismos*, which is also law in the true sense of the word: "with that most excellent leading-string of the law we must needs coöperate always"; it is needful "for the individual man to grasp the true account of these inward pulling forces and to live in accordance therewith, and . . . for the State . . . to make this into a law for itself and be guided thereby in its intercourse both with itself and with all other States." We see, then, the subordination of both individual and state to a divinely sanctioned norm. The whole scheme of morals and theology is embraced in the pregnant aphorism, a bold rephrasing of the dictum of Protagoras, "God is the measure of all things" (*Laws* 716 C) — the measure, that is to say, of the excellence of man. The very purpose of the state, as we have seen, is the production of the best possible human beings,[48] and since this is so, Plato goes so far as to declare

---

[47] This position, implicit in our ch. 6, pp. 201–232, is stated in terms on pp. 250f.

[48] *Laws* 770 C–D. Passages can be quoted from the *Laws* (as Rogers has done; cf. p. 642 below) to prove that Plato's aim was not so much to develop individual human excellence as to promote good citizenship. Thus Plato declares that true education is "training from childhood in goodness, which makes a man eagerly desirous of becoming a perfect citizen, understanding how both to rule and be ruled righteously," and again that it is "the process of drawing and guiding children toward that principle which is pronounced right by the law and confirmed as truly right by the experience of the oldest and the most just" (*Laws* 643 E and 659 D, trans. Bury, Loeb Library). But, in view of the passage we have cited in our text, it is clear that the primary aim remains moral and not political, in so far as for Plato these terms admit of separation. As Rogers himself does not deny, Plato, in stressing the "sociological," does not in his own terms remit any of the conditions demanded for the goodness of the individual soul; the qualities he would exact from the good citizen are simply those, so far as they can be attained, which define the good man, and the principles "pronounced right by the law" are, in Plato's state, to be coextensive with morality. It is

(770 D–E), it is the duty of every citizen of a state which does not adhere to this aim to "allow it to be revolutionized . . . rather than to change to a polity which naturally makes men worse." [49] Popper has told us that from Plato's equation, "good = the state's interest," there follows the obvious consequence that the state can do no wrong either against its own citizens or against other states, so long as it remains strong. Does not Plato's denial of this consequence do all that was logically necessary to prove that the alleged equation was none of his?

If this be considered still insufficient proof that the province of morality is not for Plato coterminous with the area of the state, we may turn to the *Republic*, which may be said to tell the same story in accents more philosophical and less devout, though the description of the last stages of the dialectic ascent into the transcendental sunlight of the Idea of the Good glows with a genuinely religious feeling; and in the Myth of Er, at its conclusion, we have, again, moral truths cloaked in sacred mythology. There is the same recognition that good is not a mere commodity of mortal contrivance and manufacture, but a discovery and an acknowledgment. The philosopher is he who is most pious in his admission of the authority of this cosmic morality, and most adept in its discovery and application. It follows that Plato's chief political commandment, the bringing of the philosopher into governmental command, issues in a result directly contrary to what political holism as Popper has defined it can endure. The vesting of authority in philosophic reason presents itself as the true "holism," to which all lesser wholes must bow on pain of irrationality and contradiction. The true philosopher of Plato's moral imagining is he who delivers this mandate to the community, and the well-conditioned community is that which consents most completely to its benevolent demands.[50]

---

again a case of "consilience" (cf. pp. 64, 413, 439–440, 528–529, 555–556.)

Similar considerations seem sufficient to meet the argument of Dodds (*The Greeks and the Irrational*, 1951, p. 224). Dodds sees in the religious prescriptions of the *Laws* nothing of religion *per se*, merely statecraft and an engine of social control. *Laws* 885 D and 888 B, which Dodds cites, show Plato's belief that such tenets as he imposes are necessary to ensure that men shall "do justice" and "live nobly." That such behavior would be socially useful is clear; but is it not equally clear that, to Plato, these are also prime goods for the individual citizen? And Dodds himself has stoutly maintained (e.g., pp. 234–235) that Plato stands fully committed to the essential truth of the religion he would impart. Dodds' suggested alternative, either an agent of social control,

or (like the Inquisition) a dedicated effort to save souls, is not for Plato a genuine one. It presents, rather, the two indiscerptible parts of the same whole.

[49] The translations are from Bury, Loeb Library.

[50] The "documentation" of the position maintained in the two paragraphs of the text above seems superfluous for anyone who has read the *Republic*, especially Books VI–VII, in which the metaphysical basis of Plato's ethical and social system is revealed. Even those who regard Plato as in an important sense a totalitarian can still distinguish clearly between the sort of totalitarian to whom the ultimate ground of authority is power unrestricted by morality, and Plato's manifest appeal to transcendental sanctions; see, for Crossman's recognition of this fact, our n. 26, p. 250, and for like testimony by

We shall consider, then, that we have warrant to assert that Plato is not a "political holist," a "nationalist," a "tribalist," or an "etatist," so far as this means a worshipper of the state. We have still to weigh the justice of the complaint that Plato supported the organic theory of the state and ruthlessly sacrificed to the collective the individualities and happiness of its citizens.

Elliott and McDonald, *Western Political Heritage*, 1949, pp. 12 and 97, as compared with their description of Hobbes on pp. 442 and 446. The distinction is, indeed, so palpable that one feels it necessary to ask how Popper can have managed to avoid a collision with it. The answer has been delivered to us at some length by Popper himself: he first convinces himself (pp. 143–144) that the idea of the good is mere "empty formalism" of no ethical or political utility; then by a flat misquotation of *Republic* 608 E (he translates, pp. 37 and 143, " 'good is . . . everything that preserves,' and 'evil . . . everything that destroys or corrupts,' " whereas the Greek says "good" is "that which preserves *and benefits*," etc.), he further degrades it into a mere fixative or agent of arrestment. He then reminds us of the reason he has assigned — the fear of independent thought — for Plato's delaying till the age of thirty the beginning of ethical criticism, and until that of fifty the final induction of the philosopher-kings-to-be into the highest reaches of philosophy (cf. App. XII, p. 618f.). From all these considerations he infers (p. 145) that Plato could not really have required a resident philosopher in his city merely for the purpose of knowing so barren an emptiness as the Idea of the Good and must have had some ulterior and wholly political purpose; and without more ado he assigns two such discreditable aims (cf. pp. 438 and 450 above), both local to the ideal city. We observe here Popper's readiness to suppose that because he (and Grote, whom he quotes, pp. 588–589, as being of the same opinion) can see no content in the Good of Plato, therefore Plato cannot himself have attached to it any importance, and his parallel certainty that because he himself sees the unwisdom of deferring philosophical inquiry till full maturity, therefore Plato himself must have been equally aware of it. Underlying both of these is Popper's easy assumption of Plato's duplicity, the quick conclusion that we can brush aside what Plato says and ferret out hidden motives —

discreditable, of course, else why should he have hidden them? In view of our painstaking consideration, in an earlier chapter, of all the props upon which Popper has rested his accusation of dishonesty, we feel justified in ruling out of court any of Popper's arguments which, like those just reported, require it as a premise.

This same postulate of Plato's disingenuousness with his reader has led Popper similarly (cf. our p. 358) to discount the sincerity of Plato's religious beliefs as expressed in the *Laws*. We are told that Plato was "perhaps himself an atheist," but that in any case he certainly subordinated completely to political convenience whatever religion he may have felt. (Popper's original misinterpretation, as purely political in tendency, of the passage regarding the moral unity of the World-All, was probably a result of this suspicion; see our note 45, p. 519.) It may be suggested that Popper has been assisted to his unfortunate conclusion by a failure to distinguish between Plato's outlook upon popular religious beliefs and Plato's own personal, philosophic religion. Plato deemed it necessary that popular religion should be purged of what he felt to be its crudities and impieties; thus purified, he was willing to accept it as a set of more or less adequate symbols for the expression of the deeper penetrations into the divine nature, to which alone the methods of philosophy can conduct. It is only by a radical confusion of categories that one can inquire into the honesty or dishonesty of Plato's acceptance of mythological symbols (for a discussion of Plato's attitude on such points, see n. 71, p. 429; pp. 433–435). To set right this error, we may point first to Popper's own admission, in his second edition, that Plato seriously believed in the transcendent moral whole which is the universe, and expresses this belief in the *Laws*; we may adduce the religious grandeur of the *Timaeus*, certainly not to be explained as "political opportunism"; and we may again object that there is no evidence that Plato is bent on deceiving his reader.

The greatest hindrance to a fair determination of our issue is terminological, as we shall perforce be employing terms not only difficult to define, but refractory and, so to say, determined to do our thinking for us by settling all questions in advance: "organicism," "collectivism," "anti-individualism," these resist being employed in anything less than the totality of their meaning. To attempt it is like trying to call a man one-third of a murderer. But let us, with the encouragement of Humpty-Dumpty's precedent, see which of us is master — words or we.

From the various texts which Popper has called to his support [51] we shall select as fairly representative three, one chosen from the *Republic* and two from the *Laws*. In the first, the happiness of the guardian class of the ideally "happy" city is being called in question by the respondent, Adeimantus, who feels that "Socrates" is imposing upon them unduly heavy burdens and restraints. To this challenge, gladly accepted, comes the reply,

while it would not surprise us if these men thus living prove to be the most happy, yet the object on which we fixed our eyes in the establishment of the state was not the exceptional happiness of any one class but the greatest possible happiness of the city as a whole . . . . these helpers and guardians are to be constrained and persuaded to do what will make them the best craftsmen in their own work, and similarly all the rest. And so, as the entire city develops and is ordered well, each class is to be left to the share of happiness that its nature comports.[52]

In the first passage from the *Laws*, the discussion turns not on happiness but on what is deemed the basic condition of happiness: the submission of the community as a whole to the rule of law. The division of the state into parties with rival interests, each with "a watchful eye on the other," is deplored, and it is said that "such polities we, of course, deny to be polities, just as we deny that laws are true laws unless they are enacted in the interest of the common weal of the whole State. But where the laws are enacted in the interest of a section," such "justice" is "an empty name." And again:

That State and polity come first . . . where . . . throughout the whole State . . . there is community of wives, children, and all chattels, and all that is called "private" . . . is rooted out of our life . . . and even things naturally private have become in a way "communized," — eyes, for instance . . . seem to see . . . in common, — and all men are, so far as possible, unanimous in the praise and blame they bestow, rejoicing and grieving at the same things.[53]

"The city as a whole," "the whole State," "all that is called 'private' " — in these words the major issue is brought before us, to be determined largely by the meanings we assign them. For Popper the "whole" in question is an abstract omnivorous holistic whole, that feeds upon the concrete private values of its unhappy parts; alternatively, Popper has expressed this same criticism

---

[51] Others are *Republic* 424 A, 449 B–E, 462 A–C; *Laws* 875 A, 923 B, 964 E (Popper, p. 517). On his use of *Laws* 942 A f. we shall comment below, p. 531ff.

[52] *Republic* 420 B, 421 B–C, trans. Shorey, Loeb Library.

[53] *Laws* 715 A–B, and 739 B–D, trans. Bury, Loeb Library.

by imputing to Plato the vicious aestheticism of employing the private lives of his citizens as so much insensate paint or clay in the hands of the political artist, who forces it into the rigid pattern of his archaic ideal.[54] We may pass rapidly over the impressionist reasons which apparently lie behind this interpretation, among them, presumably, the supposed exploitation and harsh repression of the "human cattle," the denial to the philosopher kings themselves of any real intellectual freedom, and the addiction of Plato to the vacuous authoritarianism of the Theory of Ideas, matters with which we have dealt elsewhere. We shall turn, instead, to a more direct consideration of Plato's meaning when he speaks thus of the individual and his relation to the whole.

Was Plato an anti-individualist? We should have learned by now that it is of little use to try to extract Plato's answer to the great problems by asking him questions to be answered with a simple "yes" or "no." Plato's outlook on the individual must be broken down into several aspects, of which the first and least disputable is his condemnation of individualist selfishness, the "private" in the sense of "mine-and-you-can't-have-it." We may feel that in setting up as his ideal for this reason, as we have seen him do, the common ownership of all property, even of wives and children, he was carrying matters to an unreasonable extreme; it is true that he himself did not attempt the complete realization of this ideal, even in the perfect city. But we may certainly sympathize with his wish to escape as far as possible the conflict of selfish interests which had been the plague of Greece, and particularly of his native city.

Plato's second disparagement of the individual — to us his chief failure here — arises from his acknowledged principle that there is but one truth, one standard of right, and his consequent failure to approve the value of the individual point of view; put in another way, this means that he did not in theory acknowledge the preciousness of individual variations, save for those variations which carry the exceptional individual closer to the ideal. Still less could he be expected to appreciate — or even tolerate — that luxuriance of individual caprice, unguided by any unifying principle, of which he has presented a lively satirical image in his portrait of the "democratic man" (*Rep.* VIII, 561 A ff.). We shall have a further word to say on this topic shortly.

Thirdly, he disapproved individualism (as is well known and truly charged against him), in the sense that he believed the average individual incapable of self-direction and in need of guidance and protection against error. Indeed, this flaw in Plato's social theory will be found to be at the heart of almost every charge we are considering in this chapter, and lends to each of these in turn whatever air of truthfulness it may possess. What has been denounced as an associated defect in Plato's treatment of the ordinary citizens

---

[54] Popper, pp. 161–163; cf. our pp. 438–439.

is his assignment to them of those "banausic" tasks which he conceived to be harmful to the body and dangerous to the soul. But as we have shown above, Plato's convictions about the high responsibilities of government on the one hand and the harmful effects of labor on the other, placed him in a dilemma from which there was no escape which could completely meet his own requirements, still less one which could have satisfied his modern critics.[55]

There are, however, other components of individualism toward which Plato is far more favorably disposed. He wished his guardians to achieve the fullest development possible to man. As individuals they were to possess not only the ability to direct others wisely but also the crowning grace of full rational self-command. Further, in the *Laws* (768 A–B) there is unmistakable recognition of a value very near the heart of individualism, when Plato affirms that all citizens shall share in prosecution of offenses against the state and shall serve their turn as judges in the popular court, giving the very individualist reason that otherwise they will have no feeling that the state is their state. Add to this that, by implication in the *Republic*, but with full explicitness in the *Laws* (720–724), Plato proposes that all citizens shall be regarded as persons having a right to be given the reasons for what is required of them

---

[55] Plato's disposition of the problem in the *Republic* is discussed on pp. 240–242; in the *Laws*, on pp. 259–261.

Plato's belief in the difficulty and precariousness of human virtue, and his consequent proposal to guard all his citizens during their formative years and all but the chosen few throughout life from enticements and distractions of the most varied kinds, have also been seen as a grave fault, indicative of a jaundiced view of human nature (Fite; cf. our p. 79), or of a totalitarian overestimate of the province of the state (Popper; cf. our n. 130, p. 557). But Plato's attitude here has another and a more engaging face. For example, in the *Theaetetus* (173 A–B), to the disparaging sketch of the addict of the law courts, with his shrewd but petty and benighted soul, Plato is careful to add that the character of such a man is a natural consequence of the environmental pressures that molded the tender young soul, warping it from its proper form. Similarly in the *Republic*, we heard (p. 79) Plato's Adeimantus declare that not innate depravity but false teaching is responsible for the worldly estimate of justice held by most men. Again, in the *Timaeus* (86 B–87 B) Plato repeats his exoneration of those whom bad education has

deprived of virtue, adding the further excuse that many wrong-doers are victims of bad physical constitutions and maladies.

In passages such as these we may measure the distance separating the idealist-reformer Plato from that cynical class-bound realist, the Old Oligarch, and we may recognize Plato's kinship to the modern liberal who seeks to abolish crime not by destroying criminals but by removing the conditions which produce them and to interpose between the younger generation and the possibility of wrong-doing a more salutary moral and physical environment. And though we should wish to draw the line between wholesome and dangerous occupations at a different point, it is still true, as the morning paper continues daily to remind us, that the performance of many socially important functions is morally too hazardous for many of our fellow citizens. We may smile at what seems to us Plato's rather naïve protectionism, but we cannot in our thoughtful moments dismiss as a mere whimsy his demand that the frailty of human virtue be reënforced by all the institutional agencies at our command, both for the sake of the individual offenders and for the welfare of the community against which they offend.

and to be patiently convinced by persuasion. The unfortunate deceptions, of which we hear so much from Plato's critics, are expedients seldom resorted to and do not touch the moral teaching which is to be imparted, teaching simplified and even sometimes couched in mythological terms, but based on standards which are those of Plato himself.

And there is another sense in which the individual, as end and not as means, is acknowledged by Plato, who has remembered that every man, or as we should say, the common man, has creaturely needs that must be met before concern with higher values becomes possible. Plato's state will guarantee to every one of its members, as Bertrand Russell has rather acidulously admitted, "enough to eat" [56] and security of life and limb. There will be freedom from exploitation and abuse — Plato is desperately in earnest in his determination to prevent the common citizens from having any just cause for feeling themselves exploited or mistreated. If anyone in the Republic is to be discriminated against economically, it is his intention that it shall be the guardian class, for whom, however, other satisfactions are provided. To talk of the nonguardian citizens as "cattle" where there is no "milking," as "sheep" where none is to be "shorn," implies a type of discrimination of which there is to be no trace. The city of the Laws, less perfect in its plan, will indeed "shear" its slaves; so did Athens; for we must remember that, though near Utopia, Plato's second-best city was still within the confines of the ancient slave-holding world. But the citizens of the Laws are not intended to batten on one another, or violate one another's rights with impunity.

But Plato is concerned with individual interests on another and higher level. He would have been guilty of the betrayal of his old master had he dropped from his heart and mind the concern for the spiritual welfare of all men within the radius of his influence. The virtue which he will enable each of his citizens to achieve, as the very health of his soul, is not, it is true, identical for everyone. The weaker soul may achieve only a vicarious participation in "the divine governing principle" which "the best man . . . has within himself" (Republic 590 C); for the average man, knowledge firm and unshakable will be replaced by true opinion which, taking over the direction of emotion and appetite, will provide his inner polity with that due order which is Platonic justice. In him it will be unable to sustain itself unaltered without the external support of good government or wise laws. But given such support, "we all," says Plato, "so far as possible may be akin and friendly, because our governance and guidance are the same.[57]

We may here notice a certain noble inconsistency which Plato introduces into his later ethical doctrine. In the Republic, as we have seen, it is neces-

---

[56] Russell, on the page (115) of his History cited in n. 24, p. 510.
[57] Republic 590 D, trans. Shorey, Loeb Library, slightly altered. Cf. our n. 202, p. 217.

sary that each man, to be accounted just, must have true knowledge or right opinion of the good; in the *Laws,* Plato goes so far as to allow a man to have that coveted appellation by merely holding fast to "the opinion of the best," though he be at the same time sadly mistaken in his beliefs, and even guilty, because of them, of "great and brutal wrongs" (*Laws* 864 A, 863 C). This passage, with its "deontological" approval of the good man tragically mistaken, registers Plato's highest flight into the stratosphere of moral individualism.

But even leaving this more radical individualism out of account as an insight with which the rest of Plato's thought was never fully aligned, we can credit to Plato a significant degree of individualism as a constant feature of his ethics. The virtues of his citizens are not identical with the mere fitness of each man to perform his civic task. They are also the inalienable personal property of their individual possessors. They would retain their full validity as a true standard of performance in any other society or in solitude, and they constitute the only wealth which a man carries with him out of this world.[58] Virtue, and its enjoyment, happiness, are the two foci of Plato's concern for his fellow men. With the partial exception of the most technical of his writings, it is true to say that every Platonic dialogue is a monument erected to his belief that individual men have a right to be considered important, and that their happiness and its enabling condition, justice done to them and by them, are the primary interests of a philosopher.

Once we recognize Plato's altruistic concern for the welfare of the individual, compromised for us though it is by its failure to include under welfare the right and duty of self-direction, we are the better prepared to follow Plato's thinking on the theme of political wholes and their relation to their members, and to measure the appropriateness of calling him a "collectivist." It is not conceivable that any serious and liberal critic could so far forget the assumptions upon which liberalism itself, along with other political faiths, is built, as to rebuke Plato for appealing to the idea of a whole, or human group, to which allegiance is due and in whose interest sacrifice is proper to be made. Dissent can begin only when the claim of the whole is believed to take serious and unnecessary toll of primary human values. Such is the case, we may agree, when the whole distorts and diminishes the individuals that compose it. And for this fault Plato's whole of the state, as we have seen, must be held in some degree accountable, though without his wish that it should be so; since what to him is full development of all the excellence that each individual is capable of attaining, is for us too often imperfection and curtailment. In the absence of freedom, at best a subservient and cloistered

---

[58] The important implications of this tenet for Plato's relation to individualism are suggested below, n. 63.

virtue can be looked for, and this, for the majority of Plato's citizens, though not for all, would be the summit of attainment.

A political whole or state is pernicious, likewise, when it is conceived as a sort of super-entity, hovering above the heads of its concrete citizens, gathering into itself all value, and depriving them individually of any title to consideration as against its sovereign claim. Of the existence of such a monster in Plato's thought we hear nothing.[58] Plato's ideal city consists simply of its citizens in action according to the plan of its constitution. There is, of course, the eternal "idea" of the city, its pattern in heaven. But to appeal to this in support of "statism" proves much too much; for in this transcendent sense, so is there also a "heavenly model" of the man and citizen. It is true, as Popper has noted,[59] that on Plato's view the dissolution of the state can come only from the imperfections and failings of its members; it is no less true — as he has failed to point out — that its perfection too is the product of the qualities of its citizens: the state is wise and brave through the wisdom and courage of the superior few, harmonious and just through the participation in virtue of all its citizens.[60] Nor has the excellence of the city of the *Laws* any other source. The religion of the superorganic state cannot be found in Plato's writings, and no quantity of Platonic references to the interest of the whole or the good of the state proves more than that Plato is mindful of the common interest and the shared good of its citizens.[61]

This position may be reënforced by some passages in which the citizens appear as beneficiaries of the operation of the principle of the whole. A review of the texts earlier quoted [62] will show that they are pervaded with a common principle, whether the "whole" in question is "moral" or political. The supposition is that wherever a right standard is established, as it necessarily is, under divine rule, in the Cosmos, and as it may and should be in a human community, a reciprocity of interest exists between the larger and the smaller terms of the relation. It is never a case of the tracks leading in and only in to the lion's den. Our familiar young atheist is told, "What is best in thy case for the All turns out best for thyself also, in accordance with the power of your common origin." [63] And the guardians, whose expansive free-

---

[58] There is, in fact, however, some hint of a superstate in Pericles' oration. See pp. 287–288 above.

[59] Popper, p. 81.

[60] *Rep.* 428 E, 429 B, 431 E, 433 C; see also *Rep.* 435 E.

[61] Our text parallels, at a respectful distance, the admirable evaluation of the political theory of the *Republic*, contained in Chapters III and IV of H. W. B. Joseph's *Essays in Ancient and Modern Philosophy*, Oxford, Clarendon Press, 1935, a book which deserves a place in any reader's medi-

cine chest as an antidote against anti-Platonic poisoning.

[62] See pp. 520 and 523 above.

[63] *Laws* 903 D, trans. Bury, Loeb Library. Cf. *Laws* 875 A, trans. Bury: "it benefits both public and private interests alike when the public interest, rather than the private, is well enacted."

Comparison of the view stated in the text with that of Solmsen, *Plato's Theology*, 1942, pp. 153–159, will reveal substantial agreement in spite of apparent divergence. The ideal of individual self-effacement for

dom and satisfactions, as these are commonly conceived, must be forgone in the execution of their duty, receive full compensation for their sacrifice: theirs is to be "a happier life than . . . that of the victors at Olympia." [64] In short, there is no Moloch here.

And finally, wholes are plainly bad when they serve as the vehicle of what Popper has called "group selfishness," a partnership of individuals willing to abandon their private interest to their group, as the price of its ability to dominate and exploit for their benefit other groups and individuals.[65] But Plato, as we have seen, has used no part of his energy in advocacy of such a whole.

When once we have overcome these false suspicions, then, like visitors to a temple in some strange land, who no longer believe it to be the shrine of a man-eating god, we should be able to look about us in Plato's city and find there something to admire. The city into which we have stepped is a whole that not only lacks the sinister quality Popper has imputed to it, but possesses positive merits in its own right. Plato does not in so many words make it a part of virtue that the good man shall feel a sense of nearness and community of interest with others, but he tacitly operates throughout with this assumption, which was presupposed also by Socrates.[66] For Plato, this unity will be most deeply felt between kinsmen, but will extend, with diminishing intensity, to fellow citizens, fellow Greeks, and beyond them, though here little more than the debt of justice is acknowledged, to mankind at large.[67] As applied to the organization of a single community, this principle is expressed in the sentence already quoted [68] from the *Laws*, which speaks of the common griefs and joys uniting the citizens of a truly ideal community. In the *Republic*, this same idea appears in the celebration of that community of feeling which exists when, "so far as may be, all the citizens rejoice and grieve alike . . . when

---

the good of the whole Solmsen believes the Greeks generally had derived from their political experience; in Plato also he finds the concept of a "Whole" whose interests are paramount and for whose sake its parts exist, a "Whole" exemplified alike in Plato's divinely ordered universe and in his ideal state. One might well infer that in Solmsen's eyes Plato is prepared to sacrifice the individual either to state or to Cosmos. On the contrary, Solmsen counts it for righteousness and for originality as well that to Plato "nothing is more essential and nothing more precious than individual souls"; unlike his predecessors Solon, Aeschylus, and Sophocles, Plato was not content to believe that the gods punish the innocent for the sins of their fathers or their fellow-citizens, but teaches that for each separate soul divine providence will secure full justice. To read Plato's political doctrines in this light will dispel sinister misconceptions of the meaning of his political "Whole."

[64] *Republic* 465 D f., trans. Shorey, Loeb Library.

[65] We are again reminded of Pericles' celebration of Athens' greatness, as proved by its hegemony over more Greeks than any other city; cf. Thucydides II, 65, and our pp. 288–289; and for Plato's rejection of this ideal, notes, p. 226.

[66] See p. 213.

[67] This statement is a generalization from widely scattered texts, many of which we have earlier discussed. See, e.g., pp. 425–431; 172f.; 173ff.; 213ff., esp. 232.

[68] On p. 523.

any one of the citizens suffers aught of good or evil." And here again Plato uses the simile which, to Popper, reveals Plato's vicious organicism, in which the state is likened to a man whose bodily organism, when one of its members is wounded, "feels the pain as a whole." [69] In the ideal city, we remember, all citizens are to be taught by the myth of the metals to regard themselves as brothers, and rulers and common citizens call each other respectively "Nurturers" and "Helpers," while within the band of guardians the names and feelings appropriate to a single family bring with them peace and concord. In the polity of the *Laws*, though the close tie of kinship is abandoned, its place is taken by the "friendship" or "dearness to itself" [70] which is among the supreme blessings of the city. It is plain that when Plato speaks of an organism, what is in his mind is not voracity, but mutuality of support and sympathy which the group enables each of its members to enjoy both as donor and as recipient.

On balance, then, while it would be a partisan misuse of language to term Plato an "individualist," that fact need not hide from us Plato's feeling for the individual as the ultimate reality here below, for the sake of whom the social framework is constructed, whose quality imparts character to the community, and whose destiny outdures that of the state which is his transitory and terrestrial home.[71] Nor will we go to war over any word, even those of

---

[69] *Republic* 462 C–D, trans. Shorey, Loeb Library.

[70] *Laws* 693 B–C. Other passages in which this concept is involved are *Rep.* 590 D, quoted on p. 526, where it is said that all inhabitants of the city will be "friendly" or "dear" to one another, being subject to the same just rule, and *Rep.* 621 C, where Socrates declares that, living righteously and wisely, we shall be "dear to ourselves" — harmonious within, like a happy city — and dear to the gods.

[71] We may in this place give some account of Popper's category of "altruistic individualism," from which he sharply distinguishes what he takes to be Plato's position. Popper (pp. 99–103) sees Plato's attitude toward the individual as altogether "anti-humanitarian and anti-Christian," and holds that Plato, by consciously attempting to represent individualism as simply selfishness, has misled guileless readers in all ages, including such Platonic critics as England and Barker, who do homage to Plato's deceptive advocacy of collectivism; thus Plato has brought confusion into speculation on ethical matters which it has been reserved for Popper to set right.

On his way to this end Popper has told us that a man may qualify as an "altruistic individualist" if he is "ready to make sacrifices in order to help individuals," and Popper has found this attitude exemplified in Dickens, who hated selfishness and felt "passionate interest in individuals with all their human weaknesses." It is found also in Pericles' recommendation of tolerance for the vagaries of fellow citizens, combined with willingness to protect them from injustice; in the Christian doctrine, "love your neighbor"; and in the Kantian doctrine that individuals must be regarded as ends, not as means only. Among these criteria, we observe more than one which would entitle Plato to membership in the group they define. For though, as we have seen, Plato did not admit the value of the individual's determination of what, for him, shall be truth, and though he did not, like Dickens, delight in individual idiosyncrasies, or like Pericles, view them with tolerance, or attach a high value to the relief of suffering, he cared for souls, and felt concern for others' happiness and mutuality of feeling and for their right to justice here on earth. An instance or two: There is the obvious paternal concern of the Platonic Socrates for the spiritual advancement of

the fighting variety, and will accordingly consent to call Plato a "collectivist," but with the all-important proviso that what he was collecting and uniting in sympathy was nothing else than as perfect and inoffensive as possible a collection of individuals.

We have now to deal with a passage from the *Laws* expressive of Plato's disapproval of one aspect of individualism, a passage of which Popper has made great and illegitimate use. His journalistic misapplication of a selection from it on the dust cover and on the title-page of Part I of his book, will be dissected in our note, where also we print the passage in full.[72] We shall here discuss his handling of it in his text.

---

his young companions, Glaucon and Adeimantus, the same attitude shown, with minor variations, in almost every dialogue from first to last (pp. 366–367), and the altruistic satisfaction taken by the "true rhetorician" in the *Phaedrus* in employing his art to procure for his pupil "the highest happiness possible to man" (cf. p. 364). In the *Laws*, despite his too strict legislation regarding slaves, there is still Plato's warning that a master is never free to forget his slaves' inalienable right to justice at his hands (777 D–E; cf. p. 179), and there is also the declaration that Zeus, the avenger of injustice, guards the stranger (729 E; cf. p. 230). We also claim the right, though Popper will not admit it, to cite Plato's altruism on behalf of his ideal citizens, who, though they figure collectively in the discussion, are yet conceived as individual recipients of the benefits he wishes to bestow. In short, Popper, having found some important aspects of altruistic individualism missing from Plato's set of values, has confused the entire issue by denying the existence of those that are really there, and has needlessly obscured, in his turn, the unity of Plato and Pericles in wishing to protect fellow citizens against injustice, the compatibility of the Kantian principle with Plato's reverence for an individual soul, and the existence of a real point of agreement between Christianity and Platonism in that love for his neighbor which, though different in kind, both teach.

[72] The Platonic passage is as follows (*Laws* 942 A–D, trans. Bury, Loeb Library): "Military organization is the subject of much consultation and of many appropriate laws. The main principle is this — that nobody, male or female, should ever be left without control, nor should anyone, wheth-

er at work or in play, grow habituated in mind to acting alone and on his own initiative, but he should live always, both in war and peace, with his eyes fixed constantly on his commander and following his lead; and he should be guided by him even in the smallest detail of his actions — for example, to stand at the word of command, and to march, and to exercise, to wash and to eat, to wake up at night for sentry-duty and despatch-carrying, and in moments of danger to wait for the commander's signal before either pursuing or retreating before an enemy; and, in a word, he must instruct his soul by habituation to avoid all thought or idea of doing anything at all apart from the rest of his company, so that the life of all shall be lived *en masse* and in common; for there is not, nor ever will be, any rule superior to this or better and more effective in ensuring safety and victory in war. This task of ruling, and being ruled by, others must be practised in peace from earliest childhood; but anarchy must be utterly removed from the lives of all mankind, and of the beasts also that are subject to man."

Popper, in citing this passage in his text, p. 102, duly emphasizes its reference to military matters, but protests simultaneously that Plato means the same "militarist principles" to be adhered to in peace as well as in war, and that they are to be applied to every area of peaceful existence rather than simply to the program of military training. He then quotes the passage with perverse mistranslations which tend to obscure its military reference (e.g., "get up," for "stand at the word of command," "move" for "march" (*poreuesthai*), "leader" for "commander" or "official" (*archôn*), and with omission of most of the phrases and clauses which point directly to military duty (e.g.,

Plato, addressing himself to the topic of military service, states the high importance of discipline for securing victory in war, insisting that every citizen-soldier, man or woman, must keep his eyes fixed on his commander — Popper translates the word as "leader" — and follow his orders in all his actions. But Plato adds that this discipline must be extended beyond serious activities to include those of play, or games, and that "this task of ruling, and being ruled by, others must be practised in peace from earliest childhood; but anarchy must be utterly removed from the lives of all mankind, and of the beasts also that are subject to man." [73] This passage Popper has made central to his accusation that for Plato in the field of politics, the individual was "the Evil One himself," to be subordinated at all costs to the collective Juggernaut, and has branded as an utterance characteristic of "totalitarian militarists and admirers of Sparta." [74]

Several corrections are urgently needed. As we have seen, Plato has no intention of directing the entire life of his state toward victory in war. What he hopes to achieve (*Laws* 829 A) is the far more difficult task of attaining complete virtue, which will in the most favorable case exempt his citizens both from civil strife and from war. And as means to this end he has designed what we have called, jocoseriously, the "Boy Scout program" of mingled religious observance, organized sport or "games," and continuous military preparedness.[75] That in the Greek world of Plato's day the need of defensive preparation for war was no idle fantasy is clear from the minimal reading of the historical record. It is as part of this program that discipline is to be observed in "games," [76] and that "ruling and being ruled" is to be practiced from childhood on.

---

the references to sentry-duty and to pursuing or retreating). The translation of the sentence in which Plato forbids independent action "*en paidiais*," "in play" or "in games," as Plato's prohibition of doing such a thing "even playfully," may have been caused by Popper's failure to note the probable reference to the military games and contests. The net result of all these changes is to make the passage appear much more applicable to the ordinary affairs of life in peace-time, and thus to exaggerate the regimentation which Plato intends.

This small unfairness is entirely eclipsed, however, by what Popper has done with the passage elsewhere. On the title-page of Part I of his book, and also on the dust jacket, he prints a carefully chosen selection from it, and beside it prints, as its very antithesis, a sentence drawn from Pericles' Funeral Oration (Thucydides, II, 40): "Though only a few may originate a policy,

we are all able to judge it." This is to print in parallel a political ideal and a proposed military regulation; yet Popper has not only failed to apprise the reader of this selection of its military reference, but employing the same mistranslations, has deleted absolutely all those parts of the passage which would reveal the fact. The unsuspecting reader is thus led to suppose that, if Plato had his way, no one throughout life should bathe, stand up, or even move, without an immediate directive to that effect from a group-leader on the Hitler model. Tactics such as these make it necessary to check in merciless detail every one of Popper's citations from the Platonic text, and reveal how far from the path of objectivity and fairness Popper has been swept.

[73] Trans. Bury, Loeb Library.
[74] Popper, pp. 102–103.
[75] See p. 516.
[76] Cf. *Laws* 829 B–C.

A further objection concerns Popper's use of the word "leader." Plato uses *"archôn,"* the same word he employs for officials of the state and for military commanders; it is clearly the latter, or the directors of the athletic contests, whom he has here in mind. In the city of the *Laws* there are only two kinds of officials or leaders: the human, who are to be selected or chosen by lot (including the military commanders) by the same persons who are to do the obeying, and who have often themselves an opportunity to become leaders in their turn, and secondly, the divine moral law and its reflection in the legislation of the city. Neither of these is at all what the word "leader" suggests in contexts where totalitarianism is in question; we have here no parallel to Hitler or to the subordinate members, appointed from above, of the Nazi hierarchy.

There is, however, something in this passage which offers a partial excuse for Popper's allergic interpretation. Plato has ended his military ordinance with an emphatic ethical pronouncement of broader reach. We have already seen at work in other regions of his thought the conviction that life should be ordered by moral principle, that everyone should at all times be serving God by performing his proper work, which might indeed be, and often was, his proper play. It was not tolerable to him to think of the privileged citizens of his colony becoming mere unworthy idlers, fattening themselves like beasts (*Laws* 807 A). No, he declares, the adorning of the soul and the body, each with its appropriate excellence, must be their employment. And to this end "a programme must be framed for all the freeborn men, prescribing how they shall pass their time continuously, from dawn to dawn and sunrise on each successive day." [77] This is the ground also of Plato's scornful disapproval of the wealthy idling Athenian who is the "democratic man" of *Republic* 561 (not, be it noted, a carpenter or a shoemaker, despite the appellation), who frivols away his days in the capricious indulgence of his variegated impulses. And this is the mood that imparts the energy of emphasis to the passage before us, with its demand for order extending even to the beasts.

Now Plato, especially that much older Plato who wrote the *Laws*, was a gravely moral man. But we should be wrong to view this demand as issuing solely from Plato's temperament. It is a demand carried further than we should feel proper in the circumstances, and yet by no means arbitrarily imposed upon the sociological situation to which he applies it. For given a society such as he is contemplating, and such as the Athens of the well-to-do in part exemplified, in which the free citizens possess a leisure which the mores forbid them to invest in "servile" or "mechanic" occupations — they toil not neither do they engage in business — is it not urgently necessary that some ordering of their days shall be interposed between them and either boredom or iniquity? It is a problem that in the opinion of some authorities

---

[77] Trans. Bury, Loeb Library.

is throwing its shadow upon the floor of our own society, as the hours of employment are reduced for millions of our citizens. Those who propose as a remedy for this situation the extension of adult education are moved by considerations not unlike Plato's own.

We have been considering an aspect of Plato's philosophy in which his zeal for the common good has led him to speak of individuals only in terms of an order by which their wayward impulses are to be controlled. As an offset to the impression thus produced we must take note of some passages, fewer and less emphatic, yet clearly expressive of their author's sincere intent, in which Plato has protested against the damage done to the interests of the individual by unrelieved regimentation, or has exhibited a concern lest the lawgiver with his eye fixed on the common interest should fail to notice the hardship that a general rule may work. Thus in the second book of the *Laws* the Athenian administers one of his most severe blows to Spartan pride when he charges the Spartans with conducting their community after the manner of a military camp and not like dwellers in cities: "you [Spartans] keep your young people massed together like a herd of colts at grass," and no Spartan takes his own colt away from the herd and "trains him . . . by all the means proper to child-nursing, so that he may turn out not only a good soldier, but able also to manage a state and cities." [78]

And in a discussion of the Greek counterpart of the levirate marriage, he offers us a particularly winsome piece of what may almost be called "anarchism" in the interests of marital compatibility. For we are told that cases may arise in which, due to some physical or mental malady or defect, the parties are unwilling to marry, and "prefer any other alternative, however painful." In such cases there is to be no summary coercion. Plato will compose a "prelude" begging the citizens thus enjoined to forgive the lawgiver his failure to provide for their varying circumstances as individuals, and begging the lawgiver to pardon "the subjects of the law inasmuch as they are naturally unable at times to carry out ordinances of the lawgiver laid down by him in ignorance," [79] and will submit the case for arbitration before a succession of the highest authorities in the state.

When one considers that these two passages are taken from the work in which, if one follows Popper, Plato's abandonment of the individual is complete, we are once more powerfully reminded of the complexity and inclusiveness of Plato's outlook and the futility of attempting to see in him the simple advocate of a particular political program.

In concluding our discussion of the individual and the whole, we may note a point of contact and a point of difference between Plato and the totalitarians. Plato's celebration of solidarity within the civic group offers an obvi-

---

[78] 666 D–E, trans. Bury, Loeb Library.   [79] 925 D–926 A, trans. Bury, Loeb Library.

ous analogy to Fascist devotion to the "Nation" or Nazi worship of the "Volk"; like the totalitarians in this respect, and we would add, in agreement with most of mankind, Plato thinks of sympathy within the group as an intrinsic good. But the contrast is hardly less obvious. Plato's ideal of community is valid for any city, attainable by men of any race. He is not celebrating devotion to a particular community conceived as standing in hostile opposition to other communities and as entitled by its superior value to outreach and override them. Plato's city is contented to take its modest place among the civilized communities of the world; its superiorities are not to be established at the price of conquest and world domination, but are moral and internal, and remain open to emulation by any other society. Without breach of allegiance to our democratic own, it should be possible for us to pay tribute to that quality of living together in fellowship which Plato praises, and which, so far as we ourselves possess it, we must value among our national treasures.

Racialism. — On many an earlier page we have had to deal obliquely with Popper's belief that he has detected in Plato a haughty racialism mingled of prejudice and hatred against barbarians, and an almost equal contempt for his fellow Greeks of nonaristocratic origin. We have sufficiently shown that Plato did not lack the idea of humanity, or scorn barbarians as such,[80] and with this charge we shall not be here concerned. But it is time at last to show against our critics [81] that Plato did not divide Greeks themselves into the nobly-born and the base, nor make it one of the principal purposes of his ideal city to preserve the pedigreed purity of its master race.

Plato's racialism, as Popper conceives it, is based upon the conviction that in any well-ordered Greek city (Athens, for instance [82]) and in particular in the ideal city of the *Republic*, there exist two racially distinct groups of citizens, aristocrats and commoners, represented metaphorically as gold and silver races, on the one hand, and copper and iron, on the other. The main principle of eugenics to be practiced by the guardians in the *Republic* is to avoid contamination of the superior group with the baser blood of the subject class; for this reason it will obviously be impossible to enroll among the guardians any individual who is of worker origin or who possesses even a trace of worker blood. A second principle is the necessity of eliminating from the superior group itself defectives or degenerates; we recollect that the "nuptial number" was supposed to be operative to this end.[83]

---

[80] See App. VII, pp. 601ff., and pp. 201–232.

[81] It will be remembered that Popper has been joined in making this complaint by Neurath and Lauwerys: cf. pp. 441–445. With Popper's thesis will also stand or fall Crossman's earlier mentioned conviction that Plato had set his heart on establish-ing a dictatorship of the "gentry."

[82] We have discussed, pp. 459ff., Popper's supposition that Plato himself claimed the right to rule in Athens on the basis of his aristocratic blood.

[83] Popper's principal statements of this position will be found on his pp. 81–82, 138–139, 496–497, 555.

To prove that a race-bound system of "castes" or groups distinguished by racial origin alone is here in question, Popper cites Plato's reference in the *Timaeus* to Egyptian caste divisions,[84] and brings into play also his own special "discovery" that in the *Republic* Plato broadly hints of the origin of the two classes by conquest.[85] The dread of contamination by worker blood Popper thinks manifested in Plato's talk of "admixtures" of particular metals in given individuals, and of the "mingling" of one metal with another which is, Plato tells us, destined in the end to overthrow the city. Popper finds this dread again expressed in Plato's figurative application to persons unfitted for the well-balanced pursuit of philosophy, of a term which may be translated as "bastard." [86] The exclusion of "bastards" from membership in the guardian class he finds reaffirmed in the assignment in the *Laws* to slave status, of children half-slave, half-free.[87] He imagines, further, that he has discovered, at *Republic* 434 A–D, a passage in which Plato has officially withdrawn the prospect of promotion proffered, in the "myth of the metals," to the gifted sons of inferiors, and has branded as the greatest injustice any attempt to cross over from below the boundaries dividing class from class. Popper has still to dispose of Plato's plain statement, in the myth aforesaid, that promotion will be accorded to children born with an admixture of one of the precious metals, which means for Popper, as we now realize, children resulting from forbidden unions between members of different classes. This he does by the familiar coupling of the pair of hypotheses, Plato's dishonesty, which is held particularly to infect the myth, and his guilty hesitancy in betraying his noble Socratic heritage.[88]

The coherence and the resourceful use of minor indications which characterize this argument are indeed impressive; but neglect of context and failure to take into account essential evidence has robbed them of effect. We have already given our reasons for rejecting many of the elements of Popper's case. To meet those that remain will require a renewal of attention to the myth of the metals, which we have paraphrased on an earlier page,[89] and a closer consideration of its genetic implications. The citizens are to be told that God, in fashioning them, has "mingled" in the generation of each one of them one or another of the four metals; any child who is "golden" or "partly golden" (*hypochrysos*) (we wish to stress that the two forms of expression are used interchangeably) shall become a ruler, and similarly silver, iron, or bronze children, or those tinged with any one of these metals, are to be assigned, each to the appropriate social station.

---

[84] See our p. 222.
[85] See n. 70, p. 426.
[86] See n. 122, p. 455, and pp. 205–206.
[87] We have pointed out the lack of true parallelism here, pp. 430–431. Popper, sure that Plato scorned both slaves and workers to an approximately equal degree, tends to overlook the distinction, basic to any Greek, between even the meanest citizen and a slave; see also n. 85, p. 173 above.
[88] See our pp. 424ff.
[89] See pp. 425–426.

The genetic theory presupposed in this myth, read in its entirety, may be analyzed for our purposes into five principles: (1) there are enormous differences in the mental and moral capacities of individual persons; (2) these differences are innate; (3) the capacities of the offspring are normally a direct inheritance from the parents; (4) even in a relatively pure strain, individuals who resemble another, related strain, may appear; (5) the child's innate capacities will become apparent at a relatively early age, even in the absence of a favoring environment. On the basis of these principles, Plato proposes that children shall be sorted out and assigned to their appropriate stations.[90]

The proposals that we have here been expounding are, it is true, embodied in a myth. But if this fact be employed by any critic to cast doubt upon the earnestness of its fundamental meaning,[91] the reply is at hand: some eight Stephanus pages later, in a passage that Popper has wholly ignored, Plato is listing the duties to be imposed upon the guardians, and refers back, as to a matter fixed and agreed upon and of basic importance, to the task "that we mentioned before when we said that if a degenerate offspring was born to the guardians he must be sent away to the other classes, and likewise if superior to the others he must be enrolled among the guardians; and the purport of this was that the other citizens too must be sent to the task for which their natures were fitted, one man to one work, in order that the entire city may come to be . . . a unity." [92]

Combining the implications of the two passages, we have the right to draw the following significant conclusions: it is Plato's serious purpose to fit each individual's capacity to the social function he is to perform. This being the

---

[90] Were we not in this section arguing specifically against Popper and those who, like him, have chosen to identify Plato's eugenic aim with that part of the Nazi program which sought to keep the blood of the preferred race free of contamination with blood of a different racial origin, we should have been obligated at this point in our text to acknowledge and comment upon the similarity of Plato's genetic principles, as here listed, and the proposals he bases upon them, to that other part of the Nazi program which sought to improve the quality of the superior race itself, considered apart from the problem of "purity." To balance the many complex and subtle similarities and differences here would require much more space and time than is at our disposal, but two points are not to be omitted: (1) both Plato and the Nazis pursued the aim of improving the human stock of their respective communities by the application of the eugenic principle of breeding from the "best"; both are open to challenge as having approved for the purpose the use of means destructive of much that is of high human value. In Plato's favor may be mentioned the lesser sacrifice he was proposing to make, by the measure of the difference between the Athenian and the modern ideal of marriage (cf. pp. 83, 135), and the broader and more universally valid criterion he has proposed for measuring what is "best" (cf. pp. 541–543); (2) Plato shared with the Nazis what is from our modern standpoint the mistaken doctrine that moral potentialities are inheritable, an error certainly more venial in his day, when genetics lay in its infantile speculative beginnings, than was the wilful erroneousness of the Nazis in making a similar supposition in the face of the formidable scientific evidence to the contrary.

[91] See pp. 431ff. for discussion of such criticism.

[92] *Republic* 423 C–D, trans. Shorey, Loeb Library.

case, it would be impossible for Plato to fix permanently the status of any child on the basis of his pedigree. The child will be provisionally thus assigned, but care will be taken to correct any error that may have occurred.[93]

Stage-direction at this point: collapse of the main pillar of Popper's argument. As the dust clears, we discern still standing two props large enough to demand special handling. The first of these is the conception that Plato, in speaking of "admixtures" and "mingling," is referring to hybridization. A scrutiny of our recent paraphrase of a portion of the myth of the metals will show that Plato has nothing of the sort in view. He is operating with a fairy-tale conception of a "soul-stuff," as it were, mixed or mingled in each particular individual with one or other of the metals, and the same generic individual who is referred to as "golden" may appear in the next sentence as "partly golden" (*hypochrysos*); again, such persons are said (*Republic* 416 E) to have "gold in their souls." There is no talk of one metal being mingled in a single soul with another metal. What serious opinion lies beneath these mythological metaphors must be elicited from what Plato says elsewhere, and examination of these passages [94] makes it probable that he had in mind a distribution of human capacities (or sets of capacities), according to what is almost a "normal curve" of frequency,[95] along a continuous scale of merit, and that his "metals" represent four ranges marked off along this scale. This being the case, an individual could not well be "mixed," though it might be possible to doubt to which of two adjoining ranges he should be assigned.

The one further misunderstandable reference to mixtures occurs at the end of the "nuptial number" passage, where the downfall of the ideal city is being described. The fatal misstep has been taken, unworthy and ill-educated persons have, for lack of better human material, been installed among the rulers, and these "will not approve themselves very efficient guardians for testing . . . our races. . . And this inter-mixture of the iron with the silver and the bronze with the gold will engender unlikeness and unharmonious unevenness, things that always beget war and enmity wherever they arise." Is this mingling, as Popper believes, the result of an interbreeding of classes, a mixture in the veins of individual guardians of "base" and "upper-class blood"? Plato's answer is not long in coming: he pictures the situation as a struggle between two groups within the guardian class, "pulling against each other, the iron and bronze toward money-making — and . . . the golden and silvern . . . trying to draw them back to virtue." [96] Plainly the "inter-mixture"

---

[93] We here make no use of *Timaeus* 19 A, where the determination to allocate children to their proper class on the basis of their innate capacities is reiterated, but in such terms that it is impossible to employ the passage either to prove or disprove Plato's intention of elevating children of workers.

[94] We mention these below, n. 99, p. 540.

[95] For this conception see *Phaedo* 89 E–90 B. The one element of it definitely present in the *Republic* is the recognition of the small number of "golden" natures that may be expected.

[96] *Republic* 546 E–547 B, trans. Shorey, Loeb Library.

of the metals and the "unevenness" here referred to consist in the presence or mingling within the guardian class of individuals belonging to the different types, and not to the presence or mingling in particular individuals of blood derived from separate classes. There is here no question of "race-poisoning," no warning against the transfer into the guardian class of those who are, as individuals, "golden" or "silvern."

There is still to be considered the passage claimed by Popper to confirm his thesis that Plato, has, "in effect, withdrawn" the earlier accorded promise of advancement. Plato, having arrived at the provisional definition of justice as "doing one's own task," is testing its validity by contemplating the results of its violation; and it is agreed between "Socrates" and Glaucon that it will do great harm to the city if "one who is by nature an artisan or . . . money-maker tempted . . . by wealth or command of votes or bodily strength or some similar advantage tries to enter into the class of the soldiers or one of the soldiers into the class of counsellors and guardians, for which he is not fitted," and that "the substitution of the one for the other" class, is "the greatest injury to a state." [97] We see that Plato does indeed lay a strict prohibition against transition from class to class. But the transitions that are in question here are specified as precisely those that violate the all-important principle of capacity. This is entirely consistent with the earlier expressed promise which Popper supposes to be rescinded here. There is no question of prohibiting the guardians from promoting a man or woman whom they judge fit for rule or for service as a soldier; as the context plainly shows, there is only prohibition against "substitution of one for the other" on any basis other than natural fitness. To rest one's angry gaze upon a sentence, as Popper has done here, in abstraction from its qualifying context — what is this if not to play anagrams with an author instead of reading him?

In the hope that we have succeeded in clearing away the clouds of misconception from Plato's theory of "race" as expressed in the *Republic*, let us ask what this removal now permits us to see. What emerges is, first, a straightforward belief that the highest human value attaches to the discovery — wherever they may be found — of the best-endowed natures and the harnessing of their energies to maximum effect for the common good. Along with this is the belief that, granted the happiest of enabling conditions, the employment of these best-endowed individuals as parents of the next generation would make possible continuous improvement. We see further Plato's belief that the potentiality of moral character forms part of the complex of transmissible traits, thus making possible the unbroken production of men who could safely be entrusted with the power of the philosopher kings. This aspiration toward developing and utilizing the highest human types is what

---

[97] *Republic* 434 A–C, trans. Shorey, Loeb Library.

we submit to be the grounds of Plato's utter rejection of racial prejudice in favor of a rational eugenic ideal.

Granted that this was Plato's ideal, it may still be asked how Plato conceived that it would be put in practice. Plato's critics [98] have pointed out that the guardians would have obvious opportunities for determining which of the children being reared as guardians were of genuine gold or silver quality and which were not, since these children would at all times be under the most careful educational surveillance. But how, it is demanded, would the guardians detect the exceptional sons of workers or money-makers whom they are enjoined to elevate? No machinery for inspection is supplied, no schools for them are even so much as mentioned. Furthermore, as any given child grew older, it would become increasingly difficult for him to make up his deficiencies in training. The only reply possible is that we have here an imperfection in Plato's scheme which, from a practical point of view, is indeed serious. Plato himself is well aware that even among the guardians, it will not be possible to distinguish with certainty until the age of fifty, a silver from a golden nature.[99] He must then have known, if he reflected on the question, that to draw the line between the abler workers and the less able guardians, would be equally difficult, and that the widening educational gap would make anything like accurate discrimination impossible. This imperfection must simply be accepted, somewhat as we today are forced to accept the danger that injustice will result from the less momentous but still difficult decision that a given young person of borderline abilities shall or shall not be admitted to high school or to college. As for the absence of any machinery for elevating children of the lower classes, this may be simply the result of the high level of generality upon which the *Republic* moves, and cannot be taken as proof that Plato did not entertain the expressed intention, any more than the absence of a Board of Censors proves that Plato did not intend to submit literature and the arts to a strict moral regulation.

It is interesting to note that Plato, before he wrote the *Politicus*, had apparently abandoned the hope that the genetic program of the *Republic* was feasible, or had, at any rate, come to believe that, should such ideal beings as the philosopher kings be brought into being, it would be impossible either to identify them on sight or to convince mankind of their superlative excellence.[100] We know from the *Laws* (951 B) that he retained the belief that men of rare and divine natures come occasionally into existence, but he offered no account of the mode of their production. What is certain is that in the *Politicus* the Statesman, that highly abstract being endowed with perfect political wisdom, attempts no more than to blend in the citizens the sober

---

[98] Crossman, p. 281; Fite, pp. 28–30.

[99] For the successive "screenings" to which the guardians are to be subjected,

see 537 B, 537 D, 539 E–540 A.

[100] *Politicus* 301 C–E.

and gentle temper with the bold and energetic, an endeavor which had formed part, it is true, in the *Republic,* of the plan for producing ideal guardians, but by no means its whole extent. Again, in the *Laws,* an attempt is to be made to persuade citizens to conduct their match-making with this same end in view. In both *Politicus* and *Laws,* Plato has abandoned the ideal entertained in the *Republic* of uniting the entire community into what is in some sense a single kinship group, and by dividing the population into the two essential functional units of slave and free,[101] he has drawn a hard and fast line, such as existed in other ancient communities, between the groups.[102] But within the citizen body itself, in neither *Politicus* nor *Laws* is there any hint of a distinction between well-born and commoner like that which he is charged with making in the city of Athens between oligarch and democrat, and with which, when it suits his purpose, Popper equates the distinction in the *Republic* between guardians and workers. In none of his three cities does Plato show any discrimination based on pedigree between citizens.

A brief comparison of Plato's eugenic objectives with those avowed by the Nazis will yield a very fair index of the contrasting value patterns that respectively inspire them. As is notorious, the Nazi breeding schedule was primarily intended to preserve the purity of the master race, an aim which we have been at some pains to show Plato did not share. The type of this race, we remember, was conceived as splendidly "Nordic" in physique, having the virtues of the warrior and the instinct and aspect of leadership. By virtue of their racial origin, thus evidenced, they would be the bearers also of cultural creativeness, and they were of course to have all the ordinary excellences of ability, energy, and so on, added unto them. In addition, maximum numbers were to be produced, to supply material for the operation of natural selection, and for the recruiting of armies of conquest.[103] With the exception of numbers,[104] and oddly enough, of mental ability, this is substantially the

---

[101] There are of course metics also in the *Laws.*

[102] Plato's line in the *Laws* between slave and free is drawn with exceptional strictness, as we have seen above, p. 186. But as we remember, Athenian law itself rendered marriage between slave and free impossible and contemplated the breeding of new citizens only by those who were themselves full citizens.

[103] W. M. McGovern, *From Luther to Hitler,* Houghton Mifflin, Boston, 1941, pp. 638–642, provides a well-documented analysis of Nazi eugenics and the racial ideal.

[104] Since Plato recommends both in the *Republic* and the *Laws* the restriction of population increase, Popper has been unable here to draw a parallel with modern

totalitarianism. He has instead ascribed to Sparta (p. 583) the endeavor to restrict population through "infanticide, birth control, and homosexuality," and has then found the same recommendations in Plato. In this charge, Popper has so scrambled historical fact with prejudicial fantasy as to make a brief exposition of his errors difficult. In the first place, it is not certain that the Spartan state (as distinct from individual Spartans) ever desired to restrict population, though it may have done so in its earlier times. Aristotle (*Pol.* II, ix, 1270 a 39 f.) says it encouraged increase, and he has apparently not been confuted by modern inquiry (cf. Busolt-Swoboda, *Griechische Staatskunde,* München, 1926, I, pp. 702–703). Popper's reference to what Aris-

program that Popper has extracted from his burrowings between the lines of the *Republic*, and presented as Plato's attempt to breed his ideal man. But if we look at the *Republic* itself, what we find is of a quite different weave.[105]

---

totle mentions as the *Cretan* "lawgiver's" reason for instituting common meals (*Ibid.*, x, 1272 a 23) is not sufficient entirely to offset this testimony. It appears that Spartan state policy sought to insure an excess of potential soldiers, regardless of the hardship inflicted on individuals. In the second place, it was for quite other reasons that the Spartan state sanctioned infanticide, and homosexuality likewise, in so far as it did so sanction it (cf. our discussion of this point, n. 33, p. 89 above). "Birth control," in the sense of refraining from begetting, the Spartans doubtless did practice: certainly unrestricted production of children was not the Spartan way. Plato, while not approving such extreme limitation as practiced by individual Spartans in his day, does recommend refraining from begetting beyond the measure required for a stationary population, saying in one place that both war and poverty will thus be avoided (*Rep.* 372 B–C, 460 A, *Laws*, 740 D). He never recommends infanticide for limiting population. Its purpose as both he and the Spartans — and also the Athenians, it appears (cf. pp. 195ff.) — conceived it, was to insure that the children reared should be sound and vigorous; for the same reason, Plato recommends abortion in certain cases (*Rep.* 461 C). Nor does Plato anywhere sanction indulgent paiderastia (cf. *infra*, Chapter 5). Finally, even though it might be shown with certainty that Sparta and Plato alike prescribed population control as a means of avoiding the necessity of expansion and conquest, what is there in this prescription to condemn? It is easy enough to imagine Popper's comments, had it been true, on the contrary, that Plato bred excess citizens and, in consequence, demanded *Lebensraum*.

[105] Plato describes at length these "golden" natures at *Republic* 485–487, and 535 A–536 A. Popper, in presenting (p. 147) what he tells us is Plato's ideal of human excellence, has characteristically selected from Plato's text only what suits his purpose. He has chosen to quote from 535 C only the phrases in which Plato lists the necessary but by no means sufficient quali-

ties of the good guardian of the lower rank, which are presupposed also in the exceptional individuals to be chosen as rulers: these must be (Shorey's translation) "the most stable, the most brave and enterprising . . . . and, so far as practicable, the most comely," and also "virile and vigorous (*blosyroi*) in temper." Popper renders *blosyroi* as "awe-inspiring," and insists (p. 559), somewhat tendentiously, that it means "grim" or "inspiring terror"; in so doing, he ignores the fact that at *Theaetetus* 149 A, Socrates half-humorously describes his mother as having been a "*blosyra*" midwife — which would seem to remove the necessity that in Plato's pages, the word shall mean "terror-inspiring." Popper then omits from his summary of Plato's description all the other qualities, moral and intellectual, which Plato says the future rulers must possess, omissions which very considerably alter the picture. He proceeds to misquote 540 C, where "Socrates" completes his description of the lives of the rulers, who, after spending their declining years in contemplation and self-denying service to the community, die and are honored, says Socrates, as "blessed and godlike men." Glaucon then exclaims to Socrates, "You have finished off your ruling men most beautifully, Socrates, like a sculptor" (Lindsay's version is here employed as showing more clearly than Shorey's how Popper's translation is related to what Plato actually says). This is the same metaphor employed at 420 C ff. for describing the ideal state as a whole; what is meant is that Socrates has depicted the rulers as beautiful, not in body alone, but in all respects, particularly in mind and character. Yet Popper, making the phrase part of Plato's description of the future rulers, represents it as referring wholly to the body, translating "sculptured in perfect beauty." In sum, by stressing vigor, "grimness," and physical beauty, and omitting entirely the intellectual and most of the moral qualities, he rouses in our minds a picture of "supermasters" which is wholly foreign to Plato's text.

Plato will seek to produce, for purposes of defense, natures not dominated by the desires and appetites, "watch-dogs" fierce to foes and gentle to friends. He includes bodily excellence, as a matter of course, but always as a subordinate end. But this is not yet his highest type, the type he desires most to produce, that of those exemplary beings, the future philosopher kings. These young men are to be balanced and gracious natures, adding to the basic qualities we have just described keen and retentive minds, and above all eager in the pursuit of theoretic truth.[106] Between them and the Nazi standard intervenes a moral distance it would be difficult to exaggerate.

The Leader and the elite. — In setting apart from the rank and file of his citizens a small minority of specially chosen and trained officials and their armed auxiliaries to constitute an elite by whom, on the topmost level, all policies are determined and through whom, at the next level of command, all decisions are carried out, Plato has been often likened to the modern totalitarians of all three varieties. It is obvious enough that in this respect there exists a structural correspondence of some kind. Just for this reason it is of the greatest importance to note the precise point to which the resemblance runs and at which it is brought to a decisive stop.

As Fite has observed, in any scheme for organizing large numbers of persons for a common purpose, where direction is lodged in one or in very few, some hierarchical structure is a necessity. Where such an organization is a government, we may add, the power of enforcement must be placed at the disposal of the executive, and unless office is hereditary, some institutional means of selecting and training future leaders must be provided. In latter-day totalitarian states, a vast and complicated array of agencies, comprising the party leaders and the party, the various armed services, storm troopers, secret police, and, in addition, special educational institutions, fulfil these functions, whereas in Plato's imagined city, only the philosopher kings and the auxiliaries are made available for all such purposes. But rough parallels can undoubtedly be drawn by anyone not overparticular in demanding exactitude between the elite groups, ancient and modern. We have fresh in our memories Plato's account of the qualities, physical and spiritual, prerequisite for membership in his elite; if now we add what he has told us of their activities, we should be ready to compare them with their modern analogues.

For the guardians of the lower degree, among whom at first are included, as yet unrecognized, those who will later be chosen as rulers, Plato has designed a rearing and education which are to bring them to the highest development of which they are capable (*Republic* 456 E). Living together, boys and girls alike, under the eye of their teachers, they listen to tales of the gods from which all

---

[106] The degree of intellectual capacity and interest which is presupposed may be inferred from our pp. 544–545 and Appendix XII, pp. 618ff.

moral crudities and frightening pictures of the after-life have been removed (377 ff.), early learn to ride (467 E), read poems in praise of gods and good men (607–608), and play the lyre, in modes both stirring and mild (399 A–B). Held to their studies by play and not by compulsion, they are to be taught the elements of mathematics (536 D–E). The shaping influence of their environment is to count for very much (400 E ff.) ; since only fair forms and characters are to be impressed upon the products of the craftsmen, they will live among sights of beauty, from which, "like a breeze that brings from wholesome places health," [107] they will receive into their souls harmony and grace. Hardened by their gymnastic (404), taken out to observe from a distance actual battle (467, 537 A),[108] but made gentle by music and persuasion and reasoned discussion (411), they grow up understanding that their duty will be to put down rebellion within the state should such occur (415 E), but disciplined to live so frugally and with such regard for the rights of others as to render such a rebellion, Plato believes, scarcely conceivable (416–417). A great lack which we observe in this education is any experience of gainful work or of handicraft; but from these Plato will resolutely debar them. Arrived at maturity and now being responsible for the safety of the state, they must, we assume, preserve their military fitness above all else; for the rest, so far as Plato tells us (412 B), they may give themselves over, like the citizens of the *Laws* described above, to hunting, athletic contests, and participation in festival dance and public worship.

For the guardians on the higher level, both men and women, there will be provided, to match their extraordinary intellectual endowment, a far more complete training, quite literally all there is available of rational education. Chosen at the age of twenty to continue their studies on a higher, more abstract plane (537 B ff.), those of them who survive the successive eliminations will spend at least half their time until they are fifty in mathematics and astronomy and in far-ranging discussion of themes logical, ethical, and metaphysical; the remainder will be spent in the practical pursuits of war and "the holding of offices suitable to youth" (539 E). They are now full-fledged rulers,

---

[107] *Republic* 401 C, trans. Shorey, Loeb Library.

[108] In qualified agreement with Fite, we may remark that it is clear, from what Plato is here proposing, that he is ascribing a positive value to warlike prowess — not, however, as Fite suggests, for the sake of foreign conquest, but because courage is a part of his conception of the totality of human excellence. In contrast to this ennobling activity stood the degradation brought by the "mechanic arts" (cf. our pp. 239ff.), with which, accordingly, Plato's young guardians are to have no concern. His distaste for these employments carries him so far that he makes "Socrates" declare the guardians-to-be shall not even imitate in dramatic presentations such activities as those of smiths and oarsmen (396 A), and no such skills are to be taught them (522 B). As we have earlier noticed (pp. 240f., pp. 259–261), this represents a survival in Plato of a prejudice he was born to, and from which he never succeeded in fully divesting himself, though one finds him in the *Laws* expressing a more adequate appreciation of the humbler arts.

and though we are told that they may devote the greater part of their time to philosophy, each in his turn must toil in the service of the state (540 A–B); nor will this alternation lead to any inconsistency in policy, for to Plato the guardians are interchangeable beings (445 D–E), conceived as knowledge and technique incarnate.

And they will need all the training they bring with them, for what awaits them is an assignment so difficult and so complex as almost to violate Plato's own much heralded principle of single function. Their duties will be on the one hand military and administrative, eugenic and educational on the other. Under the first heading it is their responsibility to see that the city shall not grow too large nor fall away (423 B f.), and shall be neither too rich nor too poor (421 D f.). They must administer justice in the courts (433 E), and formulate such laws and regulations as may be needed (425 C–427 A). Presumably they will command armies, and they will deal diplomatically with neighboring states and send embassies to Delphi.

Their second set of activities is even more demanding. They must plan and conduct the "lotteries" for marriages (459 B f.). They must inspect infants (460 B), and observe the development of every child in the city, so that he may be assigned to his proper class and even, within the worker class, to his proper occupation (423 C–D). They must "build their post of watch" in education, supervising even the children's games (424), and censoring all literature and music, maintaining standards for all the products of the craftsmen. Presumably, like the philosopher-rhetorician of the *Phaedrus*,[109] they must mold public opinion, and must also employ such temperings of truth as are required for the good of the governed (459 C–E). They must watch and test every younger guardian to see whether he (or she) is of true kingly quality (539 D–E), and not least, they must train their own successors in all the higher branches of learning and speculation (540 B), "sowing in fitting souls," to draw once more from the *Phaedrus*, words which will spring up and make their possessors blessed.[110]

Since it is inconceivable that any very small number of rulers and rulers-in-training could begin to carry out in person so formidable a schedule of duties, either Plato is intending, as Crossman has suggested,[111] to supply them with a large staff of assistants drawn from the guardians of the second class, or is intending to permit them to hire, as in the *Laws*, experts from other cities or to employ common citizens; or, as is perhaps more probable, Plato has

---

[109] *Phaedrus* 271 D f. Cf. our discussion, pp. 432–433.

[110] *Phaedrus* 276 E–277 A, trans. Fowler, Loeb Library.

[111] On our view Crossman (p. 117) has carried his analysis into greater detail than Plato, and has, in a manner, honored Plato and at the same time injured him by bestowing upon him the credit and responsibility for the conclusions reached. We find ourselves rather among those to whom, as to Jaeger, the *Republic* is not a political architect's design for a system of government bureaus, but a treatise on education set in a frame of ideas psychological, ethical, and metaphysical.

simply not concerned himself with the elaboration of details, but has left the guardians in their philosophical generality as embodied ideals of good government.

Looking back at the just-completed account, we may select from the total description those traits that are relevant to the intended comparison. The auxiliaries present an initial point of contrast. They do not appear comparable to any of the characteristic organs of a modern totalitarian regime. Unlike party members, they do not function as transmitters of ideological instruction to the masses; they are not, like the storm troopers and Gestapo, to be kept busy in serving as strong-arm men or secret police. In their aspect as guards, they resemble much rather a standing army, "established in the city," as Plato says, "with nothing to do," save to be prepared for military action at call. But Plato has not dissolved them in their function. Like the other citizens, they are conceived as living the life according to virtue, a life exemplified in them more perfectly than in the workers, in view of their considerable endowment and cultivation, but desirable in itself on every level.

Plato's philosopher kings also, and still more patently, achieve value by the mere activity of living as the most perfect vehicles of human excellence. As bearers of political power, Plato has set upon them the special seal of commitment to the impersonal decrees of reason, ability to discern and to apply disinterestedly the results of their rigorous philosophical inquiry. They are thus themselves strict subjects to an external and incorruptible authority, from which spring truth and good. And that this is no afterthought, no fraudulent garment designed to cover the nakedness of arbitrary power, is evidenced by the central and culminating position given to the vision of the Good, and by its inseparable connection with the theory of the forms, itself the mainspring of the Platonic philosophy.

In view of this subordination to a higher principle, it is no accident that the bearers of Plato's standards should not be presented to us as themselves the sources of light and bestowers of grace. Anonymous, interchangeable, belonging indifferently to either sex, there is nothing in them to suggest the mystical energies, the charismatic emanations characteristic of a Duce or a Fuehrer. They are economically dependent, possessing neither land nor private dwelling, receiving like the public slaves at Athens a salary sufficient only for their frugal maintenance. Significantly, they are not conceived as dynamic figures evoking perpetual revolution or leading their people forward toward unlimited conquests. Plato has stamped his own *ethos* upon his rulers: they are to be men in whom harmony and temperance and the strict honoring of justice are valued high above force and turbulence. Plato's elite go quietly about their tasks, in a community at rest and, so far as possible, at peace within its borders, quiet Olympians in contrast to heaven-storming Titans.

We must leave to the reader's accountancy the final appraisal of the real distance separating Plato's "leaders" and "elite" from their modern analogues. But before dismissing this topic, it is well to remember that we have all the while been comparing to the actual totalitarianisms of our time Plato's vision-ary and carefully safeguarded ideal. And we have certain knowledge that at the first departure from the ideal, from the "sacred line," as Plato calls it in the *Laws* (739 A), Plato instantly drops from his program any persons or offices such as those we have been discussing.[112] His belief in the authority of right over freedom has not abated, but there are in the second-best city no persons who are its special vehicles. Law is here the ruler (715 D). The citizens are on a virtual parity, and all alike bear arms; officials are elected and chosen by lot, and in addition are subject to a degree of accountability for their every act beyond modern practice, even under democracy (945–948). And for this abo-lition of personal control Plato gives reasons similar to those we should our-selves offer, — the inability of the mortal nature in general to resist the cor-rosions of unrestricted power (713 C, 875 A–C), and the necessity that every citizen should feel himself a member of the state (768 A–B). In Sicily we saw him recommending constitutional monarchy, with emphasis upon the "rule of law." In the face of these facts, it would be something less than justice to hold Plato responsible for the manifold evils that have issued from the reckless application of the principle of the "leader" and the "elite."

"Uniformitarianism," the "closed society," [113] indoctrination, and censor-ship. — We are about to meet what we have earlier acknowledged to be the principal unacceptable element actually present in Plato's political thought, out of which, by exaggeration and unwarrantable extension, most of the charges against him have been developed. All the detractors are at one in finding in Plato this fault, calling it by various names which do not obscure their central agreement; it appears also in some form in the lists of all our nonpartisan observers of modern totalitarianism. It is incumbent on us, there-fore, conscientiously to expound that aspect of Plato's thought upon which these criticisms converge, and taking upon ourselves, for the moment, the detractional function, to make out as strong a case against Plato as justice demands. There will be time and place later for such rebuttal as justice permits.

Looking first at the *Republic*, which has naturally been the chief target of criticism, the libertarian reader has his misgivings first awakened as early as Book II, where Plato begins his description of the education of the guardians, sketched above. For here one comes gradually to perceive that Plato is com-mending an all-embracing censorship, not indeed in direct application to

---

[112] As before, we are referring to the city of the *Laws* as it functions before the Night Council itself becomes a group of philoso-pher rulers and is made supreme over the laws; cf. n. 38, p. 517. The structure of the city's government is outlined on pp. 516–517.

[113] This term, which is applied to Plato's

political ideal by Popper in condemnation both of Plato's intended regimentation of the ordinary citizens and of Plato's sup-posed prohibition of free inquiry by the rulers of his state, is used here only in the former sense. We have repelled the latter charge elsewhere; see Appendix XII, pp. 618f., and for the *Laws*, 464–465, 517.

political affairs, but in the important sense of completely controlling the education provided for the future protectors and directors of his state. Wherever we look in this educational scheme, we find him bending and molding the young souls into the form demanded by his uncompromising moral ideal, encompassing them round and about, as we have seen, with every influence of carefully chosen and adapted tales and poems, fair sights and sounds, exercises and martial experiences, which shall attune them to a mood of steadfast courage tempered with the gentle and concessive spirit.

In pursuance of these aims, Plato will restrict and forbid. He will censor the tales told by mothers and nurses (377 B f.), and frown upon changes in children's games (424 E). He will banish from the whole city, although reluctantly and, be it noted, provisionally only, all dramatic performances and epic poetry (607–608). Artisans are to be supervised, the musical modes severely curtailed. And when once all has been rightly ordered, supreme care must be exercised lest "innovation" and "lawlessness" creep in and, ruining first the characters of men, end by destroying the laws and constitution (424 D–E).

Searching for further areas of control in Plato's state, we meet the same pattern in every quarter, with one exception. From top to bottom, this community is ordered by superior wisdom. Those who are selected to receive advanced training, it is true, are invited to pursue free inquiry, and the few who have attained the status of ruler become directors of their own consciences. Plato, conceiving that truth is one for all men, indeed presupposes that they will find at the very end of their search only what he, following the Socratic footsteps, had himself discovered, and that they will gladly submit to its authority, yet, in principle, he sets them at liberty to follow the dictates of their own reason, and it is expected that they will extend and deepen existing insights. But when once they have ascended to the vision, they become for all other citizens of the Platonic state the determiners of the very meaning of goodness. Theirs is veritably "the place of wisdom," and upon them devolve those many tasks of decision and direction which we recently described. It will be under their supervision, moreover, that the sick will be attended by physicians who are enjoined to proceed on the assumption that no member of the guardian group has leisure to be an invalid and that, like any poor carpenter in an ordinary Greek city, any guardian whose body cannot be cured must be allowed to die; and by decision of these rulers also, any whose soul is judged incurably corrupt, must be put to death. In short, the rightness of the ideal city is measured by the degree of its conformity to the guardians' commands.[114]

This, then, is the aspect of the *Republic* in which the horrified detractors have found an element truly central both to totalitarianism and to Plato's

---

[114] References for this paragraph include   *Rep.* 498 B–C, 537 D ff., esp. 538 D, 540 A–B; 405 C–408 B, 410 A.

political thought. In that strictly delimited sense of the word to which reference was made above, it makes of him a "totalitarian." [115] Plato's attempt to mold and control the citizen's every impulse, belief, and action, repels us as we imagine ourselves thus manipulated. We observe that, as in our own day, the control of opinion entails censorship of art and literature and the subordination of education to this end; and we are prone to carry further the consequences, and to imagine for ourselves other effects which we well know must have followed any attempt to actualize the *Republic*, the punishment of innovators and the deadening of all spontaneity by fear and self-righteous intolerance.

And if we turn to the *Laws* seeking a more moderate and concessive attitude, we find, surprisingly enough, that in this respect there is little to choose between the two cities.[116] Here there are, as we have seen, no philosopher kings and no auxiliaries, and there is some lessening of the state's direct control

---

[115] Considerations such as these have apparently prompted Elliott and McDonald, in their influential textbook, *Western Political Heritage*, 1949, to classify Plato (p. 12) as a totalitarian of a particular type, though distinct from any of the actual totalitarians of our day; see their pp. 626 and 851, where the imposition of ethical beliefs by the state upon its citizens is said to justify this name. It should be noted, however, that in addition to what are called "trappings" of totalitarianism, such as a one-party system and an elite, and beside the use of terror and repression (p. 858), these writers set up at least one other central and much emphasized criterion of totalitarianism, of which, as we have already recorded (n. 50, p. 521), they explicitly exonerate Plato: this is the advocacy of amoral power, which acknowledges no authority above itself. A related "totalitarian" trait, that of regarding human nature as weak, and therefore as incapable of "rational control of its environment" (p. 6), is not detected in Plato; presumably he is cleared of this imputation by his acknowledged allegiance to the pursuit of rational knowledge and his belief that his guardians, at least, would be capable of employing it for political ends. Elliott and McDonald, moreover, know Popper's book, and have taken pains (p. 86) to reject Popper's inclusion of Plato among "historicists," and to credit Plato with having held firmly to the Socratic doctrine of free moral inquiry. In short, the position taken by these writers is in general agreement with that maintained in the present book, if we except the

unfortunate use of the term "totalitarian" for a thinker who fails to exhibit traits which are justly called basic to this political outlook, and secondly, if we be granted leave to correct certain relatively slight misrepresentations of Platonic purposes which Elliott and McDonald apparently have inadvertently accepted from Popper. As examples of these we may cite their account on pp. 93–94 of the common citizens in Plato's *Republic*; rejecting emphatically, as they do, Popper's belief that Plato would not elevate able commoners, they still imply that only in this one respect is there any significant difference between the status of these citizens and that of the oppressed Spartan Helots. On pp. 94 and 98, they reproduce Popper's charge that Plato believed himself the possessor of a "secret method" of mating, which he intentionally conceals. On p. 447, Hobbes, otherwise condemned as a proto-fascist, is credited with "addressing his book to the reason of men," in contrast to the "*élitist* . . . oligarchist or aristocrat," Plato. The implication of this phrase that Plato perhaps addressed his books (as Popper sometimes implies) to the conspiratorial oligarchic underground at Athens, rather than to the "reason" of the educated Greek public of his day, is surely not intended.

[116] The *Politicus*, so far as it is possible to judge, represents a city midway between the *Laws* and the *Republic* in its institutions, but differing not at all in the degree of Plato's determination to secure unanimity in belief among its citizens.

over the citizens' lives. Yet law, laid down by the city's founders, and honored as divine reason, controlling the life of the community as gods of old shepherded the human flock, is equally authoritative. Though Plato recognizes that the march of time must entail changes, he still wishes any innovation to be regarded as unthinkable except those initiated in rare instances by the council of the Law-wardens with the consent of every citizen; and he hopes custom and public opinion will enforce still further uniformities.[117] Dramatic displays are to be permitted, even encouraged, but there is to be strict censorship, and Plato proposes to sanctify the exact dances and kinds of song appropriate to all festivals. It is in the *Laws* that Plato makes the solemn pronouncement so much stressed by Popper, that anarchy must be utterly rooted out of the lives of men. And it is in the *Laws*, too, as we recall, that Plato explicitly faces the consequences only latent in the *Republic* and accepts the necessity in extreme cases of exacting the penalty for failure to conform: death to the atheist who cannot be convinced of his error by patient argument.

Surveying the sum total of these Platonic doctrines, we are tempted, at some cost in consistency, to moderate our indignation against Plato's defamers, and to understand how as the bulldogs of modern democratic ideals they have felt called upon to growl most fiercely at this suspicious stranger from antiquity. We have before us here a most unacceptable complex of attitudes, incompatible with our own, and so built into the structure of Plato's political fabric that their removal involves the immediate collapse of the Republic, considered as a model for the distribution of powers in any actual society, and calls for fundamental changes in the polity of the *Laws*. Those of us who wish still to draw upon Plato for instruction must be prepared, in consequence, to make far-reaching adaptations and selections. The practicability of this operation we shall seek to establish in a later section. Meanwhile we shall consider the fault itself, and in uncovering the motives which led Plato to recommend such all-inclusive control, isolate its peculiar quality, and distinguish it both from the oppressions practiced by the totalitarians and from what the detractors have supposed Plato to be about.

Of prime importance is the distinction between Plato the philosopher, moving on the plane of the theoretic and the ideal, and a modern dictator, who has carried into practice what he proposed, and of whom we know that he did not draw back from the last bloody consequences of his principles. It was Plato's magnificent illusion that all substantial rights and wrongs could be identified and ranked in order of importance, and that it would then be possible to design and set forth as an ideal both the pattern of the good life and that of the good society. Among his predecessors, Hippodamas and

---

[117] The passages referred to in this sentence are *Laws* 713 E–714 A, 715 C–D; 798 A–B, 769 D f., 772 A–D, and 951 B–C. For the three sentences which follow we may cite 779, 816–817; 942 C; 907 D ff.

Phaleas had devised ideal constitutions calling for a radical reworking of existing practice, extending from the institution of functional social classes among the citizens (Hippodamas) to Phaleas' equalization of property and proposal to make municipal slaves of all artisans.[118] Among his contemporaries and fellow Socratics, perhaps Antisthenes, and certainly a little later, Xenophon, projected their moral ideals into a political romance. It is then not surprising that Plato in the *Republic* gave free rein to his moral imagination, setting himself the twofold question, "What is the best life for man and what is the character of the community whose citizens will enjoy such a way of life?"

Since, then, he was by hypothesis presenting his ideal city, he could well feel free to dictate to its citizens in all respects, or, to put it otherwise, to depict them as willing to accept complete direction; since, further, he was planning a whole society, he was at liberty to prescribe not laws only, but customs and religion as well. Thirdly, it is to be noticed that even if we take the *Republic* as in some sense presented as realizable, he was offering it to the Greek world for acceptance as an ideal, not imposing it, complete to the last logical consequence, on any actual community. As the *Laws* shows, he was presupposing that every departure from the ideal pattern of the *Republic* would entail corresponding and compensating changes in the distribution of authority within the state; the "third-best state," we may well suppose — enjoying only "third-best" rulers or laws — would have been so planned as to leave still further areas open to individual decision and control. There is no certainty that had his repressions met with resistance, he would actually have enforced them; for here another principle, the piety for fellow citizens and the horror of shedding kindred blood, might well have stayed his hand; confronted in actual practice with the necessity of employing the ancient equivalent of concentration camp and firing squad, he might well have recommended, instead, the abandonment of censorship. These considerations diminish somewhat the oppressiveness of the minutely detailed and all-pervasive regulations; they would appear to remove entirely the suggestion of personal autocracy imported into Plato's scheme by the presence of the philosopher kings, and they go far to lessen his offense in proposing the death penalty for atheists. But they do not diminish his responsibility for believing that knowledge of the right must come from above, and that it may with justice be bestowed on the less enlightened — if necessary, imposed — without their prior consent.

We have seen the importance of distinguishing Plato's exposition of ideals and proposals from the historical actualities of a modern dictatorship. A second difference between Plato and the totalitarians lies in the benefits which they respectively hoped to achieve for their citizens. In addressing himself to the designing of an ideal society, Plato did not cease to be the man whom Socrates had taught to believe the ideal coincidence of right knowing with right

---

[118] These two ideal states are described by Aristotle, *Politics* II, chapters vii and viii.

doing, and of both with happiness. There was thus laid the ground plan for a society based on the apprehension of truth and offering to its citizens as its chief contribution to their welfare access to this truth and the opportunity of living lives in accordance with it. If now we add the unfortunate conviction, also rooted in the thought of Socrates, that the true expert, the man who knows and can benefit souls, is of rare occurrence, the outlines of Plato's city begin to be clear. It will be the home of individuals, most of them communicating with truth only by proxy, but each of them thus supplied with the conditions for realizing to the full his own capacity for virtue and therefore for happiness; and as the moral expert specializes in the benefitting of souls, so every other member of the society is a specialist, and each will contribute to the common life the benefit he is peculiarly fitted to confer. It is not so much a communism and sharing of material commodities as a communism of interactive services, designed to effect the virtuous happiness of all and each. And as the communal work proceeds, the workers of every class are to be warmed with a genuine sense of mutuality, that happy breaching of the wall dividing "mine" from "thine," both for weal and woe, which we earlier noted as among the values acceptable to totalitarian and democrat alike. But the right of self-determination, as liberals would conceive it, is not for Plato's citizens. Since neither Socrates nor Plato appears ever to have doubted that every man in his deepest heart desires virtue, for them the vital question of individual choice cannot arise; freedom becomes identical with the acceptance of the pronouncements of reason, and he is most free who best obeys ideal authority.

From these principles derive the hierarchical structure of Plato's social order and the predetermined tasks of its members. These, and not the cynical opportunism, the narrow racialism, or the fanatical materialist faith of a totalitarian regime, determine the purposes to which indoctrination in Plato's city is dedicated, and set the limits within which, if we imagine it put to the test of practice, the Platonic regimentation would function. Though Plato has blurred the edges of his intention by admitting the employment of myth and the occasional medicinal lie, it cannot be doubted that his fundamental aim is the inculcation of truth, and that he has at heart not some external cause or selfish interest, but the good of the citizens themselves.

But wherever the service of these values — truth and the citizens' good — gives warrant, there Plato sanctions the intervention of wisdom united with power to control the citizens' every act and thought, and there results that obliteration of any area of individual decision which we have spread upon the record above, and which marks Plato's true kinship to the dictators.

It is only too easy to be guilty of injustice to Plato here, seeing as clearly as we do the enormous price that his proposals, if carried into effect, would exact. What we forget is that to Plato this price was almost invisible, negligible in terms not only of the community's good, but on balance, for each individual citizen likewise. The restrictions he imposed involved, as he saw the matter, no moral cost, while such values of other sorts as he was consciously preparing to resign he could scarcely weigh in the same scales with those to be achieved. He was, as he well knew, demanding that the guardians in the *Republic* should resign much that for the ordinary mortal makes life most livable; Adeimantus, voicing here the world's standpoint, protests as we have seen against the deprivations imposed upon them by their barracks existence and their poverty. Glaucon, again, is dismayed that the rulers themselves should be required to descend from the heights of speculation into the busy dust of civic affairs. And when "Socrates" provisionally banishes the poets, it is not without an expression of reluctance, as of one who suffers a personal loss. The common citizens, for their part, are called upon to abjure all participation in government, though this will be a lesser sacrifice, since (Plato believes) they will recognize and welcome the disinterested expert when he appears. In the *Laws*, too, Plato requires of the citizens much that he knows they will find difficult, at least at first.

But Plato has steeled himself against such weaknesses. With the same confident assurance with which Socrates, in the *Apology*, had declared that "no harm can befall the good man," he is implicitly asserting that no loss can accrue to those who aim at goodness. He is translating into social terms the sentence of Socrates in the *Phaedo*, denying the commensurability of calculated pleasures and pains with the one true coinage of virtue. He is proposing to require his citizens to act on the principle implied by the founder of Christianity in the question, "What shall it profit a man to gain the whole world . . .?" Here, as so often in Plato's prescriptions of social policy, we may ignore or even deplore the material content, while finding in its supporting "maxim" pure morals and high religion. Thus, if we are willing, for the moment, to regard the situation not from the standpoint of the expectable results, but in terms of Plato's aim, we can see that he believed himself to be obtaining at very small cost — a cost, moreover, which in the *Republic*, as he envisaged it, would be borne principally by those who could best afford and best sustain the loss — the highest good of all. Plato's proposals, however illiberal some of them may be, rise from genuine benevolence and aim at the realization of a high ideal.

We must now digress to consider an aspect of Plato's state only distantly related to totalitarianism as usually conceived, namely, its stability, a theme to which Popper has directed his hostile attention. To stabilize his city, or rather to "arrest" or "petrify" it, was, if we credit Popper, Plato's overriding aim.[119] In discussing the value of social stability, we are clearly in a region where rival and contradictory truisms can be only too easily interchanged, where sanity and significance depend upon a just recognition of the degree of

---

[119] See Appendix XV, which is directed against Popper's belief that, for Plato's metaphysics, change is unqualified evil.

stability to be commended, and the situation to which it is applicable. Gilbert Murray has pointedly remarked that, on the evidence of anthropology, "Inherited Conglomerates" or traditional bodies of belief, around which all societies are organized, "have practically no chance of being true or even sensible"; yet "no society can exist without them or even submit to any drastic correction of them without social danger." [120] Anthropologists and social psychologists have offered impressive descriptions of the social cost of accelerated change: the discrediting of what had been regarded as the wisdom of tradition and experience, the bewilderment and loss of social responsibility both on the part of the younger generation, deprived of guidance, and on the part of their

---

[120] Quoted from *Greek Studies*, 1946, by Gilbert Murray, p. 67, in E. R. Dodds' *The Greeks and the Irrational*, 1951, p. 192. The apparent conservatism of the sentence quoted does not prevent Murray from stoutly advocating that at least some members of a given society should make a critical examination of the "Inherited Conglomorate" from a point of view external to it. Professor Dodds' book, *The Greeks and the Irrational*, may be characterized, so far as it deals with the matters of our concern, as "two cheers" for Plato, who is roundly praised for his perception that the thin rationalism of his predecessors was an insufficient basis for morals and for his energetic attempt, especially in the *Laws*, to preserve the framework of rationalism while introducing into it provision for the training and control of the irrational element in human behavior. The third cheer is withheld from him on grounds highly reminiscent of Popper, whose book Dodds knows and cites approvingly (p. 255). Thus Dodds interprets Plato's *Laws* as a proposal for "a completely 'closed' society, to be ruled not by the illuminated reason, but (under God) by custom and religious law"; the institutions Plato has devised are little more than means to "the conditioning of human cattle" (Dodds, p. 216). And in support of these assertions, Dodds cites (p. 229) the same seemingly oppressive passage from the *Laws* (cf. our pp. 531ff.) which had been so prominently displayed by Popper; Dodds also fails to note that it forms part of Plato's discussion of military training, or to point out explicitly that in other sections of the *Laws*, Plato provides for his city, in the Night Council, a window (small though it be) open both to philosophic reason and to the experience of other societies (cf. our

p. 517). Like Popper, again, Dodds believes (pp. 223–224) that Plato would have included Socrates among his condemned atheists, and that Plato's sole reason for executing such disbelievers was the desire to save the social fabric from "contamination by dangerous thoughts"; we have argued these points on pp. 560, 521, n. 555.

It is also matter of regret to me that Dodds should have lent the authority of his name to a hazardous speculation which finds the origin of the higher philosophic education of Plato's guardians in the *Republic*, together with some experiences declared in the Platonic myths to be shared in some degree by all human souls before birth and after death, in a cross-fertilization of Socratic rationalism by an originally Asiatic "shamanism," according to which the literal detachment of the shaman's soul from his body and its journeying into distant occult regions form the basis of his esoteric wisdom and consequent supernatural authority in the community of his followers. To see in Plato's guardians, in consequence, "a new kind of rationalized shamans" is to take a long step down a path converging ultimately with Popper's explicit degradation of Plato's philosopher king into that sorry shaman — supposedly Plato himself — who traffics in breeding-taboos.

Finally, however, it is interesting to notice that, though Dodds employs many of Popper's same categories and terms — "open society," "fear of freedom," the results of his application of them to Plato are strikingly different. Plato remains, for him, an essentially admirable and nobly disinterested thinker, whose understanding of the needs of men and whose prescriptions for the solution of the social problems of his day were second to none.

elders, deprived of status and of their anticipated honors and rewards.[121] Alterations of custom and belief must always be possible in any acceptable society; it is no one's intention to deny this obvious truth; but it is equally obvious that they are more safely made if they are gradual and, at any one time, not too extensive. And in any case, the desirability of change and its approvable extent remain essentially related to the worth and quality of the particular society in question. One may easily conceive social situations in which radical surgery would be as wisely recommended as, in contrary in-stances, it might be judged unlikely to produce benefits equal to its cost. It follows that Plato's desire for stability in his ideal cities, however unwelcome some of the means proposed for securing it, will be open to censure only in so far as he has transgressed these limitations.

Plato, we must remember, had lived through the greater part of the Pelopon-nesian war, and had seen city after city, including his own, rent with faction and overcome by external force; he believed, moreover, that he had witnessed the final stages in the moral decline of Athens from the "men of Marathon" to the shrewd and selfish habitués of the courts whom he shows in the *Theaetetus*. Thus warned, he could scarcely fail to set high value upon stability as an ingredient of any admirable constitution and to give earnest consideration to means of securing it, once the presence of other values had been assured. Plato did not, as we have seen, preclude the possibility that even his perfect city might undergo change in an upward direction, and indeed provided for it in a general way; but in the case of a thing believed to be already so excellent, provision against deterioration might well appear more pressing. And yet, having chosen wisdom, like Solomon he could congratulate himself — so he believed — upon having not only happiness but stability added unto him. For the internal organization of his state, by its promotion of all forms of civic excellence, by its production of individuals inwardly harmonized and just, and by its provision for the interests of every group and member, was, in theory at least, in perfect equilibrium. Even the censorship, with its prohibition of unlicensed innovation, even the limitation of religious freedom in the *Laws*, must not be construed as mere instruments of conservation. If his community had been scheduled for dissolution before the year was out, Plato would still have wished its art and its religion to remain undefiled to its final hour. That they would also promote the city's stability was an added blessing.

This belief in a consilience of genuine goods is a recurrent feature of Plato's thought which has more than once engendered misunderstanding. Thus we found Plato believing in a kind of preëstablished harmony between the good

---

[121] For an alarming but soberly docu-mented analysis of the devastating effects of accelerated social change upon our own American culture, see Bloch, *Disintegration, Personal and Social*, 1952. A detailed case history of the virtual collapse of an Ameri-can Indian society under the stress of social forces too swift for its assimilation is pro-vided by Margaret Mead's *The Changing Culture of an Indian Tribe*, 1932.

of the well-tempered whole and the good of each of its members, a belief which Popper mistook for an exclusive concern for the whole. Similarly, we have seen that Plato believes self-benefit an inseparable concomitant of doing justice to others, a belief which Fite has mistaken for sheer self-regarding prudence. So here, Plato, maintaining that stability will inevitably wait upon the virtue of a community as a whole and of all its citizens, has again been misunderstood; in particular, his insistence that freedom from disunion within the ruling group — a necessary condition for the continued existence of any city — will go hand and hand with their scrupulous regard for the rights of their humble fellow citizens and their piety toward each other as kinsmen, has been taken by Popper as proof that he is merely advocating the arrest of change and seeking to achieve class discipline. Popper is of the opinion that for no other reason than this Plato has forbidden to the guardians private property, the private family, and the extremes either of poverty or wealth, and has endeavored to restrict them from practising the extremes of depredation upon their human cattle. As Popper interprets Plato's intention, the guardians are to be still further unified by their awareness of the enormous caste gulf which separates them from the racially and educationally inferior subject citizens, and it is only for the sake of stabilization, also, that the philosopher kings are to be elevated, like so many prestigious totem poles of mysterious superiority, above the common herd.[122]

We have earlier exposed the illusory character of this caste gulf in its racial aspect, and have reaffirmed the obvious sincerity of Plato's intention to impart the best possible higher education to his philosophers. No text supports Popper's attribution to Plato of an intention to open a psychological chasm of conscious superiority between guardian and common citizen.[123] Aristotle may have been justified in his more limited criticism, in which Popper would have been wiser to join him, that Plato's arrangements would not, in fact, have achieved the contemplated unity.[124] But as Aristotle assumes, and as we were just now urging, this would have been by no means for lack of such intention on Plato's part. Nor is it a suspicious circumstance, as Popper has whispered,[125] when Plato asks his guardians to deem "nothing more shameful than lightly to fall out with one another," and to harbor no thoughts of enmity toward kith and kin or fellow citizen;[126] it is not for the sake of mere prudence that Plato

---

[122] Popper, pp. 49, 50, 53, 54, 145–146.

[123] Popper may have in mind (though he does not here name it) that scornful attitude to the "banausic" tasks of the common citizens which, as we have seen, Plato expects his guardians to share with most well-to-do Greeks of his day and, to a considerable degree, with himself; cf. our discussion, pp. 239ff. But Plato has provided ample evidence that despite this unresolved conflict in his thought, thus reflected in the attitude he imputes to the guardians, he expects the guardians to feel obligated as kinsmen to benefit and serve the workers, and to form with them a unified city, even a "collective" of shared griefs and satisfactions.

[124] Politics II, v, 1264 a 26.

[125] Popper, p. 501.

[126] Republic 378 C, trans. Shorey, Loeb Library.

forbids them to plunder and enslave the workers. To see in this only rigid class discipline and the determination to arrest all social change more securely than did even Sparta, is to refuse Plato the right to testify to his own deepest conviction that piety, and justice to those whom it is in one's power to harm,[127] are sovereign goods.

Reverting to our theme of Plato and totalitarianism, we have now to examine his educational program, to which, as we have seen, he looked as the chief agent of his purposes. We have already exhibited some of its brighter features, its vast superiority to its supposed Spartan model, and the contrast of its intended human products with the totalitarian Leader and his elite. But there are still points to be added in Plato's favor. The modern liberal will find himself in agreement with Plato's disavowal of compulsion in the educative process, a striking parallel to his more inclusive appeal to persuasion, of which we earlier had much to say.[128] As the divine persuasion of the *Timaeus* is, in some sort, the schoolmaster to Necessity, persuading it to assume order and form, so likewise Platonic education, rejecting constraint, will employ gentler measures: "a free soul ought not to pursue any study slavishly . . . nothing that is learned under compulsion stays with the mind," says the Socrates of the *Republic* (536 E), adding the modern-sounding prohibition of which we have already spoken, "Do not . . . keep children to their studies by compulsion but by play." [129] Approvable, too, on modern principles is the Platonic recognition of the respective claims of physical and mental education, the skillful manner in which he has linked the two in a functional partnership in which the body is treated with no ascetic mortification or neglect, but nevertheless is made to serve under the direction and ultimately for the sake of its senior partner, the soul.

It is also possible to offer in terms valid for a democratic society, some justification for Plato's belief that the educational process can properly be used to mold citizens into conformity with the demands of the culture within which they are to live.[130] We must walk warily in this region of controversy,

---

[127] Cf. pp. 829–830 above, and for scrupulousness in the use of power, e.g., p. 179 and n. 133, p. 296.

[128] See pp. 431–438.

[129] Trans. Shorey, Loeb Library.

[130] The endeavor of any state to educate its citizens in accord with a moral ideal, as Plato proposes to do, has called from Popper a condemnation with which it is possible partly to agree. He argues (pp. 422–423, 459–460) that since education in our schools today is a compulsory association of pupils with the teacher, the latter has no right to try to impose a scale of values; and as we have seen (p. 419) he also maintains that the state is properly to be conceived as

a protective device, not as an agent of moral control and direction of its citizens, and that therefore it should be allowed to do little more educationally than to see that the young are "protected from . . . neglect" and that "all educational facilities are available to everybody" (pp. 109–110). To say with Crossman "that it is madness to allow the minds of children to be molded by individual taste" seems to Popper to "open wide the door to totalitarianism" (p. 129). "Too much state control in education is a fatal danger to freedom" (p. 110). While we should heartily agree to this last statement if allowed to interpret it, we also agree with Crossman; we feel that Popper

but there is a fundamental responsibility involved in the educational relationship with which the liberal must somehow make his peace. Young children are helpless to make choices for themselves, and cannot be left individually on desert islands, each to achieve his own self-development. Whether we like it or not, the social circumstances in which the child is placed will in large degree determine what he becomes, nor can the parents alone be left to determine what this shall be. It appears wiser that conscious direction, provided by society, shall intervene to guide the process as far as may be toward the socially desired ends. We differ from Plato, in our modern day, by having as our goal for every child, and at a far earlier age than Plato hoped to achieve it for his rulers, the capacity for self-direction, and the influence of this aim will work its way from the upper levels of our educational system, though with diminishing effect, down the age scale. But at the earliest ages and for many of the later school years in preponderant degree, we shall, like Plato, be seeking to mold the child as we think best for him and for our society as a whole. For this reason Plato's humane ideal of balanced adjustment of soul and body and of the harmonious integration of the soul itself, retains status even to this day, requiring to be supplemented rather than abandoned.

But even on the intermediate level and touching the very issue of political indoctrination, we believe that an armed truce can be arranged between Plato's representatives and the more reasonable of Plato's liberal critics. According to the signs of our educational times, there is a respectable and growing minority opinion in liberal quarters that "indoctrination" in the basic values of our democratic culture pattern is a necessity to the healthy survival of democracy itself. By way of fair example, we may call to witness a stanch and highly enlightened defender of the democratic process against all authoritarian attack, Professor Karl Friedrich. In *The New Belief in the Common Man* we are offered a shrewd and fresh analysis of the dangers and evils of the proposed alternatives to democracy, and, on its positive side, some constructive suggestions for the further improvement of the democratic process itself. Indoctrination is almost the villain of the piece, and Friedrich does not

---

is taking too extreme a position, and that for two reasons. He appears, first, to conceive education almost wholly as if the pupils were already adult, and thus fails to recognize the inevitable moral effect of the school. Education is not the mere provision of "educational facilities," cafeteria tables from which already mature persons select what they need. It seems clear also that "the state" of which Popper is thinking is a threatening monster, and not the beneficent agent of the public will which stands nearer to the norm of our experience. As we have blamed Plato above for subjecting the slave too much to his master and thus depriving

him of rightful access to the more impartial justice of public law, and as we have approved Plato's opposite course in respect to women, so here we believe that Plato and not Popper is more largely right: though we should conceive the state not, as Plato conceives it, as the embodiment of moral knowledge, but as the representative of its citizens in their capacity as parents, agreeing upon basic needs and minimum moral requirements, we should maintain that the state must educate its children, and must not leave them wholly to their own or their parents' private direction.

stop short of condemning the practice of educating children for democracy, if by that phrase is meant the prescription of any, even the most fundamental beliefs.[131] This would seem to be a position antipodal to Plato, but we have yet to hear a most important qualification. Our critic of prescription is convinced that "education is concerned with shaping human beings in the light of a believed-in ideal," and deems it "essential that the schools . . . step in . . . to mould as many young people . . . as possible" into the pattern required for "the conduct of its civic affairs." [132] A high educational authority, Professor Kilpatrick, in a recent article, "Crucial Issues in Educational Theory," [133] vigorously maintains that the primary task of American education is "to furnish the character traits . . . necessary to support and implement the desired civilization," with its basic ideals of the several freedoms and of equality, and declaring that the present deep division in our country and the world constitutes the major threat to contemporary civilization, he calls upon education to assist in achieving "a common outlook on life." It is apparent that in thus recognizing that education must accept the responsibility for promoting the basic values of the community, even for achieving unity and harmony, Friedrich and Kilpatrick and Plato, despite the sharp difference in political aim, are at one. Taken by itself, therefore, this trait would make Plato a democrat or a totalitarian at choice.

The censorship of art, that other major vehicle of Plato's social restrictiveness, can be more briefly dealt with. We make no defense of Plato's excessive paternalism, which would keep his citizens in aesthetic nonage all their days, sheltered from the mimicked passions and immoral acts presented by Homer and the dramatists, and from the siren sweetness of the Lydian and Ionian modes. Nor can we join him in his proscription of innovation. For us, of course, the arts are essentially a continuum of innovation, and whatever form is no longer capable of yielding some significant variation we consider as a candidate for possible canonization, but no longer fit for creative use. We can, on the other side, applaud his insight that no adequate education can neglect the aesthetic component, and his consequent concern to provide a matrix of beauty within which the human soul can grow toward its perfection. We are willing to accept a limited censorship, if kept within the bounds of the school; a modern democratic educator might wish to admit

---

[131] *The New Belief in the Common Man* by Karl J. Friedrich, Little, Brown, Boston, 1943, pp. 157, 177 f.

[132] *Ibid.*, 281–283. This "molding" of the young is the *plattein* of the *Republic*, and the principle is basic also to the primary education of the citizens of Plato's *Laws*. The Oxford scholar, Dodds, in his recent article ("Why Greek Rationalism Failed," 1952), in summary agreement with his book (*The Greeks and the Irrational*, 1951, pp. 207–224, esp. p. 219; and pp. 254–255), sees

in Plato and, after him, in Aristotle, the first "serious attempt at a rational interpretation of the irrational," and the beginnings of an educational theory which would embody the new insight; he insists on the necessity, if Reason is to survive in our own day, of employing their method of social control by what Aristotle called "*ethismos*" — habituation.

[133] William H. Kilpatrick, in *Educational Theory*, I, May 1951. The quotations are from pp. 3–5, and 8.

only such art as appeared to him at once excellent in itself and morally
above reproach, trailing no associations of irreligion or vice and calculated
to arouse generous enthusiasms such as he could wish his pupils to make
living parts of themselves. Even in the wider area of civic affairs, though
with no thought of restriction, we could follow Plato (here the good Athenian) in wishing to accept the communal responsibility of ministering in
some fashion to the sense of beauty, if only to offset the ugliness to which
many of our citizens are condemned in their daily environment, and in believing, with him, that art must not be left without attachment to the common
life.[134] And finally, it must be said that whatever Plato's fault in these matters
may be, his sins were those of the Puritan moralist and not those of the modern totalitarian using art to prove and preach racial superiority or to excite
enthusiasm for some political proposal.

We return briefly to the grim theme of Plato's condemnation of religious
heretics in the *Laws*; he provides, as we recollect, that an honest and upright disbeliever shall be imprisoned for five years in the prison adjoining the
meeting place of the Night Council, and shall be invited to participate in
their studies and investigations, but if at the end of that time he remains unconvinced, he shall die.[135] This is perhaps Plato's most unwelcome proposal,
and one which, as we have said, we trust that he would not have carried out.
Plato falls below the liberality of Athenian practice in his unremitting intention to cleanse his city of all atheism, even when only privately expressed.
Yet it was not wholly un-Athenian to persecute an atheist, nor is Plato's law
as narrow in what it forbids as the Athenian law. To say with Grote that "the
Socrates of the Platonic *Apology*" would not "be allowed to exist" by Plato
in his Republic, or in the city of the *Laws*, is to overlook a distinction:
Athens condemned those who dishonored the "gods worshipped by the city";
Plato, true to his conception of Socrates' own faith, asks only a belief in gods
(or god) who are providential and incorruptibly just.[136] The mildness of these

---

[134] Plato's name has often been linked
with that of Tolstoi in this context. As is
well known, Tolstoi after his conversion
repudiated all art as valueless or worse
which did not possess the power of "infect-
ing" mankind with approvable sentiments.
Un-Platonic are the quality of the sentiment
Tolstoi's art would convey and his standard
of "peasant appeal." The resemblance lies
in the conviction shared by the two men that
the moral or human ministry of art is sovereign over all considerations of "pleasure"
or "freedom of the artist." And there is the
further parallel that both men, each in his
own way, were prepared to make sacrifice
of their own interests, Plato, as Crossman
(p. 90) has put it (with some exaggeration,

in my judgment), in devotion "to the cause
of philosophy and of the regeneration of
Greece," allowing "the springs of his imagination to dry up," and Tolstoi disavowing
the masterly achievements for which the
world called him great.

[135] We have discussed this matter above,
pp. 355–358 and 479.

[136] Grote, *Plato*, III, pp. 240, 411. To
embroider the theme of our divergence
from Grote, let us imagine the young Socrates enrolled among the colonists in the
city of the *Laws*; what must Plato have
supposed would be his probable career?
He would see him commending himself to
all by his moral seriousness and high intelligence. At the age of 35 he is co-opted

minimum credal requirements, which represent almost the least supposed necessary by any European society until well after the Reformation, is underscored by Plato's hope of winning over the disbeliever by a five-years' course in natural theology. In the light of history we plainly see the folly of such trust in what, to him, was simply rational persuasion; yet it has a nobly Socratic aspect. These admirable elements in Plato's law lend tragedy to the spectacle of a high and serious intent brought to naught by a misplaced coercion.

One further area of restrictiveness and we have done. In the *Laws*, as we have noted, Plato is determined to insure that law shall be supreme.[137] Every citizen is to regard the law with the utmost reverence, as a thing to be, in all but the rarest instances, preserved unchanged and followed to the letter. Even the highest officers in the state are to be the servants of the law, nay rather its slaves. Every official is to be held to the strictest possible accountability; any citizen may hale him into court if he appears guilty of injustice. In this Plato is following the precedent of his native Athens, but he has greatly extended its scope. Restriction could go no further: no one shall escape it. — Yes, but does it not have another face, and, so regarded, appear also as one of the foundations of liberty under law? Plato's earnest intention of protecting the ordinary citizens in the Republic against depredation by their rulers reappears, when once the hope of ideal rulers is discarded, in a form which we as democrats can wholeheartedly accept and honor — a far cry indeed from the totalitarian substitution of administrative discretion for legal rule.[138]

Violence and inhumanity. — That Plato repudiated revolutionary violence as a means of bringing about his political reforms was evidenced at

---

as a junior member of the Night Council, at 50 elected Law-warden and chosen Commissioner of Education, in his latter years installed as Examiner, and after the completion of this *cursus honorum* honored with public burial. In short, the community would have shown him as warm a welcome as would the Republic, where he would of course have been one of those children of artisan parents enrolled among the guardians, and destined to be "king." In the city of the *Laws* he would have excited no suspicion by encouraging the citizens to care above all else for their souls, or by declaring that the gods cannot be at strife with one another; he would have had no need to go about convicting the citizens of ignorance in order to refute their complacent worldliness. And to consider an extreme unlikelihood, had some literalist in religion charged him with dishonoring the city's

gods, he would have enjoyed the protection of the carefully guarded judicial system, from which just those dangers of deceptive rhetoric, disorder, appeal to prejudice, and hasty disposition of cases of which Plato complained in the *Apology* had been sedulously excluded, and he would have been triumphantly acquitted. Plato could, in short, well feel that in the *Laws* he had designed a community preeminently safe for Socrates.

[137] We speak of the city of the *Laws* before its basic institutions are abrogated by the turning over to the Night Council of absolute power; cf. n. 38, p. 517.

[138] We acknowledge with pleasure our indebtedness to the article, "Plato and the Rule of Law" by Glenn R. Morrow (*Philosophical Review*, vol. L, March 1941), in which Morrow has discerningly celebrated Plato's great achievement in this field.

some length in an earlier chapter and need not be further argued here. We
have likewise given our reasons for regarding as calumny the charge that
violence, open or disguised, was the means whereby Plato proposed to coerce
the ordinary citizens of the Republic into subservience to their exploiting
masters.[139]

Our discussion dealt also with a distinct but related question: did Plato
advocate under legal sanctions more drastic repression of offenses against
social order than the humane conscience of the Athens of his day would
allow? We were brought to the unwelcome conclusion that in relation to some
of these offenses, notably those committed by slaves against the persons of
freemen, and in some degree also those of kinsmen against kinsmen, Plato's
legislation was excessively severe. In other respects the measure of his humanity is equal to that of his time and place, or stands above it.[140] Plato's
failings here are balanced by his recognition of the moral unity of mankind,
a principle which was destined to play its part in transforming the spiritual
values of the ancient world, and eventually to contribute substantially to the
development, in modern times, of the full-fledged concept of human freedom,
incompatible with slavery in any form.[141]

"Autarky." — Popper has found and disapproved in Plato's political
theory the attempt to achieve "autarky," i.e., as Popper defines it, self-sufficiency or independence of trade; something called by the same name, one
remembers, was a notable element in Hitler's program for the Third Reich.
The actual element in Plato's thought which Popper is thus bringing to our
attention is expressed in those passages in the *Laws* where foreign trade is
frowned upon and restricted. Thus the Athenian Stranger congratulates himself (704 D–705 B) upon the circumstance that the territory to be settled,
while producing most of the necessaries of life, produces them in no great
abundance, so that few imports will be needed and few exports will be possible;
in consequence, the city will not be flooded with wealth, that enemy of perfect
virtue. Again, only necessary imports, chiefly those required for military
purposes, are to be permitted (847 B–D) and these are to be handled by the
appropriate officials; private citizens are to be interdicted from all commercial
pursuits (919 C f.). That the same trade policy was to be followed by the
philosopher kings of the *Republic* Popper has apparently inferred, in the
absence of any specific statement, from Plato's refusal there, also, to permit
the city to grow rich and the guardians to engage in money making of any
kind. Without any supporting text, Popper lists autarky as one of the totalitarian features of the ideal city.[142]

---

[139] See pp. 344ff. and n. 70, p. 426.
[140] See pp. 186ff., especially n. 124, p.
192; and pp. 350–352.

[141] The third section of Chapter 6, pp.
201–232, is our documentation here.
[142] Popper, p. 87.

But how is all this related to the program of the modern dictators? Popper has given a very remarkable answer to this question. He sees Spartan foreign policy, as we earlier mentioned, as dominated in all respects by the purpose of "closing" the society, and lists among its aims, along with censorship, exclusion, opposition to all liberal ideals, racial pride, and limitation of population, this aim of "autarky"; he further specifies that the Spartan military aim was restricted to the domination and enslavement of neighboring states, as contrasted with the wider and more "universalistic" ambitions of Athens.[143] The narrow Spartan aims taken together, Popper declares, are truly totalitarian, and are in reality those of the modern totalitarians as well. The expansiveness and ambition to conquer the world of these latter are not properly totalitarian traits, but have been "imposed upon them, as it were, against their will" by the need, common to all tyrannies, of uniting their people in a shared enmity, and by the fact that in the modern world, all states are now neighbors. It is thus possible for Popper to declare that Plato, in decrying foreign trade, is showing his truly totalitarian color, while in their reluctant striving after conquest Hitler, poor man, and his fellow-sufferer Il Duce, were atypical!

In the face of such an extravagance we may remind ourselves, first, that Hitler's concept of the Master Race, like Il Duce's imperial ideal, was inherently dynamic and expansive, hardly to be permanently satisfied by the domination of his own people and of a few peripheral satellites. Secondly, it is to be observed that the actual content of the Nazi idea of "autarky" has hardly more than a nominal resemblance to the idea we find in Plato. Hitler's policy of "autarky" was indeed aimed at the self-sufficiency of Germany, her independence of international trade, in the sense that she would have under her control all sources of vital raw materials. But this was, during the entire period of the Nazi supremacy, an interim aim, designed to prepare Germany for successfully waging a long war of conquest.[144] A stable and permanent

---

[143] Popper, pp. 177–178. We have discussed this list of Spartan aims on pp. 311, and 322–323. Popper has also in this passage shifted again the meaning of "tyranny," which, as we have noted above (n. 115, p. 78), he sometimes describes as a governmental form based on popular support, thus bringing discredit upon Plato's admitted hatred of tyranny, and sometimes makes identical with the reactionary despotism of Critias. In this instance, he applies the term "tyranny" to the modern totalitarian states, and correctly sees in these an essential kinship with the Greek type which Plato opposed; for, as he says, they are vitiated by that same constant need of stirring up foreign wars which Plato had observed and condemned in Greek tyranny. In short, we

have here Popper's admission that Plato could never have approved the militarism of the modern totalitarians. And we may add, neither could he have approved the constant stirring up of wars against closely neighboring states, such as Popper supposes Plato approved in Sparta.

[144] I am aware that a supposedly stable self-sufficiency within a limited national territory had been proposed as a goal for Germany by several German theorists, notably Fichte, though in his formulation it was not likely to have conduced to peace. But the Nazis had no such limited objective, even in theory. Cf. *Behemoth*, by Franz Neumann, Oxford University Press, New York, 1942, pp. 329–330.

self-sufficiency can be said to have been the Nazi aim only in the sense that their ultimate goal was world domination. Plato's aim, however, was neither preparation for conquest nor the securing of independence, in the Nazi sense of that word, of foreign trade. He was proposing defense only, the securing from aggression either of his own state or of a neighbor, and the only imports he countenances and expects to continue in being are just those which Hitler most earnestly wishes to render unnecessary. Popper's choice of the word "independence" has obscured these vital differences from our view.

A further serious protest must be entered against the unsound "essentialism" inherent in Popper's conception of the foreign policy which he declares to be really totalitarian. Having identified this entity, exemplified to perfection in Sparta, he then detects it on the one hand appearing with particular clarity in Plato, and on the other hand, disguised but still recognizable in Hitlerism. Yet, as we have already shown, there is no such complete coincidence between Plato and the Spartan policy; in respect to most of the items on Popper's list, either Popper has filled in the gaps in his knowledge of Sparta by borrowing from Plato's Republic, or he has distorted Plato's meaning into a semblance of Spartanism where little or none exists.[145] Genuine similarity in the terms of his list is limited almost entirely to joint approval of exclusion and censorship, and even here there is no identity. In "autarky," Popper has found another near identity between Plato and Sparta. Yet this trait, as we have just shown, is not truly Hitlerian, and therefore fails to strengthen his triangular comparison.[146]

---

[145] See n. 170, p. 311, n. 104, p. 541, and our section on Sparta and Plato's political ideals, pp. 509ff.

[146] I do not for one moment question Popper's title to exercise the right of what was earlier (p. 417) called the "reëssentialization" of concepts. But the claimant of this privilege must observe certain minimal logical proprieties. It is clearly wrong to "reëssentialize" the same concept in two contradictory ways, as Popper has done. It will be recollected that he has earlier asked us (Popper, pp. 12–13) to condemn totalitarianism as "historicist," and to see the modern totalitarianisms of Nazism, Fascism, and Communism as based on a belief in a master race or favored nation or class, predestined to "inherit the earth"; this implies a "foreign policy" which is expansionist, to say the least. But in the passage that has just been claiming attention in our text, Popper has made clear his conviction that the essential aim of totalitarianism is to maintain unaltered a "closed," tribalistic

community behind a wall of cultural exclusiveness and isolation. This second assertion, as we have remarked in our text, p. 563, requires Popper to dismiss the expansiveness of the latter-day totalitarians as a mere circumstantial accident that forms no part of the policy of totalitarianism as such.

The second condition that must be met by anyone wishing to make material application of his reëssentialized concept is responsibility to the actual facts and a certain gentle docility in handling them. He must not push and pull and otherwise play Procrustes, as we have found Popper doing, in his effort to fit Sparta and Plato and Hitler into the same framework.

To conclude: in his handling of totalitarianism, Popper has paralleled his own treatment of historicism and of Athenian oligarchy (cf. pp. 506, 274ff., 606–608). In all three cases we have found him proving to us by example the dangers of that "methodological essentialism" against which he has entered so emphatic a warning (pp.

Efficiency. — A word is needed here in reply to Fite's disparaging discovery that the hierarchical principle on which Plato has organized his Republic is chosen solely with a view to "technological efficiency," which, it is implied, was to Plato an end in itself. (It is amusing to see Fite following this interpretation to the wilful extreme of declaring that the hierarchical order of the eternal forms, also, was but a "projection upon the sky of technological efficiency." [147]) And there is in Fite's charge also a further implication: by insisting that each shall mind his own business and by treating each person merely as a social function personified, Plato has shown callous disregard of other values which a less rigid system might have conserved. We answer that scant justice is done to Plato's Republic by anyone who permits himself to lose sight of its central aim, that of socializing the Socratic world of values. These values at once illuminated and limited Plato's vision; we may agree with Fite that much of great human worth was undreamed of in his philosophy. But we have no right to think of Plato as complacently accepting whatever means will lead to his chosen ends. The "efficiency" of the Republic is not technological, but internal and moral, and Plato's conscious sacrifice of other values, e.g., of Homer, was not prompted by technological considerations of promptitude and convenience in the carrying-out of some external purpose. The opposition of means to ends, in fact, is all but abolished in a philosophy for which living according to virtue is at once the means to the happiness of the entire community and simultaneously its final goal.

Militarism. — And now at last we must make a formal and emphatic restatement, with the addition of some further evidence, of what we have repeatedly asserted in our defense of Plato from indiscriminate attack: Plato was not a militarist, but one of the earliest advocates of the moral superiority of peace to war. We need not repeat what we have so recently written of Plato's attitude to war as expressed in the Laws, particularly the explicit rebuke administered to the Spartan polity for its central commitment to the attainment of courage and victory in war. Plato's testimony here is so unambiguous that it can be discredited only by the method, usual with Popper, of assuming that Plato has said one thing with his lips and hidden another in his heart: "many militarists have talked peace and practiced war." [148] Our general demonstration that Plato tells his reader the truth may here be supplemented by the remark that had Plato really desired to plan a state which should aim primarily at

---

34–35, 485, 624). In each case, he has set up a description or list of traits and has invested it in practice with an authority which dissolves distinctions and overrides palpable facts, much in the manner of a social stereotype which blinds its employer to observable traits and sharpens to Lyncean acuity his perception of what isn't there to be perceived, thus enabling him to condemn those who do not in fact display the disapprovable traits in the name of which the whole group is held worthy of condemnation.

[147] Fite, p. 219.

[148] Popper, p. 538.

warlike achievement, he might have said so without incurring public blame. For had not Pericles praised Athens as great beyond all other Greek states because of her far wider conquests, and was not Plato's contemporary Alcidamas free to acclaim without reservation the great Theban general Epaminondas? [149]

The *Republic,* however, requires a somewhat different handling. For we are confronted here, in addition to Popper and Neurath, by Fite, whom reading of the *Republic* has convinced that it is militarist in spirit. Unfortunately the *Republic* contains no such explicit denials as are found in the *Laws,* but it is possible to collect from scattered passages and from some general considerations sufficient evidence that no contradiction divides the earlier from the later Plato.

Anyone who does as Neurath has advised and makes an effort to pay no attention to Plato's lofty protestations of aim, but to look instead at what Plato recommends shall be done in his ideal city, will observe, without doubt, that Plato makes it his first task to recommend the provision of a corps of fearless, loyal, "athletes of war," and that he devotes much space to describing their training and education, which has as one of its basic objectives (Neurath would perhaps say its only objective) the production of effective fighting men and women. But despite the initial prominence of these soldiers, the fair-minded reader will note that in due course they are required to yield the primacy to the philosopher kings, who, though they too have received a military training, possess qualities extending into what is almost another dimension of human excellence. And it is they, we learn (*Rep.* 412 A–B, 497 C–D, 546 D–E), who are to direct the training of the soldiers which has already been described; only thus can that right education be maintained which alone can prevent the degeneration of the ideal state into Spartan militarism, which will still be able to win wars but will lose its essential allegiance to the highest values and its quality of justice to the common citizens. Though the Platonic soldiers are necessary to the continued existence of the ideal state, the philosopher rulers are, in turn, necessary to secure their distinctively Platonic character. In other words, practical assignment of tasks proves that the city of the Republic is not a war-machine.

Some particular passages will reënforce this conclusion. That war is for Plato in the *Republic* not a good *per se* is clear from the ignoble origin he assigns it. It will be remembered that on his way toward the founding of his own city, Plato drew a picture of a quasi-primitive community, living in a state of simplicity and innocence, in which war was unknown. It is only when, no longer satisfied with true and healthful pleasures, this city becomes inflamed with inordinate desires and requires more territory for their satisfaction that neighbor-city encroaches upon neighbor, and war begins.[150] Just as in the

---

[149] See our p. 143.
[150] We have summarized this section of

the *Republic* more fully on pp. 168–169 above.

Phaedo (66 C), "the acquisition of commodities" which our "slavery to the attendance of the body" brings upon us, is the source "of all wars," so here in the *Republic*, war is born of an ignoble greed and covetousness, "things from which the greatest disasters, public and private, come to states" — surely a discouraging preface to a book supposedly dedicated to the greater glory of war. It is hardly necessary to point out that a man holding this view may still without inconsistency accord an honorable position to those trained for the vigorous defense of the homeland. Inconsistency would appear if, after thus condemning the appetitive satisfactions as the cause of war, Plato had held them up none the less before his citizens as worthy objects of pursuit. But the denial of the acquisitive ideal was the very foundation of his ethical scheme.

Is Plato's state to expand by conquest at the expense of other states? This question is answered in the confident affirmative by Fite, adducing the very passage we just now mentioned, in which the luxurious city seeks to cut off a portion of its neighbor's land — strange evidence, when one considers that at the time of this offense, Plato's own city was still unborn. Neurath thinks that "the barbarians" will be the standing target of Platonic aggression; for this he has only the evidence met by our argument in an earlier passage.[151] How has Popper voted on this issue? At first it might appear that he has abstained, but a second look reveals that he has voted, "Yes, but only to a limited degree." A third look tells us why: it is, we saw, a part of the totalitarian pattern, as Popper has chosen to interpret it, to prefer control to conquest; after "enslaving" her immediate neighbors, Popper apparently supposes that Plato's city, like Sparta, would wish to remain at rest within the security of her own tribal enclosure.

In this notion Popper and the facts of the case are, we should judge, in accord to the extent of almost one-third. There is, to the best of our reading, only one passage in the *Republic* which leaves open the possibility that Plato contemplated under any conditions the enlargement of the territory of his city. At *Republic* 423 B, the question is raised "of the proper size of the city and of the territory which they" (the guardians) "should mark off for a city of that size and seek no more," and the answer given is that it shall be let grow "so long as in its growth it consents to remain a unity, but no further"; it is added that the guardians must "keep guard in every way that the city shall not be too small . . . but that it shall be a sufficient city and one." Nothing is said in this place of the means by which these ends may be achieved. One further passage must be taken into account: after explaining how the "marriages" of the guardians are to be arranged, Plato enjoins upon the rulers the duty of planning these in such a way "that they may keep the numbers of the citizens as nearly as may be the same, taking into account wars and diseases and all

---

[151] For Neurath's opinion, see p. 441;   for our discussion of the barbarian question
as raised in the *Republic*, see pp. 223ff.

such considerations, and that, so far as possible, our city may not grow too great or too small." [152]

From the first of these passages, in the absence of further context, it is only possible to say that Plato seems to be contemplating a time in the life of the city when expansion into neighboring territory might be undertaken, but whether by conquest or by peaceful incorporation of neighboring villages (synoecism), cannot be said. Athens, it will be recollected, had expanded by both methods in her earlier time. Solon's conquest of Salamis would have been a possible precedent in the mind of his kinsman Plato, and if such was the case, then plainly Plato was contemplating conquest and should be prosecuted — but he must have the privilege of trial in an Attic court. The more peaceful method of synoecism just mentioned could also have been in his mind.

In any case there was to be a limit to what was permitted in this matter: Plato in the very passage in which he is supposed by his critics to be recommending war on the barbarians, forbids his city to enslave Greek cities or fellow Greeks; those who, like Popper, habitually see in Plato the intention to emulate Sparta, should observe this prohibition. And as we saw above, when the city had grown to its optimum and very limited size, expansion was to be brought to a stop, which recalls, by the psychological association of opposites, the practice of the modern dictators. To the extent to which Plato's intention of limiting his city's expansion resembles the nonexpansionist policy of Sparta after it had conquered Messenia, Popper is right; but since Plato's nonguardian citizens are not to be Helots, and his guardians are not to be, in Spartan fashion, enslaved to the custody of their own slaves, the similarity ends abruptly. The motive of Plato's limitation is neither the enslavement of neighboring states nor the holding down of human cattle, but the furtherance of his own pacific ideal.

Plato has also offered us a glimpse into what might be called the "foreign policy" of his state; the philosopher will show that he too is a realistic statesman by providing a mildly Machiavellian policy for defense, as an offset to the city's relative inferiority in wealth and fighting strength (*Republic* 422 A– 423 B). If need of allies against threatened attack should arise, our city can easily procure them, either among neighboring cities or among the factions within the attacking city itself, by promising to them in compensation for their services all the spoils of victory. Sweet are the uses of austerity! Now it is difficult to see anything deeply criminal in this. Policies of this general nature were pursued, as the reader of Thucydides well knows, both by Athens and by Sparta. In the historical circumstances of Plato's day, the only method available to a small state of preserving its independent existence would have been

---

[152] *Republic* 460 A. Both passages in this   paragraph are taken from Shorey's trans.,
Loeb Library.

some such expedient as Plato has suggested, and suggested, be it observed, not in the interests of expansion, but solely to ward off aggression.

As final evidence in the *Republic*, we may remind the reader [153] that when Plato comes to describe timocracy, and sets it in contrast to the ideal city, of which it is the first stage of corruption, he puts in a conspicuous place, second only to its enslavement of the common people, the greater honor it bestows upon soldiers and the pursuits of war; it is not that the timocrats will be more adept in the art of war, but that, unlike the guardians of the ideal city, they will be "better suited for war than for peace," and will honor "the stratagems and contrivances of war" and "occupy themselves with war most of the time." Such statements are in themselves demonstrative indications that in Plato's state, neither oppression nor war will be the chief business of its guardians' lives.

It would not be difficult to show this same outlook from a reference to other dialogues, both earlier than the *Republic* and intermediate between the latter and the *Laws*. In the latter group, the *Politicus* alone need concern us. There, in compensation for the lost idyllic peacefulness of the age of Cronos, Plato offers us (307 E–308 A) as a theoretically attainable ideal a community of citizens in whom the balanced temperament prevails. By properly arranged marriages joining those of opposite types he would create individuals in whom the spirited element will provide a manly energy adequate to preserve the state from enslavement by her enemies, while the orderly constituent will prevent madcap militarism from endangering its welfare in the opposite fashion. Now all this is clearly little more than an elaboration of one of the principles underlying the choice and training of the junior guardians in the *Republic*, and war is being given recognition only as a means of preserving freedom, not of enlarging power.

From the dialogues commonly regarded as prior to the *Republic* we will choose the *Symposium*, and here we shall also include the *Phaedrus*,[154] dialogues which, though they are not predominately political in character, will serve to confirm those revelations of Plato's basic value schedule found in the *Republic*, rightly read. In both dialogues Plato has clearly indicated his conception of the highest goals of human life, and the direction in which they are to be pursued, while giving us at least some scattered indications of human goods of lesser rank. It would be superfluous in this place to repeat the substance of our earlier exposition of the speech of Diotima and the myth of the charioteer. These are among the great symbols of ethics and religion; the warfare to which they are relevant is that of the spirit, not the field of battle. They move in a direction contrary to the greeds and materialities for which,

---

[153] We deal with this same passage, *Rep.* 547 B ff., on pp. 510–511.

[154] For a discussion of the date of composition of the *Phaedrus*, see n. 48, p. 96.

as Plato has told us, wars are fought, and culminate in that vision of the central good and beauty which is attained, at the pinnacle of their highest education, by the philosopher kings of the *Republic*. Indeed, it is by keeping centrally before our minds the conception of an experience on this transcendental level that we are best able to realize what it was that Plato believed was infused into his city, to endow it with a quality not to be confused with either the wisdom or the power of a merely wordly state. We touch here the springs of Plato's cosmical religion.

Mention was earlier made of certain lesser goals indicated in these dialogues and relevant to our theme of war. Diotima in the *Symposium* sets on the highest level of those who are fired with noble passion, only the philosopher, and on the second level mentions the poets Homer and Hesiod, and the great legislators, Lycurgus and Solon; but among this honorable company no warrior appears. In the *Phaedrus* (248 D–E), we are offered a graduated scale of lives, listing in order the goals and occupations of those who have enjoyed with different degrees of clarity before their birth the beatific vision of the eternal Forms. At the top of the list, again, stand the philosopher and the lover of the Muses; only on the step below do we find the "lawful king or warlike ruler." Of the two pairs of lovers whom we later meet (256 A–C), the higher and the lower are, respectively, the lovers of wisdom and the seekers after honor. It is plain that we have been hearing the report of an uncommonly well organized and unified mind that everywhere preserves the firm distinction between the secondary values supplied by the warrior and the primary intrinsic excellence of philosophic wisdom.

The Verdict

Here concludes our long task of examining all the traits of totalitarianism that the several detractors have imputed to Plato and of assessing the degree of his guilt under each head. We are now ready to gather together the threads and reply to each of the detractors in turn.

To Crossman, it is plain what terms of settlement we are able to offer. We are ready to agree that Plato believed most of mankind — not merely the working people, be it noted, but all except the "golden natures" — incapable of living virtuous lives unless aided either by ideal rulers or by good laws, planned by a moral expert. But we have shown that it cannot be concluded from this that Plato sanctioned, as the second-best form of government, states headed by second-best dictators. We agree, also, that Plato approved the employment of "propaganda," but we ask that it be observed that this did not mean in general the inculcation of basic falsehood, but the mythical presentation of truth; in particular, moral values were not to be falsified or distorted. We have cleared Plato of "racialism" in the sense of an intention to make membership in the ruling group a hereditary privilege. Finally we have shown the injustice of imputing to him readiness to approve cruel and unjust state policies and propaganda devices. If these distinctions between Plato and the Fascists and Communists could be added to the vital difference in aim which Crossman recognizes, we believe Crossman would himself agree to set Plato and the modern totalitarians far apart.

It involves an unfortunate and unintended distortion of Fite's purpose in his book, to disengage from it the two points of correspondence he has mentioned between Russian Communism and Plato's thought, as if they represented the outcome of an effort on Fite's part to draw a systematic comparison. The first of these points, the authoritative imposition of opinion, we found reason to accept under the limitation that those who are to do the imposing in Plato's state are *sui generis*. The adulation of technological efficiency we have denied. Those other constituents of Plato's political program which we added on our own responsibility to Fite's list of parallels, we have shown to be either absent, or present (as the case of Spartanism) only in mild degree.

A final settlement with Popper will be more complicated. It will be remembered that in our effort to deal fairly with his conception of totalitarianism, we disposed the elements he detects in it under ten headings. Under five of these we have found cause in each case to accept a portion of the charge. Thus, first and foremost, we have agreed that Plato was proposing, in Popper's terms, to "close" his society, in so far as this denotes regimentation of the ordinary citizens; in meeting this charge, we have done little more than to enter the extenuation that what was to be thus enclosed was conceived by Plato to be something of the highest intrinsic excellence, and not the frozen image of a fancied past, valued only for stability and for the release from strain that it would confer upon its members. We have also admitted that Plato's state, by depriving most of its citizens of independent moral action and freedom of belief, would in fact harm and diminish them as human beings. We have agreed, too, that Plato would put an elite in control of his Republic, that he is entirely too harsh in the punishments imposed upon offending slaves in the *Laws*, and that, selectively, he admires Sparta, approving in particular its endeavor to attain at least a part of virtue.

Under these same headings, however, we have shown that Plato sponsored and encouraged freedom of inquiry for the philosopher kings of the Republic, and for their nearest equivalents in the city of the *Laws*, and that he contemplated change in the direction of improvement in both communities; that he never limited the criterion of morality to state interest or upheld the amoral state, and that he intended the benefit of every citizen; that he despised the oppression practised by the Spartans, the narrowness of their ideal, and the brutalizing effect of their education; that his elite was to be unified by no haughty scorn of its human cattle, his philosopher kings to be no breeder-shamans; that most of his particular inhumanities were shared with him by other enlightened Greeks of his day, while his own humanity vastly exceeded theirs in depth and in ideality of aim.

Under the five remaining headings we were able to enter unqualified denials. Plato was no historicist of any kind, no racialist — he felt indeed greater piety for those of kindred blood, but of racial scorn he was entirely free. He was scrupulous in disavowing violence, was in no modern sense an advocate of autarky, and was far rather a peace-lover than a militarist.

One wonders, in view of all these denials, whether Popper himself, if he should accept our verdicts on the several particular parts of his indictment, would continue to call Plato a totalitarian. Certainly he would have to withdraw his rebuke to Crossman and Field for supposing Plato to be morally superior to the moderns of that stripe.[155] Tested by most of Popper's own central criteria, Plato escapes the charge: the denial of political or tribal immoralism destroys close kinship with either Nazism or Fascism, the denial of racialism would seem to rule out any identity with Nazism, the removal of historicism must entail a serious loss of similarity to Communism. That Plato should be no advocate of revolutionary violence and no would-be oppressor of the common citizen, and that he should be contemplating no conquest and enslavement even of neighboring states would further reduce the parallel. The degree of his inhumanity and admiration for Sparta might be deemed insufficient to carry much weight. There is left standing in Popper's case hardly more than enough to justify his comparison of Platonism with the authoritarian Christianity of the Middle Ages. And here we may leave him, agreeing that both faiths were inspired with moral certainty and that both adopted or proposed the adoption of deplorable means of securing their universal acceptance by those subject to their sway; protesting only that at the heart of each there was a store of value, for the sake of which we can be glad that such a whole existed.

Our promise of measuring Plato's political theory by the criteria of totalitarianism as formulated by our three nonpartisan experts can be quickly kept. We have cleared Plato of Brinton's "nationalism" and "racial superiority"; the third trait, subordination to a ruler and his elite, we showed as having only a qualified correspondence to the Platonic ideal; only the "strict discipline" of the people remains. McGovern's two defining traits are both, at first view, points of agreement: the first, "a strong, forceful government," survives a second look as a genuine agreement; but "etatism," in the light of our account of "political holism," turns out to be only a partial parallel; Plato, despite his commendation of control and censorship, was no worshipper of the state, but an advocate of the subordination of political instrumentalities to moral and educational ends in the service of individuals.

Of Perry's list the last three entries were revealed as sharply un-Platonic. Especially noteworthy is the contrast between "anti-intellectualism" and the Platonic pledge, a recurring motif through the dialogues, to follow the argument wheresoever it leads. Perry's surviving trait, "uniformitarianism," turned out to be in harmony with the spirit of Plato's reforms, though we saw that

---

[155] Popper, pp. 87–88.

the uniformity that Plato was seeking was (as on Perry's specifications it has a logical right to be) a rational and universal standard. It seems, then, that no one of the three descriptions can accommodate Plato without serious injury to itself or to him.

We are brought back to a position not far from our point of departure: Plato's political ideal can be classified without distortion as a very highly differentiated one among the many varieties of authoritarian governments denoted by our generalized version of Webster's definition of totalitarianism; it can also, as we earlier agreed, be called "totalitarian" in Sabine's carefully guarded sense of a government which "obliterates the distinction between areas of private judgment and of public control." The repute of Plato as a political thinker for our time will, we submit, be dependent upon two chief considerations: (1) whether or not we take careful note of the safeguards and qualifications which Plato has, both in the *Republic* and in the *Laws*, interposed between those who are to exercise rule, and their inherent human capacity to deteriorate into the likeness of what we have in mind when the word "dictator" is set before us, and (2) whether we permit ourselves to recoil so violently from the Platonic ideal of a community controlled by a single criterion of social good, however excellent, which claims sovereignty at all points and over all individual and minority opinion, that we have no eyes left to see the perennially valid components of his thought.

Living Elements in Plato's Political Thought

We are, then, brought to ask the important question: assuming that in the warfare just ended we have repelled the fury of those who have assailed Plato as the friend of the modern enemies of our most cherished political freedoms, how much is still left standing of the noble old Platonic city through whose streets we fought? [156] We have seen that the city is no longer, without considerable remodeling, conceivable as a habitation for the good society of our time. But, one may believe, a city that has served so many generations as a place of refuge and an ideal, requiring, to be sure, some adaptation in consideration of their respective needs, may well deserve one more attempted salvaging; and it behooves us, accordingly, to ask by what alterations it might be made serviceable for present use.

In setting out on this inquiry there is one principle that must be kept in constant view: Plato, for all his concern with the political conditions of human life, was still, on our view, primarily a philosopher, and his *Republic* is not

---

[156] In undertaking to remove the outmoded historical accidents from the permanently valuable essence of Plato's thought, I invoke the inspiration and authority of Professor Ducasse, who has admirably revealed the lasting value of Aristotle's concept of "liberal education" (*Philosophy in American Education*, 1945, pp. 129–136), and the late Theodore Spencer, who has rendered a like service to Montaigne in his brilliant and charming imaginary dialogue, "Montaigne in America," 1946.

so much the plan of a city as it is a dramatically disguised essay on the True, the Good, and the Beautiful, in which is set forth its author's central convictions regarding the meaning of the world and man, the highest springs of value, and the way leading toward the vision of the eternal Good. And this is, for us aftercomers, the devotees of philosophy, the aspect of the *Republic* that far outshines all others, and which we should never permit to be made secondary to the particularities of political reform. We possess genuine rights in this matter, valid against the claims of the detractors, the specialists in the domains of history, philology, and comparative government, valid, one may even say, against Plato himself. For we lovers of philosophy are the chief heirs and administrators of his estate, a legacy which we are free to make use of as we responsibly see fit.

And along with our rights go duties: the correction of his lapses in the light of his insights, the removal from his system of all that was local and valid only for his own time and place, and even the infusion into his thought-stream of ideas and principles unknown to him and his age, but consonant with the spirit of his philosophy and prerequisite for its acceptability in the present age.

But, it may be objected, by what right are you justified in "infusing" principles unknown to Plato into his system, erasing his errors, and generally improving upon the deity you profess to worship? Our answer may be drawn from the history of religion, with which the history of some philosophical systems exhibits a striking parallel. The pattern is a familiar one. After an initial fervor of discipleship in which the word of the master is the complete and unquestioned truth, there arises first the recognition of incompleteness: the founder did not express his view on this or that issue that has now assumed an importance it did not possess in his day. It becomes necessary to extend his doctrine by discovering what he would have said had the question confronted him. And slowly it is realized, by the more thoughtful and intellectually scrupulous, that the master has expressed two opinions not possible to be brought into complete harmony with one another. The climax will be reached when, most likely in the cross-light of other doctrines, scientific or philosophic, some exceptionally discerning spirit and commonly not the least devout, discovers what appears to him a substantial gap or outright error in the traditional articles of faith.

A familiar modern instance of this rhythm of discipleship is found in the religious experience of Albert Schweitzer.[157] Historical and theological inquiries had brought this deeply devout but keen and scrupulously honest mind to a cruel dilemma between the opposing demands of faith and reason. It was not simply that the supernatural element in the Gospels was no longer possible to his belief. His special difficulty lay in his discovery of what appeared a

---

[157] See his book, *Out of My Life and   Thought,* Henry Holt and Co., New York, 1933.

major error in the belief of the Founder himself, namely "the naïve realism" [158] of his Messianic conviction that the "Time of the End" was approaching, to be signalized by a great Satanic persecution (temptation) against which Jesus directed men to pray. We cannot follow here the long struggle that brought Schweitzer to his final conclusion; it is the conclusion alone that is to our purpose. He has stated it in words that might with very little alteration be employed by a contemporary Platonist. The religion of Jesus, he declares, cannot be made "our own through the concepts in which he proclaimed it"; we "must rather translate it into those of our modern view of the world." [159] Of the success and fruitfulness of Schweitzer as a translator of those concepts, the familiar story of his life is sufficient witness.

Something less dramatic but still fairly comparable in effect has been performed, often indeed unconsciously, for the founder of their "faith," by the greater Platonists of various ages. Our opening pages were devoted to recalling the homage to Plato rendered by theologians, poets, and philosophers, a numerous company, stretching almost in an unbroken chain to our own times. Like Schweitzer, these men were making vital use of a spiritual guide to the perplexities of living and thinking in their respective times. But can we, in this present world that lies so problematically before us, still to any purpose summon Plato to our council chamber? Or must our honoring of him today be the mistaken crowning of one who is king only of the strengthless dead?

Were we commissioned by some philosophic archangel to survey the works of Plato with special attention to his "city," and to report back to him our decision, as Voltaire's Babouc was empowered to decide the fate of the city of Persepolis, we should not be at a loss. Like Babouc, we should find some elements that we could positively wish to destroy. First of all, we should wish to remove the stains that the existence of the institution of slavery have left in the fabric of his thought. We should revoke (as he himself went far toward doing in the *Laws*) the hard and fast distinction between rulers and ruled which in the *Republic* he has based upon a mistaken estimate of the capacity of the common man. We would have Plato disavow the tacit assumption against which his admissions of human fallibility were unable to take effect that he was in all essentials possessed of a final knowledge of moral truth. In the same breath we should demand a lifting of the censorship upon art, and abandonment of the prescription of a minimum religion. And we should not forget to smash the barriers that Plato has set between honorific activities and the degrading "banausic" arts. All these elements we should consign to oblivion, save in so far as it is a salutary lesson to be reminded of the errors and limitations under which it seems to be, as Whitehead has suggested, the fate of the highest and purest ideas to effect their entry into this world. And finally, we should wish to abolish a certain austere contempt in Plato's condemnation of

---

[158] *Op. cit.*, p. 37.   [159] *Ibid.*, p. 53.

whatever falls below the high standard he has set for all members of his community. We should recognize his reformer's right to moral indignation in the face of social wrongs, and still feel that Plato has not sufficiently balanced justice with mercy to satisfy our modern demand. It is here that his own principle of persuasion requires further extension and deepening in the light of the Christian principle of love and the recognition of the value of even the humblest individual lives.

But at this point we should wish to lay down the hammer of critical destruction and take up the harp of praise, asking that archangel to read with us a few of those grander passages [160] in which Plato's wings are spread and he rises to clear heights from which to survey time and existence as if from the moveless throne of the eternal truth. In such passages, Plato stirs in his reader a speechless conviction that if he has not "grasped and handled immutables," he has come within their luminous shadow; Plato has awakened in him the metaphysical faith that in some fashion which reason is pledged to make as fully intelligible as it can, existence and value are indissolubly one, and that the more we can discover of the articulation of the real, the more of ideality and value will stand revealed.

Descending from the height of such a passage and looking again at the familiar landscape of Plato's more mundane levels, are we not, like Plato's own returning inmate of the cavern, able presently to observe some things that we had not noticed before? We now see that the city we had supposed to be the dwelling-place of the philosopher kings and their wards is to the real city of which Plato is truly discoursing as the shadows on the cavern wall are to the three-dimensional bodies whose fleeting images they are. Thus not only the story of the cave but the whole *Republic* is, in some sort, a parable whose key and meaning we are directed to find, not in terms of empirical fact and material relations, but in those of an avôwedly ideal philosophy.

We are justified, then, in refusing to allow the issue to be decided in terms of the particularities of Plato's state, as if Plato's claim upon the world's attention stood or fell with his choice of three classes of citizens and two approved modes of music, and his discretion in appointing the right age for marriage. What we are seeking, as material for our test of Plato's availability in our time, will not be found among these shadows but among the principles which they imperfectly represent, especially those that lie on the intermediate levels of his thought. Let us choose some representative examples, beginning with the Platonic conviction that the fundamental business of the state is the promotion of ethical values.

We do not in these United States expect that government officials shall be moral luminaries nor look to them for the guidance of our private lives. A literal translation of Plato's panethical state we would find impossible. But

---

[160] E.g., *Phaedrus* 250 B–C, *Republic* 508 A ff., *Theaetetus* 176 A ff.

when we turn away from the realism of political practice and the techniques of administration, and begin to ask questions about the ultimate goals of political action and the standards by which our success or failure as a nation can properly be judged, it is rather surprising how suddenly the gap between us and the Greek thinker is diminished. For with him, Americans are constantly asserting that good citizenship is measured in terms of service to the community, that the community itself exists not as a mere police department or a profitable stock-company, but for the promotion of the good life and the fullest possible development of the moral capacities of all its members, that a statesman is distinguished from a mere politician by the breadth of his vision and his integrity in pursuit of ends which he himself believes valid. We want neither the "power state" with its nihilistic denial of the relevance of moral criteria to its sovereign acts, nor nineteenth-century *laissez faire*, with its conscientious indifference to the welfare, apart from the basic security, of its members. Platonic in spirit, too, are those Americans who advocate subsidies for the equalizing of educational opportunity, or the use of Federal funds for slum clearance and the endowment of scientific research. In the field of international relations our self-picture is that of a nation committed to the Platonic ideal of justice over power.

A second Platonic principle enhances the value of the first by supplying a general method for correcting its errors: the submission of all issues to the adjudication of reason. This is, for Plato, no empty formalism, with reason functioning as a synonym for whatever he may happen to believe on instinct. It is a quite definite commitment to give the deciding vote in every vital election not to the hottest appetite or the strongest impulse but to that power of the soul that is capable of rising above the flux of momentary incitements to the consideration of universals, and discovering the objective structure of the moral order. Now it is true that many contemporary minds would reject as illusory the very existence of an objective structure of this sort, taken as a reality over and above the social order that sustains it. Nevertheless Plato is here proposing a method of clarification by directed inquiry, open to all men, and thus providing an intelligible basis on which men may at the worst agree to disagree. And the possibility remains that the rationality of the method may, if persistently applied, impart something of its quality to the mentalities of all who employ it, with the result that an area of agreement may be established capable of indefinite future growth. If this hope should in the long run prove unsuccessful, it may be necessary to say that not Plato, but mankind has failed.

Meanwhile, and as one of our chief sureties against dissolution, we share with Plato a further principle, famous in British political history and much in the minds of the founders of the American Constitution, which in our tradition has been known as the "division of powers," but which Plato called the "mixed" or "tempered government," and sought in his manner to embody in the city of the *Laws*. Again, as with the *Republic*, we must not confound the letter with the spirit. Despite our many and important points of divergence from the particularities of the Platonic scheme, our acceptance of the heart of Plato's proposal makes us in this important respect Platonists all. A New England Town Meeting may well be called an echo of pure Athenian democracy, but behind and above that meeting, in the constitutional framework of our governments, in the whole body of our preponderantly traditional law, in the deliberations of our legislatures and in the sessions of our higher courts set beyond the immediate reach of the electorate, we possess a structure of diverse components, a tempering of power by power, which Plato would have viewed with fascinated delight. It is only when we forget this dimension of our political system that we are tempted to deny the debt of nurture that modern democracy owes to the reputed despiser of the democratic name.

It should not be difficult for a contemporary Platonist, pursuing strictly the principles of the *Republic* and of the *Laws*, to supply himself with as pacifistic a program as the spirit of this age will allow. He could plausibly discover the soul of Plato reincarnating itself in every whole-hearted effort to establish a peaceful international order. He will pay scant heed to the isolated utterance in the *Republic* in which a policy of war upon the non-Greek barbarians is accepted, as a preferred alternative to the war of Greeks with Greeks and with barbarians as well, and he will remember instead Plato's praise of peace and friendly feeling, so far as this could conceivably be attained. Plato's secondary and defensive "militarism" the contemporary Platonist will not, in the circumstances, dare to drop, but toward the ideal of the United Nations he will look with the same enthusiasm with which Plato looked to the coming of his philosopher kings — and for similar reasons, since the effective outlawry of war as between nations has more than a surface resemblance to the elimination of civil strife and the establishment of harmonious mutuality within a single state.

The principle, "each man active in the one work for which he is by nature fit," taken in its literal sense and applied to any complex modern society, would be either impracticable, since the assumed "one work" would scarcely be discoverable for more than the exceptionally gifted or deficient, or, if this difficulty could be supposed surmounted, would entail a dangerous extension of the existing narrow specialization or minute subdivision of labor that technology has bestowed upon us in such abundance. How then can Plato's principle be adapted to good use? Only by revising and deepening the meaning of the key words in the Platonic formula. Man, what is he, in soul and body adequately conceived? What is the proper work of man, conceived in terms of the nature that we find him to possess? We recall from the higher ranges of Plato's thought the conception of man as a "divine plant," as *au fond* a rational soul who has viewed the eternal forms and who possesses rationality as an inseparable attribute. We recall the warning against the crippling and blighting effect of certain activities; the mistaken application of this notion may now be corrected, partly at least in view of Plato's own doctrine. Every man, we shall now declare, must be regarded as a being too godlike and rational to be put to servile use. Under the conditions of contemporary civilization this will demand translation into terms of hours and conditions of work, and beyond this, commitment to an ideal already far along the road to realization, the turning of scientific knowledge to the fullest possible account in devising rational and humane techniques for the replacement of old methods of performing rough and repellent tasks. With these considerations in mind, the contemporary Platonist, observing from his study window the passing of the latest model of a motorized automatic street-sweeper, might be tempted to exclaim, "There goes Platonism on four wheels!"

But what of freedom? Is that not the fruit of another tree, which it would require wizardry to graft on Plato's stock? We think not, and for this principal reason: all those moral and social values to which Plato attached the highest worth, which were, in fact, the moving energies within his state, require freedom as a necessary condition. That Plato honored free and spontaneous performance above passive obedience and control is absolutely clear. We recall his ironical depiction of those who, having lived virtuously but only from blind custom and habit, are reborn as social harmless creatures such as bees. His contrasting ideal appears in his delineation of the philosopher kings, who enjoy the fullest freedom of inquiry and self-determination. The contemporary Platonist, then, need discover no new principle of freedom to add to Plato's store. What he must do is to extend the application of Plato's insight, and here, as in all possible fields, seek to provide for the many what once was thought possible of attainment only for the few.

And here we must leave our plea for Plato and Platonism to be decided along with the fate of the Western world with whose moral destiny they have been so intimately associated. We have sought to separate, not to confuse, Platonic light and the elements of shadow with which it has latterly been identified. Against this confusion we have everywhere contended that a great tradition, embodying a noble conception of the human spirit, can never long remain subject to control by its least illuminating insights, whether these be the result, as with Inquisitorial Christianty, of a historical betrayal of the master, or as in Platonism, the consequence of a partial eclipse of vision in the master himself. The essentials of Plato's vision still stand: the prophetic image of a social brotherhood, growing up in grace and harmony and understanding, under justice, toward an ideal perfection never quite to be reached. One need not deny that this greater Plato was, on occasion, replaced by a lesser man who was guilty of confusing things temporal with things eternal, and mistaking some of his own preferences for irremovable truth. Yet, in grateful reverence for major service rendered to the spiritual advancement of mankind, and in the hope of insights yet to be derived from his creative impact upon us, we will be wiser to keep our eyes fixed on the image of the greater man.

APPENDICES

BIBLIOGRAPHY

INDICES

Appendix **I**

Two Additional Platonic Detractors

Two rather disparate critics of Plato will share our attention here, an American professor of classics, Alban Dewes Winspear, and the widely known philosopher-historian, Arnold Toynbee.

The Genesis of Plato's Thought, by Winspear, published in 1940, appears to have been written almost entirely from the standpoint of theoretical Marxism and accordingly seeks to derive Plato's thought from the categories of class struggle between the Athenian common people and their economic enemies of the oligarchical party. Metaphysics appears as crypto-sociology, secretly directed by the hand of economic class interest; ethics loses its autonomy as rational inquiry into the structure of the good life, and sinks into the faithful handmaid of its nonmoral mistress, economics.

Professor Winspear has read, acknowledged, and turned to account Fite's book, and has reproduced much, even, of the latter's sarcastic depreciation and systematic refusal to allow Plato the benefit of any doubt. To Fite's general suspiciousness, Winspear's familiarity with the Marxist doctrine of the prevalence of "false fronts" has given a specific turn: beneath the surface of Plato's most innocent remarks, he can often discern a hidden tactic, aimed at political and economic enemies. To his Marxist suppositions, again, he is indebted for some truly astonishing opinions, far more extravagant than Fite's. Dionysius I, tyrant of Syracuse, was, we are informed, a progressive, democratic leader; Socrates was a reactionary snob. Winspear directs against Plato's political message a remarkable argument which may be summarized as follows: he maintains, first, that most of Plato's political ideals were derived from the Pythagoreans, and second, that the history of the original Pythagorean settlements in Magna Graecia and their abuse of political power in the name of aristocracy prove that Plato's ideal city, had he reduced it to practice, would have come to the same bad end; from these two premises he concludes (p. 228) that we need attach little weight

to "the idealistic aspects . . . of Plato's thinking," but may confidently reduce him to the level of an authoritarian reactionary, planning realistically to employ force, but sufficiently "subtle" (p. 248) to conceal his intention under fine phrases. Winspear here illustrates the illegitimate confusion of intensions with results against which we shall protest on other pages: it is the height of injustice to suppose that a thinker must have intended whatever the critic foresees as a probable result of the carrying out of his proposals, and then to explain his avowal of contrary aims as a mere indication of deceit. On the other hand, Winspear can find in Plato some things to admire. The reach and inclusiveness of the "synoptic vision" appeal to the admirer of the Marxist dialectic, and Plato's advocacy of self-abnegation and dedication to a cause commands the respect of one who feels himself committed to the greatest of human causes, the realization of social justice. I have not thought fit to include Professor Winspear among the necessarily small number of detractors whom I shall discuss in detail, partly because most of what is substantial in his brief is, I believe, fairly answered elsewhere in our argument, but chiefly because most of his major objections against Plato are, as we have seen, so inextricably dependent upon Marxist assumptions as to lose most of their meaning for those to whom Marxism is not, in James' phrase, a "live option."

We must not pass by unmarked, though we cannot here fully treat, the always brilliant though, I think, mutually inconsistent hyperboles of alternating laudation and damnation that Arnold Toynbee, in his *Study of History*, 1934–1939, has bestowed upon Plato: thus in one passage, comparing his teaching with that of the Gospels, he has called him "the first and greatest and most Christian of all the Hellenic philosophers" (vol. VI, p. 168), and again, because of his rejection of that very post-Periclean Athenian democracy which Toynbee himself brands as degenerate, we hear him characterized as "petulant" and "partly insincere," and taxed with "fouling his own Attic nest" (IV, p. 264)! Strictly speaking, then, it would not be possible to say precisely how Toynbee has evaluated Plato, for neither has Toynbee. But the brief account that follows may serve at least to indicate his "majority view," and will pave the way for our exposition of the case against Plato as argued by one of the major detractors, K. R. Popper, who has himself acknowledged his obligation to the British historian for many traits in his picture of Plato. The most significant of Toynbee's criticisms will be considered in later sections of our text.

Toynbee thinks of Plato as of a man who can be, on occasion, cynical, reactionary, and inhumane (I, pp. 247–249, and by clear implication, VI, p. 246), though also immensely intelligent, highly imaginative (I, p. 460), and deeply concerned for the welfare of his fellow men (VI, p. 243). This man saw in the contemporary political scene essentially what Toynbee himself sees in it: the breakdown of Hellenic society arising out of its moral incapacity (IV, p. 264). To escape the resulting "sense of drift" (V, pp. 412, 420), and to salvage what he could of Hellenic values, Plato turned to a desperate expedient: he sought a return to the simpler and more secure stability that he associated with the past, and to this end designed a scheme for "pegging" society at the level of an idealized Sparta, the Sparta of the legendary "Lycurgean" constitution, with its soldier-citizens even more rigorously trained for their separate function, and with a new caste, "in the likeness of the Athenian philosophers themselves," superimposed and given supreme authority.

That Toynbee, from his vantage point in time, would have approved a different prescription for the ills of the Greek world is understandable enough, but it is surprising to find him first granting the validity of Plato's motives and then rescinding the grant in connection with the particular means which Plato adopts to his benevolent ends. For the sake of understanding more precisely the nature of Toynbee's criticism, and in partial explanation of his animus against Plato, we must take account of the essentially formal framework within which it operates: the antithesis between "arrested" and growing societies. Toynbee has earlier (III, esp. pp. 22, 28) depicted the nomad on the steppe, with his literal dog

and cattle, and has then compared this primitive symbiosis with the "arrested" societies that result when the nomad has conquered the inhabitants of the plowland, has converted them into his "human cattle," and has trained "human watch-dogs" to assist him in managing them. Extending the parallel, through the Ottoman Turks and the Spartans, to Plato's ideal state, he now boldly applies again to its two inferior classes the original animal vocabulary (III, p. 90 ff.). We are told also that stability, "not happiness and not progress," is the sole end of such a state, in the service of which its members are to be dehumanized into the likeness of ants or bees. Toynbee also speaks very severely of the myth that Plato has recommended for promoting social solidarity; in this passage (I, pp. 247–249), which we discuss in n. 72, pp. 429–430, Plato appears in the anti-Christian role of cynical inventor of convenient and repressive racialistic lies.

The "philosopher kings" themselves, however, and Plato, whose image they reproduce, seem to escape calumny. Plato is, in fact, praised for his great altruism in sending them down from their heights of contemplation to share the light of common day with their less gifted subjects. Here again, Toynbee's Plato has taken on a Christlike character: "with a heavy heart," in conscious and conscientious self-sacrifice, he has laid upon his perfected philosophers this "grievous commandment" (VI, pp. 243–244; similarly, III, 251–252). And Plato is offered what amounts to veneration for his anticipation in the *Republic* and the *Phaedo* of the Christian "reckoning of spiritual values," in his inspiring words exalting Righteousness above wealth, honors, poetry, and all else, as the "great hope" and "splendid prize" for which the race of life is to be run.

Finally we must list a fault which Toynbee views with grave disapproval: Plato's supposed misuse of the philosophic function, manifested in his attempt to use the power at the disposal of Dionysius II for the implementation of his philosophical ideal. To Toynbee, this was Plato's confession of failure as a philosopher, whose field (Toynbee has issued this jurisdictional decree) never extends beyond "loveless and pitiless contemplation" (VI, p. 259). By thus trespassing "on the king's field of ruthless action," Plato has revealed himself as that sinister and hypocritical thing, "a saviour with the sword in disguise" (VI, p. 269). And this, be it remembered, is the same Plato who earlier was warranted as the greatest and most Christlike of Hellenic philosophers. A partial explanation of

this apparent contradiction can be found in Toynbee's own deeply felt conviction that the only salvation for mankind lies in the healing power of "the God incarnate in a man," a role which, after all, it was not given to Plato to enact.

Appendix II

Kelsen in Conflict with his Authorities

Kelsen has invoked an imposing array of authorities in confirmation of his conception of the fifth-century Athenian attitude toward homosexuality. Citation is made from *Symonds, *A Problem in Greek Ethics*, and also, always by means of parallel references, from a German version of this work, "Die Homosexualitaet in Griechenland," in Havelock Ellis and J. A. Symonds: *Das kontraere Geschlechtsgefuehl* (Bibliothek fuer Sozialwissenschaft, Herausgegeben von Hans Kurella, 7. Bd., 1896). It is Symonds whom Kelsen most frequently cites. He has made use, also of *Ivo Bruns, "Attische Liebestheorien," etc., 1900, pp. 17–37; *E. Bethe, "Die dorische Knabenliebe," etc., 1907, p. 438 ff.; *H. Gomperz, "Psychologische Beobachtungen an griechischen Philosophen," 1924; *W. Kroll, *Freundschaft und Knabenliebe*, 1927, and W. Kroll, article "Knabenliebe," in Pauly-Wissowa, *Realenzyklopaedie der klassischen Altertumswissenschaft*, 21. Bd., p. 897 ff.; and others of limited scope, dealing chiefly with the relationship between Xenophon's *Symposium* and Plato's. Those which the present writer has also been able to examine are marked with an asterisk.

We here propose to summarize briefly the stand taken by each of these writers (other than Symonds, whose opinion we have already discussed) regarding the Athenian attitude toward paiderastia, in order to determine how far Kelsen is justified in the conclusion he has drawn from them.

(a) Bruns, in the course of his comparative study of the theories of love of Plato and Xenophon, asserts (e.g., on pp. 17, 18) that approval of paiderastia, including sexual indulgence, was widespread in Plato's Athens; as evidence that men of high standing were among its advocates, he points to the speakers in Plato's *Symposium*. He states, but without documentation, that "a strong family tradition struggled against" these relationships, while "on the other hand, their ethical value in many

cases could not be overlooked"; in consequence, public opinion was divided (p. 25). Bruns believes that the issue aroused discussion involving numerous disputants on either side, most of whose identities are unknown (pp. 25, 27). Among the known opponents of the indulgent paiderastia, he lists Antisthenes, but cites as evidence only the well known fragment of Antisthenes condemning love (quoted in note 162, p. 208); and in quoting this fragment, he omits the second clause, which by its reference to the corrupting effects of love upon women, shows that the sexual passion in general, and not paiderastia, was Antisthenes' primary topic. Bruns' further argument that Antisthenes is contending against someone who had deified Eros, and therefore probably against Plato, seems to forget the place of Eros in Greek literature; cf. Sophocles' *Antigone*, 781 ff. Bruns believes that Xenophon wrote his *Symposium* primarily to assert, as against Plato's *Phaedrus* and the earlier speakers in Plato's *Symposium* (mainly Phaedrus and Pausanias) the necessity of forbidding sexual indulgence absolutely, and also to urge that love should be aroused not by the youth's beauty, but by his nobility of character; yet, being "too fully a child of his time" (p 26), Xenophon stultifies his own sermon by depicting as necessary to love the presence of this same beauty. It can, therefore, be said that Bruns believes paiderastia, even the indulgent form, to have been widely, but, he would insist, by no means universally, accepted in Plato's Athens, and to have become the subject of widespread controversy in the fourth century; even such opponents of paiderastia, however, as Xenophon, were unable to progress beyond condemning the indulgence.

(b) Bethe is primarily interested in the primitive origins of the Dorian institution, but he makes incidentally some remarks which deal with the Athenian scene. Up to the middle of the fifth century, he asserts, "Knabenliebe" (he makes no explicit distinction between its kinds), which had been spread throughout Greece by the prestige of its Dorian originators, was accepted without question, and in its indulgent form, at Athens; but at that time there arose, as a result of the general culture awakening spearheaded by the sophists, a moral opposition; as a result (p. 446), "Knabenliebe" came to be regarded at Athens, despite open advocacy, as a vice, and this though among men of high character, such as Socrates and Plato, it bore noble fruit. A second result was the prettification (pp. 438 n., and 443) by defenders of Spartan ideals like Xenophon, of the practice as it was carried on at Sparta. Bethe's statements regarding the attitude of the sophists and the change in the climate of opinion at Athens, subjects peripheral to his interest, he has not seen fit to document. Since he has not specified the grounds of his assertion, we may limit ourselves to two remarks: (1) Apart from one incidental condemnation of the degraded form of paiderastia, contained in Xenophon's report of Prodicus' moral parable (mentioned in the text, pp. 109f.) there is no textual evidence known to me that any of the sophists of the fifth century attacked paiderastia. (2) If one talks of a shift of sentiment during the latter half of this century, in the direction of condemning the relationship, this movement must be interpreted to include Socrates, who sought not to abolish but to purify the institution. We are thus brought to see the historical injustice of treating Plato as if he had been the opponent of a high-principle reform.

(c) H. Gomperz has made a deliberately modest effort to draw light from psychoanalytic theory for the understanding of traits in the personality and thought of Parmenides and Socrates. He sees in Socrates one who spent the greater part of his life in a social milieu, that of the upper classes of Athens, among whom bisexuality was "entirely customary," and the bodily possession of the beloved youth regarded as the chief end of paiderastic relationships, with the one proviso that a civilized person should desire to possess only a youth who displayed beauty of soul as well as body (pp. 62–63). To these Athenians, Socrates' demand for absolute chastity in these relations made him appear as "an unexampled, an incomparable wonder!" (p. 66). The explanation of Socrates' attitude Gomperz finds largely in his social origin from among the working people, by whom, "as we see in Attic comedy," paiderastia was regarded as something alien; it had, in fact, been adopted by Athenian "good society" from the Dorians (p. 67). For all this, Gomperz, like Bethe, supplies no documentation, except for a footnote reference to Bethe, op. cit., regarding the Dorian origin of the custom, and the bare mention of Attic comedy.

(d) Kroll, *Freundschaft u. Knabenliebe*, also dispenses almost entirely with documentation. He has read Bethe, whose central thesis he rejects as inadequate, and has also apparently read Symonds, with whom he is in closest agreement. "Knabenliebe" (again with no explicit discrimination of kinds) is shown to have been at Athens in the fifth and early fourth centuries, if not as highly honored as among the Dorians, still completely open and unashamed (p. 23). He cites the evidence of the inscriptions on walls, and on vases, which deal almost exclusively with the love of youths. Moral criticism begins with the "philosophy of the enlightenment," whose chief poet is Euripides; his opposition to the bodily aspects of paiderastia is deduced from the plot of his *Chrysippus* (p. 27.) The corresponding opposition of Antisthenes is asserted but not documented. To Socrates and Plato themselves is ascribed the chief effort to cleanse and ennoble the relationship (pp. 27–28). Socrates is seen as personally relatively indifferent to the seductions of paiderastia. Plato (far from being, as Kelsen supposes, its apologist, himself oppressed by an awareness of socially despised impulses) is seen as crusading against what was, throughout most of his lifetime, the almost universal acceptance of indulgent paiderastia.

All these authorities, therefore, and particularly Symonds, lend Kelsen's case far less aid than his appeal to them might suggest. From them all he has been able to assemble a considerable number of assertions pointing in his direction; but of these, many are undocumented or inadequately based. Kelsen has also often chosen to ignore or to discount assertions which contravene his view. On balance, his authorities constitute a reputable array of witnesses against him on the central issue, and in favor of the view that decently conducted paiderastia was, at the time considered, widely accepted among Athenians of good standing.

Among the leading advocates of this latter view may be listed one not apparently known to Kelsen. This is Hans Licht (Paul Brandt), who in his *Sexual Life in Ancient Greece*, 1932, especially in Chapter V, has devoted special attention to male homosexuality, reaching conclusions in general agreement with those of Symonds, though somewhat vitiated by lack of discrimination and caution. For Licht, "the knowledge of Greek erotic," including the special standing in Greece of the love between males, "is the indispensable assumption for a deeper knowledge of the life of ancient Greece" (p. 524). Like Symonds, Licht distinguishes sharply (pp. 446, 452–453) between the profligate and irresponsible love of boys and the widespread and respected "voluntary relationship . . . based upon mutual affection" which, despite its sensuality, is rooted (p. 440) "in the unexampled ethical valuation of the masculine character in public and private life." Having as its object the maintenance of the state and the development of civic and personal virtue, it is "an important factor in education." "We can also speak of a decided bisexuality among the Greeks" (p 445). "For them [the Greeks] paederasty, instead of a vice, was but another form of love which they regarded, not as the enemy of marriage, but as a necessary supplement to marriage, recognized by the state; and it was publicly spoken of with just as much unconcern as it was brought into the sphere of their philosophical conversations by . . . Socrates, Plato, and Aristotle" (pp. 524–525).

Licht diverges from Symonds principally in seeing a far greater degree of sensuality among the Greeks. Thus Licht detects such sensuality even in the Homeric poems, in the relationship between Achilles and Patroclus, and believes that Socrates, though he extolled purity as an ideal, was entirely tolerant of sexual indulgence between males in most cases (pp. 445–446); he treats the speeches of such characters as Phaedrus in Plato's *Symposium* as direct expressions of Plato's own attitude, and fails entirely to mention Plato's condemnation of homosexual indulgence in the *Republic* and in the *Laws*. Licht is also willing to credit the most scandalous passages in Athenaeus, and he describes Euripides (pp. 138–139) as having courted the beautiful Agathon by presenting his love in transparent symbolism before all Athens in his play *Chrysippus*. By reason of these questionable additions to his evidence, along with his failure to emphasize sufficiently the qualifications and limitations set upon the practice of paiderastia, we have preferred in the main to follow Symonds as the soberer authority.

The Murder of Slaves in Attic and Platonic Law

Comparison between Platonic and Athenian law dealing with the killing of slaves is rendered difficult by gaps and disputable interpretations on both sides. Plato's law (discussed by Morrow, *Plato's Law of Slavery*, pp. 47–56) divides all homicides into three large classes, accidental homicide, killing in anger, and deliberate murder. Under the first of these Plato is explicit, providing (*Laws* 865 A and D) that a man who kills his own slave shall undergo ritual purification only; if it be another's, he shall also restore the value of the slave, or (if he fails to do so without compulsion) he shall be liable to a suit for double the slave's value. Under the second heading difficulty of interpretation arises, since Plato provides (*Laws* 868 A) for the killer of his own slave, purification alone; while for the killer of another's slave he prescribes, without further explanation, purification and the payment of double the slave's value. Morrow interprets these penalties as identical with those imposed for accidental killing, reasoning that the double damages mentioned are simply the damages incurred, as in the former case, by failure to settle out of court. When Plato comes to deal with deliberate murder, the difficulty becomes acute, since here, where one would expect Plato to specify the penalty for all or any such killings of slaves by freemen, he specifies that the man who kills an innocent slave in order to conceal his own crime, "or for any other such reason," shall be liable to a charge of murder "exactly as if he had murdered a citizen" (*Laws* 872 C), and says no more. Morrow, reasoning that Plato has felt it unnecessary to visit any punishment above the penalty for accidental killing on the man who kills a slave in anger, extrapolates his finding and concludes that the same may well have been true of Plato's intention in the case of deliberate murder, except when, in the interests of public order, a slave informer is to be protected.

We may begin by questioning Morrow's interpretation of the penalties for killing in anger. The Platonic principle of distinguishing "harm" or "damage" from "injustice" (*Laws* 862) — the first of these to be set right by restitution, the second by admonition or punishment — has given rise to the subordinate principle that, in general, restitution shall sufficiently atone for unintentional harm. Accordingly, when a slave has been accidentally killed, this is the basic penalty, though because of the solemnity attending the shedding of blood, Plato has added ritual purification. The doing of damage in anger, since for Plato it is half-involuntary, is in general to entail double restitution, or the doubling of the consequences of accidental harm, where this is possible. That this is the general rule may be seen from *Laws* 865 E and 867 C; *Laws* 879 B and 878 B–C. When the slave killed in anger is the man's own, there is no one to whom the double restitution can appropriately be made (and there may be also involved a principle of Attic law, as we shall see below) ; the rule, therefore, is not applied. But when the slave is another's, the double payment can appropriately be awarded to the owner, and here the rule holds. The double damages mentioned, therefore, are not the penalty for litigation, but punitive damages. Once we are freed from the necessity of believing that the killing of a slave in anger, quite unlike the killing of a freeman, is treated by Plato as deserving of no penalty beyond that entailed by accidental killing, we have no reason for believing that Plato would have allowed his citizens the privilege of cheaply murdering their slaves, and we are free to fill in the gap (if there is a gap) in Plato's law of slave-murder with conjectural provisions more in keeping with Plato's standing attitude toward murder as such.

But is there actually a gap? Morrow has argued that Plato's sentence regarding slave-murder (*Laws* 872 C, paraphrased above) cannot be taken as covering murders of slaves other than potential informers, for the following reasons. Only a few sentences earlier (*Laws* 872 A) Plato has laid down the general rule that the same penalties as those for the murder of a citizen by a citizen shall apply also to the murder of "Strangers" (foreigners) by Strangers, citizens or Strangers by one another, and slaves by slaves. Now, had Plato intended to treat in precisely the same fashion all murders of slaves by freemen, he could most simply have added this type of case to his list; this, therefore, cannot have been his intention. Secondly, Plato's willingness to exclude slaves other than slave informers from such protection can be inferred from the two Platonic principles on which, as we saw in our text, Morrow chiefly relies: the autonomy of the master, and the slave as an instrument of public order.

We argue that it is perhaps arbitrary to assert that Plato must have chosen the simplest alternative, to the neglect of all other considerations. He did, in fact, intend to impose a different and more severe penalty upon the slave who had murdered a freeman; immediately after giving the list referred to, he proceeds to specify for such a slave one of those extreme penalties we have noted with regret above, a flogging at the behest of the dead man's relatives, followed by death. It may therefore have seemed to him appropriate to reserve for the final and emphatic position in his series of penalties for deliberate murder, apart from the murders of kinsmen, the penalty awaiting the freeman who murders a slave, wishing to make it clear that despite his determination to punish to the utmost the slave who kills a freeman, he is equally determined to protect the slave who is guiltless by a penalty far greater than was customary even at Athens.

Nor need we be dismayed because Plato has mentioned explicitly only one motive for the murder of a slave. In a passage in which, as Morrow has himself pointed out, Plato is being so very meticulous in listing the various possible types of murders, it is unlikely that he would knowingly have omitted a substantial group (if substantial group it was), namely: murders of slaves by freemen actuated by motives other than the one named. It is at least equally probable that Plato conceived this motive alone as likely to cause freemen deliberately to murder slaves. We

are here in accord with Ritter (cited by Morrow, *op. cit.*, p. 52), who has pointed out that some two pages earlier than the passage we are discussing, at the beginning of his legislation for murder (*Laws* 869 E–870 D), Plato has recognized three possible causes of murders, desire for wealth and pleasure, ambition, and fear of detection; of these only the last-named could ordinarily apply to slaves. We ourselves may be able to imagine situations in which other motives would be responsible, but this does not prove them to have been present to Plato's mind. And we have in the disputed sentence itself the phrase, "or for any other such reason," which may be sufficiently inclusive to cover those other remotely possible base reasons of which Plato was aware.

It must also be pointed out that the intention Morrow has ascribed to Plato in this passage of protecting simply the slave informer does not suffice to explain one prominent part of Plato's sentence, the statement that the slave whom he is concerned to protect is guiltless. A slave who shared in the guilt might have as much or more information to impart. In short, it is possible, with Ritter, to interpret the sentence simply as Plato's statement of the way in which he will deal with all deliberate murders of slaves by freemen.

The provisions of Attic law covering the killing of slaves, which, it is agreed, must serve as the chief standard by which the humanity of Plato's law is to be judged, are likewise imperfectly known and subject to disputed interpretation. Morrow, depending for evidence principally upon scattered references in the orators, and on deductions from such other sources as Plato's *Euthyphro*, has set forth the excellence of the Attic slave legislation ("The Murder of Slaves in Attic Law," 1937). At Athens, the master of a slave killed by another was entitled to bring a homicide suit on his behalf; conviction would necessarily entail "more than a fine," and might result in the exile of the slayer. The master who killed his own slave was liable to the same type of suit, which could be brought (though admittedly it seldom was brought) against him by some other member of his own family. Beyond this, Morrow sees in the *graphê hybreôs* at Athens a more potent and more generally available remedy for injuries to slaves, whether committed by someone other than the master or by the master himself. In order to establish this last point he relies heavily on the possibility that the laborer on whose behalf Euthyphro was intending to bring suit against his father was regarded as the father's slave (cf. our discussion of the *Euthyphro*, pp. 403f.); on Plato's own classification of offences by masters against their own slaves as instances of *hybris*; and on the argument that if Plato had seen the necessity of invoking stringent penalties to protect the potential slave informer against his master, Attic law must have done the same, and probably by means of the *graphê hybreôs*.

It is not possible or necessary to question Morrow's case in detail. It seems clear that Attic law was capable of inflicting heavier penalties than does Platonic law on the person, other than the slave's master, who kills a slave by accident or in rage. But its other superiorities are less well established. Thus it may be doubted whether the Attic homicide law, as distinct from the law of *hybris*, protected the slave against his master to the degree claimed. Reasons for doubting include a passage in the orator Antiphon (vi, 4) which has seemed to other authorities to imply that Attic law ordinarily prescribed for the slayer of his own slave no more than ritual purification, i.e., no more than what Plato imposed for accidental and passionate killing; this latter view is maintained by Ehrenberg (*The People of Aristophanes*, 1951, pp. 186, 188), who has not been persuaded by the force of Morrow's arguments. Nor would such a situation have been as discreditable to Athenian law as it may seem to us, since it would be possible to proceed on the assumption that under all ordinary circumstances the master would find the slave's life far more serviceable to his interests than the slave's death.

In the matter of the slave informer and *hybris* against slaves, it seems somewhat hard to have Plato's insights turned to the greater glory of Attic law and against

his own cause. Several of Morrow's arguments in favor of the probability that the Attic *graphê hybreôs* could be employed on a slave's behalf against a cruel master can with equal force be used to show that such an application of Plato's analogue to the *grâphe hybreôs*, the suit for impiety, is in the spirit of Plato's law. And the argument that since Plato clearly perceived the need of protecting a slave informer, Attic law cannot have lacked adequate devices for the purpose, seems inverted. As we know from the orators (e.g., Antiphon v, 47, 48, and 52), Athenian jurymen could be expected to regard it as entirely likely that a man might murder a slave who was able to inform against him. Attic law may, therefore, have been defective here, either because the *graphê hybreôs* was not available, or because restrictions on its use made it impracticable. Plato, by requiring the use of the private homicide suit for slave murder, and by stressing the need of protecting the slave informer, is perhaps expressing his earnest intention of supplying this very lack. In connection with one particular type of case, moreover, he provides a suggestion of a practical method of ensuring that such suits will be brought, laying it as a special intention of supplying this very lack in concern themselves with the protection of such a slave informer, and this suggestion is extensible in principle to other types of case. Plato may thus be the proper recipient of the honor Morrow has assigned conjecturally to Attic law.

If, then, we set the Attic and the Platonic provisions side by side with a view to judging their comparative excellence, we see that our knowledge of both is beset by uncertainties. Judgment in favor of one or the other will depend on the interpretation given singly to many disputed points on either side; where the benefit of the doubt is most often given, there we shall find the verdict. In such circumstances, justice to Plato may require some diminution in the degree of the contrast Morrow has found.

Antisthenes and Every Virtue Under Heaven

In order to establish his right to use Antisthenes as a foil for Plato, Popper has first rather arbitrarily chosen a number of facts and near facts from the very limited evidence available, and has then combined them in an intricate web of logically dubious relations in which the individual strands are doubtless intended to reënforce each other by convergence, but because of their inherent individual weakness, are unable to lend each other more than a spurious semblance of mutual support.

(a) The first strand depends upon the fact that Alcidamas and Lycophron, whose statements about slavery and nobility of birth we have discussed pp. 141ff., 144ff., were members of the school of Gorgias; and Antisthenes also, at one time, was a pupil of Gorgias. Now, says Popper (note 48 to chapter 8, p. 562), "we know (from Cicero, *De Natura Deorum*, and Philodemus, *De Pietate*) that Antisthenes was a monotheist; and the form in which he expressed his monotheism (there is only One God 'according to nature,' i.e., to truth, although there are many 'according to convention') shows that he had in mind the opposition *nature — convention* which, in the mind of a former member of the school of Gorgias and contemporary of Alcidamas and Lycophron . . . must have been connected with *equalitarianism*. This in itself does not of course establish the conclusion that the half-barbarian Antisthenes believed in the brotherhood of Greeks and barbarians. Yet it seems to me extremely likely that he did." Note that Popper is here being cautious, and if a little outrunning his evidence, is at any rate frankly admitting the doubtful nature of his conclusion. If he were always equally modest, we should have little quarrel with him. But in any case, we cannot accept the implication that membership in the school of Gorgias constitutes a certificate of admission to the party of the "equalitarians": cf. our pp. 154, 298.

(b) A second strand in the web: Popper states, in his text, pp. 149–150, that "we have sufficient evidence of Plato's hostility towards the equalitarian creed, a hostility which is seen in his attitude towards Antisthenes," who "seems to have extended" the equalitarianism of the school of Gorgias "into the doctrine of the brotherhood of all men." Attempting to prove this, in his note on the passage, p. 561, he argues that Antisthenes, being the only other surviving Socratic who taught at Athens, must be re-referred to somewhere in Plato's works. He then, rather strangely, makes no reference to the several places in the dialogues where common scholarly opinion finds allusion to the logical doctrines of Antisthenes (e.g., *Sophist* 251 B, 259 B); instead, following Duemmler, he points to certain passages in the *Republic*, in which Plato speaks, scornfully and in general, of would-be philosophers who bring ill repute upon philosophy by their own unworthiness, passages in which Plato uses epithets, and adds figurative descriptions (see the discussion on pp. 205f. of this book), partly compatible with known or supposed attributes of Antisthenes. Popper concludes that Plato is here *"very likely"* (italics ours) attacking Antisthenes. It is also at the beginning of this note, on p. 561, that Popper says that any discussion of Plato's relation to Antisthenes is "of course," "highly speculative," since "very little is known about Antisthenes from first-rate sources." This again is admirably cautious; but the caution is left behind in this footnote. As we have seen, in his text he states definitely that Plato's hostile attitude toward Antisthenes is known, and implies strongly that it is discreditable; he also asserts without qualification that Antisthenes is an equalitarian. The only qualified statement is that concerning the brotherhood of all men; but in due course this qualification also will vanish (see (d) below.)

(c) A third thread: Popper sets forth and approves cautiously, in note 47 to chapter 8, p. 561, the traditional view that the Cynic school descends from Antisthenes.

Now Stoicism derives, in turn, from Cynicism. Stoicism, therefore, was derived indirectly from Antisthenes, and thus the humanitarian influence which Stoicism exerted in Roman times can indirectly be credited to him (note 16 to chapter 5, pp. 510–511, and note 19 to chapter 10, p. 587). Socrates was humane, and he influenced Antisthenes (note 48 to chapter 8, pp. 563–564). Antisthenes thus is made to seem a necessary link in the transmission of the humanitarian ideal from Socrates to Stoicism, and therefore, himself, humane. But this ignores the many other channels through which ideas could pass, and reunite — e.g., Aristotle and Theophrastus (see Zeller-Nestle, 1951, p. 203) and the Platonic writings.

(d) A fourth: Antisthenes, as a monotheist, would naturally, Popper believes, be predisposed to believe in the unity of mankind (note 47 to chapter 8, p. 562). But Parmenides had been a monist, emphasizing the distinction between the One and the Many (note 37 to chapter 8, p. 560). Antisthenes' assertion of the One God who exists by nature, in contrast to the many gods of convention, suggests to Popper an affiliation with Parmenides. That there was historical connection between them is suggested by the link between Antisthenes and Gorgias, who is known to have been influenced by the logical methods of Zeno, who was Parmenides' disciple. (Note that here again, probable agreement on a particular doctrine is inferred from probable connection between two thinkers in regard to other doctrines.) Hence Popper feels free to draw what he pleases from Parmenides to fill in the blanks of our knowledge of Antisthenes. The crucial point, involving one capital confusion, is this: Parmenides had elevated his One above the Many; hence, Popper infers, Antisthenes did similarly with his one God, thus putting the many at a distance from him. Now, by a gratuitous assumption, Popper infers that the many were at an equal distance from the One, and by a sheer confusion, forgetting that Antisthenes was speaking of many *gods*, interprets the 'many' as *men*. Out of this spiral nebula of gaseous perversity emerges the preordained conclusion: Antisthenes was "probably" a believer in the brotherhood of men. Again, the "probably" is destined to drop out, in most instances, when this statement re-

appears in Popper's discussion (e.g., p. 180).

(e) Cobweb number 5: Antisthenes, asserts Popper, praised manual labor, and practiced it (note 47 to chapter 8, p. 562; note 4 to chapter 11, p. 615). From this Popper infers that he was, naturally, a great equalitarian; it corroborates the probability that the Platonic Socrates of the *Republic*, who speaks with scorn both of manual work and of slaves, is Plato's treacherous puppet, and that Antisthenes is the true continuator of the true Socrates. We show elsewhere (pp. 235–236) that Antisthenes' supposed praise of manual labor is probably founded simply on a mistake.

(f) A sixth point: Antisthenes, according to tradition, taught in the gymnasium known as the Cynosarges, a place reserved for those free men who, like Antisthenes, were not full citizens by birth. If this tradition be accepted, Popper argues, then Antisthenes must have meant to emphasize his own mixed, half-barbarian descent, which is again an affirmation of his belief in human brotherhood (note 48 to chapter 8, p. 564). Be it noted that Popper has passed over the more probable reason, namely, that Antisthenes had originally made this his athletic headquarters, and was simply not admitted elsewhere. A gymnasium was a convenient place of public resort, and, for a follower of Socrates, who had often conversed in such surroundings, a natural place for the carrying on of philosophic discussions.

(g) And finally, Antisthenes was a pupil of Socrates, his "old friend," his "old companion," "one of Socrates' closest friends," as we are told again and again (e.g., p. 95; p. 189; note 56 to chapter 10, p. 603; p. 218), without any evidence being offered beyond his presence, attested by Plato, on Socrates' last day at the prison (it is to be remembered that there were also present some dozen others, including some whose diverse development of their master's teaching was notorious). We assume that Antisthenes' presence, and his expressions of devotion to Socrates, reported in Xenophon's *Symposium*, also form part of Popper's evidence for the "friendship." It is not intended here to deny that Antisthenes was an enthusiastic admirer of Socrates; so also was Plato. What is necessary is to guard against the implication,

conveyed by the repeated phrases but quite
unproved by the available evidence, namely:
Popper's belief that Antisthenes was, on all
matters of ethical import, in the closest
accord with Socrates, far closer than his
other followers. Since Popper believes that
Socrates was a great democrat, individualist, humanitarian, and all the rest, the one
proposition that Antisthenes was in especially close accord with Socrates would go
far to establish his every excellence.

Popper's chain, or rather web, stands
now before us complete. As we review it,
we see that every strand is weakened by
some uncertainty. Of the seven, three are
entirely negligible: the supposed attacks
on Antisthenes in the *Republic*, the love of
manual labor, and the use of the Cynosarges. The connection with Parmenides is
an illusion. The affiliation with Gorgias is
inconclusive. The "close" friendship with
Socrates is a sentimental red herring. The

argument from Roman Stoicism is vitiated
by an element of special pleading.

The modest residue of Popper's argument is sufficient to support no more than
the following: It could be concluded with
reasonable confidence that Antisthenes, who
was a half-barbarian and a noncitizen,
was opposed to discrimination against persons in this situation; that he extended
this tolerance to barbarians, and that he
availed himself of the nature-convention
antithesis to assert that the distinction between Greeks and barbarians was merely
conventional, are possibilities, but nothing
more.

Popper has also adduced those affiliations of Antisthenes with Gorgias, with
Socrates, and with the Cynics and Stoics
of later date, which, when handled with
proper care, take their place, as we shall
presently see, among the accepted facts of
the history of Greek philosophy.

Nominalism, Essentialism, and Intolerance

Popper has assigned to Antisthenes a superiority to Plato in still another area, that of the logical and metaphysical foundations of scientific knowledge, setting the "nominalism" of Antisthenes in contrast to the futile "methodological essentialism" which Popper sees as the consequence, for science, of the Platonic Theory of Ideas. In thus condemning Plato (pp. 34–36), Popper is converting into a liability what historians of philosophy (who are themselves, to Popper, pp. 249–250, a pestilent tribe) commonly list among Plato's most generous contributions to the higher life of mankind. This is not the place to undertake a full discussion of the issues dividing in age-long rivalry nominalists from realists (i.e., "essentialists"). But in justice to Plato I must point out an unfairness inherent in the manner in which Popper has presented Plato in this context. Popper has set over against Plato, the methodological essentialist, the whole weight of modern science, whose progress, Popper urges, has been achieved by pursuing a nominalist method. And by adducing once again his invaluable ally, Antisthenes (pp. 218, 636–637), Popper believes he has shown that Plato could have taken warning from this "nominalist" of the dangers and sterilities to which essentialism was bound to lead. Two chief points are to be observed.

To deal first with the credit due to Antisthenes: — A formal and a material pole of nominalism must be distinguished. To Antisthenes one may at most accord (with some misgivings in the face of other views; see Field, *Plato and his Contemporaries*, 1930, esp. p. 167, who believes it unlikely that Antisthenes was "concerned with the opposition between particulars and universals in the form implied by the use of terms like Nominalism and Realism") the distinction of having been one of the first formal advocates of a method which, when in much later centuries it was applied to problems of scientific inquiry, produced results of great importance. But not even Antisthenes' most extravagant admirers have entered any material claims for him as a forerunner of modern science or even as one interested in anything bordering on scientific research. His rejection of Plato's way of inquiry did not imply that he possessed or was in pursuit of anything beyond the defense of his own method of moral intuition (see p. 208) and the logical demolition of rival views. One may grant him a shrewd eye for the epistemological difficulties in the Platonic theory of the forms, but this he may be said to have shared with the author of the *Parmenides*.

We are ourselves fully committed and prepared to award honorable recognition to the early advocates of ideas destined to play important roles in later history, as we have followed Whitehead's precedent in doing for Plato. But this principle must be applied with discretion if it is not to distort history by a confusion of the past and present tense. In the instance before us, such a confusion is achieved if we impute to Antisthenes an active and conscious waving of the scientific-nominalist banner. And for Popper, the maintenance of this view can be purchased only at the price of treating nominalism itself as a species of time-proof entity, with an "essential" nature waiting only to be unrolled, in short at the cost of falling into a form of that very "methodological essentialism" of which he so strongly disapproves.

A recent critical appraisal of Antisthenes, that of G. M. A. Grube ("Antisthenes Was No Logician," 1950), goes further than I have presumed to go in a deflationary direction. Grube finds no reason to credit Antisthenes with any fundamental contribution to logic or the theory of knowledge, his reputed discoveries dwindling to the stature of "the usual sophistic and eristic tricks which Plato exposed as contrary to all philosophic or scientific investigation" (p. 23).

To reply, now, to Popper's direct disparagement of Plato's theory of Ideas as being inimical to the advance of scientific thought: Plato's own "essentialism," for all its inadequacy to the solution of the problems of modern physics, had the great merit of sustaining faith in the order and intelligibility of natural processes. One may call it a stop-gap, or "interim" science, and credit it with considerable heuristic value. The proof of this lies not merely in the ancient world, in the fruitful results reached by members of the Academy in approaching astronomy from the realistic Platonic standpoint, and in the scientific inquiries of that incorrigible "essentialist," Aristotle. It is common knowledge that the revival of Platonism in fifteenth and sixteenth century Italy was not without importance for the founders of modern astronomy and physics, from Copernicus to Galileo. For a discussion of this influence, reference may be made to Paul Shorey's valuable essay, "Platonism and the History of Science," 1927.

One other aspect of essentialism requires a word. It is one of Popper's recurrent implications that a close and unholy tie unites essentialism and what he has chosen to call the "theory of inquisition" (Popper, pp. 189, 218–221). In favor of this view, he parades the familiar history of the dark ages of the Church beginning with Justinian, which finds its charter, he

avers, in the last books of the *Laws*; much of his earlier report on the *Republic* conveys the same impression. I think we may dismiss the charge that essentialism has a peculiar affinity with Inquisition by adducing as an important example to the contrary, Stoicism, with its doctrine of natural rights, its conviction that the entire scheme of human relations should be founded on the recognition of the essential nature of man as vested with rationality and bound by this natural relationship to fellowship with all members of his kind. That this doctrine is essentialist needs no further proof than its mere statement, which proclaims an answer to the question, "What is man"? That it is benevolent is no less obvious, and for our controversial purposes is made certain by the 587th page of Popper's book, where we read that "under the influence of Stoicism . . . Rome began to develop a very liberal and humanitarian outlook." Popper has also admitted, on his pp. 73 and 511, that what he calls "spiritual naturalism" is neutral as regards humanitarian and equalitarian principles, and that in the form given it by the proponents of "natural right," among them the Stoics, Aquinas, and Kant, it served admirable ends. Since in terms of Popper's definitions, "spiritual naturalism" is a form of "methodological essentialism," again Popper has shown that essentialism has no special tendency toward Inquisition.

Cosmopolitanism in Fifth and Fourth Century Athens

Popper does not limit to Antisthenes the credit of having entertained ideas of human unity, but believes that such "cosmopolitanism" was widely present in Plato's Athens; in this he differs markedly, as we have noted (p. 201) with Tarn. Popper associates with this cosmopolitan "movement," in the first place, that other "movement against slavery" which he believes to have prospered greatly at Athens, and which we have shown (pp. 154ff.) to have been hardly more than a general reasonableness in the treatment of slaves shown by the ordinary citizens, plus sympathy and respect for them as human beings expressed by Euripides, plus the questioning of the theoretic basis of the institution by Alcidamas and by certain unknown persons, reported by Aristotle in the mid-fourth century.

Among the direct advocates of cosmopolitanism, in addition to Antisthenes, Popper lists (pp. 562–564) Antiphon, Hippias, Euripides, Democritus, and Diogenes; he also includes (p. 566) the unexpected figure of Alcibiades. We shall speak below of the remarkable reason for which Popper thus honors Alcibiades: it is his "hopes for a universal empire of Greeks and barbarians," under his own wayward leadership. We shall also weigh and find wanting, in the main, the claims of Diogenes (p. 215). Of Antiphon enough has already been said (pp. 144ff.) to show the misinterpretation upon which his inclusion depends. Hippias' claim is based upon the one sentence discussed on pp. 147f. above. The inclusion of both Euripides and Democritus is justified apparently by the very similar fragments attributed to them (Diels believes the attribution to Democritus is probably erroneous), to the effect that "the whole earth" or "the whole universe" is "the fatherland of a noble soul" (Democritus, Fr. 247, Diels; Euripides, Fr. 1034, Nauck, 1895). To conclude from these fragments that their author or authors necessarily inferred from the ideas expressed, the proper treatment of barbarians as equals, is *a priori*

unsafe; in the case of Euripides the inference can be shown to be doubtful by passages in the plays which deny the equality of Greeks and barbarians. There is, for example, the impassioned statement of Iphigenia, a character close to Euripides' heart, as she goes to her death in order that the Greeks may conquer Troy (*Iph. Aul.* 1400) : "It is right for Greeks to rule over barbarians, . . . not barbarians over Greeks; for they are slaves, and we are free." Yet although Euripides thus did not believe barbarians entitled to equal status with the Greeks, his sympathy with individual slaves has as its corollary a sympathy with individual barbarians, since the slaves who figure in his plays were often enough non-Greeks; and he presents a Medea or a Hecuba without condescension, and even with clear approval of their case against their Greek oppressors.

Adding up, then, the total recognition of human unity credibly adduced by Popper as present in Plato's Athens, we have, in addition to the amount of antislavery sentiment which we have recognized above, two declarations of the unimportance of a purely local citizenship (Hippias, Diogenes), with the added approval, in Hippias' case, of a wider (but unspecified) allegiance; we have what appears to be a biological-immoralist universalism (Antiphon); we have sympathy for the individual barbarian (Euripides) ; and we have a statement in praise of what may be worldwide understanding between men, or may equally well be cosmic contemplation by the wise man (Euripides, perhaps Democritus). We have also the universal implications of the ethical thought of Socrates, and of his somewhat one-sided follower, Antisthenes, to both of whom we shall attempt below to do full justice.

We may add also, on our own initiative, one element in the thought of Isocrates, whom Popper does not mention in this connection. This is the notion, expressed in the *Panegyricus* and elsewhere, that Athens has achieved a Hellenism which justifies the

application of "the title 'Hellenes' . . . rather to those who share our culture than to
those who share a common blood" (*Pan.* 50,
trans. Norlin, Loeb Library). An element
of tolerance is present also in Aristophanes'
sympathy, discussed on p. 281, for those
Athenian allies and metics who did not enjoy the privileges of Athenian citizenship.
In short, the notion of human unity may be
said to have been present, so to speak, in
its scattered elements, to have been caught
hold of by this corner or by that, by more
than one thinker or poet, in much the same
fashion in which, as we shall show below,
Plato came near to conceiving it; though
his contribution to the eventual full-blown
concept, like that of Euripides, was very
great.

To his proof of the existence of a cosmopolitan movement in Athens Popper adds
(p. 563) what he calls the "attacks" of its
"enemies," the Old Oligarch and Plato. In
the Old Oligarch he finds what may well be,
under the cover of ironical praise, a deprecation of Athenian readiness to adopt foreign foods and phrases (cf. p. 278). From
the *Republic* he adduces such miscellaneous
items as Plato's objection to the improper
assumption by noncitizens of citizens' privileges, his protest against the enslaving of
captured fellow Greeks, as contrasted with
barbarians, and his ridicule of an ambition,
on the part of an Alcibiades, to rule over
both Greeks and barbarians. The two last-
named protests, as we have shown (pp.
223ff., 228f.), spring from motives quite
other than hatred or scorn of barbarian
peoples. The first of them cannot serve as
evidence of Plato's opposition to a more
humane abhorrence felt by Athenians generally against enslaving or oppressing either
Greeks or barbarians, for the simple reason
that such Athenian scruples did not exist
(cf. pp. 141ff. and pp. 319f.); it is directed
rather against the less humane actual practice of the Greeks (including the Athenians)
of enslaving fellow Greeks in addition to
barbarians. Nor need the second be taken
to prove Plato's failure to honor Alcibiades'
desire to extend to all races alike the benefits of a universalistic imperialism, since this
estimate of Alcibiades' motives is apparently a pure gift to him from Popper. The
remaining two "attacks" may indeed be
taken to show the Athenians' "cosmopolitanism" in so far as this comprised an acceptance of some foreign customs, and a

willingness to extend certain limited privileges, beyond the letter of the law, to foreigners resident in Athens. But all this as
little implies an active Athenian movement
to abolish the distinction between citizen
and noncitizen as did Athenian liberality
to slaves imply an abolition movement, nor
does it add color to the hypothesis that any
single thinker of the period had gone so far
as to proclaim in theory the equality in
rights and worth of men of every race.

In this connection it will be relevant to
survey the findings of a recent study, *The
Stranger at the Gate*, by T. J. Haarhof,
Basil Blackwell, Oxford, published in 1938,
destroyed in the bombing of London, and
reissued in 1948 (a work of which I became
aware only late in the process of preparing
this book). Haarhof has surveyed classical
literature for its revelation of attitudes
toward noncitizens and men of other races,
and also toward wider units of political organization than the *polis*, covering much of
the ground which Tarn and Popper have
traversed. His conclusions concerning the
period in which we are interested differ
from Tarn's, and superficially are more in
agreement with Popper's, in that he discovers in Greece before Alexander, partly
among the thinkers similarly cited by Popper, e.g., Alcidamas, Democritus, and Hippias, the well-attested presence of the idea
of human unity (p. 18), and condemns
Plato as having failed to advance this idea
to the degree befitting a philosopher. Haarhof has also honored as a genial cosmopolitan Herodotus, whom Popper hails as
a friend of democracy. (That Haarhof has
not sufficiently weighed the "negative instances" in Herodotus' equal treatment of
Greeks and barbarians, will be seen by con-
sulting the references given in our n. 113,
p. 289.)

But the agreement with Popper on closer
view is seen to be substantially less than
these instances would indicate. Haarhof has
included among those who show traces of
the concept of human unity, several early
figures, such as Empedocles, and among
these he puts the Pythagorean school and
Heraclitus, whom Popper would not welcome. Haarhof has denied the honor of inclusion to Antiphon (though on somewhat
different grounds from those set forth on
our pp. 144ff.), and has questioned it in the
case of Euripides. Above all, he has held up
as examples of avoidance Pericles and the

common people of Athens. Haarhof is a moderate man, not given to Popper's extremes of condemnation, yet in judging the narrow exclusiveness, the intolerance toward barbarians and foreigners, and the imperialist selfishness of Periclean Athens, he has felt that some degree of severity was required.

In his estimate of Plato, he is again close to Tarn and to Popper, yet not so condemnatory as either. He lays disapproving stress on Plato's recommendation (discussed on pp. 223ff. above), that war be waged and enslavement countenanced only against barbarians, not against Greeks, and he even follows Tarn in representing this, not correctly, as Plato's advocacy or sanctioning of truceless war against barbarians. He regrets, also, Plato's limitation of his political thought to the city state. Haarhof, however, knows something of Plato's excellences as well: the Plato he depicts abhors violence, and despite his limitation to the *polis*, does not sanction the Isocratean notion of an unprovoked war of conquest against Persia; Haarhof is aware that *"en ouranôi,"* as he puts it — that is to say, under the aspect of eternity —, Plato sees mankind as one, and that he extends protection to strangers within the gate.

In one characteristic, Haarhof's book seems closely to resemble Popper's, and thus to work Plato needless harm, though with Haarhof this is doubtless the result of inadvertence. We refer to his tendency to give the benefit of every doubt to an ancient thinker who survives only in fragments, while overlooking numerous passages in Plato which parallel these same fragments, and concentrating attention on the few passages in which Plato has definitely expressed his greater sense of loyalty to Greeks. We may illustrate this tendency by Haarhof's discovery (p. 12) of a "clear indication of the idea of world unity" in those Heraclitean fragments (Diels, Frs. 113, 114) which assert that thought is common to all and that all human laws derive from one divine source, while he passes by without mention the unitary implications of Plato's theory of ideas, with its single standard of value for men of every time and place, as well as such strong indications of uniformity as are evident in Plato's account of the creation of the human soul in the *Timaeus*. And it would not be difficult to match the universalistic implications of the

"spirit, 'holy and unutterable, that . . . penetrates the universe,' " of Empedocles (Haarhof, p. 12) with the divine providence of the tenth book of the *Laws*, which is no respecter of persons and no scorner of details, but, like the Stoic *"pronoia,"* which it so largely inspired, pervades the universe, embracing the slightest portion thereof in its benevolent and rational care. The operation of a similar differential generosity can be seen in Haarhof's judgments of some writers who have left more substantial remains, as, for example, Hippocrates, or the pseudo-Hippocrates, whom Haarhof commends for having ascribed racial differences, including differences in intellect and ethics, to variations in climate and geography. "This means," says Haarhof (p. 16), "that he ignored the current distinction between Greeks and barbarians." Similarly, Haarhof says (p. 57) of Xenophon, who chose to depict the Persian Cyrus as the ideal ruler in his *Cyropaedia*, that this proves Xenophon's freedom from any real antibarbarian prejudice: "it reduces his general acceptance of the Greek dichotomy of the world to a mere convention." Now Plato, in his *Laws* (747 C–E), ascribes the mercantile attitude of the Phoenicians and Egyptians not to race, but to climate, perhaps, or to unfortunate laws and customs (see our pp. 221–222) ; and Plato also exalts the Persian Cyrus, and the Persian Darius as well, as examples of wise rulers, who tempered despotism with democracy. Yet of these Platonic insights Haarhof takes no note, and does not admit Plato to the excuse allowed Xenophon, that his acceptance of the customary Greek-barbarian antithesis, in some passages, is offset by his more original transcendence of it in others. It is this indulgence, or rather justice, which we seek to secure for Plato.

Aside from his greater moderation and fairmindedness, the great superiority of Haarhof's approach over Popper's consists largely in his separation of the various strands of which the idea of human unity is composed, his ability to recognize the coexistence, in a given thinker or group, of parts of both the tolerant and the exclusive attitudes. This enables him to see clearly both the narrow exclusiveness of the Athenians in respect to citizenship, along with their common scorn of the barbarians, and also their willingness to welcome foreigners to their city; he need not minimize the one (indeed he goes rather further than we have cared to go in condemning the Athenian narrowness) in order to acclaim the other. As a result, he has been able to avoid Popper's dichotomy of advocates and opponents of the "open society." His picture of the complications of attitude and the slow and piecemeal emergence of the rounded ideal, is in general conformity with the pattern which this book has attempted to trace.

Appendix VII

Plato and the Idea of Mankind

In a group of extended notes, notes 46–52, pp. 561–567, Popper gives his reasons for denying that Plato possessed the concept of "humanity" or designed his political ideal to have universal application to all mankind. To several of these notes we have already devoted attention, that is, to those concerning Antisthenes, and the alleged "cosmopolitanism" of Antiphon, Antisthenes, and Diogenes. In the remaining notes, which deal primarily with the phrase "the human race" in Plato's sentence about the philosopher kings, Popper employs arguments which may be successively answered here.

Popper, as we have indicated in Chapter 1, p. 17 above, believes that Plato is a "holist," in the sense (among others; cf. our pp. 518ff.) that he hypostatizes the state, that is, considers it a "whole" which alone has independent value, as contrasted with the human individuals who compose it; their value, on this view, is merely derivative and wholly subsidiary to the state's interest. Since, as we show in Chapter 9, Plato is not in this sense a "holist," this argument cannot hold; nevertheless we may examine its development. As a "holist," Popper argues (p. 564), Plato could not casually introduce, in the phrase "the human race," occurring in the sentence referred to, the concept of this new, larger, and more comprehensive whole; had he intended to do so, he would have been impelled (a) to prepare the reader for the introduction, and would further (b) have elaborated the new idea, or at least have referred back to the concept in his subsequent discussion. In support of this, he remarks (p. 564, note 49), that in introducing the concept of the Hellenic race, in the passage about not enslaving Greeks, Plato did go into some detail. Now, granted that in the passage about not enslaving Greeks, Plato did expand somewhat his meaning, he did not "prepare," nor does he afterward refer back to it; we therefore have one instance at least of the introduction of a more

inclusive ethical whole by this "holist" Plato, without preparation.

Popper next asks whether, in his subsequent discussion of the benefits to be conferred by the philosophic rulers, Plato again mentions "mankind" or the "race of man." He presents a list of subsequent sentences, which, he says, refer back to the philosopher-kings sentence, and reports that he found in them "if anything, a withdrawal of the ambiguous expression 'race of men' "; Plato refers simply to "city" alone, or to "city" and "individual." Now we will cheerfully admit, though there is no question of "withdrawal" of the term "human race," that in several of the subsequent passages Plato speaks only of the perfection that will be attained by cities and individual men, whenever or wherever philosophy and political power coincide. The base of Popper's argument is removed if we remember what Plato is about: he is designing a model city, not an Alexandrian world empire; his thought is, therefore, naturally expressed in terms of the city and the individuals who compose it. It is in the scope of applicability that the universality of the Platonic scheme is manifest. Following through Popper's list of back references to the philosopher-kings sentence, we notice particularly one of them, in which it is said that without philosophic rulers, "neither city nor state nor man, either" shall become perfect (*Republic* 499 B); immediately after this comes the saying we have quoted in our text above, that by remote possibility, "even now, in some barbaric region," philosophic natures may be in control, and the ideal city may be in actual existence (499 C). What is it required that Plato must say, to make it clearer that he thinks not of Greeks alone, but of man, wherever he may dwell, who is to be benefited, whenever true philosophic rulers shall be constrained to rule? The truth is that Plato has not needed to prepare the reader for the introduction of this new "whole," wider than the city, because it has never been absent from his thought.

The whole ethical purpose of the *Republic*, the picture of the just man and the city which is like him, is founded on and presupposes the ethical and religious conception of mankind which is everywhere Plato's own.

Popper now seeks (p. 565) to show Plato's lack of the idea of humanity by examining his use of the terms "man" and "human." "Except in the early Socratic dialogues," and in one passage in the *Theaetetus*, 174 E ff. (an exception to which we shall revert immediately below), Popper declares that "*nowhere*" (italics ours) does Plato use these terms "to express something that transcends the distinctions of nation, race or class," or "as a moral category." Popper proceeds to bolster his assertion with a long list of examples of what he calls the "zoological" use, and the use in which things human are opposed to things divine. This contention on Popper's part is somewhat puzzling because of the extreme ease with which it can be refuted. He cannot establish his case by proving that the words sometimes bear the significations alleged; he has taken it upon himself to prove that they do not occur in a universalistic sense. This being the case, it is surprising to find that not even all of those uses which he lists bear out his assertions. In some (*Rep.* 606 E, 486 A) "men" are not contrasted with gods, but coupled; in another (*Rep.* 514 B) "men" are simply those who sit chained in the Cave of Plato's metaphor, or carry past the images which throw the shadows which they mistake for realities; in another (*Laws* 890 B) they are simply the citizens of Plato's reformed state. Nor is it easy to judge what would be considered by Popper a "humanitarian" use, unless perhaps it involved an explicit statement that all men are brothers; for of the passages listed by Popper himself, one at least refers to man generically, as an ethical agent: *Laws* 688 C, in which it is said that the confederacy of the Dorian states failed "because of ignorance about the most important concerns of men"; and looking back a few pages to see what this may mean, we discover that these "most important human concerns" are virtue, particularly wisdom, and human happiness, "that which we all wish always," "the common object of desire of all men" (*Laws* 687 C). Surely any such ethical use — and they are plentiful in Plato — transcends the distinctions of nation, race, and

class; as examples, we suggest *Rep.* 603 C, 618 B, 619 B; *Timaeus* 90 D, 937 E, 950 B–C, 951 B; a particularly impressive passage is *Laws* 770 D–E, which speaks of "the excellence of soul which is proper to man." We should add the numerous passages in which Plato speaks of man generically as God's puppet or possession, or as the most godfearing or the most divine of animals. Nor should those passages be excluded from consideration in which the words "*anthrôpos*" or "*anêr*," or their derivatives, do not occur; Plato may speak of "the just," or of "those who are to be good" as contrasted with "those who are to be rich," or, as we saw above, in the quotation from the *Laws*, he may simply say "we." But the concept of man, considered as an ethical being or as a soul, must be taken into account wherever and in whatever words it is expressed.

Popper's third proof (p. 565) of Plato's failure to conceive man generically is his attempt to show that Plato conceives, instead, "a hierarchy of 'natures'" of man. The Idea of Man comes first in excellence, then perhaps the "super-Greeks" of Plato's "city in Heaven" (the mythical, eternally subsisting form of the ideal city); then the earliest man, "the ancient primogenitor of the human race," whom, on Popper's view — please remember that Popper believes Plato to be a "historicist" in reverse (see our discussion of this idea, pp. 18–19, 622ff.) — Plato conceives to have been the best, because the first, of all mankind; then the Greeks; and finally, far at the bottom, the barbarians. For all this beautiful series, Popper has almost no evidence, and what he has is misused. It is true that Plato considers the Idea of Man and the form of the ideal city more perfect than any actual man or city. It is not true, as we shall show (pp. 628, 612ff.) that the first man or the first city is believed by Plato to have been the most perfect; if the reader will recollect our résumé of Plato's account of prehistory on p. 220 above, he will observe that there is in that account no trace of such an idea. It is true that Plato conceived of a hierarchy of human "natures," ranging from the most noble and enlightened at the top down to those poor "servitors" or "ministers," lacking in mental and moral self-control, whom Plato conceived to be able to serve the community only by bodily strength. These "natures" are not biologically pure races; even among the lower ranks, children may be born who are capable of rising to the top. The barbarians are not at the bottom of this series, nor are there, at the very top, only Greeks. In short, the supposed hierarchy is illusory — like Popper's notion of the nearly successful Athenian abolitionist movement.

Popper next tries to show (p. 566) that Plato's suggestion that the ideal city may exist among the far-off barbarians, has no importance for modifying Plato's conception of the low and slavish barbarian "nature." He says of the suggestion that it "rescinds the distinction between Greeks and barbarians no more than that between the past, the present, and the future." Why should this be rescinded? As Popper says, Plato is expressing a sweeping generalization. But the inclusion of barbarians is not thus to be disposed of. Nor does Plato add Popper's suggested phrase "in such an extremely unlikely place as" — a barbarian country. That Plato thought a love of knowledge to be prevalent chiefly in Greece, he has told us (*Republic* 436 A), in a passage to which we have referred before, where it is said, also, that a love of money is typical of Egyptians and Phoenicians, and a spirited temperament usual among the Thracians and Scythians. But Plato was in his day and in the main right about this, in the cultural-sociological sense in which he intended it, as the historical record shows. (We have discussed Plato's conception of the causes of these cultural differences on pp. 221f.) And there is in his statement that true philosophers may exist among barbarians, the definite assertion that love of knowledge, and men of truly golden natures, may be looked for also among the men of other lands and races. Plato did not think it at all likely that philosophic rulers would be established at any time, in Greece, or anywhere else, and yet he wished that it might be so; only so, he tells us, can evils cease for the cities or for the "race of men." Assuming that we have shown that "men" for Plato included men everywhere, this is to be credited to him also as an expression of good will toward men.

Popper's final argument (p. 566) is the strange contention that Plato must have felt it to be no more than an "impious absurdity" to suggest that philosopher kings might exist among the barbarians; it is regarded by Plato (so Popper holds) as a mere parallel to the greater "impious absurdity" which Plato detects in Alcibiades' ambition to rule over Greeks and barbarians. The parallel is false. Plato did regard as impious absurdity such ambition to rule; he would have regarded it as anything but impious to imagine or to wish that philosophic natures should, somewhere or anywhere, undertake the responsibility of rule, within a single city. To say that a man thinks himself fit to rule over "the whole wide world" is not the same as to say that somewhere in "the whole wide world" there may be one ideally governed city, and to desire this end.

To his long note designed to prove Plato's total lack of the idea of humanity, Popper in his second edition has added the exceptions noted above, consenting to believe, now, that "in the early Socratic dialogues" the idea may be found, and recognizing in addition (p. 566) the passage in the *Theaetetus*, 174 E ff., which we have cited in our text, pp. 263–264, and of which Popper apparently was formerly unaware. This he calls "definitely humanitarian"; but since it is, as he recognizes, "in flagrant contrast" to his own picture of Plato's state of mind, he can only propose to remove it from Plato's possession by suggesting that the *Theaetetus* is "perhaps earlier than the *Republic*" and therefore still Socratic in spirit, free of the supposed Platonic "anti-humanitarian exclusiveness." But this suggestion receives no confirmation from anything else known or reasonably conjectured about the *Theaetetus*. It is at variance with Popper's basic conviction that the early Plato had no notion of the backward abysm of past time, and is bootless in any case, since Plato as late as the *Laws* is in full possession of the concept of humanity.

For a discussion of Popper's special racial interpretation of the phrase "human race," as employed by Plato in speaking of the benefits to be conferred by his philosophic rulers, see pp. 450ff., 535ff.

Appendix VIII

On the Trustworthiness of Thucydides

Against Popper's strictures on Thucydides (mainly given on his pp. 155–158, and 248–249, notes 12 and 15 to chapter 10), and with the aid of certain modern authorities (principally J. B. Bury, *The Ancient Greek Historians*, 1909; J. H. Finley, *Thucydides*, 1942; and A. W. Gomme, *A Historical Commentary on Thucydides*, vol. I, 1945), we shall seek to confirm the truthfulness and, with indicated exceptions, the reasonableness of the historian's report upon Athenian democracy and imperialism, and thus, to supply what we shall later show to be a confirmation, with due qualifications, of Plato's right as good citizen and moral man to have felt as he did concerning the political issues of his day. On our way to this end we shall be obliged to venture certain personal opinions, but we shall avoid the temptation to settle any still disputed questions by definitive pronouncements of our own.

Popper begins his account of Thucydides (p. 173) by warning us that we must not read Thucydides without remembering that "his heart was not with Athens, his native city," that "he was certainly a member of the oligarchic party, and a friend neither of the Athenian people, the demos, who had exiled him, nor of its imperialist policy." The implications here are most questionable. Criticism of the party in power, or even of particular constitutional provisions, is not incompatible with deeper allegiance to the nation. The assumption that such must be the case, if refutation is needed, is well answered, in terms of the situation at Athens before and in the early years of the Peloponnesian war, by Gomme ("The Old Oligarch," in *Athenian Studies*, 1940, pp. 238–244). Gomme shows clearly that during the years before the death of Pericles, all classes at Athens, oligarchs as well as democrats, coöperated fully in "working" the constitution; later, as the war progressed, a small group withdrew from active participation, and contemplated revolution. But until dissatisfaction over the conduct of the war had spread to include large sec-

tions of the citizenry, they had no chances, and their existence did not seriously disturb the unity of the city. That Thucydides was among those who coöperated with the democracy is shown by his having accepted election as a general in 424. Further, Popper seems to intend the fact of Thucydides' banishment to count as strengthening the probability that he was prejudiced against the democracy, without allowing this same fact of banishment any importance as having perhaps formed part of a valid reason for Thucydides' unfavorable judgment upon that democracy. In short, we have here another instance of Popper's method, applied also throughout his book to Plato, of raising and exploiting unfavorable implications, which it is impossible to answer in detail, though we may note an occasional example.

Popper next tells us that Thucydides was "the greatest historian, perhaps, who ever lived," but that nevertheless what he has given us, in addition to the facts he records, is "an interpretation, a point of view; and in this we need not agree with him." Again we have a parallel with Popper's method of treating Plato, which involves the occasional bestowal of almost fulsome praise, which, however, does not appear to affect the final evaluation of the man as essentially unapprovable. To prove discrediting antidemocratic bias on the part of this greatest of historians, Popper adduces two major pieces of evidence:

(1) Comparing two passages from the *History* in which misdeeds against fellow citizens are recounted, in the first case committed by oligarchs, in the second by democrats, Popper alleges that the former is more lightly weighed than the latter. The first passage (Thucydides I, 107) is the brief mention of an unsuccessful attempt of certain Athenian oligarchs to end at once democracy and the building of the Long Walls of Athens, then in progress, with the aid of a Spartan expeditionary force which was operating in the neighborhood, some twenty-six years before the outbreak of the Peloponnesian war. Popper comments in

his own person, "as sometimes happens with oligarchs, class interest superseded their patriotism" (p. 174); and he notes with disapproval that Thucydides fails to censure this "most blatant treachery." He then cites as an "illustration of the strong words Thucydides could find when he wanted to describe analogous tendencies on the side of the democrats at Corcyra," Thucydides' extended comment, following his account of an oligarchically originated revolution at Corcyra, in the course of which the victorious Corcyrean demos massacred several hundred oligarchs (Thucydides III, 81–84). It is a propos of this revolution, which Thucydides says excited particular attention, being among the first of its kind in the war, that the historian inserts a solemn comment on the unhappy moral effect of the war in general — the progressive degeneration of men's loyalties, the loss of restraint and humanity, and the readiness of either side in any civic struggle to call in outside aid, either Athenian or Spartan, as the case might be. Popper, adding as further evidence of Thucydides' bias the statement that "Corcyra had been one of Athens' democratic allies" before this revolution, which had been started by the oligarchs, conceives that he has made his case for Thucydides' unfairness in this instance (Popper, p. 174).

The faults in this proof are easily observed. In the first place, it is entirely improper to assume that one can measure Thucydides' sympathies by merely noting who gets explicitly praised or blamed. This is to impute to him an essentially moralistic method of writing history that leaves out of account his recognition of the large measure of necessity in human actions, and his habitual preference for a presentation of events that leaves open and often excludes as irrelevant the question of right and wrong. This is not to deny that Thucydides had preferences and convictions, and that he sometimes shows them. It is rather a warning against inferring from the absence of an explicit comment that Thucydides approved. A warning is also needed against too hastily deciding upon a given interpretation of the historian's broader evaluations, in view of the sobering fact that differences of opinion exist among experts. As one example among many, we may point to the dispute over the "Melian debate," an episode in the History in which

Athenian envoys in the sixteenth year of the war openly express their adherence to the most cynical principles of power politics: Bury believes (op. cit., p. 140) that Thucydides is here presenting a simple if extreme instance of that absence of effective moral considerations which characterized Athenian imperialism at all times, and presumably all successful political activity at any time; Finley sees in the incident (op. cit., p. 112) the historian's picture of the moral nadir reached by the decadent democracy in the absence of wise restraints, as contrasted with that power tempered with benevolence which was at the beginning of the war the glory of Periclean imperialism. The possibility of arriving at such divergent judgments rests upon the historian's restraint, which here, as often — but here most strikingly — makes it impossible for his reader to discern his personal outlook upon the events so impersonally recorded; Popper's charge (p. 249) that Thucydides here "tries to brand Athenian imperialism" is thus, to say the least, too assured.

Furthermore, in drawing confident conclusions from the context in which Thucydides has in fact chosen to express his judgment upon the unwholesome moral effect of the war, Popper has ignored, first, Thucydides' stated reason for inserting his comment at this point; he has not observed the very much bloodier results of the Corcyrean affair than of the Athenian episode, which after all come to nothing; and he has ignored the entirely impartial application of the historian's remarks to both democrats and oligarchs. Moreover, in calling Corcyra "one of Athens' democratic allies," Popper obscures the fact that Corcyra herself, when she summoned Athens to her aid, was fighting as the champion of the expelled oligarchs of Epidamnus. It is not as simple as Popper apparently believes to judge which side, in the tangle of Greek politics, is the side of the angels. We may then add that Popper, in commenting in his own proper person, as we have seen him do, on the respective treacheries of the oligarchs and democrats, shows much more clearly than does Thucydides a readiness to blame only the side which he dislikes; could it not more fairly have been said, "as sometimes happens with men of any political persuasion, class interest superseded their patriotism"? If we are to choose

merely between interpretations or points of
view, the interpretation of the events of
Greek history offered by Thucydides would
seem at least not less objective.

But leaving Popper's attempted proof,
is it true that Thucydides unfairly weighs
the merits of the oligarchical and demo-
cratical parties, respectively, and that he
therefore is properly suspect as a guide to
sound judgment? We shall not presume to
answer this question in its finer bearings;
if pressed for an unofficial answer, we
should be inclined to say that particularly
in his judgment of individuals, Thucydides
sometimes deviates from his ideal of detached observation and nonpartisan judgment. Thus he frankly reveals (Book II,
65–67) his great admiration for Pericles,
and *per contra* is not able to avoid some
unfairness in his treatment of such a man
as Cleon; yet, as has been pointed out by
Gomperz (*Greek Thinkers*, 1901, I, p. 518),
he does not permit his personal distaste for
the man to alter in the least his reporting
of the facts, even when (as in Bk. IV, 28–
40) these are highly to the man's credit.
That his objectivity was sufficient to prevent us from being seriously deceived as to
the actions and policies of the partisans of
either side, or their practical results, is, so
far as known to us, doubted by no serious
student.

(2) Popper next objects (p. 175) that
Thucydides has represented the Athenian
empire as being, in the general opinion of
the Greeks at the beginning of the war,
"little better than a tyranny," and that, by
contrast, his criticism of Sparta is mild. It
is on the foundations of Thucydides' prejudiced appraisals, Popper avers, that "the
official judgment of 'History'" has been
built, with incalculable injury to the liberal cause throughout the generations. The
distinguished historian Eduard Meyer is
cited as an outstanding instance: he has
followed Thucydides to the foot of the letter in associating favor for the Spartan
cause with "educated" opinion, in contrast
to the support given to Athens, which is
treated as of no importance, being only that
of the uneducated masses.

Popper bolsters his assertion that Thucydides' statements on this point "are only
expressions of the anti-democratic point of
view," i.e. are untrue, by a general reference to other passages in Thucydides in
which democratic factions in various places

are shown to be hopeful of an Athenian
victory.

Yet with reference to the over-all state
of affairs, at the time of which Thucydides
speaks, what sort of justification does Popper supply for brushing aside his testimony?
None whatever, beyond, first, the assumption that Thucydides, being partisan, must
have expressed here only his own partisanship; and second, Popper's own neglect to
mention any of Thucydides' remarks which
tend to the dispraise of the Spartans. For
it would be quite simple (and to my judgment, rather nearer the truth) to prove by
parity of reasoning that Thucydides was
anti-Spartan. For this purpose it would be
sufficient to cite the reference to the violence of the Spartan Pausanias (Thucydides I, 95), and the depiction of the narrow
imagination and backward-looking Spartan
ideals as developed in the speeches in Book
I (80–86), set, as they are, in antithesis to
the noble Athenian ideals expressed in the
funeral speech of the admired Pericles
(Thucydides II, 35–47). As to Popper's
opinions of the historians, Meyer among
them, we have no wish to defend these
writers further than may be implied in the
statement that, to the extent to which they
have followed Thucydides, they have followed what is, except in the merest details,
the only sound source we have for the events
of the period in question, as well as one of
the most accurate of all sources for any period. (See Gomme, *op. cit.*, pp. 28–29;
Bury, *op. cit.*, pp. 93–99.)

As we have seen on p. 272 above, Popper
has set up a category of less extreme oligarchs who were supporters of the old values and of the old religion, and wishing to
offer partial extenuation of Thucydides, has
included him as a "representative leader"
of this group. We agree that Thucydides
was attached to certain human values in
Greek life, which might be called by Popper
"old," among them the sanctities of kinship
and civic loyalty, which partisan strife
tended to obliterate; though whether Thucydides valued them particularly for their
traditional quality — whether, as Popper
implies (p. 179), the historian viewed them
as among the blessings to be regained by
a return of the "state of our forefathers" —
is another question. But when Popper adds
the "old religion," he requires us to believe
what, to my knowledge, no accredited scholar has ever held: that Thucydides was tra-

ditionally pious. For if anything whatever is visible behind the so often impassive and sometimes subtly ironical mask of the historian, it is his scornful superiority to the "old religion," his refusal to refer happenings, toward and untoward, to the will and power of the gods, with which the old religion was inextricably involved. His frequently obtruded denials of the truth of oracles, or the monitory significance of earthquakes and astral portents, might well have brought him to answer a charge of "impiety" before the same popular Athenian court that arraigned Anaxagoras for his slanders on the sun and moon. Popper, in his effort to attach the blame of irreligion to the extreme oligarchs, "the movement itself," while still maintaining a basis for exonerating Thucydides, has been led again into his usual error of excessive system, and has ascribed to an individual whatever is necessary to make him fit into the prearranged pattern.

Popper has also charged Thucydides, as we have seen (p. 272 above), with wishing to arrest change, and with enmity to Athenian seaborne commerce; he has added as his final charge enmity to the "universalistic imperialism of the Athenian democracy" (p. 179). Since these traits are Popper's minimum definition of what it takes to make an "oligarch," this was, for him, a tactical necessity. It appears to be conceded on all hands that a mainspring of Thucydides' conception of history was a belief in the unbreakable sequence which hurries human affairs from one station to the next, admitting at the most some degree of direction by those who possess a knowledge of the recurrent patterns of events and who display the necessary promptitude of action, but never admitting of arrest. The long digression in Book I, the so-called "Archaeology," with its realistic recognition of the significance of material resources and technical development, as determinative of the particular shapes that successive stages of culture will assume, puts Thucydides once and for all in the camp of the naturalistic interpreters of history, for whom not only no return is possible, but no static preservation of the shapes assumed; he can only investigate the causes of the growth or downfall of the structures of power and value which history successively presents.

Popper's assertion that Thucydides disapproved of Athenian imperialism is a statement that cannot be called either true or false until it is given a more definite context. As Popper first makes the charge (p. 175), he is asserting that Thucydides regards unfavorably that empire as it was "at the outbreak of the Peloponnesian war," in other words, in the last years of the Periclean administration, and not what it was destined to become in the hands of Cleon and his demagogic successors. Does Popper mean that to the mind of Thucydides "imperialism" was the same thing in both cases, and if so, how will he explain the uncontested admiration shown for Pericles (Thucydides II, 65) and the equally clear distaste for the policies of the popular leader who succeeded him? Again, we find a convenient simplification imposed on the complexity of the facts. Thucydides might well have been opposed to the later treatment of the states composing the empire without being opposed to its earlier form.

Since, however, Popper makes no such distinction, but instead states in general that Thucydides wished "to fight the universalistic imperialism of the Athenian democracy," let us take him at his word. Now except for Bury, whose mercilessly objective Thucydides considers questions of value irrelevant to historical analysis, who centers his interest upon and is fascinated by "this new thing," "an empire governed by a democracy" (Bury, op. cit., pp. 77, 136–140) yet is scientifically detached, exercising a "cold independent judgment" upon its course, most contemporary authorities appear to think that Thucydides, in some sense, admired the empire. This view with some variation in kind and degree is expressed by Gomme, op. cit., pp. 90–92, and by Finley, op. cit., pp. 89–91; it is also supported by the slighter recent essay on Thucydides of D. Grene, Man in His Pride, 1950, esp. p. 55. To my reading it is difficult to escape the feeling that Thucydides has made rather a special point of the civilizing effect of sea power, viewing it as the prerequisite to any considerable political and cultural achievement. Before the rise of the naval power of Crete in earlier days, Thucydides saw only an anarchic condition of piracy; he notes the success of the great enterprise of Agamemnon as conditioned upon the strength of his fleet (Thucydides I, 4, 7, 9). It is against this background that we are presented with the Athens of Pericles, which in every line Thucydides is commending as the cultural superior to its land-bound and backward-looking Spartan rival. Not the attainment of this power but its misuse and the folly which brought it to destruction have moved the historian to reveal, implicitly but unmistakably, his adverse judgment. It is only by telescoping the story of the later stages of the war, and confusing the account of extravagances, short-sighted ruthlessness, and divided leadership, that followed the death of Pericles, with the record of the imperial Athens of Pericles, that Popper has been able to present Thucydides as the opponent of Athenian imperialism. To what appears to be his further implied charge that it is precisely the "universalistic" aspects of this imperialism which the historian opposes, we need

only reply that the contrary is more probable; certainly toward the end of the war, when the oligarchic *régime* of the Four Hundred attempted to set up similar oligarchies in the formerly democratically-governed cities of the empire, Thucydides saw plainly enough that this would not solve the problem of unifying the empire by mutual consent (Bk. VIII, 48, 64).

In sum, we have shown reason to believe that Popper has failed in his attempt to establish the unfounded and bigoted prejudice of Thucydides against change and against a universalistic ideal of empire, or explain away the authority and validity of the historian's solemn testimony to the existence of serious weaknesses in Athenian democracy.

The Political Import of the *Menexenus*

In view of Popper's conviction (cf. our n. 217, p. 336) that the section of the *Menexenus* describing the Athenian constitution (238 B–239 A) is a malicious attack upon the finest elements of Periclean-Athenian democracy, we feel called upon to determine as carefully as we can the serious meaning of what Plato has made his oratorical Socrates ironically declare. In general, we shall find that the irony in this part of the *Menexenus* takes the form of praising Athens for having what Plato believed to be a genuine excellence, but one which in his own day, he believed she did not possess; occasionally, he bestows on her the customary praise for having what is not, in his terms, a genuine and unqualified excellence.

We shall first summarize the relevant portion of the *Menexenus*, numbering the points of praise for the convenience of our later discussion: The imaginary orator undertakes to show (a) how the divinely favored Athenians fashioned themselves a form of government so excellent that it has ever since produced a corresponding excellence in its citizens. This polity, he says, (b) has remained essentially unchanged from the days of the kings; (c) it may be called "democracy" by some, but it is in very truth an "aristocracy," a rule of the best, with the approval of the multitude. (d) Power chiefly resides in the many, but (e) those who hold office are chosen solely because they are the wisest and best; (f) no man is barred by weakness or poverty or obscurity of birth. Alluding to the mythical origin of the Athenians from the soil of Attica, he affirms (g) that the citizens, since they are all children of one mother, will not endure to be masters or slaves of one another, but being by nature equal in birth, (h) seek lawfully equality in law (*isonomia*).

We observe, to begin with, that point (b) in the preceding summary has no precedent in the speech of Pericles (Thucydides II, 35–46), of which Popper supposes the *Menexenus* oration to be a parody,

and that point (g) is only distantly implied in Pericles' statement (II, 36) that the Athenians have always inhabited their land. Since point (g) is fully paralleled in Lysias' funeral oration (17–19), it can be regarded as probable that point (b), also, had its counterpart in the speech of some other orator or orators, and that, in fact, most or all of these themes were in Plato's day common property.

We may now examine the orator's points in the light thrown upon them by other Platonic writings. (a) The notion that good men establish good polities, which in turn breed good men, is in itself a commonplace of Greek thought, a premise common to Athenians and Spartans alike. Plato has given it much emphasis, especially in the *Republic*, the gold of the guardian class is qualifications elsewhere noted (cf. pp. 416 and 465), as one huge reaffirmation of this principle. The same conviction is less obviously, but none the less pervasively present in Pericles' speech, with its correlation of the excellence of the Athenian constitution with the merits of Athenian citizens. When Popper blames Plato for holding this view, he is by the same token attacking a presupposition of Periclean democracy. We must, of course, remember that here in the *Menexenus* Plato is making an ironical application of his serious conviction: despite his deep admiration of the Athenian polity which had produced the men of Marathon, he certainly did not think that in its contemporary form it was capable of nurturing the highest virtue in its citizens; good Athenians, if they arose in his day, did so of their own accord (*Republic* 496 A f., *Laws* 642 C).

(b) In asserting the unimportance of the constitutional changes that marked Athenian history from the days of the kings to the fourth century, Plato is clearly not satirizing Pericles, who did not make this particular point; Pericles probably would have been more likely to acclaim the changes, some of which he had himself sponsored. Nor do we find anywhere in

Plato a serious assertion of such an extravagance. But in his respect for Solon and the men of Marathon, and his regard for traditional pieties in modes of worship, he has shown himself not destitute of the kind of sentiment to which the claim of continuity makes its appeal. Plato is not here wholly ironical; he might have said: We Athenians have a great political tradition of which we may well be proud; but we must not blind ourselves to the importance of changes that have occurred.

(c), (e) In this claim that the democracy is the rule of the best, Platonic irony is at its peak. The orator has juggled away all trace of the actual Athens, as Plato saw it, and has transformed it by rhetorical fiat, into those "islands of the blessed" of which Socrates spoke in the introduction. There may be also an echo of Thucydides' assertion (II, 65) that while Pericles led the state, what was called the Athenian democracy was in fact the rule of the first man; or Plato may be only repeating one of the stock claims of the patriot-orators. Plato's ridicule is not here directed at the ideal evoked, that of government by the wisest and best; it is only that he was far from finding it realized at Athens. As the reader of the *Gorgias* well knows, in his eyes even the best of her statesmen had catered to her material interests, to the long-run detriment of her spiritual welfare; that the successors of these men had traveled still further from the true path, is the conviction expressed on many an indignant page of the *Republic*, the *Politicus*, and the *Laws*.

(d) With the assertion that power at Athens chiefly resided in the many, Plato could but agree, when taken as a description of fact, could but deplore, as the affirmation of an unqualified ideal. At its highest and best, he viewed politics as the enlightened, the moral art of using power in the common interest, requiring an expert for its proper exercise. That the "many," in the sense of the contemporary demos of Athens, were capable of using it rightly, was, as we have so often seen, not possible for Plato to believe. But Plato was to maintain, in the *Laws*, that the "many," properly guided and supported by stable laws and customs designed to produce virtue, must be given a large part in the operation of any state other than the ideal city of the *Republic*.

(f) Touching such external goods as wealth and birth, considered as claims to rule, we have already so fully explored Plato's views, that we may merely direct the reader to earlier pages (see pp. 261ff., 342–343). Two comments, however, may serve as reminders. Plato stood far nearer to the champions of democracy in his reluctance to admit wealth and family connections as criteria of political competence than to the oligarchs of all degrees. In Utopia, as he explained at length in the *Republic*, the gold of the guardian class is where you find it; the son of an obscure workman is to receive equal consideration as a possible future ruler of the state. Within an unreformed society, Plato seems to have recognized that a family of distinction and a certain degree of wealth were often important enabling conditions of human excellence. But his final measure was intended to be, in all cases, that excellence itself.

(g) The truly extraordinary thing about this ironic eulogy of common birth and brotherhood is that in spite of the violently unpleasant impression it first makes, as of a Plato coldly deriding the finer aspirations of his own city, whoever will look earnestly at it in the light of a general acquaintance with Plato's thought is likely to have an experience comparable to that of a person looking at a reversible illusion. As, there, the convex suddenly becomes the concave, so here the deeply Platonic quality of the ideas overwhelms our first impression, and we are instantly outside Athens, in Plato's ideal realm. Images of the *Republic* flood in: the myth of the metals, "Citizens, you are brothers and children of this land, who is your mother and your nurse"; the names that are to be given to each other by the citizens — not "masters" and "slaves," but "Preservers and Helpers," "Wagegivers and Nurturers" (condensed from *Republic* 414 E and 463 A–B). We should by now have become fully aware that Platonic irony in the *Menexenus* does not depend upon simple reversal of the vocabulary in describing things good and bad. That the sense of brotherhood uniting the citizens, imputed by the orator to the Athenian democracy, and the absence of enslavement of any group of them to any other, were in essence identical with what Plato most deeply wished for any state whose welfare he had at heart, cannot be doubted. True, he did not conceive his citizens as equal in ability and fitness for political responsibility; the kind of equality he wished for them was the equal right of all to have their welfare considered, or, in Kantian terms, to be regarded as ends, and not simply means to the ends of others. But we know from the *Republic* that in the contemporary democracy at Athens he saw, instead, a city divided against itself, in which one group of citizens, driven to penury by the extortionate greed of the moneylenders, preyed upon another group, driving them into treasonable opposition, while quieting the inattentive bulk of the citizens with some portion of their gains (564 D–565 C). Against this backdrop of actuality, Plato felt the stage picture of Athenian brotherhood to be irony at its most mordant. But once again, he has not in this played cynic to the ideal.

(h) With *isonomia* the case is a little different. This was an ideal which Plato shared so long as he could be permitted to limit its meaning. If by "equality of rights," or "equality in law," is meant the right of all actual Athenians to participate on equal terms in every function of government, then of course Plato could not sponsor any such thing. This word and its cognates and derivatives, as Plato employs it, is sometimes associated with the cry of the libertarian extremists; examples of this use of *isonomia*, *ex isou*, etc., may be seen

in *Republic* 557 A, 558 C, 561 B, 563 B. If this association is uppermost here, his use of the vocable is decidedly ironic. But *isonomia* may also mean "equality before the law," signifying that no prejudice shall enter the administration of justice to the special advantage or detriment of an individual of any class or status, as against one of any other; and to this equality before the courts, in private disputes, Pericles had explicitly referred. In this sense, Plato was decidedly an equalitarian; see, e.g., *Politicus* 305 B–C, *Laws* 945 B ff., 955 C–D. By no possibility can Plato, in the present context or elsewhere, be turning his satire against this ideal of equal justice. If this is what is meant, the irony here can only be at the expense of the rhetorical ringers of this noble but monotonous bell, or directed against what he felt to be the actual imperfections of the justice dispensed by Athenian courts.

In fine, an unprejudiced reading of this portion of the *Menexenus* reveals a Plato who, though dissident as ever from what seemed to him the hollow program of undiluted democracy, remained in essential agreement with many of the larger aims of the Athenian polity, a man whose sharpest satire is consciously directed only at the frauds and failures and never at what he felt to be the genuinely moral heart of Athenian democracy.

On Plato's Supposed Primordial City

Popper argues on many pages of his book (e.g., 41, 46–47, 55–56, 81–83, 489–490, 518–521) the existence in Plato's *Republic* of two ideal cities, the one described in Books II–IV, and again reverted to in Book VIII, the other, as far as it differs from the first, described in Books V–VII. Plato is said to be setting forth, first, his remarkably succcessful reconstruction of a tribalist society on the model of ancient Sparta; this state, Popper maintains, Plato believed to have actually existed in the past, stamped off from the Platonic idea of a state "at the beginning of time" (no very distant date, it would seem), and perfect save for one inevitable defect in its rulers' wisdom; from it, Plato conceived the only slightly imperfect Spartan and Cretan states to have descended. Plato's own ideal state, which he proposes for adoption by the Athenians, is to be identical with this first city, with the important addition of the higher education of the guardians, including the genetic number wisdom which Plato himself will supply.

Popper's elaborate theory appears to be based upon the following considerations: (1) Much ingenuity was devoted by German scholarship in the later nineteenth century to showing that the *Republic* was not originally "published" as we have it today, but that certain books or groups of books were written and appeared at different times. Of particular relevance here is one such hypothesis, referred to by Shorey (note on *Republic* 449 A) and by Adam (on 412 B), which detects traces of two ideal cities, divided as Popper has divided his two cities. The proponents of this view maintained that an earlier version of the *Republic* omitted the three central books, with their description of the "three waves" and of the higher education of the guardians, and that these were later interpolated. Adam rejects the idea of later interpolation, but sees symbolic significance in Plato's successive descriptions of three forms or levels of ideal cities, each excel-lent in its own way, and each more ideal than the former: the simple city of minimum wants (Book II, 372 A–D), then the city of moral steadfastness and intellectual activity (372 D–end of Book IV), and crowning these, the philosophic city depicted in Books V–VII; see especially Adam's notes on 410 A ff., 372 D, 543 D. All this speculation, however, has not involved the idea that the simpler city of the supposed earlier version or Adam's city of moral worth and intellect combined was believed by Plato to have been an existing primordial city. Popper has himself made this adaptation of the supposed two cities, in consonance with his thesis of Plato's "historicism," or doctrine of the progressive deterioration in time of all earthly beings, starting from an initial perfection. It is interesting to observe how Popper has apparently been influenced here by Adam's interpretation of the Platonic number (see his note on 545 C ff., and Appendix) in the light of Plato's myth in the *Politicus*. Adam, with whom we cannot here agree, has seen in the myth's description of the present epoch as a period of increasing and inevitable corruption, an explanation of the ideal city's inevitable decay and a meaning for the number itself, as representing the length of the epoch. Popper has extended the myth's significance into a serious philosophy of history, and with theoretic consistency (if at the cost of grave inconsistencies of other sorts) has removed the ideal city into the early times of our era. He has also been led into a corresponding readaptation and misinterpretation of the Platonic theory of ideas, and now presents as Plato's teaching the doctrine that the first complete embodiment of each idea, including, of course, the idea of a city, constituted the ultimate perfection of its realization, never to be surpassed, and destined only to progressive and ever more rapid degeneration. We shall show on a later page (p. 628) the weakness of this position, and its consequent inability to lend support to the theory of the two cities in the *Republic*, noting here only that the confusion between the absolutely first embodiment of an idea, and its first embodiment in the present epoch, sets the parts of Popper's argument at war with one another, and introduces unPlatonic discrepancies into Popper's version of Plato's thought.

(2) Popper also states, p. 46, that Plato makes "repeated assertions, in the *Republic*, *Timaeus*, and *Critias*, that he is describing the distant past," and, Popper adds, shows his historical intention in parallel passages in the *Laws*; all these indicate that in the main, his *Republic* is historical, and describes a city of the past. Popper subjoins in his notes, pp. 494-495, a long justification of these statements, which embodies much truth, though employed to prove mistaken conclusions. Thus Popper shows without difficulty that in many passages in the *Laws* and *Timaeus* Plato is dealing with history and the origins of things, and that he is interested in describing, at least in mythical terms, how the world was generated, and in observing how it moves, at certain times and places, toward corruption; Popper does not apparently attach any weight to Plato's recognition also of its movement at other times and places toward betterment (e.g., *Laws* 676 A and C). It is easy also for Popper to show that in the beginning of the *Timaeus* Plato says (though how seriously is another question) that an ancient Athens, later destroyed by a flood, resembled Egypt, and also resembled the ideal city of the *Republic*. But none of these facts in any way supports Popper's remarkable thesis that Plato conceived the ideal city of the *Republic*, or its near equivalent, to have come into existence at the beginning of time, or at the beginning of our epoch, and that Plato further believed this perfect society (whether one single community or a plurality, Popper leaves undetermined) to have been undergoing degeneration ever since, at varying rates, all over the world (or all over Greece), so that all existing societies were derived from it.

Popper has no Platonic text to cite in direct support of his thesis, nor from the nature of the case can we produce an explicit text to the contrary. But there are many passages which contradict it by implication, of which a few may be collected here. (a) That Plato did not conceive the first city to have been the best is implied by the way in which the discussion of the ideal state is introduced, *Rep.* 369 B ff. The origin of the simplest society is first described; this is depicted as growing into the happy city of minimum wants (372 A); this becomes the luxurious "inflamed city" (373); and from this in turn the ideal city is fashioned. This sequence of cities, while intended as conceptual rather than strictly historical, fails to confirm the idea of original perfection, followed by degeneration, and may be used to balance the parallel sequence of cities in Book VIII, which do progress from good to bad, and thus to show that this sequence too is conceptual and schematic. In other words, Plato in the *Republic* depicts development as proceeding now in one direction, now in another, as his purpose suggests, and is not limited to a downward movement. (b) When Plato declares, *Rep.* 499 C-D, that the ideal city may have existed once in all of time past, or may in the future or even now among the barbarians exist, it would seem that he implies his disbelief in its certain past existence. If it is objected that this remark is made in Book VI, and therefore implies only that Plato did not think it likely that the second ideal city, ruled by fully-trained philosophers, had existed in the past, we may point to the parallel statement in Book IX. Popper has said that at the beginning of Book VIII, Plato reverts to discussing the first and simpler ideal city of the past. Yet here at the end of Book IX (*Rep.* 592), it is said that the perfect city which has been described, the pattern of which is "laid up in heaven," may not exist on earth and may never exist. This certainly sounds like a reference to the same philosopher-ruled city spoken of in Book VI, and lends little support either to the theory of the two cities, or to the notion that, if there are indeed two, Plato regarded the one described in Book IX as an actual city of the past. (c) The historical passages in the *Laws* offer no confirmation of any belief on Plato's part that states in the past were ideal or akin to the ideal, and have since degenerated. The *Laws* (676 ff.) speaks of past time as enormously, perhaps boundlessly long. In these vast ages, cities of all sorts have flourished and perished, growing larger and smaller, better or worse. Floods and other catastrophes have many times reduced mankind in various parts of the earth to scattered hill-dwellers, and social development has had to begin again. Popper's statement (p. 490, n. 8) that Plato, though in his old age he has come to recognize the greater length of past time, nevertheless in the *Laws* "continues to believe the first settlement must be the best city" is rash indeed. For first, it brings into direct collision two parts of what Popper has presented to us as Plato's self-consistent theory of history. If Plato "continues to believe" the truly "first settlement" to have been the best, he can no longer believe it to have been the actual ancestor of Spartan institutions; now that he has, on Popper's supposition, at last become aware of the great length of past time, he must conceive it as a city incredibly distant, shrouded in the mists of antiquity. If he is assumed to mean "first in our era," where is there any mention of an era? Plato in the *Laws* speaks only of local or regional floods and catastrophes; he speaks of no periodically recurrent new eras of the world, such as are found in the *Politicus* myth. But since, as is quite apparent (Popper, p. 497) Popper is still using the words "first settlement," just as when he was discussing the *Republic*, to refer to the putative ancestor of Sparta, he can only mean that Plato when he wrote the *Laws* "continued to believe" best the city which was the "first settlement" since the most recent flood; Popper has therefore necessarily involved himself in abandoning the supposition that this city was for Plato the first embodiment of its Idea. Returning to our examination of the passage in the *Laws*, we find that Popper's assertion, even thus modified, is quite unsupported in the text: the reader may inspect *Laws* 680–684, where the early forms of settlement are described, without discovering any such statement, nor does Popper produce any. It is even difficult to guess which of the early forms of social organization described by Plato Popper has singled out as the "first settlement." Is it the patriarchal clan (680), or the settlement formed by federated clans (681 B–D)? Or is it the "city by the sea" (681 E), or perhaps the states composing the Dorian confederacy itself, the only form except the patriarchal clan about which Plato makes

complimentary remarks (683–684)? Yet Plato also condemns as badly planned the constitutions of the Dorian states, and represents the final (and still faulty) Spartan constitution as having been arrived at only after the addition of repeated improvements (684 E–686 A, 690 D–692 C). That Plato should have failed to name any of these forms as the "ideal city" seems an important weakness in Popper's case. If recourse is had to Plato's "evasiveness," how does Popper detect what Plato still believes? And the whole concept of Plato as dishonest, both in general and with particular reference to the present passage in the *Laws*, has been disproved (pp. 396–449, and n. 70, p. 426). (d) If Popper is employing as proof of Plato's belief in an early ideal city (as he seems to be doing on pp. 45, and 492–493) the state of affairs described in the *Politicus* myth (*Politicus* 271 D ff.), and again referred to in the *Laws* (713 A ff.), where before the dawn of the present era gods and daemons are said to have been the shepherds of men, he is certainly beside the point. This myth may show that Plato was sufficiently Greek to locate the not-too-seriously-believed-in golden age in the past; it does not indicate his belief in an actual first-and-best city, under human rulers, constituting the starting-point of historical political development. (e) We may also ask why, on Popper's theory, Plato should be unwilling to say in the *Laws* that a city of the past, the proto-Crete or proto-Sparta, is to be reconstructed so far as possible in second-best form. This would have been a gratifying compliment for the Athenian Stranger to pay to his Cretan and Spartan interlocutors, as compensation in part for the considerable amount of painful criticism of their respective states to which he is forced to subject them. Again at the end of the *Laws* (969), when Plato contemplates the possibility that the city they have planned may yet develop into the ideal state, he utters no word of hope that the original and best state may thus be restored to actuality, but speaks instead of a dream city hitherto existing in word only. So much reticence is on any rational hypothesis inexplicable. (f) Popper has stressed the fact (pp. 56 and 490, (3)) that in the *Laws* Plato describes the degeneration of the Persian empire and of the Dorian confederacy. We reply that

Plato does so because he wishes to avert such a fate from the new city of the *Laws*; as England has said (in his edition of the *Laws*, I, p. 344, quoted by Popper, p. 493), Plato is in search of "the secret of political vitality." Plato describes the origins of both these political forms in time, and does not conceive either of them to have been primordial; the Persian state is certainly not depicted as having arisen by degeneration from its more perfect predecessor, and as we have shown, there is no evidence that Plato believed the states of the Dorian confederacy to have arisen in this way.

(g) Not only has Popper employed his thesis of the two cities to confirm his interpretation of the passage concerning the number; the converse is also true. Thus on his interpretation, Plato's statement that the guardians will not know the number and that for success in breeding they depend upon "reasoning and observation," demonstrates that these guardians cannot be mathematically and dialectically trained, and that therefore Plato can be referring only to the rulers of the early and incomplete city. In so far, then, as we shall in the next few pages of our text disprove Popper's interpretation of the number passage, we shall *eo ipso* undermine his supposed proof that Plato describes, at any point in the *Republic*, a historical ideal city.

Appendix XI

The Mathematics of the Muses

A discussion of the nuptial number figures prominently in the not yet fully published investigation into Plato's use of mathematics of Robert S. Brumbaugh. To an obvious mastery of the technical phase of his subject, his inquiries add a freshness and fertility of procedure which command admiration even at some points where they may provoke dissent. From parts of his work having special relevance to the number ("The Role of Mathematics in Plato's Dialectic" [unpublished thesis, typescript], 1942, Appendix A; "Early Greek Theories of Sex Determination," 1949; "Note on Plato Republic IX. 587 D," 1949), supplemented by personal correspondence, I here present what he has kindly permitted me to characterize as a responsible interpretation of his general standpoint.

(1) Plato was inspired by Pythagorean and Hippocratic science with the hope of finding reliable principles according to which the higher human types required for preserving his ideal city could be bred.

(2) He believed that he possessed a theoretical knowledge of the manner in which hereditary factors, moral and intellectual, and the contributions of education and social environment, might be expected to combine in the children of parents of specified characteristics, resulting in the production of individuals fitted for specific social functions.

(3) The nuptial number, like the tyrant's number of *Rep.* 587 D, is designed as a species of diagram. If completely constructed, it would yield a three-dimensional scheme (of the combinations of four independent factors), expressing the relationships between the characteristics of children and those of their parents, and capable of serving as a guide to the production of desirable types.

(4) But Plato's genetic theory entailed the prediction that, though children of "silver" natures would be born in sufficient numbers, originating from parents of any class, the highest human types must become more rare with each successive generation. On the other hand, the empirical success of animal breeders in strengthening desired traits seemed to indicate at once the possibility that this steady decline need not occur, and the need of modifications in the theory. Plato interpreted the empirical facts as justifying the hope of improving the human breed as long as the state should continually improve its education, but believed that whenever such improvement should cease, the pessimistic prediction of the theory would be fulfilled.

(5) The irony of the Muses is occasioned by and expresses the gap between pure theory and concrete fact. The phrase *logismos met' aisthêseôs* denotes the combination of abstract mathematical theory with observation of particulars, and is descriptive of scientific method in genetics, not a scornful characterization of a method Plato regards as primitive and faulty.

It thus appears that Brumbaugh agrees with Popper in taking Plato's genetic program as Pythagorean in origin and serious in intent; Brumbaugh also takes Plato's announcement of the number through the speech of the Muses as an indication that Plato had an operationally significant number to communicate. But here the resemblance ends. Brumbaugh finds Plato's genetics inspired by a sober and scientific spirit of research capable of recognizing its own limitations and honest enough to qualify its results when these conflicted with knowledge derived from other sources. There is no suggestion that Plato hoped by his investigation to do more than increase to the utmost the stability and endurance of his best state: no magical escape from eventual decay was looked for. Plato is shown as earnestly endeavoring to implement his declared intention of assigning individual citizens to their appropriate tasks. In fine, Brumbaugh sees in these inquiries not what Popper sees, the replacement of the philosopher's function by that of the shaman-breeder, but rather the attempt within the limits of human possibility to integrate a theory of value — philosophy — with a program for its realization through the rational control of every possible agency of human betterment.

Appendix XII

Freedom of Inquiry and the Philosopher Kings

That Plato has in the *Republic* plainly declared his intention of giving his philosopher kings full freedom of inquiry is apparently not matter of dispute. Thus Crossman, taking Plato's statement at its face value, has honored him (pp. 117–118, 128) for this liberal intention; and even Popper, we judge, would agree that Plato has earnestly endeavored to give his readers just such an impression. But Popper, doubting Plato's fair words, has inspected instead the probable outcome of the practical arrangements he proposes, and in this fashion has brought himself to the conclusion (pp. 132, 145, 552–553) that Plato, "afraid of the power of thought," and knowing the inability of his inhumane doctrines to withstand fair criticism, has with open eyes made freedom of inquiry impossible within his state by forbidding his future rulers while still young to scrutinize received opinions. The special target of attack is *Republic* 537 D ff., where Plato provides that the philosophers-to-be shall not enter upon discussion of ethical principles until the age of thirty, at which time, being persons of tested stability of character, they are permitted to begin five years spent wholly in such investigations; after this, they are to descend again into the "Cave" to engage for fifteen years in practical pursuits. At the age of fifty, the now completely tested and chosen rulers will be required (540 A) to ascend to the culminating vision of the Good, and may thenceforth range the field of philosophy at will, except when called upon to serve the city.

Being under no necessity of following Popper in his search for the dishonest meaning of what Plato has said, we are free to see in Plato's provisions here an honest and regrettable error, and then to inquire into its causes and occasions. We may reject at once the notion that Plato thought his philosophy too fragile to withstand criticism, if this were competently conducted. The process of inquiry whereby truth was to be sought was, for Plato, essentially self-correcting, a process of raising the soul by successive stages to higher and higher levels of theoretic vision; the free and full continuance of the process would necessarily be attended by a growing illumination, culminating in the moment of absolute insight, wherein the highest norm to which the human community is subject, would stand revealed. An attentive reading of Book VI of the *Republic* will show that this so-called "dialectic" quest is fully autonomous, guided only by the appropriate logical and metaphysical principles, subject to no criterion of validity imposed from without.

We are brought back to the recognition, therefore, that the dangers attending the pursuit of dialectic, which Plato sought to forestall in the ideal state (and, it is likely, in his Academy), were the fallacies and confusions into which he believed ill-prepared students would inevitably fall, and the skepticism and nihilism which (*Republic* 537 E ff.) he foresaw as probable results. For these reasons he deprecated turning loose upon the abstrusities of dialectic both the unduly young and the "late learners" (*Sophist* 251 B–C, 259 C–D), persons who in either case come to philosophy without the preliminary studies necessary to the proper evaluation of arguments. He feared also the sportive eagerness of the young, who are still "puppies" (*Republic* 539 B), to tear down all established beliefs, and the ready skepticism of the self-seeking. Hence originate the age restrictions and the character tests, and also the elaborate preliminary studies required of the philosopher rulers, who, thus prepared and selected, are to be the only persons in Plato's state to whom the investigation of basic principles is allowed.

Such proposals must be unacceptable to us, who plainly see the grave evils which, though they could never find their way into the transcendental realm of Plato's ideal city, would all too certainly enter any actual political community in which his prescriptions were put literally in practice. Yet we must not forget either the complexity of the problem Plato was confronting or the genuinely moral concern to prevent the salt of his city from losing its savor that prompted him to his unfortunate solution. The principle that philosophic inquiry must be permitted only to older students of blameless moral character Plato could have derived, on the one hand, from Socrates' teaching, and on the other, from the outcome of that teaching. For Socrates, as we see him in the *Gorgias* — on our view, the historical Socrates in this respect — deplores the teaching of rhetoric in abstraction from an endeavor to effect the pupil's moral improvement and thus to fit him for the right use of his new tools (*Gorgias* 459 D–461 A, and 463–465, taken in conjunction with 527 D–E). And it may well have appeared 'to Plato, in the light of the outcome, that a similar error had all unintentionally been committed by Socrates himself. Xenophon suggests that some of those who listened to Socrates — he is speaking of Critias and Alcibiades — did so out of no intention to be "improved," but merely to acquire a skill serviceable in the pursuit of their own ends. Plato too may have noticed this possibility. To wait, under the conditions contemplated in the *Republic*, till some stability of character had been demonstrated, may have seemed to him only what social responsibility demanded; even in Athens, to take precautions against teaching skill and skepticism alone, must have seemed to him imperative. We have already discussed, pp. 365–366, how in the Academy the prohibition against early dialectical initiation was apparently replaced by the provision of antidotes against facile skepticism in the form of a shared environment and guided

discussion of moral matters in company with responsible older men.

Popper, enlarging upon a theme from Cherniss (Popper, pp. 132–133; Cherniss, *The Riddle of the Early Academy*, pp. 68–70, 79), has given a very special turn to the famous passage in the *Parmenides*, 135 C ff., in which the young Socrates is cautioned by the venerable logician not to attempt too soon the definition of the virtues, but to acquire first a skill in deducing the consequences of all metaphysical suppositions. This Popper reads as Plato's warning by proxy to his young students in the Academy, and takes as a fresh instance of Plato's dread of "originality and initiative." This motivation is not that suggested by Cherniss, who offers proof (p. 83) that Plato "did not try to impose" his own doctrines "upon his students or associates from without by the constraint of persuasion or authority, for he knew that true knowledge must come from within the soul itself"; his Academy (p. 81) "was not a school in which an orthodox metaphysical doctrine was taught," to which the members "were expected to subscribe." Popper apparently was not patient enough to listen closely to what Parmenides-Plato suggests as the reason for delaying independent metaphysical speculation, namely: that objections against a given position may seem unanswerable to a novice, who may be induced to abandon it without more ado; but that one who knows that equal or greater objections may be brought against its contradictory, can take a firmer stand, and may eventually find answers sufficient to establish it. Dialectical training of this sort was what Plato desired for his students and what he had also proposed to provide for the future rulers of the *Republic*, as a prerequisite to the making of mature judgments in the ethical domain.

Appendix XIII

The Legend of Platonic Ethics

The present note will offer comments on Fite's critique of Plato the moralist. Fite has told us (p. 6) that he intends to say as little as possible about Plato's metaphysics, but he has devoted much space (especially chapters IX, X, and XI) to the depreciation of his ethical theory. To discuss issues so large within the limits of an appendix, will be unjust to both sides, but it appears desirable at least to indicate the sources from which an adequate defense of Plato might be drawn. One further word of preface: Professor Fite is a distinguished moralist whose own contribution to ethical theory, in a contemporary perspective, has won deserved respect. We are here, however, exclusively concerned with the use he has made of it as a means of diminishing Plato.

The brunt of Fite's attack is upon Plato's alleged pseudoscientific obsession with measurement in the realm of morals, his merely prudential and calculative conception of morality, his total failure to appreciate the value of personality, and his resulting ideal of an impersonally constructed, merely efficient social order. Omitting the last-mentioned, which is dealt with on p. 565 of the text, we shall discuss Fite's highly coherent critique under the just listed aspects, as follows:

(1) The obsession with measurement. — By taking as dogmatic Platonism the "moral arithmetic" of the last part of the Protagoras (in which the Socrates of the dialogue forces Protagoras to accept the unwelcome conclusion that when a man chooses between possible acts, he seeks always to maximize pleasure and minimize pain), and by combining it in a rigidly unPlatonic way with the many praiseful things that Plato has to say about mathematical knowledge and the identity of knowledge and virtue, Fite has constructed in Plato's name a methodology of morals which I do not believe Plato would have recognized as his own. Fite chides Plato for his adoption of an absolute point of view, applicable to triangles but not to morality; for in the moral life, we must distinguish individual points of view: "this is just the kind of consideration, subjective, introspective, critical, that is most characteristic of modern philosophy and most conspicuously absent in Plato" (Fite, p. 195). He thus sees Plato as blind to the particularities of experience, which he scorns as beneath his rational dignity, and as making his appeal exclusively to abstract mathematical principles derived through an elaborate dialectical method from that which is above hypothesis (p. 220 ff.).

In contrast, Fite acclaims men like Protagoras, who travel and observe and base their notions of virtue and all else upon "what we call personal insight, and what we respect as personal experience of life" (p. 185). It is difficult briefly to sort out the unquestioned truths contained in this presentation from the element of unfairness. But it would seem almost a sufficient reply to remark that the contrast that Fite has noticed is not really between Plato and Protagoras. It is between two levels of moral knowledge, the common sense, experiential level, to which "Protagoras" is made to appeal, and that higher level of full rational apprehension of which "Socrates" is in quest. How indeed could Plato be supposed ignorant of what he so skillfully makes Protagoras expound? But he was not content to halt progress at that comfortable point. This sort of experience is there to be judged, and for that judgment Plato believed solemnly and understandably, whether rightly or wrongly, that we must rise to a plane beyond the empirical. From the standpoint of Fite's conviction that morality has its laws within the fluid domain of the shifting environment (we here follow the exposition of Fite's views given in Contemporary Ethical Theories, by T. E. Hill, 1950, p. 178) such an appeal is, of course, invalid. But in making it, Plato was revealing not his obsession with measurement, but his basic conviction that the order of human life should be modeled on the structure of the antecedently real world of Being (John Wild has made this the central thesis of his book, *Plato's Theory of Man*, cited on pp. 24–25.

(2) Prudential morality. — Throughout his devaluation of Platonic ethics, Fite has been denying that there is in it any idealistic aspiration. A striking example is his way of construing the *Gorgias*, so much "admired by idealizing interpreters" (p. 190). The supposedly Christian quality of Socrates' preference for suffering rather than committing injustice is demoted, and its principle discovered in the prudential consideration that would confirm the citizen of a well-policed state in regarding himself as "better off when his own house has been robbed than when he has robbed the house of another" (p. 194). To this one may retort: By parity of reasoning, one could as well reduce the Beatitudes to the worldly wisdom of Poor Richard's Almanack. In the Beatitudes as in the *Gorgias*, it is true, rewards are offered to the winners in the moral race. But they are spiritual rewards which the wicked would scarcely relish. It would be small satisfaction for the "sons of Belial" to be called the "sons of God," nor would Callicles, with his scorn of the powerless and his admiration for large desires ever more largely satisfied, find any of his ideals realized in the fulfilment of either Christian or Platonic promises. Plato is not proposing to pay the "good man" in a coinage of material advantage; Fite's suggestion that for Plato the good man is only the man who succeeds in getting more of what the bad man wants, is in effect a degradation of Plato's moral currency, in express violation of the warning uttered

by the Platonic Socrates in the *Phaedo* (69 A), one of Plato's noblest sentences, which may fitly here be read aloud: "My good Simmias, it may be that this is not the right exchange, by the standard of virtue, this trading of pleasures for pleasures, pains for pains . . . as if they were coins. May it not be that this alone is the right currency, in return for which we should exchange all these other things — wisdom . . . and true virtue, in all its parts."

(3) The failure to appreciate personality. — We have touched upon this theme in an earlier chapter (pp. 79–80). It is true that Plato is insufficiently aware of the full meaning of individuality as that principle has been developed in the modern world. But this limitation was generic, endemic in Greek culture of his period, as we saw (p. 288 above) in the speech of Pericles. Now in so far as Fite might have been content to show, against the generous hyperboles of Plato's admirers, that Plato's thought did not prophetically anticipate in this respect the deepest insights of later times, we might gladly have granted his point. But the value of Fite's recognition is offset by a counterexaggeration that leaves his acceptive reader with the illusion that a significant defect in Plato has been revealed.

In sum, Fite has employed his great wit and ample wisdom to a sad and wilful end. He has used the light of modern insights for the darkening of our understanding of the ultimate sources from which much of our illumination has been derived. His method is analytic, not in the sense proper to historical and critical inquiry, but rather in the chemical sense in which a powerful corrosive analyzes a valuable compound into its trivial constituents.

Appendix XIV

Was Plato a Historicist?

This note will discuss in detail Popper's charge against Plato of "historicism," and will seek to show that Popper has distorted the Platonic theory of Ideas in the interests of his charge.

1. (a) To establish the meaning which Popper has attached to this word "historicism" is our first care. We are told first that it is the belief, characteristic of certain social philosophies, that "they have discovered laws of history which enable them to prophesy the course of historical events" (p. 5); examples adduced are the Marxist prophecy that the proletariat is destined to inherit the earth, and the defeatist belief of some democrats that totalitarianism is bound to overwhelm democracy (pp. 6, 13). The consequence of such beliefs is to discourage active efforts to bring about desired changes, and to relieve men of their responsibilities (pp. 6–7). Again, at the very end of his book (p. 462), Popper inveighs against historicism as "a debased faith" which "tries to persuade us that if we merely fall into step with history everything must and will go right, and that no fundamental decision on our part is required."

Such a theory, as it stands, would be an obvious misfit for Plato. It has accordingly been tailored to fit, and we learn that Plato, though still a historicist, is different in two respects: instead of a golden future, he believes in a golden past; and he believes "that it is possible for us to break the iron law of destiny" "by a human, or rather by a superhuman effort" (which Popper, as the reader of our earlier chapters knows, supposes to be Plato's own effort) and to return to an earlier and natural form of society, which can be frozen into permanent perfection (pp. 23–24). Yet Popper will still call Plato a historicist because he believes in a cosmic trend of decay, from which he wishes to escape; this constitutes, according to Popper (pp. 27–28), the crime of having his "ends . . . determined by historicism."

Now Popper is entitled, within the covers of his book, to give to his term "historicism" the meaning which he sees fit, and may therefore deny our right to protest its application to Plato on grounds other than the factual disproof that Plato held the doctrines which Popper ascribes to him. This disproof will be our major task in what follows. But we may first point out that, as we have argued in our text, pp. 505f., Popper ought not in justice to demand that we disapprove equally both the "historicist" who has not succumbed to any fatalist temptation to resign his moral responsibilities nor worships "worldly success," and the one who exhibits these faults; if Popper is to recognize two varieties of historicist, one of which is innocent in large part of the sins of the other, two names or two evaluations are called for. Nor has Popper the right to assume what it is impossible in any case to prove, namely: that Plato's aims were determined by anything other than his judgment of what is *per se* desirable.

Another "historicist" fault detected in Plato also turns out to be on Popper's own principles either venial or on the contrary a virtue. Popper tells us (p. 26) that "the historicist is inclined to look upon social institutions mainly from the point of view of their history," while the "social engineer . . . will hardly take much interest in the origin of institutions, or in the original intentions of their founders," but will attempt rather to suggest ways of adapting them to the purpose in view. Thus Plato in the *Laws*, when he proposes to investigate the origin of constitutions and the causes which produce changes in them, by examining the changes which states have historically undergone, is held (p. 41) to reveal his "historicist methodology." To seek by the study of the past "to ascertain the driving force of historical change" (p. 46) and to find it in dissension within the ruling class, this — so it appears — is reprehensibly historicist. Now Plato's wish to discover means of adapting to given ends the complex social institution which is the state is the attitude which Popper has ascribed (pp. 25–27) to the social engineer; he has, in fact, called Plato a "Utopian" social engineer, distinguished from the admirable "piecemeal" engineer by his concern with sweeping adaptations rather than with more partial changes. We may claim, therefore, that Plato's historical survey of changes in constitutions, undertaken for the purpose named, is not "historicist," but constitutes simply a variant of that gathering of "factual information necessary for the construction or alteration of social institutions" which, Popper agrees (p. 25), must underlie the social engineer's recommendations. That Plato examines the city state as a whole rather than a limited institution such as the police force of a modern state (a type of inquiry which Popper approves) is due partly to the simpler structure and smaller scale of ancient states, partly to that custom in the Greek world to which we have often referred, the planning of new states or reorganizing of existing ones by "lawgivers" or commissions of lawmakers, appointed for the purpose. If, therefore, Plato's "ends" were not "determined" by historicism, and if, further, his supposedly "historicist" method is merely that of the fact-finding social engineer, he should at least in these respects be honored by Popper as one who in an early age attempted to develop a "social technology" to be used for ends mistaken indeed, on Popper's view, but determined solely by a belief in their intrinsic goodness.

(b) But let us have done with these hypothetical arguments and set forth our evidence that Plato was not in fact a believer in a historical law of decay, or an adulator of the past as such. Beginning with the evidence which appears to favor Popper's theory, most of which he has himself adduced, especially on pp. 487–488, we agree to list under this heading the account of the origin of the universe in *Timaeus* 30 C ff., where the Demiurge is shown looking to the eternal forms and in their image creating all beings and substances roughly in the order of their excellence, ending his own labors with the creation of the rational human soul; to the created gods he leaves the making of man's lower psychic faculties and of his body; from man, in turn, are derived by degeneration woman and all lower forms

of life. Again in the *Laws* (896 ff.), Plato speaks of soul, the self-moving motion, as first of all things which have existence, more ancient and more honorable than body. To these cosmological identifications of age with excellence may be added the mythological. Thus, as we are asked by Popper to observe, in the *Politicus* myth the present era of the world is said to be the era of the world's self-motion; bereft of the divine guidance, it trends always downward in order and in excellence, until at last, when it has become dangerously depraved, it will again be taken in hand by God and restored to its former peace and blessedness. Other instances of this mythological location of virtue and happiness in the past are found in Aristophanes' tale in the *Symposium* (189 C ff.), adduced by Popper, p. 488, describing the "double blessedness" of the globe-shaped men of the first days (cf. our p. 127). We may add to Popper's list the passage in the *Critias* (120 D ff.) where the original rulers of Atlantis, sons of Poseidon, are said to become in course of time, with the progressive dilution of their divine element by merely human blood, less just and wise. Here too may be included Popper's little quotation from the *Philebus* (16 C, trans. Fowler, Loeb Library) where Socrates introduces the philosophical method he proposes to follow as "tossed down from some divine source through the agency of a Prometheus" to "the ancients, who were better than we and lived nearer the gods," a passage clearly both mythical and poetical (it probably incorporates a latent quotation from some unknown poet) and tinctured with the playful irony of self-depreciation. Finally there is what we may call the pious honoring of age and antiquity, the many passages in which Plato commends respect and reverence for age and for parents, praises the virtues and wisdom of ancestors, or speaks of the wise lawgivers and philosophic teachers of the past.

These passages admit of explanation, first, by the observation that in cosmological discussion Plato is not necessarily talking of time at all. It is by no means certain that Plato's description of the creation is more than a mythical dramatization of ontological relationships. This position has lately been vigorously upheld by Cherniss in his *Aristotle's Criticism of Plato and the Academy*, 1944, pp. 414–431. And even were it shown that Plato had been speaking *sensu literali*, as Popper supposes, and that he displays his conviction that the world left its creator's hand perfect, to develop all its imperfections subsequently and of its own accord, this would not require him to believe, any more than did the medieval church, that continuous and progressive downward development had continued from that day forward. The argument in the *Laws* that soul is prior to body can similarly be explained as a dialectical refutation of the atomists, who had assigned that honor to matter. Especially when it is compared to the passage in the *Phaedrus* (245 D–246 A), also mentioned by Cherniss, *loc. cit.*, where soul is declared to be "ungenerated," does the dialectical nature of the proof in the *Laws* become clear. It need not, therefore, be taken as an assertion of literal, temporal relationship; but even if so taken, it would not entail the doctrine of a continuous downward trend in history.

Plato's mythical depiction of a golden past is also open to nonhistoricist interpretation. For although Plato has stored some of his most valued beliefs in his great myths, it is often Psyche's task to distinguish in them the "Dichtung" from the "Wahrheit." And certainly it is not safe to conclude that the golden past depicted in some of them was the object of Plato's literal belief, when it is considered that the Greek myths generally tell of such a past, and when, moreover, others of Plato's myths and mythohistorical passages convey quite different implications, as we shall see below. The same may be said of Plato's frequently expressed piety for age, and for the ancient traditions. These tributes were expressions of a real feeling, yet, as we shall presently see, this did not prevent him from respectfully questioning the claims of age to truth and reverence when higher interests demanded.

(c) But there is no need of remaining on the defensive in this dispute, for Plato has not left himself without a witness. We may examine first those texts that show Plato clear of historicist tendencies in situations where, were he a historicist, he could scarcely have failed to make positive indication of his view. It will be recalled that in the Myth of Er, at the conclusion of the *Republic*, Plato has described the choice of lives made by the disembodied souls who are about to descend once more to earth.

Now if Plato had had an ounce of historicist blood in his veins, would he not have spoken of the melancholy downward trend that drags each generation of souls to inevitably lower and lower levels of degradation? In the *Phaedo* myth (113 D–114 C), and again in the *Phaedrus* myth (248 E–249 D), there is no hint of any fatal lowering of the hopes of souls in later times, but always before every soul, at every incarnation, is held the hope of bettering its lot by choosing the life of virtue. Plato's whole moral message, indeed, would be stultified by any other doctrine. This moral urgency, this preaching of the great hope, the mighty importance of the choice of every soul, how could it be reconciled with the doctrine of inevitable degeneration? And which is more central to Plato's message, his picture of a mythical age of gold, or his call for moral regeneration?

(d) Plato's earnest advocacy of the life of virtue provides also the key to the meaning of the passage in the *Laws* (904 C ff.) which Popper (pp. 38, 487) has perversely misread as an account of the inevitable and progressive degeneration of the souls of men. It forms part of the exhortation, beginning at 903 B, which is imagined to be addressed to the young man who has denied that the gods concern themselves with human affairs, for the purpose of convincing him that the gods will requite virtue and vice in accord with their true natures, and that it behooves him to seek the one and shun the other. First he is told that for the sake of the "blissful existence" of the "World-all" he has been contrived, and that his own good and that of the All will be attained simultaneously by the divine plan. This does not reflect the mood of defeatism or appear to prophesy decay. Again and again (903 D, 904 D, 904 E, 905 A) the young man is told that goodness brings movement upward, toward happiness, while evil leads downward towards the abyss; there is no general downward tendency such as Popper's one-sided paraphrase suggests, no limitation of the upward movement to the "exceptional soul," in whom, as we saw (n. 135, p. 464), Popper unnecessarily discerns Plato's reference to his exceptional self. Plato does somewhat stress the horrors of the depths, for the benefit of his listener, whom he apparently regards as being in special danger of yielding to temptation; but the young man is told that the will is free (904 B–C) and there is held out to him, plain to see, the possibility of rising to the company of "better souls," or even to the "height of Heaven above." "The whole dramatic context," therefore, does not as Popper says (p. 487) imply an over-all decline, with only extraordinary exceptions. It implies rather a continuous process of upward and downward motions, with perhaps some favorable balance (the "blissful existence" of the World-all would seem to imply this), and a scale of value and happiness in which every soul has the opportunity of rising, as it has the danger of falling.

Of Popper's special translation of 904 C, "All things that share in soul," etc., it may be said, first, that it is probably wrong. The second *kata*, which he argues, is "colored" by the meaning of *katô* in the following clause, so that the soul which has changed but little is said to move "*down*" in level, may just as well mean "on," or, as Bury translates it, "over" the surface of space; England's interpretation of the sentence as a whole, in his note *ad loc.*, is different again: for him the soul which has undergone but slight change, wanders *on* or *over* the surface of the earth, in contrast to the soul which, having been either extraordinarily wicked or extraordinarily virtuous, is immediately translated either to bliss or to Hades. But England, like Bury, takes the second *kata* as meaning not "down," but "on" or "over"; so likewise do Ficino, Serranus, and Jowett. Popper's tortured rendering also yields him little advantage; for even if in these particular two sentences, Plato is stressing the downward movement which is the fate of wicked souls, in other adjoining sentences the upward movement is also declared to be possible, and every soul is said to be destined to do and suffer "what it is befitting that like should do toward like" (the translation is Bury's, like others in this paragraph), both in this life (cf. *Laws* 716 C, 728 B–D) and in the afterlife.

(e) Popper's use (p. 488) to prove Plato's discovery of "all wisdom" "in the past," of the doctrine of *anamnêsis*, or recollection, according to which the soul recognizes among the objects of earth the copies of the ideas, seen before birth, is likewise not in point; for if we take the doctrine to be literally believed in by Plato, it entails that the soul may see the ideas after death, also,

since rebirth follows rebirth, and at intervals the soul mounts once more to partake, if it is able, of the blessed vision (*Phaedrus* 249 E). Popper's argument (p. 488) that as Plato was "not less keen" than Empedocles, he must have synthesized his frequent references to Hesiodic myths into a view of the present era as one of strife, is to choose what Plato must have considered the most compelling evidence and to construct in his name a cosmic pattern which, we believe, would have seemed to him to conflict with the most salient article of faith and fact of human experience, namely the eternally open choice of virtue and knowledge.

(f) We have spoken of Plato's piety for age and antiquity, which may be regarded as evidence that he regarded the past as best. Plato, it is true, strongly believed that Athens, at least, had been more glorious and more worthy of honor in the days of Solon and of Marathon, when Athens enjoyed the balanced constitution that he praises in the *Laws*. And he believed in the pieties of kinship, in itself no very historicist attitude. But he takes no systematic view of such matters, and does not, for example, regard the Athens of the days before Solon as still better, or measure the wisdom of sages of old by the degree of their antiquity. Plato was, in fact, in somewhat of a dilemma between paying due reverence to the past, and still judging it justly and condemning when conscience bade. Thus in the *Laws* (630 B–D), the Athenian Stranger will not have it said that the Heaven-taught legislators, Lycurgus and Minos, aimed only at a part, and that the least part of virtue, in framing the laws of Sparta and of Crete; yet he himself shortly convicts the laws themselves of nearly this same fault. Plato makes the Eleatic stranger deplore the "carelessness" of earlier thinkers in failing to make their meaning clear (*Sophist* 242 C, 267 D), courteously explaining that so much may be said without offense (*Sophist* 243 A). He cannot approve the questioning of religious beliefs sanctioned by law and ancient tradition (*Timaeus* 40 D–E, *Laws* 887 C–E), yet plainly he cannot literally believe them (*Timaeus, ibid.*) and even considers them in some respects harmful (*Republic* 377 D ff., *Laws* 886 B–C, 941 B–C). He knows that the ancestral ways of educating young men to virtue were not wise (*Sophist* 229 E) and solemnly warns the aged in the *Laws* (729

B–C) that reverence is due only to those who earn it, and that the old must show reverence for the young by living blamelessly. In short, Plato indulged in no wholesale and systematic idolatry of the past.

(g) Those of Popper's arguments for Plato's historicism which are based upon Plato's supposed belief in a first and best, historically real city, the near equivalent of the ideal Republic, have already been met in Appendix X, pp. 612ff. His claim that the sequence of cities in the eighth book of the *Republic* is historical is there shown to be based on a partisan choice of considerations, to the neglect of other considerations which lie at hand (e.g., the nondegenerative series of cities in *Republic* 369 B ff.). We may here add to that refutation our strenuous objection to Popper's procedure when, in his enthusiastic support of his thesis that Plato's aim in discussing types of government is to detect their fated order of decline, he describes the logical classification of states in the *Politicus* in terms which he imports, entirely without textual support, paraphrasing Plato as saying that one type of state "changes" into another, which then "deteriorates further" (Popper, p. 45, and similarly on p. 477). This is to interpret the *Republic* series arbitrarily, then to reflect the resulting error upon the *Politicus*, which in turn is then made to appear as confirming the original misconception.

(h) Here, too, may be mentioned again the passage in the *Theaetetus* (174 E–175 B) quoted in full on our pp. 263–264, in which Plato speaks of the "unnumbered thousands of ancestors" whom every man has had, among them kings and slaves, barbarians and Greeks, and laughs at the narrow vanity of those who boast that twenty-five ancestors separate them from Heracles, son of Amphitryon. Plato's sophisticated understanding as here revealed stands in striking antithesis to the naive theory that Popper has fathered upon him.

(i) We come now to the listing of those Platonic texts which, though of course they do not deal directly with the issue — Plato had no premonition of Popper — are most strongly at variance with the historicism that Popper imputes. In the course of combatting Popper's extraordinary suggestion that Plato believed himself the destined lawgiver whose activity would initiate the new age of the world, free of all change, and statically perfect, we showed (pp. 464–

465 above) that in the *Republic*, in the *Laws*, and in the *Politicus*, Plato explicitly predicts future changes leading upward to greater perfection, respectively, in men, in the constitution of the city of the *Laws*, and in the arts and sciences generally, including the science of statecraft.

To these utterly nonhistoricist prophecies of future improvement, may be added Plato's depictions of progress made by man in past ages. We have already mentioned (p. 220, and App. X, 2 [c], p. 613) that part of the *Laws* (676 ff.) in which Plato speaks of the countless cities that have arisen and perished in the past, and proceeds to reconstruct the development of Greek culture from the most recent flood in those regions down to his own day. Popper (p. 41) has represented this whole section of the *Laws* as a story of the "decline and fall of human society," and has found within it, also, several smaller stories of "deterioration," e.g., of the primitive society of the hill shepherds (Popper, p. 477) and of the Persian Empire (p. 487). He neglects to mention also stories of the contrary movement by which all but the first of the several societies, including the Persian, have arisen. But most importantly he fails to note that, as we have shown, p. 220, Plato is subscribing to a doctrine of successive regional epochs in each of which human culture achieves a steady advance which brings much increase of evil but which alone makes possible the highest human attainments in all the arts, including government; some flood or other natural catastrophe in a limited area has then many times intervened, and development has begun anew. We are reminded that the mythical ancient Athens of the *Timaeus* (22 B ff.), destroyed by a great flood, is imagined to have constituted such a peak.

Of the isolated survivors of the most recent catastrophe in the Greek area, Plato asks (678 B, more fully quoted on p. 507 above), "Do we imagine . . . that the men of that age, who were unversed in the ways of city life — many of them noble, many ignoble, — were perfect either in virtue or in vice?" to which Clinias heartily agrees. Plato then offers an imaginary reconstruction of subsequent development, leading to the present day, assigning high honors to the simple patriarchal society of hill shepherds (679), and again to the original constitutions of Lacedaemon and its sister Dorian states (684–686), but still noting imperfections in these arising from their failure to incorporate the sovereign principle of wisdom in their laws (688 E). (And it is the incorporation of this very principle, together with internal harmony and freedom from outside domination, which the polity of the *Laws* is designed to secure (701 D).) We hear (691 D) of the happy tempering of the Lacedaemonian constitution by Lycurgus and Theopompus (leaving it, however, as we well know, from earlier books of the *Laws*, e.g., 634 ff., still defective), and of the excellence of the Persian and Athenian constitutions when they, too, stood midway between monarchy and democracy. And this tempering of the one "mother-form" of government with the other is also to characterize the city for which Plato is about to enact laws (693 D, 756 E). It is apparent that we have here no tale of degeneration, but rather the preparation for a successful solution of the problem of politics. The city of the *Laws* will be the next step in the upward series, and beyond that, at the very end of the *Laws*, Plato could not refrain from adding the suggestion that from this city the ideal Republic might be born. The whole book thus becomes, in view of the historical event, a rather pathetic promise of the fulfilment of Plato's hope for mankind.

(j) That Plato's "fear of innovation" (Popper, p. 488) in the laws and arrangements of his ideal cities, though admittedly excessive, is nevertheless based on rational considerations and not, as Popper's case requires, on superstitious dread of change *qua* change, we argue on pp. 553–557, 630–631.

(k) To sum up: Popper's thesis of Plato's historicism, resting originally, or so it seems, upon his belief that Plato's *Republic* in the main describes an actual city of the past from which existing cities are descended by degeneration, derives its further support principally from a misinterpretation of the theory of Ideas (to be discussed below), from a literal interpretation of Plato's cosmology, and from selective mention of only those Platonic passages or sentences which speak of particular downward movements in history, express veneration for the past, or recount myths of the traditional golden age. It attributes to Plato incredible naivety in the conception of time and human history, stultifies his moral message, makes

necessary the suppositions of his delusions of grandeur and his dishonesty, and involves the neglect of contiguous passages and blindness to the total movement of Plato's thought in such dialogues as the *Republic* and the *Laws*, as well as in his philosophy as a whole.

II. (a) Popper's interpretation of the theory of Ideas as the foundation of Plato's historicism is compounded of the universally accepted, the disputable which is, however, supported by a responsible body of opinion among scholars, and the original; we shall attempt to take issue only with the last of these, and even here we shall contest only those elements of Popper's view which seem vital to the question of historicism.

(b) As we have seen, I. (b) above, Popper interprets the ideas (e.g., pp. 27–28, 37–38) as prior to materially existing things in the literal sense of having existed before the origin of the universe, which he believes was to Plato a temporal event. We have shown that this is not a universally accepted view; cf. Cherniss, p. 424; Cornford, for example, whom Popper quotes often and with respect, dissents from it (cf. his *Plato's Cosmology*, 1937, p. 24 ff.). Nevertheless it need not for our purpose be disputed. Plato could have conceived the ideas as prior in this sense without being a "historicist" in the sense which Popper's argument requires, namely: one who believed that the successive material copies of the ideas, from the time of the creation down to his own day, had been progressively degenerating.

(c) Popper also lays much stress (e.g., pp. 29, 478–479) upon Plato's supposed conception of the ideas as active causes, generative principles which beget, in some sense, the material things which are their copies in the world of sense. Here also, though the particular form which his conception takes may be his own, the general view of the ideas as active principles is maintained, for example, by Zeller; nor is there need for us to dispute this view, though we do not subscribe to it. Plato could so conceive the ideas without believing the world to be decaying in time; the particular man generated today is not required by this hypothesis to be any less excellent than men generated in the distant past.

(d) Nor need we oppose Popper's contention (p. 480) that at the time he wrote

the *Republic*, Plato conceived the ideas as
immobile entities, "petrified, so to speak,"
whereas from the time of the *Sophist* onward they are more active, becoming in the
Timaeus quasi-"deified," "causes of generation." This hypothesis appears to be Popper's modification of Cornford's view (*Plato's Theory of Knowledge*, 1935, pp. 245–
248) that from the time of the *Sophist* onward, Plato conceived of Reality as including both the Ideas, which are motionless
and changeless, and the moving principle of
soul or intelligence. (We are unable in any
way to explain Popper's (p. 481) apparent
citation of Cornford, *op. cit.*, "note to 247,"
as authority for the statement that " 'Not-
being' " is by Plato "identified in the
Timaeus with Space," with which the ideas
mingle to beget particulars; Cornford in
his note on p. 247, as well as elsewhere,
says, to our reading, the exact opposite; it
is the Atomists for whom, he says, space is
'not-being.') We need point out here only
that Popper's elaborate theory of Plato's
changing conception of the Forms is self-
defeating: it deprives him of the possibility
of maintaining consistently that Plato, at
the time he wrote the *Republic*, conceived
the forms as "primogenitors"; they were
for him then, on this hypothesis, immobile
principles, useful merely for explaining the
similarities of sensible things. Yet when
Plato wrote the *Republic*, Popper has told
us (p. 41), he was already fully a historicist,
and was already employing his theory of
Ideas (pp. 33, 37–40) for explaining degenerative social change; indeed it would
appear that Popper believes the conception
of the ideas as "primogenitors" was already
a mainspring of his political thought. We
can therefore disregard Popper's hypothetical reconstruction of the development
of Plato's views, merely observing the inconsistency of ascribing to Plato at one date
a conception the premise of which he is not
supposed to have possessed until later.

(e) We may pause briefly to point out
a misleading form of statement employed
by Popper (p. 31) in expounding Plato's
theory. Popper says, truly enough, that the
usefulness of the Ideas for explaining similarities among sensibles "does not seem . . .
to be in any way connected with historicism." He then adds, "But it is; and as
Aristotle tells us, it was just this connection
which induced Plato to develop the Theory
of Ideas." Does not this imply that Aristotle

spoke of Plato's historicism, and that he
explicitly supports Popper's belief that Plato
was a historicist? Yet all that Aristotle has
done (*Metaphysics* 987 a 30–b 19, 1078 b
15) is to derive Plato's theory of ideas in
part from dissatisfaction with Heraclitus'
unknowable flux, in part from Socrates'
search for general ethical concepts, explaining that Plato extended the range of such
concepts and hypostatized them to serve as
the objects of dependable knowledge, and
adding the Pythagorean "numbers" as another model for Plato's conception. To represent this development as "historicist" is
to beg the whole question of whether Plato's
theory of hypostatized ideas is "historicist"
or not.

(f) But Popper's account of the theory
of ideas contains in addition an element
which to my knowledge is wholly his own,
and which is the point on which his whole
case depends: the supposition that Plato
believed the first material "child" of each
idea, its earliest reflection in the temporal
realm of becoming, to have been its most
perfect "child," and all subsequent "children" to have been becoming progressively
less perfect. Without this belief, Plato's
theory would not have served him as Popper
says it did (p. 33), as a "theory of change,"
or "clue to history." Yet Popper has no
proof of this. There is no Platonic, no Aristotelian text which affirms it. Popper has in
Plato's works only the mythical passage in
the *Timaeus* describing the origin of women
and animals, and the misinterpreted passage
from the *Laws*, discussed respectively in
I (b) and (d) of this note. His citation
(p. 486) of *Laws* 895 B and 966 E, in which
Plato describes "soul" as the first motion,
cannot prove that Plato conceived the first
material entities to be the most excellent
(or even that the souls of men were at first
better than they are today — if that is what
Popper wishes to maintain that Plato believed). The passage cited by Popper (p.
486) from Aristotle (*Met.* 988 a 35 and b
8 ff.), which charges the Platonists with
thinking of good as an accident of the formal cause rather than as a final cause, likewise cannot serve to prove that Plato believed the world to be decaying in time.
The contention that Plato considered the
earliest material copy of each idea to have
been the most perfect remains entirely unattested.

(g) A further remarkable feature of

Popper's whole argument remains to be mentioned. In his earlier edition Popper made it evident that he was laboring under two serious misconceptions with regard to the ideas and their entry into the actual world. The first involved Popper's depiction of the ideas as "primogenitors"; it was his unawareness that in the *Timaeus*, despite the fact that Plato employs the metaphor of parenthood to describe the relation between ideas and the material things which resemble them, he does not represent them as impressing themselves upon the Receptacle, but instead represents the Demiurge as looking to the ideas and creating the material things in their image. This error has been acknowledged and corrected in the second edition (p. 479). It is not important for our argument in this section, since, as we have said, we are limiting our discussion to the vital question of the alleged superiority of the first material copies; none the less it is remarkable that so plain a feature of the creation myth in the *Timaeus* should have been thus overlooked, and that Popper, having become aware of his oversight, should have made no change in his account of the development of Plato's thought, described in (d) above.

(h) The second misconception is directly relevant to the main issue. In his first edition Popper at least twice (pp. 188, 190) reveals his mistaken belief that Plato sets "generation" in opposition to "degenera-tion" exactly as he contrasts "the world of unchanging things or Ideas, and the world of sensible things in flux." Popper at the time he wrote his book believed, or so it would appear, that the two contrasted pairs were for Plato closely comparable. Thus he says (p. 190): "Plato often expresses the opposition as one between the world of unchanging things and the world of *corruptible* things, or between things that are *generated and those that degenerate*" (italics his). This misconception has been corrected in the second edition, and the sentence now reads impeccably (p. 486): "between *things that are ungenerated, and those that are generated and are doomed to degenerate*"; a similar correction has been made of the parallel passage on p. 483, 1. 19. Yet no further alteration has been introduced. The point to be observed is that when Popper wrote his book, he held the mistaken view that Plato distinguished sharply between "things that are generated" and "things that degenerate," supposing that Plato believed the former less corruptible (or even incorruptible) and ontologically superior. It was under this misconception that he developed his whole elaborate depiction of Plato the "historicist," the believer in the necessary superiority and relative incorruptibility of the first city, the first man, and so on. Popper has now corrected the basic error, but without abandoning or even modifying the structure reared so largely upon it.

Change and Value in Plato's Metaphysics

To his charge of enmity to political change, Popper has added the metaphysical correlate: "Plato teaches that change is evil, and that rest is divine" (pp. 37–38). Though we may grant that Plato attempts to guard his ideal city against the disturbing entry of conflicting opinions upon morals, and his improved commonwealth against any but the most carefully considered changes either in the laws or in any custom or belief, we may still protest against this notion that he assigned value to the moveless and the permanent alone. In thus depicting the Platonic metaphysic, it is true, Popper can count upon the initial assent of almost all readers. There is scarcely any piece of information concerning Plato's thought so widely distributed and advertized. The entire doctrine of the eternal Forms, the foundation of his metaphysics, seems to be fairly describable as the writing of this message across the philosophical sky. And yet, like many a genuine truth, this one has been so used as to obscure other truths and ultimately even to damage its own validity. A theoretically adequate grounding of this view is beyond our scope, but our practical purpose can be sufficiently served by a brief scrutiny of several crucial passages in the dialogues, some of which Popper has himself adduced.

In the *Timaeus* and *Laws* Plato has made it quite clear that in his universe, change, while not an attribute of reality on its highest level, is nevertheless not ranked as evil. All soul is, or is constantly participating in, motion (*Laws* 896 ff.) and even material change is a necessary means to the attainment of the highest ends contemplated by the benevolence of Mind in its eternal effort to achieve the greatest measure of order in this "only-begotten world" (*Timaeus* 29 E, 92 C). That is to say, in somewhat the sense of the word so pregnantly employed in Whitehead's title, Plato is representing change as the "process" through which "reality" effects ingression into the world of becoming. (A. E. Taylor, *Commentary on Plato's Timaeus*, 1928, esp. pp. 71–73, has

drawn parallels between Whitehead's cosmology and the *Timaeus*, stressing Whitehead's distinction between "events" and "objects." Against this interpretation Cornford, *Plato's Cosmology*, 1937, pp. xi–xii, has protested.) And if, for Plato, the process involves a negative pole of transience, this is, so to say, the price paid for value received, and in no sense a warrant for branding the totality of the process, i.e., change as a whole, as "evil." This is what is recognized and implied by Leibniz, who while using the term "metaphysical evil" to apply to every good short of the divine goodness, was trying his best to assert his optimistic faith in the "best of all possible worlds."

Popper has cited (p. 487) *Republic* 380 E ff. in support of his thesis, but examination of the passage does not confirm his view. Plato is engaged in arguing that the gods should not be represented in the traditional mythological way as transforming or disguising themselves, and employs as one of the grounds of his proof the principle that a thing superlative in excellence cannot change its nature except to become less excellent. But this principle, as we shall have occasion to remark again, does not mean that change *per se* is evil. And neither does it commend "rest," in the sense of inactivity. For the Demiurge in the *Timaeus*, having fashioned the World-All out of his desire that all things should be good, "was abiding as was his wont in his own nature" (42 E). That is to say, God acts, and the act is good, yet God is in his nature unchanged.

Popper appeals also to *Laws* 797 C ff. Here Plato is proposing to prohibit all changes in art forms, in order to prevent the contagion of change from spreading to law and custom, and in justification states the general principle, "Nothing, as we shall find, is more perilous than change in respect of everything, save only what is bad." He then illustrates his meaning by pointing to the effects upon bodily health of a change in diet: though health may be equally well maintained on either diet, the change itself from one to the other produces disturbance.

It is the same, he says, with the minds and souls of men. Yet even this apparently general assertion of the badness of change must be understood in the light of its context, and especially requires attention to the exception which it includes. Plato is describing a government and laws which he believes close to the ideal: under their guardianship, the citizens' souls are to be in good health. And since all change which affects a wholesome thing from without is disturbing to this thing, requiring readjustment if equilibrium is to be maintained, no change is to be allowed which is not in itself valuable in proportion to the value which it may disturb, i.e. the great value of the laws themselves. Plato's maxim is not "all change is bad" but "all change which endangers greater values than itself is bad." Plato's conservatism remains, but it remains subordinate to his sense of comparative values.

Finally, we may mention *Laws* 903 B ff., a passage cited in part by Popper but open to employment, instead, to prove Plato's acceptance of change. Plato here expounds an interesting theological principle comparable to some of the Christian attempts to reconcile divine providence with the existence of free will. God is said to have "designed the rule which prescribes what kind of character should be set to dwell in what kind of position and in what regions; but the causes of the generation of any special kind he left to the wills of each one of us men" (trans. Bury, Loeb Library). Here we are offered a theory of change in which each man is made the captain of his soul, whose fate will be determined in accordance with the moral law of the universe by choices of his own making. But the whole process is affirmed: it is the means to the "blissful existence" of the World-All.

Appendix XVI

Socrates and the Origins of Plato's Thought

That no view taken of Socrates and of his relation to Plato can hope to satisfy all qualified students, that indeed no detailed interpretation can hope to secure even a majority in its favor, is rendered embarrassingly obvious by the age-long history of attempts to disentangle the two men. The best that can be done, apparently, is for each writer to state clearly his "solution" and give some indication of the principal grounds on which it rests. In several sections of this book will be found partial expositions of the attitude taken toward this question, notably in passages beginning on pp. 61, 305, 399, 488, and 495. We shall not deal further in this place with the thesis upheld by Kelsen (cf. pp. 118, 466ff.), of Socrates' supposed homosexuality and resulting dominativeness, or with his relation to Plato in these two respects; nor does it appear necessary to deal directly with Winspear's and Silverberg's Socrates, who sells himself, soul and very nearly body as well, to the Athenian oligarchs (*Who Was Socrates?*, 1939). Tribute has already been paid to Socrates as humorist and teacher, and as master of persuasive argument. Focusing upon ethical and political questions, we shall bring together in summary what has been said, add some matters not dealt with elsewhere, and compare the thought of Socrates and Plato in these two departments.

It may be well, at the start, to list my "orthodoxies" in relation to the Socratic problem. The Socrates of the Platonic dialogues will be regarded here, as he is regarded by others who have addressed themselves to the question, with the exception only of Burnet and Taylor, as the spokesman, on occasion, of much that is not literally Socratic. The development which the thought of Socrates has undergone at the hand of Plato will be seen, again in the traditional way, not as a betrayal (a view Popper seems alone in holding), but as an honest endeavor on Plato's part to elicit its implications and to buttress it with consistent additions. Similarly, the *Apology*

and *Crito* will be looked to as the most hopeful sources for knowledge of the actual Socrates which we possess, to be supplemented, as is customary (here, again, Popper seems the sole exception) by the *Euthyphro* and other early dialogues of search.

The adherent of the general position just described need not be dismayed by the argument, developed with the utmost philological competence by H. Gomperz and most effectively restated, with supplementary considerations, by Oldfather ("Socrates in Court," 1938), that the speech of Socrates which constitutes Plato's *Apology* was never delivered, and that what we possess is a free imaginative construction on the part of the pupil of what his old master might and ought to have said. For on this assumption we may still look to the ideas, and particularly to what concerns moral and religious doctrine, as an undiminished source of knowing what had passed from the mind of the older into that of the younger man. And it is this reliability of understanding that, from the point of view of our inquiry, is alone at stake. No one of the major detractors except Winspear (cf. p. 446) has argued from the premise that Socrates was not the principal author of the *Apology* (nor, as it happens, is the Gomperz-Oldfather thesis noted by those students of the Socratic problem with whose works we shall have occasion to deal, since these, for the most part, were written at too early a date). Dialectically, therefore, the implications of this potentially significant thesis can be here ignored.

My divergence, however, from the larger group of recent Socratic critics will be apparent in the attempt to call attention not so much to the distinctions between the thought of Socrates and Plato (though, as remarked above, it will be recognized that these exist and are of great importance), as to those other elements which seem to me common to both, and which, when detected in Plato alone, bring Plato into disfavor with modern liberals. In the carrying out of this intention, appeal will be made to what seems almost a truism, but still a principle often overlooked in practice by those who would sharply divide the two men: Plato's failure, in any given early work such as the *Apology*, to state explicitly or attribute to Socrates some conception which is developed in another, later work, is not to be taken as proof either that Plato, at the time of writing the former, lacked the conception in question, or that Socrates himself did not maintain it; to establish this, other evidence than mere omission will be required.

As a second principle of interpretation, we shall call upon the complexity and many-sidedness of Socrates, or, as it might be expressed, the apparent inconsistencies which were held in suspension in his thought. Any credible Socrates must somehow account for and make possible the diverse interpretations put upon him by his contemporaries or near contemporaries, or at least by those who acknowledged him as master and teacher. Thus there must be found in him a point of attachment for the concern of Aristippus for attaining maximum satisfaction, a requirement which warns us against too transcendental a conception. There must be a source for Antisthenes' exaltation of "Socratic strength," of bodily toil and strenuous self-denial. We must account somehow for Xenophon's commonsense philosopher, believer in knowledge for use, and advocate of Spartan simplicity of living and law-abiding citizenship. Our "real" Socrates must have some point of similarity — though here no close relationship need be shown — with the unwashed head of the school of pseudoscience and sophistic argument depicted by Aristophanes. And he must tally above all with at least the earlier aspect of Plato's Socrates. The very list of these requirements should suffice to prove that no simple man will do, and relieve us (as Jaeger also has pointed out, *Paideia*, II, 1943, pp. 24–27) of the necessity of presenting a man who is plainly and obviously consistent.

Another principle may be derived from consideration of Socrates as he appeared to those who had the best vantage point of observation. This is the improbability that his teaching included important elements which failed to reappear in the doctrines of any of his disciples or in the portraits of him which they present, or to attract the attention of any outside observers.

A fourth principle not to be lost sight of is that Socrates cannot be reduced in scale to the size of any of the smaller "Socrateses" included in the list above. As a force is measured by the displacement, so the momentousness of a personality is shown by the influence it exerts. Our Socrates will do better to err on the side of largeness than of pettiness and mediocrity.

In view of my basic intention and the principles just listed, the Socrates to be presented will probably differ in some respect from all the others with whom the reader is conversant, in ways which will be indicated.

The first trait which Socrates must possess is clearly a predominant concern with morality and man: here we have no speculator on physical science, or student of mathematics and astronomy for their own sakes; no intellectual descendant of such a man is recorded. It seems not at all necessary to believe that in this respect the Socrates of Aristophanes is true to life; he is rather a figure displaying the picturesque Socratic traits of neglect of externals — poverty, simplicity of dress, Spartan endurance of hardship — the Socratic skill in debate, and some minor Socraticisms such as talk of midwifery to souls, all these being compounded with characteristics drawn from sophists of every sort, to form a composite scapegoat for all dissenters from traditional Athenian beliefs, and all teachers of disturbingly novel doctrines. Whoever holds this view (which agrees closely with that of Ehrenberg, *The People of Aristophanes*, 1951, pp. 275–277), clearly cannot permit Aristophanes to persuade him to join Burnet and Taylor in believing that Socrates in middle life was still primarily a student of nature. Nor need one accept the recent revival of this position sponsored by Snell ("Das früheste Zeugnis über Sokrates," 1948) and developed in detail by W. Schmid ("Das Sokratesbild der Wolken," 1948); particularly unacceptable is Snell's readiness to detect explicit references to Socrates in Euripidean aphorisms and in the Old Oligarch (ii, 19), and Schmid's assumption, pp. 212 and 215, required for the support of his position, that the Socrates of the *Apology* deliberately misrepresents his own earlier-held doctrines. At the same time, it is possible to agree with Rogers (*The Socratic Problem*, 1933, p. 90) in thinking that Socrates may have felt an early interest in

such matters, such as Plato records (*Phaedo*
96 A ff.), and even — though this appears
less certain — some residual knowledge and
interest carried forward into maturity, such
as the practical Xenophon ascribes to him
(*Mem.* IV, vii, 1–6).

From this standpoint we can now examine Popper's use of the statement made
by the Socrates of the *Apology* (19 C–D)
that he "knows nothing" at all of speculations about "things beneath the earth and
in the heavens" and "has no share" in such
"knowledge." We agree that these statements make against the Burnet-Taylor hypothesis of an early Socrates fitted to Aristophanes' specifications. But the words used
for "know" and "knowledge," *epaïô* (cf.
Crito 47 B–48 A) and *epistêmê*, both imply
expert or professional knowledge, or scientific certainty. What Socrates disclaims is
that he is in any sense an expert in, or
"professes," physical or astronomical knowledge, or has demonstrative knowledge of
either — that is, he denies that he could
have offered instruction in astronomy, which
had been specifically forbidden by the law
under which Anaxagoras was condemned.
This denial need not preclude an interest
in and acquaintance with the speculations
of other men.

Popper employs Socrates' disclaimer,
secondly (Popper, p. 599, [a]), as an aid to
proving the falseness of the "Socrates" of
the *Republic*, for the implied reason that
the latter is an advocate of the higher
mathematics as a propaedeutic to philosophy, and is obviously conversant with the
field. We should agree that Socrates the
man was almost certainly far less a student
of mathematics than Plato's Socrates of the
Republic. Yet we should make two objections to Popper here: He has himself claimed
as genuinely Socratic the mathematical
demonstration carried out with the help of
the slave in the *Meno* (cf. p. 148 above),
and therefore he cannot claim that the real
Socrates, as he conceives him, had no concern with mathematics. We are on safer
ground in leaving open the question whether mathematics as distinct from physics and
cosmology is included in Socrates' disclaimer in the *Apology*. Our second objection is
that even though the Socrates of the *Republic* is conceded to be unhistorical in the
extent of his interest in mathematics, this
is in itself neither a betrayal by Plato of
his master nor a proof that in any other

specified respect the Socrates of the *Republic* is false. What we should judge to
be the case is rather that, seeing in Socrates' method of starting from a hypothesis and examining its consequences, and
then, having amended the hypothesis as
required, repeating the process, a method
basically akin to mathematical deduction,
Plato generalized the similarity thus detected with fruitful results. In so doing he
exemplified the treatment to which he has
in so many respects subjected the Socratic
insights.

The third use which Popper has made
of the disclaimer of Socrates in the *Apology* is his argument (pp. 599 [a] and 591–
593, note 44) that since the real Socrates
had nothing to do with speculations about
"things beneath the earth or heavenly
things," he cannot have believed in an immortal soul, as does the Socrates of the
Phaedo. Socrates was not necessarily including among such matters the soul; the
context shows that he is referring to the
subject matter of cosmological inquiry,
along the lines of the Ionian physicists.
Aristotle's statement, *Met.* 989 b 34, cited
by Popper, to the effect that the Pythagorean speculations were "all about nature"
is not lightly to be taken, as Popper takes
it, to be exactly true, and to mean exactly
what he understands by it. Those to whom
the proper interpretation of this passage
seems to merit further investigation may
see Cherniss (*Aristotle's Criticism of Pre-
socratic Philosophy*, 1935, esp. pp. xii–
xiii), who shows at length the unwisdom
of treating as genuinely historical Aristotle's often highly dialectical transformations of the ideas of his philosophical predecessors; see also his discussion (pp. 237–
239) of the particular objection Aristotle
is here urging against the Pythagoreans
(namely: that their abstract numbers, conceived as first principles, cannot account
for the existence of the material universe
or the changes it undergoes), a purpose
which has colored the statement cited by
Popper. Socrates' belief in a soul as a
part of man akin to the divine, and perhaps capable of survival after death,
whether he derived the conception from
Pythagorean or from Orphic sources,
would not be disproved by his denial of
participation in cosmological and physical speculations.

The second trait which appears to characterize the Socrates of the *Apology* is a firm religious faith. There is, unmistakably, his sense of the divine guidance of his own life, first by the *daimonion* which would always halt him if he approached any evil, and second by the command of the god of Delphi (21 A ff., 28 E–29 A, 31 D, 33 C, 40 A–C, 41 D); coördinate with this is his unshakable faith in the cosmic grounding of human good (41 C–D); and it seems to me necessary to add his serene belief in the certainty, humanly speaking, of immortality. On this last point probably no more than a certain number of readers can be expected to agree that the Socrates of the *Apology* and *Crito* reveals as plainly (if less emphatically) as does the Socrates of the *Phaedo* both his belief in immortality and his reservation that this belief is not certain; it is but as certain as merely human knowledge of such matters can be, and extreme doubt of it passes into what is called in the *Phaedo* "misology" (cf. *Apology* 23 A–B, 29 A–B, 40 C ff., and *Crito* 54 E, with *Phaedo* 63 B–C, 66 E, 90 B–91 C, 107 B). True that in his concluding speech to those who have voted for his acquittal, Socrates presents death as a problematic alternative between extinction and undiminished survival, but it is noticeable that the climactic position is given to survival. So, too, in the *Crito*, the address made to Socrates by the personified laws of Athens ends with their solemn warning that he will not be well received, if he does wrong in this world, by their "brothers, the laws that govern the world to come." On this interpretation, the contrast between the *Apology* and *Crito* and the *Phaedo* is much softened, the *Phaedo* appearing as the elaboration of the simple faith of Socrates with a variety of metaphysical arguments; all three dialogues (and we may add the *Gorgias*) breathe a common air of faith in the soul as in some sense a spiritual substance, and no mere perishable accident of the body.

It is plain from Cornford's view (*Before and After Socrates*, 1932, pp. 75–77) and Jaeger's (*Paideia*, II, pp. 42, 46) that the *Apology* can be read as the utterance of an agnostic. Similarly Dodds (*The Greeks and the Irrational*, 1951, p. 210) implies his belief that it was Plato who transformed "the rational Socratic *psyche*" into an immortal soul. It is possible only

to record my own conviction, call attention to the passages on which it is based (cf. also pp. 64–65, 433–434), and list among those who see the matter in a similar (though not necessarily identical) light, e.g., A. K. Rogers (*The Socratic Problem*, 1933, pp. 75–77), R. W. Livingstone (*Portrait of Socrates*, 1938, esp. p. 75), and, somewhat ironically, one of those very skeptics in whose admired image Popper appears to have remodeled his Socrates, Bertrand Russell (*A History of Western Philosophy*, 1945, p. 89).

It appears, however, that Popper stands alone in denying to Socrates so much certainty as the affirmation that there exists an objective human good, founded in the nature of man and of the universe, and, after a fashion, accessible to knowledge. Socrates' declaration that he "recognizes that he is in truth of no account in respect to wisdom" (*Apology* 23 B), and that his wisdom, such as it is, consists in the fact "that what I do not know, I do not think I know either" (21 D, trans. Fowler, Loeb Library), cannot cancel out his assertion that "I do know that it is evil and disgraceful to do wrong and to disobey him who is better than I, whether he be god or man" (29 B, Fowler), nor, as we have argued, pp. 302ff., his certainty in affirming a schedule of values other than those of the worldling and the ordinary man in the street. (This position is in complete agreement with Rogers, *op. cit.*, pp. 76–77.) Related to this certainty is the universal validity assumed to be the property of the knowledge toward which Socrates directed his search. Socrates and his interlocutor are always engaged in seeking, not a separate truth for each, but the truth for both, valid in itself and for all men (cf. *Crito* 49, *Gorgias* 472 B–C). This truth must be accepted by any man who is to benefit by it — he must be "persuaded" of its truth; and Socrates' undogmatic method and initial assumption, in dealing with most of his interlocutors, of a greatly exaggerated ignorance is of immense importance for securing the consent of his fellow investigator to any conclusion that may be reached. And it is not to be overlooked that even in the most Socratic dialogues agreements are attained. Crito consents to Socrates' conclusions at many points, and the *Euthyphro*, to name but one example, before it reaches its final failure to define piety, has achieved unanimity between the parties to the discussion on not a few vital propositions (e.g., the "holy" is not holy because the gods love it, but of its own nature, 10 E; the gods are not in need of the services of men, 15 A). In view of these facts, Socrates' assertion that his wisdom consists in his knowledge of his own ignorance appears as an instance of those memorable but cryptic sayings characteristic of Socrates and requiring interpretation; in this case it is to be understood in the light of those passages in the *Phaedo* to which we have referred, p. 635 above, in which Socrates declares that only disembodied souls can really know (cf. also *Apology* 23 A–B, where it is said that only the god is wise), but that we may attain by reasoned argument such knowledge as is possible to man. This conclusion receives support from two of the principles with which we began our discussion: neither Plato nor the historical Socrates can be held to the requirement of developing all his views on any one occasion; and no one of his disciples, so far as we have record, maintained a skeptical or "critical dualist" position.

Closely related to the claim that Socrates believed in no objective moral truth is the claim far more frequently made on his behalf, namely: that he was an advocate of freedom of speech in general, a martyr to the right of every individual man to see his own duty or his own good and to champion it openly. This claim, persuasively urged by Grote (*Plato*, I, e.g., pp. 295, 305), has been repeated by many others, e.g., Bury, (*A History of Freedom of Thought*, 1913, pp. 33–35), Crossman (pp. 86–88), and Popper (cf. our p. 300). Yet as we have argued (pp. 304–306), there seems no reason for this attribution of a generalized liberalism to Socrates. Many a martyr has died not for any man's right to speak openly, but for the truth as he himself saw it; and in the absence of any statement of the more general principle, it is surely dangerous to supply it. There is further the absence from among the disciples of Socrates of any advocacy of such a principle or even of any discussion of it as present in the teaching of Socrates.

A further trait observable in Socrates is his faith in reason as the touchstone of truth and the means to its attainment, and in knowledge, which is virtue. The ex-

amination of oneself and of others "about virtue" (*Apology* 38 A) is the best thing in human life. The Delphic injunction "Know thyself" Socrates may be understood to have interpreted as the command to pursue this self-examination; and the knowledge "about virtue" which is to result, we may follow Plato in believing, was for Socrates the same knowledge which is virtue, because, once known in full clarity (so far as this is humanly possible), it determines the will. It cannot, therefore, consist ultimately only in the knowledge of one's own ignorance. The end of the search is not helpless uncertainty and doubt, but such certainty as Socrates himself possessed, though he did not forget that only the god is truly wise.

In this connection we may reply to Popper's charge that Plato has subtly perverted the meaning attached by Socrates to "Know thyself." For the modest Socrates, Popper asserts (pp. 551, 600–601) it meant only "Know thy own ignorance"; and for him, only those who were wise in this sense were fit to rule. But Plato in the *Philebus* (48 C–49 C), declaring that the powerful who do not know their own ignorance, but believe themselves wiser than they are, are terrible and hateful and bring injury upon others, implies his own vicious doctrine that the powerful must be wise, and Popper bids us recollect that wisdom for Plato consists in "initiation into the deeper mysteries of dialectic philosophy" or "training in the Royal Science of politics."

Now it is not disputed that by "Know thyself," the Greeks in general most commonly had meant "Know your own measure," "Recognize the limits of your moral qualities and powers," as is attested by E. G. Wilkins, in her thesis *"Know Thyself" in Greek Literature*, University of Chicago Libraries, 1917, pp. 12–13, 15. And Socrates would naturally start from this meaning, giving it often (though by no means always) the specific sense of "Know the limits of your knowledge." Thus in the *Apology* Socrates doubtless has "Know thyself" in mind when he declares (23 A–B) that his "service to the god" has made him wise in knowing the limitations upon his own wisdom (cf. p. 635 above), in respect to which he is "of no account." And those who suppose themselves wise when they are not, exemplify for him the lack of self-knowledge at its worst. But even in the *Apology*, as we have seen, Socrates does not declare that he knows nothing; there are several vastly important items of his knowledge which have survived his sharpest scrutiny. It is hard to believe that the Socrates of the *Apology* would have dissented from the doctrine that the wise are those who, doubting their own worldly wisdom, know unshakably the supreme importance of caring for their souls, and acknowledge objective justice and right as standing above all other goods.

Turning to the other half of Popper's charge, we may assert that wisdom in this very sense is for Plato the proper qualification for the possession of power. True that Plato believes the practice of dialectic — the "examination of life," and "talking about virtue," as Socrates (*Apology* 38 A) had called his version of this process — the proper avenue to stable wisdom of this sort; true that such investigation of truth and acquisition of virtue constitute for Plato training in the art of politics (cf. pp. 364f.) ; and in both these convictions Plato is still Socratic in very large measure. We may doubt that Plato's proposed methods of training, or those of Socrates either, for that matter, are the only or even the best devices for producing an unshakable dedication to right action. But this leaves standing and without reproach Plato's conviction that those who lack wisdom thus defined are hateful and harmful as rulers.

From the Socratic faith in reason springs another Socratic tenet, his belief in the expert, the man who knows. In every field of human endeavor, Socrates argues in the *Apology* (25 A–B), some few men excel; the rest are laymen. Even in matters of morality the rule should hold; he would expect to find one Athenian or at best a few who are able to make young men better. Such a man the record shows he considered himself to be, modestly and hesitantly but yet forced to it by his inability to discover a better. He alone was fully aware of the true schedule of values, the true means to the fulfillment of god's will. Those who were able even to accept his teaching were few, and would always be so (*Crito* 49 D) ; the many remained unconvinced, hostile, ready to silence and condemn him. Out of the spiritual inequality thus exemplified could develop the doctrine of the varying spiritual capacities of men which we find in the *Phaedrus* and in the *Republic*. Whether it is itself Socratic or Platonic we cannot say; but it has its roots in Socrates.

The aim of the expert in the care of souls is to assist men in attaining virtue, or the excellence proper to man. And inseparable from the Socratic conception of such virtue is its ultimate and universal desirability. Compared with it, all other benefits or advantages are of no account. To do injustice, this is true misfortune, from which if he could Socrates would wish to save his judges (*Apology* 30 C–D), and which he himself will at all costs avoid (*Crito* 47 D–48 A). But the man who keeps himself thus unspotted can suffer no real harm. Toward this ultimate security, the god himself has specially enjoined upon Socrates the obligation to assist others, but it does not rest on him alone. He urges those of his judges who have voted for his acquittal, if they would deal justly with him, after his death to admonish his sons to care for their souls (*Apology* 41 E). He does not say so, but he implies that such concern for others' true welfare is owed by all men, and particularly by kinsmen and fellow citizens, to one another.

Before considering the political outlook of Socrates we may pause to sum up the moral teaching we have been expounding: the central concern with man, the sense of man's nearness to the divine and of the momentousness of his moral choices, the belief that for all men one good is appointed and one path to this good, namely reason, and the call for the moral expert who knows how to minister to souls. From all these there results, as concerns the few who have received the call (and this includes Antisthenes as well as Plato), the obligation to benefit others morally, to destroy error, and to give birth in reasoned discussion to true knowledge; for themselves and for these others also there results the good for man, the soul well cared for.

The first characteristic of Socrates as a "politician," as we see him in the *Apology* and *Crito* (and also in Xenophon), is certainly his "apolity," his abstinence from direct participation in the political affairs of Athens. He tells us in the *Apol-*

ogy 31 D–32 A, that he has conceived it to be no part of his duty to court death by opposing the popular will, which, as he says, he would certainly have been compelled by his principles to do on more occasions than the one famous instance of the trial of the Arginusae generals (cf. our p. 318). We wish to point out that when Popper (p. 152) calls the expression of a similar reason for refraining from politics, made by the "Socrates" of the *Republic*, "sour and most un-Socratic," he is overlooking this passage in the *Apology*. We have here a characteristic instance of Popper's double standard, applied on the one hand to the Socrates of the *Apology* and on the other to him of the *Republic*, on the basis of which the two are made to appear as saint and sinner.

This abstinence of Socrates from politics, however, must not be assumed to mean abstinence also from the discussion of the statesman's art or of the ideal form of government. As we have remarked, p. 305, the Socrates of the Socratic dialogues, unless we include the *Euthydemus* and the *Gorgias*, does not directly discuss political theory; the situation in both the *Apology* and *Crito* would render the raising of such theoretical questions inappropriate. But Xenophon (for what his testimony is worth) freely represents him as doing so (*Mem.* e.g., I, ii, *passim*; III, ix, 10). And the interest of both Xenophon and Plato, and perhaps also Antisthenes (cf. p. 210), in planning ideal states ruled over by dedicated experts in the art of government suggests, as does the similar appearance in several disciples of an interest in feminism, a common source in Socrates.

Highly important for determining Socrates' political outlook are his recurrent strictures in both *Apology* and *Crito*, on the "many" or on "multitudes." As we have shown, p. 304, the "many" in the political sense are spoken of as lawless and irresponsible, and dangerous to good men (*Apol.* 28 A–B); they are, moreover, incompetent in that most important function of the moral expert, the ability to make men more wise (*Crito* 44 D). It is not the opinions of the majority of men, the laymen in virtue, which can guide us in settling questions of right and wrong (44 C, 47 A f., 49 D). Nor are ethical questions for the Socrates of the *Apology*

sharply distinct from those of politics, as they are for some of his modern interpreters; this we shall discuss further below. It is for this reason that we cannot accept Rogers' argument (*op. cit.*, p. 71) that Socrates could not have spoken as he does (*Apology* 31 C–E) of his abstinence from politics, if he "had been indulging in propaganda" against democracy; what Socrates had to say on moral questions, as in this question of the "many," could not have been without bearing on political questions. The *Gorgias* also, if we are allowed to cite it as evidence, ascribes to Socrates a vigorous condemnation of the moral standard of all the "citizens and Strangers" of Athens, and a decisive rejection of the settling of questions in ethics by the majority vote of any group (471 E–472 C). There is an obvious consistency between all these positions and that approval of a political art parallel to the art of medicine which the Socrates of the *Gorgias* goes on to express, and which the *Republic* carries to its logical conclusion. That Plato himself believed the man Socrates to have been essentially engaged in investigating the foundations of such an art of politics is testified by Plato again in the *Politicus* (299 B f.), where he compares the Athenian condemnation of Socrates to the actions of persons who should forbid on pain of death all attempts to advance the arts of medicine or navigation.

Correlative with Socrates' disparagement of the "many" is the indication visible in the *Apology* that Socrates did not share the admiration for "equality" which underlay the use of the lot, and which formed the rallying cry of the extremer Athenian democrats. Socrates' emphatic declaration, already quoted, — "I do know that it is evil and disgraceful to act unjustly and to disobey him who is better than I, be he god or man" (29 B) — implies the same belief in the rightful authority of the better man, with the proviso that he shall be truly better, which we find expressed in many a later dialogue. And as we have seen, p. 416, Socrates does not defend the equation of justice with simple equality, as Popper supposes he does, in the *Gorgias*.

Some importance may properly be attached, also, to Socrates' opinion of Spartan institutions, though not as much as

Popper would maintain. We should not forget that despite its objectionable features, Sparta could be viewed as a modified democracy, and that such a "moderate democrat" as Isocrates considered it admirable in this respect. However this may be, Socrates in the *Crito* (52 E, 53 B), explaining that he has been well pleased with the laws of Athens, says that he has preferred them even to those of Crete and Sparta, though he has always praised these states as being "well-governed" (*eunomeisthai*); he adds that since Thebes and Megara, too, are "well-governed," they will not welcome a lawbreaker such as Crito urges him, Socrates, to become. This does not sound like opposition on principle to any form of government not democratic. It implies approval both of the respect for law which, he says, characterizes all the states mentioned, and of the laws themselves of Crete and Sparta.

We note further that though Socrates had associates who were democrats, none of his philosophical continuators came forward as a sturdy advocate of the Athenian form of government of that day. Not Plato alone, but Xenophon also, who in later life was glad once more to be acceptable to his countrymen, played critic to Athenian democracy, and in differing degrees and with differing effect, both men showed approval of aspects of Sparta. And as we have seen, pp. 210f., it is as probable as anything we know of Antisthenes that he too called in question democratic principles and perhaps was also an admirer of Sparta.

To depict Socrates as a convinced supporter of the extreme Athenian democracy in the face of all these facts would seem impossible, yet, as we have seen, Popper energetically affirms it (pp. 188, 596, 600, 602), and in so doing he has on his side the weight of Rogers' opinion (*op. cit.*, pp. 72–73). The chief justification for this claim is the presence in Socrates' thought of a third principle, expressed in the *Crito* with great solemnity, that of his obligation to obey the laws of Athens. He affirms that as a son of Athens he is bound by piety to do so; secondly, he is obligated because he has chosen freely to remain a citizen of Athens and has approved its laws above all others, though it was open to him to have lived as an alien elsewhere; he has not even gone abroad or sought to

know the laws of other states (50 C ff., esp. 51 E–52 A). The laws of Athens have given him also the opportunity either of "persuading" them of "what is really just" or of obeying; one or other of these it was his duty to do (51 B–C, E). This last statement has been interpreted by Rogers (p. 72) and also by Popper (p. 596) as Socrates' testimony that Athens provided each of her citizens with the constitutional right to work politically for the repeal or revision of laws which seemed to him as an individual to be unjust. On these grounds Rogers and Popper conclude that if the *Crito* is truly Socratic in the sentiments it expresses, we have here Socrates' own heartfelt statement that he approves the Athenian constitution (which was certainly democratic), and that he will die rather than injure it.

The case for Socrates' approval of Athenian democracy is further bolstered with several slighter arguments, ranging from Rogers' mention of Aristophanes' failure in the *Clouds* to attribute any antidemocratic sympathies to Socrates, to what Popper sees as Socrates' own claim in the *Apology*, to sympathy with democratic persons and "democratic legality," and Socrates' eulogy in the *Crito*, again on Popper's view (p. 596), of virtue, justice, and "institutions and laws (those of Athens) as the best things among men."

Yet this conflict between Socratic approval and disapproval of Athenian democracy is not beyond solution. I can only indicate what seems to me a fully adequate solution. The context in the *Crito* makes it entirely clear that the "laws and institutions" which Socrates includes among the most precious human possessions are those of well-governed cities in general, including Thebes and Megara; Socrates, therefore, whether he approves or disapproves democracy, believes laws precious, even when they are imperfect. Secondly, his approval of Athenian laws does not preclude his approval also of those of Crete and Sparta; again we have no exclusive affirmation of the Athenian form of democracy as such. When we examine the particular Athenian laws which he has occasion to acknowledge as excellent, we find that they are the laws of marriage and those which directed his parents in nurturing him and educating him in gymnastic and music (50 D–E); he says that he has seen and approved also how the laws "dispense justice and in other respects administer the city" (51 D–E) ; he praises the permission which Athens accords her citizens to depart at will, taking with them their possessions, and that other right to a hearing or trial which, as we shall explain below, we hold to be what is meant by the opportunity to "persuade" the laws (51 D–52 A). None of these laws is necessarily part of the democratic constitution in the stricter sense. Finally, Socrates' filial relation to the laws, a relation which he also likens to that of a slave to his master, and the general principle that it is never right to do wrong even in requital of wrong, bind him to his own city (49 C–52 E) ; these arguments, too, are not at all specific to democracy. In short, Socrates in honoring above all others the laws of Athens honors that sum total of laws and customs which inform with character the whole Athenian way of life and not the democratic constitution as such. It is quite within the evidence to believe that he considers the laws in some respects seriously imperfect and in need of reform, even that he believes them in some ways less perfect than those of Sparta, though he concedes to his native city as to a parent the right to be honored and protected by her sons even when they believe her mistaken in her way of life, and feels a particular regard for the welfare of his kinsmen, his fellow citizens (cf. *Apology* 30 A).

Once the possibility of this reading of the *Crito* is established, we can deal with the more specific arguments which have been brought to support the hypothesis of Socrates' special sympathy for democracy. It is most improbable that *Crito* 51 B–E, where Socrates speaks of having been given the opportunity to "persuade" the laws, is a reference to the possibility of reforming Athenian laws by constitutional methods. Far more likely is the interpretation of this metaphor as a reference to the citizen's right, whenever a charge is brought against him or a duty is laid upon him by the city, to have his day in court, and to persuade the jury, if he can, to acquit him. That this is what Socrates has in mind is made more probable by the use of the same word, "persuade" or "convince" (*peithein*) at *Apology* 37 A–B, where Socrates attributes his failure to "persuade" his judges of his innocence to the shortness of the time given him for his defense; in some other cities, he says (Sparta is one of these), several days are allotted to the decision of a capital case. Now it is true that here he finds fault with a provision of the Athenian law, whereas at the end of the *Crito* (54 C–D) he declares that he is the victim of men, not of the laws of Athens, thus separating the laws from his accusers or from the jurymen who condemned him. But an extended metaphor such as the personification of the laws of Athens cannot be expected to achieve detailed correspondence with all the facts; if the laws are to be likened collectively to a parent or a master, scant provision can be made in such a figure of speech for nice distinctions between the laws as a whole and particular laws which are regarded as faulty, or between the law and the accusers and judges. The improbability that Socrates is speaking of the possibility that he might have worked for the repeal of an unjust law is greatly increased by his own statement that he was compelled to abstain from participation in the political process at Athens by the danger of death, should he oppose the *dêmos* on principle, and moreover by the obstacle which, as we know from other sources (cf. our p. 318), the *graphê paranomôn* seems to have set in the path of legal change.

Among slighter arguments we may answer first the one based by Rogers, p. 73, upon Aristophanes' silence as to antidemocratic bias in Socrates. Aristophanes is scarcely, either in our opinion or in Rogers', a generally reliable witness to the real intentions of Socrates; Rogers will agree that Aristophanes omits much which is most essential. The playwright himself was no admirer of the extreme democracy, and would therefore have seen no occasion to pillory Socrates for holding similar views. Finally, such opinions were neither picturesque nor comic. The comedian has, therefore, plentiful reasons for his silence. Popper's companion remark (p. 600) that Aristophanes, by linking Socrates with the sophists, "most" of whom "were democrats," implies that Socrates too was a democrat, is not only unsound as regards the sophists, but also seems, as with Rogers' argument, to involve too great reliance on Aristophanes: the playwright links Socrates with those sophists who taught natural science and dishonest skill in rhetoric; are we to believe these similarities too? Popper has also employed (p. 596) Xenophon's testimony in the *Anabasis* (III, i, 5) that Socrates had advised him against joining Cyrus, on the ground that Athens might well look askance at a citizen who joined a former ally of Sparta against Athens. This argument does not touch what we are maintaining, namely: that Socrates was loyal to Athens, and urged others to be so, without approving the extreme democracy of her constitution. Popper's identification of Athens with the democratic constitution, even with its extremer provisions, has blinded him to this possibility.

Of Popper's remaining arguments, two are based upon the *Apology*. Reference is made (20 E–21 A) to Chaerophon, an ardent Socratic to whom the Delphic oracle had given the momentous reply that no one was wiser than Socrates; in reminding the jury of Chaerophon's democratic sympathies, argues Popper (p. 602), Socrates "emphasizes" his own "intimacy with an ardent democrat," something we must not suspect him of doing "without being truly sympathetic with the democratic cause." Similarly, Popper asserts (*ibid.*) that in describing to the jury his refusal to yield either to the democratic Assembly or to the Thirty Tyrants when ordered to act unjustly, Socrates "emphasizes his faith in democratic legality." Popper in making the first of these points overlooks the possibility that Socrates is interested in showing what was in fact the truth, that he has had friends among both democrats and oligarchs. Later in the *Apology* (33 D f.) he has occasion to call to witness several of his young associates who are present in court along with their fathers or elder relatives, to whom, as Socrates argues, he does not seem to be a corrupter of youth. Among these he does not scruple to name Plato and his brother Adeimantus, who, as close kinsmen of Critias and Charmides, well-remembered for oligarchic villainy, were in themselves sufficient to offset mention of several ardent democrats. Popper's second point is similarly one-sided in what it calls upon us to notice. Socrates is pointing out his faith in legality, not in democratic legality. By what right does Popper allocate to the Athenian democrats alone this admired quality?

The final argument which Popper adduces to prove the partisan democratic sympathies of Socrates is indeed a dangerous one: he proposes (p. 596) to regard as an interpolation, either by a later hand or by Plato's own treachery, the clause in the *Crito* (52 E) where Socrates says he has always praised the laws of Crete and Sparta. This clause is in conflict, Popper urges, with Socrates' other statement (*Crito* 52 B–C) that he has not desired to go abroad or to "know" the laws of other states, and even more in conflict with his general acceptance of Athenian laws. Popper here overlooks the meaning which is given to the word "know" by the context of travel abroad, that of "knowing-as-a-result-of-personal-acquaintance." But even were Popper's particular objection well grounded, his suggested remedy is extreme. The questioning of clauses in the Platonic text is not practised by careful interpreters in general in the absence of technical indications, such as manuscript variants or grammatical difficulties. And to propose alternatively that even in the *Crito* we be suspicious of Plato's misrepresenting hand is to risk invalidating the dialogue as a basis for any judgment whatsoever upon Socrates as distinct from Plato, and in particular to weaken what is after all the only respectable evidence that exists anywhere for Socrates' approval of the Athenian (democratic) constitution, namely: his statement in the *Crito* that he has found the laws of Athens acceptable to him his whole life long. Thus Popper, in his effort to avoid accepting an unwelcome passage, is logically driven to the far more unwelcome alternative of breaching one of his major strongholds.

We have stressed Socrates' distrust in the verdict of the equal "many" whether in the political or in the philosophic sense, and have pointed out his holding up in both the *Apology* and the *Crito* of the ideal of the moral expert, and in the *Gorgias*, the ideal of the statesman-physician; we have even maintained that in some respects he was an earnest admirer of Sparta. Yet we have not, it will be observed, denied that he considered Athenian laws excellent among actual laws, and in many respects above reproach. This unstable equilibrium in the Socratic attitude as depicted in these early dialogues is paralleled in the movement of Plato's thought throughout his life, as we see him now attempting to work out the consequences of the ideal, as in the *Republic* and the *Politicus*, now starting from the actual Athenian laws and attempting to reform them to meet the Socratic criticisms of them, as in the *Laws*. Our discussion tends, therefore, to the conclusion that in the early dialogues either we have a Socrates who thus sets the problem and provides the starting point for Plato's political thought, or we must conclude, so great is the consistency, that we have no Socrates at all, but only Plato's own early adumbration of all the main lines of his later development.

We may further illustrate the relationship between Socrates and Plato in relation to politics by citing several points at which the *Apology* and *Crito* anticipate thoughts expressed, to the scandal of Plato's critics, in the *Laws*. Rogers, as we have said, sees Socrates as prodemocratic, Plato as antidemocratic; he further contrasts (p. 111) the Socratic conviction that "the goodness which true wisdom presupposes is a condition of the human soul" with Plato's belief that it is "this as well, but even more fundamentally it is social, a goodness for citizenship." In proof of Plato's attitude he cites *Laws* 643 E and 659 D, from both of which we shall quote immediately below. Popper, as we have explained, pp. 299ff. and pp. 396ff., holds a view of Socrates similar to Rogers', and in Plato's case maintains simply that he identifies virtue with subservience to the state's interest. We have already, on pp. 520ff. above, in meeting Popper's arguments, shown that for Plato goodness is not, as Rogers avers, "more fundamentally . . . goodness for citizenship." Starting, now, by acepting the other half of Rogers' statement, that for Plato goodness is good citizenship "as well" (to the extent that the laws of the state are such as to foster virtue), we shall seek to show that the same view is held by the Socrates who speaks to us in the *Apology* and *Crito*.

To match the sentence cited by Rogers from Plato's *Laws*, 643 E, where true education is said to be "training from childhood in goodness, which makes a man eagerly desirous of becoming a perfect

citizen" (trans. Bury, Loeb Library), we remind ourselves first of those other passages in the *Laws* which set as the aim of the entire city the attainment by its citizens of the highest human excellence, and then call attention to a passage in the *Apology* near the beginning (20 A–B), in which Socrates describes how, on meeting a friend who had sons, he had commented to him that if the boys were colts or calves, it would be no hard task to discover a trainer competent to produce in them the excellence befitting such animals; but "since they are human beings," who, he had asked, shall impart to them "the kind of excellence which is that of a man and a citizen?" We have here the same identification of human goodness and "goodness for citizenship" which is supposed to be specifically non-Socratic.

The same parallel with Plato's opinion in the *Laws* can be detected in the principles governing the actions of Socrates as described in the two early dialogues. Socrates here draws for us the line between the citizen's duty of rebellion against the constituted authority of the state, and the duty of submission. In the one, we see him setting above the state his service to the god, or, as it might be put, his duty to foster virtue, to tend both his own soul and those of his fellow citizens; in the other dialogue, we learn that no other cause can justify the citizen in weakening by his disobedience the law of his city. In Plato's *Laws*, in the passage cited on p. 521, the same duty to hold the cause of virtue preëminent over allegiance to the city is laid upon the citizens by Plato. Even in *Laws* 659 D, the second of the passages cited by Rogers to show Plato's identification of virtue with citizenship, quoted in our n., p. 520, Plato makes the confirmation of those who are "oldest and most just" necessary to give full validity to the law which is to serve as moral standard for his citizens. If now it be argued that Plato held himself competent to enunciate such law, so too did Socrates believe himself competent to declare a universal and cosmically valid standard of moral good. The self-exaltation here implied is only that which necessarily attaches to anyone who believes himself clearly to perceive the universal good, and which attaches in equal measure to those who, like Popper, preach the necessity that all men should make responsible choice of the goals which he points out to them.

It has been held to Plato's discredit that he conceives the state as an educational institution designed to produce moral excellence in its citizens; he conceives that even the best of men, so Popper has argued, "depend upon society, upon the state," and "can reach perfection only through the state and in the state"; Socrates, in contrast, proclaims the "autarky" or "self-sufficiency of the good man" (Popper, pp. 76, 515, 639). It is difficult to meet this charge as stated, since it appears obvious that all of us do in fact "depend upon society" both materially and morally to a very large extent, and one would not wish to deny that Plato was aware of this fact. Nor need we deny that Plato held good laws (or ideal rulers) to be the sole means whereby most men can attain virtue, and desirable for the protection of even the best natures, since many of these must be corrupted in an unwholesome environment. We even find Plato in one passage (*Rep.* 497 A) speaking of the "greater stature" that the few true devotees of philosophy (including Socrates himself) might attain in an ideal state; we may associate this with Plato's suggestion (*Rep.* 424 A) of the continuous upward evolution in human quality that might result from the interaction of better men and better nurture. But if in his charge against Plato Popper means to mean that, for Plato, no man could attain true moral excellence outside of the perfect state, we have shown the contrary on pp. 416, 465, 520f., and we may add *Theaet.* 176 B and *Symp.* 211 B–212 A; there are also the inescapable implications of his exaltation of Socrates. Plato's ability to combine in one scheme of values these two poles, the dependence on society and the transpolitical "appeal to Heaven" is, as we view it, a reproduction of the same duality in the allegiance of the historical Socrates. No one questions the presence in Socrates of the transpolitical appeal; whoever doubts the dependence upon society should observe once more the Socrates of the *Crito*. In acknowledging his debt to the laws of Athens, he does not commend them for their hands-off policy, their scrupulous refraining from interference in the moral training given him by his parents and teachers, and in his own subsequent moral development. He represents them as solemnly reminding

him that he is their child and their nursling, that they have educated him and given him what share they could of all that was fair and good (51 C–D). Here is no honoring of a state which does not educate its citizens for virtue.

Plato has been condemned as setting the state higher than the individual, in contrast to the "individualist" Socrates. We have seen that Plato does not do so; he sets the moral welfare of each and every citizen above the material concern of the individual or of the group, and the material welfare of the group above the material (but not the spiritual) welfare of the individual. But in this place we may call attention to the strong terms in which in the *Crito* Socrates states the claim of the state to the citizen's submission. Plato in the *Laws*, preparing to enact a law limiting severely the right of bequest, can be found declaring to the aged testator, "You yourself and this your property are not your own, but belong to the whole of your race, both past and future, and . . . still more truly does all your race and its property belong to the State" (923 A, trans. Bury, Loeb Library). But Socrates in the *Crito* makes the laws say, "You are our offspring and our slave, you yourself and your ancestors," and "your country is more to be revered . . . than your mother and your father and all your ancestors" (50 E–51 B, trans. Fowler, Loeb Library).

We may note in passing that in these sentences is also contained, as elsewhere in the *Crito* (52 C–D), an affirmation of the master's claim to rule over his slave, who is also obligated to submit even to abuse. This shows that same acceptance of the institution of slavery which is held reprehensible in Plato. And in both *Crito* (51 B) and *Apology* (28 D–E) Socrates acknowledges the state's unquestionable right to demand of its citizens their services in war, an obligation which is called "militarism" when enjoined by Plato in the *Laws*.

A contrast has been drawn, again, by Cornford (*op. cit.*, pp. 43–49, 82–83) and with more emphasis, by Popper (e.g., p. 601), between Socrates' readiness to talk to the young, his criticism in their presence of the supposed wisdom of the self-satisfied citizens of Athens, and the principle affirmed by Plato in the *Laws* (and similarly in the *Republic*) that the moral teachings of the city shall not be questioned in the presence of the young, nor, for that matter, examined by most of the citizens even in their later years. Dodds also (*The Greeks and the Irrational*, 1951, p. 212) has recently called attention to what he thinks Plato's breach at this point with his old master. Now, it would be idle to deny that Socrates and Plato differ here; yet, if the position we have been defending is tenable, their different attitudes derive from a common principle subsisting at a deeper level of conviction.

That this is so may perhaps still require careful demonstration, in view of the several pronouncements of Socrates which are customarily otherwise interpreted. There is the famous sentence, "The unexamined life is unworthy of a man" (*Apology* 38 A), and there is Socrates' comparison of himself to the gadfly who goes about arousing the citizens from their dogmatic certainty (30 E–31 A). Here it seems that the questioning of moral values is treated as itself a value. But as we have pointed out, pp. 305–306, the actual situation of Socrates differed from the imagined situation of Plato. Socrates had serious objections to make against the value schedule which, he felt, the Athenians of his day honored by their actions and taught by example to their sons. It was against the uncritical acceptance of this morality of convenience that his mission was directed; this was the slumber from which the gadfly was to awaken his fellow citizens, this the conceit of wisdom against which his examination and refutation were directed. Socrates has been misunderstood by those who fail to observe the immediate sequel of every such refutation, the exhortation to adopt forthwith the Socratic scorn of that fear which thinks it knows that death is an evil, and to embrace the Socratic certainty that justice alone is truly good. This may be observed at *Apology* 29 E–30 A, 31 A–B, and 41 D–E, and is not controverted by 38 A. We find here no skepticism directed to proving that death may, after all, be the greatest evil, no refutation of persons who suppose themselves wise in knowing the supreme importance of virtue. Socrates feels himself secure in urging the questioning of customary moral beliefs, first because he believes their inadequacy will thus be exposed, second because he believes the truth must be wholeheartedly accepted by anyone who is to benefit by it, and third (a position

in accord with that of Cornford) because he believes there is an objective moral truth which will infallibly be uncovered by the persistent application of reason to human affairs.

Since this is so, we need not hesitate to see in Plato's *Laws* a city in which (so Plato intends) the Socratic schedule of values is to be embodied in law and universally accepted, and in which, therefore, no gadfly and no examination and refutation of complacently worldly citizens will be needed. All will live, if not the personally examined life, the life which has been examined and found good, and "to talk every day about virtue," which, in the *Apology* Socrates declares to be, along with the examining, the "greatest good for man," will be transformed into that constant "charming" of themselves with the praises of goodness which is to be among the chief duties of the citizens (*Laws* 663 B ff., esp. 665 C). Socrates, living, so to speak, in the City of Destruction, had need to preach constantly the pilgrimage to the Celestial City. But Plato, imagining that blessed city to be attained, must change his text.

Popper's charge that Plato has betrayed Socrates has been met, if by "betray" is meant consciously to attribute to him doctrines known to be abhorrent to him. But if it is reduced to mean only the attribution to him of developments and extensions of his thought held by Popper, though not by Plato, to be discreditable — against this there is no defense; for who is to say that the most reverent disciple may not be guilty, in the judgment of some observer, of this fault? And thus in building on a Socratic base the theory of ideas, in depicting Socrates as requiring the study of higher mathematics as a prerequisite to philosophy, and in approving the construction, in the *Timaeus*, of a teleological cosmology, Plato doubtless, in the opinion of some critics, has brought discredit upon Socrates. So, too, in constructing the plans of ideal cities, and proposing there to give to the moral imperatives of Socrates the force of coercive civil law, Plato may have gone beyond Socrates in a direction we ourselves deplore. But if Plato believed, as he manifestly did, that Socrates had hold of the true good, the one and only good, how could he think it possible or right to deny it to mankind? There is error here, but sublime error, in the transformation of Socrates, coming to each of the Athenians, as he says (*Apology* 31 B, trans. Fowler, Loeb Library), "like a father or an elder brother and urging you to care for virtue," into those laws which, as Plato says (*Laws* 859 A, trans. Bury, Loeb Library), are to "give counsel about what is noble, good and just," and to "resemble persons moved by love and wisdom, such as a father and mother."

Bibliography

Adam, James, *The Republic of Plato* (edition), Cambridge University Press, 1905.

Aiken, H. D., review of *The Open Society and Its Enemies, Journal of Philosophy*, XLIV, 1947.

Allendy, René, *Treason Complex*, English trans., Social Science Publishers, New York, 1949.

Anderson, Maxwell, *Barefoot in Athens*, Wm. Sloane Associates, New York, 1951.

Barker, Ernest, *Greek Political Theory*, London, 1947.

Becker, W. A., *Charicles*, Longmans, Green, London, 1899.

Bethe, E., "Die Dorische Knabenliebe, ihre Ethik und ihre Idee," *Rhienisches Museum*, Neue Folge, 62. Bd., 1907.

Blanshard, Brand, C. J. Ducasse, *et al.*, *Philosophy in American Education*, Harper and Brothers, New York, 1945.

Blass, F., *Die Attische Beredsamkeit*, Teubner, Leipzig, 1892.

Bloch, Herbert A., *Disorganization, Personal and Social*, Knopf, New York, 1952.

Bluck, R. S., *Plato's Life and Thought*, Routledge and Kegan Paul, London, 1949.

—— *Plato's Seventh and Eighth Letters*, Cambridge, 1947.

Boas, George, "Fact and Legend in the Biography of Plato," *Philosophical Review*, LVII, 1948.

Bolkestein, H., "The Exposure of Children at Athens and the *Engchytristriai*," *Classical Philology*, XVII, 1922.

Bonner, R. J., and Gertrude Smith, *The Administration of Justice from Homer to Aristotle*, University of Chicago Press, Chicago, 1938.

Bowra, C. M., *Ancient Greek Literature*, Home University Library, Oxford University Press, London, 1933.

—— *Early Greek Elegists*, Harvard University Press, Cambridge, 1938.

Brandt, Paul (see Licht, Hans).

Brinton, Crane, *Ideas and Men*, Prentice-Hall, New York, 1940.

Brumbaugh, R. S., "The Role of Mathematics in Plato's Dialectic" (unpublished thesis, typescript), University of Chicago, 1942.

—— "Early Greek Theories of Sex Determination," *Journal of Heredity*, XL, Feb. 1949.

—— "Note on Plato *Republic* IX. 587 D," *Classical Philology*, XLIV, July 1949.

Bruns, Ivo, "Attische Liebestheorien und die zeitliche Folge des platonischen *Phaedrus*, sowie der beiden Symposien," *Neue Jahrbuecher fuer das Klassischen Altertum*, V, 1900.

Burnet, John, *Plato's Phaedo* (edition), Clarendon Press, Oxford, 1911.

—— *Greek Philosophy from Thales to Plato*, Macmillan, London, 1914.

—— *Plato's Euthyphro, Apology of Socrates, and Crito* (edition), Clarendon Press, Oxford, 1924.

Bury, J. B., *The Ancient Greek Historians*, Macmillan, New York, 1909.

—— *A History of Freedom of Thought*, Henry Holt, New York, 1913.

—— *History of Greece*, London, Macmillan, 1931.

Bury, R. G., *The Symposium of Plato* (edition), Cambridge, 1932.

Busolt-Swoboda, *Griechische Staatskunde*, Muenchen, 1926.

Calhoun, G. M., *Athenian Clubs in Politics and Litigation*, Bulletin of the University of Texas, Austin, Texas, 1931.

Cambridge Ancient History, ed. Bury, J. B., *et al.*, Macmillan, New York, 1927, vols. V, VI.

Cameron, A., "The Exposure of Children and Greek Ethics," *Classical Review*, XLVI, 1932.

Capek, Karel, *Masaryk on Thought and Life, Conversations with Karel Capek*, George Allen and Unwin, Ltd., London, 1938.

Cassirer, Ernst, *The Myth of the State*, Yale University Press, New Haven, 1946.

Chapman, John Jay, *Lucian, Plato and Greek Morals*, Houghton Mifflin, Boston, 1931.

Chase, A., "The Influence of Athenian Institutions upon the *Laws* of Plato," in *Harvard Studies in Classical Philology*, XLIV, Harvard University Press, Cambridge, 1933.

Cherniss, Harold, *Aristotle's Criticism of Presocratic Philosophy*, Johns Hopkins Press, Baltimore, 1935.

—— *Aristotle's Criticism of Plato and the Academy*, vol. I, Johns Hopkins Press, Baltimore, 1944.

—— *The Riddle of the Early Academy*, University of California Press, 1945.

Cohen, Morris, *Reason and Nature*, Harcourt, Brace, New York, 1931.

Cornford, F. M., *Before and After Socrates*, Cambridge University Press, 1932.

—— *Plato's Theory of Knowledge*, Kegan Paul, London, 1935.

—— *Plato's Cosmology*, Harcourt, Brace, New York, 1937.

Crossman, R. H. S., *Plato Today*, Oxford University Press, New York, 1939.

Decharme, Paul, *Euripides and the Spirit of His Dramas*, New York, 1906.

De Morgan, Augustus, *A Budget of Paradoxes*, London, 1872.

Diels, H., *Die Fragmente der Vorsokratiker*, Weidmannsche Buchhandlung, Berlin, 1922.

Dodds, E. R., *The Greeks and the Irrational*, University of California Press, Berkeley and Los Angeles, 1951.

Ducasse, Curt J. (see Blanshard, Brand).

Dudley, D. R., *A History of Cynicism*, Methuen, London, 1937.

Duemmler, F., "Die *Ath. Pol* des Kritias," *Hermes*, XXVII, 1892.

Earp, F. R., *The Greek Way of Life*, Oxford University Press, London, 1929.

Ehrenberg, Victor, *The People of Aristophanes*, Basil Blackwell, Oxford, 1951.

Elliott, W. Y., and N. A. McDonald, *Western Political Heritage*, Prentice-Hall, New York, 1949.

Emerson, R. W., *Representative Men*, Houghton Mifflin, Boston, 1876.

England, E. B., *The Laws of Plato*, University Press, Manchester, 1921.

Field, G. C., *Plato and his Contemporaries*, Methuen, London, 1930.

—— "On Misunderstanding Plato," *Philosophy*, XIX, 1944.

—— *The Philosophy of Plato*, Oxford University Press, London, 1949.

Finley, John H., *Thucydides*, Harvard University Press, Cambridge, 1942.

Fite, Warner, *The Platonic Legend*, Scribner, New York, 1934.

—— *Jesus the Man*, Harvard University Press, Cambridge, 1946.

Freeman, E. A., *History of Federal Government in Greece and Italy*, Macmillan, London, 1893.

Friedrich, Karl J., *The New Belief in the Common Man*, Little, Brown, Boston, 1943.

Fritz, Kurt von, and E. Kapp, *Aristotle's Constitution of Athens*, Hafner Publishing Co., New York, 1950.

Fromm, Erich, *Escape from Freedom*, Farrar and Rinehart, New York, 1941.

—— "Conscience," in *Moral Principles of Action*, ed. R. N. Anshen, Harper, New York, 1952.

Frutiger, Percival, *Les Mythes de Platon*, Paris, 1930.

Glotz, G., *Ancient Greece at Work*, Kegan Paul, London, 1926.

Gomme, A. W., *The Population of Athens in the Fifth and Fourth Centuries B.C.*, Basil Blackwell, Oxford, 1933.

—— "Two Problems in Athenian Citizenship Law," *Classical Philology*, XXIX, 1934.

—— "The Old Oligarch," in *Athenian Studies, Harvard Studies in Classical Philology*, Harvard University Press, Cambridge, 1940.

—— *A Historical Commentary on Thucydides*, vol. I, Clarendon Press, Oxford, 1945.

Gomperz, H., "Psychologische Beobachtungen an griechischen Philosophen," *Imago*, X, 1924.

—— "Sokrates Haltung vor seinen Richtern," *Wiener Studien*, LIV, 1936.

Gomperz, Theodor, *Greek Thinkers*, Scribner, New York, 1901.

Grene, D., *Man in His Pride*, University of Chicago Press, 1950.

Grote, George, *Plato and the Other Companions of Socrates*, John Murray, London, 1865.

—— *A History of Greece* (condensed), ed. Mitchell and Caspari, Routledge, London, 1907.

Grube, G. M. A., *Plato's Thought*, Methuen, London, 1935.

—— "Antisthenes Was No Logician," *Transactions of the American Philological Association*, LXXXI, 1950.

Haarhof, T. J., *The Stranger at the Gate*, Basil Blackwell, Oxford, 1948.

Hackforth, R., *Plato's Phaedrus*, Cambridge University Press, 1952.

Hadas, Moses, *History of Greek Literature*, Columbia University Press, New York, 1950.

Hamilton, Edith, *The Great Age of Greek Literature*, Norton, New York, 1942.

Heitland, W. E., *Agricola*, Cambridge, 1921.

Herzberg, A., *The Psychology of Philosophers*, Harcourt, Brace, New York, 1929.

Hill, T. E., *Contemporary Ethical Theories*, Macmillan, New York, 1950.

Hitler, Adolf, *Mein Kampf*, translated by R. Manheim, Houghton Mifflin, Boston, 1943.

How, W. W., and J. Wells, *A Commentary on Herodotus*, Clarendon Press, Oxford, 1936.

Howald, Ernst, *Die platonische Akademie und die moderne Universitas Litterarum*, Zurich, 1921.

Jaeger, Werner, *Aristotle*, Clarendon Press, Oxford, 1934.

——*Paideia*, Oxford University Press, New York, vol. I, 1939; vol. II, 1943; vol. III, 1944.

——*Theology of the Early Greek Philosophers*, Clarendon Press, Oxford, 1947.

Jebb, R. C., *The Attic Orators*, Macmillan, London, 1893.

Jenkins, Richard L., M.D., "Psychiatry at the Crossroads," *American Journal of Psychiatry*, Nov., 1949.

Joseph, H. W. B., *Essays in Ancient and Modern Philosophy*, Clarendon Press, Oxford, 1935.

Kardiner, Abram, *et al.*, *Psychological Frontiers of Society*, Columbia University Press, N. Y., 1945.

Kelsen, Hans, "Platonic Justice," *International Journal of Ethics*, XLVIII, 1937–1938.

——"Platonic Love," *American Imago*, III, April, 1942.

Kilpatrick, William H., "Crucial Issues in Educational Theory," *Educational Theory*, I, May 1951.

Kitto, H. D. F., *The Greeks*, Penguin Books, London, 1951.

Kock, Th., *Comicorum Atticorum Fragmenta*, Leipzig, 1880.

Kroll, W., *Freundschaft und Knabenliebe* (Tusculum-Schriften, IV. Heft), Muechen, 1927.

Lagerborg, Rolf, *Die platonische Liebe*, Leipzig, 1926.

Licht, Hans (Brandt, Paul), *Sexual Life in Ancient Greece*, George Routledge and Sons, London, 1932.

Lindsay, A. D., review of *The Open Society and Its Enemies*, *Manchester Guardian*, Dec. 5, 1945.

Linforth, I. M., *Solon the Athenian*, University of California Press, Berkeley, 1919.

Livingstone, R. W., *Portrait of Socrates*, Clarendon Press, Oxford, 1938.

Locke, John, *The Second Treatise of Civil Government* and *A Letter concerning Toleration*, ed. J. W. Gough, Basil Blackwell, Oxford, 1946.

Lodge, R. C., *Plato's Theory of Education*, Kegan Paul, London, 1947.

Marcuse, Ludwig, *Plato and Dionysius, a Double Biography*, Knopf, New York, 1947.

McGovern, W. M., *From Luther to Hitler*, Houghton Mifflin, Boston, 1941.

Mead, Margaret, *The Changing Culture of an Indian Tribe*, Columbia University Press, New York, 1932.

Meritt, B. D., H. T. Wade-Gery, and M. F. McGregor, *The Athenian Tribute Lists*, The American School of Classical Studies at Athens, Princeton, N. J., vol. II, 1949, and III, 1950.

Meyer, Eduard, *Geschichte des Altertums*, Stuttgart and Berlin, 1902.

Milton, John, *Apology for Smectymnuus*, *Works*, Columbia University Press, New York, 1931.

Minar, E. L., *Early Pythagorean Politics*, Waverly Press, Baltimore, 1942.

Mises, Richard von, *Positivism*, Harvard University Press, Cambridge, 1951.

More, Paul Elmer, *Hellenistic Philosophies*, Princeton U. Press, Princeton, 1923.

Morrow, Glenn, "Studies in the Platonic Epistles," *Illinois Studies in Language and Literature*, XVIII, 1935.

——"The Murder of Slaves in Attic Law," *Classical Philology*, XXXII, 1937.

——"Plato and Greek Slavery," *Mind*, XLVIII, 1939.

——"Plato's Law of Slavery," *Illinois Studies in Language and Literature*, XXV, 1939–40.

——"Plato and the Rule of Law," *Philosophical Review*, L, March, 1941.

——"Plato and the Law of Nature," in *Essays in Political Theory*, Cornell University Press, Ithaca, 1948.

Mowrer, O. H., "Dynamic Theory of Personality," in *Personality and the Behavior Disorders*, ed. J. McV. Hunt, Ronald Press, New York, 1944.

Murphy, Gardner, *Personality*, Harper, New York, 1947.

Murray, Gilbert, *Rise of the Greek Epic*, Clarendon Press, Oxford, 1911.

—— *Greek Studies*, Clarendon Press, Oxford, 1946.

Murray, H. A., *Explorations in Personality*, Oxford University Press, New York, 1938.

Neil, R. A., *The Knights of Aristophanes* (edition), Cambridge, 1901.

Nestle, Wilhelm, "Untersuchungen ueber die philosophischen Quellen des Euripides," *Philologus*, Suppl. VIII, Leipzig, 1902.

—— *Sokratiker* (*Die Griechischen Philosophen*, II), Diederichs, Jena, 1923.

—— *Vom Mythos zum Logos*, Alfred Kroener, Stuttgart, 1942.

Neumann, Franz, *Behemoth*, Oxford University Press, New York, 1942.

Neurath, Otto, and Lauwerys, J. A., "Nazi Textbooks and the Future, II," *Journal of Education* (British), LXXVI, Dec. 1944; and "Plato's *Republic* and German Education," *Ibid.*, LXXVII, Feb. 1945. (Also the controversy in the same journal, April–Aug., 1945.)

Newman, W. L., *The Politics of Aristotle*, Clarendon Press, Oxford, 1887.

Norwood, Gilbert, *Greek Comedy*, Methuen and Co., London, 1931.

Oldfather, W. A., "Socrates in Court," *Classical Weekly*, XXXI, April 1938.

Perry, R. B., "The Philosophical Roots of Totalitarianism," in *The Roots of Totalitarianism*, by R. M. MacIver, M. J. Bonn, and R. B. Perry, James-Patten Rowe Pamphlet Series No. 9, American Academy of Political and Social Science, Philadelphia, 1940.

Piaget, Jean, "The Child and Moral Realism," in *Moral Principles of Action*, ed. R. N. Anshen, Harper, New York, 1952.

Pickard-Cambridge, A. W., *Select Fragments of the Greek Comic Poets*, Clarendon Press, Oxford, 1900.

Plutarch: The Lives of the Noble Grecians and Romans, translated by John Dryden, and revised by Arthur Hugh Clough, Modern Library, New York, 1932.

Pohlenz, M., *Aus Platon's Werdezeit*, Berlin, 1913.

Popper, K. R., *The Open Society and Its Enemies*, George Routledge and Sons, London, 1945; Princeton Press, Princeton, 1950.

Post, L. A., *Thirteen Epistles of Plato*, Clarendon Press, Oxford, 1925.

Rank, Otto, *Das Inzestmotiv in Dichtung und Sage*, Leipzig u. Wien, 1912.

Robinson, Richard, *Plato's Earlier Dialectic*, Cornell University Press, Ithaca, N. Y., 1941.

—— "Dr. Popper's Defence of Democracy," *Philosophical Review*, LX, 1951.

Rogers, A. K., *The Socratic Problem*, Yale University Press, New Haven, 1933.

Ross, Sir David, *Plato's Theory of Ideas*, Clarendon Press, Oxford, 1951.

Russell, Bertrand, *A History of Western Philosophy*, Simon and Schuster, New York, 1945.

Sabine, George H., *A History of Political Theory*, Henry Holt and Co., New York, 1950.

Sandburg, Carl, *Cornhuskers*, Henry Holt and Co., New York, 1918.

Sanford, R. Nevitt, "Personality Patterns in School Children," in *Child Behavior and Development*, ed. R. G. Barker, J. S. Kounin, and H. F. Wright, McGraw-Hill, New York, 1943.

Scheidweiler, Felix, "Zum Alexandros des Euripides," *Philologus*, XCVII, 1948.

Schilder, Paul, *Goals and Desires of Man*, Columbia University Press, New York, 1942.

Schiller, F. C. S., *Studies in Humanism*, Macmillan, London, 1912.

Schmid, Wolfgang, "Das Sokratesbild der Wolken," *Philologus*, XCVII, 1948.

Schwartz, Eduard, *Ethik der Griechen*, K. F. Koehler, Stuttgart, 1951.

Schweitzer, Albert, *Out of My Life and Thought*, Henry Holt and Co., New York, 1933.

Shaw, Bernard, *The Intelligent Woman's Guide to Socialism and Capitalism*, Brentano's, New York, 1928.

Shorey, Paul, *The Unity of Plato's Thought*, University of Chicago Press, 1903.

—— "Platonism and the History of Science," *American Philosophical Society Proceedings*, LXVI, 1927.

—— "The Question of the Socratic Element in Plato," *Proceedings of the Sixth International Congress of Philosophy*, ed. E. S. Brightman, Longmans, Green and Co., New York, 1927.

—— *What Plato Said*, University of Chicago Press, 1933.

Snell, Bruno, "Euripides Alexandros," *Hermes*, Einzelschriften, Heft 5, 1937.

—— "Das frühste Zeugnis über Sokrates," *Philologus*, XCVII, 1948.

Solmsen, Friedrich, *Plato's Theology*, Cornell University Press, Ithaca, 1942.

Spencer, Theodore, "Montaigne in America," *Atlantic Monthly*, March 1946.

Stenzel, Julius, *Platon der Erzieher*, Felix Meiner, Leipzig, 1928.

—— *Plato's Method of Dialectic*, translated and edited by D. J. Allan, Clarendon, Oxford, 1940.

Stephans, Dorothy, *Critias, Life and Literary Remains*, University of Cincinnati Dissertation, 1939.

Stewart, J. A., *The Myths of Plato*, Macmillan, London, 1905.

Symonds, John A., *A Problem in Greek Ethics* (first published 1883), privately printed, London, 1901.

Tarn, W. W., "Alexander the Great and the Unity of Mankind," *Proc. of the British Academy*, XIX, 1933.

—— "Alexander, Cynics, and Stoics," *American Journal of Philology*, LX, 1939.

Taylor, A. E., *Plato, the Man and His Work*, Lincoln MacVeagh, The Dial Press, Inc., New York, 1927; also the same, 1929.

—— *Commentary on Plato's Timaeus*, Clarendon Press, Oxford, 1928.

—— *Plato: Timaeus and Critias* (translation), Methuen and Co., London, 1929.

—— *The Laws of Plato* (translation), J. M. Dent, London, 1934.

—— "The Decline and Fall of the State in *Republic*, VIII," *Mind*, XLVIII, 1939.

Theiss, Edwin L., "Hostility to Plato in Antiquity," typewritten, unpublished doctoral thesis, University of Chicago, 1916.

Thompson, W. E., *The Phaedrus of Plato* (edition), London, 1868.

Thomson, A. D., *Euripides and the Attic Orators*, Macmillan, New York, 1898.

Thucydides, *History*, Crawley translation, Modern Library, New York, 1934.

Toynbee, Arnold, *A Study of History*, Oxford, London, 1934–9.

Ueberweg-Praechter, *Die Philosophie des Altertums*, Mittler, Berlin, 1926.

Van Hook, La Rue, "The Exposure of Infants at Athens," *Transactions of the American Philological Association*, LI, 1920.

Vinogradoff, Paul, *Outlines of Historical Jurisprudence*, Oxford University Press, London, 1922.

Vlastos, Gregory, "Slavery in Plato's Thought," *Philosophical Review*, L, 1941.

Westermann, W. L., article "Sklaverei," Pauly-Wissowa, Supplement-Bd. VI.

—— "Athenaeus and the Slaves of Athens," in *Athenian Studies*, Harvard University Press, 1940.

Whitehead, A. N., *Adventures of Ideas*, Macmillan, New York, 1933.

Wilamowitz-Moellendorf, U. von, *Die Griechische und Lateinische Literatur*, u.s.w., Teubner, Leipzig, 1912.

—— *Platon*, Weidmann, Berlin, 1920; also the same, Berlin, 1948.

Wild, John, *Plato's Theory of Man*, Harvard University Press, Cambridge, Mass., 1946.

Wilkins, E. G., *"Know Thyself" in Greek Literature*, privately printed, University of Chicago Libraries, 1917.

Winspear, A., and T. Silverberg, *Who Was Socrates?* The Cordon Press, 1939.

Winspear, A. D., *The Genesis of Plato's Thought*, Dryden Press, New York, 1940.

Woodbridge, F. J. E., *The Son of Apollo*, Houghton Mifflin, Boston, 1929.

Zeller, Eduard, *Plato and the Earlier Academy*, English trans., Longmans, Green, London, 1888.

—— *Outlines of the History of Greek Philosophy*, revised by Wilhelm Nestle, English trans., Humanities Press, New York, 1951.

Zimmern, Alfred, *The Greek Commonwealth*, Oxford, fourth edition, 1924.

Index of Persons